EDITION
11

Intermediate Financial Management

EUGENE F. BRIGHAM
University of Florida

PHILLIP R. DAVES
University of Tennessee

SOUTH-WESTERN
CENGAGE Learning®

Australia • Brazil • Japan • Korea • Mexico • Singapore • Spain • United Kingdom • United States

SOUTH-WESTERN
CENGAGE Learning

Intermediate Financial Management, Eleventh Edition

Eugene F. Brigham and Phillip R. Daves

VP/Editorial Director:
Jack W. Calhoun

Editor-in-Chief:
Joe Sabatino

Executive Editor:
Mike Reynolds

Developmental Editor:
Kendra Brown

Sr. Editorial Assistant:
Adele Scholtz

Sr. Marketing Communications Manager:
Jim Overly

Marketing Manager:
Nathan Anderson

Marketing Coordinator:
Suellen Ruttkay

Content Project Managers:
Scott Dillon & Jacquelyn K Featherly

Supervising Media Editor:
Scott Fidler

Manufacturing Planner:
Kevin Kluck

Production House/Compositor:
Cenveo Publisher Services

Sr. Rights Specialist:
John Hill

Sr. Art Director:
Michelle Kunkler

Internal Designer:
Plan-It-Publishing

Cover Designer:
Rose Alcorn

Cover Image:
© Nikada/iStockphoto.com

For product information and technology assistance, contact us at
Cengage Learning Customer & Sales Support, 1-800-354-9706

For permission to use material from this text or product,
submit all requests online at **www.cengage.com/permissions**
Further permissions questions can be emailed to
permissionrequest@cengage.com

ExamView® and ExamView Pro® are registered trademarks of FSCreations, Inc. Windows is a registered trademark of the Microsoft Corporation used herein under license. Macintosh and Power Macintosh are registered trademarks of Apple Computer, Inc. used herein under license.

Library of Congress Control Number: 2011945042

Student Edition ISBN 13: 978-1-111-53025-9

Student Edition ISBN 10: 1-111-53025-4

Package Student Edition ISBN 13: 978-1-111-53026-6

Package Student Edition ISBN 10: 1-111-53026-2

South-Western Cengage Learning

5191 Natorp Boulevard
Mason, OH 45040
USA

Cengage Learning products are represented in Canada by Nelson Education, Ltd.

For your course and learning solutions, visit **www.cengage.com**

Purchase any of our products at your local college store or at our preferred online store **www.cengagebrain.com**

Printed in Canada
1 2 3 4 5 6 7 16 15 14 13 12

Brief Contents

APPENDIXES

WEB CHAPTERS & WEB EXTENSIONS

Students: Access the Web Chapters and Web Extensions by visiting **www.cengagebrain.com**, searching ISBN 9781111530266, and clicking "Access Now" under "Study Tools" to go to the student textbook companion site.

Instructors: Access the Web Chapters, Web Extensions, and other instructor resources by going to **login.cengage.com**, logging in with your faculty account username and password, and using ISBN 9781111530266 to search for and to add resources to your account "Bookshelf."

WEB CHAPTERS

Contents

Web Chapters

Web Extensions

Much has happened in finance recently. Years ago, when the body of knowledge was smaller, the fundamental principles could be covered in a one-term lecture course and then reinforced in a subsequent case course. This approach is no longer feasible. There is simply too much material to cover in one lecture course.

As the body of knowledge expanded, we and other instructors experienced increasing difficulties. Eventually, we reached these conclusions:

- The introductory course should be designed for all business students, not just for finance majors, and it should provide a broad overview of finance. Therefore, a text designed for the first course should cover key concepts but avoid confusing students by going beyond basic principles.
- Finance majors need a second course that provides not only greater depth on the core issues of valuation, capital budgeting, capital structure, cost of capital, and working capital management but also covers such special topics as mergers, multinational finance, leasing, risk management, and bankruptcy.
- This second course should also utilize cases that show how finance theory is used in practice to help make better financial decisions.

When we began teaching under the two-course structure, we tried two types of existing books, but neither worked well. First, there were books that emphasized theory, but they were unsatisfactory because students had difficulty seeing the usefulness of the theory and consequently were not motivated to learn it. Moreover, these books were of limited value in helping students deal with cases. Second, there were books designed primarily for the introductory MBA course that contained the required material, but they also contained too much introductory material. We eventually concluded that a new text was needed, one designed specifically for the second financial management course, and that led to the creation of *Intermediate Financial Management*, or *IFM* for short.

The Next Level: *Intermediate Financial Management*

In your introductory finance course you learned a number of terms and concepts. However, an intro course cannot make you "operational" in the sense of actually "doing" financial management. For one thing, introductory courses necessarily focus on individual chapters and even sections of chapters, and first-course exams generally consist of relatively simple problems plus short-answer questions. As a result, it is hard to get a good sense of how the various parts of financial management interact with one another. Second, there is not enough time in the intro course to allow students to set up and work out realistic problems, nor is there time to delve into actual cases that illustrate how finance theory is applied in practice.

© Nikada/iStockphoto.com

Now it is time to move on. In *Intermediate Financial Management,* we first review materials that were covered in the introductory course, then take up new material. The review is absolutely essential, because no one can remember everything that was covered in the first course, yet all of the introductory material is essential for a good understanding of the more advanced material. Accordingly, we revisit topics such as the net present value (NPV) and internal rate of return (IRR) methods, but now we delve into them more deeply, considering how to streamline and automate the calculations, how to obtain the necessary data, and how errors in the data might affect the outcome. We also relate the topics covered in different chapters to one another, showing, for example, how cost of capital, capital structure, dividend policy, and capital budgeting combine forces to affect the firm's value.

Also, because spreadsheets such as *Excel,* not financial calculators, are used for most real-world calculations, students need to be proficient with spreadsheets so that they will be more marketable after graduation. Therefore, we explain how to do various types of financial analysis with *Excel.* Working with *Excel* actually has two important benefits: (1) a knowledge of *Excel* is important in the workplace and the job market, and (2) setting up spreadsheet models and analyzing the results also provide useful insights into the implications of financial decisions.

Corporate Valuation as a Unifying Theme

Management's goal is to maximize firm value. Job candidates who understand the theoretical underpinning for value maximization and have the practical skills to analyze business decisions within this context make better, more valuable employees. Our goal is to provide you with both this theoretical underpinning and a practical skill set. To this end we have developed several integrating features that will help you to keep the big picture of value maximization in mind while you are honing your analytical skills:

- Every chapter starts off with a series of integrating *Beginning of Chapter Questions* that will help you to place the material in the broader context of financial management.
- Most chapters have a valuation graphic and description that show exactly how the material relates to corporate valuation.
- Each chapter has a *Mini Case* that provides a business context for the material.
- Each chapter has an *Excel* spreadsheet *Tool Kit* that steps through all of the calculations in the chapter.
- Each chapter has a spreadsheet *Build-a-Model* that steps you through constructing an *Excel* model to work problems. We've designed these features and tools so that you'll finish your course with the skills to analyze business decisions and the understanding of how these decisions impact corporate value.

Design of the Book

Based on more than 30 years working on *Intermediate Financial Management* and teaching the advanced undergraduate financial management course, we have concluded that the book should include the following features:

- *Completeness.* Because *IFM* is designed for finance majors, it should be self-contained and suitable for reference purposes. Therefore, we specifically and purposely included (a) some material that overlaps with introductory finance texts and (b) more material than can realistically be covered in a single course. We included in Chapters 2 through 5 some fundamental materials borrowed directly from other Cengage Learning texts. If an instructor chooses to cover this material, or if an individual student feels a need to cover it on his or her own, it is available. In other chapters, we included relatively brief reviews of first-course topics. This was necessary both to put *IFM* on a stand-alone basis and to help students who have a delay between their introductory and second financial management courses get up to speed before tackling new material. This review is particularly important for working capital management and such "special topics" as mergers, lease analysis, and convertibles—all of which are often either touched on only lightly or skipped in the introductory course. Thus, the variety of topics covered in the text provides adopters with a choice of materials for the second course, and students can use materials that were not covered for reference purposes. We note, though, that instructors must be careful not to bite off more than their students can chew.

- *Theory and applications.* Financial theory is useful to financial decision makers, both for the insights it provides and for direct application in several important decision areas. However, theory can seem sterile and pointless unless its usefulness is made clear. Therefore, in *IFM*, we present theory in a decision-making context, which motivates students by showing them how theory can lead to better decisions. The combination of theory and applications also makes the text more usable as a reference for case courses as well as for real-world decision making.

- *Computer orientation.* Today, a business that does not use computers in its financial planning is about as competitive as a student who tries to take a finance exam without a financial calculator. Throughout the text we provide computer spreadsheet examples for the calculations and spreadsheet problems for the students to work. This emphasis on spreadsheets both orients students to the business environment they will face upon graduation and helps them understand key financial concepts better.

- *Global perspective.* Successful businesses know that the world's economies are rapidly converging, that business is becoming globalized, and that it is difficult to remain competitive without being a global player. Even purely domestic firms cannot escape the influence of the global economy, because international events have a significant effect on domestic interest rates and economic activity. All of this means that today's finance students—who are tomorrow's financial executives—must develop a global perspective. To this end, *IFM* also contains an entire chapter on multinational financial management. In addition, to help students "think global," we provide examples throughout the text that focus on the types of global problems companies face. Of course, we cannot make multinational finance experts out of students in a conventional corporate finance course, but we can help them recognize that insular decision making is insufficient in today's world.

Beginning of Chapter Questions

We start each chapter with several Beginning of Chapter (BOC) questions. You will be able to answer some of the questions before you even read the chapter, and you will be able to give better answers after you have read it. Other questions are harder, and you won't feel truly comfortable answering them until after they have been discussed in class. We considered putting the questions at the ends of the chapters, but we concluded that they would best serve our purposes if placed at the beginning. Here is a summary of our thinking as we wrote the questions:

- The questions indicate to you the key issues covered in the chapter and the things you should know when you complete the chapter.
- Some of the questions were designed to help you remember terms and concepts that were covered in the introductory course. Others indicate where we will be going beyond the intro course.
- You need to be able to relate different parts of financial management to one another, so some of the BOC questions were designed to get you to think about how the various chapters are related to one another. These questions tend to be harder, and they can be answered more completely after a classroom discussion.
- You also need to think about how financial concepts are applied in the real world, so some of the BOC questions focus on the application of theories to the decision process. Again, complete answers to these questions require a good bit of thought and discussion.
- Some of the BOC questions are designed to help you see how *Excel* can be used to make better financial decisions. These questions have accompanying models that provide tutorials on *Excel* functions and commands. The completed models are available on the textbook's website. Going through them will help you learn how to use *Excel* as well as give you valuable insights into the financial issues covered in the chapter. We have also provided an "*Excel* Tool Locater," which is an index of all of the *Excel* skills that the BOC models go over. This index is in the *Excel* file, **Excel Locations.xls.** Because recruiters like students who are good with *Excel,* this will also help you as you look for a good job. It will also help you succeed once you are in the workplace.

We personally have used the BOC questions in several different ways:

- In some classes we simply told students to use the BOC questions or not, as they wished. Some students did study them and retrieve the *Excel* models from the Web, but many just ignored them.
- We have also assigned selected BOC questions and then used them, along with the related *Excel* models, as the basis for some of our lectures.
- Most recently, we literally built our course around the BOC questions.[1] Here we informed students on day one that we would start each class by calling on them randomly and grading them on their answers.[2] We also informed them that our exams would be taken verbatim from the BOC questions. They complained a bit about the quizzes, but the students' course evaluations stated that the quizzes should be continued because without them they would have come to class less well prepared and hence would have learned much less than they did.
- The best way to prepare for the course as we taught it was by first reading the questions, then reading the chapter, and then writing out notes outlining answers to the questions in preparation for the oral quiz. We expected students to give complete answers to "easy" questions, but we gave them good grades if

---

[1]Actually, we broke our course into two segments, one where we covered selected text chapters and another where we covered cases that were related to and illustrated the text chapters. For the case portion of the course, students made presentations and discussed the cases. All of the cases required them to use *Excel.*

[2]Most of our students were graduating seniors who were interviewing for jobs. We excused them from class (and the quizzes) if they informed us by e-mail before class that they were interviewing.

they could say enough about the harder questions to demonstrate that they had thought about how to answer them. We would then discuss the harder questions in lieu of a straight lecture, going into the related *Excel* models both to explain *Excel* features and to provide insights into different issues.

- Our midterm and final exams consisted of five of the harder BOC questions, of which three had to be answered in two hours in an essay format. It took a much more complete answer to earn a good grade than would have been required on the oral quizzes. We also allowed students to use a four-page "cheat sheet" on the exams.[3] That reduced time spent trying to memorize things as opposed to understanding them. Also, students told us that making up the cheat sheets was a great way to study.

Major Changes in the Eleventh Edition

As in every revision, we updated and clarified sections throughout the text. Specifically, we also made the following changes in content:

References to, implications of, and explanations for the global economic crisis.

The text has been updated in almost every chapter to include real-world examples of the impact of the global economic crisis on financial markets and financial management. Many chapters have focused "Global Economic Crisis" boxes that discuss particularly important issues.

Updated big-picture graphics at the start of each chapter.

One of the major challenges students face in this second corporate finance course is seeing how all of the topics fit together. To aid the students' integration of the material from chapter-to-chapter and across their finance curriculum, we've included a graphic at the beginning of each chapter and in each PowerPoint show that clearly illustrates where the chapter's topics fit into the big picture.

Additional integration of the textbook and the accompanying *Excel Tool Kit* spreadsheet models for each chapter.

Many figures in the textbook are actually screen shots from the chapter's *Excel Tool Kit* model. This serves two purposes. First, it makes the analysis more transparent to the student; the student or instructor can go to the *Tool Kit* and see exactly how all of the numbers in a figure were calculated. Second, it provides an additional resource for students and instructors to use in learning *Excel*.

Significant Changes in Selected Chapters

We made many small improvements within each chapter; some of the more notable ones are discussed below.

Chapter 1: An Overview of Financial Management and the Financial Environment

We added a new box on globalization, "Columbus Was Wrong—the World Is Flat! And Hot, And Crowded," and a new box on the global economic crisis, "Say Hello to the Global Economic Crisis!" We completely rewrote the section on financial securities, including a discussion of securitization, and added a new section on the global crisis. New figures showing the national debt, trade balances, federal budget

---

[3]We did require that students make up their own "cheat sheets," and we required them to turn their sheets in with their exams so we could check for independence.

deficits, and the Case-Shiller real estate index help us better illustrate different aspects of the global crisis.

Chapter 2: Risk and Return: Part I

We added a new box on the risk that remains even for long-term investors, "What Does Risk Really Mean?" We added two additional boxes on risk, "How Risky Is a Large Portfolio of Stocks?" and "Another Kind of Risk: The Bernie Madoff Story."

Chapter 3: Risk and Return: Part II

We added a box on *The Wall Street Journal* contest between dart throwers and investors, "Skill or Luck?" We expanded our discussion of the Fama-French three-factor model and included a table showing returns of portfolios formed by sorting on size and the book-to-market ratio.

Chapter 4: Bond Valuation

We added five new boxes related to the global economic crisis: (1) "Betting With or Against the U.S. Government: The Case of Treasury Bond Credit Default Swaps," (2) "Insuring with Credit Default Swaps: Let the Buyer Beware!" (3) "U.S. Treasury Bonds Downgraded!" (4) "The Few, the Proud, the ... AAA-Rated Companies!" and (5) "Are Investors Rational?" We also added a new table summarizing corporate bond default rates and annual changes in ratings.

Chapter 5: Basic Stock Valuation

We added a new box on behavioral issues, "Rational Behavior versus Animal Spirits, Herding, and Anchoring Bias." We also added a new section, "The Market Stock Price versus Intrinsic Value."

Chapter 6: Financial Options

We completely rewrote the description of the binomial option pricing model. In addition to the hedge portfolio, we also discuss replicating portfolios. We now provide the binomial formula, and we show the complete solution to the two-period model. To provide greater continuity, the company used to illustrate the binomial example is now the same company used to illustrate the Black-Scholes model. Our discussion of put options now includes the Black-Scholes put formula.

Chapter 7: Accounting for Financial Management

We added a new box on the global economic crisis that explains the problems associated with off-balance-sheet assets, "Let's Play Hide-and-Seek!" We added a new figure illustrating the uses of free cash flow. We now have two end-of-chapter spreadsheet problems, one focusing on the articulation between the income statement and statement of cash flows and one focusing on free cash flow.

Chapter 8: Analysis of Financial Statements

We added a new box on marking to market, "The Price Is Right! (Or Wrong!)," and a new box on international accounting standards, "The World Might Be Flat, but Global Accounting Is Bumpy! The Case of IFRS versus FASB." We have included discussion of the price/EBITDA ratio, gross profit margin, and operating profit margin; we also explain how to use the statement of cash flows in financial analysis.

Chapter 9: Financial Planning and Forecasting Financial Statements

It is difficult to do financial planning without using spreadsheet software, so we completely rewrote the chapter and explicitly integrated the text and the *Excel Tool Kit* model. We illustrate the ways that financial policies (i.e., dividend payout and capital structure choices) affect financial projections, including ways to ensure that balance sheets balance. The *Excel Tool Kit* model now shows a very simple way to incorporate financing feedback effects.

Chapter 10: Determining the Cost of Capital

We added a new figure to highlight the similarities and differences among capital structure weights based on book values, market values, and target values. We added a new box, "GE and Warren Buffett: The Cost of Preferred Stock." We completely rewrote our discussion of the market risk premium, which now includes the impact of stock repurchases on estimating the market risk premium. We also present data from surveys identifying the market risk premia used by CFOs and professors.

Chapter 11: Corporate Valuation and Value-Based Management

We added three new boxes. The first describes corporate governance issues at IBM, "Let's Go to Miami! IBM's 2009 Annual Meeting." The second discusses leadership at bailout recipients, "Would the U.S. Government Be an Effective Board Director?" The third discusses the 2009 proxy season, "Shareholder Reactions to the Crisis."

Chapter 12: Capital Budgeting: Decision Criteria

We reworked the numerical examples in this chapter and the next so that they represent a single, consistent company. We also added a new box, "Why NPV Is Better Than IRR."

Chapter 13: Capital Budgeting: Estimating Cash Flow and Analyzing Risk

We reworked the numerical examples in this chapter and in the previous one so they represent a single, consistent company. We also incorporated two additional decimal places in the MACRS depreciation schedules to reflect the actual rates in the federal tax tables. We now show how to use tornado diagrams in sensitivity analysis. We rewrote our discussion of Monte Carlo simulation and show how to conduct a simulation analysis without using add-ins but instead using only *Excel*'s built-in features (Data Tables and random number generators). We have included an example of replacement analysis and an example of a decision tree showing abandonment. We added a new box, "Are Bank Stress Tests Stressful Enough?"

Chapter 15: Capital Structure Decisions: Part I

We improved our discussion of recapitalizations within the context of the FCF valuation model. We added a new box, "Deleveraging," that discusses the changes in leverage many companies and individuals are making in light of the global economic crisis.

Chapter 17: Distributions to Shareholders: Dividends and Repurchases

We consolidated the coverage of stock repurchases that had been spread over two chapters and located it here. We also use the FCF valuation model to illustrate the different impacts of stock repurchases versus dividend payments. We added two new boxes. The first discusses recent dividend cuts, "Will Dividends Ever Be the Same?" and the second discusses Sun Microsystem's stock splits and recent reverse split, "Talk About a Split Personality!"

Chapter 18: Initial Public Offerings, Investment Banking, and Financial Restructuring

We added a new section on investment banking activities. We added a new box on "Investment Banks and the Global Economic Crisis."

Chapter 19: Lease Financing

A new box addresses the FASB/IASB movement to capitalize all leases, "Off-Balance Sheet Financing: Is It Going to Disappear?"

Chapter 20: Hybrid Financing: Preferred Stock, Warrants, and Convertibles

A new box discusses the use of payment-in-kind preferred stock in the merger of Dow Chemical Company and Rohm & Haas, "The Romance Had No Chemistry, but It Had a Lot of Preferred Stock!"

Chapter 21: Working Capital Management

We reorganized the chapter so that we now discuss working capital holdings and financing before discussing the cash conversion cycle. We rewrote our coverage of the cash conversion cycle to explain the general concepts and then apply them to actual financial statement data. We added three new boxes, "Some Firms Operate with Negative Working Capital!" "Your Check Isn't in the Mail," and "A Wag of the Finger or Tip of the Hat? The Colbert Report and Small Business Payment Terms." We added a new section on the cost of bank loans.

Chapter 24: Derivatives and Risk Management

We added a new box on "Value at Risk and Enterprise Risk Management." Throughout the chapter we discuss the failure of risk management during the global economic crisis.

Chapter 25: Bankruptcy, Reorganization, and Liquidation

We added a new box on personal and small business bankruptcies, "A Nation of Defaulters?"

Chapter 26: Mergers, LBOs, Divestitures, and Holding Companies

We added a section explaining how the stock-swap ratio is determined for mergers where the payment is in the form of the acquiring company's stock.

Chapter 27: Multinational Financial Management

We added two new boxes. The first is on regulating international bribery and taxation, "Greasing the Wheels of International Business." The second new box discusses the wave of foreign companies partnering with Chinese banks to provide consumer finance services, "Consumer Finance in China."

Test Bank

The instructor's test bank has been updated and revised with many new questions and problems.

Other Ways the Book Can be Used

The second corporate finance course can be taught in a variety of other ways, depending on a school's curriculum structure and the instructor's personal preferences. We have been focusing on the BOC questions and discussions, but we have used alternative formats, and all can work out very nicely. Therefore, we designed the book so that it can be flexible.

Mini Cases as a framework for lectures. We originally wrote the Mini Cases specifically for use in class. We had students read the chapter and the Mini Case, and then we systematically went through it in class to "explain" the chapter. (See the section titled "The Instructional Package" later in this Preface for a discussion of lecture aids available from Cengage Learning.) Here we use a *PowerPoint* slide show, which is provided on the Instructor's Resource CD and on the Instructors website, and which we make available to students on our own course website. Students bring a printout of the slides to class, which makes it easier to take good notes. Generally, it takes us about two hours to frame the issues with the opening questions and then go through a Mini Case, so we allocate that much time. We want to facilitate questions and class discussion, and the Mini Case format stimulates both.

The Mini Cases themselves provide case content, so it is not as necessary to use regular cases as it would be if we used lectures based entirely on text chapters. Still, we like to use a number of the free-standing cases that are available from TextChoice, Cengage Learning's online case library, at **www.textchoice2.com/casenet**, and we have teams of students present their findings in class. The presenters play the role of consultants teaching newly hired corporate staff members (the rest of the class) how to analyze a particular problem, and we as instructors play the role of "chief consultant"—normally silent but available to answer questions if the student "consultants" don't know the answers (which is rare). We use this format because it is more realistic to have students think about *how to analyze* problems than to focus on the final decision, which is really the job of corporate executives with far more experience than undergraduate students.

To ensure that nonpresenting students actually study the case, we call on them randomly before the presentation begins, we grade them on class participation, and our exams are patterned closely after the material in the cases. Therefore, nonpresenting students have an incentive to study and understand the cases and to participate when the cases are discussed in class. This format has worked well, and we have obtained excellent results with a relatively small amount of preparation time. Indeed, some of our Ph.D. students with no previous teaching experience have taught the course entirely on their own, following our outline and format, and also obtained excellent results.

An emphasis on basic material. If students have not gained a thorough understanding of the basic concepts from their earlier finance courses, instructors may want to place more emphasis on the basics and thus cover Chapters 2 through 5 in detail rather than merely as a review. We even provide a chapter (Web Chapter 28) on time value of money skills on the textbook's website for students who need an even more complete review. Then, Chapters 6 through 17 can be covered in detail, and any remaining time can be used to cover some of the other chapters. This approach gives students a sound background on the core of financial management, but it does not leave sufficient time to cover a number of interesting and important topics. However, because the book is written in a modular format, if students understand the fundamental core topics they should be able to cover the remaining chapters on their own, if and when the need arises.

A case-based course. At the other extreme, where students have an exceptionally good background, hence little need to review topics that were covered in the basic finance course, instructors can spend less time on the early chapters and concentrate on advanced topics. When we take this approach, we assign Web Chapter 29 as a quick review and then assign cases that deal with the topics covered in the early chapters. We tell students to review the other relevant chapters on their own to the extent necessary to work the cases, thus freeing up class time for the more advanced material. This approach works best with relatively mature students, including evening students with some business experience.

Comprehensive Learning Solutions

Intermediate Financial Management includes a broad range of ancillary materials designed both to enhance students' learning and to help instructors prepare for and conduct classes.

Supplemental Student Resources

Students: Access all of the below resources [except the Study Guide] by visiting **www.cengagebrain.com**, searching ISBN 9781111530266, and clicking "Access Now" under "Study Tools" to go to the student textbook companion site.

Beginning of chapter (BOC) spreadsheets. Many of the integrative questions that appear at the start of each chapter have a spreadsheet model that illustrates the topic. There is also an index of the *Excel* techniques covered in the BOC *Excel* models. This index is in the *Excel* file, ***Excel Locations.xls,*** and it provides a quick way to locate examples of *Excel* programming techniques

End-of-chapter Build-A-Model spreadsheet problems. In addition to the Tool Kits and Beginning of Chapter models, most chapters have a "Build a Model" spreadsheet problem. These spreadsheets contain financial data plus instructions for solving a particular problem. The model is partially completed, with headings but no formulas, so the models must literally be built. The partially completed spreadsheets for these "Build a Model" problems are on the student companion website, with the completed versions available to instructors.

Mini Case spreadsheets. These *Excel* spreadsheets do all the calculations required in the Mini Cases. They are similar to the Tool Kits for the chapter, except (a) the numbers in the examples correspond to the Mini Case rather than to the chapter per se, and (b) there are some features that make it possible to do "what-if" analyses on a real-time basis in class.

Web Chapters and Web Extensions. Web chapters provide a chapter-length discussion of specialized topics that are not of sufficient general interest to warrant inclusion in the printed version of the text. Web extensions provide additional discussion or examples pertaining to material that is in the text.

Study Guide (ISBN 9781111530273). This printed supplement outlines the key sections of each chapter, and it provides sets of questions and problems similar to those in the text, along with worked-out solutions.

Instructor Resources

Instructors: Access the above chapter resources and the following instructor ancillaries [except the ExamView Test Bank and Study Guide] by going to **login.cengage .com**, logging in with your faculty account username and password, and using ISBN 9781111530266 to search for and to add resources to your account "Bookshelf."

Unless otherwise noted, all resources and ancillaries are available on both the instructor companion site and the Instructor Resource CD (IRCD).

Instructor's Resource CD (ISBN 9781111530389). The IRCD contains electronic versions of the Instructor's Manual, Test Bank, and Study Guide in Microsoft Word® format. It also has the PPT slides and all of the student companion site spreadsheet content with applicable solutions.

- ***Instructor's Manual (ISBN 9781111530280).*** This comprehensive manual contains answers to all the Beginning of Chapter Questions, end-of-chapter questions and problems, and Mini Cases. The Instructor's Manual is also available in print format.

- **PowerPoint® slides.** Created by the authors, the PowerPoint® slides cover essential topics for each chapter. Graphs, tables, and lists are developed sequentially for your convenience and can be easily modified for your needs. There are *also* slides that are specifically based on each chapter's Mini Case and in which graphs, tables, lists, and calculations are developed sequentially.
- **Test Bank (ISBN 9781111530297).** The *Test Bank* that contains more than 1,200 class-tested questions and problems. Information regarding the topic and degree of difficulty, along with the complete solution for all numerical problems, is provided with each question. The Test Bank is also available in print format.

ExamView® Test Bank (ISBN 9781111530310). This easy-to-use, computerized test creation software contains all of the questions in the Microsoft Word® Test Bank and is compatible with Microsoft® Windows®. Add or edit questions, instructions, and answers, and select questions by previewing them on the screen, selecting them randomly, or selecting them by number. Instructors can also create and administer quizzes online, whether over the Internet, a local area network (LAN), or a wide area network (WAN). Contact your Cengage Learning representative for more information. The ExamView® Test Bank is only available as a standalone CD.

Additional Course Tools

New! Aplia for *Intermediate Financial Management*.

Engage, prepare and educate your students with this ideal online learning solution. Aplia™ Finance improves comprehension and outcomes by increasing student effort and engagement. Students stay on top of coursework with regularly scheduled homework assignments while automatic grading provides detailed, immediate feedback. Aplia™ assignments match the language, style, and structure of the text which allows your students to apply what they learn directly to homework. Find out more at **www.aplia.com/finance**.

- Grade It Now
- End-of-Chapter Problems
- Auto-Graded Problem Sets
- Preparing for Finance Tutorials
- News Analyses
- Course Management System
- Digital Textbook

CengageNOW™ for *Intermediate Financial Management*. Designed by instructors for instructors, CengageNOW™ mirrors your natural workflow and provides time-saving, performance-enhancing tools for you and your students—all in one program!

CengageNOW™ takes the best of current technology tools including online homework management; fully customizable algorithmic end-of-chapter problems and test bank; and course support materials such as online quizzing, videos, and tutorials to support your course goals and save you significant preparation and grading time!

- **Plan** student assignments with an easy online homework management component
- **Manage** your grade book with ease
- **Teach** today's student using valuable course support materials
- **Reinforce** student comprehension with Personalized Study
- **Test** with customizable algorithmic end-of-chapter problems and test bank
- **Grade** automatically for seamless, immediate results

TextChoice. More than 100 cases written by Eugene F. Brigham, Linda Klein, and Chris Buzzard are now available via TextChoice, Cengage Learning's online case library. Cases are organized in a database that allows instructors to select individual cases or to create customized casebooks. Most cases have optional spreadsheet models that reduce number crunching, which allows more time for students to consider conceptual issues. The models also show students how computers can be used to make better financial decisions. Cases that we have found particularly useful for the different chapters are listed in the end-of-chapter references. The cases, case solutions, and spreadsheet models can be previewed and ordered by professors at **www.textchoice2.com/casenet**.

Cengage Learning Custom Solutions. Whether you need print, digital, or hybrid course materials, Cengage Learning Custom Solutions can help you create your perfect learning solution. Draw from Cengage Learning's extensive library of texts and collections, add or create your own original work, and create customized media and technology to match your learning and course objectives. Our editorial team will work with you through each step, allowing you to concentrate on the most important thing—your students. Learn more about all our services at **www.cengage.com/custom**.

The Cengage Global Economic Watch (GEW) Resource Center. This is your source for turning today's challenges into tomorrow's solutions. This online portal houses the most current and up-to-date content concerning the economic crisis.

Organized by discipline, the GEW Resource Center offers the solutions instructors and students need in an easy-to-use format. Included are an overview and timeline of the historical events leading up to the crisis, links to the latest news and resources, discussion and testing content, an instructor feedback forum, and a Global Issues Database. Visit **www.cengage.com/thewatch** for more information.

Acknowledgments

This book reflects the efforts of a great many people over a number of years. First, we would like to thank Fred Weston, Joel Houston, Mike Ehrhardt, and Scott Besley, who worked with us on other books published by Cengage Learning from which we borrowed liberally to create *IFM*. We also owe Lou Gapenski special thanks for his many past contributions to earlier editions of this text.

The following professors and professionals, who are experts on specific topics, provided extensive feedback on this edition. We are grateful for their insights.

Thomas J. Alexander
Z. Ayca Altintig
Onur Arugaslan
Steve Beach
Kevin K. Boeh
Mary R. Brown
James J. Cordeiro
Tony Crawford
Ross Dickens
David A. Dumpe
Theodore Engel
John Griffith
Axel Grossmann

George Hachey
Thomas Hall
Tim Jares
Young Kim
Merouane Lakehal-Ayat
Richard N. LaRocca
Yingchou Lin
Barbara MacLeod
Ohaness Paskelian
Bruce Payne
Edward Pyatt
Howard Qi
Alicia Rodriguez

Kenneth Roskelley
Atul Saxena
Mark Sipper
Stephen V. Smith
G. Kevin Spellman
Tom Stuckey
Diane Rizzuto Suhler
Qian Sun
Denver Swaby
A. Tessmer
Manish Tewari

In addition, we would like to thank the following people, whose reviews and comments on prior editions and companion books have contributed to this edition: Mike Adler, Syed Ahmad, Sadhana M. Alangar, Edward I. Altman, Mary Schary Amram, Bruce Anderson, Ron Anderson, Bob Angell, Vince Apilado, Henry Arnold, Nasser Arshadi, Bob Aubey, Abdul Aziz, Gil Babcock, Peter Bacon, Kent Baker, Tom Bankston, Les Barenbaum, Charles Barngrover, John R. Becker-Blease, Bill Beedles, Moshe Ben-Horim, William (Bill) Beranek, Tom Berry, Bill Bertin, Roger Bey, Dalton Bigbee, John Bildersee, Lloyd P. Blenman, Russ Boisjoly, Keith Boles, Gordon R. Bonner, Geof Booth, Kenneth Boudreaux, Helen Bowers, Lyle Bowlin, Oswald Bowlin, Don Boyd, G. Michael Boyd, Pat Boyer, Ben S. Branch, Joe Brandt, Elizabeth Brannigan, Greg Brauer, Mary Broske, Dave Brown, David T. Brown, Kate Brown, Bill Brueggeman, Kirt Butler, Robert Button, Julie Cagle, Bill (B. J.) Campsey, Bob Carleson, Severin Carlson, David Cary, Steve Celec, Don Chance, Antony Chang, Susan Chaplinsky, Jay Choi, S. K. Choudhury, Lal Chugh, Maclyn Clouse, Margaret Considine, Phil Cooley, Joe Copeland, David Cordell, John Cotner, Charles Cox, David Crary, John Crockett, Roy Crum, Brent Dalrymple, Bill Damon, William H. Dare, Joel Dauten, Steve Dawson, Sankar De, Miles Delano, Fred Dellva, Anand Desai, Bernard Dill, Greg Dimkoff, Les Dlabay, Mark Dorfman, Gene Drycimski, Dean Dudley, David Durst, Ed Dyl, Dick Edelman, Charles Edwards, John Ellis, Dave Ewert, John Ezzell, Richard Fendler, Michael Ferri, Jim Filkins, John Finnerty, Susan Fischer, Mark Flannery, Steven Flint, Russ Fogler, Jennifer Foo, E. Bruce Frederickson, Dan French, Tina Galloway, Phil Gardial, Michael Garlington, Jim Garvin, Adam Gehr, Jim Gentry, Philip Glasgo, Rudyard Goode, Myron Gordon, Walt Goulet, Bernie Grablowsky, Theoharry Grammatikos, Ed Grossnickle, John Groth, Alan Grunewald, Manak Gupta, Sam Hadaway, Don Hakala, Sally Hamilton, Gerald Hamsmith, William Hardin, Joel Harper, John Harris, Paul Hastings, Bob Haugen, Steve Hawkey, Del Hawley, Hal Heaton, Robert Hehre, John Helmuth, K. L. Henebry, George Hettenhouse, Hans Heymann, Kendall Hill, Roger Hill, Tom Hindelang, Linda Hittle, Ralph Hocking, J. Ronald Hoffmeister, Jim Horrigan, John Houston, John Howe, Keith Howe, Jim Hsieh, Hugh Hunter, Steve Isberg, James E. Jackson, Jim Jackson, Vahan Janjigian, Kose John, Craig Johnson, Keith H. Johnson, Ramon Johnson, Ken Johnston, Ray Jones, Manuel Jose, Tejendra Kalia, Gus Kalogeras, Mike Keenan, Bill Kennedy, Joe Kiernan, Robert Kieschnick, Rick Kish, Linda Klein, Don Knight, Dorothy Koehl, Raj K. Kohli, Jaroslaw Komarynsky, Duncan Kretovich, Harold Krogh, Charles Kroncke, Joan Lamm, P. Lange, Howard Lanser, Martin Laurence, Ed Lawrence, Richard LeCompte, Wayne Lee, Jim LePage, Ilene Levin, Jules Levine, John Lewis, Kartono Liano, James T. Lindley, Chuck Linke, Bill Lloyd, Susan Long, Judy Maese, Bob Magee, Ileen Malitz, Phil Malone, Terry Maness, Chris Manning, Terry Martell, D. J. Masson, John Mathys, John McAlhany, Andy McCollough, Bill McDaniel, Robin McLaughlin, Tom McCue, Jamshid Mehran, Ilhan Meric, Larry Merville, Rick Meyer, Stuart Michelson, Jim Millar, Ed Miller, John Mitchell, Carol Moerdyk, Bob Moore, Barry Morris, Gene Morris, Fred Morrissey, Chris Muscarella, David Nachman, Tim Nantell, Don Nast, Bill Nelson, Bob Nelson, Bob Niendorf, Tom O'Brien, Dennis O'Connor, John O'Donnell, Jim Olsen, Robert Olsen, R. Daniel Pace, Coleen Pantalone, Jim Pappas, Stephen Parrish, Glenn Petry, Jim Pettijohn, Rich Pettit, Dick Pettway, Hugo Phillips, John Pinkerton, Gerald Pogue, Ralph A. Pope, R. Potter, Franklin Potts, R. Powell, Chris Prestopino, Jerry Prock, Howard Puckett, Herbert Quigley, George Racette, Bob Radcliffe, Allen Rappaport, Bill Rentz, Ken Riener, Charles Rini, John Ritchie, Jay Ritter, Pietra Rivoli, Fiona Robertson, Antonio Rodriguez, E. M. Roussakis, Dexter Rowell, Michael Ryngaert, Jim Sachlis, Abdul Sadik, Thomas Scampini, Kevin Scanlon, Frederick Schadler,

James Schallheim, Mary Jane Scheuer, Carl Schweser, John Settle, Alan Severn, Sol Shalit, Frederic Shipley, Dilip Shome, Ron Shrieves, Neil Sicherman, J. B. Silvers, Clay Singleton, Joe Sinkey, Stacy Sirmans, Jaye Smith, Steve Smith, Don Sorenson, David Spears, Andrew Spieler, Ken Stanly, Ed Stendardi, Alan Stephens, Don Stevens, Jerry Stevens, G. Bennett Stewart, Glen Strasburg, Robert Strong, Philip Swensen, Ernie Swift, Paul Swink, Eugene Swinnerton, Robert Taggart, Gary Tallman, Dennis Tanner, Russ Taussig, Richard Teweles, Ted Teweles, Andrew Thompson, Jonathan Tiemann, Sheridan Titman, George Trivoli, George Tsetsekos, Alan L. Tucker, Mel Tysseland, David Upton, Howard Van Auken, Pretorious Van den Dool, Pieter Vanderburg, Paul Vanderheiden, David Vang, Jim Verbrugge, Patrick Vincent, Steve Vinson, Susan Visscher, John Wachowicz, Joe Walker, Mike Walker, Sam Weaver, Kuo Chiang Wei, Bill Welch, Gary R. Wells, Fred Weston, Norm Williams, Tony Wingler, Ed Wolfe, Larry Wolken, Annie Wong, Bob G. Wood, Jr., Don Woods, Thomas Wright, Michael Yonan, Miranda Zhang, Zhong-guo Zhou, David Ziebart, Dennis Zocco, and Kent Zumwalt.

Special thanks are due to Fred Weston, Myron Gordon, Merton Miller, and Franco Modigliani, who have done much to help develop the field of financial management and who provided us with instruction and inspiration; to Roy Crum, who coauthored the multinational finance chapter; to Jay Ritter, who helped us with the materials on financial markets and IPOs; to Larry Wolken, who offered his hard work and advice for the development of the *PowerPoint* slides; to Dana Aberwald Clark, Susan Ball, and Chris Buzzard, who helped us develop the spread-sheet models; and to Susan Whitman, Amelia Bell, Stephanie Hodge, and Kirsten Benson, who provided editorial support.

Both our colleagues and our students at the Universities of Florida and Tennessee gave us many useful suggestions, and the Cengage Learning and Cenveo Publisher Services staffs—especially Scott Dillon, Jaci Featherly, Lori Hazzard, Kendra Brown, Nate Anderson, Michelle Kunkler, Scott Fidler, Adele Scholtz, Suellen Ruttkay, and Mike Reynolds of Cengage Learning—helped greatly with all phases of text development, production, and marketing.

Errors in the Text

At this point, authors generally say something like this: "We appreciate all the help we received from the people listed above, but any remaining errors are, of course, our own responsibility." And in many books, there are plenty of remaining errors. Having experienced difficulties with errors ourselves, both as students and as instructors, we resolved to avoid this problem in *Intermediate Financial Management*. As a result of our error detection procedures, we are convinced that the book is relatively free of mistakes.

Partly because of our confidence that few such errors remain, but primarily because we want to detect those errors that may have slipped by to correct them in subsequent printings, we decided to offer a reward of $10 per error to the first person who reports it to us. For purposes of this reward, errors are defined as misspelled words, nonrounding numerical errors, incorrect statements, and any other error that inhibits comprehension. Typesetting problems such as irregular spacing and differences in opinion regarding grammatical or punctuation conventions do not qualify for this reward. Finally, any qualifying error that has follow-through effects is counted as two errors only. Please report any errors to Phillip Daves at the following email address: pdaves@utk.edu.

Conclusion

Finance is, in a real sense, the cornerstone of the free enterprise system. Good financial management is therefore vitally important to the economic health of business firms, hence to the nation and the world. Because of its importance, financial management should be thoroughly understood. However, this is easier said than done. The field is relatively complex, and it is undergoing constant change in response to shifts in economic conditions. All of this makes financial management stimulating and exciting, but also challenging and sometimes perplexing. We sincerely hope that the Eleventh Edition of *Intermediate Financial Management* will help you understand the financial problems faced by businesses today, as well as the best ways to solve those problems.

Eugene F. Brigham
College of Business Administration
University of Florida
Gainesville, Florida 32611-7167
gene.brigham@cba.ufl.edu

Phillip R. Daves
College of Business Administration
University of Tennessee
Knoxville, Tennessee 37996-0540
pdaves@utk.edu

March 2012

Intermediate Financial Management

PART I

Fundamental Concepts of Corporate Finance

Chapter 1

An Overview of Financial Management and the Financial Environment

This book is designed to explain what "financial management" is all about and to show how it can be used to help increase the value of a firm. It is intended for use in a second-level finance course, following the introductory course. Only the basic course is prerequisite, so if students have taken other finance courses, especially on investments or capital markets, they will find some of the material a review.

The book is often used in a "capstone" course taken during the last term before graduation. This is an exhilarating time for students, with graduation looming and a job search under way. It is also a good time to step back from the technical skills developed in the classroom and to look at the big picture of why financial management is so important. Spending the time now to develop a good overview of financial management can be tremendously valuable to your career. Why is financial management so valuable? In a nutshell, because it explains both how managers can increase their firms' value and why it is essential for them to do so.

Today's business environment is more complicated than ever. Investors are increasingly forcing managers to focus on value maximization, but events ranging from the scandals at Enron, WorldCom, Tyco, and a host of other companies during the early 2000s to the global financial meltdown and recession at the end of that decade have shown that ethical behavior and managerial accountability are crucial prerequisites. Mastering the technical details of financial management and understanding its role within the firm is important to graduating students because companies want to hire people who can make decisions with the broad corporate goal of value maximization in mind. Therefore, students who understand the principles of value maximization have a major advantage in the job market over students who do not. Demonstrating that you understand all this can make a big difference in both the quality of your initial job and your subsequent career path.

Beginning of Chapter Questions

As you read the chapter, consider how you would answer the following questions. You *should not* necessarily be able to answer the questions before you read the chapter. Rather, you should use them to get a sense of the issues covered in the chapter. After reading the chapter, you should be able to give at least partial answers to the questions, and you should be able to give better answers after the chapter has been discussed in class. Note, too, that it is often useful, when answering conceptual questions, to use hypothetical data to illustrate your answer. For example, your answer to Question 2 would probably be better if it were illustrated with numbers. We have done this, using *Excel;* our model is available on the textbook's Web site. Accessing the model and working through it is a useful exercise.

1. What is presumed to be the **primary goal** of financial management? How is this goal related to other societal goals and considerations? Is this goal consistent with the basic assumptions of microeconomics? Are managers' actions always consistent with this goal?

2. Finance is all about **valuation**—how to estimate asset values and what to do to increase them. We develop and use *Excel* models throughout the book. We start that process in this chapter with simple models used to value bonds, stocks, and capital budgeting projects. Working through the model will give you a refresher in valuation plus a refresher on (or preview of) *Excel*. The model can be accessed on the textbook's Web site under the "Chapter Models" section. If you have never used *Excel* at all, then you should not attempt to use it to help answer this question, or if you do, you should not get frustrated if you have trouble.

   a. Explain how to find the value of a bond given the rate of interest it pays (its coupon rate), its par value (assume $1,000), and the going rate of interest on bonds with the same risk and maturity.

   b. Explain how to find the value of a stock given its last dividend, its expected growth rate, and its required rate of return.

   c. Explain how to find the value of a capital budgeting project given its cost, its expected annual net cash flows, its life, and its cost of capital.

   d. In each of the above cases, discuss how changes in the inputs would affect the output. Would it matter if the outputs were highly sensitive to changes in the inputs?

3. What are the advantages of the corporate form over a sole proprietorship or a partnership? What are the disadvantages of this form?

4. What are the various factors that affect the cost of money and hence interest rates? How will changes in these components affect asset prices?

5. What is securitization? How is securitization supposed to help banks and S&Ls manage risks and increase homeowners' access to capital?

6. What was the global economic crisis? This is a really big question, so, more specifically, explain how in our interconnected global economy a decrease in housing prices in large U.S. cities ended up bankrupting Norwegian retirees.

1.1 How to Use This Text

In your introductory finance course, you learned a number of terms and concepts, and you now have an idea of what financial management is all about. However, you probably focused on individual chapters, or sections of chapters, and you probably prepared for exams that consisted of relatively simple problems and short-answer questions, often given in a multiple-choice format. That was a necessary part of the learning process, but now it is time to move on.

In *Intermediate Financial Management*, we go back over much of what you covered in the introductory course, plus introduce new material. However, our focus now is different. At this point we want you to learn how to *apply* the concepts, how to obtain the data necessary to implement the various decision models, and how to relate the various parts of finance to one another. So, while we revisit topics such as the net present value (NPV) and internal rate of return (IRR) methods, we delve into them more deeply, considering how to streamline and automate the calculations, how to obtain the necessary data, and how errors in the data affect the outcome. We also spend more time comparing the topics covered in different chapters to one another. For example, you probably did not spend much time considering how the cost of capital, capital structure, dividend policy, and capital budgeting are related to one another, but we now discuss these critically important relationships.

Also, since spreadsheets such as *Excel,* not financial calculators, are used to analyze actual business decisions, you need to be proficient with spreadsheets to get many good jobs and certainly to succeed in those jobs. Therefore, we explain how to do the most common types of financial analyses using *Excel.* This focus has two benefits: Knowledge of *Excel* is useful per se, and setting up and analyzing the output from spreadsheet models will also teach you a lot about financial concepts.

To help sharpen your focus, we start each chapter with several *Beginning of Chapter Questions.* Some of these questions are designed to help you see how the chapter ties in with other chapters, while others will help you think about how the concepts are applied in the real world. You probably won't be able to answer all of the questions when you start working through the chapter, but that's fine! The questions aren't a pre-test. Their purpose is to help guide you through the material, and having them in mind when you read will help you understand the chapter in a more integrative and relevant way.

Most of the chapters have two spreadsheet models, which are available on the textbook's Web site. The first is a "Tool Kit," which contains the *Excel* models used to generate most of the tables and examples in the chapter. The second is a model that deals with specific Beginning of Chapter Questions. Both models contain notes and comments that explain the *Excel* procedures we used, so they can be used as a tutorial for learning more about both *Excel* and finance. Again, since recruiters prefer students who are good with *Excel,* learning more about it will help you get a better job and then succeed in it.

THE GLOBAL ECONOMIC CRISIS

What Is the Global Economic Crisis?
Imagine a story of greed and reckless daring, of fortunes made and fortunes lost, of enormous corporations failing and even governments brought to the brink of ruin. No, this isn't a box-office blockbuster, but instead is the situation that faced the world's financial markets and economies in 2008 and 2009.

What exactly was the crisis? At the risk of oversimplification, many of the world's individuals, financial institutions, and governments borrowed too much money and used those borrowed funds to make speculative investments. Those investments turned out to be worth less than the amounts owed by the borrowers, forcing widespread bankruptcies, buyouts, and restructurings for both borrowers and lenders. This in turn reduced the supply of available funds that financial institutions normally lent to creditworthy individuals, manufacturers, and retailers. Without access to credit, consumers bought less, manufacturers produced less, and retailers sold less—all of which led to layoffs. According to the National Bureau of Economic Research, the resulting recession lasted from December 2007 through June 2009, and as of the writing of this chapter in mid-2011, the U.S. economy is still not growing very quickly. As we progress through this chapter and the rest of the book, we will discuss different aspects of the crisis. For real-time updates, go to the Global Economic Crisis (GEC) Resource Center at **www.cengage.com/gec** and log in.

1.2 The Corporate Life Cycle

Many major corporations, including Apple Computer and Hewlett-Packard, began life in a garage or basement. How is it possible for such companies to grow into the giants we see today? No two companies develop in exactly the same way, but the following sections describe some typical stages in the corporate life cycle.

1.2a Starting Up as a Proprietorship

Many companies begin as a **proprietorship**, which is an unincorporated business owned by one individual. Starting a business as a proprietor is easy—one merely begins business operations after obtaining any required city or state business licenses. The proprietorship has three important advantages: (1) it is easily and inexpensively formed, (2) it is subject to few government regulations, and (3) its income is not subject to corporate taxation but is taxed as part of the proprietor's personal income.

However, the proprietorship also has three important limitations: (1) it may be difficult for a proprietorship to obtain the capital needed for growth; (2) the proprietor has unlimited personal liability for the business's debts, which can result in losses that exceed the money invested in the company (creditors may even be able to seize a proprietor's house or other personal property!); and (3) the life of a proprietorship is limited to the life of its founder. For these three reasons, sole proprietorships are used primarily for small businesses. In fact, proprietorships account for only about 13% of all sales, based on dollar values, even though about 80% of all companies are proprietorships.

COLUMBUS WAS WRONG—THE WORLD *IS* FLAT! AND HOT! AND CROWDED!

In his best-selling book *The World Is Flat*, Thomas L. Friedman argues that many of the barriers that long protected businesses and employees from global competition have been broken down by dramatic improvements in communication and transportation technologies. The result is a level playing field that spans the entire world. As we move into the information age, any work that can be digitized will flow to those able to do it at the lowest cost, whether they live in San Jose's Silicon Valley or Bangalore, India. For physical products, supply chains now span the world. For example, raw materials might be extracted in South America, fabricated into electronic components in Asia, and then used in computers assembled in the United States, with the final product being sold in Europe.

Similar changes are occurring in the financial markets, as capital flows across the globe to those who can best use it. Indeed, China raised more money through initial public offerings in 2010 than both Europe and the United States together, and the euro is becoming the currency of choice for denominating global bond issues.

Unfortunately, a dynamic world can bring runaway growth, which can lead to significant environmental problems and energy shortages. Friedman describes these problems in another bestseller, *Hot, Flat, and Crowded*. In a flat world, the keys to success are knowledge, skills, and a great work ethic. In a flat, hot, and crowded world, these factors must be combined with innovation and creativity to deal with truly global problems.

1.2b More Than One Owner: A Partnership

Some companies start with more than one owner, and some proprietors decide to add a partner as the business grows. A **partnership** exists whenever two or more persons or entities associate to conduct a noncorporate business for profit. Partnerships may operate under different degrees of formality, ranging from informal, oral understandings to formal agreements filed with the secretary of the state in which the partnership was formed. Partnership agreements define the ways any profits and losses are shared between partners. A partnership's advantages and disadvantages are generally similar to those of a proprietorship.

Regarding liability, the partners can potentially lose all of their personal assets, even assets not invested in the business, because under partnership law, each partner is liable for the business's debts. Therefore, in the event the partnership goes bankrupt, if any partner is unable to meet his or her pro rata liability then the remaining partners must make good on the unsatisfied claims, drawing on their personal assets to the extent necessary. To avoid this, it is possible to limit the liabilities of some of the partners by establishing a **limited partnership**, wherein certain partners are designated **general partners** and others **limited partners**. In a limited partnership, the limited partners can lose only the amount of their investment in the partnership, while the general partners have unlimited liability. However, the limited partners typically have no control—it rests solely with the general partners—and their returns are likewise limited. Limited partnerships are common in real estate, oil, equipment leasing ventures, and venture capital. However, they are not widely used in general business situations because usually no partner is willing to be the general partner and thus accept the majority of the business's risk, and no partners are willing to be limited partners and give up all control.

In both regular and limited partnerships, at least one partner is liable for the debts of the partnership. However, in a **limited liability partnership (LLP)**, sometimes called a **limited liability company (LLC)**, all partners enjoy limited liability with regard to the business's liabilities, and their potential losses are limited to their investment in the LLP. Of course, this arrangement increases the risk faced by an LLP's lenders, customers, and suppliers.

1.2c Many Owners: A Corporation

Most partnerships have difficulty attracting substantial amounts of capital. This is generally not a problem for a slow-growing business, but if a business's products or services really catch on, and if it needs to raise large sums of money to capitalize on its opportunities, then the difficulty in attracting capital becomes a real drawback. Thus, many growth companies, such as Hewlett-Packard and Microsoft, began life as a proprietorship or partnership, but at some point their founders decided to convert to a corporation. On the other hand, some companies, in anticipation of growth, actually begin as corporations. A **corporation** is a legal entity created under state laws, and it is separate and distinct from its owners and managers. This separation gives the corporation three major advantages: (1) *unlimited life*—a corporation can continue after its original owners and managers are deceased; (2) *easy transferability of ownership interest*—ownership interests are divided into shares of stock, which can be transferred far more easily than can proprietorship or partnership interests; and (3) *limited liability*—losses are limited to the actual funds invested.

To illustrate limited liability, suppose you invested $10,000 in a partnership that then went bankrupt and owed $1 million. Because the owners are liable for the debts of a partnership, you could be assessed for a share of the company's debt, and you could be held liable for the entire $1 million if your partners could not pay their shares. On the other hand, if you invested $10,000 in the stock of a corporation that went bankrupt, your potential loss on the investment would be limited to your $10,000 investment.[1] Unlimited life, easy transferability of ownership interest, and limited liability make it much easier for corporations than proprietorships or partnerships to raise money in the financial markets and grow into large companies.

The corporate form offers significant advantages over proprietorships and partnerships, but it also has two disadvantages: (1) Corporate earnings may be subject to double taxation—the earnings of the corporation are taxed at the corporate level, and then earnings paid out as dividends are taxed again as income to the stockholders. (2) Setting up a corporation involves preparing a charter, writing a set of bylaws, and filing the many required state and federal reports, which is more complex and time-consuming than creating a proprietorship or a partnership.

The **charter** includes the following information: (1) name of the proposed corporation, (2) types of activities it will pursue, (3) amount of capital stock, (4) number of directors, and (5) names and addresses of directors. The charter is filed with the secretary of the state in which the firm will be incorporated, and when it is approved, the corporation is officially in existence.[2] After the corporation begins operating, quarterly and annual employment, financial, and tax reports must be filed with state and federal authorities.

The **bylaws** are a set of rules drawn up by the founders of the corporation. Included are such points as (1) how directors are to be elected (all elected each year or perhaps one-third each year for 3-year terms); (2) whether the existing stockholders will have the first right to buy any new shares the firm issues; and (3) procedures for changing the bylaws themselves, should conditions require it.

There are actually several different types of corporations. Professionals such as doctors, lawyers, and accountants often form a **professional corporation (PC)** or a **professional association (PA)**. These types of corporations do not relieve the participants of professional (malpractice) liability. Indeed, the primary motivation behind the professional corporation was to provide a way for groups of professionals to incorporate and thus avoid certain types of unlimited liability yet still be held responsible for professional liability.

Finally, if certain requirements are met, particularly with regard to size and number of stockholders, owners can establish a corporation but elect to be taxed as if the business were a proprietorship or partnership. Such firms, which differ not in organizational form but only in how their owners are taxed, are called **S corporations**.

1.2d Growing and Managing a Corporation

Once a corporation has been established, how does it evolve? When entrepreneurs start a company, they usually provide all the financing from their personal resources, which may include savings, home equity loans, or even credit cards. As the corporation grows, it will need factories, equipment, inventory, and other resources to support its growth. In time, the entrepreneurs usually deplete their own resources and must turn to external financing. Many young companies are too risky for

---

1. In the case of very small corporations, the limited liability may be fiction because lenders frequently require personal guarantees from the stockholders.
2. More than 60% of major U.S. corporations are chartered in Delaware, which has, over the years, provided a favorable legal environment for corporations. It is not necessary for a firm to be headquartered, or even to conduct operations, in its state of incorporation, or even in its country of incorporation.

banks, so the founders must sell stock to outsiders, including friends, family, private investors (often called angels), or venture capitalists. If the corporation continues to grow, it may become successful enough to attract lending from banks, or it may even raise additional funds through an **initial public offering (IPO)** by selling stock to the public at large. After an IPO, corporations support their growth by borrowing from banks, issuing debt, or selling additional shares of stock. In short, a corporation's ability to grow depends on its interactions with the financial markets, which we describe in much more detail later in this chapter.

For proprietorships, partnerships, and small corporations, the firm's owners are also its managers. This is usually not true for a large corporation, which means that large firms' stockholders, who are its owners, face a serious problem. What is to prevent managers from acting in their own best interests, rather than in the best interests of the stockholder/owners? This is called an **agency problem**, because managers are hired as agents to act on behalf of the owners. Agency problems can be addressed by a company's **corporate governance**, which is the set of rules that controls the company's behavior towards its directors, managers, employees, shareholders, creditors, customers, competitors, and community. We will have much more to say about agency problems and corporate governance throughout the book, especially in Chapters 11, 15, and 17.[3]

Self Test	What are the key differences between proprietorships, partnerships, and corporations?
	Describe some special types of partnerships and corporations, and explain the differences among them.

1.3 The Primary Objective of the Corporation: Value Maximization

Shareholders are the owners of a corporation, and they purchase stocks because they want to earn a good return on their investment without undue risk exposure. In most cases, shareholders elect directors, who then hire managers to run the corporation on a day-to-day basis. Because managers are supposed to be working on behalf of shareholders, they should pursue policies that enhance shareholder value. Consequently, throughout this book we operate on the assumption that management's primary objective is *stockholder wealth maximization.*[4]

---

3. The classic work on agency theory is Michael C. Jensen and William H. Meckling's "Theory of the Firm, Managerial Behavior, Agency Costs, and Ownership Structure," *Journal of Financial Economics,* October 1976, 305–360. Another article by Jensen specifically addresses these issues; see "Value Maximization, Stakeholder Theory, and the Corporate Objective Function," *Journal of Applied Corporate Finance,* Fall 2001, 8–21. For an overview of corporate governance, see Stuart Gillan, "Recent Developments in Corporate Governance: An Overview," *Journal of Corporate Finance,* June 2006, 381–402.

4. This is a reasonable assumption when management has significant ownership in the company or when there is a well-designed management compensation plan. However, it is probably fair to say that when a management compensation plan is poorly designed, *management wealth maximization* may take over and lead to decisions that are inconsistent with shareholder wealth maximization. A good rule of thumb is that when a managerial decision appears to be at odds with shareholder wealth maximization, the explanation is either management's compensation plan or oddities in tax regulations.

The **market price** is the stock price that we observe in the financial markets. We later explain in detail how stock prices are determined, but for now it is enough to say that a company's market price incorporates the information available to investors. If the market price reflects all *relevant* information, then the observed price is also the **intrinsic, or fundamental, price**. However, investors rarely have all relevant information. For example, companies report most major decisions, but they sometimes withhold selected information to prevent competitors from gaining strategic advantages.

Unfortunately, some managers deliberately mislead investors by taking actions to make their companies appear more valuable than they truly are. Sometimes these actions are illegal, such as those taken by the senior managers at Enron. Sometimes the actions are legal but are taken to push the current market price above its fundamental price in the short term. For example, suppose a utility's stock price is equal to its fundamental price of $50 per share. What would happen if the utility substantially reduced its tree-trimming program but didn't tell investors? This would lower current costs and thus boost current earnings and current cash flow, but it would also lead to major expenditures in the future when falling limbs damage the lines. If investors were told about the major repair costs facing the company, the market price would immediately drop to a new fundamental value of $45. But if investors were kept in the dark, they might misinterpret the higher-than-expected current earnings, and the market price might go up to $52. Investors would eventually understand the situation when the company later incurred large costs to repair the damaged lines; when that happened, the price would fall to its fundamental value of $45.

Consider this hypothetical sequence of events for the company above. The managers deceived investors, and the price rose to $52 when it would have fallen to $45 if not for the deception. Of course, this benefited those who owned the stock at the time of the deception, including managers with stock options. But when the deception came to light, those stockholders who still owned the stock suffered a significant loss, ending up with stock worth less than its original fundamental value. If the managers cashed in their stock options prior to this, then only the stockholders were hurt by the deception. Because the managers were hired to act in the interests of stockholders, their deception was a breach of their fiduciary responsibility. In addition, the managers' deception would damage the company's reputation, making it harder to raise capital in the future.

Therefore, when we say management's objective should be to maximize stockholder wealth, we really mean it is to *maximize the fundamental price of the firm's common stock*, not just the current market price. Firms do, of course, have other objectives; in particular, the managers who make the actual decisions are interested in their own personal satisfaction, in their employees' welfare, and in the good of their communities and of society at large. Still, for the reasons set forth in the following sections, *maximizing intrinsic stock value is the most important objective for most corporations.*

1.3a Intrinsic Stock Value Maximization and Social Welfare

If a firm attempts to maximize its intrinsic stock value, is this good or bad for society? In general, it is good. Aside from such illegal actions as fraudulent accounting, exploiting monopoly power, violating safety codes, and failing to meet

ETHICS FOR INDIVIDUALS AND BUSINESSES

A firm's commitment to business ethics can be measured by the tendency of its employees, from the top down, to adhere to laws, regulations, and moral standards relating to product safety and quality, fair employment practices, fair marketing and selling practices, the use of confidential information for personal gain, community involvement, and illegal payments to obtain business.

Ethical Dilemmas. When conflicts arise between profits and ethics, sometimes legal and ethical considerations make the choice obvious. At other times the right choice isn't clear. For example, suppose Norfolk Southern's managers know that its trains are polluting the air, but the amount of pollution is within legal limits and further reduction would be costly, causing harm to their shareholders. Are the managers ethically bound to reduce pollution? Aren't they also ethically bound to act in their shareholders' best interests? This is clearly a dilemma.

Ethical Responsibility. Over the past few years, illegal ethical lapses have led to a number of bankruptcies, which have raised this question: Were the *companies* unethical, or was it just a few of their *employees*? Arthur Andersen, an accounting firm, audited Enron, WorldCom, and several other companies that committed accounting fraud. The U.S. Justice Department concluded that Andersen itself was guilty because it fostered a climate in which unethical behavior was permitted, and it built an incentive system that made such behavior profitable to both the perpetrators and the firm itself. As a result, Andersen went out of business. Andersen was later judged to be not guilty, but by the time the judgment was rendered the company was already out of business. People simply did not want to deal with a tainted accounting firm.

Protecting Ethical Employees. If employees discover questionable activities or are given questionable orders, should they obey their bosses' orders, refuse to obey those orders, or report the situation to a higher authority, such as the company's board of directors, its auditors, or a federal prosecutor? In 2002 Congress passed the Sarbanes-Oxley Act, with a provision designed to protect "whistle-blowers." If an employee reports corporate wrongdoing and later is penalized, he or she can ask the Occupational Safety and Health Administration to investigate the situation, and if the employee was improperly penalized, the company can be required to reinstate the person, along with back pay and a sizable penalty award. Several big awards have been handed out since the act was passed.

environmental standards, *the same actions that maximize intrinsic stock values also benefit society.* Here are some of the reasons:

1. **To a large extent, the owners of stock *are* society.** Seventy-five years ago this was not true, because most stock ownership was concentrated in the hands of a relatively small segment of society consisting of the wealthiest individuals. Since then, there has been explosive growth in pension funds, life insurance companies, and mutual funds. These institutions now own more than 61% of all stock, which means that most individuals have an indirect stake in the stock market. In addition, more than 47% of all U.S. households now own stock or bonds directly, as compared with only 32.5% in 1989. Thus, most members of society now have an important stake in the stock market, either directly or indirectly. Therefore, when a manager takes actions to maximize the stock price, this improves the quality of life for millions of ordinary citizens.
2. **Consumers benefit.** Stock price maximization requires efficient, low-cost businesses that produce high-quality goods and services at the lowest possible cost. This means that companies must develop products and services that consumers want and need, which leads to new technology and new products. Also, companies that maximize their stock price must generate growth in sales by

creating value for customers in the form of efficient and courteous service, adequate stocks of merchandise, and well-located business establishments.

People sometimes argue that firms, in their efforts to raise profits and stock prices, increase product prices and gouge the public. In a reasonably competitive economy, which we have, prices are constrained by competition and consumer resistance. If a firm raises its prices beyond reasonable levels, it will simply lose its market share. Even giant firms such as Dell and Coca-Cola lose business to domestic and foreign competitors if they set prices above the level necessary to cover production costs plus a "normal" profit. Of course, firms *want* to earn more, and they constantly try to cut costs, develop new products, and so on, and thereby earn above-normal profits. Note, though, that if they are indeed successful and do earn above-normal profits, those very profits will attract competition, which will eventually drive prices down. So again, the main long-term beneficiary is the consumer.

3. **Employees benefit.** There are situations where a stock increases when a company announces plans to lay off employees, but viewed over time this is the exception rather than the rule. In general, companies that successfully increase stock prices also grow and add more employees, thus benefiting society. Note too that many governments across the world, including U.S. federal and state governments, are privatizing some of their state-owned activities by selling these operations to investors. Perhaps not surprisingly, the sales and cash flows of recently privatized companies generally improve. Moreover, studies show that newly privatized companies tend to grow and thus require more employees when they are managed with the goal of stock price maximization.

One of *Fortune* magazine's key criteria in determining its list of most-admired companies is a company's ability to attract, develop, and retain talented people. The results consistently show high correlations among admiration for a company, its ability to satisfy employees, and its creation of value for shareholders. Employees find that it is both fun and financially rewarding to work for successful companies. Thus, successful companies get the cream of the employee crop, and skilled, motivated employees are one of the keys to corporate success.

1.3b Managerial Actions to Maximize Shareholder Wealth

What types of actions can managers take to maximize shareholder wealth? To answer this question, we first need to ask, "What determines a firm's value?" In a nutshell, it is *a company's ability to generate cash flows now and in the future.*

We address different aspects of this in detail throughout the book, but we can lay out three basic facts now: (1) any financial asset, including a company's stock, is valuable only to the extent that it generates cash flows; (2) the timing of cash flows matters—cash received sooner is better; and (3) investors are averse to risk, so all else equal, they will pay more for a stock whose cash flows are relatively certain than for one whose cash flows are more risky. Because of these three facts, managers can enhance their firm's value by increasing the size of the expected cash flows, by speeding up their receipt, and by reducing their risk.

The cash flows that matter are called **free cash flows (FCF)**, not because they are free, but because they are available (or free) for distribution to all of the company's investors, including creditors and stockholders. You will learn how to calculate free cash flows in Chapter 7, but for now you should know that free cash flow is:

$$FCF = \text{Sales revenues} - \text{Operating costs} - \text{Operating taxes}$$
$$- \text{Required investments in operating capital}$$

Corporate Scandals and Maximizing Stock Price

The list of corporate scandals seems to go on forever: Sunbeam, Enron, ImClone, WorldCom, Tyco, Adelphia . . . . At first glance, it's tempting to say, "Look what happens when managers care only about maximizing stock price." But a closer look reveals a much different story. In fact, if these managers were trying to maximize stock price, they failed dismally, given the resulting values of these companies.

Although details vary from company to company, a few common themes emerge. First, managerial compensation was linked to the *short-term* performance of the stock price via poorly designed stock option and stock grant programs. This provided managers with a powerful incentive to drive up the stock price at the option vesting date without worrying about the future. Second, it is virtually impossible to take *legal and ethical* actions that drive up the stock price in the short term without harming it in the long term because the value of a company is based on all of its future free cash flows and not just cash flows in the immediate future. Because legal and ethical actions to quickly drive up the stock price didn't exist (other than the old-fashioned ones, such as increasing sales, cutting costs, or reducing capital requirements), these managers began bending a few rules. Third, as they initially got away with bending rules, it seems that their egos and hubris grew to such an extent that they felt they were above all rules, so they began breaking even more rules.

Stock prices did go up, at least temporarily, but as Abraham Lincoln said, "You can't fool all of the people all of the time." As the scandals became public, the stocks' prices plummeted, and in some cases the companies were ruined.

There are several important lessons to be learned from these examples. First, people respond to incentives, and poorly designed incentives can cause disastrous results. Second, ethical violations usually begin with small steps, so if stockholders want managers to avoid large ethical violations, then they shouldn't let them make the small ones. Third, there is no shortcut to creating lasting value. It takes hard work to increase sales, cut costs, and reduce capital requirements, but this is the formula for success.

Brand managers and marketing managers can increase sales (and prices) by truly understanding their customers and then designing goods and services that customers want. Human resource managers can improve productivity through training and employee retention. Production and logistics managers can improve profit margins, reduce inventory, and improve throughput at factories by implementing supply chain management, just-in-time inventory management, and lean manufacturing. In fact, all managers make decisions that can increase free cash flows.

One of the financial manager's roles is to help others see how their actions affect the company's ability to generate cash flow and, hence, its intrinsic value. Financial managers also must decide *how to finance the firm*. In particular, they must choose the mix of debt and equity that should be used and the specific types of debt and equity securities that should be issued. They must also decide what percentage of current earnings should be retained and reinvested rather than paid out as dividends. Along with these financing decisions, the general level of interest rates in the economy, the risk of the firm's operations, and stock market investors' overall attitude toward risk determine the rate of return that is required to satisfy a firm's investors. This rate of return from an investor's perspective is a cost from the company's point of view. Therefore, the rate of return required by investors is called the **weighted average cost of capital (WACC)**.

The relationship between a firm's fundamental value, its free cash flows, and its cost of capital is defined by the following equation:

$$\text{Value} = \frac{\text{FCF}_1}{(1 + \text{WACC})^1} + \frac{\text{FCF}_2}{(1 + \text{WACC})^2} + \frac{\text{FCF}_3}{(1 + \text{WACC})^3} + \cdots + \frac{\text{FCF}_\infty}{(1 + \text{WACC})^\infty} \qquad (1\text{–}1)$$

We will explain how to use this equation in later chapters, but for now note that (1) a growing firm often needs to raise external funds in the financial markets and (2) the actual price of a firm's stock is determined in those markets. Therefore, the rest of this chapter focuses on financial markets.

Self Test

What should be management's primary objective?

How does maximizing the fundamental stock price benefit society?

Free cash flow depends on what three factors?

How is a firm's fundamental value related to its free cash flows and its cost of capital?

1.4 Financial Securities

The variety of financial securities is limited only by human creativity, ingenuity, and governmental regulations. At the risk of oversimplification, we can classify most financial securities by the type of claim and the time until maturity. In addition, some securities actually are created from packages of other securities. We discuss the key aspects of financial securities in this section.

www

You can access current and historical interest rates and economic data from the Federal Reserve Economic Data (FRED) site at **www.stls.frb.org/fred**.

1.4a Type of Claim: Debt, Equity, or Derivatives

Financial securities are simply pieces of paper with contractual provisions that entitle their owners to specific rights and claims on specific cash flows or values. Debt instruments typically have specified payments and a specified maturity. For example, an Alcoa bond might promise to pay 10% interest for 30 years, at which time it promises to make a $1,000 principal payment. If debt matures in more than a year, it is called a *capital market security*. Thus, the Alcoa bond in this example is a capital market security.

If the debt matures in less than a year, it is a *money market security*. For example, Home Depot might expect to receive $300,000 in 75 days, but it needs cash now. Home Depot might issue commercial paper, which is essentially an IOU. In this example, Home Depot might agree to pay $300,000 in 75 days in exchange for $297,000 today. Thus, commercial paper is a money market security.

Equity instruments are a claim upon a residual value. For example, Alcoa's stockholders are entitled to the cash flows generated by Alcoa after its bondholders, creditors, and other claimants have been satisfied. Because stock has no maturity date, it is a capital market security.

Notice that debt and equity represent claims upon the cash flows generated by real assets, such as the cash flows generated by Alcoa's factories and operations.

WEB

For an overview of derivatives, see **Web Extension 1A** on the textbook's Web site.

In contrast, **derivatives** are securities whose values depend on, or are *derived* from, the values of some other traded assets. For example, options and futures are two important types of derivatives, and their values depend on the prices of other assets. An option on Alcoa stock or a futures contract to buy pork bellies are examples of derivatives. We discuss options in Chapter 6 and in *Web Extension 1A*, which provides a brief overview of options and other derivatives.

Some securities are a mix of debt, equity, and derivatives. For example, preferred stock has some features like debt and some like equity, while convertible debt has both debt-like and option-like features.

We discuss these and other financial securities in detail later in the book, but Table 1-1 provides a summary of the most important conventional financial securities. We discuss rates of return later in this chapter, but notice now in Table 1-1 that interest rates tend to increase with the maturity and risk of the security.

Some securities are created from packages of other securities, a process called *securitization*. The misuse of securitized assets is one of the primary causes of the global financial crisis, so we discuss securitization next.

1.4b The Process of Securitization

Many types of assets can be securitized, but we will focus on mortgages because they played such an important role in the global financial crisis. At one time, most mortgages were made by **savings and loan associations (S&Ls)**, which took in the vast majority of their deposits from individuals who lived in nearby neighborhoods. The S&Ls pooled these deposits and then lent money to people in the neighborhood in the form of fixed-rate mortgages, which were pieces of paper signed by borrowers promising to make specified payments to the S&L. The new homeowners paid principal and interest to the S&L, which then paid interest to its depositors and reinvested the principal repayments in other mortgages. This was clearly better than having individuals lend directly to aspiring homeowners, because a single individual might not have enough money to finance an entire house or the expertise to know if the borrower was creditworthy. Note that the S&Ls were government-chartered institutions, and they obtained money in the form of immediately withdrawable deposits and then invested most of it in the form of mortgages with fixed interest rates and on individual homes. Also, initially the S&Ls were not permitted to have branch operations—they were limited to one office so as to maintain their local orientation.

These restrictions had important implications. First, in the 1950s there was a massive migration of people to the west, so there was a strong demand for funds in that area. However, the wealthiest savers were in the east. That meant that mortgage interest rates were much higher in California and other western states than in New York and the east. This created disequilibrium, something that can't exist forever in financial markets.

Second, note that the S&Ls' assets consisted mainly of long-term, fixed-rate mortgages, but their liabilities were in the form of deposits that could be withdrawn immediately. The combination of long-term assets and short-term liabilities created another problem. If the overall level of interest rates increased, the S&Ls would have to increase the rates they paid on deposits or else savers would take their money elsewhere. However, the S&Ls couldn't increase the rates on their outstanding mortgages because these mortgages had fixed interest rates. This problem came to a head in the 1960s, when the Vietnam War led to inflation, which pushed up interest rates. At this point, the "money market fund" industry was born, and it literally sucked money out of the S&Ls, forcing many of them into bankruptcy.

TABLE 1-1   Summary of Major Financial Instruments

Instrument	Major Participants	Risk	Original Maturity	Rates of Return on 5/10/11[a]
U.S. Treasury bills	Sold by U.S. Treasury	Default-free	91 days to 1 year	0.07%
Bankers' acceptances	A firm's promise to pay, guaranteed by a bank	Low if strong bank guarantees	Up to 180 days	0.33%
Commercial paper	Issued by financially secure firms to large investors	Low default risk	Up to 270 days	0.17%
Negotiable certificates of deposit (CDs)	Issued by major banks to large investors	Depends on strength of issuer	Up to 1 year	0.30%
Money market mutual funds	Invest in short-term debt; held by individuals and businesses	Low degree of risk	No specific maturity (instant liquidity)	0.62%
Eurodollar market time deposits	Issued by banks outside the United States	Depends on strength of issuer	Up to 1 year	0.30%
Consumer credit loans	Loans by banks/credit unions/ finance companies	Risk is variable	Variable	Variable
Commercial loans	Loans by banks to corporations	Depends on borrower	Up to 7 years	Tied to prime rate (3.25%) or LIBOR (0.42%)[b]
U.S. Treasury notes and bonds	Issued by U.S. government	No default risk, but price falls if interest rates rise	2 to 30 years	3.17%
Mortgages	Loans secured by property	Risk is variable	Up to 30 years	3.94%
Municipal bonds	Issued by state and local governments to individuals and institutions	Riskier than U.S. government bonds, but exempt from most taxes	Up to 30 years	3.95%
Corporate bonds	Issued by corporations to individuals and institutions	Riskier than U.S. government debt; depends on strength of issuer	Up to 40 years[c]	4.97%
Leases	Similar to debt; firms lease assets rather than borrow and then buy them	Risk similar to corporate bonds	Generally 3 to 20 years	Similar to bond yields
Preferred stocks	Issued by corporations to individuals and institutions	Riskier than corporate bonds	Unlimited	6% to 9%
Common stocks[d]	Issued by corporations to individuals and institutions	Riskier than preferred stocks	Unlimited	9% to 15%

© Cengage Learning 2013

[a]Data are from *The Wall Street Journal* (**online.wsj.com**) or the *Federal Reserve Statistical Release* (**www.federalreserve.gov/ releases/H15/update**). Bankers' acceptances assume a 3-month maturity. Money market rates are for the Merrill Lynch Ready Assets Trust. The corporate bond rate is for AAA-rated bonds.

[b]The prime rate is the rate U.S. banks charge to good customers. LIBOR (London Interbank Offered Rate) is the rate that U.K. banks charge one another.

[c]A few corporations have issued 100-year bonds; however, most have issued bonds with maturities of less than 40 years.

[d]Common stocks are expected to provide a "return" in the form of dividends and capital gains rather than interest. Of course, if you buy a stock, your *actual* return may be considerably higher or lower than your *expected* return.

The government responded by giving the S&Ls broader lending powers, permitting nationwide branching and allowing them to obtain funds as long-term debt in addition to immediately withdrawable deposits. Unfortunately, these changes had another set of unintended consequences. S&L managers who had previously dealt with a limited array of investments and funding choices in local communities were suddenly allowed to expand their scope of operations. Many of these inexperienced S&L managers made poor business decisions and the result was disastrous—virtually the entire S&L industry collapsed, with many S&Ls going bankrupt or being acquired in shotgun mergers with commercial banks.

The demise of the S&Ls created another financial disequilibrium—a higher demand for mortgages than the supply of available funds from the mortgage lending industry. Savings were accumulating in pension funds, insurance companies, and other institutions, not in S&Ls and banks, the traditional mortgage lenders.

This situation led to the development of "mortgage securitization," a process whereby banks, the remaining S&Ls, and specialized mortgage originating firms would originate mortgages and then sell them to investment banks, which would bundle them into packages and then use these packages as collateral for bonds that could be sold to pension funds, insurance companies, and other institutional investors. Thus, individual loans were bundled and then used to back a bond—a "security"—that could be traded in the financial markets.

Congress facilitated this process by creating two stockholder-owned but government-sponsored entities, the Federal National Mortgage Association (Fannie Mae) and the Federal Home Loan Mortgage Corporation (Freddie Mac). Fannie Mae and Freddie Mac were financed by issuing a relatively small amount of stock and a huge amount of debt.

To illustrate the securitization process, suppose an S&L or bank is paying its depositors 5% but is charging its borrowers 8% on their mortgages. The S&L can take hundreds of these mortgages, put them in a pool, and then sell the pool to Fannie Mae. The mortgagees can still make their payments to the original S&L, which will then forward the payments (less a small handling fee) to Fannie Mae.

Consider the S&L's perspective. First, it can use the cash it receives from selling the mortgages to make additional loans to other aspiring homeowners. Second, the S&L is no longer exposed to the risk of owning mortgages. The risk hasn't disappeared—it has been transferred from the S&L (and its federal deposit insurers) to Fannie Mae. This is clearly a better situation for aspiring homeowners and perhaps also for taxpayers.

Fannie Mae can take the mortgages it just bought, put them into a very large pool, and sell bonds backed by the pool to investors. The homeowner will pay the S&L, the S&L will forward the payment to Fannie Mae, and Fannie Mae will use the funds to pay interest on the bonds it issued, to pay dividends on its stock, and to buy additional mortgages from S&Ls, which can then make additional loans to aspiring homeowners. Notice that the mortgage risk has been shifted from Fannie Mae to the investors who now own the mortgage-backed bonds.

How does the situation look from the perspective of the investors who own the bonds? In theory, they own a share in a large pool of mortgages from all over the country, so a problem in a particular region's real estate market or job market won't affect the whole pool. Therefore, their expected rate of return should be very close to the 8% rate paid by the home-owning mortgagees. (It will be a little less due to handling fees charged by the S&L and Fannie Mae and to the small amount of expected losses from the homeowners who could be expected to default on their mortgages.) These investors could have deposited their money at an S&L and earned a virtually risk-free 5%. Instead, they chose to accept more risk in hopes of the higher 8% return. Note too that mortgage-backed bonds are more liquid than individual mortgage loans, so the securitization process increases liquidity, which is desirable. The bottom line is that risk has been reduced by the pooling process and then allocated to those who are willing to accept it in return for a higher rate of return.

Thus, in theory it is a win–win–win situation: More money is available for aspiring homeowners, S&Ls (and taxpayers) have less risk, and there are opportunities for investors who are willing to take on more risk to obtain higher potential returns. Although the securitization process began with mortgages, it is now being used with car loans, student loans, credit card debt, and other loans. The details vary for different assets, but the processes and benefits are similar to those with mortgage securitization: (1) increased supplies of lendable funds; (2) transfer of risk to those who are willing to bear it; and (3) increased liquidity for holders of the debt.

Mortgage securitization was a win–win situation in theory, but as practiced in the last decade it has turned into a lose–lose situation. We will have more to say about securitization and the global economic crisis later in this chapter, but first let's take a look at the cost of money.

1.5 The Cost of Money

In a free economy, capital from those with available funds is allocated through the price system to users who have a need for funds. The interaction of the providers' supply and the users' demand determines the cost (or price) of money, which is the rate users pay to providers. For debt, we call this price the **interest rate**. For equity, we call it the **cost of equity**, and it consists of the dividends and capital gains stockholders expect. Keep in mind that the "price" of money is a cost from a user's perspective but a return from the provider's point of view.

Notice in Table 1-1 that a financial instrument's rate of return generally increases as its maturity and risk increase. We will have much more to say about the relationships among an individual security's features, risk, and return later in the book, but there are some fundamental factors and economic conditions that affect all financial instruments.

1.5a Fundamental Factors That Affect the Cost of Money

The four most fundamental factors affecting the cost of money are (1) **production opportunities**, (2) **time preferences for consumption**, (3) **risk**, and (4) **inflation**. By production opportunities, we mean the ability to turn capital into benefits. If a business raises capital, the benefits are determined by the expected rates of return on its production opportunities. If a student borrows to finance his or her education, the benefits are higher expected future salaries (and, of course, the sheer joy of learning!). If a homeowner borrows, the benefits are the pleasure from living in his or her own home, plus any expected appreciation in the value of the home. Observe that the expected rates of return on these "production opportunities" put an upper limit on how much users can pay to providers.

Providers can use their current funds for consumption or saving. By saving, they give up consumption now in the expectation of having more consumption in the future. If providers have a strong preference for consumption now, then it takes high interest rates to induce them to trade current consumption for future consumption. Therefore, the time preference for consumption has a major impact on the cost of money. Notice that the time preference for consumption varies for different individuals, for different age groups, and for different cultures. For example, people in Japan have a lower time preference for consumption than those in the United States, which partially explains why Japanese families tend to save more than U.S. families even though interest rates are lower in Japan.

If the expected rate of return on an investment is risky, then providers require a higher expected return to induce them to take the extra risk, which drives up the cost of money. As you will see later in this book, the risk of a security is determined by market conditions and the security's particular features.

Inflation also leads to a higher cost of money. For example, suppose you earned 10% one year on your investment but inflation caused prices to increase by 20%. This means you can't consume as much at the end of the year as when you originally invested your money. Obviously, if you had expected 20% inflation, you would have required a higher rate of return than 10%.

1.5b Economic Conditions and Policies That Affect the Cost of Money

www

The home page for the Board of Governors of the Federal Reserve System can be found at **www .federalreserve.gov**. You can access general information about the Federal Reserve, including press releases, speeches, and monetary policy.

Economic conditions and policies also affect the cost of money. These include: (1) Federal Reserve policy; (2) the federal budget deficit or surplus; (3) the level of business activity; and (4) international factors, including the foreign trade balance, the international business climate, and exchange rates.

Federal Reserve Policy

If the Federal Reserve Board wants to stimulate the economy, it most often uses open market operations to purchase Treasury securities held by banks. Because banks are selling some of their securities, the banks will have more cash, which increases their supply of loanable funds, which in turn makes banks willing to lend more money at lower interest rates. In addition, the Fed's purchases represent an increase in the demand for Treasury securities. As for anything that is for sale, increased demand causes Treasury securities' prices to go up and interest rates to go down. The net result is a reduction in interest rates, which stimulates the economy by making it less costly for companies to borrow for new projects or for individuals to borrow for major purchases or other expenditures.

When banks sell their holdings of Treasury securities to the Fed, the banks' reserves go up, which increases the money supply. A larger money supply ultimately leads to an increase in expected inflation, which eventually pushes interest rates up. Thus, the Fed can stimulate the economy in the short term by driving down interest rates and increasing the money supply, but this creates longer-term inflationary pressures. This is exactly the dilemma facing the Fed in mid-2011. If the Fed wishes to slow down the economy and reduce inflation, the Fed reverses the process. Instead of purchasing Treasury securities, the Fed sells Treasury securities to banks, which causes an increase in short-term interest rates but a decrease in long-term inflationary pressures.

Budget Deficits or Surpluses

If the federal government spends more than it takes in from tax revenues then it's running a deficit, and that deficit must be covered either by borrowing or by printing money (increasing the money supply). The government borrows by issuing new Treasury securities. All else held equal, this creates a greater supply of Treasury securities, which leads to lower security prices and higher interest rates. Other federal government actions that increase the money supply also increase expectations for future inflation, which drives up interest rates. Thus, the larger the federal deficit, other things held constant, the higher the level of interest rates. Since 1962, the federal government has run a deficit every year except two (2000 and 2001). Annual deficits in the mid-1990s were in the $250 billion range, while the 2009 and 2010 deficits were about six times that level at $1.5 and $1.4 trillion. These huge deficits have contributed to the cumulative federal debt, which as of mid-2011 stands at over $14 trillion.

Business Activity

Figure 1-1 shows interest rates, inflation, and recessions. Notice that interest rates and inflation typically rise prior to a recession and fall afterward. There are several reasons for this pattern.

Consumer demand slows during a recession, keeping companies from increasing prices, which reduces price inflation. Companies also cut back on hiring, which reduces wage inflation. Less disposable income causes consumers to reduce their purchases of homes and automobiles, reducing consumer demand for loans. Companies reduce investments in new operations, which reduces their demand for funds. The cumulative effect is downward pressure on inflation and interest rates. The Federal Reserve is also active during recessions, trying to stimulate the economy by driving down interest rates.

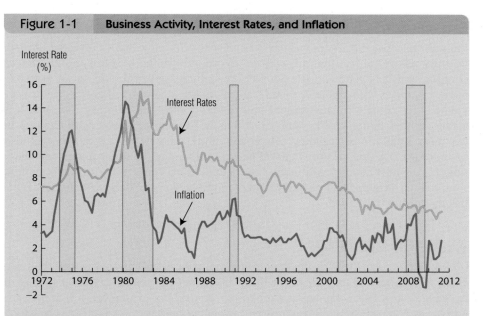

Figure 1-1   Business Activity, Interest Rates, and Inflation

Notes:
1. Tick marks represent January 1 of the year.
2. The shaded areas designate business recessions as defined by the National Bureau of Economic Research; see **www.nber.org/cycles**.
3. Interest rates are for AAA corporate bonds; see the St. Louis Federal Reserve Web site: **http://research.stlouisfed.org/fred/**. These rates reflect the average rate during the month ending on the date shown.
4. Inflation is measured by the annual rate of change for the Consumer Price Index (CPI) for the preceding 12 months; see **http://research.stlouisfed.org/fred/**.

© Cengage Learning 2013

International Trade Deficits or Surpluses

Businesses and individuals in the United States buy from and sell to people and firms in other countries. If we buy more than we sell (that is, if we import more than we export), we are said to be running a *foreign trade deficit*. When trade deficits occur, they must be financed, and the main source of financing is debt. In other words, if we import $200 billion of goods but export only $90 billion, we run a trade deficit of $110 billion, and we will probably borrow the $110 billion.[5] Therefore, the larger our trade deficit, the more we must borrow, and increased borrowing drives up interest rates. Also, international investors are willing to hold U.S. debt if and only if the risk-adjusted rate paid on this debt is competitive with interest rates in other countries. Therefore, if the Federal Reserve attempts to lower interest rates in the United States, causing our rates to fall below rates abroad (after adjustments for expected changes in the exchange rate), then international investors will sell U.S. bonds, which will depress bond prices and result in higher U.S. rates. Thus, if the trade deficit is large relative to the size of the overall economy, it will hinder the Fed's ability to reduce interest rates and combat a recession.

The United States has been running annual trade deficits since the mid-1970s, and the cumulative effect of trade deficits and budget deficits is that the United States has become the largest debtor nation of all time. As noted earlier, this federal debt exceeds *$14 trillion!* As a result, our interest rates are very much influenced by interest rates in other countries around the world.

International Country Risk

International risk factors may increase the cost of money that is invested abroad. **Country risk** is the risk that arises from investing or doing business in a particular country, and it depends on the country's economic, political, and social environment. Countries with stable economic, social, political, and regulatory systems provide a safer climate for investment and therefore have less country risk than less stable nations. Examples of country risk include the risk associated with changes in tax rates, regulations, currency conversion, and exchange rates. Country risk also includes the risk that (1) property will be expropriated without adequate compensation; (2) the host country will impose new stipulations concerning local production, sourcing, or hiring practices; and (3) there might be damage or destruction of facilities due to internal strife.

Exchange Rate Risk

International securities frequently are denominated in a currency other than the dollar, which means that the value of an investment depends on what happens to exchange rates. This is known as **exchange rate risk**. For example, if a U.S. investor purchases a Japanese bond, interest will probably be paid in Japanese yen, which must then be converted to dollars if the investor wants to spend his or her money in the United States. If the yen weakens relative to the dollar, then the yen will buy fewer dollars when it comes time for the investor to convert the Japanese bond's payout. Alternatively, if the yen strengthens relative to the dollar, the investor will earn higher dollar returns. It therefore follows that the effective rate of return on a

---

5. The deficit could also be financed by selling assets, including gold, corporate stocks, entire companies, and real estate. The United States has financed its massive trade deficits by all of these means in recent years, but the primary method has been by borrowing from foreigners.

foreign investment will depend on both the performance of the foreign security in its home market and on what happens to exchange rates over the life of the investment. We discuss exchange rates in detail in Chapter 27.

1.6 The Global Economic Crisis

Although the global economic crisis has many causes, mortgage securitization in the 2000s is certainly one culprit, so we begin with it.

1.6a The Globalization of Mortgage Market Securitization

A national TV program ran a documentary on the travails of Norwegian retirees resulting from defaults on Florida mortgages. Your first reaction might be to wonder how Norwegian retirees became financially involved with risky Florida mortgages. We will break the answer to that question into two parts. First, we will identify the different links in the financial chain between the retirees and mortgagees. Second, we will explain why there were so many weak links.

In the movie *Jerry Maguire,* Tom Cruise said, "Show me the money!" That's a good way to start identifying the financial links, starting with a single home purchase in Florida.

Home Purchase

In exchange for cash, a seller in Florida turned over ownership of a house to a buyer.

Mortgage Origination

To get the cash used to purchase the house, the home buyer signed a mortgage loan agreement and gave it to an "originator." Years ago the originator would probably have been an S&L or a bank, but more recently the originators have been specialized mortgage brokers, which was true in this case. The broker gathered and examined the borrower's credit information, arranged for an independent appraisal of the house's value, handled the paperwork, and received a fee for these services.

Securitization and Resecuritization

In exchange for cash, the originator sold the mortgage to a securitizing firm. For example, Merrill Lynch's investment banking operation was a major player in securitizing loans. It would bundle large numbers of mortgages into pools and then create new securities that had claims on the pools' cash flows. Some claims were simple, such as a proportional share of a pool, and some claims were more complex, such as a claim on all interest payments during the first 5 years or a claim on only principal payments. More complicated claims were entitled to a fixed payment, while other claims would receive payments only after the "senior" claimants had been paid. These slices of the pool were called "tranches," which comes from a French word for slice.

Some of the tranches were themselves re-combined and then re-divided into securities called collateralized debt obligations (CDOs), some of which were themselves combined and subdivided into other securities, commonly called CDOs-squared. For example, Lehman Brothers often bought different tranches, split them into CDOs of differing risk, and then had the different CDOs rated by an agency like Moody's or Standard & Poor's.

There are two very important points to notice. First, the process didn't change the *total amount of risk* embedded in the mortgages, but it did make it possible to create some securities that were less risky than average and some that were more risky. Second, each time a new security was created or rated, fees were being earned by the investment banks and rating agencies.

The Investors

In exchange for cash, the securitizing firms sold the newly created securities to individual investors, hedge funds, college endowments, insurance companies, and other financial institutions, including a pension fund in Norway. Keep in mind that financial institutions are themselves funded by individuals, so cash begins with individuals and flows through the system until it is eventually received by the seller of the home. If all goes according to plan, payments on the mortgages eventually return to the individuals who originally provided the cash. But in this case, the chain was broken by a wave of mortgage defaults, resulting in problems for Norwegian retirees.

Students and managers often ask us, "What happened to all the money?" The short answer is "It went from investors to home sellers, with fees being skimmed off all along the way."

Although the process is complex, in theory there is nothing inherently wrong with it. In fact, it should, in theory, provide more funding for U.S. home purchasers, and it should allow risk to be shifted to those best able to bear it. Unfortunately, this isn't the end of the story.

1.6b The Dark Side of Securitization: The Sub-Prime Mortgage Meltdown

What caused the financial crisis? Entire books have been written on this subject, but we can identify a few of the culprits.

Regulators Approved Sub-Prime Standards

In the 1980s and early 1990s, regulations did not permit a nonqualifying mortgage to be securitized, so most originators mandated that borrowers meet certain requirements, including having at least a certain minimum level of income relative to the mortgage payments and a minimum down payment relative to the size of the mortgage. But in the mid-1990s, Washington politicians wanted to extend home ownership to groups that traditionally had difficulty obtaining mortgages. To accomplish this, regulations were relaxed so that nonqualifying mortgages could be securitized. Such loans are commonly called sub-prime or Alt-A mortgages. Thus, riskier mortgages were soon being securitized and sold to investors. Again, there was nothing inherently wrong, provided the two following questions were being answered in the affirmative: One, were home buyers making sound decisions regarding their ability to repay the loans? And two, did the ultimate investors recognize the additional risk? We now know that the answer to both questions is a resounding "no." Homeowners were signing mortgages that they could not hope to repay, and investors treated these mortgages as if they were much safer than they actually were.

The Fed Helped Fuel the Real Estate Bubble

With more people able to get a mortgage, including people who should not have obtained one, the demand for homes increased. This alone would have driven up house prices. However, the Fed also slashed interest rates to historic lows after the terrorist attacks of 9/11 to prevent a recession, and it kept them low for a long time. These low rates made mortgage payments lower, which made home owner-ship seem even more affordable, again contributing to an increase in the demand for housing. Figure 1-2 shows that the combination of lower mortgage qualifi-cations and lower interest rates caused house prices to skyrocket. Thus, the Fed contributed to an artificial bubble in real estate.

Home Buyers Wanted More for Less

Even with low interest rates, how could sub-prime borrowers afford the mortgage payments, especially with house prices rising? First, most sub-prime borrowers chose an adjustable rate mortgage (ARM) with an interest rate based on a short-term rate, such as that on 1-year Treasury bonds, to which the lender added a couple of percentage points. Because the Fed had pushed short-term rates so low, the initial rates on ARMs were very low.

With a traditional fixed-rate mortgage, the payments remain fixed over time. But with an ARM, an increase in market interest rates triggers higher monthly pay-ments, so an ARM is riskier than a fixed-rate mortgage. However, many borrowers

Figure 1-2   The Real Estate Boom: Housing Prices and Mortgage Rates

Notes:

1. The real estate index is the Case-Shiller composite index for house prices in 10 real estate markets, available at **www.standardandpoors.com/indices/sp-case-shiller-home-price-indices/en/us/?indexId=spusa**.

2. Interest rates are for 30-year conventional fixed-rate mortgages, available from the St. Louis Federal Reserve: **http://research.stlouisfed.org/fred/**.

© Cengage Learning 2013

chose an *even riskier* mortgage, the "option ARM," where the borrower can choose to make such low payments during the first couple of years that they don't even cover the interest, causing the loan balance to actually increase each month! At a later date, the payments would be reset to reflect both the current market interest rate and the higher loan balance. For example, in some cases a monthly payment of $948 for the first 32 months was reset to $2,454 for the remaining 328 months.

Why would anyone who couldn't afford to make a $2,454 monthly payment choose an option ARM? Here are three possible reasons. First, some borrowers simply didn't understand the situation and were victims of predatory lending practices by brokers eager to earn fees regardless of the consequences. Second, some borrowers thought that the home price would go up enough to allow them to sell at a profit or else refinance with another low-payment loan. Third, some people were simply greedy and short-sighted, and they wanted to live in a better home than they could afford.

Mortgage Brokers Didn't Care

Years ago, S&Ls and banks had a vested interest in the mortgages they originated because they held them for the life of the loan—up to 30 years. If a mortgage went bad, the bank or S&L would lose money, so they were careful to verify that the borrower would be able to repay the loan. In the bubble years, though, over 80% of mortgages were arranged by independent mortgage brokers who received a commission. Thus, the broker's incentive was to complete deals even if the borrowers couldn't make the payments after the soon-to-come reset. So it's easy to understand (but not to approve!) why brokers pushed deals onto borrowers who were almost certain to default eventually.

Real Estate Appraisers Were Lax

The relaxed regulations didn't require the mortgage broker to verify the borrower's income, so these loans were called "liar loans" because the borrowers could overstate their income. But even in these cases, the broker had to get an appraisal showing that the house's value was greater than the loan amount. Many real estate appraisers simply assumed that house prices would keep going up, so they were willing to appraise houses at unrealistically high values. Like the mortgage brokers, they were paid at the time of their service. Other than damage to their reputations, they weren't concerned if the borrower later defaulted and the value of the house turned out to be less than the remaining loan balance, causing a loss for the lender.

Originators and Securitizers Wanted Quantity, Not Quality

Originating institutions like Countrywide Financial and New Century Mortgage made money when they sold the mortgages, long before any of the mortgages defaulted. The same is true for securitizing firms such as Bear Stearns, Merrill Lynch, and Lehman Brothers. Their incentives were to generate volume originating loans, not to make sure the loans should have been made. This started at the top—CEOs and other top executives received stock options and bonuses based on their firms' profits, and profits depended on volume. Thus, the top officers pushed their subordinates to generate volume, those subordinates pushed the originators to write more mortgages, and the originators pushed the appraisers to come up with high values.

Rating Agencies Were Lax

Investors who purchased the complicated mortgage-backed securities wanted to know how risky they were, so they insisted on seeing the bonds' "ratings." Rating agencies were paid to investigate the details of each bond and to assign a rating that reflected the security's risk. The securitizing firms paid the rating agencies to do the ratings. For example, Lehman Brothers hired Moody's to rate some of their CDOs. Indeed, the investment banks would actually pay for advice from the rating agencies as they were designing the securities. The rating and consulting activities were extremely lucrative for the agencies, which ignored the obvious conflict of interest: The investment bank wanted a high rating, the rating agency got paid to help design securities that would qualify for a high rating, and high ratings led to continued business for the raters.

Insurance Wasn't Insurance

To provide a higher rating and make these mortgage-backed securities look even more attractive to investors, the issuers would frequently purchase a type of insurance policy on the security called a **credit default swap**. For example, suppose you had wanted to purchase a CDO from Lehman Brothers but were worried about the risk. What if Lehman Brothers had agreed to pay an annual fee to an insurance company like AIG, which would guarantee the CDO's payments if the underlying mortgages defaulted? You probably would have felt confident enough to buy the CDO.

But any similarity to a conventional insurance policy ends here. Unlike home insurance, where there is a single policyholder and a single insurer, totally uninvolved speculators can also make bets on your CDO by either selling or purchasing credit default swaps on the CDO. For example, a hedge fund could buy a credit default swap on your CDO if it thinks the CDO will default; or an investment bank like Bear Stearns could sell a swap, betting that the CDO won't default. In fact, the International Swaps and Derivatives Association estimates that in mid-2008 there was about $54 trillion in credit default swaps. This staggering amount was approximately 7 times the value of all U.S. mortgages, over 4 times the level of the U.S. national debt, and over twice the value of the entire U.S. stock market.

Another big difference is that home insurance companies are highly regulated, but there was virtually no regulation in the credit default swap market. The players traded directly among themselves, with no central clearinghouse. It was almost impossible to tell how much risk any of the players had taken on, making it impossible to know whether or not counterparties like AIG would be able to fulfill their obligations in the event of a CDO default. And that made it impossible to know the value of CDOs held by many banks, which in turn made it impossible to judge whether or not those banks were de facto bankrupt.

Rocket Scientists Had Poor Rearview Mirrors

Brilliant financial experts, often trained in physics and hired from rocket science firms, built elegant models to determine the value of these new securities. Unfortunately, a model is only as good as its inputs. The experts looked at the high growth rates of recent real estate prices (see Figure 1-2) and assumed that future growth rates also would be high. These high growth rates caused models to calculate very high CDO prices, at least until the real estate market crumbled.

Investors Wanted More for Less

In the early 2000s, low-rated debt (including mortgage-backed securities), hedge funds, and private equity funds produced great rates of return. Many investors jumped into this debt to keep up with the Joneses. As shown in Chapter 4 when we discuss bond ratings and bond spreads, investors began lowering the premium they required for taking on extra risk. Thus, investors focused primarily on returns and largely ignored risk. In fairness, some investors assumed the credit ratings were accurate, and they trusted the representatives of the investment banks selling the securities. In retrospect, however, Warren Buffett's maxim that "I only invest in companies I understand" seems wiser than ever.

The Emperor Has No Clothes

In 2006, many of the option ARMs began to reset, borrowers began to default, and home prices first leveled off and then began to fall. Things got worse in 2007 and 2008, and by early 2009, almost 1 out of 10 mortgages was in default or foreclosure, resulting in displaced families and virtual ghost towns of new subdivisions. As homeowners defaulted on their mortgages, so did the CDOs backed by the mortgages. That brought down the counterparties like AIG who had insured the CDOs via credit default swaps. Virtually overnight, investors realized that mortgage-backed security default rates were headed higher and that the houses used as collateral were worth less than the mortgages. Mortgage-backed security prices plummeted, investors quit buying newly securitized mortgages, and liquidity in the secondary market disappeared. Thus, the investors who owned these securities were stuck with pieces of paper that were substantially lower than the values reported on their balance sheets.

1.6c From Sub-Prime Meltdown to Liquidity Crisis to Economic Crisis

Like the Andromeda strain, the sub-prime meltdown went viral, and it ended up infecting almost all aspects of the economy. Financial institutions were the first to fall. Many originating firms had not sold all of their sub-prime mortgages, and they failed. For example, New Century declared bankruptcy in 2007, IndyMac was placed under FDIC control in 2008, and Countrywide was acquired by Bank of America in 2008 to avoid bankruptcy.

Securitizing firms also crashed, partly because they kept some of the new securities they created. For example, Fannie Mae and Freddie Mac had huge losses on their portfolio assets, causing them to be virtually taken over by the Federal Housing Finance Agency in 2008. In addition to big losses on their own sub-prime portfolios, many investment banks also had losses related to their positions in credit default swaps. Thus, Lehman Brothers was forced into bankruptcy, Bear Stearns was sold to JPMorgan Chase, and Merrill Lynch was sold to Bank of America, with huge losses to their stockholders.

Because Lehman Brothers defaulted on some of its commercial paper, investors in the Reserve Primary Fund, a big money market mutual fund, saw the value of its investments "break the buck," dropping to less than a dollar per share. To avoid panic and a total lockdown in the money markets, the U.S. Treasury agreed to insure some investments in money market funds.

AIG was the largest backer of credit default swaps, and it operated worldwide. In 2008 it became obvious that AIG could not honor its commitments as a counterparty, so the Fed effectively nationalized AIG to avoid a domino effect in which AIG's failure would topple hundreds of other financial institutions.

In normal times, banks provide liquidity to the economy and funding for creditworthy businesses and individuals. These activities are absolutely crucial for a well-functioning economy. However, the financial contagion spread to commercial banks because some owned mortgage-backed securities, some owned commercial paper issued by failing institutions, and some had exposure to credit default swaps. As banks worried about their survival in the fall of 2008, they stopped providing credit to other banks and businesses. The market for commercial paper dried up to such an extent that the Fed began buying new commercial paper from issuing companies.

Banks also began hoarding cash rather than lending it. The Fed requires banks to keep 10% of the funds they raise from depositors on "reserve." Banks use the other 90% to make loans or to buy securities. In aggregate, there usually has been about $9 billion in excess reserves—that is, reserves over and above the 10% they are required to keep on hand. However, at the end of 2008, banks held over $770 billion in excess reserves compared to $75 billion in required reserves. As of May 2011, excess reserves stand at almost double this figure, $1.4 trillion. This hoarding may reduce the banks' risk, but it deprives the economy of much-needed capital.

The reduction in construction, manufacturing, retailing, and consumption caused job losses in 2008 and 2009, exacerbated the recession that began in late 2007, and weakened the recovery that nominally began in June 2009. The recession itself was the worst recession since the Great Depression of the 1930s and was international in its scope.

Briefly describe some of the mistakes that were made by participants in the sub-prime mortgage process.

1.7 The Big Picture

Finance has a lot of vocabulary and tools that might be new to you. To help you avoid getting bogged down in the trenches, Figure 1-3 presents the "big picture." A manager's primary job is to increase the company's intrinsic value, but how exactly does one go about doing that? The equation in the center of Figure 1-3 shows that

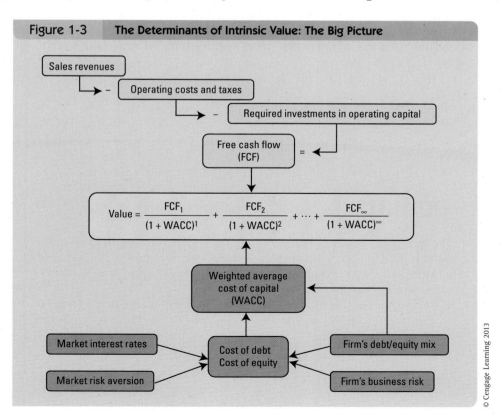

Figure 1-3 The Determinants of Intrinsic Value: The Big Picture

$$\text{Value} = \frac{\text{FCF}_1}{(1 + \text{WACC})^1} + \frac{\text{FCF}_2}{(1 + \text{WACC})^2} + \cdots + \frac{\text{FCF}_\infty}{(1 + \text{WACC})^\infty}$$

© Cengage Learning 2013

intrinsic value is the present value of the firm's expected free cash flows, discounted at the weighted average cost of capital. Thus, there are two approaches for increasing intrinsic value: Improve FCF or reduce the WACC. Observe that several factors affect FCF and several factors affect the WACC. In the rest of the book's chapters, we will typically focus on only one of these factors, systematically building the vocabulary and tools that you will use after graduation to improve your company's intrinsic value. It is true that every manager needs to understand financial vocabulary and be able to apply financial tools, but really successful managers also understand how their decisions affect the big picture. So as you read this book, keep in mind where each topic fits into the big picture.

e-Resources

The textbook's Web site contains several types of files that will be helpful to you:

1. It contains *Excel* files, called *Tool Kits,* that provide well-documented models for almost all of the text's calculations. Not only will these *Tool Kits* help you with this finance course, they also will serve as tool kits for you in other courses and in your career.
2. There are problems at the end of the chapters that require spreadsheets, and the Web site contains the models you will need to begin work on these problems.

When we think it might be helpful for you to look at one of the Web site's files, we'll show an icon in the margin like the one shown here.

Other resources are also on the Web site, including Cyberproblems and problems that use the Thomson ONE—Business School Edition Web site. The textbook's Web site also contains an electronic library that contains Adobe PDF files for "extensions" to many chapters that cover additional useful material related to the chapter.

Summary

- The three main forms of business organization are the **proprietorship**, the **partnership**, and the **corporation**. Although each form of organization offers advantages and disadvantages, *corporations conduct much more business than the other forms.*
- The primary objective of management should be to *maximize stockholders' wealth,* and this means *maximizing the company's* **fundamental**, or **intrinsic**, **stock price.** Legal actions that maximize stock prices usually increase social welfare.

- **Free cash flows (FCFs)** are the cash flows available for distribution to all of a firm's investors (shareholders and creditors) after the firm has paid all expenses (including taxes) and has made the required investments in operations to support growth.
- The **weighted average cost of capital (WACC)** is the average return required by all of the firm's investors. It is determined by the firm's *capital structure* (the firm's relative amounts of debt and equity), *interest rates*, the firm's *risk*, and the *market's attitude toward risk*.
- The value of a firm depends on the size of the firm's free cash flows, the timing of those flows, and their risk. A **firm's fundamental**, or **intrinsic, value** is defined by

$$\text{Value} = \frac{FCF_1}{(1 + WACC)^1} + \frac{FCF_2}{(1 + WACC)^2} + \frac{FCF_3}{(1 + WACC)^3} + \cdots + \frac{FCF_\infty}{(1 + WACC)^\infty}$$

- Four fundamental factors affect the cost of money: (1) **production opportunities**, (2) **time preferences for consumption**, (3) **risk**, and (4) **inflation**.
- **Derivatives**, such as options, are claims on other financial securities. In **securitization**, new securities are created from claims on packages of other securities.
- *Web Extension 1A* discusses derivatives, and *Web Extension 1B* provides some background coverage of stock markets.

Questions

1–1 Define each of the following terms:
   a. Proprietorship; partnership; corporation
   b. Limited partnership; limited liability partnership; professional corporation
   c. Stockholder wealth maximization
   d. Production opportunities; time preferences for consumption
   e. Foreign trade deficit
   f. Securitization

1–2 What are the three principal forms of business organization? What are the advantages and disadvantages of each?

1–3 What is a firm's fundamental, or intrinsic, value? What might cause a firm's intrinsic value to be different than its actual market value?

1–4 Edmund Enterprises recently made a large investment to upgrade its technology. Although these improvements won't have much of an impact on performance in the short run, they are expected to reduce future costs significantly. What impact will this investment have on Edmund Enterprises's earnings per share this year? What impact might this investment have on the company's intrinsic value and stock price?

MINI CASE

Assume that you recently graduated and have just reported to work as an investment advisor at the brokerage firm of Balik and Kiefer Inc. One of the firm's clients is Michelle DellaTorre, a professional tennis player who has just come to the United States from Chile. DellaTorre is a highly ranked tennis player who would like to start a company to produce and market apparel she designs. She also expects to invest substantial amounts of money through Balik and Kiefer. DellaTorre is very bright, and she would like to understand in general terms what will happen to her money. Your boss has developed the following set of questions you must answer to explain the U.S. financial system to DellaTorre.

a. Why is corporate finance important to all managers?

b. Describe the organizational forms a company might have as it evolves from a start-up to a major corporation. List the advantages and disadvantages of each form.

c. How do corporations go public and continue to grow? What are agency problems? What is corporate governance?

d. What should be the primary objective of managers?
   (1) Do firms have any responsibilities to society at large?
   (2) Is stock price maximization good or bad for society?
   (3) Should firms behave ethically?

e. What three aspects of cash flows affect the value of any investment?

f. What are free cash flows?

g. What is the weighted average cost of capital?

h. How do free cash flows and the weighted average cost of capital interact to determine a firm's value?

i. What do we call the price that a borrower must pay for debt capital? What is the price of equity capital? What are the four most fundamental factors that affect the cost of money, or the general level of interest rates, in the economy?

j. What are some economic conditions (including international aspects) that affect the cost of money?

k. What are financial securities? Describe some financial instruments.

l. Briefly explain mortgage securitization and how it contributed to the global economic crisis.

Chapter 2

Risk and Return: Part I

In this chapter, we start from the basic premise that investors like returns and dislike risk. Therefore, people will invest in relatively risky assets only if they expect to receive relatively high returns—the higher the perceived risk, the higher the expected rate of return an investor will demand. We define exactly what the term *risk* means as it relates to investments, we examine procedures used to measure risk, and we discuss more precisely the relationship between risk and required returns. In later chapters we extend these relationships to show how risk and return interact to determine security prices. Managers must understand and apply these concepts as they plan the actions that will shape their firms' futures, and investors must understand them in order to make appropriate investment decisions.

WEB

The textbook's Web site contains an *Excel* file that will guide you through the chapter's calculations. The file for this chapter is **Ch02 Tool Kit.xls**, and we encourage you to open the file and follow along as you read the chapter.

Beginning of Chapter Questions

As you read the chapter, consider how you would answer the following questions. You *should not* necessarily be able to answer the questions before you read the chapter. Rather, you should use them to get a sense of the issues covered in the chapter. After reading the chapter, you should be able to give at least partial answers to the questions, and you should be able to give better answers after the chapter has been discussed in class. Note, too, that it is often useful, when answering conceptual questions, to use hypothetical data to illustrate your answer. We illustrate the answers with an *Excel* model that is available on the textbook's Web site. Accessing the model and working through it is a useful exercise, and it provides insights that are useful when answering the questions.

1. Differentiate between (a) **stand-alone risk** and (b) **risk in a portfolio context.** How are they measured, and are both concepts relevant for investors?

2. Can an investor eliminate **market risk** from a portfolio of common stocks? How many stocks must a portfolio contain to be "reasonably well diversified"? Do all portfolios with, say, 50 stocks have about the same amount of risk?

3. a. Differentiate between the terms **expected rate of return, required rate of return,** and **historical rate of return** as they are applied to common stocks.
   b. If you found values for each of these returns for several different stocks, would the values for each stock most likely be the same or different; that is, would Stock A's expected, required, and historical rates of return be equal to one another? Why?

4. What does the term **risk aversion** mean, and how is risk aversion related to the expected return on a stock?

5. What is the **Capital Asset Pricing Model (CAPM)?** What are some of its key assumptions? Has it been empirically verified? What is the role of the **Security Market Line** in the CAPM? Suppose you had to estimate the required rate of return on a stock using the CAPM. What data would you need, where would you get the data, and how confident would you be of your estimate?

6. Suppose you have data that show the rates of return earned by Stock X, Stock Y, and the market over the last 5 years, along with the risk-free rate of return and the required return on the market. You also have estimates of the expected returns on X and Y.
   a. How could you decide, based on these expected returns, if Stocks X and Y are good deals, bad deals, or in equilibrium?
   b. Now suppose in Year 6 the market is quite strong. Stock X has a high positive return, but Stock Y's price falls because investors suddenly become quite concerned about its future prospects; that is, it becomes riskier, and like a bond that suddenly becomes risky, its price falls. Based on the CAPM and using the most recent 5 years of data, would Stock Y's required return as calculated just after the end of Year 6 rise or fall? What can you say about these results?

2.1 Returns on Investments

With most investments, an individual or business spends money today with the expectation of earning even more money in the future. The concept of *return* provides investors with a convenient way to express the financial performance of an investment. To illustrate, suppose you buy 10 shares of a stock for $1,000. The stock pays no dividends, but at the end of 1 year you sell the stock for $1,100. What is the return on your $1,000 investment?

One way to express an investment's return is in *dollar terms:*

$$\text{Dollar return} = \text{Amount to be received} - \text{Amount invested}$$
$$= \$1,100 - \$1,000$$
$$= \$100$$

INTRINSIC VALUE, RISK, AND RETURN

The intrinsic value of a company is the present value of its expected future free cash flows (FCF) discounted at the weighted average cost of capital (WACC). This chapter shows you how to measure a firm's risk and the rate of return expected by shareholders, which affects the WACC. All else held equal, higher risk increases the WACC, which reduces the firm's value.

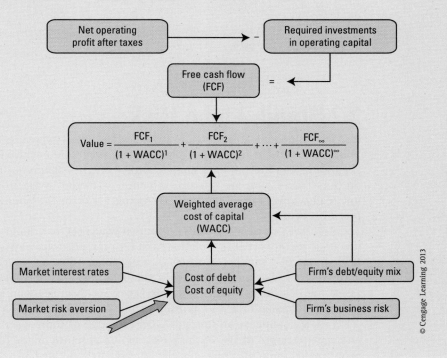

© Cengage Learning 2013

If at the end of the year you sell the stock for only $900, your dollar return will be −$100.

Although expressing returns in dollars is easy, two problems arise: (1) to make a meaningful judgment about the return, you need to know the scale (size) of the investment; a $100 return on a $100 investment is a great return (assuming the investment is held for 1 year), but a $100 return on a $10,000 investment would be a poor return. (2) You also need to know the timing of the return; a $100 return on a $100 investment is a great return if it occurs after 1 year, but the same dollar return after 20 years is not very good.

The solution to these scale and timing problems is to express investment results as *rates of return,* or *percentage returns.* For example, the rate of return on the 1-year stock investment, when $1,100 is received after 1 year, is 10%:

$$\text{Rate of return} = \frac{\text{Amount received} - \text{Amount invested}}{\text{Amount invested}}$$

$$= \frac{\text{Dollar return}}{\text{Amount invested}} = \frac{\$100}{\$1,000}$$

$$= 0.10 = 10\%$$

The rate of return calculation "standardizes" the dollar return by considering the annual return per unit of investment. Although this example has only one outflow and one inflow, the annualized rate of return can easily be calculated in situations where multiple cash flows occur over time by using time value of money concepts as discussed in Chapter 28.

Self Test

Differentiate between dollar returns and rates of return.

Why are rates of return superior to dollar returns when comparing different potential investments? (*Hint:* Think about size and timing.)

If you pay $500 for an investment that returns $600 in 1 year, what is your annual rate of return? **(20%)**

2.2 Stand-Alone Risk

Risk is defined in *Webster's* as "a hazard; a peril; exposure to loss or injury." Thus, risk refers to the chance that some unfavorable event will occur. If you go skydiving, you are taking a chance with your life—skydiving is risky. If you bet on horse races, you are risking your money. If you invest in speculative stocks (or, really, *any* stock), then you are taking a risk in the hope of earning an appreciable return.

An asset's risk can be analyzed in two ways: (1) on a stand-alone basis, where the asset is considered in isolation, and (2) on a portfolio basis, where the asset is held as one of a number of assets in a portfolio. Thus, an asset's **stand-alone risk** is the risk an investor would face if she held only this one asset. Obviously, most assets are held in portfolios, but it is necessary to understand stand-alone risk in order to understand risk in a portfolio context.

To begin, suppose an investor buys $100,000 of short-term Treasury bills with an expected return of 5%. In this case, the rate of return on the investment, 5%, can be estimated quite precisely, and the investment is defined as being essentially *risk free*. However, if the $100,000 were invested in the stock of a company just being organized to prospect for oil in the mid-Atlantic, then the investment's return could not be estimated precisely. One might analyze the situation and conclude that the *expected* rate of return, in a statistical sense, is 20%, but the investor should recognize that the *actual* rate of return could range from, say, +1,000% to −100%. Because there is a significant danger of actually earning much less than the expected return, this stock would be relatively risky.

No investment should be undertaken unless the expected rate of return is high enough to compensate for the perceived risk. In our example, it is clear that few if any investors would be willing to buy the oil company's stock if its expected return were 5%, the same as that of the T-bill.

Risky assets rarely produce their exact expected rates of return; in general, risky assets earn either more or less than was originally expected. Indeed, if assets always produced their expected returns, they would not be risky. Investment risk, then, is related to the probability of actually earning a low or negative return: The greater the chance of a low or negative return, and the larger the potential loss, the riskier the investment. However, risk can be defined more precisely, and we do so in the next section.

2.2a Distributions

An event's *probability* is defined as the chance that the event will occur. For example, a weather forecaster might state: "There is a 40% chance of rain today and a 60% chance that it will not rain." If all possible events, or outcomes, are listed, and if a probability is assigned to each event, then the listing is called a **probability distribution.** Keep in mind that the probabilities must sum to 1.0, or 100%.

With this in mind, consider the possible rates of return—due to dividends or stock price changes—that you might earn next year on a $10,000 investment in the stock of either Sale.com or Basic Foods Inc. Sale.com is an Internet company that offers deep discounts on factory seconds and overstocked merchandise. Because it faces intense competition, its new services may or may not be competitive in the marketplace, so its future earnings cannot be predicted very well. Indeed, some new company could develop better services and literally bankrupt Sale.com. Basic Foods, on the other hand, distributes essential food staples to grocery stores, and its sales and profits are relatively stable and predictable.

The rate-of-return probability distributions for the two companies are shown in Figure 2-1. There is a 30% chance of strong demand, in which case both companies will have high earnings, pay high dividends, and enjoy capital gains. There is a 40% probability of normal demand and moderate returns and a 30% probability of weak demand, which will mean low earnings and dividends as well as capital losses. Notice, however, that Sale.com's rate of return could vary far more widely than that of Basic Foods. There is a fairly high probability that the value of Sale.com's stock will drop substantially, resulting in a 70% loss, while there is a much smaller possible loss for Basic Foods.[1]

2.2b Expected Rate of Return

If we multiply each possible outcome by its probability of occurrence and then sum these products, as in Figure 2-2, the result is a *weighted average* of outcomes. The weights are the probabilities, and the weighted average is the **expected rate of return, $\hat{r}$,** called "r-hat."[2] The expected rates of return for both Sale.com and Basic Foods are shown in Figure 2-2 to be 15%. This type of table is known as a *payoff matrix.*

Figure 2-1	Probability Distributions for Sale.com and Basic Foods			
	A	B	C	D
26	Demand for the Company's Products	Probability of this Demand Occurring	Rate of Return on Stock if this Demand Occurs	
27				
28			Sale.com	Basic Foods
29	Strong	0.30	90%	45%
30	Normal	0.40	15%	15%
31	Weak	0.30	−60%	−15%
32		1.00		
33				

© Cengage Learning 2013

---

1. Note that the following discussion of risk applies to all random variables, not just stock returns.
2. In other chapters, we will use $\hat{r}_d$ and $\hat{r}_s$ to signify expected returns on bonds and stocks, respectively. However, this distinction is unnecessary in this chapter, so we just use the general term, $\hat{r}$, to signify the expected return on an investment.

Figure 2-2   Calculation of Expected Rates of Return: Payoff Matrix

	A	B	C	D	E	F
41	Demand for the Company's Products (1)	Probability of this Demand Occurring (2)	Sale.com		Basic Foods	
42			Rate of Return (3)	Product (2) x (3) = (4)	Rate of Return (5)	Product (2) x (5) = (6)
43						
44	Strong	0.3	90%	27%	45%	13.5%
45	Normal	0.4	15%	6%	15%	6.0%
46	Weak	0.3	−60%	−18%	−15%	−4.5%
47		1.0				
48	Expected Rate of Return = Sum of Products =		$\hat{r}$ =	15%	$\hat{r}$ =	15%
49						

WEB

See **Ch02 Tool Kit.xls** on the textbook's Web site.

The calculation for expected rate of return can also be expressed as an equation that does the same thing as the payoff matrix table:

(2–1)

$$\text{Expected rate of return} = \hat{r} = P_1 r_1 + P_2 r_2 + \cdots + P_n r_n$$

$$= \sum_{i=1}^{n} P_i r_i$$

Here r_i is the return if outcome i occurs, P_i is the probability that outcome i occurs, and n is the number of possible outcomes. Thus, $\hat{r}$ is a weighted average of the possible outcomes (the r_i values), with each outcome's weight being its probability of occurrence. Using the data for Sale.com, we obtain its expected rate of return as follows:

$$\hat{r} = P_1(r_1) + P_2(r_2) + P_3(r_3)$$

$$= 0.3(90\%) + 0.4(15\%) + 0.3(-60\%)$$

$$= 15\%$$

Basic Foods's expected rate of return is also 15%:

$$\hat{r} = 0.3(45\%) + 0.4(15\%) + 0.3(-15\%)$$

$$= 15\%$$

We can graph the rates of return to obtain a picture of the variability of possible outcomes; this is shown in the bar charts of Figure 2-3. The height of each bar signifies the probability that a given outcome will occur. The range of probable returns for Sale.com is from −60% to +90%, with an expected return of 15%. The expected return for Basic Foods is also 15%, but its range is much narrower.

Thus far, we have assumed that only three situations can exist: strong, normal, and weak demand. Actually, of course, demand could range from a deep depression to a fantastic boom, and there are unlimited possibilities in between. Suppose we had the time and patience to assign a probability to each possible level of demand (with the sum of the probabilities still equaling 1.0) and to assign a rate of return to each stock for each level of demand. We would have a table similar to Figure 2-2, except it would have many more entries in each column. This table could be used

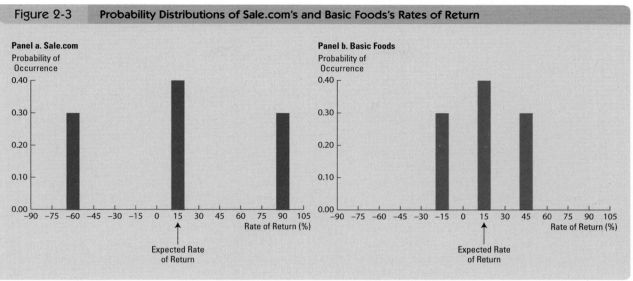

Figure 2-3   **Probability Distributions of Sale.com's and Basic Foods's Rates of Return**

Figure 2-4   **Approximate Continuous Probability Distributions of Sale.com's and Basic Foods's Rates of Return**

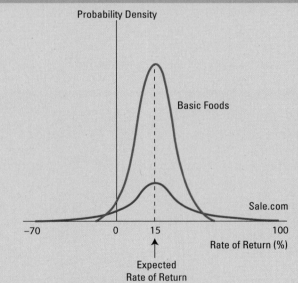

Note: The assumptions regarding the probabilities of various outcomes have been changed from those in Figure 2-3. There the probability of obtaining exactly 15% was 40%; here it is *much smaller* because there are many possible outcomes instead of just three. With continuous distributions, it is more appropriate to ask what the probability is of obtaining at least some specified rate of return than to ask what the probability is of achieving exactly that rate. This topic is covered in detail in statistics courses.

to calculate expected rates of return using the same approach as shown previously. In fact, the probabilities and outcomes could be approximated by continuous curves such as those presented in Figure 2-4.

The tighter (or more peaked) the probability distribution, the more likely it is that the actual outcome will be close to the expected value, and hence the less likely it is that the actual return will end up far below the expected return. Thus, *the tighter the probability distribution, the lower the risk assigned to a stock.* Since Basic Foods has a relatively tight probability distribution, its *actual return* is likely to be closer to its 15% *expected return* than that of Sale.com.

2.2c Measuring Stand-Alone Risk: The Standard Deviation

Risk is a difficult concept to grasp, and a great deal of controversy has surrounded attempts to define and measure it. However, a common definition that is satisfactory for many purposes is stated in terms of probability distributions such as those presented in Figure 2-4: *The tighter the probability distribution of expected future returns, the smaller the risk of a given investment.* According to this definition, Basic Foods is less risky than Sale.com because there is a smaller chance that its actual return will end up far below its expected return.

To be most useful, any measure of risk should have a definite value—we need a measure of the tightness of the probability distribution. One such measure is the **standard deviation,** the symbol for which is σ, pronounced "sigma." The smaller the standard deviation, the tighter the probability distribution and, accordingly, the less risky the stock. To calculate the standard deviation, we proceed as shown in Figure 2-5, taking the following steps:[3]

1. Calculate the expected rate of return:

$$\text{Expected rate of return} = \hat{r} = \sum_{i=1}^{n} P_i r_i$$

For Sale.com, we previously found $\hat{r} = 15\%$.

Figure 2-5   **Calculating Sale.com's and Basic Foods's Standard Deviations**

	A	B	C	D	E	F
89						
90	Panel a.			Sale.com		
	Probability of Occurrence	Rate of Return on Stock	Expected Return	Deviation from Expected Return	Squared Deviation	Sq. Dev. × Prob.
91	(1)	(2)	(3)	(2) − (3) = (4)	$(4)^2$ = (5)	(5) × (1) = (6)
92	0.3	90%	15%	75.0%	56.25%	16.88%
93	0.4	15%	15%	0.0%	0.00%	0.00%
94	0.3	−60%	15%	−75.0%	56.25%	16.88%
95	1.0				Sum = Variance =	33.75%
96				Std. Dev. = Square root of variance =		58.09%
97						
98	Panel b.			Basic Foods		
	Probability of Occurrence	Rate of Return on Stock	Expected Return	Deviation from Expected Return	Squared Deviation	Sq. Dev. × Prob.
99	(1)	(2)	(3)	(2) − (3) = (4)	$(4)^2$ = (5)	(5) × (1) = (6)
100	0.3	45%	15%	30.0%	9.00%	2.70%
101	0.4	15%	15%	0.0%	0.00%	0.00%
102	0.3	−15%	15%	−30.0%	9.00%	2.70%
103	1.0				Sum = Variance =	5.40%
104				Std. Dev. = Square root of variance =		23.24%
105						

---

3. These equations are valid for any random variable from a discrete probability distribution, not just for returns.

2. Subtract the expected rate of return ($\hat{r}$) from each possible outcome (r_i) to obtain a set of deviations about $\hat{r}$ as shown in Column 4 of Figure 2-5:

$$\text{Deviation}_i = r_i - \hat{r}$$

3. Square each deviation as shown in Column 5. Then multiply the squared deviations in Column 5 by the probability of occurrence for its related outcome; these products are shown in Column 6. Sum these products to obtain the **variance** of the probability distribution:

$$\text{Variance} = \sigma^2 = \sum_{i=1}^{n} (r_i - \hat{r})^2 P_i \qquad \text{(2–2)}$$

4. Finally, find the square root of the variance to obtain the standard deviation:

$$\text{Standard deviation} = \sigma = \sqrt{\sum_{i=1}^{n} (r_i - \hat{r})^2 P_i} \qquad \text{(2–3)}$$

Thus, the standard deviation is essentially a weighted average of the deviations from the expected value, and it provides an idea of how far above or below the expected value the actual value is likely to be. If we use this procedure, Sale .com's standard deviation is seen in Figure 2-5 to be $\sigma = 58.09\%$; we likewise find Basic Foods's standard deviation to be 23.24%. Sale.com has the larger standard deviation, which indicates a greater variation of returns and thus a greater chance that the actual return will turn out to be substantially lower than the expected return. Therefore, Sale.com is a riskier investment than Basic Foods when held alone.[4]

If we have a **normal distribution**, then the *actual* return will be within ± 1 standard deviation of the *expected* return 68.26% of the time. Figure 2-6 illustrates this point, and it also shows the situation for $\pm 2\sigma$ and $\pm 3\sigma$. For Sale.com, $\hat{r} = 15\%$ and $\sigma = 58.09\%$, whereas for Basic Foods $\hat{r} = 15\%$ and $\sigma = 23.24\%$. Thus, if the two distributions were normal, there would be a 68.26% probability that Sale.com's actual return would be in the range of $15\% \pm 58.09\%$, or from -43.09% to 73.09%. For Basic Foods, the 68.26% range is $15\% \pm 23.24\%$, or from -8.24% to 38.24%.

WEB

See **Ch02 Tool Kit.xls** on the textbook's Web site for all calculations.

---

4. As *Ch02 Tool Kit.xls* shows, it is easy to calculate the standard deviation in *Excel*. Calculating by hand is tedious and error-prone:

$$\sigma = \sqrt{(0.3)(0.90 - 0.15)^2 + (0.4)(0.15 - 0.15)^2 + (0.3)(-0.60 - 0.15)^2} = 0.5809$$

Most financial calculators have no built-in formula for finding the expected value or variance for discrete probability distributions, except for the special case in which the probabilities for all outcomes are equal. Therefore, you must go through the processes outlined in Figures 2-2 and 2-5 (i.e., Equations 2-1 and 2-3). For an example of this process using a financial calculator, see Richard W. Taylor, "Discrete Probability Analysis with the BAII Plus Professional Calculator," *Journal of Financial Education,* Winter 2005, pp. 100–106.

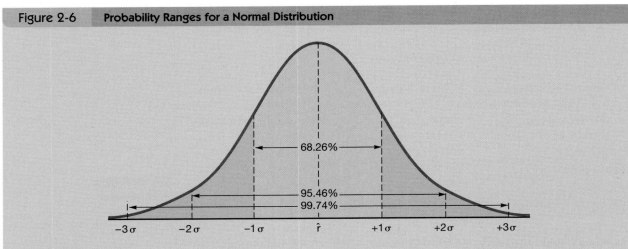

Figure 2-6 Probability Ranges for a Normal Distribution

Notes:
a. The area under the normal curve always equals 1.0, or 100%. Thus, the areas under any pair of normal curves drawn on the same scale, whether they are peaked or flat, must be equal.
b. Half of the area under a normal curve is to the left of the mean, indicating that there is a 50% probability that the actual outcome will be less than the mean, and half is to the right of $\hat{r}$, indicating a 50% probability that it will be greater than the mean.
c. Of the area under the curve, 68.26% is within $\pm 1\sigma$ of the mean, indicating that the probability is 68.26% that the actual outcome will be within the range $\hat{r} - \sigma$ to $\hat{r} + \sigma$.

WHAT DOES RISK REALLY MEAN?

As explained in the text, the probability of being within 1 standard deviation of the expected return is 68.26%, so the probability of being further than 1 standard deviation from the mean is 31.74%. There is an equal probability of being above or below the range, so there is a 15.87% chance of being more than 1 standard deviation below the mean, which is roughly equal to a 1 in 6 chance (1 in 6 is 16.67%).

For the average firm listed on the New York Stock Exchange, σ has been in the range of 35% to 40% in recent years, with an expected return of around 8% to 12%. One standard deviation below this expected return is about 10% − 35% = −25%. This means that, for a typical stock in typical year, there is about a 1 in 6 chance of having a 25% loss. You might be thinking that 1 in 6 is a pretty low probability, but what if your chance of getting hit by a car when you crossed a street were 1 in 6? When put that way, 1 in 6 sounds pretty scary.

You might also correctly be thinking that there would be a 1 in 6 chance of getting a return higher than 1 stan-dard deviation above the mean, which would be about 45% for a typical stock. A 45% return is great, but human nature is such that most investors would dislike a 25% loss a whole lot more than they would enjoy a 45% gain.

You might also be thinking that you'll be okay if you hold stock long enough. But even if you buy and hold a diversified portfolio for 10 years, there is still roughly a 10% chance that you will lose money. If you hold it for 20 years, there is about a 4% chance of losing. Such odds wouldn't be worrisome if you were engaged in a game of chance that could be played multiple times, but you have only one life to live and just a few rolls of the dice.

We aren't suggesting that investors shouldn't buy stocks; indeed, we own stock ourselves. But we do believe investors should understand more clearly exactly how much risk stock investing entails.

2.2d Using Historical Data to Measure Risk

WEB

For more discussion of probability distributions, see **Web Extension 2A**, available on the text-book's Web site.

In our previous example, we described the procedure for finding the mean and standard deviation when the data are in the form of a known probability distribution. This implies that the distribution includes all data points, not a sample of data points from a broader universe of returns. Suppose, however, that only a sample of returns over some past period is available. These past **realized rates of return** are denoted as $\bar{r}_t$ ("r bar t"), where t designates the time period. The average annual return over the last n years is then denoted as $\bar{r}_{Avg}$:

$$\bar{r}_{Avg} = \frac{\sum\limits_{t=1}^{n} \bar{r}_t}{n} \qquad (2\text{-}4)$$

The standard deviation of the sample of returns can then be estimated using this formula:[5]

$$\text{Estimated } \sigma = S = \sqrt{\frac{\sum\limits_{t=1}^{n} (\bar{r}_t - \bar{r}_{Avg})^2}{n-1}} \qquad (2\text{-}5)$$

When estimated from past data, the standard deviation is often denoted by S.

To illustrate, consider the historical returns in Figure 2-7. Using Equations 2-4 and 2-5, the estimated average and standard deviation are, respectively,

$$\bar{r}_{Avg} = \frac{15\% - 5\% + 20\%}{3} = 10.0\%$$

$$\text{Estimated } \sigma \text{ (or S)} = \sqrt{\frac{(15\% - 10\%)^2 + (-5\% - 10\%)^2 + (20\% - 10\%)^2}{3-1}}$$

$$= 13.2\%$$

Figure 2-7   Standard Deviation Based on a Sample of Historical Data

	A	B	C	D
120				Realized
121			Year	return
122			2010	15.0%
123			2011	−5.0%
124			2012	20.0%
125				
126	Average =AVERAGE(D122:D124) =			10.0%
127	Standard deviation =STDEV(D122:D124) =			13.2%
128				

---

5. Because we are estimating the standard deviation from a sample of observations, the denominator in Equation 2-5 is "n − 1" and not just "n." Equations 2-4 and 2-5 are built into all financial calculators. For example, to find the sample standard deviation, enter the rates of return into the calculator and press the key marked S (or S_x) to get the standard deviation. See our tutorials on the textbook's Web site or your calculator's manual for details.

WEB

See **Ch02 Tool Kit.xls** on the textbook's Web site.

The average and standard deviation can also be calculated using *Excel*'s built-in functions, shown below using numerical data rather than cell ranges as inputs:

$$=\text{AVERAGE}(0.15, -0.05, 0.20) = 10.0\%$$

$$=\text{STDEV}(0.15, -0.05, 0.20) = 13.2\%$$

The historical standard deviation is often used as an estimate of the future variability. Because past variability is likely to be repeated, past variability may be a reasonably good estimate of future risk. However, it is usually incorrect to use $\bar{r}_{\text{Avg}}$ based on a past period as an estimate of $\hat{r}$, the expected future return. For example, just because a stock had a 75% return in the past year, there is no reason to expect a 75% return this year.

2.2e Measuring Stand-Alone Risk: The Coefficient of Variation

If a choice has to be made between two investments that have the same expected returns but different standard deviations, most people would choose the one with the lower standard deviation and, therefore, the lower risk. Similarly, given a choice between two investments with the same risk (standard deviation) but different expected returns, investors would generally prefer the investment with the higher expected return. To most people, this is common sense—return is "good," risk is "bad," and consequently investors want as much return and as little risk as possible. But how do we choose between two investments if one has a higher expected return and the other a lower standard deviation? To help answer this question, we often use another measure of risk, the **coefficient of variation (CV)**, which is the standard deviation divided by the expected return:

(2–6)
$$\text{Coefficient of variation} = \text{CV} = \frac{\sigma}{\hat{r}}$$

The coefficient of variation shows the risk per unit of return, and it provides a more meaningful basis for comparison than σ when the expected returns on two alternatives are different. Since Basic Foods and Sale.com have the same expected return, 15%, the coefficient of variation is not necessary in this case: The firm with the larger standard deviation, Sale.com, must have the larger coefficient of variation when the means are equal. In fact, the coefficient of variation for Sale.com is 58.09/15 = 3.87 and that for Basic Foods is 23.24/15 = 1.55. Thus, Sale.com is more than twice as risky as Basic Foods on the basis of this criterion. Because the coefficient of variation captures the effects of both risk and return, it is a better measure than the standard deviation when evaluating stand-alone risk in situations in which different investments have substantially different expected returns.

2.2f Risk Aversion and Required Returns

Suppose you have worked hard and saved $1 million, which you now plan to invest for 1 year. You can buy a 5% U.S. Treasury security, and at the end of the year you will have a sure $1.05 million, which is your original investment plus $50,000 in interest. Alternatively, you can buy stock in Genetic Advances Inc. If Genetic Advances's research programs are successful, your stock will increase in

THE TRADE-OFF BETWEEN RISK AND RETURN

The table accompanying this box summarizes the historical trade-off between risk and return for different classes of investments. The assets that produced the highest average returns also had the highest standard deviations and the widest ranges of returns. For example, small-company stocks had the highest average annual return, but their standard deviation of returns was also the highest. In contrast, U.S. Treasury bills had the lowest standard deviation, but they also had the lowest average return.

Note that a T-bill is riskless *if you hold it until maturity,* but if you invest in a rolling portfolio of T-bills and hold the portfolio for a number of years, then your investment income will vary depending on what happens to the level of interest rates in each year. You can be sure of the return you will earn on an individual T-bill, but you cannot be sure of the return you will earn on a portfolio of T-bills held over a number of years.

	Small-Company Stocks	Large-Company Stocks	Long-Term Corporate Bonds	Long-Term Government Bonds	U.S. Treasury Bills	Inflation
Distribution of Realized Returns, 1926–2010						
Average return	16.7%	11.9%	6.2%	5.9%	3.7%	3.1%
Standard deviation	32.6%	20.4%	8.3%	9.5%	3.1%	4.2%
Excess return over T-bonds[a]	10.8%	6.0%	0.3%			

[a]The excess return over T-bonds is called the "historical risk premium." This excess return will also be the current risk premium that is reflected in security prices if and only if investors expect returns in the future to be similar to returns earned in the past.

Source: Based on *Stocks, Bonds, Bills, and Inflation: Valuation Edition 2011 Yearbook* (Chicago: Ibbotson Associates, 2011).

value to $2.1 million. However, if the research is a failure, the value of your stock will go to zero, and you will be penniless. You regard Genetic Advances's chances of success or failure as being 50-50, so the expected value of the stock investment is 0.5($0) + 0.5($2,100,000) = $1,050,000. Subtracting the $1 million cost of the stock leaves an expected profit of $50,000, or an expected (but risky) 5% rate of return: $50,000/$1,000,000 = 0.05 = 5%.

Thus, you have a choice between a sure $50,000 profit (representing a 5% rate of return) on the Treasury security and a risky expected $50,000 profit (also representing a 5% expected rate of return) on the Genetic Advances stock. Which one would you choose? *If you choose the less risky investment, you are risk averse. Most investors are indeed risk averse, and certainly the average investor is risk averse with regard to his "serious money." Because this is a well-documented fact, we shall assume* **risk aversion** *throughout the remainder of the book.*

What are the implications of risk aversion for security prices and rates of return? The answer is that, other things held constant, the higher a security's risk, the lower its price and the higher its required return. To see how risk aversion affects security prices, consider again Basic Foods and Sale.com. Suppose each stock is expected to pay an annual dividend of $15 forever. We know that the dividend could be higher or lower, but $15 is our best guess. Under these conditions, the price of each stock can be found as the present value of a perpetuity. If each stock had an expected return of 15%, then each stock's price must be P = $15/0.15 = $100. However, investors are averse to risk, so under these conditions there would be a general preference for Basic Foods—it has the same expected return as Sale.com but less risk. People with money to invest would bid for Basic Foods rather than Sale. com stock, and Sale.com stockholders would start selling their stock and using the money to buy Basic Foods. Buying pressure would drive up Basic Foods's stock price, and selling pressure would simultaneously cause Sale.com's price to decline.

These price changes, in turn, would cause changes in the expected rates of return on the two securities. Suppose, for example, that Basic Foods's stock price was bid up from $100 to $150, whereas Sale.com's stock price declined from $100 to $75. This would cause Basic Foods's expected return to fall to 10%, while Sale. com's expected return would rise to 20%.[6] The difference in returns, 20% − 10% = 10%, is a **risk premium, RP,** which represents the additional compensation investors require for assuming the additional risk of Sale.com stock.

This example demonstrates a fundamentally important principle: *In a market dominated by risk-averse investors, riskier securities must have higher expected returns, as estimated by the marginal investor, than less risky securities. If this situation does not already exist, then buying and selling in the marketplace will force it to occur.* We will consider the question of how much higher the returns on risky securities must be later in the chapter, after we see how diversification affects risk and the way it should be measured. Then, in later chapters, we will see how risk-adjusted rates of return affect the prices that investors are willing to pay for bonds and stocks.

Self Test

What does "investment risk" mean?

Set up an illustrative probability distribution for an investment.

What is a payoff matrix?

Which of the two stocks graphed in Figure 2-4 is less risky? Why?

How does one calculate the standard deviation?

Which is a better measure of risk when assets have different expected returns: (1) the standard deviation or (2) the coefficient of variation? Why?

Discuss the following statement: "Most investors are risk averse."

How does risk aversion affect rates of return on securities?

An investment has a 20% chance of producing a 25% return, a 60% chance of producing a 10% return, and a 20% chance of producing a −15% return. What is its expected return? **(8%)** What is its standard deviation? **(12.9%)**

A stock's returns for the past 3 years were 10%, −15%, and 35%. What is the historical average return? **(10%)** What is the historical sample standard deviation? **(25%)**

An investment has an expected return of 15% and a standard deviation of 30%. What is its coefficient of variation? **(2.0)**

---

6. Recall that the present value of a perpetuity is P = PMT/I, where PMT is the constant annual cash flow of the perpetuity and I is the rate of return. For stocks, we use r for the expected rate of return. Solving for r, the expected return for Basic Foods is $15/$150 = 0.10 = 10% and that for Sale.com is $15/$75 = 0.20 = 20%.

2.3 Risk in a Portfolio Context

In the preceding section we considered the risk of assets held in isolation. Now we analyze the risk of assets held in portfolios. As we shall see, an asset held as part of a portfolio is less risky than the same asset held in isolation. Therefore, most financial assets are actually held as parts of portfolios. Banks, pension funds, insurance companies, mutual funds, and other financial institutions are required by law to hold diversified portfolios. Even individual investors—at least those whose security holdings constitute a significant part of their total wealth—generally hold portfolios, not the stock of only one firm. This being the case, from an investor's standpoint the fact that a particular stock goes up or down is not the key issue: What's important are the portfolio's return and its risk. Logically, then, the risk and return of an individual security should be analyzed in terms of how that security affects the risk and return of the portfolio in which it is held.

To illustrate, Pay Up Inc. collects debts for other firms and operates nationwide through 37 offices. The company is not well known, its stock is not very liquid, its earnings have fluctuated quite a bit in the past, and it doesn't pay a dividend. All this suggests that Pay Up is risky and that the required rate of return on its stock should be relatively high. However, Pay Up's required rate of return in 2011, and all other years, was quite low relative to those of most other companies. Thus, investors regard Pay Up as being a low-risk company in spite of its uncertain profits. This is counterintuitive, but it is caused by diversification and its effect on risk. Pay Up's earnings rise during recessions, whereas most other companies' earnings tend to decline when the economy slumps. The stock is like a fire insurance policy—it pays off when other things go badly. Therefore, adding Pay Up to a portfolio of "normal" stocks tends to stabilize returns on the entire portfolio, thus making the portfolio less risky.

2.3a Portfolio Returns

The **expected return on a portfolio, $\hat{r}_p$**, is simply the weighted average of the expected returns on the individual assets in the portfolio. Suppose there are n stocks. The expected return on Stock i is $\hat{r}_i$. The fraction of the portfolio's dollar value invested in Stock i (that is, the value of the investment in Stock i divided by the total value of the portfolio) is w_i, and all the w_i must sum to 1.0. The expected return on the portfolio is

$$\hat{r}_p = w_1\hat{r}_1 + w_2\hat{r}_2 + \ldots + w_n\hat{r}_n$$

$$= \sum_{i=1}^{n} w_i\hat{r}_i$$

(2–7)

To illustrate, assume that a security analyst estimated the upcoming year's returns on the stocks of four large companies, as shown in Figure 2-8. A client wishes to invest $1 million, divided among the stocks as shown in the figure. Notice that the $300,000 investment in Southwest Airlines means that its

Figure 2-8   Expected Returns on a Portfolio of Stocks

	A	B	C	D	E
150	Stock	Amount of Investment	Portfolio Weight	Expected Return	Weighted Expected Return
151	Southwest Airlines	$300,000	0.3	15.0%	4.5%
152	Starbucks	$100,000	0.1	12.0%	1.2%
153	FedEx	$200,000	0.2	10.0%	2.0%
154	Dell	$400,000	0.4	9.0%	3.6%
155	Total investment =	$1,000,000	1.0		
156					
157				Portfolio's Expected Return =	11.3%

© Cengage Learning 2013

WEB

See *Ch02 Tool Kit.xls* on the textbook's Web site.

weight in the portfolio is $0.3 = \$300,000/\$1,000,000$. The expected portfolio return is:

$$\hat{r}_p = w_1\hat{r}_1 + w_2\hat{r}_2 + w_3\hat{r}_3 + w_4\hat{r}_4$$

$$= 0.3(15\%) + 0.1(12\%) + 0.2(10\%) + 0.4(9\%)$$

$$= 11.3\%$$

Of course, the actual realized rates of return almost certainly will be different from their expected values, so the realized portfolio return, $\bar{r}_p$, will be different from the expected return. For example, Starbucks might double and provide a return of +100%, whereas Dell might have a terrible year, fall sharply, and have a return of −75%. Note, though, that those two events would be somewhat offsetting, so the portfolio's return might still be close to its expected return.

2.3b Portfolio Risk

As we just saw, the expected return on a portfolio is simply the weighted average of the expected returns on the individual assets in the portfolio. However, unlike returns, the risk of a portfolio, σ_p, is generally not the weighted average of the standard deviations of the individual assets in the portfolio. Indeed, the portfolio's standard deviation will (almost always) be smaller than the assets' weighted standard deviations, and it is theoretically possible to combine stocks that are individually quite risky as measured by their standard deviations and form a portfolio that is completely riskless, with $\sigma_p = 0$.

To illustrate the effect of combining assets, consider first the situation in Figure 2-9. The bottom section gives data on rates of return for Stocks W and M as well as for a portfolio invested 50% in each stock. (*Note:* These stocks are called W and M because the graphs of their returns in Figure 2-9 resemble a W and an M.) The three graphs plot the data in a time-series format. Note that the portfolio's return is 15% in every year. Therefore, although the two stocks would be quite risky if they were held in isolation, when combined to form Portfolio WM they are not risky at all.

The reason Stocks W and M can be combined to form a riskless portfolio is that their returns move countercyclically to each other—when W's returns fall, those of M rise, and vice versa. The tendency of two variables to move together is called **correlation**,

Figure 2-9   **Rates of Return for Two Perfectly Negatively Correlated Stocks
($\rho = -1.0$) and for Portfolio WM**

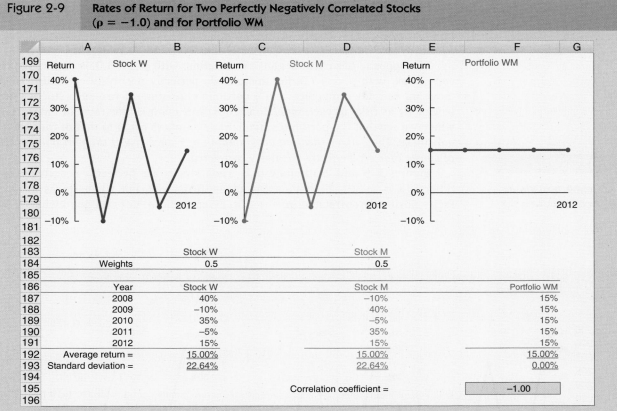

	Stock W		Stock M			Portfolio WM
Weights	0.5		0.5			

Year	Stock W	Stock M	Portfolio WM
2008	40%	−10%	15%
2009	−10%	40%	15%
2010	35%	−5%	15%
2011	−5%	35%	15%
2012	15%	15%	15%
Average return =	15.00%	15.00%	15.00%
Standard deviation =	22.64%	22.64%	0.00%
		Correlation coefficient =	−1.00

© Cengage Learning 2013

and the **correlation coefficient** measures this tendency.[7] The symbol for the correlation coefficient is the Greek letter rho, ρ (pronounced roe). In statistical terms, we say that the returns on Stocks W and M are *perfectly negatively correlated,* with $\rho = -1.0$.

The estimate of correlation from a sample of historical data is often called "R." Here is the formula to estimate the correlation between stocks i and j ($\bar{r}_{i,t}$ is the actual return for Stock i in period t, and $\bar{r}_{i,Avg}$ is the average return during the n-period sample; similar notation is used for stock j):

WEB

See **Ch02 Tool Kit.xls** on the textbook's Web site.

$$\text{Estimated } \rho = R = \frac{\sum_{t=1}^{n}(\bar{r}_{i,t} - \bar{r}_{i,Avg})(\bar{r}_{j,t} - \bar{r}_{j,Avg})}{\sqrt{\left[\sum_{t=1}^{n}(\bar{r}_{i,t} - \bar{r}_{i,Avg})^2\right]\left[\sum_{t=1}^{n}(\bar{r}_{j,t} - \bar{r}_{j,Avg})^2\right]}}$$

(2–8)

---

7. The correlation coefficient, ρ, can range from +1.0, denoting that the two variables move up and down in perfect synchronization, to −1.0, denoting that the variables always move in exactly opposite directions. A correlation coefficient of zero indicates that the two variables are not related to each other—that is, changes in one variable are independent of changes in the other.

Fortunately, it is easy to estimate the correlation coefficients with a financial calculator or *Excel*. With a calculator, simply enter the returns of the two stocks and then press a key labeled "r."[8] In *Excel*, use the CORREL function. See *Ch02 Tool Kit.xls*, where we calculate the correlation between Stocks W and M.

The opposite of perfect negative correlation, with $\rho = -1.0$, is *perfect positive correlation*, with $\rho = +1.0$. Returns on two perfectly positively correlated stocks move up and down together, and a portfolio consisting of two such stocks would be exactly as risky as each individual stock. This point is illustrated in Figure 2-10, where we see that the portfolio's standard deviation is equal to that of the individual stocks. Thus, *diversification does nothing to reduce risk if the portfolio consists of stocks that are perfectly positively correlated.*

Figures 2-9 and 2-10 show that when stocks are perfectly negatively correlated ($\rho = -1.0$), all risk can be diversified away, but when stocks are perfectly positively correlated ($\rho = +1.0$), diversification does no good whatsoever.

WEB

See *Ch02 Tool Kit.xls* on the textbook's Web site.

Figure 2-10   **Rates of Return for Two Perfectly Positively Correlated Stocks ($\rho = +1.0$) and for Portfolio WW'**

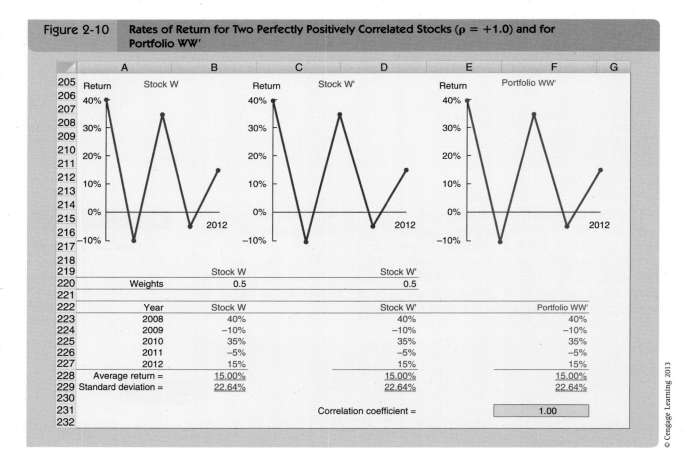

	Stock W		Stock W'	
Weights	0.5		0.5	

Year	Stock W		Stock W'	Portfolio WW'
2008	40%		40%	40%
2009	−10%		−10%	−10%
2010	35%		35%	35%
2011	−5%		−5%	−5%
2012	15%		15%	15%
Average return =	15.00%		15.00%	15.00%
Standard deviation =	22.64%		22.64%	22.64%
		Correlation coefficient =		1.00

© Cengage Learning 2013

---

8. See our tutorial or your calculator manual for the exact steps. Also, note that the correlation coefficient is often denoted by the term "r." We use ρ here to avoid confusion with r, which is used to denote the rate of return.

In reality, virtually all stocks are positively correlated, but not perfectly so. Past studies have estimated that, on average, the correlation coefficient for the monthly returns on two randomly selected stocks is in the range of 0.28 to 0.35.[9] *Under this condition, combining stocks into portfolios reduces but does not completely eliminate risk.* Figure 2-11 illustrates this point with two stocks whose correlation coefficient is $\rho = +0.35$. The portfolio's average return is 15%, which is exactly the same as the average return for our other two illustrative portfolios, but its standard deviation is 18.6%, which is between the other two portfolios' standard deviations.

These examples demonstrate that in one extreme case ($\rho = -1.0$), risk can be completely eliminated, while in the other extreme case ($\rho = +1.0$), diversification

WEB

See **Ch02 Tool Kit.xls** on the textbook's Web site.

Figure 2-11 Rates of Return for Two Partially Correlated Stocks ($\rho = +0.35$) and for Portfolio WY

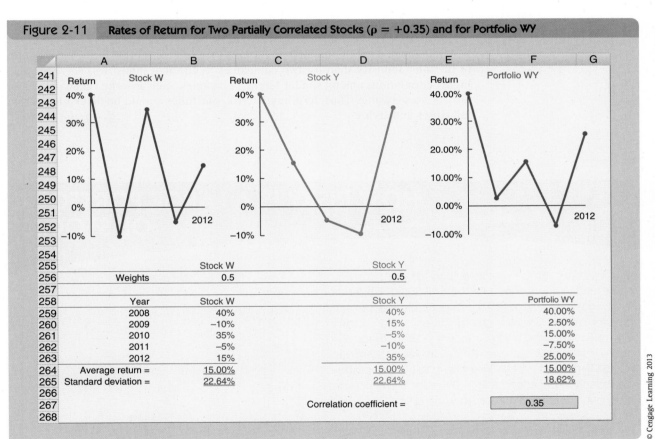

	Stock W		Stock Y	
Weights	0.5		0.5	

Year	Stock W	Stock Y	Portfolio WY
2008	40%	40%	40.00%
2009	−10%	15%	2.50%
2010	35%	−5%	15.00%
2011	−5%	−10%	−7.50%
2012	15%	35%	25.00%
Average return =	15.00%	15.00%	15.00%
Standard deviation =	22.64%	22.64%	18.62%
		Correlation coefficient =	0.35

© Cengage Learning 2013

---

9. During the period 1968–1998, the average correlation coefficient between two randomly selected stocks was 0.28, while the average correlation coefficient between two large-company stocks was 0.33; see Louis K. C. Chan, Jason Karceski, and Josef Lakonishok, "On Portfolio Optimization: Forecasting Covariance and Choosing the Risk Model," *The Review of Financial Studies,* Vol. 12, No. 5, Winter 1999, pp. 937–974. The average correlation fell from around 0.35 in the late 1970s to less than 0.10 by the late 1990s; see John Y. Campbell, Martin Lettau, Burton G. Malkiel, and Yexiao Xu, "Have Individual Stocks Become More Volatile? An Empirical Exploration of Idiosyncratic Risk," *Journal of Finance,* February 2001, pp. 1–43.

does not affect risk at all. The real world lies between these extremes, so combining stocks into portfolios reduces—but does not eliminate—the risk inherent in the individual stocks. Also, we should note that in the real world it is *impossible* to find stocks like W and M, whose returns are expected to be perfectly negatively correlated. Therefore, *it is impossible to form completely riskless stock portfolios.* Diversification can reduce risk but not eliminate it, so the real world is similar to the situation depicted in Figure 2-11.

What would happen if we included more than two stocks in the portfolio? As a rule, *the risk of a portfolio declines as the number of stocks in the portfolio increases.* If we added enough partially correlated stocks, could we completely eliminate risk? The answer is "no," but adding stocks to a portfolio reduces its risk to an extent that depends on the *degree of correlation* among the stocks: The smaller the stocks' correlation coefficients, the lower the portfolio's risk. If we could find stocks with correlations of −1.0, all risk could be eliminated. However, *in the real world the correlations among the individual stocks are generally positive but less than +1.0, so some (but not all) risk can be eliminated.*

In general, there are higher correlations between the returns on two companies in the same industry than for two companies in different industries. There are also higher correlations among similar "style" companies, such as large versus small and growth versus value. Thus, to minimize risk, portfolios should be diversified across industries and styles.

HOW RISKY IS A LARGE PORTFOLIO OF STOCKS?

Many investors, including the authors of this text, buy "index" mutual funds that hold the S&P 500. Such funds are obviously well diversified. However, as you can see from the accompanying graph, diversification didn't help much when the market crashed in 2008. In just 2½ months, the market lost over 40% of its value. Someone with a $1 million nest egg invested in this "safe" portfolio suddenly experienced a $411,000 loss. Diversification helps, but it doesn't eliminate stock market risk.

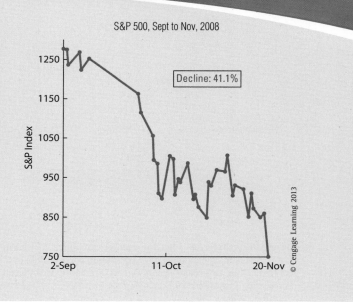

S&P 500, Sept to Nov, 2008

Decline: 41.1%

© Cengage Learning 2013

2.3c Diversifiable Risk versus Market Risk

As already mentioned, it's difficult if not impossible to find stocks whose expected returns are negatively correlated—most stocks tend to do well when the national economy is strong and badly when it is weak. Thus, even very large portfolios end up with a substantial amount of risk, but not as much risk as if all the money were invested in only one stock.

To see more precisely how portfolio size affects portfolio risk, consider Figure 2-12, which shows how portfolio risk is affected by forming larger and larger portfolios of randomly selected New York Stock Exchange (NYSE) stocks. Standard deviations are plotted for an average one-stock portfolio, an average two-stock portfolio, and so on, up to a portfolio consisting of all 2,000-plus common stocks that were listed on the NYSE at the time the data were plotted. The graph illustrates that, in general, the risk of a portfolio consisting of large-company stocks tends to decline and to approach some limit as the size of the portfolio increases. According to data accumulated in recent years, σ_1, the standard deviation of a one-stock portfolio (or an average stock), is approximately 35%. However, a portfolio consisting of all stocks, which is called the **market portfolio**, would have a standard deviation, σ_M, of only about 20%, which is shown as the horizontal dashed line in Figure 2-12.

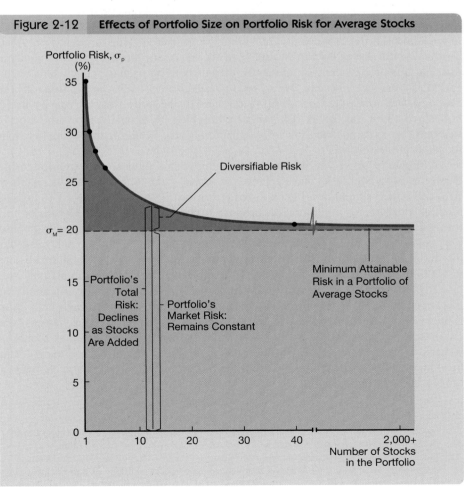

Figure 2-12	Effects of Portfolio Size on Portfolio Risk for Average Stocks

Portfolio Risk, σ_p (%)

Diversifiable Risk

σ_M = 20

Portfolio's Total Risk: Declines as Stocks Are Added

Portfolio's Market Risk: Remains Constant

Minimum Attainable Risk in a Portfolio of Average Stocks

Number of Stocks in the Portfolio

Thus, *almost half of the risk inherent in an average individual stock can be eliminated if the stock is held in a reasonably well-diversified portfolio, which is one containing 40 or more stocks in a number of different industries.* Some risk always remains—terrorists can attack, recessions can get out of hand, meteors can strike, and so forth—so it is impossible to diversify away the effects of broad stock market movements that affect virtually all stocks.

The part of a stock's risk that *can* be eliminated is called *diversifiable risk,* while the part that *cannot* be eliminated is called *market risk.*[10] The fact that a large part of the risk of any individual stock can be eliminated is vitally important, because rational investors *will* eliminate it and thus render it irrelevant.

Diversifiable risk is caused by such random events as lawsuits, strikes, successful and unsuccessful marketing programs, winning or losing a major contract, and other events that are unique to a particular firm. Because these events are random, their effects on a portfolio can be eliminated by diversification—bad events in one firm will be offset by good events in another. **Market risk,** on the other hand, stems from factors that systematically affect most firms: war, inflation, recessions, and high interest rates. Because most stocks are negatively affected by these factors, market risk cannot be eliminated by diversification.

We know that investors demand a premium for bearing risk; that is, the higher the risk of a security, the higher its expected return must be to induce investors to buy (or to hold) it. However, if investors are primarily concerned with the risk of their *portfolios* rather than the risk of the individual securities in the portfolio, then how should the risk of an individual stock be measured? One answer is provided by the **Capital Asset Pricing Model (CAPM)**, an important tool used to analyze the relationship between risk and rates of return.[11] The primary conclusion of the CAPM is this: *The relevant risk of an individual stock is its contribution to the risk of a well-diversified portfolio.* A stock might be quite risky if held by itself, but—since about half of its risk can be eliminated by diversification—the stock's **relevant risk** is its *contribution to the portfolio's risk,* which is much smaller than its stand-alone risk.

A simple example will help make this point clear. Suppose you are offered the chance to flip a coin. If it comes up heads, you win $20,000, but if it's tails, you lose $16,000. This is a good bet—the expected return is 0.5($20,000) + 0.5(−$16,000) = $2,000. However, it's a highly risky proposition because you have a 50% chance of losing $16,000. Thus, you might well refuse to make the bet. Alternatively, suppose that you were to flip 100 coins and that you would win $200 for each head but lose $160 for each tail. It is theoretically possible that you would flip all heads and win $20,000, and it is also theoretically possible that you would flip all tails and lose $16,000, but the chances are very high that you would actually flip about 50 heads and about 50 tails, winning a net of about $2,000. Although each individual flip is a risky bet, collectively you have a low-risk proposition because most of the risk has been diversified away. This is the idea behind holding portfolios of stocks rather than just one stock. The difference is that, with stocks, not all of the risk can be eliminated by diversification—those risks related to broad, systematic changes in the stock market will remain.

---

10. Diversifiable risk is also known as *company-specific,* or *unsystematic,* risk. Market risk is also known as *nondiversifiable, systematic,* or *beta,* risk; it is the risk that remains after diversification.
11. Indeed, Nobel Prizes were awarded to the developers of the CAPM, Professors Harry Markowitz and William F. Sharpe. The CAPM is a relatively complex theory, and only its basic elements are presented in this chapter.

THE BENEFITS OF DIVERSIFYING OVERSEAS

Figure 2-12 shows that an investor can significantly reduce portfolio risk by holding a large number of stocks. The figure accompanying this box suggests that investors may be able to reduce risk even further by holding stocks from all around the world, because the returns on domestic and international stocks are not perfectly correlated.

Although U.S. investors have traditionally been relatively reluctant to hold international assets, it is a safe bet that in the years ahead U.S. investors will shift more and more of their assets to overseas investments.

Source: For further reading, see Kenneth Kasa, "Measuring the Gains from International Portfolio Diversification," *Federal Reserve Bank of San Francisco Weekly Letter,* no. 94-14 (April 8, 1994).

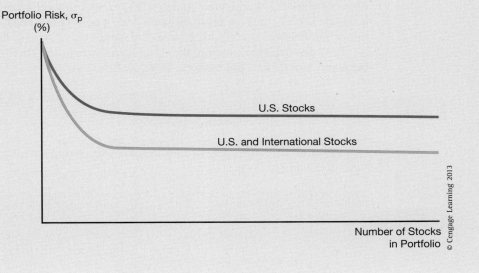

Are all stocks equally risky in the sense that adding them to a well-diversified portfolio will have the same effect on the portfolio's risk? The answer is "no." Different stocks will affect the portfolio differently, so different securities have different degrees of relevant risk. How can the relevant risk of an individual stock be measured? As we have seen, all risk except that related to broad market movements can, and presumably will, be diversified away. After all, why accept risk that can be eliminated easily? *The risk that remains after diversifying is called market risk, the risk that is inherent in the market.* In the next section, we develop a measure of a stock's market risk and then, in a later section, we introduce an equation for determining the required rate of return on a stock, given its market risk.

2.3d Contribution to Market Risk: Beta

The primary conclusion reached in the preceding section is that the relevant risk of an individual stock is the amount of risk the stock contributes to a well-diversified portfolio. The benchmark for a well-diversified stock portfolio is the market portfolio, which is a portfolio containing all stocks. Therefore, the relevant risk of an individual stock, which is measured by its **beta coefficient,** is defined under the CAPM as the amount of risk that the stock contributes to the market portfolio. In CAPM terminology, ρ_{iM} is the correlation between Stock i's return and the market return, σ_i is the standard deviation of Stock i's return, and σ_M is the standard deviation of the market's return. The beta coefficient of Stock i, denoted by b_i, is found as follows:

(2–9)
$$b_i = \left(\frac{\sigma_i}{\sigma_M}\right) \rho_{iM}$$

This tells us that a stock with a high standard deviation, σ_i, will tend to have a high beta, which means that, other things held constant, the stock contributes a lot of risk to a well-diversified portfolio. This makes sense, because a stock with high stand-alone risk will tend to destabilize the portfolio. Note too that a stock with a high correlation with the market, ρ_{iM}, will also tend to have a large beta and hence be risky. This also makes sense, because a high correlation means that diversification is not helping much, with most of the stock's risk affecting the portfolio's risk.

It is also useful to transform the variables in Equation 2-9 to form the **covariance between Stock i and the market, COV$_{iM}$,** defined as[12]

(2–10)
$$COV_{iM} = \rho_{iM}\sigma_i\sigma_M$$

Substituting Equation 2-10 into 2-9 provides another frequently used expression for calculating beta:

(2–11)
$$b_i = \frac{COV_{iM}}{\sigma_M^2}$$

Calculators and spreadsheets can calculate the components of Equation 2-9 (ρ_{iM}, σ_i, and σ_M), which can then be used to calculate beta, but there is another way. Suppose you plotted the stock's returns on the y-axis of a graph and the market portfolio's returns on the x-axis. The formula for the slope of a regression line is exactly equal to the formula for beta in Equation 2-11. Therefore, to estimate beta for a security, you can just estimate a regression with the stock's returns on the y-axis and the market's returns on the x-axis, which we do in the next section.

So what, exactly, does it mean for a stock to have a low or a high beta? A low beta stock's returns are relatively unrelated to the market's return. It also might have low total risk, as measured by its standard deviation, but if its correlation with the market

---

12. Using historical data, the sample covariance can be calculated as

Sample covariance from historical data $= COV_{iM} = \dfrac{\sum\limits_{t=1}^{n} (\bar{r}_{i,t} - \bar{r}_{i,Avg})(\bar{r}_{M,t} - \bar{r}_{M,Avg})}{n-1}$

Calculating the covariance is somewhat easier than calculating the correlation. So if you have already calculated the standard deviations, it is easier to calculate the covariance and then calculate the correlation as $\rho_{iM} = COV_{iM}/(\sigma_i\sigma_M)$.

is low enough, it could have a large standard deviation but still a low beta. Because the low beta stock's returns are relatively unrelated to the market's returns, it contributes little risk to a well-diversified portfolio. On the other hand, a high beta stock's returns are more closely related to the market's returns. When the market is doing well, the high beta stock tends to do well, and when the market does poorly, it also does poorly. The high beta stock also is likely to have a large standard deviation and total risk. Thus, the high beta stock contributes a good deal of risk to a well-diversified portfolio.

Self Test

Explain the following statement: "An asset held as part of a portfolio is generally less risky than the same asset held in isolation."

What is meant by *perfect positive correlation, perfect negative correlation,* and *zero correlation?*

In general, can the risk of a portfolio be reduced to zero by increasing the number of stocks in the portfolio? Explain.

What is the average beta? If a stock has the average beta, what does that imply about its risk relative to the market?

Why is beta the theoretically correct measure of a stock's risk?

If you plotted the returns on a particular stock versus those on the Dow Jones Index over the past 5 years, what would the slope of the regression line tell you about the stock's market risk?

2.4 Calculating Beta Coefficients

The CAPM is an *ex ante* model, which means that all of the variables represent before-the-fact, *expected* values. In particular, the beta coefficient used by investors should reflect the relationship between a stock's expected return and the market's return during some *future* period. However, people generally calculate betas using data from some *past* period and then assume that the stock's risk will be the same in the future as it was in the past.

Table 2-1 shows the betas for some well-known companies as provided by two different financial organizations, Value Line and Yahoo! Finance. Notice that their estimates of beta usually differ because they calculate it in slightly different ways. Given these differences, many analysts choose to calculate their own betas or else average the published betas.

Recall from the previous section how betas can be calculated. The actual historical returns for a company are plotted on the y-axis, and the market portfolio's returns are plotted on the x-axis. A regression line is then fitted through the points, and the slope of that line provides an estimate of the stock's beta. It is possible to compute beta coefficients with a calculator, but in the real world a computer is typically used, either with a statistical software program or a spreadsheet program. The chapter's *Excel Tool Kit* model shows how GE's beta can be calculated using *Excel*'s regression function.[13]

The first step in a regression analysis is getting the data. Most analysts use 4 to 5 years of monthly data, although some use 52 weeks of weekly data. We decided to use 4 years (48 months) of monthly data, so we began by downloading 49 months of

WEB

See *Ch02 Tool Kit.xls* on the textbook's Web site.

---

13. For an explanation of computing beta with a financial calculator, see *Web Extension 2B* on the textbook's Web site.

TABLE 2-1	Beta Coefficients for Some Actual Companies	
Stock (Ticker Symbol)	**Value Line**	**Yahoo! Finance**
Amazon.com (AMZN)	1.05	1.07
Cisco Systems (CSCO)	0.95	1.21
Dell Computer (DELL)	0.95	1.36
Microsoft Corp. (MSFT)	0.80	1.02
General Electric (GE)	1.20	1.71
Empire District Electric (EDE)	0.70	0.65
Coca-Cola (KO)	0.60	0.59
Heinz (HNZ)	0.65	0.57
Energen Corp. (EGN)	1.10	1.02
Procter & Gamble (PG)	0.60	0.52

Sources: **www.valueline.com** and **finance.yahoo.com**, January 2011.

stock prices for GE from the Yahoo! Finance Web site (we needed 49 months of data to get 48 rates of return). We used the S&P 500 Index as the market portfolio because it is representative of the market and because many analysts use this index. Figure 2-13 shows a portion of these data; the full data set is in the chapter's *Tool Kit*.

Figure 2-13   **Stock Return Data for General Electric and the S&P 500 Index**

	A	B	C	D	E
395	Month	Market Level (S&P 500 Index) at Month End	Market's Return	GE Adjusted Stock Price at Month End	GE's Return
396	January 2011	1,286.12	2.3%	$20.14	10.1%
397	December 2010	1,257.64	6.5%	$18.29	16.4%
398	November 2010	1,180.55	−0.2%	$15.71	−1.1%
399	October 2010	1,183.26	3.7%	$15.89	−1.4%
441	April 2007	1,482.37	4.3%	$31.65	4.2%
442	March 2007	1,420.86	1.0%	$30.37	1.3%
443	February 2007	1,406.82	−2.2%	$29.98	−2.4%
444	January 2007	1,438.24	NA	$30.72	NA
445					
446	Description of Data				
447	Average return (annual):		−0.8%		−2.4%
448	Standard deviation (annual):		19.7%		40.1%
449	Minimum monthly return:		−16.9%		−27.8%
450	Maximum monthly return:		9.4%		25.1%
451	Correlation between GE and the market:				0.82
452	Beta: $b_{GE} = \rho_{GE,M} (\sigma_{GE} / \sigma_M)$				1.66
453					
454	Beta (using the SLOPE function):				1.66
455	Intercept (using the INTERCEPT function):				0.00
456	R^2 (using the RSQ function):				0.67

Note: The data for May 2007 through September 2010 are not shown but are included in all calculations.

The second step is to convert the stock prices into rates of return. For example, to find the January 2011 return for GE, we find the percentage change from the previous month: ($20.14 − $18.29)/$18.29 = 0.101 = 10.1%.[14] We also find the percent change of the S&P Index level and use this as the market return.

As the lower portion of Figure 2-13 shows, GE had an average annual return of −2.4% during this 4-year period, while the market had an average annual return of −0.8%. As we noted before, it is usually unreasonable to think that the future expected return for a stock will equal its average historical return over a relatively short period, such as 4 years. If this were not true, then why would anyone buy either the S&P or GE if they expected the same negative returns as were earned in the past? However, we might well expect past volatility to be a reasonable estimate of future volatility, at least during the next couple of years. Note that the annualized standard deviation for GE's return during this period was 40.1% versus 19.7% for the market. The range between GE's minimum and maximum returns is also greater than the corresponding range for the market. Thus, GE's volatility is greater than the market's volatility. This is what we would expect, since the market is a well-diversified portfolio and so much of its risk has been diversified away. The correlation between GE's stock returns and the market returns is 0.82, which is somewhat higher than the correlation between a typical stock and the market.

We obtained inputs from Figure 2-13 and used Equation 2-9 to approximate GE's beta:

$$b_i = \left(\frac{\sigma_i}{\sigma_M}\right) \rho_{iM} = \left(\frac{0.401}{0.197}\right)(0.82) = 1.669 \approx 1.66$$

Other than a small difference due to rounding in intermediate steps, this is the same result reported in Figure 2-14.

A picture is worth a thousand words, so Figure 2-14 shows a plot of GE's returns against the market returns. As you will notice if you look in the *Excel Tool Kit* file, we used the *Excel* chart feature to add a trend line and to display the equation and R² value on the chart itself. We also could have used the *Excel* regression analysis feature, which would have provided more detailed data.

Figure 2-14 indicates that GE's estimated beta is about 1.66, as shown by the slope coefficient in the regression equation displayed on the chart. This means that GE's beta is greater than the 1.0 average beta. Therefore, GE's returns tend to move up and down (on average) by more than the market's returns. Note, however, that the points are only loosely clustered around the regression line. Sometimes GE does much better than the market, while at other times it does much worse. The R² value shown in the chart measures the degree of dispersion about the regression line. Statistically speaking, it measures the percentage of the variance that is explained

---

14. The prices reported in Yahoo! Finance are adjusted for dividends and stock splits, so we can calculate the return as the percentage change in the adjusted price. If you use a source that reports actual market prices, then you must make the adjustment yourself when calculating returns. For example, suppose the stock price is $100 in January, the company has a 2-for-1 split, and the actual price is then $60 in February. The reported adjusted price for February would be $60, but the reported adjusted price for January would be lowered to $50 to reflect the stock split. This gives an accurate stock return of 20%: ($60 − $50)/$50 = 20%, the same as if there had not been a split, in which case the return would have been ($120 − $100)/$100 = 20%. Or suppose the actual price in March was $50, the company paid a $10 dividend, and the actual price in April was $60. Shareholders have earned a return of ($60 + $10 − $50)/$50 = 40%. Yahoo! Finance reports an adjusted price of $60 for April and an adjusted price of $42.857 for March, which gives a return of ($60 – $42.857)/$42.857 = 40%. Again, the percentage change in the adjusted price accurately reflects the actual return.

Figure 2-14 | **Stock Return Data for General Electric and the S&P 500 Index**

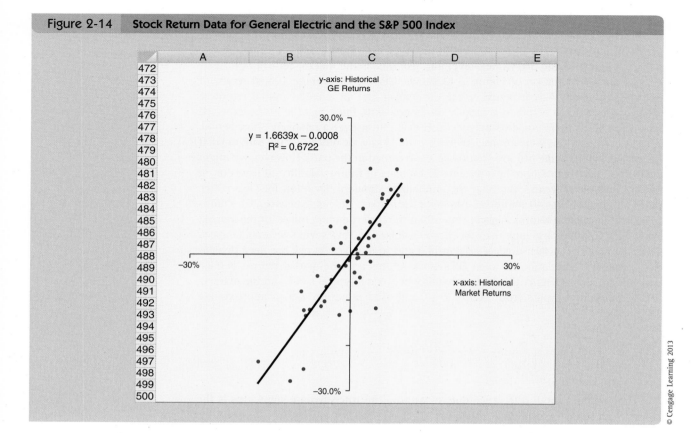

by the regression equation. An R^2 of 1.0 indicates that all points lie exactly on the line and hence that all of the variations in the y-variable are explained by the x-variable. GE's R^2 is about 0.67, which is somewhat higher than the typical stock R^2 of 0.32. This indicates that about 67% of the variance in GE's returns is explained by the market returns versus only 32% of the explained variance of a typical stock. If we had done a similar analysis for a portfolio of 40 randomly selected stocks, then the points would probably have been clustered tightly around the regression line and the R^2 probably would have exceeded 0.90.

Finally, observe that the intercept shown in the regression equation on the chart is −0.0008. This indicates that GE's average monthly return was −0.08% less than that of a typical company during these 4 years, or 12(−0.08%) = −0.96% less per year as a result of factors other than the general decline in stock prices.

2.4a Portfolio Betas

An important aspect of the CAPM is that the beta of a portfolio is a weighted average of its individual securities' betas:

(2–12)

$$b_p = w_1 b_1 + w_2 b_2 + \ldots + w_n b_n$$

$$= \sum_{i=1}^{n} w_i b_i$$

Here b_p is the beta of the portfolio, which shows its tendency to move with the market; w_i is the fraction of the portfolio invested in Stock i; and b_i is the beta coefficient of Stock i. For example, suppose an investor holds a $100,000 portfolio consisting of $33,333.33 invested in each of three stocks; each of the stocks has a beta of 0.70. The weight of each stock in the portfolio is $33,333.33/$100,000 = 0.3333. The portfolio's beta will be b_p = 0.70:

$$b_p = 0.3333(0.70) + 0.3333(0.70) + 0.3333(0.70) = 0.70$$

Such a portfolio will be less risky than the market, so it should experience relatively narrow price swings and have relatively small fluctuations in its rates of return. In terms of Figure 2-14, the slope of its regression line would be 0.70, which is less than that for a portfolio of average stocks.

Now suppose that one of the existing stocks is sold and replaced by a stock with b_i = 2.00. This action will increase the beta of the portfolio from b_{p1} = 0.70 to b_{p2} = 1.13:

$$b_{p2} = 0.3333(0.70) + 0.3333(0.70) + 0.3333(2.00)$$

$$= 1.13$$

Had a stock with b_i = 0.20 been added, the portfolio beta would have declined from 0.70 to 0.53. Adding a low-beta stock, therefore, would reduce the risk of the portfolio. Consequently, adding new stocks to a portfolio can change the risk of that portfolio. *Since a stock's beta measures its contribution to the risk of a portfolio, beta is the theoretically correct measure of the stock's risk.*

2.4b Some Other Points Related to Beta

The preceding analysis of risk in a portfolio context is part of the CAPM, and we highlight the key points below.

1. A stock's risk consists of two components, market risk and diversifiable risk.
2. Diversifiable risk can be eliminated by diversification, and most investors do indeed diversify, either by holding large portfolios or by purchasing shares in a mutual fund. We are left, then, with market risk, which is caused by general movements in the stock market and which reflects the fact that most stocks are systematically affected by events like war, recessions, and inflation. Market risk is the only risk relevant to a rational, diversified investor because such an investor can eliminate diversifiable risk.
3. Investors must be compensated for bearing risk: The greater the risk of a stock, the higher its required return. However, compensation is required only for risk that cannot be eliminated by diversification. If stocks had risk premiums due to diversifiable risk, then well-diversified investors would start buying those securities (which the investors would not consider especially risky) and bidding up their prices. The stocks' final (equilibrium) expected returns would reflect only nondiversifiable market risk.
4. The market risk of a stock is measured by its beta coefficient, and beta is the proper measure of the stock's relevant risk. If b equals 1.0, then the stock is about as risky as the market, assuming it is held in a diversified portfolio. If b is less than 1.0, then the stock is less risky than the market; if beta is greater than 1.0, the stock is more risky.

5. The beta of a portfolio is a weighted average of the individual securities' betas.
6. *Since a stock's beta coefficient determines how the stock affects the risk of a diversified portfolio, beta is the most relevant measure of any stock's risk.*

What types of data are needed to calculate a beta coefficient for an actual company?

What does the R^2 measure? What is the R^2 for a typical company?

An investor has a three-stock portfolio with $25,000 invested in Dell, $50,000 invested in Ford, and $25,000 invested in Wal-Mart. Dell's beta is estimated to be 1.20, Ford's beta is estimated to be 0.80, and Wal-Mart's beta is estimated to be 1.0. What is the estimated beta of the investor's portfolio? **(0.95)**

2.5 The Relationship between Risk and Return

In the preceding section we saw that, under the CAPM theory, beta is the proper measure of a stock's relevant risk. However, we need to quantify how risk affects required returns: For a given level of risk as measured by beta, what rate of return do investors require to compensate them for bearing that risk? To begin, let us define the following terms.

$\hat{r}_i$ = *Expected* rate of return on Stock i.

r_i = *Required* rate of return on Stock i. This is the minimum expected return that is required to induce an average investor to purchase the stock.

$\bar{r}$ = Realized, after-the-fact return.

r_{RF} = Risk-free rate of return. In this context, r_{RF} is generally measured by the expected return on long-term U.S. Treasury bonds.

b_i = Beta coefficient of Stock i.

r_M = Required rate of return on a portfolio consisting of all stocks, which is called the *market portfolio*.

RP_M = Risk premium on "the market." $RP_M = (r_M - r_{RF})$ is the additional return over the risk-free rate required to induce an average investor to invest in the market portfolio.

RP_i = Risk premium on Stock i: $RP_i = (RP_M)b_i$.

The **market risk premium, RP_M**, is the premium that investors require for bearing the risk of an average stock, and it depends on the degree of risk aversion that investors on average have. Assume that Treasury bonds yield r_{RF} = 6% and that the stock market has a required return of r_M = 11%. Under these conditions, the market risk premium, RP_M, is 5%:

$$RP_M = r_M - r_{RF} = 11\% - 6\% = 5\%$$

We can measure a stock's relative risk by its beta coefficient and then calculate its individual risk premium as follows:

$$\text{Risk premium for Stock i} = RP_i = (RP_M)b_i \qquad (2\text{–}13)$$

For example, if $b_i = 0.5$ and $RP_M = 5\%$, then RP_i is 2.5%:

$$RP_i = (5\%)(0.5)$$
$$= 2.5\%$$

The required return for any investment can be expressed in general terms as

$$\text{Required return} = \text{Risk-free return} + \text{Premium for risk}$$

Here the risk-free return includes a premium for expected inflation, and we assume that the assets under consideration have similar maturities and liquidity. Under these conditions, the relationship between risk and required returns can be found as specified in the **Security Market Line (SML)**:

$$\text{SML equation:} \quad \begin{pmatrix}\text{Required return} \\ \text{on Stock i}\end{pmatrix} = \begin{pmatrix}\text{Risk-free} \\ \text{rate}\end{pmatrix} + \begin{pmatrix}\text{Market risk} \\ \text{premium}\end{pmatrix}\begin{pmatrix}\text{Beta of} \\ \text{Stock i}\end{pmatrix}$$
$$r_i = r_{RF} + (r_M - r_{RF})b_i$$
$$= r_{RF} + (RP_M)b_i \qquad (2\text{–}14)$$

The required return for our illustrative Stock i is then found as follows:

$$r_i = 6\% + 5\%(0.5)$$
$$= 8.5\%$$

If some other Stock j were riskier than Stock i and had $b_j = 2.0$, then its required rate of return would be 16%:

$$r_j = 6\% + (5\%)2.0 = 16\%$$

An average stock, with $b = 1.0$, would have a required return of 11%, the same as the market return:

$$r_A = 6\% + (5\%)1.0 = 11\% = r_M$$

Equation 2-14 is called the Security Market Line (SML) equation, and it is often expressed in graph form; see Figure 2-15, which shows the SML when $r_{RF} = 6\%$ and $RP_M = 5\%$. Note the following points:

1. Required rates of return are shown on the vertical axis, while risk as measured by beta is shown on the horizontal axis. This graph is quite different from the regression line shown in Figure 2-14, where the returns on individual stocks were plotted

Figure 2-15   The Security Market Line (SML)

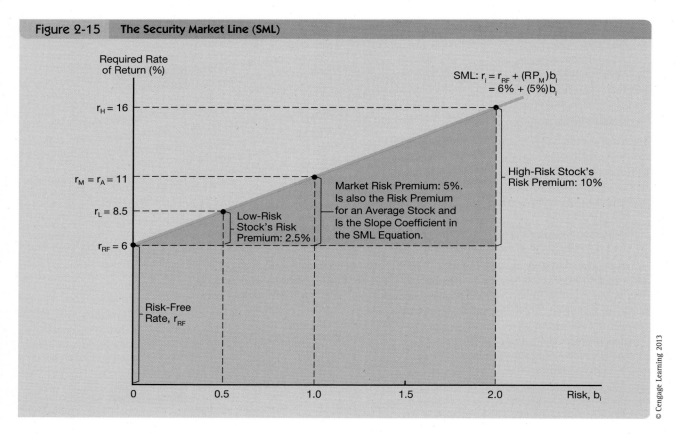

on the vertical axis and returns on the market index were shown on the horizontal axis. Here, the slope of the regression line from an analysis such as that conducted in Figure 2-14 is plotted as beta on the horizontal axis of Figure 2-15.

2. Riskless securities have $b_i = 0$; therefore, r_{RF} appears as the vertical axis intercept in Figure 2-15. If we could construct a portfolio that had a beta of zero, then it would have a required return equal to the risk-free rate.

3. The slope of the SML (5% in Figure 2-15) reflects the degree of risk aversion in the economy: The greater the average investor's aversion to risk, then (a) the steeper the slope of the line, (b) the greater the risk premium for all stocks, and (c) the higher the required rate of return on all stocks.[15] These points are discussed further in a later section.

4. The values we worked out for stocks with $b_i = 0.5$, $b_i = 1.0$, and $b_i = 2.0$ agree with the values shown on the graph for r_L, r_A, and r_H.

5. Negative betas are rare, but they can occur. For example, some stocks associated with gold, such as a mining operation, occasionally have a negative beta. Based on the SML, a stock with a negative beta should have a required return less than the risk-free rate. In fact, a stock with a very large but negative beta

---

15. Students sometimes confuse beta with the slope of the SML. This is a mistake. The slope of any straight line is equal to the "rise" divided by the "run," or $(Y_1 - Y_0)/(X_1 - X_0)$. Consider Figure 2-15. If we let Y = r and X = beta and if we go from the origin to b = 1.0, then we see that the slope is $(r_M - r_{RF})/(b_M - b_{RF}) = (11\% - 6\%)/(1 - 0) = 5\%$. Thus, the slope of the SML is equal to $(r_M - r_{RF})$, the market risk premium. In Figure 2-15, $r_i = 6\% + 5\%(b_i)$, so an increase of beta from 1.0 to 2.0 would produce a 5-percentage-point increase in r_i.

might have negative required return! This means that when the market is doing well, this stock will do poorly. But it also implies the opposite: When the market is doing poorly, a negative-beta stock should have a positive return. In other words, the negative-beta stock acts like an insurance policy. Therefore, an investor might be willing to accept a negative return on the stock during good times if it is likely to provide a positive return in bad times.

What would happen if a stock's expected return, $\hat{r}_i$, were greater than its required return, r_i? In other words, suppose investors thought they could get a 14% return even though the stock's risk only justified an 11% return? If all investors felt this way, then demand for the stock would soar as investors tried to purchase it. But if everyone tried to buy the stock, its price would go up. As the price went up, the extra expected returns would evaporate until the expected return equaled the required return. The reverse would happen if the expected return were less than the required return. Therefore, it seems reasonable to expect that investors' actions would tend to drive the expected return toward the required return.

Unexpected news about a stock's cash flow prospects would certainly change the stock's expected return. A stock's required return can also change because the Security Market Line and a company's position on it can change over time as a result of changes in interest rates, investors' aversion to risk, and individual companies' betas. Such changes are discussed in the following sections.

2.5a The Impact of Changes in Inflation and Interest Rates

Interest is the same as "rent" on borrowed money, or the price of money. Thus, r_{RF} is the price of money to a riskless borrower. The risk-free rate as measured by the rate on U.S. Treasury securities is called the *nominal,* or *quoted, rate,* and it consists of two elements: (1) a *real inflation-free rate of return, r**; and (2) an *inflation premium, IP,* equal to the anticipated rate of inflation.[16] Thus, $r_{RF} = r^* + IP$. The real rate on long-term Treasury bonds has historically ranged from 2% to 4% with a mean of about 3%. Therefore, the 6% r_{RF} shown in Figure 2-15 might be thought of as consisting of a 3% real risk-free rate of return plus a 3% inflation premium: $r_{RF} = r^* + IP = 3\% + 3\% = 6\%$.

The nominal risk-free rate could change as a result of changes in anticipated inflation or changes in the real interest rate. Consider a recession, such as the one that began in 2007. If consumers and businesses decide to cut back on spending, this will reduce the demand for funds, and that will, other things held constant, lower the risk-free rate and thus the required return on other investments.[17] A key point to note is that a change in r_{RF} will not necessarily cause a change in the market risk premium. Thus, as r_{RF} changes, so will the required return on the market, and this will, other things held constant, keep the market risk premium stable.

---

16. In addition to anticipated inflation, the inflation premium may also include a premium for bearing inflation risk. Long-term Treasury bonds also contain a maturity risk premium, MRP. Here we include the MRP in r* to simplify the discussion. See Chapter 4 for more on bond pricing and bond risk premiums.

17. Think of a sailboat floating in a harbor. The distance from the ocean floor to the ocean surface is like the risk-free rate, and it moves up and down with the tides. The distance from the top of the ship's mast to the ocean floor is like the required market return: It too moves up and down with the tides. The distance from the mast-top to the ocean surface is like the market risk premium—it stays the same, even though tides move the ship up and down. Thus, other things held constant, a change in the risk-free rate also causes an identical change in the required market return, r_M, resulting in a relatively stable market risk premium, $r_M - r_{RF}$.

Figure 2-16   Shift in the SML Caused by an Increase in Interest Rates

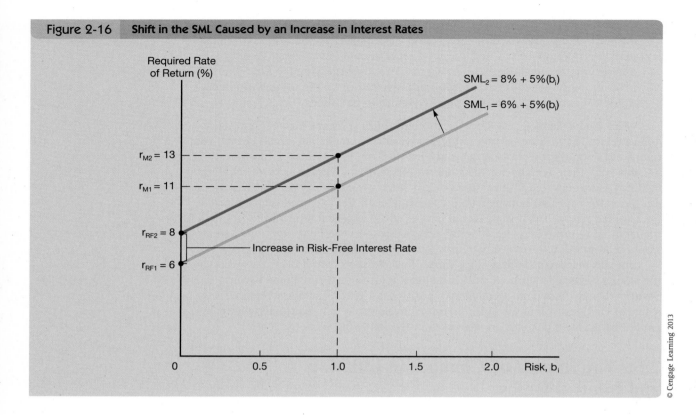

Suppose the risk-free interest rate increases to 8% from some combination of an increase in real rates and in anticipated inflation. Such a change is shown in Figure 2-16. Notice that, under the CAPM, the increase in r_{RF} leads to an *identical* increase in the rate of return on all assets, because the same risk-free rate is built into the required rate of return on all assets. For example, the rate of return on an average stock, r_M, increases from 11% to 13%. Other risky securities' returns also rise by 2 percentage points.

2.5b Changes in Risk Aversion

The slope of the Security Market Line reflects the extent to which investors are averse to risk: The steeper the slope of the line, the greater the average investor's aversion to risk. Suppose all investors were indifferent to risk—that is, suppose they were *not* risk averse. If r_{RF} were 6%, then risky assets would also provide an expected return of 6%, because if there were no risk aversion then there would be no risk premium, and the SML would be plotted as a horizontal line. As risk aversion increases, so does the risk premium, and this causes the slope of the SML to become steeper.

Figure 2-17 illustrates an increase in risk aversion. The market risk premium rises from 5% to 7.5%, causing r_M to rise from $r_{M1} = 11\%$ to $r_{M2} = 13.5\%$. The returns on other risky assets also rise, and the effect of this shift in risk aversion is greater for riskier securities. For example, the required return on a stock with $b_i = 0.5$ increases by only 1.25 percentage points, from 8.5% to 9.75%; that on a stock with $b_i = 1.0$ increases by 2.5 percentage points, from 11.0% to 13.5%; and that on a stock with $b_i = 1.5$ increases by 3.75 percentage points, from 13.5% to 17.25%.

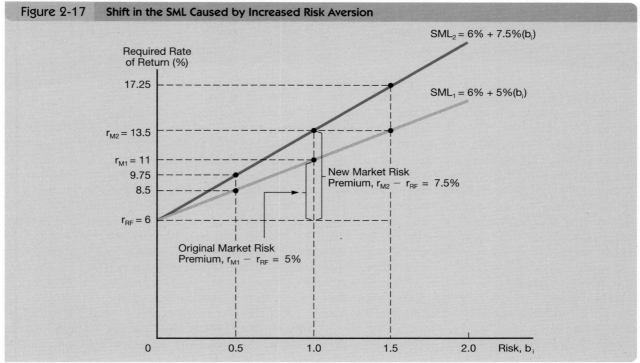

Figure 2-17 Shift in the SML Caused by Increased Risk Aversion

2.5c Changes in a Stock's Beta Coefficient

Given risk aversion and a positively sloped SML as in Figure 2-17, the higher a stock's beta, the higher its required rate of return. As we shall see later in the book, a firm can influence its beta through changes in the composition of its assets and also through its use of debt: Acquiring riskier assets will increase beta, as will a change in capital structure that calls for a higher debt ratio. A company's beta can also change as a result of external factors such as increased competition in its industry, the expiration of basic patents, and the like. When such changes lead to a higher or lower beta, the required rate of return will also change.

Self Test

Differentiate among the expected rate of return ($\hat{r}$), the required rate of return (r), and the realized, after-the-fact return ($\bar{r}$) on a stock. Which must be larger to get you to buy the stock, $\hat{r}$ or r? Would $\hat{r}$, r, and $\bar{r}$ typically be the same or different for a given company, say on January 1, 2012?

What are the differences between the relative returns graph (the regression line in Figure 2-14), where "betas are made," and the SML graph (Figure 2-15), where "betas are used"? Discuss both how the graphs are constructed and the information they convey.

What happens to the SML graph in Figure 2-15 when inflation increases or decreases?

What happens to the SML graph when risk aversion increases or decreases? What would the SML look like if investors were completely indifferent to risk—that is, had zero risk aversion?

How can a firm influence its market risk as reflected in its beta?

A stock has a beta of 1.4. Assume that the risk-free rate is 5.5% and that the market risk premium is 5%. What is the stock's required rate of return? **(12.5%)**

ANOTHER KIND OF RISK: THE BERNIE MADOFF STORY

In the fall of 2008, Bernard Madoff's massive Ponzi scheme was exposed, revealing an important type of risk that's not dealt with in this chapter. Madoff was a money manager in the 1960s, and apparently through good luck he produced above-average results for several years. His clients then told their friends about Madoff's success, and those friends sent in money for him to invest. Madoff's actual returns then dropped, but he didn't tell his clients that they were losing money. Rather, he told them that returns were holding up well, and he used new incoming money to pay dividends and meet withdrawal requests. The idea of using new money to pay off old investors is called a Ponzi scheme, named after Charles Ponzi, a Bostonian who set up the first widely publicized such scheme in the early 1900s.

Madoff perfected the system, ran his scheme for about 40 years, and attracted about $50 billion of investors' funds. His investors ranged from well-known billionaires to retirees who invested their entire life savings. His advertising was strictly word-of-mouth, and clients telling potential clients about the many wealthy and highly regarded people who invested with him certainly helped. All of his investors assumed that someone else had done the "due diligence" and found the operation to be clean. A few investors who actually did some due diligence were suspicious and didn't invest with him, but for the most part, people just blindly followed the others.

The hedge fund boom that began in the 1990s was a big help. "Funds of funds," which are hedge funds set up to investigate and then invest in other hedge funds, gained momentum, and some of those funds were Madoff's biggest investors. They were a scam in their own right, taking fees to investigate other hedge funds and money managers to find the best of them, but really doing virtually no investigating on their own and simply sending the money entrusted to them to Bernie Madoff. Madoff also paid some "finders" to frequent country club bars, brag about how well they were doing in the market, and induce other fish to swim into his net.

All Ponzi schemes crash when something occurs that causes some investors to seek to withdraw funds in amounts greater than the incoming funds from new investors. Someone tries to get out, can't do it, tells others who worry and try to get out too, and almost overnight the scam unravels. That happened to Madoff in 2008, when the stock market crash caused some of his investors to seek withdrawals and few new dollars were coming in. In the end, his investors lost billions; some lost their entire life savings, and several have committed suicide. Moreover, the Madoff revelations have led to the exposure of other, similar (but smaller) frauds. Indeed, people—especially the rich and famous—are reluctant to admit they've been taken, so it's likely that lots of frauds are never reported.

How can you guard against a fraud like Madoff's? For a scheme as sophisticated as that of Madoff, it's not easy, but there are some steps that can and should be taken.

1. *Use your basic financial knowledge and some common sense.* Earlier in this chapter we gave you an idea about the kinds of returns that have been earned in the past on different classes of investments with different risk profiles. If someone offers you an investment that seems too good to be true, it probably is, so you should drill deep to see if it is really what its sponsor says it is before you invest. If you don't have the time and expertise for such investigation, you should probably avoid the investment.
2. *Deal with reputable institutions.* We hate to recommend avoiding small and new organizations, but unless you have the ability to check out an investment manager carefully, that's probably a good idea. There are institutions with the expertise to conduct such investigations, so you might be wise to leave the too-good-to-be-true investments to them.
3. *Diversify.* Many people were burned by Bernie Madoff, but the ones who were hurt worst were those who trusted most or all of their funds to him. Those who diversified their holdings were hurt, but they weren't wiped out. So diversify!

2.6 Some Concerns about Beta and the CAPM

www

Kenneth French's Web site, **http://mba.tuck .dartmouth.edu/pages/ faculty/ken.french/ index.html** is an excellent resource for data and information regarding factors related to stock returns.

The Capital Asset Pricing Model is more than just an abstract theory described in textbooks. It has great intuitive appeal, and it is widely used by analysts, investors, and corporations. However, a number of studies have raised concerns about its validity. For example, a study by Eugene Fama of the University of Chicago and Kenneth French of Dartmouth found no historical relationship between stocks' returns and their market betas, confirming a position long held by some professors and stock market analysts.[18]

As an alternative to the traditional CAPM, researchers and practitioners are developing models with more explanatory variables than just beta. These multi-factor models represent an attractive generalization of the traditional CAPM model's insight that market risk—risk that cannot be diversified away—underlies the pricing of assets. In the multi-variable models, risk is assumed to be caused by a number of different factors, including size of firm, market/book ratios, measures of liquidity, and the like, whereas the CAPM gauges risk only relative to returns on the market portfolio. The multi-variable models represent a potentially important step forward in finance theory, but they also have some deficiencies when applied in practice. As a result, the basic CAPM is still the most widely used method for thinking about required rates of return on stocks.

> Have there been any studies that question the validity of the CAPM? Explain.

Self Test

2.7 Some Concluding Thoughts: Implications for Corporate Managers and Investors

The connection between risk and return is an important concept, and it has numerous implications for both corporate managers and investors. As we will see in later chapters, corporate managers spend a great deal of time assessing the risk and returns of individual projects. Indeed, given their concerns about the risk of individual projects, it might be fair to ask why we spend so much time discussing the riskiness of stocks. Why not begin by looking at the riskiness of such business assets as plant and equipment? The reason is that, *for a management whose primary goal is to maximize intrinsic value, the overriding consideration is the riskiness of the firm's stock, and the relevant risk of any physical asset must be measured in terms of its effect on the stock's risk as seen by investors.* For example, suppose the luxury retailer Saks Fifth Avenue is considering a major investment in a new outlet mall enterprise that specializes in low-cost, affordable clothes and sensible personal items, and provides lay-away financing for more expensive items. Sales, and hence

---

18. See Eugene F. Fama and Kenneth R. French, "The Cross-Section of Expected Stock Returns," *Journal of Finance,* Vol. 47 (1992), pp. 427–465; and Eugene F. Fama and Kenneth R. French, "Common Risk Factors in the Returns on Stocks and Bonds," *Journal of Financial Economics,* Vol. 33 (1993), pp. 3–56. They found that stock returns are related to firm size and market/book ratios. Small firms and those firms with low market/book ratios had higher returns; however, they found no relationship between returns and beta.

earnings, at stores such as these are highly uncertain, so on a stand-alone basis this new venture is quite risky. However, suppose that profits and stock returns in this industry are negatively correlated with luxury retail profits. When times are good and people have plenty of money, they are more likely to splurge on luxury items. When times are bad, they tend to be more frugal, shopping for more sensible personal items. Therefore, returns would be high on regular operations and low on the outlet division during good times, but the opposite would be true during recessions. The result might be a pattern like that shown earlier in Figure 2-9 for Stocks W and M. Thus, what appears to be a risky investment when viewed on a stand-alone basis might not be so risky when viewed within the context of the company as a whole.

This analysis can be extended to the corporation's stockholders. Because Saks's stock is owned by diversified stockholders, the real issue each time management makes an investment decision is this: How will this investment affect the risk of our stockholders? Again, the stand-alone risk of an individual project may look quite high; however, when viewed in the context of the project's effect on stockholder risk, it may not be as large. We will address this issue again in Chapter 13, where we examine the effects of capital budgeting on companies' beta coefficients and thus on stockholders' risks.

These concepts are obviously important for individual investors, but they are also important for corporate managers. Here we summarize some key ideas that all investors should consider.

1. *There is a trade-off between risk and return.* The average investor likes higher returns but dislikes risk. It follows that higher-risk investments need to offer investors higher expected returns. Put another way: If you are seeking higher returns, you must be willing to assume higher risks.

2. *Diversification is crucial.* By diversifying wisely, investors can dramatically reduce risk without reducing their expected returns. Don't put all of your money in one or two stocks, or in one or two industries. A huge mistake many people make is to invest a high percentage of their funds in their employer's stock. Then, if the company goes bankrupt, they lose not only their job but also their invested capital. Although no stock is completely riskless, you can smooth out the bumps somewhat by holding a well-diversified portfolio.

3. *Real returns are what matters.* All investors should understand the difference between nominal and real returns. When assessing performance, the real return (what you have left after inflation) is what really matters. It follows that, as expected inflation increases, investors need to earn higher nominal returns.

4. *The risk of an investment often depends on how long you plan to hold the investment.* Common stocks, for example, can be extremely risky for short-term investors. However, over the long haul the bumps tend to even out, so stocks are less risky when held as part of a long-term portfolio. Indeed, in his best-selling book, *Stocks for the Long Run,* Jeremy Siegel of the University of Pennsylvania concludes: "The safest long-term investment for the preservation of purchasing power has clearly been stocks, not bonds."

5. The past gives us insights into the risk and returns on various investments, but *there is no guarantee that the future will repeat the past.* Stocks that have performed well in recent years might tumble, while stocks that have struggled may rebound. The same thing can hold true for the stock market as a whole. Even Jeremy Siegel, who has preached that stocks have historically been good long-term investments, has also argued that there is no assurance that returns in the future will be as strong as they have been in the past. More importantly, when purchasing a stock you always need to ask: "Is this stock fairly valued, or is it currently priced too high?" We discuss this issue more completely in the next chapter.

Explain the following statement: "The stand-alone risk of an individual corporate project may be quite high, but viewed in the context of its effect on stockholders' risk, the project's true risk may be much lower."

How does the correlation between returns on a project and returns on the firm's other assets affect the project's risk?

What are some important concepts for individual investors to consider when evaluating the risk and returns of various investments?

Summary

This chapter focuses on the trade-off between risk and return. We began by discussing how to estimate risk and return for both individual assets and portfolios. In particular, we differentiated between stand-alone risk and risk in a portfolio context, and we explained the benefits of diversification. Finally, we introduced the CAPM, which describes how risk affects rates of return. In the chapters that follow, we will give you the tools to estimate the required rates of return for bonds, preferred stock, and common stock, and we will explain how firms use these rates of return to estimate their costs of capital. As you will see, the cost of capital is a basic element in the capital budgeting process. The key concepts covered in this chapter are listed below.

- **Risk** can be defined as the chance that some unfavorable event will occur.
- The risk of an asset's cash flows can be considered on a **stand-alone basis** (each asset all by itself) or in a **portfolio context,** in which the investment is combined with other assets and its risk is reduced through **diversification.**
- Most rational investors hold **portfolios of assets,** and they are more concerned with the risk of their portfolios than with the risk of individual assets.
- The **expected return** on an investment is the mean value of its probability distribution of returns.
- The **greater the probability** that the actual return will be far below the expected return, the **greater the asset's stand-alone risk.**
- The average investor is **risk averse,** which means that he or she must be compensated for holding risky assets. Therefore, riskier assets have higher required returns than less risky assets.
- An asset's risk has two components: (1) **diversifiable risk,** which can be eliminated by diversification, and (2) **market risk,** which cannot be eliminated by diversification.
- Market risk is measured by the standard deviation of returns on a well-diversified portfolio, one that consists of all stocks traded in the market. Such a portfolio is called the **market portfolio.**
- The **relevant risk** of an individual asset is its contribution to the risk of a well-diversified portfolio. Since market risk cannot be eliminated by diversification, investors must be compensated for bearing it.

- A stock's **beta coefficient, b,** is a measure of its market risk. Beta measures the extent to which the stock's returns move relative to the market.
- A **high-beta stock** has stock returns that tend to move up and down by more than the returns on an average stock, while the opposite is true for a **low-beta stock.** An average stock has b = 1.0, as does the market portfolio.
- The **beta of a portfolio** is a **weighted average** of the betas of the individual securities in the portfolio.
- The **Security Market Line (SML)** equation shows the relationship between a security's market risk and its required rate of return. The return required for any security i is equal to the **risk-free rate** plus the **market risk premium** multiplied by the security's **beta:** $r_i = r_{RF} + (RP_M)b_i$.
- In equilibrium, the expected rate of return on a stock must equal its required return. However, a number of things can happen to cause the required rate of return to change: (1) **the risk-free rate can change** because of changes in either real rates or expected inflation, (2) **a stock's beta can change,** and (3) **investors' aversion to risk can change.**
- Because returns on assets in different countries are not perfectly correlated, **global diversification** may result in lower risk for multinational companies and globally diversified portfolios.
- The CAPM is conceptually based on **expected returns.** However, only historical returns are available to test it. Various tests have been conducted, and none has "proved" that the CAPM actually describes how investors behave. Indeed, evidence exists to suggest that investors regard factors other than just beta when analyzing risk. The 2008–2009 market crash suggests that, in addition to risk as measured by beta, liquidity is important as well.
- Two web extensions accompany this chapter: *Web Extension 2A* provides a discussion of **continuous probability distributions,** and *Web Extension 2B* shows how to calculate beta with a financial calculator.

Questions

2–1 Define the following terms, using graphs or equations to illustrate your answers where feasible.
  a. Risk in general; stand-alone risk; probability distribution and its relation to risk
  b. Expected rate of return, $\hat{r}$
  c. Continuous probability distribution
  d. Standard deviation, σ; variance, σ^2; coefficient of variation, CV
  e. Risk aversion; realized rate of return, $\bar{r}$
  f. Risk premium for Stock i, RP_i; market risk premium, RP_M
  g. Capital Asset Pricing Model (CAPM)
  h. Expected return on a portfolio, $\hat{r}_p$; market portfolio
  i. Correlation as a concept; correlation coefficient, ρ
  j. Market risk; diversifiable risk; relevant risk
  k. Beta coefficient, b; average stock's beta
  l. Security Market Line (SML); SML equation
  m. Slope of SML and its relationship to risk aversion
2–2 The probability distribution of a less risky return is more peaked than that of a riskier return. What shape would the probability distribution have for (a) completely certain returns and (b) completely uncertain returns?

2–3 Security A has an expected return of 7%, a standard deviation of returns of 35%, a correlation coefficient with the market of −0.3, and a beta coefficient of −1.5. Security B has an expected return of 12%, a standard deviation of returns of 10%, a correlation with the market of 0.7, and a beta coefficient of 1.0. Which security is riskier? Why?

2–4 Suppose you owned a portfolio consisting of $250,000 of U.S. government bonds with a maturity of 30 years.
a. Would your portfolio be riskless?
b. Now suppose you hold a portfolio consisting of $250,000 of 30-day Treasury bills. Every 30 days your bills mature, and you reinvest the principal ($250,000) in a new batch of bills. Assume that you live on the investment income from your portfolio and that you want to maintain a constant standard of living. Is your portfolio truly riskless?
c. Can you think of any asset that would be completely riskless? What security comes closest to being riskless? Explain.

2–5 If investors' aversion to risk *increased*, would the risk premium on a high-beta stock increase by more or less than that on a low-beta stock? Explain.

2–6 If a company's beta were to double, would its expected return double?

2–7 In the real world, is it possible to construct a portfolio of stocks that has an expected return equal to the risk-free rate?

Problems   Answers Appear in Appendix B

Easy Problems 1–3

2–1 **Portfolio Beta** Your investment club has only two stocks in its portfolio; $20,000 is invested in a stock with a beta of 0.7, and $35,000 is invested in a stock with a beta of 1.3. What is the portfolio's beta?

2–2 **Required Rate of Return** AA Industries's stock has a beta of 0.8. The risk-free rate is 4%, and the expected return on the market is 12%. What is the required rate of return on AA's stock?

2–3 **Required Rates of Return** What is the required return on the market, on a stock with a beta of 1.0, and on a stock with a beta of 1.7? Assume that the risk-free rate is 5% and that the market risk premium is 7%.

Intermediate Problems 4–9

2–4 **Expected Return: Discrete Distribution** A stock's return has the following distribution:

Demand for the Company's Products	Probability of This Demand Occurring	Rate of Return if This Demand Occurs (%)
Weak	0.1	−50%
Below average	0.2	−5
Average	0.4	16
Above average	0.2	25
Strong	0.1	60
	1.0	

Calculate the stock's expected return, standard deviation, and coefficient of variation.

2-5 Expected Returns: Discrete Distribution The market and Stock J have the following probability distributions:

Probability	r_M	r_J
0.3	15%	20%
0.4	9	5
0.3	18	12

a. Calculate the expected rates of return for the market and Stock J.
b. Calculate the standard deviations for the market and Stock J.
c. Calculate the coefficients of variation for the market and Stock J.

2-6 Required Rate of Return Suppose $r_{RF} = 5\%$, $r_M = 10\%$, and $r_A = 12\%$.
a. Calculate Stock A's beta.
b. If Stock A's beta were 2.0, then what would be A's new required rate of return?

2-7 Required Rate of Return As an equity analyst you are concerned with what will happen to the required return to Universal Toddler Industries's stock as market conditions change. Suppose $r_{RF} = 5\%$, $r_M = 12\%$, and $b_{UTI} = 1.4$.
a. Under current conditions, what is r_{UTI}, the required rate of return on UTI stock?
b. Now suppose r_{RF} (1) increases to 6% or (2) decreases to 4%. The slope of the SML remains constant. How would this affect r_M and r_{UTI}?
c. Now assume r_{RF} remains at 5% but r_M (1) increases to 14% or (2) falls to 11%. The slope of the SML does not remain constant. How would these changes affect r_{UTI}?

2-8 Portfolio Beta Your retirement fund consists of a $5,000 investment in each of 15 different common stocks. The portfolio's beta is 1.20. Now, suppose you sell one of the stocks with a beta of 0.8 for $5,000 and use the proceeds to buy another stock whose beta is 1.6. Calculate your portfolio's new beta.

2-9 Portfolio Required Return Suppose you manage a $4 million fund that consists of four stocks with the following investments:

Stock	Investment	Beta
A	$ 400,000	1.50
B	600,000	−0.50
C	1,000,000	1.25
D	2,000,000	0.75

If the market's required rate of return is 14% and the risk-free rate is 6%, what is the fund's required rate of return?

Challenging Problems 10–13

2-10 Portfolio Beta You have a $2 million portfolio consisting of a $100,000 investment in each of 20 different stocks. The portfolio has a beta of 1.1. You are considering selling $100,000 worth of one stock with a beta of 0.9 and using the proceeds to purchase another stock with a beta of 1.4. What will the portfolio's new beta be after these transactions?

2-11 Required Rate of Return Stock R has a beta of 1.5, Stock S has a beta of 0.75, the expected rate of return on an average stock is 13%, and the risk-free rate is 7%.

By how much does the required return on the riskier stock exceed that on the less risky stock?

2-12 **Historical Realized Rates of Return** You are considering an investment in either individual stocks or a portfolio of stocks. The two stocks you are researching, stocks A and B, have the following historical returns:

Year	$\overline{r}_A$	$\overline{r}_B$
2008	−20.00%	−5.00%
2009	42.00	15.00
2010	20.00	−13.00
2011	−8.00	50.00
2012	25.00	12.00

a. Calculate the average rate of return for each stock during the 5-year period.

b. Suppose you had held a portfolio consisting of 50% of Stock A and 50% of Stock B. What would have been the realized rate of return on the portfolio in each year? What would have been the average return on the portfolio during this period?

c. Calculate the standard deviation of returns for each stock and for the portfolio.

d. Calculate the coefficient of variation for each stock and for the portfolio.

e. If you are a risk-averse investor then, assuming these are your only choices, would you prefer to hold Stock A, Stock B, or the portfolio? Why?

2-13 **Historical Returns: Expected and Required Rates of Return** You have observed the following returns over time:

Year	Stock X	Stock Y	Market
2008	14%	13%	12%
2009	19	7	10
2010	−16	−5	−12
2011	3	1	1
2012	20	11	15

Assume that the risk-free rate is 6% and the market risk premium is 5%.

a. What are the betas of Stocks X and Y?

b. What are the required rates of return on Stocks X and Y?

c. What is the required rate of return on a portfolio consisting of 80% of Stock X and 20% of Stock Y?

d. If Stock X's expected return is 22%, is Stock X under- or overvalued?

Spreadsheet Problem

2-14 **Evaluating Risk and Return** Start with the partial model in the file *Ch02 P14 Build a Model.xls* on the textbook's Web site. The file contains hypothetical data for working this problem. Goodman Industries's and Landry Incorporated's stock prices and dividends, along with the Market Index, are shown below. Stock prices are reported for December 31 of each year, and dividends reflect those paid during the year. The market data are adjusted to include dividends.

Year	Goodman Industries Stock Price	Dividend	Landry Incorporated Stock Price	Dividend	Market Index Includes Dividends
2012	$25.88	$1.73	$73.13	$4.50	17,495.97
2011	22.13	1.59	78.45	4.35	13,178.55
2010	24.75	1.50	73.13	4.13	13,019.97
2009	16.13	1.43	85.88	3.75	9,651.05
2008	17.06	1.35	90.00	3.38	8,403.42
2007	11.44	1.28	83.63	3.00	7,058.96

a. Use the data given to calculate annual returns for Goodman, Landry, and the Market Index, and then calculate average annual returns for the two stocks and the index. (*Hint:* Remember, returns are calculated by subtracting the beginning price from the ending price to get the capital gain or loss, adding the dividend to the capital gain or loss, and then dividing the result by the beginning price. Assume that dividends are already included in the index. Also, you cannot calculate the rate of return for 2007 because you do not have 2006 data.)

b. Calculate the standard deviations of the returns for Goodman, Landry, and the Market Index. (*Hint:* Use the sample standard deviation formula given in the chapter, which corresponds to the STDEV function in *Excel.*)

c. Now calculate the coefficients of variation for Goodman, Landry, and the Market Index.

d. Construct a scatter diagram graph that shows Goodman's returns on the vertical axis and the Market Index's returns on the horizontal axis. Construct a similar graph showing Landry's stock returns on the vertical axis.

e. Estimate Goodman's and Landry's betas as the slopes of regression lines with stock return on the vertical axis (y-axis) and market return on the horizontal axis (x-axis). (*Hint:* Use *Excel's* SLOPE function.) Are these betas consistent with your graph?

f. The risk-free rate on long-term Treasury bonds is 6.04%. Assume that the market risk premium is 5%. What is the required return on the market? Now use the SML equation to calculate the two companies' required returns.

g. If you formed a portfolio that consisted of 50% Goodman stock and 50% Landry stock, what would be its beta and its required return?

h. Suppose an investor wants to include some Goodman Industries stock in his portfolio. Stocks A, B, and C are currently in the portfolio, and their betas are 0.769, 0.985, and 1.423, respectively. Calculate the new portfolio's required return if it consists of 25% Goodman, 15% Stock A, 40% Stock B, and 20% Stock C.

 THOMSON REUTERS

Use the Thomson ONE–Business School Edition online database to work this chapter's questions.

Using Past Information to Estimate Required Returns

In the Capital Asset Pricing Model (CAPM) discussion, beta is identified as the correct measure of risk for diversified shareholders. Recall that beta measures the extent to which the returns of a given stock move with the stock market. When using the CAPM to estimate required returns, we would ideally like to know how the stock will move with the market in the future, but since we don't have a crystal ball we generally use historical data to estimate this relationship.

As noted in the chapter, beta can be estimated by regressing the individual stock's returns against the returns of the overall market. As an alternative to running our own regressions, we can instead rely on reported betas from a variety of sources. These published sources make it easy to obtain beta estimates for most large publicly traded corporations. However, a word of caution is in order. Beta estimates can often be quite sensitive to the time period in which the data are estimated, the market index used, and the frequency of the data used. Therefore, it is not uncommon to find a wide range of beta estimates among the various published sources. Indeed, Thomson ONE reports multiple beta estimates. These multiple estimates reflect the fact that Thomson ONE puts together data from a variety of different sources.

Discussion Questions

1. Begin by taking a look at the historical performance of the overall stock market. If you want to see, for example, the performance of the S&P 500, select INDICES and enter S&PCOMP. Click on PERFORMANCE and you will immediately see a quick summary of the market's performance in recent months and years. How has the market performed over the past year? The past 3 years? The past 5 years? The past 10 years?

2. Now let's take a closer look at the stocks of four companies: Colgate Palmolive (CL), Gillette (G), Heinz (HNZ), and Microsoft (MSFT). Before looking at the data, which of these companies would you expect to have a relatively high beta (greater than 1.0), and which of these companies would you expect to have a relatively low beta (less than 1.0)?

3. Select one of the four stocks listed in question 2 by selecting COMPANIES, entering the company's ticker symbol, and clicking on GO. On the overview page, you should see a chart that summarizes how the stock has done relative to the S&P 500 over the past 6 months. Has the stock outperformed or underperformed the overall market during this time period?

4. Return to the overview page for the stock you selected. If you scroll down the page you should see an estimate of the company's beta. What is the company's beta? What was the source of the estimated beta?

5. Click on the tab labeled PRICES. What is the company's current dividend yield? What has been its total return to investors over the past 6 months? Over the past year? Over the past 3 years? (Remember that total return includes the dividend yield plus any capital gains or losses.)

6. What is the estimated beta on this page? What is the source of the estimated beta? Why might different sources produce different estimates of beta? (*Note:* if you want to see even more beta estimates, click OVERVIEWS on the second line of tabs and then select SEC DATABASE MARKET DATA. Scroll through the STOCK OVERVIEW SECTION and you will see a range of different beta estimates.)

7. Select a beta estimate that you believe is best. (If you are not sure, you may want to consider an average of the given estimates.) Assume that the risk-free rate is 5% and that the market risk premium is 6%. What is the required return on the company's stock?

8. Repeat the same exercise for each of the three remaining companies. Do the reported betas confirm your earlier intuition? In general, do you find that the higher-beta stocks tend to do better in up markets and worse in down markets? Explain.

MINI CASE

Assume that you recently graduated with a major in finance and that you just landed a job as a financial planner with Barney Smith Inc., a large financial services corporation. Your first assignment is to invest $100,000 for a client. Because the funds are to be invested in a new business that the client plans to start at the end of 1 year, you have been instructed to plan for a 1-year holding period. Further, your boss has restricted you to the investment alternatives shown in the table below. (Disregard for now the items at the bottom of the data; you will fill in the blanks later.)

Barney Smith's economic forecasting staff has developed probability estimates for the state of the economy, and its security analysts have developed a sophisticated computer program that was used to estimate the rate of return on each alternative under each state of the economy. Alta Industries is an electronics firm, Repo Men Inc. collects past-due debts, and American Foam manufactures mattresses and various other foam products. Barney Smith also maintains an "index fund" that owns a market-weighted fraction of all publicly traded stocks; you can invest in that fund and thus obtain average stock market results. Given the situation as described, answer the following questions.

Estimated Returns on Alternative Investments

State of the Economy	Probability	T-Bills	Alta Industries	Repo Men	American Foam	Market Portfolio	2-Stock Portfolio
Recession	0.1	8.0%	−22.0%	28.0%	10.0%[a]	−13.0%	3.0%
Below average	0.2	8.0	−2.0	14.7	−10.0	1.0	
Average	0.4	8.0	20.0	0.0	7.0	15.0	10.0
Above average	0.2	8.0	35.0	−10.0	45.0	29.0	
Boom	0.1	8.0	50.0	−20.0	30.0	43.0	15.0
r̂		8.0%	_____	1.7%	13.8%	15.0%	_____
σ		0.0%	_____	13.4%	18.8%	15.3%	_____
CV			_____	7.9	1.4	1.0	_____
b			_____	−0.86	0.68		_____

[a]Note that the estimated returns of American Foam do not always move in the same direction as the overall economy. For example, when the economy is below average, consumers purchase fewer mattresses than they would if the economy were stronger. However, if the economy is in a flat-out recession, a large number of consumers who were planning to purchase a more expensive inner spring mattress may purchase, instead, a cheaper foam mattress. Under these circumstances, we would expect American Foam's stock price to be higher if there is a recession than if the economy was just below average.

a. What are investment returns? What is the return on an investment that costs $1,000 and is sold after 1 year for $1,100?

b. (1) Why is the T-bill's return independent of the state of the economy? Do T-bills promise a completely risk-free return? (2) Why are Alta Industries's returns expected to move with the economy whereas Repo Men's are expected to move counter to the economy?

c. Calculate the expected rate of return on each alternative, and fill in the blanks in the row for $\hat{r}$ in the table.

d. You should recognize that basing a decision solely on expected returns is appropriate only for risk-neutral individuals. Because your client, like virtually everyone, is risk averse, the riskiness of each alternative is an important aspect of the decision. One possible measure of risk is the standard deviation of returns. (1) Calculate this value for each alternative, and fill in the blank in the row for σ in the table. (2) What type of risk is measured by the standard deviation? (3) Draw a graph that shows *roughly* the shape of the probability distributions for Alta Industries, American Foam, and T-bills.

e. Suppose you suddenly remembered that the coefficient of variation (CV) is generally regarded as being a better measure of stand-alone risk than the standard deviation when the alternatives being considered have widely differing expected returns. Calculate the missing CVs, and fill in the blanks in the row for CV in the table. Does the CV produce the same risk rankings as the standard deviation?

f. Suppose you created a two-stock portfolio by investing $50,000 in Alta Industries and $50,000 in Repo Men. (1) Calculate the expected return ($\hat{r}_p$), the standard deviation (σ_p), and the coefficient of variation (CV_p) for this portfolio, and fill in the appropriate blanks in the table. (2) How does the risk of this two-stock portfolio compare with the risk of the individual stocks if they were held in isolation?

g. Suppose an investor starts with a portfolio consisting of one randomly selected stock. As more and more randomly selected stocks are added to the portfolio, what happens to the portfolio's risk and its expected return? What is the implication for investors? Draw a graph of the two portfolios to illustrate your answer.

h. (1) Should portfolio effects influence how investors think about the risk of individual stocks? (2) If you decided to hold a one-stock portfolio and consequently were exposed to more risk than diversified investors, could you expect to be compensated for all of your risk; that is, could you earn a risk premium on that part of your risk that you could have eliminated by diversifying?

i. How is market risk measured for individual securities? How are beta coefficients calculated?

j. Suppose you have the following historical returns for the stock market and for the company P. Q. Unlimited. Explain how to calculate beta, and use the historical stock returns to calculate the beta for PQU. Interpret your results.

Year	Market	PQU
1	25.7%	40.0%
2	8.0	−15.0
3	−11.0	−15.0
4	15.0	35.0
5	32.5	10.0
6	13.7	30.0
7	40.0	42.0
8	10.0	−10.0
9	−10.8	−25.0
10	−13.1	25.0

k. The expected rates of return and the beta coefficients of the alternatives, as supplied by Barney Smith's computer program, are as follows:

Security	Return ($\hat{r}$)	Risk (Beta)
Alta Industries	17.4%	1.30
Market	15.0	1.00
American Foam	13.8	0.89
T-bills	8.0	0.00
Repo Men	1.7	−0.87

(1) Do the expected returns appear to be related to each alternative's market risk? (2) Is it possible to choose among the alternatives on the basis of the information developed thus far?

l. (1) Write out the Security Market Line (SML) equation, use it to calculate the required rate of return on each alternative, and then graph the relationship between the expected and required rates of return.

(2) How do the expected rates of return compare with the required rates of return? (3) Does it make sense that Repo Men has an expected return that is less than the T-bill rate? (4) What would be the market risk and the required return of a 50-50 portfolio of Alta Industries and Repo Men? Of Alta Industries and American Foam?

m. (1) Suppose investors raised their inflation expectations by 3 percentage points over current estimates as reflected in the 8% T-bill rate. What effect would higher inflation have on the SML and on the returns required on high- and low-risk securities? (2) Suppose instead that investors' risk aversion increased enough to cause the market risk premium to increase by 3 percentage points. (Assume inflation remains constant.) What effect would this have on the SML and on returns of high- and low-risk securities?

Selected Additional Cases

The following cases from TextChoice, *Cengage Learning's online case library, cover many of the concepts discussed in this chapter and are available at* **www.textchoice2.com/casenet.**

Klein-Brigham Series:
Case 2, "Peachtree Securities, Inc. (A)."

Brigham-Buzzard Series:
Case 2, "Powerline Network Corporation (Risk and Return)."

Chapter 3

Risk and Return: Part II

In Chapter 2, we presented the key elements of risk and return analysis. There we saw that much of a stock's risk can be eliminated by diversification, so rational investors should hold portfolios of stocks rather than shares of a single stock. We also introduced the Capital Asset Pricing Model (CAPM), which links risk and required rates of return and uses a stock's beta coefficient as the relevant measure of risk. In this chapter, we extend these concepts and explain portfolio theory. We then present an in-depth treatment of the CAPM, including a more detailed look at how betas are calculated. We discuss two other asset pricing models, the Arbitrage Pricing Theory model and the Fama-French three-factor model. Finally, we introduce a relatively new but fast-growing field, behavioral finance.

WEB

The textbook's Web site contains an *Excel* file that will guide you through the chapter's calculations. The file for this chapter is ***Ch03 Tool Kit.xls***, and we encourage you to open the file and follow along as you read the chapter.

Beginning of Chapter Questions

As you read the chapter, consider how you would answer the following questions. You *should not* necessarily be able to answer the questions before you read the chapter. Rather, you should use them to get a sense of the issues covered in the chapter. After reading the chapter, you should be able to give at least partial answers to the questions, and you should be able to give better answers after the chapter has been discussed in class. Note, too, that it is often useful, when answering conceptual questions, to use hypothetical data to illustrate your answer. We illustrate the answers with an *Excel* model that is available on the textbook's Web site. Accessing the model and working through it is a useful exercise, and it provides insights that are useful when answering the questions.

1. In general terms, what is the **Capital Asset Pricing Model (CAPM)?** What assumptions were made when it was derived?
2. Define the terms **covariance** and **correlation coefficient.** How are they related to one another, and how do they affect the required rate of return on a stock? Would correlation affect its required rate of return if a stock were held (say, by the company's founder) in a one-asset portfolio?
3. What is an **efficient portfolio?** What is the **Capital Market Line (CML),** how is it related to efficient portfolios, and how does it interface with an investor's indifference curve to determine the investor's optimal portfolio? Is it possible that two rational investors could agree as to the specifications of the Capital Market Line, but one would hold a portfolio heavily weighted with Treasury securities while the other held only risky stocks bought on margin?

4. What is the **Security Market Line (SML)?** What information is developed in the Capital Market Line analysis and then carried over and used to help specify the SML? For practical applications as opposed to theoretical considerations, which is more relevant, the CML or the SML?
5. What is the difference between a **historical beta,** an **adjusted beta,** and a **fundamental beta?** Does it matter which beta is used, and if so, which is best?
6. Has the validity of the CAPM been confirmed through empirical tests?
7. What is the difference between a **diversifiable risk** and a **nondiversifiable risk?** Should stock portfolio managers try to eliminate both types of risk?
8. If a publicly traded company has a large number of undiversified investors, along with some who are well diversified, can the undiversified investors earn a rate of return high enough to compensate them for the risk they bear? Does this affect the company's cost of capital?

3.1 Efficient Portfolios

Recall from Chapter 2 the important role in portfolio risk that is played by the correlation between assets. One important use of portfolio risk concepts is to select **efficient portfolios,** defined as those portfolios that provide the highest expected return for any degree of risk—or the lowest degree of risk for any expected return. We begin with the two-asset case and then extend it to the general case of N assets.

3.1a The Two-Asset Case

Consider two assets, A and B. Suppose we have estimated the expected returns ($\hat{r}_A$ and $\hat{r}_B$), the standard deviations (σ_A and σ_B) of returns, and the correlation coefficient (ρ_{AB}) for returns.[1] The expected return and standard deviation (SD) for a portfolio containing these two assets are

---

1. See Chapter 2 for definitions using historical data to estimate the expected return, standard deviation, covariance, and correlation.

INTRINSIC VALUE, RISK, AND RETURN

In Chapter 1, we told you that managers should strive to make their firms more valuable and that the value of a firm is determined by the size, timing, and risk of its free cash flows (FCF). In Chapter 2, we discussed risk, which affects WACC and value.

Now we provide additional insights into how to manage a portfolio's risk and measure a firm's risk.

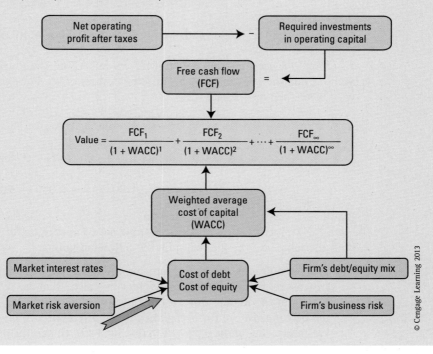

© Cengage Learning 2013

$$\hat{r}_p = w_A \hat{r}_A + (1 - w_A)\hat{r}_B$$

(3–1)

and

$$\text{Portfolio SD} = \sigma_p = \sqrt{w_A^2 \sigma_A^2 + (1 - w_A)^2 \sigma_B^2 + 2w_A(1 - w_A)\rho_{AB}\sigma_A\sigma_B}$$

(3–2)

Here w_A is the fraction of the portfolio invested in Security A, so $(1 - w_A)$ is the fraction invested in Security B.

To illustrate, suppose we can allocate our funds between A and B in any proportion. Suppose Security A has an expected rate of return of $\hat{r}_A = 5\%$ and a standard deviation of returns of $\sigma_A = 4\%$, while $\hat{r}_B = 8\%$ and $\sigma_B = 10\%$. Our first task is to determine the set of *attainable* portfolios and then, from this attainable set, to select the *efficient* subset.

To construct the attainable set, we need data on the degree of correlation between the two securities' expected returns, ρ_{AB}. Let us work with three different assumed degrees of correlation—namely, $\rho_{AB} = +1.0$, $\rho_{AB} = 0$, and $\rho_{AB} = -1.0$—and use them to develop the portfolios' expected returns, $\hat{r}_p$, and standard deviations, σ_p. (Of course, only one correlation can exist; our example simply shows three alternative situations that could occur.)

To calculate $\hat{r}_p$, we use Equation 3-1: Substitute the given values for $\hat{r}_A$ and $\hat{r}_B$, and then calculate $\hat{r}_p$ for different values of w_A. For example, if $w_A = 0.75$, then $\hat{r}_p = 5.75\%$:

$$\hat{r}_p = w_A \hat{r}_A + (1 - w_A)\hat{r}_B$$
$$= 0.75(5\%) + 0.25(8\%) = 5.75\%$$

Other values of $\hat{r}_p$ are found similarly and are shown in the third column of Figure 3-1.

Next, we use Equation 3-2 to find σ_p. Substitute the given values for σ_A, σ_B, and ρ_{AB}, and then calculate σ_p for different values of w_A. For example, if $\rho_{AB} = 0$ and $w_A = 0.75$, then $\sigma_p = 3.9\%$:

$$\sigma_p = \sqrt{w_A^2 \sigma_A^2 + (1 - w_A)^2 \sigma_B^2 + 2w_A(1 - w_A)\rho_{AB}\sigma_A\sigma_B}$$

$$= \sqrt{(0.75^2)(0.04^2) + (1 - 0.75)^2(0.10^2) + 2(0.75)(1 - 0.75)(0)(0.04)(0.10)}$$

$$= \sqrt{0.0009 + 0.000625 + 0} = \sqrt{0.001525} = 0.039 = 3.9\%$$

Figure 3-1 gives $\hat{r}_p$ and σ_p values for $w_A = 1.00$, 0.75, 0.50, 0.25, and 0.00, and Figure 3-2 plots $\hat{r}_p$, σ_p, and the attainable set of portfolios for each correlation. In both the table and the graphs, note the following points.

1. The three graphs across the top row of Figure 3-2 designate Case I, where the two assets are perfectly positively correlated; that is, $\rho_{AB} = +1.0$. The three graphs in the middle row are for the case of zero correlation, and the three in the bottom row are for perfect negative correlation.
2. We rarely encounter $\rho_{AB} = -1.0$, 0.0, or $+1.0$. Generally, ρ_{AB} is in the range of $+0.5$ to $+0.7$ for most stocks. Case II (zero correlation) produces graphs that, pictorially, most closely resemble real-world examples.
3. The left column of graphs shows how the *expected portfolio returns* vary with different combinations of A and B. We see that these graphs are identical in each of the three cases: The portfolio return, $\hat{r}_p$, is a linear function of w_A, and it does not depend on the correlation coefficients. This is also seen from the $\hat{r}_p$ column in Figure 3-1.

WEB

See *Ch3 Tool Kit.xls* on the textbook's Web site for all calculations.

Figure 3-1 $\hat{r}_p$ and σ_p under Various Assumptions

	A	B	C	D	E	F
	Proportion of Portfolio in Security A	Proportion of Portfolio in Security B			σ_p	
				Case I	Case II	Case III
	(Value of w_A)	(Value of 1-w_A)	$\hat{r}_P$	$\rho_{AB} = +1.0$	$\rho_{AB} = 0.0$	$\rho_{AB} = -1.0$
146	1.00	0.00	5.00%	4.0%	4.0%	4.0%
147	0.75	0.25	5.75%	5.5%	3.9%	0.5%
148	0.50	0.50	6.50%	7.0%	5.4%	3.0%
149	0.25	0.75	7.25%	8.5%	7.6%	6.5%
150	0.00	1.00	8.00%	10.0%	10.0%	10.0%

Figure 3-2	Illustrations of Portfolio Returns, Risk, and the Attainable Set of Portfolios

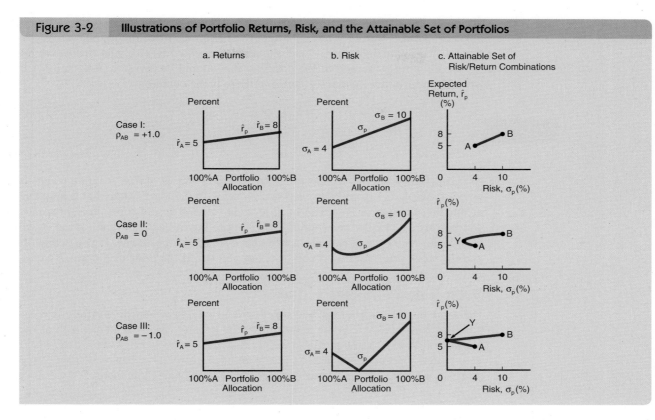

a. Returns   b. Risk   c. Attainable Set of Risk/Return Combinations

4. The middle column of graphs shows how risk is affected by the portfolio mix. Starting from the top, we see that portfolio risk, σ_p, increases linearly in Case I, where $\rho_{AB} = +1.0$; it is nonlinear in Case II; and Case III shows that risk can be completely diversified away if $\rho_{AB} = -1.0$. Thus σ_p, unlike $\hat{r}_p$, *does* depend on correlation.

5. Note that in both Cases II and III, but not in Case I, someone holding only Stock A could sell some A and buy some B, thus increasing expected return and lowering risk as well.

6. The right column of graphs shows the attainable, or feasible, set of portfolios constructed with different mixes of Securities A and B. Unlike the other columns, which plotted return and risk versus the portfolio's composition, each of these three graphs was plotted from pairs of $\hat{r}_p$ and σ_p, as shown in Figure 3-1. For example, Point A in the upper right graph is the point $\hat{r}_p = 5\%$, $\sigma_p = 4\%$ from the Case I data. All other points on the curves were plotted similarly. With only two securities in the portfolio, the attainable set is a curve or line, and we can achieve each risk/return combination on the relevant curve by some allocation of our investment funds between Securities A and B.

7. Are all combinations on the attainable set equally good? The answer is "no." Only that part of the attainable set from Y to B in Cases II and III is defined as *efficient*. The part from A to Y is inefficient because, for any degree of risk on the line segment AY, a higher return can be found on segment YB. Thus, no rational investor would hold a portfolio that lies on segment AY. In Case I, however, the entire feasible set is efficient—no combination of the securities can be ruled out.

From these examples we see that in one extreme case ($\rho = -1.0$), risk can be completely eliminated, while in the other extreme case ($\rho = +1.0$), diversification does no good whatsoever. In between these extremes, combining two stocks into a portfolio reduces but does not eliminate the risk inherent in the individual stocks. If we differentiate Equation 3-2, set the derivative equal to zero, and then solve for w_A, we obtain the fraction of the portfolio that should be invested in Security A if we wish to form the least-risky portfolio. Here is the equation:

(3–3)

$$\text{Minimum risk portfolio: } w_A = \frac{\sigma_B(\sigma_B - \rho_{AB}\sigma_A)}{\sigma_A^2 + \sigma_B^2 - 2\rho_{AB}\sigma_A\sigma_B}$$

As a rule, we limit w_A to the range 0 to +1.0; that is, if the solution value is $w_A > 1.0$, set $w_A = 1.0$, and if w_A is negative, set $w_A = 0.0$. A w_A value that is negative means that Security A is sold short; if w_A is positive, B is sold short. In a short sale, you borrow a stock and then sell it, expecting to buy it back later (at a lower price) in order to repay the person from whom the stock was borrowed. If you sell short and the stock price rises then you lose, but you win if the price declines.

3.1b The N-Asset Case

The same principles from the two-asset case also apply when the portfolio is composed of N assets. Here is the notation for the N-asset case: The percentage of the investment in asset i (the portfolio weight) is w_i, the expected return for asset i is $\hat{r}_i$, the standard deviation of asset i is σ_i, and the correlation between asset i and asset j is ρ_{ij}. The expected return for a portfolio with N assets is then

(3–4)

$$\hat{r}_p = \sum_{i=1}^{N} w_i \hat{r}_i$$

and the variance of the portfolio is

(3–5)

$$\sigma_p^2 = \sum_{i=1}^{N} \sum_{j=1}^{N} w_i w_j \sigma_i \sigma_j \rho_{ij}$$

For the case in which $i = j$, the correlation is $\rho_{ij} = \rho_{ii} = 1$. Notice also that when $i = j$, the product $\sigma_i \sigma_j = \sigma_i \sigma_i = \sigma_i^2$.

One way to apply Equation 3-5 is to set up a table with a row and column for each asset. Give the rows and columns labels showing the assets' weights and standard deviations. Then fill in each cell in the table by multiplying the values in the row and column headings by the correlation between the assets, as shown below:

	$w_1\sigma_1$ (1)	$w_2\sigma_2$ (2)	$w_3\sigma_3$ (3)
$w_1\sigma_1$ (1)	$w_1\sigma_1 w_1\sigma_1 \rho_{11} = w_1^2\sigma_1^2$	$w_1\sigma_1 w_2\sigma_2 \rho_{12}$	$w_1\sigma_1 w_3\sigma_3 \rho_{13}$
$w_2\sigma_2$ (2)	$w_2\sigma_2 w_1\sigma_1 \rho_{21}$	$w_2\sigma_2 w_2\sigma_2 \rho_{22} = w_2^2\sigma_2^2$	$w_2\sigma_2 w_3\sigma_3 \rho_{23}$
$w_3\sigma_3$ (3)	$w_3\sigma_3 w_1\sigma_1 \rho_{31}$	$w_3\sigma_3 w_2\sigma_2 \rho_{32}$	$w_3\sigma_3 w_3\sigma_3 \rho_{33} = w_3^2\sigma_3^2$

The portfolio variance is the sum of the nine cells. For the diagonal, we have substituted the values for the case in which $i = j$. Notice that some of the cells have identical values. For example, the cell for Row 1 and Column 2 has the same value as the cell for Column 1 and Row 2. This suggests an alternative formula:

$$\sigma_p^2 = \sum_{i=1}^{N} w_i^2 \sigma_i^2 + \sum_{i=1}^{N} \sum_{\substack{j=1 \\ j \neq i}}^{N} w_i \sigma_i \, w_j \sigma_j \rho_{ij}$$

(3–5a)

The main thing to remember when calculating portfolio standard deviations is simply this: Do not leave out any terms. Using a table like the one above can help.

Self Test

What is meant by the term "attainable set"?

Within the attainable set, which portfolios are "efficient"?

Stock A has an expected return of 10% and a standard deviation of 35%. Stock B has an expected return of 15% and a standard deviation of 45%. The correlation coefficient between Stock A and B is 0.3. What are the expected return and standard deviation of a portfolio invested 60% in Stock A and 40% in Stock B? **(12.0%; 31.5%)**

3.2 Choosing the Optimal Portfolio

With only two assets, the feasible set of portfolios is a line or curve, as shown in the third column of graphs in Figure 3-2. However, by increasing the number of assets, we obtain an area, such as the shaded region in Figure 3-3. The points A, H, G, and E represent single securities (or portfolios containing only one security).

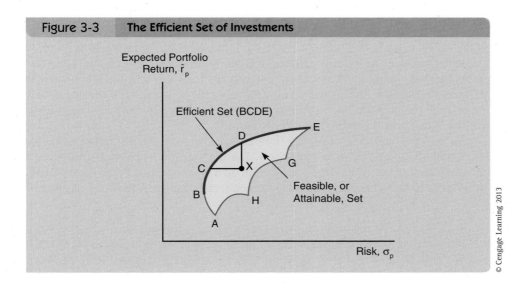

Figure 3-3   The Efficient Set of Investments

© Cengage Learning 2013

All the other points in the shaded area and its boundaries, which comprise the feasible set, represent portfolios of two or more securities. Each point in this area represents a particular portfolio with a risk of σ_p and an expected return of $\hat{r}_p$. For example, point X represents one such portfolio's risk and expected return, as do each of points B, C, and D.

Given the full set of potential portfolios that could be constructed from the available assets, which portfolio should actually be held? This choice involves two separate decisions: (1) determining the efficient set of portfolios and (2) choosing from the efficient set the single portfolio that is best for the specific investor.

3.2a The Efficient Frontier

In Figure 3-3, the boundary line BCDE defines the efficient set of portfolios, which is also called the **efficient frontier**.[2] Portfolios to the left of the efficient set are not possible because they lie outside the attainable set. Portfolios to the right of the boundary line (interior portfolios) are inefficient because some other portfolio would provide either a higher return for the same degree of risk or a lower risk for the same rate of return. For example, Portfolio X is *dominated* in this sense by all portfolios on the curve CD.

3.2b Risk-Return Indifference Curves

Given the efficient set of portfolios, which specific portfolio should an investor choose? To determine the optimal portfolio for a particular investor, we must know the investor's attitude toward risk as reflected in his or her risk–return trade-off function, or **indifference curve**.

An investor's risk–return trade-off function is based on the standard economic concepts of utility theory and indifference curves, which are illustrated in Figure 3-4. The curves labeled I_Y and I_Z represent the indifference curves of Individuals Y and Z. Ms. Y's curve indicates indifference between the riskless 5% portfolio, a portfolio with an expected return of 6% but a risk of $\sigma_p = 1.4\%$, and so on. Mr. Z's curve indicates indifference between a riskless 5% return, an expected 6% return with risk of $\sigma_p = 3.3\%$, and so on.

Note that Ms. Y requires a higher expected rate of return as compensation for any given amount of risk; thus, Ms. Y is said to be more **risk averse** than Mr. Z. Her higher risk aversion causes Ms. Y to require a higher **risk premium**—defined here as the difference between the 5% riskless return and the expected return required to compensate for any specific amount of risk—than Mr. Z requires. Thus, Ms. Y requires a risk premium (RP_Y) of 2.5% to compensate for a risk of $\sigma_p = 3.3\%$, whereas Mr. Z's risk premium for this degree of risk is only $RP_Z = 1.0\%$. *As a generalization, the steeper the slope of an investor's indifference curve, the more risk averse the investor.* Thus, Ms. Y is more risk averse than Mr. Z.

Each individual has a "map" of indifference curves; the indifference maps for Ms. Y and Mr. Z are shown in Figure 3-5. The higher curves denote a greater level of satisfaction (or utility). Thus, I_{Z2} is better than I_{Z1} because, for any level of risk, Mr. Z has a higher expected return and hence greater utility. An infinite number of

---

2. A computational procedure for determining the efficient set of portfolios was developed by Harry Markowitz and first reported in his article "Portfolio Selection," *Journal of Finance,* March 1952, pp. 77–91. In this article, Markowitz developed the basic concepts of portfolio theory, and he later won the Nobel Prize in economics for his work.

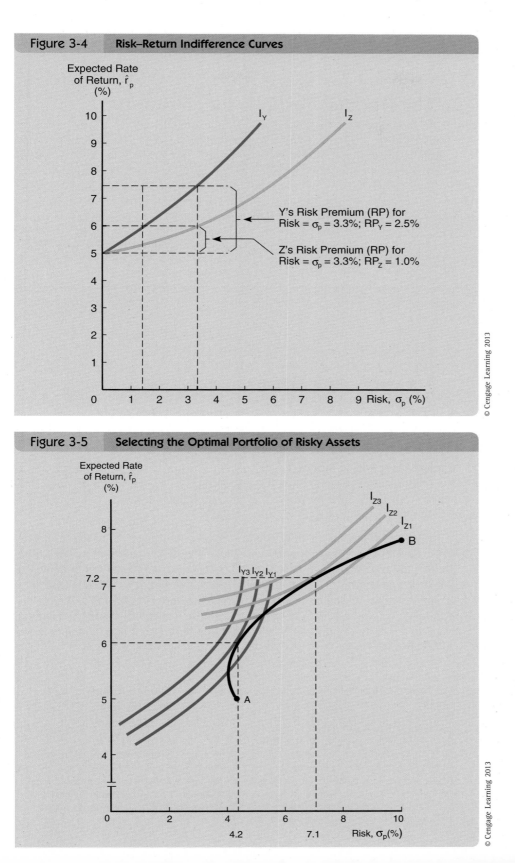

Figure 3-4   Risk–Return Indifference Curves

Expected Rate
of Return, r̂_p
(%)

Y's Risk Premium (RP) for
Risk = σ_p = 3.3%; RP_Y = 2.5%

Z's Risk Premium (RP) for
Risk = σ_p = 3.3%; RP_Z = 1.0%

Risk, σ_p (%)

© Cengage Learning 2013

Figure 3-5   Selecting the Optimal Portfolio of Risky Assets

Expected Rate
of Return, r̂_p
(%)

Risk, σ_p(%)

© Cengage Learning 2013

indifference curves could be drawn in the map for each individual, and each individual has a unique map.

3.2c The Optimal Portfolio for an Investor

Figure 3-5 also shows the feasible set of portfolios for the two-asset case, under the assumption that $\rho_{AB} = 0$, as it was developed in Figure 3-2. The optimal portfolio for each investor is found at the tangency point between the efficient set of portfolios and one of the investor's indifference curves. This tangency point marks the highest level of satisfaction the investor can attain. Ms. Y, who is more risk averse than Mr. Z, chooses a portfolio with a lower expected return (about 6%) but a risk of only $\sigma_p = 4.2\%$. Mr. Z picks a portfolio that provides an expected return of about 7.2% but has a risk of about $\sigma_p = 7.1\%$. Ms. Y's portfolio is more heavily weighted with the less risky security, while Mr. Z's portfolio contains a larger proportion of the more risky security.[3]

Self Test	What is the efficient frontier?
	What are indifference curves?
	Conceptually, how does an investor choose his or her optimal portfolio?

3.3 The Basic Assumptions of the Capital Asset Pricing Model

The **Capital Asset Pricing Model (CAPM)**, which was introduced in Chapter 2, specifies the relationship between risk and required rates of return on assets when they are held in well-diversified portfolios. The assumptions underlying the CAPM's development are summarized in the following list.[4]

1. All investors focus on a single holding period, and they seek to maximize the expected utility of their terminal wealth by choosing among alternative portfolios on the basis of each portfolio's expected return and standard deviation.
2. All investors can borrow or lend an unlimited amount at a given risk-free rate of interest, r_{RF}, and there are no restrictions on short sales of any asset.
3. All investors have identical estimates of the expected returns, variances, and covariances among all assets (that is, investors have homogeneous expectations).

---

3. Ms. Y's portfolio would contain 67% of Security A and 33% of Security B, whereas Mr. Z's portfolio would consist of 27% of Security A and 73% of Security B. These percentages can be determined with Equation 3-1 by simply seeing what percentage of the two securities is consistent with $\hat{r}_p = 6.0\%$ and 7.2%. For example, $w_A(5\%) + (1 - w_A)(8\%) = 7.2\%$, and solving for w_A, we obtain $w_A = 0.27$ and $(1 - w_A) = 0.73$.

4. The CAPM was originated by William F. Sharpe in his article "Capital Asset Prices: A Theory of Market Equilibrium under Conditions of Risk," *Journal of Finance,* September 1964, pp. 425–442. Professor Sharpe won the Nobel Prize in economics for his work on capital asset pricing. The assumptions inherent in Sharpe's model were spelled out by Michael C. Jensen in "Capital Markets: Theory and Evidence," *Bell Journal of Economics and Management Science,* Autumn 1972, pp. 357–398.

4. All assets are perfectly divisible and perfectly liquid (that is, marketable at the going price).
5. There are no transaction costs.
6. There are no taxes.
7. All investors are price takers (that is, all investors assume that their own buying and selling activity will not affect stock prices).
8. The quantities of all assets are given and fixed.

Theoretical extensions in the literature have relaxed some of these assumptions, and in general, these extensions have led to conclusions that are reasonably consistent with the basic theory. However, the validity of any model can be established only through empirical tests, which we discuss later in the chapter.

What are the key assumptions of the CAPM?	Self Test

3.4 The Capital Market Line and the Security Market Line

Figure 3-5 showed the set of portfolio opportunities for the two-asset case, and it illustrated how indifference curves can be used to select the optimal portfolio from the feasible set. In Figure 3-6, we show a similar diagram for the many-asset case, but here we also include a risk-free asset with a return r_{RF}. The riskless asset by definition has zero risk, $\sigma = 0\%$, so it is plotted on the vertical axis.

Figure 3-6   Investor Equilibrium: Combining the Risk-Free Asset with the Market Portfolio

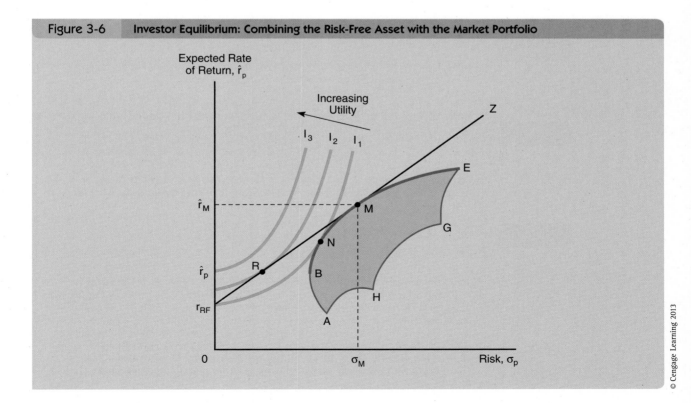

The figure shows both the feasible set of portfolios of risky assets (the shaded area) and a set of indifference curves (I_1, I_2, I_3) for a particular investor. Point N, where indifference curve I_1 is tangent to the efficient set, represents a possible portfolio choice; it is the point on the efficient set of risky portfolios where the investor obtains the highest possible return for a given amount of risk and the smallest degree of risk for a given expected return.

However, the investor can do better than Portfolio N by reaching a higher indifference curve. In addition to the feasible set of risky portfolios, we now have a risk-free asset that provides a riskless return, r_{RF}. Given the risk-free asset, investors can create new portfolios that combine the risk-free asset with a portfolio of risky assets. This enables them to achieve any combination of risk and return on the straight line connecting r_{RF} with M, the point of tangency between that straight line and the efficient frontier of risky asset portfolios.[5] Some portfolios on the line r_{RF}MZ will be preferred to risky portfolios on the efficient frontier BNME, so the points on the line r_{RF}MZ now represent the best attainable combinations of risk and return.

Given the new opportunities along line r_{RF}MZ, our investor will move from Point N to Point R, which is on her highest attainable risk–return indifference curve. Note that any point on the old efficient frontier BNME (except the point of tangency M) is dominated by some point along the line r_{RF}MZ. In general, since investors can purchase some of the risk-free security and some of the risky portfolio (M), it will be possible to move to a point such as R. In addition, if the investor can borrow as well as lend (lending is equivalent to buying

---

5. The risk–return combinations between a risk-free asset and a risky asset (a single stock or a portfolio of stocks) will always be linear. To see this, consider the following equations, which were developed earlier, for return ($\hat{r}_p$) and risk (σ_p) for any combination w_{RF} and $(1 - w_{RF})$:

(3–1a)
$$\hat{r}_p = w_{RF}r_{RF} + (1 - w_{RF})\,\hat{r}_M$$

and

(3–2a)
$$\sigma_P = \sqrt{w_{RF}^2\sigma_{RF}^2 + (1 - w_{RF})^2\sigma_M^2 + 2w_{RF}(1 - w_{RF})\rho_{RF,M}\sigma_{RF}\sigma_M}$$

Equation 3-1a is linear. As for Equation 3-2a, we know that r_{RF} is the risk-free asset, so $\sigma_{RF} = 0$; hence, σ_{RF}^2 is also zero. Using this information, we can simplify Equation 3-2a as follows:

(3–2b)
$$\sigma_p = \sqrt{(1 - w_{RF})^2\sigma_M^2} = (1 - w_{RF})\sigma_M$$

Thus, σ_p is also linear when a riskless asset is combined with a portfolio of risky assets.

If expected returns, as measured by $\hat{r}_p$, and risk, as measured by σ_p, are both linear functions of w_{RF}, then the relationship between $\hat{r}_p$ and σ_p, when graphed as in Figure 3-6, must also be linear. For example, if 100% of the portfolio is invested in r_{RF} with a return of 8%, then the portfolio return will be 8% and σ_p will be 0. If 100% is invested in M with $r_M = 12\%$ and $\sigma_M = 10\%$, then $\sigma_p = 1.0(10\%) = 10\%$ and $\hat{r}_p = 0(8\%) + 1.0(12\%) = 12\%$. If 50% of the portfolio is invested in M and 50% in the risk-free asset, then $\sigma_p = 0.5(10\%) = 5\%$ and $\hat{r}_p = 0.5(8\%) + 0.5(12\%) = 10\%$. Plotting these points will reveal the linear relationship given as r_{RF}MZ in Figure 3-6.

risk-free debt securities) at the riskless rate r_{RF}, then it is possible to move out on the line segment MZ; an investor would do so if his indifference curve were tangent to $r_{RF}MZ$, to the right of Point M.[6]

All investors should hold portfolios lying on the line $r_{RF}MZ$ under the conditions assumed in the CAPM. This implies that they should hold portfolios that are combinations of the risk-free security and the risky Portfolio M. Thus, the addition of the risk-free asset totally changes the efficient set: The efficient set now lies along line $r_{RF}MZ$ rather than along the curve BNME. Note also that if the capital market is to be in equilibrium, then M must be a portfolio that contains every risky asset in exact proportion to that asset's fraction of the total market value of all assets. In other words, if Security i is X percent of the total market value of all securities, then X percent of the market portfolio M must consist of Security i. (That is, M is the market value–weighted portfolio of *all* risky assets in the economy.) Thus, all investors should hold portfolios that lie on the line $r_{RF}MZ$, with the particular location of a given individual's portfolio being determined by the point at which his indifference curve is tangent to the line.

The line $r_{RF}MZ$ in Figure 3-6 is called the **Capital Market Line (CML)**. It has an intercept of r_{RF} and a slope of $(\hat{r}_M - r_{RF})/\sigma_M$.[7] Therefore, the equation for the Capital Market Line may be expressed as follows:

$$\text{CML: } \hat{r}_p = r_{RF} + \left(\frac{\hat{r}_M - r_{RF}}{\sigma_M} \right) \sigma_p$$

(3-6)

The expected rate of return *on an efficient portfolio* is equal to the riskless rate plus a risk premium that is equal to $(\hat{r}_M - r_{RF})/\sigma_M$ multiplied by the portfolio's standard deviation, σ_p. Thus, the CML specifies a linear relationship between an efficient portfolio's expected return and risk, where the slope of the CML is equal to the expected return on the market portfolio of risky stocks $(\hat{r}_M)$ *minus* the risk-free rate (r_{RF}), which is called the **market risk premium**, all divided by the standard deviation of returns on the market portfolio, σ_M:

$$\text{Slope of the CML} = (\hat{r}_M - r_{RF})/\sigma_M$$

For example, suppose $r_{RF} = 10\%$, $\hat{r}_M = 15\%$, and $\sigma_M = 15\%$. In this case, the slope of the CML would be $(15\% - 10\%)/15\% = 0.33$, and if a particular efficient portfolio had $\sigma_p = 10\%$, then its $\hat{r}_p$ would be

$$\hat{r}_p = 10\% + 0.33(10\%) = 13.3\%$$

---

6. An investor who is highly averse to risk will have a steep indifference curve and will end up holding only the riskless asset or perhaps a portfolio at a point such as R (i.e., holding some of the risky market portfolio and some of the riskless asset). An investor who is only slightly averse to risk will have a relatively flat indifference curve, which will cause her to move out beyond M toward Z, borrowing to do so. This investor might buy stocks on margin, which means borrowing and using the stocks as collateral. If individuals' borrowing rates are higher than r_{RF}, then the line $r_{RF}MZ$ will tilt down (i.e., be less steep) beyond M. This condition would invalidate the basic CAPM or at least require that it be modified. Therefore, the assumption of being able to borrow or lend at the same rate is crucial to CAPM theory.

7. Recall that the slope of any line is measured as $\Delta Y/\Delta X$, or the change in height associated with a given change in horizontal distance. Here r_{RF} is at 0 on the horizontal axis, so $\Delta X = \sigma_M - 0 = \sigma_M$. The vertical axis difference associated with a change from r_{RF} to $\hat{r}_M$ is $\hat{r}_M - r_{RF}$. Therefore, slope $= \Delta Y/\Delta X = (\hat{r}_M - r_{RF})/\sigma_M$.

Figure 3-7   **The Capital Market Line (CML)**

Note: We did not draw it in, but you can visualize the shaded space shown in Figure 3-6 in this graph and the CML as the line formed by connecting r_{RF} with the tangent to the shaded space.

A (riskier) portfolio with $\sigma_p = 20\%$ would have $\hat{r}_p = 10\% + 0.33(20\%) = 16.6\%$.

The CML is graphed in Figure 3-7. It is a straight line with an intercept at r_{RF} and a slope equal to the market risk premium $(r_M - r_{RF})$ divided by σ_M. The slope of the CML reflects the aggregate attitude of investors toward risk.

Recall that an efficient portfolio is one that is well diversified; hence all of its unsystematic risk has been eliminated and its only remaining risk is market risk. Therefore, unlike individual stocks, the risk of an efficient portfolio is measured by its standard deviation, σ_p. The CML equation specifies the relationship between risk and return for such efficient portfolios—that is, for portfolios that lie on the CML—and in the CML equation and graph, risk is measured by portfolio standard deviation.

The CML specifies the relationship between risk and return for an efficient portfolio, but investors and managers are more concerned about the relationship between risk and return for *individual assets*. To develop the risk–return relationship for individual securities, note in Figure 3-6 that all investors are assumed to hold Portfolio M, so M must be the market portfolio (i.e., the one that contains all stocks). Note also that M is an *efficient* portfolio. Thus, the CML defines the relationship between the market portfolio's expected return and its standard deviation. Equations 3-4 and 3-5 show the formulas for the expected return and standard deviation for a multi-asset portfolio, including the market portfolio. It is possible to take the equations for the expected return and standard deviation of a multi-asset portfolio and show that the required return for each individual Stock i must conform to the following equation in order for the CML to hold for the market portfolio:[8]

---

8. For consistency with most investment textbooks, we let Cov(r_i, r_M) denote the covariance between the returns of assets i and M. Using the notation in Chapter 2, we would have denoted the covariance as $COV_{i,M}$.

$$r_i = r_{RF} + \frac{(r_M - r_{RF})}{\sigma_M}\left(\frac{Cov(r_i, r_M)}{\sigma_M}\right)$$

(3–7)

$$= r_{RF} + (r_M - r_{RF})\left(\frac{Cov(r_i, r_M)}{\sigma_M^2}\right)$$

The CAPM defines Company i's beta coefficient, b_i, as follows:

$$b_i = \frac{\text{Covariance between Stock i and the market}}{\text{Variance of market returns}} = \frac{Cov(r_i, r_M)}{\sigma_M^2}$$

(3–8)

$$= \left(\frac{\rho_{iM}\sigma_i\sigma_M}{\sigma_M^2}\right) = \rho_{iM}\left(\frac{\sigma_i}{\sigma_M}\right)$$

Recall that the risk premium for the market, RP_M, is $r_M - r_{RF}$. Using this definition and substituting Equation 3-8 into Equation 3-7 gives the **Security Market Line (SML)**:

$$\text{SML: } r_i = r_{RF} + (r_M - r_{RF})b_i$$

(3–9)

$$= r_{RF} + (RP_M)b_i$$

The SML tells us that an individual stock's required return is equal to the risk-free rate plus a premium for bearing risk. The premium for risk is equal to the risk premium for the market, RP_M, multiplied by the risk of the individual stock, as measured by its beta coefficient. The beta coefficient measures the amount of risk that the stock contributes to the market portfolio.

Unlike the CML for a well-diversified portfolio, the SML tells us that the standard deviation (σ_i) of an individual stock should not be used to measure its risk, because some of the risk as reflected by σ_i can be eliminated by diversification. Beta reflects risk after taking diversification benefits into account, and so beta, rather than σ_i, is used to measure individual stocks' risks to investors. Be sure to keep in mind the distinction between the SML and the CML and why that distinction exists.

Self Test

Draw a graph showing the feasible set of risky assets, the efficient frontier, the risk-free asset, and the CML.

Write out the equation for the CML and explain its meaning.

Write out the equation for the SML and explain its meaning.

What is the difference between the CML and the SML?

The standard deviation of stock returns of Park Corporation is 60%. The standard deviation of the market return is 20%. If the correlation between Park and the market is 0.40, what is Park's beta? **(1.2)**

SKILL OR LUCK?

That's the question *The Wall Street Journal's* Investment Dartboard Contest sought to answer by comparing the actual investment results of professional analysts against amateurs and dart throwers. Here's how the contest worked. First, *The Wall Street Journal (WSJ)* picked four professional analysts, and each of those pros formed a portfolio by picking four stocks. Second, amateurs could enter the contest by e-mailing their pick of a single stock to the *WSJ*, which then picked four amateurs at random and combined their choices to make a four-stock portfolio. Third, a group of *WSJ* editors formed a portfolio by throwing four darts at the stock tables. At the beginning of each contest, the *WSJ* announced the six resulting portfolios, and at the end of 6 months, the paper announced the results. The top two pros were invited back for the next contest.

Since 1990 there have been 142 completed contests. The pros beat the darts 87 times and lost 55 times. The pros also beat the Dow Jones Industrial Average (DJIA) in 54% of the contests. The pros had an average 6-month portfolio return of 10.2%, much higher than either the DJIA 6-month average of 5.6% or the darts' return of only 3.5%. The readers, meantime, lost an average of 4% ver-

sus a same-period (30 contests) gain of 7.2% for the pros.

Do these results mean that skill is more important than luck when it comes to investing in stocks? Not necessarily, according to Burton Malkiel, an economics professor at Princeton and the author of the widely read book, *A Random Walk Down Wall Street*. Since the dart-selected portfolios consist of randomly chosen stocks, they should have average risk. However, the pros consistently picked high-risk stocks. Because there was a bull market during most of the contest, one would expect high-risk stocks to outperform the average stock. According to Malkiel, the pros' performance could be due as much to a rising market as to superior analytical skills. The *WSJ* discontinued that contest in 2002, so we can't know for sure whether Malkiel was right or wrong.

The *WSJ* now runs a new contest, pitting six amateurs against six darts. In the recently completed Contest No. 40, the readers averaged a 14% gain versus the darts' 21% gain (the Dow Jones Industrial Average was up 18%). Overall, readers have won 14 contests, and the darts have won 26. If you would like to enter the contest, e-mail your stock pick to **sundaydartboard@wsj.com**.

3.5 Calculating Beta Coefficients

Equation 3-8 defines beta, but recall from Chapter 2 that this equation for beta is also the formula for the slope coefficient in a regression of the stock return against the market return. Therefore, beta can be calculated by plotting the historical returns of a stock on the y-axis of a graph versus the historical returns of the market portfolio on the x-axis and then fitting the regression line. In his 1964 article that set forth the CAPM, Sharpe called this regression line the **characteristic line.** Thus, a stock's beta is the slope of its characteristic line. In Chapter 2, we used this approach to calculate the beta for General Electric. In this chapter, we perform a more detailed analysis of the calculation of beta for General Electric, and we also perform a similar analysis for a portfolio of stocks, Fidelity's Magellan Fund.

3.5a Calculating the Beta Coefficient for a Single Stock: General Electric

WEB

See *Ch03 Tool Kit.xls* on the textbook's Web site.

Table 3-1 shows a summary of the data used in this analysis; the full data set is in the file *Ch03 Tool Kit.xls* and has monthly returns for the 4-year period February 2007–January 2011. Table 3-1 shows the market returns (defined as the percentage price change of the

TABLE 3-1	Summary of Data for Calculating Beta (February 2007–January 2011)			
	r_M, **Market Return (S&P 500 Index)**	r_i, **GE Return**	r_p, **Fidelity Magellan Fund Return**	r_{RF}, **Risk-Free Rate (Monthly Return on 3-Month T-Bill)**
Average return (annual)	−0.8%	−2.4%	1.7%	1.4%
Standard deviation (annual)	19.7%	40.1%	25.0%	0.5%
Correlation with market return, ρ		0.82	0.95	−0.07

© Cengage Learning 2013

S&P 500), the stock returns for GE, and the returns on the Magellan Fund (which is a well-diversified portfolio). The table also shows the risk-free rate, defined as the rate on a short-term (3-month) U.S. Treasury bill, which we will use later in this analysis.

As Table 3-1 shows, GE had an average annual return of −2.4% during this 4-year period, while the market had an average annual return of −0.8%. As we noted before, it is usually unreasonable to think that the future expected return for a stock will equal its average historical return over a relatively short period, such as 4 years. However, we might well expect past volatility to be a reasonable estimate of future volatility, at least during the next couple of years. Observe that the standard deviation for GE's return during this period was 40.1%, versus 19.7% for the market. Thus, the market's volatility is less than that of GE. This is what we would expect, since the market is a well-diversified portfolio and thus much of its risk has been diversified away. The correlation between GE's stock returns and the market returns is about 0.82, which is a little higher than the correlation for a typical stock.

Figure 3-8 shows a plot of GE's returns against the market's returns. We used the *Excel* regression analysis feature to estimate the regression. Table 3-2 reports

WEB

See **Ch03 Tool Kit.xls** on the textbook's Web site for all calculations.

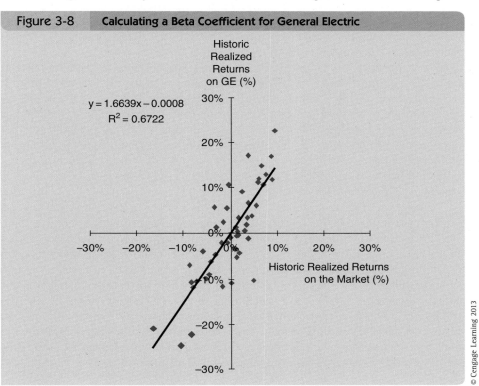

Figure 3-8   **Calculating a Beta Coefficient for General Electric**

$y = 1.6639x − 0.0008$
$R^2 = 0.6722$

Historic Realized Returns on GE (%)

Historic Realized Returns on the Market (%)

© Cengage Learning 2013

TABLE 3-2	Regression Results for Calculating Beta				
	Regression Coefficient	t-Statistic	Probability of t-Statistic	Lower 95% Confidence Interval	Upper 95% Confidence Interval
Panel a: General Electric (Market model)					
Intercept	0.00	−0.09	0.93	−0.02	0.02
Slope (beta)	1.66	9.71	0.00	1.32	2.01
Panel b: Magellan Fund (Market model)					
Intercept	0.00	0.70	0.49	0.00	0.01
Slope (beta)	1.20	21.10	0.00	1.09	1.32
Panel c: General Electric (CAPM: Excess returns)					
Intercept	0.00	−0.01	0.99	−0.02	0.02
Slope (beta)	1.66	9.70	0.00	1.32	2.01

Note: The market model uses actual historical returns; the CAPM model uses returns in excess of the risk-free rate.

some of the regression results for GE. Its estimated beta, which is the slope coefficient, is about 1.66. As with all regression results, 1.66 is just an estimate of beta, not necessarily the true value of beta. Table 3-2 also shows the t-statistic and the probability that the true beta is zero. For GE, this probability is approximately equal to zero. This means that there is virtually a zero chance that the true beta is equal to zero. Since this probability is less than 5%, statisticians would say that the slope coefficient, beta, is "statistically significant." The output of the regression analysis also gives us the 95% confidence interval for the estimate of beta. For GE, the results tell us that we can be 95% confident that the true beta is between 1.32 and 2.01. This is an extremely wide range, but it is typical for most individual stocks. Therefore, the regression estimate for the beta of any single company is highly uncertain.

Observe also that the points in Figure 3-8 are not clustered very tightly around the regression line. Sometimes GE does much better than the market; other times it does much worse. The R^2 value shown in the chart measures the degree of dispersion about the regression line. Statistically speaking, it measures the percentage of variance that is explained by the regression equation. An R^2 of 1.0 indicates that all points lie exactly on the line; in this case, all of the variance in the y variable is explained by the x variable. The R^2 for GE is about 0.67, which is typical for most individual stocks. This indicates that about 67% of the variance in GE's returns is explained by the overall market return.

Finally, note that the intercept shown in the regression equation displayed on the chart is about −0.0008. Since the regression equation is based on monthly data, this means that GE had a −0.96% average annual return that was not explained by the CAPM model. However, the regression results in Table 3-2 also show that the probability of the t-statistic is much greater than 5%, meaning that the "true" intercept might be zero. Therefore, most statisticians would say that this intercept is not statistically significant—the returns of GE are so volatile that we cannot be sure the true intercept is not equal to zero. Translating statistician-speak into plain English, this means that the part of GE's average monthly return that is *not* explained by the CAPM could, in fact, be zero. Thus, the CAPM might very well explain all of GE's average monthly returns.

3.5b The Market Model versus the CAPM

When we estimated beta, we used the following regression equation:

$$\overline{r}_{i,t} = a_i + b_i \overline{r}_{M,t} + e_{i,t}$$

(3–10)

where

$\overline{r}_{i,t}$ = Historical (realized) rate of return on Stock i in period t.
$\overline{r}_{M,t}$ = Historical (realized) rate of return on the market in period t.
a_i = Vertical axis intercept term for Stock i.
b_i = Slope, or beta coefficient, for Stock i.
$e_{i,t}$ = Random error, reflecting the difference between the actual return on Stock i in a given period and the return as predicted by the regression line.

Equation 3-10 is called the **market model,** because it regresses the stock's return against the market's return. However, the SML of the CAPM for realized returns is a little different from Equation 3-10:

$$\text{SML for realized returns: } \overline{r}_{i,t} = \overline{r}_{RF,t} + b_i(\overline{r}_{M,t} - \overline{r}_{RF,t}) + e_{i,t}$$

(3–11)

where $\overline{r}_{RF,t}$ is the historical (realized) risk-free rate in period t.

In order to use the CAPM to estimate beta, we must rewrite Equation 3-11 as a regression equation by adding an intercept, a_i. The result is

$$(\overline{r}_i - \overline{r}_{RF,t}) = a_i + b_i(\overline{r}_{M,t} - \overline{r}_{RF,t}) + e_{i,t}$$

(3–12)

Therefore, to be theoretically correct when estimating beta, we should use the stock's return in excess of the risk-free rate as the y variable and use the market's return in excess of the risk-free rate as the x variable. We did this for GE using the data in Table 3-1, and the results were reported in Panel c of Table 3-2. Note that there are no appreciable differences between the results in Panel a, the market model, and in Panel c, the CAPM model. This typically is the case, so we will use the market model in the rest of the book.

3.5c Calculating the Beta Coefficient for a Portfolio: The Magellan Fund

Let's calculate beta for the Magellan Fund, which is a well-diversified portfolio. Figure 3-9 shows the plot of Magellan's monthly returns versus the market's monthly returns. Note the differences between this chart and the one for GE shown in Figure 3-8. The points for Magellan are tightly clustered around the regression line, indicating that the vast majority of Magellan's variability is explained by the stock market. The R^2 of over 0.90 confirms this visual conclusion. We can also see from Table 3-1 that the Magellan Fund has a standard deviation of 25.0%, which is higher than the 19.7% standard deviation of the market.

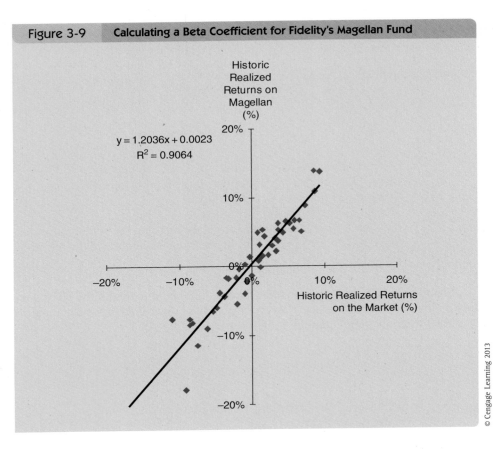

Figure 3-9   **Calculating a Beta Coefficient for Fidelity's Magellan Fund**

WEB

See ***Ch03 Tool Kit.xls***
on the textbook's Web
site for all calculations for
these measures.

As Table 3-2 shows, the estimated beta is 1.20, and the 95% confidence interval is from 1.09 to 1.32, which is much tighter than the one for GE. The intercept is virtually zero, and the probability of the intercept's t-statistic is greater than 5%. Therefore, the intercept is statistically insignificant, indicating that the CAPM explains the average monthly return of the Magellan Fund very well.

Mutual fund managers are often evaluated by their risk-adjusted performance. The three most widely used measures are *Jensen's alpha, Sharpe's reward-to-variability ratio,* and *Treynor's reward-to-volatility ratio.* **Jensen's alpha**, which is the intercept in a CAPM regression of excess returns, is 2.99% per year for Magellan, which seems to indicate that the Magellan fund had slightly superior performance. However, this intercept was not statistically significantly different from zero. Its t-statistic is 0.77, which is so low a value that it could happen about 44% of the time by chance even if the intercept were truly zero. When this probability is greater than 5%, as is the case for Magellan, then most statisticians would be reluctant to conclude that Magellan's *estimated* excess return of 2.99% is not *actually* equal to zero.

Sharpe's reward-to-variability ratio is defined as the portfolio's average return (in excess of the risk-free rate) divided by its standard deviation. Sharpe's ratio for Magellan during the past 4 years is 0.01, which is greater than the S&P's measure of −0.11; but neither is very large, since Magellan just barely outperformed a risk-free investment over the period and the market underperformed a risk-free investment.

Treynor's reward-to-volatility ratio is defined as the portfolio's average return (in excess of the risk-free rate) divided by its beta. For Magellan, this is 0.3%, which is a little better than the S&P 500's ratio of −2.2%. All in all, the Magellan fund seems to have slightly outperformed the market, but perhaps not by a statistically significant amount. Although it's not clear whether Magellan "beat the market," it did dramatically reduce the risk faced by investors as compared with the risk inherent in a randomly chosen individual stock.

3.5d Additional Insights into Risk and Return

The CAPM provides some additional insights into the relationship between risk and return.

1. The relationship between a stock's total risk, market risk, and diversifiable risk can be expressed as follows:

$$\text{Total risk} = \text{Variance} = \text{Market risk} + \text{Diversifiable risk}$$
$$\sigma_i^2 = b_i^2 \sigma_M^2 + \sigma_{e_i}^2$$

(3–13)

Here σ_i^2 is the variance (or total risk) of Stock i, σ_M^2 is the variance of the market, b_i is Stock i's beta coefficient, and $\sigma_{e_i}^2$ is the variance of Stock i's regression error term.

2. If all the points in Figure 3-8 had plotted exactly on the regression line, then the variance of the error term, $\sigma_{e_i}^2$, would have been zero and all of the stock's total risk would have been market risk. On the other hand, if the points were widely scattered about the regression line, then much of the stock's total risk would be diversifiable. The shares of a large, well-diversified mutual fund will plot very close to the regression line.

3. Beta is a measure of relative market risk, but the *actual* market risk of Stock i is $b_i^2 \sigma_M^2$. Market risk can also be expressed in standard deviation form, $b_i \sigma_M$. The higher a stock's beta, the higher its market risk. If beta were zero, the stock would have no market risk; whereas if beta were 1.0, then the stock would be exactly as risky as the market—assuming the stock is held in a diversified portfolio—and the stock's market risk would be σ_M.

3.5e Advanced Issues in Calculating Beta

Betas are generally estimated from the stock's characteristic line by running a linear regression between past returns on the stock in question and past returns on some market index. We define betas developed in this manner as **historical betas**. However, in most situations, it is the *future* beta that is needed. This has led to the development of two different types of betas: (1) adjusted betas and (2) fundamental betas.

Adjusted betas grew largely out of the work of Marshall E. Blume, who showed that true betas tend to move toward 1.0 over time.[9] Therefore, we can begin with a firm's pure historical statistical beta, make an adjustment for the expected future movement toward 1.0, and produce an adjusted beta that will, on average, be a

---

9. See Marshall E. Blume, "Betas and Their Regression Tendencies," *Journal of Finance*, June 1975, pp. 785–796, and Marshall E. Blume, "On the Assessment of Risk," *Journal of Finance*, March 1971, pp. 1–10.

better predictor of the future beta than the unadjusted historical beta would be. *Value Line* publishes betas based on approximately this formula:

$$\text{Adjusted beta} = 0.67(\text{Historical beta}) + 0.35(1.0).$$

Consider American Camping Corporation, a retailer of supplies for outdoor activities. ACC's historical beta is 1.2. Therefore, its adjusted beta is

$$\text{Adjusted beta} = 0.67(1.2) + 0.35(1.0) = 1.15.$$

Other researchers have extended the adjustment process to include such fundamental risk variables as financial leverage, sales volatility, and the like. The end product here is a **fundamental beta,** which is constantly adjusted to reflect changes in a firm's operations and capital structure. In contrast, with historical betas (including adjusted ones), such changes might not be reflected until several years after the company's "true" beta had changed.

Adjusted betas obviously are heavily dependent on unadjusted historical betas, and so are fundamental betas as they are actually calculated. Therefore, the plain old historical beta, calculated as the slope of the characteristic line, is important even if one goes on to develop a more exotic version. With this in mind, it should be noted that several different sets of data can be used to calculate historical betas, and the different data sets produce different results. Here are some of the details:

1. Betas can be based on historical periods of different lengths. For example, data for the past 1 year, 3 years, 5 years, or even 10 years may be used. Many people who calculate betas today use 5 years of data; but this choice is arbitrary, and different lengths of time usually alter significantly the calculated beta for a given company.

2. Returns may be calculated over holding periods of different lengths—a day, a week, a month, a quarter, a year, and so on. For example, if it has been decided to analyze data on NYSE stocks over a 5-year period, then we might obtain $52(5) = 260$ weekly returns on each stock and on the market index. We could also use $12(5) = 60$ monthly returns, or $1(5) = 5$ annual returns. The set of returns on each stock, however large the set turns out to be, would then be regressed on the corresponding market returns to obtain the stock's beta. In statistical analysis, it is generally better to have more rather than fewer observations, because using more observations generally leads to greater statistical confidence. This suggests the use of weekly returns and, say, 5 years of data for a sample size of 260, or even daily returns for a still larger sample size. However, the shorter the holding period, the more likely the data are to exhibit random "noise." Also, the greater the number of years of data, the more likely it is that the company's basic risk position has changed. Thus, the choice of both the number of years of data and the length of the holding period for calculating rates of return involves trade-offs between the preference for many observations and a desire to rely on more recent and thus more relevant data.

3. The value used to represent "the market" is also an important consideration, because the index that is used can have a significant effect on the calculated beta. Many analysts today use the New York Stock Exchange Composite Index (based on more than 2,000 common stocks, weighted by the value of each company), but others use the S&P 500 Index. In theory, the broader the index, the better the beta. Indeed, the theoretical index should include returns on all stocks, bonds, leases, private businesses, real estate, and even "human capital."

As a practical matter, however, we cannot get accurate returns data on most other types of assets, so measurement problems largely restrict us to stock indexes.

Where does this leave financial managers regarding the proper beta? They must "pay their money and take their choice." Some managers calculate their own betas using whichever procedure seems most appropriate under the circumstances. Others use betas calculated by organizations such as Yahoo! Finance or *Value Line,* perhaps using one service or perhaps averaging the betas of several services. The choice is a matter of judgment and data availability, for there is no "right" beta. Generally, though, the betas derived from different sources will, for a given company, be reasonably close together. If they are not, then our confidence in using the CAPM will be diminished.

Self Test

Explain the meaning and significance of a stock's beta coefficient. Illustrate your explanation by drawing, on one graph, the characteristic lines for stocks with low, average, and high risk. (*Hint:* Let your three characteristic lines intersect at $\bar{r}_i = \bar{r}_M = 6\%$, the assumed risk-free rate.)

What is a typical R^2 for the characteristic line of an individual stock? For a portfolio?

What is the market model? How is it different from the SML for the CAPM?

How are total risk, market risk, and diversifiable risk related?

3.6 Empirical Tests of the CAPM

Does the CAPM's SML produce reasonable estimates for a stock's required return? The literature dealing with empirical tests of the CAPM is quite extensive, so we can give here only a synopsis of some of the key work.

3.6a Tests of the Stability of Beta Coefficients

According to the CAPM, the beta used to estimate a stock's market risk should reflect investors' estimates of the stock's *future* variability in relation to that of the market. Obviously, we do not know now how a stock will be related to the market in the future, nor do we know how the average investor views this expected future relative variability. All we have are data on past variability, which we can use to plot the characteristic line and to calculate *historical betas*. If historical betas have been stable over time, then there would seem to be reason for investors to use past betas as estimators of future variability. For example, if Stock i's beta had been stable in the past, then its historical b_i would probably be a good proxy for its *ex ante,* or expected, beta. By "stable" we mean that if b_i were calculated with data from the period of, say, 2008 to 2012, then this same beta (approximately) should be found from 2013 to 2017.

Robert Levy, Marshall Blume, and others have studied in depth the question of beta stability.[10] Levy calculated betas for individual securities, as well as for

---

10. See Robert A. Levy, "On the Short-Term Stationarity of Beta Coefficients," *Financial Analysts Journal,* November/December 1971, pp. 55–62; and Marshall E. Blume, "Betas and Their Regression Tendencies," *Journal of Finance,* June 1975, pp. 785–796.

portfolios of securities, over a range of time intervals. He concluded (1) that the betas of individual stocks are unstable and hence past betas for *individual securities* are *not* good estimators of their future risk, but (2) that betas of portfolios of ten or more randomly selected stocks are reasonably stable and hence past *portfolio* betas are good estimators of future portfolio volatility. In effect, the errors in individual securities' betas tend to offset one another in a portfolio. The work of Blume and others supports this position.

The conclusion that follows from the beta stability studies is that the CAPM is a better concept for structuring investment portfolios than it is for estimating the required return for individual securities.[11]

3.6b Tests of the CAPM Based on the Slope of the SML

The CAPM states that a linear relationship exists between a security's required rate of return and its beta. Moreover, when the SML is graphed, the vertical axis intercept should be r_{RF} and the required rate of return for a stock (or portfolio) with $b = 1.0$ should be r_M, the required rate of return on the market. Various researchers have attempted to test the validity of the CAPM by calculating betas and realized rates of return, plotting these values in graphs such as that in Figure 3-10, and then observing whether or not (1) the intercept is equal to r_{RF}, (2) the plot is linear, and (3) the line passes through the point $b = 1.0$, r_M. Monthly or daily historical rates of return are generally used for stocks, and both 30-day Treasury bill rates and long-term Treasury bond rates have been used to estimate the value of r_{RF}. Also, most of the studies actually analyzed portfolios rather than individual securities because security betas are so unstable.

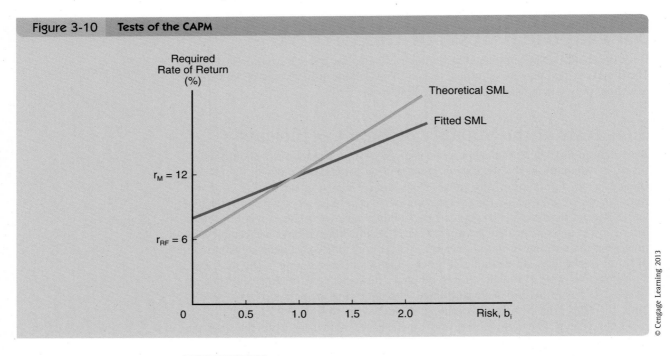

Figure 3-10   Tests of the CAPM

© Cengage Learning 2013

11. For more on beta stability, see Robert W. Kolb and Ricardo J. Rodriguez, "The Regression Tendencies of Betas: A Reappraisal," *The Financial Review,* May 1989, pp. 319–334. Also see Robert Kolb, "Is the Distribution of Betas Stationary?" *Journal of Financial Research,* Winter 1990, pp. 279–283.

Before discussing the results of the tests, it is critical to recognize that although the CAPM is an *ex ante,* or forward-looking, model, the data used to test it are entirely historical. This presents a problem, for there is no reason to believe that *realized* rates of return over past holding periods are necessarily equal to the rates of return people *expect* in the future. Also, historical betas may or may not reflect expected future risk. This lack of *ex ante* data makes it extremely difficult to test the CAPM, but for what it's worth, here is a summary of the key results.

1. The evidence generally shows a significant positive relationship between realized returns and beta. However, the slope of the relationship is usually less than that predicted by the CAPM.
2. The relationship between risk and return appears to be linear. Empirical studies give no evidence of significant curvature in the risk–return relationship.
3. Tests that attempt to assess the relative importance of market and company-specific risk do not yield conclusive results. The CAPM implies that company-specific risk should not be relevant, yet both kinds of risk appear to be positively related to security returns; that is, higher returns seem to be required to compensate for diversifiable as well as market risk. However, it may be that the observed relationships reflect statistical problems rather than the true nature of capital markets.
4. Richard Roll has questioned whether it is even conceptually possible to test the CAPM.[12] Roll showed that the linear relationship that prior researchers had observed in graphs like Figure 3-10 resulted from the mathematical properties of the models being tested; therefore, a finding of linearity would prove nothing whatsoever about the CAPM's validity. Roll's work did not disprove the CAPM, but it did demonstrate the virtual impossibility of proving that investors behave in accordance with its predictions.
5. If the CAPM were completely valid, then it should apply to all financial assets, including bonds. In fact, when bonds are introduced into the analysis, they do *not* plot on the SML. This is worrisome, to say the least.

3.6c Current Status of the CAPM

The CAPM is extremely appealing on an intellectual level: It is logical and rational, and once someone works through and understands the theory, his reaction is usually to accept it without question. However, doubts begin to arise when one thinks about the assumptions upon which the model is based, and these doubts are as much reinforced as reduced by the empirical tests. Our own views on the CAPM's current status are as follows.

1. The CAPM framework, with its focus on market as opposed to stand-alone risk, is clearly a useful way to think about the risk of assets. Thus, as a conceptual model, the CAPM is of truly fundamental importance.
2. When applied in practice, the CAPM appears to provide neat, precise answers to important questions about risk and required rates of return. However, the answers are less clear than they seem. The simple truth is that we do not know precisely how to measure any of the inputs required to implement the CAPM. These inputs should all be *ex ante,* yet only *ex post* data are available. Furthermore, historical data on $\bar{r}_M$, r_{RF}, and betas vary greatly depending on the time

---

12. See Richard Roll, "A Critique of the Asset Pricing Theory's Tests," *Journal of Financial Economics,* March 1977, pp. 129–176.

period studied and the methods used to estimate them. Thus, even though the CAPM appears to be precise, estimates of r_i found through its use are subject to potentially large errors.[13]

3. Because the CAPM is logical in the sense that it represents the way risk-averse people ought to behave, the model is a useful conceptual tool.

4. It is appropriate to think about many financial problems in a CAPM framework. However, it is important to recognize the limitations of the CAPM when using it in practice.

Self Test

What are the two major types of tests that have been performed to test the validity of the CAPM? (**Beta stability; slope of the SML**) Explain their results.

Are there any reasons to question the validity of the CAPM? Explain.

3.7 Arbitrage Pricing Theory

The CAPM is a single-factor model. That is, it specifies risk as a function of only one factor, the security's beta coefficient. Perhaps the risk–return relationship is more complex, with a stock's required return a function of more than one factor. For example, what if investors, because personal tax rates on capital gains are lower than those on dividends, value capital gains more highly than dividends? Then, if two stocks had the same market risk, the stock paying the higher dividend would have the higher required rate of return. In that case, required returns would be a function of two factors, market risk and dividend policy.

Further, what if many factors are required to specify the equilibrium risk–return relationship rather than just one or two? Stephen Ross has proposed an approach called the **Arbitrage Pricing Theory (APT)**.[14] The APT can include any number of risk factors, so the required return could be a function of two, three, four, or more factors. We should note at the outset that the APT is based on complex mathematical and statistical theory that goes far beyond the scope of this text. Also, although the APT model is widely discussed in academic literature, practical usage to date has been limited. However, such use may increase, so students should at least have an intuitive idea of what the APT is all about.

The SML states that each stock's required return is equal to the risk-free rate plus the product of the market risk premium times the stock's beta coefficient. If stocks are in equilibrium, then the required return will be equal to the expected return:

$$\hat{r}_i = r_i = r_{RF} + (r_M - r_{RF})b_i$$

The historical realized return, $\bar{r}_i$, which will generally be different from the expected return, can be expressed as follows:[15]

(3–14)

$$\bar{r}_i = \hat{r}_i + (\bar{r}_M - \hat{r}_M)b_i + e_i$$

---

13. For an article supporting a positive link between market risk and expected return, see Felicia Marston and Robert S. Harris, "Risk and Return: A Revisit Using Expected Returns," *The Financial Review*, February 1993, pp. 117–137.

14. See Stephen A. Ross, "The Arbitrage Theory of Capital Asset Pricing," *Journal of Economic Theory*, December 1976, pp. 341–360.

15. To avoid cluttering the notation, we have dropped the subscript t to denote a particular time period.

Thus, the realized return, $\overline{r}_i$, will be equal to the expected return, $\hat{r}_i$, plus a positive or negative increment, $(\overline{r}_M - \hat{r}_M)b_i$, which depends jointly on the stock's beta and on whether the market did better or worse than was expected, plus a random error term, e_i.

The market's realized return, $\overline{r}_M$, is in turn determined by a number of factors, including domestic economic activity as measured by gross domestic product (GDP), the strength of the world economy, the level of inflation, changes in tax laws, and so forth. Further, different groups of stocks are affected in different ways by these fundamental factors. So, rather than specifying a stock's return as a function of one factor (return on the market), one could specify required and realized returns on individual stocks as a function of various fundamental economic factors. If this were done, we would transform Equation 3-14 into 3-15:

$$\overline{r}_i = \hat{r}_i + (\overline{F}_1 - \hat{F}_1)b_{i1} + \cdots + (\overline{F}_j - \hat{F}_j)b_{ij} + e_i \qquad \text{(3–15)}$$

Here,

$\overline{r}_i$ = Realized rate of return on Stock i.
$\hat{r}_i$ = Expected rate of return on Stock i.
$\overline{F}_j$ = Realized value of economic Factor j.
$\hat{F}_j$ = Expected value of Factor j.
b_{ij} = Sensitivity of Stock i to economic Factor j.
e_i = Effect of unique events on the realized return of Stock i.

Equation 3-15 shows that the realized return on any stock is the sum of: (1) the stock's expected return; (2) increases or decreases that depend on unexpected changes in fundamental economic factors, multiplied by the sensitivity of the stock to these changes; and (3) a random term that reflects changes unique to the firm.

Certain stocks or groups of stocks are most sensitive to Factor 1, others to Factor 2, and so forth, and every portfolio's returns depend on what happened to the different fundamental factors. Theoretically, one could construct a portfolio such that (1) the portfolio was riskless and (2) the net investment in it was zero (some stocks would be sold short, with the proceeds from the short sales being used to buy the stocks held long). Such a zero-investment portfolio must have a zero expected return, or else arbitrage operations would occur and cause the prices of the underlying assets to change until the portfolio's expected return became zero. Using some complex mathematics and a set of assumptions that include the possibility of short sales, the APT equivalent of the CAPM's Security Market Line can be developed from Equation 3-15 as follows:[16]

$$r_i = r_{RF} + (r_1 - r_{RF})b_{i1} + \cdots + (r_j - r_{RF})b_{ij} \qquad \text{(3–16)}$$

Here r_j is the required rate of return on a portfolio that is sensitive only to economic Factor j ($b_{pj} = 1.0$) and has zero sensitivity to all other factors. Thus, for example, $(r_2 - r_{RF})$ is the risk premium on a portfolio with $b_{p2} = 1.0$ and all other $b_{pj} = 0.0$. Note that Equation 3-16 is identical in form to the SML, but it permits a stock's required return to be a function of multiple factors.

---

16. See Thomas E. Copeland, J. Fred Weston, and Kuldeep Shastri, *Financial Theory and Corporate Policy*, 4th ed. (Reading, MA: Addison-Wesley, 2005).

To illustrate the APT concept, assume that all stocks' returns depend on only three risk factors: inflation, industrial production, and the aggregate degree of risk aversion (the cost of bearing risk, which we assume is reflected in the spread between the yields on Treasury and low-grade bonds). Further, suppose that: (1) the risk-free rate is 8.0%; (2) the required rate of return is 13% on a portfolio with unit sensitivity (b = 1.0) to inflation and zero sensitivities (b = 0.0) to industrial production and degree of risk aversion; (3) the required return is 10% on a portfolio with unit sensitivity to industrial production and zero sensitivities to inflation and degree of risk aversion; and (4) the required return is 6% on a portfolio (the risk-bearing portfolio) with unit sensitivity to the degree of risk aversion and zero sensitivities to inflation and industrial production. Finally, assume that Stock i has factor sensitivities (betas) of 0.9 to the inflation portfolio, 1.2 to the industrial production portfolio, and −0.7 to the risk-bearing portfolio. Stock i's required rate of return, according to the APT, would be 16.3%:

$$r_i = 8\% + (13\% - 8\%)0.9 + (10\% - 8\%)1.2 + (6\% - 8\%)(-0.7)$$

$$= 16.3\%$$

Note that if the required rate of return on the market were 15.0% and if Stock i had a CAPM beta of 1.1, then its required rate of return, according to the SML, would be 15.7%:

$$r_i = 8\% + (15\% - 8\%)1.1 = 15.7\%$$

The primary theoretical advantage of the APT is that it permits several economic factors to influence individual stock returns, whereas the CAPM assumes that the effect of all factors, except those that are unique to the firm, can be captured in a single measure: the variability of the stock with respect to the market portfolio. Also, the APT requires fewer assumptions than the CAPM and hence is more general. Finally, the APT does not assume that all investors hold the market portfolio, a CAPM requirement that is clearly not met in practice.

However, the APT faces several major hurdles in implementation, the most severe of which is that the theory does not actually identify the relevant factors. The APT does not tell us what factors influence returns, nor does it even indicate how many factors should appear in the model. There is some empirical evidence that only three or four factors are relevant: perhaps inflation, industrial production, the spread between low- and high-grade bonds, and the term structure of interest rates—but no one knows for sure.

The APT's proponents argue that it is not actually necessary to identify the relevant factors. Researchers use a statistical procedure called **factor analysis** to develop the APT parameters. Basically, they start with hundreds, or even thousands, of stocks and then create several different portfolios, where the returns on each portfolio are not highly correlated with returns on the other portfolios. Thus, each portfolio is apparently more heavily influenced by one of the unknown factors than are the other portfolios. Then, the required rate of return on each portfolio becomes the estimate for that unknown economic factor, shown as r_j in Equation 3-16. The sensitivities of each individual stock's returns to the returns on that portfolio are the factor sensitivities (betas). Unfortunately, the results of factor analysis are not easily interpreted; hence it does not provide significant insights into the underlying economic determinants of risk.[17]

---

17. For additional discussion of the APT, see Edward L. Bubnys, "Simulating and Forecasting Utility Stock Returns: Arbitrage Pricing Theory vs. Capital Asset Pricing Model," *The Financial Review,* February 1990, pp. 1–23; David H. Goldenberg and Ashok J. Robin, "The Arbitrage Pricing Theory and Cost-of-Capital Estimation: The Case of Electric Utilities," *Journal of Financial Research,* Fall 1991, pp. 181–196; and Ashok Robin and Ravi Shukla, "The Magnitude of Pricing Errors in the Arbitrage Pricing Theory," *Journal of Financial Research,* Spring 1991, pp. 65–82.

>
> What is the primary difference between the APT and the CAPM?
>
> What are some disadvantages of the APT?
>
> An analyst has modeled the stock of Brown Kitchen Supplies using a two-factor APT model. The risk-free rate is 5%, the required return on the first factor (r_1) is 10%, and the required return on the second factor (r_2) is 15%. If $b_{i1} = 0.5$ and $b_{i2} = 1.3$, what is Brown's required return? **(20.5%)**

3.8 The Fama-French Three-Factor Model

Table 3-3 reports the returns for 25 portfolios, commonly called the Fama-French portfolios because Professors Eugene Fama and Kenneth French were the first to form them. These portfolios are based on the company's size as measured by the market value of its equity (MVE) and the company's book-to-market ratio (B/M), defined as the book value of equity divided by the market value of equity. Each row shows portfolios with similarly sized companies; each column shows portfolios whose companies have similar B/M ratios. Notice that if you look across each row, the average return tends to increase as the B/M ratio increases. In other words, stocks with high B/M ratios have higher returns. If you look up each column (except for the column with the lowest B/M ratios), stock returns tend to increase: Small companies have higher returns.

TABLE 3-3	Average Annual Returns for the Fama-French Portfolios Based on Size and Book Equity to Market Equity, 1927–2010				
	Book Equity to Market Equity				
Size	**Low**	**2**	**3**	**4**	**High**
Small	11.7%	19.6%	21.0%	23.9%	30.3%
2	11.8	17.1	19.0	18.9	19.8
3	12.3	15.8	16.9	17.4	19.4
4	12.4	13.5	15.2	16.5	17.9
Big	10.9	12.4	13.3	13.9	15.0

Source: Professor Kenneth French, **http://mba.tuck.dartmouth.edu/pages/faculty/ ken.french/data_library.html**. These are equal-weighted annual returns. Following is a description from Professor French's Web site describing the construction of the portfolios: "The portfolios, which are constructed at the end of each June, are the intersections of 5 portfolios formed on size (market equity, ME) and 5 portfolios formed on the ratio of book equity to market equity (BE/ME). The size breakpoints for year t are the NYSE market equity quintiles at the end of June of t. BE/ME for June of year t is the book equity for the last fiscal year end in $t - 1$ divided by ME for December of $t - 1$. The BE/ME breakpoints are NYSE quintiles. The portfolios for July of year t to June of $t + 1$ include all NYSE, AMEX, and NASDAQ stocks for which we have market equity data for December of $t - 1$ and June of t, and (positive) book equity data for $t - 1$."

What might explain this pattern? If the market value is larger than the book value, then investors are optimistic about the stock's future. On the other hand, if the book value is larger than the market value, then investors are pessimistic about the stock's future, and it is likely that a ratio analysis will reveal that the company is experiencing impaired operating performance and possibly even financial distress. In other words, a stock with a high B/M ratio might be risky, in which case investors would require a higher expected return to induce them to invest in such a stock.

Small companies have less access to capital markets than do large companies, which subjects small companies to greater risk in the event of a credit crunch—such as the one that occurred during the global economic crisis that began in 2007. With greater risk, investors would require a higher expected return to induce them to invest in small companies.

As we mentioned in Chapter 2, the results of two studies by Eugene F. Fama and Kenneth R. French seriously challenge the CAPM.[18] In the first of these studies, published in 1992, Fama and French hypothesized that the SML should have three factors. The first is the stock's CAPM beta, which measures the market risk of the stock. The second is the size of the company, measured by the market value of its equity (MVE). The third factor is the book-to-market ratio (B/M).

When Fama and French tested their hypotheses, they found that small companies and companies with high B/M ratios had higher rates of return than the average stock, just as they hypothesized. Somewhat surprisingly, however, they found no relation between beta and return. After taking into account the returns due to the company's size and B/M ratio, high-beta stocks did not have higher than average returns and low-beta stocks did not have lower than average returns.

In the second of their two studies, published in 1993, Fama and French developed a three-factor model based on their previous results. The first factor in the **Fama-French three-factor model** is the market risk premium, which is the market return, $\bar{r}_M$, minus the risk-free rate, $\bar{r}_{RF}$. Thus, their model begins like the CAPM, but they go on to add a second and third factor.[19] To form the second factor, they ranked all actively traded stocks by size and then divided them into two portfolios, one consisting of small stocks and one consisting of big stocks. They calculated the return on each of these two portfolios and created a third portfolio by subtracting the return on the big portfolio from that of the small one. They called this the SMB (small minus big) portfolio. This portfolio is designed to measure the variation in stock returns that is caused by the size effect.

To form the third factor, they ranked all stocks according to their book-to-market ratios (B/M). They placed the 30% of stocks with the highest ratios into a portfolio they called the H portfolio (for high B/M ratios) and placed the 30% of stocks with the lowest ratios into a portfolio called the L portfolio (for low B/M ratios). Then they subtracted the return of the L portfolio from that of the H portfolio to derive the HML (high minus low) portfolio. Their resulting model is shown here:

(3–17)

$$(\bar{r}_i - \bar{r}_{RF}) = a_i + b_i(\bar{r}_M - \bar{r}_{RF}) + c_i(\bar{r}_{SMB}) + d_i(\bar{r}_{HML}) + e_i$$

18. See Eugene F. Fama and Kenneth R. French, "The Cross-Section of Expected Stock Returns," *Journal of Finance,* Vol. 47, 1992, pp. 427–465. Also see Eugene F. Fama and Kenneth R. French, "Common Risk Factors in the Returns on Stocks and Bonds," *Journal of Financial Economics,* Vol. 33, 1993, pp. 3–56.

19. Although our description captures the essence of their process for forming factors, their actual procedure is a little more complicated. The interested reader should see their 1993 paper, cited in footnote 18.

where

> $\bar{r}_i$ = Historical (realized) rate of return on Stock i.
> $\bar{r}_{RF}$ = Historical (realized) rate of return on the risk-free rate.
> $\bar{r}_M$ = Historical (realized) rate of return on the market.
> $\bar{r}_{SMB}$ = Historical (realized) rate of return on the small-size portfolio minus the big-size portfolio.
> $\bar{r}_{HML}$ = Historical (realized) rate of return on the high-B/M portfolio minus the low-B/M portfolio.
> a_i = Vertical axis intercept term for Stock i.
> $b_i, c_i,$ and d_i = Slope coefficients for Stock i.
> e_i = Random error, reflecting the difference between the actual return on Stock i in a given period and the return as predicted by the regression line.

The Fama-French three-factor model version of the CAPM Security Market Line for the required return on a stock is

$$r_i = r_{RF} + a_i + b_i(r_M - r_{RF}) + c_i(r_{SMB}) + d_i(r_{HML})$$ (3–18)

where $r_M - r_{RF}$ is the market risk premium, r_{SMB} is the expected value (i.e., premium) for the size factor, and r_{HML} is the expected value (i.e., premium) for the book-to-market factor.

Here is how you might apply this model. Suppose you ran the regression in Equation 3-17 for a stock and estimated the following regression coefficients: $a_i = 0.0$, $b_i = 0.9$, $c_i = 0.2$, and $d_i = 0.3$. Assume that the expected market risk premium is 6% (i.e., $r_M - r_{RF} = 6\%$) and that the risk-free rate is 6.5%. Suppose the expected value of r_{SMB} is 3.2% and the expected value of r_{HML} is 4.8%.[20] Using the Fama-French three-factor model, the required return is

$$r_i = r_{RF} + a_i + b_i(r_M - r_{RF}) + c_i(r_{SMB}) + d_i(r_{HML})$$
$$= 6.5\% + 0.0 + 0.9(6\%) + 0.2(3.2\%) + 0.3(4.8\%)$$ (3–18a)
$$= 13.98\%$$

To date, the Fama-French three-factor model has been used primarily by academic researchers rather than by managers of actual companies, the majority of whom are still using the CAPM. Part of this difference was due at one time to the lack of available data. Most professors had access to the type of data required to calculate the factors, but data for the size factor and the B/M factor were not readily available to the general public. To help alleviate this problem, Professor French has made the required historical data available on his Web site.[21] However, it is still difficult to estimate the expected values of the size factor and the B/M factor. Although we know the historical average returns for these factors, we don't know whether the past historical returns are good estimators of the future expected returns. In other

---

20. These are the average returns found by Fama and French in their sample period for r_{SMB} and r_{HML}.
21. Professor French's Web site, **http://mba.tuck.dartmouth.edu/pages/faculty/ken.french/data_library.html#Research**, now provides time-series data for the returns on the factors ($\bar{r}_M - \bar{r}_{RF}$, $\bar{r}_{SMB}$, and $\bar{r}_{HML}$).

words, we don't know the risk premium associated with the size and book/market sources of risk. Finally, many managers choose to wait and adopt a new theory only after it has been widely accepted by the academic community.

And that isn't the case right now. In fact, there are a number of subsequent studies indicating that the Fama-French model is not correct.[22] Several of these studies suggest that the size effect no longer influences stock returns, that there never was a size effect (the previous results were caused by peculiarities in the data sources), or that the size effect doesn't apply to most companies. Other studies suggest that the book-to-market effect is not as significant as first supposed and/or that the book-to-market effect is not a function of risk. Another study shows that if the composition of a company's assets were changing over time with respect to the mix of physical assets and growth opportunities (involving, e.g., R&D or patents), then this would be enough to make it *appear* as though there were size and book-to-market effects. In other words, even if the returns on the individual assets conform to the CAPM, changes in the mix of assets would cause the firm's beta to change over time in such a way that the firm would appear to have size and book-to-market effects.[23]

Self Test	What are the factors in the Fama-French model?
	How can the model be used to estimate the required return on a stock?
	Why isn't the model widely used by managers at actual companies?
	An analyst has modeled the stock of a company using a Fama-French three-factor model. The risk-free rate is 5%, the required market return is 11%, the risk premium for small stocks (r_{SMB}) is 3.2%, and the risk premium for value stocks (r_{HML}) is 4.8%. If $a_i = 0$, $b_i = 0.7$, $c_i = 1.2$, and $d_i = 0.7$, then what is the stock's required return? **(16.4%)**

3.9 An Alternative Theory of Risk and Return: Behavioral Finance

The Efficient Markets Hypothesis (EMH) is one of the cornerstones of modern finance theory. It implies that, on average, assets trade at prices equal to their intrinsic values. As we note in Chapter 5, the logic behind the EMH is straightforward. If a stock's price is "too low," then rational traders will quickly take advantage of this opportunity and will buy the stock, and these actions will quickly push prices back to their equilibrium level. Likewise, if a stock's price is "too high," then rational

---

22. See Peter J. Knez and Mark J. Ready, "On the Robustness of Size and Book-to-Market in the Cross-Sectional Regressions," *Journal of Finance,* September 1997, pp. 1355–1382; Dongcheol Kim, "A Reexamination of Firm Size, Book-to-Market, and Earnings Price in the Cross-Section of Expected Stock Returns," *Journal of Financial and Quantitative Analysis,* December 1997, pp. 463–489; Tyler Shumway and Vincent A. Warther, "The Delisting Bias in CRSP's Nasdaq Data and Its Implications for the Size Effect," *Journal of Finance,* December 1999, pp. 2361–2379; Tim Loughran, "Book-to-Market across Firm Size, Exchange, and Seasonality: Is There an Effect?" *Journal of Financial and Quantitative Analysis,* September 1997, pp. 249–268; and Ilia D. Dichev, "Is the Risk of Bankruptcy a Systematic Risk?" *Journal of Finance,* June 1998, pp. 1131–1147.

23. See Jonathan B. Berk, Richard C. Green, and Vasant Naik, "Optimal Investment, Growth Options, and Security Returns," *Journal of Finance,* October 1999, pp. 1553–1608.

traders will sell it, pushing the price down to its equilibrium level. Proponents of the EMH argue that prices cannot be systematically wrong unless you believe that market participants are unable or unwilling to take advantage of profitable trading opportunities.

The logic behind the EMH is compelling, but some events seem to be inconsistent with the hypothesis. First, there is some evidence that stocks may have short-term momentum. Stocks that perform poorly tend to continue performing poorly over the next 3 to 12 months, and stocks that perform well tend to continue performing well in the short-term future. On the other hand, there is some evidence that stocks have long-term reversals. In particular, stocks that have the lowest returns in a 5-year period tend to outperform the market during the next 5 years. The opposite is true for stocks that outperform the market during a 5-year period: They tend to have lower than average returns during the next 5-year period.[24]

In response to such observations, a number of researchers are blending psychology with finance, creating a new field called **behavioral finance.** A large body of evidence in the field of psychology indicates that people don't behave rationally in many areas of their lives, so some argue that we should not expect people to behave rationally with their investments.[25] Pioneers in this field include psychologists Daniel Kahneman and Amos Tversky, along with University of Chicago finance professor Richard Thaler. Their work has encouraged a growing number of scholars to work in this promising area of research.

Professor Thaler and his colleague Nicholas Barberis have summarized much of this research.[26] They argue that behavioral finance theory rests on two important building blocks. First, mispricing can persist because it is often difficult or risky for traders to take advantage of mispriced assets. For example, even if it is clear that a stock's price is too low because investors have overreacted to recent bad news, a trader with limited capital may be reluctant to buy the stock for fear that the same forces that pushed the price down may work to keep it artificially low for a long period of time. On the other side, during the stock market bubble that burst in 2000, many traders who believed (correctly!) that stock prices were too high lost a lot of money selling stocks in the early stages of the bubble, because stock prices climbed even higher before they eventually collapsed. In other words, there is no reliable way to take advantage of mispricing.

While the first building block explains *why* mispricings may persist, the second tries to understand *how* mispricings occur in the first place. This is where the insights from psychology come into play. For example, Kahneman and Tversky suggest that individuals view potential losses and potential gains very differently.[27] If you ask an average person whether he or she would rather have $500 with certainty or flip a fair coin and receive $1,000 if it comes up heads and nothing if it comes up tails, most would prefer the certain $500 gain, which suggests an aversion to risk. However, if you ask the same person whether he or she would rather pay $500 with certainty or flip a coin and pay $1,000 if it's heads and nothing if it's tails, most

24. N. Jegadeesh and S. Titman, "Returns to Buying Winners and Selling Losers: Implications for Stock Market Efficiency," *Journal of Finance,* March 1993, pp. 69–91; and W. F. M. DeBondt and R. H. Thaler, "Does the Stock Market Overreact?" *Journal of Finance,* July 1985, pp. 793–808.

25. See Brian O'Reilly, "Why Johnny Can't Invest," *Fortune,* November 9, 1998, pp. 173–178.

26. Nicholas Barberis and Richard Thaler, "A Survey of Behavioral Finance," in *Handbook of the Economics of Finance,* George Constantinides, Milt Harris, and René Stulz, eds. (Amsterdam: Elsevier/North-Holland, 2003), Chapter 18.

27. Daniel Kahneman and Amos Tversky, "Prospect Theory: An Analysis of Decision under Risk," *Econometrica,* March 1979, pp. 263–292.

would indicate that they prefer to flip the coin. But this implies a preference for risk. In other words, people appear to dislike risk when it comes to possible gains but will take on risk in order to avoid sure losses. Other experiments have reinforced this idea that most people experience "loss aversion," or a strong desire to avoid realizing losses. In irrational, but common, mental bookkeeping, a loss isn't really a loss until the losing investment is actually sold. This leads investors to sell losers much less frequently than winners even though this is suboptimal for tax purposes.[28]

Not only do most people view risky gains and losses differently, but other studies suggest that people's willingness to take a gamble depends on recent past performance. Gamblers who are ahead tend to take on more risks (i.e., they are playing with the house's money), whereas those who are behind tend to become more conservative. These experiments suggest that investors and managers behave differently in down markets than they do in up markets, in which they are playing with the "house's" money.

Many psychological tests also show that people are overconfident with respect to their own abilities relative to the abilities of others, which is the basis of Garrison Keillor's joke about a town where all the children are above average. Barberis and Thaler point out:

> Overconfidence may in part stem from two other biases, self attribution bias and hindsight bias. Self attribution bias refers to people's tendency to ascribe any success they have in some activity to their own talents, while blaming failure on bad luck, rather than on their ineptitude. Doing this repeatedly will lead people to the pleasing but erroneous conclusion that they are very talented. For example, investors might become overconfident after several quarters of investing success [Gervais and Odean (2001)[29]]. Hindsight bias is the tendency of people to believe, after an event has occurred, that they predicted it before it happened. If people think they predicted the past better than they actually did, they may also believe that they can predict the future better than they actually can. (2003, p. 1066)

Some researchers have hypothesized that the combination of overconfidence and biased self-attribution leads to overly volatile stock markets, short-term momentum, and long-term reversals.[30] In other words, stock returns reflect the (predictably) irrational behavior of humans. Behavioral finance also has implications for corporate finance. Research by Ulrike Malmendier and Geoffrey Tate suggests that overconfidence leads managers to overestimate their abilities and the quality of their projects.[31] This result may explain why so many corporate projects fail to live up to their stated expectations.

| **Self Test** | What is short-term momentum? What are long-term reversals? |
| | What is behavioral finance? |

28. See Terrance Odean, "Are Investors Reluctant to Realize Their Losses?" *Journal of Finance,* October 1998, pp. 1775–1798.

29. See Terrance Odean and Simon Gervais, "Learning to Be Overconfident," *Review of Financial Studies,* Spring 2001, pp. 1–27.

30. See Terrance Odean, "Volume, Volatility, Price, and Profit When All Traders Are Above Average," *Journal of Finance,* December 1998, pp. 1887–1934; and Kent Daniel, David Hirshleifer, and Avanidhar Subrahmanyam, "Investor Psychology and Security Market Under- and Overreactions," *Journal of Finance,* December 1998, pp. 1839–1885.

31. See Ulrike Malmendier and Geoffrey Tate, "CEO Overconfidence and Corporate Investment," *Journal of Finance,* December 2005, pp. 2661–2700.

Summary

The primary goal of this chapter was to extend your knowledge of risk and return concepts. The key concepts covered are listed below.

- The **feasible set** of portfolios represents all portfolios that can be constructed from a given set of assets.
- An **efficient portfolio** is one that offers the most return for a given amount of risk or the least risk for a given amount of return.
- The **optimal portfolio** for an investor is defined by the investor's highest possible **indifference curve** that is tangent to the **efficient set** of portfolios.
- The **Capital Asset Pricing Model (CAPM)** describes the relationship between market risk and required rates of return.
- The **Capital Market Line (CML)** describes the risk–return relationship for efficient portfolios—that is, for portfolios consisting of a mix of the market portfolio and a riskless asset.
- The **Security Market Line (SML)** is an integral part of the CAPM, and it describes the risk–return relationship for individual assets. The required rate of return for any Stock i is equal to the **risk-free rate** plus the **market risk premium** multiplied by the stock's **beta coefficient**: $r_i = r_{RF} + (r_M - r_{RF})b_i$.
- Stock i's **beta coefficient, b_i,** is a measure of the stock's **market risk.** Beta measures the **variability** of returns on a security **relative to returns on the market,** which is the portfolio of all risky assets.
- The beta coefficient is measured by the slope of the stock's **characteristic line,** which is found by regressing historical returns on the stock versus historical returns on the market.
- Although the CAPM provides a convenient framework for thinking about risk and return issues, it *cannot be proven empirically* and its parameters are extremely difficult to estimate. Thus, the required rate of return for a stock as estimated by the CAPM may not be exactly equal to the true required rate of return.
- In contrast to the CAPM, the **Arbitrage Pricing Theory (APT)** hypothesizes that expected stock returns are due to more than one factor.
- The **Fama-French three-factor model** has one factor for the **market return,** a second factor for the **size effect,** and a third factor for the **book-to-market effect.**
- **Behavioral finance** assumes that investors don't always behave rationally.

Questions

3-1 Define the following terms, using graphs or equations to illustrate your answers wherever feasible:
   a. Portfolio; feasible set; efficient portfolio; efficient frontier
   b. Indifference curve; optimal portfolio
   c. Capital Asset Pricing Model (CAPM); Capital Market Line (CML)
   d. Characteristic line; beta coefficient, b
   e. Arbitrage Pricing Theory (APT); Fama-French three-factor model; behavioral finance

3-2 Security A has an expected rate of return of 6%, a standard deviation of returns of 30%, a correlation coefficient with the market of −0.25, and a beta coefficient of −0.5. Security B has an expected return of 11%, a standard deviation of returns of 10%, a correlation with the market of 0.75, and a beta coefficient of 0.5. Which security is more risky? Why?

Problems   Answers Appear in Appendix B

Easy Problems 1–3

3-1 **Beta** The standard deviation of stock returns for Stock A is 40%. The standard deviation of the market return is 20%. If the correlation between Stock A and the market is 0.70, then what is Stock A's beta?

3-2 **APT** An analyst has modeled the stock of Crisp Trucking using a two-factor APT model. The risk-free rate is 6%, the expected return on the first factor (r_1) is 12%, and the expected return on the second factor (r_2) is 8%. If $b_{i1} = 0.7$ and $b_{i2} = 0.9$, what is Crisp's required return?

3-3 **Fama-French Three-Factor Model** An analyst has modeled the stock of a company using the Fama-French three-factor model. The risk-free rate is 5%, the required market return is 10%, the risk premium for small stocks (r_{SMB}) is 3.2%, and the risk premium for value stocks (r_{HML}) is 4.8%. If $a_i = 0$, $b_i = 1.2$, $c_i = -0.4$, and $d_i = 1.3$, what is the stock's required return?

Intermediate Problems 4–6

3-4 **Two-Asset Portfolio** Stock A has an expected return of 12% and a standard deviation of 40%. Stock B has an expected return of 18% and a standard deviation of 60%. The correlation coefficient between Stocks A and B is 0.2. What are the expected return and standard deviation of a portfolio invested 30% in Stock A and 70% in Stock B?

3-5 **SML and CML Comparison** The beta coefficient of an asset can be expressed as a function of the asset's correlation with the market as follows:

$$b_i = \frac{\rho_{iM}\sigma_i}{\sigma_M}$$

a. Substitute this expression for beta into the Security Market Line (SML), Equation 3-9. This results in an alternative form of the SML.

b. Compare your answer to part a with the Capital Market Line (CML), Equation 3-6. What similarities are observed? What conclusions can be drawn?

3-6 **CAPM and the Fama-French Three-Factor Model** Suppose you are given the following information: The beta of Company i, b_i, is 1.1; the risk-free rate, r_{RF}, is 7%; and the expected market premium, $r_M - r_{RF}$, is 6.5%. Assume that $a_i = 0.0$.

a. Use the Security Market Line (SML) of the CAPM to find the required return for this company.

b. Because your company is smaller than average and more successful than average (that is, it has a low book-to-market ratio), you think the Fama-French three-factor model might be more appropriate than the CAPM. You estimate the additional coefficients from the Fama-French three-factor model: The coefficient for the size effect, c_i, is 0.7, and the coefficient for

the book-to-market effect, d_i, is −0.3. If the expected value of the size factor is 5% and the expected value of the book-to-market factor is 4%, what
is the required return using the Fama-French three-factor model?

Challenging Problems 7–8

3-7 Characteristic Line and Security Market Line You are given the following set
of data:

| | Historical Rates of Return | |
Year	NYSE	Stock X
1	−26.5%	−14.0%
2	37.2	23.0
3	23.8	17.5
4	−7.2	2.0
5	6.6	8.1
6	20.5	19.4
7	30.6	18.2

a. Use a spreadsheet (or a calculator with a linear regression function) to determine Stock X's beta coefficient.
b. Determine the arithmetic average rates of return for Stock X and the NYSE
over the period given. Calculate the standard deviations of returns for both
Stock X and the NYSE.
c. Assume that the situation during Years 1 to 7 is expected to prevail in the
future (i.e., $\hat{r}_X = \bar{r}_{X,Average}$, $\hat{r}_M = \bar{r}_{M,Average}$, and both σ_X and b_X in the future
will equal their past values). Also assume that Stock X is in equilibrium—
that is, it plots on the Security Market Line. What is the risk-free rate?
d. Plot the Security Market Line.
e. Suppose you hold a large, well-diversified portfolio and are considering adding
to that portfolio either Stock X or another stock, Stock Y, which has the same
beta as Stock X but a higher standard deviation of returns. Stocks X and Y have
the same expected returns: $\hat{r}_X = \hat{r}_Y = 10.6\%$. Which stock should you choose?

3-8 Characteristic Line You are given the following set of data:

| | Historical Rates of Return | |
Year	NYSE	Stock Y
1	4.0%	3.0%
2	14.3	18.2
3	19.0	9.1
4	−14.7	−6.0
5	−26.5	−15.3
6	37.2	33.1
7	23.8	6.1
8	−7.2	3.2
9	6.6	14.8
10	20.5	24.1
11	30.6	18.0
	Mean = 9.8%	9.8%
	σ = 19.6%	13.8%

a. Construct a scatter diagram showing the relationship between returns on Stock Y and the market. Use a spreadsheet or a calculator with a linear regression function to estimate beta.

b. Give a verbal interpretation of what the regression line and the beta coefficient show about Stock Y's volatility and relative risk as compared with those of other stocks.

c. Suppose the regression line were exactly as shown by your graph from part b but the scatter plot of points more spread out. How would this affect (1) the firm's risk if the stock is held in a one-asset portfolio and (2) the actual risk premium on the stock if the CAPM holds exactly?

d. Suppose the regression line were downward sloping and the beta coefficient were negative. What would this imply about (1) Stock Y's relative risk, (2) its correlation with the market, and (3) its probable risk premium?

Spreadsheet Problem

3-9 **Feasible Portfolios** Start with the partial model in the file *Ch03 P09 Build a Model.xls* from the textbook's Web site. Following is information for the required returns and standard deviations of returns for A, B, and C:

Stock	r_i	σ_i
A	7.0%	33.11%
B	10.0	53.85
C	20.0	89.44

The correlation coefficients for each pair are shown below in a matrix, with each cell in the matrix giving the correlation between the stock in that row and column. For example, $\rho_{AB} = 0.1571$ is in the row for A and the column for B. Notice that the diagonal values are equal to 1 because a variable is always perfectly correlated with itself.

	A	B	C
A	1.0000	0.1571	0.1891
B	0.1571	1.0000	0.1661
C	0.1891	0.1661	1.0000

a. Suppose a portfolio has 30% invested in A, 50% in B, and 20% in C. What are the expected return and standard deviation of the portfolio?

b. The partial model lists six different combinations of portfolio weights. For each combination of weights, find the required return and standard deviation.

c. The partial model provides a scatter diagram showing the required returns and standard deviations already calculated. This provides a visual indicator of the feasible set. If you seek a return of 10.5%, then what is the smallest standard deviation that you must accept?

MINI CASE

Answer the following questions.

a. Suppose Asset A has an expected return of 10% and a standard deviation of 20%. Asset B has an expected return of 16% and a standard deviation of 40%. If the correlation between A and B is 0.35, what are the expected return and standard deviation for a portfolio consisting of 30% Asset A and 70% Asset B?

b. Plot the attainable portfolios for a correlation of 0.35. Now plot the attainable portfolios for correlations of +1.0 and −1.0.

c. Suppose a risk-free asset has an expected return of 5%. By definition, its standard deviation is zero, and its correlation with any other asset is also zero. Using only Asset A and the risk-free asset, plot the attainable portfolios.

d. Construct a plausible graph that shows risk (as measured by portfolio standard deviation) on the x-axis and expected rate of return on the y-axis. Now add an illustrative feasible (or attainable) set of portfolios and show what portion of the feasible set is efficient. What makes a particular portfolio efficient? Don't worry about specific values when constructing the graph—merely illustrate how things look with "reasonable" data.

e. Add a set of indifference curves to the graph created for part b. What do these curves represent? What is the optimal portfolio for this investor? Add a second set of indifference curves that leads to the selection of a different optimal portfolio. Why do the two investors choose different portfolios?

f. What is the Capital Asset Pricing Model (CAPM)? What are the assumptions that underlie the model?

g. Now add the risk-free asset. What impact does this have on the efficient frontier?

h. Write out the equation for the Capital Market Line (CML), and draw it on the graph. Interpret the plotted CML. Now add a set of indifference curves and illustrate how an investor's optimal portfolio is some combination of the risky portfolio and the risk-free asset. What is the composition of the risky portfolio?

i. What is a characteristic line? How is this line used to estimate a stock's beta coefficient? Write out and explain the formula that relates total risk, market risk, and diversifiable risk.

j. What are two potential tests that can be conducted to verify the CAPM? What are the results of such tests? What is Roll's critique of CAPM tests?

k. Briefly explain the difference between the CAPM and the Arbitrage Pricing Theory (APT).

l. Suppose you are given the following information: The beta of a company, b_i, is 0.9; the risk-free rate, r_{RF}, is 6.8%; and the expected market premium, $r_M − r_{RF}$, is 6.3%. Because your company is larger than average and more successful than average (that is, it has a lower book-to-market ratio), you think the Fama-French three-factor model might be more appropriate than the CAPM. You estimate the additional coefficients from the Fama-French three-factor model: The coefficient for the size effect, c_i, is −0.5, and the coefficient for the book-to-market effect, d_i, is −0.3. If the expected value of the size factor is 4% and the expected value of the book-to-market factor is 5%, then what is the required return using the Fama-French three-factor model? (Assume that $a_i = 0.0$.) What is the required return using CAPM?

Selected Additional Case

The following case from TextChoice, Cengage Learning's online case library, covers many of the concepts discussed in this chapter and is available at **www.textchoice2.com/casenet.**

Klein-Brigham Series:
Case 2, "Peachtree Securities, Inc. (A)."

Chapter 4

Bond Valuation

Growing companies must acquire land, buildings, equipment, inventory, and other operating assets. The debt markets are a major source of funding for such purchases. Therefore, every manager should have a working knowledge of the types of bonds that companies and government agencies issue, the terms that are contained in bond contracts, the types of risks to which both bond investors and issuers are exposed, and procedures for determining the values of and rates of return on bonds.

Beginning of Chapter Questions

As you read the chapter, consider how you would answer the following questions. You *should not* necessarily be able to answer the questions before you read the chapter. Rather, you should use them to get a sense of the issues covered in the chapter. After reading the chapter, you should be able to give at least partial answers to the questions, and you should be able to give better answers after the chapter has been discussed in class. Note, too, that it is often useful, when answering conceptual questions, to use hypothetical data to illustrate your answer. We illustrate the answers with an *Excel* model that is available on the textbook's Web site. Accessing the model and working through it is a useful exercise, and it provides insights that are useful when answering the questions.

1. Define and discuss how to calculate a bond's **coupon rate, current yield, expected capital gains yield for the current year, yield to maturity (YTM),** and **yield to call (YTC).** What might be some representative numbers for a strong company like GE today? Are these rates fixed for the life of the bond, or do they change over time?

2. Define the terms **interest rate risk** and **reinvestment rate risk.** How are these risks affected by maturities, call provisions, and coupon rates? Why might different types of investors view these risks differently? How would they affect the yield curve? Illustrate your answers with bonds with different maturities and different coupon rates, but just discuss the effects of call provisions.

3. Would a bond be more or less desirable if you learned that it has a **sinking fund** that requires the company to redeem, say, 10% of the original issue each year beginning in 2015, either through open market purchases or by calling the redeemed bonds at par? How would it affect your answer if you learned that the bond was selling at a high premium, say, 130% of par, or at a large discount, say, 70% of par?

4. What is a **bond rating,** and how do ratings affect bonds' prices and yields? Who rates bonds, and what are some of the factors the rating agencies consider? Is it possible for a given company to have several different bonds outstanding that have different ratings? Explain.

5. Financial assets such as mortgages, credit card receivables, and auto loan receivables are often bundled up, placed in a bank trust department, and then used as collateral for publicly traded bonds. Bond prices typically rise when interest rates decline, but bonds backed by mortgages frequently fall when rates decline. Why might this happen?

4.1 Who Issues Bonds?

A **bond** is a long-term contract under which a borrower agrees to make payments of interest and principal, on specific dates, to the holders of the bond. For example, on January 5, 2013, MicroDrive Inc. borrowed $50 million by issuing $50 million of bonds. For convenience, we assume that MicroDrive sold 50,000 individual bonds for $1,000 each. Actually, it could have sold one $50 million bond, 10 bonds with a $5 million face value, or any other combination that totals to $50 million. In any event, MicroDrive received the $50 million, and in exchange it promised to make annual interest payments and to repay the $50 million on a specified maturity date.

Investors have many choices when investing in bonds, but bonds are classified into four main types: Treasury, corporate, municipal, and foreign. Each type differs with respect to expected return and degree of risk.

WEB

The textbook's Web site contains an *Excel* file that will guide you through the chapter's calculations. The file for this chapter is ***Ch04 Tool Kit.xls***, and we encourage you to open the file and follow along as you read the chapter.

INTRINSIC VALUE AND THE COST OF DEBT

This chapter explains bond pricing and bond risk, which affect the return demanded by a firm's bondholders. A bondholder's return is a cost from the company's point of view. This cost of debt affects the firm's weighted average cost of capital (WACC), which in turn affects the company's intrinsic value. Therefore, it is important for all managers to understand the cost of debt, which we explain in this chapter.

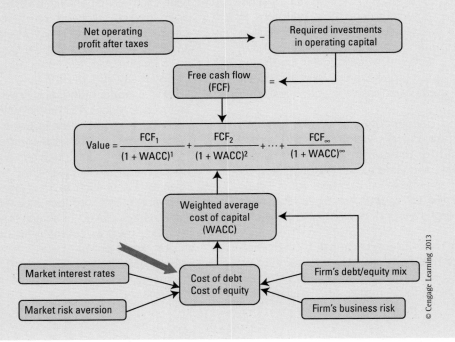

© Cengage Learning 2013

Treasury bonds, sometimes referred to as *government bonds,* are issued by the U.S. federal government.[1] It is reasonable to assume that the federal government will make good on its promised payments, so these bonds have almost no default risk. However, Treasury bond prices decline when interest rates rise, so they are not free of all risks.

Federal agencies and other government-sponsored entities (GSEs) include the Tennessee Valley Authority, the Small Business Administration, Fannie Mae, Freddie Mac, and the Federal Home Loan Bank System, among others. **Agency debt** and **GSE debt** are not officially backed by the full faith and credit of the U.S. government, but investors assume that the government implicitly guarantees this debt, so these bonds carry interest rates only slightly higher than Treasury bonds. In 2008, the implicit guarantee became much more explicit as the

---

1. The U.S. Treasury actually issues three types of securities: "bills," "notes," and "bonds." A bond makes an equal payment every 6 months until it matures, at which time it makes an additional lump-sum payment. If the maturity at the time of issue is less than 10 years, the security is called a note rather than a bond. A T-bill has a maturity of 52 weeks or less at the time of issue, and it makes no payments at all until it matures. Thus, T-bills are sold initially at a discount to their face, or maturity, value.

government placed several GSEs into conservatorship, including Fannie Mae and Freddie Mac.

Corporate bonds, as the name implies, are issued by corporations. Unlike Treasury bonds, corporate bonds are exposed to default risk—if the issuing company gets into trouble, it may be unable to make the promised interest and principal payments. Different corporate bonds have different levels of default risk, depending on the issuing company's characteristics and the terms of the specific bond. Default risk is often referred to as "credit risk," and the larger the credit risk, the higher the interest rate the issuer must pay.

Municipal bonds, or "munis," are issued by state and local governments. Like corporate bonds, munis have default risk. However, munis offer one major advantage: The interest earned on most municipal bonds is exempt from federal taxes and also from state taxes if the holder is a resident of the issuing state. Consequently, municipal bonds carry interest rates that are considerably lower than those on corporate bonds with the same default risk.

Foreign bonds are issued by foreign governments or foreign corporations. Foreign corporate bonds are, of course, exposed to default risk, and so are some foreign government bonds. An additional risk exists if the bonds are denominated in a currency other than that of the investor's home currency. For example, if a U.S. investor purchases a corporate bond denominated in Japanese yen and if the yen subsequently falls relative to the dollar, then the investor will lose money even if the company does not default on its bonds.

Self Test

What is a bond?

What are the four main types of bonds?

Why are U.S. Treasury bonds not riskless?

To what types of risk are investors of foreign bonds exposed?

THE GLOBAL ECONOMIC CRISIS

Betting With or Against the U.S. Government: The Case of Treasury Bond Credit Default Swaps

It might be hard to believe, but there is actually a market for U.S. Treasury bond insurance. In early 2009, a credit default swap (CDS) on a 5-year T-bond was selling for 71 basis points (a basis point is 1 percentage point). This means that you could pay $7.10 a year to a counterparty who would promise to insure $1,000 of T-bond principal against default. Considering that the T-bond pays only $18.75 a year in interest, the insurance would eat up a lot of the annual interest for an investor who owned the bond. However, most of the trading in this CDS is by speculators and hedgers who don't even own the T-bond but are simply betting for or against the financial soundness of the U.S. government.

But it does make you wonder: "If the United States fails, who will be around to pay off the CDS?"

4.2 Key Characteristics of Bonds

Although all bonds have some common characteristics, they do not always have identical contractual features, as described below.

4.2a Par Value

The **par value** is the stated face value of the bond; for illustrative purposes, we generally assume a par value of $1,000. In practice, some bonds have par values that are multiples of $1,000 (for example, $5,000) and some have par values of less than $1,000 (Treasury bonds can be purchased in multiples of $100). The par value generally represents the amount of money the firm borrows and promises to repay on the maturity date.

4.2b Coupon Interest Rate

www

An excellent site for information on many types of bonds is the Yahoo! Finance bond site, which can be found at **finance.yahoo.com/ bonds**. The site has a great deal of information about corporates, municipals, Treasuries, and bond funds. It includes free bond searches, through which the user specifies the attributes desired in a bond and then the search returns the publicly traded bonds meeting the criteria. The site also includes a bond calculator and an excellent glossary of bond terminology.

MicroDrive's bonds require the company to pay a fixed number of dollars of interest every year (or, more typically, every 6 months). When this **coupon payment**, as it is called, is divided by the par value, the result is the **coupon interest rate**. For example, MicroDrive's bonds have a $1,000 par value, and they pay $100 in interest each year. The bond's coupon interest is $100, so its coupon interest rate is $100/$1,000 = 10%. The coupon payment, which is fixed at the time the bond is issued, remains in force during the life of the bond.[2] Typically, at the time a bond is issued, its coupon payment is set at a level that will enable the bond to be issued at or near its par value.

In some cases, a bond's coupon payment will vary over time. For these **floating-rate bonds**, the coupon rate is set for, say, the initial 6-month period, after which it is adjusted every 6 months based on some market rate. Some corporate issues are tied to the Treasury bond rate; other issues are tied to other rates, such as LIBOR (the London Interbank Offered Rate). Many additional provisions can be included in floating-rate issues. For example, some are convertible to fixed-rate debt, whereas others have upper and lower limits ("caps" and "floors") on how high or low the rate can go.

Floating-rate debt is popular with investors who are worried about the risk of rising interest rates, since the interest paid on such bonds increases whenever market rates rise. This causes the market value of the debt to be stabilized, and it also provides institutional buyers, such as banks, with income that is better geared to their own obligations. Banks' deposit costs rise with interest rates, so the income on floating-rate loans they have made rises at the same time as their deposit costs rise. The savings and loan industry was almost destroyed as a result of its former practice of making fixed-rate mortgage loans but borrowing on floating-rate terms. If you are earning 6% fixed but paying 10% floating (which they were), you will soon go bankrupt (which they did). Moreover, floating-rate debt appeals to corporations that want to issue long-term debt without committing themselves to paying a historically high interest rate for the entire life of the loan.

---

2. At one time, bonds literally had a number of small coupons attached to them, and on each interest payment date the owner would clip off the coupon for that date and either cash it at the bank or mail it to the company's paying agent, who would then mail back a check for the interest. For example, a 30-year, semiannual bond would start with 60 coupons. Today, most new bonds are *registered*—no physical coupons are involved, and interest checks automatically are mailed to the registered owners or directly deposited in their bank accounts.

Some bonds pay no coupons at all but are offered at a substantial discount below their par values and hence provide capital appreciation rather than interest income. These securities are called **zero coupon bonds** ("zeros"). Most zero coupon bonds are Treasury bonds, although a few corporations, such as Coca-Cola, have zero coupon bonds outstanding. Some bonds are issued with a coupon rate too low for the bond to be issued at par, so the bond is issued at a price less than its par value. In general, any bond originally offered at a price significantly below its par value is called an **original issue discount (OID) bond**.

Some bonds don't pay cash coupons but pay coupons consisting of additional bonds (or a percentage of an additional bond). These are called **payment-in-kind bonds**, or just **PIK bonds**. PIK bonds are usually issued by companies with cash flow problems, which makes them risky.

Some bonds have a step-up provision: If the company's bond rating is downgraded, then it must increase the bond's coupon rate. Step-ups are more popular in Europe than in the United States, but that is beginning to change. Note that a step-up is quite dangerous from the company's standpoint. The downgrade means that it is having trouble servicing its debt, and the step-up will exacerbate the problem. This combination has led to a number of bankruptcies.

WEB

For more on zero coupon bonds, including U.S. Treasury STRIP bonds, see **Web Extension 4A** on the textbook's Web site.

4.2c Maturity Date

Bonds generally have a specified **maturity date** on which the par value must be repaid. MicroDrive bonds issued on January 5, 2013, will mature on January 5, 2028; thus, they have a 15-year maturity at the time they are issued. Most bonds have **original maturities** (the maturity at the time the bond is issued) ranging from 10 to 40 years, but any maturity is legally permissible.[3] Of course, the effective maturity of a bond declines each year after it has been issued. Thus, MicroDrive's bonds have a 15-year original maturity, but in 2014, a year later, they will have a 14-year maturity, and so on.

4.2d Provisions to Call or Redeem Bonds

Most corporate bonds contain a **call provision**, which gives the issuing corporation the right to call the bonds for redemption.[4] The call provision generally states that the company must pay the bondholders an amount greater than the par value if they are called. The additional sum, which is termed a **call premium**, is often set equal to 1 year's interest if the bonds are called during the first year, and the premium declines at a constant rate of INT/N each year thereafter (where INT = annual interest and N = original maturity in years). For example, the call premium on a $1,000 par value, 10-year, 10% bond would generally be $100 if it were called during the first year, $90 during the second year (calculated by reducing the $100, or 10%, premium by one-tenth), and so on. However, bonds are often not callable until several years (generally 5 to 10) after they are issued. This is known as a **deferred call**, and the bonds are said to have **call protection**.

Suppose a company sold bonds when interest rates were relatively high. Provided the issue is callable, the company could sell a new issue of low-yielding

---

3. In July 1993, Walt Disney Co., attempting to lock in a low interest rate, issued the first 100-year bonds to be sold by any borrower in modern times. Soon after, Coca-Cola became the second company to stretch the meaning of "long-term bond" by selling $150 million of 100-year bonds.

4. A majority of municipal bonds also contain call provisions. Although the U.S. Treasury no longer issues callable bonds, some past Treasury issues were callable.

securities if and when interest rates drop. It could then use the proceeds of the new issue to retire the high-rate issue and thus reduce its interest expense. This process is called a **refunding operation**.

A call provision is valuable to the firm but potentially detrimental to investors. If interest rates go up, the company will not call the bond, and the investor will be stuck with the original coupon rate on the bond, even though interest rates in the economy have risen sharply. However, if interest rates fall, the company *will* call the bond and pay off investors, who then must reinvest the proceeds at the current market interest rate, which is lower than the rate they were getting on the original bond. In other words, the investor loses when interest rates go up but doesn't reap the gains when rates fall. To induce an investor to take this type of risk, a new issue of callable bonds must provide a higher coupon rate than an otherwise similar issue of noncallable bonds.

Bonds that are **redeemable at par** at the holder's option protect investors against a rise in interest rates. If rates rise, the price of a fixed-rate bond declines. However, if holders have the option of turning their bonds in and having them redeemed at par, then they are protected against rising rates. If interest rates have risen, holders will turn in the bonds and reinvest the proceeds at a higher rate.

Event risk is the chance that some sudden event will occur and increase the credit risk of a company, hence lowering the firm's bond rating and the value of its outstanding bonds. Investors' concern over event risk means that those firms deemed most likely to face events that could harm bondholders must pay extremely high interest rates. To reduce this interest rate, some bonds have a covenant called a **super poison put**, which enables a bondholder to turn in, or "put," a bond back to the issuer at par in the event of a takeover, merger, or major recapitalization.

Some bonds have a **make-whole call provision**. This allows a company to call the bond, but it must pay a call price that is essentially equal to the market value of a similar noncallable bond. This provides companies with an easy way to repurchase bonds as part of a financial restructuring, such as a merger.

4.2e Sinking Funds

Some bonds include a **sinking fund provision** that facilitates the orderly retirement of the bond issue. On rare occasions the firm may be required to deposit money with a trustee, which invests the funds and then uses the accumulated sum to retire the bonds when they mature. Usually, though, the sinking fund is used to buy back a certain percentage of the issue each year. A failure to meet the sinking fund requirement causes the bond to be thrown into default, which may force the company into bankruptcy.

In most cases, the firm is given the right to administer the sinking fund in either of two ways.

1. The company can call in for redemption (at par value) a certain percentage of the bonds each year; for example, it might be able to call 5% of the total original amount of the issue at a price of $1,000 per bond. The bonds are numbered serially, and those called for redemption are determined by a lottery administered by the trustee.
2. The company may buy the required number of bonds on the open market.

The firm will choose the least-cost method. If interest rates have risen, causing bond prices to fall, then it will buy bonds in the open market at a discount; if interest rates have fallen, it will call the bonds. Note that a call for sinking fund purposes is quite different from a refunding call as discussed previously. A sinking fund call typically requires no call premium, but only a small percentage of the issue is normally callable in any one year.[5]

Although sinking funds are designed to protect bondholders by ensuring that an issue is retired in an orderly fashion, you should recognize that sinking funds can work to the detriment of bondholders. For example, suppose that the bond carries a 10% interest rate but that yields on similar bonds have fallen to 7.5%. A sinking fund call at par would require an investor to give up a bond that pays $100 of interest and then to reinvest in a bond that pays only $75 per year. This obviously harms those bondholders whose bonds are called. On balance, however, bonds that have a sinking fund are regarded as being safer than those without such a provision, so at the time they are issued sinking fund bonds have lower coupon rates than otherwise similar bonds without sinking funds.

4.2f Other Provisions and Features

Owners of **convertible bonds** have the option to convert the bonds into a fixed number of shares of common stock. Convertibles offer investors the chance to share in the upside if a company does well, so investors are willing to accept a lower coupon rate on convertibles than on an otherwise identical but nonconvertible bond.

Warrants are options that permit the holder to buy stock at a fixed price, thereby providing a gain if the price of the stock rises. Some bonds are issued with warrants. As with convertibles, bonds with warrants have lower coupon rates than straight bonds.

An **income bond** is required to pay interest only if earnings are high enough to cover the interest expense. If earnings are not sufficient, then the company is not required to pay interest and the bondholders do not have the right to force the company into bankruptcy. Therefore, from an investor's standpoint, income bonds are riskier than "regular" bonds.

Indexed bonds, also called **purchasing power bonds**, first became popular in Brazil, Israel, and a few other countries plagued by high inflation rates. The interest payments and maturity payment rise automatically when the inflation rate rises, thus protecting the bondholders against inflation. In January 1997, the U.S. Treasury began issuing indexed bonds called TIPS, short for Treasury Inflation-Protected Securities. Later in this chapter we show how TIPS can be used to estimate the risk-free rate.

4.2g Bond Markets

Corporate bonds are traded primarily in electronic/telephone markets rather than in organized exchanges. Most bonds are owned by and traded among a relatively small number of very large financial institutions, including banks, investment banks, life insurance companies, mutual funds, and pension funds. Although these institutions buy and sell very large blocks of bonds, it is relatively easy for bond dealers to arrange transactions because there are relatively few players in this market as compared with stock markets.

Information on bond trades is not widely published, but a representative group of bonds is listed and traded on the bond division of the NYSE and is reported on the bond market page of *The Wall Street Journal*. Bond data are also available on the Internet at sites such as **finance.yahoo.com**.

---

5. Some sinking funds require the issuer to pay a call premium.

Define "floating-rate bonds" and "zero coupon bonds."

Why is a call provision advantageous to a bond issuer?

What are the two ways a sinking fund can be handled? Which method will be chosen by the firm if interest rates have risen? If interest rates have fallen?

Are securities that provide for a sinking fund regarded as being riskier than those without this type of provision? Explain.

What are income bonds and indexed bonds?

Why do convertible bonds and bonds with warrants have lower coupons than similarly rated bonds that do not have these features?

4.3 Bond Valuation

The value of any financial asset—a stock, a bond, a lease, or even a physical asset such as an apartment building or a piece of machinery—is simply the present value of the cash flows the asset is expected to produce. The cash flows from a specific bond depend on its contractual features, as described in the previous section. For a standard coupon-bearing bond such as the one issued by MicroDrive, the cash flows consist of interest payments during the life of the bond plus the amount borrowed when the bond matures (usually a $1,000 par value):

The notation in the time line is explained below.

r_d = The bond's required rate of return, which is the market rate of interest for that type of bond. This is the discount rate that is used to calculate the present value of the bond's cash flows. It is also called the "yield" or "going rate of interest." Note that r_d is *not* the coupon interest rate. It is equal to the coupon rate only if (as in this case) the bond is selling at par. Generally, most coupon bonds are issued at par, which implies that the coupon rate is set at r_d. Thereafter, interest rates, as measured by r_d, will fluctuate, but the coupon rate is fixed, so r_d will equal the coupon rate only by chance. We use the term "i" or "I" to designate the interest rate for many calculations because those terms are used on financial calculators, but "r," with the subscript "d" to designate the rate on a debt security, is normally used in finance.

N = Number of years until the bond matures. Note that N declines each year after the bond was issued, so a bond that had a maturity of 15 years when it was issued (original maturity = 15) will have N = 14 after 1 year, N = 13 after 2 years, and so on. Note also that for the sake of simplicity we assume the bond pays interest once a year, or annually, so N is measured in years. We consider bonds with semian-nual payment bonds later in the chapter.

INT = Dollars of interest paid each year = (Coupon rate)(Par value). For a bond with a 10% coupon and a $1,000 par value, the annual interest is 0.10($1,000) = $100. In calculator terminology, INT = PMT = 100. If the bond had been a semiannual payment bond, the payment would have been $50 every 6 months.

M = Par, or maturity, value of the bond. This amount must be paid off at maturity, and it is often equal to $1,000.

The following general equation, written in several forms, can be used to find the value of any bond, V_B:

$$V_B = \frac{INT}{(1 + r_d)^1} + \frac{INT}{(1 + r_d)^2} + \cdots + \frac{INT}{(1 + r_d)^N} + \frac{M}{(1 + r_d)^N}$$

$$= \sum_{t=1}^{N} \frac{INT}{(1 + r_d)^t} + \frac{M}{(1 + r_d)^N}$$

(4–1)

$$= INT\left[\frac{1}{r_d} - \frac{1}{r_d(1 + r_d)^N}\right] + \frac{M}{(1 + r_d)^N}$$

Observe that the cash flows consist of an annuity of N years plus a lump-sum payment at the end of Year N. Equation 4-1 can be solved by using (1) a formula, (2) a financial calculator, or (3) a spreadsheet.

4.3a Solving for the Bond Price

Recall that MicroDrive issued a 15-year bond with an annual coupon rate of 10% and a par value of $1,000. To find the value of MicroDrive's bond by using a formula, insert values for MicroDrive's bond into Equation 4-1:

$$V_B = \sum_{t=1}^{15} \frac{\$100}{(1 + 0.10)^t} + \frac{\$1,000}{(1 + 0.10)^{15}}$$

$$= \$100\left[\frac{1}{0.10} - \frac{1}{0.10(1 + 0.10)^{15}}\right] + \frac{\$1,000}{(1 + 0.10)^{15}}$$

(4–1a)

$$= \$1,000$$

You could use the first line of Equation 4-1a to discount each cash flow back to the present and then sum these PVs to find the bond's value; see Figure 4-1. This procedure is not very efficient, especially if the bond has many years to maturity. Alternatively, you could use the formula in the second line of Equation 4-1a with a simple or scientific calculator, although this would still be somewhat cumbersome.

A financial calculator is ideally suited for finding bond values. Here is the setup for MicroDrive's bond:

Inputs:	15	10		100	1000
	N	**I/YR**	**PV**	**PMT**	**FV**
Output:			−1000		

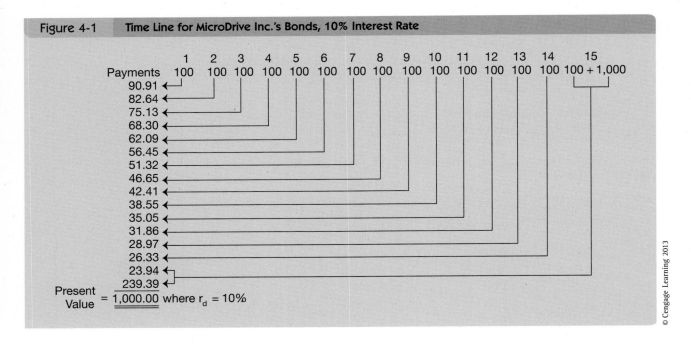

Figure 4-1   Time Line for MicroDrive Inc.'s Bonds, 10% Interest Rate

Input N = 15, I/YR = r_d = 10, INT = PMT = 100, and M = FV = 1000; then press the PV key to find the value of the bond, $1,000. Since the PV is an outflow to the investor, it is shown with a negative sign. The calculator is programmed to solve Equation 4-1: It finds the PV of an annuity of $100 per year for 15 years, discounted at 10%, then it finds the PV of the $1,000 maturity payment, and then it adds these two PVs to find the value of the bond. Notice that even though the time line in Figure 4-1 shows a total of $1,100 at Year 15, you should not enter FV = 1100! When you entered N = 15 and PMT = 100, you told the calculator that there is a $100 payment at Year 15. Thus, setting FV = 1000 accounts for any *extra* payment at Year 15, above and beyond the $100 payment.

With *Excel*, it is easiest to use the PV function: **=PV(I,N,PMT,FV,0)**. For Micro-Drive's bond, the function is **=PV(0.10,15,100,1000,0)** with a result of −$1,000. Like the financial calculator solution, the bond value is negative because PMT and FV are positive.

Excel also provides specialized functions for bond prices based on actual dates. For example, in *Excel* you could find the MicroDrive bond value as of the date it was issued by using the function wizard to enter this formula:

$$= \text{PRICE(DATE}(2013,1,5),\text{DATE}(2028,1,5),10\%,10\%,100,1,1)$$

The first two arguments in the function are *Excel*'s DATE function. The DATE function takes the year, month, and day as inputs and converts them into a date. The first argument is the date on which you want to find the price, and the second argument is the maturity date. The third argument in the PRICE function is the bond's coupon rate, followed by the required return on the bond, r_d. The fifth argument, 100, is the redemption value of the bond at maturity per $100 of face value; entering "100" means that the bond pays 100% of its face value when it matures. The sixth argument is the number of payments per year. The last argument, 1, tells the program to base the price on the actual number of days in each

WEB

See *Ch04 Tool Kit.xls* on the textbook's Web site.

© Cengage Learning 2013

month and year. This function produces a result based upon a face value of $100. In other words, if the bond pays $100 of face value at maturity, then the PRICE function result is the price of the bond. Because MicroDrive's bond pays $1,000 of face value at maturity, we must multiply the PRICE function's result by 10. In this example, the PRICE function returns a result of $100. When we multiply it by 10, we get the actual price of $1,000. This function is essential if a bond is being evaluated between coupon payment dates. See *Ch04 Tool Kit.xls* on the textbook's Web site for an example.[6]

4.3b Interest Rate Changes and Bond Prices

In this example, the bond is selling at a price equal to its par value. Whenever the going market rate of interest, r_d, is equal to the coupon rate, a *fixed-rate* bond will sell at its par value. Normally, the coupon rate is set at the going rate when a bond is issued, causing it to sell at par initially.

The coupon rate remains fixed after the bond is issued, but interest rates in the market move up and down. Looking at Equation 4-1, we see that an *increase* in the market interest rate (r_d) will cause the price of an outstanding bond to *fall*, whereas a *decrease* in rates will cause the bond's price to *rise*. For example, if the market interest rate on MicroDrive's bond increased to 15% immediately after it was issued, we would recalculate the price with the new market interest rate as follows:

Inputs: 15   15   100   1000

Output: −707.63

The price would fall to $707.63. Notice that the bond would then sell at a price below its par value. Whenever the going rate of interest *rises above* the coupon rate, a fixed-rate bond's price will *fall below* its par value, and it is called a **discount bond**.

On the other hand, bond prices rise when market interest rates fall. For example, if the market interest rate on MicroDrive's bond decreased to 5%, then we would once again recalculate its price:

Inputs: 15   5   100   1000

Output: −1518.98

---

6. The bond prices quoted by brokers are calculated as described. However, if you bought a bond between interest payment dates, you would have to pay the basic price plus accrued interest. Thus, if you purchased a MicroDrive bond 6 months after it was issued, your broker would send you an invoice stating that you must pay $1,000 as the basic price of the bond plus $50 interest, representing one-half the annual interest of $100. The seller of the bond would receive $1,050. If you bought the bond the day before its interest payment date, you would pay $1,000 + (364/365)($100) = $1,099.73. Of course, you would receive an interest payment of $100 at the end of the next day. For more on the valuation of bonds between payment dates, see Richard Taylor, "The Valuation of Semiannual Bonds between Interest Payment Dates," *The Financial Review,* August 1988, pp. 365–368, and K. S. Maurice Tse and Mark A. White, "The Valuation of Semiannual Bonds between Interest Payment Dates: A Correction," *Financial Review,* November 1990, pp. 659–662.

In this case, the price rises to $1,518.98. In general, whenever the going interest rate *falls below* the coupon rate, a fixed-rate bond's price will *rise above* its par value, and it is called a **premium bond**.

Self Test	Why do the prices of fixed-rate bonds fall if expectations for inflation rise?

Why do the prices of fixed-rate bonds fall if expectations for inflation rise?

What is a discount bond? A premium bond?

A bond that matures in 6 years has a par value of $1,000, an annual coupon payment of $80, and a market interest rate of 9%. What is its price? (**$955.14**)

A bond that matures in 18 years has a par value of $1,000, an annual coupon of 10%, and a market interest rate of 7%. What is its price? (**$1,301.77**)

4.4 Changes in Bond Values over Time

At the time a coupon bond is issued, the coupon is generally set at a level that will cause the market price of the bond to equal its par value. If a lower coupon were set then investors would not be willing to pay $1,000 for the bond, and if a higher coupon were set then investors would clamor for the bond and bid its price up over $1,000. Investment bankers can judge quite precisely the coupon rate that will cause a bond to sell at its $1,000 par value.

A bond that has just been issued is known as a **new issue**. (Investment bankers classify a bond as a new issue for about a month after it has first been issued. New issues are usually actively traded and are called "on-the-run" bonds.) Once the bond has been on the market for a while, it is classified as an **outstanding bond**, also called a **seasoned issue**. Newly issued bonds generally sell very close to par, but the prices of seasoned bonds vary widely from par. Except for floating-rate bonds, coupon payments are constant, so when economic conditions change, a 10% coupon bond with a $100 coupon that sold at par when it was issued will sell for more or less than $1,000 thereafter.

MicroDrive's bonds with a 10% coupon rate were originally issued at par. If r_d remained constant at 10%, what would the value of the bond be 1 year after it was issued? Now the term to maturity is only 14 years—that is, N = 14. With a financial calculator, just override N = 15 with N = 14, press the PV key, and you find a value of $1,000. If we continued, setting N = 13, N = 12, and so forth, we would see that the value of the bond will remain at $1,000 as long as the going interest rate remains constant at the coupon rate, 10%.

Now suppose interest rates in the economy fell after the MicroDrive bonds were issued and, as a result, r_d *fell below the coupon rate,* decreasing from 10% to 5%. Both the coupon interest payments and the maturity value remain constant, but now 5% would have to be used for r_d in Equation 4-1. The value of the bond at the end of the first year would be $1,494.93:

$$V_B = \sum_{t=1}^{14} \frac{\$100}{(1+0.05)^t} + \frac{\$1,000}{(1+0.05)^{14}}$$

$$= \$100 \left[\frac{1}{0.05} - \frac{1}{0.05(1+0.05)^{14}} \right] + \frac{\$1,000}{(1+0.05)^{14}}$$

$$= \$1,494.93$$

With a financial calculator, just change r_d = I/YR from 10 to 5, and then press the PV key to get the answer, $1,494.93. Thus, if r_d fell *below* the coupon rate, the bond would sell *above* par, or at a **premium**.

The arithmetic of the bond value increase should be clear, but what is the logic behind it? Because r_d has fallen to 5%, with $1,000 to invest you could buy new bonds like MicroDrive's (every day some 10 to 12 companies sell new bonds), except that these new bonds would pay $50 of interest each year rather than $100. Naturally, you would prefer $100 to $50, so you would be willing to pay more than $1,000 for a MicroDrive bond to obtain its higher coupons. All investors would react similarly; as a result, the MicroDrive bonds would be bid up in price to $1,494.93, at which point they would provide the same 5% rate of return to a potential investor as the new bonds.

Assuming that interest rates remain constant at 5% for the next 14 years, what would happen to the value of a MicroDrive bond? It would fall gradually from $1,494.93 at present to $1,000 at maturity, when MicroDrive will redeem each bond for $1,000. This point can be illustrated by calculating the value of the bond 1 year later, when it has 13 years remaining to maturity. With a financial calculator, simply input the values for N, I/YR, PMT, and FV, now using N = 13, and press the PV key to find the value of the bond, $1,469.68. Thus, the value of the bond will have fallen from $1,494.93 to $1,469.68, or by $25.25. If you were to calculate the value of the bond at other future dates, the price would continue to fall as the maturity date approached.

Note that if you purchased the bond at a price of $1,494.93 and then sold it 1 year later with r_d still at 5%, you would have a capital loss of $25.25, or a total return of $100.00 − $25.25 = $74.75. Your percentage rate of return would consist of the rate of return due to the interest payment (called the **current yield**) and the rate of return due to the price change (called the **capital gains yield**). This total rate of return is often called the bond yield, and it is calculated as follows:

Interest, or current, yield	=	$100/$1,494.93 =	0.0669 =	6.69%
Capital gains yield	=	−$25.25/$1,494.93 =	−0.0169 =	−1.69%
Total rate of return, or yield	=	$74.75/$1,494.93 =	0.0500 =	5.00%

Had interest rates risen from 10% to 15% during the first year after issue (rather than falling from 10% to 5%), then you would enter N = 14, I/YR = 15, PMT = 100, and FV = 1000, and then press the PV key to find the value of the bond, $713.78. In this case, the bond would sell below its par value, or at a discount. The total expected future return on the bond would again consist of an expected return due to interest and an expected return due to capital gains or capital losses. In this situation, the capital gains yield would be *positive*. The total return would be 15%. To see this, calculate the price of the bond with 13 years left to maturity, assuming that interest rates remain at 15%. With a calculator, enter N = 13, I/YR = 15, PMT = 100, and FV = 1000; then press PV to obtain the bond's value, $720.84.

Note that the capital gain for the year is the difference between the bond's value at Year 2 (with 13 years remaining) and the bond's value at Year 1 (with 14 years remaining), or $720.84 − $713.78 = $7.06. The interest yield, capital gains yield, and total yield are calculated as follows:

Interest, or current, yield	=	$100/$713.78 = 0.1401 =	14.01%
Capital gains yield	=	$7.06/$713.78 = 0.0099 =	0.99%
Total rate of return, or yield	=	$107.06/$713.78 = 0.1500 =	15.00%

Figure 4-2 graphs the value of the bond over time, assuming that interest rates in the economy (1) remain constant at 10%, (2) fall to 5% and then remain constant at that level, or (3) rise to 15% and remain constant at that level. Of course, if interest rates do *not* remain constant, then the price of the bond will fluctuate. However, regardless of what future interest rates do, the bond's price will approach $1,000 as it nears the maturity date (barring bankruptcy, in which case the bond's value might fall dramatically).

Figure 4-2 illustrates the following key points.

WEB

See **Ch04 Tool Kit.xls** for all calculations.

1. Whenever the going rate of interest, r_d, is equal to the coupon rate, a *fixed-rate* bond will sell at its par value. Normally, the coupon rate is set equal to the going rate when a bond is issued, causing it to sell at par initially.
2. Interest rates do change over time, but the coupon rate remains fixed after the bond has been issued. Whenever the going rate of interest *rises above* the coupon rate, a fixed-rate bond's price will *fall below* its par value. Such a bond is called a discount bond.
3. Whenever the going rate of interest *falls below* the coupon rate, a fixed-rate bond's price will *rise above* its par value. Such a bond is called a premium bond.
4. Thus, an *increase* in interest rates will cause the prices of outstanding bonds to *fall,* whereas a *decrease* in rates will cause bond prices to *rise.*
5. The market value of a bond will always approach its par value as its maturity date approaches, provided the firm does not go bankrupt.

These points are very important, for they show that bondholders may suffer capital losses or make capital gains depending on whether interest rates rise or fall after the bond is purchased.

Figure 4-2	**Time Path of the Value of a 10% Coupon, $1,000 Par Value Bond When Interest Rates Are 5%, 10%, and 15%**

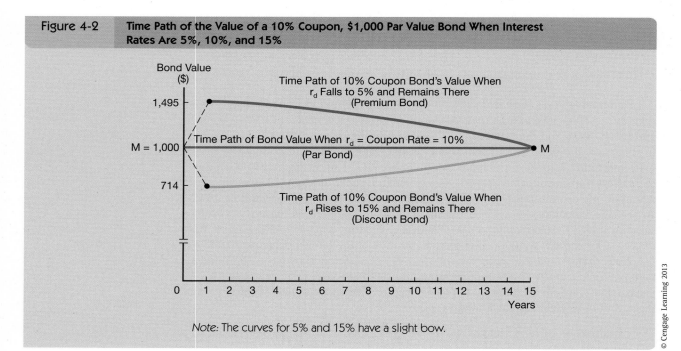

Note: The curves for 5% and 15% have a slight bow.

What is meant by the terms "new issue" and "seasoned issue"?

Last year, a firm issued 30-year, 8% annual coupon bonds at a par value of $1,000. (1) Suppose that 1 year later the going rate drops to 6%. What is the new price of the bonds, assuming that they now have 29 years to maturity? **($1,271.81)** (2) Suppose instead that 1 year after issue the going interest rate increases to 10% (rather than dropping to 6%). What is the price? **($812.61)**

4.5 Bonds with Semiannual Coupons

Although some bonds pay interest annually, the vast majority actually pay interest semiannually. To evaluate semiannual payment bonds, we must modify the valuation model as follows.

1. Divide the annual coupon interest payment by 2 to determine the dollars of interest paid every 6 months.
2. Multiply the years to maturity, N, by 2 to determine the number of semiannual periods.
3. Divide the nominal (quoted) interest rate, r_d, by 2 to determine the periodic (semiannual) interest rate.

By making these changes, we obtain the following equation for finding the value of a bond that pays interest semiannually:

$$V_B = \sum_{t=1}^{2N} \frac{INT/2}{(1 + r_d/2)^t} + \frac{M}{(1 + r_d/2)^{2N}}$$

(4–2)

To illustrate, assume now that MicroDrive's bonds pay $50 interest every 6 months rather than $100 at the end of each year. Each semiannual interest payment is only

DRINKING YOUR COUPONS

In 1996, Chateau Teyssier, an English vineyard, was looking for some cash to purchase additional vines and to modernize its production facilities. Their solution? With the assistance of a leading underwriter, Matrix Securities, the vineyard issued 375 bonds, each costing 2,650 British pounds. The issue raised nearly 1 million pounds, or roughly $1.5 million.

What makes these bonds interesting is that, instead of paying with something boring like money, they paid their investors back with wine. Each June until 2002, when the bond matured, investors received their "coupons." Between 1997 and 2001, each bond provided six cases of the vineyard's rosé or claret. Starting in 1998 and continuing through maturity in 2002, investors also received four cases of its prestigious Saint Emilion Grand Cru. Then, in 2002, they got their money back.

The bonds were not without risk. The vineyard's owner, Jonathan Malthus, acknowledged that the quality of the wine "is at the mercy of the gods."

Source: Steven Irvine, "My Wine Is My Bond, and I Drink My Coupons," *Euromoney,* July 1996, p. 7.

half as large, but there are twice as many of them. The nominal, or quoted, coupon rate is "10%, semiannual payments."[7]

When the going (nominal) rate of interest is 5% with semiannual compounding, the value of this 15-year bond is found as follows:

Inputs: 30   2.5   50   1000

N   I/YR   PV   PMT   FV

Output: −1523.26

Enter $N = 30$, $r_d = I/YR = 2.5$, $PMT = 50$, $FV = 1000$, and then press the PV key to obtain the bond's value, $1,523.26. The value with semiannual interest payments is slightly larger than $1,518.98, the value when interest is paid annually. This higher value occurs because interest payments are received somewhat faster under semiannual compounding.

Self Test

Describe how the annual bond valuation formula is changed to evaluate semiannual coupon bonds. Write out the revised formula.

A bond has a 25-year maturity, an 8% annual coupon paid semiannually, and a face value of $1,000. The going nominal *annual* interest rate (r_d) is 6%. What is the bond's price? **($1,257.30)**

4.6 Bond Yields

Unlike the coupon interest rate, which is fixed, the bond's *yield* varies from day to day depending on current market conditions. Moreover, the yield can be calculated in three different ways, and three "answers" can be obtained. These different yields are described in the following sections.

4.6a Yield to Maturity

Suppose you were offered a 14-year, 10% annual coupon, $1,000 par value bond at a price of $1,494.93. What rate of interest would you earn on your investment if you bought the bond and held it to maturity? This rate is called the bond's **yield to maturity (YTM)**, and it is the interest rate generally discussed by investors when they talk about rates of return. The yield to maturity is usually the same as the market rate of interest, r_d. To find the YTM for a bond with annual interest payments, you must solve Equation 4-1 for r_d:[8]

---

7. In this situation, the coupon rate of "10% paid semiannually" is the rate that bond dealers, corporate treasurers, and investors generally would discuss. Of course, if this bond were issued at par, then its *effective annual rate* would be higher than 10%:

$$\text{EAR} = \text{EFF\%} = \left(1 + \frac{r_{NOM}}{M}\right)^M - 1 = \left(1 + \frac{0.10}{2}\right)^2 - 1 = (1.05)^2 - 1 = 10.25\%$$

Because 10% with annual payments is quite different from 10% with semiannual payments, we have assumed a change in effective rates in this section from the situation described in Section 4.3, where we assumed 10% with annual payments.

8. If the bond has semiannual payments, you must solve Equation 4-2 for r_d.

$$\text{Bond price} = \sum_{t=1}^{N} \frac{\text{INT}}{(1+\text{YTM})^t} + \frac{M}{(1+\text{YTM})^N} \qquad (4\text{–}3)$$

For MicroDrive's yield, you must solve this equation:

$$\$1,494.93 = \frac{\$100}{(1+r_d)^1} + \cdots + \frac{\$100}{(1+r_d)^{14}} + \frac{\$1,000}{(1+r_d)^{14}}$$

You could substitute values for r_d until you found a value that "works" and forces the sum of the PVs on the right side of the equal sign to equal $1,494.93, but this would be tedious and time-consuming.[9] As you might guess, it is much easier with a financial calculator. Here is the setup:

Inputs: 14   −1494.93   100   1000

Output: 5

Simply enter N = 14, PV = −1494.93, PMT = 100, and FV = 1000, and then press the I/YR key for the answer of 5%.

You could also find the YTM with a spreadsheet. In *Excel,* you would use the RATE function for this bond, inputting N = 14, PMT = 100, PV = −1494.93, FV = 1000, 0 for Type, and leave Guess blank: **=RATE(14,100,−1494.93,1000,0)**. The result is 5%. The RATE function works only if the current date is immediately after either the issue date or a coupon payment date. To find bond yields on other dates, use *Excel*'s YIELD function. See the *Ch04 Tool Kit.xls* file for an example.

The yield to maturity can be viewed as the bond's *promised rate of return,* which is the return that investors will receive if all the promised payments are made. However, the yield to maturity equals the *expected rate of return* only if (1) the probability of default is zero and (2) the bond cannot be called. If there is some default risk or if the bond may be called, then there is some probability that the promised payments to maturity will not be received, in which case the calculated yield to maturity will differ from the expected return.

The YTM for a bond that sells at par consists entirely of an interest yield, but if the bond sells at a price other than its par value, then the YTM will consist of the interest yield plus a positive or negative capital gains yield. Note also that a bond's yield to maturity changes whenever interest rates in the economy change, and this is almost daily. If you purchase a bond and hold it until it matures, you will receive the YTM that existed on the purchase date, but the bond's calculated YTM will change frequently between the purchase date and the maturity date.[10]

---

9. Alternatively, you can substitute values of r_d into the third form of Equation 4-1 until you find a value that works.

10. We often are asked by students if the purchaser of a bond will receive the YTM if interest rates subsequently change. The answer is definitely "yes" provided the question means "Is the realized rate of return on the investment in the bond equal to the YTM?" This is because the realized rate of return on an investment is the rate that sets the present value of the realized cash flows equal to the price. If instead the question means "Is the realized rate of return on the investment in the bond and the subsequent reinvestment of the coupons equal to the YTM?", then the answer is definitely "no." Thus, the question really is one about strategy and timing. The bond, in combination with a reinvestment strategy, is really two investments, and clearly the realized rate on this combined strategy depends on the reinvestment rate (see *Web Extension 4C* for more on investing for a target future value). For the

4.6b Yield to Call

If you purchased a bond that was callable and the company called it, you would not have the option of holding the bond until it matured. Therefore, the yield to maturity would not be earned. For example, if MicroDrive's 10% coupon bonds were callable and if interest rates fell from 10% to 5%, then the company could call in the 10% bonds, replace them with 5% bonds, and save $100 − $50 = $50 interest per bond per year. This would be good for the company but not for the bondholders.

If current interest rates are well below an outstanding bond's coupon rate, then a callable bond is likely to be called, and investors will estimate its expected rate of return as the **yield to call (YTC)** rather than as the yield to maturity. To calculate the YTC, solve this equation for r_d:

(4–4)
$$\text{Price of callable bond} = \sum_{t=1}^{N} \frac{\text{INT}}{(1 + r_d)^t} + \frac{\text{Call price}}{(1 + r_d)^N}$$

Here N is the number of years until the company can call the bond, r_d is the YTC, and "Call price" is the price the company must pay in order to call the bond (it is often set equal to the par value plus 1 year's interest).

To illustrate, suppose MicroDrive's bonds had a provision that permitted the company, if it desired, to call the bonds 10 years after the issue date at a price of $1,100. Suppose further that 1 year after issuance the going interest rate had declined, causing the price of the bonds to rise to $1,494.93. Here is the time line and the setup for finding the bond's YTC with a financial calculator:

The YTC is 4.21%—this is the return you would earn if you bought the bond at a price of $1,494.93 and it was called 9 years from today. (The bond could not be called until 10 years after issuance, and 1 year has gone by, so there are 9 years left until the first call date.)

Do you think MicroDrive *will* call the bonds when they become callable? MicroDrive's actions depend on the going interest rate when the bonds become callable. If the going rate remains at r_d = 5%, then MicroDrive could save 10% − 5% = 5%, or $50 per bond per year, by calling them and replacing the 10% bonds

---

rest of the book, we assume that an investment in a bond is just that, an investment only in the bond, and not a combination of the bond and a reinvestment strategy; this means the investor earns the expected YTM if the bond is held to maturity.

with a new 5% issue. There would be costs to the company to refund the issue, but the interest savings would probably be worth the cost, so MicroDrive would probably refund the bonds. Therefore, you would probably earn YTC = 4.21% rather than YTM = 5% if you bought the bonds under the indicated conditions.

In the balance of this chapter, we assume that bonds are not callable unless otherwise noted. However, some of the end-of-chapter problems deal with yield to call.

4.6c Current Yield

If you examine brokerage house reports on bonds, you will often see reference to a bond's **current yield**. The current yield is the annual interest payment divided by the bond's current price. For example, if MicroDrive's bonds with a 10% coupon were currently selling at $985, then the bond's current yield would be $100/$985 = 0.1015 = 10.15%.

Unlike the yield to maturity, the current yield does not represent the rate of return that investors should expect on the bond. The current yield provides information regarding the amount of cash income that a bond will generate in a given year, but it does not provide an accurate measure of the bond's total expected return, the yield to maturity. In fact, here is the relation between current yield, capital gains yield (which can be negative for a capital loss), and the yield to maturity:

$$\text{Current yield} + \text{Capital gains yield} = \text{Yield to maturity} \qquad (4\text{--}5)$$

4.6d The Cost of Debt and Intrinsic Value

The "Intrinsic Value" Box at the beginning of this chapter highlights the cost of debt, which affects the weighted average cost of capital (WACC), which in turn affects the company's intrinsic value. The pre-tax cost of debt from the company's perspective is the required return from the debtholder's perspective. Therefore, the pre-tax cost of debt is the yield to maturity (or the yield to call if a call is likely). But why do different bonds have different yields to maturity? The following sections answer this question.

Self Test

Explain the difference between the yield to maturity and the yield to call.

How does a bond's current yield differ from its total return?

Could the current yield exceed the total return?

A bond currently sells for $850. It has an 8-year maturity, an annual coupon of $80, and a par value of $1,000. What is its yield to maturity? **(10.90%)** What is its current yield? **(9.41%)**

A bond currently sells for $1,250. It pays a $110 annual coupon and has a 20-year maturity, but it can be called in 5 years at $1,110. What are its YTM and its YTC? **(8.38%, 6.85%)** Is the bond likely to be called if interest rates don't change?

4.7 The Pre-Tax Cost of Debt: Determinants of Market Interest Rates

Up until now we have given you r_d, the going market rate. But as we showed in Chapter 1, different debt securities often have very different market rates. What explains these differences? In general, the quoted (or nominal) interest rate on a debt security, r_d, is composed of a real risk-free rate of interest, r^*, plus several premiums that reflect inflation, the risk of the security, and the security's marketability (or liquidity). A conceptual framework is shown below:

$$\text{Quoted market interest rate} = r_d = r^* + IP + DRP + LP + MRP$$
$$= r_{RF} + DRP + LP + MRP$$

(4–6)

Here are definitions of the variables in Equation 4-6:

r_d = Quoted, or nominal, rate of interest on a given security.[11] There are many different securities and hence many different quoted interest rates.

r^* = Real risk-free rate of interest. Pronounced "r-star," r^* is the rate that would exist on a riskless security if zero inflation were expected.

IP = Inflation premium, which is equal to the average expected inflation rate over the life of the security. The expected future inflation rate is not necessarily equal to the current inflation rate, so IP is not necessarily equal to current inflation.

r_{RF} = $r^* + IP$, and it is the quoted risk-free rate of interest on a security such as a U.S. Treasury bill, which is very liquid and also free of most risks. Note that r_{RF} includes the premium for expected inflation because $r_{RF} = r^* + IP$.

DRP = Default risk premium. This premium reflects the possibility that the issuer will not pay interest or principal at the stated time and in the stated amount. The DRP is zero for U.S. Treasury securities, but it rises as the riskiness of issuers increases.

LP = Liquidity, or marketability, premium. This is a premium charged by lenders to reflect the fact that some securities cannot be converted to cash on short notice at a "reasonable" price. The LP is very low for Treasury securities and for securities issued by large, strong firms, but it is relatively high on securities issued by very small firms.

---

11. The term *nominal* as it is used here means the *stated* rate as opposed to the *real* rate, which is adjusted to remove inflation effects. Suppose you bought a 10-year Treasury bond with a quoted, or nominal, rate of about 4.6%. If inflation averages 2.5% over the next 10 years, then the real rate would be about 4.6% − 2.5% = 2.1%. To be technically correct, we should find the real rate by solving for r^* in the following equation: $(1 + r^*)(1 + 0.025) = (1 + 0.046)$. Solving the equation, we find $r^* = 2.05\%$. Since this is very close to the 2.1% just calculated, we will continue to approximate the real rate in this chapter by subtracting inflation from the nominal rate.

> MRP = Maturity risk premium. As we will explain later, longer-term bonds (even Treasury bonds) are exposed to a significant risk of price declines, and a maturity risk premium is charged by lenders to reflect this risk.

We discuss the components whose sum makes up the quoted, or nominal, rate on a given security in the following sections.

Self Test

Write out an equation for the nominal interest rate on any debt security.

4.8 The Real Risk-Free Rate of Interest, r*

The **real risk-free rate of interest, r***, is defined as the interest rate that would exist on a riskless security if no inflation were expected, and it may be thought of as the rate of interest on *short-term* U.S. Treasury securities in an inflation-free world. The real risk-free rate is not static—it changes over time depending on economic conditions, especially (1) the rate of return corporations and other borrowers expect to earn on productive assets and (2) people's time preferences for current versus future consumption.[12]

In addition to its regular bond offerings, in 1997, the U.S. Treasury began issuing **indexed bonds**, with payments linked to inflation. These bonds are called **TIPS**, short for **Treasury Inflation-Protected Securities**. Because the payments (including the principal) are tied to inflation, the yield on TIPS is a good estimate of the real risk-free rate. In early 2011, the TIPS with about 1 year remaining until maturity had a −1.15% yield.[13] This is a pretty good estimate of the real risk-free rate, r*, although ideally we would prefer a TIPS with an even shorter time until maturity. We will have more to say about how to use TIPS when we discuss the inflation premium in the next section. For details on how TIPS are adjusted to protect against inflation, see *Web Extension 4B* on the textbook's Web site.

WWW

See **www.bloomberg .com** and select MARKET DATA. Then select RATES AND BONDS for a partial listing of indexed Treasury bonds and their interest rates. See **online.wsj .com** for a complete set of Treasury quotes. See **www.treasurydirect .gov/indiv/products/ products.htm** for a complete listing of all Treasury securities.

Self Test

What security provides a good estimate of the real risk-free rate?

---

12. The real rate of interest as discussed here is different from the *current* real rate as often discussed in the press. The current real rate is often estimated as the current interest rate minus the current (or most recent) inflation rate, whereas the real rate, as used here (and in the fields of finance and economics generally) without the word "current," is the current interest rate minus the *expected future* inflation rate over the life of the security. For example, suppose the current quoted rate for a 1-year Treasury bill is 5%, inflation during the previous year was 2%, and inflation expected for the coming year is 4%. Then the *current* real rate would be approximately 5% − 2% = 3%, but the *expected* real rate would be approximately 5% − 4% = 1%.

13. Negative *nominal* rates are pretty much impossible—investors would just hold cash instead of investing in a negative-rate bond. But negative real rates are possible. In spring 2008, the combination of stagnant economic growth, a high level of investor uncertainty, fears of inflation, and the Federal Reserve's reduction in nominal short-term interest rates caused the real rate to fall below zero, as measured by negative yields on several short-term TIPS. The situation was repeated in January 2011 as well.

4.9 The Inflation Premium (IP)

Inflation has a major effect on interest rates because it erodes the purchasing power of the dollar and lowers the real rate of return on investments. To illustrate, suppose you invest $3,000 in a default-free zero coupon bond that matures in 1 year and pays a 5% interest rate. At the end of the year, you will receive $3,150—your original $3,000 plus $150 of interest. Now suppose that the inflation rate during the year is 10% and that it affects all items equally. If gas had cost $3 per gallon at the beginning of the year, it would cost $3.30 at the end of the year. Therefore, your $3,000 would have bought $3,000/$3 = 1,000 gallons at the beginning of the year but only $3,150/$3.30 = 955 gallons at the end. In *real terms,* you would be worse off—you would receive $150 of interest, but it would not be sufficient to offset inflation. You would thus be better off buying 1,000 gallons of gas (or some other storable asset) than buying the default-free bond.

Investors are well aware of inflation's effects on interest rates, so when they lend money, they build in an **inflation premium (IP)** equal to the average expected inflation rate over the life of the security. For a short-term, default-free U.S. Treasury bill, the actual interest rate charged, $r_{\text{T-bill}}$, would be the real risk-free rate, r^*, plus the inflation premium (IP):

$$r_{\text{T-bill}} = r_{\text{RF}} = r^* + IP$$

Therefore, if the real short-term risk-free rate of interest were $r^* = 0.6\%$ and if inflation were expected to be 1.0% (and hence IP = 1.0%) during the next year, then the quoted rate of interest on 1-year T-bills would be 0.6% + 1.0% = 1.6%.

It is important to note that the inflation rate built into interest rates is *the inflation rate expected in the future,* not the rate experienced in the past. Thus, the latest reported figures might show an annual inflation rate of 2%, but that is for the *past* year. If people on average expect a 6% inflation rate in the future, then 6% would be built into the current interest rate.

Note also that the inflation rate reflected in the quoted interest rate on any security is the *average rate of inflation expected over the security's life.* Thus, the inflation rate built into a 1-year bond is the expected inflation rate for the next year, but the inflation rate built into a 30-year bond is the average rate of inflation expected over the next 30 years. If I_t is the expected inflation during year t, then the inflation premium for an N-year bond's yield (IP_N) can be approximated as

(4–7)
$$IP_N = \frac{I_1 + I_2 + \cdots + I_N}{N}$$

For example, if investors expect inflation to average 3% during Year 1 and 5% during Year 2, then the inflation premium built into a 2-year bond's yield can be approximated by[14]

$$IP_2 = \frac{I_1 + I_2}{2} + \frac{3\% + 5\%}{2} = 4\%$$

In the previous section, we saw that the yield on an inflation-indexed Treasury bond (TIPS) is a good estimate of the real interest rate. We can also use TIPS

---

14. To be theoretically correct, we should take the *geometric average*: $(1 + IP_2)^2 = (1 + I_1)(1 + I_2)$. In this example, we have $(1 + IP_2)^2 = (1 + 0.03)(1 + 0.05)$. Solving for IP_2 yields 3.9952, which is close to our approximation of 4%.

to estimate inflation premiums. For example, in early 2011 the yield on a 5-year nonindexed T-bond was 2.22% and the yield on a 5-year TIPS was 0.10%. Thus, the 5-year inflation premium was 2.22% − 0.10% = 2.12%, implying that investors expected inflation to average 2.12% over the next 5 years.[15] Similarly, the rate on a 20-year nonindexed T-bond was 4.35% and the rate on a 20-year indexed T-bond was 1.92%. Thus, the 20-year inflation premium was approximately 4.35% − 1.92% = 2.43%, implying that investors expected inflation to average 2.43% over the long term.[16] These calculations are summarized below:

	Maturity	
	5 Years	**20 Years**
Yield on nonindexed U.S. Treasury bond	2.22%	4.35%
Yield on TIPS	0.10	1.92
Inflation premium	2.12%	2.43%

Expectations for future inflation are closely, but not perfectly, correlated with rates experienced in the recent past. Therefore, if the inflation rate reported for last month increases, people often raise their expectations for future inflation, and this change in expectations will cause an increase in interest rates.

Note that Germany, Japan, and Switzerland have, over the past several years, had lower inflation rates than the United States, so their interest rates have generally been lower than ours. South Africa, Brazil, and most South American countries have experienced higher inflation, which is reflected in their interest rates.

Self Test

Explain how a TIPS and a nonindexed Treasury security can be used to estimate the inflation premium.

The yield on a 15-year TIPS is 3% and the yield on a 15-year Treasury bond is 5%. What is the inflation premium for a 15-year security? **(2%)**

4.10 The Nominal, or Quoted, Risk-Free Rate of Interest, r_{RF}

The **nominal**, or **quoted, risk-free rate**, r_{RF}, is the real risk-free rate plus a premium for expected inflation: $r_{RF} = r^* + IP$. To be strictly correct, the risk-free rate should mean the interest rate on a totally risk-free security—one that has no risk of default,

---

15. To be theoretically precise, we should use a *geometric average* by solving the following equation: (1 + IP)(1.001) = 1.0222. Solving for IP gives IP = 2.12%, which is the same as our approximation.

    Note, though, that the difference in yield between a T-bond and a TIPS of the same maturity reflects both the expected inflation *and* any risk premium for bearing inflation risk. So the difference in yields is really an upper limit on the expected inflation.

16. There are several other sources for the estimated inflation premium. The Congressional Budget Office regularly updates the estimates of inflation that it uses in its forecasted budgets; see **www.cbo.gov**; select Economic Projections. A second source is the University of Michigan's Institute for Social Research, which regularly polls consumers regarding their expectations for price increases during the next year; see **www.sca.isr.umich.edu** for the survey.

    We prefer using inflation premiums derived from indexed and nonindexed Treasury securities, as described in the text, since these are based on how investors actually spend their money, not on theoretical models or opinions.

no maturity risk, no liquidity risk, no risk of loss if inflation increases, and no risk of any other type. There is no such security, so there is no observable truly risk-free rate. When the term "risk-free rate" is used without either the modifier "real" or the modifier "nominal," people generally mean the quoted (nominal) rate, and we will follow that convention in this book. Therefore, when we use the term "risk-free rate, r_{RF}," we mean the nominal risk-free rate, which includes an inflation premium equal to the average expected inflation rate over the life of the security. In general, we use the T-bill rate to approximate the short-term risk-free rate and use the T-bond rate to approximate the long-term risk-free rate (even though it also includes a maturity premium). So, whenever you see the term "risk-free rate," assume that we are referring either to the quoted U.S. T-bill rate or to the quoted T-bond rate.

Since $r_{RF} = r^* + IP$, we can express the quoted rate as

(4-8)
$$\text{Nominal, or quoted, rate} = r_d = r_{RF} + DRP + LP + MRP$$

Self Test

What security is a good approximation of the nominal risk-free rate?

4.11 The Default Risk Premium (DRP)

If the issuer defaults on a payment, investors receive less than the promised return on the bond. The quoted interest rate includes a default risk premium (DRP)—the greater the default risk, the higher the bond's yield to maturity.[17] The default risk on Treasury securities is virtually zero, but default risk can be substantial for corporate and municipal bonds. In this section, we consider some issues related to default risk.

4.11a Bond Contract Provisions That Influence Default Risk

Default risk is affected by both the financial strength of the issuer and the terms of the bond contract, especially whether collateral has been pledged to secure the bond. Several types of contract provisions are discussed next.

Bond Indentures

An **indenture** is a legal document that spells out the rights of both bondholders and the issuing corporation. A **trustee** is an official (usually a bank) who represents the bondholders and makes sure the terms of the indenture are carried out. The indenture may be several hundred pages in length, and it will include **restrictive covenants** that cover such points as the conditions under which the issuer can pay off the bonds prior to maturity, the levels at which certain ratios must be maintained if the company is to issue additional debt, and restrictions against the payment of dividends unless earnings meet certain specifications.

---

17. Suppose two bonds have the same promised cash flows, coupon rate, maturity, liquidity, and inflation exposure, but one bond has more default risk than the other. Investors will naturally pay less for the bond with the greater chance of default. As a result, bonds with higher default risk will have higher interest rates.

The Securities and Exchange Commission (1) approves indentures and (2) makes sure that all indenture provisions are met before allowing a company to sell new securities to the public. A firm will have different indentures for each of the major types of bonds it issues, but a single indenture covers all bonds of the same type. For example, one indenture will cover a firm's first mortgage bonds, another its debentures, and a third its convertible bonds.

Mortgage Bonds

A corporation pledges certain assets as security for a **mortgage bond**. The company might also choose to issue *second-mortgage bonds* secured by the same assets that were secured by a previously issued mortgage bond. In the event of liquidation, the holders of these second mortgage bonds would have a claim against the property, but only after the first mortgage bondholders had been paid off in full. Thus, second mortgages are sometimes called *junior mortgages,* because they are junior in priority to the claims of *senior mortgages,* or *first-mortgage bonds.* All mortgage bonds are subject to an indenture that usually limits the amount of new bonds that can be issued.

Debentures and Subordinated Debentures

A **debenture** is an unsecured bond, and as such it provides no lien against specific property as security for the obligation. Debenture holders are, therefore, general creditors whose claims are protected by property not otherwise pledged.

The term *subordinate* means "below," or "inferior to"; thus, in the event of bankruptcy, subordinated debt has claims on assets only after senior debt has been paid off. **Subordinated debentures** may be subordinated either to designated notes payable (usually bank loans) or to all other debt. In the event of liquidation or reorganization, holders of subordinated debentures cannot be paid until all senior debt, as named in the debentures' indentures, has been paid.

Development Bonds

Some companies may be in a position to benefit from the sale of either **development bonds** or **pollution control bonds.** State and local governments may set up both *industrial development agencies* and *pollution control agencies.* These agencies are allowed, under certain circumstances, to sell **tax-exempt bonds** and then make the proceeds available to corporations for specific uses deemed (by Congress) to be in the public interest. For example, a Detroit pollution control agency might sell bonds to provide Ford with funds for purchasing pollution control equipment. Because the income from the bonds would be tax exempt, the bonds would have relatively low interest rates. Note, however, that these bonds are guaranteed by the corporation that will use the funds, not by a governmental unit, so their rating reflects the credit strength of the corporation using the funds.

Municipal Bond Insurance

Municipalities can have their bonds insured, which means that an insurance company guarantees to pay the coupon and principal payments should the issuer default. This reduces risk to investors, who will thus accept a lower coupon rate for an insured bond than for a comparable but uninsured one. Even though the municipality must pay a fee to have its bonds insured, its savings due to the lower coupon rate often make insurance cost-effective. Keep in mind that the insurers are private companies, and the value added by the insurance depends on the creditworthiness of the insurer. The larger insurers are strong companies, and their own ratings are AAA.

THE GLOBAL ECONOMIC CRISIS

Insuring with Credit Default Swaps:
Let the Buyer Beware!

A credit default swap (CDS) is like an insurance policy. The purchaser of the CDS agrees to make annual payments to a counterparty that agrees to pay if a particular bond defaults. During the 2000s, investment banks often would purchase CDS for the mortgage-backed securities (MBS) they were creating in order to make the securities more attractive to investors. But how good was this type of insurance? As it turned out, not very. For example, Lehman Brothers might have bought a CDS from AIG in order to sell a Lehman-created MBS to an investor. But when the MBS began defaulting, neither Lehman nor AIG was capable of making full restitution to the investor.

4.11b Bond Ratings

Since the early 1900s, bonds have been assigned quality ratings that reflect their probability of going into default. The three major rating agencies are Moody's Investors Service (Moody's), Standard & Poor's Corporation (S&P), and Fitch Ratings. As shown in Columns (3) and (4) of Table 4-1, triple-A and double-A bonds are extremely safe, rarely defaulting even within 5 years of being assigned a rating.

TABLE 4-1   Bond Ratings, Default Risk, and Yields

Rating Agency[a]		Percent Defaulting Within:[b]		Median Ratios[c]		Percent Upgraded or Downgraded in 2009[b]		
S&P and Fitch (1)	Moody's (2)	1 year (3)	5 years (4)	Return on capital (5)	Total debt/ Total capital (6)	Down (7)	Up (8)	Yield[d] (9)
Investment-grade bonds								
AAA	Aaa	0.0%	0.0%	27.6%	12.4%	27.8%	NA	3.92%
AA	Aa	0.0	0.1	27.0	28.3	25.8	0.0	4.45
A	A	0.1	0.7	17.5	37.5	18.4	0.9	4.48
BBB	Baa	0.3	2.8	13.4	42.5	9.5	1.2	5.13
Junk bonds								
BB	Ba	1.5	7.5	11.3	53.7	15.2	6.4	5.87
B	B	2.7	9.3	8.7	75.9	14.6	5.4	7.38
CCC	Caa	26.4	35.3	3.2	113.5	59.3	1.9	10.09

© Cengage Learning 2013

[a]The ratings agencies also use "modifiers" for bonds rated below triple-A. S&P and Fitch use a plus and minus system; thus, A+ designates the strongest A-rated bonds and A− the weakest. Moody's uses a 1, 2, or 3 designation, with 1 denoting the strongest and 3 the weakest; thus, within the double-A category, Aa1 is the best, Aa2 is average, and Aa3 is the weakest.
[b]Default data are from Fitch Ratings Global Corporate Finance 2009 Transition and Default Study, March 18, 2010: see **www.fitchratings.com/creditdesk/reports/report_frame.cfm?rpt_id=505006**.
[c]Median ratios are from Standard & Poor's 2006 Corporate Ratings Criteria, April 23, 2007: see **www2.standardandpoors.com/ spf/pdf/fixedincome/Corporate_Ratings_2006.pdf**.
[d]Composite yields for 10-year AAA, AA, and A bonds can be found at **finance.yahoo.com/bonds/composite_bond_rates**. Representative yields for 10-year BBB, BB, B, and CCC bonds can be found using the bond screener at **screen.yahoo.com/ bonds.html**.

Single-A and triple-B bonds are also strong enough to be called **investment-grade bonds**, and they are the lowest-rated bonds that many banks and other institutional investors are permitted by law to hold. Double-B and lower bonds are speculative, or **junk bonds**. These bonds have a significant probability of defaulting.

4.11c Bond Rating Criteria, Upgrades, and Downgrades

Bond ratings are based on both quantitative and qualitative factors, as we describe below.

1. **Financial Ratios.** Many ratios potentially are important, but the return on invested capital, debt ratio, and interest coverage ratio are particularly valuable for predicting financial distress. For example, Columns (1), (5), and (6) in Table 4-1 show a strong relationship between ratings and the return on capital and the debt ratio.
2. **Bond Contract Terms.** Important provisions for determining the bond's rating include whether the bond is secured by a mortgage on specific assets, whether the bond is subordinated to other debt, any sinking fund provisions, guarantees by some other party with a high credit ranking, and *restrictive covenants* such as requirements that the firm keep its debt ratio below a given level or that it keep its times interest earned ratio above a given level.
3. **Qualitative Factors.** Included here would be such factors as sensitivity of the firm's earnings to the strength of the economy, how it is affected by inflation, whether it is having or is likely to have labor problems, the extent of its international operations (including the stability of the countries in which it operates), potential environmental problems, potential antitrust problems, and so on. Today (2011), a critical factor is exposure to sub-prime loans, including the difficulty of determining the extent of this exposure owing to the complexity of the assets backed by such loans.

Rating agencies review outstanding bonds on a periodic basis and re-rate if necessary. Columns (7) and (8) in Table 4-1 show the percentages of companies in each rating category that were downgraded or upgraded in 2009 by Fitch Ratings. The year 2009 was a difficult one, as more bonds were downgraded than upgraded.

Over the long run, ratings agencies have done a reasonably good job of measuring the average credit risk of bonds and of changing ratings whenever there is a significant change in credit quality. However, it is important to understand that ratings do not adjust immediately to changes in credit quality, and in some cases there can be a considerable lag between a change in credit quality and a change in rating. For example, Enron's bonds still carried an investment-grade rating on a Friday in December 2001, but the company declared bankruptcy 2 days later, on Sunday. Many other abrupt downgrades occurred in 2007 and 2008, leading to calls by Congress and the SEC for changes in rating agencies and the way they rate bonds. Clearly, improvements can be made, but there will always be occasions when completely unexpected information about a company is released, leading to a sudden change in its rating.

4.11d Bond Ratings and the Default Risk Premium

Why are bond ratings so important? First, most bonds are purchased by institutional investors rather than individuals, and many institutions are restricted to investment-grade securities. Thus, if a firm's bonds fall below BBB, it will have a difficult time selling new bonds because many potential purchasers will not be allowed to buy them. Second, many bond covenants stipulate that the coupon rate on the bond automatically increases if the rating falls below a specified level. Third,

THE GLOBAL ECONOMIC CRISIS

U.S. Treasury Bonds Downgraded!

The worsening recession that began at the end of 2007 led Congress to pass a huge economic stimulus package in early 2009. The combination of the stimulus package and the government's bailouts of financial institutions has caused the U.S. government to increase its borrowing substantially. The Congressional Budget Office reports that by of the end of 2010, federal debt held by the public exceeded $9 trillion and is projected to exceed $16 trillion by 2020, or almost 70% of U.S. GDP. This is a lot of money, even by Washington standards!

With so much debt outstanding and enormous annual deficits continuing, in mid-2011 Congress was faced with the need to increase the amount of debt the federal government is allowed to issue. Although Congress had increased the debt ceiling 74 times previously, and 10 times since 2001, partisan and heated debate seriously delayed approval of the measure and brought the federal government to the brink of default on its obligations by August. At the last minute, Congress approved a debt ceiling increase,

narrowly avoiding a partial government shutdown. However, the deficit reduction package that accompanied the legislation was small, doing little to address the structural revenue and spending imbalance the federal government faces going forward.

On August 5, 2011, the combination of a dysfunctional political process apparently incapable of reliably performing basic financial housekeeping chores, and the lack of a clear plan to address future deficits, raised enough questions about the U.S. government's financial stability to induce Standard & Poors (S&P), the credit rating agency, to downgrade U.S. public debt from AAA to AA1, effectively removing it from its list of risk-free investments. Financial markets quickly responded to this dark assessment with the Dow Jones Industrial Average plunging some 13% over the next week. Moody's and Fitch, the other two major rating agencies, however, kept their ratings of U.S. public debt at their highest levels. With 2 out of 3 agencies rating U.S. debt at the highest level, is the yield on U.S. debt still a proxy for the riskless rate? What do you think?

because a bond's rating is an indicator of its default risk, the rating has a direct, measurable influence on the bond's yield. Column (9) of Table 4-1 shows that an AAA bond has a yield of 3.92% and that yields increase as the rating falls. In fact, an investor would earn 10.09% on a CCC bond if it didn't default.

A **bond spread** is the difference between a bond's yield and the yield on some other security of the same maturity. Unless specified differently, the term "spread" generally means the difference between a bond's yield and the yield on a Treasury bond of similar maturity.

Figure 4-3 shows the spreads between an index of AAA bonds and a 10-year Treasury bond; it also shows spreads for an index of BBB bonds relative to the T-bond. Figure 4-3 illustrates three important points. First, the BAA spread always is greater than the AAA spread. This is because a BAA bond is riskier than a AAA bond, so BAA investors require extra compensation for their extra risk. The same is true for other ratings: Lower-rated bonds have higher yields.

Second, the spreads are not constant over time. For example, look at the AAA spread. It was exceptionally low during the boom years of 2005–2007 but rose dramatically as the economy subsequently declined.

Third, the difference between the BAA spread and the AAA spread isn't constant over time. The two spreads were quite close to one another in early 2000 but were very far apart in early 2009. In other words, BAA investors didn't require much extra return over that of an AAA bond to induce them to take on that extra

Figure 4-3	**Bond Spreads**

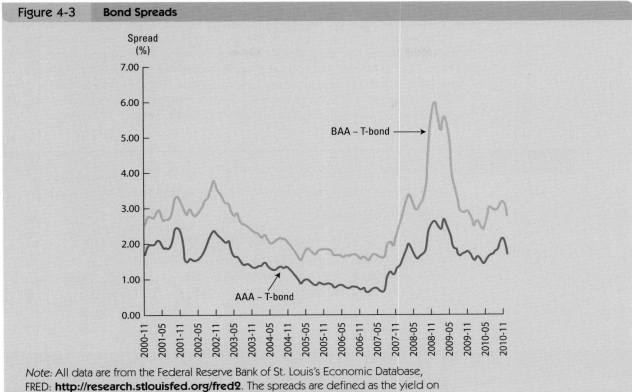

Note: All data are from the Federal Reserve Bank of St. Louis's Economic Database, FRED: **http://research.stlouisfed.org/fred2**. The spreads are defined as the yield on the risky bond (AAA or BAA) minus the yield on a 10-year Treasury bond.

THE FEW, THE PROUD, THE...
AAA-RATED COMPANIES!

AAA-rated companies are members of an elite group. Over the last 20 years, this cream of the crop has included such powerhouses as 3M, Abbott Labs, BellSouth, ExxonMobil, GE, Kellogg, Microsoft, and UPS. Only large companies with stable cash flows make it into this group, and for years they guarded their AAA ratings vigilantly. In recent years, however, the nonfinancial AAA-rated corporation has become a vanishing breed. In February 2011, the major ratings agencies (Fitch, S&P, and Moody's) only agreed on the highest rating for two nonfinancial companies without government backing: ExxonMobil and Johnson & Johnson. Restricting the selection criterion to being highest-rated by only two of the ratings agencies adds only Microsoft and XTO Energy (a subsidiary of ExxonMobil). When the list is expanded to more than just nonfinancials, it is interesting to note that many of the powerhouses are not-for-profits. For example, Saddleback Valley Commu-nity Church, a megachurch located in Southern California, has a top rating, as do MIT and Princeton University.

Why do so few companies have AAA ratings? One reason may be that the recent financial crisis and recession have hurt the creditworthiness of even large, stable companies. A more likely explanation, however, is that in recent years large, stable companies have increased their debt levels to take greater advantage of the tax savings that they afford. With higher debt levels, these companies are no longer eligible for the highest rating. In essence, they have sacrificed their AAA rating for lower taxes. Does this sound like a good tradeoff to you? We will discuss how companies choose the level of debt in Chapter 15.

Source: **www.finra.org/Investors/InvestmentChoices/Bonds**.

risk now (2011) or for most of the previous decade, but in 2009 they required a very large risk premium.

Not only do spreads vary with the rating of the security, they also usually increase as maturity increases. This should make sense. If a bond matures soon, investors are able to forecast the company's performance fairly well. But if a bond has a long time until it matures, investors have a difficult time forecasting the likelihood that the company will fall into financial distress. This extra uncertainty creates additional risk, so investors demand a higher required return.

Self Test

Differentiate between mortgage bonds and debentures.

Name the major rating agencies, and list some factors that affect bond ratings.

What is a bond spread?

How do bond ratings affect the default risk premium?

A 10-year T-bond has a yield of 6%. A 10-year corporate bond with a rating of AA has a yield of 7.5%. If the corporate bond has excellent liquidity, what is an estimate of the corporate bond's default risk premium? **(1.5%)**

THE GLOBAL ECONOMIC CRISIS

Are Investors Rational?

The figure in this box shows the yield on junk bonds during the recent past. Observe that the yields were less than 10% from mid-2003 through the end of 2007, and then again after 2009. During the run-up to the 2008 financial crisis, 10-year T-bonds yielded an average of about 4.4%. Thus, the spread on junk bonds over Treasuries was only about 5.4% during these boom years, which is exceptionally low by historic standards. In other words, investors had a voracious appetite for risk and simply didn't require much extra return to induce them to buy very risky securities—investors almost ignored risk during the boom years. But as the economy began to deteriorate in 2008, investors reversed course and became extremely risk averse, with junk-bond yields climbing as high as 25% and the spread exceeding 21%. Interestingly, the pre-financial crisis situation has reappeared even in the midst of a severe recession (as of January 2011), with junk bonds again earning low yields

and investors apparently relatively unconcerned with risk. Such drastic changes in investors' risk aversion are hard to reconcile with careful, deliberate, and rational behavior!

Source: Financial Industry Regulatory Authority, January 28, 2011, High Yield Index (NBBH) Yields: see **http://cxa.marketwatch.com/finra/BondCenter/ActiveUSCorpBond.aspx**.

4.12 The Liquidity Premium (LP)

A "liquid" asset can be converted to cash quickly and at a "fair market value." Financial assets are generally more liquid than real assets. Because liquidity is important, investors include **liquidity premiums (LPs)** when market rates of securities are established. Although it is difficult to measure liquidity premiums accurately, a differential of at least 2 percentage points (and perhaps up to 4 or 5 percentage points) exists between the least liquid and the most liquid financial assets of similar default risk and maturity. Corporate bonds issued by small companies are traded less frequently than those issued by large companies, so small-company bonds tend to have a higher liquidity premium.

For example, liquidity in the market for mortgage-backed securities evaporated in 2008 and early 2009. The few transactions that occurred were priced such that the yields on these MBS were extremely high, which was partially due to a much higher liquidity premium caused by the extremely low liquidity of MBS.

Self Test

Which bond usually will have a higher liquidity premium: One issued by a large company or one issued by a small company?

4.13 The Maturity Risk Premium (MRP)

All bonds, even Treasury bonds, are exposed to two additional sources of risk: interest rate risk and reinvestment risk. The net effect of these two sources of risk upon a bond's yield is called the **maturity risk premium, MRP**. The following sections explain how interest rate risk and reinvestment risk affect a bond's yield.

4.13a Interest Rate Risk

Interest rates go up and down over time, and an increase in interest rates leads to a decline in the value of outstanding bonds. This risk of a decline in bond values due to rising interest rates is called **interest rate risk**. To illustrate, suppose you bought some 10% MicroDrive bonds at a price of $1,000 and then interest rates rose in the following year to 15%. As we saw earlier, the price of the bonds would fall to $713.78, so you would have a loss of $286.22 per bond.[18] Interest rates can and do rise, and rising rates cause a loss of value for bondholders. Thus, bond investors are exposed to risk from changing interest rates.

One's exposure to interest rate risk is higher on bonds with long maturities than on those maturing in the near future.[19] This point can be demonstrated by showing

WEB

For more on bond risk, including duration analysis, see **Web Extension 4C** on the textbook's Web site.

---

18 You would have an *accounting* (and tax) loss only if you sold the bond; if you held it to maturity, you would not have such a loss. However, even if you did not sell, you would still have suffered a *real economic loss in an opportunity cost sense* because you would have lost the opportunity to invest at 15% and would be stuck with a 10% bond in a 15% market. In an economic sense, "paper losses" are just as bad as realized accounting losses.

19 Actually, a bond's maturity and coupon rate each affect interest rate risk. Low coupons mean that most of the bond's return will come from repayment of principal, whereas on a high-coupon bond with the same maturity, more of the cash flows will come in during the early years because of the relatively large coupon payments. A measurement called "duration," which finds the average number of years that the bond's PV of cash flows remains outstanding, has been developed to combine maturity and coupons. A zero coupon bond, which has no interest payments and whose payments all come at maturity, has a duration equal to the bond's maturity. Coupon bonds all have durations that are shorter than maturity, and the higher the coupon rate, the shorter the duration. Bonds with longer duration are exposed to more interest rate risk. *Excel*'s DURATION function provides an easy way to calculate a bond's duration. See *Web Extension 4C* and *Ch04 Tool Kit.xls* for more on duration.

how the value of a 1-year bond with a 10% annual coupon fluctuates with changes in r_d and then comparing these changes with those on a 25-year bond. The 1-year bond's value for $r_d = 5\%$ is shown below:

Inputs: 1   5   100   1000

Output (Bond Value):   −1047.62

Using either a calculator or a spreadsheet, you could calculate the bond values for a 1-year and a 25-year bond at several current market interest rates; these results are plotted in Figure 4-4. Note how much more sensitive the price of the 25-year bond is to changes in interest rates. At a 10% interest rate, both the 25-year and the 1-year bonds are valued at $1,000. When rates rise to 15%, the 25-year bond falls to $676.79 but the 1-year bond falls only to $956.52.

For bonds with similar coupons, this differential sensitivity to changes in interest rates always holds true: The longer the maturity of the bond, the more its price changes in response to a given change in interest rates. Thus, even if the risk of default on two bonds is exactly the same, the one with the longer maturity is exposed to more risk from a rise in interest rates.

The explanation for this difference in interest rate risk is simple. Suppose you bought a 25-year bond that yielded 10%, or $100 a year. Now suppose interest rates on bonds of comparable risk rose to 15%. You would be stuck with only $100 of interest for the next 25 years. On the other hand, had you bought a 1-year bond, you would have a low return for only 1 year. At the end of the year, you would get your $1,000 back, and you could then reinvest it and receive a 15% return ($150) for the next year. Thus, interest rate risk reflects the length of time one is committed to a given investment.

WEB

See **Ch04 Tool Kit.xls.**

Figure 4-4   **Value of Long- and Short-Term 10% Annual Coupon Bonds at Different Market Interest Rates**

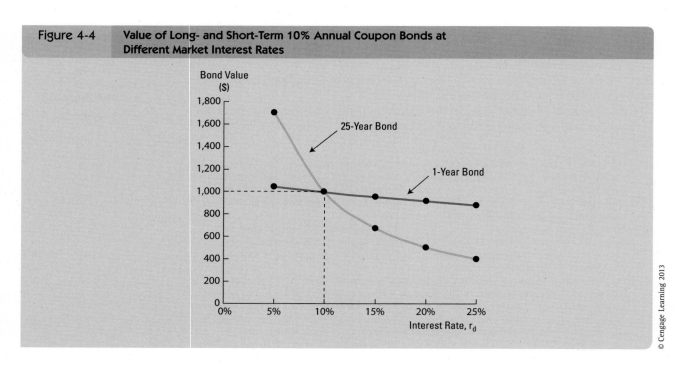

4.13b Reinvestment Rate Risk

As we saw in the preceding section, an *increase* in interest rates will hurt bond-holders because it will lead to a decline in the value of a bond portfolio. But can a *decrease* in interest rates also hurt bondholders? The answer is "yes," because if interest rates fall then a bondholder may suffer a reduction in his or her income. For example, consider a retiree who has a portfolio of bonds and lives off the income they produce. The bonds, on average, have a coupon rate of 10%. Now suppose that interest rates decline to 5%. The short-term bonds will mature, and when they do, they will have to be replaced with lower-yielding bonds. In addition, many of the remaining long-term bonds may be called, and as calls occur, the bondholder will have to replace 10% bonds with 5% bonds. Thus, our retiree will suffer a reduction of income.

The risk of an income decline due to a drop in interest rates is called **reinvestment rate risk**. Reinvestment rate risk is obviously high on callable bonds. It is also high on short-maturity bonds, because the shorter the maturity of a bond, the fewer the years when the relatively high old interest rate will be earned and the sooner the funds will have to be reinvested at the new low rate. Thus, retirees whose primary holdings are short-term securities, such as bank CDs and short-term bonds, are hurt badly by a decline in rates, but holders of long-term bonds continue to enjoy their old high rates.

4.13c Comparing Interest Rate Risk and Reinvestment Rate Risk: The Maturity Risk Premium

Note that interest rate risk relates to the *value* of the bonds in a portfolio, while reinvestment rate risk relates to the *income* the portfolio produces. If you hold long-term bonds then you will face a lot of interest rate risk, because the value of your bonds will decline if interest rates rise; but you will not face much rein-vestment rate risk, so your income will be stable. On the other hand, if you hold short-term bonds, you will not be exposed to much interest rate risk because the value of your portfolio will be stable, but you will be exposed to considerable reinvestment rate risk because your income will fluctuate with changes in interest rates. We see, then, that no fixed-rate bond can be considered totally riskless—even most Treasury bonds are exposed to both interest rate risk and reinvestment rate risk.[20]

Bond prices reflect the trading activities of the marginal investors, defined as those who trade often enough and with large enough sums to determine bond prices. Although one particular investor might be more averse to reinvestment risk than to interest rate risk, the data suggest that the marginal investor is more averse to interest rate risk than to reinvestment risk. To induce the marginal investor to take on interest rate risk, long-term bonds must have a higher expected rate of return than short-term bonds. Holding all else equal, this additional return is the maturity risk premium (MRP).

---

20 Although indexed Treasury bonds are almost riskless, they pay a relatively low real rate. Note also that risks have not disappeared—they have simply been transferred from bondholders to taxpayers.

Differentiate between interest rate risk and reinvestment rate risk.

To which type of risk are holders of long-term bonds more exposed? Short-term bondholders?

Assume that the real risk-free rate is $r^* = 3\%$ and that the average expected inflation rate is 2.5% for the foreseeable future. The DRP and LP for a bond are each 1%, and the applicable MRP is 2%. What is the bond's yield? **(9.5%)**

4.14 The Term Structure of Interest Rates

The **term structure of interest rates** describes the relationship between long-term and short-term rates. The term structure is important both to corporate treasurers deciding whether to borrow by issuing long-term or short-term debt and to investors who are deciding whether to buy long-term or short-term bonds.

Interest rates for bonds with different maturities can be found in a variety of publications, including *The Wall Street Journal* and the *Federal Reserve Bulletin*, as well as on a number of Web sites, including Bloomberg, Yahoo!, CNN Financial, and the Federal Reserve Board. Using interest rate data from these sources, we can determine the term structure at any given point in time. For example, Figure 4-5 presents interest rates for different maturities on three different dates. The set of data for a given date, when plotted on a graph such as Figure 4-5, is called the **yield curve** for that date.

As the figure shows, the yield curve changes both in position and in slope over time. In March 1980, all rates were quite high because high inflation was expected. However, the rate of inflation was expected to decline, so the inflation premium (IP) was larger for short-term bonds than for long-term bonds. This caused short-term yields to be higher than long-term yields, resulting in a *downward-sloping*

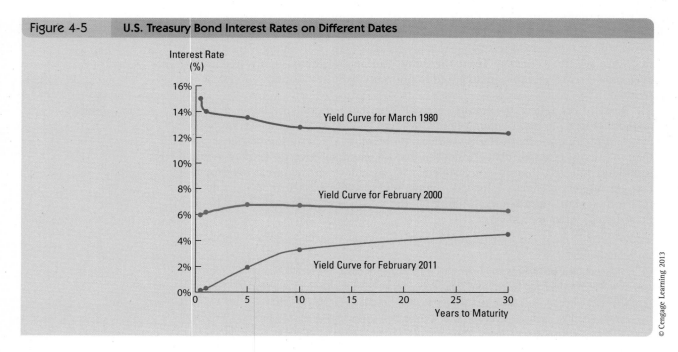

Figure 4-5   U.S. Treasury Bond Interest Rates on Different Dates

yield curve. By February 2000, inflation had indeed declined and thus all rates were lower. The yield curve had become **humped**—medium-term rates were higher than either short- or long-term rates. By February 2011, all rates had fallen below the 2000 levels. Because short-term rates had dropped below long-term rates, the yield curve was *upward sloping*.

Historically, long-term rates are generally higher than short-term rates owing to the maturity risk premium, so the yield curve usually slopes upward. For this reason, people often call an upward-sloping yield curve a **"normal" yield curve** and a yield curve that slopes downward an **inverted**, or **"abnormal,"** curve. Thus, in Figure 4-5 the yield curve for March 1980 was inverted, whereas the yield curve in February 2011 was normal. As stated above, the February 2000 curve was humped.

A few academics and practitioners contend that large bond traders who buy and sell securities of different maturities each day dominate the market. According to this view, a bond trader is just as willing to buy a 30-year bond to pick up a short-term profit as to buy a 3-month security. Strict proponents of this view argue that the shape of the yield curve is therefore determined only by market expectations about future interest rates, a position that is called the **pure expectations theory**, or sometimes just the **expectations theory**. If this were true, then the maturity risk premium (MRP) would be zero and long-term interest rates would simply be a weighted average of current and expected future short-term interest rates. See *Web Extension 4D* for a more detailed discussion of the expectations theory.

WEB

For a discussion of the expectations theory, see *Web Extension 4D* on the textbook's Web site.

Self Test

What is a yield curve, and what information would you need to draw this curve?

Distinguish among the shapes of a "normal" yield curve, an "abnormal" curve, and a "humped" curve.

If the interest rates on 1-, 5-, 20-, and 30-year bonds are (respectively) 4%, 5%, 6%, and 7%, then how would you describe the yield curve? How would you describe it if the rates were reversed?

4.15 Financing with Junk Bonds

Recall that bonds rated less than BBB are noninvestment-grade debt, also called junk bonds or high-yield debt. There are two ways that a bond can become a junk bond. First, the bond might have been investment-grade debt when it was issued but its rating declined because the issuing corporation had fallen on hard times. Such bonds are called "fallen angels," and there are many such bonds as we write this in 2011.

Some bonds are junk bonds at the time they are issued, but this was not always true. Prior to the 1980s, fixed-income investors such as pension funds and insurance companies were generally unwilling to buy risky bonds, so it was almost impossible for risky companies to raise capital in the public bond markets. Then, in the late 1970s, Michael Milken of the investment banking firm Drexel Burnham Lambert, relying on historical studies that showed risky bonds yielded more than enough to compensate for their risk, convinced institutional investors that junk bond yields were worth their risk. Thus was born the junk bond market.

In the 1980s, large investors like T. Boone Pickens and Henry Kravis thought that certain old-line, established companies were run inefficiently and were financed too conservatively. These corporate raiders were able to put in some of their own money, borrow the rest via junk bonds, and take over the target company, usually taking the company private. The fact that interest on the bonds was tax deductible, combined with the much higher debt ratios of the restructured firms, also increased after-tax cash flows and helped make the deals feasible. Because these deals used lots of debt, they were called **leveraged buyouts (LBOs)**.

In recent years, private equity firms have conducted transactions very similar to the LBOs of the 1980s, taking advantage of historically low junk-bond rates to help finance their purchases. For example, in 2007 the private equity firm Kohlberg Kravis Roberts and Company (KKR) took the discount retailer Dollar General private in a $6.9 billion deal. As part of the transaction, Dollar General issued $1.9 billion in junk bonds. So KKR financed approximately 73% of the deal with its own cash (coming from its own equity and from money it had borrowed on its own account) and about 27% of the deal with money that Dollar General raised, for a net investment of about $5 billion. In late 2009, KKR took Dollar General public again at $21 per share with a resulting market value of equity of $7.1 billion and a very tidy gain!

Self Test	What are junk bonds?

4.16 Bankruptcy and Reorganization

When a business becomes *insolvent,* it does not have enough cash to meet its interest and principal payments. A decision must then be made whether to dissolve the firm through *liquidation* or to permit it to *reorganize* and thus stay alive. These issues are addressed in Chapters 7 and 11 of the federal bankruptcy statutes, and the final decision is made by a federal bankruptcy court judge.

The decision to force a firm to liquidate versus permit it to reorganize depends on whether the value of the reorganized firm is likely to be greater than the value of the firm's assets if they are sold off piecemeal. In a reorganization, the firm's creditors negotiate with management on the terms of a potential reorganization. The reorganization plan may call for a *restructuring* of the firm's debt, in which case the interest rate may be reduced, the term to maturity lengthened, or some of the debt may be exchanged for equity. The point of the restructuring is to reduce the financial charges to a level that the firm's cash flows can support. Of course, the common stockholders also have to give up something: They often see their position diluted as a result of additional shares being given to debtholders in exchange for accepting a reduced amount of debt principal and interest. In fact, the original common stockholders often end up with nothing. A trustee may be appointed by the court to oversee the reorganization, but generally the existing management is allowed to retain control.

Liquidation occurs if the company is deemed to be too far gone to be saved—if it is worth more dead than alive. If the bankruptcy court orders liquidation, then assets are sold off and the cash obtained is distributed as specified in Chapter 7 of the Bankruptcy Act. Here is the priority of claims: (1) past-due property taxes; (2) secured creditors who are entitled to the proceeds from the sale of collateral; (3) the trustee's costs of administering and operating the bankrupt firm; (4) expenses incurred after bankruptcy was filed; (5) wages due workers, up to a limit of $2,000 per worker; (6) claims for unpaid contributions to employee benefit plans (with wages and claims not to exceed $2,000 per worker); (7) unsecured claims for customer deposits up to $900 per customer; (8) federal, state, and local taxes due; (9) unfunded pension plan liabilities (although some limitations exist); (10) general unsecured creditors; (11) preferred stockholders (up to the par value of their stock); and (12) common stockholders (although usually nothing is left).

The key points for you to know are: (1) the federal bankruptcy statutes govern both reorganization and liquidation, (2) bankruptcies occur frequently, and (3) a priority of the specified claims must be followed when distributing the assets of a liquidated firm. We discuss bankruptcy in more detail in Chapter 25.

Self Test

Differentiate between a Chapter 7 liquidation and a Chapter 11 reorganization.

List the priority of claims for the distribution of a liquidated firm's assets.

Summary

This chapter described the different types of bonds that governments and corporations issue, explained how bond prices are established, and discussed how investors estimate the rates of return they can expect to earn. The rate of return required by debtholders is the company's pre-tax cost of debt, and this rate depends on the risk that investors face when they buy bonds.

- A **bond** is a long-term promissory note issued by a business or governmental unit. The issuer receives money in exchange for promising to make interest payments and to repay the principal on a specified future date.
- Some special types of long-term financing include **zero coupon bonds**, which pay no annual interest but are issued at a discount; see *Web Extension 4A* for more on zero coupon bonds. Other types are **floating-rate debt**, whose interest payments fluctuate with changes in the general level of interest rates; and **junk bonds**, which are high-risk, high-yield instruments issued by firms that use a great deal of financial leverage.
- A **call provision** gives the issuing corporation the right to redeem the bonds prior to maturity under specified terms, usually at a price greater than the maturity value (the difference is a **call premium**). A firm will typically call a bond if interest rates fall substantially below the coupon rate.
- A **sinking fund** is a provision that requires the corporation to retire a portion of the bond issue each year. The purpose of the sinking fund is to provide for the orderly retirement of the issue. A sinking fund typically requires no call premium.
- The **value of a bond** is found as the present value of an **annuity** (the interest payments) plus the present value of a lump sum (the **principal**). The bond is evaluated at the appropriate periodic interest rate over the number of periods for which interest payments are made.
- The equation used to find the value of an annual coupon bond is

$$V_B = \sum_{t=1}^{N} \frac{INT}{(1 + r_d)^t} + \frac{M}{(1 + r_d)^N}$$

- An adjustment to the formula must be made if the bond pays interest **semiannually**: divide INT and r_d by 2, and multiply N by 2.
- The expected rate of return on a bond held to maturity is defined as the bond's **yield to maturity (YTM)**:

$$\text{Bond price} = \sum_{t=1}^{N} \frac{\text{INT}}{(1+\text{YTM})^t} + \frac{M}{(1+\text{YTM})^N}$$

- The expected rate of return on a callable bond held to its call date is defined as the **yield to call (YTC)**.
- The **nominal** (or **quoted**) **interest rate** on a debt security, r_d, is composed of the real risk-free rate, r*, plus premiums that reflect inflation (IP), default risk (DRP), liquidity (LP), and maturity risk (MRP):

$$r_d = r* + \text{IP} + \text{DRP} + \text{LP} + \text{MRP}$$

- The **risk-free rate of interest, r_{RF},** is defined as the real risk-free rate, r*, plus an inflation premium, IP: $r_{RF} = r* + \text{IP}$.
- **Treasury Inflation-Protected Securities (TIPS)** are U.S. Treasury bonds that have no inflation risk. See *Web Extension 4B* for more discussion of TIPS.
- The longer the maturity of a bond, the more its price will change in response to a given change in interest rates; this is called **interest rate risk**. However, bonds with short maturities expose investors to high **reinvestment rate risk**, which is the risk that income from a bond portfolio will decline because cash flows received from bonds will be rolled over at lower interest rates.
- **Duration** is a measure of interest rate risk. See *Web Extension 4C* for a discussion of duration.
- Corporate and municipal bonds have **default risk**. If an issuer defaults, investors receive less than the promised return on the bond. Therefore, investors should evaluate a bond's default risk before making a purchase.
- Bonds are assigned **ratings** that reflect the probability of their going into default. The highest rating is AAA, and they go down to D. The higher a bond's rating, the lower its risk and therefore its interest rate.
- The relationship between the yields on securities and the securities' maturities is known as the **term structure of interest rates**, and the **yield curve** is a graph of this relationship.
- The shape of the yield curve depends on two key factors: (1) *expectations about future inflation* and (2) *perceptions about the relative risk of securities with different maturities*.
- The yield curve is normally **upward sloping**—this is called a **normal yield curve**. However, the curve can slope downward (an **inverted yield curve**) if the inflation rate is expected to decline. The yield curve also can be **humped**, which means that interest rates on medium-term maturities are higher than rates on both short- and long-term maturities.
- The **expectations theory** states that yields on long-term bonds reflect expected future interest rates. *Web Extension 4D* discusses this theory.

Questions

4-1 Define each of the following terms:
    a. Bond; Treasury bond; corporate bond; municipal bond; foreign bond
    b. Par value; maturity date; coupon payment; coupon interest rate

c. Floating-rate bond; zero coupon bond; original issue discount bond (OID)

d. Call provision; redeemable bond; sinking fund

e. Convertible bond; warrant; income bond; indexed, or purchasing power, bond

f. Premium bond; discount bond

g. Current yield (on a bond); yield to maturity (YTM); yield to call (YTC)

h. Indentures; mortgage bond; debenture; subordinated debenture

i. Development bond; municipal bond insurance; junk bond; investment-grade bond

j. Real risk-free rate of interest, r*; nominal risk-free rate of interest, r_{RF}

k. Inflation premium (IP); default risk premium (DRP); liquidity; liquidity premium (LP)

l. Interest rate risk; maturity risk premium (MRP); reinvestment rate risk

m. Term structure of interest rates; yield curve

n. "Normal" yield curve; inverted ("abnormal") yield curve

4-2 "Short-term interest rates are more volatile than long-term interest rates, so short-term bond prices are more sensitive to interest rate changes than are long-term bond prices." Is this statement true or false? Explain.

4-3 The rate of return you would get if you bought a bond and held it to its maturity date is called the bond's yield to maturity. If interest rates in the economy rise after a bond has been issued, what will happen to the bond's price and to its YTM? Does the length of time to maturity affect the extent to which a given change in interest rates will affect the bond's price?

4-4 If you buy a *callable* bond and interest rates decline, will the value of your bond rise by as much as it would have risen if the bond had not been callable? Explain.

4-5 A sinking fund can be set up in one of two ways. Discuss the advantages and disadvantages of each procedure from the viewpoint of both the firm and its bondholders.

Problems   Answers Appear in Appendix B

Easy Problems 1–6

4-1 **Bond Valuation with Annual Payments** Jackson Corporation's bonds have 12 years remaining to maturity. Interest is paid annually, the bonds have a $1,000 par value, and the coupon interest rate is 8%. The bonds have a yield to maturity of 9%. What is the current market price of these bonds?

4-2 **Yield to Maturity for Annual Payments** Wilson Wonders's bonds have 12 years remaining to maturity. Interest is paid annually, the bonds have a $1,000 par value, and the coupon interest rate is 10%. The bonds sell at a price of $850. What is their yield to maturity?

4-3 **Current Yield for Annual Payments** Heath Foods's bonds have 7 years remaining to maturity. The bonds have a face value of $1,000 and a yield to maturity of 8%. They pay interest annually and have a 9% coupon rate. What is their current yield?

4-4 **Determinant of Interest Rates** The real risk-free rate of interest is 4%. Inflation is expected to be 2% this year and 4% during the next 2 years. Assume that the maturity risk premium is zero.

What is the yield on 2-year Treasury securities? What is the yield on 3-year Treasury securities?

4-5 Default Risk Premium A Treasury bond that matures in 10 years has a yield of 6%. A 10-year corporate bond has a yield of 9%. Assume that the liquidity premium on the corporate bond is 0.5%. What is the default risk premium on the corporate bond?

4-6 Maturity Risk Premium The real risk-free rate is 3%, and inflation is expected to be 3% for the next 2 years. A 2-year Treasury security yields 6.3%. What is the maturity risk premium for the 2-year security?

Intermediate Problems 7–20

4-7 Bond Valuation with Semiannual Payments Renfro Rentals has issued bonds that have a 10% coupon rate, payable semiannually. The bonds mature in 8 years, have a face value of $1,000, and a yield to maturity of 8.5%. What is the price of the bonds?

4-8 Yield to Maturity and Call with Semiannual Payments Thatcher Corporation's bonds will mature in 10 years. The bonds have a face value of $1,000 and an 8% coupon rate, paid semiannually. The price of the bonds is $1,100. The bonds are callable in 5 years at a call price of $1,050. What is their yield to maturity? What is their yield to call?

4-9 Bond Valuation and Interest Rate Risk The Garraty Company has two bond issues outstanding. Both bonds pay $100 annual interest plus $1,000 at maturity. Bond L has a maturity of 15 years, and Bond S has a maturity of 1 year.
   a. What will be the value of each of these bonds when the going rate of interest is (1) 5%, (2) 8%, and (3) 12%? Assume that there is only one more interest payment to be made on Bond S.
   b. Why does the longer-term (15-year) bond fluctuate more when interest rates change than does the shorter-term bond (1 year)?

4-10 Yield to Maturity and Required Returns The Brownstone Corporation's bonds have 5 years remaining to maturity. Interest is paid annually, the bonds have a $1,000 par value, and the coupon interest rate is 9%.
   a. What is the yield to maturity at a current market price of (1) $829 or (2) $1,104?
   b. Would you pay $829 for one of these bonds if you thought that the appropriate rate of interest was 12%—that is, if r_d = 12%? Explain your answer.

4-11 Yield to Call and Realized Rates of Return Seven years ago, Goodwynn & Wolf Incorporated sold a 20-year bond issue with a 14% annual coupon rate and a 9% call premium. Today, G&W called the bonds. The bonds originally were sold at their face value of $1,000. Compute the realized rate of return for investors who purchased the bonds when they were issued and who surrender them today in exchange for the call price.

4-12 Bond Yields and Rates of Return A 10-year, 12% semiannual coupon bond with a par value of $1,000 may be called in 4 years at a call price of $1,060. The bond sells for $1,100. (Assume that the bond has just been issued.)
   a. What is the bond's yield to maturity?
   b. What is the bond's current yield?
   c. What is the bond's capital gain or loss yield?
   d. What is the bond's yield to call?

4-13 Yield to Maturity and Current Yield You just purchased a bond that matures in 5 years. The bond has a face value of $1,000 and has an 8% annual coupon. The bond has a current yield of 8.21%. What is the bond's yield to maturity?

4-14 Current Yield with Semiannual Payments A bond that matures in 7 years sells for $1,020. The bond has a face value of $1,000 and a yield to maturity of 10.5883%. The bond pays coupons semiannually. What is the bond's current yield?

4-15 Yield to Call, Yield to Maturity, and Market Rates Absalom Motors's 14% coupon rate, semiannual payment, $1,000 par value bonds that mature in 30 years are callable 5 years from now at a price of $1,050. The bonds sell at a price of $1,353.54, and the yield curve is flat. Assuming that interest rates in the economy are expected to remain at their current level, what is the best estimate of the nominal interest rate on new bonds?

4-16 Interest Rate Sensitivity A bond trader purchased each of the following bonds at a yield to maturity of 8%. Immediately after she purchased the bonds, interest rates fell to 7%. What is the percentage change in the price of each bond after the decline in interest rates? Fill in the following table:

	Price @ 8%	Price @ 7%	Percentage Change
10-year, 10% annual coupon	_____	_____	_____
10-year zero	_____	_____	_____
5-year zero	_____	_____	_____
30-year zero	_____	_____	_____
$100 perpetuity	_____	_____	_____

4-17 Bond Value as Maturity Approaches An investor has two bonds in his portfolio. Each bond matures in 4 years, has a face value of $1,000, and has a yield to maturity equal to 9.6%. One bond, Bond C, pays an annual coupon of 10%; the other bond, Bond Z, is a zero coupon bond. Assuming that the yield to maturity of each bond remains at 9.6% over the next 4 years, what will be the price of each of the bonds at the following time periods? Fill in the following table:

t	Price of Bond C	Price of Bond Z
0	_____	_____
1	_____	_____
2	_____	_____
3	_____	_____
4	_____	_____

4-18 Determinants of Interest Rates The real risk-free rate is 2%. Inflation is expected to be 3% this year, 4% next year, and then 3.5% thereafter. The maturity risk premium is estimated to be $0.0005 \times (t - 1)$, where t = number of years to maturity. What is the nominal interest rate on a 7-year Treasury security?

4-19 **Maturity Risk Premiums** Assume that the real risk-free rate, r*, is 3% and that inflation is expected to be 8% in Year 1, 5% in Year 2, and 4% thereafter. Assume also that all Treasury securities are highly liquid and free of default risk. If 2-year and 5-year Treasury notes both yield 10%, what is the difference in the maturity risk premiums (MRPs) on the two notes; that is, what is MRP_5 minus MRP_2?

4-20 **Inflation Risk Premiums** Because of a recession, the inflation rate expected for the coming year is only 3%. However, the inflation rate in Year 2 and thereafter is expected to be constant at some level above 3%. Assume that the real risk-free rate is $r* = 2\%$ for all maturities and that there are no maturity premiums. If 3-year Treasury notes yield 2 percentage points more than 1-year notes, what inflation rate is expected after Year 1?

Challenging Problems 21–23

4-21 **Bond Valuation and Changes in Maturity and Required Returns** Suppose Hillard Manufacturing sold an issue of bonds with a 10-year maturity, a $1,000 par value, a 10% coupon rate, and semiannual interest payments.
  a. Two years after the bonds were issued, the going rate of interest on bonds such as these fell to 6%. At what price would the bonds sell?
  b. Suppose that 2 years after the initial offering, the going interest rate had risen to 12%. At what price would the bonds sell?
  c. Suppose that 2 years after the issue date (as in part a) interest rates fell to 6%. Suppose further that the interest rate remained at 6% for the next 8 years. What would happen to the price of the bonds over time?

4-22 **Yield to Maturity and Yield to Call** Arnot International's bonds have a current market price of $1,200. The bonds have an 11% annual coupon payment, a $1,000 face value, and 10 years left until maturity. The bonds may be called in 5 years at 109% of face value (call price = $1,090).
  a. What is the yield to maturity?
  b. What is the yield to call if they are called in 5 years?
  c. Which yield might investors expect to earn on these bonds, and why?
  d. The bond's indenture indicates that the call provision gives the firm the right to call them at the end of each year beginning in Year 5. In Year 5, they may be called at 109% of face value, but in each of the next 4 years the call percentage will decline by 1 percentage point. Thus, in Year 6 they may be called at 108% of face value, in Year 7 they may be called at 107% of face value, and so on. If the yield curve is horizontal and interest rates remain at their current level, when is the latest that investors might expect the firm to call the bonds?

4-23 **Determinants of Interest Rates** Suppose you and most other investors expect the inflation rate to be 7% next year, to fall to 5% during the following year, and then to remain at a rate of 3% thereafter. Assume that the real risk-free rate, r*, will remain at 2% and that maturity risk premiums on Treasury securities rise from zero on very short-term securities (those that mature in a few days) to a level of 0.2 percentage points for 1-year securities. Furthermore, maturity risk premiums increase 0.2 percentage points for each year to maturity, up to a limit of 1.0 percentage point on 5-year or longer-term T-notes and T-bonds.
  a. Calculate the interest rate on 1-, 2-, 3-, 4-, 5-, 10-, and 20-year Treasury securities, and plot the yield curve.

b. Now suppose ExxonMobil's bonds, rated AAA, have the same maturities as the Treasury bonds. As an approximation, plot an ExxonMobil yield curve on the same graph with the Treasury bond yield curve. (*Hint:* Think about the default risk premium on ExxonMobil's long-term versus its short-term bonds.)

c. Now plot the approximate yield curve of Long Island Lighting Company, a risky nuclear utility.

Spreadsheet Problem

4-24 **Build a Model: Bond Valuation** Start with the partial model in the file *Ch04 P24 Build a Model.xls* on the textbook's Web site. A 20-year, 8% semiannual coupon bond with a par value of $1,000 may be called in 5 years at a call price of $1,040. The bond sells for $1,100. (Assume that the bond has just been issued.)

a. What is the bond's yield to maturity?

b. What is the bond's current yield?

c. What is the bond's capital gain or loss yield?

d. What is the bond's yield to call?

e. How would the price of the bond be affected by a change in the going market interest rate? (*Hint:* Conduct a sensitivity analysis of price to changes in the going market interest rate for the bond. Assume that the bond will be called if and only if the going rate of interest *falls below* the coupon rate. This is an oversimplification, but assume it anyway for purposes of this problem.)

f. Now assume the date is October 25, 2012. Assume further that a 12%, 10-year bond was issued on July 1, 2012, pays interest semiannually (on January 1 and July 1), and sells for $1,100. Use your spreadsheet to find the bond's yield.

MINI CASE

Sam Strother and Shawna Tibbs are vice presidents of Mutual of Seattle Insurance Company and co-directors of the company's pension fund management division. An important new client, the North-Western Municipal Alliance, has requested that Mutual of Seattle present an investment seminar to the mayors of the represented cities, and Strother and Tibbs, who will make the actual presentation, have asked you to help them by answering the following questions.

a. What are the key features of a bond?

b. What are call provisions and sinking fund provisions? Do these provisions make bonds more or less risky?

c. How does one determine the value of any asset whose value is based on expected future cash flows?

d. How is the value of a bond determined? What is the value of a 10-year, $1,000 par value bond with a 10% annual coupon if its required rate of return is 10%?

e. (1) What would be the value of the bond described in part d if, just after it had been issued, the expected inflation rate rose by 3 percentage points, causing investors to require a 13% return? Would we now have a discount or a premium bond?

(2) What would happen to the bond's value if inflation fell and r_d declined to 7%? Would we now have a premium or a discount bond?

(3) What would happen to the value of the 10-year bond over time if the required rate of return remained at 13%? If it remained at 7%? (*Hint:* With a financial calculator, enter PMT, I/YR, FV, and N, and then change N to see what happens to the PV as the bond approaches maturity.)

f. (1) What is the yield to maturity on a 10-year, 9% annual coupon, $1,000 par value bond that sells for $887.00? That sells for $1,134.20? What does the fact that a bond sells at a discount or at a premium tell you about the relationship between r_d and the bond's coupon rate?

(2) What are the total return, the current yield, and the capital gains yield for the discount bond? (Assume the bond is held to maturity and the company does not default on the bond.)

g. How does the equation for valuing a bond change if semiannual payments are made? Find the value of a 10-year, semiannual payment, 10% coupon bond if the nominal r_d = 13%.

h. Suppose a 10-year, 10% semiannual coupon bond with a par value of $1,000 is currently selling for $1,135.90, producing a nominal yield to maturity of 8%. However, the bond can be called after 5 years for a price of $1,050.

(1) What is the bond's *nominal* yield to call (YTC)?

(2) If you bought this bond, do you think you would be more likely to earn the YTM or the YTC? Why?

i. Write a general expression for the yield on any debt security (r_d) and define these terms: real risk-free rate of interest (r*), inflation premium (IP), default risk premium (DRP), liquidity premium (LP), and maturity risk premium (MRP).

j. Define the nominal risk-free rate (r_{RF}). What security can be used as an estimate of r_{RF}?

k. Describe a way to estimate the inflation premium (IP) for a t-year bond.

l. What is a *bond spread* and how is it related to the default risk premium? How are bond ratings related to default risk? What factors affect a company's bond rating?

m. What is *interest rate* (or *price*) *risk?* Which bond has more interest rate risk: an annual payment 1-year bond or a 10-year bond? Why?

n. What is *reinvestment rate risk?* Which has more reinvestment rate risk: a 1-year bond or a 10-year bond?

o. How are interest rate risk and reinvestment rate risk related to the maturity risk premium?

p. What is the term structure of interest rates? What is a yield curve?

q. Briefly describe bankruptcy law. If a firm were to default on its bonds, would the company be liquidated immediately? Would the bondholders be assured of receiving all of their promised payments?

Selected Additional Cases

The following cases from TextChoice, Cengage Learning's online case library, cover many of the concepts discussed in this chapter and are available at **www.textchoice2.com/casenet.**

Klein-Brigham Series:
Case 3, "Peachtree Securities, Inc. (B)"; Case 72, "Swan Davis"; and Case 78, "Beatrice Peabody."

Brigham-Buzzard Series:
Case 3, "Powerline Network Corporation (Bonds and Preferred Stock)."

Chapter 5

Basic Stock Valuation

In Chapter 2, we examined stocks' risks and the factors that affect their required returns. In this chapter, we use those findings to estimate the *intrinsic value* of a stock. The concepts and models developed here will also be used when we estimate the cost of capital in Chapter 10, a key concept used in many important decisions, especially decisions to invest or not invest in new assets.

Some companies are so small that their common stocks are not actively traded; they are owned by only a few people, usually the companies' managers. The stock in such firms is said to be closely held. In contrast, the stocks of most large companies are owned by many investors, most of whom are not active in management. These are publicly held stocks. Institutions such as pension plans, mutual funds, hedge funds, foreign investors, and insurance companies hold about half the market value of all stocks and buy and sell relatively actively. As a result, they account for about 75% of all transactions and thus have a heavy influence on the valuation of individual stocks. But before plunging into stock valuation, it is useful to begin with a closer look at what it means to be a stockholder.

WEB

The textbook's Web site contains an *Excel* file that will guide you through the chapter's calculations. The file for this chapter is ***Ch05 Tool Kit.xls***, and we encourage you to open the file and follow along as you read the chapter.

Beginning of Chapter Questions

As you read the chapter, consider how you would answer the following questions. You *should not* necessarily be able to answer the questions before you read the chapter. Rather, you should use them to get a sense of the issues covered in the chapter. After reading the chapter, you should be able to give at least partial answers to the questions, and you should be able to give better answers after the chapter has been discussed in class. Note, too, that it is often useful, when answering conceptual questions, to use hypothetical data to illustrate your answer. We illustrate the answers with an *Excel* model that is available on the textbook's Web site. Accessing the model and working through it is a useful exercise, and it provides insights that are useful when answering the questions.

1. Assuming that the required rate of return is determined by the CAPM, explain how you would use the dividend growth model to estimate the price for Stock i. Indicate what data you would need, and give an example of a "reasonable" value for each data input.

2. How would the stock's calculated price be affected if g, r_{RF}, IP (the premium for inflation), r_M, and b_i each (a) "improved" or (b) "became worse" by some arbitrary but "reasonable" amount? "Improved" means caused the stock price to increase, and "became worse" means lowered the price. "Reasonable" means that the condition has existed in the recent past for the economy and/or some particular company. You can look at our model for examples.

3. How could you use the nonconstant growth model to find the value of the stock? Here you can assume that the expected growth rate starts at a high level, then declines for several years, and finally reaches a steady state where growth is constant.

4. Suppose you were offered a chance to buy a stock at a specified price. The stock paid a dividend last year, and the dividend is expected to grow at a very high rate for several years, at a moderate rate for several more years, and at a constant rate from then on. How could you estimate the expected rate of return on the stock?

5. In general, what are some characteristics of stocks for which a dividend growth model is appropriate? What are some characteristics of stocks for which these models are not appropriate? How could you evaluate this second type of stock?

6. What does each of the three forms of the Efficient Markets Hypothesis say about each of the following?
   a. Technical trading rules—that is, rules based on past movements in the stock
   b. Fundamental analysis—that is, trying to identify undervalued or overvalued stocks based on publicly available financial information
   c. Insider trading
   d. Hot tips from (1) Internet chat rooms, (2) close friends unconnected with the company, or (3) close friends who work for the company

5.1 Legal Rights and Privileges of Common Stockholders

The common stockholders are the *owners* of a corporation, and as such they have certain rights and privileges as discussed in this section.

5.1a Control of the Firm

A firm's common stockholders have the right to elect its directors, who, in turn, elect the officers who manage the business. In a small firm, the largest stockholder typically serves as president and chairperson of the board. In a large, publicly owned firm, the managers typically have some stock, but their personal holdings are generally

CORPORATE VALUATION AND STOCK PRICES

In Chapter 1, we told you that managers should strive to maximize intrinsic value and that the value of a firm is determined by the size, timing, and risk of its free cash flows (FCF). Recall that one use of FCF is to pay dividends. One way to estimate the intrinsic value of stock is to discount the cash flows to stockholders (dividends, D_t) at the rate of return required by stockholders (r_s). The result is the intrinsic value to stockholders.

You may say, "But what about capital gains? Don't investors buy stocks expecting to realize capital gains?" The answer is "yes," but we will see that this model actually incorporates capital gains.

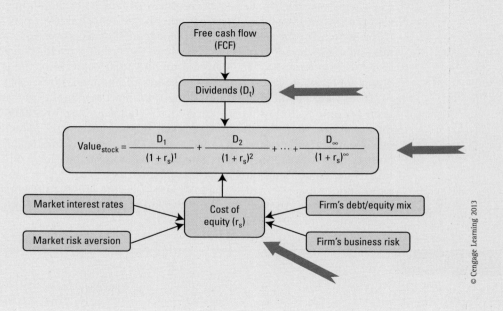

insufficient to give them voting control. Thus, the managers of most publicly owned firms can be removed by the stockholders if the management team is not effective.

Corporations must hold periodic elections to select directors, usually once a year, with the vote taken at the annual meeting. At some companies, all directors are elected each year for a 1-year term. At other companies, the terms are staggered. For example, one-third of the directors are elected each year for a 3-year term.

Each share of stock has one vote, so the owner of 1,000 shares has 1,000 votes for each director.[1] Stockholders can appear at the annual meeting and vote in

---

1. In the situation described, a 1,000-share stockholder could cast 1,000 votes for each of three directors if there were three contested seats on the board. An alternative procedure that may be prescribed in the corporate charter calls for *cumulative voting*. Here the 1,000-share stockholder would get 3,000 votes if there were three vacancies, and he or she could cast all of them for one director. Cumulative voting helps minority stockholders (i.e., those who do not own a majority of the shares) get representation on the board.

person, but typically they transfer their right to vote to another party by means of a **proxy.** Management always solicits stockholders' proxies and usually gets them. However, if earnings are poor and stockholders are dissatisfied, an outside group may solicit the proxies in an effort to overthrow management and take control of the business. This is known as a **proxy fight.** Proxy fights are discussed in detail in Chapter 11.

5.1b The Preemptive Right

Common stockholders often have the right, called the **preemptive right,** to purchase any additional shares sold by the firm. In some states, the preemptive right is automatically included in every corporate charter; in others, it is used only if it is specifically inserted into the charter.

The preemptive right enables current stockholders to maintain control, and it also prevents a transfer of wealth from current stockholders to new stockholders. If it were not for this safeguard, the management of a corporation could issue additional shares at a low price and purchase these shares itself. Management could thereby seize control of the corporation and steal value from the current stockholders. For example, suppose 1,000 shares of common stock, each with a price of $100, were outstanding, making the total market value of the firm $100,000. If an additional 1,000 shares were sold at $50 a share, or for $50,000, this would raise the total market value to $150,000. When total market value is divided by new total shares outstanding, a value of $75 a share is obtained. The old stockholders thus lose $25 per share, and the new stockholders have an instant profit of $25 per share. Thus, selling common stock at a price below the market value would dilute its price and transfer wealth from the present stockholders to those who were allowed to purchase the new shares. The preemptive right prevents such occurrences.

Self Test

What is a proxy fight?

What are the two primary reasons for using preemptive rights?

---

www

Note that **finance.yahoo .com** provides an easy way to find stocks meeting specified criteria. Under the Investing tab, select Stocks and then Stock Screener. To find the largest companies in terms of market value, for example, choose More Preset Screens, then select Largest Market Cap. You can also create custom screens to find stocks meeting other criteria.

5.2 Types of Common Stock

Although most firms have only one type of common stock, in some instances **classified stock** is used to meet a company's special needs. Generally, when special classifications are used, one type is designated *Class A,* another *Class B,* and so on. Small, new companies seeking funds from outside sources frequently use different types of common stock. For example, when Genetic Concepts went public, its Class A stock was sold to the public and paid a dividend, but this stock had no voting rights for 5 years. Its Class B stock, which was retained by the firm's organizers, had full voting rights for 5 years, but the legal terms stated that dividends could not be paid on the Class B stock until the company had established its earning power and built up retained earnings to a designated level. The use of classified stock thus enabled the public to take a position in a conservatively financed growth company without sacrificing income, while the founders retained absolute control during the crucial early stages of the firm's development. At the same time, outside investors were protected against excessive withdrawals of funds by the original owners. As is often the case in such situations, the Class B stock was called **founders' shares.**[2]

As these examples illustrate, the right to vote is often a distinguishing characteristic between different classes of stock. Suppose two classes of stock differ in only one respect: One class has voting rights but the other does not. As you would expect, the stock with voting rights would be more valuable. In the United States, which has a legal system with fairly strong protection for minority stockholders (that is, noncontrolling stockholders), voting stock typically sells at a price 4% to 6% above that of otherwise similar nonvoting stock. Thus, if a stock with no voting rights sold for $50, then one with voting rights would probably sell for $52 to $53. In countries with legal systems that provide less protection for minority stockholders, the right to vote is far more valuable. For example voting stock in Israel sells for 45% more on average than nonvoting stock, and voting stock in Italy has an 82% higher value than nonvoting stock.

Some companies have multiple lines of business, with each line having very different growth prospects. Because cash flows for all business lines are mingled on financial statements, some companies worry that investors are not able to value the high-growth business lines correctly. To separate the cash flows and to allow separate valuations, occasionally a company will have classes of stock with dividends tied to a particular part of a company. This is called **tracking stock,** or **target stock.** For example, in 2006 Liberty Media Corporation, a conglomerate that owned such entertainment assets as the Starz movie channel and investments in Time Warner, issued two different tracking stocks to track the two different lines of its business. One of these, Liberty Interactive tracking stock, was designed to track the performance of its QVC home shopping network and other high-growth Internet-based interactive assets. The other, Liberty Capital Group, comprised slower-growth holdings like the Starz Entertainment Group. The idea was that investors would assign a higher value to the high-growth portion of the company if it traded separately.

However, many analysts are skeptical as to whether tracking stock increases a company's total market value. Companies still report consolidated financial statements for the entire company and have considerable leeway in allocating costs, deploying capital, and reporting the financial results for the various divisions, even those with tracking stock. Thus, a tracking stock is far from identical to the stock of an independent, stand-alone company.

What are some reasons why a company might use classified stock?

Self Test

5.3 The Market Stock Price versus Intrinsic Value

We saw in Chapter 1 that managers should seek to maximize the value of their firms' stocks. In that chapter, we also emphasized the difference between stock price and intrinsic value. The stock price is simply the current market price, and it is easily observed for publicly traded companies. By contrast, intrinsic value, which

---

2. Note that "Class A," "Class B," and so on have no standard meanings. Most firms have no classified shares, but a firm that does could designate its Class B shares as founders' shares and its Class A shares as those sold to the public and another firm might reverse these designations.

represents the "true" value of the company's stock, cannot be directly observed and must instead be estimated. Figure 5-1 illustrates the connection between stock price and intrinsic value.

As the figure suggests, market equilibrium occurs when the stock's price equals its intrinsic value. If the stock market is reasonably efficient, then gaps between the stock price and intrinsic value should not be very large, and they should not persist for very long. However, there are cases when an individual stock price may be much higher or lower than its intrinsic value, and such divergence may persist for quite a while. During several years leading up to the crash of 2008–2009, most of the large investment banks were reporting record profits and selling at record prices. However, much of those earnings were illusory in that they did not reflect the huge risks that existed in the sub-prime mortgages they were buying. So, with hindsight, we now know that the market prices of most financial firms' stocks exceeded their intrinsic values just prior to 2008. Then, when the market realized what was happening, those stock prices crashed. Citigroup, Merrill Lynch, and others lost over 80% of their value in a few short months, and others suffered even worse declines. It clearly pays to question market prices at times!

5.3a Why Do Investors and Companies Care about Intrinsic Value?

The remainder of this chapter focuses primarily on different approaches for estimating a stock's intrinsic value. Before describing these approaches, it is worth asking why it is important for investors and companies to understand how to estimate intrinsic values.

When investing in common stocks, the goal is to purchase stocks that are undervalued (i.e., the price is below the stock's intrinsic value) and avoid stocks that are overvalued. Consequently, Wall Street analysts, institutional investors who control mutual funds and pension funds, and even many individual investors are

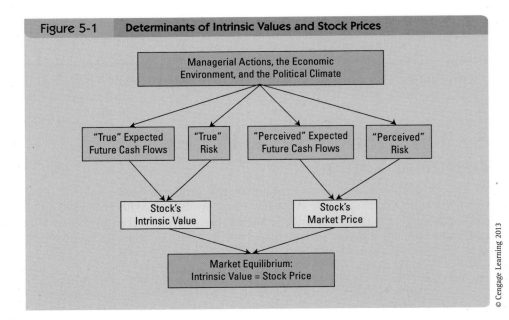

Figure 5-1   Determinants of Intrinsic Values and Stock Prices

quite interested in finding reliable models that help predict intrinsic value. Investors obviously care about intrinsic value, but managers also must understand how intrinsic value is estimated. First, managers need to know how alternative actions are likely to affect stock prices, and the models of intrinsic value that we cover help demonstrate the connection between managerial decisions and firm value. Second, managers should consider whether their stock is significantly undervalued or overvalued before making certain decisions. For example, firms should consider carefully the decision to issue new shares if they believe their stock is undervalued, and an estimate of their stock's intrinsic value is the key to such decisions.

Two basic models are used to estimate intrinsic values: The *discounted dividend model* and the *corporate valuation model*. The dividend model focuses on dividends, while the corporate model drills down below dividends and focuses on sales, costs, and free cash flows. We cover the discounted dividend model in this chapter and the corporate valuation model in Chapter 11.

What's the difference between a stock's price and its intrinsic value?

Why do investors and managers need to understand how a firm's intrinsic value is estimated?

Self Test

5.4 Stock Market Reporting

Fifty years ago, investors who wanted real-time information would sit in brokerage firms' offices watching a "ticker tape" go by that displayed prices of stocks as they were traded. Those who did not need current information could find the previous day's prices from the business section of a daily newspaper like *The Wall Street Journal*. Today, though, one can get quotes throughout the day from many different Internet sources, including Yahoo![3] Figure 5-2 shows the quote for General Electric, which is traded on the NYSE under the symbol GE, on February 8, 2011. GE ended the regular trading day (4 p.m. EST) at $21.28, up $0.41, which was a 1.96% increase from the previous day. However, the stock rose by 4 cents in after-hours trading. The data also show that GE opened the day at $20.96 and traded in a range from $20.91 to $21.31. If this quote had been obtained during trading hours, it would also have provided information about the quotes at which the stock could be bought (the Ask quote) or sold (the Bid quote). During the past year, the price hit a high of $21.31 and a low of $13.75. A total of 54.94 million GE shares traded that day, which was a little below the average trading volume of 59.2 million shares.

The screen with the stock quote information also gives the total market value of GE's common stock (the Market Cap); the dividend and dividend yield; the most recent "ttm," or "trailing twelve months," EPS and P/E ratios; and a graph showing the stock's performance during the day. (However, the graph can be changed to show the stock's performance over a number of time periods up to and including 5 years.) In addition to this information, the Web page has links to financial

---

3. Most free sources actually provide quotes that are delayed by 20 minutes, but if you subscribe to a paid site like *The Wall Street Journal*'s online service, or if you have a brokerage account, you can generally get online real-time quotes.

Figure 5-2   **Stock Quote and Other Key Data for GE, February 8, 2011**

Source: **finance.yahoo.com.**

statements, research reports, historical ratios, analysts' forecasts of EPS and EPS growth rates, and a wealth of other data.

5.5 Valuing Common Stocks

Common stocks are expected to provide a stream of future cash flows, and a stock's value is found the same way as the values of other financial assets—namely, as the present value of its expected future cash flow stream. The expected cash flows consist of two elements: (1) the dividends expected in each year and (2) the price investors expect to receive when they sell the stock. The expected final stock price includes the return of the original investment plus an expected capital gain.

5.5a Definitions of Terms Used in Stock Valuation Models

We saw in Chapter 1 that a manager should seek to maximize the intrinsic value of the firm's stock. To do this, a manager needs to know how her actions are likely to affect the stock's price. Therefore, we develop some models in this section to show how the value of a share of stock is determined, and we begin by defining some key terms as follows.

D_t = Dividend the stockholder *expects* to receive at the end of Year t. D_0 is the most recent dividend, which has already been paid; D_1 is the first dividend expected, which will be paid at the end of this year; D_2 is the dividend expected at the end of Year 2; and so forth. D_1 represents the first cash flow that a new purchaser of the stock will receive, because D_0 has just been paid. D_0 is known with certainty, but all future dividends are expected values, so the estimate of D_t may differ among investors.[4]

P_0 = Actual **market price** of the stock today.

$\hat{P}_t$ = Expected price of the stock at the end of each Year t (pronounced "P hat t"). $\hat{P}_0$ is the **intrinsic,** or **fundamental, value** of the stock today as seen by the particular investor doing the analysis; $\hat{P}_1$ is the price expected at the end of 1 year; and so on. Note that $\hat{P}_0$ is the intrinsic value of the stock today based on a particular investor's estimate of the stock's expected dividend stream and the risk of that stream. Hence, whereas the market price P_0 is fixed and is identical for all investors, $\hat{P}_0$ could differ among investors depending on how optimistic they are regarding the company. The caret, or "hat," is used to indicate that $\hat{P}_t$ is an estimated future value. $\hat{P}_0$, the individual investor's estimate of the intrinsic value today, could be above or below P_0, the current stock price, but an investor would buy the stock only if his estimate of $\hat{P}_0$ were equal to or greater than P_0.

Since there are many investors in the market, there can be many values for $\hat{P}_0$. However, we can think of a group of "average," or "marginal," investors whose actions actually determine the market price. For these marginal investors, P_0 must equal $\hat{P}_0$; otherwise, a disequilibrium would exist, and buying and selling in the market would cause P_0 to change until $P_0 = \hat{P}_0$ as seen by the marginal investor.

D_1/P_0 = Expected **dividend yield** during the coming year. If the stock is expected to pay a dividend of $D_1 = \$1$ during the next 12 months and if its current price is $P_0 = \$10$, then the expected dividend yield is $\$1/\$10 = 0.10 = 10\%$.

$\dfrac{\hat{P}_1 - P_0}{P_0}$ = Expected **capital gains yield** during the coming year. If the stock sells for $10 today and if it is expected to rise to $10.50 at the end of one year, then the expected capital gain is $\hat{P}_1 - P_0 = \$10.50 - \$10.00 = \$0.50$, and the expected capital gains yield is $\$0.50/\$10 = 0.05 = 5\%$.

g = Expected **growth rate** in dividends as predicted by a marginal investor. If dividends are expected to grow at a constant rate, then g is also the expected rate of growth in earnings and the stock's price. Different investors may use different values of g to evaluate a firm's stock, but the market price, P_0, is set on the basis of g as estimated by the marginal investor.

---

4. Stocks generally pay dividends quarterly, so theoretically we should evaluate them on a quarterly basis. However, in stock valuation, most analysts work on an annual basis because the data generally are not precise enough to warrant refinement to a quarterly model. For additional information on the quarterly model, see Robert Brooks and Billy Helms, "An N-Stage, Fractional Period, Quarterly Dividend Discount Model," *Financial Review,* November 1990, pp. 651–657.

r_s = Minimum acceptable return, or **required rate of return,** on the stock, considering both its risk and the returns available on other investments. Again, this term generally relates to the marginal investor. The primary determinants of r_s include the real rate of return, expected inflation, and risk.

$\hat{r}_s$ = **Expected rate of return** that an investor who buys the stock expects to receive in the future. $\hat{r}_s$ (pronounced "r hat s") could be above or below r_s, but one would buy the stock only if $\hat{r}_s \geq r_s$. Note that the expected return ($\hat{r}_s$) is equal to the expected dividend yield (D_1/P_0) plus the expected capital gains yield ($[\hat{P}_1 - P_0]/P_0$). In our example, $\hat{r}_s = 10\% + 5\% = 15\%$.

$\bar{r}_s$ = **Actual,** or **realized,** *after-the-fact* **rate of return,** pronounced "r bar s." You may *expect* to obtain a return of $\hat{r}_s = 15\%$ if you buy Exxon-Mobil today, but if the market declines then you may end up next year with an actual realized return that is much lower and perhaps even negative.

5.5b Expected Dividends as the Basis for Stock Values

Like all financial assets, the value of a stock is estimated by finding the present value of a stream of expected future cash flows. What are the cash flows that corporations are expected to provide to their stockholders? First, think of yourself as an investor who buys a stock with the intention of holding it (in your family) forever. In this case, all that you (and your heirs) will receive is a stream of dividends, and the value of the stock today is calculated as the present value of an infinite stream of dividends:

(5–1)

$$\text{Value of stock} = \hat{P}_0 = \text{PV of expected future dividends}$$

$$= \frac{D_1}{(1+r_s)^1} + \frac{D_2}{(1+r_s)^2} + \cdots + \frac{D_\infty}{(1+r_s)^\infty}$$

$$= \sum_{t=1}^{\infty} \frac{D_t}{(1+r_s)^t}$$

What about the more typical case, where you expect to hold the stock for a finite period and then sell it—what is the value of $\hat{P}_0$ in this case? Unless the company is likely to be liquidated or sold and thus to disappear, *the value of the stock is again determined by Equation 5-1*. To see this, recognize that for any individual investor, the expected cash flows consist of expected dividends plus the expected sale price of the stock. However, the sale price a current investor receives will depend on the dividends some future investor expects. Therefore, for all present and future investors in total, expected cash flows must be based on expected future dividends. Put another way, unless a firm is liquidated or sold to another concern, the cash flows it provides to its stockholders will consist only of a stream of dividends. Therefore, the value of a share of its stock must be the present value of that expected dividend stream.

The general validity of Equation 5-1 can also be confirmed by solving the following problem. Suppose I buy a stock and expect to hold it for 1 year. I will receive dividends during the year plus the value $\hat{P}_1$ when I sell at the end of the year. But what will determine the value of $\hat{P}_1$? The answer is that it will be determined as the present value of the dividends expected during Year 2 plus the stock price at the end of that year, which, in turn, will be determined as the present value of another set of future dividends and an even more distant stock price. This process can be continued ad infinitum, and the ultimate result is Equation 5-1.[5]

Self Test

What are the two components of most stocks' expected total return?

How does one calculate the capital gains yield and the dividend yield of a stock?

If D_1 = $3.00, P_0 = $50, and $\hat{P}_1$ = $52, what are the stock's expected dividend yield, expected capital gains yield, and expected total return for the coming year? (**6%, 4%, 10%**)

5.6 Valuing a Constant Growth Stock

Equation 5-1 is a generalized stock valuation model in that the time pattern of D_t can be anything: D_t can be rising, falling, fluctuating randomly, or even zero for several years, yet Equation 5-1 will still hold. With a computer spreadsheet we can easily use this equation to find a stock's intrinsic value for any pattern of dividends.[6] In practice, the hard part is getting an accurate forecast of the future dividends. However, in many cases the stream of dividends is expected to grow at a constant rate, and if so then Equation 5-1 can be rewritten as follows:

$$\hat{P}_0 = \frac{D_0(1+g)^1}{(1+r_s)^1} + \frac{D_0(1+g)^2}{(1+r_s)^2} + \cdots + \frac{D_0(1+g)^\infty}{(1+r_s)^\infty}$$

$$= D_0 \sum_{t=1}^{\infty} \frac{(1+g)^t}{(1+r_s)^t} \qquad (5\text{–}2)$$

$$= \frac{D_0(1+g)}{r_s - g} = \frac{D_1}{r_s - g}$$

---

5. It is ironic that investors periodically lose sight of the long-run nature of stocks as investments and forget that, in order to sell a stock at a profit, one must find a buyer who will pay the higher price. If you analyze a stock's value in accordance with Equation 5-1, conclude that the stock's market price exceeds a reasonable value, and then buy the stock anyway, then you would be following the "bigger fool" theory of investment—you think that you may be a fool to buy the stock at its excessive price, but you think that when you get ready to sell it, you can find someone who is an even bigger fool. The bigger fool theory was widely followed in the spring of 2000, just before the Nasdaq market lost more than one-third of its value, and then again in the housing market before it peaked in mid-2006.

6. Actually, we can only find an approximate price. However, if we project dividends for 100 or so years, the present value of that finite dividend stream is approximately equal to the present value of the infinite dividend stream.

WEB

The last term in Equation 5-2 is derived in **Web Extension 5A** on the textbook's Web site.

The last term of Equation 5-2 is called the **constant growth model**, or the **Gordon model**, after Myron J. Gordon, who did much to develop and popularize it.

A necessary condition for the validity of Equation 5-2 is that r_s be greater than g. Look back at the second form of Equation 5-2. If g is larger than r_s, then $(1 + g)^t/(1 + r_s)^t$ must always be greater than 1. In this case, the second line of Equation 5-2 is the sum of an infinite number of terms, with each term being larger than 1. Therefore, if g were constant and greater than r_s, the resulting stock price would be infinite! Since no company is worth an infinite amount, it is impossible to have a constant growth rate that is greater than r_s forever. Similarly, a student will occasionally plug a value for g that is greater than r_s into the last form of Equation 5-2 and report a negative stock price. This is nonsensical. The last form of Equation 5-2 is valid only when g is less than r_s. *If g is greater than r_s then the constant growth model cannot be used, and the answer you would get from using Equation 5-2 would be wrong and misleading.*

5.6a Illustration of a Constant Growth Stock

Assume that MicroDrive just paid a dividend of $1.15 (that is, D_0 = $1.15). Its stock has a required rate of return, r_s, of 13.4%, and investors expect the dividend to grow at a constant 8% rate in the future. The estimated dividend 1 year hence would be D_1 = $1.15(1.08) = $1.24; D_2 would be $1.34; and the estimated dividend 5 years hence would be $1.69:

$$D_t = D_0(1 + g)^t = \$1.15(1.08)^5 = \$1.69$$

We could use this procedure to estimate each future dividend and then use Equation 5-1 to determine the current stock value, $\hat{P}_0$. In other words, we could find each expected future dividend, calculate its present value, and then sum all the present values to find the intrinsic value of the stock.

Such a process would be time-consuming, but we can take a shortcut—just insert the illustrative data into Equation 5-2 to find the stock's intrinsic value, $23:

$$\hat{P}_0 = \frac{\$1.15(1.08)}{0.134 - 0.08} = \frac{\$1.242}{0.054} = \$23.00$$

The concept underlying the valuation process for a constant growth stock is graphed in Figure 5-3. Dividends are growing at the rate g = 8%, but because r_s > g, the present value of each future dividend is declining. For example, the dividend in Year 1 is $D_1 = D_0(1 + g)^1 = \$1.15(1.08) = \$1.242$. However, the present value of this dividend, discounted at 13.4%, is $PV(D_1) = \$1.242/(1.134)^1 = \$1.095$. The dividend expected in Year 2 grows to $1.242(1.08) = $1.341, but the present value of this dividend falls to $1.043. Continuing, D_3 = $1.449 and $PV(D_3)$ = $0.993, and so on. Thus, the expected dividends are growing, but the present value of each successive dividend is declining, because the dividend growth rate (8%) is less than the rate used for discounting the dividends to the present (13.4%).

If we summed the present values of each future dividend, this summation would be the value of the stock, $\hat{P}_0$. When g is a constant, this summation is equal to $D_1/(r_s - g)$, as shown in Equation 5-2. Therefore, if we extended the lower step-function curve in Figure 5-3 on out to infinity and added up the present values of each future dividend, the summation would be identical to the value given by Equation 5-2, $23.00.

Although Equation 5-2 assumes there are *infinite* time periods, most of the value is based on dividends during a *finite* time period. In our example, 70% of the

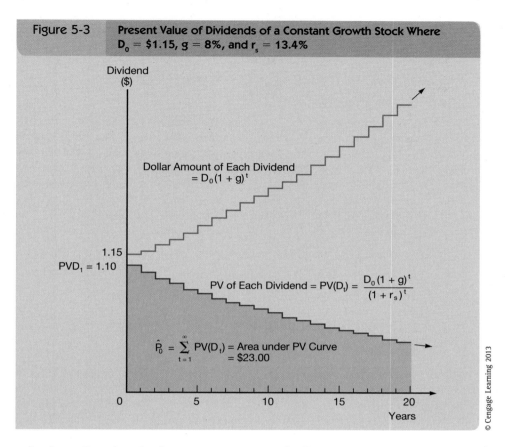

Figure 5-3 **Present Value of Dividends of a Constant Growth Stock Where $D_0 = \$1.15$, $g = 8\%$, and $r_s = 13.4\%$**

value is attributed to the first 25 years, 91% to the first 50 years, and 99.4% to the first 100 years. This means that companies don't have to survive forever to justify using the Gordon growth model.

5.6b Dividend and Earnings Growth

Because a stock price depends on *all future dividends*, not just next year's dividend, increasing next year's dividend will not have much impact on stock price unless investors expect the dividend increase to be sustainable. Dividends are paid with cash, which means sustainable dividend growth must come from sustainable cash flow growth. The cash flow that is available for distribution to shareholders depends on profitability, investments in operating capital, and the level of debt. Dividends, profitability, capital investments, and capital structure are all interrelated, especially in the long term. A dollar used to pay dividends can't be used for reinvestment in the firm or to pay down debt, so everything else equal, higher dividends must be associated with lower growth or a higher debt level. Growth in dividends can be supported by increasing debt, but to avoid unacceptably high levels of debt, long-term dividend growth must be limited to long-term earnings growth.

Earnings per share (EPS) growth depends on economy-wide factors (such as recessions and inflation), industry-wide factors (such as technological innovations), and firm-specific factors (management skill, brand identity, patent protection, etc.). For a firm to grow faster than the economy, either the industry must become a bigger part of the economy or the firm must take market share from its competitors. In the long run, competition and market saturation will tend to limit EPS growth to the sum of population growth and inflation. And as we just explained, the long-term dividend growth rate cannot exceed the long-term EPS growth rate.

5.6c Do Stock Prices Reflect Long-Term or Short-Term Events?

Managers often complain that the stock market is shortsighted and that investors care only about conditions over the next few years. Let's use the constant growth model to test this assertion. MicroDrive's most recent dividend was $1.15, and it is expected to grow at a rate of 8% per year. Since we know the growth rate, we can forecast the dividends for each of the next 5 years and then find their present values:

$$
\begin{aligned}
PV &= \frac{D_0(1+g)^1}{(1+r_s)^1} + \frac{D_0(1+g)^2}{(1+r_s)^2} + \frac{D_0(1+g)^3}{(1+r_s)^3} + \frac{D_0(1+g)^4}{(1+r_s)^4} + \frac{D_0(1+g)^5}{(1+r_s)^5} \\
&= \frac{\$1.15(1.08)^1}{(1.134)^1} + \frac{\$1.15(1.08)^2}{(1.134)^2} + \frac{\$1.15(1.08)^3}{(1.134)^3} + \frac{\$1.15(1.08)^4}{(1.134)^4} + \frac{\$1.15(1.08)^5}{(1.134)^5} \\
&= \frac{\$1.242}{(1.134)^1} + \frac{\$1.341}{(1.134)^2} + \frac{\$1.449}{(1.134)^3} + \frac{\$1.565}{(1.134)^4} + \frac{\$1.690}{(1.134)^5} \\
&= 1.095 + 1.043 + 0.993 + 0.946 + 0.901 \\
&\approx \$5.00
\end{aligned}
$$

Recall that MicroDrive's stock price is $23.00. Therefore, only $5.00, or $5/$23 = 0.22 = 22%, of the $23.00 stock price is attributable to short-term cash flows. This means that MicroDrive's managers will affect the stock price more by working to increase long-term cash flows than by focusing on short-term flows. This situation holds for most companies. Indeed, a number of professors and consulting firms have used actual company data to show that more than 80% of a typical company's stock price is due to cash flows expected farther than 5 years in the future.

This brings up an interesting question. If most of a stock's value is due to long-term cash flows, then why do managers and analysts pay so much attention to quarterly earnings? Part of the answer lies in the information conveyed by short-term earnings. For example, when actual quarterly earnings are lower than expected not because of fundamental problems but only because a company has increased its research and development (R&D) expenditures, studies have shown that the stock price probably won't decline and may actually increase. This makes sense, because R&D should increase future cash flows. On the other hand, if quarterly earnings are lower than expected because customers don't like the company's new products, then this new information will have negative implications for future values of g, the long-term growth rate. As we show later in this chapter, even small changes in g can lead to large changes in stock prices. Therefore, quarterly earnings themselves might not be that important, but the information they convey about future prospects can be extremely important.

Another reason many managers focus on short-term earnings is that some firms pay managerial bonuses on the basis of current earnings rather than stock prices (which reflect future earnings). For these managers, the concern with quarterly earnings is not due to their effect on stock prices—it's due to their effect on bonuses.[7]

---

7. Many apparent puzzles in finance can be explained either by managerial compensation systems or by peculiar features of the Tax Code. So, if you can't explain a firm's behavior in terms of economic logic, look to compensation procedures or taxes as possible explanations.

5.6d When Can the Constant Growth Model Be Used?

The constant growth model is most appropriate for mature companies with a stable history of growth. Expected growth rates vary somewhat among companies, but dividend growth for most mature firms is generally expected to continue in the future at about the same rate as nominal gross domestic product (real GDP plus inflation). On this basis, one might expect the dividends of an average, or "normal," company to grow at a rate of 5% to 8% a year. Note, though, that the 2008–2009 recession caused many analysts to lower their expectations for long-run growth, and those lowered expectations contributed mightily to the stock market crash.

Note too that Equation 5-2 is sufficiently general to handle the case of a **zero growth stock,** where the dividend is expected to remain constant over time. If $g = 0$, then Equation 5-2 reduces to Equation 5-3:

$$\hat{P}_0 = \frac{D}{r_s}$$ (5–3)

This is essentially the equation for a perpetuity, and it is simply the dividend divided by the discount rate.

Self Test
Write out and explain the valuation formula for a constant growth stock.
Are stock prices affected more by long-term or short-term performance? Explain.
A stock is expected to pay a dividend of $2 at the end of the year. The required rate of return is $r_s = 12\%$. What would the stock's price be if the constant growth rate in dividends were 4%? (**$25.00**) What would the price be if $g = 0\%$? (**$16.67**)

5.7 Expected Rate of Return on a Constant Growth Stock

When using Equation 5-2, we first estimated D_0 and r_s, the *required* rate of return on the stock; then we solved for the stock's intrinsic value, which we compared to its actual market price. We can also reverse the process, observing the actual stock price, substituting it into Equation 5-2, and solving for the rate of return. In doing so, we are finding the *expected* rate of return, which will also equal the *required* rate of return, $\hat{r}_s = r_s$, if the market is in equilibrium:[8]

$$\begin{aligned}\hat{r}_s &= \begin{array}{c}\text{Expected rate}\\\text{of return}\end{array} = \begin{array}{c}\text{Expected}\\\text{dividend yield}\end{array} + \begin{array}{c}\text{Expected capital}\\\text{gains yield}\end{array}\\[6pt] &= \begin{array}{c}\text{Expected}\\\text{dividend yield}\end{array} + \begin{array}{c}\text{Expected}\\\text{growth rate}\end{array}\\[6pt] &= \frac{D_1}{P_0} + g\end{aligned}$$ (5–4)

---

8. We say that a stock is in *equilibrium* when $r_s = \hat{r}_s$ and $\hat{P}_0 = P_0$. We discuss this in more detail later in the chapter.

Thus, if you buy a stock for a price $P_0 = \$23$, and if you expect the stock to pay a dividend $D_1 = \$1.242$ 1 year from now and to grow at a constant rate $g = 8\%$ in the future, then your expected rate of return will be 13.4%:

$$\hat{r}_s = \frac{\$1.242}{\$23} + 8\% = 5.4\% + 8\% = 13.4\%$$

In this form, we see that $\hat{r}_s$ is the *expected total return* and that it consists of an *expected dividend yield*, $D_1/P_0 = 5.4\%$, plus an *expected growth rate* (which is also the *expected capital gains yield*) of $g = 8\%$.

Suppose that the current price, P_0, is equal to $23 and that the Year-1 expected dividend, D_1, is equal to $1.242. What is the expected price at the end of the first year, immediately after D_1 has been paid? First, we can estimate the expected Year-2 dividend as $D_2 = D_1(1 + g) = \$1.242(1.08) = \$1.3414$. Then we can apply a version of Equation 5-2 that is shifted ahead by 1 year, using D_2 instead of D_1 and solving for $\hat{P}_1$ instead of $\hat{P}_0$:

$$\hat{P}_1 = \frac{D_2}{r_s - g} + \frac{\$1.3414}{0.134 - 0.08} = \$24.84$$

Even easier, notice that $\hat{P}_1$ must be 8% larger than $23, the price found 1 year earlier for P_0:

$$\$23(1.08) = \$24.84$$

Either way, we expect a capital gain of $24.84 - $23.00 = $1.84 during the year, which is a capital gains yield of 8%:

$$\text{Capital gains yield} = \frac{\text{Capital gains}}{\text{Beginning price}} = \frac{\$1.84}{\$23.00} = 0.08 = 8\%$$

We could extend the analysis, and in each future year the expected capital gains yield would always equal g, the expected dividend growth rate.

The dividend yield during the year could be estimated as follows:

$$\text{Dividend yield} = \frac{D_2}{\hat{P}_1} = \frac{\$1.3414}{\$24.84} = 0.054 = 5.4\%$$

The dividend yield for the following year could also be calculated, and again it would be 5.4%. Thus, *for a constant growth stock*, the following conditions must hold:

1. The dividend is expected to grow forever at a constant rate, g.
2. The stock price will also grow at this same rate.
3. The expected dividend yield is constant.
4. The expected capital gains yield is also constant and is equal to g, the dividend (and stock price) growth rate.
5. The expected total rate of return, $\hat{r}_s$, is equal to the expected dividend yield plus the expected growth rate: $\hat{r}_s =$ dividend yield $+ g$.

The term *expected* should be clarified—it means "expected" in a probabilistic sense, as the "statistically expected" outcome. Thus, if we say the growth rate is expected to remain constant at 8%, we mean that the best prediction for the growth rate in any future year is 8%, not that we literally expect the growth rate to be exactly 8% in each future year. In this sense, the constant growth assumption is a reasonable one for many large, mature companies.

Self Test

What conditions must hold in order for a stock to be evaluated using the constant growth model?

What does the term "expected" mean when we say "expected growth rate"?

If D_0 = \$4.00, r_s = 9%, and g = 5% for a constant growth stock, what are the stock's expected dividend yield and capital gains yield for the coming year? **(4%, 5%)**

5.8 Valuing Nonconstant Growth Stocks

For many companies, it is not appropriate to assume that dividends will grow at a constant rate. Firms typically go through *life cycles*. During their early years, their growth is much faster than that of the economy as a whole; then they match the economy's growth; and finally their growth is slower than that of the economy.[9] Automobile manufacturers in the 1920s, software companies such as Microsoft in the 1990s, and technology firms such as Cisco in the 2000s are examples of firms in the early part of the cycle; these firms are called **supernormal,** or **nonconstant, growth** firms. Figure 5-4 illustrates nonconstant growth and also compares it with normal growth, zero growth, and negative growth.[10]

In Figure 5-4, the dividends of the nonconstant growth firm are expected to grow at a 30% rate for 3 years, after which the growth rate is expected to fall to 8%, the assumed average for the economy. The value of this firm, like any other, is the present value of its expected future dividends as determined by Equation 5-1. When D_t is growing at a constant rate, we simplify Equation 5-1 to $\hat{P}_0 = D_1/(r_s - g)$. In the nonconstant case, however, the expected growth rate is not a constant—it declines at the end of the nonconstant growth period.

Because Equation 5-2 requires a constant growth rate, we obviously cannot use it to value stocks that have nonconstant growth. However, assuming a company currently experiencing nonconstant growth will eventually slow down and become a constant growth stock, we can use Equation 5-2 to help find the stock's value. First,

---

9. The concept of life cycles could be broadened to *product cycle,* which would include both small start-up companies and large companies like Apple, which periodically introduce new products that give sales and earnings a boost. We should also mention *business cycles,* which alternately depress and boost sales and profits. The growth rate just after a major new product has been introduced, or just after a firm emerges from the depths of a recession, is likely to be much higher than the "expected long-run average growth rate," which is the number that should be used in a DCF analysis.

10. A negative growth rate indicates a declining company. A mining company whose profits are falling because of a declining ore body is an example. Someone buying such a company would expect its earnings, and consequently its dividends and stock price, to decline each year, and this would lead to capital losses rather than capital gains. Obviously, a declining company's stock price will be relatively low, and its dividend yield must be high enough to offset the expected capital loss and still produce a competitive total return. Students sometimes argue that they would never be willing to buy a stock whose price was expected to decline. However, if the annual dividends are large enough to *more than offset* the falling stock price, the stock could still provide a fair return.

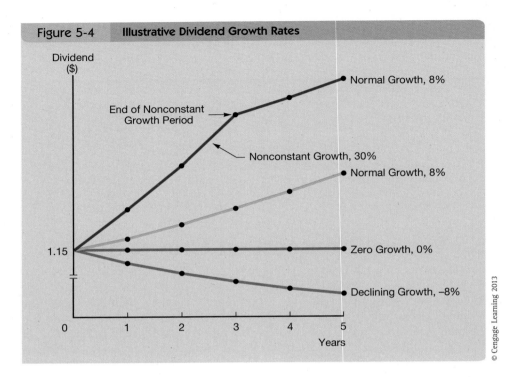

Figure 5-4   Illustrative Dividend Growth Rates

we assume that the dividend will grow at a nonconstant rate (generally a relatively high rate) for N periods, after which it will grow at a constant rate, g. Often N is called the **horizon date** or the **terminal date**.

Recall that a stock's current intrinsic value, $\hat{P}_0$, is the present value of all dividends after Time 0, discounted back to Time 0. Similarly, the intrinsic value of a stock at Time N is the present value of all dividends beyond Time N, discounted back to Time N. When dividends beyond Time N are expected to grow at a constant rate, we can use a variation of the constant growth formula, Equation 5-2, to estimate the stock's intrinsic value at Time N. The intrinsic value at Time N is often called the **horizon value** or the **terminal value**:

(5–5)
$$\text{Horizon value} = \hat{P}_N = \frac{D_{N+1}}{r_s - g} = \frac{D_N(1 + g)}{r_s - g}$$

A stock's intrinsic value today, $\hat{P}_0$, is the present value of the dividends during the nonconstant growth period plus the present value of the dividends after the horizon date:

$$\hat{P}_0 = \underbrace{\frac{D_1}{(1 + r_s)^1} + \frac{D_2}{(1 + r_s)^2} + \cdots + \frac{D_N}{(1 + r_s)^N}}_{\substack{\text{PV of dividends during the} \\ \text{nonconstant growth period} \\ t = 1 \text{ to } N}} + \underbrace{\frac{D_{N+1}}{(1 + r_s)^{N+1}} + \cdots + \frac{D_\infty}{(1 + r_s)^\infty}}_{\substack{\text{PV of dividends during the} \\ \text{constant growth period} \\ t = N + 1 \text{ to } \infty}}$$

The horizon value is the value of all dividends beyond Time N discounted back to Time N. Discounting the horizon value from Time N to Time 0 provides an estimate of the present value of all dividends beyond the nonconstant growth period. Thus, the stock's current intrinsic value is the present value of all dividends during the nonconstant growth period plus the present value of the horizon value:

$$\hat{P}_0 = \left[\frac{D_1}{(1+r_s)^1} + \frac{D_2}{(1+r_s)^2} + \cdots + \frac{D_N}{(1+r_s)^N} \right] + \frac{\hat{P}_N}{(1+r_s)^N}$$

$$= \left[\frac{D_1}{(1+r_s)^1} + \frac{D_2}{(1+r_s)^2} + \cdots + \frac{D_N}{(1+r_s)^N} \right] + \frac{[(D_{N+1})/(r_s - g)]}{(1+r_s)^N}$$

(5–6)

To implement Equation 5-6, we go through the following three steps.

1. Estimate the expected dividends for each year during the period of nonconstant growth.
2. Find the expected price of the stock at the end of the nonconstant growth period, at which point it has become a constant growth stock.
3. Find the present values of the expected dividends during the nonconstant growth period and the present value of the expected stock price at the end of the nonconstant growth period. Their sum is the intrinsic value of the stock, $\hat{P}_0$.

To illustrate the process for valuing nonconstant growth stocks, we make the following assumptions.

r_s = Stockholders' required rate of return = 13.4%. This rate is used to discount all the cash flows.

N = Years of nonconstant growth = 3.

$g_{t,t+1}$ = Rate of growth in both earnings and dividends during the nonconstant growth period from period t to the next period. $g_{0,1}$ = 30%, $g_{1,2}$ = 20%, and $g_{2,3}$ = 10%. These rates are shown directly on the time line.

g_L = Rate of constant long-term growth after the nonconstant period = 8%. This rate is also shown on the time line, between Years 3 and 4.

D_0 = Last dividend the company paid = $1.15.

WEB

See *Ch05 Tool Kit.xls* on the textbook's Web site.

The valuation process as diagrammed in Figure 5-5 is explained in the steps set forth below the time line. The estimated value of the nonconstant growth stock is $31.13.

Self Test

Explain how one would find the value of a nonconstant growth stock.

Explain what is meant by the terms "horizon (terminal) date" and "horizon (terminal) value."

Suppose D_0 = $5.00 and r_s = 10%. The expected growth rate from Year 0 to Year 1 (g_1) = 20%, the expected growth rate from Year 1 to Year 2 (g_2) = 10%, and the constant growth rate beyond Year 2 is g_L = 5%. What are the expected dividends for Year 1 and Year 2? **($6.00 and $6.60)** What is the expected horizon value price at Year 2 ($\hat{P}_2$)? **($138.60)** What is $\hat{P}_0$? **($125.45)**

Figure 5-5 **Process for Finding the Value of a Nonconstant Growth Stock**

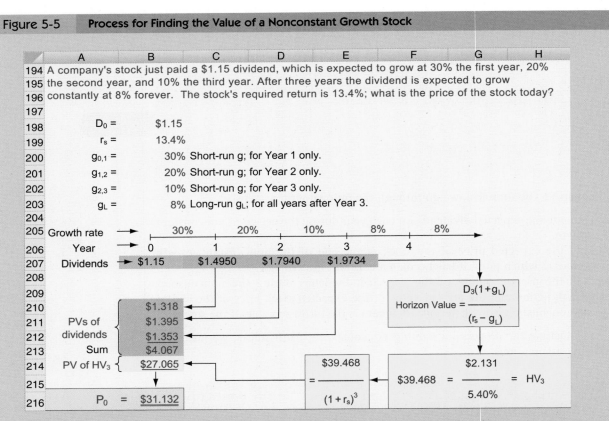

194 A company's stock just paid a $1.15 dividend, which is expected to grow at 30% the first year, 20%
195 the second year, and 10% the third year. After three years the dividend is expected to grow
196 constantly at 8% forever. The stock's required return is 13.4%; what is the price of the stock today?

$D_0 =$ $1.15

$r_s =$ 13.4%

$g_{0,1} =$ 30% Short-run g; for Year 1 only.

$g_{1,2} =$ 20% Short-run g; for Year 2 only.

$g_{2,3} =$ 10% Short-run g; for Year 3 only.

$g_L =$ 8% Long-run g_L; for all years after Year 3.

Growth rate: 30% 20% 10% 8% 8%

Year: 0 1 2 3 4

Dividends: $1.15 $1.4950 $1.7940 $1.9734

$$\text{Horizon Value} = \frac{D_3(1+g_L)}{(r_s - g_L)}$$

PVs of dividends:
$1.318
$1.395
$1.353

Sum: $4.067

PV of HV$_3$: $27.065

$$= \frac{\$39.468}{(1 + r_s)^3}$$

$$\$39.468 = \frac{\$2.131}{5.40\%} = HV_3$$

$P_0 =$ $31.132

Notes:

Step 1: Calculate the dividends expected at the end of each year during the nonconstant growth period. Calculate the first dividend, $D_1 = D_0(1 + g_{0,1}) = \$1.15(1.30) = \$1.4950$. Here $g_{0,1}$ is the growth rate (30%) during the first year of the nonconstant growth period. Show the $1.4950 on the time line as the cash flow at Year 1. Then calculate $D_2 = D_1(1 + g_{1,2}) = \$1.4950(1.20) = \$1.7940$ and then $D_3 = D_2(1 + g_{2,3}) = \$1.7940(1.10) = \$1.9734$. (The figure shows the values rounded to four decimal places, but all calculations used nonrounded values.) Show these values on the time line as the cash flows at Year 2 and Year 3. Note that D_0 is used only to calculate D_1.

Step 2: At Year 3, the stock becomes a constant growth stock. Therefore, we can use the constant growth formula to find $\hat{P}_3$, which is the PV of the dividends from Year 4 to infinity as evaluated at Year 3. First we determine $D_4 = \$1.9734(1.08) = \$2.1313$ for use in the formula, and then we calculate $\hat{P}_3$ as follows:

$$\hat{P}_3 = \frac{D_4}{r_s - g_n} = \frac{\$2.1313}{0.134 - 0.08} = \$39.4680$$

We show this $39.468 on the time line as a second cash flow at Year 3. The $39.468 is a Year-3 cash flow in the sense that the owner of the stock could sell it for $39.468 at Year 3 and also in the sense that $39.468 is the value at Year 3 of the dividend cash flows from Year 4 to infinity.

Step 3: Now that the cash flows have been placed on the time line, we can discount each cash flow at the required rate of return, $r_s = 13.4\%$. This produces the PVs shown to the left below the time line, and the sum of the PVs is the value of the nonconstant growth stock, $31.13.

In the figure we show the setup for an *Excel* solution. With a financial calculator, you could use the cash flow (CFLO) register of your calculator. Enter 0 for CF_0 because you get no cash flow at Time 0, $CF_1 = 1.495$, $CF_2 = 1.7940$, and $CF_3 = 1.9734 + 39.468 = 41.4414$. Then enter I/YR = 13.4 and press the NPV key to find the value of the stock, $31.1315.

5.9 Stock Valuation by the Free Cash Flow Approach

The box at the beginning of the chapter showed that the value of a firm is the present value of its future expected free cash flows (FCFs) discounted at the weighted average cost of capital (WACC). The following example illustrates how the firm's total value can be used to find the value of its stock.

Suppose Crum Inc. had a free cash flow of $200 million at the end of the most recent year. Chapter 9 shows how to forecast financial statements and free cash flows, but for now let's assume that Crum's FCFs are expected to grow at a constant rate of 5% per year forever. Chapter 10 explains how to estimate the weighted average cost of capital, but for now let's assume that Crum's WACC is 9%. The present value of the expected future free cash flows is the PV of a growing annuity, so we can use a variation of Equation 5-2, the value of a constantly growing stream of dividends:

$$V = \frac{FCF(1+g)}{WACC-g} = \frac{\$200(1.05)}{0.09-0.05} = \$5,250 \text{ million} \qquad (5\text{–}7)$$

FCF is the cash flow available for distribution to *all* of the firm's investors, bondholders as well as stockholders. Also, the WACC is the average rate of return required by *all* of the firm's investors, not just shareholders. Therefore, V is the value of the entire firm's operations, not just the value of its equity. If the firm had any nonoperating assets, such as short-term investments in marketable securities, then we would add them to V to find the firm's total value. Crum has no nonoperating assets, so its total value is $5,250 million. To find the value of its equity, subtract the value of claims held by all investors other than common shareholders, such as debtholders and preferred stockholders. If the value of debt plus preferred stock is $2,000 million, then Crum's common equity has a value of $5,250 − $2,000 = $3,250 million. If 325 million shares of stock are outstanding, then the intrinsic value of the stock is $3,250/325 = $10 per share. This example should give you the general idea behind the free cash flow approach to stock price valuation, but see Chapter 11 for a more comprehensive example, including a situation in which free cash flows are growing at a nonconstant rate.

Self Test

Explain how to find a firm's stock price using the free cash flow approach.

5.10 Market Multiple Analysis

If a company is publicly traded, then we can simply look up its most recent stock price to get an estimate of the stock's value. However, we must take another approach if the firm is privately owned. We could estimate the firm's cost of equity based on data for a sample of companies, forecast its earnings and dividends, and apply the DCF method to find the value of its stock. However, another method, **market multiple analysis,** can and generally would be used. Here we would take a metric for the firm—say, its EPS—and then multiply by a market-determined multiple such as the average P/E ratio for a sample of similar companies. This would give us an estimate of the stock's intrinsic value. Market multiples can also be applied to total net income, to sales, to book value, or to number of subscribers for businesses such as cable TV or cellular telephone systems. Whereas the discounted dividend method applies valuation concepts in a precise manner by focusing on expected cash flows, market multiple analysis is more judgmental.

To illustrate the concept, suppose Tapley Products is a privately held firm whose forecasted earnings per share are $7.70, and suppose the average price/earnings (P/E) ratio for a set of similar publicly traded companies is 12. To estimate the intrinsic value of Tapley's stock we would simply multiply its $7.70 EPS by the multiple 12, obtaining the value $7.70(12) = $92.40.

Another commonly used metric is *earnings before interest, taxes, depreciation, and amortization (EBITDA)*. The EBITDA *multiple* is the total value of a company (the market value of its equity plus that of its debt) divided by EBITDA. This multiple is based on total value, since EBITDA is used to compensate the firm's stockholders and bondholders. Therefore, it is called an **entity multiple.** The EBITDA market multiple is the average EBITDA multiple for a group of similar publicly traded companies. This procedure gives an estimate of the company's total value, and to find the estimated intrinsic value of the stock we would subtract the value of the debt from total value and then divide by the shares of stock outstanding.

As suggested previously, in some businesses, such as cable TV and cellular telephone, a critical factor is the number of customers the company has. For example, when a telephone company acquires a cellular operator, it might pay a price that is based on the number of customers. Managed care companies such as HMOs have applied similar logic in acquisitions, basing valuations primarily on the number of people insured. Some Internet companies have been valued by the number of "eyeballs," which is the number of hits on the site.

If you examine the prospectus for a firm that is having an IPO, or information regarding the acquisition of one firm by another, you will almost certainly see references to market multiple analysis. Security analysts also use this approach, sometimes as a primary measure and sometimes as a supplement to a DCF analysis, when estimating firms' intrinsic values.

Self Test

What is market multiple analysis?

What is an entity multiple?

5.11 Preferred Stock

Preferred stock is a *hybrid*—it's similar to bonds in some respects and to common stock in others. Like bonds, preferred stock has a par value, and a fixed amount of dividends must be paid before dividends can be paid on the common stock. However, if the preferred dividend is not earned, the directors can omit (or "pass") it without throwing the company into bankruptcy. So, although preferred stock has a fixed payment like bonds, a failure to make this payment will not lead to bankruptcy.

The dividends on preferred stocks are fixed, and if they are scheduled to go on forever, the issue is a perpetuity whose value is found as follows:

(5–8)

$$V_{ps} = \frac{D_{ps}}{r_{ps}}$$

V_{ps} is the value of the preferred stock, D_{ps} is the preferred dividend, and r_{ps} is the required rate of return. MicroDrive has preferred stock outstanding that pays a dividend of $10 per year. If the required rate of return on this preferred stock is 10%, then its value is $100:

$$V_{ps} = \frac{\$10.00}{0.10} = \$100.00$$

If we know the current price of a preferred stock and its dividend, we can transpose terms and solve for the expected rate of return as follows:

$$\hat{r}_{ps} = \frac{D_{ps}}{V_{ps}}$$

(5–9)

Some preferred stocks have a stated maturity, say, 50 years. If a firm's preferred stock matures in 50 years, pays a $10 annual dividend, has a par value of $100, and has a required return of 8%, then we can find its price using a financial calculator: Enter N = 50, I/YR = 8, PMT = 10, and FV = 100. Then press PV to find the price, V_{ps} = $124.47. If you know the price of a share of preferred stock, you can solve for I/YR to find the expected rate of return, $\hat{r}_{ps}$.

Most preferred stocks pay dividends quarterly. This is true for MicroDrive, so we could find the effective rate of return on its preferred stock as follows:

$$EFF\% = EAR = \left(1 + \frac{r_{NOM}}{M}\right)^M - 1 = \left(1 + \frac{0.10}{4}\right)^4 - 1 = 10.38\%$$

If an investor wanted to compare the returns on MicroDrive's bonds and its preferred stock, it would be best to convert the nominal rates on each security to effective rates and then compare these "equivalent annual rates."

Self Test

Explain the following statement: "Preferred stock is a hybrid security."

Is the equation used to value preferred stock more like the one used to evaluate perpetual bonds or the one used for common stock? Explain.

A preferred stock has an annual dividend of $5. The required return is 8%. What is the V_{ps}? (**$62.50**)

5.12 Stock Market Equilibrium

Recall that r_i, the required return on Stock i, can be found using the Capital Asset Pricing Model (CAPM) as discussed in Chapter 2:

$$r_i = r_{RF} + (RP_M)b_i$$

If the risk-free rate of return is 8%, the market risk premium, RP_M, is 4%, and Stock i has a beta of 2, then its required rate of return is 16%:

$$r_i = 8\% + (4\%)2.0$$

$$= 16\%$$

The **marginal investor** will want to buy Stock i if its expected rate of return is more than 16%, will want to sell it if the expected rate of return is less than 16%, and will be indifferent—and hence will hold but not buy or sell it—if the expected rate of return is exactly 16%.

Now suppose a typical investor's portfolio contains Stock i, and suppose she analyzes the stock's prospects and concludes that its earnings, dividends, and price can be expected to grow at a constant rate of 5% per year. The last dividend was $D_0 = \$2.8571$, so the next expected dividend is

$$D_1 = \$2.8571(1.05) = \$3$$

Our investor observes that the present price of the stock, P_0, is $30. Should she purchase more of Stock i, sell the stock, or maintain the present position?

The investor can calculate Stock i's *expected rate of return* as follows:

$$\hat{r}_i = \frac{D_1}{P_0} + g = \frac{\$3}{\$30} + 5\% = 15\%$$

Because the expected rate of return, 15%, is less than the required return, 16%, the investor would want to sell the stock, as would most other holders if this one is typical. However, few people would want to buy at the $30 price, so the present owners would be unable to find buyers unless they cut the price of the stock. Thus, the price would decline, and this decline would continue until the price reached $27.27, at which point the stock would be in **equilibrium**, defined as the price at which the expected rate of return, 16%, is equal to the required rate of return as seen by the marginal investor:

$$\hat{r}_i = \frac{\$3}{\$27.27} + 5\% = 11\% + 5\% = 16\% = r_i$$

Had the stock initially sold for less than $27.27, say, for $25, then events would have been reversed. Investors would have wanted to buy the stock because its expected rate of return would have exceeded its required rate of return, and buy orders would have driven the stock's price up to $27.27.

To summarize, in equilibrium two related conditions must hold:

1. A stock's expected rate of return as seen by the marginal investor must equal its required rate of return: $\hat{r}_i = r_i$.
2. The actual market price of the stock must equal its intrinsic value as estimated by the marginal investor: $P_0 = \hat{P}_0$.

Of course, some individual investors probably believe that $\hat{r}_i > r_i$ and $\hat{P}_0 > P_0$, hence they would invest in the stock, while other investors have the opposite view and would sell all of their shares. However, it is the marginal investor who establishes the actual market price, and for the marginal investor we must have $\hat{r}_i = r_i$ and $P_0 = \hat{P}_0$. If these conditions do not hold, trading will occur until they do.

5.12a Changes in Equilibrium Stock Prices and Market Volatility

Stock prices are not constant—as we demonstrated earlier in this chapter and elsewhere, they undergo violent changes at times. Indeed, many stocks declined by 80% or more during 2008, and a few enjoyed gains of up to 200% or even more. At the risk of understatement, the stock market is volatile!

To see how such changes can occur, assume that Stock i is in equilibrium, selling at a price of $27.27. If all expectations are met exactly, during the next year the price would gradually rise by 5%, to $28.63. However, many different events could occur to cause a change in the equilibrium price. To illustrate, consider again the set of inputs used to develop Stock i's price of $27.27, along with a new set of expected inputs:

	Variable Value	
	Original	**New**
Risk-free rate, r_{RF}	8%	7%
Market risk premium, $r_M - r_{RF}$	4%	3%
Stock i's beta coefficient, b_i	2.0	1.0
Stock i's expected growth rate, g_i	5%	6%
D_0	$2.8571	$2.8571
Price of Stock i	$27.27	?

Now give yourself a test: Would each of the indicated changes, by itself, lead to an increase, a decrease, or no change in the price, and what is your guess as to the new stock price?

Every change, taken alone, would lead to a higher price. Taken together, the first three would lower r_i from 16% to 10%:

$$\text{Original } r_i = 8\% + 4\%(2.0) = 16\%$$
$$\text{New } r_i = 7\% + 3\%(1.0) = 10\%$$

Using these values together with the new g = 6%, we find that $\hat{P}_0$ rises from $27.27 to $75.71:[11]

$$\text{Original } \hat{P}_0 = \frac{\$2.8571(1.05)}{0.16 - 0.05} = \frac{\$3}{0.11} = \$27.27$$

$$\text{New } \hat{P}_0 = \frac{\$2.8571(1.06)}{0.10 - 0.06} = \frac{\$3.0285}{0.04} = \$75.71$$

---

11   A price change of this magnitude is by no means rare. The prices of *many* stocks double or halve during any given year. For example, IDT Corporation, a provider of domestic and international long distance calling cards, increased 571% in 2010, while DJSP Enterprises, a company that specialized in providing non-legal support to the home foreclosure industry, lost 93.3% of its value.

At the new price, the expected and required rates of return are equal:[12]

$$\hat{r}_i = \frac{\$3.0285}{\$75.71} + 6\% = 10\% = r_i$$

This indicates that the stock is in equilibrium at the new and higher price. As this example illustrates, even small changes in the size of expected future dividends or in their risk, as reflected in the required return, can cause large changes in stock prices as the price moves from one equilibrium condition to another. What might cause investors to change their expectations about future dividends? It could be new information about the company, such as preliminary results for an R&D program, initial sales of a new product, or the discovery of harmful side effects from the use of an existing product. Or new information that will affect many companies could arrive, such as the collapse of the debt markets in 2008. Given the existence of computers and telecommunications networks, new information hits the market on an almost continuous basis, and it causes frequent and sometimes large changes in stock prices. In other words, *ready availability of information causes stock prices to be volatile.*

If a stock's price is stable, this probably means that little new information is arriving. But if you think it's risky to invest in a volatile stock, imagine how risky it would be to invest in a company that rarely releases new information about its sales or operations. It may be bad to see your stock's price jump around, but it would be a lot worse to see a stable quoted price most of the time and then to see huge moves on the rare days when new information is released.[13] Fortunately, in our economy timely information is readily available, and evidence suggests that stocks—especially those of large companies—adjust rapidly to new information. Consequently, equilibrium ordinarily exists for any given stock, and required and expected returns are generally equal. Stock prices certainly change, sometimes violently and rapidly, but this simply reflects changing conditions and expectations.

There are times, of course, when a stock appears to react for several months to favorable or unfavorable developments. However, this does not necessarily signify a long adjustment period; rather, it could simply indicate that, as more new pieces of information about the situation come out, the market adjusts to them. The ability of the market to adjust to new information is discussed in the next section.

Self Test

What two conditions must hold for a stock to be in equilibrium?

Why doesn't a volatile stock price imply irrational pricing?

---

12   It should be obvious by now that *actual realized* rates of return are not necessarily equal to expected and required returns. Thus, an investor might have *expected* to receive a return of 15% if he had bought IDT stock, but after the fact, the realized return was far above 15% in 2010. On the other hand, the 2010 actual realized return on DJSP stock was far below 15%.

13   Note, however, that if information came out infrequently, stock prices would probably be stable for a time and then experience large price swings when news did come out. This would be a bit like not having a lot of little earthquakes (frequent new information) that relieve stress along the fault and instead building up stress for a number of years before a massive earthquake.

5.13 The Efficient Markets Hypothesis

A body of theory called the **Efficient Markets Hypothesis (EMH)** asserts that (1) stocks are always in equilibrium and (2) it is impossible for an investor to "beat the market" and consistently earn a higher rate of return than is justified by the stock's risk. Those who believe in the EMH note that there are 100,000 or so full-time, highly trained, professional analysts and traders operating in the market, while there are fewer than 3,000 major stocks. Therefore, if each analyst followed 30 stocks (which is about right, as analysts tend to specialize in a specific industry), there would on average be 1,000 analysts following each stock. Furthermore, these analysts work for organizations such as Morgan Stanley, Goldman Sachs, CALPERS, Prudential Financial, and the like, which have billions of dollars available with which to take advantage of bargains. In addition, as a result of SEC disclosure requirements and electronic information networks, as new information about a stock becomes available, these analysts generally receive and evaluate it at the same time. Therefore, the price of a stock will adjust almost immediately to any new development. That, in a nutshell, is the logic behind the efficient markets hypothesis. However, there are variations on the theory, as we discuss next.

5.13a Weak-Form Efficiency

Technical analysts believe that past trends or patterns in stock prices can be used to predict future stock prices. In contrast, those who believe in the **weak form** of the EMH argue that all information contained in past price movements is fully reflected in current market prices. If the weak form were true, then information about recent trends in stock prices would be of no use in selecting stocks—the fact that a stock has risen for the past three days, for example, would give us no useful clues as to what it will do today or tomorrow. Those who believe that weak-form efficiency exists also believe that technical analysts, also known as "chartists," are wasting their time.

To illustrate the arguments, after studying the past history of the stock market, a technical analyst might "discover" the following pattern: If a stock falls for three consecutive days, its price typically rises by 10% the following day. The technician would then conclude that investors could make money by purchasing a stock whose price has fallen three consecutive days.

Weak-form advocates argue that if this pattern truly existed then other investors would soon discover it, and if so, why would anyone be willing to sell a stock after it had fallen for three consecutive days? In other words, why sell if you know that the price is going to increase by 10% the next day? Those who believe in weak-form efficiency argue that if the stock were really likely to rise to $44 tomorrow, then its price *today, right now,* would actually rise to somewhere close to $44, thereby eliminating the trading opportunity. Consequently, weak-form efficiency implies that any information that comes from past stock prices is rapidly incorporated into the current stock price.

5.13b Semistrong-Form Efficiency

The **semistrong form** of the EMH states that current market prices reflect all *publicly available* information. Therefore, if semistrong-form efficiency exists, it would do no good to pore over annual reports or other published data because market prices would have adjusted to any good or bad news contained in such reports back when the news came out. With semistrong-form efficiency, investors should expect to earn returns commensurate with risk, but they should not expect to do any better or worse other than by chance.

Another implication of semistrong-form efficiency is that whenever information is released to the public, stock prices will respond only if the information is different from what had been expected. For example, if a company announces a 30% increase in earnings and if that increase is about what analysts had been expecting, then the announcement should have little or no effect on the company's stock price. On the other hand, the stock price would probably fall if analysts had expected earnings to increase by more than 30%, but it probably would rise if they had expected a smaller increase.

5.13c Strong-Form Efficiency

The **strong form** of the EMH states that current market prices reflect all pertinent information, whether publicly available or privately held. If this form holds, even insiders would find it impossible to earn consistently abnormal returns in the stock market.

5.13d Is the Stock Market Efficient?

Many empirical studies have been conducted to test the validity of the three forms of market efficiency. Most empirical studies are joint tests of the EMH and an asset pricing model (usually the CAPM, discussed in Chapter 2 or the Fama-French three-factor model, discussed in Chapter 3). They are joint tests in the sense that they examine whether a particular strategy can beat the market, where "beating the market" means earning a return higher than that predicted by the particular asset pricing model. Most studies suggest that the stock market is highly efficient in the weak form and reasonably efficient in the semistrong form, at least for the larger and more widely followed stocks.[14] The evidence suggests that the strong form EMH does not hold, because those who possessed inside information could and did (illegally) make abnormal profits.

However, skeptics of the EMH point to the stock market bubbles that burst in 2000 and 2008 and suggest that, at the height of these booms, the stocks of many companies—especially in the technology sector—vastly exceeded their intrinsic values. These skeptics suggest that investors are not simply machines that rationally process all available information; rather, a variety of psychological and perhaps irrational factors also come into play. Indeed, researchers have begun to incorporate elements of cognitive psychology in an effort to better understand how individuals and entire

---

14. The vast majority of academic studies have shown that no excess returns (defined as returns above those predicted by the CAPM or other asset pricing models) can be earned with technical analysis—that is, using past stock prices to predict future stock prices—especially after considering transactions costs. A possible exception is in the area of long-term reversals, where several studies show that portfolios of stocks with poor past long-term performance tend to do slightly better than average in the future long term, and vice versa. Another possible exception is in the area of momentum, where studies show that stocks with strong performance in the short-term past tend to do slightly better than average in the short-term future, and likewise for weak performance. For example, see N. Jegadeesh and S. Titman, "Returns to Buying Winners and Selling Losers: Implications for Stock Market Efficiency," *Journal of Finance,* March 1993, pp. 69–91, and W. F. M. DeBondt and R. H. Thaler, "Does the Stock Market Overreact?" *Journal of Finance,* July 1985, pp. 793–808. However, when a way to "beat" the market becomes known, the actions of investors tend to eliminate it.

markets respond to different circumstances. In other words, if people aren't rational in their daily decisions, why should we expect them to be rational in their financial decisions? For example, studies show that investors tend to hold on too long to stocks that have performed poorly in the past (i.e., losers) but that they sell winners too quickly. This field of study is called *behavioral finance.*[15]

Keep in mind that the EMH does not assume that all investors are rational. Instead, it assumes that stock market prices track intrinsic values fairly closely. As we described earlier, new information should cause a stock's intrinsic value to move rapidly to a new level that reflects the new information. The EMH also assumes that if stock prices deviate from their intrinsic values, investors will *quickly* take advantage of this mispricing by buying undervalued stocks and selling overvalued stocks. Thus, investors' actions work to drive prices to their new equilibrium level based on new information. Even if some investors behave irrationally, as by holding losers too long and/or selling winners too quickly, this does not imply that the markets are not efficient. Thus, it is possible to have irrational investors in a rational market.

On the other hand, if the market itself is inherently irrational (i.e., if mispricings persist for long periods), then rational investors can lose a lot of money even if they are ultimately proven to be correct. For example, a "rational" investor in mid-1999 might have concluded that the Nasdaq was overvalued when it was trading at 3,000. If such an investor had acted on that assumption and sold stock short, he would have lost a lot of money the following year, when the Nasdaq soared to over 5,000 as "irrational exuberance" pushed the prices of already overvalued stocks to even higher levels. Ultimately, if our "rational investor" had the courage, patience, and financial resources to hold on, he would have been vindicated in the long run, because the Nasdaq subsequently fell from over 5,000 to about 1,300. But as the economist John Maynard Keynes said, "In the long run we are all dead."

What is the bottom line on market efficiency? Based on our reading of the evidence, we believe that for most stocks, for most of the time, it is generally safe to assume that the market is reasonably efficient in the sense that the intrinsic price is approximately equal to the actual market price ($\hat{P}_0 \approx P_0$). However, major shifts can and do occur periodically, causing most stocks to move strongly up or down. In the early 1980s, inflation was running over 10% per year and interest rates on AAA corporate bonds hit 15%. That knocked most stocks way below their intrinsic values, so when inflation fears receded, stock prices roared ahead. A similar situation, but in reverse, may have occurred in 2008 and 2009. Stock prices fell sharply, probably to a level below their intrinsic values, since they recovered substantially by 2011. In other words, we may have experienced a "reverse bubble."

5.13e Implications of Market Efficiency for Financial Decisions

What bearing does the EMH have on financial decisions? First, many investors have given up trying to beat the market because the professionals who manage

---

15. Three noteworthy sources for students interested in behavioral finance are: Richard H. Thaler, Editor, *Advances in Behavioral Finance* (New York: Russell Sage Foundation, 1993); Andrei Shleifer, *Inefficient Markets: An Introduction to Behavioral Finance* (New York: Oxford University Press, 2000); and Nicholas Barberis and Richard Thaler, "A Survey of Behavioral Finance," Chapter 18 in *Handbook of the Economics of Finance,* edited by George Constantinides, Milt Harris, and René Stulz (Amsterdam: Elsevier/North-Holland, 2003). Students interested in learning more about the Efficient Markets Hypothesis should consult Burton G. Malkiel, *A Random Walk Down Wall Street* (New York: W.W. Norton & Company, 2007).

mutual fund portfolios, on average, do not outperform the overall stock market as measured by an index like the S&P 500.[16] Indeed, the relatively poor performance of actively managed mutual funds helps explain the growing popularity of index funds, where administrative costs are lower than for actively managed funds. Rather than spending time and money trying to find undervalued stocks, index funds try instead to match overall market returns by buying the basket of stocks that makes up a particular index, such as the S&P 500.

Second, market efficiency also has important implications for managerial decisions, especially stock issues, stock repurchases, and tender offers. If the market prices stocks fairly, then managerial decisions based on the premise that a stock is undervalued or overvalued might not make sense. Managers may have better information about their

RATIONAL BEHAVIOR VERSUS ANIMAL SPIRITS, HERDING, AND ANCHORING BIAS

If investors were completely rational, they would carefully analyze all the available information about stocks and then make well-informed decisions to buy, sell, or hold them. Most academics have argued that investors with enough clout to move the market behave in this manner. However, the stock market bubbles of 2000 and 2008 suggest that something other than pure rationality is alive and well.

The great economist John Maynard Keynes, writing during the 1920s and 1930s, suggested that **animal spirits** influence markets. After a period of rising prosperity and stock prices, Keynes believed that investors begin to think that the good times will last forever, a feeling that is driven by happy talk and high spirits rather than cool reasoning. Indeed, psychologists have demonstrated that many people do in fact anchor too closely on recent events when predicting future events, a phenomenon called **anchoring bias.** Therefore, when the market is performing better than average, they tend to think it will continue to perform better than average. Even worse, when one group of investors does well, other investors begin to emulate them, acting like a herd of sheep following one another merrily down the road. Such **herding behavior** makes it easy for hedge funds to raise enormous sums and for con men like Bernie Madoff to find new marks.

Overinflated markets and bubbles eventually burst, and when they do, the same psychological factors act in reverse, often causing bigger declines than can be explained by rational models. Eventually, though, markets bottom out, and before long the next bubble starts to inflate. Historically, such cycles have existed for as far back as our data go, and these cycles are inconsistent with the idea of rational, data-driven investors. This is the realm of behavioral finance as discussed earlier in the chapter.

How can we reconcile theories that assume investors and decision makers are rational and data-driven with the fact that businesses and the stock market are influenced by people subject to animal spirits and herding instincts? Our conclusion is that there is some truth in both theories—markets are rational to a large extent, but they are also subject to irrational behavior at times. Our advice is to do careful, rational analyses, using the tools and techniques described in this book, but also to recognize that actual prices can differ from intrinsic values—sometimes by large amounts and for long periods. That's the bad news. The good news is that differences between actual prices and intrinsic values provide wonderful opportunities for those able to capitalize on them.

---

16. For a discussion of the performance of actively managed funds, see Jonathan Clements, "Resisting the Lure of Managed Funds," *The Wall Street Journal,* February 27, 2001, p. C1.

own companies than outsiders, but it would be illegal to use this information for their own advantage, and they cannot deliberately defraud investors by knowingly putting out false information.

What is the Efficient Markets Hypothesis (EMH)?

What are the differences among the three forms of the EMH?

What are the implications of the EMH for financial decisions?

Summary

Corporate decisions should be analyzed in terms of how alternative courses of action are likely to affect a firm's value. However, it is necessary to know how stock prices are established before attempting to measure how a given decision will affect a firm's value. This chapter showed how stock values are determined and also how investors go about estimating the rates of return they expect to earn. The key concepts covered are listed below.

- A **proxy** is a document that gives one person the power to act for another, typically the power to vote shares of common stock. A **proxy fight** occurs when an outside group solicits stockholders' proxies in an effort to overthrow the current management.
- A **takeover** occurs when a person or group succeeds in ousting a firm's management and takes control of the company.
- Stockholders often have the right to purchase any additional shares sold by the firm. This right, called the **preemptive right**, protects the present stockholders' control and prevents dilution of their value.
- Although most firms have only one type of common stock, in some instances **classified stock** is used to meet the special needs of the company. One type is **founders' shares.** This is stock owned by the firm's founders that carries sole voting rights but restricted dividends for a specified number of years.
- A **closely held company** is one whose stock is owned by a few individuals who are typically associated with the firm's management.
- A **publicly held company** is one whose stock is owned by a relatively large number of individuals who are not actively involved in the firm's management. Publicly held companies are generally regulated by the SEC or other governmental bodies.
- The **intrinsic value of a share of stock** is calculated as the **present value of the stream of dividends** the stock is expected to provide in the future.

- The equation used to find the **intrinsic, or expected, value of a constant growth stock** is

$$\hat{P}_0 = \frac{D_1}{r_s - g}$$

  Web Extension 5A provides a derivation of this formula.
- The **expected total rate of return** from a stock consists of an **expected dividend yield** plus an **expected capital gains yield.** For a constant growth firm, both the dividend yield and the capital gains yield are expected to remain constant in the future.
- The equation for $\hat{r}_s$, the **expected rate of return on a constant growth stock,** is

$$\hat{r}_s = \frac{D_1}{P_0} + g$$

- A **zero growth stock** is one whose future dividends are not expected to grow at all. A **nonconstant growth stock** is one whose earnings and dividends are expected to grow much faster than the economy as a whole over some specified time period and then to grow at the "normal" rate.
- To find the **present value of a nonconstant growth stock,** (1) find the dividends expected during the nonconstant growth period, (2) find the price of the stock at the end of the nonconstant growth period, (3) discount the dividends and the projected price back to the present, and (4) sum these PVs to find the current intrinsic, or expected, value of the stock, $\hat{P}_0$.
- The **horizon (terminal) date** is the date when individual dividend forecasts are no longer made because the dividend growth rate is assumed to be constant thereafter.
- The **horizon (terminal) value** is the value at the horizon date of all future dividends after that date:

$$\hat{P}_N = \frac{D_{N+1}}{r_s - g}$$

- **Preferred stock** is a hybrid security having some characteristics of debt and some of equity.
- The **value of a share of perpetual preferred stock** is found as the dividend divided by the required rate of return:

$$V_{ps} = \frac{D_{ps}}{r_{ps}}$$

- **Preferred stock** that has a finite maturity is evaluated with a formula that is identical in form to the bond value formula.
- The **marginal investor** is a representative investor whose actions reflect the beliefs of those people who are currently trading a stock. It is the marginal investor who determines a stock's price.
- **Equilibrium** is the condition under which the expected return on a security as seen by the marginal investor is just equal to its required return, $\hat{r}_s = r_s$. Also, the stock's intrinsic value must be equal to its market price, $\hat{P}_0 = P_0$.

- The **Efficient Markets Hypothesis (EMH)** holds that (1) stocks are always in equilibrium and (2) it is impossible for an investor who does not have inside information to consistently "beat the market." Therefore, according to the EMH, stocks are always fairly valued ($\hat{P}_0 = P_0$) and have a required return equal to their expected return ($r_s = \hat{r}_s$).
- **Animal spirits** refers to the tendency of investors to become excited and let their emotions affect their behavior; **herding instincts** refers to the tendency of investors to follow the crowd, relying on others rather than their own analysis; and **anchoring bias** is the human tendency to "anchor" too closely on recent events when predicting future events. These three factors can interfere with basing decisions on pure rational analysis.

Questions

5-1 Define each of the following terms:
a. Proxy; proxy fight; takeover; preemptive right; classified stock; founders' shares
b. Closely held stock; publicly owned stock
c. Intrinsic value ($\hat{P}_0$); market price (P_0)
d. Required rate of return, r_s; expected rate of return, $\hat{r}_s$; actual, or realized, rate of return, $\bar{r}_s$
e. Capital gains yield; dividend yield; expected total return
f. Normal, or constant, growth; nonconstant growth; zero growth stock
g. Preferred stock
h. Equilibrium; Efficient Markets Hypothesis (EMH); three forms of EMH
i. Purely rational behavior; animal spirits; herding instincts; anchoring; behavioral finance

5-2 Two investors are evaluating General Electric's stock for possible purchase. They agree on the expected value of D_1 and also on the expected future dividend growth rate. Further, they agree on the risk of the stock. However, one investor normally holds stocks for 2 years and the other normally holds stocks for 10 years. On the basis of the type of analysis done in this chapter, they should both be willing to pay the same price for General Electric's stock. True or false? Explain.

5-3 A bond that pays interest forever and has no maturity date is a perpetual bond, also called a perpetuity or a consol. In what respect is a perpetual bond similar to (1) a no-growth common stock and (2) a share of preferred stock?

5-4 In this chapter and elsewhere we have argued that a stock's market price can deviate from its intrinsic value. Discuss the following question: If all investors attempt to behave in an entirely rational manner, could these differences still exist? In answering this question, think about information that's available to insiders versus outsiders, the difficulty of estimating the probabilities of financial events versus physical events, and the validity of the concepts of animal spirits, herding, and anchoring.

Problems   Answers Appear in Appendix B

Easy Problems 1–5

5-1 **DPS Calculation** Thress Industries just paid a dividend of $1.50 a share (i.e., $D_0 = \$1.50$). The dividend is expected to grow 5% a year for the next 3 years and then 10% a year thereafter. What is the expected dividend per share for each of the next 5 years?

5-2 **Constant Growth Valuation** Boehm Incorporated is expected to pay a $1.50 per share dividend at the end of this year (i.e., $D_1 = \$1.50$). The dividend is expected to grow at a constant rate of 6% a year. The required rate of return on the stock, r_s, is 13%. What is the value per share of Boehm's stock?

5-3 **Constant Growth Valuation** Woidtke Manufacturing's stock currently sells for $22 a share. The stock just paid a dividend of $1.20 a share (i.e., $D_0 = \$1.20$), and the dividend is expected to grow forever at a constant rate of 10% a year. What stock price is expected 1 year from now? What is the required rate of return on Woidtke's stock?

5-4 **Preferred Stock Valuation** Nick's Enchiladas Incorporated has preferred stock outstanding that pays a dividend of $5 at the end of each year. The preferred sells for $50 a share. What is the stock's required rate of return?

5-5 **Nonconstant Growth Valuation** A company currently pays a dividend of $2 per share ($D_0 = \$2$). It is estimated that the company's dividend will grow at a rate of 20% per year for the next 2 years, then at a constant rate of 7% thereafter. The company's stock has a beta of 1.2, the risk-free rate is 7.5%, and the market risk premium is 4%. What is your estimate of the stock's current price?

Intermediate Problems 6–16

5-6 **Constant Growth Rate, g** A stock is trading at $80 per share. The stock is expected to have a year-end dividend of $4 per share ($D_1 = \$4$), and it is expected to grow at some constant rate g throughout time. The stock's required rate of return is 14%. If markets are efficient, what is your forecast of g?

5-7 **Constant Growth Valuation** Crisp Cookware's common stock is expected to pay a dividend of $3 a share at the end of this year ($D_1 = \$3.00$); its beta is 0.8; the risk-free rate is 5.2%; and the market risk premium is 6%. The dividend is expected to grow at some constant rate g, and the stock currently sells for $40 a share. Assuming the market is in equilibrium, what does the market believe will be the stock's price at the end of 3 years (i.e., what is $\hat{P}_3$)?

5-8 **Preferred Stock Rate of Return** What is the nominal rate of return on a preferred stock with a $50 par value, a stated dividend of 7% of par, and a current market price of (a) $30, (b) $40, (c) $50, and (d) $70?

5-9 **Declining Growth Stock Valuation** Brushy Mountain Mining Company's coal reserves are being depleted, so its sales are falling. Also, environmental costs increase each year, so its costs are rising. As a result, the company's earnings and dividends are declining at the constant rate of 4% per year. If $D_0 = \$6$ and $r_s = 14\%$, what is the value of Brushy Mountain's stock?

5-10 Rates of Return and Equilibrium The beta coefficient for Stock C is $b_c = 0.4$ and that for Stock D is $b_D = -0.5$. (Stock D's beta is negative, indicating that its rate of return rises whenever returns on most other stocks fall. There are very few negative-beta stocks, although collection agency and gold mining stocks are sometimes cited as examples.)

   a. If the risk-free rate is 9% and the expected rate of return on an average stock is 13%, what are the required rates of return on Stocks C and D?

   b. For Stock C, suppose the current price, P_0, is $25; the next expected dividend, D_1, is $1.50; and the stock's expected constant growth rate is 4%. Is the stock in equilibrium? Explain, and describe what would happen if the stock were not in equilibrium.

5-11 Nonconstant Growth Stock Valuation Assume that the average firm in your company's industry is expected to grow at a constant rate of 6% and that its dividend yield is 7%. Your company is about as risky as the average firm in the industry, but it has just successfully completed some R&D work that leads you to expect that its earnings and dividends will grow at a rate of 50% $[D_1 = D_0(1 + g) = D_0(1.50)]$ this year and 25% the following year, after which growth should return to the 6% industry average. If the last dividend paid (D_0) was $1, what is the value per share of your firm's stock?

5-12 Nonconstant Growth Stock Valuation Simpkins Corporation does not pay any dividends because it is expanding rapidly and needs to retain all of its earnings. However, investors expect Simpkins to begin paying dividends, with the first dividend of $0.50 coming 3 years from today. The dividend should grow rapidly—at a rate of 80% per year—during Years 4 and 5. After Year 5, the company should grow at a constant rate of 7% per year. If the required return on the stock is 16%, what is the value of the stock today?

5-13 Preferred Stock Valuation Several years ago, Rolen Riders issued preferred stock with a stated annual dividend of 10% of its $100 par value. Preferred stock of this type currently yields 8%. Assume dividends are paid annually.

   a. What is the value of Rolen's preferred stock?

   b. Suppose interest rate levels have risen to the point where the preferred stock now yields 12%. What would be the new value of Rolen's preferred stock?

5-14 Return on Common Stock You buy a share of The Ludwig Corporation stock for $21.40. You expect it to pay dividends of $1.07, $1.1449, and $1.2250 in Years 1, 2, and 3, respectively, and you expect to sell it at a price of $26.22 at the end of 3 years.

   a. Calculate the growth rate in dividends.

   b. Calculate the expected dividend yield.

   c. Assuming that the calculated growth rate is expected to continue, you can add the dividend yield to the expected growth rate to obtain the expected total rate of return. What is this stock's expected total rate of return?

5-15 Constant Growth Stock Valuation Investors require a 13% rate of return on Brooks Sisters's stock ($r_s = 13\%$).

   a. What would the value of Brooks's stock be if the previous dividend were $D_0 = \$3.00$ and if investors expect dividends to grow at a constant annual rate of (1) −5%, (2) 0%, (3) 5%, and (4) 10%?

   b. Using data from part a, what is the constant growth model's value for Brooks Sisters's stock if the required rate of return is 13% and the expected growth rate is (1) 13% or (2) 15%? Are these reasonable results? Explain.

   c. Is it reasonable to expect that a constant growth stock would have $g > r_s$?

5-16 **Equilibrium Stock Price** The risk-free rate of return, r_{RF}, is 11%; the required rate of return on the market, r_M, is 14%; and Schuler Company's stock has a beta coefficient of 1.5.

 a. If the dividend expected during the coming year, D_1, is $2.25, and if g is a constant 5%, then at what price should Schuler's stock sell?

 b. Now suppose that the Federal Reserve Board increases the money supply, causing a fall in the risk-free rate to 9% and in r_M to 12%. How would this affect the price of the stock?

 c. In addition to the change in part b, suppose investors' risk aversion declines; this fact, combined with the decline in r_{RF}, causes r_M to fall to 11%. At what price would Schuler's stock now sell?

 d. Suppose Schuler has a change in management. The new group institutes policies that increase the expected constant growth rate to 6%. Also, the new management stabilizes sales and profits and thus causes the beta coefficient to decline from 1.5 to 1.3. Assume that r_{RF} and r_M are equal to the values in part c. After all these changes, what is Schuler's new equilibrium price? (*Note:* D_1 goes to $2.27.)

Challenging Problems 17–19

5-17 **Constant Growth Stock Valuation** You are analyzing Jillian's Jewelry (JJ) stock for a possible purchase. JJ just paid a dividend of $1.50 *yesterday*. You expect the dividend to grow at the rate of 6% per year for the next 3 years; if you buy the stock, you plan to hold it for 3 years and then sell it.

 a. What dividends do you expect for JJ stock over the next 3 years? In other words, calculate D_1, D_2, and D_3. Note that $D_0 = $1.50.

 b. JJ's stock has a required return of 13%, and so this is the rate you'll use to discount dividends. Find the present value of the dividend stream; that is, calculate the PV of D_1, D_2, and D_3, and then sum these PVs.

 c. JJ stock should trade for $27.05 3 years from now (i.e., you expect $\hat{P}_3 = $27.05). Discounted at a 13% rate, what is the present value of this expected future stock price? In other words, calculate the PV of $27.05.

 d. If you plan to buy the stock, hold it for 3 years, and then sell it for $27.05, what is the most you should pay for it?

 e. Use the constant growth model to calculate the present value of this stock. Assume that g = 6% and is constant.

 f. Is the value of this stock dependent on how long you plan to hold it? In other words, if your planned holding period were 2 years or 5 years rather than 3 years, would this affect the value of the stock today, $\hat{P}_0$? Explain your answer.

5-18 **Nonconstant Growth Stock Valuation** Reizenstein Technologies (RT) has just developed a solar panel capable of generating 200% more electricity than any solar panel currently on the market. As a result, RT is expected to experience a 15% annual growth rate for the next 5 years. By the end of 5 years, other firms will have developed comparable technology, and RT's growth rate will slow to 5% per year indefinitely. Stockholders require a return of 12% on RT's stock. The most recent annual dividend (D_0), which was paid yesterday, was $1.75 per share.

 a. Calculate RT's expected dividends for t = 1, t = 2, t = 3, t = 4, and t = 5.

 b. Calculate the intrinsic value of the stock today, $\hat{P}_0$. Proceed by finding the present value of the dividends expected at t = 1, t = 2, t = 3, t = 4, and t = 5 plus the present value of the stock price that should exist at t = 5, $\hat{P}_5$. The $\hat{P}_5$ stock price can be found by using the constant growth equation. Note that to find $\hat{P}_5$ you use the dividend expected at t = 6, which is 5% greater than the t = 5 dividend.

c. Calculate the expected dividend yield $(D_1/\hat{P}_0)$, the capital gains yield expected during the first year, and the expected total return (dividend yield plus capital gains yield) during the first year. (Assume that $\hat{P}_0 = P_0$, and recognize that the capital gains yield is equal to the total return minus the dividend yield.) Also calculate these same three yields for t = 5 (e.g., $D_6/\hat{P}_5$).

d. If your calculated intrinsic value differed substantially from the current market price, and if your views are consistent with those of most investors (the marginal investor), what would happen in the marketplace? What would happen if your views were *not* consistent with those of the marginal investor and you turned out to be correct?

5-19 **Nonconstant Growth Stock Valuation**   Conroy Consulting Corporation (CCC) has been growing at a rate of 30% per year in recent years. This same nonconstant growth rate is expected to last for another 2 years ($g_{0,1} = g_{1,2} = 30\%$).

a. If $D_0 = \$2.50$, $r_s = 12\%$, and $g_L = 7\%$, then what is CCC's stock worth today? What is its expected dividend yield and its capital gains yield at this time?

b. Now assume that CCC's period of nonconstant growth is to last another 5 years rather than 2 years ($g_{0,1} = g_{1,2} = g_{2,3} = g_{3,4} = g_{4,5} = 30\%$). How would this affect its price, dividend yield, and capital gains yield? Answer in words only.

c. What will CCC's dividend yield and capital gains yield be once its period of nonconstant growth ends? (*Hint:* These values will be the same regardless of whether you examine the case of 2 or 5 years of nonconstant growth, and the calculations are very easy.)

d. Of what interest to investors is the relationship over time between dividend yield and capital gains yield?

Spreadsheet Problem

5-20 **Build a Model: Nonconstant Growth and Corporate Valuation**   Start with the partial model in the file *Ch05 P20 Build a Model.xls* on the textbook's Web site. Rework parts a, b, and c of Problem 5-19 using a spreadsheet model. For part b, calculate the price, dividend yield, and capital gains yield as called for in the problem.

 THOMSON REUTERS

Use the Thomson ONE–Business School Edition online database to work this chapter's questions.

Estimating ExxonMobil's Intrinsic Stock Value

In this chapter we described the various factors that influence stock prices and the approaches analysts use to estimate a stock's intrinsic value. By comparing these intrinsic value estimates to the current price, an investor can assess whether it makes sense to buy or sell a particular stock. Stocks trading at a price far below their estimated intrinsic values may be good candidates for purchase, whereas stocks trading at prices far in excess of their intrinsic value may be good stocks to avoid or sell.

Although estimating a stock's intrinsic value is a complex exercise that requires reliable data and good judgment, we can use the data available in Thomson ONE to arrive at a quick "back of the envelope" calculation of intrinsic value.

Discussion Questions

1. For the purposes of this exercise, let's take a closer look at the stock of Exxon-Mobil Corporation (XOM). Looking at the COMPANY OVERVIEW, we can immediately see the company's current stock price and its performance relative to the overall market in recent months. What is ExxonMobil's current stock price? How has the stock performed relative to the market over the past few months?

2. Click on the "NEWS" tab to see the recent news stories for the company. Have there been any recent events affecting the company's stock price, or have things been relatively quiet?

3. To provide a starting point for gauging a company's relative valuation, analysts often look at a company's price-to-earnings (P/E) ratio. Returning to the COMPANY OVERVIEW page, you can see XOM's current P/E ratio. To put this number in perspective, it is useful to compare this ratio with other companies in the same industry and to take a look at how this ratio has changed over time. If you want to see how XOM's P/E ratio stacks up to its peers, click on the tab labeled PEERS. Click on FINANCIALS on the next row of tabs and then select KEY FINANCIAL RATIOS. Toward the bottom of the table you should see information on the P/E ratio in the section titled Market Value Ratios. Toward the top, you should see an item that says CLICK HERE TO SELECT NEW PEER SET—do this if you want to compare XOM to a different set of firms.

   For the most part, is XOM's P/E ratio above or below that of its peers? Off the top of your head, can these factors explain why XOM's P/E ratio differs from its peers?

4. To see how XOM's P/E ratio has varied over time, return to the COMPANY OVERVIEW page. Next click FINANCIALS—GROWTH RATIOS and then select WORLDSCOPE—INCOME STATEMENT RATIOS. Is XOM's current P/E ratio well above or well below its historical average? If so, do you have any explanation for why the current P/E deviates from its historical trend? On the basis of this information, does XOM's current P/E suggest that the stock is undervalued or overvalued? Explain.

5. In the text, we discussed using the dividend growth model to estimate a stock's intrinsic value. To keep things as simple as possible, let's assume at first that XOM's dividend is expected to grow at some constant rate over time. Then its intrinsic value would equal $D_1/(r_s - g)$, where D_1 is the expected annual dividend 1 year from now, r_s is the stock's required rate of return, and g is the dividend's constant growth rate. To estimate the dividend growth rate, it's helpful first to look at XOM's dividend history. Staying on the current Web page (WORLDSCOPE—INCOME STATEMENT RATIOS), you should immediately find the company's annual dividend for the past several years. On the basis of this information, what has been the average annual dividend growth rate? Another

way to obtain estimates of dividend growth rates is to look at analysts' forecasts for future dividends, which can be found on the ESTIMATES tab. Scrolling down the page, you should see an area marked Consensus Estimates and a tab under Available Measures. Here you click on the down arrow key and select Dividends Per Share (DPS). What is the median year-end dividend forecast? You can use this as an estimate of D_1 in your measure of intrinsic value. You can also use this forecast along with the historical data to arrive at a measure of the forecasted dividend growth rate, g.

6. The required return on equity, r_s, is the final input needed to estimate intrinsic value. For our purposes you can either assume a number (say, 8% or 9%) or use the CAPM to calculate an estimated cost of equity using the data available in Thomson ONE. (For more details, take a look at the Thomson ONE exercise for Chapter 2). Having decided on your best estimates for D_1, r_s, and g, you can then calculate XOM's intrinsic value. How does this estimate compare with the current stock price? Does your preliminary analysis suggest that XOM is undervalued or overvalued? Explain.

7. Often it is useful to perform a sensitivity analysis, in which you show how your estimate of intrinsic value varies according to different estimates of D_1, r_s, and g. To do so, recalculate your intrinsic value estimate for a range of different estimates for each of these key inputs. One convenient way to do this is to set up a simple data table in *Excel*. Refer to the *Excel* tutorial accessed through the textbook's Web site for instructions on data tables. On the basis of this analysis, what inputs justify the current stock price?

8. On the basis of the dividend history you uncovered in question 5 and your assessment of XOM's future dividend payout policies, do you think it is reasonable to assume that the constant growth model is a good proxy for intrinsic value? If not, how would you use the available data in Thomson ONE to estimate intrinsic value using the nonconstant growth model?

9. Finally, you can also use the information in Thomson ONE to value the entire corporation. This approach requires that you estimate XOM's annual free cash flows. Once you estimate the value of the entire corporation, you subtract the value of debt and preferred stock to arrive at an estimate of the company's equity value. Divide this number by the number of shares of common stock outstanding, which yields an alternative estimate of the stock's intrinsic value. This approach may take some more time and involve more judgment concerning forecasts of future free cash flows, but you can use the financial statements and growth forecasts in Thomson ONE as useful starting points. Go to Worldscope's Cash Flow Ratios Report (which you find by clicking on FINANCIALS, FUNDAMENTAL RATIOS, and WORLDSCOPE RATIOS) to find an estimate of "free cash flow per share." Although this number is useful, Worldscope's definition of free cash flow subtracts out dividends per share; therefore, to make it comparable to the measure used in this text, you must add back dividends. To see Worldscope's definition of free cash flow (or any term), click on SEARCH FOR COMPANIES from the left toolbar and then select the ADVANCED SEARCH tab. In the middle of your screen, on the right-hand side, you will see a dialog box with terms. Use the down arrow to scroll through the terms, highlighting the term for which you would like to see a definition. Then, click on the DEFINITION button immediately below the dialog box.

MINI CASE

Sam Strother and Shawna Tibbs are senior vice presidents of Mutual of Seattle. They are co-directors of the company's pension fund management division, with Strother having responsibility for fixed income securities (primarily bonds) and Tibbs responsible for equity investments. A major new client, the Northwestern Municipal Alliance, has requested that Mutual of Seattle present an investment seminar to the mayors of the cities in the association, and Strother and Tibbs, who will make the actual presentation, have asked you to help them.

To illustrate the common stock valuation process, Strother and Tibbs have asked you to analyze the Temp Force Company, an employment agency that supplies word processor operators and computer programmers to businesses with temporarily heavy workloads. You are to answer the following questions.

a. Describe briefly the legal rights and privileges of common stockholders.

b. (1) Write out a formula that can be used to value any stock, regardless of its dividend pattern.

   (2) What is a constant growth stock? How are constant growth stocks valued?

   (3) What happens if a company has a constant g that exceeds its r_s? Will many stocks have expected $g > r_s$ in the short run (i.e., for the next few years)? In the long run (i.e., forever)?

c. Assume that Temp Force has a beta coefficient of 1.2, that the risk-free rate (the yield on T-bonds) is 7.0%, and that the market risk premium is 5%. What is the required rate of return on the firm's stock?

d. Assume that Temp Force is a constant growth company whose last dividend (D_0, which was paid yesterday) was $2.00 and whose dividend is expected to grow indefinitely at a 6% rate.

   (1) What is the firm's expected dividend stream over the next 3 years?

   (2) What is the firm's current intrinsic stock price?

   (3) What is the stock's expected value 1 year from now?

(4) What are the expected dividend yield, the expected capital gains yield, and the expected total return during the first year?

e. Now assume that the stock is currently selling at $30.29. What is its expected rate of return?

f. What would the stock price be if the dividends were expected to have zero growth?

g. Now assume that Temp Force's dividend is expected to experience nonconstant growth of 30% from Year 0 to Year 1, 25% from Year 1 to Year 2, and 15% from Year 2 to Year 3. After Year 3, dividends will grow at a constant rate of 6%. What is the stock's intrinsic value under these conditions? What are the expected dividend yield and capital gains yield during the first year? What are the expected dividend yield and capital gains yield during the fourth year (from Year 3 to Year 4)?

h. Is the stock price based more on long-term or short-term expectations? Answer this by finding the percentage of Temp Force's current stock price that is based on dividends expected more than 3 years in the future.

i. Suppose Temp Force is expected to experience zero growth during the first 3 years and then to resume its steady-state growth of 6% in the fourth year. What is the stock's intrinsic value now? What are its expected dividend yield and its capital gains yield in Year 1? In Year 4?

j. Now suppose that Temp Force's earnings and dividends are expected to decline by a constant 6% per year forever—that is, g = −6%. Why would anyone be willing to buy such a stock, and at what price should it sell? What would be the dividend yield and capital gains yield in each year?

k. What is market multiple analysis?

l. Temp Force recently issued preferred stock that pays an annual dividend of $5 at a price of $50 per share. What is the expected return to an investor who buys this preferred stock?

m. Why do stock prices change? Suppose the expected D_1 is $2, the growth rate is 5%, and r_s is 10%. Using the constant growth model, what is the stock's price? What is the impact on the stock price if g falls to 4% or rises to 6%? If r_s increases to 9% or to 11%?

n. What does market equilibrium mean?

o. If equilibrium does not exist, how will it be established?

p. What is the Efficient Markets Hypothesis, what are its three forms, and what are its implications?

q. Assume that all the growth rates used in the preceding answers were averages of the growth rates published by well-known and respected security analysts. Would you then say that your results are based on a purely rational analysis? If not, what factors might have led to "irrational results"?

Selected Additional Cases

The following cases from TextChoice, *Cengage Learning's online case library, cover many of the concepts discussed in this chapter and are available at* **www.textchoice2.com/casenet.**

Klein-Brigham Series:
Case 3, "Peachtree Securities, Inc. (B)"; Case 71, "Swan Davis"; Case 78, "Beatrice Peabody"; and Case 101, "TECO Energy."

Brigham-Buzzard Series:
Case 4, "Powerline Network Corporation (Stocks)."

Chapter **6**

Financial Options

WEB

The textbook's Web site contains an *Excel* file that will guide you through the chapter's calculations. The file for this chapter is ***Ch06 Tool Kit.xls***, and we encourage you to open the file and follow along as you read the chapter.

There are two fundamental approaches to valuing assets. The first is the *discounted cash flow* (DCF) approach, which we covered in previous chapters: An asset's value is the present value of its cash flows. The second is the *option pricing* approach. It is important that every manager understands the basic principles of option pricing, for the following reasons. First, many projects allow managers to make strategic or tactical changes in plans as market conditions change. The existence of these "embedded options" often means the difference between a successful project and a failure. Understanding basic financial options can help you manage the value inherent in these real options. Second, many companies use derivatives to manage risk; many derivatives are types of financial options, so an understanding of basic financial options is necessary before tackling derivatives. Third, option pricing theory provides insights into the optimal debt/equity choice, especially when convertible securities are involved. And fourth, understanding financial options will help you better understand any employee stock options that you receive.

Beginning of Chapter Questions

As you read the chapter, consider how you would answer the following questions. You *should not* necessarily be able to answer the questions before you read the chapter. Rather, you should use them to get a sense of the issues covered in the chapter. After reading the chapter, you should be able to give at least partial answers to the questions, and you should be able to give better answers after the chapter has been discussed in class. Note, too, that it is often useful, when answering conceptual questions, to use hypothetical data to illustrate your answer. We illustrate the answers with an *Excel* model that is available on the textbook's Web site. Accessing the model and working through it is a useful exercise, and it provides insights that are useful when answering the questions.

1. How is the value of a financial option affected by (a) the current price of the underlying asset, (b) the exercise (or strike) price, (c) the risk-free rate, (d) the time until expiration (or maturity), and (e) the variance of returns on the asset?

2. Should options given as part of compensation packages be reported on the income statement as an expense? What are some pros and cons relating to this issue?

3. The rationale behind granting stock options is to induce employees to work harder and be more productive. As the stock price increases (presumably due to their hard work), the employees share in this added wealth. Another way to share this wealth would be to grant shares of stock, rather than options. What are the advantages and disadvantages of using stock options rather than shares of stock as employee incentives?

4. The stockholders' claim in a levered firm can be viewed as a call option; stockholders have the option to purchase the firm's assets by paying off its debt. What incentives does this provide to stockholders and managers in choosing investment projects?

THE INTRINSIC VALUE OF STOCK OPTIONS

In previous chapters we showed that the intrinsic value of an asset is the present value of its cash flows. This time value of money approach works great for stocks and bonds, but we must use another approach for options and derivatives. If we can find a portfolio of stocks and risk-free bonds that replicates an option's cash flows, then the intrinsic value of the option must be identical to the value of the replicating portfolio.

© Cengage Learning 2013

6.1 Overview of Financial Options

In general, an **option** is a contract that gives its owner the right to buy (or sell) an asset at some predetermined price within a specified period of time. However, there are many types of options and option markets.[1] Consider the options reported in Table 6-1, which is an extract from a Listed Options Quotations table as it might appear on a Web site or in a daily newspaper. The first column reports the closing stock price. For example, the table shows that General Computer Corporation's (GCC) stock price closed at $53.50 on January 6, 2012.

A **call option** gives its owner the right to *buy* a share of stock at a fixed price, which is called the **strike price** (sometimes called the **exercise price** because it is the price at which you exercise the option). A **put option** gives its owner the right to *sell* a share of stock at a fixed strike price. For example, the first row in Table 6-1 is for GCC's options that have a $50 strike price. Observe that the table has columns for call options and for put options with this strike price.

Each option has an **expiration date,** after which the option may not be exercised. Table 6-1 reports data for options that expire in February, March, and May (the expiration date is the Friday before the third Saturday of the exercise month). If the option can be exercised any time before the expiration, then it is called an **American option**; if it can be exercised only on its expiration date, it is a **European option**. All of GCC's options are American options. The first row shows that GCC has a call option with a strike price of $50 that expires on May 18 (the third Saturday in May 2012 is the 19th). The quoted price for this option is $5.50.[2]

When the current stock price is greater than the strike price, the option is **in-the-money.** For example, GCC's $50 (strike) May call option is in-the-money by $53.50 − $50 = $3.50. Thus, if the option were immediately exercised, it would have a payoff of $3.50. On the other hand, GCC's $55 (strike) May call is **out-of-the-money** because the current $53.50 stock price is below the $55 strike price. Obviously, you currently would not want to exercise this option by paying the $55 strike price for a share of stock selling for $53.50. Therefore, the **exercise value,** which is any profit from immediately exercising an option, is[3]

(6–1)
$$\text{Exercise value} = \text{MAX}[\text{Current price of the stock} - \text{Strike price, 0}]$$

An American option's price always will be greater than (or equal to) its exercise value. If the option's price were less, you could buy the option and immediately exercise it, reaping a sure gain. For example, GCC's May call with a $50 strike price sells for $5.50, which is greater than its exercise value of $3.50. Also, GCC's out-of-the-money May call with a strike price of $55 sells for $3.15 even though it would be worthless if it had to be exercised immediately. An option always will be worth more than zero as long as there is still any chance at all that it will end up in-the-money: Where there is life, there is hope! The difference between the option's price

---

1. For an in-depth treatment of options, see Don M. Chance and Robert Brooks, *An Introduction to Derivatives and Risk Management,* 8th ed. (Mason, OH: South-Western, Cengage Learning, 2010), or John C. Hull, *Options, Futures, and Other Derivatives,* 7th ed. (Upper Saddle River, NJ: Prentice-Hall, 2009).
2. Option contracts are generally written in 100-share multiples, but we focus on the cost and payoffs of a single option.
3. MAX means choose the maximum. For example, MAX[15, 0] = 15 and MAX[−10, 0] = 0.

TABLE 6-1	Listed Options Quotations for January 6, 2012						
		CALLS—LAST QUOTE			PUTS—LAST QUOTE		
Closing Price	Strike Price	February	March	May	February	March	May
General Computer Corporation (GCC)							
53.50	50	4.25	4.75	5.50	0.65	1.40	2.20
53.50	55	1.30	2.05	3.15	2.65	r	4.50
53.50	60	0.30	0.70	1.50	6.65	r	8.00

Note: r means not traded on January 6.

and its exercise value is called the **time value** because it represents the extra amount over the option's immediate exercise value that a purchaser will pay for the chance the stock price will appreciate over time.[4] For example, GCC's May call with a $50 strike price sells for $5.50 and has an exercise value of $3.50, so its time value is $5.50 − $3.50 = $2.00.

Suppose you bought GCC's $50 (strike) May call option for $5.50 and then the stock price increased to $60. If you exercised the option by purchasing the stock for the $50 strike price, you could immediately sell the share of stock at its market price of $60, resulting in a payoff of $60 − $50 = $10. Notice that the stock itself had a return of 12.1% = ($60 − $53.50)/$53.50, but the option's return was 81.8% = ($10 − $5.50)/$5.50. Thus, the option offers the possibility of a higher return.

However, if the stock price fell to $50 and stayed there until the option expired, the stock would have a return of −6.5% = ($50.00 − $53.50)/$53.50, but the option would have a 100% loss (it would expire worthless). As this example shows, call options are a lot riskier than stocks. This works to your advantage if the stock price goes up but to your disadvantage if the stock price falls.

Suppose you bought GCC's May put option (with a strike price of $50) for $2.20 and then the stock price fell to $45. You could buy a share of stock for $45 and exercise the put option, which would allow you to sell the share of stock at its strike price of $50. Your payoff from exercising the put would be $5 = $50 − $45. Stockholders would lose money because the stock price fell, but a put holder would make money. In this example, your rate of return would be 127.3% = ($5 − $2.20)/$2.20. So if you think a stock price is going to fall, you can make money by purchasing a put option. On the other hand, if the stock price doesn't fall below the strike price of $50 before the put expires, you would lose 100% of your investment in the put option.[5]

Options are traded on a number of exchanges, with the Chicago Board Options Exchange (CBOE) being the oldest and the largest. Existing options can be traded in the secondary market in much the same way that existing shares of stock are traded in secondary markets. But unlike new shares of stock that are issued by corporations, new options can be "issued" by investors. This is called **writing** an option.

---

4. Among traders, an option's market price is also called its "premium." This is particularly confusing since for all other securities the word *premium* means the excess of the market price over some base price. To avoid confusion, we will not use the word *premium* to refer to the option price.

5. Most investors don't actually exercise an option prior to expiration. If they want to cash in the option's profit or cut its losses, they sell the option to some other investor. As you will see later in the chapter, the cash flow from selling the option before its expiration is always greater than (or equal to) the profit from exercising the option.

WWW

The Chicago Board Options Exchange provides 20-minute delayed quotes for equity, index, and LEAPS options at **www.cboe.com**.

For example, you could write a call option and sell it to some other investor. You would receive cash from the option buyer at the time you wrote the option, but you would be obligated to sell a share of stock at the strike price if the option buyer later decided to exercise the option.[6] Thus, each option has two parties, the writer and the buyer, with the CBOE (or some other exchange) acting as an intermediary. Other than commissions, the writer's profits are exactly opposite those of the buyer. An investor who writes call options against stock held in his or her portfolio is said to be selling **covered options.** Options sold without the stock to back them up are called **naked options.**

In addition to options on individual stocks, options are also available on several stock indexes such as the NYSE Index and the S&P 100 Index. Index options permit one to hedge (or bet) on a rise or fall in the general market as well as on individual stocks.

The leverage involved in option trading makes it possible for speculators with just a few dollars to make a fortune almost overnight. Also, investors with sizable portfolios can sell options against their stocks and earn the value of the option (less brokerage commissions) even if the stock's price remains constant. Most important, though, options can be used to create *hedges* that protect the value of an individual stock or portfolio.[7]

Conventional options are generally written for 6 months or less, but a type of option called a **Long-Term Equity AnticiPation Security (LEAPS)** is different. Like conventional options, LEAPS are listed on exchanges and are available on both individual stocks and stock indexes. The major difference is that LEAPS are long-term options, having maturities of up to almost 3 years. One-year LEAPS cost about twice as much as the matching 3-month option, but because of their much longer time to expiration, LEAPS provide buyers with more potential for gains and offer better long-term protection for a portfolio.

Corporations on whose stocks the options are written have nothing to do with the option market. Corporations do not raise money in the option market, nor do they have any direct transactions in it. Moreover, option holders do not vote for corporate directors or receive dividends. There have been studies by the SEC and others as to whether option trading stabilizes or destabilizes the stock market and whether this activity helps or hinders corporations seeking to raise new capital. The studies have not been conclusive, but research on the impact of option trading is ongoing.

Self Test	
	What is an option? A call option? A put option?
	Define a call option's exercise value. Why is the market price of a call option usually above its exercise value?
	Brighton Memory's stock is currently trading at $50 a share. A call option on the stock with a $35 strike price currently sells for $21. What is the exercise value of the call option? **($15.00)** What is the time value? **($6.00)**

---

6. Your broker would require collateral to ensure that you kept this obligation.
7. Insiders who trade illegally generally buy options rather than stock because the leverage inherent in options increases the profit potential. However, it is illegal to use insider information for personal gain, and an insider using such information would be taking advantage of the option seller. Insider trading, in addition to being unfair and essentially equivalent to stealing, hurts the economy: Investors lose confidence in the capital markets and raise their required returns because of an increased element of risk, and this raises the cost of capital and thus reduces the level of real investment.

FINANCIAL REPORTING FOR EMPLOYEE STOCK OPTIONS

When granted to executives and other employees, options are a "hybrid" form of compensation. At some companies, especially small ones, option grants may be a substitute for cash wages: Employees are willing to take lower cash salaries if they have options. Options also provide an incentive for employees to work harder. Whether issued to motivate employees or to conserve cash, options clearly have value at the time they are granted, and they transfer wealth from existing shareholders to employees to the extent that they do not reduce cash expenditures or increase employee productivity enough to offset their value at the time of issue.

Companies like the fact that an option grant requires no immediate cash expenditure, although it might dilute shareholder wealth if later it is exercised. Employees, and especially CEOs, like the potential wealth they receive when they are granted options. When option grants were relatively small, they didn't show up on investors' radar screens. However, as the high-tech sector began making mega-grants in the 1990s, and as other industries followed suit in the heavy use of options, stockholders began to realize that large grants were making some CEOs filthy rich at the stockholders' expense.

Before 2005, option grants were barely visible in companies' financial reports. Even though such grants are clearly a wealth transfer to employees, companies were required only to footnote the grants and could ignore them when reporting their income statements and balance sheets. The Financial Accounting Standards Board now requires companies to show option grants as an expense on the income statement. To do this, the value of the options is estimated at the time of the grant and then expensed during the vesting period, which is the amount of time the employee must wait before being allowed to exercise the options. For example, if the initial value is $100 million and the vesting period is 2 years, the company would report a $50 million expense for each of the next 2 years. This approach isn't perfect, because the grant is not a cash expense; nor does the approach take into account changes in the option's value after the initial grant. However, it does make the option grant more visible to investors, which is a good thing.

6.2 The Single-Period Binomial Option Pricing Approach

We can use a model like the Capital Asset Pricing Model (CAPM) to calculate the required return on a stock and then use that required return to discount its expected future cash flows to find its value. No such model exists for the required return on options, so we must use a different approach to find an option's value. In Section 6.5 we describe the Black-Scholes option pricing model, but in this section we explain the binomial option pricing model. The idea behind this model is different from that of the DCF model used for stock valuation. Instead of discounting cash flows at a required return to obtain a price, as we did with the stock valuation model, we will use the option, shares of stock, and the risk-free rate to construct a portfolio whose value we already know and then deduce the option's price from this portfolio's value.

The following sections describe and apply the binomial option pricing model to Western Cellular, a manufacturer of cell phones. Call options exist that permit the holder to buy 1 share of Western at a strike price, X, of $35. Western's options will expire at the end of 6 months (t is the number of years until expiration, so t = 0.5 for Western's options). Western's stock price, P, is currently $40 per share. Given this background information, we will use the binomial model to determine the call option's value. The first step is to determine the option's possible payoffs, as described in the next section.

6.2a Payoffs in a Single-Period Binomial Model

In general, the time until expiration can be divided into many periods, with n denoting the number of periods. But in a single-period model, which we describe in this section, there is only one period. We assume that, at the end of the period, the stock's price can take on only one of two possible values, so this is called the **binomial approach**. For this example, Western's stock will either go up (u) by a factor of 1.25 or go down (d) by a factor of 0.80. If we were considering a riskier stock, then we would have assumed a wider range of ending prices; we will show how to estimate this range later in the chapter. If we let u = 1.25 and d = 0.80, then the ending stock price will be either P(u) = $40(1.25) = $50 or P(d) = $40(0.80) = $32. Figure 6-1 illustrates the stock's possible price paths and contains additional information about the call option that is explained in what follows.

When the option expires at the end of the year, Western's stock will sell for either $50 or $32. As shown in Figure 6-1, if the stock goes up to $50 then the option will have a payoff, C_u, of $15 at expiration because the option is in-the-money: $50 − $35 = $15. If the stock price goes down to $32 then the option's payoff, C_d, will be zero because the option is out-of-the-money.

6.2b The Hedge Portfolio Approach

Suppose we created a portfolio by writing 1 call option and purchasing 1 share of stock. As Figure 6-1 shows, if the stock price goes up then our portfolio's stock will be worth $50 but we will owe $15 on the option, so our portfolio's net payoff is $35 = $50 − $15. If the stock price goes down then our portfolio's stock will

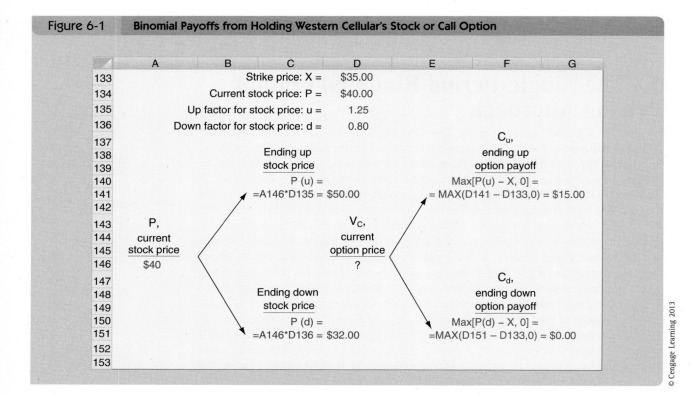

Figure 6-1   Binomial Payoffs from Holding Western Cellular's Stock or Call Option

© Cengage Learning 2013

be worth only \$32, but the amount we owe on the written option also will fall to zero, leaving the portfolio's net payoff at \$32. The portfolio's end-of-period price range is smaller than if we had just owned the stock, so writing the call option reduces the portfolio's price risk. Taking this further: Is it possible for us to choose the number of shares held by our portfolio so that it will have the same net payoff whether the stock goes up or down? If so, then our portfolio is hedged and will have a riskless payoff when the option expires. Therefore, it is called a **hedge portfolio.**

We are not really interested in investing in the hedge portfolio, but we want to use it to help us determine the value of the option. Notice that if the hedge portfolio has a riskless net payoff when the option expires, then we can find the present value of this payoff by discounting it at the risk-free rate. Our current portfolio value must equal this present value, which allows us to determine the option's value. The following example illustrates the steps in this approach.

1. Find N_s, the Number of Shares of Stock in the Hedge Portfolio

We want the portfolio's payoff to be the same whether the stock goes up or down. If we write 1 call option and buy N_s shares of stock, then the portfolio's stock will be worth $N_s(P)(u)$ should the stock price go up, so its net payoff will be $N_s(P)(u) - C_u$. The portfolio's stock will be worth $N_s(P)(d)$ if the stock price goes down, so its net payoff will be $N_s(P)(d) - C_d$. Setting these portfolio payoffs equal to one another and then solving for N_s yields

$$N_s = \frac{C_u - C_d}{P(u) - P(d)} = \frac{C_u - C_d}{P(u - d)} \qquad (6\text{--}2)$$

For Western, the hedge portfolio has 0.83333 share of stock:[8]

$$N_s = \frac{C_u - C_d}{P(u) - P(d)} = \frac{\$15 - \$0}{\$50 - \$32} = 0.83333$$

2. Find the Hedge Portfolio's Payoff

Our next step is to find the hedge portfolio's payoff when the stock price goes up (you will get the same result if instead you find the portfolio's payoff when the stock goes down). Recall that the hedge portfolio has N_s shares of stock and that we have written the call option, so the call option's payoff must be subtracted:

$$\text{Hedge portfolio's payoff if stock is up} = N_s\, P(u) - C_u$$
$$= 0.83333(\$50) - \$15$$
$$= \$26.6665$$

---

8. An easy way to remember this formula is to notice that N_s is equal to the range in possible option payoffs divided by the range in possible stock prices.

Figure 6-2   Hedge Portfolio with Riskless Payoffs

	A	B	C	D	E	F
180					Strike price: X =	$35.00
181					Current stock price: P =	$40.00
182					Up factor for stock price: u =	1.25
183					Down factor for stock price: d =	0.80
184					Up option payoff: C_u = MAX[0,P(u)–X] =	$15.00
185					Down option payoff: C_d =MAX[0,P(d)–X] =	$0.00
186		Number of shares of stock in portfolio: N_s = (C_u – C_d) / P(u–d) =				0.83333
187						
188				Stock price = P (u) = $50.00		
189	P,			Portfolio's stock payoff: = P(u)(N_s) =		$41.67
190	current			Subtract option's payoff: C_u =		$15.00
191	stock price			Portfolio's net payoff = P(u)N_s – C_u =		$26.67
192	$40					
193						
194						
195						
196				Stock price = P (d) = $32.00		
197				Portfolio's stock payoff: = P(d)(N_s) =		$26.67
198				Subtract option's payoff: C_d =		$0.00
199				Portfolio's net payoff = P(d)N_s – C_d =		$26.67

© Cengage Learning 2013

$$\text{Hedge portfolio's payoff if stock is down} = N_s P(d) - C_d$$
$$= 0.83333(\$32) - \$0$$
$$= \$26.6665$$

WEB

See *Ch06 Tool Kit.xls* on the textbook's Web site.

Figure 6-2 illustrates the payoffs of the hedge portfolio.

3. Find the Present Value of the Hedge Portfolio's Payoff

Because the hedge portfolio's payoff is riskless, the current value of the hedge portfolio must be equal to the present value of its riskless payoff. Option pricing models usually assume continuous compounding, which we discuss in *Web Extension 28C* on the textbook's Web site, but daily compounding works well. For a 1-period model, the time to expiration also is the time until the payoff occurs. In a later section we consider more than 1 period prior to expiration, so the time that we discount the payoff is equal to the time until expiration (t) divided by the number of periods until expiration (n). In our example, t = 0.5 and n = 1. Therefore, the present value of the hedge portfolio's payoff is

$$\text{PV of riskless payoff} = \frac{\$26.6665}{\left(1 + \dfrac{r_{RF}}{365}\right)^{365(t/n)}} = \frac{\$26.6665}{\left(1 + \dfrac{0.08}{365}\right)^{365(0.5/1)}}$$

$$= \$25.621$$

4. Find the Option's Value

The current value of the hedge portfolio is the value of the stock, $N_s(P)$, less the value of the call option we wrote. Because the payoff is riskless, the current value of the hedge portfolio must also equal the present value of the riskless payoff:

Current value of hedge portfolio $= N_s P - V_C =$ Present value of riskless payoff

Solving for the call option's value, we get

$$V_C = N_s P - \text{Present value of riskless payoff}$$

For Western's option, this is

$$\begin{aligned} V_C &= 0.83333(\$40) - \$25.621 \\ &= \$7.71 \end{aligned}$$

6.2c Hedge Portfolios and Replicating Portfolios

In our previous derivation of the call option's value, we combined an investment in the stock with writing a call option to create a risk-free investment. We can modify this approach and create a portfolio that replicates the call option's payoffs. For example, suppose we formed a portfolio by purchasing 0.83333 shares of Western's stock and borrowing $25.621 at the risk-free rate (this is equivalent to selling a T-bill short). In 6 months, we would repay $25.621(1 + 0.08/365)^{365(0.5/1)} = \$26.6665$. If the stock goes up, our net payoff would be $0.83333(\$50) - \$26.6665 = \$15.00$. If the stock goes down, our net payoff would be $0.83333(\$32) - \$26.6665 = \$0$. The portfolio's payoffs are exactly equal to the option's payoffs as shown in Figure 6-1, so our portfolio of 0.83333 shares of stock and the $25.621 that we borrowed would exactly replicate the option's payoffs. Therefore, this is called a **replicating portfolio**. Our cost to create this portfolio is the cost of the stock less the amount we borrowed:

$$\text{Cost of replicating portfolio} = 0.83333(\$40) - \$25.621 = \$7.71$$

If the call option did not sell for exactly $7.71, then a clever investor could make a sure profit. For example, suppose the option sold for $8. The investor would write an option, which would provide $8 of cash now but would obligate the investor to pay either $15 or $0 in 6 months when the option expires. However, the investor could use the $8 to create the replicating portfolio, leaving the investor with $8 – $7.71 = $0.29. In 6 months, the replicating portfolio will pay either $15 or $0. Thus, the investor isn't exposed to any risk—the payoffs received from the replicating portfolio exactly offset the payoffs owed on the option. The investor uses none of his own money, has no risk, has no net future obligations, but has $0.29 in cash. This is **arbitrage**, and if such an arbitrage opportunity existed then the investor would scale it up by writing thousands of options.[9]

Such arbitrage opportunities don't persist for long in a reasonably efficient economy because other investors will also see the opportunity and will try to do the same thing. With so many investors trying to write (i.e., sell) the option, its price will fall; with so many investors trying to purchase the stock, its price will increase. This will continue until the option and replicating portfolio have identical prices. And because our financial markets are really quite efficient, you would never observe the derivative security and the replicating portfolio trading for different prices—they would always have the same price and there would

---

9. If the option sold for less than the replicating portfolio, the investor would raise cash by shorting the portfolio and use the cash to purchase the option, again resulting in arbitrage profits.

be no arbitrage opportunities. What this means is that, by finding the price of a portfolio that replicates a derivative security, we have also found the price of the derivative security itself!

6.3 The Single-Period Binomial Option Pricing Formula[10]

The hedge portfolio approach works well if you only want to find the value of one type of option with one period until expiration. But in all other situations, the step-by-step approach becomes tedious very quickly. The following sections describe a formula that replaces the step-by-step approach.

6.3a The Binomial Option Pricing Formula

With a little (or a lot!) of algebra, we can derive a single formula for a call option. After programming it into *Excel,* which we did for this chapter's *Tool Kit,* it is easy to change inputs and determine the new value of a call option. Here is the binomial option pricing formula:

(6–3)

$$V_c = \frac{C_u \left[\dfrac{(1 + r_{RF}/365)^{365(t/n)} - d}{u - d} \right] + C_d \left[\dfrac{u - (1 + r_{RF}/365)^{365(t/n)}}{u - d} \right]}{(1 + r_{RF}/365)^{365(t/n)}}$$

---

10. The material in this section is relatively technical, and some instructors may choose to skip it with no loss in continuity.

We can apply this formula to Western's call option:

$$V_c = \frac{\$15\left[\dfrac{(1+0.08/365)^{365(0.5/1)}-0.80}{1.25-0.80}\right] + \$0\left[\dfrac{1.25-(1+0.08/365)^{365(0.5/1)}}{1.25-0.80}\right]}{(1+0.08/365)^{365(0.5/1)}}$$

$$= \frac{\$15(0.5351)+\$0(0.2092)}{1.040806} = \$7.71$$

Notice that this is the same value that resulted from the step-by-step process shown earlier.

The binomial option pricing formula in Equation 6-3 does not include the actual probabilities that the stock will go up or down, nor does it include the expected stock return, which is not what one might expect. After all, the higher the stock's expected return, the greater the chance that the call will be in-the-money at expiration. Note, however, that the stock's expected return is already indirectly incorporated into the stock price.

If we want to value other Western call options or puts that expire in 6 months, then we can again use Equation 6-3. Observe that for options with the same time left until expiration, C_u and C_d are the only variables that depend on the option itself. The other variables depend only on the stock process (u and d), the risk-free rate, the time until expiration, and the number of periods until expiration. If we group these variables together, we can then define π_u and π_d as

$$\pi_u = \frac{\left[\dfrac{(1+r_{RF}/365)^{365(t/n)}-d}{u-d}\right]}{(1+r_{RF}/365)^{365(t/n)}} \qquad (6\text{-}4)$$

and

$$\pi_d = \frac{\left[\dfrac{u-(1+r_{RF}/365)^{365(t/n)}}{u-d}\right]}{(1+r_{RF}/365)^{365(t/n)}} \qquad (6\text{-}5)$$

By substituting these values into Equation 6-3, we obtain an option pricing model that can be applied to all of Western's 6-month options:

$$V_c = C_u\,\pi_u + C_d\,\pi_d \qquad (6\text{-}6)$$

In this example, π_u and π_d are

$$\pi_u = \frac{\left[\dfrac{(1+0.08/365)^{365(0.5/1)}-0.80}{1.25-0.80}\right]}{(1+0.08/365)^{365(0.5/1)}} = 0.5141$$

and

$$\pi_d = \frac{\left[\dfrac{1.25 - (1 + 0.08/365)^{365(0.5/1)}}{1.25 - 0.80}\right]}{(1 + 0.08/365)^{365(0.5/1)}} = 0.4466$$

Using Equation 6-6, the value of Western's 6-month call option with a strike price of $35 is

$$V_C = C_u \, \pi_u + C_d \, \pi_d$$
$$= \$15(0.5141) + \$0(0.4466)$$
$$= \$7.71$$

Sometimes these π's are called *primitive securities* because π_u is the price of a simple security that pays $1 if the stock goes up and nothing if it goes down; π_d is the opposite. This means that we can use these π's to find the price of any 6-month option on Western. For example, suppose we want to find the value of a 6-month call option on Western but with a strike price of $30. Rather than reinvent the wheel, all we have to do is find the payoffs of this option and use the same values of π_u and π_d in Equation 6-6. If the stock goes up to $50, the option will pay $50 − $30 = $20; if the stock falls to $32, the option will pay $32 − $30 = $2. The value of the call option is:

$$\text{Value of 6-month call with \$30 strike price} = C_u \, \pi_u + C_d \, \pi_d$$
$$= \$20(0.5141) + \$2(0.4466)$$
$$= \$11.18$$

It is a bit tedious initially to calculate π_u and π_d, but once you save them it is easy to find the value of any 6-month call or put option on the stock. In fact, you can use these π's to find the value of any security with payoffs that depend on Western's 6-month stock prices, which makes them a very powerful tool.

Self Test

Yegi's Fine Phones has a current stock price of $30. You need to find the value of a call option with a strike price of $32 that expires in 3 months. Use the binomial model with one period until expiration. The factor for an increase in stock price is u = 1.15; the factor for a downward movement is d = 0.85. What are the possible stock prices at expiration? (**$34.50 or $25.50**) What are the option's possible payoffs at expiration? (**$2.50 or $0**) What are π_u and π_d? (**0.5422 and 0.4429**) What is the current value of the option (assume each month is 1/12 of a year)? (**$1.36**)

6.4 The Multi-Period Binomial Option Pricing Model[11]

Clearly, the one-period example is simplified. Although you could duplicate buying 0.8333 share and writing one option by buying 8,333 shares and writing 10,000 options, the stock price assumptions are unrealistic—Western's stock price could be almost anything after 6 months, not just $50 or $32. However, if we allowed

---

11. The material in this section is relatively technical, and some instructors may choose to skip it with no loss in continuity.

the stock to move up or down more often, then a more realistic range of ending prices would result. In other words, dividing the time until expiration into more periods would improve the realism of the resulting prices at expiration. The key to implementing a multi-period binomial model is to keep the stock return's annual standard deviation the same no matter how many periods you have during a year. In fact, analysts typically begin with an estimate of the standard deviation and use it to determine u and d. The derivation is beyond the scope of a financial management textbook, but the appropriate equations are

$$u = e^{\sigma\sqrt{t/n}}$$

(6–7)

$$d = \frac{1}{u}$$

(6–8)

where σ is the annualized standard deviation of the stock's return, t is the time in years until expiration, and n is the number of periods until expiration.

The standard deviation of Western's stock returns is 31.5573%, and application of Equations 6-7 and 6-8 confirms the values of u and d that we used previously:

$$u = e^{0.315573\sqrt{0.5/1}} = 1.25 \quad \text{and} \quad d = \frac{1}{1.25} = 0.80$$

Now suppose we allow stock prices to change every 3 months (which is 0.25 years). Using Equations 6-7 and 6-8, we estimate u and d to be

$$u = e^{0.31573\sqrt{0.5/2}} = 1.1709 \quad \text{and} \quad d = \frac{1}{1.1709} = 0.8540$$

At the end of the first 3 months, Western's price would either rise to $40(1.1709) = \$46.84$ or fall to $40(0.8540) = \$34.16$. If the price rises in the first 3 months to $46.84, then it would either go up to $46.84(1.1709) = \$54.84$ or go down to $46.84(0.8540) = \$40$ at expiration. If instead the price initially falls to $40(0.8540) = \$34.16$ during the first 3 months, then it would either go up to $34.16(1.1709) = \$40$ or go down to $34.16(0.8540) = \$29.17$ by expiration. This pattern of stock price movements is called a **binomial lattice** and is shown in Figure 6-3.

Because the interest rate and the volatility (as defined by u and d) are constant for each period, we can calculate π_u and π_d for any period and apply these same values for each period:[12]

$$\pi_u = \frac{\left[\dfrac{(1 + 0.08/365)^{365(0.5/2)} - 0.8540}{1.1709 - 0.8540}\right]}{(1 + 0.08/365)^{365(0.5/2)}} = 0.51400$$

---

12. These values were calculated in *Excel*, so there may be small differences due to rounding in intermediate steps.

Figure 6-3   **Two-Period Binomial Lattice and Option Valuation**

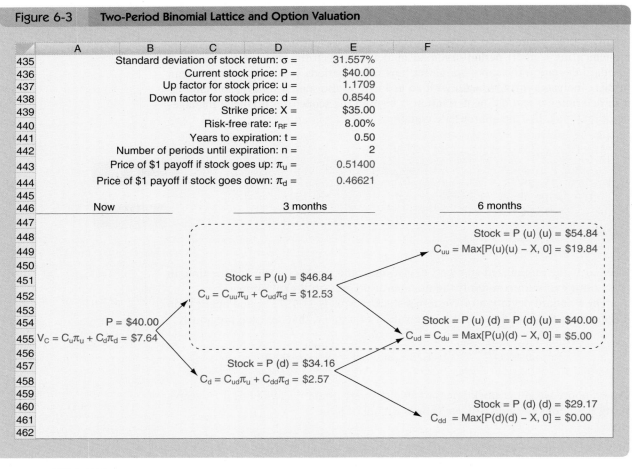

	A	B	C	D	E	F
435		Standard deviation of stock return: σ =			31.557%	
436		Current stock price: P =			$40.00	
437		Up factor for stock price: u =			1.1709	
438		Down factor for stock price: d =			0.8540	
439		Strike price: X =			$35.00	
440		Risk-free rate: r_{RF} =			8.00%	
441		Years to expiration: t =			0.50	
442		Number of periods until expiration: n =			2	
443		Price of $1 payoff if stock goes up: π_u =			0.51400	
444		Price of $1 payoff if stock goes down: π_d =			0.46621	

Now — 3 months — 6 months

Stock = P (u) (u) = $54.84
C_{uu} = Max[P(u)(u) − X, 0] = $19.84

Stock = P (u) = $46.84
$C_u = C_{uu}\pi_u + C_{ud}\pi_d$ = $12.53

P = $40.00
$V_C = C_u\pi_u + C_d\pi_d$ = $7.64

Stock = P (u) (d) = P (d) (u) = $40.00
$C_{ud} = C_{du}$ = Max[P(u)(d) − X, 0] = $5.00

Stock = P (d) = $34.16
$C_d = C_{ud}\pi_u + C_{dd}\pi_d$ = $2.57

Stock = P (d) (d) = $29.17
C_{dd} = Max[P(d)(d) − X, 0] = $0.00

© Cengage Learning 2013

WEB

See *Ch06 Tool Kit.xls* on the textbook's Web site.

$$\pi_d = \frac{\left[\dfrac{1.1709 - (1 + 0.08/365)^{365(0.5/2)}}{1.1709 - 0.8540}\right]}{(1 + 0.08/365)^{365(0.5/2)}} = 0.46621$$

These values are shown in Figure 6-3.

The lattice shows the possible stock prices at the option's expiration and we know the strike price, so we can calculate the option payoffs at expiration. Figure 6-3 also shows the option payoffs at expiration. If we focus only on the upper right portion of the lattice shown inside the dotted lines, then it is similar to the single-period problem we solved in Section 6.3. In fact, we can use the binomial option pricing model from Equation 6-6 to determine the value of the option in 3 months given that the stock price increased to $46.84. As shown in Figure 6-3, the option will be worth $12.53 in 3 months if the stock price goes up to $46.84. We can repeat this procedure on the lower right portion of Figure 6-3 to determine the call option's value in 3 months if the stock price falls to $34.16; in this case, the call's value would be $2.57. Finally, we can use Equation 6-6 and the 3-month option values just calculated to determine the current price of the option, which is $7.64. Thus, we are able to find the current option price by solving three simple binomial problems.

If we broke the year into smaller periods and allowed the stock price to move up or down more often, then the lattice would have an even more realistic range of possible ending stock prices. Of course, estimating the current option price would require solving lots of binomial problems within the lattice, but each problem is simple and computers can solve them rapidly. With more outcomes, the resulting estimated option price is more accurate. For example, if we divide the year into 15 periods then the estimated price is $7.42. With 50 periods, the price is $7.39. With 100 periods it is still $7.39, which shows that the solution converges to its final value within a relatively small number of steps. In fact, as we break the time to expiration into smaller and smaller periods, the solution for the binomial approach converges to the Black-Scholes solution, which is described in the next section.

The binomial approach is widely used to value options with more complicated payoffs than the call option in our example, such as employee stock options. This is beyond the scope of a financial management textbook, but if you are interested in learning more about the binomial approach then you should take a look at the textbooks by Don Chance and John Hull cited in footnote 1.

Self Test

Ringling Cycle's stock price is now $20. You need to find the value of a call option with a strike price of $22 that expires in 2 months. You want to use the binomial model with 2 periods (each period is a month). Your assistant has calculated that u = 1.1553, d = 0.8656, π_u = 0.4838, and π_d = 0.5095. Draw the binomial lattice for stock prices. What are the possible prices after 1 month? **($23.11 or $17.31)** After 2 months? **($26.69, $20, or $14.99)** What are the option's possible payoffs at expiration? **($4.69, $0, or $0)** What will the option's value be in 1 month if the stock goes up? **($2.27)** What will the option's value be in 1 month if the stock price goes down? **($0)** What is the current value of the option (assume each month is 1/12 of a year)? **($1.10)**

6.5 The Black-Scholes Option Pricing Model (OPM)

The **Black-Scholes option pricing model (OPM)**, developed in 1973, helped give rise to the rapid growth in options trading. This model, which has even been programmed into some handheld and Web-based calculators, is widely used by option traders.

6.5a OPM Assumptions and Equations

In deriving their option pricing model, Fischer Black and Myron Scholes made the following assumptions.

1. The stock underlying the call option provides no dividends or other distributions during the life of the option.
2. There are no transaction costs for buying or selling either the stock or the option.
3. The short-term, risk-free interest rate is known and is constant during the life of the option.
4. Any purchaser of a security may borrow any fraction of the purchase price at the short-term, risk-free interest rate.
5. Short selling is permitted, and the short seller will receive immediately the full cash proceeds of today's price for a security sold short.
6. The call option can be exercised only on its expiration date.
7. Trading in all securities takes place continuously, and the stock price moves randomly.

WWW

For a Web-based option calculator, see **www .cboe.com/LearnCenter/ OptionCalculator.aspx**.

The derivation of the Black-Scholes model rests on the same concepts as the binomial model, except time is divided into such small increments that stock prices change continuously. The Black-Scholes model consists of the following three equations:

(6–9)
$$V_C = P[N(d_1)] - X[e^{-r_{RF}t}][N(d_2)]$$

(6–10)
$$d_1 = \frac{\ln(P/X) + [r_{RF} + (\sigma^2/2)]t}{\sigma\sqrt{t}}$$

(6–11)
$$d_2 = d_1 - \sigma\sqrt{t}$$

The variables used in the Black-Scholes model are explained below.

V_C = Current value of the call option.
P = Current price of the underlying stock.
$N(d_i)$ = Probability that a deviation less than d_i will occur in a standard normal distribution. Thus, $N(d_1)$ and $N(d_2)$ represent areas under a standard normal distribution function.
X = Strike price of the option.
$e \approx 2.7183$.
r_{RF} = Risk-free interest rate.[13]
t = Time until the option expires (the option period).
$\ln(P/X)$ = Natural logarithm of P/X.
σ = Standard deviation of the rate of return on the stock.

WWW

Robert's Online Option Pricer can be accessed at **www.intrepid.com/ robertl/index.html**. The site is designed to provide a financial service over the Internet to small investors for option pricing, giving anyone a means to price option trades without having to buy expensive software and hardware.

The value of the option is a function of five variables: (1) P, the stock's price; (2) t, the option's time to expiration; (3) X, the strike price; (4) σ, the standard deviation of the underlying stock; and (5) r_{RF}, the risk-free rate. We do not derive the Black-Scholes model—the derivation involves some extremely complicated mathematics that go far beyond the scope of this text. However, it is not difficult to use the model. Under the assumptions set forth previously, if the option price is different from the one found by Equation 6-9, then this would provide the opportunity for arbitrage profits, which would force the option price back to the value indicated by the model.[14] As we noted earlier, the Black-Scholes model is widely used by traders because actual option prices conform reasonably well to values derived from the model.

---

13. The risk-free rate should be expressed as a continuously compounded rate. If r is a continuously compounded rate, then the effective annual yield is $e^r - 1.0$. An 8% continuously compounded rate of return yields $e^{0.08} - 1 = 8.33\%$. In all of the Black-Scholes option pricing model examples, we will assume that the rate is expressed as a continuously compounded rate.
14. *Programmed trading,* in which stocks are bought and options are sold (or vice versa), is an example of arbitrage between stocks and options.

6.5b Application of the Black-Scholes Option Pricing Model

The current stock price (P), the exercise price (X), and the time to maturity (t) can all be obtained from a newspaper, such as *The Wall Street Journal,* or from the Internet, such as the CBOE's Web site. The risk-free rate (r_{RF}) is the yield on a Treasury bill with a maturity equal to the option expiration date. The annualized standard deviation of stock returns (σ) can be estimated from daily stock prices. First, find the stock return for each trading day for a sample period, such as each trading day of the past year. Second, estimate the variance of the daily stock returns. Third, multiply this estimated daily variance by the number of trading days in a year, which is approximately 250.[15] Take the square root of the annualized variance, and the result is an estimate of the annualized standard deviation.

We will use the Black-Scholes model to estimate Western's call option that we discussed previously. Here are the inputs:

$$P = \$40$$
$$X = \$35$$
$$t = 6 \text{ months (0.5 years)}$$
$$r_{RF} = 8.0\% = 0.080$$
$$\sigma = 31.557\% = 0.31557$$

Given this information, we first estimate d_1 and d_2 from Equations 6-10 and 6-11:

WEB

See **Ch06 Tool Kit.xls** on the textbook's Web site for all calculations.

$$d_1 = \frac{\ln(\$40/\$35) + [0.08 + ((0.31557^2)/2)](0.5)}{0.31557\sqrt{0.5}}$$

$$= \frac{0.13353 + 0.064896}{0.22314} = 0.8892$$

$$d_2 = d_1 - 0.31557\sqrt{0.5} = 0.6661$$

Note that $N(d_1)$ and $N(d_2)$ represent areas under a standard normal distribution function. The easiest way to calculate this value is with *Excel.* For example, we can

---

15. If stocks traded every day of the year, then each return covers a 24-hour period; you would simply estimate the variance of the 1-day returns with your sample of daily returns and then multiply this estimate by 365 for an estimate of the annual variance. However, stocks don't trade every day because of weekends and holidays. If you measure returns from the close of one trading day until the close of the next trading day (called "trading-day returns"), then some returns are for 1 day (such as Thursday close to Friday close) and some are for longer periods, like the 3-day return from Friday close to Monday close. It might seem reasonable that the 3-day returns have 3 times the variance of a 1-day return and should be treated differently when estimating the daily return variance, but that is not the case. It turns out that the 3-day return over a weekend has only slightly higher variance than a 1-day return, and so it is reasonable to treat all of the trading-day returns the same. With roughly 250 trading days in a year, most analysts take the estimate of the variance of daily returns and multiply by 250 (or 252, depending on the year, to be more precise) to obtain an estimate of the annual variance. See John C. Hull, *Options, Futures, and Other Derivatives,* 7th ed. (Upper Saddle River, NJ: Prentice-Hall, 2009) p. 285.

use the function **=NORMSDIST(0.8892)**, which returns a value of $N(d_1) = N(0.8892) = 0.8131$. Similarly, the **NORMSDIST** function returns a value of $N(d_2) = 0.7473$.[16] We can use those values to solve Equation 6-9:

$$V_c = \$40[N(0.8892)] - \$35e^{-(0.08)(0.5)}[N(0.6661)]$$
$$= \$7.39$$

handwritten: 35.568   24.26494   .04   0.96079

Thus, the value of the option is $7.39. This is the same value we found using the binomial approach with 100 periods in the year.

6.5c The Five Factors That Affect Call Option Prices

The Black-Scholes model has five inputs, so there are five factors that affect call option prices. As we will see in the next section, these five inputs also affect put option prices. Figure 6-4 shows how three of Western Cellular's call options are affected by Western's stock price (all three options have a strike price of $35). The three options expire in 1 year, in 6 months (0.5 years, like the option in our example), and in 3 months (or 0.25 years), respectively.

Figure 6-4 offers several insights regarding option valuation. Notice that for all stock prices, the call option prices are always above the exercise value. Also, when the stock price falls far below the strike price, call option prices fall toward zero. In other words, options lose value as they become more and more out-of-the-money. When the stock price greatly exceeds the strike price, call option prices fall toward the exercise value. Thus, for very high stock prices, call options tend to move up and down by about the same amount as does the stock price.

WEB

See **Ch06 Tool Kit.xls** on the textbook's Web site.

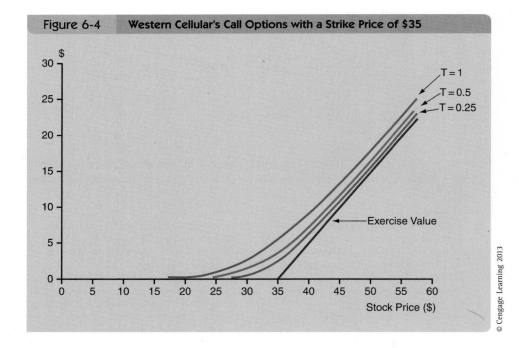

Figure 6-4   Western Cellular's Call Options with a Strike Price of $35

© Cengage Learning 2013

---

16. If you do not have access to *Excel,* then you can use the table in Appendix A. For example, the table shows that the value for $d_1 = 0.88$ is $0.5000 + 0.3106 = 0.8106$ and that the value for $d_1 = 0.89$ is $0.5000 + 0.3133 = 0.8133$, so $N(0.8892)$ lies between 0.8106 and 0.8133. You could interpolate to find a closer value, but we suggest using *Excel* instead.

Call option prices increase if the stock price increases. This is because the strike price is fixed, so an increase in stock price increases the chance that the option will be in-the-money at expiration. Although we don't show it in the figure, an increase in the strike price would obviously cause a decrease in the call option's value because higher strike prices mean a lower chance of being in-the-money at expiration.

The 1-year call option always has a greater value than the 6-month call option, which always has a greater value than the 3-month call option; thus, the longer a call option has until expiration, the greater its value. This is because stock prices move up on average, so a longer time until expiration means a greater chance for the option to be in-the-money by its expiration date, making the option more valuable.

Option prices are higher when the stock is more volatile. Shown in the following table are the Black-Scholes model prices for Western's call option with the original inputs except for standard deviation, which is allowed to vary.

WEB

See *Ch06 Tool Kit.xls* for all calculations.

Standard Deviation (σ)	Call Option Price
0.001%	$ 6.37
10.000	6.38
31.557	7.39
40.000	8.07
60.000	9.87
90.000	12.70

The first row shows the option price if there is very little stock volatility.[17] Notice that as volatility increases, so does the option price. Therefore, the riskier the underlying security, the more valuable the option. To see why this makes sense, suppose you bought a call option with a strike price equal to the current stock price. If the stock had no risk (which means $\sigma = 0$), then there would be a zero probability of the stock going up, hence a zero probability of making money on the option. On the other hand, if you bought an option on a high-variance stock, there would be a higher probability that the stock would go way up and hence that you would make a large profit on the option. Of course, a high-variance stock could go way down, but as an option holder your losses would be limited to the price paid for the option—only the right-hand side of the stock's probability distribution counts. Put another way, an increase in the price of the stock helps option holders more than a decrease hurts them, so the greater the stock's volatility, the greater the value of the option. This makes options on risky stocks more valuable than those on safer,

---

17. With such a low standard deviation, the current stock price of $40 is unlikely to change very much before expiration, so the option will be in-the-money at expiration and the owner will certainly pay the strike price and exercise the option at that time. This means that the present value of the strike price is the cost of exercising expressed in today's dollars. The present value of a stock's expected cash flows is equal to the current stock price. So the value of the option today is approximately equal to the current stock price of $40 less the present value of the strike price that must be paid when the stock is exercised at expiration. If we assume daily compounding, then the current option price should be:

$$V_c (\text{for } \sigma = 0.001\%) \approx \$40 - \frac{\$35}{\left(1 + \dfrac{0.08}{365}\right)^{365(0.5)}} = \$6.37$$

Observe that this is the same value given by the Black-Scholes model, even though we calculated it more directly. This approach only works if the volatility is almost zero.

low-risk stocks. For example, an option on Cisco should have a greater value than an otherwise identical option on Kroger, the grocery store chain.

The risk-free rate also has a relatively small impact on option prices. Shown below are the prices for Western's call option with the original inputs except for the risk-free rate, which is allowed to vary.

WEB

See **Ch06 Tool Kit.xls** for all calculations.

Risk-Free Rate (r_{RF})	Call Option Price
0%	$6.41
4	6.89
8	7.39
12	7.90
20	8.93

As the risk-free rate increases, the value of the option increases. The principal effect of an increase in r_{RF} is to reduce the present value of the exercise price, which increases the current value of the option. Option prices in general are not very sensitive to interest rate changes, at least not to changes within the ranges normally encountered.

TAXES AND STOCK OPTIONS

If an employee stock option grant meets certain conditions, it is called a "tax-qualifying grant" or sometimes an "Incentive Stock Option"; otherwise, it is a "nonqualifying grant." For example, suppose you receive a grant of 1,000 options with an exercise price of $50. If the stock price goes to $110 and you exercise the options, you must pay $50(1,000) = $50,000 for stock that is worth $110,000, which is a sweet deal. But what is your tax liability? If you receive a nonqualifying grant, then you are liable for ordinary income taxes on 1,000($110 − $50) = $60,000 when you exercise the option. But if it is a tax-qualified grant, you owe no regular taxes when exercised. By waiting at least a year and then selling the stock for, say, $150, you would have a long-term capital gain of 1,000($150 − $50) = $100,000, which would be taxed at the lower capital gains rate.

Before you gloat over your newfound wealth, you had better consult your accountant. Your "profit" when you exercise the tax-qualified options isn't taxable under the regular tax code, but it is under the Alternative Minimum Tax (AMT) code. With an AMT tax rate of up to 28%, you might owe as much as 0.28($110 − $50)(1,000) = $16,800. Here's where people get into trouble. The AMT tax isn't due until the following April, so you might think about waiting until then to sell some stock to pay your AMT tax (so that the sale will qualify as a long-term capital gain).

But what happens if the stock price falls to $5 by next April? You can sell your stock, which raises only $5(1,000) = $5,000 in cash. Without going into the details, you will have a long-term capital loss of 1,000($50 − $5) = $45,000 but IRS regulations limit your net capital loss in a single year to $3,000. In other words, the cash from the sale and the tax benefit from the capital loss aren't nearly enough to cover the AMT tax. You may be able to reduce your taxes in future years because of the AMT tax you pay this year and the carryforward of the remaining long-term capital loss, but that doesn't help right now. You lost $45,000 of your original $50,000 investment, you now have very little cash, and—adding insult to injury—the IRS will insist that you also pay the $16,800 AMT tax.

This is exactly what happened to many people who made paper fortunes in the dot-com boom only to see them evaporate in the ensuing bust. They were left with worthless stock but multimillion-dollar AMT tax obligations. In fact, many still have IRS liens garnishing their wages until they eventually pay their AMT tax. So if you receive stock options, we congratulate you. But unless you want to be the next poster child for poor financial planning, we advise you to settle your AMT tax when you incur it.

Myron Scholes and Robert Merton (who also was a pioneer in the field of options) were awarded the 1997 Nobel Prize in Economics, and Fischer Black would have been a co-recipient had he still been living. Their work provided analytical tools and methodologies that are widely used to solve many types of financial problems, not just option pricing. Indeed, the entire field of modern risk management is based primarily on their contributions. Although the Black-Scholes model was derived for a European option that can be exercised only on its maturity date, it also applies to American options that don't pay any dividends prior to expiration. The textbooks by Don Chance and John Hull (cited in footnote 1) show adjusted models for dividend-paying stocks.

Self Test

What is the purpose of the Black-Scholes option pricing model?

Explain what a "riskless hedge" is and how the riskless hedge concept is used in the Black-Scholes OPM.

Describe the effect of a change in each of the following factors on the value of a call option: (1) stock price, (2) exercise price, (3) option life, (4) risk-free rate, and (5) stock return standard deviation (i.e., risk of stock).

Using an *Excel* worksheet, what is the value of a call option with these data: P = \$35, X = \$25, r_{RF} = 6%, t = 0.5 (6 months), and σ = 0.6? **(\$12.05)**

6.6 The Valuation of Put Options

A put option gives its owner the right to sell a share of stock. If the stock pays no dividends and the option can be exercised only upon its expiration date, what is its value? Rather than reinventing the wheel, consider the payoffs for two portfolios at expiration date T, as shown in Table 6-2. The first portfolio consists of a put option and a share of stock; the second has a call option (with the same strike price and expiration date as the put option) and some cash. The amount of cash is equal to the present value of the strike price discounted at the continuously compounded risk-free rate, which is $X e^{-r_{RF}t}$. At expiration, the value of this cash will equal the strike price, X.

If P_T, the stock price at expiration date T, is less than X, the strike price, when the option expires, then the value of the put option at expiration is $X - P_T$.

TABLE 6-2	Portfolio Payoffs		
		Payoff at Expiration If:	
		$P_T < X$	$P_T \geq X$
Put		$X - P_T$	0
Stock		P_T	P_T
	Portfolio 1:	X	P_T
Call		0	$P_T - X$
Cash		X	X
	Portfolio 2:	X	P_T

© Cengage Learning 2013

Therefore, the value of Portfolio 1, which contains the put and the stock, is equal to X minus P_T plus P_T, or just X. For Portfolio 2, the value of the call is zero at expiration (because the call option is out-of-the-money), and the value of the cash is X, for a total value of X. Notice that both portfolios have the same payoffs if the stock price is less than the strike price.

What if the stock price is greater than the strike price at expiration? In this case, the put is worth nothing, so the payoff of Portfolio 1 is equal to P_T, the stock price at expiration. The call option is worth $P_T - X$, and the cash is worth X, so the payoff of Portfolio 2 is P_T. Hence the payoffs of the two portfolios are equal regardless of whether the stock price is below or above the strike price.

If the two portfolios have identical payoffs, then they must have identical values. This is known as the **put–call parity relationship**:

$$\text{Put option} + \text{Stock} = \text{Call option} + \text{PV of exercise price.}$$

If V is the Black-Scholes value of the call option, then the value of a put is[18]

(6–12)
$$\text{Put option} = V_c - P + Xe^{-r_{RF}t}$$

For example, consider a put option written on the stock discussed in the previous section. If the put option has the same exercise price and expiration date as the call, then its price is

$$\begin{aligned} \text{Put option} &= \$7.39 - \$40 + \$35\,e^{-0.08(0.5)} \\ &= \$7.39 - \$40 + \$33.63 = \$1.02 \end{aligned}$$

It is also possible to modify the Black-Scholes call option formula to obtain a put option formula:

(6–13)
$$\text{Put option} = P[N(d_1) - 1] - Xe^{-r_{RF}t}[N(d_2) - 1]$$

The only difference between this formula for puts and the formula for calls is the subtraction of 1 from $N(d_1)$ and $N(d_2)$ in the call option formula.

6.6a The Five Factors That Affect Put Option Prices

Just like with call options, the exercise price, the underlying stock price, the time to expiration, the stock's standard deviation, and the risk-free rate affect the price of a put option. Since a put pays off when the stock price declines below the exercise price, the impact of the underlying stock price and exercise price and risk-free rate on the put are opposite that of the call option. That is, put prices are higher when the stock price is lower and when the exercise price is higher. Put prices are

18. This model cannot be applied to an American put option or to a European option on a stock that pays a dividend prior to expiration. For an explanation of valuation approaches in these situations, see the books by Chance and Hull cited in footnote 1.

also lower when the risk-free rate is higher, mostly because a higher risk-free rate reduces the present value of the exercise price, which for a put is a payout to the option holder when the option is exercised.

On the other hand, put options are affected by the stock's standard deviation just like call options. Both put and call option prices are higher when the stock's standard deviation is higher. This is true for put options because the higher the standard deviation, the bigger the chance of a large stock price decline and a large put payoff. The effect of the time to maturity on the put option price is indeterminate. A call option is more valuable the longer the maturity, but some puts are more valuable the longer to maturity, and some are less valuable. For example, consider an in-the-money put option (the stock price is below the exercise price) on a stock with a low standard deviation. In this case a longer maturity put option is less valuable than a shorter maturity put option because the longer the time to maturity, the more likely the stock is to grow and erode the put's payoff. But if the stock's standard deviation is high, then the longer maturity put option will be more valuable since the likelihood of the stock declining even more and resulting in a high payoff to the put is greater.

Self Test

In words, what is put–call parity?

A put option written on the stock of Taylor Enterprises (TE) has an exercise price of $25 and 6 months remaining until expiration. The risk-free rate is 6%. A call option written on TE has the same exercise price and expiration date as the put option. TE's stock price is $35. If the call option has a price of $12.05, then what is the price (i.e., value) of the put option? **($1.31)**

Explain why both put and call options are worth more if the stock return standard deviation is higher, but put and call options are affected oppositely by the stock price.

6.7 Applications of Option Pricing in Corporate Finance

Option pricing is used in four major areas of corporate finance: (1) real options analysis for project evaluation and strategic decisions, (2) risk management, (3) capital structure decisions, and (4) compensation plans.

6.7a Real Options

Suppose a company has a 1-year proprietary license to develop a software application for use in a new generation of wireless cellular telephones. Hiring programmers and marketing consultants to complete the project will cost $30 million. The good news is that if consumers love the new cell phones, there will be a tremendous demand for the software. The bad news is that if sales of the new cell phones are low, the software project will be a disaster. Should the company spend the $30 million and develop the software?

Because the company has a license, it has the option of waiting for a year, at which time it might have a much better insight into market demand for the new cell phones. If demand is high in a year, then the company can spend the

$30 million and develop the software. If demand is low, it can avoid losing the $30 million development cost by simply letting the license expire. Notice that the license is analogous to a call option: It gives the company the right to buy something (in this case, software for the new cell phones) at a fixed price ($30 million) at any time during the next year. The license gives the company a **real option**, because the underlying asset (the software) is a real asset and not a financial asset.

There are many other types of real options, including the option to increase capacity at a plant, to expand into new geographical regions, to introduce new products, to switch inputs (such as gas versus oil), to switch outputs (such as producing sedans versus SUVs), and to abandon a project. Many companies now evaluate real options with techniques that are similar to those described earlier in the chapter for pricing financial options.

6.7b Risk Management

Suppose a company plans to issue $400 million of bonds in 6 months to pay for a new plant now under construction. The plant will be profitable if interest rates remain at current levels, but if rates rise then it will be unprofitable. To hedge against rising rates, the company could purchase a put option on Treasury bonds. If interest rates go up then the company would "lose" because its bonds would carry a high interest rate, but it would have an offsetting gain on its put options. Conversely, if rates fall then the company would "win" when it issues its own low-rate bonds, but it would lose on the put options. By purchasing puts, the company has hedged the risk due to possible interest rate changes that it would otherwise face.

Another example of risk management is a firm that bids on a foreign contract. For example, suppose a winning bid means that the firm will receive a payment of 12 million euros in 9 months. At a current exchange rate of $1.57 per euro, the project would be profitable. But if the exchange rate falls to $1.10 per euro, the project would be a loser. To avoid exchange rate risk, the firm could take a short position in a forward contract that allows it to convert 12 million euros into dollars at a fixed rate of $1.50 per euro in 9 months, which would still ensure a profitable project. This eliminates exchange rate risk if the firm wins the contract, but what if the firm loses the contract? It would still be obligated to sell 12 million euros at a price of $1.50 per euro, which could be a disaster. For example, if the exchange rate rises to $1.75 per euro, then the firm would have to spend $21 million to purchase 12 million euros at a price of $1.75/€ and then sell the euros for $18 million = ($1.50/€)(€12 million), a loss of $3 million.

To eliminate this risk, the firm could instead purchase a currency put option that allows it to sell 12 million euros in 9 months at a fixed price of $1.50 per euro. If the company wins the bid, it will exercise the put option and sell the 12 million euros for $1.50 per euro if the exchange rate has declined. If the exchange rate hasn't declined, then it will sell the euros on the open market for more than $1.50 and let the option expire. On the other hand, if the firm loses the bid, then it has no reason to sell euros and could let the option contract expire. Note, however, that even if the firm doesn't win the contract, it still is gambling on the exchange rate because it owns the put; if the price of euros declines below $1.50, the firm will still make some money on the option. Thus, the company can lock in the future exchange rate if it wins the bid and can avoid any net payment at all if it loses the bid. The total cost in either scenario is equal to the initial cost of the option. In other words, the cost of the option is like insurance that guarantees the exchange rate if the company wins the bid and guarantees no net obligations if it loses the bid.

Many other applications of risk management involve futures contracts and other complex derivatives rather than calls and puts. However, the principles used in pricing derivatives are similar to those used earlier in this chapter for pricing options. Thus, financial options and their valuation techniques play key roles in risk management.

6.7c Capital Structure Decisions

Decisions regarding the mix of debt and equity used to finance operations are quite important. One interesting aspect of the capital structure decision is based on option pricing. For example, consider a firm with debt requiring a final principal payment of $60 million in 1 year. If the company's value 1 year from now is $61 million, then it can pay off the debt and have $1 million left for stockholders. If the firm's value is less than $60 million, then it may well file for bankruptcy and turn over its assets to creditors, resulting in stockholders' equity of zero. In other words, the value of the stockholders' equity is analogous to a call option: The equity holders have the right to buy the assets for $60 million (which is the face value of the debt) in 1 year (when the debt matures).

Suppose the firm's owner-managers are considering two projects. One project has very little risk, and it will result in an asset value of either $59 million or $61 million. The other has high risk, and it will result in an asset value of either $20 million or $100 million. Notice that the equity will be worth zero if the assets are worth less than $60 million, so the stockholders will be no worse off if the assets end up at $20 million than if they end up at $59 million. On the other hand, the stockholders would benefit much more if the assets were worth $100 million rather than $61 million. Thus, the owner-managers have an incentive to choose risky projects, which is consistent with an option's value rising with the risk of the underlying asset. Potential lenders recognize this situation, so they build covenants into loan agreements that restrict managers from making excessively risky investments.

Not only does option pricing theory help explain why managers might want to choose risky projects (consider, for example, the cases of Enron, Lehman Brothers, and AIG) and why debtholders might want restrictive covenants, but options also play a direct role in capital structure choices. For example, a firm could choose to issue convertible debt, which gives bondholders the option to convert their debt into stock if the value of the company turns out to be higher than expected. In exchange for this option, bondholders charge a lower interest rate than for nonconvertible debt. Because owner-managers must share the wealth with convertible-bond holders, they have a smaller incentive to gamble with high-risk projects.

6.7d Compensation Plans

Many companies use stock options as a part of their compensation plans. It is important for boards of directors to understand the value of these options before they grant them to employees. We discuss compensation issues associated with stock options in more detail in Chapter 11.

| Describe four ways that option pricing is used in corporate finance. | **Self Test** |

Summary

In this chapter, we discussed option pricing topics, which included the following:

- **Financial options** are instruments that (1) are created by exchanges rather than firms, (2) are bought and sold primarily by investors, and (3) are of importance to both investors and financial managers.
- The two primary types of financial options are (1) **call options**, which give the holder the right to purchase a specified asset at a given price (the **exercise**, or **strike**, **price**) for a given period of time, and (2) **put options**, which give the holder the right to sell an asset at a given price for a given period of time.
- A call option's **exercise value** is defined as the maximum of zero or the current price of the stock less the strike price.
- The **Black-Scholes option pricing model (OPM)** or the **binomial model** can be used to estimate the value of a call option.
- The five inputs to the Black-Scholes model are (1) P, the current stock price; (2) X, the strike price; (3) r_{RF}, the risk-free interest rate; (4) t, the remaining time until expiration; and (5) σ, the standard deviation of the stock's rate of return.
- A call option's value increases if P increases, X decreases, r_{RF} increases, t increases, or σ increases.
- The **put–call parity relationship** states that

  Put option + Stock = Call option + PV of exercise price.

Questions

6-1 Define each of the following terms:
   a. Option; call option; put option
   b. Exercise value; strike price
   c. Black-Scholes option pricing model
6-2 Why do options sell at prices higher than their exercise values?
6-3 Describe the effect on a call option's price that results from an increase in each of the following factors: (1) stock price, (2) strike price, (3) time to expiration, (4) risk-free rate, and (5) standard deviation of stock return.

Problems   Answers Appear in Appendix B

Easy Problems 1–2

6-1 **Options** A call option on the stock of Bedrock Boulders has a market price of $7. The stock sells for $30 a share, and the option has a strike price of $25 a share. What is the exercise value of the call option? What is the option's time value?

6-2 **Options** The exercise price on one of Flanagan Company's options is $15, its exercise value is $22, and its time value is $5. What are the option's market value and the price of the stock?

Intermediate Problems 3–4

6-3 **Black-Scholes Model** Assume that you have been given the following information on Purcell Industries:

Current stock price = $15   Strike price of option = $15
Time to maturity of option = 6 months   Risk-free rate = 6%
Variance of stock return = 0.12

d_1 = 0.24495 $N(d_1)$ = 0.59675
d_2 = 0.00000 $N(d_2)$ = 0.50000

According to the Black-Scholes option pricing model, what is the option's value?

6-4 **Put–Call Parity** The current price of a stock is $33, and the annual risk-free rate is 6%. A call option with a strike price of $32 and with 1 year until expiration has a current value of $6.56. What is the value of a put option written on the stock with the same exercise price and expiration date as the call option?

Challenging Problems 5–7

6-5 **Black-Scholes Model** Use the Black-Scholes Model to find the price for a call option with the following inputs: (1) current stock price is $30, (2) strike price is $35, (3) time to expiration is 4 months, (4) annualized risk-free rate is 5%, and (5) variance of stock return is 0.25.

6-6 **Binomial Model** The current price of a stock is $20. In 1 year, the price will be either $26 or $16. The annual risk-free rate is 5%. Find the price of a call option on the stock that has a strike price of $21 and that expires in 1 year. (*Hint:* Use daily compounding.)

6-7 **Binomial Model** The current price of a stock is $15. In 6 months, the price will be either $18 or $13. The annual risk-free rate is 6%. Find the price of a call option on the stock that has a strike price of $14 and that expires in 6 months. (*Hint:* Use daily compounding.)

Spreadsheet Problem

6-8 **Build a Model: Black-Scholes Model** Start with the partial model in the file *Ch06 P08 Build a Model.xls* on the textbook's Web site. You have been given the following information for a call option on the stock of Puckett Industries: $P = \$65.00$, $X = \$70.00$, $t = 0.50$, $r_{RF} = 5.00\%$, and $\sigma = 50.00\%$.

a. Use the Black-Scholes option pricing model to determine the value of the call option.

b. Suppose there is a put option on Puckett's stock with exactly the same inputs as the call option. What is the value of the put?

MINI CASE

Assume that you have just been hired as a financial analyst by Triple Play Inc., a mid-sized California company that specializes in creating high-fashion clothing. Because no one at Triple Play is familiar with the basics of financial options, you have been asked to prepare a brief report that the firm's executives can use to gain at least a cursory understanding of the topic.

To begin, you gathered some outside materials on the subject and used these materials to draft a list of pertinent questions that need to be answered. In fact, one possible approach to the report is to use a question-and-answer format. Now that the questions have been drafted, you have to develop the answers.

a. What is a financial option? What is the single most important characteristic of an option?

b. Options have a unique set of terminology. Define the following terms:

(1) Call option
(2) Put option
(3) Strike price or exercise price
(4) Expiration date
(5) Exercise value
(6) Option price
(7) Time value

(8) Writing an option
(9) Covered option
(10) Naked option
(11) In-the-money call
(12) Out-of-the-money call
(13) LEAPS

c. Consider Triple Play's call option with a $25 strike price. The following table contains historical values for this option at different stock prices:

Stock Price	Call Option Price
$25	$ 3.00
30	7.50
35	12.00
40	16.50
45	21.00
50	25.50

(1) Create a table that shows (a) stock price, (b) strike price, (c) exercise value, (d) option price, and (e) the time value, which is the option's price less its exercise value.

(2) What happens to the time value as the stock price rises? Why?

d. Consider a stock with a current price of P = $27. Suppose that over the next 6 months the stock price will either go up by a factor of 1.41 or down by a factor of 0.71. Consider a call option on the stock with a strike price of $25 that expires in 6 months. The risk-free rate is 6%.

(1) Using the binomial model, what are the ending values of the stock price? What are the payoffs of the call option?

(2) Suppose you write 1 call option and buy N_s shares of stock. How many shares must you buy to create a portfolio with a riskless payoff (i.e., a hedge portfolio)? What is the payoff of the portfolio?

(3) What is the present value of the hedge portfolio? What is the value of the call option?

(4) What is a replicating portfolio? What is arbitrage?

e. In 1973, Fischer Black and Myron Scholes developed the Black-Scholes option pricing model (OPM).

(1) What assumptions underlie the OPM?

(2) Write out the three equations that constitute the model.

(3) According to the OPM, what is the value of a call option with the following characteristics?
Stock price = $27.00
Strike price = $25.00
Time to expiration = 6 months = 0.5 years
Risk-free rate = 6.0%
Stock return standard deviation = 0.49

f. What impact does each of the following parameters have on the value of a call option?

(1) Current stock price

(2) Strike price

(3) Option's term to maturity

(4) Risk-free rate

(5) Variability of the stock price

g. What is put–call parity?

Chapter 7

Accounting for Financial Management

A manager's primary goal is to maximize the fundamental, or intrinsic, value of the firm's stock. This value is based on the stream of cash flows the firm is expected to generate in the future. But how does an investor go about estimating future cash flows, and how does a manager decide which actions are most likely to increase cash flows? The first step is to understand the financial statements that publicly traded firms must provide to the public. Thus, we begin with a discussion of financial statements, including how to interpret them and how to use them. Because value depends on usable, after-tax cash flows, we highlight the difference between accounting income and cash flow. In fact, it is *after-tax* cash flow that is important, so we also provide an overview of the federal income tax system.

Beginning of Chapter Questions

As you read the chapter, consider how you would answer the following questions. You *should not* necessarily be able to answer the questions before you read the chapter. Rather, you should use them to get a sense of the issues covered in the chapter. After reading the chapter, you should be able to give at least partial answers to the questions, and you should be able to give better answers after the chapter has been discussed in class. Note, too, that it is often useful, when answering conceptual questions, to use hypothetical data to illustrate your answer. We illustrate the answers with an *Excel* model that is available on the textbook's Web site. Accessing the model and working through it is a useful exercise, and it provides insights that are useful when answering the questions.

1. How are the balance sheet and the income statement *related* to one another? How would you explain to a layperson the *primary purpose* of each of the statements? Which of the numbers in the income statement is considered to be most important?

2. WorldCom capitalized some costs that should, under standard accounting practices, have been expensed. Enron and some other companies took similar actions to inflate their reported income and to hide debts. (a) Explain how such improper and illegal actions would affect the firms' financial statements and stock prices. (b) What effect did the revelations about these actions have on the specific companies' stock prices and the prices of other stocks? (c) Could such actions affect the entire economy?

3. How could (accurate) balance sheet and income statement information be used, along with

other information, to make a **statement of cash flows?** What is the primary purpose of this statement?

4. Differentiate between **net income, EPS, EBITDA, net cash flow, NOPAT, free cash flow, MVA,** and **EVA.** What is the primary purpose of each item; that is, when and how is it used?

5. How and why are regular accounting data *modified* for use in financial management? (*Hint:* Think about cash and operations.)

6. The **income statement** shows "flows" over a period of time, while the **balance sheet** shows accounts at a given point in time. Explain how these two concepts are combined when we calculate **free cash flow.**

7. **Taxes** affect many financial decisions. Explain how (a) **interest and dividend payments** are treated for tax purposes, from both a company's and an investor's perspective, and (b) how **dividends and capital gains** are treated for tax purposes by individuals. In your answers, explain how these tax treatments influence corporations' and investors' behavior.

8. If Congress wants to *stimulate* the economy, explain how it might alter each of the following: (a) **personal and corporate tax rates,** (b) **depreciation schedules,** and (c) the **differential between the tax rate on personal income and long-term capital gains.** How would these changes affect corporate profitability and free cash flow? How would they affect investors' choices regarding which securities to hold in their portfolios? Might any of these actions affect the general level of interest rates?

7.1 Financial Statements and Reports

A company's **annual report** usually begins with the chairman's description of the firm's operating results during the past year and a discussion of new developments that will affect future operations. The annual report also presents four basic financial statements—the *balance sheet,* the *income statement,* the *statement of stockholders' equity,* and the *statement of cash flows.*[1]

WEB

The textbook's Web site contains an *Excel* file that will guide you through the chapter's calculations. The file for this chapter is ***Ch07 Tool Kit.xls,*** and we encourage you to open the file and follow along as you read the chapter.

---

1. Firms also provide less comprehensive quarterly reports. Larger firms file even more detailed statements, giving breakdowns for each major division or subsidiary, with the Securities and Exchange Commission (SEC). These reports, called *10-Q* and *10-K reports,* are available on the SEC's Web site at **www.sec.gov** under the heading "EDGAR."

INTRINSIC VALUE, FREE CASH FLOW, AND FINANCIAL STATEMENTS

In Chapter 1, we told you that managers should strive to make their firms more valuable and that the intrinsic value of a firm is determined by the present value of its free cash flows (FCF) discounted at the weighted average cost of capital (WACC). This chapter focuses on FCF, including its calculation from financial statements and its interpretation when evaluating a company and manager.

www

A source for links to the annual reports of many companies is **www.annualreportservice.com**.

The quantitative and written materials are equally important. The financial statements report *what has actually happened* to assets, earnings, dividends, and cash flows during the past few years, whereas the written materials attempt to explain why things turned out the way they did.

For illustrative purposes, we use a hypothetical company, MicroDrive Inc., which produces hard drives for microcomputers. Formed in 1982, MicroDrive has grown steadily and has a reputation as one of the best firms in the microcomputer components industry.

Self Test

What is the annual report, and what two types of information are given in it?

What four types of financial statements are typically included in the annual report?

7.2 The Balance Sheet

Table 7-1 shows MicroDrive's most recent **balance sheets**, which represent "snapshots" of its financial position on the last day of each year. Although most companies report their balance sheets only on the last day of a given period, the

TABLE 7-1	MicroDrive Inc.: December 31 Balance Sheets (Millions of Dollars)					
Assets	**2012**	**2011**	**Liabilities and Equity**		**2012**	**2011**
Cash and equivalents	$ 10	$ 15	Accounts payable		$ 60	$ 30
Short-term investments	0	65	Notes payable		110	60
Accounts receivable	375	315	Accruals		140	130
Inventories	615	415	Total current liabilities		$ 310	$ 220
Total current assets	$1,000	$ 810	Long-term bonds		754	580
Net plant and equipment	1,000	870	Total liabilities		$1,064	$ 800
			Preferred stock (400,000 shares)		40	40
			Common stock (50,000,000 shares)		130	130
			Retained earnings		766	710
			Total common equity		$ 896	$ 840
Total assets	$2,000	$1,680	Total liabilities and equity		$2,000	$1,680

"snapshot" actually changes daily as inventories are bought and sold, as fixed assets are added or retired, or as loan balances are increased or paid down. Moreover, a retailer will have much larger inventories before Christmas than later in the spring, so balance sheets for the same company can look quite different at different times during the year.

The left side of a balance sheet lists assets, which are the "things" the company owns. They are listed in order of "liquidity," or length of time it typically takes to convert them to cash at fair market values. The right side lists the claims that various groups have against the company's value, listed in the order in which they must be paid. For example, suppliers may have a claim called "accounts payable" that is due within 30 days, banks may have claims called "notes payable" that are due within 90 days, and bondholders may have claims that are not due for 20 years or more.

Stockholders come last, for two reasons. First, their claim represents ownership (or equity) and need never be "paid off." Second, they have a residual claim in the sense that they may receive payments only if the other claimants have already been paid. The nonstockholder claims are liabilities from the stockholders' perspective. The amounts shown on the balance sheets are called **book values** because they are based on the amounts recorded by bookkeepers when assets are purchased or liabilities are issued. As you will see throughout this textbook, book values may be very different from **market values**, which are the current values as determined in the marketplace.

WEB

See **Ch07 Tool Kit.xls** for details.

Self Test

What is the balance sheet, and what information does it provide?

What determines the order of the information shown on the balance sheet?

Why might a company's December 31 balance sheet differ from its June 30 balance sheet?

A firm has $8 million in total assets. It has $3 million in current liabilities, $2 million in long-term debt, and $1 million in preferred stock. What is the total value of common equity? (**$2 million**)

THE GLOBAL ECONOMIC CRISIS

Let's Play Hide-and-Seek!

In a shameful lapse of regulatory accountability, banks and other financial institutions were allowed to use "structured investment vehicles" (SIVs) to hide assets and liabilities off their balance sheets and simply not report them. Here's how SIVs worked and why they subsequently failed. The SIV was set up as a separate legal entity that the bank owned and managed. The SIV would borrow money in the short-term market (backed by the credit of the bank) and then invest in long-term securities. As you might guess, many SIVs invested in mortgage-backed securities. When the SIV paid only 3% on its borrowings but earned 10% on its investments, the managing bank was able to report fabulous earnings, especially if it also earned fees for creating the mortgage securities that went into the SIV.

But this game of hide-and-seek doesn't have a happy ending. Mortgage-backed securities began defaulting in 2007 and 2008, causing the SIVs to pass losses through to the banks. SunTrust, Citigroup, Bank of America, and Northern Rock are just a few of the many banks that reported enormous losses in the SIV game. Investors, depositors, and the government eventually found the hidden assets and liabilities, but by then the assets were worth a lot less than the liabilities.

In a case of too little and too late, regulators are closing these loopholes, and it doesn't look like there will be any more SIVs in the near future. But the damage has been done, and the entire financial system is at risk in large part because of this high-stakes game of hide-and-seek.

7.3 The Income Statement

WEB

See **Ch07 Tool Kit.xls** for details.

Table 7-2 shows the **income statements** for MicroDrive. Income statements can cover any period of time, but they are usually prepared monthly, quarterly, and annually. Unlike the balance sheet, which is a snapshot of a firm at a point in time, the income statement reflects performance during the period.

Subtracting operating costs from net sales but excluding depreciation and amortization results in **EBITDA**, which stands for earnings before interest, taxes, depreciation, and amortization. Depreciation and amortization are annual charges that reflect the estimated costs of the assets used up each year. Depreciation applies to tangible assets, such as plant and equipment, whereas amortization applies to intangible assets such as patents, copyrights, trademarks, and goodwill.[2] Because neither depreciation nor amortization is paid in cash, some analysts claim that EBITDA is a better measure of financial strength than is net income. However, as we show later in the chapter, EBITDA is not as important as free cash flow. In fact, some financial wags have stated that EBITDA really stands for "earnings before anything bad happens."

The net income available to common shareholders, which is revenues less expenses, taxes, and preferred dividends (but before paying common dividends), is generally referred to as **net income**, although it is also called **profit** or **earnings**,

---

2. The accounting treatment of goodwill resulting from mergers has changed in recent years. Rather than an annual charge, companies are required to periodically evaluate the value of goodwill and reduce net income only if the goodwill's value has decreased materially ("become impaired," in the language of accountants). For example, in 2002 AOL Time Warner wrote off almost $100 billion associated with the AOL merger. It doesn't take too many $100 billion expenses to really hurt net income!

TABLE 7-2	MicroDrive Inc.: Income Statements for Years Ending December 31 (Millions of Dollars, Except for Per Share Data)		
		2012	**2011**
Net sales		$3,000	$2,850
Operating costs excluding depreciation and amortization		2,617	2,500
Earnings before interest, taxes, depreciation, and amortization (EBITDA)		$ 383	$ 350
Depreciation and amortization		100	90
Earnings before interest and taxes (EBIT, or operating income)		$ 283	$ 260
Less interest		88	60
Earnings before taxes (EBT)		$ 195	$ 200
Taxes (40%)		78	80
Net income before preferred dividends		$ 117	$ 120
Preferred dividends		4	4
Net income		$ 113	$ 116
Additional Information			
Common dividends		$ 57	$ 53
Addition to retained earnings		$ 56	$ 63
Per Share Data			
Common stock price		$23.00	$26.00
Earnings per share (EPS)		$ 2.26	$ 2.32
Dividends per share (DPS)		$ 1.14	$ 1.06
Book value per share (BVPS)		$17.92	$16.80
Cash flow per share (CFPS)		$ 4.26	$ 4.12

Notes:
There are 50,000,000 shares of common stock outstanding. Note that EPS is based on earnings after preferred dividends—that is, on net income available to common stockholders. Calculations of the most recent EPS, DPS, BVPS, and CFPS values are as follows:

$$\text{Earnings per share} = \text{EPS} = \frac{\text{Net income}}{\text{Common shares outstanding}} = \frac{\$113,000,000}{50,000,000} = \$2.26$$

$$\text{Dividends per share} = \text{DPS} = \frac{\text{Dividends paid to common stockholders}}{\text{Common shares outstanding}} = \frac{\$57,000,000}{50,000,000} = \$1.14$$

$$\text{Book value per share} = \text{BVPS} = \frac{\text{Total common equity}}{\text{Common shares outstanding}} = \frac{\$896,000,000}{50,000,000} = \$17.92$$

$$\text{Cash flow per share} = \text{CFPS} = \frac{\text{Net income} + \text{Depreciation} + \text{Amortization}}{\text{Common shares outstanding}} = \frac{\$213,000,000}{50,000,000} = \$4.26$$

particularly in the news or financial press. Dividing net income by the number of shares outstanding gives earnings per share (EPS), which is often called "the bottom line." Throughout this book, unless otherwise indicated, net income means net income available to common stockholders.[3]

Self Test	
	What is an income statement, and what information does it provide?
	What is often called "the bottom line?"
	What is EBITDA?
	Regarding the time period reported, how does the income statement differ from the balance sheet?
	A firm has $2 million in earnings before taxes. The firm has an interest expense of $300,000 and depreciation of $200,000; it has no amortization. What is its EBITDA? **($2.5 million)**

7.4 Statement of Stockholders' Equity

Changes in stockholders' equity during the accounting period are reported in the **statement of stockholders' equity.** Table 7-3 shows that MicroDrive earned $113 million during 2012, paid out $57 million in common dividends, and plowed $56 million back into the business. Thus, the balance sheet item "Retained earnings" increased from $710 million at year-end 2011 to $766 million at year-end 2012.[4] The last column shows the beginning stockholders' equity, any changes, and the end-of-year stockholders' equity.

Note that "retained earnings" does not represent assets but is instead a *claim against assets.* In 2012, MicroDrive's stockholders allowed it to reinvest $56 million instead of distributing the money as dividends, and management spent this money on new assets. Thus, retained earnings, as reported on the balance sheet, does not represent cash and is not "available" for the payment of dividends or anything else.[5]

---

3. Companies also report "comprehensive income," which is the sum of net income and any "comprehensive" income item, such as unrealized gain or loss when an asset is marked-to-market. For our examples, we assume that there are no comprehensive income items.

   Some companies also choose to report "pro forma income." For example, if a company incurs an expense that it doesn't expect to recur, such as the closing of a plant, it might calculate pro forma income as though it had not incurred the one-time expense. There are no hard-and-fast rules for calculating pro forma income, so many companies find ingenious ways to make pro forma income higher than traditional income. The SEC and the Public Company Accounting Oversight Board (PCAOB) are taking steps to reduce deceptive uses of pro forma reporting.

4. If they had been applicable, then columns would have been used to show "Additional Paid-in Capital" and "Treasury Stock." Also, additional rows would have contained information on such things as new issues of stock, treasury stock acquired or reissued, stock options exercised, and unrealized foreign exchange gains or losses.

5. The amount reported in the retained earnings account is *not* an indication of the amount of cash the firm has. Cash (as of the balance sheet date) is found in the cash account, an asset account. A positive number in the retained earnings account indicates only that in the past the firm earned some income, but its dividends paid were less than its earnings. Even though a company reports record earnings and shows an increase in its retained earnings account, it still may be short of cash.

   The same situation holds for individuals. You might own a new BMW (no loan), lots of clothes, and an expensive stereo—and hence have a high net worth—but if you have only 23 cents in your pocket plus $5 in your checking account, you will still be short of cash.

TABLE 7-3	MicroDrive Inc.: Statement of Stockholders' Equity, December 31, 2012 (Millions of Dollars)			
	Common Stock (Millions)			
	Shares	**Amount**	**Retained Earnings**	**Total Equity**
Balances, Dec. 31, 2011	50	$130	$710	$840
Net income			$113	$113
Cash dividends			(57)	(57)
Issuance of common stock	0	0		
Balances, Dec. 31, 2012	50	$130	$766	$896

© Cengage Learning 2013

WEB

See **Ch07 Tool Kit.xls** for details.

Note: Here and throughout the book, parentheses are used to denote negative numbers.

Self Test

What is the statement of stockholders' equity, and what information does it provide?

Why do changes in retained earnings occur?

Explain why the following statement is true: "The retained earnings reported on the balance sheet does not represent cash and is not available for the payment of dividends or anything else."

A firm had a retained earnings balance of $3 million in the previous year. In the current year, its net income is $2.5 million. If it pays $1 million in common dividends in the current year, what is its resulting retained earnings balance? **($4.5 million)**

7.5 Net Cash Flow

A business's **net cash flow** generally differs from its *accounting profit* because some of the revenues and expenses listed on the income statement were not received or paid in cash during the year. The relationship between net cash flow and net income is:

$$\text{Net cash flow} = \text{Net income} - \text{Noncash revenues} + \text{Noncash charges} \qquad (7\text{--}1)$$

The primary examples of noncash charges are depreciation and amortization. These items reduce net income but are not paid out in cash, so we add them back to net income when calculating net cash flow. Another example of a noncash charge is deferred taxes. In some instances, companies are allowed to defer tax payments to a later date even though the tax payment is reported as an expense on the income statement. Therefore, deferred tax payments are added to net income when calculating net cash flow.[6] Sometimes a customer will purchase services or products that

---

6. Deferred taxes may arise, for example, if a company uses accelerated depreciation for tax purposes but straight-line depreciation for reporting its financial statements to investors. If deferred taxes are increasing, then the company is paying less in taxes than it reports to the public.

FINANCIAL ANALYSIS ON THE WEB

A wide range of valuable financial information is available on the Web. With just a couple of clicks, an investor can easily find the key financial statements for most publicly traded companies. Here's a partial (by no means a complete) list of places you can go to get started.

- One of the very best sources of financial information is Thomson Financial. Go to the textbook's Web site and follow the directions to access Thomson ONE—Business School Edition. An especially useful feature is the ability to download up to 10 years of financial statements in spreadsheet form. First, enter the ticker for a company and click Go. From the menu at left (in dark blue), select Financials. A new menu (in light blue) will expand and selecting Thomson Financials under the Financial Statements heading will reveal Balance Sheets, Income Statements, and Cash Flow Statements items. Select any of these and a menu item for 5YR and 10YR statements will pop up. Select the 10YR item and 10 years of the selected financial statements will be displayed. To download the financial statements into a spreadsheet, click on the *Excel* icon toward the right of the light blue row at the top of the Thomson ONE panel. This will bring up a dialog box that lets you download the *Excel* file to your computer.
- Try Yahoo! Finance's Web site, **finance.yahoo .com**. Here you will find updated market information along with links to a variety of interesting research sites. Enter a stock's ticker symbol, click GET QUOTES, and you will see the stock's current price along with recent news about the company. The panel on the left has links to key statistics and to the company's income statement, balance sheet, statement of cash flows, and more.

The Web site also has a list of insider transactions, so you can tell if a company's CEO and other key insiders are buying or selling their company's stock. In addition, there is a message board where investors share opinions about the company, and there is a link to the company's filings with the SEC. Note that, in most cases, a more complete list of the SEC filings can be found at **www.sec.gov**.

- Other sources for up-to-date market information are **http://money.cnn.com** and **www.zacks.com**. These sites also provide financial statements in standardized formats.
- Both **www.bloomberg.com** and **www.marketwatch .com** have areas where you can obtain stock quotes along with company financials, links to Wall Street research, and links to SEC filings.
- If you are looking for charts of key accounting variables (for example, sales, inventory, depreciation and amortization, and reported earnings) as well as financial statements, take a look at **www.smartmoney .com**.
- Another good place to look is **www.investor .reuters.com**. Here you can find links to analysts' research reports along with the key financial statements.
- Zacks (already mentioned) and **www.hoovers.com** have free research available along with more detailed information provided to subscribers.

In addition to this information, you may be looking for sites that provide opinions regarding the direction of the overall market and views regarding individual stocks. Two popular sites in this category are The Motley Fool's Web site, **www.fool.com**, and the Web site for The Street .com, **www.thestreet.com**.

extend beyond the reporting date, such as iPhone subscriptions at Apple. Even if the company collects the cash at the time of the purchase, the company will spread the reported revenues over the life of the purchase. This causes income to be lower than cash flow in the first year and higher in any subsequent years, so adjustments are made when calculating net cash flow.

Depreciation and amortization usually are the largest noncash items, and in many cases the other noncash items roughly net out to zero. For this reason, many analysts assume that net cash flow equals net income plus depreciation and amortization:

$$\text{Net cash flow} = \text{Net income} + \text{Depreciation and amortization} \qquad (7\text{--}2)$$

We will generally assume that Equation 7-2 holds. However, you should remember that Equation 7-2 will not accurately reflect net cash flow when there are significant noncash items other than depreciation and amortization.

We can illustrate Equation 7-2 with 2012 data for MicroDrive taken from Table 7-2:

$$\text{Net cash flow} = \$113 + \$100 = \$213 \text{ million}$$

To illustrate depreciation's effect, suppose a machine with a life of 5 years and zero expected salvage value was purchased in late 2011 for $100,000 and placed into service in early 2012. This $100,000 cost is not expensed in the purchase year; rather, it is charged against production over the machine's 5-year depreciable life. If the depreciation expense were not taken, then profits would be overstated and taxes would be too high. Therefore, the annual depreciation charge is deducted from sales revenues, along with such other costs as labor and raw materials, to determine income. However, because the $100,000 was actually expended back in 2011, the depreciation charged against income in 2012 and subsequent years is not a cash outflow. *Depreciation is a noncash charge, so it must be added back to net income to obtain the net cash flow.* If we assume that all other noncash items (including amortization) sum to zero, then net cash flow is simply equal to net income plus depreciation.

Self Test

Differentiate between net cash flow and accounting profit.

A firm has net income of $5 million. Assuming that depreciation of $1 million is its only noncash expense, what is the firm's net cash flow? **($6 million)**

7.6 Statement of Cash Flows

Even if a company reports a large net income during a year, the *amount of cash* reported on its year-end balance sheet may be the same or even lower than its beginning cash. The reason is that its net income can be used in a variety of ways, not just kept as cash in the bank. For example, the firm may use its net income to pay dividends, to increase inventories, to finance accounts receivable, to invest in fixed assets, to reduce debt, or to buy back common stock. Indeed, the company's *cash position* as reported on its balance sheet is affected by a great many factors, which include the following.

1. **Net income before preferred dividends.** Other things held constant, a positive net income will lead to more cash in the bank. However, as we shall discuss, other things generally are not held constant.

2. **Noncash adjustments to net income.** To calculate cash flow, it is necessary to adjust net income to reflect noncash revenues and expenses, such as depreciation and deferred taxes, as shown previously in the calculation of net cash flow.

3. **Changes in working capital.** Increases in current assets other than cash (such as inventories and accounts receivable) decrease cash, whereas decreases in these accounts increase cash. For example, if inventories are to increase, then the firm must use some of its cash to acquire the additional inventory. Conversely, if inventories decrease, this generally means the firm is selling inventories and not replacing all of them, hence generating cash. On the other hand, if payables increase then the firm has received additional credit from its suppliers, which saves cash, but if payables decrease, this means it has used cash to pay off its suppliers. Therefore, increases in current liabilities such as accounts payable increase cash, whereas decreases in current liabilities decrease cash.

4. **Investments.** If a company invests in fixed assets or short-term financial investments, this will reduce its cash position. On the other hand, if it sells some fixed assets or short-term investments, this will increase cash.

5. **Security transactions and dividend payments.** If a company issues stock or bonds during the year, the funds raised will increase its cash position. On the other hand, if the company uses cash to buy back outstanding stock or to pay off debt, or if it pays dividends to its shareholders, this will reduce cash.

Each of these five factors is reflected in the **statement of cash flows,** which summarizes the changes in a company's cash position. The statement separates activities into three categories, plus a summary section, as follows.

1. **Operating activities,** which includes net income, depreciation, changes in current assets and liabilities other than cash, short-term investments, and short-term debt.

2. **Investing activities,** which includes investments in or sales of fixed assets and short-term financial investments.

3. **Financing activities,** which includes raising cash by issuing short-term debt, long-term debt, or stock. Also, because dividend payments, stock repurchases, and principal payments on debt reduce a company's cash, such transactions are included here.

Accounting texts explain how to prepare the statement of cash flows, but the statement is used to help answer questions such as these: Is the firm generating enough cash to purchase the additional assets required for growth? Is the firm generating any extra cash that can be used to repay debt or to invest in new products? Such information is useful both for managers and investors, so the statement of cash flows is an important part of the annual report.

Table 7-4 shows MicroDrive's statement of cash flows as it would appear in the company's annual report. The top section shows cash generated by and used in operations—for MicroDrive, operations provided net cash flows of *minus* $3 million. This subtotal, the minus $3 million net cash flow provided by operating activities, is in many respects the most important figure in any of the financial statements. Profits as reported on the income statement can be "doctored" by such tactics as depreciating assets too slowly, not recognizing bad debts promptly, and the like. However, it is far more difficult to simultaneously doctor profits and the working capital accounts. Therefore, it is not uncommon for a company to report positive net income right up to the day it declares bankruptcy. In such cases, however, the net cash flow from operations almost always began to deteriorate much earlier, and analysts who kept an eye on cash flow could have predicted trouble. Therefore, if you are ever analyzing a

TABLE 7-4	MicroDrive Inc.: Statement of Cash Flows for 2012 (Millions of Dollars)	
		Cash Provided or Used
Operating Activities		
Net income before preferred dividends		$117
Adjustments:		
Noncash adjustments:		
Depreciation and amortization[a]		100
Due to changes in working capital:[b]		
Increase in accounts receivable		(60)
Increase in inventories		(200)
Increase in accounts payable		30
Increase in accruals		10
Net cash provided (used) by operating activities		($ 3)
Investing Activities		
Cash used to acquire fixed assets[c]		($230)
Sale of short-term investments		$ 65
Net cash provided (used) by investing activities		($165)
Financing Activities		
Increase in notes payable		$ 50
Increase in bonds outstanding		174
Payment of preferred and common dividends		(61)
Net cash provided (used) by financing activities		$163
Summary		
Net change in cash		($ 5)
Cash at beginning of year		15
Cash at end of year		$ 10

© Cengage Learning 2013

[a]Depreciation and amortization is a noncash expense that was deducted when calculating net income. It must be added back to show the correct cash flow from operations.
[b]An increase in a current asset *decreases* cash. An increase in a current liability *increases* cash. For example, inventories increased by $200 million and therefore reduced cash by a like amount.
[c]The net increase in fixed assets is $130 million; however, this net amount is after a deduction for the year's depreciation expense. Depreciation expense would have to be added back to find the increase in gross fixed assets. From the company's income statement, we see that the 2012 depreciation expense is $100 million; thus, expenditures on fixed assets were actually $230 million.

company and are pressed for time, look first at the trend in net cash flow provided by operating activities, because it will tell you more than any other number.

The second section shows investing activities. MicroDrive purchased fixed assets totaling $230 million and sold $65 million of short-term investments, for a net cash flow from investing activities of *minus* $165 million.

FILLING IN THE GAAP

While U.S. companies adhere to "Generally Accepted Accounting Principles," or GAAP, when preparing financial statements, most other developed countries use "International Financial Reporting Standards," or IFRS. The U.S. GAAP system is "rules-based," with thousands of instructions, or "guidances," for how individual transactions should be reported in financial statements. IFRS, on the other hand, is a "principles-based" system in which myriad detailed instructions are replaced by fewer overall guiding principles. For example, whereas GAAP provides extensive and detailed rules about when to recognize revenue from any conceivable activity, IFRS provides just four categories of revenue and two overall principles for timing recognition. This means that even the most basic accounting measure, revenue, is different under the two standards—Total Revenue, or Sales, under GAAP won't typically equal Total Revenue under IFRS. Thus, financial statements prepared under GAAP cannot be compared directly to IFRS financial statements, making comparative financial analysis of U.S. and international companies difficult. Perhaps more problematic is that the IFRS principles allow for more company discretion in recording transactions. This means that two different companies may treat an identical transaction differently when using IFRS, which makes company-to-company comparisons more difficult.

The U.S. Financial Accounting Standards Board (FASB) and the International Accounting Standards Board (IASB) have been working on a project to merge the two standards since 2002. If the current timetable holds, the joint standards will be completed by the end of 2011, with adoption by U.S. firms by 2015.

What does this mean for you? There will still be an income statement, a balance sheet, and an equivalent to the statement of cash flows. Line item summary measures may change a bit, and the technical details about how individual transactions are recorded will certainly change. Accounting systems will be re-programmed, accounting texts will be re-written, and CPAs will have to re-train. The end result, though, will be a better ability to compare U.S. and international companies' financial statements.

To keep abreast of developments in IFRS/GAAP convergence, visit the IASB Web site at **www.iasb.org** and the FASB Web site at **www.fasb.org**. For discussions of the issues companies face with convergence, see **www.pwc.com/us/en/issues/ifrs-reporting/publications/ifrs-and-us-gaap-similarities-and-differences-september-2010.jhtml** and **www.ey.com/Publication/vwLUAssets/IFRS_v_GAAP_basics_Jan09/$file/IFRS_v_GAAP_basics_Jan09.pdf**.

The third section, financing activities, includes borrowing from banks (notes payable), selling new bonds, and paying dividends on common and preferred stock. Micro-Drive raised $224 million by borrowing, but it paid $61 million in preferred and common dividends. Therefore, its net inflow of funds from financing activities was $163 million.

In the summary, when all of these sources and uses of cash are totaled, we see that MicroDrive's cash outflows exceeded its cash inflows by $5 million during 2012; that is, its net change in cash was a *negative* $5 million.

MicroDrive's statement of cash flows should be worrisome to its managers and to outside analysts. The company had a $3 million cash shortfall from operations, it spent an additional $230 million on new fixed assets, and it paid out another $61 million in dividends. It covered these cash outlays by borrowing heavily and by liquidating $65 million of short-term investments. Obviously, this situation cannot continue year after year, so something will have to be done. In Chapter 9, when we discuss financial planning, we consider some of the actions that MicroDrive's financial staff might recommend.[7]

---

7. For a more detailed discussion of financial statement analysis, see Lyn M. Fraser and Aileen Ormiston, *Understanding Financial Statements*, 9th ed. (Upper Saddle River, NJ: Prentice-Hall, 2010).

What types of questions does the statement of cash flows answer?

Identify and briefly explain the three different categories of activities shown in the statement of cash flows.

A firm has inventories of $2 million for the previous year and $1.5 million for the current year. What impact does this have on net cash provided by operations? **(Increase of $500,000)**

7.7 Modifying Accounting Data for Managerial Decisions

Thus far in the chapter we have focused on financial statements as they are presented in the annual report. When you studied income statements in accounting, the emphasis was probably on the firm's net income, which is its **accounting profit.** However, the intrinsic value of a company's operations is determined by the stream of cash flows that the operations will generate now and in the future. To be more specific, the value of operations depends on all the future expected **free cash flows (FCF),** defined as after-tax operating profit minus the amount of new investment in working capital and fixed assets necessary to sustain the business. *Therefore, the way for managers to make their companies more valuable is to increase free cash flow now and in the future.*

Notice that FCF is the cash flow *available for distribution to all the company's investors after the company has made all investments necessary to sustain ongoing operations.* How well have MicroDrive's managers done in generating FCF? In this section, we will calculate MicroDrive's FCF and evaluate the performance of MicroDrive's managers.

Figure 7-1 shows the five steps in calculating free cash flow. As we explain each individual step in the following sections, refer back to Figure 7-1 to keep the big picture in mind.

7.7a Net Operating Profit after Taxes (NOPAT)

If two companies have different amounts of debt and hence different amounts of interest charges, they could have identical operating performances but different net incomes—the one with more debt would have a lower net income. Net income is certainly important, but it does not always reflect the true performance of a company's operations or the effectiveness of its operating managers. A better measurement for comparing managers' performance is **net operating profit after taxes,** or **NOPAT,** which is the amount of profit a company would generate if it had no debt and held no financial assets. NOPAT is defined as follows:[8]

---

8. For firms with a more complicated tax situation, it is better to define NOPAT as follows: NOPAT = (Net income before preferred dividends) + (Net interest expense)(1 − Tax rate). Also, if firms are able to defer paying some of their taxes, perhaps by the use of accelerated depreciation, then NOPAT should be adjusted to reflect the taxes that the company actually paid on its operating income. See P. Daves, M. Ehrhardt, and R. Shrieves, *Corporate Valuation: A Guide for Managers and Investors* (Mason, OH: Thomson South-Western, 2004) for a detailed explanation of these and other adjustments. Also see Tim Koller, Marc Goedhart, and David Wessels, *Valuation: Measuring and Managing the Value of Companies* (Hoboken, NJ: Wiley, 2005), and G. Bennett Stewart, *The Quest for Value* (New York: Harper Collins, 1991).

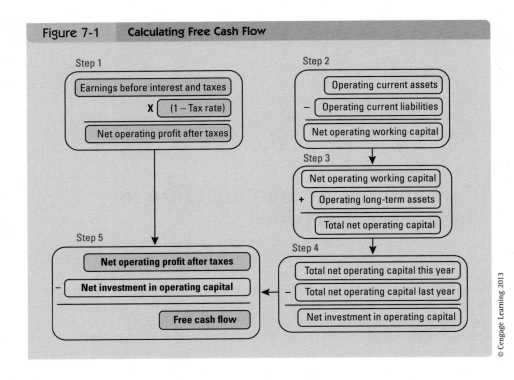

Figure 7-1 Calculating Free Cash Flow

(7–3)

$$NOPAT = EBIT(1 - \text{Tax rate})$$

Using data from the income statements of Table 7-2, MicroDrive's 2012 NOPAT is

$$NOPAT = \$283(1 - 0.4) = \$283(0.6) = \$169.8 \text{ million}$$

This means MicroDrive generated an after-tax operating profit of $169.8 million, a little better than its previous NOPAT of $260(0.6) = $156.0 million. However, the income statements in Table 7-2 show that MicroDrive's earnings per share actually declined. This decrease in EPS was caused by an increase in interest expense, and not by a decrease in operating profit.

7.7b Net Operating Working Capital

Most companies need some current assets to support their operating activities. For example, all companies must carry some cash to "grease the wheels" of their operations. Companies continuously receive checks from customers and write checks to suppliers, employees, and so on. Because inflows and outflows do not coincide perfectly, a company must keep some cash in its bank account. In other words, some cash is required to conduct operations. The same is true for most other current assets, such as inventory and accounts receivable, which are required for normal operations. The short-term assets normally used in a company's operating activities are called **operating current assets**.

For the previous year, its total net operating capital was

$$\text{Total net operating capital} = \$585 + \$870$$
$$= \$1,455 \text{ million}$$

Notice that we have defined total net operating capital as the sum of net operating working capital and operating long-term assets. In other words, our definition is in terms of operating assets and liabilities. However, we can also calculate total net operating capital by adding up the funds provided by investors, such as notes payable, long-term bonds, preferred stock, and common equity. For MicroDrive, the total capital provided by investors at year-end 2011 was $60 + $580 + $40 + $840 = $1,520 million. Of this amount, $65 million was tied up in short-term investments, which are not directly related to MicroDrive's operations. Therefore, only $1,520 − $65 = $1,455 million of investor-supplied capital was used in operations. Notice that this is exactly the same value as calculated before. This shows that we can calculate total net operating capital either from net operating working capital and operating long-term assets or from the investor-supplied funds. We usually base our calculations on operating data because this approach allows us to analyze a division, factory, or work center, whereas the approach based on investor-supplied capital is applicable only for the entire company.

The expression "total net operating capital" is a mouthful, so we often call it *operating capital* or even just *capital*. Also, unless we specifically say "investor-supplied capital," we are referring to total net operating capital.

7.7d Net Investment in Operating Capital

As calculated previously, MicroDrive had $1,455 million of total net operating capital at the end of 2011 and $1,800 million at the end of 2012. Therefore, during 2012, it made a **net investment in operating capital** of

$$\text{Net investment in operating capital} = \$1,800 - \$1,455 = \$345 \text{ million}$$

Most of this investment was made in net operating working capital, which rose from $585 million to $800 million, or by $215 million. This 37% increase in net operating working capital, in view of a sales increase of only 5% (from $2,850 to $3,000 million), should set off warning bells in your head: Why did MicroDrive tie up so much additional cash in working capital? Is the company gearing up for a big increase in sales, or are inventories not moving and receivables not being collected? We will address these questions in detail in Chapter 8, when we cover ratio analysis.

7.7e Calculating Free Cash Flow

Free cash flow is defined as

$$\text{FCF} = \text{NOPAT} - \text{Net investment in operating capital} \qquad \text{(7-6)}$$

MicroDrive's free cash flow in 2012 was

$$\text{FCF} = \$169.8 - (\$1,800 - \$1,455)$$
$$= \$169.8 - \$345$$
$$= -\$175.2 \text{ million}$$

Although we prefer this approach to calculating FCF, sometimes the financial press calculates FCF with a different approach. The results are the same either way, but you should be aware of this alternative approach. The difference lies in how depreciation is treated. To see this, notice that net fixed assets rose from $870 to $1,000 million, or by $130 million. However, MicroDrive reported $100 million of depreciation, so its gross investment in fixed assets was $130 + $100 = $230 million for the year. With this background, the **gross investment in operating capital** is

$$(7\text{-}7) \qquad \begin{array}{c}\text{Gross investment} \\ \text{in operating capital}\end{array} = \begin{array}{c}\text{Net investment in} \\ \text{operating capital}\end{array} + \text{Depreciation}$$

For MicroDrive, the gross investment in operating capital was:

$$\begin{array}{c}\text{Gross investment} \\ \text{in operating capital}\end{array} = \$345 + \$100 = \$445 \text{ million}$$

Because depreciation is a noncash expense, some analysts calculate **operating cash flow** as

$$(7\text{-}8) \qquad \text{Operating cash flow} = \text{NOPAT} + \text{Depreciation}$$

MicroDrive's most recent operating cash flow is

$$\text{Operating cash flow} = \text{NOPAT} + \text{Depreciation} = \$169.8 + \$100 = \$269.8$$

An algebraically equivalent expression for free cash flow in terms of operating cash flow and gross investment in operating capital is

$$(7\text{-}9) \qquad \begin{aligned} \text{FCF} &= (\text{NOPAT} + \text{Depreciation}) - \left(\begin{array}{c}\text{Net investment in} \\ \text{operating capital}\end{array} + \text{Depreciation} \right) \\[2mm] &= \begin{array}{c}\text{Operating} \\ \text{cash flow}\end{array} - \begin{array}{c}\text{Gross investment in} \\ \text{operating capital}\end{array} \\[2mm] &= \begin{array}{c}\text{Operating} \\ \text{cash flow}\end{array} - \begin{array}{c}\text{Gross investment in} \\ \text{long-term operating assets}\end{array} - \begin{array}{c}\text{Investment} \\ \text{in NOWC}\end{array} \end{aligned}$$

For MicroDrive, this definition produces FCF of −$175.2, the same value as found earlier:

$$\begin{aligned} \text{FCF} &= (\$169.8 + \$100) - \$445 \\ &= -\$175.2 \text{ million} \end{aligned}$$

Equations 7-6 and 7-9 are equivalent because depreciation is added to both NOPAT and net investment in Equation 7-6 to arrive at Equation 7-9. We usually use Equation 7-6, because it saves us this step, but you should be aware of this alternative approach.

7.7f The Uses of FCF

Recall that free cash flow (FCF) is the amount of cash that is available for distribution to all investors, including shareholders and debtholders. There are five good uses for FCF:

1. Pay interest to debtholders, keeping in mind that the net cost to the company is the after-tax interest expense.
2. Repay debtholders; that is, pay off some of the debt.
3. Pay dividends to shareholders.
4. Repurchase stock from shareholders.
5. Buy short-term investments or other nonoperating assets.

Consider MicroDrive, with its FCF of –$175.2 million in 2012. How did MicroDrive use the FCF?

MicroDrive's income statement shows an interest expense of $88 million. With a tax rate of 40%, the after-tax interest payment for the year is

$$\text{After-tax interest payment} = \$88(1 - 40\%) = \$52.8 \text{ million}$$

The net amount of debt that is repaid is equal to the amount at the beginning of the year minus the amount at the end of the year. This includes notes payable and long-term debt. If the amount of ending debt is less than the beginning debt, the company paid down some of its debt. But if the ending debt is greater than the beginning debt, the company actually borrowed additional funds from creditors. In that case, it would be a negative use of FCF. For MicroDrive, the net debt repayment for 2012 is

$$\text{Net reduction in debt} = (\$60 + \$580) - (\$754 + \$110) = -\$224 \text{ million}$$

This is a "negative use" of FCF because it increased the debt balance. This is typical of most companies because growing companies usually add debt each year.

MicroDrive paid $4 million in preferred dividends and $57 in common dividends for a total of

$$\text{Dividend payments} = \$4 + \$57 = \$61 \text{ million}$$

The net amount of stock that is repurchased is equal to the amount at the beginning of the year minus the amount at the end of the year. This includes preferred stock and common stock. If the amount of ending stock is less than the beginning stock, then the company made net repurchases. But if the ending stock is greater than the beginning stock, the company actually made net issuances. In that case, it would be a negative use of FCF. Even though MicroDrive neither issued nor repurchased stock during the year, many companies use FCF to repurchase stocks as a replacement for or supplement to dividends, as we discuss in Chapter 17.

The amount of net purchases of short-term investments is equal to the amount at the end of the year minus the amount at the beginning of the year. If the amount of ending investments is greater than the beginning investments, then the company made net purchases. But if the ending investments are less than the beginning investments, the company actually sold investments. In that case, it would be a negative use of FCF. MicroDrive's net purchases of short-term investments in 2012 are:

$$\text{Net purchases of short-term investments} = \$0 - \$65 = -\$65 \text{ million}$$

Notice that this is a "negative use" because MicroDrive sold short-term investments instead of purchasing them.

We combine these individual uses of FCF to find the total uses.

1. After-tax interest:		$ 52.8
2. Net debt repayments:		−224.0
3. Dividends:		61.0
4. Net stock repurchases:		0.0
5. Net purchases of ST investments:		−65.0
Total uses of FCF:		−$175.2

The −$175.2 total for uses of FCF is identical to the value of FCF from operations that we calculated previously. If it were not equal, then we would have made an error somewhere in our calculations.

Observe that a company does not use FCF to acquire operating assets, because the calculation of FCF already takes into account the purchase of operating assets needed to support growth. Unfortunately, there is evidence to suggest that some companies with high FCF tend to make unnecessary investments that don't add value, such as paying too much to acquire another company. Thus, high FCF can cause waste if managers fail to act in the best interests of shareholders. As discussed in Chapter 1, this is called an agency cost, since managers are hired as agents to act on behalf of stockholders. We discuss agency costs and ways to control them in Chapter 11, where we discuss value-based management and corporate governance, and in Chapter 15, where we discuss the choice of capital structure.

7.7g FCF and Corporate Value

Free cash flow is the amount of cash available for distribution to investors; so the fundamental value of a company to its investors depends on the present value of its expected future FCFs, discounted at the company's weighted average cost of capital (WACC). Subsequent chapters will develop the tools needed to forecast FCFs and evaluate their risk. Chapter 11 ties all this together with a model that is used to calculate the value of a company. Even though you do not yet have all the tools to apply the model, it's important that you understand this basic concept: *FCF is the cash flow available for distribution to investors. Therefore, the fundamental value of a firm primarily depends on its expected future FCF.*

7.7h Evaluating FCF, NOPAT, and Operating Capital

Even though MicroDrive had a positive NOPAT, its very high investment in operating assets resulted in a negative FCF. Because free cash flow is the cash flow available for distribution to investors, MicroDrive's negative FCF meant that MicroDrive had to sell short-term investments and so investors actually had to provide *additional* money to keep the business going.

Is a negative free cash flow always bad? The answer is, "Not necessarily; it depends on why the free cash flow was negative." It's a bad sign if FCF was negative because NOPAT was negative, since then the company is probably experiencing operating problems. However, many high-growth companies have positive NOPAT but negative FCF because they are making large investments in operating assets to support growth. There is nothing wrong with profitable growth, even if it causes negative cash flows.

One way to determine whether growth is profitable is by examining the **return on invested capital (ROIC),** which is the ratio of NOPAT to total operating capital. If the ROIC exceeds the rate of return required by investors, then a negative free cash flow caused by high growth is nothing to worry about. Chapter 11 discusses this in detail.

To calculate the ROIC, we first calculate NOPAT and operating capital. The return on invested capital is a performance measure that indicates how much NOPAT is generated by each dollar of operating capital:

$$\text{ROIC} = \frac{\text{NOPAT}}{\text{Operating capital}}$$

(7–10)

If ROIC is greater than the rate of return that investors require, which is the weighted average cost of capital (WACC), then the firm is adding value.

As noted previously, a negative FCF is not necessarily bad, provided it is due to high, profitable growth.[10] For example, Qualcomm's sales grew by 26% in 2008, which led to large capital investments and an FCF of *negative* $4.6 billion. However, its ROIC was about 29%, so the growth was profitable. Qualcomm experienced negative growth in 2009 and only slow growth in 2010 as a result of the global recession, and with slower growth came smaller capital requirements and higher FCF; FCF soared to about $2.5 billion in 2010 with an ROIC of 14%. Certainly Qualcomm would have preferred to maintain its 26% growth rate and high ROIC, but the silver lining behind the decline in growth was the substantial increase in FCF.

MicroDrive had an ROIC in 2012 of 9.43%: $169.8/$1,800 = 0.0943. Is this enough to cover its cost of capital? We'll answer that question in the next section.

Self Test

What is net operating working capital? Why does it exclude most short-term investments and also notes payable?

What is total net operating capital? Why is it important for managers to calculate a company's capital requirements?

Why is NOPAT a better performance measure than net income?

What is free cash flow? Why is it important?

A firm's total net operating capital for the previous year was $2 million. For the current year, its total net operating capital is $2.5 million and its NOPAT is $1.2 million. What is its free cash flow for the current year? **($700,000)**

---

10. If g is the growth rate in capital, then with a little (or a lot of!) algebra, free cash flow is

$$\text{FCF} = \text{Capital}\left(\text{ROIC} - \frac{g}{1+g}\right)$$

This shows that when the growth rate gets almost as high as ROIC, then FCF will be negative.

7.8 MVA and EVA

Neither traditional accounting data nor the modified data discussed in the preceding section incorporates stock prices, even though the primary goal of management is to maximize the firm's stock price. Financial analysts have therefore developed two additional performance measures, Market Value Added (MVA) and Economic Value Added (EVA). These concepts are discussed in this section.[11]

7.8a Market Value Added (MVA)

The primary goal of most firms is to maximize shareholders' wealth. This goal obviously benefits shareholders, but it also helps to ensure that scarce resources are allocated efficiently, which benefits the economy. Shareholder wealth is maximized by maximizing the *difference* between the market value of the firm's stock and the amount of equity capital that was supplied by shareholders. This difference is called the **Market Value Added (MVA):**

(7–11)

$$\text{MVA} = \text{Market value of stock} - \text{Equity capital supplied by shareholders}$$
$$= (\text{Shares outstanding})(\text{Stock price}) - \text{Total common equity}$$

For an updated estimate of Coca-Cola's MVA, go to **finance.yahoo.com**, enter KO, and click GO. This shows the market value of equity, called Mkt Cap. To get the book value of equity, select Balance Sheet from the left panel.

To illustrate, consider Coca-Cola. In December 2010, its total market equity value was $152.0 billion while its balance sheet showed that stockholders had put up only $24.8 billion. Thus, Coca-Cola's MVA was $152.0 − $24.8 = $127.2 billion. This $127.2 billion represents the difference between the money that Coca-Cola's stockholders have invested in the corporation since its founding—including indirect investment by retaining earnings—and the cash they could get if they sold the business. The higher its MVA, the better the job management is doing for the firm's shareholders.

Sometimes MVA is defined as the total market value of the company minus the total amount of investor-supplied capital:

(7–11a)

$$\text{MVA} = \text{Total market value} - \text{Total investor-supplied capital}$$
$$= (\text{Market value of stock} + \text{Market value of debt})$$
$$- \text{Total investor-supplied capital}$$

For most companies, the total amount of investor-supplied capital is the sum of equity, debt, and preferred stock. We can calculate the total amount of investor-supplied capital directly from their reported values in the financial statements. The total market value of a company is the sum of the market values of common equity, debt, and preferred stock. It is easy to find the market value of equity, since stock prices are readily available, but it is not always easy to find the market value of debt. Hence, many analysts use the value of debt that is reported in the financial statements, which is the debt's book value, as an estimate of its market value.

For Coca-Cola, the total amount of reported debt was about $23.9 billion, and Coca-Cola had no preferred stock. Using this as an estimate of the market value

---

11. The concepts of EVA and MVA were developed by Joel Stern and Bennett Stewart, co-founders of the consulting firm Stern Stewart & Company. Stern Stewart copyrighted the terms "EVA" and "MVA," so other consulting firms have given other names to these values. Still, EVA and MVA are the terms most commonly used in practice.

of debt, Coke's total market value was $152.0 + $23.9 = $175.9 billion. The total amount of investor-supplied funds was $24.8 + $23.9 = $48.7 billion. Using these total values, the MVA was $175.9 − $48.7 = $127.2 billion. Note that this is the same answer as when we used the previous definition of MVA. Both methods will give the same result if the market value of debt is approximately equal to its book value.

7.8b Economic Value Added (EVA)

Whereas MVA measures the effects of managerial actions since the very inception of a company, **Economic Value Added (EVA)** focuses on managerial effectiveness in a given year. The basic EVA formula is:

$$
\begin{aligned}
\text{EVA} &= \text{Net operating profit after taxes (NOPAT)} \\
&\quad - \text{After-tax dollar cost of capital used to support operations} \\
&= \text{EBIT}(1 - \text{Tax rate}) - (\text{Total net operating capital})(\text{WACC})
\end{aligned}
$$

 (7–12)

We can also calculate EVA in terms of ROIC:

$$
\text{EVA} = (\text{Operating capital})(\text{ROIC} - \text{WACC})
$$

(7–13)

As this equation shows, a firm adds value—that is, has a positive EVA—if its ROIC is greater than its WACC. If WACC exceeds ROIC, then new investments in operating capital will reduce the firm's value.

Economic Value Added is an estimate of a business's true economic profit for the year, and it differs sharply from accounting profit.[12] EVA represents the residual income that remains after the cost of *all* capital, including equity capital, has been deducted, whereas accounting profit is determined without imposing a charge for equity capital. As we discuss in Chapter 10, equity capital has a cost because shareholders give up the opportunity to invest and earn returns elsewhere when they provide capital to the firm. This cost is an *opportunity cost* rather than an *accounting cost,* but it is quite real nevertheless.

Note that when calculating EVA we do not add back depreciation. Although it is not a cash expense, depreciation is a cost because worn-out assets must be replaced, and it is therefore deducted when determining both net income and EVA. Our calculation of EVA assumes that the true economic depreciation of the company's fixed assets exactly equals the depreciation used for accounting and tax purposes. If this were not the case, adjustments would have to be made to obtain a more accurate measure of EVA.

Economic Value Added measures the extent to which the firm has increased shareholder value. Therefore, if managers focus on EVA, this will help to ensure that they operate in a manner that is consistent with maximizing shareholder wealth. Note too that EVA can be determined for divisions as well as for the company as a

---

12. The most important reason EVA differs from accounting profit is that the cost of equity capital is deducted when EVA is calculated. Other factors that could lead to differences include adjustments that might be made to depreciation, to research and development costs, to inventory valuations, and so on. These other adjustments also can affect the calculation of investor-supplied capital, which affects both EVA and MVA. See Stewart, *The Quest for Value,* cited in footnote 8.

TABLE 7-5	MVA and EVA for MicroDrive Inc. (Millions of Dollars)		
		2012	**2011**
MVA Calculation			
Price per share		$ 23.0	$ 26.0
Number of shares (millions)		50.0	50.0
Market value of equity = Share price × Number of shares		$1,150.0	$1,300.0
Book value of equity		$ 896.0	$ 840.0
MVA = Market value − Book value		$ 254.0	$ 460.0
EVA Calculation			
EBIT		$ 283.0	$ 260.0
Tax rate		40.0%	40.0%
NOPAT = EBIT(1 − T)		$ 169.8	$ 156.0
Total investor-supplied operating capital[a]		$1,800.0	$1,455.0
Weighted average cost of capital, WACC (%)		11.0%	10.8%
Dollar cost of capital = Operating capital × WACC		$ 198.0	$ 157.1
EVA = NOPAT − Dollar cost of capital		($ 28.2)	($ 1.1)
ROIC = NOPAT ÷ Operating capital		9.43%	10.72%
ROIC − Cost of capital = ROIC − WACC		(1.57%)	(0.08%)
EVA = Operating capital × (ROIC − WACC)		($ 28.2)	($ 1.1)

© Cengage Learning 2013

[a]Investor-supplied operating capital equals the sum of notes payable, long-term debt, preferred stock, and common equity, less short-term investments. It could also be calculated as total liabilities and equity minus accounts payable, accruals, and short-term investments. It is also equal to total net operating capital.

WEB

See *Ch07 Tool Kit.xls* for details.

whole, so it provides a useful basis for determining managerial performance at all levels. Consequently, EVA is being used by an increasing number of firms as the primary basis for determining managerial compensation.

Table 7-5 shows how MicroDrive's MVA and EVA are calculated. The stock price was $23 per share at year-end 2012, down from $26 per share the previous year. Its WACC, which is the percentage after-tax cost of capital, was 10.8% in 2011 and 11.0% in 2012, and its tax rate was 40%. Other data in Table 7-5 were given in the basic financial statements provided earlier in the chapter.

Note first that the lower stock price and the higher book value of equity (due to retaining earnings during 2012) combined to reduce the MVA. The 2012 MVA is still positive, but $460 − $254 = $206 million of stockholders' value was lost during the year.

Economic Value Added for 2011 was virtually zero, and in 2012 it was negative. Operating income (NOPAT) rose, but EVA still declined, primarily because the amount of capital rose more sharply than NOPAT—by about 24% versus 9%—and the cost of this additional capital pulled EVA down.

Recall also that net income fell, but not nearly so dramatically as the decline in EVA. Net income does not reflect the amount of equity capital employed, but EVA does. Because of this omission, net income is not as useful as EVA for setting corporate goals and measuring managerial performance.

SARBANES-OXLEY AND FINANCIAL FRAUD

Investors need to be cautious when they review financial statements. Although companies are required to follow generally accepted accounting principles (GAAP), managers still have quite a lot of discretion in deciding how and when to report certain transactions. Consequently, two firms in exactly the same operating situation may report financial statements that convey different impressions about their financial strength. Some variations may stem from legitimate differences of opinion about the correct way to record transactions. In other cases, managers may choose to report numbers in a way that helps them present either higher earnings or more stable earnings over time. As long as they follow GAAP, such actions are not illegal, but these differences make it harder for investors to compare companies and gauge their true performances.

Unfortunately, there have also been cases where managers overstepped the bounds and reported fraudulent statements. Indeed, a number of high-profile executives have faced criminal charges because of their misleading accounting practices. For example, in June 2002 it was discovered that WorldCom (now called MCI) had committed the most massive accounting fraud of all time by recording over $7 billion of ordinary operating costs as capital expenditures, thus overstating net income by the same amount.

WorldCom's published financial statements fooled most investors—investors bid the stock price up to $64.50, and banks and other lenders provided the company with more than $30 billion of loans. Arthur Andersen, the firm's auditor, was faulted for not detecting the fraud. WorldCom's CFO and CEO were convicted, and Arthur Andersen went bankrupt. But that didn't help the investors who relied on the published financial statements.

In response to these and other abuses, Congress passed the Sarbanes-Oxley Act of 2002. One of its provisions requires both the CEO and the CFO to sign a statement certifying that the "financial statements and disclosures fairly represent, in all material respects, the operations and financial condition" of the company. This will make it easier to haul off in handcuffs a CEO or CFO who has been misleading investors. Whether this will prevent future financial fraud remains to be seen.

We will have more to say about both MVA and EVA later in the book, but we can close this section with two observations. First, there is a relationship between MVA and EVA, but it is not a direct one. If a company has a history of negative EVAs, then its MVA will probably be negative; conversely, its MVA probably will be positive if the company has a history of positive EVAs. However, the stock price, which is the key ingredient in the MVA calculation, depends more on expected future performance than on historical performance. Therefore, a company with a history of negative EVAs could have a positive MVA, provided investors expect a turnaround in the future.

The second observation is that when EVAs or MVAs are used to evaluate managerial performance as part of an incentive compensation program, EVA is the measure that is typically used. The reasons are: (1) EVA shows the value added during a given year, whereas MVA reflects performance over the company's entire life, perhaps even including times before the current managers were born; and (2) EVA can be applied to individual divisions or other units of a large corporation, whereas MVA must be applied to the entire corporation.

7.9 The Federal Income Tax System

The value of any financial asset (including stocks, bonds, and mortgages), as well as most real assets such as plants or even entire firms, depends on the after-tax stream of cash flows produced by the asset. The following sections describe the key features of corporate and individual taxation.

7.9a Corporate Income Taxes

The corporate tax structure, shown in Table 7-6, is relatively simple. The **marginal tax rate** is the rate paid on the last dollar of income, while the **average tax rate** is the average rate paid on all income. To illustrate, if a firm had $65,000 of taxable income, its tax bill would be

$$\text{Taxes} = \$7,500 + 0.25(\$65,000 - \$50,000)$$
$$= \$7,500 + \$3,750 = \$11,250$$

Its marginal rate would be 25%, and its average tax rate would be $11,250/$65,000 = 17.3%. Note that corporate income above $18,333,333 has an average and marginal tax rate of 35%.[13]

---

13. Prior to 1987, many large, profitable corporations such as General Electric and Boeing paid no income taxes. The reasons for this were as follows: (1) expenses, especially depreciation, were defined differently for calculating taxable income than for reporting earnings to stockholders, so some companies reported positive profits to stockholders but losses—hence no taxes—to the Internal Revenue Service; and (2) some companies that did have tax liabilities used various tax credits to offset taxes that would otherwise have been payable. This situation was effectively eliminated in 1987.

The principal method used to eliminate this situation is the Alternative Minimum Tax (AMT). Under the AMT, both corporate and individual taxpayers must figure their taxes in two ways, the "regular" way and the AMT way, and then pay the higher of the two. The AMT is calculated as follows: (1) Figure your regular taxes. (2) Take your taxable income under the regular method and then add back certain items, especially income on certain municipal bonds, depreciation in excess of straight-line depreciation, certain research and drilling costs, itemized or standard deductions (for individuals), and a number of other items. (3) The income determined in (2) is defined as AMT income, and it must then be multiplied by the AMT tax rate to determine the tax due under the AMT system. An individual or corporation must then pay the higher of the regular tax or the AMT tax. In 2011, there were two AMT tax rates for individuals (26% and 28%, depending on the level of AMT income and filing status). Most corporations have an AMT of 20%. However, there is no AMT for very small companies, defined as those that have had average sales of less than $7.5 million for the past 3 years. Even with the AMT, however, GE, for example, still pays taxes at a rate well under 20% due to other loopholes in the tax code.

TABLE 7-6	Corporate Tax Rates as of January 2011		
If a Corporation's Taxable Income Is	**It Pays This Amount on the Base of the Bracket**	**Plus This Percentage on the Excess Over the Base**	**Average Tax Rate at Top of Bracket**
Up to $50,000	$ 0	15%	15.0%
$50,000–$75,000	$ 7,500	25	18.3
$75,000–$100,000	$ 13,750	34	22.3
$100,000–$335,000	$ 22,250	39	34.0
$335,000–$10,000,000	$ 113,900	34	34.0
$10,000,000–$15,000,000	$3,400,000	35	34.3
$15,000,000–$18,333,333	$5,150,000	38	35.0
Over $18,333,333	$6,416,667	35	35.0

Interest and Dividend Income Received by a Corporation

Interest income received by a corporation is taxed as ordinary income at regular corporate tax rates. However, *70% of the dividends received by one corporation from another is excluded from taxable income, while the remaining 30% is taxed at the ordinary tax rate.*[14] Thus, a corporation earning more than $18,333,333 and paying a 35% marginal tax rate would pay only $(0.30)(0.35) = 0.105 = 10.5\%$ of its dividend income as taxes, so its effective tax rate on dividends received would be 10.5%. If this firm had $10,000 in pre-tax dividend income, then its after-tax dividend income would be $8,950:

$$\frac{\text{After-tax}}{\text{income}} = \frac{\text{Before-tax}}{\text{income}} - \text{Taxes}$$

$$= \frac{\text{Before-tax}}{\text{income}} - \left(\frac{\text{Before-tax}}{\text{income}}\right)(\text{Effective tax rate})$$

$$= \left(\frac{\text{Before-tax}}{\text{income}}\right)(1 - \text{Effective tax rate})$$

$$= \$10,000[1 - (0.30)(0.35)]$$

$$= \$10,000(1 - 0.105) = \$10,000(0.895) = \$8,950$$

WEB

See **Ch07 Tool Kit.xls** for details.

If the corporation pays its own after-tax income out to its stockholders as dividends, then the income is ultimately subjected to *triple taxation:* (1) the original corporation is first taxed, (2) the second corporation is then taxed on the dividends it received, and (3) the individuals who receive the final dividends are taxed again. This is the reason for the 70% exclusion on intercorporate dividends.

If a corporation has surplus funds that can be invested in marketable securities, the tax treatment favors investment in stocks, which pay dividends, rather than

---

14. The size of the dividend exclusion actually depends on the degree of ownership. Corporations that own less than 20% of the stock of the dividend-paying company can exclude 70% of the dividends received; firms that own more than 20% but less than 80% can exclude 80% of the dividends; and firms that own more than 80% can exclude the entire dividend payment. We will, in general, assume a 70% dividend exclusion.

in bonds, which pay interest. For example, suppose Home Depot had $100,000 to invest, and suppose it could buy either bonds that paid interest of $8,000 per year or preferred stock that paid dividends of $7,000. Home Depot is in the 35% tax bracket; therefore, its tax on the interest, if it bought bonds, would be 0.35($8,000) = $2,800, and its after-tax income would be $5,200. If it bought preferred (or common) stock, its tax would be 0.35[(0.30)($7,000)] = $735, and its after-tax income would be $6,265. Other factors might lead Home Depot to invest in bonds, but the tax treatment certainly favors stock investments when the investor is a corporation.[15]

Interest and Dividends Paid by a Corporation

A firm's operations can be financed with either debt or equity capital. If the firm uses debt then it must pay interest on this debt, but if the firm uses equity then it is expected to pay dividends to the equity investors (stockholders). The interest *paid* by a corporation is deducted from its operating income to obtain its taxable income, but dividends paid are not deductible. Therefore, a firm needs $1 of pre-tax income to pay $1 of interest, but if it is in the 40% federal-plus-state tax bracket, it must earn $1.67 of pre-tax income to pay $1 of dividends:

$$\text{Pre-tax income needed to pay \$1 of dividends} = \frac{\$1}{1 - \text{Tax rate}} = \frac{\$1}{0.60} = \$1.67$$

Working backward, if a company has $1.67 in pre-tax income, it must pay $0.67 in taxes: (0.4)($1.67) = $0.67. This leaves the firm with after-tax income of $1.00.

Of course, it is generally not possible to finance exclusively with debt capital, and the risk of doing so would offset the benefits of the higher expected income. Still, *the fact that interest is a deductible expense has a profound effect on the way businesses are financed: Our corporate tax system favors debt financing over equity financing.* This point is discussed in more detail in Chapters 10 and 15.

Corporate Capital Gains

Before 1987, corporate long-term capital gains were taxed at lower rates than corporate ordinary income, so the situation was similar for corporations and individuals. Under current law, however, corporations' capital gains are taxed at the same rates as their operating income.

Corporate Loss Carryback and Carryforward

Ordinary corporate operating losses can be carried back (**carryback**) to each of the preceding 2 years and forward (**carryforward**) for the next 20 years and thus be used to offset taxable income in those years. For example, an operating loss in 2012 could be carried back and used to reduce taxable income in 2010 and 2011 as well as forward, if necessary, to reduce taxes in 2013, 2014, and so on, to the year 2032.

---

15. This illustration demonstrates why corporations favor investing in lower-yielding preferred stocks over higher-yielding bonds. When tax consequences are considered, the yield on the preferred stock, [1 − 0.35(0.30)](7.0%) = 6.265%, is higher than the yield on the bond, (1 − 0.35)(8.0%) = 5.2%. Also, note that corporations are restricted in their use of borrowed funds to purchase other firms' preferred or common stocks. Without such restrictions, firms could engage in *tax arbitrage,* whereby the interest on borrowed funds reduces taxable income on a dollar-for-dollar basis while taxable income is increased by only $0.30 per dollar of dividend income. Thus, current tax laws reduce the 70% dividend exclusion in proportion to the amount of borrowed funds used to purchase the stock.

After carrying back 2 years, any remaining loss is typically carried forward first to the next year, then to the one after that, and so on, until losses have been used up or the 20-year carryforward limit has been reached.

To illustrate, suppose Apex Corporation had $2 million of *pre-tax* profits (taxable income) in 2010 and 2011, and then, in 2012, Apex lost $12 million. Also, assume that Apex's federal-plus-state tax rate is 40%. As shown in Table 7-7, the company would use the carryback feature to recompute its taxes for 2010, using $2 million of the 2012 operating losses to reduce the 2010 pre-tax profit to zero. This would permit it to recover the taxes paid in 2010. Therefore, in 2012 Apex would receive a refund of its 2010 taxes because of the loss experienced in 2012. Because $10 million of the unrecovered losses would still be available, Apex would repeat this procedure for 2011. Thus, in 2012 the company would pay zero taxes for 2012 and also would receive a refund for taxes paid in 2010 and 2011. Apex would still have $8 million of unrecovered losses to carry forward, subject to the 20-year limit. This $8 million could be used to offset future taxable income. The purpose of this loss treatment is to avoid penalizing corporations whose incomes fluctuate substantially from year to year.

Improper Accumulation to Avoid Payment of Dividends

Corporations could refrain from paying dividends and thus permit their stockholders to avoid personal income taxes on dividends. To prevent this, the Tax Code contains an **improper accumulation** provision that states that earnings accumulated by a corporation are subject to penalty rates *if the purpose of the accumulation is to enable stockholders to avoid personal income taxes.* A cumulative total of $250,000 (the balance sheet item "retained earnings") is by law exempted from the improper accumulation tax for most corporations. This is a benefit primarily to small corporations.

WEB

See **Ch07 Tool Kit.xls** for details.

TABLE 7-7	Apex Corporation: Calculation of $12 Million Loss Carryback and Amount Available for Carryforward		
	Past Year 2010	**Past Year 2011**	**Current Year 2012**
Original taxable income	$2,000,000	$2,000,000	−$12,000,000
Carryback credit	2,000,000	2,000,000	
Adjusted profit	$ 0	$ 0	
Taxes previously paid (40%)	800,000	800,000	
Difference = Tax refund due	$ 800,000	$ 800,000	
Total tax refund received			$ 1,600,000
Amount of loss carryforward available			
Current loss			−$12,000,000
Carryback losses used			4,000,000
Carryforward losses still available			−$ 8,000,000

© Cengage Learning 2013

The improper accumulation penalty applies only if the retained earnings in excess of $250,000 are *shown by the IRS to be unnecessary to meet the reasonable needs of the business.* A great many companies do indeed have legitimate reasons for retaining more than $250,000 of earnings. For example, earnings may be retained and used to pay off debt, to finance growth, or to provide the corporation with a cushion against possible cash drains caused by losses. How much a firm should be allowed to accumulate for uncertain contingencies is a matter of judgment. We shall consider this matter again in Chapter 17, which deals with corporate dividend policy.

Consolidated Corporate Tax Returns

If a corporation owns 80% or more of another corporation's stock, then it can aggregate income and file one consolidated tax return; thus, the losses of one company can be used to offset the profits of another. (Similarly, one division's losses can be used to offset another division's profits.) No business ever wants to incur losses (you can go broke losing $1 to save 35¢ in taxes), but tax offsets do help make it more feasible for large, multidivisional corporations to undertake risky new ventures or ventures that will suffer losses during a developmental period.

Taxes on Overseas Income

Many U.S. corporations have overseas subsidiaries, and those subsidiaries must pay taxes in the countries where they operate. Often, foreign tax rates are lower than U.S. rates. As long as foreign earnings are reinvested overseas, no U.S. tax is due on those earnings. However, when foreign earnings are repatriated to the U.S. parent, they are taxed at the applicable U.S. rate, less a credit for taxes paid to the foreign country. As a result, U.S. corporations such as IBM, Coca-Cola, and Microsoft have been able to defer billions of dollars of taxes. This procedure has stimulated overseas investments by U.S. multinational firms—they can continue the deferral indefinitely, but only if they reinvest the earnings in their overseas operations.[16]

7.9b Taxation of Small Businesses: S Corporations

The Tax Code provides that small businesses that meet certain restrictions may be set up as corporations and thus receive the benefits of the corporate form of organization—especially limited liability—yet still be taxed as proprietorships or partnerships rather than as corporations. These corporations are called **S corporations.** ("Regular" corporations are called C corporations.) If a corporation elects S corporation status for tax purposes, then all of the business's income is reported as personal income by its stockholders, on a pro rata basis, and thus is taxed at the rates that apply to individuals. This is an important benefit to the owners of small corporations in which

---

16. This is a contentious political issue. U.S. corporations argue that our tax system is similar to systems in the rest of the world, and if they were taxed immediately on all overseas earnings then they would be at a competitive disadvantage vis-à-vis their global competitors. Others argue that taxation encourages overseas investments at the expense of domestic investments, contributing to the jobs outsourcing problem and also to the federal budget deficit.

all or most of the income earned each year will be distributed as dividends, because then the income is taxed only once, at the individual level.

7.9c Personal Taxes

Web Extension 7A provides a more detailed treatment of individual taxation, but the key elements are presented here. **Ordinary income** consists primarily of wages or profits from a proprietorship or partnership, plus investment income. For the 2010 tax year, individuals with less than $8,375 of taxable income are subject to a federal income tax rate of 10%. For those with higher income, tax rates increase and go up to 35%, depending on the level of income. This is called a **progressive tax,** because the higher one's income, the larger the percentage paid in taxes.

WEB

See *Web Extension 7A* on the textbook's Web site for details concerning personal taxation.

As noted before, individuals are taxed on investment income as well as earned income, but with a few exceptions and modifications. For example, interest received from most state and local government bonds, called **municipals** or **"munis,"** is not subject to federal taxation. However, interest earned on most other bonds or lending is taxed as ordinary income. This means that a lower-yielding muni can provide the same after-tax return as a higher-yielding corporate bond. For a taxpayer in the 35% marginal tax bracket, a muni yielding 5.5% provides the same after-tax return as a corporate bond with a pre-tax yield of 8.46%: $8.46\%(1 - 0.35) = 5.5\%$.

Assets such as stocks, bonds, and real estate are defined as capital assets. If you own a capital asset and its price goes up, then your wealth increases, but you are not liable for any taxes on your increased wealth until you sell the asset. If you sell the asset for more than you originally paid, the profit is called a **capital gain;** if you sell it for less, then you suffer a **capital loss.** The length of time you owned the asset determines the tax treatment. If held for less than 1 year, then your gain or loss is simply added to your other ordinary income. If held for more than a year, then gains are called *long-term capital gains* and are taxed at a lower rate. See *Web Extension 7A* for details, but the long-term capital gains rate is 15% for most situations.

Under the 2003 tax law changes, dividends are now taxed as though they were capital gains. As stated earlier, corporations may deduct interest payments but not dividends when computing their corporate tax liability, which means that dividends are taxed twice, once at the corporate level and again at the personal level. This differential treatment motivates corporations to use debt relatively heavily and to pay small (or even no) dividends. The 2003 tax law did not eliminate the differential treatment of dividends and interest payments from the corporate perspective, but it did make the tax treatment of dividends more similar to that of capital gains from investors' perspectives. To see this, consider a company that doesn't pay a dividend but instead reinvests the cash it could have paid. The company's stock price should increase, leading to a capital gain, which would be taxed at the same rate as the dividend. Of course, the stock price appreciation isn't actually taxed until the stock is sold, whereas the dividend is taxed in the year it is paid, so dividends will still be more costly than capital gains for many investors.

Finally, note that the income of S corporations *and* noncorporate businesses is reported as income by the firms' owners. Since there are far more S corporations, partnerships, and proprietorships than C corporations (which are subject to the corporate tax), individual tax considerations play an important role in business finance.

Explain what is meant by this statement: "Our tax rates are progressive."

If a corporation has $85,000 in taxable income, what is its tax liability? **($17,150)**

Explain the difference between marginal tax rates and average tax rates.

What are municipal bonds, and how are these bonds taxed?

What are capital gains and losses, and how are they taxed?

How does the federal income tax system treat dividends received by a corporation versus those received by an individual?

What is the difference in the tax treatment of interest and dividends paid by a corporation? Does this factor favor debt or equity financing?

Briefly explain how tax loss carryback and carryforward procedures work.

Summary

The primary purposes of this chapter were (1) to describe the basic financial statements, (2) to present some background information on cash flows, and (3) to provide an overview of the federal income tax system. The key concepts covered are listed below.

- The four basic statements contained in the **annual report** are the balance sheet, the income statement, the statement of stockholders' equity, and the statement of cash flows.
- The **balance sheet** shows assets on the left-hand side and liabilities and equity, or claims against assets, on the right-hand side. (Sometimes assets are shown at the top and claims at the bottom of the balance sheet.) The balance sheet may be thought of as a snapshot of the firm's financial position at a particular point in time.
- The **income statement** reports the results of operations over a period of time, and it shows earnings per share as its "bottom line."
- The **statement of stockholders' equity** shows the change in retained earnings between balance sheet dates. Retained earnings represent a claim against assets, not assets per se.
- The **statement of cash flows** reports the effect of operating, investing, and financing activities on cash flows over an accounting period.
- **Net cash flow** differs from **accounting profit** because some of the revenues and expenses reflected in accounting profits may not have been received or paid out in cash during the year. Depreciation is typically the largest noncash item, so net cash flow is often expressed as net income plus depreciation.
- **Operating current assets** are the current assets that are used to support operations, such as cash, inventory, and accounts receivable. They do not include short-term investments.

- **Operating current liabilities** are the current liabilities that occur as a natural consequence of operations, such as accounts payable and accruals. They do not include notes payable or any other short-term debts that charge interest.
- **Net operating working capital** is the difference between operating current assets and operating current liabilities. Thus, it is the working capital acquired with investor-supplied funds.
- **Operating long-term assets** are the long-term assets used to support operations, such as net plant and equipment. They do not include any long-term investments that pay interest or dividends.
- **Total net operating capital** (which means the same as **operating capital** and **net operating assets**) is the sum of net operating working capital and operating long-term assets. It is the total amount of capital needed to run the business.
- **NOPAT** is net operating profit after taxes. It is the after-tax profit a company would have if it had no debt and no investments in nonoperating assets. Because it excludes the effects of financial decisions, it is a better measure of operating performance than is net income.
- **Free cash flow (FCF)** is the amount of cash flow remaining after a company makes the asset investments necessary to support operations. In other words, FCF is the amount of cash flow available for distribution to investors, so *the value of a company is directly related to its ability to generate free cash flow.* FCF is defined as NOPAT minus the net investment in operating capital.
- **Market Value Added (MVA)** represents the difference between the total market value of a firm and the total amount of investor-supplied capital. If the market values of debt and preferred stock equal their values as reported on the financial statements, then MVA is the difference between the market value of a firm's stock and the amount of equity its shareholders have supplied.
- **Economic Value Added (EVA)** is the difference between after-tax operating profit and the total dollar cost of capital, including the cost of equity capital. EVA is an estimate of the value created by management during the year, and it differs substantially from accounting profit because no charge for the use of equity capital is reflected in accounting profit.
- Interest income received by a corporation is taxed as **ordinary income**; however, 70% of the dividends received by one corporation from another are excluded from **taxable income**.
- Because interest paid by a corporation is a **deductible expense** whereas dividends are not, our tax system favors debt over equity financing.
- Ordinary corporate operating losses can be **carried back** to each of the preceding 2 years and **carried forward** for the next 20 years in order to offset taxable income in those years.
- **S corporations** are small businesses that have the limited-liability benefits of the corporate form of organization yet are taxed as partnerships or proprietorships.
- In the United States, tax rates are **progressive**—the higher one's income, the larger the percentage paid in taxes.
- Assets such as stocks, bonds, and real estate are defined as **capital assets**. If a capital asset is sold for more than its cost, the profit is called a **capital gain**; if the asset is sold for a loss, it is called a **capital loss**. Assets held for more than a year provide **long-term gains** or **losses**.
- Dividends are taxed as though they were capital gains.
- **Personal taxes** are discussed in more detail in *Web Extension 7A.*

Questions

7-1 Define each of the following terms:
  a. Annual report; balance sheet; income statement
  b. Common stockholders' equity, or net worth; retained earnings
  c. Statement of stockholders' equity; statement of cash flows
  d. Depreciation; amortization; EBITDA
  e. Operating current assets; operating current liabilities; net operating working capital; total net operating capital
  f. Accounting profit; net cash flow; NOPAT; free cash flow
  g. Market Value Added; Economic Value Added
  h. Progressive tax; taxable income; marginal and average tax rates
  i. Capital gain or loss; tax loss carryback and carryforward
  j. Improper accumulation; S corporation

7-2 What four statements are contained in most annual reports?

7-3 If a "typical" firm reports $20 million of retained earnings on its balance sheet, can the firm definitely pay a $20 million cash dividend?

7-4 Explain the following statement: "Whereas the balance sheet can be thought of as a snapshot of the firm's financial position *at a point in time,* the income statement reports on operations *over a period of time.*"

7-5 What is operating capital, and why is it important?

7-6 Explain the difference between NOPAT and net income. Which is a better measure of the performance of a company's operations?

7-7 What is free cash flow? Why is it the most important measure of cash flow?

7-8 If you were starting a business, what tax considerations might cause you to prefer to set it up as a proprietorship or a partnership rather than as a corporation?

Problems   Answers Appear in Appendix B

Note: By the time this book is published, Congress may have changed rates and/or other provisions of current tax law—as noted in the chapter, such changes occur fairly often. Work all problems on the assumption that the information in the chapter is applicable.

Easy Problems 1–6

7-1 **Personal After-Tax Yield** An investor recently purchased a corporate bond that yields 9%. The investor is in the 36% combined federal and state tax bracket. What is the bond's after-tax yield?

7-2 **Personal After-Tax Yield** Corporate bonds issued by Johnson Corporation currently yield 8%. Municipal bonds of equal risk currently yield 6%. At what tax rate would an investor be indifferent between these two bonds?

7-3 **Income Statement** Molteni Motors Inc. recently reported $6 million of net income. Its EBIT was $13 million, and its tax rate was 40%. What was its interest expense? (*Hint:* Write out the headings for an income statement and then fill in the known values. Then divide $6 million net income by $1 - T = 0.6$ to find the pre-tax income. The difference between EBIT and taxable income must be the interest expense. Use this same procedure to work some of the other problems.)

7-4 Income Statement Talbot Enterprises recently reported an EBITDA of $8 million and net income of $2.4 million. It had $2.0 million of interest expense, and its corporate tax rate was 40%. What was its charge for depreciation and amortization?

7-5 Net Cash Flow Kendall Corners Inc. recently reported net income of $3.1 million and depreciation of $500,000. What was its net cash flow? Assume it had no amortization expense.

7-6 Statement of Retained Earnings In its most recent financial statements, Del-Castillo Inc. reported $70 million of net income and $900 million of retained earnings. The previous retained earnings were $855 million. How much in dividends was paid to shareholders during the year?

Intermediate Problems 7–11

7-7 Corporate Tax Liability The Talley Corporation had a taxable income of $365,000 from operations after all operating costs but before (1) interest charges of $50,000, (2) dividends received of $15,000, (3) dividends paid of $25,000, and (4) income taxes. What are the firm's income tax liability and its after-tax income? What are the company's marginal and average tax rates on taxable income?

7-8 Corporate Tax Liability The Wendt Corporation had $10.5 million of taxable income.
a. What is the company's federal income tax bill for the year?
b. Assume the firm receives an additional $1 million of interest income from some bonds it owns. What is the tax on this interest income?
c. Now assume that Wendt does not receive the interest income but does receive an additional $1 million as dividends on some stock it owns. What is the tax on this dividend income?

7-9 Corporate After-Tax Yield The Shrieves Corporation has $10,000 that it plans to invest in marketable securities. It is choosing among AT&T bonds, which yield 7.5%, state of Florida muni bonds, which yield 5% (but are not taxable), and AT&T preferred stock, with a dividend yield of 6%. Shrieves's corporate tax rate is 35%, and 70% of the dividends received are tax exempt. Find the after-tax rates of return on all three securities.

7-10 Cash Flows The Moore Corporation has operating income (EBIT) of $750,000. The company's depreciation expense is $200,000. Moore is 100% equity financed, and it faces a 40% tax rate. What is the company's net income? What is its net cash flow?

7-11 Income and Cash Flow Analysis The Berndt Corporation expects to have sales of $12 million. Costs other than depreciation are expected to be 75% of sales, and depreciation is expected to be $1.5 million. All sales revenues will be collected in cash, and costs other than depreciation must be paid for during the year. Berndt's federal-plus-state tax rate is 40%. Berndt has no debt.
a. Set up an income statement. What is Berndt's expected net cash flow?
b. Suppose Congress changed the tax laws so that Berndt's depreciation expenses doubled. No changes in operations occurred. What would happen to reported profit and to net cash flow?
c. Now suppose that Congress, instead of doubling Berndt's depreciation, reduced it by 50%. How would profit and net cash flow be affected?
d. If this were your company, would you prefer Congress to cause your depreciation expense to be doubled or halved? Why?

Challenging Problems 12–13

7-12 **Free Cash Flows** Using Rhodes Corporation's financial statements (shown below), answer the following questions.
a. What is the net operating profit after taxes (NOPAT) for 2012?
b. What are the amounts of net operating working capital for both years?
c. What are the amounts of total net operating capital for both years?
d. What is the free cash flow for 2012?
e. What is the ROIC for 2012?
f. How much of the FCF did Rhodes use for each of the following purposes: after-tax interest, net debt repayments, dividends, net stock repurchases, and net purchases of short-term investments? (*Hint:* Remember that a net use can be negative.)

Rhodes Corporation: Income Statements for Year Ending December 31 (Millions of Dollars)

	2012	2011
Sales	$11,000	$10,000
Operating costs excluding depreciation	9,360	8,500
Depreciation and amortization	380	360
Earnings before interest and taxes	$ 1,260	$ 1,140
Less interest	120	100
Earnings before taxes	$ 1,140	$ 1,040
Taxes (40%)	456	416
Net income available to common stockholders	$ 684	$ 624
Common dividends	$ 220	$ 200

Rhodes Corporation: Balance Sheets as of December 31 (Millions of Dollars)

	2012	2011
Assets		
Cash	$ 550	$ 500
Short-term investments	110	100
Accounts receivable	2,750	2,500
Inventories	1,650	1,500
Total current assets	$5,060	$4,600
Net plant and equipment	3,850	3,500
Total assets	$8,910	$8,100

	2012	2011
Liabilities and Equity		
Accounts payable	$1,100	$1,000
Accruals	550	500
Notes payable	384	200
Total current liabilities	$2,034	$1,700
Long-term debt	1,100	1,000
Total liabilities	$3,134	$2,700
Common stock	4,312	4,400
Retained earnings	1,464	1,000
Total common equity	$5,776	$5,400
Total liabilities and equity	$8,910	$8,100

7-13 **Loss Carryback and Carryforward** The Bookbinder Company has made
$150,000 before taxes during each of the last 15 years, and it expects to make
$150,000 a year before taxes in the future. However, in 2012 the firm incurred
a loss of $650,000. The firm will claim a tax credit at the time it files its 2012
income tax return, and it will receive a check from the U.S. Treasury. Show how
it calculates this credit, and then indicate the firm's tax liability for each of the
next 5 years. Assume a 40% tax rate on *all* income to ease the calculations.

Spreadsheet Problems

7-14 **Build a Model: Financial Statements, EVA, and MVA** Begin with the partial
model in the file *Ch07 P14 Build a Model.xls* on the textbook's Web site.
   a. Cumberland Industries's 2012 sales were $455,000,000; operating costs
   (excluding depreciation) were equal to 85% of sales; net fixed assets were
   $67,000,000; depreciation amounted to 10% of net fixed assets; interest
   expenses were $8,550,000; the state-plus-federal corporate tax rate was 40%;
   and Cumberland paid 25% of its net income out in dividends. Given this information, construct Cumberland's 2012 income statement. Also calculate total
   dividends and the addition to retained earnings. (*Hint:* Start with the partial
   model in the file and report all dollar figures in thousands to reduce clutter.)
   b. Cumberland Industries's partial balance sheets are shown below. Cumberland
   issued $10,000,000 of new common stock in 2012. Using this information and
   the results from part a, fill in the missing values for common stock, retained
   earnings, total common equity, and total liabilities and equity.

Cumberland Industries: Balance Sheets as of December 31 (Thousands of Dollars)

	2012	2011
Assets		
Cash	$ 91,450	$ 74,625
Short-term investments	11,400	15,100
Accounts receivable	108,470	85,527
Inventories	38,450	34,982
Total current assets	$249,770	$210,234
Net fixed assets	67,000	42,436
Total assets	$316,770	$252,670

	2012	2011
Liabilities and Equity		
Accounts payable	$ 30,761	$ 23,109
Accruals	30,405	22,656
Notes payable	12,717	14,217
Total current liabilities	$ 73,883	$ 59,982
Long-term debt	80,263	63,914
Total liabilities	$154,146	$123,896
Common stock	?	$ 90,000
Retained earnings	?	38,774
Total common equity	?	$128,774
Total liabilities and equity	?	$252,670

    c. Construct the statement of cash flows for 2012.

7-15 **Build a Model: Free Cash Flows, EVA, and MVA** Begin with the partial model in the file *Ch07 P15 Build a Model.xls* on the textbook's Web site.

    a. Using the financial statements shown below for Lan & Chen Technologies, calculate net operating working capital, total net operating capital, net operating profit after taxes, free cash flow, and return on invested capital for 2012. (*Hint:* Start with the partial model in the file and report all dollar figures in thousands to reduce clutter.)

    b. Assume there were 15 million shares outstanding at the end of 2012, the year-end closing stock price was $65 per share, and the after-tax cost of capital was 8%. Calculate EVA and MVA for 2012.

Lan & Chen Technologies: Income Statements for Year Ending December 31 (Thousands of Dollars)

	2012	2011
Sales	$945,000	$900,000
Expenses excluding depreciation and amortization	812,700	774,000
EBITDA	$132,300	$126,000
Depreciation and amortization	33,100	31,500
EBIT	$ 99,200	$ 94,500
Interest expense	10,470	8,600
EBT	$ 88,730	$ 85,900
Taxes (40%)	35,492	34,360
Net income	$ 53,238	$ 51,540
Common dividends	$ 43,300	$ 41,230
Addition to retained earnings	$ 9,938	$ 10,310

Lan & Chen Technologies: December 31 Balance Sheets (Thousands of Dollars)

	2012	**2011**
Assets		
Cash and cash equivalents	$ 47,250	$ 45,000
Short-term investments	3,800	3,600
Accounts receivable	283,500	270,000
Inventories	141,750	135,000
Total current assets	$476,300	$453,600
Net fixed assets	330,750	315,000
Total assets	$807,050	$768,600
Liabilities and Equity		
Accounts payable	$ 94,500	$ 90,000
Accruals	47,250	45,000
Notes payable	26,262	9,000
Total current liabilities	$168,012	$144,000
Long-term debt	94,500	90,000
Total liabilities	$262,512	$234,000
Common stock	444,600	444,600
Retained earnings	99,938	90,000
Total common equity	$544,538	$534,600
Total liabilities and equity	$807,050	$768,600

 # THOMSON REUTERS

Use the Thomson ONE–Business School Edition online database to work this chapter's questions.

Exploring Starbucks's Financial Statements

Over the past decade, Starbucks coffee shops have become an increasingly familiar part of the urban landscape. The Thomson ONE–Business School Edition online database can provide a wealth of financial information for companies such as Starbucks. Begin by entering the company's ticker symbol, SBUX, and then selecting GO. The opening screen includes a summary of what Starbucks does, a chart of its recent stock price, EPS estimates, some recent news stories, and a list of key financial data and ratios.

For recent stock price performance, look at the top of the Stock Price Chart and click on the section labeled Interactive Chart. From this point, we are able to obtain a chart of the company's stock price performance relative to the overall market, as measured by the S&P 500. To obtain a 10-year chart, go to Time Frame, click on the down arrow, and select 10 years. Then click on Draw, and a 10-year price chart should appear.

You can also find Starbucks's recent financial statements. On the left side of your screen, click on the Financials tab to find the company's balance sheet, income statement, and statement of cash flows for the past 5 years. Clicking on the Microsoft *Excel* icon downloads these statements directly to a spreadsheet.

Discussion Questions

1. Looking at the most recent year available, what is the amount of total assets on Starbucks's balance sheet? What percentage is fixed assets, such as plant and equipment, and what percentage is current assets? How much has the company grown over the years shown?
2. Does Starbucks have a lot of long-term debt? What are Starbucks's primary sources of financing?
3. Looking at the statement of cash flows, what factors can explain the change in the company's cash position over the last couple of years?
4. Looking at the income statement, what are the company's most recent sales and net income? Over the past several years, what has been the sales growth rate? What has been the growth rate in net income?

MINI CASE

Jenny Cochran, a graduate of the University of Tennessee with 4 years of experience as an equities analyst, was recently brought in as assistant to the chairman of the board of Computron Industries, a manufacturer of computer components.

The company doubled its plant capacity, opened new sales offices outside its home territory, and launched an expensive advertising campaign. Computron's results were not satisfactory, to put it mildly. Its board of directors, which consisted of its president and vice-president plus its major stockholders (who were all local businesspeople), was most upset when directors learned how the expansion was going. Suppliers were being paid late and were unhappy, and the bank was complaining about the deteriorating situation and threatening to cut off credit. As a result, Robert Edwards, Computron's president, was informed that changes would have to be made—and quickly—or he would be fired. At the board's insistence, Jenny Cochran was given the job of assistant to Gary Meissner, a retired banker who was Computron's chairman and largest stockholder. Meissner agreed to give up a few of his golfing days and to help nurse the company back to health, with Cochran's assistance.

Cochran began by gathering financial statements and other data.

	2011	2012
Balance Sheets		
Assets		
Cash	$ 9,000	$ 7,282
Short-term investments	48,600	20,000
Accounts receivable	351,200	632,160
Inventories	715,200	1,287,360
Total current assets	$1,124,000	$1,946,802
Gross fixed assets	491,000	1,202,950
Less: Accumulated depreciation	146,200	263,160
Net fixed assets	$ 344,800	$ 939,790
Total assets	$1,468,800	$2,886,592
Liabilities and Equity		
Accounts payable	$ 145,600	$ 324,000
Notes payable	200,000	720,000
Accruals	136,000	284,960
Total current liabilities	$ 481,600	$1,328,960
Long-term debt	323,432	1,000,000
Common stock (100,000 shares)	460,000	460,000
Retained earnings	203,768	97,632
Total equity	$ 663,768	$ 557,632
Total liabilities and equity	$1,468,800	$2,886,592

	2011	2012
Income Statements		
Sales	$3,432,000	$5,834,400
Cost of goods sold	2,864,000	4,980,000
Other expenses	340,000	720,000
Depreciation and amortization	18,900	116,960
Total operating costs	$3,222,900	$5,816,960
EBIT	$ 209,100	$ 17,440
Interest expense	62,500	176,000
EBT	$ 146,600	($ 158,560)
Taxes (40%)	58,640	(63,424)
Net income	$ 87,960	($ 95,136)

(Continued)

	2011	2012
Other Data		
Stock price	$ 8.50	$ 6.00
Shares outstanding	100,000	100,000
EPS	$ 0.880	($ 0.951)
DPS	$ 0.220	$ 0.110
Tax rate	40%	40%

	2012
Statement of Cash Flows	
Operating Activities	
Net income	($ 95,136)
Adjustments:	
Noncash adjustments:	
Depreciation and amortization	116,960
Changes in working capital:	
Change in accounts receivable	(280,960)
Change in inventories	(572,160)
Change in accounts payable	178,400
Change in accruals	148,960
Net cash provided (used) by operating activities	($ 503,936)
Investing Activities	
Cash used to acquire fixed assets	($ 711,950)
Change in short-term investments	28,600
Net cash provided (used) by investing activities	($ 683,350)
Financing Activities	
Change in notes payable	$ 520,000
Change in long-term debt	676,568
Change in common stock	—
Payment of cash dividends	(11,000)
Net cash provided (used) by financing activities	$1,185,568
Summary	
Net change in cash	($ 1,718)
Cash at beginning of year	9,000
Cash at end of year	$ 7,282

Assume that you are Cochran's assistant and that you must help her answer the following questions for Meissner.

   a. What effect did the expansion have on sales and net income? What effect did the expansion have on the asset side of the balance sheet? What effect did it have on liabilities and equity?

   b. What do you conclude from the statement of cash flows?

   c. What is free cash flow? Why is it important? What are the five uses of FCF?

   d. What is Computron's net operating profit after taxes (NOPAT)? What are operating current assets? What are operating current liabilities? How much net operating working capital and total net operating capital does Computron have?

   e. What is Computron's free cash flow (FCF)? What are Computron's "net uses" of its FCF?

   f. Calculate Computron's return on invested capital. Computron has a 10% cost of capital (WACC). Do you think Computron's growth added value?

   g. Cochran also has asked you to estimate Computron's EVA. She estimates that the after-tax cost of capital was 10% in both years.

   h. What happened to Computron's Market Value Added (MVA)?

   i. Assume that a corporation has $100,000 of taxable income from operations plus $5,000 of interest income and $10,000 of dividend income. What is the company's federal tax liability?

   j. Assume that you are in the 25% marginal tax bracket and that you have $5,000 to invest. You have narrowed your investment choices down to California bonds with a yield of 7% or equally risky ExxonMobil bonds with a yield of 10%. Which one should you choose and why? At what marginal tax rate would you be indifferent to the choice between California and ExxonMobil bonds?

Chapter 8

Analysis of Financial Statements

WEB

The textbook's Web site contains an *Excel* file that will guide you through the chapter's calculations. The file for this chapter is ***Ch08 Tool Kit.xls***, and we encourage you to open the file and follow along as you read the chapter.

Financial statement analysis involves (1) comparing a firm's performance with that of other firms in the same industry and (2) evaluating trends in the firm's financial position over time. Managers use financial analysis to identify situations needing attention; potential lenders use financial analysis to determine whether a company is creditworthy; and stockholders use financial analysis to help predict future earnings, dividends, and free cash flow. As we explain in this chapter, there are similarities and differences among these uses.[1]

---

1. Widespread accounting fraud has cast doubt on whether all firms' published financial statements can be trusted. New regulations by the SEC and the exchanges, as well as new laws enacted by Congress, have improved oversight of the accounting industry and increased the criminal penalties on management for fraudulent reporting.

Beginning of Chapter Questions

As you read the chapter, consider how you would answer the following questions. You *should not* necessarily be able to answer the questions before you read the chapter. Rather, you should use them to get a sense of the issues covered in the chapter. After reading the chapter, you should be able to give at least partial answers to the questions, and you should be able to give better answers after the chapter has been discussed in class. Note, too, that it is often useful, when answering conceptual questions, to use hypothetical data to illustrate your answer. We illustrate the answers with an *Excel* model that is available on the textbook's Web site. Accessing the model and working through it is a useful exercise, and it provides insights that are useful when answering the questions.

1. Why are **financial ratios** used? Name five categories of ratios, and then list several ratios in each category. Would a bank loan officer, a bond analyst, a stock analyst, and a manager be likely to put the same emphasis and interpretation on each ratio?

2. Suppose a company has a DSO that is considerably higher than its industry average. If the company could reduce its accounts receivable to the point where its DSO was equal to the industry average *without affecting its sales or its operating costs,* how would this affect (a) its **free cash flow,** (b) **its return on common equity,** (c) its **debt ratio,** (d) its **times-interest-earned ratio,** (e) its **loan/EBITDA ratio,** (f) **its price/earnings ratio,** and (g) its **market/book ratio?**

3. How do managers, bankers, and security analysts use (a) **trend analysis,** (b) **benchmarking,** (c) **percent change analysis,** and (d) **common size analysis?**

4. Explain how **ratio analysis** in general, and the **Du Pont model** in particular, can be used by managers to help maximize their firms' stock prices.

5. How would each of the following factors affect ratio analysis? (a) The firm's sales are highly seasonal. (b) The firm uses some type of window dressing. (c) The firm issues more debt and uses the proceeds to repurchase stock. (d) The firm leases more of its fixed assets than most firms in its industry. (e) In an effort to stimulate sales, the firm eases its credit policy by offering 60-day credit terms rather than the current 30-day terms. How might one use sensitivity analysis to help quantify the answers?

6. How might one establish norms (or target values) for the financial ratios of a company that is just getting started? Where might data for this purpose be obtained? Could information of this type be used to help determine how much debt and equity capital a new firm would require?

8.1 Financial Analysis

When we perform a financial analysis, we conduct the following steps.

8.1a Gather Data

The first step in financial analysis is to gather data. As we discussed in Chapter 7, financial statements can be downloaded from many different Web sites. One of our favorites is Zacks Investment Research, which provides financial statements in a standardized format. If you cut and paste financial statements from Zacks into a spreadsheet and then perform a financial analysis, you can quickly repeat the analysis on a different company by simply pasting that company's financial statements into the same cells as the original company's statements. In other words, there is no need to reinvent the wheel each time you analyze a company.

8.1b Examine the Statement of Cash Flows

Some financial analysis can be done with virtually no calculations. For example, we always look to the statement of cash flows first, particularly the net cash provided

www

See **www.zacks.com** for a source of standardized financial statements.

INTRINSIC VALUE AND ANALYSIS OF FINANCIAL STATEMENTS

The intrinsic value of a firm is determined by the present value of the expected future free cash flows (FCF) when discounted at the weighted average cost of capital (WACC). This chapter explains how to use financial statements to evaluate a company's profitability, required capital investments, business risk, and mix of debt and equity.

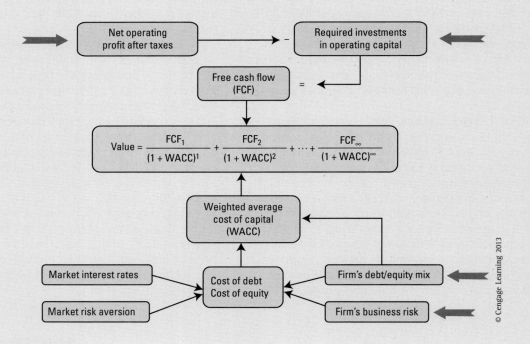

by operating activities. Downward trends or negative net cash flow from operations almost always indicate problems. The statement of cash flows section on investing activities shows whether the company has made a big acquisition, especially when compared with the prior years' net cash flows from investing activities. A quick look at the section on financing activities also reveals whether or not a company is issuing debt or buying back stock; in other words, is the company raising capital from investors or returning it to them?

8.1c Calculate and Examine the Return on Invested Capital

After examining the statement of cash flows, we calculate the return on invested capital (ROIC) as described in Chapter 7. The ROIC provides a vital measure of a firm's overall performance. If ROIC is greater than the company's weighted average cost of capital (WACC), then the company usually is adding value. If ROIC is less than WACC, then the company usually has serious problems. No matter what ROIC tells us about the firm's overall performance, it is important to examine specific areas within the firm, and for that we use ratios.

8.1d Begin Ratio Analysis

Financial ratios are designed to extract important information that might not be obvious simply from examining a firm's financial statements. For example, suppose Firm A owes $5 million of debt while Firm B owes $50 million of debt. Which company is in a stronger financial position? It is impossible to answer this question without first standardizing each firm's debt relative to total assets, earnings, and interest. Such standardized comparisons are provided through *ratio analysis*.

We will calculate the 2012 financial ratios for MicroDrive Inc., using data from the balance sheets and income statements given in Table 8-1. We will also evaluate the ratios in relation to the industry averages. Note that dollar amounts are in millions.

8.2 Liquidity Ratios

As shown in Table 8-1, MicroDrive has current liabilities of $310 million that must be paid off within the coming year. Will it have trouble satisfying those obligations? **Liquidity ratios** attempt to answer this type of question: We discuss two commonly used liquidity ratios in this section.

WEB

See *Ch08 Tool Kit.xls* for all calculations.

8.2a The Current Ratio

The **current ratio** is calculated by dividing current assets by current liabilities:

$$\text{Current ratio} = \frac{\text{Current assets}}{\text{Current liabilities}}$$

$$= \frac{\$1,000}{\$310} = 3.2$$

Industry average $= 4.2$

Current assets normally include cash, marketable securities, accounts receivable, and inventories. Current liabilities consist of accounts payable, short-term notes payable, current maturities of long-term debt, accrued taxes, and other accrued expenses.

MicroDrive has a lower current ratio than the average for its industry. Is this good or bad? Sometimes the answer depends on who is asking the question. For example, suppose a supplier is trying to decide whether to extend credit to MicroDrive. In general, creditors like to see a high current ratio. If a company is getting into financial difficulty, it will begin paying its bills (accounts payable) more slowly, borrowing from its bank, and so on, so its current liabilities will be increasing. If current liabilities are rising faster than current assets then the current ratio will fall, and this could spell trouble. Because the current ratio provides the best single indicator of the extent to which the claims of short-term creditors are covered by assets that are expected to be converted to cash fairly quickly, it is the most commonly used measure of short-term solvency.

TABLE 8-1	MicroDrive Inc.: Balance Sheets and Income Statements for Years Ending December 31 (Millions of Dollars, Except for Per Share Data)					
Assets	**2012**	**2011**	**Liabilities and Equity**	**2012**	**2011**
Cash and equivalents	$ 10	$ 15	Accounts payable	$ 60	$ 30
Short-term investments	0	65	Notes payable	110	60
Accounts receivable	375	315	Accruals	140	130
Inventories	615	415	Total current liabilities	$ 310	$ 220
Total current assets	$1,000	$ 810	Long-term bonds[a]	754	580
Net plant and equipment	1,000	870	Total liabilities	$1,064	$ 800
			Preferred stock (400,000 shares)	40	40
			Common stock (50,000,000 shares)	130	130
			Retained earnings	766	710
			Total common equity	$ 896	$ 840
Total assets	$2,000	$1,680	Total liabilities and equity	$2,000	$1,680

	2012	**2011**
Net sales	$3,000	$2,850
Operating costs excluding depreciation and amortization[b]	2,617	2,500
Earnings before interest, taxes, depreciation, and amortization (EBITDA)	$ 383	$ 350
Depreciation and amortization	100	90
Earnings before interest and taxes (EBIT, or operating income)	$ 283	$ 260
Less interest	88	60
Earnings before taxes (EBT)	$ 195	$ 200
Taxes (40%)	78	80
Net income before preferred dividends	$ 117	$ 120
Preferred dividends	4	4
Net income	$ 113	$ 116
Common dividends	$ 57	$ 53
Addition to retained earnings	$ 56	$ 63
Per-Share Data		
Common stock price	$ 23.00	$ 26.00
Earnings per share (EPS)	$ 2.26	$ 2.32
Book value per share (BVPS)	$ 17.92	$ 16.80
Cash flow per share (CFPS)	$ 4.26	$ 4.12

[a]The bonds have a sinking fund requirement of $20 million a year.
[b]The costs include lease payments of $28 million a year.

Now consider the current ratio from the perspective of a shareholder. A high current ratio could mean that the company has a lot of money tied up in nonproductive assets, such as excess cash or marketable securities. Or perhaps the high current ratio is due to large inventory holdings, which might well become obsolete before they can be sold. Thus, shareholders might not want a high current ratio.

An industry average is not a magic number that all firms should strive to maintain—in fact, some very well-managed firms will be above the average, while other good firms will be below it. However, if a firm's ratios are far removed from the averages for its industry, this is a red flag, and analysts should be concerned about why the variance occurs. For example, suppose a low current ratio is traced to low inventories. Is this a competitive advantage resulting from the firm's mastery of just-in-time inventory management, or is it an Achilles' heel that is causing the firm to miss shipments and lose sales? Ratio analysis doesn't answer such questions, but it does point to areas of potential concern.

8.2b The Quick, or Acid Test, Ratio

The **quick, or acid test, ratio** is calculated by deducting inventories from current assets and then dividing the remainder by current liabilities:

$$\text{Quick, or acid test, ratio} = \frac{\text{Current assets} - \text{Inventories}}{\text{Current liabilities}}$$

$$= \frac{\$385}{\$310} = 1.2$$

Industry average $= 2.1$

A **liquid asset** is one that trades in an active market and hence can be converted quickly to cash at the going market price. Inventories are typically the least liquid of a firm's current assets; hence they are the current assets on which losses are most likely to occur in a bankruptcy. Therefore, a measure of the firm's ability to pay off short-term obligations without relying on the sale of inventories is important.

The industry average quick ratio is 2.1, so MicroDrive's 1.2 ratio is low in comparison with other firms in its industry. Still, if the accounts receivable can be collected, the company can pay off its current liabilities without having to liquidate its inventory.

Self Test

Identify two ratios that are used to analyze a firm's liquidity position, and write out their equations.

What are the characteristics of a liquid asset? Give some examples.

Which current asset is typically the least liquid?

A company has current liabilities of $800 million, and its current ratio is 2.5. What is its level of current assets? (**$2,000 million**) If this firm's quick ratio is 2, how much inventory does it have? (**$400 million**)

8.3 Asset Management Ratios

Asset management ratios measure how effectively a firm is managing its assets. If a company has excessive investments in assets, then its operating capital will be unduly high, which will reduce its free cash flow and ultimately its stock price. On the other hand, if a company does not have enough assets then it will lose sales, which will hurt profitability, free cash flow, and the stock price. Therefore, it is important to have the *right* amount invested in assets. Ratios that analyze the different types of assets are described in this section.

8.3a Evaluating Inventories: The Inventory Turnover Ratio

The **inventory turnover ratio** is defined as sales divided by inventories:

$$\text{Inventory turnover ratio} = \frac{\text{Sales}}{\text{Inventories}}$$

$$= \frac{\$3,000}{\$615} = 4.9$$

Industry average $= 9.0$

As a rough approximation, each item of MicroDrive's inventory is sold out and restocked, or "turned over," 4.9 times per year.[2]

MicroDrive's turnover of 4.9 is much lower than the industry average of 9.0. This suggests that MicroDrive is holding too much inventory. High levels of inventory add to net operating working capital (NOWC), which reduces FCF, which leads to lower stock prices. In addition, MicroDrive's low inventory turnover ratio makes us wonder whether the firm is actually holding obsolete goods not worth their stated value.[3]

Note that sales occur over the entire year, whereas the inventory figure is measured at a single point in time. For this reason, it is better to use an average inventory measure.[4]

---

2. "Turnover" is a term that originated many years ago with the old Yankee peddler who would load up his wagon with goods and then go off to peddle his wares. If he made 10 trips per year, stocked 100 pans, and made a gross profit of $5 per pan, his annual gross profit would be (100)($5)(10) = $5,000. If he "turned over" (i.e., sold) his inventory faster and made 20 trips per year, then his gross profit would double, other things held constant. So, his turnover directly affected his profits.

3. A problem arises when calculating and analyzing the inventory turnover ratio. Sales are stated at market prices, so if inventories are carried at cost, as they generally are, then the calculated turnover overstates the true turnover ratio. Therefore, it would be more appropriate to use cost of goods sold in place of sales in the formula's numerator. However, established compilers of financial ratio statistics such as Dun & Bradstreet use the ratio of sales to inventories carried at cost. To develop a figure that can be compared with those published by Dun & Bradstreet and similar organizations, it is necessary to measure inventory turnover with sales in the numerator, as we do here.

4. Preferably, the average inventory value should be calculated by summing the monthly figures during the year and dividing by 12. If monthly data are not available, one can add the beginning and ending annual figures and divide by 2. However, most industry ratios are calculated as shown here, using end-of-year values.

THE GLOBAL ECONOMIC CRISIS

The Price Is Right! (Or Wrong!)

How much is an asset worth if no one is buying or selling? The answer to that question matters because an accounting practice called "mark to market" requires that some assets be adjusted on the balance sheet to reflect their "fair market value." The accounting rules are complicated, but the general idea is that if an asset is available for sale, then the balance sheet would be most accurate if it showed the asset's market value. For example, suppose a company purchased $100 million of Treasury bonds and the value of those bonds later fell to $90 million. With mark to market, the company would report the bonds' value on the balance sheet as $90 million, not the original purchase price of $100 million. Notice that marking to market can have a significant impact on financial ratios and thus on investors' perception of a firm's financial health.

But what if the assets are mortgage-backed securities that were originally purchased for $100 million? As defaults increased during 2008, the value of such securities fell rapidly, and then investors virtually stopped trading them. How should the company report them? At the $100 million original price, at a $60 million price that was observed before the market largely dried up, at $25 million when a hedge fund in desperate need for cash to avoid a costly default sold a few of these securities, or at $0, since there are no current quotes? Or should they be reported at a price generated by a computer model or in some other manner?

The answer to this question is especially important during times of economic stress. Congress, the SEC, FASB, and the U.S. Treasury all are working to find the right answers. If they come up with a price that is too low, it could cause investors mistakenly to believe that some companies are worth much less than their intrinsic values, and this could trigger runs on banks and bankruptcies for companies that might otherwise survive. But if the price is too high, some "walking dead" or "zombie" companies could linger on and later cause even larger losses for investors, including the U.S. government, which is now the largest investor in many financial institutions. Either way, an error in pricing could perhaps trigger a domino effect that might topple the entire financial system. So let's hope the price is right!

If the firm's business is highly seasonal, or if there has been a strong upward or downward sales trend during the year, then it is especially useful to make some such adjustment. To maintain comparability with industry averages, however, we did not use the average inventory figure.

8.3b Evaluating Receivables: The Days Sales Outstanding

Days sales outstanding (DSO), also called the "average collection period" (ACP), is used to appraise accounts receivable, and it is calculated by dividing accounts receivable by average daily sales to find the number of days' sales that are tied up in receivables.[5] Thus, the DSO represents the average length of time that the firm

---

5. It would be better to use *average* receivables, but we have used year-end values for comparability with the industry average.

must wait after making a sale before receiving cash, which is the average collection period. MicroDrive's DSO is 46, well above the 36-day industry average:

$$\text{DSO} = \frac{\text{Days sales}}{\text{outstanding}} = \frac{\text{Receivables}}{\text{Average sales per day}} = \frac{\text{Receivables}}{\text{Annual sales}/365}$$

$$= \frac{\$375}{\$3,000/365} = \frac{\$375}{\$8.2192} = 45.6 \text{ days} \approx 46 \text{ days}$$

Industry average = 36 days

MicroDrive's sales terms call for payment within 30 days. The fact that 46 days of sales are outstanding indicates that customers, on average, are not paying their bills on time. As with inventory, high levels of accounts receivable cause high levels of NOWC, which hurts FCF and stock price.

A customer who is paying late may well be in financial trouble, in which case MicroDrive may have a hard time ever collecting the receivable. Therefore, if the trend in DSO has been rising but the credit policy has not been changed, steps should be taken to review credit standards and to expedite the collection of accounts receivable.

8.3c Evaluating Fixed Assets: The Fixed Assets Turnover Ratio

The **fixed assets turnover ratio** measures how effectively the firm uses its plant and equipment. It is the ratio of sales to net fixed assets:

$$\text{Fixed assets turnover ratio} = \frac{\text{Sales}}{\text{Net fixed assets}}$$

$$= \frac{\$3,000}{\$1,000} = 3.0$$

Industry average = 3.0

MicroDrive's ratio of 3.0 is equal to the industry average, indicating that the firm is using its fixed assets about as intensively as are other firms in its industry. Therefore, MicroDrive seems to have about the right amount of fixed assets in relation to other firms.

A potential problem can exist when interpreting the fixed assets turnover ratio. Recall from accounting that fixed assets reflect the historical costs of the assets. Inflation has caused the current value of many assets that were purchased in the past to be seriously understated. Therefore, if we were comparing an old firm that had acquired many of its fixed assets years ago at low prices with a new company that had acquired its fixed assets only recently, we would probably find that the old firm had the higher fixed assets turnover ratio. However, this would be more reflective of the difficulty accountants have in dealing with inflation than of any inefficiency on the part of the new firm. You should be alert to this potential problem when evaluating the fixed assets turnover ratio.

8.3d Evaluating Total Assets:
The Total Assets Turnover Ratio

The **total assets turnover ratio** is calculated by dividing sales by total assets:

$$\text{Total assets turnover ratio} = \frac{\text{Sales}}{\text{Total assets}}$$

$$= \frac{\$3,000}{\$2,000} = 1.5$$

Industry average $= 1.8$

MicroDrive's ratio is somewhat below the industry average, indicating that the company is not generating a sufficient volume of business given its total asset investment. Sales should be increased, some assets should be sold, or a combination of these steps should be taken.

Self Test

Identify four ratios that are used to measure how effectively a firm is managing its assets, and write out their equations.

What problem might arise when comparing different firms' fixed assets turnover ratios?

A firm has annual sales of $200 million, $40 million of inventory, and $60 million of accounts receivable. What is its inventory turnover ratio? **(5)** What is its DSO based on a 365-day year? **(109.5 days)**

8.4 Debt Management Ratios

The extent to which a firm uses debt financing, or **financial leverage,** has three important implications: (1) By raising funds through debt, stockholders can maintain control of a firm without increasing their investment. (2) If the firm earns more on investments financed with borrowed funds than it pays in interest, then its shareholders' returns are magnified, or "leveraged," but their risks are also magnified. (3) Creditors look to the equity, or owner-supplied funds, to provide a margin of safety, so the higher the proportion of funding supplied by stockholders, the less risk creditors face. Chapter 15 explains the first two points in detail, while the following ratios examine leverage from a creditor's point of view.

8.4a How the Firm Is Financed:
Total Liabilities to Total Assets

The ratio of total liabilities to total assets is called the **debt ratio,** or sometimes the **total debt ratio.** It measures the percentage of funds provided by current liabilities and long-term debt:

$$\text{Debt ratio} = \frac{\text{Total liabilities}}{\text{Total assets}}$$

$$= \frac{\$310 + \$754}{\$2,000} = \frac{\$1,064}{\$2,000} = 53.2\%$$

Industry average $= 40.0\%$

Creditors prefer low debt ratios because the lower the ratio, the greater the cushion against creditors' losses in the event of liquidation. Stockholders, on the other hand, may want more leverage because it magnifies their return, as we explain in Section 8.8 when we discuss the Du Pont model.

MicroDrive's debt ratio is 53.2% but its debt ratio in the previous year was 47.6%, which means that creditors are now supplying more than half the total financing. In addition to an upward trend, the level of the debt ratio is well above the industry average. Creditors may be reluctant to lend the firm more money because a high debt ratio is associated with a greater risk of bankruptcy.

Some sources report the debt-to-equity ratio, defined as:

$$\text{Debt-to-equity ratio} = \frac{\text{Total liabilities}}{\text{Total assets} - \text{Total liabilities}}$$

$$= \frac{\$310 + \$754}{\$2,000 - (\$310 + \$754)} = \frac{\$1,064}{\$936} = 1.14$$

$$\text{Industry average} = 0.67$$

The debt-to-equity ratio and the debt ratio contain the same information but present that information slightly differently.[6] The debt-to-equity ratio shows that MicroDrive has $1.14 of debt for every dollar of equity, whereas the debt ratio shows that 53.2% of MicroDrive's financing is in the form of liabilities. We find it more intuitive to think about the percentage of the firm that is financed with debt, so we usually use the debt ratio. However, the debt-to-equity ratio is also widely used, so you should know how to interpret it.

Sometimes it is useful to express debt ratios in terms of market values. It is easy to calculate the market value of equity, which is equal to the stock price multiplied by the number of shares. MicroDrive's market value of equity is $23(50) = $1,150. Often it is difficult to estimate the market value of liabilities, so many analysts define the market debt ratio as

$$\text{Market debt ratio} = \frac{\text{Total liabilities}}{\text{Total liabilities} + \text{Market value of equity}}$$

$$= \frac{\$1,064}{\$1,064 + (\$23 \times 50)} = \frac{\$1,064}{\$2,214} = 48.1\%$$

MicroDrive's market debt ratio in the previous year was 38.1%. The big increase was due to two major factors: Liabilities increased and the stock price fell. The stock price reflects a company's prospects for generating future cash flows, so a decline in stock price indicates a likely decline in future cash flows. Thus, the market debt ratio reflects a source of risk that is not captured by the conventional book debt ratio.

---

6. The debt ratio and debt-to-equity ratios are simply transformations of each other:

$$\text{Debt-to-equity} = \frac{\text{Debt ratio}}{1 - \text{Debt ratio}} \text{ and Debt ratio} = \frac{\text{Debt-to-equity}}{1 + \text{Debt-to-equity}}$$

If you use a debt ratio that you did not calculate yourself, be sure to find out how the ratio was defined. Some sources define the numerator to be only long-term debt, others define it to be all interest-bearing debt, while others do as we do, which is to define it to be total liabilities, so be sure to check your source's definition.

8.4b Ability to Pay Interest: Times-Interest-Earned Ratio

The **times-interest-earned (TIE) ratio**, also called the **interest coverage ratio**, is determined by dividing earnings before interest and taxes (EBIT in Table 8-1) by the interest expense:

$$\text{Times-interest-earned (TIE) ratio} = \frac{\text{EBIT}}{\text{Interest expense}}$$

$$= \frac{\$283}{\$88} = 3.2$$

Industry average $= 6.0$

The TIE ratio measures the extent to which operating income can decline before the firm is unable to meet its annual interest costs. Failure to meet this obligation can bring legal action by the firm's creditors, possibly resulting in bankruptcy. Note that earnings before interest and taxes, rather than net income, is used in the numerator. Because interest is paid with pre-tax dollars, the firm's ability to pay current interest is not affected by taxes.

MicroDrive's interest is covered 3.2 times. The industry average is 6, so Micro-Drive is covering its interest charges by a relatively low margin of safety. Thus, the TIE ratio reinforces the conclusion from our analysis of the debt ratio that MicroDrive would face difficulties if it attempted to borrow additional funds.

8.4c Ability to Service Debt: EBITDA Coverage Ratio

The TIE ratio is useful for assessing a company's ability to meet interest charges on its debt, but this ratio has two shortcomings: (1) Interest is not the only fixed financial charge—companies must also reduce debt on schedule, and many firms lease assets and thus must make lease payments. If they fail to repay debt or meet lease payments, they can be forced into bankruptcy. (2) EBIT does not represent all the cash flow available to service debt, especially if a firm has high depreciation and/or amortization charges. The **EBITDA coverage ratio** accounts for these deficiencies:[7]

---

7. Different analysts define the EBITDA coverage ratio in different ways. For example, some omit the lease payment information; others "gross up" principal payments by dividing them by $1 - T$ since these payments are not tax deductions and hence must be made with after-tax cash flows. We included lease payments because for many firms they are quite important, and failing to make them can lead to bankruptcy just as surely as can failure to make payments on "regular" debt. We did not gross up principal payments because, if a company is in financial difficulty, then its tax rate will probably be zero; hence the gross up is not necessary whenever the ratio is really important.

$$\text{EBITDA coverage ratio} = \frac{\text{EBITDA} + \text{Lease payments}}{\text{Interest} + \text{Principle payments} + \text{Lease payments}}$$

$$= \frac{\$383 + \$28}{\$88 + \$20 + \$28} = \frac{\$411}{\$136} = 3.0$$

Industry average = 4.3

MicroDrive had $383 million of earnings before interest, taxes, depreciation, and amortization (EBITDA). Also, lease payments of $28 million were deducted while calculating EBITDA. That $28 million was available to meet financial charges; hence it must be added back, bringing the total available to cover fixed financial charges to $411 million. Fixed financial charges consisted of $88 million of interest, $20 million of sinking fund payments, and $28 million for lease payments, for a total of $136 million.[8] Therefore, MicroDrive covered its fixed financial charges by 3.0 times. However, if EBITDA declines then the coverage will fall, and EBITDA certainly can decline. Moreover, MicroDrive's ratio is well below the industry average, so again the company seems to have a relatively high level of debt.

The EBITDA coverage ratio is most useful for relatively short-term lenders such as banks, which rarely make loans (except real estate-backed loans) for longer than about 5 years. Over a relatively short period, depreciation-generated funds can be used to service debt. Over a longer time, those funds must be reinvested to maintain the plant and equipment or else the company cannot remain in business. Therefore, banks and other relatively short-term lenders focus on the EBITDA coverage ratio, whereas long-term bondholders focus on the TIE ratio.

Self Test

How does the use of financial leverage affect current stockholders' control position?

Explain the following statement: "Analysts look at both balance sheet and income statement ratios when appraising a firm's financial condition."

Name three ratios that are used to measure the extent to which a firm uses financial leverage, and write out their equations.

A company has EBITDA of $600 million, interest payments of $60 million, lease payments of $40 million, and required principal payments (due this year) of $30 million. What is its EBITDA coverage ratio? **(4.9)**

8.5 Profitability Ratios

Profitability is the net result of a number of policies and decisions. The ratios examined thus far provide useful clues as to the effectiveness of a firm's operations, but the **profitability ratios** go on to show the combined effects of liquidity, asset management, and debt on operating results.

---

8. A sinking fund is a required annual payment designed to reduce the balance of a bond or preferred stock issue.

8.5a Net Profit Margin

The **net profit margin**, which is also called the **profit margin on sales**, is calculated by dividing net income by sales. It gives the profit per dollar of sales:

$$\text{Net profit margin} = \frac{\text{Net income available to common stockholders}}{\text{Sales}}$$

$$= \frac{\$113}{\$3,000} = 3.8\%$$

$$\text{Industry average} = 5.0\%$$

MicroDrive's net profit margin is below the industry average of 5%, but why is this so? Is it due to inefficient operations, high interest expenses, or both?

Instead of just comparing net income to sales, many analysts also break the income statement into smaller parts to identify the sources of a low net profit margin. For example, the **operating profit margin** is defined as

$$\text{Operating profit margin} = \frac{\text{EBIT}}{\text{Sales}}$$

The operating profit margin identifies how a company is performing with respect to its operations before the impact of interest expenses is considered. Some analysts drill even deeper by breaking operating costs into their components. For example, the **gross profit margin** is defined as

$$\text{Gross profit margin} = \frac{\text{Sales} - \text{Cost of goods sold}}{\text{Sales}}$$

The gross profit margin identifies the gross profit per dollar of sales before any other expenses are deducted.

Rather than calculate each type of profit margin here, later in the chapter we will use common size analysis and percent change analysis to focus on different parts of the income statement. In addition, we will use the Du Pont equation to show how the ratios interact with one another.

Sometimes it is confusing to have so many different types of profit margins. To help simplify the situation, we will focus primarily on the net profit margin throughout the book and simply call it the "profit margin."

8.5b Basic Earning Power (BEP) Ratio

The **basic earning power (BEP) ratio** is calculated by dividing earnings before interest and taxes (EBIT) by total assets:

$$\text{Basic earning power (BEP) ratio} = \frac{\text{EBIT}}{\text{Total assets}}$$

THE WORLD MIGHT BE FLAT, BUT GLOBAL ACCOUNTING ISN'T: IFRS VERSUS FASB

In a flat world, distance is no barrier. Work flows to where it can be accomplished most efficiently, and capital flows to where it can be invested most profitably. If a radiologist in India is more efficient than one in the United States, then images will be e-mailed to India for diagnosis; if rates of return are higher in Brazil, then investors throughout the world will provide funding for Brazilian projects. One key to "flattening" the world is agreement on common standards. For example, there are common Internet standards so that users throughout the world are able to communicate.

A glaring exception to standardization is in accounting. The Securities and Exchange Commission (SEC) in the United States requires firms to comply with standards set by the Financial Accounting Standards Board (FASB). But the European Union requires all EU-listed companies to comply with the International Financial Reporting Standards (IFRS) as defined by the International Accounting Standards Board (IASB).

IFRS tends to rely on general principles, whereas FASB standards are rules-based. As the recent accounting scandals demonstrate, many U.S. companies have been able to comply with U.S. rules while violating the principle, or intent, underlying the rules. The United States is likely to adopt IFRS, or a slightly modified IFRS, but the question is "When?" The SEC estimated that a large company is likely to incur costs of up to $32 million when switching to IFRS. So even though a survey by the accounting firm KPMG indicates that most investors and analysts favor adoption of IFRS, the path to adoption is likely to be bumpy.

Sources: See the Web sites of the IASB and the FASB, **www.iasb.org.uk** and **www.fasb.org**. Also see David M. Katz and Sarah Johnson, "Top Obama Advisers Clash on Global Accounting Standards," January 15, 2009, at **www.cfo.com**; and "Survey Favors IFRS Adoption," February 3, 2009, at **www.webcpa.com**.

$$= \frac{\$283}{\$2,000} = 14.2\%$$

Industry average $= 17.2\%$

This ratio shows the raw earning power of the firm's assets before the influence of taxes and leverage, and it is useful for comparing firms with different tax situations and different degrees of financial leverage. Because of its low turnover ratios and low profit margin on sales, MicroDrive is not getting as high a return on its assets as is the average company in its industry.[9]

---

9. Notice that EBIT is earned throughout the year, whereas the total assets figure is an end-of-the-year number. Therefore, it would be better, conceptually, to calculate this ratio as EBIT/(Average assets) = EBIT/[(Beginning assets + Ending assets)/2]. We have not made this adjustment because the published ratios used for comparative purposes do not include it. However, when we construct our own comparative ratios, we do make this adjustment. The same adjustment would also be appropriate for the next two ratios, ROA and ROE.

8.5c Return on Total Assets

The ratio of net income to total assets measures the **return on total assets** (**ROA**) after interest and taxes. This ratio is also called the **return on assets** and is defined as follows:

$$\text{Return on total assets} = \text{ROA} = \frac{\text{Net income available to common stockholders}}{\text{Total assets}}$$

$$= \frac{\$113}{\$2,000} = 5.7\%$$

Industry average = 9.0%

MicroDrive's 5.7% return is well below the 9% average for the industry. This low return is due to (1) the company's low basic earning power and (2) high interest costs resulting from its above-average use of debt; both of these factors cause Micro Drive's net income to be relatively low.

8.5d Return on Common Equity

The ratio of net income to common equity measures the **return on common equity** (**ROE**):

$$\text{Return on common equity} = \text{ROE} = \frac{\text{Net income available to common stockholders}}{\text{Common equity}}$$

$$= \frac{\$113}{\$896} = 12.6\%$$

Industry average = 15.0%

Stockholders invest to earn a return on their money, and this ratio tells how well they are doing in an accounting sense. MicroDrive's 12.6% return is below the 15% industry average, but not as far below as its return on total assets. This somewhat better result is due to the company's greater use of debt, a point that we explain in detail later in the chapter.

Self Test

Identify and write out the equations for four profitability ratios.

Why is the basic earning power ratio useful?

Why does the use of debt lower ROA?

What does ROE measure?

A company has $200 billion of sales and $10 billion of net income. Its total assets are $100 billion, financed half by debt and half by common equity. What is its profit margin? **(5%)** What is its ROA? **(10%)** What is its ROE? **(20%)** Would ROA increase if the firm used less leverage? **(Yes)** Would ROE increase? **(No)**

8.6 Market Value Ratios

Market value ratios relate a firm's stock price to its earnings, cash flow, and book value per share. Market value ratios are a way to measure the value of a company's stock relative to that of another company.

8.6a Price/Earnings Ratio

The **price/earnings (P/E) ratio** shows how much investors are willing to pay per dollar of reported profits. MicroDrive's stock sells for $23, so with an earnings per share (EPS) of $2.27 its P/E ratio is 10.2:

$$\text{Price/earnings (P/E) ratio} = \frac{\text{Price per share}}{\text{Earnings per share}}$$

$$= \frac{\$23.00}{\$2.26} = 10.2$$

Industry average $= 12.5$

Price/earnings ratios are higher for firms with strong growth prospects, other things held constant, but they are lower for riskier firms. Because MicroDrive's P/E ratio is below the average, this suggests that the company is regarded as being somewhat riskier than most, as having poorer growth prospects, or both. In early 2011, the average P/E ratio for firms in the S&P 500 was 18.12, indicating that investors were willing to pay $18.12 for every dollar of earnings.

8.6b Price/Cash Flow Ratio

Stock prices depend on a company's ability to generate cash flows. Consequently, investors often look at the **price/cash flow ratio**, where cash flow is defined as net income plus depreciation and amortization:

$$\text{Price/cash flow ratio} = \frac{\text{Price per share}}{\text{Cash flow per share}}$$

$$= \frac{\$23.00}{\$4.26} = 5.4$$

Industry average $= 6.8$

MicroDrive's price/cash flow ratio is also below the industry average, once again suggesting that its growth prospects are below average, its risk is above average, or both.

The **price/EBITDA ratio** is similar to the price/cash flow ratio, except the price/EBITDA ratio measures performance before the impact of interest expenses and taxes, making it a better measure of operating performance. MicroDrive's EBITDA per share is $383/50 = $7.66, so its price/EBITDA is $23/$7.66 = 3.0. The industry average price/EBITDA ratio is 4.6, so we see again that MicroDrive is below the industry average.

Note that some analysts look at other multiples as well. For example, depending on the industry, some may look at measures such as price/sales or price/customers. Ultimately, though, value depends on free cash flows, so if these "exotic" ratios do not forecast future free cash flow, they may turn out to be misleading. This was true in the case of the dot-com retailers before they crashed and burned in 2000, costing investors many billions.

8.6c Market/Book Ratio

The ratio of a stock's market price to its book value gives another indication of how investors regard the company. Companies with relatively high rates of return on equity generally sell at higher multiples of book value than those with low returns. First, we find MicroDrive's book value per share:

$$\text{Book value per share} = \frac{\text{Common equity}}{\text{Shares outstanding}}$$

$$= \frac{\$896}{50} = \$17.92$$

Now we divide the market price by the book value to get a **market/book (M/B) ratio** of 1.3 times:

$$\text{Market/book ratio} = \text{M/B} = \frac{\text{Market price per share}}{\text{Book value per share}}$$

$$= \frac{\$23.00}{\$17.92} = 1.3$$

$$\text{Industry average} = 1.7$$

Investors are willing to pay relatively little for a dollar of MicroDrive's book value.

The average company in the S&P 500 had a market/book ratio of about 2.90 in early 2011. Since M/B ratios typically exceed 1.0, this means that investors are willing to pay more for stocks than their accounting book values. The book value is a record of the past, showing the cumulative amount that stockholders have invested, either directly by purchasing newly issued shares or indirectly through retaining earnings. In contrast, the market price is forward-looking, incorporating investors' expectations of future cash flows. For example, in early 2011 Bank of America had a market/book ratio of only 0.68, reflecting the financial services industry's problems, whereas Apple's market/book ratio was 6.22, indicating that investors expected Apple's past successes to continue.

Table 8-2 summarizes MicroDrive's financial ratios. As the table indicates, the company has many problems.

Self Test

Describe three ratios that relate a firm's stock price to its earnings, cash flow, and book value per share, and write out their equations.

What does the price/earnings (P/E) ratio show? If one firm's P/E ratio is lower than that of another, what are some factors that might explain the difference?

How is book value per share calculated? Explain why book values often deviate from market values.

A company has $6 billion of net income, $2 billion of depreciation and amortization, $80 billion of common equity, and 1 billion shares of stock. If its stock price is $96 per share, what is its price/earnings ratio? **(16)** Its price/cash flow ratio? **(12)** Its market/book ratio? **(1.2)**

TABLE 8-2	MicroDrive Inc.: Summary of Financial Ratios (Millions of Dollars)					

Ratio	Formula	Calculation		Ratio	Industry Average	Comment
Liquidity						
Current	$\dfrac{\text{Current assets}}{\text{Current liabilities}}$	$\dfrac{\$1,000}{\$310}$	=	3.2	4.2	Poor
Quick	$\dfrac{\text{Current assets} - \text{Inventories}}{\text{Current liabilities}}$	$\dfrac{\$385}{\$310}$	=	1.2	2.1	Poor
Asset Management						
Inventory turnover	$\dfrac{\text{Sales}}{\text{Inventories}}$	$\dfrac{\$3,000}{\$615}$	=	4.9	9.0	Poor
Days sales outstanding (DSO)	$\dfrac{\text{Receivables}}{\text{Annual sales}/365}$	$\dfrac{\$375}{\$8.219}$	=	45.6	36.0	Poor
Fixed assets turnover	$\dfrac{\text{Sales}}{\text{Net fixed assets}}$	$\dfrac{\$3,000}{\$1,000}$	=	3.0	3.0	OK
Total assets turnover	$\dfrac{\text{Sales}}{\text{Total assets}}$	$\dfrac{\$3,000}{\$2,000}$	=	1.5	1.8	Poor
Debt Management						
Debt ratio	$\dfrac{\text{Total liabilities}}{\text{Total assets}}$	$\dfrac{\$1,064}{\$2,000}$	=	53.2%	40.0%	High (risky)
Times-interest-earned (TIE)	$\dfrac{\text{Earings before interest and taxes (EBIT)}}{\text{Interest charges}}$	$\dfrac{\$283}{\$88}$	=	3.2	6.0	Low (risky)
EBITDA coverage	$\dfrac{\text{EBITDA} + \text{Lease pmts.}}{\text{Interest} + \text{Principle payments} + \text{Lease pmts.}}$	$\dfrac{\$411}{\$136}$	=	3.0	4.3	Low (risky)
Profitability						
Profit margin on sales	$\dfrac{\text{Net income available to common stockholders}}{\text{Sales}}$	$\dfrac{\$113}{\$3,000}$	=	3.8%	5.0%	Poor
Basic earning power (BEP)	$\dfrac{\text{Earnings before interest and taxes (EBIT)}}{\text{Total assets}}$	$\dfrac{\$283}{\$2,000}$	=	14.2%	17.2%	Poor
Return on total assets (ROA)	$\dfrac{\text{Net income available to common stockholders}}{\text{Total assets}}$	$\dfrac{\$113}{\$2,000}$	=	5.7%	9.0%	Poor
Return on common equity (ROE)	$\dfrac{\text{Net income available to common stockholders}}{\text{Common equity}}$	$\dfrac{\$113}{\$896}$	=	12.6%	15.0%	Poor
Market Value						
Price/earnings (P/E)	$\dfrac{\text{Price per share}}{\text{Earnings per share}}$	$\dfrac{\$23.00}{\$2.26}$	=	10.2	12.5	Low
Price/cash flow	$\dfrac{\text{Price per share}}{\text{Cash flow per shares}}$	$\dfrac{\$23.00}{\$4.26}$	=	5.4	6.8	Low
Market/book (M/B)	$\dfrac{\text{Market price per share}}{\text{Book value per share}}$	$\dfrac{\$23.00}{\$17.92}$	=	1.3	1.7	Low

8.7 Trend Analysis, Common Size Analysis, and Percentage Change Analysis

Trends give clues as to whether a firm's financial condition is likely to improve or deteriorate. To do a **trend analysis**, you examine a ratio over time, as shown in Figure 8-1. This graph shows that MicroDrive's rate of return on common equity has been declining since 2009, even though the industry average has been relatively stable. All the other ratios could be analyzed similarly.

In a **common size analysis**, all income statement items are divided by sales and all balance sheet items are divided by total assets. Thus, a common size income statement shows each item as a percentage of sales, and a common size balance sheet shows each item as a percentage of total assets.[10] The advantage of common size analysis is that it facilitates comparisons of balance sheets and income statements over time and across companies.

Common size statements are easy to generate if the financial statements are in a spreadsheet. In fact, if you obtain your data from a source that uses standardized financial statements, then it is easy to cut and paste the data for a new company over your original company's data, and all of your spreadsheet formulas will be valid for the new company. We generated Figure 8-2 in the *Excel* file ***Ch08 Tool Kit.xls***. Figure 8-2 shows MicroDrive's 2011 and 2012 common size income statements, along with the composite statement for the industry. (*Note:* Rounding may cause

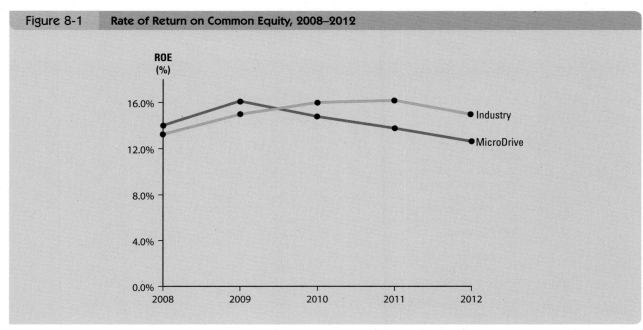

Figure 8-1   **Rate of Return on Common Equity, 2008–2012**

© Cengage Learning 2013

---

10. Some sources of industry data, such as Risk Management Associates (formerly known as Robert Morris Associates), are presented exclusively in common size form.

WEB

See *Ch08 Tool Kit.xls.*

addition/subtraction differences in Figures 8-2, 8-3, and 8-4.) MicroDrive's EBIT is slightly below average, and its interest expenses are slightly above average. The net effect is a relatively low profit margin.

Figure 8-3 shows MicroDrive's common size balance sheets along with the industry composite. Its accounts receivable are significantly higher than the industry average, its inventories are significantly higher, and it uses much more debt than the average firm.

Figure 8-2 MicroDrive Inc.: Common Size Income Statement

	A	B	C	Industry Composite 2012	MicroDrive 2012	2011
167				Industry Composite	MicroDrive	
168				2012	2012	2011
169	Net sales			100.0%	100.0%	100.0%
170	Operating costs			87.6%	87.2%	87.7%
171	Earnings before interest, taxes, depr. & amort. (EBITDA)			12.4%	12.8%	12.3%
172	Depreciation and amortization			2.8%	3.3%	3.2%
173	Earnings before interest and taxes (EBIT)			9.6%	9.4%	9.1%
174	Less interest			1.3%	2.9%	2.1%
175	Earnings before taxes (EBT)			8.3%	6.5%	7.0%
176	Taxes (40%)			3.3%	2.6%	2.8%
177	Net income before preferred dividends			5.0%	3.9%	4.2%
178	Preferred dividends				0.1%	0.1%
179	Net income available to common stockholders (profit margin)			5.0%	3.8%	4.1%
180						

© Cengage Learning 2013

Figure 8-3 MicroDrive Inc.: Common Size Balance Sheet

	A	B	Industry Composite 2012	MicroDrive 2012	2011
185			Industry Composite	MicroDrive	
186			2012	2012	2011
187	*Assets*				
188	Cash and equivalents		1.0%	0.5%	0.9%
189	Short-term investments		2.2%	0.0%	3.9%
190	Accounts receivable		17.8%	18.8%	18.8%
191	Inventories		19.8%	30.8%	24.7%
192	Total current assets		40.8%	50.0%	48.2%
193	Net plant and equipment		59.2%	50.0%	51.8%
194	Total assets		100.0%	100.0%	100.0%
195					
196	*Liabilities and equity*				
197	Accounts payable		1.8%	3.0%	1.8%
198	Notes payable		4.4%	5.5%	3.6%
199	Accruals		3.6%	7.0%	7.7%
200	Total current liabilities		9.8%	15.5%	13.1%
201	Long-term bonds		30.2%	37.7%	34.5%
202	Total liabilities		40.0%	53.2%	47.6%
203	Preferred stock		0.0%	2.0%	2.4%
204	Total common equity		60.0%	44.8%	50.0%
205	Total liabilities and equity		100.0%	100.0%	100.0%
206					

© Cengage Learning 2013

Figure 8-4 **MicroDrive Inc.: Income Statement Percentage Change Analysis**

	A	B	C	D
				Percent
213	Base year = 2011			Change in
214				2012
215	Net sales			5.3%
216	Operating costs			4.7%
217	Earnings before interest, taxes, depr. & amort. (EBITDA)			9.4%
218	Depreciation and amortization			11.1%
219	Earnings before interest and taxes (EBIT)			8.8%
220	Less interest			46.7%
221	Earnings before taxes (EBT)			(2.5%)
222	Taxes (40%)			(2.5%)
223	Net income before preferred dividends			(2.5%)
224	Preferred dividends			0.0%
225	Net income available to common stockholders			(2.6%)
226				

© Cengage Learning 2013

In **percentage change analysis**, growth rates are calculated for all income statement items and balance sheet accounts relative to a base year. To illustrate, Figure 8-4 contains MicroDrive's income statement percentage change analysis for 2012 relative to 2011. Sales increased at a 5.3% rate during 2012, but EBITDA increased by 9.4%. This "good news" was offset by a 46.7% increase in interest expense. The significant growth in interest expense caused growth in net income to be negative. Thus, the percentage change analysis points out that the decrease in net income in 2012 resulted almost exclusively from an increase in interest expense. This conclusion could be reached by analyzing dollar amounts, but percentage change analysis simplifies the task. We apply the same type of analysis to the balance sheets (see the file *Ch08 Tool Kit.xls*), which shows that inventories grew at a whopping 48.2% rate. With only a 5.3% growth in sales, the extreme growth in inventories should be of great concern to MicroDrive's managers.

WEB

See *Ch08 Tool Kit.xls* for details.

Self Test

What is a trend analysis, and what important information does it provide?

What is common size analysis?

What is percentage change analysis?

8.8 Tying the Ratios Together: The Du Pont Equation

In ratio analysis, it is sometimes easy to miss the forest for all the trees. The **Du Pont equation** provides a framework that ties together a firm's profitability, asset efficiency, and use of debt. The return on assets (ROA) can be expressed as the profit margin multiplied by the total assets turnover ratio:

$$
\begin{aligned}
\text{ROA} &= \text{Profit margin} \times \text{Total assets turnover} \\
&= \frac{\text{Net income}}{\text{Sales}} \times \frac{\text{Sales}}{\text{Total assets}}
\end{aligned}
\tag{8-1}
$$

For MicroDrive, the ROA is

$$\text{ROA} = 3.77\% \times 1.5 = 5.65\%$$

MicroDrive made 3.8%, or 3.8 cents, on each dollar of sales, and its assets were turned over 1.5 times during the year. Therefore, the company earned a return of 5.65% on its assets.

To find the return on equity (ROE), multiply the ROA by the *equity multiplier,* which is the ratio of assets to common equity:

$$
\text{Equity multiplier} = \frac{\text{Total assets}}{\text{Common equity}}
\tag{8-2}
$$

Firms that have a lot of leverage (i.e., a lot of liabilities or preferred stock) have a high equity multiplier because the assets are financed with a relatively smaller amount of equity. Therefore, the return on equity (ROE) depends on the ROA and the use of leverage:

$$
\begin{aligned}
\text{ROE} &= \text{ROA} \times \text{Equity multiplier} \\
&= \frac{\text{Net income}}{\text{Total assets}} \times \frac{\text{Total assets}}{\text{Common equity}}
\end{aligned}
\tag{8-3}
$$

MicroDrive's ROE is

$$
\begin{aligned}
\text{ROE} &= 5.65\% \times \$2{,}000/\$896 \\
&= 5.65\% \times 2.23 \\
&= 12.6\%
\end{aligned}
$$

Combining Equations 8-1 and 8-3 gives the *extended, or modified, Du Pont equation,* which shows how the profit margin, the total assets turnover ratio, and the equity multiplier combine to determine the ROE:

$$
\begin{aligned}
\text{ROE} &= (\text{Profit margin})(\text{Total assets turnover})(\text{Equity multiplier}) \\
&= \frac{\text{Net income}}{\text{Sales}} \times \frac{\text{Sales}}{\text{Total assets}} \times \frac{\text{Total assets}}{\text{Common equity}}
\end{aligned}
\tag{8-4}
$$

For MicroDrive, we have

$$\text{ROE} = (3.77\%)(1.5)(2.23)$$
$$= 12.6\%$$

The insights provided by the Du Pont model are valuable, and the model can be used for "quick and dirty" estimates of the impact that operating changes have on returns. For example, holding all else equal, if MicroDrive can implement lean production techniques and increase to 1.8 its ratio of sales to total assets, then its ROE will improve to $(3.77\%)(1.8)(2.23) = 15.13\%$. For a more complete "what if" analysis, most companies use a forecasting model such as the one described in Chapter 9.

Self Test

Explain how the extended, or modified, Du Pont equation can be used to reveal the basic determinants of ROE.

What is the equity multiplier?

A company has a profit margin of 6%, a total asset turnover ratio of 2, and an equity multiplier of 1.5. What is its ROE? **(18%)**

8.9 Comparative Ratios and Benchmarking

Ratio analysis involves comparisons. A company's ratios are compared with those of other firms in the same industry—that is, with industry average figures. However, like most firms, MicroDrive's managers go one step further: They also compare their ratios with those of a smaller set of the leading computer companies. This technique is called **benchmarking**, and the companies used for the comparison are called **benchmark companies**. For example, MicroDrive benchmarks against five other firms that its management considers to be the best-managed companies with operations similar to its own.

Many companies also benchmark various parts of their overall operation against top companies, whether they are in the same industry or not. For example, Micro-Drive has a division that sells hard drives directly to consumers through catalogs and the Internet. This division's shipping department benchmarks against L.L.Bean, even though they are in different industries, because L.L.Bean's shipping department is one of the best. MicroDrive wants its own shippers to strive to match L.L.Bean's record for on-time shipments.

Comparative ratios are available from a number of sources, including *Value Line*, Dun and Bradstreet (D&B), and the *Annual Statement Studies* published by Risk Management Associates, which is the national association of bank loan officers. Table 8-3 reports selected ratios from Reuters for Apple and its industry, revealing that Apple has a much higher profit margin and lower debt ratio than its peers.

Each data-supplying organization uses a somewhat different set of ratios designed for its own purposes. For example, D&B deals mainly with small firms, many of which are proprietorships, and it sells its services primarily to banks and other lenders. Therefore, D&B is concerned largely with the creditor's viewpoint, and its ratios emphasize current assets and liabilities, not market value ratios. So, when you select a comparative

www

To find quick information about a company, go to **www.reuters.com** Here you can find company profiles, stock price and share information, and several key ratios.

TABLE 8-3	Comparative Ratios for Apple Inc., the Computer Hardware Industry, the Technology Sector, and the S&P 500			
Ratio	**Apple**	**Computer Hardware Industry**[a]	**Technology Sector**[b]	**S&P 500**
P/E ratio	21.43	16.00	24.84	18.12
Market to book	6.22	2.27	3.87	2.90
Price to tangible book	6.38	4.55	4.68	7.54
Price to cash flow	19.80	9.16	9.88	10.99
Net profit margin	21.48	4.35	10.52	10.84
Quick ratio	1.96	1.10	1.16	0.66
Current ratio	2.01	1.49	2.23	0.98
Long-term debt to equity	0.00	22.71	14.85	119.81
Total debt to equity	0.00	58.07	23.33	175.73
Interest coverage (TIE)[c]	–	0.28	1.44	16.50
Return on assets	22.84	7.27	10.10	5.88
Return on equity	35.28	17.90	15.57	17.36
Inventory turnover	52.51	12.14	239.32	6.61
Asset turnover	1.06	1.98	0.82	0.54

© Cengage Learning 2013

[a]The computer hardware industry is composed of fifty firms, including IBM, Dell, Apple, Sun Microsystems, Gateway, and Silicon Graphics.
[b]The technology sector contains eleven industries, including communications equipment, computer hardware, computer networks, semiconductors, and software and programming.
[c]Apple had more interest income than interest expense.

Source: Adapted from **www.reuters.com**, December 28, 2010.

data source, you should be sure that your own emphasis is similar to that of the agency whose ratios you plan to use. Additionally, there are often definitional differences in the ratios presented by different sources, so before using a source, be sure to verify the exact definitions of the ratios to ensure consistency with your own work.

Self Test

Differentiate between trend analysis and comparative ratio analysis.

What is benchmarking?

8.10 Uses and Limitations of Ratio Analysis

Ratio analysis provides useful information concerning a company's operations and financial condition, but it has limitations that necessitate care and judgment. Some potential problems include the following.

1. Many large firms operate different divisions in different industries, and for such companies it is difficult to develop a meaningful set of industry averages. Therefore, industry averages are more applicable to small, narrowly focused firms than to large, multidivisional ones.

2. To set goals for high-level performance, it is best to benchmark on the industry *leaders'* ratios rather than the industry *average* ratios.

3. Inflation may have badly distorted firms' balance sheets—reported values are often substantially different from "true" values. Further, because inflation affects depreciation charges and inventory costs, reported profits are also affected. Thus, inflation can distort a ratio analysis for one firm over time or a comparative analysis of firms of different ages.

4. Seasonal factors can also distort a ratio analysis. For example, the inventory turnover ratio for a food processor will be radically different if the balance sheet figure used for inventory is the one just before versus the one just after the close of the canning season. This problem can be minimized by using monthly averages for inventory (and receivables) when calculating turnover ratios.

5. Firms can employ **"window dressing" techniques** to make their financial statements look stronger. To illustrate, suppose a company takes out a 2-year loan in late December. Because the loan is for more than 1 year, it is not included in current liabilities even though the cash received through the loan is reported as a current asset. This improves the current and quick ratios and makes the year-end balance sheet look stronger. If the company pays the loan back in January, then the transaction was strictly window dressing.

6. Companies' choices of different accounting practices can distort comparisons. For example, choices of different inventory valuation and depreciation methods affect financial statements differently, making comparisons among companies less meaningful. As another example, if one firm leases a substantial amount of its productive equipment, then its assets may appear low relative to sales (because leased assets often do not appear on the balance sheet) and its debt may appear low (because the liability associated with the lease obligation may not be shown as debt).[11]

In summary, conducting ratio analysis in a mechanical, unthinking manner is dangerous, but when ratio analysis is used intelligently and with good judgment, it can provide useful insights into a firm's operations and identify the right questions to ask.

RATIO ANALYSIS ON THE WEB

A great source for comparative ratios is **www.reuters.com**. Enter a company's ticker at the top of the page. This brings up a table with the stock quote, company information, and additional links. Select Financials, which brings up a page with a detailed ratio analysis for the company and includes comparative ratios for other companies in the same sector, the same industry, and the S&P 500. (*Note:* You may have to register to get extra features, but registration is free.)

---

11. This may change when FASB and IASB complete their joint project on leasing. As of the middle of 2011, the FASB and IASB plan to provide a draft of the revised standards by the end of 2011. See **72.3.243.42/project/leases.shtml** for updates.

8.11 Looking beyond the Numbers

Sound financial analysis involves more than just calculating and comparing ratios—qualitative factors must be considered. Here are some questions suggested by the American Association of Individual Investors (AAII).

1. To what extent are the company's revenues tied to one key customer or to one key product? To what extent does the company rely on a single supplier? Reliance on single customers, products, or suppliers increases risk.
2. What percentage of the company's business is generated overseas? Companies with a large percentage of overseas business are exposed to risk of currency exchange volatility and political instability.
3. What are the probable actions of current competitors and the likelihood of additional new competitors?
4. Do the company's future prospects depend critically on the success of products currently in the pipeline or on existing products?
5. How does the legal and regulatory environment affect the company?

Summary

This chapter explained techniques used by investors and managers to analyze financial statements. The key concepts covered are listed below.

- **Liquidity ratios** show the relationship of a firm's current assets to its current liabilities and thus its ability to meet maturing debts. Two commonly used liquidity ratios are the **current ratio** and the **quick, or acid test, ratio.**
- **Asset management ratios** measure how effectively a firm is managing its assets. These ratios include **inventory turnover, days sales outstanding, fixed assets turnover,** and **total assets turnover.**
- **Debt management ratios** reveal (1) the extent to which the firm is financed with debt and (2) its likelihood of defaulting on its debt obligations. They include the **debt ratio,** the **times-interest-earned ratio,** and the **EBITDA coverage ratio.**
- **Profitability ratios** show the combined effects of liquidity, asset management, and debt management policies on operating results. They include the **net profit margin** (also called the **profit margin on sales**), the **basic earning power ratio,** the **return on total assets,** and the **return on common equity.**

- **Market value ratios** relate the firm's stock price to its earnings, cash flow, and book value per share, thus giving management an indication of what investors think of the company's past performance and future prospects. These include the **price/earnings ratio**, the **price/cash flow ratio**, and the **market/book ratio**.
- **Trend analysis**, in which one plots a ratio over time, is important because it reveals whether the firm's condition has been improving or deteriorating over time.
- The **Du Pont model** is designed to show how the profit margin on sales, the assets turnover ratio, and the use of debt all interact to determine the rate of return on equity. The firm's management can use the Du Pont model to analyze ways of improving performance.
- **Benchmarking** is the process of comparing a particular company with a group of similar successful companies.

Ratio analysis has limitations, but when used with care and judgment it can be very helpful.

Questions

8-1 Define each of the following terms:
  a. *Liquidity ratios:* current ratio; quick, or acid test, ratio
  b. *Asset management ratios:* inventory turnover ratio; days sales outstanding (DSO); fixed assets turnover ratio; total assets turnover ratio
  c. *Financial leverage ratios:* debt ratio; times-interest-earned (TIE) ratio; coverage ratio
  d. *Profitability ratios:* profit margin on sales; basic earning power (BEP) ratio; return on total assets (ROA); return on common equity (ROE)
  e. *Market value ratios:* price/earnings (P/E) ratio; price/cash flow ratio; market/book (M/B) ratio; book value per share
  f. Trend analysis; comparative ratio analysis; benchmarking
  g. Du Pont equation; window dressing; seasonal effects on ratios

8-2 Financial ratio analysis is conducted by managers, equity investors, long-term creditors, and short-term creditors. What is the primary emphasis of each of these groups in evaluating ratios?

8-3 Over the past year, M. D. Ryngaert & Co. has realized an increase in its current ratio and a drop in its total assets turnover ratio. However, the company's sales, quick ratio, and fixed assets turnover ratio have remained constant. What explains these changes?

8-4 Profit margins and turnover ratios vary from one industry to another. What differences would you expect to find between a grocery chain such as Safeway and a steel company? Think particularly about the turnover ratios, the profit margin, and the Du Pont equation.

8-5 How might (a) seasonal factors and (b) different growth rates distort a comparative ratio analysis? Give some examples. How might these problems be alleviated?

8-6 Why is it sometimes misleading to compare a company's financial ratios with those of other firms that operate in the same industry?

Problems   Answers Appear in Appendix B

Easy Problems 1–5

8-1 Days Sales Outstanding Greene Sisters has a DSO of 20 days. The company's average daily sales are $20,000. What is the level of its accounts receivable? Assume there are 365 days in a year.

8-2 Debt Ratio Vigo Vacations has an equity multiplier of 2.5. The company's assets are financed with some combination of long-term debt and common equity. What is the company's debt ratio?

8-3 Market/Book Ratio Winston Washers's stock price is $75 per share. Winston has $10 billion in total assets. Its balance sheet shows $1 billion in current liabilities, $3 billion in long-term debt, and $6 billion in common equity. It has 800 million shares of common stock outstanding. What is Winston's market/book ratio?

8-4 Price/Earnings Ratio Reno Revolvers has an EPS of $1.50, a cash flow per share of $3.00, and a price/cash flow ratio of 8.0. What is its P/E ratio?

8-5 ROE Needham Pharmaceuticals has a profit margin of 3% and an equity multiplier of 2.0. Its sales are $100 million and it has total assets of $50 million. What is its ROE?

Intermediate Problems 6–10

8-6 Du Pont Analysis Gardial & Son has an ROA of 12%, a 5% profit margin, and a return on equity equal to 20%. What is the company's total assets turnover? What is the firm's equity multiplier?

8-7 Current and Quick Ratios Ace Industries has current assets equal to $3 million. The company's current ratio is 1.5, and its quick ratio is 1.0. What is the firm's level of current liabilities? What is the firm's level of inventories?

8-8 Profit Margin and Debt Ratio Assume you are given the following relationships for the Haslam Corporation:

Sales/total assets	1.2
Return on assets (ROA)	4%
Return on equity (ROE)	7%

Calculate Haslam's profit margin and debt ratio.

8-9 Current and Quick Ratios The Nelson Company has $1,312,500 in current assets and $525,000 in current liabilities. Its initial inventory level is $375,000, and it will raise funds as additional notes payable and use them to increase inventory. How much can Nelson's short-term debt (notes payable) increase without pushing its current ratio below 2.0? What will be the firm's quick ratio after Nelson has raised the maximum amount of short-term funds?

8-10 Times-Interest-Earned Ratio The Morris Corporation has $600,000 of debt outstanding, and it pays an interest rate of 8% annually. Morris's annual sales are $3 million, its average tax rate is 40%, and its net profit margin on sales is 3%. If the company does not maintain a TIE ratio of at least 5 to 1, then its bank will refuse to renew the loan and bankruptcy will result. What is Morris's TIE ratio?

Challenging Problems 11–14

8-11 Balance Sheet Analysis Complete the balance sheet and sales information in the table that follows for J. White Industries using the following financial data:

Debt ratio: 40%
Quick ratio: 0.80
Total assets turnover: 1.5
Days sales outstanding: 36.5 days[a]
Gross profit margin on sales: (Sales − Cost of goods sold)/Sales = 25%
Inventory turnover ratio: 5.0

[a]Calculation is based on a 365-day year.

Balance Sheet

Cash	_____	Accounts payable	_____
Accounts receivable	_____	Long-term debt	50,000
Inventories	_____	Common stock	_____
Fixed assets	_____	Retained earnings	100,000
Total assets	$400,000	Total liabilities and equity	
Sales		Cost of goods sold	

8-12 Comprehensive Ratio Calculations The Kretovich Company had a quick ratio of 1.4, a current ratio of 3.0, an inventory turnover of 6 times, total current assets of $810,000, and cash and marketable securities of $120,000. What were Kretovich's annual sales and its DSO? Assume a 365-day year.

8-13 Comprehensive Ratio Analysis Data for Lozano Chip Company and its industry averages follow.

a. Calculate the indicated ratios for Lozano.
b. Construct the extended Du Pont equation for both Lozano and the industry.
c. Outline Lozano's strengths and weaknesses as revealed by your analysis.
d. Suppose Lozano had doubled its sales as well as its inventories, accounts receivable, and common equity during 2012. How would that information affect the validity of your ratio analysis? (*Hint:* Think about averages and the effects of rapid growth on ratios if averages are not used. No calculations are needed.)

Lozano Chip Company: Balance Sheet as of December 31, 2012 (Thousands of Dollars)

Cash	$ 225,000	Accounts payable	$ 601,866
Receivables	1,575,000	Notes payable	326,634
Inventories	1,125,000	Other current liabilities	525,000
Total current assets	$2,950,000	Total current liabilities	$1,453,500
Net fixed assets	1,350,000	Long-term debt	1,068,750
		Common equity	1,752,750
Total assets	$4,275,000	Total liabilities and equity	$4,275,000

Lozano Chip Company: Income Statement for Year Ended December 31, 2012 (Thousands of Dollars)

Sales	$ 7,500,000
Cost of goods sold	6,375,000
Selling, general, and administrative expenses	825,000
Earnings before interest and taxes (EBIT)	$ 300,000
Interest expense	111,631
Earnings before taxes (EBT)	$ 188,369
Federal and state income taxes (40%)	75,348
Net income	$ 113,022

Ratio	Lozano	Industry Average
Current assets/Current liabilities	_____	2.0
Days sales outstanding[a]	_____	35.0 days
Sales/Inventory	_____	6.7
Sales/Fixed assets	_____	12.1
Sales/Total assets	_____	3.0
Net income/Sales	_____	1.2%
Net income/Total assets	_____	3.6%
Net income/Common equity	_____	9.0%
Total liabilities/Total assets	_____	60.0%

[a]Calculation is based on a 365-day year.

8-14 **Comprehensive Ratio Analysis** The Jimenez Corporation's forecasted 2013 financial statements follow, along with some industry average ratios.

a. Calculate Jimenez's 2013 forecasted ratios, compare them with the industry average data, and comment briefly on Jimenez's projected strengths and weaknesses.

b. What do you think would happen to Jimenez's ratios if the company initiated cost-cutting measures that allowed it to hold lower levels of inventory and substantially decreased the cost of goods sold? No calculations are necessary; think about which ratios would be affected by changes in these two accounts.

Jimenez Corporation: Forecasted Balance Sheet as of December 31, 2013

Assets	
Cash	$ 72,000
Accounts receivable	439,000
Inventories	894,000
Total current assets	$ 1,405,000
Fixed assets	431,000
Total assets	$ 1,836,000
Liabilities and Equity	
Accounts and notes payable	$ 432,000
Accruals	170,000
Total current liabilities	$ 602,000
Long-term debt	404,290
Common stock	575,000
Retained earnings	254,710
Total liabilities and equity	$ 1,836,000

Jimenez Corporation: Forecasted Income Statement for 2013

Sales	$4,290,000
Cost of goods sold	3,580,000
Selling, general, and administrative expenses	370,320
Depreciation and amortization	159,000
Earnings before taxes (EBT)	$ 180,680
Taxes (40%)	72,272
Net income	$ 108,408

Per Share Data

EPS	$ 4.71
Cash dividends per share	$ 0.95
P/E ratio	5.0
Market price (average)	$ 23.57
Number of shares outstanding	23,000

Industry Financial Ratios (2012)[a]

Quick ratio	1.0
Current ratio	2.7
Inventory turnover[b]	7.0
Days sales outstanding[c]	32.0 days
Fixed assets turnover[b]	13.0
Total assets turnover[b]	2.6
Return on assets	9.1%
Return on equity	18.2%
Debt ratio	50.0%
Profit margin on sales	3.5%
P/E ratio	6.0
Price/Cash flow ratio	3.5

[a]Industry average ratios have been constant for the past 4 years.
[b]Based on year-end balance sheet figures.
[c]Calculation is based on a 365-day year.

Spreadsheet Problem

8-15 **Build a Model: Ratio Analysis** Start with the partial model in the file *Ch08 P15 Build a Model.xls* from the textbook's Web site. Joshua & White (J&W) Technologies's financial statements are also shown below. Answer the following questions. (*Note:* Industry average ratios are provided in *Ch08 P15 Build a Model.xls.*)

a. Has J&W's liquidity position improved or worsened? Explain.

b. Has J&W's ability to manage its assets improved or worsened? Explain.

c. How has J&W's profitability changed during the last year?

d. Perform an extended Du Pont analysis for J&W for 2011 and 2012. What do these results tell you?

e. Perform a common size analysis. What has happened to the composition (that is, percentage in each category) of assets and liabilities?

f. Perform a percentage change analysis. What does this tell you about the change in profitability and asset utilization?

Joshua & White Technologies: December 31 Balance Sheets (Thousands of Dollars)

Assets	2012	2011	Liabilities & Equity	2012	2011
Cash and cash equivalents	$ 21,000	$ 20,000	Accounts payable	$ 33,600	$ 32,000
Short-term investments	3,759	3,240	Accruals	12,600	12,000
Accounts receivable	52,500	48,000	Notes payable	19,929	6,480
Inventories	84,000	56,000	Total current liabilities	$ 66,129	$ 50,480
Total current assets	$161,259	$127,240	Long-term debt	67,662	58,320
Net fixed assets	218,400	200,000	Total liabilities	$133,791	$108,800
Total assets	$379,659	$327,240	Common stock	183,793	178,440
			Retained earnings	62,075	40,000
			Total common equity	$245,868	$218,440
			Total liabilities & equity	$379,659	$327,240

Joshua & White Technologies December 31 Income Statements (Thousands of Dollars)

	2012	2011
Sales	$420,000	$400,000
Expenses excluding depreciation and amortization	327,600	320,000
EBITDA	$ 92,400	$ 80,000
Depreciation and amortization	19,660	18,000
EBIT	$ 72,740	$ 62,000
Interest expense	5,740	4,460
EBT	$ 67,000	$ 57,540
Taxes (40%)	26,800	23,016
Net income	$ 40,200	$ 34,524
Common dividends	$ 18,125	$ 17,262

Other Data	2012	2011
Year-end stock price	$ 90.00	$ 96.00
Number of shares (Thousands)	4,052	4,000
Lease payment (Thousands of Dollars)	$20,000	$20,000
Sinking fund payment (Thousands of Dollars)	$ 0	$ 0

THOMSON REUTERS

Use the Thomson ONE—Business School Edition online database to work this chapter's questions.

Analysis of Ford's Financial Statements

Use Thomson ONE to analyze Ford Motor Company. Enter Ford's ticker symbol (F) and select GO. By selecting the menu at left labeled Financials, you can find Ford's key financial statements for the past several years. Under the Financial Ratios heading select Thomson Ratios and then Annual Ratios to see an in-depth summary of Ford's various ratios over the past 5 years.

Click on the Comparables menu at left and scroll down to find the submenu items for Key Financials and Key Financial Ratios for Ford and a few of its peers. If you scroll up, still in the Comparables menu, you can select a different the list of peer firms to be included in the analysis. The default group is "Peers by SIC code."

Discussion Questions

1. What has happened to Ford's liquidity position over the past 3 years? How does Ford's liquidity compare with its peers? (*Hint:* You may use both the peer key financial ratios and liquidity comparison to answer this question.)
2. Take a look at Ford's inventory turnover ratio. How does this ratio compare with its peers? Have there been any interesting changes over time in this measure? Do you consider Ford's inventory management to be a strength or a weakness?
3. Construct a simple Du Pont analysis for Ford and its peers. What are Ford's strengths and weaknesses relative to its competitors?

MINI CASE

The first part of the case, presented in Chapter 7, discussed the situation of Computron Industries after an expansion program. A large loss occurred in 2012, rather than the expected profit. As a result, its managers, directors, and investors are concerned about the firm's survival.

Jenny Cochran was brought in as assistant to Gary Meissner, Computron's chairman, who had the task of getting the company back into a sound financial position. Computron's 2011 and 2012 balance sheets and income statements, together with projections for 2013, are shown in the following tables. The tables also show the 2011 and 2012 financial ratios, along with industry average data. The 2013 projected financial statement data represent Cochran's and Meissner's best guess for 2013 results, assuming that some new financing is arranged to get the company "over the hump."

Balance Sheets

	2011	2012	2013E
Assets			
Cash	$ 9,000	$ 7,282	$ 14,000
Short-term investments	48,600	20,000	71,632
Accounts receivable	351,200	632,160	878,000
Inventories	715,200	1,287,360	1,716,480
Total current assets	$1,124,000	$1,946,802	$2,680,112
Gross fixed assets	491,000	1,202,950	1,220,000
Less: Accumulated depreciation	146,200	263,160	383,160
Net fixed assets	$ 344,800	$ 939,790	$ 836,840
Total assets	$1,468,800	$2,886,592	$3,516,952
Liabilities and Equity			
Accounts payable	$ 145,600	$ 324,000	$ 359,800
Notes payable	200,000	720,000	300,000
Accruals	136,000	284,960	380,000
Total current liabilities	$ 481,600	$1,328,960	$1,039,800
Long-term debt	323,432	1,000,000	500,000
Common stock (100,000 shares)	460,000	460,000	1,680,936
Retained earnings	203,768	97,632	296,216
Total equity	$ 663,768	$ 557,632	$1,977,152
Total liabilities and equity	$1,468,800	$2,886,592	$3,516,952

Note: "E" denotes "estimated"; the 2013 data are forecasts.

Income Statements

	2011	2012	2013E
Sales	$3,432,000	$5,834,400	$7,035,600
Cost of goods sold	2,864,000	4,980,000	5,800,000
Other expenses	340,000	720,000	612,960
Depreciation and amortization	18,900	116,960	120,000
Total operating costs	$3,222,900	$5,816,960	$6,532,960
EBIT	$ 209,100	$ 17,440	$ 502,640
Interest expense	62,500	176,000	80,000
EBT	$ 146,600	($ 158,560)	$ 422,640
Taxes (40%)	58,640	(63,424)	169,056
Net income	$ 87,960	($ 95,136)	$ 253,584
Other Data			
Stock price	$ 8.50	$ 6.00	$ 12.17
Shares outstanding	100,000	100,000	250,000

	2011	2012	2013E
EPS	$ 0.880	($ 0.951)	$ 1.014
DPS	$ 0.220	0.110	0.220
Tax rate	40%	40%	40%
Book value per share	$ 6.638	$ 5.576	$ 7.909
Lease payments	$40,000	$40,000	$40,000

Note: "E" denotes "estimated"; the 2013 data are forecasts.

Ratio Analysis

	2011	2012	2013E	Industry Average
Current	2.3	1.5	_____	2.7
Quick	0.8	0.5	_____	1.0
Inventory turnover	4.8	4.5	_____	6.1
Days sales outstanding	37.3	39.6	_____	32.0
Fixed assets turnover	10.0	6.2	_____	7.0
Total assets turnover	2.3	2.0	_____	2.5
Debt ratio	54.8%	80.7%	_____	50.0%
TIE	3.3	0.1	_____	6.2
EBITDA coverage	2.6	0.8	_____	8.0
Profit margin	2.6%	−1.6%	_____	3.6%
Basic earning power	14.2%	0.6%	_____	17.8%
ROA	6.0%	−3.3%	_____	9.0%
ROE	13.3%	−17.1%	_____	17.9%
Price/Earnings (P/E)	9.7	−6.3	_____	16.2
Price/Cash flow	8.0	27.5	_____	7.6
Market/Book	1.3	1.1	_____	2.9

Note: "E" denotes "estimated."

Cochran must prepare an analysis of where the company is now, what it must do to regain its financial health, and what actions should be taken. Your assignment is to help her answer the following questions. Provide clear explanations, not yes or no answers.

a. Why are ratios useful? What three groups use ratio analysis and for what reasons?

b. Calculate the 2013 current and quick ratios based on the projected balance sheet and income statement data. What can you say about the company's liquidity position in 2011, 2012, and as projected for 2013? We often think of ratios as being useful (1) to managers to help run business, (2) to bankers for credit analysis, and (3) to stockholders for stock valuation. Would these different types of analysts have an equal interest in the liquidity ratios?

c. Calculate the 2013 inventory turnover, days sales outstanding (DSO), fixed assets turnover, and total assets turnover. How does Computron's utilization of assets stack up against that of other firms in its industry?

d. Calculate the 2013 debt, times-interest-earned, and EBITDA coverage ratios. How does Computron compare with the industry with respect to financial leverage? What can you conclude from these ratios?

e. Calculate the 2013 profit margin, basic earning power (BEP), return on assets (ROA), and return on equity (ROE). What can you say about these ratios?

f. Calculate the 2013 price/earnings ratio, price/cash flow ratio, and market/book ratio. Do these ratios indicate that investors are expected to have a high or low opinion of the company?

g. Perform a common size analysis and percentage change analysis. What do these analyses tell you about Computron?

h. Use the extended Du Pont equation to provide a summary and overview of Computron's financial condition as projected for 2013. What are the firm's major strengths and weaknesses?

i. What are some potential problems and limitations of financial ratio analysis?

j. What are some qualitative factors that analysts should consider when evaluating a company's likely future financial performance?

Selected Additional Cases

The following cases from TextChoice, *Cengage Learning's online case library, cover many of the concepts discussed in this chapter and are available at* **www.textchoice2.com/casenet.**

Klein-Brigham Series:
Case 35, "Mark X Company (A)," which illustrates the use of ratio analysis in the evaluation of a firm's existing and potential financial positions; Case 36, "Garden State Container Corporation," which is similar in content to Case 35; Case 51, "Safe Packaging Corporation," which updates Case 36; Case 68, "Sweet Dreams Inc.," which also updates Case 36; and Case 71, "Swan-Davis, Inc.," which illustrates how financial analysis—based on both historical statements and forecasted statements—is used for internal management and lending decisions.

PART II

Corporate Valuation

Chapter 9

Financial Planning and Forecasting Financial Statements

Our primary objective in this book is to explain how financial managers can make their companies more valuable. However, value creation is impossible unless the company has well-designed strategic and tactical operating plans. As Yogi Berra once said, "You've got to be careful if you don't know where you're going, because you might not get there." An important component of these operating plans is financial projections.

Managers use **pro forma,** or **projected, financial statements** in four ways: (1) By looking at projected statements, they can assess whether the firm's anticipated performance is in line with the firm's own general targets and with investors' expectations. (2) Pro forma statements can be used to estimate the effect of proposed operating changes, enabling managers to conduct "what if" analyses. (3) Managers use pro forma statements to anticipate the firm's future financing needs. (4) Managers forecast free cash flows under different operating plans, forecast their capital requirements, and then choose the plan that maximizes shareholder value. Security analysts make the same types of projections, forecasting future earnings, cash flows, and stock prices.

Beginning of Chapter Questions

As you read the chapter, consider how you would answer the following questions. You *should not* necessarily be able to answer the questions before you read the chapter. Rather, you should use them to get a sense of the issues covered in the chapter. After reading the chapter, you should be able to give at least partial answers to the questions, and you should be able to give better answers after the chapter has been discussed in class. Note, too, that it is often useful, when answering conceptual questions, to use hypothetical data to illustrate your answer. We illustrate the answers with an *Excel* model that is available on the textbook's Web site. Accessing the model and working through it is a useful exercise, and it provides insights that are useful when answering the questions.

1. List and discuss briefly the major components of a firm's **strategic plan.** What role do projections of financial statements play in the development of the strategic plan?

2. One forecasting technique is called the **forecasted financial statement approach,** and it is used to forecast future financial statements. If you had a company's balance sheets and income statements for the past 5 years but no other information, how could you use the forecasted financial statement approach to forecast the following items for the coming year? (a) Its sales revenues. (b) Its financial statements. (c) Its

funds requirements (AFN). (d) Its financial condition and profitability as shown by its ROE and other key ratios.

3. If you had a set of industry average ratios for the firm you were analyzing, how might you use these data?

4. All forecasts are subject to error. Do you think top managers would be concerned about the effects on the firm if sales revenues or unit costs, for example, turned out to be different from the forecasted level? How could you provide information on the effects of such errors?

5. Define the following terms and then explain the role they might play in your forecast. (a) **Economies of scale.** (b) **Lumpy assets.** (c) **Excess capacity.**

6. The funds requirement can be forecasted by the forecasted financial statement approach, but you could also use the **AFN equation.** What is this equation, and how does it operate? What are its advantages and disadvantages relative to the financial statement method?

7. For most firms, there is some sales growth rate at which they could grow without needing any external financing, that is, where AFN = $0. How could you determine that growth rate? What variables under management's control would affect this **sustainable growth rate?**

9.1 Overview of Financial Planning

Most companies have strategic plans, operating plans, and financial plans.

9.1a Strategic Plans

Strategic plans usually have statements for mission, corporate scope, corporate objectives, and strategies.

Mission Statement

Strategic plans usually begin with a *mission statement*, which is a statement of the firm's overall purpose. Many companies are very clear about their corporate mission, and for most this is typical: "Our mission is to maximize shareowner value over time." Before the economic crisis of 2008 and 2009, many companies forgot

WEB

The textbook's Web site contains an *Excel* file that will guide you through the chapter's calculations. The file for this chapter is *Ch09 Tool Kit.xls*, and we encourage you to open the file and follow along as you read the chapter.

CORPORATE VALUATION AND FINANCIAL PLANNING

The value of a firm is determined by the size, timing, and risk of its expected future free cash flows (FCF). This chapter explains how to project financial statements and use them to calculate expected future free cash flows

under different operating plans. The next chapter takes the analysis further, showing how to identify optimal plans and then design incentive compensation systems that will lead to optimal results.

© Cengage Learning 2013

about the "over time" part, focusing instead on "maximizing the stock price on the date the CEO's options vest." Stockholders and directors have, fortunately, brought "over time" back into focus.

The goal of creating wealth for the company's owners is not as common abroad as it is in the United States. For example, Veba AG (now part of the German energy company E.ON), one of Germany's largest companies, created a stir when it made the following statement in its annual report: "Our commitment is to create value for you, our shareholders." This was quite different from the usual German model, because German companies generally have representatives from labor on their boards of directors and explicitly state their commitments to labor and a variety of other stakeholders. As one might expect, Veba's stock consistently outperformed the average German stock. As the trend in international investing continues, more and more non-U.S. companies are adopting a corporate purpose similar to that of Veba.

Corporate Scope

A firm's corporate scope defines its line or lines of business and its geographic area of operations. For example, Coca-Cola limits its products to soft drinks, but it operates on a global scale. PepsiCo followed Coke's lead by spinning off its food service businesses, as several studies have found that the market tends to value focused firms more highly than diversified ones.[1] During the bull market that led up to the 2008–2009 crash, many companies expanded into areas management knew little about, seeking sales growth as much or more than profits. For example, electric utilities bought insurance companies, and conservative banks bought shady mortgage originators. Those misguided ventures led to many disasters, so today companies are paying more attention to having a well-defined and reasonable corporate scope.

Statement of Corporate Objectives

This statement sets forth specific goals or targets to help operating managers focus on the firm's primary objectives. Most organizations have both quantitative and qualitative objectives. A typical quantitative objective might be attaining a 50% market share, a 20% ROE, and a 10% earnings growth rate. Qualitatively, their stated objective might be: "To provide better information systems to lower the cost and improve the efficiency of the U.S. medical system."

Corporate Strategies

Once a firm has defined its purpose, scope, and objectives, it must develop a strategy for achieving its goals. Corporate strategies are broad approaches rather than detailed plans. For example, one airline may have a strategy of offering no-frills service to a limited number of cities, while another's strategy may be to offer "a stateroom in the sky." Any such strategy should, of course, be compatible with the firm's purpose, scope, and objectives.

Overall, the strategic plan provides a "vision" of what the firm's top management expects, and without such a vision, the firm is not likely to be successful.

9.1b Operating Plans

Operating plans provide detailed implementation guidance to help the firm realize its strategic vision. These plans can be developed for any time horizon, but most companies use a 5-year horizon, with the plan being quite detailed for the first year but less and less specific for each succeeding year. The plan explains who is responsible for each particular function, when specific tasks are to be accomplished, targets for sales and profits, and the like. Large, multidivisional companies such as General Electric break their operating plans down by divisions, so each division has its own goals, mission, and plan for meeting its objectives. These plans are then consolidated to form the overall corporate plan.

---

1. See, for example, Philip G. Berger and Eli Ofek, "Diversification's Effect on Firm Value," *Journal of Financial Economics,* January 1995, pp. 39–66; and Larry Lang and René Stulz, "Tobin's Q, Corporate Diversification, and Firm Performance," *Journal of Political Economy,* Vol. 102, 1994, pp. 1248–1280.

9.1c The Financial Plan

The financial planning process generally involves five steps.

1. The firm forecasts financial statements under alternative versions of the operating plan in order to analyze the effects of different operating procedures on projected profits and financial ratios.
2. Next, it determines the amount of capital that will be needed to support the plan; that is, it finds out how much the new assets needed to achieve the target sales will cost, since without adequate capital, the plan obviously cannot be realized.
3. Then the firm forecasts the funds that will be generated internally. If internal funds are insufficient to cover the required new investment, then it must identify sources from which the required external capital can be raised, taking account of any constraints due to bond covenants that limit its debt ratio and other financial ratios. Market conditions must also be recognized. For example, in 2009 banks reduced many firms' lines of credit and also increased the fees and interest rates on such lines. This surprised firms that were not keeping up with conditions in financial markets.
4. The firm establishes a performance-based management compensation system that rewards employees for creating shareholder wealth. The emphasis here should be on the long run, not on profits over the next few quarters or even years. A failure in this area was an important factor leading to the worldwide financial and economic crisis that hit in 2008 and 2009.
5. Finally, management must monitor operations after implementing the plan to spot any deviations and then take corrective actions. Computer software is helping greatly here, and it's changing the way companies do business. In particular, corporate information systems are reducing the need for "middle managers" and flattening firms' management structures.

In the remainder of this chapter, we explain how to create a financial plan, including its three key components: (1) the sales forecast, (2) forecasted financial statements, and (3) methods for raising any needed external financing. Later, in Chapter 11, we discuss in more detail the relationships among incentives, compensation, and performance.

Self Test

Briefly explain the following terms: (1) mission statement, (2) corporate scope, (3) corporate objectives, and (4) corporate strategies.

Briefly describe the key elements of an operating plan.

Identify the five steps involved in the financial planning process as discussed in this section.

9.2 Sales Forecast

The **sales forecast** generally starts with a review of sales during the past 5 to 10 years, expressed in a graph such as that in Figure 9-1. The first part of the graph shows 5 years of historical sales for MicroDrive, the fictional firm we discussed in Chapters 7 and 8. The graph could have contained 10 years of sales data, but MicroDrive typically focuses on sales for the latest 5 years because its studies have shown that its future growth is more closely related to recent events than to the distant past.

Entire courses are devoted to forecasting sales, so we only touch on the basic elements here. However, forecasting the future sales growth rate always begins with

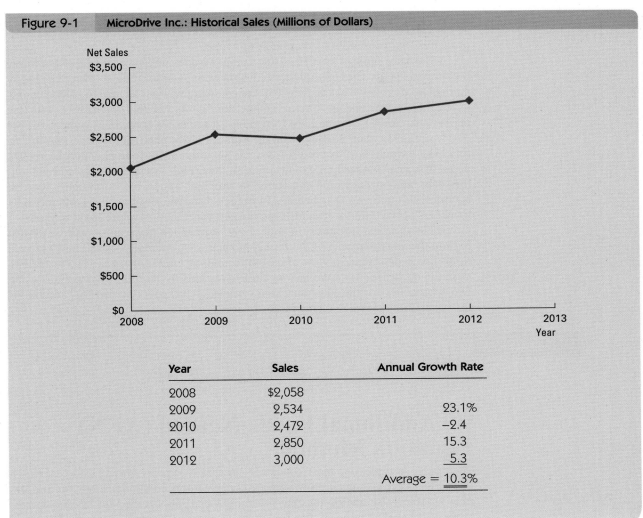

Figure 9-1   MicroDrive Inc.: Historical Sales (Millions of Dollars)

Year	Sales	Annual Growth Rate
2008	$2,058	
2009	2,534	23.1%
2010	2,472	−2.4
2011	2,850	15.3
2012	3,000	5.3
		Average = 10.3%

a look at past growth. MicroDrive's recent annual growth rates have averaged 10.3%, and the compound growth rate from 2008 to 2012 is the value for g in this equation:[2]

$$\$2,058(1 + g)^4 = \$3,000$$

The value of g can be found by solving the equation with a financial calculator. Enter N = 4, PV = −2058, PMT = 0, and FV = 3000; then, press I/YR to get g = 9.9%.[3]

No sensible manager would ever just forecast a continuation of past sales growth without taking account of current conditions in both the national and global economies, the firm's and its competitors' new products, planned advertising programs, and so on. But in the end, a sales forecast will emerge. In MicroDrive's case,

---

2. Unless we indicate otherwise, we report values from MicroDrive's financial statements in millions of dollars, as shown in Figure 9-1.
3. See this chapter's *Excel Tool Kit* for an explanation of projecting sales using a trend line or the average exponential growth rate.

the conclusion is that sales are most likely to grow at a 10% rate. Note, though, that actual sales could turn out to be materially higher or lower, depending on a number of factors that cannot be forecasted at this time.

If the sales forecast is off and the company does not have sufficient flexibility built into its plans, the consequences could be serious. First, if the market expands by *more* than MicroDrive has anticipated, the company will not be able to meet demand. Its customers will end up buying competitors' products, and MicroDrive will lose market share that might be hard to regain. On the other hand, if its projections are overly optimistic then it could wind up with too much plant, equipment, and inventory, which would hurt its profits, free cash flow, and intrinsic stock value. Moreover, if the firm had financed an expansion with debt, high interest charges and mandatory debt repayments would compound its problem. Thus, an accurate sales forecast is critical to the firm's well-being. After much discussion and analysis, MicroDrive's managers decided that a 10% increase in sales was the most appropriate forecast.

The firm's next questions include these: How much new capital will be needed to fund the increased sales? Can this capital be raised internally, or will new external funds be needed? And in view of current economic conditions, will it be feasible to raise the needed capital? We answer these questions in the following sections using two approaches: (1) the additional funds needed (AFN) equation method, and (2) the forecasted financial statements method.

Self Test	List some factors that should be considered when developing a sales forecast.
	Why is an accurate sales forecast critical to profitability?

9.3 Additional Funds Needed (AFN) Equation Method

MicroDrive is typical of most companies in that it expects growth in sales, which means its assets also must grow. Asset growth requires additional funds, so the firm may have to raise additional external capital if it has insufficient internal funds. If we assume that none of the firm's ratios will change (an assumption that we later modify), we can use a simple approach, the **additional funds needed (AFN)** equation method, to forecast financial requirements. The logic of the AFN equation approach is discussed in the next few sections.

9.3a Required Increase in Assets

In a steady-state situation in which no excess capacity exists, the firm must have additional plant and equipment, more delivery trucks, higher inventories, and so forth if sales are to increase. In addition, more sales will lead to more accounts receivable, and those receivables must be financed from the time of the sale until they are collected. Therefore, both fixed and current assets must increase if sales are to increase. Of course, if assets are to increase, liabilities and equity must also increase by a like amount to make the balance sheet balance.

9.3b Spontaneous Liabilities

The first sources of expansion funding are the "spontaneous" increases that will occur in MicroDrive's accounts payable and accrued wages and taxes. The company's suppliers give it 10 days to pay for inventory purchases, and since purchases will increase with sales, accounts payable will automatically rise. For example, if sales rise by 10% then inventory purchases will also rise by 10%, and this will cause accounts payable to rise spontaneously by the same 10%. Similarly, because the company pays workers every 2 weeks, more workers and a larger payroll will mean more accrued wages payable. Finally, higher expected income will mean more accrued income taxes, and its higher wage bill will mean more accrued withholding taxes. No interest normally is paid on these spontaneous funds, but their amount is limited by credit terms, contracts with workers, and tax laws. Therefore, *spontaneous funds will thus be used to the extent possible, but there is little flexibility in their usage.*

9.3c Addition to Retained Earnings

The second source of funds for expansion comes from net income. Part of MicroDrive's profit will be paid out in dividends, but the remainder will be reinvested in operating assets, as shown in the Assets section of the balance sheet; a corresponding amount will be reported as an addition to retained earnings in the Liabilities and equity section of the balance sheet. There is some flexibility in the amount of funds that will be generated from new reinvested earnings because dividends can be increased or decreased, but if the firm plans to hold its dividend steady or to increase it at a target rate, as most do, then flexibility is limited.

9.3d Calculating Additional Funds Needed (AFN)

If we start with the required new assets and then subtract both spontaneous funds and additions to retained earnings, we are left with the additional funds needed, or AFN. The AFN must come from *external sources*; hence it is sometimes called EFN. The typical sources of external funds are bank loans, new long-term bonds, new preferred stock, and newly issued common stock. The mix of the external funds used should be consistent with the firm's financial policies, especially its target debt ratio.

9.3e Using MicroDrive's Data to Implement the AFN Equation Method

Figure 9-2 reports MicroDrive's 2011 and 2012 financial statements.

Equation 9-1 summarizes the logic underlying the AFN equation method. Figure 9-3 defines the notation in Equation 9-1 and applies it to identify Micro-Drive's AFN. The **additional funds needed (AFN) equation** is:

$$
\begin{array}{llll}
\text{Required} & \text{Increase in} & \text{Increase in} & \text{Additional} \\
\text{increase} - & \text{spontaneous} - & \text{retained} & = \text{funds} \\
\text{in assets} & \text{liabilities} & \text{earnings} & \text{needed}
\end{array}
$$

$$(A_0^*/S_0)\Delta S - (L_0^*/S_0)\Delta S - S_1 \times M \times (1 - \text{Payout Ratio}) = \text{AFN}$$

(9–1)

We see from Part II of Figure 9-3 that, for sales to increase by $300 million, MicroDrive must increase assets by $200 million. Therefore, liabilities and capital must also increase by $200 million. Of this total, $20 million will come from spontaneous liabilities, and another $61.6 million will come from new retained earnings. The remaining $118.4 million must be raised from external sources—probably some

Figure 9-2	MicroDrive's Most Recent Financial Statements (Millions of Dollars, Except for Per Share Data)

	A	B	C	D	E	F	G	H
103	INCOME STATEMENTS		2011	2012	BALANCE SHEETS		2011	2012
104					*Assets*			
105	Sales		$2,850.0	$3,000.0	Cash		$15.0	$10.0
106	Costs except depreciation		2,500.0	2,617.0	ST Investments		65.0	0.0
107	Depreciation		90.0	100.0	Accounts receivable		315.0	375.0
108	Total operating costs		$2,590.0	$2,717.0	Inventories		415.0	615.0
109	EBIT		260.0	283.0	Total current assets		$810.0	$1,000.0
110	Less interest (INT)		60.0	88.0	Net plant and equip.		870.0	1,000.0
111	Earnings before taxes (EBT)		$200.0	$195.0	Total assets		$1,680.0	$2,000.0
112	Taxes (40%)		80.0	78.0				
113	Income before pref. dividends		$120.0	$117.0	*Liabilities and equity*			
114	Preferred dividends		4.0	4.0	Accounts payable		$30.0	$60.0
115	Net income for common (NI)		$116.0	$113.0	Accruals		130.0	140.0
116					Notes payable		60.0	110.0
117	Dividends to common (DIVs)		$53.0	$57.0	Total current liab.		$220.0	$310.0
118	Add. to retained earnings:				Long-term bonds		580.0	754.0
119	(NI – DIVs)		$63.0	$56.0	Total liabilities		$800.0	$1,064.0
120	Shares of common stock		50	50	Preferred stock		40.0	40.0
121	Earnings per share (EPS)		$2.32	$2.26	Common stock		130.0	130.0
122	Dividends per share (DPS)		$1.06	$1.14	Retained earnings		710.0	766.0
123	Price per share (P)		$26.00	$23.00	Total common equity		$840.0	$896.0
124					Total liab. & equity		$1,680.0	$2,000.0
125								

combination of short-term bank loans, long-term bonds, preferred stock, and common stock.

9.3f Key Factors in the AFN Equation

The AFN equation shows that external financing requirements depend on five key factors.

1. **Sales growth (g).** Rapidly growing companies require large increases in assets and a corresponding large amount of external financing, other things held constant. When capital is in short supply, as was the case during the financial crisis of 2009, companies may be forced to limit their growth.

2. **Capital intensity (A_0^*/S_0).** The amount of assets required per dollar of sales, A_0^*/S_0, is the **capital intensity ratio**, which has a major effect on capital requirements. Companies with relatively high assets-to-sales ratios require a relatively large amount of new assets for any given increase in sales; hence they have a greater need for external financing. If a firm can find a way to lower this ratio—for instance, by adopting a just-in-time inventory system, by going to two shifts in its manufacturing plants, or by outsourcing rather than manufacturing parts—then it can achieve a given level of growth with fewer assets and thus less new external capital.

3. **Spontaneous liabilities-to-sales ratio (L_0^*/S_0).** If a company can increase its spontaneously generated liabilities, this will reduce its need for external financing. One way of raising this ratio is by paying suppliers in, say, 20 days rather than 10 days. Such a change may be possible but, as we shall see in Chapter 21, it would probably have serious adverse consequences.

Figure 9-3   Additional Funds Needed (AFN) (Millions of Dollars)

	A	B	C	D	E	F	G	H	I
131	Part I. Inputs and Definitions								
132	S_0:		Last year's sales, i.e., 2012 sales:						$3,000
133	g:		Forecasted growth rate in sales:						10.00%
134	S_1:		Coming year's sales, i.e., 2013 sales = $S_0 \times (1 + g)$:						$3,300
135	gS_0:		Change in sales = $S_1 - S_0 = \Delta S$:						$300
136	A_0^*:		Assets that must increase to support the increase in sales:						$2,000
137	A_0^* / S_0:		Required assets per dollar of sales:						66.67%
138	L_0^*:		Last year's spontaneous liabilities i.e., payables + accruals:						$200
139	L_0^* / S_0:		Spontaneous liabilities per dollar of sales:						6.67%
140	Profit margin (M):		2012 profit margin = net income/sales:						3.77%
141	Payout ratio (POR):		Last year's dividends / net income = % of income paid out:						50.44%
142									
143	Part II. Additional Funds Needed (AFN) to Support Growth								
144									
145	AFN =	Required Increase in Assets		–	Spontaneous Increase		–	Addition to Retained	
146	=	$(A_0^*/S_0)\Delta S$		–	$(L_0^*/S_0)\Delta S$		–	$S_1 \times M \times (1 - POR)$	
147				–			–		
148	=	$(A_0^*/S_0)(gS_0)$		–	$(L_0^*/S_0)(gS_0)$		–	$(1+g)S_0 \times M \times (1 - POR)$	
149				–			–		
150	=	(0.667)($300)		–	(0.067)($300)		–	$3,300(0.0377)(1 – 0.504)	
151	=	$200		–	$20.00		–	$61.60	
152	AFN =	$118.40 million							

Notes:
1. Under the assumed conditions, the firm must raise $118.42 million externally to support its planned growth. However, the model assumes (1) that no excess capacity existed in 2012, so all assets were needed to produce the indicated sales; and (2) that the key ratios will remain constant at their 2012 levels. We explain later how to relax these assumptions, but it is better to use forecasted financial statements to deal with these issues, as we do on *Tab 2* of the *Excel Tool Kit* model.
2. Under the conditions set forth in Figure 9-3, a growth rate of 3.21% could be achieved without any AFN. This 3.21% is called the "sustainable growth rate," and we explain how it is calculated in a later section and also in the chapter's *Excel Tool Kit* model.

4. **Profit margin (M = Net Income/Sales)**. The higher the profit margin, the more net income is available to support increases in assets—and hence the less the need for external financing. A firms' profit margin is normally as high as management can get it, but sometimes a change in operations can boost the sales price or reduce costs, thus raising the margin further. If so, this will permit a faster growth rate with less external capital.

5. **Payout ratio (POR = DPS/EPS)**. The less of its income a company distributes as dividends, the larger its addition to retained earnings—and hence the less its need for external capital. Companies typically like to keep their dividends stable or to increase them at a steady rate—stockholders like stable, dependable dividends, so such a dividend policy will generally lower the cost of equity and thus maximize the stock price. So even though reducing the dividend is one way a company can reduce its need for external capital, companies generally resort to this method only if they are under financial duress.

9.3g The Self-Supporting Growth Rate

One interesting question is: "What is the maximum growth rate the firm could achieve if it had no access to external capital?" This rate is called the "self-supporting growth rate," and it can be found as the value of g that, when used in the AFN equation, results in an AFN of zero. We first replace ΔS in the AFN equation with gS_0 and S_1 with $(1+g)S_0$ so that the only unknown is g; we then solve for g to obtain the following equation for the self-supporting growth rate:

(9-2)

$$\text{Self-supporting g} = \frac{M(1 - POR)(S_0)}{A_0^* - L_0^* - M(1 - POR)(S_0)}$$

The definitions of the terms used in this equation are shown in Figure 9-3.

If the firm has any positive earnings and pays out less than 100% in dividends, then it will have some additions to retained earnings, and those additions could be combined with spontaneous funds to enable the company to grow at some rate without having to raise external capital. As explained in the chapter's *Excel* **Tool Kit**, this value can be found either algebraically or with *Excel*'s Goal Seek function. For MicroDrive, the self-supporting growth rate is 3.21%; this means it could grow at that rate even if capital markets dried up completely, with everything else held constant.

WEB

See **Ch09 Tool Kit.xls** on the textbook's Web site for details.

9.3h A Potential Problem with the AFN Equation: Excess Capacity

As noted previously, when we use the AFN equation we are implicitly assuming that the key ratios remain constant at their base-year levels. However, this assumption may not always be true. For example, in 2010 many firms were operating at significantly less than their full capacity because of the recession. Let's suppose MicroDrive had been operating its fixed assets at only 50% of capacity. It could then double its sales, which is a 100% increase, without adding any fixed assets at all. Similarly, if it had 25% more inventories at the start of the year than it required, it could increase sales by 25% without increasing its inventories. We could adjust the AFN equation to account for excess capacity, and we explain how to do so in the **Tool Kit**. However, a far better procedure is simply to recognize that while the AFN is useful for quickly obtaining a "back of the envelope" estimate of external financing requirements, the forecasted financial statements method, which is explained in the next section, is vastly superior for realistic financial planning.

Self Test

If all ratios are expected to remain constant, an equation can be used to forecast AFN. Write out the equation and briefly explain it.

Describe how the following factors affect external capital requirements: (1) payout ratio, (2) capital intensity, (3) profit margin.

In what sense do accounts payable and accruals provide "spontaneous funds" to a growing firm?

Is it possible for the calculated AFN to be negative? If so, what would this imply?

Refer to data in the MicroDrive example presented, but now assume that MicroDrive's growth rate in sales is forecasted to be 15% rather than 10%. If all ratios remain constant, what would the AFN be? (**$205.6 million**)

9.4 Forecasted Financial Statements Method

As its name implies, the objective of the **forecasted financial statements (FFS) method** is to project a complete set of financial statements. Because financial statements contain numerous accounts, forecasting is almost always done using computer software such as *Excel*. There are many different ways to do this, and entire books have been written on the topic.[4] In the following analysis, we explain one particular approach that we have found to be effective, particularly for a company considering changes to its capital structure or dividend policy.[5] In addition, it is easy to modify this forecasting approach to incorporate changes in assumptions.

Forecasting financial statements is conceptually similar to the AFN equation, but it is easy to get lost in the details. *Excel*'s calculations don't necessarily follow this sequence, but keep these conceptual steps in mind as we describe MicroDrive's forecasted financial statements.

1. Forecast the operating items on the income statement and balance sheet; these include sales, costs, operating assets, and spontaneous operating liabilities. Notice that these are the items required to calculate free cash flow.
2. Forecast items that depend on the firm's choice of financial policies, such as the dividend payout policy and the planned financing from debt and equity.
3. Forecast interest expense and preferred dividends, given the levels of debt and preferred stock that were forecast according to the financing plan.
4. Use the forecasted interest expense and preferred dividends to complete the income statement.
5. Determine the total common dividend payments.
6. Issue or repurchase additional common stock to make the balance sheets balance.
7. Calculate AFN as the amount of funding needed in excess of the amount of funding planned.

Forecasting is an iterative process. It begins with a set of initial operating assumptions and financial policies. The resulting forecasted statements are used to estimate free cash flow, EPS, and financial ratios. Managers then go through a set of "what if" questions and examine their operating assumptions and financial policies, as we describe next.

9.4a Background on the Company and the Forecast

MicroDrive's board recently installed a new management team: A new CEO, CFO, marketing manager, sales manager, inventory manager, and credit manager—only

---

4. For a much more detailed treatment of financial forecasting, see P. Daves, M. Ehrhardt, and R. Shrieves, *Corporate Valuation: A Guide for Managers and Investors* (Mason, OH: Thomson/South-Western, 2004).

5. One point about *Excel* models is worth noting. It is generally fairly easy to set up a model to study a given issue, but the complexity of the model rises exponentially as you attempt to deal with more and more different issues within the model. Therefore, in our experience it's generally better to develop limited-scope, single-issue models and then modify them to create new models—rather than trying to develop one model that can "do everything." Also, and crucially, it's much easier to debug single-purpose models than all-inclusive ones. Furthermore, if others are planning to use and perhaps modify the model, it's far easier for them to work with a simple model. There have been numerous occasions when we were given a complex model, had a hard time understanding it, and then abandoned it to make our own model that could do what we needed. These statements about "keeping it simple" are, of course, more appropriate for time-constrained students than for business people.

the production manager was retained. The new team was charged with improving the company's performance. As we noted in Chapter 8, many of MicroDrive's ratios are below industry averages.

The management team met in late 2012, when the industry was in a recession, for a 3-day retreat. The new CFO developed an *Excel* model to forecast financial statements under several different sets of assumptions, or scenarios. The first scenario assumes that operations maintain the status quo, the second that operations improve, and the third that conditions deteriorate. During the 3-day meeting, the CFO developed a fourth scenario based on discussions among the managers regarding changes that could be made to improve the firm's performance. (We report the details of these discussions in a later section.) They concluded that many changes could be implemented almost immediately and that the effects of those changes would be reflected in the 2013 results.

WEB

See *Ch09 Tool Kit.xls* on the textbook's Web site for details.

9.4b Input Data for the Forecast: Alternative Scenarios

The forecast begins with Figure 9-4, which shows the data used in the three preliminary forecasts as well as the final forecast. Industry averages and MicroDrive's actual operating and financial data for the most recent year are given in Columns C and D. Ignore Column E for the moment and look at Columns F, G, H, and I, which show the inputs used in four alternative scenarios.

Inputs for the Status Quo Scenario

The Status Quo scenario in Column F assumes that the firm in 2013 has essentially the same operating and financial ratios as it had in 2012, except that its rate of sales growth increases from 5.26% to 10%. Operating costs, operating assets, and operating spontaneous liabilities are assumed to be the same percentage of sales in 2013 as in 2012. Depreciation is assumed to be a fixed percentage of the net plant and equipment.

The components of MicroDrive's investor-supplied capital are notes payable, long-term bonds, preferred stock, and common equity. For this initial forecast, the target proportions of these components as percentages of total investor-supplied capital are held constant. The interest rates on its debt and the dividend rate on its preferred stock are assumed to remain at 2012 levels. The payout ratio for total common dividends is also assumed to stay at approximately the 2012 level in the Status Quo scenario.

If additional financing is needed, it is assumed that new shares of common stock can be issued at $23 per share, the 2012 year-end price. If a surplus of funds arises, then MicroDrive will pay down some of its debt and repurchase shares of preferred and common stock.

Inputs for the Best-Case Scenario

The data in Column G are for the Best case. Here the CEO assumes that MicroDrive is able to achieve industry average operating results immediately. However, the CEO also assumes that the company continues to use its current capital structure, which calls for more debt than the industry average. The improved operating performance would lower the costs of debt and preferred stock. However, the higher than average debt level would offset this factor to some extent, so the end result would be somewhat higher than industry average cost rates for notes payable, long-term debt, and preferred stock.

Figure 9-4   Input Data for the Forecast (Millions, Except for Percentages and Per Share Data)

	A	B	C	D	E	F	G	H	I
84									
85			2012 Actual Values		2013 Forecasted Input Values for Scenarios				
86	Inputs		2012 Actual Values		2013 Forecasted Input Values for Scenarios				
87					Active Scenario: Final				
88			Industry	MicroDrive	Active Scenario: Final	Status Quo	Best	Worst	Final
89	Operating Ratios:		Industry	MicroDrive	Final	Status Quo	Best	Worst	Final
90	Growth rate in sales		10.00%	5.26%	10.00%	10.00%	10.00%	−10.00%	10.00%
91	Op costs except depr'n / Sales		83.00%	87.23%	86.00%	87.23%	83.00%	92.21%	86.00%
92	Depr'n / Net plant & equip.		10.20%	10.00%	10.20%	10.00%	10.00%	10.00%	10.20%
93	Cash / Sales		0.25%	0.33%	0.25%	0.33%	0.33%	0.33%	0.25%
94	Accounts Rec. / Sales		9.80%	12.50%	11.00%	12.50%	9.80%	15.00%	11.00%
95	Inventory / Sales		11.11%	20.50%	16.00%	20.50%	11.11%	25.50%	16.00%
96	Net plant & equip. / Sales		33.33%	33.33%	33.33%	33.33%	33.33%	40.00%	33.33%
97	Accounts Pay. / Sales		2.00%	2.00%	2.00%	2.00%	2.00%	2.00%	2.00%
98	Accruals / Sales		4.00%	4.67%	4.00%	4.67%	2.00%	4.67%	4.00%
99	Tax rate:		40.00%	40.00%	40.00%	40.00%	40.00%	40.00%	40.00%
100	Financing Data:								
101	Notes payable/Investor-sup cap		5.00%	6.11%	5.00%	6.11%	6.11%	6.11%	5.00%
102	LT bonds/Investor-sup capital		32.00%	41.89%	37.00%	41.89%	41.89%	41.89%	37.00%
103	Pref. stock/Investor-sup cap.		3.00%	2.22%	3.00%	2.22%	2.22%	2.22%	3.00%
104	Comm equity/Investor-sup cap		60.00%	49.78%	55.00%	49.78%	49.78%	49.78%	55.00%
105	Interest rate on notes payable		8.00%	9.00%	8.50%	9.00%	8.50%	11.00%	8.50%
106	Interest rate on L-T bonds		10.00%	11.00%	10.50%	11.00%	10.50%	11.50%	10.50%
107	Dividend rate on pfd stock		9.00%	10.00%	9.50%	10.00%	9.50%	10.00%	9.50%
108	Target dividend payout ratio		40.00%	50.44%	40.00%	50.67%	50.67%	50.67%	40.00%
109			2012 MicroDrive	2013 Final	2013 Status Quo	2013 Best	2013 Worst	2013 Final	
110	Key Results		2012 MicroDrive	2013 Final	2013 Status Quo	2013 Best	2013 Worst	2013 Final	
111	Free cash flow (FCF)		−$175.20	$208.63	$6.98	$401.59	−$141.01	$208.63	
112	Return on inv. capital (ROIC)		9.43%	11.65%	9.44%	16.21%	3.07%	11.65%	
113	Earnings per share (EPS)		$2.26	$3.11	$2.42	$5.07	−$0.10	$3.11	
114	Return on equity (ROE)		12.61%	15.70%	12.60%	25.97%	−0.55%	15.70%	
115	# Shares, end-of-year		50.00	50.06	51.23	42.54	54.62	50.06	
116	Dividends per share (DPS)		$1.14	$1.24	$1.23	$2.57	$0.00	$1.24	

Inputs for the Worst-Case Scenario

The data in Column H, the Worst case, assume a continued long, bad recession, in which case the growth rate would be negative and the operating and financial ratios would be poor. It is likely that the stock price would decline during the year, but the CFO assumes that new shares could still have been issued at the beginning of the year for $23 per share, before investors and managers learned how bad things were going to get.

Inputs for the Final Scenario

The fourth set of input data, given in Column I and called "Final," was developed during the 3-day management conference held in late 2012. All of the operating executives were there, and all aspects of the business (including the ratios shown in Figure 9-4) were discussed. Some of the executives were relatively optimistic while others were relatively pessimistic, but all tried their best to be realistic. We will discuss these Final inputs in the next section.

Inputs for the Active Scenario

Now look at Column E in Figure 9-4, the one labeled "Active Scenario: Final." With *Excel*'s Scenario Manager, you choose a scenario and *Excel* replaces the input data in Column E with the data for the chosen scenario (we had chosen the Final scenario when we created Figure 9-4, so that is the scenario showing in Column E). These inputs are then linked to the section of the spreadsheet where the financial statements are forecast. (The forecasted statements are shown in Figure 9-5.)

After forecasting the financial statements, the model calculates performance measures, including the forecasted free cash flow (FCF), return on invested capital (ROIC), EPS, ROE, number of shares at the end of the year, and DPS. These six key results also are shown at the bottom of Figure 9-4; we will discuss them later.

9.4c Discussion of the Forecasted Operating Input Data

The CFO had taken a two-part computer course in college. The first module was taught by a computer science expert who focused on the mechanics of programming and computer usage in general. The second module was taught by an economist who discussed how to apply computers to specific tasks, including various types of forecasting. The economist's favorite term was GIGO, which stands for "garbage in, garbage out," and she repeated it constantly. No matter how well a model is set up, if the inputs used aren't accurate then the output won't be accurate, either. The CFO began the discussion by reminding the management team of this critical fact.

The sales growth rate is the first input item shown in Figure 9-4 and is followed by the most important driver of profitability, the ratio of operating costs (excluding depreciation) to sales. MicroDrive's 2012 operating cost ratio was 87.23%, well above the 83% industry average. This ratio is affected by operating costs, sales prices, and unit sales, and it was discussed at length during the planning conference. The CFO showed the forecasted results for the status quo, best-case, and worst-case scenarios, after which the CEO led a discussion of what the firm could actually achieve in 2013. After much discussion, the management team concluded that, because of licensing fees and other costs, it was not feasible for the firm to achieve the industry average operating cost ratio of 83% in the foreseeable future. However, the team believed that a figure of 86%, down from 2012's 87.23%, was "attainable." They agreed that over time it might be possible to reduce this ratio a bit further, but that 86% was the most realistic choice to use in the forecast.

Intrinsic value is affected by many factors, including the level of inventory. If MicroDrive carries too much inventory then storage costs, deterioration, and obsolescence will drive up operating costs. The CFO had studied the inventory/sales ratio earlier and had pointed out that MicroDrive had almost twice as much inventory for its sales as an average firm in the industry. The CEO stated that the production, sales, and purchasing managers were jointly responsible for inventory in MicroDrive's supply chain. The managers said that they had already been working on a plan to fix this problem. Because MicroDrive's production facilities are farther from their suppliers and customers than are those of most other firms in the industry, MicroDrive must hold a higher than average level of inventory to avoid running out of stock if sales surge. In the end, it was agreed that the inventory/sales ratio could be lowered from 20.5% to 16%, a significant improvement but still above the 11.11% industry average.

The CFO also pointed out that accounts receivable were much higher than the industry average level. This meant that too much capital was tied up in receivables. If a firm continues to sell to a customer who does not pay on time, the account balance will rise significantly, and if the customer then defaults, the selling firm will suffer a larger bad debt loss than if it had stopped selling to the customer sooner. In addition, collection costs rise with the amount of old receivables, which is another reason to keep a tight rein on credit operations. During the discussion, the sales manager noted that tightening its credit policy would lose the firm some sales. However, the lost sales would not be excessive, because most of the late-paying customers were financially sound but were just taking advantage of the "float" MicroDrive was giving them. After the discussion, the credit manager, sales manager, and treasurer jointly agreed that it would be feasible to reduce the receivables/sales ratio to 11% in 2013. That was still above the 9.8% industry average but below MicroDrive's 2012 level of 12.5%. Therefore, 11% was built into the final forecast.

The CFO also brought up the net plant/sales ratio but noted that this ratio was in line with the industry average—the production manager, who was not replaced during the management change, had been forecasting sales accurately and holding equipment purchases to the level actually required. This was facilitated by the outsourcing of production to make up for shortfalls if more orders came during a given period than had been expected. This smart use of outsourcing enabled the firm to operate without carrying excess capacity in "normal" times in order to meet demand when orders surged. Thus, the 2012 ratio of 33.3% for net plant and equipment to sales was used in the forecast.

9.4d Financial Policy Issues

The discussion next turned to two key financial policies: capital structure and dividends. The CFO noted that MicroDrive's debt ratio was significantly above the industry average. This high leverage boosted ROE and EPS during good times, but it also raised the interest rates for debt as well as the required return on common stock. Further, an excessive amount of debt increased the risk of bankruptcy and reduced the firm's ability to maintain stable operations in times of stress. The treasurer noted that the company's banks were concerned about its high debt usage and that banks nationwide were reducing the credit lines of companies deemed to have too much debt. MicroDrive's credit lines had not been reduced to date, but if the firm were to have even one bad quarter then a reduction might well occur, and that would be devastating. Credit is the lifeblood of a business, and if its credit were curtailed then MicroDrive might not be able to purchase supplies, pay workers, and so on, which would be fatal. After this discussion, the decision was made to increase the common equity ratio from its current 49.8% level of investor-supplied capital to 55.0%.[6]

The discussion then turned to dividend policy. In recent years, MicroDrive has been increasing the dividend by about 8% per year, and the board of directors has stated that it would like to continue this policy. However, the CFO recently disclosed to the board that many companies that formerly increased their dividends at a steady rate had re-examined that policy and had lowered the targeted rate of increase. An 8% annual increase during the long boom from the 1980s until 2008 had been feasible, but in the current and likely future economic climate a different policy might be necessary. The CFO also pointed out that the average mature firm in the industry was distributing about 40% of its earnings as dividends, compared with MicroDrive's 50.4%. At the conclusion of this discussion, it was decided to use the 40% industry average payout for the forecast, determine the resulting dividend per share, review the resulting

---

6. Capital structure decisions are discussed in detail in Chapter 15.

performance measures, and then discuss the dividend policy recommendation with the board. The CEO agreed with this plan but clearly hoped that the forecast would support a dividend growth rate of 8% or more.

The next item discussed was the timing of new financing. The treasurer argued that it would be best to issue any required new stock early in the year to ensure that these funds would be available—stock prices are volatile, and the market for new stock could slam shut later in the year. Also, if the firm raised equity early, that would make it easier to issue new debt later. The CFO and CEO agreed, so the decision was made to sell any required new stock early and to borrow throughout the year as needed.

A question was asked about the price at which new stock would be sold. The CFO noted that the most recent price was $23 per share, and that was the most likely price at which new shares could be sold early in the year. Interest rates on the existing debt floated, moving up and down with rates in the general economy and the company's financial condition.[7] The CFO thought interest rates probably would fluctuate to some extent, but there was no more reason to believe that rates would go up than go down. However, by mid-year the company's own financial condition would be known sufficiently well to influence its cost of debt. Therefore, as indicated in Figure 9-4, the rates vary depending on the scenarios—low rates under good conditions and high rates under bad conditions. The preferred dividend also floated, so its rate also varied with the scenarios.

Based on an earlier back-of-the-envelope calculation using the AFN model, the CFO had concluded that if operations improved significantly, the firm might not need any new external funds and might even have a surplus. For example, if the profit margin could be increased, this would lower external capital requirements. Even more importantly, if the ratios of inventories and accounts receivable to sales could be lowered, as the management team had discussed earlier, then this would greatly reduce the need for new capital, especially during 2013. Those considerations prompted the CEO to raise the following question: "If excess funds become available, what should we do with them?" The CFO had actually considered several possibilities: (1) increase the dividend, (2) repurchase stock and repay debt in amounts that would keep the capital structure constant, (3) invest excess funds in marketable securities, or (4) embark on a merger program to acquire other firms. They decided that the best alternative for modeling purposes was to simply use surplus funds to repay debt and buy back stock. If the surplus was projected to extend on into the long run, then a strategic decision would have to be made regarding what to do with it, but that would require input from the board.

Debt could be repaid at book value and preferred stock repurchased at close to book value. If the common stock repurchase occurred early in the year, then it could probably be bought at close to the current price. This brought up the question of when any surplus funds would actually be available—would they be available early or late, or would they come in regularly throughout the year? It might make sense to *raise* new funds early, but excess funds could not be *used* until they were actually in hand, and that would probably occur throughout the year. The decision was made to repurchase stock early in the year and repay debt later in the year. The CFO also planned to revisit this issue when developing the projected 2013 cash budget. (Cash budgets are discussed in Chapter 21; they are typically done on a monthly basis.)

---

7. All of the debt—both short-term bank loans and long-term bonds—had floating rates. The spread between the bank loan rate and the London Interbank Offered Rate (LIBOR) was based on the firm's interest coverage ratio (EBIT to interest charges). The long-term bond rate was determined similarly. The bank loan rate was reset quarterly, and the long-term rate was reset every 6 months.

9.4e The Forecasted Financial Statements

Using input from the Final scenario as shown in column E of Figure 9-4, MicroDrive's forecasted financial statements (balance sheet and income statement) are reported in Figure 9-5.[8] The following points explain how to forecast the statements shown in Figure 9-5.

WEB

See **Ch09 Tool Kit.xls** on the textbook's Web site for details.

1. Forecast next year's sales based on the assumed growth rate: $S_{2013} = S_{2012} \times (1 + g)$.
2. Forecast each of the operating assets (cash, accounts receivable, inventories, and net plant and equipment) and the spontaneous current liabilities (accounts payable and accruals) as a percentage of forecasted sales. This completes the assets section of the balance sheet and partially completes the liabilities section.
3. Use the forecasted operating data from Step 2 to calculate the required investor-supplied capital, which is found as Total assets – (Accounts payable + Accruals). Note that this amount of investor-supplied capital is precisely the amount of funding that, when combined with Accounts payable and Accruals, will make the balance sheet balance.
4. Multiply the investor-supplied capital found in Step 3 by the inputs for the target capital structure percentages shown in Figure 9-4 to forecast the amounts of notes payable, long-term bonds, preferred stock, and total common equity. This completes the balance sheet except for dividing the forecasted total common equity into its two components, common stock and retained earnings.
5. Calculate operating costs as a percentage of forecasted sales and calculate depreciation as a percentage of forecasted net plant and equipment. Subtract these costs from sales to find EBIT.
6. It is assumed that new debt will be borrowed throughout the year, so interest expenses will be based on the average amount of debt outstanding during the year. This amount is equal to the average of the beginning-of-year debt and the end-of-year debt forecast in Step 4. Multiply this average by the interest rate to determine the forecasted interest expense. Note that we have separate lines for notes payable interest expense and long-term bond interest expense since their interest rates differ.
7. Subtract interest expense from EBIT to find taxable income (EBT). Calculate taxes and subtract them from EBT to get net income before preferred dividends.
8. Forecast preferred dividends in a similar manner as the forecasted interest expense in Step 6: (1) find the average amount of preferred stock outstanding during the year and then (2) multiply it by the preferred stock's dividend rate.
9. Subtract the forecasted preferred dividends from the net income before preferred dividends to find the net income available to common stockholders.
10. Multiply the net income by the target payout ratio to forecast the total amount of common dividends paid. If net income is negative, set common dividends to zero.
11. Subtract common dividends from net income to find the addition to retained earnings.
12. The forecasted total retained earnings shown on the balance sheet is equal to the prior year's retained earnings plus the addition to retained earnings calculated in Step 11.
13. The forecasted total common stock must be equal to the difference between forecasted total common equity from Step 4 and the forecasted retained earnings balance from Step 12: Common stock = Total common equity – Retained earnings.

---

8. Columns E and I are identical in Figure 9-4. *Excel*'s Scenario Manager replaces the values in Column E with the values shown in Column I when the Final scenario is selected. Similarly, the Scenario Manager replaces data in Column E with the values shown in Columns F, G, or H when those scenarios are selected.

Figure 9-5	Forecasted Financial Statements (Millions of Dollars, Except for Per Share Data)

	A	B	C	D	E	F	G
129	Scenario Shown: Final						Final
130			Most Recent				Forecast
131	Part 1. Balance Sheet		2012	Factors	Basis for 2013 Forecast		2013
132	*Assets*						
133	Cash		$10.0	0.25%	Factor × 2013 Sales		$8.25
134	Accounts receivable		375.0	11.00%	Factor × 2013 Sales		$363.00
135	Inventories		615.0	16.00%	Factor × 2013 Sales		$528.00
136	Total current assets		$1,000.0				$899.25
137	Net plant and equipment		1,000.0	33.33%	Factor × 2013 Sales		$1,100.00
138	Total assets (TA)		$2,000.0				$1,999.25
139	*Liabilities and equity*						
140	Accounts payable		$60.0	2.00%	Factor × 2013 Sales		$66.00
141	Accruals		140.0	4.00%	Factor × 2013 Sales		$132.00
142	Notes payable[a]		110.0	5.00%	% of investor-sup. cap.		$90.06
143	Total current liabilities		$310.0				$288.06
144	Long-term bonds[a]		754.0	37.00%	% of investor-sup. cap.		$666.46
145	Total liabilities		$1,064.0				$954.52
146	Preferred stock[a]		$40.0	3.00%	% of investor-sup. cap.		$54.04
147	Common stock		130.0		Tot. Com. Eq – Ret. Earn		$131.35
148	Retained earnings		766.0		Old RE + Add. to RE		$859.34
149	Total common equity[a]		$896.0	55.00%	% of investor-sup. cap.		$990.69
150	Total liabilities and equity		$2,000.0				$1,999.25
151	[a] Investor-supplied capital		$1,800.0		TA – accts. pay. – accruals		$1,801.25
152	Scenario Shown: Final						Final
153			Most Recent				Forecast
154	Part 2. Income Statement		2012	Factor	Basis for 2013 Forecast		2013
155	Sales		$3,000.0	110%	Factor × 2012 Sales		$3,300.00
156	Costs except depreciation		2,617.0	86.00%	Factor × 2013 Sales		$2,838.00
157	Depreciation		100.0	10.20%	Factor × 2013 Net plant		$112.20
158	Total operating costs		$2,717.0				$2,950.20
159	EBIT		$283.0				$349.80
160	Less: Interest on notes		9.9	8.50%	Interest rate × Avg notes		$8.50
161	Interest on bonds		78.1	10.50%	Interest rate × Avg bonds		$74.57
162	Earnings before taxes (EBT)		$195.0				$266.72
163	Taxes (40%)		78.0	40.00%	Tax rate × 2013 EBT		$106.69
164	NI before preferred dividends		$117.0				$160.03
165	Preferred dividends		4.0	9.50%	Pfd div rate × Avg preferred		$4.47
166	NI available to common		$113.0				$155.57
167	Dividends paid out		$57.0	40.00%	Net income × Payout rate		$62.23
168	Addition to retained earnings		$56.0		Net income – Dividends		$93.34
169	Change in shares outstanding				(Change in Com. stk.)/P_{2012}		0.06
170	Ending shares outstanding		50.00		$Shares_{2012} + \Delta$ shares		50.06
171	Earnings per share, EPS		$2.26		Net income/Total shares		$3.11
172	Dividends per share, DPS		$1.14		Total dividends/Total shares		$1.24

Note: Calculations in the model have been shown to one decimal, so rounding differences may occur.

14. The required additional dollars of common stock issued or repurchased are equal to the change in common stock: Additional dollars of stock issued or repurchased = Common stock in 2013 – Common stock in 2012. If the amount is negative, it means that stock will be repurchased rather than issued.

15. The number of new shares either issued or repurchased is equal to the additional dollars of common stock found in Step 14 divided by the price per share. Because the stock is assumed to be sold at the beginning of 2013, the assumed stock price is $23, the price at the end of 2012. We calculate this as: Change in shares = (Additional dollars of common stock) ÷ (Stock price at the beginning of the year).

16. The number of shares outstanding at the end of the year is equal to the number of outstanding shares at the beginning of the year plus the change in the number of shares calculated in Step 15.

9.4f Analyzing the Forecasted Results

After the Final set of inputs had been chosen, the CFO created a summary sheet showing key results for the different scenarios, as shown in Figure 9-6. After projecting the key results on a big screen, the team discussed each of the scenarios. Everyone dismissed the worst-case results, because if things started getting that bad there would be an emergency meeting in which actions would be taken to modify the plan. Similarly, the status quo and best-case results were given short shrift, and then the team focused on the Final scenario results.

The jump in EPS looked good, and even with the assumed 40% payout ratio, DPS rose by about 9%, which pleased the CEO.

The ROE improved nicely, rising from 12.6% to 15.7%, which exceeded the industry average. However, the CFO pointed out that the firm's debt ratio, even after the capital structure change, still exceeded the industry average, and that its greater leverage was largely responsible for the above-average ROE.

Free cash flow was projected to make a tremendous improvement, from −$175 million in 2012 to +$209 million in 2013. The CFO noted, though, that a similar improvement would not occur in the future, because most of the gain in free cash flow

Figure 9-6   Summary of Key Results for Forecasted Scenarios (Millions, Except for Per Share Data)

	A	B	2012 Actual		2013 Forecasts			
			Industry	MicroDrive				
242 Key Results					Final	Status Quo	Best	Worst
243 Net operating profit after taxes			NA	$170	$210	$187	$271	$61
244 Net operating working capital			NA	$800	$701	$880	$569	$922
245 Total operating capital			NA	$1,800	$1,801	$1,980	$1,669	$2,002
246 FCF = NOPAT − Δ op. capital			NA	−$175	$209	$7	$402	−$141
247 Return on invested capital			11.0%	9.4%	11.7%	9.5%	16.2%	3.1%
248 EPS			NA	$2.26	$3.11	$2.43	$5.07	−$0.10
249 DPS			NA	$1.14	$1.24	$1.23	$2.57	$0.00
250 Return on equity (ROE)			15.0%	12.6%	15.7%	12.6%	26.0%	−0.5%
251 Return on assets (ROA)			9.0%	5.7%	7.8%	5.7%	12.0%	−0.2%
252 Inventory turnover			9.0	4.9	6.3	4.9	9.0	3.9
253 Days sales outstanding			36.0	45.6	40.2	45.6	35.8	54.8
254 Total liabilities / TA			46.0%	53.2%	47.7%	53.2%	51.8%	52.3%
255 Times interest earned			6.0	3.2	4.2	3.2	5.3	1.0
256 Shares outstanding			NA	50.00	50.06	51.22	42.54	54.62
257 Payout ratio			40.0%	50.4%	40.0%	50.7%	50.7%	0.0%
258 AFN[a]			NA	$224	−$92	$118	−$237	$208

[a]The AFN equation calculates the additional financing required compared to the most recent year. With forecasted financial statements, AFN is the additional financing over the planned amount of financing and is calculated as AFN = required assets − planned liabilites and equity = TA − Accts. pay. − Accruals − Planned NP − Planned LT bonds − Planned pf. stk − Planned common stk − RE. Here, planned NP, bonds, pf. stk, and common stock are equal to their current levels.

was attributable to the one-time reduction in inventories and accounts receivable. AFN, the last item in Figure 9-6, is the additional funding that would be required if no additional notes payable, bonds, preferred stock, or common stock were issued. AFN is negative, indicating a surplus of funds in 2013, and is negative for the same reason free cash flow is positive—the reduction in inventories and accounts receivable. The lower payout and higher profit margin also helped reduce the AFN, but the one-time reduction in inventories and receivables was the key driver here.

The forecasted statement of cash flows in Figure 9-7 tells a similar story: (1) cash flow from operations is positive and large (with large cash flows resulting from improved asset utilization); (2) cash flow from investments is negative because of the expansion in fixed assets needed to support growth; and (3) the cash flow from financing activities shows that MicroDrive would be able to pay large dividends and reduce its debt.

At the conclusion of the CFO's summary, the CEO said that the firm would be in great shape and that nice bonuses and stock options would result if the targets were met and maintained over the long run.

9.4f Alternative Financial Policies and Multi-Year Forecasts

When the CEO and CFO presented the plan to the board of directors, the board was pleased overall but had a few questions. Several board members, including the

Figure 9-7	Forecasted Statement of Cash Flows (Millions of Dollars, Except for Per Share Data)

	A	B	C	D	E	F
					Actual	Forecast
268	Scenario Shown: Final					
269					2012	2013
270	Operating Activities					
271	Net Income before preferred dividends				$117.0	$160.0
272	Noncash adjustments					
273	Depreciation and amortization				100.0	112.2
274	Due to changes in working capital					
275	Increase(−)/Decrease(+) in accounts receivable				−60.0	12.0
276	Increase(−)/Decrease(+) in inventories				−200.0	87.0
277	Increase(−)/Decrease(+) in payables				30.0	6.0
278	Increase(−)/Decrease(+) in accruals				10.0	−8.0
279	Net cash provided by operating activities				−$3.0	$369.2
280						
281	Long-term investing activities					
282	Cash used to acquire fixed assets				−$230.0	−$212.2
283	Sale of short-term investments				65.0	0.0
284	Net cash provided by investing activities				−$165.0	−$212.2
285						
286	Financing Activities					
287	Increase(+)/Decrease(−) in notes payable				$50.0	−$19.9
288	Increase(+)/Decrease(−) in bonds				174.0	−87.5
289	Preferred stock issue(+)/repurchase(−)				0.0	14.0
290	Payment of common and preferred dividends				−61.0	−66.7
291	Common stock issue(+)/repurchase(−)				0.0	1.3
292	Net cash provided by financing activities				$163.0	−$158.8
293						
294	Net cash flow				−$5.0	−$1.7
295	Cash at beginning of the year				15.0	10.0
296	Cash at end of the year				$10.0	$8.3

chairman and founder of the company, were concerned that the plan included issu-ing new shares of common stock. They were also uneasy about the assumed price at which shares of stock could be repurchased later in the year if there were surplus funds. In addition, the board thought that determining dividends as a fixed percent-age payout of net income might introduce quite a bit of volatility in DPS. Because of these concerns, the board asked the CFO to provide forecasted statements using the following different assumptions regarding the financial policies.

For the purposes of this additional forecast, the board specified the following financial policies: (1) let the regular DPS grow at a specified rate; (2) do not change the level of existing notes payable; and (3) do not issue or repurchase bonds, preferred stock, or common stock. If additional financing is needed, the board suggested fore-casting the AFN as a draw against an existing line of credit on a temporary basis (even though the interest rate would be high) until the board could meet and decide on a final financing plan. If instead a surplus of funds is available at the end of the year, the board suggested that the surplus be paid to shareholders in the form of a special dividend.[9]

Figure 9-8	One-Year Forecasted Financial Statements under an Alternative Financial Policy: Scenario = Maintain (Millions, Except for Per Share Data)

	A	B	C	D	E	F	G	H
94	Scenario Shown:	Maintain				Planned		With
95		Actual	Factor	Basis for		(w/o AFN)	AFN	AFN
96	Balance Sheet	2012	or Rate	2013 Forecast		2013	Adjust.	2013
97	*Assets*							
98	Cash	$10.0	0.33% ×	2013 Sales		$11.0		$11.0
99	Acc. rec.	375.0	12.50% ×	2013 Sales		412.5		412.5
100	Inventories	615.0	20.50% ×	2013 Sales		676.5		676.5
101	Total CA	$1,000.0				$1,100.0		$1,100.0
102	Net plant & equip.	1,000.0	33.33% ×	2013 Sales		1,100.0		1,100.0
103	Total assets (TA)	$2,000.0				$2,200.0		$2,200.0
104	*Liab. & equity*							
105	Accounts payable	$60.0	2.00% ×	2013 Sales		$66.0		$66.0
106	Accruals	140.0	4.67% ×	2013 Sales		154.1		154.1
107	Notes pay. (NP)	110.0		Carry over		110.0		110.0
108	Line of credit (LOC)[a]			Blank			$109.3	109.3
109	Total CL	$310.0				$330.1		$439.4
110	LT bonds	754.0		Carry over		754.0		754.0
111	Tot. liab.	$1,064.0				$1,084.1		$1,193.4
112	Pref. stock	40.0		Carry over		40.0		40.0
113	Com. stock	130.0		Carry over		130.0		130.0
114	Ret. earnings	766.0		2012 RE + ΔRE		836.5		836.5
115	Total CE	$896.0				$966.5		$966.5
116	Total L&E	$2,000.0				$2,090.6		$2,200.0
117								
118	AFN[b]	=	TA – Planned total liabilities & equity				$109.3	
119	Line of credit[c]	=	AFN if AFN > 0 (additional financing needed)				$109.3	
120	Special dividend[d]	=	–AFN if AFN ≤ 0 (surplus funds available)				$0.0	
121								

(Continued)

---

9. In actuality, the board would decide at that time whether to repurchase shares of stock instead, if that seemed preferable given the prevailing stock price.

Figure 9-8   **One-Year Forecasted Financial Statements under an Alternative Financial Policy: Scenario = Maintain (Millions, Except for Per Share Data)** *(Continued)*

	A	B	C	D	E	F	G	H
122	Scenario Shown: Maintain					Planned		With
123		Actual	Factor	Basis for		(w/o AFN)	AFN	AFN
124	Income Statement	2012	or Rate	2013 Forecast		2013	Adjust.	2013
125	Sales	$3,000.0	1.10 ×	2012 Sales		$3,300.0		$3,300.0
126	Costs (excl. depr.)	2,617.0	87.21% ×	2013 Sales		2,877.9		2,877.9
127	Depreciation	100.0	10.00% ×	2013 Net plant		110.0		110.0
128	Total op. costs	$2,717.0				$2,987.9		$2,987.9
129	EBIT	$283.0				$312.1		$312.1
130	Int. on planned NP	9.9	9.00% ×	Avg notes		9.9		9.9
131	Int. on planned bonds	78.1	11.00% ×	Avg bonds		82.9		82.9
132	Int. on LOC[e]		9.00%	Blank			$0.0	0.0
133	EBT	$195.0				$219.2		$219.2
134	Taxes (T = 40%)	78.0	40.00% ×	2013 EBT		87.7		87.7
135	NI before pref. div.	$117.0				$131.5		$131.5
136	Pref. div.	4.0	10.00% ×	Avg preferred		4.0		4.0
137	NI to common	$113.0				$127.5		$127.5
138								
139	# of shares (n)	50.0		Carry over		50.0		50.0
140	Regular DPS	$1.14	1.00 ×	2012 DPS		$1.14		$1.14
141	Regular dividends	$57.0		n × 2013 DPS		$57.0		$57.0
142	Special dividend[f]	0.0				0.0	$0.0	0.0
143	Add. To RE (ΔRE)	$56.0		NI – Dividends		$70.5		$70.5

[a]If additional financing is needed, the line of credit will be used on a temporary basis.
[b]The AFN in forecasted financial statements is equal to the required assets minus the planned liabilities and equity (i.e., the liabilities and equity assuming AFN is zero).
[c]If AFN > 0, then additional financing will be raised by borrowing via the line of credit.
[d]If AFN ≤ 0, then surplus funds will be used to pay a special dividend.
[e]This forecast assumes that any temporary borrowing will be undertaken at the end of the year; thus, there will be no additional interest expense.
[f]Any surplus funds will be paid out as a special dividend.

© Cengage Learning 2013

The board asked to see two scenarios. The first is similar to the Status Quo scenario previously discussed, except that the board's three financial policies just described are employed (the board suggested a zero growth rate for regular DPS). Because there is no change in operating performance, this is called the Maintain scenario. The second scenario is similar to the Final scenario discussed earlier, except that the board's financial policy is applied (the board suggested an 8% growth in regular DPS for this scenario). Because there are significant improvements in operating performance, this is called the Improve scenario. The board asked to see the Maintain scenario first, which is shown in Figure 9-8 (see *Tab 3* in ***Ch09 Tool Kit.xls*** for details).

The operating items are forecasted in the same way as shown before. All liabilities and equity accounts (except the line of credit) are planned in the sense that they are specified by the financial policies. For the policies used here, there are no changes in notes payable, bonds, or common stock; in addition, regular dividends are specified, so the addition to retained earnings is specified. Column F in Figure 9-8 shows these planned forecasts, but notice that the balance sheets don't balance: The total assets line equals $2,200, but total liabilities and equity sum only to $2,090.6. Thus, there is a $2,200 − $2,090.6 = $109.3 million shortfall. In other words, the AFN is $109.3, as shown in Row 118. Because additional financing is needed, there will be an adjustment to the statements by borrowing $109.3 through the line of credit, as shown in Column G. Because we assume that the borrowing occurs at the end of the year, there will be no additional interest in this forecast. Column H shows the forecasted statements after including the AFN.

Figure 9-9 reports the forecasted statements for the Improve scenario. The balance sheets in Column F again do not balance, but this is because there is more financing (total liabilities and equity = $2,089.4) than assets (total assets = $1,999.2). Thus, Row 118 shows a negative AFN, −$90.2 million. This will be paid out as a special dividend, as shown in Column G. Column H reports the forecasted statements after including the AFN.

The board expressed two additional concerns. First, they thought it unrealistic to assume that the line of credit was only used on the last day of the year and thus caused no additional interest expense. The board felt it would be more appropriate to assume that the line of credit was accessed at regular intervals

Figure 9-9   **One-Year Forecasted Financial Statements under an Alternative Financial Policy: Scenario = Improve (Millions, Except for Per Share Data)**

	A	B	C	D	E	F	G	H
94	Scenario Shown:	Improve				Planned		With
95		Actual	Factor	Basis for		(w/o AFN)	AFN	AFN
96	Balance Sheet	2012	or Rate	2013 Forecast		2013	Adjust.	2013
97	*Assets*							
98	Cash	$10.0	0.25% ×	2013 Sales		$8.3		$8.3
99	Acc. rec.	375.0	11.00% ×	2013 Sales		363.0		363.0
100	Inventories	615.0	16.00% ×	2013 Sales		528.0		528.0
101	Total CA	$1,000.0				$899.3		$899.3
102	Net plant & equip.	1,000.0	33.33% ×	2013 Sales		1,100.0		1,100.0
103	Total assets (TA)	$2,000.0				$1,999.2		$1,999.2
104	*Liab. & equity*							
105	Accounts payable	$60.0	2.00% ×	2013 Sales		$66.0		$66.0
106	Accruals	140.0	4.00% ×	2013 Sales		132.0		132.0
107	Notes pay. (NP)	110.0		Carry over		110.0		110.0
108	Line of credit (LOC)[a]			Blank			$0.0	0.0
109	Total CL	$310.0				$308.0		$308.0
110	LT bonds	754.0		Carry over		754.0		754.0
111	Tot. liab.	$1,064.0				$1,062.0		$1,062.0
112	Pref. stock	40.0		Carry over		40.0		40.0
113	Com. stock	130.0		Carry over		130.0		130.0
114	Ret. earnings	766.0		2012 RE + ΔRE		857.4		767.2
115	Total CE	$896.0				$987.4		$897.2
116	Total L&E	$2,000.0				$2,089.4		$1,999.2
117								
118	AFN[b]		=	TA − Planned total liabilities & equity			−$90.2	
119	Line of credit[c]		=	AFN if AFN > 0 (additional financing needed)			$0.0	
120	Special dividend[d]		=	−AFN if AFN ≤ 0 (surplus funds available)			$90.0	
121								

(Continued)

© Cengage Learning 2013

Figure 9-9 **One-Year Forecasted Financial Statements under an Alternative Financial Policy: Scenario = Improve (Millions, Except for Per Share Data)** *(Continued)*

	A	B	C	D	E	F	G	H
122	Scenario Shown:	Improve				Planned		With
123		Actual	Factor	Basis for		(w/o AFN)	AFN	AFN
124	Income Statement	2012	or Rate	2013 Forecast		2013	Adjust.	2013
125	Sales	$3,000.0	1.10 ×	2012 Sales		$3,300.0		$3,300.0
126	Costs (excl. depr.)	2,617.0	86.00% ×	2013 Sales		2,838.0		2,838.0
127	Depreciation	100.0	10.20% ×	2013 Net plant		112.2		112.2
128	Total op. costs	$2,717.0				$2,950.2		$2,950.2
129	EBIT	$283.0				$349.8		$349.8
130	Int. on planned NP	9.9	8.50% ×	Avg notes		9.4		9.4
131	Int. on planned bonds	78.1	10.50% ×	Avg bonds		79.2		79.2
132	Int. on LOC[e]		8.50%	Blank			$0.0	0.0
133	EBT	$195.0				$261.3		$261.3
134	Taxes (T = 40%)	78.0	40.00% ×	2013 EBT		104.5		104.5
135	NI before pref. div.	$117.0				$156.8		$156.8
136	Pref. div.	4.0	9.50% ×	Avg preferred		3.8		3.8
137	NI to common	$113.0				$153.0		$153.0
138								
139	# of shares (n)	50.0		Carry over		50.0		50.0
140	Regular DPS	$1.14	1.08 ×	2012 DPS		$1.23		$1.23
141	Regular dividends	$57.0		n × 2013 DPS		$61.6		$61.6
142	Special dividend[f]	0.0				0.0	$90.2	90.2
143	Add. To RE (ΔRE)	$56.0		NI – Dividends		$91.4		$1.2

[a]If additional financing is needed, the line of credit will be used on a temporary basis.
[b]The AFN in forecasted financial statements is equal to the required assets minus the planned liabilities and equity (i.e., the liabilities and equity assuming AFN is zero).
[c]If AFN > 0, then additional financing will be raised by borrowing via the line of credit.
[d]If AFN ≤ 0, then surplus funds will be used to pay a special dividend.
[e]This forecast assumes that any temporary borrowing will be undertaken at the end of the year; thus, there will be no additional interest expense.
[f]Any surplus funds will be paid out as a special dividend.

throughout the year, which would lead to additional interest expense. The CFO explained that when the AFN leads to additional interest expense it reduces net income, which reduces the addition to retained earnings and then increases the AFN, with the cycle being repeated in a circular manner. This is called **financing feedback,** and there are a variety of ways to incorporate feedback effects into the forecast. The CFO agreed that adding debt throughout the year was a more realistic assumption but said that the end-of-year assumption usually produced results fairly close to those that incorporated feedback effects. However, the CFO agreed to incorporate financing feedback in the next set of forecasts, but rather than use valuable board time explaining feedback adjustments in detail, the CFO suggested that interested board members take a look at *Tab 4* in *Ch09 Tool Kit.xls*.

The board also wanted to see multi-year projections. After updating the forecasting model to incorporate feedback effects and multi-year forecasts, the CFO returned to the board meeting and presented the results shown in Figure 9-10. (See *Tab 5* in *Ch09 Tool Kit.xls* for calculations.)

Figure 9-10   Summary of Forecasted Key Results for the "Improve" Scenario (Millions, Except for Percentages and Per Share Data)

	A	B	C	D	E	F	G	H	I
					Forecast	Forecast	Forecast	Forecast	Forecast
211			Actual		2013	2014	2015	2016	2017
212			2012						
213			Industry	MicroDrive	Improve	Improve	Improve	Improve	Improve
214	Key Results								
215	Net operating profit after taxes		NA	$170	$210	$231	$254	$279	$307
216	Net operating working capital		NA	$800	$701	$771	$849	$933	$1,027
217	Total operating capital		NA	$1,800	$1,801	$1,981	$2,180	$2,397	$2,637
218	FCF = NOPAT − Δ op capital		NA	−$175	$209	$51	$56	$61	$68
219	Return on invested capital		11.0%	9.4%	11.7%	11.7%	11.7%	11.7%	11.7%
220	EPS		NA	$2.26	$3.06	$3.43	$3.79	$4.19	$4.63
221	DPS		NA	$1.14	$1.23	$1.33	$1.44	$1.55	$1.68
222	Return on equity (ROE)		15.0%	12.6%	17.0%	17.1%	16.9%	16.7%	16.5%
223	Return on assets (ROA)		9.0%	5.7%	7.7%	7.8%	7.8%	7.9%	7.9%
224	Inventory turnover		9.0	4.9	6.3	6.3	6.3	6.3	6.3
225	Days sales outstanding		36.0	45.6	40.2	40.2	40.2	40.2	40.2
226	Total liabilities / TA		46.0%	53.2%	53.1%	52.6%	52.1%	51.5%	50.8%
227	Times interest earned		6.0	3.2	4.0	4.3	4.8	5.3	5.8
228	Shares outstanding		NA	50.00	50.00	50.00	50.00	50.00	50.00
229	Payout ratio		40.0%	50.4%	40.2%	38.8%	37.9%	37.0%	36.2%
230	AFN		NA	$224	−$90	$75	$156	$242	$334
231	Line of credit balance		NA	$0	$0	$75	$156	$242	$334
232	Special dividend		NA	$0	$90	$0	$0	$0	$0

The dramatic increase in FCF during 2013 would be a result of the improved operations, including less inventory and fewer receivables. After this one-time improvement, FCF drops in 2014 but then increases each year. The improved operations are reflected in the increased return on invested capital, which in turn leads to strong growth in EPS and thus enables growth in DPS. With the projected increase in the times interest earned ratio and the decrease in the ratio of total liabilities to total assets, the board discussed whether MicroDrive could support more debt. They decided to discuss a possible recapitalization at their next meeting, in which MicroDrive might issue bonds and use the proceeds to pay off the line of credit and possibly repurchase shares of stock, topics we discuss in Chapters 15 and 17.

Self Test

Is the AFN as calculated using the forecasted financial statements method, with all the ratios held constant, the same (except for rounding errors) as the AFN found using the AFN equation? Explain.

Why does the text argue that the forecasted financial statements method is preferable to the AFN equation method?

What does the acronym GIGO stand for? Is this important for forecasting?

9.5 Forecasting When the Ratios Change

The AFN equation assumes that the ratios of assets and liabilities to sales (A_0^*/S_0 and L_0^*/S_0) remain constant over time. This assumption can be relaxed when we use the forecasted financial statement method, but in our forecast we made a one-time change in these ratios and then held them constant thereafter. This implies that each "spontaneous" asset and liability item increases at the same rate as sales. In graph form, this implies the type of relationship shown in Panel a of Figure 9-11, a relationship whose graph (1) is linear and (2) passes through the origin. Under those conditions, if the company's sales increase from $200 million to $400 million, or by 100%, then inventory will also increase by 100%, from $100 million to $200 million.

The assumption of constant ratios and identical growth rates is appropriate at times, but there are times when it is incorrect. Three such conditions are described in the following sections.

Figure 9-11   Four Possible Ratio Relationships (Millions of Dollars)

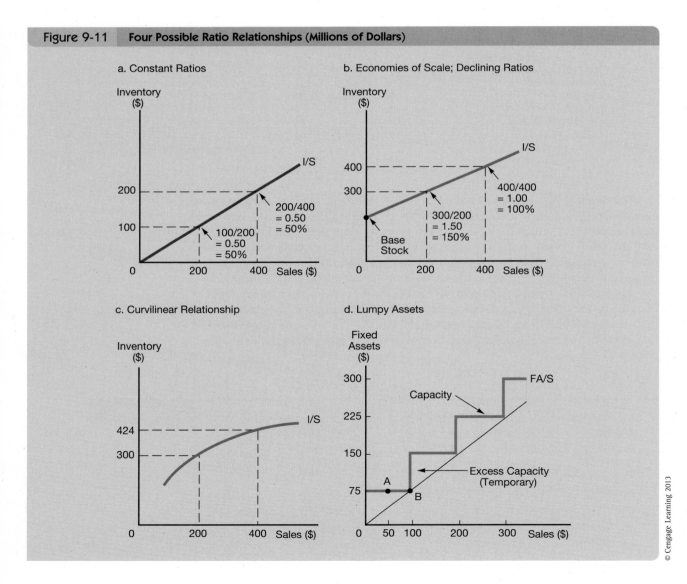

9.5a Economies of Scale

There are economies of scale in the use of many kinds of assets, and when economies of scale occur, the ratios are likely to change over time as the size of the firm increases. For example, retailers often need to maintain base stocks of different inventory items even if current sales are quite low. As sales expand, inventories may then grow less rapidly than sales, so the ratio of inventory to sales (I/S) declines. This situation is depicted in Panel b of Figure 9-11. Here we see that the inventory/sales ratio is 1.5 (or 150%) when sales are $200 million but declines to 1.0 when sales climb to $400 million.

The relationship in Panel b is linear, but nonlinear relationships often exist. Indeed, if the firm uses one popular model for establishing inventory levels (the Economic Ordering Quantity, or EOQ, model), its inventories will rise with the *square root* of sales. This situation is shown in Panel c of Figure 9-11, which shows a curved line whose slope decreases at higher sales levels. In this situation, very large increases in sales would require very little additional inventory.[10]

9.5b Lumpy Assets

In many industries, technological considerations dictate that if a firm is to be competitive, it must add fixed assets in large, discrete units; such assets are often referred to as **lumpy assets**. In the paper industry, for example, there are strong economies of scale in basic paper mill equipment, so when a paper company expands capacity, it must do so in large, lumpy increments. This type of situation is depicted in Panel d of Figure 9-11. Here we assume that the minimum economically efficient plant has a cost of $75 million, and that such a plant can produce enough output to reach a sales level of $100 million. If the firm is to be competitive, it simply must have at least $75 million of fixed assets.

Lumpy assets have a major effect on the ratio of fixed assets to sales (FA/S) at different sales levels and, consequently, on financial requirements. At Point A in Panel d, which represents a sales level of $50 million, the fixed assets are $75 million and so the ratio FA/S = $75/$50 = 1.5. Sales can expand by $50 million, out to $100 million, with no additions to fixed assets. At that point, represented by Point B, the ratio FA/S = $75/$100 = 0.75. However, since the firm is operating at capacity (sales of $100 million), even a small increase in sales would require a doubling of plant capacity, so a small projected sales increase would bring with it a large financial requirement.[11]

---

10. See **Web Extension 09A** for more on forecasting when things like inventories are not constant in relation to sales.

11. Several other points should be noted about Panel d of Figure 9-11. First, if the firm is operating at a sales level of $100 million or less, then any expansion that calls for a sales increase of more than $100 million would require a *doubling* of the firm's fixed assets. A much smaller percentage increase would be involved if the firm were large enough to be operating a number of plants. Second, firms generally go to multiple shifts and take other actions to minimize the need for new fixed asset capacity as they approach Point B. However, these efforts can only go so far, and eventually a fixed asset expansion will be required. Third, firms often make arrangements to share excess capacity with other firms in their industry. For example, the situation in the electric utility industry is very much like that depicted in Panel d. However, electric companies often build jointly owned plants, or else they "take turns" building plants, and then they buy power from or sell power to other utilities to avoid building new plants that would be underutilized.

9.5c Excess Capacity Adjustments

If a firm has excess capacity, then sales can grow before the firm must add capacity. The level of full capacity sales is

(9-3)
$$\text{Full capacity sales} = \frac{\text{Actual sales}}{\text{Percentage of capacity at which fixed assets were operated}}$$

For example, consider MicroDrive and use the data from its financial statements in Figure 9-2, but now assume that excess capacity exists in fixed assets. Specifically, assume that fixed assets in 2012 were being utilized to only 96% of capacity. If fixed assets had been used to full capacity, then 2012 sales could have been as high as $3,125 million versus the $3,000 million in actual sales:

$$\text{Full capacity sales} = \frac{\text{Actual sales}}{\text{Percentage of capacity at which fixed assets were operated}}$$

$$= \frac{\$3,000 \text{ million}}{0.96} = \$3,125 \text{ million}$$

The target fixed assets/sales ratio can be defined in terms of the full capacity sales:

(9-4)
$$\text{Target fixed assets/Sales} = \frac{\text{Actual fixed sales}}{\text{Full capacity sales}}$$

MicroDrive's target fixed assets/sales ratio should be 32% rather than 33.3%:

$$\text{Target fixed assets/Sales} = \frac{\text{Actual fixed assets}}{\text{Full capacity sales}}$$

$$= \frac{\$1,000}{\$3,125} = 0.32 = 32\%$$

The required level of fixed assets depends upon this target fixed assets/sales ratio:

(9-5)
$$\text{Required level of fixed assets} = \left(\frac{\text{Target fixed assets}}{\text{Sales}} \right) \left(\begin{array}{c} \text{Projected} \\ \text{sales} \end{array} \right)$$

Therefore, if MicroDrive's sales increase to $3,300 million, its fixed assets would have to increase to $1,056 million:

$$\text{Required level of fixed assets} = \left(\frac{\text{Target fixed assets}}{\text{Sales}} \right) \left(\begin{array}{c} \text{Projected} \\ \text{sales} \end{array} \right)$$

$$= 0.32(\$3,300) = \$1,056 \text{ million}$$

We previously forecasted that MicroDrive would need to increase fixed assets at the same rate as sales, or by 10%. That meant an increase of $100 million, from $1,000 million to $1,100 million. Under the new assumptions, the actual required increase in fixed assets is only from $1,000 million to $1,056 million, or $56 million. Thus, the capacity-adjusted forecast is $100 − $56 = $44 million less than the earlier forecast. With a smaller fixed asset requirement, the projected AFN would decline from an estimated $118 million to $118 − $44 = $74 million.

Note also that when excess capacity exists, sales can grow to the capacity sales as calculated above with no increase in fixed assets, but sales beyond that level would require additions of fixed assets as in our example. The same situation could occur with respect to inventories, and the required additions would be determined in exactly the same manner as for fixed assets. Theoretically, the same situation could occur with other types of assets, but as a practical matter excess capacity normally exists only with respect to fixed assets and inventories.

How do economies of scale and lumpy assets affect financial forecasting?

Self Test

Summary

- **Financial forecasting** generally begins with a forecast of the firm's sales in terms of both units and dollars.
- Either the **forecasted financial statements (FFS) method** or the **additional funds needed (AFN) equation** can be used to forecast financial requirements. If conditions are likely to change, the financial statements method is more reliable, and it also provides ratios and other data that can be used to evaluate alternative business plans. The AFN equation is typically used to arrive at an approximation for AFN.
- A firm can determine its **AFN** by estimating the amount of new assets necessary to support the forecasted level of sales and then subtracting from this amount the spontaneous funds that will be generated from operations. The firm can then plan how to raise the AFN most efficiently.
- The higher a firm's **sales growth rate** and the higher its **payout ratio**, the greater will be its need for additional financing.
- The greatest benefit of the forecasted financial statements method is its use in planning to optimize operations and thereby increase the firm's intrinsic value and thus its stock price.
- Adjustments must be made if **economies of scale** exist in the use of assets, if **excess capacity** exists, or if growth must occur in large increments (**lumpy assets**).
- **Linear regression** and **excess capacity adjustments** can be used to forecast asset requirements in situations in which assets are not expected to grow at the same rate as sales. See *Web Extension 9A* for more discussion of these issues.

Questions

9–1 Define each of the following terms:
  a. Mission statement; corporate scope; statement of corporate objectives; corporate strategies
  b. Operating plan; financial plan; sales forecast
  c. Spontaneous liabilities; profit margin; payout ratio
  d. Additional funds needed (AFN); AFN equation; capital intensity ratio; self-supporting growth rate
  e. Forecasted financial statement approach
  f. Excess capacity; lumpy assets; economies of scale
  g. Full capacity sales; target fixed assets/sales ratio; required level of fixed assets
  h. Financing feedback effects

9–2 Some liability and net worth items increase spontaneously with increases in sales. Put a check (✓) by those items listed below that typically increase spontaneously:

Accounts payable   _____   Mortgage bonds   _____
Notes payable to banks   _____   Common stock   _____
Accrued wages   _____   Retained earnings   _____
Accrued taxes   _____

9–3 The following equation is sometimes used to forecast financial requirements:

$$AFN = (A_0^*/S_0)(\Delta S) - (L_0^*/S_0)(\Delta S) - MS_1(1 - POR)$$

What key assumption do we make when using this equation? Under what conditions might this assumption not hold true?

9–4 Name five key factors that affect a firm's external financing requirements.

9–5 What is meant by the term "self-supporting growth rate"? How is this rate related to the AFN equation, and how can that equation be used to calculate the self-supporting growth rate?

9–6 Suppose a firm makes the policy changes listed below. If a change means that external, nonspontaneous financial requirements (AFN) will increase, indicate this by a (+); indicate a decrease by a (−); and indicate no effect or an indeterminate effect by a (0). Think in terms of the *immediate, short-run* effect on funds requirements.
  a. The dividend payout ratio is increased.   _____
  b. The firm decides to pay all suppliers on delivery, rather than after a 30-day delay, to take advantage of discounts for rapid payment.   _____
  c. The firm begins to offer credit to its customers, whereas previously all sales had been on a cash basis.   _____
  d. The firm's profit margin is eroded by increased competition, although sales hold steady.   _____
  e. The firm sells its manufacturing plants for cash to a contractor and simultaneously signs an outsourcing contract to purchase from that contractor goods that the firm formerly produced.   _____
  f. The firm negotiates a new contract with its union that lowers its labor costs without affecting its output.   _____

9-7 Assume that you recently received your MBA and now work as assistant to the CFO of a relatively large corporation. Your boss has asked you to prepare a financial forecast for the coming year, using an *Excel* model, and then to present your forecast to the firm's executive committee. Describe how you would deal with the following issues.

a. Would you want to set up the model with a number of scenarios whose results could be presented to the executives?

b. What are "financing feedbacks," and what are the pros and cons of incorporating such feedbacks into your model?

c. What are the pros and cons of assuming that all necessary outside funds are obtained from a single source (such as a bank loan) versus assuming that a mix of funds is raised so as to keep the capital structure at its target level?

d. What are the pros and cons of providing the capability to examine the results of changing dividend policy and capital structure policy as well as various operating policies such as credit policy, outsourcing policy, and so forth?

e. What does the acronym GIGO stand for, and how important is this for someone who is developing a financial model? For someone using a forecasting model? How might post-audits and incentive compensation plans help reduce GIGO?

Answers Appear in Appendix B

Problems

Easy Problems 1–3

9-1 AFN Equation Broussard Skateboard's sales are expected to increase by 15% from $8 million in 2012 to $9.2 million in 2013. Its assets totaled $5 million at the end of 2012. Broussard is already at full capacity, so its assets must grow at the same rate as projected sales. At the end of 2012, current liabilities were $1.4 million, consisting of $450,000 of accounts payable, $500,000 of notes payable, and $450,000 of accruals. The after-tax profit margin is forecasted to be 6%, and the forecasted payout ratio is 40%. Use the AFN equation to forecast Broussard's additional funds needed for the coming year.

9-2 AFN Equation Refer to Problem 9-1. What would be the additional funds needed if the company's year-end 2012 assets had been $7 million? Assume that all other numbers, including sales, are the same as in Problem 9-1 and that the company is operating at full capacity. Why is this AFN different from the one you found in Problem 9-1? Is the company's "capital intensity" ratio the same or different?

9-3 AFN Equation Refer to Problem 9-1. Return to the assumption that the company had $5 million in assets at the end of 2012, but now assume that the company pays no dividends. Under these assumptions, what would be the additional funds needed for the coming year? Why is this AFN different from the one you found in Problem 9-1?

Intermediate Problems 4–6

9–4 Sales Increase Maggie's Muffins, Inc., generated $5,000,000 in sales during 2012, and its year-end total assets were $2,500,000. Also, at year-end 2012, current liabilities were $1,000,000, consisting of $300,000 of notes payable, $500,000 of accounts payable, and $200,000 of accruals. Looking ahead to 2013, the company estimates that its assets must increase at the same rate as sales, its spontaneous liabilities will increase at the same rate as sales, its profit margin will be 7%, and its payout ratio will be 80%. How large a sales increase can the company achieve without having to raise funds externally; that is, what is its self-supporting growth rate?

9–5 Long-Term Financing Needed At year-end 2012, Wallace Landscaping's total assets were $2.17 million and its accounts payable were $560,000. Sales, which in 2012 were $3.5 million, are expected to increase by 35% in 2013. Total assets and accounts payable are proportional to sales, and that relationship will be maintained. Wallace typically uses no current liabilities other than accounts payable. Common stock amounted to $625,000 in 2012, and retained earnings were $395,000. Wallace has arranged to sell $195,000 of new common stock in 2013 to meet some of its financing needs. The remainder of its financing needs will be met by issuing new long-term debt at the end of 2013. (Because the debt is added at the end of the year, there will be no additional interest expense due to the new debt.) Its net profit margin on sales is 5%, and 45% of earnings will be paid out as dividends.

a. What were Wallace's total long-term debt and total liabilities in 2012?

b. How much new long-term debt financing will be needed in 2013? (*Hint:* AFN − New stock = New long-term debt.)

9–6 Additional Funds Needed The Booth Company's sales are forecasted to double from $1,000 in 2012 to $2,000 in 2013. Here is the December 31, 2012, balance sheet:

Cash	$ 100	Accounts payable	$ 50
Accounts receivable	200	Notes payable	150
Inventories	200	Accruals	50
Net fixed assets	500	Long-term debt	400
		Common stock	100
		Retained earnings	250
Total assets	$1,000	Total liabilities and equity	$1,000

Booth's fixed assets were used to only 50% of capacity during 2012, but its current assets were at their proper levels in relation to sales. All assets except fixed assets must increase at the same rate as sales, and fixed assets would also have to increase at the same rate if the current excess capacity did not exist. Booth's after-tax profit margin is forecasted to be 5% and its payout ratio to be 60%. What is Booth's additional funds needed (AFN) for the coming year?

Challenging Problems 7–9

9–7 Forecasted Statements and Ratios Upton Computers makes bulk purchases of small computers, stocks them in conveniently located warehouses, ships them to its chain of retail stores, and has a staff to advise customers and help them set up their new computers. Upton's balance sheet as of December 31, 2012, is shown here (millions of dollars):

Cash	$ 3.5	Accounts payable	$ 9.0
Receivables	26.0	Notes payable	18.0
Inventories	58.0	Accruals	8.5
Total current assets	$ 87.5	Total current liabilities	$ 35.5
Net fixed assets	35.0	Mortgage loan	6.0
		Common stock	15.0
		Retained earnings	66.0
Total assets	$122.5	Total liabilities and equity	$122.5

Sales for 2012 were $350 million and net income for the year was $10.5 million, so the firm's profit margin was 3.0%. Upton paid dividends of $4.2 million to common stockholders, so its payout ratio was 40%. Its tax rate is 40%, and it operated at full capacity. Assume that all assets/sales ratios, spontaneous liabilities/sales ratios, the profit margin, and the payout ratio remain constant in 2013.

a. If sales are projected to increase by $70 million, or 20%, during 2013, use the AFN equation to determine Upton's projected external capital requirements.

b. Using the AFN equation, determine Upton's self-supporting growth rate. That is, what is the maximum growth rate the firm can achieve without having to employ nonspontaneous external funds?

c. Use the forecasted financial statement method to forecast Upton's balance sheet for December 31, 2013. Assume that all additional external capital is raised as a bank loan at the end of the year and is reflected in notes payable (because the debt is added at the end of the year, there will be no additional interest expense due to the new debt). Assume Upton's profit margin and dividend payout ratio will be the same in 2013 as they were in 2012. What is the amount of notes payable reported on the 2013 forecasted balance sheets? (*Hint:* You don't need to forecast the income statements because you are given the projected sales, profit margin, and dividend payout ratio; these figures allow you to calculate the 2013 addition to retained earnings for the balance sheet.)

9–8 **Additional Funds Needed** Stevens Textiles's 2012 financial statements are shown below:

Balance Sheet as of December 31, 2012 (Thousands of Dollars)

Cash	$ 1,080	Accounts payable	$ 4,320
Receivables	6,480	Accruals	2,880
Inventories	9,000	Notes payable	2,100
Total current assets	$16,560	Total current liabilities	$ 9,300
Net fixed assets	12,600	Mortgage bonds	3,500
		Common stock	3,500
		Retained earnings	12,860
Total assets	$29,160	Total liabilities and equity	$29,160

Income Statement for December 31, 2012 (Thousands of Dollars)

Sales	$36,000
Operating costs	32,440
Earnings before interest and taxes	$ 3,560
Interest	460
Earnings before taxes	$ 3,100
Taxes (40%)	1,240
Net income	$ 1,860
Dividends (45%)	$ 837
Addition to retained earnings	$ 1,023

a. Suppose 2013 sales are projected to increase by 15% over 2012 sales. Use the forecasted financial statement method to forecast a balance sheet and income statement for December 31, 2013. The interest rate on all debt is 10%, and cash earns no interest income. Assume that all additional debt is added at the end of the year, which means that you should base the forecasted interest expense on the balance of debt at the beginning of the year. Use the forecasted income statement to determine the addition to retained earnings. Assume that the company was operating at full capacity in 2012, that it cannot sell off any of its fixed assets, and that any required financing will be borrowed as notes payable. Also, assume that assets, spontaneous liabilities, and operating costs are expected to increase by the same percentage as sales. Determine the additional funds needed.

b. What is the resulting total forecasted amount of notes payable?

c. In your answers to Parts a and b, you should not have charged any interest on the additional debt added during 2013 because it was assumed that the new debt was added at the end of the year. But now suppose that the new debt is added throughout the year. Don't do any calculations, but how would this change the answers to parts a and b?

9–9 **Additional Funds Needed** Garlington Technologies Inc.'s 2012 financial statements are shown below:

Balance Sheet as of December 31, 2012

Cash	$ 180,000	Accounts payable	$ 360,000
Receivables	360,000	Notes payable	156,000
Inventories	720,000	Accruals	180,000
Total current assets	$1,260,000	Total current liabilities	$ 696,000
Fixed assets	1,440,000	Common stock	1,800,000
		Retained earnings	204,000
Total assets	$2,700,000	Total liabilities and equity	$2,700,000

Income Statement for December 31, 2012

Sales	$3,600,000
Operating costs	3,279,720
EBIT	$ 320,280
Interest	18,280
EBT	$ 302,000
Taxes (40%)	120,800
Net income	$ 181,200
Dividends	$ 108,000

Suppose that in 2013 sales increase by 10% over 2012 sales and that 2013 dividends will increase to $112,000. Forecast the financial statements using the forecasted financial statement method. Assume the firm operated at full capacity in 2012. Use an interest rate of 13%, and assume that any new debt will be added at the end of the year (so forecast the interest expense based on the debt balance at the beginning of the year). Cash does not earn any interest income. Assume that the AFN will be in the form of notes payable.

Spreadsheet Problems

9-10 **Build a Model: Forecasting Financial Statements** Start with the partial model in the file *Ch09 P10 Build a Model.xls* on the textbook's Web site, which contains the 2012 financial statements of Zieber Corporation. Forecast Zeiber's 2013 income statement and balance sheets. Use the following assumptions: (1) Sales grow by 6%. (2) The ratios of expenses to sales, depreciation to fixed assets, cash to sales, accounts receivable to sales, and inventories to sales will be the same in 2013 as in 2012. (3) Zeiber will not issue any new stock or new long-term bonds. (4) The interest rate is 9% for short-term debt and 11% for long-term debt. (5) No interest is earned on cash. (6) Dividends grow at an 8% rate. (6) Calculate the additional funds needed (AFN). If new financing is required, assume it will be raised as notes payable. Assume that any new notes payable will be borrowed on the last day of the year, so there will be no additional interest expense for the new notes payable. If surplus funds are available, pay a special dividend.
   a. What are the forecasted levels of notes payable and special dividends?
   b. Now assume that the growth in sales is only 3%. What are the forecasted levels of notes payable and special dividends?

9-11 **Build a Model: Forecasting Financial Statements** Start with the partial model in the file *Ch09 P11 Build a Model.xls* on the textbook's Web site, which shows Matthews Industries's most recent balance sheet, income statement, and other data. Matthews Industries's financial planners must forecast the company's financial results for the coming year. The forecast will be based on the forecasted financial statement method, and any additional funds needed will be obtained by using notes payable. Complete the partial model and answer the following questions.
   a. Assume that the firm's 2012 profit margin, payout ratio, capital intensity ratio, and spontaneous liabilities-to-sales ratio remain constant. If sales grow by 10% in 2013, what is the required external capital the firm will need in 2013 as calculated by the AFN equation?
   b. If 2012 ratios remain constant, what is Matthews's self-supporting growth rate? Describe how the self-supporting growth rate will change in response to each of the following: (1) the profit margin declines, (2) the payout ratio increases, (3) the capital intensity ratio declines.
   c. Matthews's management has reviewed its financial statements and arrived at two possible scenarios for 2013. The first scenario assumes a steady state while the second scenario, the target scenario, shows some improvement in ratios toward industry average values. Forecasted values for the scenarios are shown in the partially completed file *Ch09 P11 Build a Model.xls*. If Matthews assumes that external financing is achieved through notes payable and that financing feedbacks are not considered because the new notes

payable are added at the end of the year, then what are the firm's forecasted AFN, EPS, DPS, and year-end stock price under each scenario?

d. Matthews's management realizes that interest for additional notes payable should be included in the analysis. Assume that notes will be issued midway through the year, so that interest on these notes is incurred for only half the year. If Matthews assumes now that external financing is achieved through notes payable and if financing feedbacks are considered, then what are the firm's forecasted AFN, EPS, DPS, and year-end stock price under each scenario?

 THOMSON REUTERS

Use the Thomson ONE–Business School Edition online database to work this chapter's questions.

Forecasting the Future Performance of Abercrombie & Fitch

Clothing retailer Abercrombie & Fitch enjoyed phenomenal success in the late 1990s. Between 1996 and 2000, its sales grew almost fourfold, from $335 million to more than $1.2 billion, and its stock price soared by more than 500%. More recently, however, its growth rate has begun to slow down, and Abercrombie has had a hard time meeting its quarterly earnings targets. These problems were compounded by the global recession in 2009 with the stock price in November 2009 falling by 90% from its high 1 year before. Abercrombie's struggles resulted from increased competition, a sluggish economy, and the challenges of staying ahead of the fashion curve.

Since 2009, the company's stock has rebounded strongly but questions remain about the firm's long-term growth prospects. Given the questions about Abercrombie's future growth rate, analysts have focused on the company's earnings reports. Thomson ONE provides a convenient and detailed summary of the company's recent earnings history along with a summary of analysts' earnings forecasts.

To access this information, we begin by entering the company's ticker symbol, ANF, on Thomson ONE's main screen and then selecting GO. This takes us to an overview of the company's recent performance. After checking out the overview, you should click on the tab labeled Estimates, near the top of your screen. Here you will find a wide range of information about the company's past and projected earnings.

Discussion Questions

1. What are the mean and median forecasts for Abercrombie's earnings per share over the next fiscal year?
2. Based on analysts' forecasts, what is the firm's expected long-term growth rate in earnings?
3. Have analysts made any significant changes to their forecasted earnings for Abercrombie & Fitch in the past few months?
4. Historically, have Abercrombie's reported earnings generally met, exceeded, or fallen short of analysts' forecasted earnings?
5. How has Abercrombie's stock performed this year relative to the S&P 500?

MINI CASE

Hatfield Medical Supplies's stock price had been lagging its industry averages, so its board of directors brought in a new CEO, Adam Lee. Lee asked for the company's long-run strategic plan; when he learned that no formal plan existed, he decided to develop one himself. Lee had brought in Rick Novak, a finance MBA who had been working for a consulting company, to replace the old CFO, and he asked Rick to develop the financial planning section of the strategic plan. In his previous job, Novak's primary task had been to help clients develop financial forecasts, and that was one reason Lee hired him.

Novak began as he always did, by comparing Hatfield's financial ratios to the industry averages. If any ratio was substandard, he discussed it with the responsible manager to see what could be done to improve the situation. Figure 9-MC-1 provides Hatfield's latest financial statements plus some ratios and other data that Novak plans to use in his analysis. Notice that the figure is extracted from an *Excel* spreadsheet. Novak learned back in his university days that, because of interactions among variables, any realistic financial forecast must be based on a computer model. (The model is available to your instructor on the textbook's Web site.) Of course, he is also aware of the well-known computer axiom—garbage in, garbage out (GIGO). Novak therefore plans to discuss the model's inputs carefully with Hatfield's operating managers, individually and also collectively in the company's financial planning conference.

a. Do you think Adam Lee should develop a strategic plan for the company? Why? What are the central elements of such a plan? What is the role of finance in a strategic plan?

b. Given the data in Figure 9-MC-1, how well run would you say Hatfield appears to be in comparison with other firms in its industry? What are its primary strengths and weaknesses? Be specific in your answer, and point to various ratios that support your position. Also, use the Du Pont equation (see Chapter 8) as one part of your analysis.

c. Use the AFN equation to estimate Hatfield's required new external capital for 2013 if the 15% expected growth takes place. Assume that the firm's 2012 ratios will remain the same in 2013.

d. Define the term *capital intensity*. Explain how a decline in capital intensity would affect the AFN, other things held constant. Would economies of scale combined with rapid growth affect capital intensity, other things held constant? Also, explain how changes in each of the following would affect AFN, holding other things constant: the growth rate, the amount of accounts payable, the profit margin, and the payout ratio.

e. Define the term *self-supporting growth rate*. Based on the Figure 9-MC-1 data, what is Hatfield's self-supporting growth rate? Would the self-supporting growth rate be affected by a change in the capital intensity ratio or the other factors mentioned in question d? Other things held constant, would the calculated capital intensity ratio change over time if the company were growing and were also subject to economies of scale and/or lumpy assets?

f. Forecast the financial statements for 2013 using the following assumptions. (1) Operating ratios remain unchanged. (2) No additional notes payable, LT bonds, or common stock will be issued. (3) The interest rate on all debt is 10%. (4) If additional financing is needed, then it will be raised through a line of credit. The line of credit would be tapped on the last day of the year, so it would create no additional interest expenses for that year. (5) Interest expenses for notes payable and LT bonds are based on the average balances during the year. (6) If surplus funds are available, the surplus will be paid out as a special dividend payment. (7) Regular dividends will grow by 15%. (8) Sales will grow by 15%. We call this the Steady scenario because operations remain unchanged.

(1) How much new capital will the firm need (i.e., what is the forecasted AFN); how does

Figure 9-MC-1 Financial Statements and Other Data (Millions, Except for Per Share Data)

	A	B	C		D	E	F	G
4	Balance Sheet, Hatfield, 12/31/12					Income Statement, Hatfield, 2012		
5	Cash and securities		$20			Sales		$2,000
6	Accounts receivable		290			Total operating costs		1,900
7	Inventories		390			EBIT		$100
8	Total current assets		$700			Interest		60
9	Net fixed assets		500			EBT		$40
10	Total assets		$1,200			Taxes (40%)		16
11						Net income		$24
12	Accounts pay. + accruals		$100			Dividends		$9
13	Notes payable		80			Add. to retain. earnings		$15
14	Total current liabilities		$180			Shares outstanding		10
15	Long-term debt		520			EPS		$2.40
16	Total liabilities		$700			DPS		$0.90
17	Common stock		300			Year-end stock price		$24.00
18	Retained earnings		200					
19	Total common equity		$500					
20	Total liab. & equity		$1,200					
21								
22	Selected Ratios and Other Data, 2012				Hatfield	Industry		
23	Sales, 2012 (S_0):				$2,000	$2,000		Sales set equal to
24	Expected growth in sales:				15.0%	15.0%		Hatfield to make the
25	Profit margin (M):				1.2%	2.74%		data comparable.
26	Assets/Sales (A_0^*/S_0):				60.0%	50.0%		
27	Payout ratio (POR):				37.5%	35.0%		
28	Equity multiplier (Assets/Equity):				2.40	2.13		
29	Total liability/Total assets				58.3%	53.0%		
30	Times interest earned (EBIT/Interest):				1.67	5.20		
31	Increase in sales ($\Delta S = gS_0$):				$300	$300		
32	(Payables + Accruals)/Sales (L_0^*/S_0):				5.0%	4.0%		
33	Operating costs/Sales:				95.0%	93.0%		
34	Cash/Sales:				1.0%	1.0%		
35	Receivables/Sales:				14.5%	11.0%		
36	Inventories/Sales:				19.5%	15.0%		
37	Fixed assets/Sales:				25.0%	23.0%		
38	Tax rate:				40.0%	40.0%		
39	Interest rate on all debt:				10.00%	9.5%		
40	Price/Earning (P/E):				10.0	12.0		
41	ROE (Net income/Common equity):				4.80%	11.64%		

Note: Hatfield was operating at full capacity in 2012.

it compare with the amount you calculated using the AFN equation; and why does any difference exist?

(2) Calculate the firm's free cash flow, return on invested capital, EPS, DPS, ROE, and any other ratios you think would be useful in considering the situation.

(3) Assuming all of the inputs turn out to be exactly correct, would these answers also be exactly correct? If not, why not?

g. Repeat the analysis performed for Question f but now assume that Hatfield is able to achieve industry averages for the following input variables: operating costs/sales, receivables/sales, inventories/sales, and fixed assets/sales. Answer parts (1) and (2) of Question f under the new assumptions.

h. Could a strategic plan that included an incentive compensation program affect the firm's ability to move toward industry average operating performance?

i. What is financing feedback?

Selected Additional Cases

The following cases from TextChoice, *Cengage Learning's online case library, cover many of the concepts discussed in this chapter and are available at* **www.textchoice2.com/casenet.**

Klein-Brigham Series:

Case 37, "Space-Age Materials, Inc."; Case 38, "Automated Banking Management, Inc."; Case 52, "Expert Systems"; and Case 69, "Medical Management Systems, Inc."

Chapter **10**

Determining the Cost of Capital

WEB

The textbook's Web site contains an *Excel* file that will guide you through the chapter's calculations. The file for this chapter is ***Ch10 Tool Kit.xls***, and we encourage you to open the file and follow along as you read the chapter.

Businesses require capital to develop new products, build factories and distribution centers, install information technology, expand internationally, and acquire other companies. For each of these actions, a company must estimate the total investment required and then decide whether the expected rate of return exceeds the cost of the capital. The cost of capital is also a factor in compensation plans, with bonuses dependent on whether the company's return on invested capital exceeds the cost of that capital. This cost is also a key factor in choosing the firm's mixture of debt and equity and in decisions to lease rather than buy assets. As these examples illustrate, the cost of capital is a critical element in many business decisions.[1]

---

1. The cost of capital is also an important factor in the regulation of electric, gas, and water companies. These utilities are natural monopolies in the sense that one firm can supply service at a lower cost than could two or more firms. Because it has a monopoly, an unregulated electric or water company could exploit its customers. Therefore, regulators (1) determine the cost of the capital investors have provided the utility and then (2) set rates designed to permit the company to earn its cost of capital, no more and no less.

Beginning of Chapter Questions

As you read the chapter, consider how you would answer the following questions. You *should not* necessarily be able to answer the questions before you read the chapter. Rather, you should use them to get a sense of the issues covered in the chapter. After reading the chapter, you should be able to give at least partial answers to the questions, and you should be able to give better answers after the chapter has been discussed in class. Note, too, that it is often useful, when answering conceptual questions, to use hypothetical data to illustrate your answer. We illustrate the answers with an *Excel* model that is available on the textbook's Web site. Accessing the model and working through it is a useful exercise, and it provides insights that are useful when answering the questions.

1. What are the main **components of a company's cost of capital?** Rank these components from lowest to highest cost (a) on a before-tax and (b) on an after-tax cost basis, and explain why these differences exist.

2. How are the component costs combined to form a **weighted average cost of capital (WACC),** and why is it necessary to use the WACC in capital budgeting?

3. What weights should be used when you calculate the WACC? Discuss the choice between book value and market value weights, and the role of the "target" capital structure for a firm whose actual capital structure is far removed from the target.

4. Describe each of the following methods for estimating the cost of equity: (a) the **CAPM,** (b) **DCF,** and (c) the **bond-yield-plus-risk-premium.** Where can you obtain inputs for each of these methods, and how accurate are estimates based on each procedure? Can you state categorically that one method is better than the others, or does the "best" method depend on the circumstances?

5. How do **flotation costs** affect the cost of capital? Are these costs about the same for each of the three capital components? How do they change as the firm raises larger and larger amounts of capital, and how do flotation costs affect the way a company raises capital from year to year?

6. For a given firm, **why does WACC change over time?** Can the firm control the factors that lead to changes in the WACC and thus determine its WACC?

7. At any one time, should the **same WACC** be used to evaluate each of a company's capital budgeting projects? If not, how should the WACC be adjusted for the different projects?

10.1 The Weighted Average Cost of Capital

If a firm's only investors were common stockholders, then its cost of capital would be the required rate of return on its equity. However, most firms employ different types of capital, and because of their differences in risk, the different securities have different required rates of return. The required rate of return on each capital component is called its **component cost,** and the cost of capital used to analyze capital budgeting decisions is found as a *weighted average* of the various components' costs. We call this weighted average just that, the **weighted average cost of capital,** or **WACC.**

National Computer Corporation (NCC) is a mid-sized manufacturer of mainframe computers. We will estimate NCC's cost of capital in this chapter. We begin by providing some basic information in Figure 10-1, including: (1) balance sheets; (2) percentages of total liabilities and equity comprised by each item (Column F); (3) percentages of financing in the form of "costly" capital supplied by investors, including banks, bondholders, and stockholders (Column H reports percentages based on book values from the financial statements); (4) percentages of investor-supplied capital based on current market values (Columns I and J); and (5) target capital

CORPORATE VALUATION AND THE COST OF CAPITAL

In Chapter 1, we told you that managers should strive to make their firms more valuable and that the value of a firm is determined by the size, timing, and risk of its free cash flows (FCF). Indeed, a firm's intrinsic value is found as the present value of its FCFs, discounted at the weighted average cost of capital (WACC). In previous chapters, we examined the major sources of financing (stocks, bonds, and preferred stock) and the costs of those instruments. In this chapter, we put those pieces together and estimate the WACC that is used to determine intrinsic value.

structure weights that management plans to use when raising new capital in the future (Column L). Following is a brief discussion of this information.

Notice that we exclude accounts payable and accruals from Columns G to L. Capital is provided by *investors*—interest-bearing debt, preferred stock, and common equity. Accounts payable and accruals arise from operating decisions, not from financing decisions. For example, payables and accruals increase automatically when sales increase, so the impact of payables and accruals is incorporated into a firm's free cash flows and a project's cash flows rather than into the cost of capital. Therefore, we consider only investor-supplied capital when we calculate the cost of capital.

Notice that Figure 10-1 (in Columns H, J, and L) reports percentages of financing based on book values, market values, and target weights. We examine the choice of target weights in more detail in Chapter 15, where we discuss the optimal capital structure, which is one financed with percentages of debt, preferred stock, and common equity that maximize the firm's value. As shown in the last column of Figure 10-1, NCC has concluded that it should use 30% debt, 10% preferred stock, and 60% common equity in its target capital structure, and it plans to raise capital in those

Figure 10-1   **National Computer Corporation: Book Values, Market Values, and Target Capital Structure (Millions of Dollars, December 31, 2012)**

	A	B	C	D	E	F	G	H	I	J	K L
							Investor-Supplied Capital				Target Capital Structure
35	Balance Sheets						Book		Market		
36											
37						Percent	Book	Percent	Market	Percent	
38	Assets		Liabilities and Equity			of Total	Value	of Total	Value	of Total	
39											
40	Cash	$ 65	Accounts payable		$ 650	6.5%					
41	S-T investments	10	Accruals		399	4.0%					
42	Receivables	1,800	Spontaneous liabilities		$1,049	10.5%					
43	Inventories	3,100	Notes payable		350	3.5%	$ 350	3.9%	$ 350	2.2%	
44	Total C.A.	$4,975	Total C.L.		$1,399	14.0%					
45			Long-term debt		4,200	42.0%	4,200	46.9%	4,200	26.0%	
46	Net fixed assets	5,020	Total liabilities		$5,599	56.0%	$4,550	50.9%	$ 4,550	28.2%	w_d = 30.0%
47			Preferred stock		1,200	12.0%	1,200	13.4%	1,200	7.4%	w_{ps} = 10.0%
48			Common stock		650	6.5%	650	7.3%			
49			Retained earnings		2,546	25.5%	2,546	28.5%			
50			Total common equity		$3,196	32.0%	$3,196	35.7%	10,400	64.4%	w_s = 60.0%
51	Total assets	$9,995	Total liabilities and equity		$9,995	100.0%	$8,946	100.0%	$16,150	100.0%	100.0%
52											

Notes:

1. The market value of the notes payable is equal to the book value. Some of NCC's long-term bonds sell at a discount and some sell at a premium, but their aggregate market value is approximately equal to their aggregate book value.
2. The common stock price is $32 per share. There are 325 million shares outstanding, for a total market cap of $32(325) = $10,400 million.
3. The preferred stock price is $100 per share. There are 12 million shares outstanding, for a total market value of $100(12) = $1,200 million.
4. When establishing the target capital structure, no distinction is made between common equity raised by issuing stock versus retaining earnings.
5. The firm assumes that it will eventually replace most notes payable with long-term bonds and that the costs of notes payable and long-term debt are approximately the same; hence it simply uses a 30% weight for all investor-supplied debt (i.e., for the combined notes payable and long-term debt).
6. Accounts payable and accruals are not sources of investor-supplied capital, so we exclude them when calculating the WACC. However, we include the effects of payables and accruals on free cash flow and on a project's cash flows, so we do not ignore payables and accruals when estimating the value of a company or project. See Chapter 21 for more discussion of payables in the context of working capital management.
7. When deciding on a target capital structure, managers consider the firm's current and recent past book and market value structures as well as those of benchmark firms. They also perform stress tests by forecasting financial statements under different assumptions regarding capital structures and different states of the economy. See Chapter 15 for more on setting the target capital structure weights.

proportions in the future. Therefore, we use those target weights when calculating NCC's weighted average cost of capital.[2]

2. We should also note that the weights could be based on either the book or market values of the capital components. The market value of the equity is found by multiplying the stock's price by the number of shares outstanding. Market value weights are theoretically superior. However, accountants show assets on a book value basis, bond rating agencies and security analysts generally focus on book values, and market value weights are quite unstable because stock prices fluctuate so much. If a firm's book and market values differ widely, then often it appears as though management sets *target* weights as a blend of book and market weights. We discuss this more in Chapter 15, but for now just accept the target weights provided in this chapter as determined by management.

What is a component cost?

What is a target capital structure?

10.2 Basic Definitions

Now we define the key terms used in this chapter. Later we describe how to estimate the values of these variables and how to combine them to form the weighted average cost of capital, but an early overview is useful.

r_d = Interest rate on the firm's new debt = before-tax component cost of debt. It can be found in several ways, including calculating the yield to maturity on the firm's currently outstanding bonds.

$r_d(1 - T)$ = After-tax component cost of debt, where T is the firm's marginal tax rate. *$r_d(1 - T)$ is the debt cost used to calculate the weighted average cost of capital.* As we shall see, the after-tax cost of debt is lower than its before-tax cost because interest is tax deductible.

r_{ps} = Component cost of preferred stock, found as the yield investors expect to earn on the preferred stock. Preferred dividends are not tax deductible, so the before-tax and after-tax costs of preferred stock are equal.

r_s = Component cost of common equity raised by retaining earnings, or *internal equity*. It is the r_s developed in Chapter 5, where it is defined as the rate of return that investors require on a firm's common stock. Most firms, once they have become well established, obtain all of their new equity by retaining earnings.

r_e = component cost of *external equity*, or common equity raised by issuing new stock. As we will see, r_e is equal to r_s plus a factor that reflects the cost of issuing new stock. Note, though, that established firms like NCC rarely issue new stock; hence r_e is rarely a relevant consideration except for very young, rapidly growing firms.

w = w_d, w_{ps}, w_s, w_e = target weights of debt, preferred stock, internal equity (by retaining earnings), and external equity (new issues of common stock). The weights are the percentages of the different types of capital the firm plans to use when it raises capital in the future. Target weights may differ from actual current weights.

WACC = the firm's weighted average, or overall, cost of capital.

The target proportions of debt (w_d), preferred stock (w_{ps}), and common equity (w_s)—along with the costs of those components—are used to calculate the firm's **weighted average cost of capital, WACC**[3]:

---

3. We assume at this point that all new common equity is raised internally by retaining earnings, as is true for most companies with moderate or slow sales growth, so the cost of common equity is r_s.

$$WACC = \begin{pmatrix} \% \\ \text{of} \\ \text{debt} \end{pmatrix} \begin{pmatrix} \text{After-tax} \\ \text{cost of} \\ \text{debt} \end{pmatrix} + \begin{pmatrix} \% \text{ of} \\ \text{preferred} \\ \text{stock} \end{pmatrix} \begin{pmatrix} \text{Cost of} \\ \text{preferred} \\ \text{stock} \end{pmatrix} + \begin{pmatrix} \% \text{ of} \\ \text{common} \\ \text{equity} \end{pmatrix} \begin{pmatrix} \text{Cost of} \\ \text{common} \\ \text{equity} \end{pmatrix} \quad (10\text{-}1)$$

$$= \quad w_d r_d (1 - T) \quad + \quad w_{ps} r_{ps} \quad + \quad w_s r_s$$

In the following sections, we explain how to estimate the various components' costs.

Self Test

Identify the firm's three major capital structure components, and give the symbols for their respective costs and weights.

What are the two possible sources of new common equity (and hence two possible costs of common equity)? Which one is normally relevant, and why is this so?

10.3 Cost of Debt, $r_d(1 - T)$

The first step in estimating the cost of debt is to determine the rate of return debt-holders require, or r_d. Although estimating r_d is conceptually straightforward, some problems arise in practice. Companies use both fixed- and floating-rate debt, both straight and convertible debt, both long- and short-term debt, as well as debt with and without sinking funds. Each type of debt may have a somewhat different cost.

It is unlikely that the financial manager will know at the beginning of a planning period the exact types and amounts of debt that will be used during the period. The type or types used will depend on the specific assets to be financed and on capital market conditions as they develop over time. Even so, the financial manager does know what types of debt are typical for his firm. For example, NCC typically issues commercial paper to raise short-term money to finance working capital, and it issues 30-year bonds to raise long-term debt used to help finance its capital budgeting projects. Since the WACC is used primarily in capital budgeting, NCC's treasurer uses the cost of 30-year bonds in her WACC estimate.

Assume that it is January 2013 and that NCC's treasurer is estimating the WACC for the coming year. How should she calculate the component cost of debt? Most financial managers begin by discussing current and prospective interest rates with their investment bankers. Assume NCC's bankers believe that a new, 30-year, noncallable, straight bond issue would require a 9% coupon rate with semiannual payments. It can be offered to the public at its $1,000 par value. Therefore, their estimate of r_d is 9%.[4]

Note that 9% is the cost of **new, or marginal, debt**, and it will probably not be the same as the average rate on NCC's previously issued debt, which is called the **historical, or embedded, rate.** The embedded cost is important for some decisions but not for others. For example, the average cost of all the capital raised in the past and still outstanding is used by regulators when they determine the rate of return that a public utility should be allowed to earn. However, in financial management

---

4. The effective annual rate is $(1 + 0.09/2)^2 - 1 = 9.2\%$, but NCC and most other companies use nominal rates for all component costs.

the WACC is used primarily to make investment decisions, and these decisions hinge on projects' expected future returns versus the cost of the new, or marginal, capital that will be used to finance those projects. *Thus, for our purposes, the relevant cost is the marginal cost of new debt to be raised during the planning period.*

Suppose NCC has issued debt in the past and the bonds are publicly traded. The financial staff can use the market price of the bonds to find the yield to maturity (or yield to call, if the bonds sell at a premium and are likely to be called). This yield is the rate of return that current bondholders expect to receive, and it is also a good estimate of r_d, the rate of return that new bondholders will require.

For example, suppose NCC has outstanding bonds with an 8% annual coupon rate, 22 years remaining until maturity, and a face value of $1,000. The bonds make semiannual coupon payments and currently are trading in the market at a price of $904.91. We can find the yield to maturity by using a financial calculator with these inputs: N = 44, PV = −904.91, PMT = 40, and FV = 1000. Solving for the rate, we find I/YR = 4.5%. This is a semiannual periodic rate, so the nominal annual rate is 9.0%. This is consistent with the investment bankers' estimated rate, so 9% is a reasonable estimate for r_d. If NCC had no publicly traded debt, then its staff could still look at the yields on publicly traded debt of similar firms for a reasonable estimate of r_d.

The required return to debtholders, r_d, is not equal to the company's cost of debt because interest payments are deductible, which means the government in effect pays part of the total cost. As a result, the weighted average cost of capital is calculated using the **after-tax cost of debt,** $r_d(1 − T)$**,** which is the interest rate on debt, r_d, less the tax savings that result because interest is deductible. Here T is the firm's marginal tax rate.[5]

(10–2)

$$\text{After-tax component cost of debt} = \text{Interest rate} - \text{Tax savings}$$
$$= r_d - r_d T$$
$$= r_d(1 - T)$$

If we assume that NCC's marginal federal-plus-state tax rate is 40%, then its after-tax cost of debt is 5.4%:[6]

$$r_d(1 - T) = 9\%(1.0 - 0.4)$$
$$= 9\%(0.6)$$
$$= 5.4\%$$

10.3a Flotation Costs and the Cost of Debt

Most debt offerings have very low flotation costs, especially for privately placed debt. Because flotation costs are usually low, most analysts ignore them when estimating

---

5. The federal tax rate for most corporations is 35%. However, most corporations are also subject to state income taxes, so the marginal tax rate on most corporate income is about 40%. For illustrative purposes, we assume that the effective federal-plus-state tax rate on marginal income is 40%. The effective tax rate is *zero* for a firm with such large current or past losses that it does not pay taxes. In this situation, the after-tax cost of debt is equal to the pre-tax interest rate.
6. Strictly speaking, the after-tax cost of debt should reflect the *expected* cost of debt. Although NCC's bonds have a promised return of 9%, there is some chance of default and so its bondholders' expected return (and consequently NCC's cost) is a bit less than 9%. However, for a relatively strong company such as NCC, this difference is quite small.

the after-tax cost of debt. However, the following example illustrates the procedure for incorporating flotation costs as well as their impact on the after-tax cost of debt.

Suppose NCC can issue 30-year debt with an annual coupon rate of 9%, with coupons paid semiannually. The flotation costs, F, are equal to 1% of the value of the issue. Instead of finding the pre-tax yield based upon pre-tax cash flows and then adjusting it to reflect taxes, as we did before, we can find the after-tax, flotation-adjusted cost by using this formula:

$$M(1-F) = \sum_{t=1}^{N} \frac{INT(1-T)}{[1 + r_d(1-T)]^t} + \frac{M}{[1 + r_d(1-T)]^N} \qquad (10\text{--}3)$$

Here M is the bond's maturity (or par) value, F is the **percentage flotation cost** (i.e., the percentage of proceeds paid to the investment bankers), N is the number of payments, T is the firm's tax rate, INT is the dollars of interest per period, and $r_d(1-T)$ is the after-tax cost of debt adjusted for flotation costs. With a financial calculator, enter N = 60, PV = $-1000(1 - 0.01)$ = -990, PMT = $45(1 - 0.40)$ = 27, and FV = 1000. Solving for I/YR, we find I/YR = $r_d(1 - T)$ = 2.73%, which is the semiannual after-tax component cost of debt. The nominal after-tax cost of debt is 5.46%. Note that this is quite close to the original 5.40% after-tax cost, so in this instance adjusting for flotation costs doesn't make much difference.[7]

However, the flotation adjustment would be higher if F were larger or if the bond's life were shorter. For example, if F were 10% rather than 1%, then the nominal annual flotation-adjusted $r_d(1 - T)$ would be 6.13%. With N at 1 year rather than 30 years and F still equal to 1%, the nominal annual $r_d(1 - T)$ = 6.45%. Finally, if F = 10% and N = 1, then the nominal annual $r_d(1 - T)$ = 16.67%. In all of these cases, the effect of flotation costs would be too large to ignore.

As an alternative to adjusting the cost of debt for flotation costs, in some situations it makes sense to instead adjust the project's cash flows. For example, **project financing** is a special situation in which a large project, such as an oil refinery, is financed with debt plus other securities that have a specific claim on the project's cash flows. This is different from the usual debt offering, in which the debt has a claim on all of the corporation's cash flows. Because project financing is funded by securities with claims tied to a particular project, the flotation costs can be included with the project's other cash flows when evaluating the project's value. However, project financing is relatively rare, so when we incorporate the impact of flotation costs, we usually do so by adjusting the component cost of the new debt.

10.3b The Cost of Short-Term Debt

As we mentioned earlier, most U.S. companies use short-term debt primarily to finance seasonal working capital needs. Seasonal debt fluctuates during the year, often dropping close to zero, so it is not a permanent source of financing for most U.S. companies. Therefore, we usually do not include short-term debt when estimating the cost of capital.

---

7. Equation 10-3 produces the correct after-tax cost of debt only for bonds issued at par. For bonds with a price other than par, the after-tax cash flows must be adjusted to take into account the actual taxation of the discount or premium. See *Web Extension 4A* on the textbook's Web site for a discussion of the taxation of original issue discount bonds. Also, we ignored the tax shield due to amortization of flotation costs because it has very little effect on the cost of debt; see *Ch10 Tool Kit.xls* for an example that incorporates the amortization tax shield.

However, some U.S. companies and many international companies, especially those in Japan, do use relatively large amounts of short-term debt on a consistent basis. For such companies, we should include short-term debt as a capital component when estimating the WACC. Most short-term debt is in the form of bank loans, often with an interest rate that is tied to the prime rate or to the London Interbank Offered Rate (LIBOR). The interest rate on short-term debt is its pre-tax cost, and it must be adjusted to determine its after-tax cost. Also, there are normally no flotation costs for short-term debt, so flotation adjustments are not required.

Self Test	Why is the after-tax cost of debt, rather than its before-tax cost, used to calculate the weighted average cost of capital?
	Is the relevant cost of debt when calculating the WACC the interest rate on already *outstanding* debt or the rate on *new* debt? Why?
	A company has outstanding long-term bonds with a face value of $1,000, a 10% coupon rate, 25 years remaining until maturity, and a current market value of $1,214.82. If it pays interest semiannually, then what is the nominal annual pre-tax cost of debt? **(8%)** If the company's tax rate is 40%, what is the after-tax cost of debt? **(4.8%)**

10.4 Cost of Preferred Stock, r_{ps}

Many firms (including NCC) use, or plan to use, preferred stock as part of their financing mix. Preferred dividends are not tax deductible, so the company bears their full cost. Therefore, *no tax adjustment is used when calculating the cost of preferred stock*. Some preferred stocks are issued without a stated maturity date, but today most have a sinking fund that effectively limits their life. Finally, although it is not mandatory that preferred dividends be paid, firms generally have every intention of doing so, because otherwise (1) they cannot pay dividends on their common stock, (2) they will find it difficult to raise additional funds in the capital markets, and (3) in some cases preferred stockholders can take control of the firm.

The **component cost of preferred stock, r_{ps}**, is the cost used in the WACC calculation. For preferred stock with a stated maturity date, we use the same approach as in the previous section for the cost of debt, keeping in mind that a firm has no tax savings with preferred stock. For preferred stock without a stated maturity date, r_{ps} is

(10–4)

$$\text{Component cost of preferred stock} = r_{ps} = \frac{D_{ps}}{P_{ps}(1 - F)}$$

Here D_{ps} is the preferred dividend, P_{ps} is the preferred stock price, and F is the flotation cost as a percentage of proceeds.

To illustrate the calculation, assume NCC has preferred stock that pays an $8 dividend per share and sells for $100 per share. If NCC issued new shares of preferred then it would incur an underwriting (or flotation) cost of 2.5%, or $2.50 per share, so it would net $97.50 per share. Therefore, NCC's cost of preferred stock is 8.2%:

$$r_{ps} = \$8/\$97.50 = 8.2\%$$

GE AND WARREN BUFFETT: THE COST OF PREFERRED STOCK

In October 2008, GE was in serious trouble. Its stock price had been crashing, its sales and earnings were declining, it was having trouble rolling over its commercial paper, and there were rumors that its bonds were about to be downgraded, which would raise its interest expense and exacerbate all its other problems. Then Warren Buffett came to the rescue. Buffett agreed to buy $3 billion of a new GE preferred stock, and he publicly expressed his confidence by asserting that "GE will continue to be successful in the years to come." GE needed a boost, and Buffett's money and endorsement provided it.

However, Buffett didn't exactly give GE something for nothing. The preferred stock carried a 10% coupon, it had a 10% call premium, and it was convertible into GE's common stock during the next 5 years at a rate of 4.4944 shares of common per share of preferred. GE incurred no flotation costs because the deal was worked out between the two parties rather than being sold by underwriters. GE had been financing with commercial paper (until that market dried up) at an after-tax cost of about 2%, and its AAA-rated bonds were yielding about 8%, for an after-tax cost of about 4.8% because interest is tax deductible. So the 10% coupon cost of Buffett's preferred stock was not cheap.

Buffett actually expected to earn more than 10% on the deal. We don't know what he assumed the stock would do over the next 5 years, but he might have expected it to grow at a rate of 13.3% per year, which would move the stock from its then-current price of $24.50 to $45.74. Given that growth rate, Buffett could earn a tidy 23.3% on his investment by converting to common stock at the end of Year 5. Even if the stock appreciated at only 6% he would still earn 16.78% per year, and if the stock actually declined then he would still earn 10%—provided GE didn't go bankrupt. (The rate of return on the convertible preferred stock is calculated in the GE Pfd Stk worksheet in **Ch10 Tool Kit.xls**.) Two and a half years into the deal, GE is trading at about $20, which is a substantial improvement over its low of $7 in March 2009—but lower than when the preferred was issued. If GE continues to recover as it has since its low, Buffett stands to make a substantial profit on the investment.

Buffett's return is the mirror image of GE's cost. Because GE had been doing most of its financing with commercial paper and long-term debt at much lower rates, using convertible preferred instead was a real shock to its system. Obviously, this raised GE's weighted average cost of capital, and that presumably affected its required return on new assets and thus its capital budget.

If we had not incorporated flotation costs, we would have incorrectly estimated $r_{ps} = \$8/\$100 = 8.0\%$, which is too big a difference to ignore. Therefore, analysts usually include flotation costs when estimating the firm's cost of preferred stock.

Although preferred stock is riskier than debt, NCC's preferred stock has a lower return to investors than does its debt: 8% versus 9%. However, recall that most preferred stock is held by other companies, which are allowed to exclude 70% of preferred stocks' dividends from taxation. Thus, the after-tax return to these investors is higher for preferred stock than for debt, which is consistent with preferred stock being riskier than debt.

Self Test

Does the component cost of preferred stock include or exclude flotation costs? Explain.

Why is no tax adjustment made to the cost of preferred stock?

A company's preferred stock currently trades for $50 per share and pays a $3 annual dividend. Flotation costs are equal to 3% of the gross proceeds. If the company issues preferred stock, what is the cost of that stock? **(6.19%)**

10.5 Cost of Common Stock, r$_s$

Companies can raise common equity in two ways: (1) by selling newly issued shares to the public, and (2) by retaining and reinvesting earnings. If new shares are issued, what rate of return must the company earn to satisfy the new stockholders? In previous chapters we have seen that investors require a return of r$_s$. However, a company must earn more than r$_s$ on new external equity to provide this rate of return to investors, because there are flotation costs when a firm issues new equity.

Few firms with moderate or slow growth issue new shares of common stock through public offerings.[8] In fact, less than 2% of all new corporate funds come from the external public equity market. There are three reasons for this.

1. As we noted earlier, flotation costs can be quite high.
2. Investors perceive the issuance of common stock as a negative signal about the true value of the company's stock. Investors believe that managers have superior knowledge about companies' future prospects and that managers are most likely to issue new stock when they think the current stock price is above its intrinsic value. Suppose a company has an extremely profitable new project but will have to finance it with external capital. If the firm finances the project with common stock, the new stockholders will share in the windfall when the new project's profits start rolling in. Therefore, it is logical to think that managers will want to finance really good new projects with debt, temporarily increasing the debt ratio but planning to sell stock when profits rise and pull up the stock price. On the other hand, if things look bad, management might want to finance with stock to let new shareholders share in the pain. The net result is that if a mature company announces plans to issue additional shares, investors typically take this as a signal of bad news; as a result, the stock declines.
3. Even without the signaling effect, an increase in the supply of stock will put pressure on the stock's price, forcing the company to sell the new stock at a lower price than existed before the new issue was announced.

In the remainder of this section, we assume that the company does not plan to issue new shares.[9] We will address the impact of flotation costs on the cost of equity in Section 10.10.

Does new equity capital raised by reinvesting earnings have a cost? The answer is a resounding "yes!" If earnings are reinvested, then stockholders will incur an **opportunity cost**—the earnings could have been paid out as dividends or used to repurchase stock, and in either case stockholders would have received funds that they could reinvest in other securities. *Thus, the firm should earn on its reinvested earnings at least as much as its stockholders themselves could earn on alternative investments of equivalent risk.*

What rate of return could stockholders expect to earn on equivalent-risk investments? The answer is r$_s$, because they could presumably earn that return by simply buying the stock of the firm in question or that of a similar firm. *Therefore, r$_s$ is the cost of common equity raised internally as reinvested earnings.* If a company

---

8. A few companies issue new shares through new-stock dividend reinvestment plans, which we discuss in Chapter 17. Many companies sell stock to their employees, and companies occasionally issue stock to finance huge projects or mergers. Also, some utilities regularly issue common stock.

9. There are times when companies should issue stock in spite of these problems; hence, we discuss stock issues and the cost of equity later in the chapter.

can't earn at least r_s on reinvested earnings, then it should pass those earnings on to its stockholders and let them invest the money themselves in assets that do yield r_s.

Whereas debt and preferred stock are contractual obligations that have easily determined costs, it is more difficult to estimate r_s. However, we can employ the principles described in Chapters 2 and 5 to produce reasonably good estimates for the cost of equity. Three methods are typically used: (1) the Capital Asset Pricing Model (CAPM), (2) the discounted cash flow (DCF) method, and (3) the own-bond-yield-plus-judgmental-risk-premium approach. These methods are not mutually exclusive: When estimating a company's cost of equity, we generally use all three methods and then use an average, weighted on the basis of our confidence in the data used for each method.

Self Test

What are the two primary sources of equity capital?

Why do most established firms not issue additional shares of common equity?

Explain why there is a cost to using reinvested earnings; that is, why aren't reinvested earnings a free source of capital?

10.6 The CAPM Approach

To estimate the cost of common stock using the Capital Asset Pricing Model as discussed in Chapter 2, we proceed as follows.

1. Estimate the risk-free rate, r_{RF}.
2. Estimate the current market risk premium, RP_M, which is the required market return minus the risk-free rate.
3. Estimate the stock's beta coefficient, b_i, which measures the stock's relative risk. The subscript i signifies Stock i's beta.
4. Use these three values in Equation 10-5 to estimate the stock's required rate of return:

$$r_s = r_{RF} + (RP_M)b_i \qquad (10\text{--}5)$$

Equation 10-5 shows that the CAPM estimate of r_s begins with the risk-free rate, r_{RF}. We then add a risk premium that is equal to the risk premium on the market, RP_M, scaled up or down to reflect the particular stock's risk as measured by its beta coefficient. The following sections explain how to implement this four-step process.

10.6a Estimating the Risk-Free Rate

The starting point for the CAPM cost-of-equity estimate is r_{RF}, the risk-free rate. There is no such thing as a truly riskless asset in the U.S. economy. Treasury securities are essentially free of default risk; however, nonindexed long-term T-bonds will suffer capital losses if interest rates rise, indexed long-term bonds will decline if the real rate rises, and a portfolio of short-term T-bills will provide a volatile earnings stream because the rate earned on T-bills varies over time.

Since we cannot, in practice, find a truly riskless rate upon which to base the CAPM, what rate should we use? A survey of highly regarded companies shows that

WWW

To find the rate on a T-bond, go to **www .federalreserve.gov**. Select "Economic Research & Data" and then select "Statistical Releases and Historical Data." Click on "Daily" for "H.15: Selected Interest Rates."

about two-thirds of them use the rate on 10-year Treasury bonds.[10] We agree with their choice, and here are our reasons.

1. Common stocks are long-term securities and—although a particular stockholder may not have a long investment horizon—most stockholders do invest on a relatively long-term basis. Therefore, it is reasonable to think that stock returns embody relatively long-term inflation expectations similar to those reflected in bonds rather than the short-term expectations in bills.
2. Short-term Treasury bill rates are more volatile than are long-term Treasury bond rates and, most experts agree, are more volatile than r_s.[11]
3. In theory, the CAPM is supposed to measure the required return over a particular holding period. When it is used to estimate the cost of equity for a project, the theoretically correct holding period is the life of the project. Since a time period of 10 years is a reasonable average for projects' lives, the return on a 10-year T-bond is a logical choice for the risk-free rate.

T-bond rates can be found in *The Wall Street Journal*, the *Federal Reserve Bulletin*, or on the Internet. Although most analysts use the yield on a 10-year T-bond as a proxy for the risk-free rate, yields on 20- or 30-year T-bonds are also reasonable proxies.

10.6b Estimating the Market Risk Premium

Recall from Chapter 2 that the market risk premium, RP_M, is the required return on the stock market minus the risk-free rate, where the risk-free rate usually is defined as the yield on a 10-year Treasury bond. This is also called the **equity risk premium**, or just the **equity premium**. Since most investors are risk averse, they require a higher anticipated return (a risk premium) to induce them to invest in risky equities versus a Treasury bond. Unfortunately, the required return on the market, and hence the equity premium, is not directly observable. Three approaches may be used to estimate the market risk premium: (1) calculate historical premiums and use them to estimate the current premium; (2) use the current value of the market to estimate forward-looking premiums; and (3) survey experts. We proceed with an explanation of each approach.

Historical Risk Premium

Historical risk premium data for U.S. securities, updated annually, are available from many sources, including Ibbotson Associates.[12] Using data from 1926 through the most recent year, Ibbotson calculates the actual realized rate of return each year for the stock market and for long-term government bonds. Ibbotson defines the annual equity risk premium as the difference between the historical realized

---

10. See Robert E. Bruner, Kenneth M. Eades, Robert S. Harris, and Robert C. Higgins, "Best Practices in Estimating the Cost of Capital: Survey and Synthesis," *Financial Practice and Education,* Spring/Summer 1998, pp. 13–28.
11. Economic events usually have a larger impact on short-term rates than on long-term rates. For example, see the analysis of the 1995–1996 debt-limit disagreement between the White House and Congress provided in Srinivas Nippani, Pu Liu, and Craig T. Schulman, "Are Treasury Securities Free of Default?" *Journal of Financial and Quantitative Analysis,* June 2001, pp. 251–266.
12. See *Ibbotson Stocks, Bonds, Bills, and Inflation: 2011 Valuation Yearbook* (Chicago: Morningstar, Inc., 2011) for the most recent estimates.

returns on stocks and the historical returns on long-term T-bonds.[13] Ibbotson's 2011 book reported a 6.0% arithmetic average historical risk premium and a 4.0% geometric average. If investor risk aversion had actually been constant during the sample period, then the arithmetic average would be the best estimate for next year's risk premium, whereas the geometric average would be the best estimate for the longer-term risk premium, say, for the next 20 years.

There are several problems with using historical averages to estimate the current risk premium. First, stock returns are quite volatile, which leads to low confidence in estimated averages. For example, the estimated historical average premium is 6.0%, but the 95% confidence interval ranges from less than 2% to more than 10%. In other words, there is a very good chance that the true risk premium is much different from the calculated 6.0% average.

Second, the historical average is extremely sensitive to the period over which it is calculated. Just 11 years ago the historical average premium was 8.1%, which is substantially different from the current 6.0% average. In fact, in many years the average T-bond return has been higher than the average stock return, resulting in a negative historical premium for those years. However, the expected premium can't be negative—no one would invest in the stock market expecting to get a return that is less than the risk-free rate.

Third, changes in the risk premium can occur if investors' tolerance for risk changes. This causes problems in interpreting historical returns because a change in the required risk premium causes an *opposite change in the observed* premium. For example, an increase in the required premium means that investors have become more risk averse and require a higher return on stocks. But applying a higher discount rate to a stock's future cash flows causes a decline in stock price. Thus, an *increase* in the required premium causes a simultaneous *decrease* in the observed premium. Part of the market's precipitous decline in 2008 and 2009 surely was due to investors' increased risk aversion.

Forward-Looking Risk Premiums

An alternative to the historical risk premium is the forward-looking, or ex ante, risk premium. Again, the market risk premium is $RP_M = r_M - r_{RF}$, but r_M and r_{RF} are measured using forward-looking rather than historical data. As explained previously, we can use the yield to maturity on a 10-year T-bond as an estimate of the risk-free rate, which was 3.34% when we wrote this in January 2011. The challenge is to estimate the required return on the market, r_M. The most common approach is to assume that the market is in equilibrium, in which case the required return is equal to the expected return: $r_M = \hat{r}_M$. We can use the discounted cash flow (DCF) model from Chapter 5 to estimate the expected market rate of return, $\hat{r}_M$. If we assume that the market dividend will grow at a constant rate and that the firms that make up the market pay out as dividends all the funds available for distribution (i.e., the firms make no stock repurchases or purchases of short-term investments), then the required return is:

$$\text{Required rate of return} = r_M = \text{Expected rate of return} = \hat{r}_M = \frac{D_1}{P_0} + g \qquad (10\text{–}6)$$

---

13. The risk premium should be defined using the yield on T-bonds, so Ibbotson actually uses the return on T-bonds due to coupons rather than the total bond return (which includes capital gains and appreciation) as a proxy for the yield.

www

For current estimates from Standard & Poor's, go to **www .standardandpoors.com** and select SP 500 under Categories and Index Earnings under Download Data.

www

Go to the Federal Reserve Web site at **www.federal reserve.gov/releases/ h15/update** for current yields on T-bonds and TIPS.

Thus, the required return on the market can be estimated as the sum of the market's expected dividend yield plus the expected constant growth rate in dividends.

It is easy to obtain the market's actual dividend yield; in January 2011, Reuters.com reported a dividend yield of 1.54% for the S&P 500. It is a little more difficult, but not impossible, to find an estimate of the expected dividend yield. In January 2011, Standard & Poor's reported a projected dividend yield of 1.84% for the S&P 500.

We have an estimate of the expected dividend yield to use in Equation 10-6, but where can we get an estimate of the constant dividend growth rate, g? There is no definitive answer to that question, but neither are we totally in the dark. In the long run, constant dividend growth is driven by constant earnings growth, which in turn is driven by constant sales growth; hence it is reasonable to use an estimate of the market's long-term growth rate of sales as a proxy for the dividend growth rate.

Sales revenue growth is determined by growth in prices and units sold. In the long run, price growth will follow inflation. Historically, the average inflation rate has been about 3%. We can get a forward estimate of inflation by subtracting the real interest rate from the yield on a 10-year T-bond. The yield of an inflation-protected Treasury bond (called a TIPS) is a good estimate of the real interest rate. In January 2011, the yield on a 10-year TIPS was 0.97%, so a forward estimate of inflation is 3.34% − 0.97% = 2.37%.[14] This suggests that a reasonable estimate of expected inflation is somewhere between 2.37% and the historical average of 3%. In the long run, quantity growth will be driven by population growth. What is a reasonable estimate of sustainable population growth? There is no definitive answer, but somewhere around 1% to 2.5% is reasonable. Combining long-term population growth with expected inflation suggests that the long-term constant growth rate in sales is around 3.37% to 5.5%.[15]

Using the mid-point of our inflation and population growth estimates, a reasonable estimate of g is about 4.44%. When we combine this with the market's projected dividend yield, our estimate of the expected market risk return is

$$r_M = \hat{r}_M = \frac{D_1}{P_0} + g$$
$$= 1.84\% + 4.44\%$$
$$= 6.28\%$$

Given the 10-year T-bond yield of 3.34%, the estimated forward-looking market risk premium is therefore

$$RP_M = r_M - r_{RF}$$
$$= 6.28\% - 3.34\%$$
$$= 2.94\%$$

---

14. The difference in the yield on a T-bond and a TIPS of the same maturity actually includes a risk premium for bearing inflation risk as well as the anticipated inflation, but we assume that anticipated inflation makes up most of the difference.

15. Our estimates might be a little low because they ignore potential innovation and sustainable productivity growth. Will innovation create net increases in the quantity sold as new products hit the market, or will new products simply replace old products, resulting in no net increase in quantity sold? Real productivity (measured as per capita GDP) in the United States has grown at an average annual rate of about 1.5% to 2.5%. Will this continue, or will the law of diminishing returns cause productivity eventually to level off? If you are optimistic about the positive prospects of innovation and productivity, then you might want to add about 1% to our estimates of long-term sales growth. Keep in mind, though, that there's a reason economics is called "the dismal science"!

This probably underestimates the market risk premium because it relies on two unrealistic assumptions: (1) firms will not repurchase any stock and (2) growth in dividends will be constant. Let's examine each of these assumptions and see how to incorporate them into the forward-looking approach.

In recent years, companies in the S&P 500 have distributed roughly as much cash to shareholders in the form of stock repurchases as in dividends.[16] We define Rep/Div as the dollars used to repurchase stock divided by the dollars paid out in dividends and define Rep_1 as the expected repurchases at Year 1. In this notation, the total dollars paid out in dividends and repurchases will be $(1 + Rep/Div)(Div)$. When stocks are repurchased each year, the number of outstanding shares declines each year, so the long-term growth rate in dividends per share (DPS) no longer is equal to the growth rate in sales. Let g be the long-term growth rate in total payouts (which should be the same as the long-term growth rate in sales and earnings), and let g_{DPS} be the long-term growth in DPS. The expected market return is given by

$$r_M = \hat{r}_M = (1 + Rep/Div)\frac{D_1}{P_0} + g$$

$$= \frac{D_1}{P_0} + \frac{Rep_1}{P_0} + g$$ (10–7)

$$= \frac{D_1}{P_0} + g_{DPS}$$

where the actual growth rate in dividends per share, g_{DPS}, is the sum of the repurchase yield (Rep_1/P_0) and the long-term growth rate in sales. All three versions of Equation 10-7 are equivalent, but we usually work with the first line because it's easier to obtain the necessary inputs.

If we assume that companies will, in aggregate, distribute about as many dollars via repurchases as via cash dividends in the future as they have in the recent past, then Rep/Div ≈ 1. Using our previous estimates of the dividend yield and the long-term growth rate, the expected market return and risk premium are

$$r_M = \hat{r}_M = (1 + Rep/Div)\frac{D_1}{P_0} + g$$

$$= (1 + 1)(1.84\%) + 4.44\% = 8.12\%$$

$$RP_M = r_M - r_{RF} = 8.12\% - 3.34\% = 4.78\%$$

As these equations show, it is fairly easy to incorporate the impact of stock repurchases into our estimated market risk premium. We can also incorporate nonconstant payouts. We do this in **Web Extension 10A** and in the **Tab Web 10A** in **Ch10 Tool Kit.xls**. Allowing for nonconstant growth and stock repurchases, we estimate that the required market return is about 7.87%. This would imply a market risk premium of

$$RP_M = r_M - r_{RF} = 7.87\% - 3.34\% = 4.53\%$$

---

16. For example, see the analysis by Douglas J. Skinner, "The Evolving Relation between Earnings, Dividends, and Stock Repurchases," *Journal of Financial Economics*, Vol. 87, 2008, pp. 582–609. We discuss payout strategies in more detail in Chapter 17.

Although this is our best estimate of the market risk premium as of January 2011, the forward-looking approach has some potential problems. First, analysts (and professors!) have a hard time accurately predicting sales, earnings, and payouts for more than a few quarters into the future. Second, the accuracy (and truthfulness) of analysts who work for investment banking firms has been questioned in recent years. This suggests it might be better to use the forecasts of independent analysts, such as those who work for publications like *Value Line,* rather than those who work for the large investment banking firms who sell stocks for a living. Third, different analysts have different estimates for growth, and we don't know which estimate, if any, truly represents the views of the marginal investor.

Surveys of Experts

What do the experts think about the market risk premium? Two professors at Duke University, John Graham and Campbell Harvey (now working in conjunction with *CFO* magazine), have surveyed CFOs quarterly beginning in 2000.[17] One survey question asks CFOs what they expect the S&P 500 return to be over the next year and over the next 10 years. Their answers through the end of 2010 have implied an average expected risk premium of about 3.7% for the 10-year investment horizon, and only about 1.7% for the 1-year investment horizon.

According to recent surveys of professors, the expected market risk premium is around 5.0% to 6.5%, with most professors in 2007 and 2008 indicating that they believe the risk premium has fallen somewhat since 2000.[18]

To muddy the water a bit further, some academics have recently argued for a much lower market risk premium. Professors Eugene Fama and Kenneth French examined earnings and dividend growth rates during the period from 1951 to 2000 and estimated the forward-looking market risk premium to be 2.55%. Similarly, Professor Jay Ritter from the University of Florida argues that the forward-looking market risk premium should be based on inflation-adjusted expected returns, which would make it even lower—closer to 1%.[19]

Our View on the Market Risk Premium

After reading the previous sections, you might well be confused about the best way to estimate the market risk premium. Here's our opinion: The risk premium is driven primarily by investors' attitudes toward risk, and there are good reasons to believe that investors' risk aversion changes over time. Some factors suggest that the premium has declined. The introduction of pension plans, Social Security, health insurance, and disability insurance over the last 50 years means that people today can take more chances with their investments, which should make them less risk averse. Moreover, many households have dual incomes, which also allows

---

17. See John Graham and Campbell Harvey, "The Equity Risk Premium in 2008," Working Paper, Duke University, 2008. For updates on the survey, see **www.cfosurvey.org.**

18. See Ivo Welch, "Views of Financial Economists on The Equity Premium and Other Issues," *The Journal of Business,* October 2000, pp. 501–537, with 2009 updates at **http://welch.econ.brown. edu/academics/equpdate-results2009.html.** Also see Pablo Fernández, "Market Risk Premium Used in 2008 by Professors: A Survey with 1,400 Answers" (April 16, 2009), at SSRN: **http:// ssrn.com/abstract=1344209.**

19. See Eugene F. Fama and Kenneth R. French, "The Equity Premium," *Journal of Finance,* April 2002, pp. 637–659; and Jay Ritter, "The Biggest Mistakes We Teach," *Journal of Financial Research,* Summer 2002, pp. 159–168.

investors to take more chances. Finally, the historical average return on the market as Ibbotson measures it is probably too high for two reasons. The first is survivorship bias: The companies that fail had low returns, so excluding them raises the average historical return on stocks, which in turn raises the historical risk premium. The second reason is that increases in required returns cause decreases in observed returns, and vice versa.

On the other hand, we have recently seen a huge plunge in stock and home prices, most of us know people who have recently lost their jobs, and the pundits speak of investors exiting the stock market as a result of recent losses and fears of more losses. And some analysts who were recently extolling the virtues of "stocks for the long run" are now recommending T-bonds and other low-risk assets rather than stock.

Putting it all together, we conclude that the true risk premium in 2011 is lower than Ibbotson's long-term historical average, but it is certainly not negative as suggested by some recent data. But just how low is it? In our consulting, we currently (spring 2011) use a risk premium of about 6%, but we would have a hard time arguing with someone who used a risk premium anywhere in the range of 3.5% to 6.5%. We believe that investors' aversion to risk is relatively stable much of the time, but it is not absolutely constant from year to year and is certainly not constant during periods of great stress, such as during the 2008–2009 financial crisis. When stock prices are relatively high, investors feel less risk averse, so we would use a risk premium at the low end of our range. Conversely, when prices are depressed, we would use a premium at the high end of the range. The bottom line is that there is no way to prove that a particular risk premium is either right or wrong, though we'd be suspicious of an estimated market premium that is less than 3.0% or greater than 6.5%.[20]

10.6c Estimating Beta

Recall from Chapter 2 that beta can be estimated as the slope coefficient in a regression, with the company's stock returns on the y-axis and market returns on the x-axis. The result is called the *historical beta* because it is based on historical data. Although this approach is conceptually straightforward, complications quickly arise in practice.

First, there is no theoretical guidance as to the correct holding period for measuring returns. The returns for a company can be calculated using daily, weekly, or monthly periods, and the resulting betas will differ. Beta is also sensitive to the number of years of data that are used. With too few years, there will be few observations and the regression will not be statistically significant. On the other hand, with too many years the statistical significance may be improved but the "true" beta may have changed over the sample period. In practice, it is common to use either 3 to 5 years of monthly returns, or perhaps 1 to 2 years of weekly returns. Unfortunately, betas calculated in different ways can be different, and it is impossible to know for certain which is correct.

A second problem is that the market return should, in theory, reflect returns on every single asset—even human capital as reflected in people's earning power. In practice, however, it is common to use only an index of common stocks such as

WWW

To find an estimate of beta, go to **www.reuters .com** and then enter the ticker symbol for a stock quote. Or go to Thomson ONE—Business School Edition. Beta is shown in the Key Fundamentals section.

---

20. For more on estimating the risk premium, see Robert S. Harris and Felicia C. Marston, "Estimating Shareholder Risk Premia Using Analysts' Growth Forecasts," *Financial Management*, Summer 1992, pp. 63–70.

the S&P 500, the NYSE Composite, or the Wilshire 5000. Even though these indexes are correlated with one another, using different indexes in the regression will result in a different beta, and we would surely obtain a different beta if we broadened the index to include real estate and other assets.

Third, some organizations modify the calculated historical beta in order to produce what they deem to be a more accurate estimate of the "true" beta, where the true beta is the one that reflects the risk perceptions of the marginal investor. One modification, called an *adjusted beta,* attempts to correct a possible statistical bias by adjusting the historical beta to make it closer to the known average beta of 1.0. A second modification is to estimate a *fundamental beta,* which incorporates known information such as any changes in the company's product lines or capital structure.

Fourth, the estimate of beta for any individual company is statistically imprecise. The average company has an estimated beta of 1.0, but the 95% confidence interval ranges from about 0.6 to 1.4. For most companies, if your regression produces an estimated beta of 1.0, then in general you can only be 95% sure that the true beta lies within the range from 0.6 to 1.4. This isn't a big problem with well-diversified portfolios, but it does add another element of uncertainty when calculating the cost of equity for a single company.

The preceding discussion refers to conditions in the United States and other countries with well-developed financial markets where relatively good data are available. When we consider countries with less-developed financial markets, we are much less certain about the true size of a company's beta. Moreover, further complications arise when we are dealing with multinational companies, especially those that raise equity capital in different parts of the world. We might, for example, be relatively confident in the beta calculated for the parent company in its home country but less confident of the betas for subsidiaries located in other countries. When such complications arise, we are often forced to make "educated guesses" as to the appropriate beta. It would be nice to have exact, precise numbers for everything and thus be able to make decisions with a great deal of confidence, but that's not the way the world is—we are often forced to use judgment and to make educated guesses. Still, our discussion should help improve your judgment regarding the choice of beta for use in cost-of-capital studies, and it should also keep you from being too dogmatic about the accuracy of your beta and therefore your estimated cost of capital.

10.6d One More Caveat Regarding the CAPM Approach

We should point out one more potential problem with the CAPM: It has never been proven that investors base their required rates of return on the equation $r_M = r_{RF} + (RP_M)b_i$. Hundreds, perhaps thousands of studies have been conducted to test the validity of the CAPM, but there have been no definitive answers. The principal problem is that the CAPM itself deals only with *expectations,* yet the tests of the theory (such as the Fama-French work described in Chapter 2) have necessarily relied on historical data.

Still, we do know that security analysts and portfolio managers rely on the CAPM for much of their work, and betas are widely publicized. In addition, the CAPM's focus on diversification and systematic risk is quite logical, so it makes sense for people to use it when they make investment decisions. Therefore, it is reasonable to use the CAPM when you estimate the cost of equity, as most academics recommend and most corporate practitioners do. Just recognize that there may be other factors at work and so—even if you could estimate r_{RF}, b_i, and RP_M exactly—your estimate of r_s might still not be exact.

10.6e An Illustration of the CAPM Approach

To illustrate the CAPM approach, assume that $r_{RF} = 5\%$, $RP_M = 5.5\%$, and NCC's $b_i = 1.2$. Therefore, NCC is riskier than an average company, and its cost of equity is about 11.6%:

$$
\begin{aligned}
r_s &= 5\% + (5.5\%)(1.2) \\
    &= 5\% + 6.6\% \\
    &= 11.6\%
\end{aligned}
$$

It should be obvious by now that, although the CAPM approach appears to yield precise estimates of r_s, it is impossible to know with certainty the correct values of the required inputs to make it operational; this is because (1) it is impossible to estimate the required inputs precisely and (2) even if we knew the correct inputs, it might still turn out that the CAPM does not perfectly reflect the views of the marginal investor. Still, in our judgment, it is possible to develop "reasonable" estimates of the required variables, and we believe that investors do use the CAPM concept when making decisions and, thus, that it can be used to obtain reasonable estimates of the cost of equity capital. Indeed, despite the difficulties we have pointed out, surveys indicate that the CAPM is the dominant choice for the vast majority of companies in the United States and around the world.

Self Test

What is generally considered to be the more appropriate estimate of the risk-free rate: the yield on a short-term T-bill or the yield on a 10-year T-bond?

Explain both the historical and the forward-looking approach to estimating the market risk premium.

Describe some problems one encounters when estimating beta.

A company's beta is 1.4, the yield on a 10-year T-bond is 4%, and the market risk premium is 4.5%. What is r_s? (**10.3%**)

10.7 Dividend-Yield-Plus-Growth-Rate, or Discounted Cash Flow (DCF), Approach

In Chapter 5, we saw that if an investor expects dividends to grow at a constant rate and if the company makes all payouts in the form of dividends (the company does not repurchase stock), then the price of a stock can be found as follows:

$$
\hat{P}_0 = \frac{D_1}{r_s - g}
$$

 (10–8)

Here $\hat{P}_0$ is the intrinsic value of the stock for the investor, D_1 is the dividend expected to be paid at the end of Year 1, g is the expected growth rate in dividends, and r_s is the required rate of return. For the marginal investor, the required return is equal to the expected return. If this investor is the marginal investor then $\hat{P}_0 = P_0$, the market price of the stock, and we can solve for r_s to obtain the required rate of return on common equity:

(10–9)

$$\hat{r}_s = r_s = \frac{D_1}{P_0} + \text{Expected g}$$

Thus, investors expect to receive a dividend yield, D_1/P_0, plus a capital gain, g, for a total expected return of $\hat{r}_s$. In equilibrium this expected return is also equal to the required return, r_s. This method of estimating the cost of equity is called the **discounted cash flow, or DCF, method.** Henceforth, we will assume that markets are at equilibrium (which means that $r_s = \hat{r}_s$), and this permits us to use the terms r_s and $\hat{r}_s$ interchangeably.

10.7a Estimating Inputs for the DCF Approach

Three inputs are required to use the DCF approach: the current stock price, the current dividend, and the marginal investor's expected dividend growth rate. The stock price and the dividend are easy to obtain, but the expected growth rate is difficult to estimate, as we will see in the following sections.

Historical Growth Rates

If earnings and dividend growth rates have been relatively stable in the past, and if investors expect these trends to continue, then the past realized growth rate may be used as an estimate of the expected future growth rate. This is a reasonable proposition, but such situations occur only at a handful of very mature, slow-growing companies. Unfortunately, this limits the usefulness of historical growth rates as predictors of future growth rates for most companies.

Retention Growth Model

Most firms pay out some of their net income as dividends and reinvest, or retain, the rest. The more they retain, and the higher the earned rate of return on those retained earnings, the larger their growth rate. This is the idea behind the retention growth model.

The **payout ratio** is the percent of net income that the firm pays out in dividends, and the **retention ratio** is the complement of the payout ratio: Retention ratio = (1 − Payout ratio). NCC's payout ratio has averaged 63% over the past 15 years, so its retention rate has averaged 1.0 − 0.63 = 0.37 = 37%. Also, NCC's return on equity (ROE) has averaged 14.5% over the past 15 years. We know that, other things held constant, the earnings growth rate depends on the amount of income the firm retains and the rate of return it earns on those retained earnings, and the **retention growth equation** can be expressed as follows:

(10–10)

$$g = \text{ROE(Retention ratio)}$$

When we use this equation to estimate the DCF growth rate, we are implicitly making four important assumptions: (1) we expect the payout rate, and thus the retention rate, to remain constant; (2) we expect the ROE on new investments to remain constant and equal to the ROE on existing assets; (3) the firm is not expected to repurchase or issue new common stock, or, if it does, this new stock will be sold at a price equal to its book value; and (4) future projects are expected to have the same degree of risk as the firm's existing assets. Under these assumptions, the earnings growth rate will be constant, and it will also be the dividend growth rate.

Using NCC's 14.5% average ROE and its 37% retention rate, we can use Equation 10-10 to find the estimated g:

$$g = 14.5\%(0.37) = 5.365 \approx 5.4\%$$

Analysts' Forecasts

A third technique calls for using security analysts' forecasts. As we discussed earlier, analysts publish earnings' growth rate estimates for most of the larger publicly owned companies. For example, *Value Line* provides such forecasts on about 1,700 companies, and all of the larger brokerage houses provide similar forecasts. Further, several companies compile analysts' forecasts on a regular basis and provide summary information such as the median and range of forecasts on widely followed companies. These growth rate summaries, such as those compiled by Zacks or by Thomson ONE—BSE, can be found on the Internet. These earnings growth rates are often used as proxies for dividend growth rates.

Note, however, that analysts' forecasts often involve nonconstant growth. For example, one widely followed analyst forecasted that NCC would have a 10.4% annual growth rate in earnings and dividends over the next 5 years, after which the growth rate would decline to 5%. Such nonconstant growth forecasts can be converted to an approximate constant growth rate. Computer simulations indicate that dividends beyond Year 50 contribute very little to the value of any stock—the present value of all dividends beyond Year 50 is virtually zero, so for practical purposes we can ignore anything beyond 50 years. If we consider only a 50-year horizon, then we can develop a weighted average growth rate and use it as a constant growth rate for cost-of-capital purposes. In the NCC case, we assume a growth rate of 10.4% for 5 years followed by a growth rate of 5% for 45 years. We weight the short-term growth by 5/50 = 10% and the long-term growth by 45/50 = 90%. This produces an average growth rate of 0.10(10.4%) + 0.90(5%) = 5.54% ≈ 5.5%.[21]

www

For example, see
www.zacks.com.

Applying the DCF Approach

To illustrate the DCF approach, suppose NCC's stock sells for $32, its next expected dividend is $1.82, and its expected growth rate is 5.5%. NCC is not expected to repurchase any stock. NCC's stock is thought to be in equilibrium, so its expected and required rates of return are equal. Based on these assumptions, its estimated DCF cost of common equity is 11.2%:

$$\hat{r}_s = r_s = \frac{\$1.82}{\$32.00} + 5.5\%$$
$$= 5.7\% + 5.5\%$$
$$= 11.2\%$$

---

21. Instead of converting nonconstant growth estimates into an approximate average growth rate, it is possible to use the nonconstant growth estimates to estimate directly the required return on common stock. See *Web Extension 10A* on the textbook's Web site for an explanation of this approach; all calculations are in the worksheet *Web 10A* in the file *Ch10 Tool Kit.xls*.

10.7b Evaluating the Methods for Estimating Growth

Observe that the DCF approach finds the cost of common equity as the dividend yield (the expected dividend divided by the current price) plus the growth rate. The dividend yield can be estimated without much error, but there is uncertainty in the growth estimate. We would like to know the expected average growth rate as forecasted by the marginal investor, but that rate simply cannot be observed. However, we have considered three methods that can be used to estimate expected future growth: (1) historical growth rates, which implicitly assume that investors expect past results to be repeated in the future; (2) the retention growth model, which implicitly assumes that investors expect historical payout ratios and ROEs to be repeated; and (3) analysts' forecasts. Of these three methods, the third is the most logical. Moreover, studies have also shown that analysts' forecasts usually predict actual future growth better than the other methods. We recommend a primary reliance on analysts' forecasts for the growth rate in DCF cost of capital estimates.[22]

Self Test

What inputs are required for the DCF method?

What are three ways to estimate the expected dividend growth rate, and which of these methods is likely to provide the best estimate?

A company's estimated growth rate in dividends is 6%, its current stock price is $40, and its expected annual dividend is $2. Using the DCF approach, what is the firm's r_s? (**11%**)

10.8 Own-Bond-Yield-Plus-Judgmental-Risk-Premium Approach

Some analysts use a subjective, ad hoc procedure to estimate a firm's cost of common equity: They simply add a judgmental risk premium of 3% to 5% to the interest rate on the firm's own long-term debt. It is logical to think that firms with risky, low-rated, and hence high–interest rate debt will also have risky, high-cost equity, and the procedure for basing the cost of equity on a readily observable debt cost utilizes this logic. In this approach,

(10–11)
$$r_s = \text{Company's own bond yield} + \text{Judgmental risk premium}$$

NCC's bonds yield 9.0%, so if its judgmental risk premium is estimated as 3% then its estimated cost of equity is 12%:

$$r_s = 9\% + 3\% = 12\%$$

---

22. See Robert Harris, "Using Analysts' Growth Rate Forecasts to Estimate Shareholder Required Rates of Return," *Financial Management,* Spring 1986, pp. 58–67.

Because the risk premium is a judgmental estimate, the estimated value of r_s is also judgmental. Similarly, though, a lot of judgment goes into the CAPM and DCF estimates of r_s. Empirical work suggests that the risk premium over a firm's own bond yield generally has ranged from 3 to 5 percentage points.[23] Therefore, this method is not likely to produce a precise cost of equity, but it can help "get us into the ballpark."

Explain the reasoning behind the bond-yield-plus-judgmental-risk-premium approach.

A company's bond yield is 7%. If the appropriate own-bond-yield risk premium is 3.5%, then what is r_s? (**10.5%**)

10.9 Comparison of the CAPM, DCF, and Own-Bond-Yield-Plus-Judgmental-Risk-Premium Methods

We have discussed three methods for estimating the cost of common stock. For NCC, the CAPM estimate is 11.6%, the DCF constant growth estimate is 11.2%, and the own-bond-yield-plus-judgmental-risk-premium estimate is 12%. The overall average of these three methods is (11.6% + 11.2% + 12%)/3 = 11.6%. These results are unusually close, so it would make little difference which one we used. However, if the methods produced widely varied estimates, then a financial analyst would have to use his or her own best judgment regarding the relative merits of each estimate and then choose one that seemed reasonable under the circumstances.

Recent surveys indicate that the CAPM is by far the most widely used method. Although most firms use more than one method, almost 74% of respondents in one survey (and 85% in another) used the CAPM.[24] This is in sharp contrast to a 1982 survey, which found that only 30% of respondents used the CAPM.[25] Only 16% now use the DCF approach, down from 31% in 1982. The bond-yield-plus-judgmental-risk-premium is relied upon primarily by companies that are not publicly traded.

People experienced in estimating the cost of equity recognize that both careful analysis and sound judgment are required. It would be nice to pretend that judgment

23. Analysts have surveyed portfolio managers, asking how much more they would have to expect to earn on a firm's stock versus its bonds to induce them to buy the stock. The range we have seen is 3% to 5%, which is what we use. Discussions with financial executives indicate that most are comfortable with this range. All this is purely judgmental, but that's the case for much of finance.

24. See John R. Graham and Campbell Harvey, "The Theory and Practice of Corporate Finance: Evidence from the Field," *Journal of Financial Economics,* 2001, pp. 187–243, and the paper cited in footnote 10. It is interesting that a growing number of firms (about 34%) also are using CAPM-type models with more than one factor. Of these firms, over 40% include factors for interest rate risk, foreign exchange risk, and business cycle risk (proxied by gross domestic product). More than 20% of these firms include a factor for inflation, size, and exposure to particular commodity prices. Less than 20% of these firms make adjustments due to distress factors, book-to-market ratios, or momentum factors.

25. See Lawrence J. Gitman and Vincent Mercurio, "Cost of Capital Techniques Used by Major U.S. Firms: Survey Analysis of *Fortune's* 1000," *Financial Management,* 1982, pp. 21–29.

is unnecessary and to specify an easy, precise way of determining the exact cost of equity capital. Unfortunately, this is not possible—finance is in large part a matter of judgment, and we simply must face that fact.[26]

Self Test

Which approach for estimating the required return on common stock is used most often by businesses today?

10.10 Adjusting the Cost of Equity for Flotation Costs

As explained earlier, most mature companies rely primarily on reinvesting a large portion of their earnings and hence rarely issue new common stock. However, for those that do, the **cost of new common equity, r_e,** or external equity, is higher than the cost of equity raised internally by reinvesting earnings, r_s, because of the **flotation costs** involved in issuing new common stock. What rate of return must be earned on new investments to make issuing stock worthwhile? Put another way, what is the cost of new common stock?

The answer, for a constant growth firm, is found by applying this formula:

(10–12)

$$r_e = \hat{r}_e = \frac{D_1}{P_0(1 - F)} + g$$

In Equation 10-12, F is the percentage flotation cost incurred in selling the new stock, so here $P_0(1 - F)$ is the net price per share received by the company.

Using the same inputs as when we estimated NCC's cost of common equity using the DCF approach—but assuming that NCC incurs a flotation cost of 12.5% to sell new common stock—its cost of new outside equity is calculated as follows:

$$r_e = \frac{\$1.82}{\$32(1 - 0.125)} + 5.5\%$$

$$= 6.5\% + 5.5\% = 12.0\%$$

As we calculated earlier using the DCF model (but ignoring flotation costs), NCC's stockholders require a return of $r_s = 11.2\%$. However, because of flotation costs the company must earn *more* than 11.2% on the net funds it has to invest if investors are to receive an 11.2% return on the money they actually contributed. Specifically,

---

26. One senior executive told us that, in his judgment, the CAPM's popularity was partly the result of lower-level staffers wanting to use methods that can be defended by reference to the finance literature and to "hard" numbers based on published data, like historical betas and risk premiums. His conclusion was that the CAPM's use with historical data is widely discussed in the finance literature and taught in MBA programs, so the result is sort of a self-fulfilling prophecy. He went on to say that in his opinion a great deal of judgment is required; in his company, lower-level staffers derived relatively precise results and then experienced, senior managers applied judgment when making decisions based on those results. He thought this procedure worked out well for his company.

if the firm earns 12.0% on net funds obtained by issuing new stock, then earnings per share will remain at the previously expected level, the firm's expected dividend can be maintained, and so the price per share will not decline. If it earns less than 12.0% then earnings, dividends, and growth will fall below expectations, which will cause a decline in the stock price. If it earns more than 12.0%, the stock price will rise.

As we noted previously, most analysts use the CAPM to estimate the cost of equity. In an earlier section, we estimated NCC's CAPM cost of equity as 11.6%. How would the analyst incorporate flotation costs into a CAPM cost estimate? If application of the DCF methodology gives a cost of internally generated equity of 11.2% but a cost of 12.0% when flotation costs are involved, then the flotation costs add 0.8 percentage points to the cost of equity. To incorporate flotation costs into the CAPM estimate, we would simply add 0.8% to the 11.6% CAPM estimate, resulting in a 12.4% estimated cost of external equity. As an alternative, you could find the average of the CAPM, DCF, and own-bond-yield-plus-judgmental-risk-premium costs of equity (ignoring flotation costs) and then add to it the 0.8 percentage points to adjust for flotation costs.

Table 10-1 shows the average flotation costs for debt and equity issued by U.S. corporations in the 1990s. The common stock flotation costs are for non-IPO issues. For IPOs, flotation costs are higher: about 17% higher if less than $10 million is raised and higher still as issue size increases. The data in Table 10-1 include both utility and nonutility companies; if utilities had been excluded, the reported flotation costs would have been higher. Table 10-1 shows that flotation costs are significantly higher for equity than for debt. Notice that all flotation costs, as a *percentage* of capital raised, fall as the *amount* of capital raised increases.

The lower cost for issuing debt results from two factors. First, debt is a contractual obligation; hence returns are more predictable, which makes selling debt easier. Second, corporate debt is sold mainly in large blocks to institutional investors, whereas common stock is sold in smaller amounts to many different investors; this

TABLE 10-1	Average Flotation Costs for Debt and Equity	
Amount of Capital Raised (Millions of Dollars)	Average Flotation Cost for Common Stock (% of Total Capital Raised)	Average Flotation Cost for New Debt (% of Total Capital Raised)
2–9.99	13.28%	4.39%
10–19.99	8.72	2.76
20–39.99	6.93	2.42
40–59.99	5.87	2.32
60–79.99	5.18	2.34
80–99.99	4.73	2.16
100–199.99	4.22	2.31
200–499.99	3.47	2.19
500 and up	3.15	1.64

Source: Inmoo Lee, Scott Lochhead, Jay Ritter, and Quanshui Zhao, "The Costs of Raising Capital," *The Journal of Financial Research,* Spring 1996, pp. 59–74. Reprinted with permission.

imposes higher costs on the investment banks, who pass these costs on to the issuing company.

Self Test

What are flotation costs?

Why are flotation costs higher for stock than for debt?

A firm has common stock with $D_1 = \$3.00$; $P_0 = \$30$; $g = 5\%$; and $F = 4\%$. If the firm must issue new stock, what is its cost of external equity, r_e? (**15.42%**)

10.11 Composite, or Weighted Average, Cost of Capital, WACC

As we saw earlier in this chapter (and as we discuss in more detail in Chapter 15), each firm has an optimal capital structure, which is defined as the mix of debt, preferred, and common equity that maximizes its stock price. Therefore, a value-maximizing firm must attempt to find its *target (or optimal) capital structure* and then raise new capital in a manner that will keep the actual capital structure on target over time. In this chapter, we assume that the firm has identified its optimal capital structure, that it uses this optimum as the target, and that it finances so as to remain constantly on target. How the target is established is examined in Chapter 15. The target proportions of debt, preferred stock, and common equity, along with the component costs of capital, are used to calculate the WACC, as shown previously in Equation 10-1:

(10–1)	$$\text{WACC} = w_d r_d (1 - T) + w_{ps} r_{ps} + w_s r_s$$

Here w_d, w_{ps}, and w_s are the target weights for debt, preferred, and common equity, respectively.[27]

To illustrate, we first note that NCC has a target capital structure calling for 30% debt, 10% preferred stock, and 60% common equity. Its before-tax cost of debt, r_d, is 9%; its cost of preferred stock, r_{ps}, is 8.2%; its cost of common equity, r_s, is 11.6%; its marginal tax rate is 40%; and all of its new equity will come from reinvested earnings. We can now calculate NCC's weighted average cost of capital as follows:

$$\text{WACC} = 0.3(9.0\%)(1 - 0.4) + 0.1(8.2\%) + 0.6(11.6\%)$$
$$= 9.4\%$$

Three points should be noted. First, the WACC is the cost the company would incur to raise each new, or *marginal,* dollar of capital—it is not the average cost of dollars raised in the past. Second, the percentages of each capital component, called *weights,*

---

27. If a company also used short-term debt as a permanent source of financing, then its cost of capital would be:

(10–1a)	$$\text{WACC} = w_d r_d (1 - T) + w_{STD} r_{STD} (1 - T) + w_{ps} r_{ps} + w_s r_s$$

where w_{STD} is the percentage of the firm that is financed with short-term debt and r_{STD} is the cost of short-term debt.

should be based on management's target capital structure, not on the particular sources of financing in any single year. Third, the target weights should be based on market values and not on book values. We discuss these points in what follows.

10.11a Marginal Rates versus Historical Rates

The required rates of return for a company's investors, whether they are new or old, are always marginal rates. For example, a stockholder might have invested in a company last year when the risk-free interest rate was 6% and the required return on equity was 12%. If the risk-free rate subsequently falls and is now 4%, then the investor's required return on equity is now 10% (holding all else constant). This is the same required rate of return that a new equity holder would have, whether the new investor bought stock in the secondary market or through a new equity offering. In other words, whether the shareholders are already equity holders or are brand-new equity holders, they all have the same required rate of return, which is the current required rate of return on equity. The same reasoning applies for the firm's bondholders. All bondholders, whether old or new, have a required rate of return equal to today's yield on the firm's debt, which is based on current market conditions.

Because investors' required rates of return are based on *current* market conditions, not on market conditions when they purchased their securities, it follows that the cost of capital depends on current conditions and not on past market conditions.

10.11b Target Weights versus Annual Financing Choices

We have heard managers (and students!) say, "Our debt has a 5% after-tax cost versus a 10% WACC and a 14% cost of equity. Therefore, since we will finance only with debt this year, we should evaluate this year's projects at a 5% cost." There are two flaws in this line of reasoning.

First, suppose the firm exhausts its capacity to issue low-cost debt this year to take on projects with after-tax returns as low as 5.1% (which is slightly higher than the after-tax cost of debt). Then next year, when the firm must finance with common equity, it will have to turn down projects with returns as high as 13.9% (which is slightly lower than the cost of equity). To avoid this problem, a firm that plans to remain in business indefinitely should evaluate all projects using the 10% WACC.

Second, both existing and new investors have claims on *all* future cash flows. For example, if a company raises debt and also invests in a new project that same year, the new debtholders don't have a specific claim on that specific project's cash flows (assuming it is not non-recourse project financing). In fact, new debtholders receive a claim on the cash flows being generated by existing as well as new projects, while old debtholders (and equity holders) have claims on both new and existing projects. Thus, the decision to take on a new project should depend on the project's ability to satisfy all of the company's investors, not just the new debtholders, even if only debt is being raised that year.

10.11c Weights for Component Costs: Book Values versus Market Values versus Targets

Our primary reason for calculating the WACC is to use it in capital budgeting or corporate valuation, since we need to compare the expected returns on projects and companies with the cost of the funds used to finance them. As Figure 10-1 showed, accountants report financial statements in book value terms, but financial analysts can convert those numbers into market values.

At one time academics—and, to a lesser extent, financial executives—debated whether we should use book value versus market value weights when estimating the cost of capital. The main arguments in favor of book weights were (1) these are the numbers shown on financial statements, (2) the bond rating agencies seem to focus on book weights, and (3) book values are more stable than market values, so book value weights produce more stable inputs for use in capital budgeting. The main arguments in favor of market value weights were (1) firms raise funds by selling securities at their market values, not at book values, and (2) market values are more consistent with the idea of value maximization.

Market value supporters won the argument, as they should have, but in a dynamic world it is simply not feasible to blindly and mechanically focus on current market value weights (i.e., on the market value weights given in Column J of Figure 10-1). As a result of the stock market crash of 2008–2009, many firms saw their equity ratios drop from about 75% to near 10%, and managers concluded that neither the book value nor market value numbers represented how they wanted to finance in the future. Thus, they didn't want to use either book value or market value weights.

What they did, as we discuss in Chapter 15, was focus on a less mechanical, more judgmental capital structure—the **target capital structure**. At the target structure, the firm uses enough debt to gain the benefits of interest tax shields and also leverages up earnings per share. However, the amount of debt is not so great that it subjects the firm to a high probability of financial distress during a period of economic recession. Managements have some flexibility in setting their target capital structures, but they are also subject to constraints and market forces. Firms compare their data with those of benchmark firms in their industry; this allows firms to see how they are doing relative to other firms in their industry. If a company uses too little debt then its earnings will be lower than they could have been without subjecting the firm to undue risk, and individual stockholders, private equity firms, or hedge firms will probably challenge management and force it toward the optimal structure. If a

GLOBAL VARIATIONS IN THE COST OF CAPITAL

For U.S. firms to be competitive with foreign companies, they must have a cost of capital no greater than that faced by their international competitors. In the past, many experts argued that U.S. firms were at a disadvantage. In particular, Japanese firms enjoyed a very low cost of capital, which lowered their total costs and thus made it hard for U.S. firms to compete with them. Recent events, however, have considerably narrowed cost-of-capital differences between U.S. and Japanese firms. In particular, the U.S. stock market has outperformed the Japanese market in recent years, which has made it easier and cheaper for U.S. firms to raise equity capital.

As capital markets become increasingly integrated, cross-country differences in the cost of capital are declining. Today, most large corporations raise capital throughout the world; hence, we are moving toward one global capital market instead of distinct capital markets in each country. Government policies and market conditions can affect the cost of capital within a given country, but this primarily affects smaller firms that do not have access to global capital markets, and even these differences are becoming less important as time passes. What matters most is the risk of the individual firm, not the market in which it raises capital.

company uses too much debt, then lenders will raise interest rates or perhaps refuse to lend at all, rating agencies and analysts will report on its risky situation, the intrinsic value of the firm's stock will decline, and its market value will suffer. Thus, forces exist to compel firms to set their target capital structures at levels that will maximize their intrinsic values and thus their stock prices.

Finally, note that an optimal capital structure in one economic environment may not be optimal under different market conditions. In a dynamic economy it is important to constantly monitor the situation and make adjustments to the target capital structure as circumstances change.

Self Test

How is the weighted average cost of capital calculated? Write out the equation.

Should the weights used to calculate the WACC be based on book values, market values, or something else? Explain.

A firm has the following data: target capital structure of 25% debt, 10% preferred stock, and 65% common equity; tax rate = 40%; r_d = 7%; r_{ps} = 7.5%; and r_s = 11.5%. Assume the firm will not issue new stock. What is this firm's WACC? **(9.28%)**

10.12 Factors That Affect the WACC

The cost of capital is affected by some factors that are under a firm's control and some that are not.

10.12a Three Factors the Firm Cannot Control

Three key determinants of WACC are beyond a firm's control: (1) the state of the financial markets, including stock prices in general and the level of interest rates; (2) investors' aversion to risk and thus the market risk premium; and (3) tax rates as set by Congress.

Stock and Bond Markets

The stock and bond markets, and the market for short-term debt, are normally in equilibrium and thus fairly stable. However, at times the markets are disrupted, making it virtually impossible for a firm to raise capital at reasonable rates. This happened in 2008 and 2009, before the U.S. Treasury and the Federal Reserve intervened to open up the capital markets. During such times, firms tend to cut back on growth plans; if they must raise capital, its cost can be extraordinarily high. For example, see the box "GE and Warren Buffett: The Cost of Preferred Stock" presented earlier in the chapter.

Note also that if interest rates in the economy rise, the costs of both debt and equity will increase. The firm will have to pay bondholders a higher interest rate to obtain debt capital; and, as indicated in our discussion of the CAPM, higher interest rates also increase the cost of equity. Interest rates are heavily influenced by inflation. When inflation hit historic highs in the early 1980s, interest rates followed, but they trended mostly down for 25 years through the recession accompanying the 2008 financial crisis. Strong actions by the federal government in the spring of 2009 brought rates even lower, which contributed to the official ending of the recession in June 2009. These actions encouraged investment, and there is little doubt that they will eventually lead to stronger growth. However, many observers fear that the government's actions will also reignite long-run inflation, which would lead to higher interest rates.[28]

Market Risk Premium

Investors' aversion to risk determines the market risk premium. Individual firms have no control over the RP_M, which affects the cost of equity and thus the WACC.

Tax Rates

Tax rates, which are influenced by the president and set by Congress, have an important effect on the cost of capital. They are used when we calculate the after-tax cost of debt for use in the WACC. In addition, the lower tax rate on dividends and capital gains than on interest income favors financing with stock rather than bonds, as we discuss in detail in Chapter 15.

10.12b Three Factors the Firm Can Control

A firm can affect its cost of capital through (1) its capital structure policy, (2) its dividend policy, and (3) its investment (capital budgeting) policy.

Capital Structure Policy

In this chapter, we assume that the firm has a given target capital structure, and we use weights based on that target to calculate its WACC. However, a firm can change its capital structure, and such a change can affect its cost of capital. For example, the after-tax cost of debt is lower than the cost of equity, so if the firm decides to use more debt and less common equity, then this increase in debt will tend to lower the WACC. However, an increased use of debt will increase the risk of debt and the equity, offsetting to some extent the effect due to a greater weighting of debt. In Chapter 15 we discuss this in more depth, and we demonstrate that the optimal capital structure is the one that minimizes the WACC and simultaneously maximizes the intrinsic value of the stock.

Dividend Policy

As we will see in Chapter 17, the percentage of earnings paid out in dividends may affect a stock's required rate of return, r_s. Also, if the payout ratio is so high that the firm must issue new stock to fund its capital budget, then the resulting flotation costs will also affect the WACC.

Investment Policy

When we estimate the cost of capital, we use as the starting point the required rates of return on the firm's outstanding stock and bonds, which reflect the risks inherent in the

---

28. Other things held constant, if the government doubles the money supply then there would be twice as many dollars chasing the same amount of goods, and this would eventually lead to inflation. So one cost of the stimulus program may be higher inflation.

existing assets. Therefore, we are implicitly assuming that new capital will be invested in assets with the same degree of risk as existing assets. This assumption is generally correct, because most firms do invest in assets similar to those they currently use. However, the equal risk assumption is incorrect if a firm dramatically changes its investment policy. For example, if a company invests in an entirely new line of business, then its marginal cost of capital should reflect the risk of that new business. With hindsight we can therefore see that GE's huge investments in the TV and movie businesses, as well as its investment in mortgages, increased its risk and thus its cost of capital.

Name some factors that are generally beyond the firm's control but still affect its cost of capital.

What three policies that are under the firm's control affect its cost of capital?

Explain how a change in interest rates in the economy would be expected to affect each component of the weighted average cost of capital.

10.13 Adjusting the Cost of Capital for Risk

As we have calculated it, the weighted average cost of capital reflects the average risk and overall capital structure of the entire firm. No adjustments are needed when using the WACC as the discount rate when estimating the value of a company by discounting its cash flows. However, adjustments for risk are often needed when evaluating a division or project. For example, what if a firm has divisions in several business lines that differ in risk? Or what if a company is considering a project that is much riskier than its typical project? It is not logical to use the overall cost of capital to discount divisional or project-specific cash flows that don't have the same risk as the company's average cash flows. The following sections explain how to adjust the cost of capital for divisions and for specific projects.

10.13a Divisional Costs of Capital

Consider Starlight Sandwich Shops, a company with two divisions—a bakery operation and a chain of cafes. The bakery division is low-risk and has a 10% WACC. The cafe division is riskier and has a 14% WACC. Each division is approximately the same size, so Starlight's overall cost of capital is 12%. The bakery manager has a project with an 11% expected rate of return, and the cafe division manager has a project with a 13% expected return. Should these projects be accepted or rejected? Starlight will create value if it accepts the bakery's project, since its rate of return is greater than its cost of capital (11% > 10%), but the cafe project's rate of return is less than its cost of capital (13% < 14%), so it should reject that project. However, if management simply compared the two projects' returns with Starlight's 12% overall cost of capital, then the bakery's value-adding project would be rejected while the cafe's value-destroying project would be accepted.

Many firms use the CAPM to estimate the cost of capital for specific divisions. To begin, recall that the Security Market Line (SML) equation expresses the risk–return relationship as follows:

$$r_s = r_{RF} + (RP_M)b_i$$

As an example, consider the case of Huron Steel Company, an integrated steel producer operating in the Great Lakes region. For simplicity, assume that Huron has only one division and uses only equity capital, so its cost of equity is also its corporate cost of capital, or WACC. Huron's beta = b = 1.1, r_{RF} = 5%, and RP_M = 6%. Thus, Huron's cost of equity (and WACC) is 11.6%:

$$r_s = 5\% + (6\%)1.1 = 11.6\%$$

This suggests that investors should be willing to give Huron money to invest in new, average-risk projects if the company expects to earn 11.6% or more on this money. By "average risk" we mean projects having risk similar to the firm's existing division.

Now suppose Huron creates a new transportation division consisting of a fleet of barges to haul iron ore, and suppose barge operations typically have betas of 1.5 rather than 1.1. The barge division, with b = 1.5, has a 14.0% cost of capital:

$$r_{Barge} = 5\% + (6\%)1.5 = 14.0\%$$

On the other hand, if Huron adds a low-risk division, such as a new distribution center with a beta of only 0.5, then that division's cost of capital would be 8%:

$$r_{Center} = 5\% + (6\%)0.5 = 8.0\%$$

A firm itself may be regarded as a "portfolio of assets," and since the beta of a portfolio is a weighted average of the betas of its individual assets, adding the barge and distribution center divisions will change Huron's overall beta. The exact value of the new corporate beta would depend on the size of the investments in the new divisions relative to Huron's original steel operations. If 70% of Huron's total value ends up in the steel division, 20% in the barge division, and 10% in the distribution center, then its new corporate beta would be calculated as follows:

$$\text{New beta} = 0.7(1.1) + 0.2(1.5) + 0.1(0.5) = 1.12$$

Thus, investors in Huron's stock would require a return of

$$r_{Huron} = 5\% + (6\%)1.12 = 11.72\%$$

Even though investors require an overall return of 11.72%, they should expect a rate of return on projects in each division at least as high as the division's required return based on the SML. In particular, they should expect a return of at least 11.6% from the steel division, 14.0% from the barge division, and 8.0% from the distribution center.

Obviously, our example suggests a level of precision that is much higher than firms can obtain in the real world. Still, managers should be aware of the logic of our example, and they should strive to measure the required inputs as well as possible.

10.13b Techniques for Measuring Divisional Betas

In Chapter 2 we discussed the estimation of betas for stocks and indicated how difficult it is to measure beta precisely. Estimating divisional betas is much more difficult, primarily because divisions do not have their own publicly traded stock.[29] Therefore, we must estimate the beta that the division would have if it were an independent, publicly traded company. Two approaches can be used to estimate divisional betas: the pure play method and the accounting beta method.

The Pure Play Method

In the **pure play method,** the company tries to find the betas of several publicly held specialized companies in the same line of business as the division being evaluated, and it then averages those betas to determine the cost of capital for its own division. For example, suppose Huron found three companies devoted exclusively to operating barges, and suppose that Huron's management believes its barge division would be subject to the same risks as those firms. Then Huron could use the average beta of those firms as a proxy for its barge division's beta.[30]

The Accounting Beta Method

As noted above, it may be impossible to find specialized publicly traded firms suitable for the pure play approach. If that is the case, we may be able to use the **accounting beta method.** Betas are normally found by regressing the returns of a particular company's *stock* against returns on a *stock market index.* However, we could run a regression of the division's *accounting return on assets* against the *average return on assets* for a large sample of companies, such as those included in the S&P 500. Betas determined in this way (that is, by using accounting data rather than stock market data) are called **accounting betas.**

10.13c Estimating the Cost of Capital for Individual Projects

In Chapter 13 we examine ways to estimate the risk inherent in individual projects, but at this point it is useful to consider how project risk is reflected in measures of the firm's cost of capital. First, although it is intuitively clear that riskier projects have a higher cost of capital, it is difficult to measure projects' relative risks. Also, note that three separate and distinct types of risk can be identified as follows.

1. **Stand-alone risk,** which is the variability of the project's expected returns.
2. **Corporate,** or **within-firm, risk,** which is the variability the project contributes to the corporation's returns, giving consideration to the fact that the project represents only one asset of the firm's portfolio of assets and so some of its risk will be diversified away.
3. **Market,** or **beta, risk,** which is the risk of the project as seen by a well-diversified stockholder who owns many different stocks. A project's market risk is measured by its effect on the firm's overall beta coefficient.

---

29. This same problem applies to privately held companies, which we discuss in Section 10.14.
30. If the pure play firms employ different capital structures than that of Huron, then this must be addressed by adjusting the beta coefficients. See Chapter 15 for a discussion of this aspect of the pure play method. For a technique that can be used when pure play firms are not available, see Yatin Bhagwat and Michael Ehrhardt, "A Full Information Approach for Estimating Divisional Betas," *Financial Management,* Summer 1991, pp. 60–69.

Taking on a project with a high degree of either stand-alone or corporate risk will not necessarily increase the corporate beta. However, if the project has highly uncertain returns and if those returns are highly correlated with returns on the firm's other assets and with most other assets in the economy, then the project will have a high degree of all types of risk. For example, consider General Motors's decision to undertake a major expansion to build electric autos. GM is not sure how its technology will work on a mass production basis, so there is much risk in the venture—its stand-alone risk is high. Management also estimates that the project will do best if the economy is strong, for then people will have more money to spend on automobiles. This means that the project will tend to do well if GM's other divisions are doing well but will do poorly if other divisions are doing poorly. This being the case, the project will also have a high degree of corporate risk. Finally, since GM's profits are highly correlated with those of most other firms, the project's beta will also be high. Thus, this project will be risky under all three definitions of risk.

Of the three measures, market risk is theoretically the most relevant because of its direct effect on stock prices. Unfortunately, the market risk for a project is also the most difficult to estimate. In practice, most decision makers consider all three risk measures in a subjective manner.

The first step is to determine the divisional cost of capital before grouping divisional projects into subjective risk categories. Then, using the divisional WACC as a starting point, **risk-adjusted costs of capital** are developed for each category. For example, a firm might establish three risk classes—high, average, and low—and then assign average-risk projects the divisional cost of capital, higher-risk projects an above-average cost, and lower-risk projects a below-average cost. Thus, if a division's WACC were 10%, its managers might use 10% to evaluate average-risk projects in the division, 12% for high-risk projects, and 8% for low-risk projects. Although this approach is better than ignoring project risk, these adjustments are necessarily subjective and somewhat arbitrary. Unfortunately, given the data, there is no completely satisfactory way to specify exactly how much higher or lower we should go in setting risk-adjusted costs of capital.

Self Test

Based on the CAPM, how would one adjust the corporation's overall cost of capital to establish the required return for most projects in a low-risk division and in a high-risk division?

Describe the pure play and the accounting beta methods for estimating divisional betas.

What are the three types of risk to which projects are exposed? Which type of risk is theoretically the most relevant? Why?

Describe a procedure firms can use to establish costs of capital for projects with differing degrees of risk.

10.14 Privately Owned Firms and Small Businesses

Up until now, our discussion of the cost of common equity has been focused on publicly owned corporations. When we estimated the rate of return required by public stockholders, we used stock prices as input data for the DCF method and used stock returns to estimate beta as an input for the CAPM approach. But how can one measure the cost of equity for a firm whose stock is not traded? Most analysts begin by identifying one or more publicly traded firms that are in the same industry and that are approximately the same size as the privately owned firm.[31] The analyst then estimates the betas for these publicly traded firms and uses their average beta as an estimate of the beta of the privately owned firm. This is similar to the pure play method discussed earlier for estimating divisional betas. With an estimate of beta, the cost of equity can be estimated using the CAPM approach.

The stock of a privately held firm is less liquid than that of a publicly held firm. Just as investors demand a liquidity premium on thinly traded bonds, they also add a liquidity premium to obtain the required return on a privately held firm's stock.[32] Many analysts make an ad hoc adjustment to reflect this lack of liquidity by adding 1 to 3 percentage points to the firm's cost of equity. This "rule of thumb" is not theoretically satisfying because we don't know exactly how large the liquidity premium should be, but it is logical and is also a common practice.[33]

In addition to the difficulty of estimating the cost of equity for small and privately held firms, there are also problems in estimating their proper capital structure weights. These weights should take account of the firm's market value weights. However, a privately held firm can't directly observe its market value, so it can't directly observe its market value weights. To resolve this problem, many analysts begin by making a trial guess as to the value of the firm's equity. The analysts then use this estimated value of equity to estimate the cost of capital, next use the cost of capital to estimate the value of the firm, and finally complete the circle by using the estimated value of the firm to estimate the value of its equity.[34] If this newly estimated equity value is different from their trial guess, analysts repeat the process but start the iteration with the newly estimated equity value as the trial value of equity. After several iterations, the trial value of equity and the resulting estimated equity value usually converge. Although somewhat tedious, this process provides consistent estimates of the weights and the cost of capital.

> **Self Test**
>
> Identify some problems that occur when estimating the cost of capital for a privately held firm. What are some solutions to these problems?

10.15 Four Mistakes to Avoid

We often see managers and students make the following mistakes when estimating the cost of capital. Although we have discussed these errors previously at separate places in the chapter, they are worth repeating here.

1. *Never base the cost of debt on the coupon rate on a firm's existing debt.* The cost of debt must be based on the interest rate the firm would pay if it issued new debt today.

---

31. In Chapter 15, we show how to adjust for differences in capital structures.
32. See Yakov Amihud and Haim Mendelson, "Liquidity and Cost of Capital: Implications for Corporate Management," *Journal of Applied Corporate Finance,* Fall 1989, pp. 65–73.
33. In fact, some analysts make a similar liquidity adjustment for any small firm's cost of common equity even if the firm is publicly traded. Ibbotson Association's data, discussed earlier in the chapter in connection with historical risk premiums, support this position: The smaller the firm, the larger the historical risk premiums.
34. See Chapter 11 for more discussion on estimating the value of a firm.

WWW

To find the current S&P 500 Market-to-Book ratio, go to **www.reuters.com**, get the stock quote for any company, and select "Ratios." Then look for the Price-to-Book ratio.

2. *When estimating the market risk premium for the CAPM method, never use the historical average return on stocks in conjunction with the current return on T-bonds.* The historical average return on bonds should be subtracted from the past average return on stocks to calculate the *historical market risk premium.* On the other hand, it is appropriate to subtract today's yield on T-bonds from an estimate of the expected future return on stocks to obtain the *forward-looking market risk premium.* A case can be made for using either the historical or the current risk premium, but it would be wrong to take the *historical* rate of return on stocks, subtract from it the *current* rate on T-bonds, and then use the difference as the market risk premium.

3. *Never use the current book value capital structure to obtain the weights when estimating the WACC.* Your first choice should be to use the firm's target capital structure for the weights. However, if you are an outside analyst and do not know the target weights, it would probably be best to estimate weights based on the current market values of the capital components. If the company's debt is not publicly traded, then it is reasonable to use the book value of debt to estimate the weights because book and market values of debt, especially short-term debt, are usually close to one another. However, stocks' market values in recent years have generally been at least 2–3 times their book values, so using book values for equity could lead to serious errors. The bottom line: If you don't know the target weights then use the market value, not the book value, of equity when calculating the WACC.

4. *Always remember that capital components are funds that come from investors.* If it's not from an investor, then it's not a capital component. Sometimes the argument is made that accounts payable and accruals should be included in the calculation of the WACC. However, these funds are not provided by investors. Instead, they arise from operating relationships with suppliers and employees. Such funds are not included when calculating free cash flows, and they are not included when we calculate the amount of capital needed in a capital budgeting analysis. Therefore, they should not be included when we calculate the WACC.

| **Self Test** | What four mistakes are commonly made when estimating the WACC? |

Summary

This chapter discussed how the cost of capital is developed for use in capital budgeting. The key points covered are listed below.

- Much of the chapter was devoted to pointing out the problems encountered when estimating the cost of capital. Although these problems are not trivial, the state of the art in cost-of-capital estimation is really not in bad shape. The procedures outlined in this chapter can be used to obtain cost-of-capital estimates that are sufficiently accurate for practical purposes.

- The cost of capital used in capital budgeting is a **weighted average** of the types of capital the firm uses—typically debt, preferred stock, and common equity.
- The **component cost of debt** is the **after-tax cost of new debt.** It is found by multiplying the interest rate paid on new debt by $1 - T$, where T is the firm's marginal tax rate: $r_d(1 - T)$.
- Most debt is raised directly from lenders without the use of investment bankers; hence no flotation costs are incurred. However, a **debt flotation cost adjustment** should be made if large flotation costs are incurred. We reduce the bond's issue price by the flotation expenses, reduce the bond's cash flows to reflect taxes, and then solve for the after-tax yield to maturity.
- The **component cost of preferred stock** is calculated as the preferred dividend divided by the net price the firm receives after deducting flotation costs: $r_{ps} = D_{ps}/[P_{ps}(1 - F)]$. Flotation costs on preferred stock are usually fairly high, so we typically include the impact of flotation costs when estimating r_{ps}. Also note that if the preferred stock is convertible into common stock, then the true cost of the preferred stock will exceed the flotation-adjusted yield of the preferred dividend.
- The **cost of common equity, r_s,** also called the **cost of common stock**, is the rate of return required by the firm's stockholders, and it can be estimated in three ways: (1) the **CAPM**; (2) the **dividend-yield-plus-growth-rate**, or **DCF, approach**; and (3) the **own-bond-yield-plus-judgmental-risk-premium approach.**
- To use the **CAPM approach,** we (1) estimate the firm's beta, (2) multiply this beta by the market risk premium to obtain the firm's risk premium, and then (3) add the firm's risk premium to the risk-free rate to obtain its cost of common stock: $r_s = r_{RF} + (RP_M)b_i$.
- The best proxy for the **risk-free rate** is the yield on long-term T-bonds, with 10 years the maturity used most frequently.
- To use the **dividend-yield-plus-growth-rate approach,** which is also called the **discounted cash flow (DCF) approach,** add the firm's expected dividend growth rate to its expected dividend yield: $r_s = \hat{r}_s = D_1/P_0 + g$. *Web Extension 10A* shows how to estimate the DCF cost of equity if dividends are not growing at a constant rate.
- The growth rate for use in the DCF model can be based on security analysts' **published forecasts,** on **historical growth rates** of earnings and dividends, or on the **retention growth model,** $g = (1 - \text{Payout})(\text{Return on equity})$.
- The **own-bond-yield-plus-judgmental-risk-premium approach** calls for adding a subjective risk premium of 3 to 5 percentage points to the interest rate on the firm's own long-term debt: $r_s = \text{Bond yield} + \text{Judgmental risk premium}$.
- When calculating the **cost of new common stock, r_e,** the DCF approach can be used to estimate the flotation cost. For a constant growth stock, the flotation-adjusted cost can be expressed as $r_e = \hat{r}_e = D_1/[P_0(1 - F)] + g$. Note that flotation costs cause r_e to be greater than r_s. We can find the difference between r_e and r_s and then add this differential to the CAPM estimate of r_s to find the CAPM estimate of r_e.

- Each firm has a **target capital structure**, which is defined as the mix of debt, preferred stock, and common equity that minimizes its **weighted average cost of capital (WACC)**:

$$\text{WACC} = w_d r_d (1 - T) + w_{ps} r_{ps} + w_s r_s$$

- We discuss in Chapter 15 how the target weights are determined, but keep in mind that if you don't know the target weights, it's better to calculate WACC using market value than book value weights.
- **Various factors affect a firm's cost of capital.** Some are determined by the financial environment, but the firm can influence others through its financing, investment, and dividend policies.
- Many firms estimate **divisional costs of capital** that reflect each division's risk and capital structure.
- The **pure play** and **accounting beta methods** can be used to estimate betas for large projects or for divisions.
- A project's **stand-alone risk** is the risk the project would have if it were the firm's only asset and if stockholders held only that one stock. Stand-alone risk is measured by the variability of the asset's expected returns.
- **Corporate**, or **within-firm, risk** reflects the effect of a project on the firm's risk, and it is measured by the project's effect on the firm's earnings variability.
- **Market**, or **beta, risk** reflects the effects of a project on stockholders' risk, assuming they hold diversified portfolios. Market risk is measured by the project's effect on the firm's beta coefficient.
- Most decision makers consider all three risk measures in a subjective manner and then classify projects into risk categories. Using the firm's WACC as a starting point, risk-adjusted costs of capital are developed for each category. The **risk-adjusted cost of capital** is the cost of capital appropriate for a given project, given its risk. The greater a project's risk, the higher its cost of capital.
- Firms may be able to use the CAPM to estimate the cost of capital for specific projects or divisions. However, estimating betas for projects is difficult and subjective; hence, project risk adjustments tend to be more subjective than precisely measured.

The cost of capital as developed in this chapter is used in the next two chapters to evaluate potential capital budgeting projects, and it is used later in the text to determine the value of a corporation.

Questions

10-1 Define each of the following terms:
    a. Weighted average cost of capital, WACC; after-tax cost of debt, $r_d(1 - T)$
    b. Cost of preferred stock, r_{ps}; cost of common equity (or cost of common stock), r_s
    c. Target capital structure
    d. Flotation cost, F; cost of new external common equity, r_e

10-2 How can the WACC be both an average cost and a marginal cost?

10-3 How would each of the factors in the following table affect a firm's cost of debt, $r_d(1 - T)$; its cost of equity, r_s; and its weighted average cost of capital, WACC? Indicate by a plus (+), a minus (−), or a zero (0) if the factor would raise, lower, or have an indeterminate effect on the item in question. Assume that all other factors are held constant. Be prepared to justify your answer, but recognize that several of the parts probably have no single correct answer; these questions are designed to stimulate thought and discussion.

| | Effect on: | | |
	$r_d(1 - T)$	r_s	WACC
a. The corporate tax rate is lowered.	_____	_____	_____
b. The Federal Reserve tightens credit.	_____	_____	_____
c. The firm uses more debt.	_____	_____	_____
d. The firm doubles the amount of capital it raises during the year.	_____	_____	_____
e. The firm expands into a risky new area.	_____	_____	_____
f. Investors become more risk averse.	_____	_____	_____

10-4 Distinguish between beta (or market) risk, within-firm (or corporate) risk, and stand-alone risk for a potential project. Of the three measures, which is theoretically the most relevant, and why?

10-5 Suppose a firm estimates its overall cost of capital for the coming year to be 10%. What might be reasonable costs of capital for average-risk, high-risk, and low-risk projects?

Problems   Answers Appear in Appendix B

Easy Problems 1–8

10-1 **After-Tax Cost of Debt** Calculate the after-tax cost of debt under each of the following conditions:
   a. Interest rate of 13%, tax rate of 0%
   b. Interest rate of 13%, tax rate of 20%
   c. Interest rate of 13%, tax rate of 35%

10-2 **After-Tax Cost of Debt** LL Incorporated's currently outstanding 11% coupon bonds have a yield to maturity of 8%. LL believes it could issue new bonds at par that would provide a similar yield to maturity. If its marginal tax rate is 35%, what is LL's after-tax cost of debt?

10-3 **Cost of Preferred Stock** Duggins Veterinary Supplies can issue perpetual preferred stock at a price of $50 a share with an annual dividend of $4.50 a share. Ignoring flotation costs, what is the company's cost of preferred stock, r_{ps}?

10-4 **Cost of Preferred Stock with Flotation Costs** Burnwood Tech plans to issue some $60 par preferred stock with a 6% dividend. A similar stock is selling on the market for $70. Burnwood must pay flotation costs of 5% of the issue price. What is the cost of the preferred stock?

10-5 **Cost of Equity: DCF** Summerdahl Resort's common stock is currently trading at $36 a share. The stock is expected to pay a dividend of $3.00 a share at the end of the year ($D_1 = \$3.00$), and the dividend is expected to grow at a constant rate of 5% a year. What is its cost of common equity?

10-6 **Cost of Equity: CAPM** Booher Book Stores has a beta of 0.8. The yield on a 3-month T-bill is 4%, and the yield on a 10-year T-bond is 6%. The market risk premium is 5.5%, and the return on an average stock in the market last year was 15%. What is the estimated cost of common equity using the CAPM?

10-7 **WACC** Shi Importers's balance sheet shows $300 million in debt, $50 million in preferred stock, and $250 million in total common equity. Shi's tax rate is 40%, $r_d = 6\%$, $r_{ps} = 5.8\%$, and $r_s = 12\%$. If Shi has a target capital structure of 30% debt, 5% preferred stock, and 65% common stock, what is its WACC?

10-8 **WACC** David Ortiz Motors has a target capital structure of 40% debt and 60% equity. The yield to maturity on the company's outstanding bonds is 9%, and the company's tax rate is 40%. Ortiz's CFO has calculated the company's WACC as 9.96%. What is the company's cost of equity capital?

Intermediate Problems 9–14

10-9 **Bond Yield and After-Tax Cost of Debt** A company's 6% coupon rate, semi-annual payment, $1,000 par value bond that matures in 30 years sells at a price of $515.16. The company's federal-plus-state tax rate is 40%. What is the firm's after-tax component cost of debt for purposes of calculating the WACC? (*Hint:* Base your answer on the *nominal* rate.)

10-10 **Cost of Equity** The earnings, dividends, and stock price of Shelby Inc. are expected to grow at 7% per year in the future. Shelby's common stock sells for $23 per share, its last dividend was $2.00, and the company will pay a dividend of $2.14 at the end of the current year.
   a. Using the discounted cash flow approach, what is its cost of equity?
   b. If the firm's beta is 1.6, the risk-free rate is 9%, and the expected return on the market is 13%, then what would be the firm's cost of equity based on the CAPM approach?
   c. If the firm's bonds earn a return of 12%, then what would be your estimate of r_s using the own-bond-yield-plus-judgmental-risk-premium approach? (*Hint:* Use the midpoint of the risk premium range.)
   d. On the basis of the results of parts a through c, what would be your estimate of Shelby's cost of equity?

10-11 **Cost of Equity** Radon Homes's current EPS is $6.50. It was $4.42 5 years ago. The company pays out 40% of its earnings as dividends, and the stock sells for $36.
   a. Calculate the historical growth rate in earnings. (*Hint:* This is a 5-year growth period.)
   b. Calculate the *next* expected dividend per share, D_1. (*Hint:* $D_0 = 0.4(\$6.50) = \$2.60$.) Assume that the past growth rate will continue.
   c. What is Radon's cost of equity, r_s?

10-12 **Calculation of g and EPS** Spencer Supplies's stock is currently selling for $60 a share. The firm is expected to earn $5.40 per share this year and to pay a year-end dividend of $3.60.

    a. If investors require a 9% return, what rate of growth must be expected for Spencer?

    b. If Spencer reinvests earnings in projects with average returns equal to the stock's expected rate of return, then what will be next year's EPS? (*Hint:* g = ROE × Retention ratio.)

10-13 **The Cost of Equity and Flotation Costs** Messman Manufacturing will issue common stock to the public for $30. The expected dividend and the growth in dividends are $3.00 per share and 5%, respectively. If the flotation cost is 10% of the issue's gross proceeds, what is the cost of external equity, r_e?

10-14 **The Cost of Debt and Flotation Costs** Suppose a company will issue new 20-year debt with a par value of $1,000 and a coupon rate of 9%, paid annually. The tax rate is 40%. If the flotation cost is 2% of the issue proceeds, then what is the after-tax cost of debt? Disregard the tax shield from the amortization of flotation costs.

Challenging Problems 15–17

10-15 **WACC Estimation** On January 1, the total market value of the Tysseland Company was $60 million. During the year, the company plans to raise and invest $30 million in new projects. The firm's present market value capital structure, shown below, is considered to be optimal. There is no short-term debt.

Debt	$30,000,000
Common equity	30,000,000
Total capital	$60,000,000

New bonds will have an 8% coupon rate, and they will be sold at par. Common stock is currently selling at $30 a share. The stockholders' required rate of return is estimated to be 12%, consisting of a dividend yield of 4% and an expected constant growth rate of 8%. (The next expected dividend is $1.20, so the dividend yield is $1.20/$30 = 4%.) The marginal tax rate is 40%.

    a. In order to maintain the present capital structure, how much of the new investment must be financed by common equity?

    b. Assuming there is sufficient cash flow for Tysseland to maintain its target capital structure without issuing additional shares of equity, what is its WACC?

    c. Suppose now that there is not enough internal cash flow and the firm must issue new shares of stock. Qualitatively speaking, what will happen to the WACC? No numbers are required to answer this question.

10-16 Market Value Capital Structure Suppose the Schoof Company has this *book value* balance sheet:

Current assets	$30,000,000	Current liabilities	$10,000,000
Fixed assets	50,000,000	Long-term debt	30,000,000
		Common stock	
		(1 million shares)	1,000,000
		Retained earnings	39,000,000
Total assets	$80,000,000	Total liabilities and equity	$80,000,000

The current liabilities consist entirely of notes payable to banks, and the interest rate on this debt is 10%, the same as the rate on new bank loans. These bank loans are not used for seasonal financing but instead are part of the company's permanent capital structure. The long-term debt consists of 30,000 bonds, each with a par value of $1,000, an annual coupon interest rate of 6%, and a 20-year maturity. The going rate of interest on new long-term debt, r_d, is 10%, and this is the present yield to maturity on the bonds. The common stock sells at a price of $60 per share. Calculate the firm's *market value* capital structure.

10-17 WACC Estimation The table below gives the balance sheet for Travellers Inn Inc. (TII), a company that was formed by merging a number of regional motel chains.

Travellers Inn: December 31, 2012 (Millions of Dollars)

Cash	$ 10	Accounts payable	$ 10
Accounts receivable	20	Accruals	10
Inventories	20	Short-term debt	5
Current assets	$ 50	Current liabilities	$ 25
Net fixed assets	50	Long-term debt	30
		Preferred stock	5
		Common equity	
		Common stock	$ 10
		Retained earnings	30
		Total common equity	$ 40
Total assets	$100	Total liabilities and equity	$100

The following facts also apply to TII.

(1) Short-term debt consists of bank loans that currently cost 10%, with interest payable quarterly. These loans are used to finance receivables and inventories on a seasonal basis, so bank loans are zero in the off-season.

(2) The long-term debt consists of 20-year, semiannual payment mortgage bonds with a coupon rate of 8%. Currently, these bonds provide a yield to investors of $r_d = 12\%$. If new bonds were sold, they would have a 12% yield to maturity.

(3) TII's perpetual preferred stock has a $100 par value, pays a quarterly dividend of $2, and has a yield to investors of 11%. New perpetual preferred would have to provide the same yield to investors, and the company would incur a 5% flotation cost to sell it.

(4) The company has 4 million shares of common stock outstanding. $P_0 =$ $20, but the stock has recently traded in the price range from $17 to $23. $D_0 = 1 and $EPS_0 = 2. ROE based on average equity was 24% in 2012, but management expects to increase this return on equity to 30%; however, security analysts and investors generally are not aware of management's optimism in this regard.

(5) Betas, as reported by security analysts, range from 1.3 to 1.7; the T-bond rate is 10%; and RP_M is estimated by various brokerage houses to be in the range from 4.5% to 5.5%. Some brokerage house analysts report forecasted dividend growth rates in the range of 10% to 15% over the foreseeable future.

(6) TII's financial vice president recently polled some pension fund investment managers who hold TII's securities regarding what minimum rate of return on TII's common would make them willing to buy the common rather than TII bonds, given that the bonds yielded 12%. The responses suggested a risk premium over TII bonds of 4 to 6 percentage points.

(7) TII is in the 40% federal-plus-state tax bracket.

(8) TII's principal investment banker predicts a decline in interest rates, with r_d falling to 10% and the T-bond rate to 8%, although the bank acknowledges that an increase in the expected inflation rate could lead to an increase rather than a decrease in interest rates.

Assume that you were recently hired by TII as a financial analyst and that your boss, the treasurer, has asked you to estimate the company's WACC under the assumption that no new equity will be issued. Your cost of capital should be appropriate for use in evaluating projects that are in the same risk class as the assets TII now operates.

Spreadsheet Problem

10-18 **Build a Model: WACC** Start with the partial model in the file *Ch10 P18 Build a Model.xls* on the textbook's Web site. The stock of Gao Computing sells for $50, and last year's dividend was $2.10. A flotation cost of 10% would be required to issue new common stock. Gao's preferred stock pays a dividend of $3.30 per share, and new preferred could be sold at a price to net the company $30 per share. Security analysts are projecting that the common dividend will grow at a rate of 7% a year. The firm can issue additional long-term debt at an interest rate (or a before-tax cost) of 10%, and its marginal tax rate is 35%. The market risk premium is 6%, the risk-free rate is 6.5%, and Gao's beta is 0.83. In its cost-of-capital calculations, Gao uses a target capital structure with 45% debt, 5% preferred stock, and 50% common equity.

 a. Calculate the cost of each capital component—in other words, the after-tax cost of debt, the cost of preferred stock (including flotation costs), and the cost of equity (ignoring flotation costs). Use both the DCF method and the CAPM method to find the cost of equity.

 b. Calculate the cost of new stock using the DCF model.

 c. What is the cost of new common stock based on the CAPM? (*Hint:* Find the difference between r_e and r_s as determined by the DCF method and then add that difference to the CAPM value for r_s.)

    d. Assuming that Gao will not issue new equity and will continue to use the same target capital structure, what is the company's WACC?

    e. Suppose Gao is evaluating three projects with the following characteristics.

       (1) Each project has a cost of $1 million. They will all be financed using the target mix of long-term debt, preferred stock, and common equity. The cost of the common equity for each project should be based on the beta estimated for the project. All equity will come from reinvested earnings.

       (2) Equity invested in Project A would have a beta of 0.5 and an expected return of 9.0%.

       (3) Equity invested in Project B would have a beta of 1.0 and an expected return of 10.0%.

       (4) Equity invested in Project C would have a beta of 2.0 and an expected return of 11.0%.

    f. Analyze the company's situation and explain why each project should be accepted or rejected.

THOMSON REUTERS

Use the Thomson ONE–Business School Edition online database to work this chapter's questions.

Calculating 3M's Cost of Capital

In this chapter we described how to estimate a company's WACC, which is the weighted average of its costs of debt, preferred stock, and common equity. Most of the data we need to do this can be found in Thomson ONE. Here, we walk through the steps used to calculate Minnesota Mining & Manufacturing's (MMM) WACC.

Discussion Questions

1. As a first step, we need to estimate what percentage of MMM's capital comes from long-term debt, preferred stock, and common equity. If we click on FINANCIALS, we can see immediately from the balance sheet the amount of MMM's long-term debt and common equity (as of mid-2012, MMM had no preferred stock). Alternatively, you can click on FUNDAMENTAL RATIOS in the next row of tabs below and then select WORLDSCOPE'S BALANCE SHEET RATIOS. Here, you will also find a recent measure of long-term debt as a percentage of total capital.

    Recall that the weights used in the WACC are based on the company's target capital structure. If we assume the company wants to maintain the same mix of capital that it currently has on its balance sheet, then what weights should you use to estimate the WACC for MMM? (In Chapter 15, we will see that we might arrive at different estimates for these weights if we assume that MMM bases its target capital structure on the market values, rather than the book values, of debt and equity.)

2. Once again, we can use the CAPM to estimate MMM's cost of equity. Thomson ONE provides various estimates of beta; select the measure that you believe is

best and combine this with your estimates of the risk-free rate and the market risk premium to obtain an estimate of its cost of equity. (See the Thomson ONE exercise in Chapter 2 for more details.) What is your estimate for the cost of equity? Why might it not make much sense to use the DCF approach to estimate MMM's cost of equity?

3. Next, we need to calculate MMM's cost of debt. Unfortunately, Thomson ONE doesn't provide a direct measure of the cost of debt. However, we can use different approaches to estimate it. One approach is to take the company's long-term interest expense and divide it by the amount of long-term debt. This approach works only if the historical cost of debt equals the yield to maturity in today's market (that is, only if MMM's outstanding bonds are trading at close to par). This approach may produce misleading estimates in the years during which MMM issues a significant amount of new debt.

   For example, if a company issues a lot of debt at the end of the year, then the full amount of debt will appear on the year-end balance sheet, yet we still may not see a sharp increase in interest expense on the annual income statement because the debt was outstanding for only a small portion of the entire year. When this situation occurs, the estimated cost of debt will likely understate the true cost of debt.

   Another approach is to try to find this number in the notes to the company's annual report by accessing the company's home page and its Investor Relations section. Remember that you need the after-tax cost of debt to calculate a firm's WACC, so you will need MMM's average tax rate (which has been about 37% in recent years). What is your estimate of MMM's after-tax cost of debt?

4. Putting all this information together, what is your estimate of MMM's WACC? How confident are you in this estimate? Explain your answer.

MINI CASE

During the last few years, Harry Davis Industries has been too constrained by the high cost of capital to make many capital investments. Recently, though, capital costs have been declining, and the company has decided to look seriously at a major expansion program proposed by the marketing department. Assume that you are an assistant to Leigh Jones, the financial vice president. Your first task is to estimate Harry Davis's cost of capital. Jones has provided you with the following data, which she believes may be relevant to your task:

(1) The firm's tax rate is 40%.

(2) The current price of Harry Davis's 12% coupon, semiannual payment, noncallable bonds with 15 years remaining to maturity is $1,153.72. Harry Davis does not use short-term interest-bearing debt on a permanent basis. New bonds would be privately placed with no flotation cost.

(3) The current price of the firm's 10%, $100 par value, quarterly dividend, perpetual preferred stock is $116.95. Harry Davis would incur flotation costs equal to 5% of the proceeds on a new issue.

(4) Harry Davis's common stock is currently selling at $50 per share. Its last dividend (D_0) was $3.12, and dividends are expected to grow at a constant rate of 5.8% in the foreseeable future. Harry Davis's beta is 1.2, the yield on T-bonds is 5.6%, and the market risk premium is estimated to be 6%. For the own-bond-yield-plus-judgmental-risk-premium approach, the firm uses a 3.2% risk premium.

(5) Harry Davis's target capital structure is 30% long-term debt, 10% preferred stock, and 60% common equity.

To help you structure the task, Leigh Jones has asked you to answer the following questions.

a. (1) What sources of capital should be included when you estimate Harry Davis's weighted average cost of capital?

(2) Should the component costs be figured on a before-tax or an after-tax basis?

(3) Should the costs be historical (embedded) costs or new (marginal) costs?

b. What is the market interest rate on Harry Davis's debt, and what is the component cost of this debt for WACC purposes?

c. (1) What is the firm's cost of preferred stock?

(2) Harry Davis's preferred stock is riskier to investors than its debt, yet the preferred's yield to investors is lower than the yield to maturity on the debt. Does this suggest that you have made a mistake? (Hint: Think about taxes.)

d. (1) What are the two primary ways companies raise common equity?

(2) Why is there a cost associated with reinvested earnings?

(3) Harry Davis doesn't plan to issue new shares of common stock. Using the CAPM approach, what is Harry Davis's estimated cost of equity?

e. (1) What is the estimated cost of equity using the discounted cash flow (DCF) approach?

(2) Suppose the firm has historically earned 15% on equity (ROE) and has paid out 62% of earnings, and suppose investors expect similar values to obtain in the future. How could you use this in-formation to estimate the future dividend growth rate, and what growth rate would you get? Is this consistent with the 5.8% growth rate given earlier?

(3) Could the DCF method be applied if the growth rate were not constant? How?

f. What is the cost of equity based on the own-bond-yield-plus-judgmental-risk-premium method?

g. What is your final estimate for the cost of equity, r_s?

h. What is Harry Davis's weighted average cost of capital (WACC)?

i. What factors influence a company's WACC?

j. Should the company use the overall, or composite, WACC as the hurdle rate for each of its divisions?

k. What procedures can be used to estimate the risk-adjusted cost of capital for a particular division? What approaches are used to measure a division's beta?

l. Harry Davis is interested in establishing a new division that will focus primarily on developing new Internet-based projects. In trying to determine the cost of capital for this new division, you discover that specialized firms involved in similar projects have, on average, the following characteristics: (1) their capital structure is 10% debt and 90% common equity; (2) their cost of debt is typically 12%; and (3) they have a beta of 1.7. Given this information, what would your estimate be for the new division's cost of capital?

m. What are three types of project risk? How can each type of risk be considered when thinking about the new division's cost of capital?

n. Explain in words why new common stock that is raised externally has a higher percentage cost than equity that is raised internally by retaining earnings.

o. (1) Harry Davis estimates that if it issues new common stock, the flotation cost will be 15%. Harry Davis incorporates the flotation costs into the DCF approach. What is the estimated cost of newly issued common stock, taking into account the flotation cost?

(2) Suppose Harry Davis issues 30-year debt with a par value of $1,000 and a coupon rate of 10%, paid annually. If flotation costs are 2%, what is the after-tax cost of debt for the new bond issue?

p. What four common mistakes in estimating the WACC should Harry Davis avoid?

Selected Additional Cases

The following cases from TextChoice, *Cengage Learning's online case library, cover many of the concepts discussed in this chapter and are available at* **www.textchoice2.com/casenet.**

Klein-Brigham Series:

Case 6, "Randolph Corporation"; Case 42, "West Coast Semiconductor"; Case 54, "Ace Repair"; Case 55, "Premier Paint & Body"; Case 75, "The Western Company"; and Case 81, "Pressed Paper Products."

Brigham-Buzzard Series:

Case 5, "Powerline Network Corporation (Determining the Cost of Capital)."

Chapter 11

Corporate Valuation and Value-Based Management

© Nikada/iStockPhoto.com

WEB

The textbook's *Web* site contains an *Excel* file that will guide you through the chapter's calculations. The file for this chapter is *Ch11 Tool Kit.xls*, and we encourage you to open the file and follow along as you read the chapter.

As we have emphasized throughout the book, maximizing intrinsic value should be management's primary objective. However, to maximize value, managers need a tool for estimating the effects of alternative strategies. In this chapter, we develop and illustrate such a tool—the **corporate valuation model**, which is the present value of expected future free cash flows discounted at the weighted average cost of capital. In a sense, the corporate valuation model is the culmination of all the material covered thus far, because it pulls together financial statements, cash flows, financial projections, time value of money, risk, and the cost of capital. Some companies practice **value-based management** by systematically using the corporate valuation model to guide their decisions. The degree to which a company employs principles of value-based management often depends on its **corporate governance**, which is the set of laws, rules, and procedures that influence its operations and the decisions made by its managers. This chapter addresses all these topics, beginning with corporate valuation.

Beginning of Chapter Questions

As you read the chapter, consider how you would answer the following questions. You *should not* necessarily be able to answer the questions before you read the chapter. Rather, you should use them to get a sense of the issues covered in the chapter. After reading the chapter, you should be able to give at least partial answers to the questions, and you should be able to give better answers after the chapter has been discussed in class. Note, too, that it is often useful, when answering conceptual questions, to use hypothetical data to illustrate your answer. We illustrate the answers with an *Excel* model that is available on the textbook's Web site. Accessing the model and working through it is a useful exercise, and it provides insights that are useful when answering the questions.

1. What's the difference between **operating** and **nonoperating assets,** and between **net operating working capital** and **net working capital?** Why are these distinctions important to someone who is estimating the value of a business?

2. What is the definition of **free cash flow (FCF),** and how is it related to the **value of a firm's operations** as determined using the **corporate valuation model?**

3. What is **value-based management,** and how is it related to the corporate valuation model? Is value-based management a good way to run a business, or can you think of alternative systems that are likely to produce better results?

4. Define **EVA** and **MVA,** and indicate how those concepts are related to value-based management.

5. Why is **corporate governance** important to investors? Explain how each of the following is related to corporate governance: (a) management entrenchment, (b) hostile takeovers, (c) incentive compensation plans, (d) greenmail, (e) poison pills, (f) strong boards of directors, (g) vesting periods for options, and (h) ESOPs.

6. How does the **free cash flow model** differ from the **dividend growth model,** and what are the advantages and disadvantages of each model? Do these models produce the same answers to the total value of a firm and the value of its stock?

7. How have events such as the accounting frauds at AIG, Enron, WorldCom, and several other companies affected people's ideas about corporate governance, the government's role in corporate governance, and the use of options for management compensation?

11.1 Overview of Corporate Valuation

As stated earlier, managers should evaluate the effects of alternative strategies on their firms' values. This really means forecasting financial statements under alternative strategies, finding the present value of each strategy's cash flow stream, and then choosing the strategy that provides the maximum value. The financial statements should be projected using the techniques and procedures discussed in Chapter 9, and the discount rate should be the risk-adjusted cost of capital as discussed in Chapter 10. But what model should managers use to discount the cash flows? One possibility is the dividend growth model from Chapter 5. However, that model is often unsuitable for managerial purposes. For example, suppose a start-up company is formed to develop and market a new product. Its managers will focus on product development, marketing, and raising capital. They will probably be thinking about an eventual IPO, or perhaps the sale of the company to a larger firm—Cisco, Microsoft, Intel, IBM, or another of the industry leaders that buy hundreds of successful new companies each year. For the managers of such a start-up, the decision to initiate dividend payments in the foreseeable future will be totally off the radar screen. Thus, the dividend growth model is not useful for valuing most start-up companies.

Also, many established firms pay no dividends. Investors may expect them to pay dividends sometime in the future—but when, and how much? As long as internal

CORPORATE VALUATION: PUTTING THE PIECES TOGETHER

The intrinsic value of a firm is determined by the size, timing, and risk of its expected future free cash flows (FCF). Chapter 9 showed how to project financial statements, and Chapter 7 showed how to calculate free cash flows. Chapter 10 explained how to estimate the weighted average cost of capital. This chapter puts the pieces together and shows how to calculate the value of a firm. It also shows how to use the valuation model as a guide for choosing among different corporate strategies and operating tactics.

opportunities and acquisitions are so attractive, the initiation of dividends will be postponed, and this makes the dividend growth model of little use. Even Microsoft, one of the world's most successful companies, paid no dividends until 2003.

Finally, the dividend growth model is generally of limited use for internal management purposes, even for a dividend-paying company. If the firm consisted of just one big asset and if that asset produced all of the cash flows used to pay dividends, then alternative strategies could be judged through the use of the dividend growth model. However, most firms have several different divisions with many assets, so the corporation's value depends on the cash flows from many different assets and on the actions of many managers. These managers need a way to measure the effects of their decisions on corporate value, but the discounted dividend model isn't very useful because individual divisions don't pay dividends.

Fortunately, the corporate valuation model does not depend on dividends, and it can be applied to divisions and subunits as well as to the entire firm.

Another important aspect of value-based management is the concept of corporate governance. The corporate valuation model shows how corporate decisions affect *stockholders*. However, corporate decisions are made by managers, not stockholders, and maximizing shareholder wealth is not the same as individual managers maximizing their own "satisfaction." Thus, a key aspect of value-based management is making sure that managers focus on the goal of maximizing stockholder wealth. The set of laws, rules, and procedures that influence a company's operations and motivate its managers falls under the general heading of *corporate governance*.

This chapter discusses the corporate valuation model, value-based management, and corporate governance, beginning with the corporate valuation model.

Self Test

Why is the corporate valuation model applicable in more circumstances than the dividend growth model?

What is value-based management?

What is corporate governance?

11.2 The Corporate Valuation Model

There are two types of corporate assets: **operating** and **nonoperating**. Operating assets, in turn, take two forms: **assets-in-place** and **growth options**. Assets-in-place include such tangible assets as land, buildings, machines, and inventory as well as intangible assets such as patents, customer lists, reputation, and general know-how. Growth options are opportunities to expand that arise from the firm's current operating knowledge, experience, and other resources. The assets-in-place provide an expected stream of cash flows, and so do the growth options. For instance, Wal-Mart has stores, inventory, widespread name recognition, a reputation for low prices, and considerable expertise in business processes. These tangible and intangible assets produce current sales and cash flows, and they also provide opportunities for new investments that will produce additional cash flows in the future. Similarly, Merck owns manufacturing plants, patents, and other real assets; it also has a knowledge base that facilitates the development of new drugs and thus new cash flow streams.

Most companies also own some nonoperating assets, which come in two forms. The first is a marketable securities portfolio over and above the cash needed to operate the business. For example, Ford Motor Company's automotive operation held about $14.2 billion in marketable securities at the end of December 2010, and this was in addition to $6.3 billion in cash. Second, Ford also had $2.4 billion of investments in other businesses, which were reported on the asset side of the balance sheet as "Equity in Net Assets of Affiliated Companies." In total, Ford had $14.2 + $2.4 = $16.6 billion of nonoperating assets, amounting to 26% of its $64.6 billion of total automotive assets. For most companies, the percentage is much lower. For example, as of the end of October 2010, Wal-Mart's percentage of nonoperating assets was less than 1%, which is more typical.

We see, then, that for most companies operating assets are far more important than nonoperating assets. Moreover, companies can influence the values of their operating assets, whereas the values of nonoperating assets are largely beyond their direct control. Therefore, value-based management—and hence this chapter—focuses on operating assets.

11.2a Estimating the Value of Operations

Figures 11-1 and 11-2 contain the actual 2012 and projected 2013 to 2016 financial statements for MagnaVision Inc., which produces optical systems for use in medical photography. (See Chapter 9 for more details on how to project financial statements.) Growth has been rapid in the past, but the market is becoming saturated, so the sales growth rate is expected to decline from 21% in 2013 to a sustainable rate of 5% in 2016 and beyond. Profit margins are expected to improve as the production process becomes more efficient and because MagnaVision will no longer be incurring marketing costs associated with the introduction of a major product. All items on the financial statements are projected to grow at a 5% rate after 2016. Note that the company does not pay a dividend, but it is expected to start paying out about 75% of its earnings beginning in 2015. (Chapter 17 explains in more detail how companies decide how much to pay out in dividends.)

Recall that free cash flow (FCF) is the cash from operations that is actually available for distribution to investors, including stockholders, bondholders, and preferred stockholders. The value of operations is the present value of the free cash flows the firm is expected to generate out into the future. Therefore, MagnaVision's value can be calculated as the present value of its expected future free cash flows from operations, discounted at its weighted average cost of capital (WACC), plus the value of its nonoperating assets. Here is the equation for the value of operations, which is the firm's value as a going concern:

Figure 11-1   MagnaVision Inc.: Income Statements (Millions of Dollars, Except for Per Share Data)

	A	B	C	D	E	F	G
			Actual		Projected		
26			2012	2013	2014[a]	2015	2016
28	Net Sales		$700.0	$850.0	$1,000.0	$1,100.0	$1,155.0
29	Costs (except depreciation)		599.0	734.0	911.0	935.0	982.0
30	Depreciation		28.0	31.0	34.0	36.0	38.0
31	Total operating costs		$627.0	$765.0	$945.0	$971.0	$1,020.0
32	Earning before int. & tax (EBIT)		$73.0	$85.0	$55.0	$129.0	$135.0
33	Less: Net interest[b]		13.0	15.0	16.0	17.0	19.0
34	Earning before taxes		$60.0	$70.0	$39.0	$112.0	$116.0
35	Taxes (40%)		24.0	28.0	15.6	44.8	46.4
36	Net income before pref. div.		$36.0	$42.0	$23.4	$67.2	$69.6
37	Preferred div.		6.0	7.0	7.4	8.0	8.3
38	Net income avail. for com. div.		$30.0	$35.0	$16.0	$59.2	$61.3
39	Common dividends		$0.0	$0.0	$0.0	$44.2	$45.3
40	Addition to retained earnings		$30.0	$35.0	$16.0	$15.0	$16.0
41							
42	Number of shares		100	100	100	100	100
43	Dividends per share		$0.000	$0.000	$0.000	$0.442	$0.453

[a]Net income is projected to decline in 2014. This is due to the projected cost for a one-time marketing program in that year.
[b]"Net interest" is interest paid on debt minus interest earned on marketable securities. Both items could be shown separately on the income statements, but for this example we combine them and show net interest. MagnaVision pays more interest than it earns; hence its net interest is subtracted.

Figure 11-2   MagnaVision Inc.: Balance Sheets (Millions of Dollars)

	A	B	C	D	E	F	G
			Actual		Projected		
52			2012	2013	2014	2015	2016
53	Assets						
54	Cash		$17.0	$20.0	$22.0	$23.0	$24.0
55	Marketable Securities[a]		63.0	70.0	80.0	84.0	88.0
56	Accounts receivable		85.0	100.0	110.0	116.0	121.0
57	Inventories		170.0	200.0	220.0	231.0	243.0
58	Total current assets		$335.0	$390.0	$432.0	$454.0	$476.0
59	Net plant and equipment		279.0	310.0	341.0	358.0	376.0
60	Total Assets		$614.0	$700.0	$773.0	$812.0	$852.0
61							
62	Liabilities and Equity						
63	Accounts Payable		$16.0	$20.0	$22.0	$23.0	$24.0
64	Notes payable		123.0	140.0	160.0	168.0	176.0
65	Accruals		44.0	50.0	55.0	58.0	61.0
66	Total current liabilities		$183.0	$210.0	$237.0	$249.0	$261.0
67	Long-term bonds		124.0	140.0	160.0	168.0	176.0
68	Preferred stock		62.0	70.0	80.0	84.0	88.0
69	Common Stock[b]		$200.0	$200.0	$200.0	$200.0	$200.0
70	Retained earnings		45.0	80.0	96.0	111.0	127.0
71	Common equity		$245.0	$280.0	$296.0	$311.0	$327.0
72	Total liabilities and equity		$614.0	$700.0	$773.0	$812.0	$852.0

[a]All assets except marketable securities are operating assets required to support sales. The marketable securities are financial assets not required in operations.
[b]Par plus paid-in capital.

Value of operations $= V_{op} =$ PV of expected future free cash flows

$$= \frac{FCF_1}{(1 + WACC)^1} + \frac{FCF_2}{(1 + WACC)^2} + \cdots + \frac{FCF_\infty}{(1 + WACC)^\infty} \qquad (11\text{--}1)$$

$$= \sum_{t=1}^{\infty} \frac{FCF_t}{(1 + WACC)^t}$$

MagnaVision's cost of capital is 10.84%. To find its value of operations as a going concern, we use an approach similar to the nonconstant dividend growth model for stocks in Chapter 5 and proceed as follows.

1. Assume that the firm will experience nonconstant growth for N years, after which it will grow at some constant rate.
2. Calculate the expected free cash flow for each of the N nonconstant growth years.
3. Recognize that growth after Year N will be constant, so we can use the constant growth formula to find the firm's value at Year N. This is the sum of the PVs for year N + 1 and all subsequent years, discounted back to Year N.
4. Find the PV of the free cash flows for each of the N nonconstant growth years. Also, find the PV of the firm's value at Year N.
5. Now sum all the PVs, those of the annual free cash flows during the nonconstant period plus the PV of the Year-N value, to find the firm's value of operations.

Figure 11-3   Calculating MagnaVision's Expected Free Cash Flow (Millions of Dollars)

	A	B	C	D	E	F	G
81			Actual		Projected		
82	Step 1: Calculate FCF		2012	2013	2014[b]	2015	2016
83	1. Net operating working capital[a]		$212.0	$250.0	$275.0	$289.0	$303.0
84	2. Net plant and equipment		279.0	310.0	341.0	358.0	376.0
85	3. Net operating capital		$491.0	$560.0	$616.0	$647.0	$679.0
86	4. Investment in operating capital			69.0	56.0	31.0	32.0
87	5. NOPAT		$43.8	$51.0	$33.0	$77.4	$81.0
88	6. Less: Investment in op. capital			69.0	56.0	31.0	32.0
89	7. Free cash flow			-$18.0	-$23.0	$46.4	$49.0

[a]We use the terms "total net operating capital," "operating capital," and "net operating assets" interchangeably.
[b]NOPAT declines in 2014 because of a marketing expenditure projected for that year. See Note a in Figure 11-1.

© Cengage Learning 2013

Figure 11-3 calculates free cash flow for each year, using procedures discussed in Chapter 7. Line 1, with data for 2013 from the balance sheets in Figure 11-2, shows the required net operating working capital, or operating current assets minus operating current liabilities, for 2012:

$$\begin{array}{c} \text{Required net} \\ \text{operating} \\ \text{working capital} \end{array} = \left(\begin{array}{c} \text{Cash} \\ + \text{ Accounts receivable} \\ + \text{ Inventories} \end{array} \right) - \left(\begin{array}{c} \text{Accounts payable} \\ + \text{ Accruals} \end{array} \right)$$

$$= (\$17.00 + \$85.00 + \$170.00) - (\$16.00 + \$44.00)$$
$$= \$212.00$$

Line 2 shows required net plant and equipment; Line 3, which is the sum of Lines 1 and 2, shows the required net operating assets, also called total net operating capital or just operating capital. For 2012, operating capital is $212 + $279 = $491 million.

Line 4 shows the required annual addition to operating capital, found as the change in operating capital from the previous year. For 2013, the required investment in operating capital is $560 − $491 = $69 million.

Line 5 shows NOPAT, or net operating profit after taxes. Note that EBIT is operating earnings *before* taxes, while NOPAT is operating earnings *after* taxes. Therefore, NOPAT = EBIT(1 − T). With a 2013 EBIT of $85 million (as shown in Figure 11-1) and a tax rate of 40%, the NOPAT projected for 2013 is $51 million:

$$\text{NOPAT} = \text{EBIT}(1 - T) = \$85(1.0 - 0.4) = \$51 \text{ million}$$

Although MagnaVision's operating capital is projected to produce $51 million of after-tax profits in 2013, the company must invest $69 million in new operating capital in 2013 to support its growth plan. Therefore, the free cash flow for 2013, shown on Line 7, is a negative $18 million:

$$\text{Free cash flow (FCF)} = \$51 - \$69 = -\$18 \text{ million}$$

This negative free cash flow in the early years is typical for young, high-growth companies. Even though net operating profit after taxes (NOPAT) is positive in all years, free cash flow is negative because of the need to invest in operating assets. The negative free cash flow means the company will have to obtain new funds from investors, and the balance sheets in Figure 11-2 show that notes payable, long-term bonds, and preferred stock all increase from 2012 to 2013. Stockholders will also help fund MagnaVision's growth–they will receive no dividends until 2015, so all of the net income from 2013 and 2014 will be reinvested. However, as growth slows, free cash flow will become positive, and MagnaVision plans to use some of its FCF to pay dividends beginning in 2015.[1]

A variant of the constant growth dividend model is shown as Equation 11-2. This equation can be used to find the value of MagnaVision's operations at time N, when its free cash flows stabilize and begin to grow at a constant rate. This is the value of all FCFs beyond time N, discounted back to time N (which is 2016 for MagnaVision):

$$V_{op(\text{at time N})} = \sum_{t=N+1}^{\infty} \frac{FCF_t}{(1+WACC)^{t-N}}$$

$$= \frac{FCF_{N+1}}{WACC-g} = \frac{FCF_N(1+g)}{WACC-g}$$

(11–2)

Based on a 10.84% cost of capital, $49 million of free cash flow in 2016, and a 5% growth rate, the value of MagnaVision's operations as of December 31, 2016, is forecasted to be $880.99 million:

$$V_{op(12/31/16)} = \frac{FCF_{12/31/16}(1+g)}{WACC-g}$$

$$= \frac{\$49(1+0.05)}{0.1084-0.05} = \frac{\$51.45}{0.1084-0.05} = \$880.99$$

(11–2a)

This $880.99 million figure is called the company's **horizon value** because it is the value at the end of the forecast period. It is also sometimes called a **continuing value** or **terminal value**. It is the amount that MagnaVision could expect to receive if it sold its operating assets on December 31, 2016.

Figure 11-4 shows the free cash flow for each year during the nonconstant growth period along with the horizon value of operations in 2016. To find the value of operations as of "today," December 31, 2012, we find the PV of the horizon value and each annual free cash flow in Figure 11-4, discounting at the 10.84% cost of capital:

$$V_{op(12/31/12)} = \frac{-\$18.00}{(1+0.1084)^1} + \frac{-\$23.00}{(1+0.1084)^2} + \frac{\$46.40}{(1+0.1084)^3} + \frac{\$49.00}{(1+0.1084)^4} + \frac{\$880.99}{(1+0.1084)^4}$$

$$= \$615.27$$

WEB

See **Ch11 Tool Kit.xls** on the textbook's Web site.

---

1. MagnaVision plans to increase its debt and preferred stock each year so as to maintain a constant capital structure. We discuss capital structure in detail in Chapter 15.

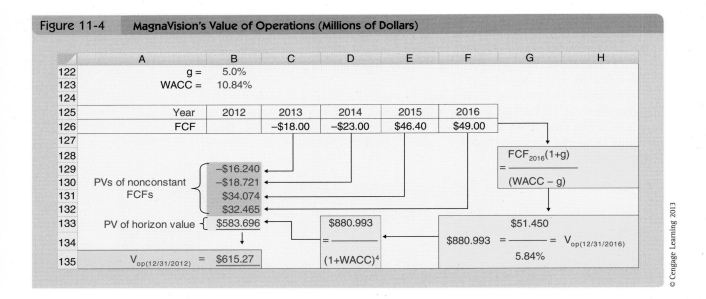

Figure 11-4 MagnaVision's Value of Operations (Millions of Dollars)

© Cengage Learning 2013

The sum of the PVs is approximately $615 million, and it represents an estimate of the price MagnaVision could expect to receive if it sold its operating assets "today," December 31, 2012.

11.2b Estimating the Price Per Share

The total value of any company is the value of its operations plus the value of its nonoperating assets.[2] As shown in the Figure 11-2 balance sheet for December 31, 2012, MagnaVision had $63 million of marketable securities on that date. Unlike for operating assets, we don't need to calculate a present value for marketable securities because short-term financial assets as reported on the balance sheet are at (or close to) their market value. Therefore, MagnaVision's total value on December 31, 2012, is $615.27 + $63 = $678.27 million.

If the company's total value on December 31, 2012, is $678.27 million, then what is the value of its common equity? First, the sum of notes payable and long-term debt is $123 + $124 = $247 million, and these securities have the first claim on assets and income.[3] The preferred stock has a claim of $62 million, and it also ranks above the common. Therefore, the value left for common stockholders is $678.27 − $247 − $62 = $369.27 million.

Figure 11-5 is a bar chart that provides a breakdown of MagnaVision's value. The left bar shows the company's total value as the sum of its nonoperating assets and its value of operations. Next, the middle bar shows the claim of each class of investors on that total value. Debtholders have the highest priority claim, and Magna Vision owes $123 million on notes payable and $124 million on long-term bonds for a total of $247 million. The preferred stockholders have the next claim, $62 million. The remaining value belongs to the common equity, and it amounts to

---

2. The total value also includes the value of growth options not associated with assets-in-place, but MagnaVision has no such options.

3. Accounts payable and accruals were part of the calculation of FCF, so their impact on value is already incorporated into the valuation of the company's operations. It would be double-counting to subtract them now from the value of operations.

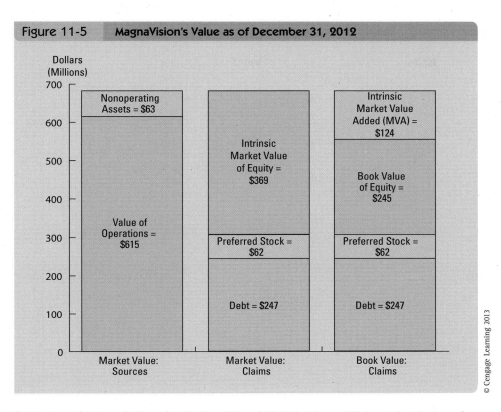

Figure 11-5   MagnaVision's Value as of December 31, 2012

$678.27 − $247 − $62 = $369.27 million.[4] This is MagnaVision's intrinsic value of equity.

In Chapter 7, we defined the Market Value Added (MVA) as the difference between the market value of equity and the book value of equity capital supplied by shareholders. Here we focus on the *intrinsic* MVA, which is the difference between the intrinsic market value of stock and the book value of equity. The bar on the right side of Figure 11-5 divides the estimated market value of equity into these two components.

Figure 11-6 summarizes the calculations used to find MagnaVision's stock value. There are 100 million shares outstanding, and their total intrinsic value is $369.27 million. Therefore, the intrinsic value of a single share is $369.27/100 = $3.69.

11.2c The Dividend Growth Model Applied to MagnaVision

MagnaVision has not yet begun to pay dividends. However, as we saw in Figure 11-1, a cash dividend of $0.442 per share is forecasted for 2015. The dividend is expected to grow by about 2.5% in 2016 and at a constant 5% rate thereafter. MagnaVision's cost of equity is 14%. In this situation, we can apply the nonconstant dividend growth model as developed earlier in Chapter 5. Figure 11-7 shows that the value of MagnaVision's stock, based on this model, is $3.70 per share,

---

4. When estimating the intrinsic market value of equity, it would be better to subtract the market values of debt and preferred stock rather than their book values. However, in most cases (including this one), the book values of fixed-income securities are close to their market values. When this is true, one can simply use book values.

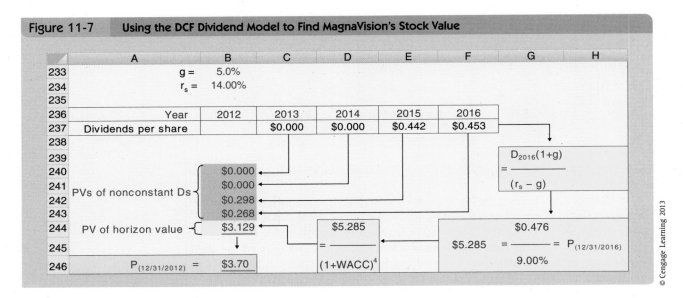

Figure 11-6 Finding the Value of MagnaVision's Intrinsic Stock Price (Millions, Except for Per Share Data)

	A	B	C	D
196		Process	MagnaVision	
197				
198		Value of operations	$615.27	
199		+ Value of nonoperating assets	63.00	
200		Total intrinsic value of firm	$678.27	
201		– Debt	247.00	
202		– Preferred stock	62.00	
203		Intrinsic value of equity	$369.27	
204		÷ Number of shares	100.00	
205				
206		Intrinsic stock price per share =	$3.69	

© Cengage Learning 2013

Figure 11-7 Using the DCF Dividend Model to Find MagnaVision's Stock Value

	A	B	C	D	E	F	G	H
233	g =	5.0%						
234	r_s =	14.00%						
235								
236	Year	2012	2013	2014	2015	2016		
237	Dividends per share		$0.000	$0.000	$0.442	$0.453		
238								
239							$\dfrac{D_{2016}(1+g)}{(r_s - g)}$	
240		$0.000						
241	PVs of nonconstant Ds	$0.000						
242		$0.298						
243		$0.268						
244	PV of horizon value	$3.129		$5.285			$0.476	
245				=		$5.285	= $\dfrac{0.476}{9.00\%}$ = $P_{(12/31/2016)}$	
246	$P_{(12/31/2012)}$ =	$3.70		$(1+WACC)^4$				

© Cengage Learning 2013

WEB

See **Ch11 Tool Kit.xls** on the textbook's Web site.

which is the same (except for a rounding difference) as the value found using the corporate valuation model.[5]

11.2d Comparing the Corporate Valuation and Dividend Growth Models

Because the corporate valuation and dividend growth models give the same answer, does it matter which model you choose? In general, it does. For example, if you were a financial analyst estimating the value of a mature company whose dividends are expected to grow steadily in the future, it would probably be more efficient to use the dividend growth model. In this case you would need to estimate only the growth rate in dividends, not the entire set of forecasted financial statements.

However, if a company is paying a dividend but is still in the high-growth stage of its life cycle, you would need to project the future financial statements

---

5. The small difference is due to rounding the cost of capital to four significant digits.

before you could make a reasonable estimate of future dividends. Then, because you would have already estimated future financial statements, it would be a toss-up as to whether the corporate valuation model or the dividend growth model would be easier to apply. Intel, which pays a dividend of about 78 cents per share on earnings of about $2.31 per share, is an example of a company to which you could apply either model.

Now suppose you were trying to estimate the value of a company that has never paid a dividend, or a new firm that is about to go public, or a division that GE or some other large company is planning to sell. In each of these situations there would be no choice: You would have to estimate future financial statements and use the corporate valuation model.

Actually, much can be learned from the corporate valuation model even if a company is paying steady dividends; hence, many analysts today use it for all valuation analyses. The process of projecting future financial statements can reveal quite a bit about a company's operations and financing needs. Also, such an analysis can provide insights into actions that might be taken to increase the company's value. This is the essence of value-based management, which we discuss in the next section.[6]

Self Test

Give some examples of assets-in-place, growth options, and nonoperating assets.

Write out the equation for the value of operations.

What is the *horizon value*? Why is it also called the *terminal value* or *continuing value*?

Explain how to estimate the price per share using the corporate valuation model.

A company expects FCF of −$10 million at Year 1 and FCF of $20 million at Year 2; after Year 2, FCF is expected to grow at a 5% rate. If the WACC is 10%, then what is the horizon value of operations, $V_{op(Year\ 2)}$? (**$420 million**) What is the current value of operations, $V_{op(Year\ 0)}$? (**$354.55 million**)

A company has a current value of operations of $800 million, and it holds $100 million in short-term investments. If the company has $400 million in debt and has 10 million shares outstanding, what is the price per share? (**$50.00**)

11.3 Value-Based Management

WEB

See *Ch11 Tool Kit.xls* on the textbook's Web site.

Bell Electronics Inc. has two divisions, Memory and Instruments, with total sales of $1.5 billion and operating capital of $1.07 billion. Based on its current stock and bond prices, the company's total market value is about $1.215 billion, giving it an MVA of $145 million: $1.215 − $1.070 = $0.145 billion = $145 million. Because it has a positive MVA, Bell has created value for its investors. Even so, management

---

6. For a more detailed explanation of corporate valuation, see P. Daves, M. Ehrhardt, and R. Shrieves, *Corporate Valuation: A Guide for Managers and Investors* (Mason, OH: Thomson/ South-Western, 2004).

is considering several new strategic plans in its efforts to increase the firm's value. All of Bell's assets are used in operations.

The Memory division produces memory chips for such handheld electronic devices as smart phones, while the Instruments division produces devices for measuring and controlling sewage and water treatment facilities. Table 11-1 shows the latest financial results for the two divisions and for the company as a whole.

As the table shows, Bell Memory is the larger of the two divisions, with higher sales and more operating capital. Bell Memory is also more profitable, with a NOPAT/Sales ratio of 7.9% versus 7.2% for Bell Instruments. This year, as in other recent years, the focus of the initial strategic planning sessions was on the Memory division. Bell Memory has grown rapidly because of the phenomenal growth in consumer electronics, and this division rocketed past Instruments several years ago. Although Memory's growth has tapered off, senior management generally agreed that this division should receive the lion's share of corporate attention and resources because it is larger, more profitable, and, frankly, more exciting. After all, Bell Memory is associated with the glamorous market for telecommunications and personal electronic devices, whereas Bell Instruments is associated with sewage and sludge.

The financial assumptions and projections associated with the preliminary strategic plans for the two divisions are shown in Figures 11-8 and 11-9. The initial strategic plans project that each division will have 5% annual growth for the next 5 years and thereafter. These plans also assume that the cost structures of the two divisions will remain unchanged from the current year, 2012. Only partial financial projections are shown in Figures 11-8 and 11-9. However, when Bell's management decides on a final strategic plan, it will develop complete financial statements for the company as a whole and use them to determine financing requirements, as described in Chapter 9.

To evaluate the plans, Bell's management applied the corporate valuation model to each division, thus valuing them using the free cash flow valuation technique. Each division has a WACC of 10.5%, and Figure 11-10 shows the results. The three key items are NOPAT, the required investment in operating capital, and the resulting free cash flows for each year. In addition, the table shows each division's horizon value of operations at 2017, which is the end of the 5 years of explicit forecasts, as calculated via Equation 11-2. The value of operations at 2012 is the present value of the free cash flows and the horizon value, discounted at the weighted average cost of capital. As expected, Bell Memory has the greater value of operations, $709.6 million versus $505.5 million for Bell Instruments. However, the managers were surprised to see that Bell Memory's Market Value Added (MVA) is *negative*:

TABLE 11-1	2012 Financial Results for Bell Electronics Inc. (Millions of Dollars, Except for Percentages)		
	Division 1: Bell Memory	Division 2: Bell Instruments	Total Company
Sales	$1,000.0	$500.0	$1,500.0
Operating capital	870.0	200.0	1,070.0
Earnings before interest and taxes (EBIT)	131.0	60.0	191.0
Net operating profit after taxes (NOPAT)	78.6	36.0	114.6
Operating profitability (NOPAT/Sales)	7.9%	7.2%	7.6%

Figure 11-8   Initial Projections for the Bell Memory Division (Millions of Dollars, Except for Percentages)

	A	B	C	D	E	F	G
13		Actual	Projected	Projected	Projected	Projected	Projected
14	Panel A: Inputs	2012	2013	2014	2015	2016	2017
15	Sales Growth Rate		5%	5%	5%	5%	5%
16	Costs / Sales	81%	81%	81%	81%	81%	81%
17	Depreciation / Net plant & equip.	10%	10%	10%	10%	10%	10%
18	Cash / Sales	1%	1%	1%	1%	1%	1%
19	Acct. Rec. / Sales	8%	8%	8%	8%	8%	8%
20	Inventories / Sales	30%	30%	30%	30%	30%	30%
21	Net plant & equip. / Sales	59%	59%	59%	59%	59%	59%
22	Acct. Pay. / Sales	5%	5%	5%	5%	5%	5%
23	Accruals / Sales	6%	6%	6%	6%	6%	6%
24	Tax rate	40%	40%	40%	40%	40%	40%
25							
26	Panel 2: Partial Income Statement	2012	2013	2014	2015	2016	2017
27	Net Sales	$1,000.0	$1,050.0	$1,102.5	$1,157.6	$1,215.5	$1,276.3
28	Costs (except depreciation)	$810.0	$850.5	$893.0	$937.7	$984.6	$1,033.8
29	Depreciation	59.0	62.0	65.0	68.3	71.7	75.3
30	Total operating costs	$869.0	$912.5	$958.1	$1,006.0	$1,056.3	$1,109.1
31	Op. profit before int. & tax	$131.0	$137.6	$144.4	$151.6	$159.2	$167.2
32							
33	Panel C: Partial Balance Sheets						
34	Operating Assets	2012	2013	2014	2015	2016	2017
35	Cash	$10.0	$10.5	$11.0	$11.6	$12.2	$12.8
36	Accounts receivable	80.0	84.0	88.2	92.6	97.2	102.1
37	Inventories	300.0	315.0	330.8	347.3	364.7	382.9
38	Operating current assets	$390.0	$409.5	$430.0	$451.5	$474.0	$497.7
39	Net plant and equipment	$590.0	$619.5	$650.5	$683.0	$717.1	$753.0
40							
41	Operating Liabilities						
42	Accounts Payable	$50.0	$52.5	$55.1	$57.9	$60.8	$63.8
43	Accruals	60.0	63.0	66.2	69.5	72.9	76.6
44	Operating current liabilities	$110.0	$115.5	$121.3	$127.3	$133.7	$140.4

$709.6 value of operations − $870.0 operating capital = −$160.4 million.[7] In contrast, Bell Instruments's MVA is positive: $505.5 value of operations − $200 operating capital = $305.5 million.

A second strategic planning meeting was called to address this unexpected result. In it, Bell Memory's managers proposed a $20 million marketing campaign to boost

WEB

See **Ch11 Tool Kit.xls** on the textbook's Web site.

---

7. Earlier in this chapter, we estimated MVA as the estimated value of equity minus the book value of equity. We can also define MVA as

$$MVA = \text{Total market value} - \text{Total investor-supplied capital}$$

(see Chapter 7). By subtracting the value of any short-term investments from total market value, we get the value of operations. If we subtract short-term investments from total capital, we get investor-supplied operating capital. Therefore, MVA can be estimated as

$$MVA = \text{Value of operations} - \text{Investor-supplied operating capital}$$

Recall from Chapter 7 that investor-supplied operating capital is equal to total net operating capital, which we also call total capital. Therefore, we can estimate MVA for a division or for a privately held company as

$$MVA = \text{Value of operations} - \text{Total operating capital}$$

Figure 11-9   Initial Projections for the Bell Instruments Division (Millions of Dollars, Except for Percentages)

	A	B	C	D	E	F	G
49		Actual	*Projected*	*Projected*	*Projected*	*Projected*	*Projected*
50	Panel A: Inputs	2012	2013	2014	2015	2016	2017
51	Sales Growth Rate		5%	5%	5%	5%	5%
52	Costs / Sales	85%	85%	85%	85%	85%	85%
53	Depreciation / Net plant & equip.	10%	10%	10%	10%	10%	10%
54	Cash / Sales	1%	1%	1%	1%	1%	1%
55	Acct. Rec. / Sales	5%	5%	5%	5%	5%	5%
56	Inventories / Sales	15%	15%	15%	15%	15%	15%
57	Net plant & equipment / Sales	30%	30%	30%	30%	30%	30%
58	Acct. Pay. / Sales	5%	5%	5%	5%	5%	5%
59	Accruals / Sales	6%	6%	6%	6%	6%	6%
60	Tax rate	40%	40%	40%	40%	40%	40%
61							
62	Panel B: Partial Income Statement	2012	2013	2014	2015	2016	2017
63	Net Sales	$500.0	$525.0	$551.3	$578.8	$607.8	$638.1
64	Costs (except depreciation)	425.0	446.3	468.6	492.0	516.6	542.4
65	Depreciation	15.0	15.8	16.5	17.4	18.2	19.1
66	Total operating costs	$440.0	$462.0	$485.1	$509.4	$534.8	$561.6
67	Earning before int. & tax	$60.0	$63.0	$66.2	$69.5	$72.9	$76.6
68							
69	Panel C: Partial Balance Sheets						
70	Operating Assets	2012	2013	2014	2015	2016	2017
71	Cash	$5.0	$5.3	$5.5	$5.8	$6.1	$6.4
72	Accounts receivable	25.0	26.3	27.6	28.9	30.4	31.9
73	Inventories	75.0	78.8	82.7	86.8	91.2	95.7
74	Operating current assets	$105.0	$110.3	$115.8	$121.6	$127.6	$134.0
75	Net plant and equipment	$150.0	$157.5	$165.4	$173.6	$182.3	$191.4
76							
77	Operating Liabilities						
78	Accounts Payable	$25.0	$26.3	$27.6	$28.9	$30.4	$31.9
79	Accruals	30.0	31.5	33.1	34.7	36.5	38.3
80	Operating current liabilities	$55.0	$57.8	$60.6	$63.7	$66.9	$70.2

their sales growth rate from 5% to 6%. They argued that because Bell Memory is so profitable, its value would be much higher if they could push up sales. Before accepting this proposal, though, the proposed changes were run through the valuation model. The managers changed the Bell Memory division's growth rate from 5% to 6%; see the file **Ch11 Tool Kit.xls** on the textbook's Web site for details. To their surprise, the division's value of operations fell to $691.5 million, and its MVA also declined, from −$160.4 million to −$178.5 million. Although Bell Memory was profitable, increasing its sales growth actually reduced its value!

To better understand these results, we can express the firm's value in terms of four fundamental wealth drivers:

$$g = \text{Growth in sales}$$
$$OP = \text{Operating profitability (OP)} = \text{NOPAT/Sales}$$
$$CR = \text{Capital requirements (CR)} = \text{Operating capital/Sales}$$
$$WACC = \text{Weighted average cost of capital}$$

Figure 11-10   Initial FCF Valuation of Each Division (Millions of Dollars, Except for Percentages)

	A	B	C	D	E	F	G
87	Panel A: FCF Valuation of the						
88	Bell Memory Division	Actual	Projected	Projected	Projected	Projected	Projected
89	Calculation of FCF:	2012	2013	2014	2015	2016	2017
90	Net operating working capital	$280.0	$294.0	$308.7	$324.1	$340.3	$357.4
91	Net plant & equipment	590.0	619.5	650.5	683.0	717.1	753.0
92	Net operating capital	$870.0	$913.5	$959.2	$1,007.1	$1,057.5	$1,110.4
93	Investment in operating capital		$43.5	$45.7	$48.0	$50.4	$52.9
94	NOPAT (Tax rate = 40%)	$78.6	$82.5	$86.7	$91.0	$95.5	$100.3
95	Free cash flow (FCF)		$39.0	$41.0	$43.0	$45.2	$47.4
96	Growth in FCF			5%	5%	5%	5%
97	Value of Operations:						
98	WACC	10.5%					
99	Horizon value						$905.7
100	Total cash flow		$ 39.0	$ 41.0	$ 43.0	$ 45.2	$953.1
101	Value of operations =	$709.6					
102	Divisional MVA						
103	(Val. of ops - total op. capital) =	($160.4)					
104							
105	Panel B: FCF Valuation of the						
106	Bell Instruments Division	Actual	Projected	Projected	Projected	Projected	Projected
107	Calculation of FCF	2012	2013	2014	2015	2016	2017
108	Net operating working capital	$50.0	$52.5	$55.1	$57.9	$60.8	$63.8
109	Net plant & equipment	150.0	157.5	165.4	173.6	182.3	191.4
110	Net operating capital	$200.0	$210.0	$220.5	$231.5	$243.1	$255.3
111	Investment in operating capital		$10.0	$10.5	$11.0	$11.6	$12.2
112	NOPAT (Tax rate = 40%)	$36.0	$37.8	$39.7	$41.7	$43.8	$45.9
113	Free cash flow (FCF)		$27.8	$29.2	$30.6	$32.2	$33.8
114	Growth in FCF			5%	5%	5%	5%
115	Value of Operations						
116	WACC	10.5%					
117	Horizon value						$645.1
118	Total cash flow		$ 27.8	$ 29.2	$ 30.6	$ 32.2	$678.9
119	Value of operations =	$505.5					
120	Divisional MVA						
121	(Val. of ops - total op. capital) =	$305.5					
122							

Notes: The WACC is 10.5% for each division. The horizon value (HV) at 2017 is calculated using Equation 11-2, the constant growth formula for free cash flows:

$$HV_{2017} = [FCF_{2017}(1 + g)] \div (WACC - g)$$

The value of operations is the present value of the horizon value and the free cash flows discounted at the WACC; it is calculated in a manner similar to Figure 11-3. Projected figures may not total exactly because of rounding. See **Ch11 Tool Kit.xls** on the textbook's Web site for all calculations.

How do these drivers affect the value of a firm? First, the sales growth rate usually (but not always) has a positive effect on value, provided the company is profitable enough. However, the effect can be negative if growth requires a great deal of capital and if the cost of capital is high. Second, operating profitability, which measures the after-tax profit per dollar of sales, always has a positive effect—the higher the better. Third, the capital requirements ratio, which measures how much operating capital is needed to generate a dollar of sales, also has a consistent effect: The lower the CR the better, since a low CR means that the company can generate new sales with smaller amounts of new capital. Finally, the fourth factor, the WACC, also has a consistent effect: The lower it is, the higher the firm's value.

Another important metric in the corporate valuation model is the **expected return on invested capital (EROIC)**, defined as the expected NOPAT for the coming year divided by the amount of operating capital at the beginning of the year (which is the end of the preceding year). It can also be defined in terms of the fundamental value drivers for profitability (OP) and capital requirements (CR). Thus, EROIC represents the expected return on the capital that has already been invested:

(11–3)

$$\text{EROIC}_N = \frac{\text{NOPAT}_{N+1}}{\text{Capital}_N}$$

$$= \frac{\text{OP}_{N+1}}{\text{CR}_N}$$

To illustrate, the EROIC of the Bell Memory division for 2017, the last year in the forecast period, is

WEB

See **Ch11 Tool Kit.xls** on the textbook's Web site for details.

$$\text{EROIC}_{2017} = \frac{\text{NOPAT}_{2018}}{\text{Capital}_{2017}} = \frac{\text{NOPAT}_{2017}(1+g)}{\text{Capital}_{2017}} = \frac{\$100.3(1.05)}{\$1,110.4} = 9.5\%$$

To see exactly how the four value drivers and EROIC determine value for a constant growth firm, we can start with Equation 11-2 (which we repeat here),

$$V_{op(\text{at time }N)} = \frac{\text{FCF}_{N+1}}{\text{WACC} - g}$$

and rewrite it in terms of the value drivers:

(11–4)

$$V_{op(\text{at time }N)} = \text{Capital}_N + \left\{ \left[\frac{\text{Sales}_N(1+g)}{\text{WACC} - g} \right] \left[\text{OP} - \text{WACC}\left(\frac{\text{CR}}{1+g} \right) \right] \right\}$$

Equation 11-4 shows that the value of operations can be divided into two components: (1) the dollars of operating capital that investors have provided; and (2) the additional value that management has added or subtracted, which is equivalent to MVA.

Note that the first [bracketed] fraction in Equation 11-4 represents the present value of growing sales, discounted at the WACC. This would be the MVA of a firm that has no costs and that never needs to invest additional capital. But firms do have costs and capital requirements, and their effect is captured by the term in the second set of brackets. Here we see that, holding g constant, MVA will improve if operating profitability (OP) increases, if WACC decreases, and/or if capital requirements (CR) decrease.

Observe that an increase in growth will not necessarily increase value. OP could be positive, but if CR is quite high—meaning that a lot of new capital is needed to support a given increase in sales—then the second bracketed term can be negative. In this situation, growth causes the first bracketed term to increase; however, since it's being multiplied by a negative term (the second bracket), the net result will be a decrease in MVA.

We can also rewrite Equation 11-2 in terms of EROIC (or profitability and capital requirements) as follows:

$$V_{op(at\ time\ N)} = Capital_N + \frac{Capital_N\,(EROIC_N - WACC)}{WACC - g}$$

$$= Capital_N + \frac{Capital_N\left(\dfrac{OP_{N+1}}{CR_N} - WACC\right)}{WACC - g}$$

(11–5)

Equation 11-5 also breaks value into two components, the value of capital and the MVA, shown in the second term. This term for MVA shows that value depends on the EROIC, the WACC, and the spread between the expected return on invested capital. Notice that the EROIC in turn depends on profitability and required capital. If the combination of profitability and required capital produces an EROIC greater than WACC, then the return on capital is greater than the return investors expect and management is adding value. In this case, an increase in the growth rate causes value to go up. If EROIC is exactly equal to WACC then the firm is, in an economic sense, "breaking even." It has positive accounting profits and cash flow, but these cash flows are just sufficient to satisfy investors, causing value to exactly equal the amount of capital that has been provided. If EROIC is less than WACC then the term in parentheses is negative, management is destroying value, and growth is harmful. This is one case where the faster the growth rate, the lower the firm's value.

We should also note that the insights from Equations 11-4 and 11-5 apply to all firms, but the equations themselves can be applied only to relatively stable firms whose growth has leveled out at a constant rate. For example, in 2010 World Fuel Services's sales grew at 69% per year, so we cannot apply Equations 11-4 and 11-5 directly (although we could always apply Equation 11-1). World Fuel Services is an extremely low-margin business and its NOPAT/Sales ratio was only 0.8%, but it was nonetheless quite profitable. Despite its profits, it had a negative free cash flow of about $276 million! If World Fuel Services can maintain profitability as its growth slows to sustainable levels, it will generate huge amounts of FCF. This explains why its MVA was over $1.3 billion in 2010 even though its FCF was negative.

Table 11-2 shows the value drivers for Bell's two divisions as measured at 2017, the end of the forecast period. We report these for the *end* of the forecast period because ratios can change during the forecast period in response to input changes. By the end of the forecast period, however, all inputs and ratios should be stable.

Both divisions have the same growth rate and the same WACC, as shown in Table 11-2. Bell Memory is more profitable, but it also has much higher capital requirements. The result is that Bell Memory's EROIC is only 9.5%, well below its 10.5% WACC. Thus, growth doesn't help Bell Memory—indeed, it reduces the division's value.

TABLE 11-2	Bell Electronics's Forecasted Value Drivers for 2017	
	Division 1: **Bell Memory**	**Division 2:** **Bell Instruments**
Growth: g	5.0%	5.0%
Profitability: ($NOPAT_{2017}/Sales_{2017}$)	7.9	7.2
Capital requirement: ($Capital_{2017}/Sales_{2017}$)	87.0	40.0
WACC	10.5	10.5
Expected return on invested capital, EROIC: $NOPAT_{2017}(1 + g)/Capital_{2017}$	9.5	18.9

Based on this analysis, Bell Memory's managers decided not to request funds for a marketing campaign. Instead, they developed a plan to reduce capital requirements. The new plan called for spending $50 million on an integrated supply chain information system that would allow them to cut their inventory/sales ratio from 30% to 20% and also reduce the ratio of net plant to sales from 59% to 50%. Table 11-3 shows projected operating results based on this new plan. The value of operations would increase from $709.6 million to $1.1574 billion, or by $447.8 million. Because this amount is well over the $50 million required to implement the plan, top management decided to approve it. Note also that the plan shows MVA becoming positive at $287.4 million (a substantial improvement on the preliminary plan's negative $160.4 million) and the divisional EROIC rising to 13.0%, well over the 10.5% WACC.

Bell Instruments's managers also used the valuation model to assess changes in plans for their division. Given their high EROIC, the Instruments division proposed

TABLE 11-3	Comparison of the Preliminary and Final Plans (Millions of Dollars, Except for Percentages)				
		Bell Memory		**Bell Instruments**	
		Preliminary	**Final**	**Preliminary**	**Final**
Inputs					
Sales growth rate, g		5%	5%	5%	6%
Inventories/Sales		30	20	15	16
Net plant/Sales		59	50	30	30
Results					
EROIC (2017)[a]		9.5%	13.0%	18.9%	18.6%
Invested (operating) capital (2017)[a]		$1,110.4	$ 867.9	$255.3	$274.3
Current value of operations (2012)[b]		709.6	1,157.4	505.5	570.1
Current MVA (2012)[b]		(160.4)	287.4	305.5	370.1

[a]We report EROIC and capital for the end of the forecast period because ratios can change during the forecast period if inputs change during that period. By the end of the forecast period, however, all inputs and ratios should be stable.
[b]We report the value of operations and the MVA as of the current date, 2012, because we want to see what effect the proposed plans would have on the current value of the two divisions.

(1) an aggressive marketing campaign and (2) an increase in inventories that would allow faster delivery and fewer stockouts. Together, these changes would boost the growth rate from 5% to 6%. The direct cost to implement the plan was $20 million, but there was also an indirect cost in that more inventories would have to be carried: The ratio of inventories to sales was forecasted to increase from 15% to 16%.

Should Instruments's new plan be implemented? Table 11-3 shows the forecasted results. The capital requirements associated with the increased inventory caused the EROIC to fall from 18.9% to 18.6%, but (1) the 18.6% return greatly exceeds the 10.5% WACC, and (2) the spread between 18.6% and 10.5% would be earned on additional capital. This caused the forecasted value of operations to increase from $505.5 to $570.1 million, or by $64.6 million. An 18.6% return on $274.3 million of capital is more valuable than an 18.9% return on $255.3 million of capital.[8] (To see this, note that you, or one of Bell's stockholders, would surely rather have an asset that provides a 50% return on an investment of $1,000 than one that provides a 100% return on an investment of $1.) Therefore, the new plan should be accepted, even though it lowers the Instruments division's EROIC.

Sometimes companies focus on their profitability and growth without giving adequate consideration to their capital requirements. This is a big mistake—*all* the wealth creation drivers, not just growth, must be taken into account. Fortunately for Bell's investors, the revised plan was accepted. However, as this example illustrates, it is easy for a company to mistakenly focus only on profitability and growth. They are important, but so are the other value drivers: capital requirements and the weighted average cost of capital. Value-based management explicitly includes the effects of all the value drivers because it uses the corporate valuation model, and the drivers are all embodied in that model.[9]

Self Test

What are the four drivers of value?

How is it possible for sales growth to *decrease* the value of a profitable firm?

You are given the following forecasted information for a constant growth company: sales = $10 million, operating profitability (OP) = 5%, capital requirements (CR) = 40%, growth (g) = 6%, and the weighted average cost of capital (WACC) = 10%. What is the current level of capital? (**$4 million**) What is the current level of NOPAT? (**$0.5 million**) What is the EROIC? (**13.25%**) What is the value of operations? (**$7.25 million**)

---

8. A potential fly in the ointment is that Bell's compensation plan might be based on rates of return and not on changes in wealth. In such a plan, which is fairly typical, the managers might reject the new proposed strategic plan if it lowers ROIC and hence their bonuses, even though the plan is good for the company's stockholders. We discuss the effect of compensation plans in more detail later in the chapter.

9. For more on corporate valuation and value-based management, see Sheridan Titman and John D. Martin, *Valuation: The Art and Science of Corporate Investment Decisions*, 2nd ed. (Boston: Prentice Hall, 2011); Tim Koller, Marc Goedhart, and David Wessels, *Valuation: Measuring and Managing the Value of Companies*, 4th ed. (Hoboken, NJ: John Wiley & Sons, 2005); John D. Martin and J. William Petty, *Value Based Management: The Corporate Response to the Shareholder Revolution* (Boston: Harvard Business School Press, 2000); John D. Martin, J. William Petty, and James S. Wallace, *Value Based Management with Corporate Social Responsibility* (New York: Oxford University Press, 2009); James M. McTaggart, Peter W. Kontes, and Michael C. Mankins, *The Value Imperative* (New York: The Free Press, 1994); and G. Bennett Stewart, *The Quest for Value* (New York: Harper Collins, 1991). For an application to small-firm valuation, see Michael S. Long and Thomas A. Bryant, *Valuing the Closely Held Firm* (New York: Oxford University Press, 2008).

www

For excellent discussions of corporate governance, see the Web pages of CalPERS (the California Public Employees' Retirement System), **www.calpers.org**, and TIAA-CREF (Teachers Insurance and Annuity Association College Retirement Equity Fund), **www.tiaa-cref.org**.

11.4 Managerial Behavior and Shareholder Wealth

Shareholders want companies to hire managers who are able and willing to take legal and ethical actions to maximize intrinsic stock prices.[10] This obviously requires managers with technical competence, but it also requires managers who are willing to put forth the extra effort necessary to identify and implement value-adding activities. However, managers are people, and people have both personal and corporate goals. Logically, therefore, managers can be expected to act in their own self-interests, and if their self-interests are not aligned with those of stockholders, then corporate value will not be maximized. There are six ways in which a manager's behavior might harm a firm's intrinsic value.

1. Managers might not expend the time and effort required to maximize firm value. Rather than focusing on corporate tasks, they might spend too much time on external activities, such as serving on boards of other companies, or on nonproductive activities, such as golfing, lunching, and traveling.
2. Managers might use corporate resources on activities that benefit themselves rather than shareholders. For example, they might spend company money on such perquisites as lavish offices, memberships at country clubs, museum-quality art for corporate apartments, large personal staffs, and corporate jets. Because these perks are not actually cash payments to the managers, they are called **nonpecuniary benefits**.
3. Managers might avoid making difficult but value-enhancing decisions that harm friends in the company. For example, a manager might not close a plant or terminate a project if the manager has personal relationships with those who are adversely affected by such decisions, even if termination is the economically sound action.
4. Managers might take on too much risk or they might not take on enough risk. For example, a company might have the opportunity to undertake a risky project with a positive NPV. If the project turns out badly, then the manager's reputation will be harmed and the manager might even be fired. Thus, a manager might choose to avoid risky projects even if they are desirable from a shareholder's point of view. On the other hand, a manager might take on projects with too much risk. Consider a project that is not living up to expectations. A manager might be tempted to invest even more money in the project rather than admit that the project is a failure. Or a manager might be willing to take on a second project with a negative NPV if it has even a slight chance of a very positive outcome, since hitting a home run with this second project might cover up the first project's poor performance. In other words, the manager might throw good money after bad.

---

10. Notice that we said both legal and ethical actions. The accounting frauds perpetrated by Enron, WorldCom, and others that were uncovered in 2002 raised stock prices in the short run, but only because investors were misled about the companies' financial positions. Then, when the correct financial information was finally revealed, the stocks tanked. Investors who bought shares based on the fraudulent financial statements lost tens of billions of dollars. Releasing false financial statements is illegal. Aggressive earnings management and the use of misleading accounting tricks to pump up reported earnings is unethical, and executives can go to jail as a result of their shenanigans. When we speak of taking actions to maximize stock prices, we mean making operational or financial changes designed to maximize intrinsic stock value, not fooling investors with false or misleading financial reports.

5. If a company is generating positive free cash flow, a manager might "stockpile" it in the form of marketable securities instead of returning FCF to investors. This potentially harms investors because it prevents them from allocating these funds to other companies with good growth opportunities. Even worse, positive FCF often tempts a manager into paying too much for the acquisition of another company. In fact, most mergers and acquisitions end up as break-even deals, at best, for the acquiring company because the premiums paid for the targets are often very large.

   Why would a manager be reluctant to return cash to investors? First, extra cash on hand reduces the company's risk, which appeals to many managers. Second, a large distribution of cash to investors is an admission that the company doesn't have enough good investment opportunities. Slow growth is normal for a maturing company, but it isn't very exciting for a manager to admit this. Third, there is a lot of glamour associated with making a large acquisition, and this can provide a large boost to a manager's ego. Fourth, compensation usually is higher for executives at larger companies; cash distributions to investors make a company smaller, not larger.

6. Managers might not release all the information that is desired by investors. Sometimes, they might withhold information to prevent competitors from gaining an advantage. At other times, they might try to avoid releasing bad news. For example, they might "massage" the data or "manage the earnings" so that the news doesn't look so bad. If investors are unsure about the quality of information provided by managers, they tend to discount the company's expected free cash flows at a higher cost of capital, which reduces the company's intrinsic value.

   If senior managers believe there is little chance that they will be removed, we say that they are *entrenched*. Such a company faces a high risk of being poorly run, because entrenched managers are able to act in their own interests rather than in the interests of shareholders.

Name six types of managerial behaviors that can reduce a firm's intrinsic value.	**Self Test**

11.5 Corporate Governance

A key requirement for successful implementation of value-based management is to influence executives and other managers so that they do not behave in the ways described in the previous section but instead behave in a way that maximizes a firm's intrinsic value. Corporate governance can provide just such an influence. Corporate governance can be defined as the set of laws, rules, and procedures that influence a company's operations and the decisions made by its managers. At the risk of oversimplification, most corporate governance provisions come in two forms, sticks and carrots. The primary stick is the *threat of removal*, either as a decision by the board of directors or as the result of a hostile takeover. If a firm's managers are maximizing the value of the resources entrusted to them, they need not fear the loss of their jobs. On the other hand, if managers are not maximizing value, they should be removed by their own boards of directors, by dissident stockholders, or by other companies seeking to profit by installing a better management team. The main carrot is *compensation*. Managers have greater incentives to maximize intrinsic stock value if their compensation is linked to their firm's performance rather than being strictly in the form of salary.

Almost all corporate governance provisions affect either the threat of removal or compensation. Some provisions are internal to a firm and are under its control.[11] These internal provisions and features can be divided into five areas: (1) monitoring and discipline by the board of directors, (2) charter provisions and bylaws that affect the likelihood of hostile takeovers, (3) compensation plans, (4) capital structure choices, and (5) accounting control systems. In addition to the corporate governance provisions that are under a firm's control, there are also environmental factors outside of a firm's control, such as the regulatory environment, block ownership patterns, competition in the product markets, the media, and litigation. Our discussion begins with the internal provisions.

11.5a Monitoring and Discipline by the Board of Directors

Shareholders are a corporation's owners, and they elect the board of directors to act as agents on their behalf. In the United States, it is the board's duty to monitor senior managers and discipline them if they do not act in the interests of shareholders, either by removal or by a reduction in compensation.[12] This is not necessarily the case outside the United States. For example, many companies in Europe are required to have employee representatives on the board. Also, many European and Asian companies have bank representatives on the board. But even in the United States, many boards fail to act in the shareholders' best interests. How can this be?

Consider the election process. The board of directors has a nominating committee. These directors choose the candidates for the open director positions, and the ballot for a board position usually lists only one candidate. Although outside candidates can run a "write-in" campaign, only those candidates named by the board's nominating committee are on the ballot.[13] At many companies, the CEO is also the chairman of the board and has considerable influence on this nominating committee. This means that in practice it often is the CEO who, in effect, nominates candidates for the board. High compensation and prestige go with a position on the board of a major company, so board seats are prized possessions. Board members typically want to retain their positions, and they are grateful to whomever helped get them on the board. Thus, the nominating process often results in a board that is favorably disposed to the CEO.

At most companies, a candidate is elected simply by having a majority of votes cast. The proxy ballot usually lists all candidates, with a box for each candidate to check if the shareholder votes "For" the candidate and a box to check if the shareholder "Withholds" a vote on the candidate—you can't actually vote "No"; you can only withhold your vote. In theory, a candidate could be elected with a single "For" vote if all other votes were withheld. In practice, though, most shareholders either vote "For" or assign to management their right to vote (proxy is defined as the authority to act for another, which is why it is called a proxy statement). In practice,

---

11. We have adapted this framework from the one provided by Stuart L. Gillan, "Recent Developments in Corporate Governance: An Overview," *Journal of Corporate Finance,* June 2006, pp. 381–402. Gillan provides an excellent discussion of the issues associated with corporate governance, and we highly recommend this article to the reader who is interested in an expanded discussion of the issues in this section.

12. There are a few exceptions to this rule. For example, some states have laws allowing the board to take into consideration the interests of other stakeholders, such as employees and members of the community.

13. There is currently (early 2011) a movement under way to allow shareholders to nominate candidates for the board, but only time will tell whether this movement is successful.

then, the nominated candidates virtually always receive a majority of votes and are thus elected.

Occasionally there is a "Just vote no" campaign in which a large investor (usually an institution such as a pension fund) urges stockholders to withhold their votes for one or more directors. Although such campaigns do not directly affect the director's election, they do provide a visible way for investors to express their dissatisfaction. Recent evidence shows that "Just vote no" campaigns at poorly performing firms lead to better subsequent firm performance and a greater probability that the CEO will be dismissed.[14]

Voting procedures also affect the ability of outsiders to gain positions on the board. If the charter specifies cumulative voting, then each shareholder is given a number of votes equal to his or her shares multiplied by the number of board seats up for election. For example, the holder of 100 shares of stock will receive 1,000 votes if 10 seats are to be filled. Then, the shareholder can distribute those votes however he or she sees fit. One hundred votes could be cast for each of 10 candidates, or all 1,000 votes could be cast for one candidate. If noncumulative voting is used, our hypothetical stockholder cannot concentrate votes in this way—no more than 100 votes can be cast for any one candidate.

With noncumulative voting, if management controls 51% of the shares then they can fill every seat on the board, leaving dissident stockholders without any representation on the board. With cumulative voting, however, if 10 seats are to be filled then dissidents could elect a representative, provided they have 10% plus 1 additional share of the stock.

Note also that bylaws specify whether the entire board is to be elected annually or if directors are to have staggered terms with, say, one-third of the seats to be

LET'S GO TO MIAMI! IBM'S 2009 ANNUAL MEETING

IBM invited its stockholders to its annual meeting held on April 28, 2009, in Miami. The agenda included election of each board member for a 1-year term, ratification of PricewaterhouseCoopers as its independent auditing firm, approval of long-term incentive plans for executives, and three stockholder proposals: (1) adopt cumulative voting; (2) remove consideration of pension income that does not reflect operating performance from the measure of income used for bonuses; (3) adopt an advisory shareholder vote each year ratifying (or not) executive compensation. IBM's board recommended that shareholders vote against all three proposals.

About 8 pages of the proxy statement described nominees for the board and their compensation, about 53 pages explained executive compensation, and about 4½ pages covered the stockholders' proposals, with much of that being management's explanation for why it opposed them.

Stockholders were permitted to vote over the Web, by telephone, by mail, or in person at the meeting. When the result were tallied, IBM revealed that all board nominees had been elected by a majority and that all three stockholder proposals had been defeated, although the last two proposals garnered over 43% of the votes in their favor.

IBM's annual meeting might not have been as exciting as the TV show *CSI: Miami*, but we think the evidence shows that there will be more stockholder proposals in the future and that many will win approval.

---

14. See Diane Del Guercio, Laura Seery, and Tracie Woidtke, "Do Boards Pay Attention When Institutional Investor Activists 'Just Vote No'?" *Journal of Financial Economics,* October 2008, pp. 84–103.

filled each year and directors to serve 3-year terms. With staggered terms, fewer seats come up each year, making it harder for dissidents to gain representation on the board. Staggered boards are also called **classified boards**.

Many board members are "insiders"—that is, people who hold managerial positions within the company, such as the CFO. Because insiders report to the CEO, it may be difficult for them to oppose the CEO at a board meeting. To help mitigate this problem, several exchanges, such as the NYSE and Nasdaq, now require that listed companies have a majority of outside directors.

Some "outside" board members often have strong connections with the CEO through professional relationships, personal friendships, and consulting or other fee-generating activities. In fact, outsiders sometimes have very little expert business knowledge but have "celebrity" status from nonbusiness activities. Some companies also have **interlocking boards of directors,** where Company A's CEO sits on Company B's board and B's CEO sits on A's board. In these situations, even the outside directors are not truly independent and impartial.

Large boards (those with more than about ten members) often are less effective than smaller boards. As anyone who has been on a committee can attest, individual participation tends to fall as committee size increases. Thus, there is a greater likelihood that members of a large board will be less active than those on smaller boards.

The compensation of board members has an impact on the board's effectiveness. When board members have exceptionally high compensation, the CEO also tends to have exceptionally high compensation. This suggests that such boards tend to be too lenient with the CEO.[15] The form of board compensation also affects board performance. Rather than compensating board members with only salary, many companies now include restricted stock grants or stock options in an effort to better align board members with stockholders.

Studies show that corporate governance usually improves if (1) the CEO is not also the chairman of the board, (2) the board has a majority of true outsiders who bring some type of business expertise to the board and are not too busy with other activities, (3) the board is not too large, and (4) board members are compensated appropriately (not too high and not all cash, but including exposure to equity risk through options or stock). The good news for the shareholder is that the boards at many companies have made significant improvements in these directions during the past decade. Fewer CEOs are also board chairmen and, as power has shifted from CEOs to boards as a whole, there has been a tendency to replace insiders with strong, independent outsiders. Today, the typical board has about one-third insiders and two-thirds outsiders, and most outsiders are truly independent. Moreover, board members are compensated primarily with stock or options rather than a straight salary. These changes clearly have decreased the patience of boards with poorly performing CEOs. Within the past several years the CEOs of Wachovia, Sprint Nextel, Gap, Hewlett-Packard, Home Depot, Citigroup, Pfizer, Ford, and Dynegy, to name just a few, have been removed by their boards. This would have been unheard of 30 years ago.

11.5b Charter Provisions and Bylaws That Affect the Likelihood of Hostile Takeovers

Hostile takeovers usually occur when managers have not been willing or able to maximize the profit potential of the resources under their control. In such a

---

15. See I. E. Brick, O. Palmon, and J. Wald, "CEO Compensation, Director Compensation, and Firm Performance: Evidence of Cronyism?" *Journal of Corporate Finance,* June 2006, pp. 403–423.

situation, another company can acquire the poorly performing firm, replace its managers, increase free cash flow, and improve MVA. The following paragraphs describe some provisions that can be included in a corporate charter to make it harder for poorly performing managers to remain in control.[16]

A shareholder-friendly charter should ban **targeted share repurchases,** also known as **greenmail.** For example, suppose a company's stock is selling for $20 per share. Now a hostile bidder, or raider, who plans to replace management if the takeover is successful, buys 5% of the company's stock at the $20 price.[17] The raider then makes an offer to purchase the remainder of the stock for $30 per share. The company might offer to buy back the raider's stock at a price of, say, $35 per share. This is called a targeted share repurchase since the stock will be purchased only from the raider and not from any other shareholders. A raider who paid only $20 per share for the stock would be making a quick profit of $15 per share, which could easily total several hundred million dollars. As a part of the deal, the raider would sign a document promising not to attempt to take over the company for a specified number of years; hence the buyback also is called greenmail. Greenmail hurts shareholders in two ways. First, they are left with $20 stock when they could have received $30 per share. Second, the company purchased stock from the bidder at $35 per share, which represents a direct loss by the remaining shareholders of $15 for each repurchased share.

Managers who buy back stock in targeted repurchases typically argue that their firms are worth more than the raiders offered and that, in time, the "true value" will be revealed in the form of a much higher stock price. This situation might be true if a company were in the process of restructuring itself, or if new products with high potential were in the pipeline. But if the old management had been in power for a long time and had a history of making empty promises, then one should question whether the true purpose of the buyback was to protect stockholders or management.

Another characteristic of a stockholder-friendly charter is that it does not contain a **shareholder rights provision,** better described as a **poison pill.** These provisions give the shareholders of target firms the right to buy a specified number of shares in the company at a very low price if an outside group or firm acquires a specified percentage of the firm's stock. Therefore, if a potential acquirer tries to take over a company, its other shareholders will be entitled to purchase additional shares of stock at a bargain price, thus seriously diluting the holdings of the raider. For this reason, these clauses are called poison pills, because if they are in the charter, the acquirer will end up swallowing a poison pill if the acquisition is successful. Obviously, the existence of a poison pill makes a takeover more difficult, and this helps to entrench management.

A third management entrenchment tool is a **restricted voting rights** provision, which automatically cancels the voting rights of any shareholder who owns more

16. Some states have laws that go further than others to protect management. This is one reason that many companies are incorporated in manager-friendly Delaware. Some companies have even shifted their state of incorporation to Delaware because their managers felt that a hostile takeover attempt was likely. Note that a "shareholder-friendly charter" could and would waive the company's right to strong anti-takeover protection, even if the state allowed it.

17. Someone can, under the law, acquire up to 5% of a firm's stock without announcing the acquisition. Once the 5% limit has been hit, the acquirer has 10 days to "announce" the acquisition by filing Schedule 13D with the SEC. Schedule 13D reports not only the acquirer's number of shares but also his or her intentions, such as a passive investment or a takeover. These reports are monitored closely, so as soon as one is filed, management is alerted to the possibility of an imminent takeover.

THE GLOBAL ECONOMIC CRISIS

Would the U.S. Government Be an Effective Board Director?

In response to the global economic crisis that began with the recession of 2007, many governments are becoming major stakeholders in heretofore publicly traded companies. For example, the U.S. government has invested billions in Fannie Mae and Freddie Mac, taking them into conservatorship and having a direct say in the companies' leadership and operations, including the dismissal of former Fannie Mae CEO Daniel Mudd in 2008.

The U.S. government has made multibillon-dollar investments in banks (among them, Citigroup, Bank of America, JPMorgan Chase, and Wells Fargo), insurance companies, AIG (spectacularly), and auto companies (GM and Chrysler). Much of this has been in the form of

preferred stock, which does not give the government any direct voting or decision-making authority. However, the government has certainly applied moral suasion, as evidenced by the removal of GM's former CEO Rick Wagoner. The government also imposed limits on executive compensation at firms receiving additional government funds.

For the most part, however, the government does not have voting rights at bailout recipients, nor does it have representation on their boards of directors. It will be interesting to see if this changes and if the government takes a more direct role in corporate governance.

Source: See **http://projects.nytimes.com/creditcrisis/recipients/table** for updates on TARP recipients.

than a specified amount of the company's stock. The board can grant voting rights to such a shareholder, but this is unlikely if that shareholder plans to take over the company.

11.5c Using Compensation to Align Managerial and Shareholder Interests

The typical CEO today receives a fixed salary, a cash bonus based on the firm's performance, and stock-based compensation, either in the form of stock grants or option grants. Cash bonuses often are based upon short-run operating factors, such as this year's growth in earnings per share, or medium-term operating performance, such as earnings growth over the past 3 years.

Stock-based compensation is often in the form of options. Chapter 6 explains option valuation in detail, but here we discuss how a standard **stock option compensation plan** works. Suppose IBM decides to grant an option to an employee, allowing her to purchase a specified number of IBM shares at a fixed price, called the **strike price** (or **exercise price**), regardless of the actual price of the stock. The strike price is usually set equal to the current stock price at the time the option is granted. Thus, if IBM's current price were $100, then the option would have an exercise price of $100. Options usually cannot be exercised until after some specified period (the **vesting period**), which is usually 1 to 5 years. Some grants have **cliff vesting,** which means that all the granted options vest at the same date, such as 3 years after the grant. Other grants have **annual vesting,** which means that a certain percentage vest each year. For example, one-third of the options in the grant might vest each year. The options have an **expiration date,** usually 10 years after issue. For our IBM example, assume that the options have cliff vesting in 3 years and have an expiration date in 10 years. Thus, the employee can exercise the option 3 years after issue or wait as long as 10 years. Of course, the employee would not exercise unless IBM's stock is above the $100 exercise price, and if the price never rose above $100, the option would expire unexercised. However, if the stock price were above $100 on the expiration date, the option would surely be exercised.

Suppose the stock price had grown to $134 after 5 years, at which point the employee decided to exercise the option. She would buy stock from IBM for $100, so IBM would get only $100 for stock worth $134. The employee would (probably) sell the stock the same day she exercised the option and hence would receive in cash the $34 difference between the $134 stock price and the $100 exercise price. There are two important points to note in this example. First, most employees sell stock soon after exercising the option. Thus, the incentive effects of an option grant typically end when the option is exercised. Second, option pricing theory shows that it is not optimal to exercise a conventional call option on stock that does not pay dividends before the option expires: An investor is always better off selling the option in the marketplace rather than exercising it. But because employee stock options are not tradable, grantees often exercise the options well before they expire. For example, people often time the exercise of options to the purchase of a new home or some other large expenditure. But early exercise occurs not just for liquidity reasons, such as needing cash to purchase a house, but also because of behavioral reasons. For example, exercises occur more frequently after stock run-ups, which suggests that grantees view the stock as overpriced.

In theory, stock options should align a manager's interests with those of shareholders, influencing the manager to behave in a way that maximizes the company's value. But in practice there are two reasons why this does not always occur.

First, suppose a CEO granted options on 1 million shares. If we use the same stock prices as in our previous example then the grantee would receive $34 for each option, or a total of $34 million. Keep in mind that this is in addition to an annual salary and cash bonuses. The logic behind employee options is that they motivate people to work harder and smarter, thus making the company more valuable and benefiting shareholders. But take a closer look at this example. If the risk-free rate is 5.5%, the market risk premium is 6%, and IBM's beta is 1.19, then the expected return, based on the CAPM, is 5.5% + 1.19(6%) = 12.64%. IBM's dividend yield is only 0.8%, so the expected annual price appreciation must be about 11.84% (12.64% − 0.8% = 11.84%). Now note that if IBM's stock price grew from $100 to $134 over 5 years, that would translate to an annual growth rate of only 6%, not the 11.84% shareholders expected. Thus, the executive would receive $34 million for helping run a company that performed below shareholders' expectations. As this example illustrates, standard stock options do not necessarily link executives' wealth with that of shareholders.

Second, and even worse, the events of the early 2000s showed that some executives were willing to illegally falsify financial statements in order to drive up stock prices just prior to exercising their stock options.[18] In some notable cases, the subsequent stock

---

18. Several academic studies show that option-based compensation leads to a greater likelihood of earnings restatements (which means having to refile financial statements with the SEC because there was a material error) and outright fraud. See A. Agrawal and S. Chadha, "Corporate Governance and Accounting Scandals," *Journal of Law and Economics,* 2006, pp. 371–406; N. Burns and S. Kedia, "The Impact of Performance-Based Compensation on Misreporting," *Journal of Financial Economics,* January 2006, pp. 35–67; and D. J. Denis, P. Hanouna, and A. Sarin, "Is There a Dark Side to Incentive Compensation?" *Journal of Corporate Finance,* June 2006, pp. 467–488.

price drop and loss of investor confidence have forced firms into bankruptcy. Such behavior is certainly not in shareholders' best interests!

As a result, companies today are experimenting with different types of compensation plans that involve different vesting periods and different measures of performance. For example, from a legal standpoint it is more difficult to manipulate EVA (Economic Value Added) than earnings per share.[19] Therefore, many companies incorporate EVA-type measures in their compensation systems. Also, many companies have quit granting options and instead are granting restricted stock that cannot be sold until it has vested.

Just as "all ships rise in a rising tide," so too do most stocks rise in a bull market such as that of 2003–2007. In a strong market, even the stocks of companies whose performance ranks in the bottom 10% of their peer group can rise and thus trigger handsome executive bonuses. This situation is leading to compensation plans that are based on *relative* as opposed to *absolute* stock price performance. For example, some compensation plans have indexed options whose exercise prices depend on the performance of the market or a subset of competitors.

Finally, the empirical results from academic studies show that the correlation between executive compensation and corporate performance is mixed. Some studies suggest that the type of compensation plan used affects company performance, while others find little effect, if any. But we can say with certainty that managerial compensation plans will continue to receive lots of attention from researchers, the popular press, and boards of directors.

11.5d Capital Structure and Internal Control Systems

Capital structure decisions can affect managerial behavior. As the debt level increases, so does the probability of bankruptcy. This increased threat of bankruptcy brings with it two effects on behavior. First, as discussed earlier in this chapter, managers may waste money on unnecessary expenditures and perquisites. This behavior is more likely when times are good and firms are flush with cash; it is less likely in the face of high debt levels and possible bankruptcy. Thus high levels of debt tend to reduce managerial waste. Second, however, high levels of debt may also reduce a manager's willingness to undertake positive-NPV but risky projects. Most managers have their personal reputation and wealth tied to a single company. If that company has a lot of debt then a particularly risky project, even if it has a positive NPV, may be just too risky for the manager to tolerate because a bad outcome could lead to bankruptcy and loss of the manager's job. Stockholders, on the other hand, are diversified and would want the manager to invest in positive-NPV projects even if they are risky. When managers forgo risky but value-adding projects, the resulting **underinvestment problem** reduces firm value. So increasing debt might increase firm value by reducing wasteful expenditures, but it also might reduce value by inducing underinvestment by managers. Empirical tests have not been able to establish exactly which effect dominates.

Internal control systems have become an increasingly important issue since the passage of the Sarbanes-Oxley Act of 2002. Section 404 of the act requires companies to establish effective internal control systems. The Securities and Exchange Commission,

---

19. For a discussion of EVA, see Al Ehrbar, *EVA: The Real Key to Creating Wealth* (New York: John Wiley & Sons, 1998); and Pamela P. Peterson and David R. Peterson, *Company Performance and Measures of Value Added* (The Research Foundation of the Institute of Chartered Financial Analysts, 1996).

THE GLOBAL ECONOMIC CRISIS

Shareholder Reactions to the Crisis

It is safe to say that shareholders were dismayed by the market's decline in 2008, and it looks like they are seeking more control. RiskMetrics Group provides data on the shareholder proposals that are included in proxy statements, with votes tallied at the annual meetings. The 2009 proxy season saw an enormous number of proposals related to corporate governance, especially compensation, as shown below.

	Number of proposals
Executive Pay Issues	
Advisory vote on compensation	85
Vote on golden parachutes	9
Anti–gross-ups policy	2
Vote on executive death benefits	12
Retention period for stock awards	14
Establish bonus banks	3
Board Issues	
Independent board chairman	33
Allow for cumulative voting	34
Require majority vote to elect directors	51
Takeover Defenses/Other	
Right to call special meeting	61
End supermajority vote requirement	15
Repeal classified board	71

It will be interesting to see how companies respond to these votes and whether more shareholder power translates into better performance.

Source: RiskMetrics Group, **www.riskmetrics.com/knowledge/proxy_season_scorecard_2009**.

which is charged with the implementation of Sarbanes-Oxley, defines an effective internal control system as one that provides "reasonable assurance regarding the reliability of financial reporting and the preparation of financial statements for external purposes in accordance with generally accepted accounting principles." In other words, investors should be able to trust a company's reported financial statements.

11.5e Environmental Factors Outside of a Firm's Control

As noted earlier, corporate governance is also affected by environmental factors that are outside of a firm's control, including the regulatory/legal environment, block ownership patterns, competition in the product markets, the media, and litigation.

THE SARBANES-OXLEY ACT OF 2002 AND CORPORATE GOVERNANCE

In 2002, Congress passed the Sarbanes-Oxley Act, known in the industry as SOX, as a measure to improve transparency in financial accounting and to prevent fraud. SOX consists of eleven chapters, or *titles*, which establish wide-ranging new regulations for auditors, CEOs and CFOs, boards of directors, investment analysts, and investment banks. These regulations are designed to ensure that (a) companies that perform audits are sufficiently independent of the companies that they audit, (b) a key executive in each company *personally* certifies that the financial statements are complete and accurate, (c) the board of directors's audit committee is relatively independent of management, (d) financial analysts are relatively independent of the companies they analyze, and (e) companies publicly and promptly release all important information about their financial condition. The individual titles are briefly summarized below.

Title I establishes the Public Company Accounting Oversight Board, whose charge is to oversee auditors and establish quality control and ethical standards for audits.

Title II requires that auditors be independent of the companies that they audit. Basically this means they can't provide consulting services to the companies they audit. The purpose is to remove financial incentives for auditors to help management cook the books.

Title III requires that the board of directors's audit committee must be composed of "independent" members. Section 302 requires that the CEO and CFO must review the annual and quarterly financial statements and reports and personally certify that they are complete and accurate. Penalties for certifying reports that executives know are false range up to a $5 million fine, 20 years in prison, or both. Under Section 304, if the financial statements turn out to be false and must be *restated,* then certain bonuses and equity-based compensation that executives earn must be reimbursed to the company.

Title IV's Section 401(a) requires prompt disclosure and more extensive reporting on off–balance sheet transactions. Section 404 requires that management evaluate its internal financial controls and report whether they are "effective." The external auditing firm must also indicate whether it agrees with management's evaluation of its internal controls. Section 409 requires that a company disclose to the public promptly and *in plain English* any material changes to its financial condition. Title IV also places restrictions on the loans that a company can make to its executives.

Title V addresses the relationship between financial analysts, the investment banks they work for, and the companies they cover. It requires that analysts and brokers who make stock recommendations disclose any conflicts of interest they might have concerning the stocks they recommend.

Titles VI and VII are technical in nature, dealing with the SEC's budget and powers and requiring that several studies be undertaken by the SEC.

Title VIII establishes penalties for destroying or falsifying audit records. It also provides "whistle-blower protection" for employees who report fraud.

Title IX increases the penalties for a variety of white-collar crimes associated with securities fraud, such as mail and wire fraud. Section 902 also makes it a crime to alter, destroy, or hide documents that might be used in an investigation. It also makes it a crime to conspire to do so.

Title X requires that the CEO sign the company's federal income tax return.

Title XI provides penalties for obstructing an investigation and grants the SEC authority to remove officers or directors from a company if they have committed fraud.

Regulations and Laws

The regulatory/legal environment includes the agencies that regulate financial markets, such as the SEC. Even though the fines and penalties levied on firms for financial misrepresentation by the SEC are relatively small, the damage to a firm's reputation can have significant costs, leading to extremely large reductions in the firm's value.[20] Thus, the regulatory system has an enormous impact on corporate governance and firm value.

The regulatory/legal environment also includes the laws and legal system under which a company operates. These vary greatly from country to country. Studies show that firms located in countries with strong legal protection for investors have stronger corporate governance and that this is reflected in better access to financial markets, a lower cost of equity, increases in market liquidity, and less noise in stock prices.[21]

Block Ownership Patterns

Prior to the 1960s, most U.S. stock was owned by a large number of individual investors, each of whom owned a diversified portfolio of stocks. Because each individual owned a small amount of any given company's stock, there was little that he or she could do to influence its operations. Also, with such a small investment, it was not cost effective for the investor to monitor companies closely. Indeed dissatisfied stockholders would typically just "vote with their feet" by selling the stock. This situation began to change as institutional investors such as pension funds and mutual funds gained control of larger and larger shares of investment capital—and as they then acquired larger and larger percentages of all outstanding stock. Given their large block holdings, it now makes sense for institutional investors to monitor management, and they have the clout to influence the board. In some cases, they have actually elected their own representatives to the board. For example, when TIAA-CREF, a huge private pension fund, became frustrated with the performance and leadership of Furr's/Bishop, a cafeteria chain, the fund led a fight that ousted the entire board and then elected a new board consisting only of outsiders.

In general, activist investors with large blocks in companies have been good for all shareholders. They have searched for firms with poor profitability and then replaced management with new teams that are well versed in value-based management techniques, thereby improving profitability. Not surprisingly, stock prices usually rise on the news that a well-known activist investor has taken a major position in an underperforming company.

Note that activist investors can improve performance even if they don't go so far as to take over a firm. More often, they either elect their own representatives to the board or simply point out the firm's problems to other board members. In such cases, boards often change their attitudes and become less tolerant when they realize that the management team is not following the dictates of value-based management. Moreover, the firm's top managers recognize what will happen if they don't whip the company into shape, and they go about doing just that.

---

20. For example, see Jonathan M. Karpoff, D. Scott Lee, and Gerald S. Martin, "The Cost to Firms of Cooking the Books," *Journal of Financial and Quantitative Analysis,* September 2008, pp. 581–612.
21. For example, see R. La Porta, F. Lopez-de-Silanes, A. Shleifer, and R. Vishny, "Legal Determinants of External Finance," *Journal of Finance,* January 1997, pp. 1131–1150; Hazem Daouk, Charles M. C. Lee, and David Ng, "Capital Market Governance: How Do Security Laws Affect Market Performance?" *Journal of Corporate Finance,* June 2006, pp. 560–593; and Li Jin and Stewart C. Myers, "R^2 Around the World: New Theory and New Tests," *Journal of Financial Economics,* February 2006, pp. 257–292.

Competition in Product Markets

The degree of competition in a firm's product market has an impact on its corporate governance. For example, companies in industries with lots of competition don't have the luxury of tolerating poorly performing CEOs. As might be expected, CEO turnover is higher in competitive industries than in those with less competition.[22] When most firms in an industry are fairly similar, you might expect it to be easier to find a qualified replacement from another firm for a poorly performing CEO. This is exactly what the evidence shows: As industry homogeneity increases, so does the incidence of CEO turnover.[23]

The Media and Litigation

Corporate governance, especially compensation, is a hot topic in the media. The media can have a positive impact by discovering or reporting corporate problems, such as the Enron scandal. Another example is the extensive coverage that was given to option backdating, in which the exercise prices of executive stock options were set *after* the options officially were granted. Because the exercise prices were set at the lowest stock price during the quarter in which the options were granted, the options were in-the-money and more valuable when their "official" lives began. Several CEOs have already lost their jobs over this practice, and more firings are likely.

However, the media can also hurt corporate governance by focusing too much attention on a CEO. Such "superstar" CEOs often command excessive compensation packages and spend too much time on activities outside the company, resulting in too much pay for too little performance.[24]

In addition to penalties and fines from regulatory bodies such as the SEC, civil litigation also occurs when companies are suspected of fraud. Recent research indicates that such suits lead to improvements in corporate governance.[25]

Self Test

What are the two primary forms of corporate governance provisions that correspond to the stick and the carrot?

What factors improve the effectiveness of a board of directors?

What are three provisions in many corporate charters that deter takeovers?

Describe how a typical stock option plan works. What are some problems with a typical stock option plan?

---

22. See M. De Fond and C. Park, "The Effect of Competition on CEO Turnover," *Journal of Accounting and Economics,* Vol. 27, 1999, pp. 35–56; and T. Fee and C. Hadlock, "Management Turnover and Product Market Competition: Empirical Evidence from the U.S. Newspaper Industry," *Journal of Business,* April 2000, pp. 205–243.
23. See R. Parrino, "CEO Turnover and Outside Succession: A Cross-Sectional Analysis," *Journal of Financial Economics,* Vol. 46, 1997, pp. 165–197.
24. See U. Malmendier and G. A. Tate, "Superstar CEOs," *Quarterly Journal of Economics,* November 2009, pp. 1593–1638.
25. For example, see D. B. Farber, "Restoring Trust after Fraud: Does Corporate Governance Matter?" *Accounting Review,* April 2005, pp. 539–561; and Stephen P. Ferris, Tomas Jandik, Robert M. Lawless, and Anil Makhija, "Derivative Lawsuits as a Corporate Governance Mechanism: Empirical Evidence on Board Changes Surrounding Filings," *Journal of Financial and Quantitative Analysis,* March 2007, pp. 143–166.

INTERNATIONAL CORPORATE GOVERNANCE

Corporate governance includes the following factors: (1) the likelihood that a poorly performing firm can be taken over; (2) whether the board of directors is dominated by insiders or outsiders; (3) the extent to which most of the stock is held by a few large "blockholders" versus many small shareholders; and (4) the size and form of executive compensation. An interesting study compared corporate governance in Germany, Japan, and the United States.

First, note from the accompanying table that the threat of a takeover serves as a stick in the United States but not in Japan or Germany. This threat, which reduces management entrenchment, should benefit shareholders in the United States relative to the other two countries. Second, German and Japanese boards are larger than those in the United States. Japanese boards consist primarily of insiders, unlike German and American boards, which have similar inside/outside mixes. It should be noted, though, that the boards of most large German corporations include representatives of labor, whereas U.S. boards represent only shareholders. Thus, it would appear that U.S. boards, with a higher percentage of outsiders, would have interests most closely aligned with those of shareholders.

German and Japanese firms are also more likely to be controlled by large blocks of stock than those in the United States. Although pension and mutual funds, as well as other institutional investors, are increasingly important in the United States, block ownership is still less prevalent than in Germany and Japan. In both Germany and Japan, banks often own large blocks of stock, something that is not permitted by law in the United States, and corporations also own large blocks of stock in other corporations. In Japan, combinations of companies, called *keiretsus*, have cross-ownership of stock among the member companies, and these interlocking blocks distort the definition of an outside board member. For example, when the performance of a company in a keiretsu deteriorates, new directors are often appointed from the staffs of other members of the keiretsu. Such appointees might be classified officially as insiders, but they represent interests other than those of the troubled company's CEO.

In general, large blockholders are better able to monitor management than are small investors, so one might expect the blockholder factor to favor German and Japanese shareholders. However, these blockholders have other relationships with the company that might be detrimental to outside shareholders. For example, if one company buys from another, transfer pricing might be used to shift wealth to a favored company, or a company might be forced to buy from a sister company in spite of the availability of lower-cost resources from outside the group.

Executive compensation packages differ dramatically across the three countries, with U.S. executives receiving by far the highest compensation. However, compensation plans are remarkably similar in terms of how sensitive total compensation is to corporate performance.

Which country's system of corporate governance is best from the standpoint of a shareholder whose goal is stock price maximization? There is no definitive answer. U.S. stocks have had the best performance in recent years. Moreover, German and Japanese companies are slowly moving toward the U.S. system with respect to size of compensation, and compensation plans in all three countries are being linked ever more closely to performance. At the same time, however, U.S. companies are moving toward the others in the sense of having larger ownership blocks; because those blocks are primarily held by pension and mutual funds (rather than banks and related corporations), they better represent the interests of shareholders.

Source: Steven N. Kaplan, "Top Executive Incentives in Germany, Japan, and the USA: A Comparison," in *Executive Compensation and Shareholder Value*, Jennifer Carpenter and David Yermack, eds. (Boston: Kluwer Academic Publishers, 1999), pp. 3–12.

International Characteristics of Corporate Governance

	Germany	Japan	United States
Threat of a takeover	Moderate	Low	High
Board of directors			
Size of board	26	21	14
Percent insiders	27%	91%	33%
Percent outsiders	73%	9%	67%
Are large blocks of stock typically owned by			
A controlling family?	Yes	No	No
Another corporation?	Yes	Yes	No
A bank?	Yes	Yes	No
Executive compensation			
Amount of compensation	Moderate	Low	High
Sensitivity to performance	Low to moderate	Low to moderate	Low to moderate

www

See **www.esopasso-ciation.org** for more on ESOPs.

11.6 Employee Stock Ownership Plans (ESOPs)

Studies show that 90% of the employees who receive stock under option plans sell the stock as soon as they exercise their options, so the plans motivate employees only for a limited period.[26] Moreover, many companies limit their stock option plans to key managers and executives. To help provide long-term productivity gains and improve retirement incomes for all employees, Congress authorized the use of **Employee Stock Ownership Plans (ESOPs)**. Today about 9,000 privately held companies and 1,000 publicly held firms have ESOPs, and more are being created every day. Typically, the ESOP's major asset is shares of the common stock of the company that created it, and of the 10,000 total ESOPs, about 2,500 of them actually own a majority of their company's stock.[27]

To illustrate how an ESOP works, consider Gallagher & Abbott Inc. (G&A), a construction company located in Knoxville, Tennessee. G&A's simplified balance sheet is shown below:

G&A's Balance Sheet prior to ESOP (Millions of Dollars)

Assets		Liabilities and Equity	
Cash	$ 10	Debt	$100
Other	190	Equity (1 million shares)	100
Total	$200	Total	$200

Now G&A creates an ESOP, which is a new legal entity. The company issues 500,000 shares of new stock at $100 per share, or $50 million in total, which it

---

26. See Gary Laufman, "To Have and Have Not," *CFO,* March 1998, pp. 58–66.
27. See Eugene Pilotte, "Employee Stock Ownership Plans, Management Motives, and Shareholder Wealth: A Review of the Evidence," *Journal of Financial Education,* Spring 1997, pp. 41–46; and Daniel Eisenberg, "No ESOP Fable," *Time,* May 10, 1999, p. 95.

sells to the ESOP. The company's employees are the ESOP's stockholders, and each employee receives an ownership interest based on the size of his or her salary and years of service. The ESOP borrows the $50 million to buy the newly issued stock.[28] Financial institutions are willing to lend the ESOP the money because G&A signs a guarantee for the loan. Here is the company's new balance sheet:

G&A's Balance Sheet after the ESOP (Millions of Dollars)

Assets		Liabilities and Equity	
Cash	$ 60	Debt[a]	$100
Other	190	Equity (1.5 million shares)	150
Total	$250	Total	$250

[a]The company has guaranteed the ESOP's loan, and it has promised to make payments to the ESOP sufficient to retire the loan, but this does not show up on the balance sheet.

The company now has an additional $50 million of cash and $50 million more of book equity, but it has a de facto liability owing to its guarantee of the ESOP's debt. It could use the cash to finance an expansion, but many companies use the cash to repurchase their own common stock, so we assume that G&A will do likewise. The company's new balance sheets, and that of the ESOP, are shown below:

G&A's Balance Sheet after the ESOP and Share Repurchase (Millions of Dollars)

Assets		Liabilities and Equity	
Cash	$ 10	Debt	$100
Other	190	Equity (1 million shares)	150
		Treasury stock	(50)
Total	$200	Total	$200

ESOP's Initial Balance Sheet (Millions of Dollars)

Assets		Liabilities and Equity	
G&A stock	$50	Debt	$50
		Equity	0
Total	$50	Total	$50

Note that although the company's balance sheet looks exactly as it did initially, there is actually a huge difference—the company has guaranteed the ESOP's debt and hence it has an off–balance sheet liability of $50 million. Moreover, because the ESOP has no equity, the guarantee is very real indeed. Finally, observe that operating assets have not been increased at all, but the total debt outstanding supported by those assets has increased by $50 million.[29]

---

28. Our description is somewhat simplified. Technically, the stock would be placed in a suspense account and then be allocated to employees as the debt is repaid.
29. We assumed that the company used the $50 million paid to it by the ESOP to repurchase common stock and thus to increase its de facto debt. It could have used the $50 million to retire debt, in which case its true debt ratio would remain unchanged, or it could have used the money to support an expansion.

If this were the whole story, then there would be no reason to have an ESOP. However, G&A has promised to make payments to the ESOP in sufficient amounts to enable the ESOP to pay interest and principal charges on the debt, amortizing it over 15 years. Thus, after 15 years, the debt will be paid off and the ESOP's equity holders (the employees) will have equity with a book value of $50 million and a market value that could be much higher if G&A's stock increases, as it should over time. Then, as employees retire, the ESOP will distribute a pro rata amount of the G&A stock to each employee, who can then use it as a part of his or her retirement plan.

An ESOP is clearly beneficial for employees, but why would a company want to establish one? There are five primary reasons.

1. Congress passed the enabling legislation in hopes of enhancing employees' productivity and thus making the economy more efficient. In theory, employees who have equity in the enterprise will work harder and smarter. Note too that if employees are more productive and creative then this will benefit outside shareholders, because productivity enhancements that benefit ESOP shareholders also benefit outside shareholders.

2. The ESOP represents additional compensation to employees: In our example, there is a $50 million (or more) transfer of wealth from existing shareholders to employees over the 15-year period. Presumably, if the ESOP were not created then some other form of compensation would have been required, and that alternative compensation might not have the secondary benefit of enhancing productivity. Also note that the ESOP's payments to employees (as opposed to the payment by the company) come primarily at retirement, and Congress wanted to boost retirement incomes.

3. Depending on when an employee's rights to the ESOP are vested, the ESOP may help the firm retain employees.

4. There are strong tax incentives that encourage a company to form an ESOP. First, Congress decreed that when the ESOP owns 50% or more of the company's common stock, financial institutions that lend money to ESOPs can exclude from taxable income 50% of the interest they receive on the loan. This improves the financial institutions' after-tax returns, which allows them to lend to ESOPs at below-market rates. Therefore, a company that establishes an ESOP can borrow through the ESOP at a lower rate than would otherwise be available—in our example, the $50 million of debt would be at a reduced rate.

   There is also a second tax advantage. If the company were to borrow directly, it could deduct interest but not principal payments from its taxable income. However, companies typically make the required payments to their ESOPs in the form of cash dividends. Dividends are not normally deductible from taxable income, but *cash dividends paid on ESOP stock are deductible if the dividends are paid to plan participants or are used to repay the loan.* Thus, companies whose ESOPs own 50% of their stock can in effect borrow on ESOP loans at subsidized rates and then deduct both the interest and principal payments made on the loans. American Airlines and Publix Supermarkets are two of the many firms that have used ESOPs to obtain this benefit, along with motivating employees by giving them an equity interest in the enterprise.

5. A less desirable use of ESOPs is to help companies avoid being acquired by another company. The company's CEO, or someone appointed by the CEO, typically acts as trustee for its ESOP, and the trustee is supposed to vote the ESOP's shares according to the will of the plan participants. Moreover, the

participants, who are the company's employees, usually oppose takeovers because they frequently involve labor cutbacks. Therefore, if an ESOP owns a significant percentage of the company's shares, then management has a powerful tool for warding off takeovers. This is not good for outside stockholders.

Are ESOPs good for a company's shareholders? In theory, ESOPs motivate employees by providing them with an ownership interest. That should increase productivity and thereby enhance stock values. Moreover, tax incentives mitigate the costs associated with some ESOPs. However, an ESOP can be used to help entrench management, and that could hurt stockholders. How do the pros and cons balance out? The empirical evidence is not entirely clear, but certain findings are worth noting. First, if an ESOP is established to help defend against a takeover, then the firm's stock price typically falls when plans for the ESOP are announced. The market does not like the prospect of entrenching management and having to give up the premium normally associated with a takeover. However, if the ESOP is established for tax purposes and/or to motivate employees, the stock price generally goes up at the time of the announcement. In these cases, the company typically has a subsequent improvement in sales per employee and other long-term performance measures, which stimulates the stock price. Indeed, a study showed that companies with ESOPs enjoyed a 26% average annual stock return compared to a return of only 19% for peer companies without ESOPs.[30] It thus appears that ESOPs, if used appropriately, can be a powerful tool for creating shareholder value.

What are ESOPs? What are some of their advantages and disadvantages?	**Self Test**

Summary

- **Corporate assets** consist of operating assets and financial, or nonoperating, assets.
- **Operating assets** take two forms: assets-in-place and growth options.
- **Assets-in-place** include the land, buildings, machines, and inventory that the firm uses in its operations to produce products and services.
- **Growth options** refer to opportunities the firm has to increase sales. They include opportunities arising from R&D expenditures, customer relationships, and the like.
- **Nonoperating assets** are distinguished from operating assets and include **financial assets** such as investments in marketable securities and noncontrolling interests in the stock of other companies.
- The **value of nonoperating assets** is usually close to the figure reported on the balance sheet.

---

30.   See Daniel Eisenberg, "No ESOP Fable," *Time*, May 10, 1999, p. 95.

- The **value of operations** is the present value of all the future free cash flows expected from operations when discounted at the weighted average cost of capital:

$$V_{op(at\ time\ 0)} = \sum_{t=1}^{\infty} \frac{FCF_t}{(1 + WACC)^t}$$

- The **horizon value** is the value of operations at the end of the explicit forecast period. It is also called the **terminal value** or **continuing value,** and it is equal to the present value of all free cash flows beyond the forecast period, discounted back to the end of the forecast period at the weighted average cost of capital:

$$Continuing\ value = V_{op(at\ time\ N)} = \frac{FCF_{N+1}}{WACC - g} = \frac{FCF_N(1 + g)}{WACC - g}$$

- The **corporate valuation model** can be used to calculate the total value of a company by finding the value of operations plus the value of nonoperating assets.
- The intrinsic **value of equity** is the total value of the company minus the value of the debt and preferred stock. The intrinsic **price per share** is the total value of the equity divided by the number of shares.
- **Value-based management** involves the systematic use of the corporate valuation model to evaluate a company's potential decisions.
- The four **value drivers** are (1) the growth rate (g) of sales; (2) operating profitability (OP), which is measured by the ratio of NOPAT to sales; (3) capital requirements (CR), as measured by the ratio of operating capital to sales; and (4) the weighted average cost of capital (WACC).
- **Expected return on invested capital (EROIC)** is equal to expected NOPAT divided by the amount of capital that is available at the beginning of the year.
- A company creates value when the spread between EROIC and WACC is positive—that is, when EROIC – WACC > 0.
- **Corporate governance** involves the manner in which shareholders' objectives are implemented, and it is reflected in a company's policies and actions.
- The two primary mechanisms used in corporate governance are (1) the threat of removal of a poorly performing CEO and (2) the type of plan used to compensate executives and managers.
- Poorly performing managers can be removed either by a takeover or by the company's own board of directors. Provisions in the corporate charter affect the difficulty of a successful takeover, and the composition of the board of directors affects the likelihood of a manager being removed by the board.
- **Managerial entrenchment** is most likely when a company has a weak board of directors coupled with strong anti-takeover provisions in its corporate charter. In this situation, the likelihood that badly performing senior managers will be fired is low.
- **Nonpecuniary benefits** are noncash perks such as lavish offices, memberships at country clubs, corporate jets, foreign junkets, and the like. Some of these expenditures may be cost effective, but others are wasteful and simply reduce profits. Such fat is almost always cut after a hostile takeover.

- **Targeted share repurchases,** also known as **greenmail,** occur when a company buys back stock from a potential acquirer at a price higher than the market price. In return, the potential acquirer agrees not to attempt to take over the company.
- **Shareholder rights provisions,** also known as **poison pills,** allow existing shareholders to purchase additional shares of stock at a price lower than the market value if a potential acquirer purchases a controlling stake in the company.
- A **restricted voting rights** provision automatically deprives a shareholder of voting rights if he or she owns more than a specified amount of stock.
- **Interlocking boards of directors** occur when the CEO of Company A sits on the board of Company B and also B's CEO sits on A's board.
- A **stock option** provides for the purchase of a share of stock at a fixed price, called the **exercise price,** no matter what the actual price of the stock is. Stock options have an **expiration date,** after which they cannot be exercised.
- An **Employee Stock Ownership Plan (ESOP)** is a plan that facilitates employees' ownership of stock in the company for which they work.

Questions

11–1 Define each of the following terms:
    a. Assets-in-place; growth options; nonoperating assets
    b. Net operating working capital; operating capital; NOPAT; free cash flow
    c. Value of operations; horizon value; corporate valuation model
    d. Value-based management; value drivers; EROIC
    e. Managerial entrenchment; nonpecuniary benefits
    f. Greenmail; poison pills; restricted voting rights
    g. Stock option; ESOP

11–2 Explain how to use the corporate valuation model to find the price per share of common equity.

11–3 Explain how it is possible for sales growth to decrease the value of a profitable company.

11–4 What are some actions an entrenched management might take that would harm shareholders?

11–5 How is it possible for an employee stock option to be valuable even if the firm's stock price fails to meet shareholders' expectations?

Problems   Answers Appear in Appendix B

Easy Problems 1–5

11–1 **Free Cash Flow** Use the following income statements and balance sheets to calculate Garnet Inc.'s free cash flow for 2012.

Garnet Inc.

	2013	2012
Income Statement (Millions of Dollars)		
Net sales	$530.0	$500.0
Costs (except depreciation)	400.0	380.0
Depreciation	30.0	25.0
Total operating costs	$430.0	$405.0
Earnings before interest and taxes (EBIT)	100.0	95.0
Less interest	23.0	21.0
Earnings before taxes	$ 77.0	$ 74.0
Taxes (40%)	30.8	29.6
Net income	$ 46.2	$ 44.4

Balance Sheet	2013	2012
Assets		
Cash	$ 28.0	$ 27.0
Marketable securities	69.0	66.0
Accounts receivable	84.0	80.0
Inventories	112.0	106.0
Total current assets	$293.0	$279.0
Net plant and equipment	281.0	265.0
Total assets	$574.0	$544.0
Liabilities and Equity		
Accounts payable	$ 56.0	$ 52.0
Notes payable	138.0	130.0
Accruals	28.0	28.0
Total current liabilities	$222.0	$210.0
Long-term bonds	173.0	164.0
Common stock	100.0	100.0
Retained earnings	79.0	70.0
Common equity	$179.0	$170.0
Total liabilities and equity	$574.0	$544.0

11-2 **Value of Operations of Constant Growth Firm** EMC Corporation has never paid a dividend. Its current free cash flow of $400,000 is expected to grow at a constant rate of 5%. The weighted average cost of capital is WACC = 12%. Calculate EMC's value of operations.

11-3 **Horizon Value** Current and projected free cash flows for Radell Global Operations are shown below. Growth is expected to be constant after 2014, and the weighted average cost of capital is 11%. What is the horizon (continuing) value at 2014?

	Actual	Projected		
	2012	2013	2014	2015
Free cash flow (millions of dollars)	$606.82	$667.50	$707.55	$750.00

11-4 **EROIC and MVA of Constant Growth Firm** A company has capital of $200 million. It has an EROIC of 9%, forecasted constant growth of 5%, and a WACC of 10%. What is its value of operations? What is its intrinsic MVA? (*Hint:* Use Equation 11-5.)

11-5 **Value Drivers and Horizon Value of Constant Growth Firm** You are given the following forecasted information for the year 2016: sales = $300,000,000, operating profitability (OP) = 6%, capital requirements (CR) = 43%, growth (g) = 5%, and the weighted average cost of capital (WACC) = 9.8%. If these values remain constant, what is the horizon value (i.e., the 2016 value of operations)? (*Hint:* Use Equation 11-4.)

Intermediate Problems 6–7

11-6 **Value of Operations** Brooks Enterprises has never paid a dividend. Free cash flow is projected to be $80,000 and $100,000 for the next 2 years, respectively; after the second year, FCF is expected to grow at a constant rate of 8%. The company's weighted average cost of capital is 12%.
   a. What is the terminal, or horizon, value of operations? (*Hint:* Find the value of all free cash flows beyond Year 2 discounted back to Year 2.)
   b. Calculate the value of Brooks's operations.

11-7 **Corporate Valuation** Dozier Corporation is a fast-growing supplier of office products. Analysts project the following free cash flows (FCFs) during the next 3 years, after which FCF is expected to grow at a constant 7% rate. Dozier's weighted average cost of capital is WACC = 13%.

	Year		
	1	**2**	**3**
Free cash flow ($ millions)	−$20	$30	$40

   a. What is Dozier's terminal, or horizon, value? (*Hint:* Find the value of all free cash flows beyond Year 3 discounted back to Year 3.)
   b. What is the current value of operations for Dozier?
   c. Suppose Dozier has $10 million in marketable securities, $100 million in debt, and 10 million shares of stock. What is the intrinsic price per share?

Challenging Problems 8–10

11-8 **Value of Equity** The balance sheet of Hutter Amalgamated is shown below. If the 12/31/2012 value of operations is $756 million, what is the 12/31/2012 intrinsic market value of equity?

Balance Sheet, December 31, 2012 (Millions of Dollars)

Assets		Liabilities and Equity	
Cash	$ 20.0	Accounts payable	$ 19.0
Marketable securities	77.0	Notes payable	151.0
Accounts receivable	100.0	Accruals	51.0
Inventories	200.0	Total current liabilities	$221.0
Total current assets	$397.0	Long-term bonds	190.0
Net plant and equipment	279.0	Preferred stock	76.0
		Common stock	100.0
		(par plus PIC)	
		Retained earnings	89.0
		Common equity	$189.0
Total assets	$676.0	Total liabilities and equity	$676.0

11-9 **Price per Share** The balance sheet of Roop Industries is shown below. The 12/31/2012 value of operations is $651 million, and there are 10 million shares of common equity. What is the intrinsic price per share?

Balance Sheet, December 31, 2012 (Millions of Dollars)

Assets		Liabilities and Equity	
Cash	$ 20.0	Accounts payable	$ 19.0
Marketable securities	47.0	Notes payable	65.0
Accounts receivable	100.0	Accruals	51.0
Inventories	200.0	Total current liabilities	$135.0
Total current assets	$367.0	Long-term bonds	131.0
Net plant and equipment	279.0	Preferred stock	33.0
		Common stock	160.0
		(par plus PIC)	
		Retained earnings	187.0
		Common equity	$347.0
Total assets	$646.0	Total liabilities and equity	$646.0

11-10 **Corporate Valuation** The financial statements of Lioi Steel Fabricators are shown below—both the actual results for 2012 and the projections for 2013. Free cash flow is expected to grow at a 6% rate after 2013. The weighted average cost of capital is 11%.
   a. If operating capital as of 12/31/2012 is $502.2 million, what is the free cash flow for 12/31/2013?
   b. What is the horizon value as of 12/31/2013?
   c. What is the value of operations as of 12/31/2012?
   d. What is the total value of the company as of 12/31/2012?
   e. What is the intrinsic price per share for 12/31/2012?

Income Statements for the Year Ending December 31
(Millions of Dollars Except for Per Share Data)

	Actual 2012	Projected 2013
Net sales	$500.0	$530.0
Costs (except depreciation)	360.0	381.6
Depreciation	37.5	39.8
Total operating costs	$397.5	$421.4
Earnings before interest and taxes	$102.5	$108.6
Less interest	13.9	16.0
Earnings before taxes	$ 88.6	$ 92.6
Taxes (40%)	35.4	37.0
Net income before preferred dividends	$ 53.2	$ 55.6
Preferred dividends	6.0	7.4
Net income available for common dividends	$ 47.2	$ 48.2
Common dividends	$ 40.8	$ 29.7
Addition to retained earnings	$ 6.4	$ 18.5
Number of shares	10.0	10.0
Dividends per share	$ 4.08	$ 2.97

Balance Sheets for December 31
(Millions of Dollars)

	Actual 2012	Projected 2013
Assets		
Cash	$ 5.3	$ 5.6
Marketable securities	49.9	51.9
Accounts receivable	53.0	56.2
Inventories	106.0	112.4
Total current assets	$214.2	$226.1
Net plant and equipment	375.0	397.5
Total assets	$589.2	$623.6
Liabilities and Equity		
Accounts payable	$ 9.6	$ 11.2
Notes payable	69.9	74.1
Accruals	27.5	28.1
Total current liabilities	$107.0	$113.4
Long-term bonds	140.8	148.2
Preferred stock	35.0	37.1
Common stock (par plus PIC)	160.0	160.0
Retained earnings	146.4	164.9
Common equity	$306.4	$324.9
Total liabilities and equity	$589.2	$623.6

Spreadsheet Problem

11-11 Build a Model: Corporate Valuation Start with the partial model in the file *Ch11 P11 Build a Model.xls* on the textbook's Web site. The Henley Corporation is a privately held company specializing in lawn care products and services. The most recent financial statements are shown below.

Income Statement for the Year Ending December 31
(Millions of Dollars Except for Per Share Data)

	2012
Net sales	$800.0
Costs (except depreciation)	576.0
Depreciation	60.0
Total operating costs	$636.0
Earnings before interest and taxes	$164.0
Less interest	32.0
Earnings before taxes	$132.0
Taxes (40%)	52.8
Net income before preferred dividends	$ 79.2
Preferred dividends	1.4
Net income available for common dividends	$ 77.9
Common dividends	$ 31.1
Addition to retained earnings	$ 46.7
Number of shares (in millions)	10.0
Dividends per share	$ 3.11

Balance Sheet for December 31 (Millions of Dollars)

Assets	2012	Liabilities and Equity	2012
Cash	$ 8.0	Accounts payable	$ 16.0
Marketable securities	20.0	Notes payable	40.0
Accounts receivable	80.0	Accruals	40.0
Inventories	160.0	Total current liabilities	$ 96.0
Total current assets	$268.0	Long-term bonds	300.0
Net plant and equipment	600.0	Preferred stock	15.0
		Common stock (par plus PIC)	257.0
		Retained earnings	200.0
		Common equity	$457.0
Total assets	$868.0	Total liabilities and equity	$868.0

Projected ratios and selected information for the current and projected years are shown below.

	Actual	Projected			
	2012	2013	2014	2015	2016
Sales growth rate		15%	10%	6%	6%
Costs/Sales	72%	72	72	72	72
Depreciation/Net PPE	10	10	10	10	10
Cash/Sales	1	1	1	1	1
Accounts receivable/Sales	10	10	10	10	10

(Continued)

	Actual	Projected			
	2012	**2013**	**2014**	**2015**	**2016**
Inventories/Sales	20	20	20	20	20
Net PPE/Sales	75	75	75	75	75
Accounts payable/Sales	2	2	2	2	2
Accruals/Sales	5	5	5	5	5
Tax rate	40	40	40	40	40
Weighted average cost of capital (WACC)	10.5	10.5	10.5	10.5	10.5

a. Forecast the parts of the income statement and balance sheet that are necessary for calculating free cash flow.

b. Calculate free cash flow for each projected year. Also calculate the growth rates of free cash flow each year to verify that there is constant growth (that is, the same as the constant growth rate in sales) by the end of the forecast period.

c. Calculate operating profitability (OP = NOPAT/Sales), capital requirements (CR = Operating capital/Sales), and expected return on invested capital (EROIC = Expected NOPAT/Operating capital at beginning of year). Based on the spread between EROIC and WACC, do you think that the company will have a positive Market Value Added (MVA = Market value of company – Book value of company = Value of operations – Operating capital)?

d. Calculate the value of operations and MVA. (*Hint:* First calculate the horizon value at the end of the forecast period, which is equal to the value of operations at the end of the forecast period.) Assume that the annual growth rate beyond the horizon is 6%.

e. Calculate the price per share of common equity as of 12/31/2012.

MINI CASE

You have been hired as a consultant to Kulpa Fishing Supplies (KFS), a company that is seeking to increase its value. The company's CEO and founder, Mia Kulpa, has asked you to estimate the value of two privately held companies that KFS is considering acquiring. But first, the senior management of KFS would like for you to explain how to value companies that don't pay any dividends. You have structured your presentation around the following items.

a. List the two types of assets that companies own.

b. What are assets-in-place? How can their value be estimated?

c. What are nonoperating assets? How can their value be estimated?

d. What is the total value of a corporation? Who has claims on this value?

e. The first acquisition target is a privately held company in a mature industry owned by two brothers, each with 5 million shares of stock. The company currently has free cash flow of $24 million. Its WACC is 11%, and the FCF is expected to grow at a constant rate of 5%. The company owns marketable securities of $100 million. It is financed with $200 million of debt, $50 million of preferred stock, and $210 million of book equity.

   (1) What is its value of operations?

   (2) What is its total corporate value?

   (3) What is its intrinsic value of equity?

   (4) What is its intrinsic stock price per share?

   (5) What is its intrinsic MVA (MVA = Total corporate value − Total book value of capital supplied by investors)?

f. The second acquisition target is a privately held company in a growing industry. The target has recently borrowed $40 million to finance its expansion; it has no other debt or preferred stock. It pays no dividends and currently has no marketable securities. KFS expects the company to produce free cash flows of −$5 million in 1 year, $10 million in 2 years, and $20 million in 3 years. After 3 years, free cash flow will grow at a rate of 6%. The target's WACC is 10% and it currently has 10 million shares of stock outstanding.

   (1) What is the company's horizon value (i.e., its value of operations at Year 3)? What is its current value of operations (i.e., at Time 0)?

   (2) What is its intrinsic value of equity on a price-per-share basis?

g. KFS is also interested in applying value-based management to its own divisions. Explain what value-based management is.

h. What are the four value drivers? How does each of them affect value?

i. What is the expected return on invested capital (EROIC)? Why is the spread between EROIC and WACC so important?

j. KFS has two divisions. Both have current sales of $1,000 million, current expected growth of 5%, and a WACC of 10%. Division A has high profitability (OP = 6%) but high capital requirements (CR = 78%). Division B has low profitability (OP = 4%) but low capital requirements (CR = 27%). Given the current growth rate of 5%, determine the intrinsic MVA of each division. What is the intrinsic MVA of each division if growth is instead 6%?

k. What is the EROIC of each division for 5% growth and for 6% growth? How is this related to intrinsic MVA?

l. List six potential managerial behaviors that can harm a firm's value.

m. The managers at KFS have heard that corporate governance can affect shareholder value. What is corporate governance? List five corporate governance provisions that are internal to a firm and are under its control.

n. What characteristics of the board of directors usually lead to effective corporate governance?

o. List three provisions in the corporate charter that affect takeovers.

p. Briefly describe the use of stock options in a compensation plan. What are some potential problems with stock options as a form of compensation?

q. What is block ownership? How does it affect corporate governance?

r. Briefly explain how regulatory agencies and legal systems affect corporate governance.

Selected Additional Cases

The following cases from TextChoice, Cengage Learning's online case library, cover many of the concepts discussed in this chapter and are available at **www.textchoice2.com/casenet.**

Klein-Brigham Series:
Case 41, "Advanced Fuels Corporation," and Case 93, "Electro Technology Corporation," discuss financing and valuing a new venture.

Brigham-Buzzard Series:
Case 14, "Maris Distributing Company," discusses valuation techniques used in a court case.

PART III

Project Valuation

Chapter 12

Capital Budgeting: Decision Criteria

© Mike-dee/Shutterstock.com

WEB

The textbook's Web site contains an *Excel* file that will guide you through the chapter's calculations. The file for this chapter is ***Ch12 Tool Kit.xls***, and we encourage you to open the file and follow along as you read the chapter.

In Chapters 12 and 13, we discuss *capital budgeting*. Here *capital* refers to long-term assets used in production, and a *budget* is a plan that outlines projected expenditures during a future period. Thus, *the capital budget* is a summary of planned investments of assets that will last for more than a year, and **capital budgeting** is the whole process of analyzing projects and deciding which ones to accept and thus include in the capital budget. Chapter 12 focuses on the basics of capital budgeting, especially the primary criteria used to evaluate projects, and it explains why one method—the net present value (NPV)—is the best single criterion. We use simplified examples in this chapter to explain the basic theory and then, in Chapter 13, we go on to discuss how cash flows are estimated, how risk is measured, and how capital budgeting decisions are actually made.

Beginning of Chapter Questions

As you read the chapter, consider how you would answer the following questions. You *should not* necessarily be able to answer the questions before you read the chapter. Rather, you should use them to get a sense of the issues covered in the chapter. After reading the chapter, you should be able to give at least partial answers to the questions, and you should be able to give better answers after the chapter has been discussed in class. Note, too, that it is often useful, when answering conceptual questions, to use hypothetical data to illustrate your answer. We illustrate the answers with an *Excel* model that is available on the textbook's Web site. Accessing the model and working through it is a useful exercise, and it provides insights that are useful when answering the questions.

1. Describe the **six primary capital budgeting decision criteria.** What are their pros and cons, and how are they related to maximizing shareholder wealth? Should managers use just one criterion, or are there good reasons for using two or more criteria in the decision process?

2. Why do conflicts sometimes arise between the **net present value (NPV)** and **internal rate of return (IRR)** methods; that is, what conditions can lead to conflicts? Can similar conflicts arise between **modified internal rate of return (MIRR)** and NPV rankings, or between rankings by the MIRR and IRR methods?

3. If management's goal is to maximize shareholder wealth, should it focus on the regular IRR or the MIRR? Explain your answer.

4. Under what conditions might you find more than one IRR for a project? How would you decide whether or not to accept the project? If you were comparing two mutually exclusive projects, one with a single IRR of 12% and the other with two different IRRs of 10% and 15%, how should you choose between the projects?

5. What is the **unequal life problem,** under what conditions is it relevant, and how should it be dealt with?

6. What is a **post-audit,** and what is the purpose of this audit?

7. What is **capital rationing,** what conditions lead to it, and how should it be dealt with?

12.1 An Overview of Capital Budgeting

Capital budgeting is based on the same procedures used in the corporate valuation model, but with one major difference. Whereas we used the corporate valuation model to evaluate existing companies or divisions, capital budgeting involves both analyzing and creating investment projects. If companies execute their plans well, then capital budgeting projects will be successful, but poor execution will lead to project failures. Still, in both corporate valuation and capital budgeting, we forecast a set of cash flows, find the present value of those flows, and then make the investment if and only if the PV of the expected future cash flows exceeds the investment's cost.

A firm's growth, and even its ability to remain competitive and to survive, depends on a constant flow of ideas for new products, improvements in existing products, and ways to operate more efficiently. Accordingly, well-managed firms go to great lengths to develop good capital budgeting proposals. For example, the executive vice president of one successful corporation told us that his company takes the following steps to generate projects.

Our R&D department constantly searches for new products and ways to improve existing products. In addition, our Executive Committee, which consists of senior executives in marketing, production, and finance, identifies the products and markets in which our company should compete, and the Committee sets long-run targets for each division. These targets, which are spelled out in the corporation's strategic business plan, provide a general guide to the operating executives who must meet them. The operating

CORPORATE VALUATION AND CAPITAL BUDGETING

You can calculate the cash flows (CF) for a project in much the same way as for a firm. When the project's cash flows are discounted at the appropriate risk-adjusted weighted average cost of capital ("r" for simplicity), the result is the project's value. Note that when valuing an entire firm we discount its free cash flows at the overall weighted average cost of capital, but when valuing a project we discount its cash flows at the project's own risk-adjusted cost of capital. Note also that the firm's free cash flows are the total of all the net cash flows from its past projects. Thus, if a project is accepted and put into operation, it will provide cash flows that add to the firm's free cash flows and thus to the firm's value.

Subtracting the initial cost of the project from the discounted future expected cash flows gives the project's net present value (NPV). A project that has a positive NPV adds value to the firm. In fact, the firm's Market Value Added (MVA) is the sum of all its projects' NPVs. The key point, though, is that the process of evaluating projects, or capital budgeting, is absolutely critical for a firm's success.

© Cengage Learning 2013

executives then seek new products, set expansion plans for existing products, and look for ways to reduce production and distribution costs. Since bonuses and promotions are based on each unit's ability to meet or exceed its targets, these economic incentives encourage our operating managers to seek out profitable investment opportunities.

While our senior executives are judged and rewarded on the basis of how well their units perform, people further down the line are given bonuses and stock options for suggestions that lead to profitable investments. Additionally, a percentage of our corporate profit is set aside for distribution to nonexecutive employees, and we have an Employees' Stock Ownership Plan (ESOP) to provide further incentives. Our objective is to encourage employees at all levels to keep an eye out for good ideas, especially those that lead to capital investments.

Analyzing capital expenditure proposals is not costless—benefits can be gained, but analysis does have a cost. For certain types of projects, an extremely detailed analysis may be warranted, whereas simpler procedures are adequate for other projects. Accordingly, firms generally categorize projects and analyze those in each category somewhat differently:

1. *Replacement needed to continue profitable operations.* An example would be an essential pump on a profitable offshore oil platform. The platform manager could make this investment without an elaborate review process.
2. *Replacement to reduce costs.* An example would be the replacement of serviceable but obsolete equipment in order to lower costs. A fairly detailed analysis would be needed, with more detail required for larger expenditures.
3. *Expansion of existing products or markets.* These decisions require a forecast of growth in demand, so a more detailed analysis is required. Go/no-go decisions are generally made at a higher level than are replacement decisions.
4. *Expansion into new products or markets.* These investments involve strategic decisions that could change the fundamental nature of the business. A detailed analysis is required, and the final decision is made by top officers, possibly with board approval.
5. *Contraction decisions.* Especially during bad recessions, companies often find themselves with more capacity than they are likely to need in the foreseeable future. Then, rather than continue to operate plants at, say, 50% of capacity and incur losses as a result of excessive fixed costs, they decide to downsize. That generally requires payments to laid off workers and additional costs for shutting down selected operations. These decisions are made at the board level.
6. *Safety and/or environmental projects.* Expenditures necessary to comply with environmental orders, labor agreements, or insurance policy terms fall into this category. How these projects are handled depends on their size, with small ones being treated much like the Category 1 projects and large ones requiring expenditures that might even cause the firm to abandon the line of business.
7. *Other.* This catch-all includes items such as office buildings, parking lots, and executive aircraft. How they are handled varies among companies.
8. *Mergers.* Buying a whole firm (or division) is different from buying a machine or building a new plant. Still, basic capital budgeting procedures are used when making merger decisions.

Relatively simple calculations, and only a few supporting documents, are required for most replacement decisions, especially maintenance investments in profitable plants. More detailed analyses are required as we move on to more complex expansion decisions, especially for investments in new products or areas. Also, within each category projects are grouped by their dollar costs: Larger investments require increasingly detailed analysis and approval at higher levels. Thus, a plant manager might be authorized to approve maintenance expenditures up to $10,000 using a simple payback analysis, but the full board of directors might have to approve decisions that involve either amounts greater than $1 million or expansions into new products or markets.

If a firm has capable and imaginative executives and employees, and if its incentive system is working properly, then many ideas for capital investment will be forthcoming. Some ideas will be good and should be funded, but others should be killed. Therefore, the following procedures have been established for screening projects and deciding which to accept or reject:[1]

1. Net Present Value (NPV)
2. Internal Rate of Return (IRR)
3. Modified Internal Rate of Return (MIRR)

---

1. One other rarely used criterion, the Accounting Rate of Return, is covered in the chapter's *Excel Tool Kit* model and *Web Extension 12A*.

4. Profitability Index (PI)
5. Regular Payback
6. Discounted Payback

As we shall see, the NPV is the best single criterion, primarily because it is directly related to the firm's central goal of maximizing the stock's intrinsic value. However, all of the methods provide some useful information, and all are used in practice.

In the sections that follow, we will use these six procedures to analyze the decisions that Guyton Products Company (GPC) faces. GPC is a high-tech "lab-bench-to-market" development company that takes cutting-edge research advances and translates them into consumer products. GPC has recently licensed a nano-fabrication coating technology from a university that promises to significantly increase the efficiency with which solar energy can be harvested and stored as heat. GPC is considering using this technology in two different product lines. In the first, code-named "Project S" for "solid," the technology would be used to coat rock and concrete structures to be used as passive heat sinks and sources for energy-efficient residential and commercial buildings. In the second, code-named "Project L" for "liquid," it would be used to coat the collectors in a high-efficiency solar water heater. GPC must decide whether to undertake either of these two projects.

In Chapter 13, we will discuss in detail how to estimate the cash flows for Project L and how to deal with uncertainty and risk in making capital budgeting decisions, but for now we will take the two projects' cash flows as given so that we can focus on how to use the six procedures.[2]

Self Test

How is capital budgeting similar to security valuation? How is it different?

What are some ways that firms generate ideas for capital projects?

Identify the major project classification categories, and explain how and why they are used.

List six procedures used for screening projects and deciding which to accept or reject.

12.2 Net Present Value (NPV)

The **net present value (NPV)**, defined as the present value of a project's cash inflows minus the present value of its costs, tells us how much the project contributes to shareholder wealth—the larger the NPV, the more value the project adds and thus the higher the stock's price. NPV is generally regarded as the best single screening criterion. We use the data for GPC's Projects S and L shown in Figure 12-1 to illustrate the calculations for the NPV and the other criteria. Although Projects S and L are GPC's "solid" and "liquid" projects, you may also find it helpful to think of S and L as standing for *Short* and *Long*: Project S is a short-term project in the sense that most of its cash inflows come in relatively soon; Project L has more total cash inflows, but most are realized in the later years.

The projects are equally risky, and they both have a 10% cost of capital. Furthermore, the cash flows have been adjusted to incorporate the impact of depreciation,

---

2. We will see in Chapter 13 that the cash flows we analyze are, in fact, free cash flows as calculated in Chapters 8 and 9 and analyzed in Chapter 11.

Figure 12-1   Cash Flows (CF$_t$) and Selected Evaluation Criteria for Projects S and L

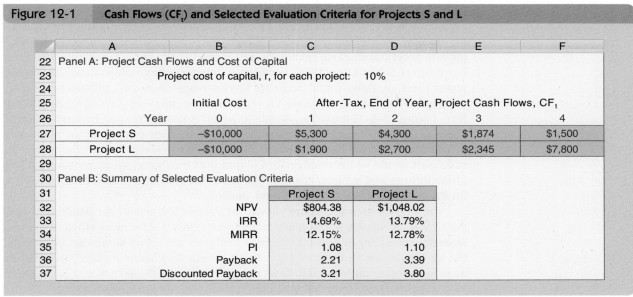

	A	B	C	D	E	F
22	Panel A: Project Cash Flows and Cost of Capital					
23		Project cost of capital, r, for each project:	10%			
24						
25		Initial Cost		After-Tax, End of Year, Project Cash Flows, CF$_t$		
26	Year	0	1	2	3	4
27	Project S	–$10,000	$5,300	$4,300	$1,874	$1,500
28	Project L	–$10,000	$1,900	$2,700	$2,345	$7,800
29						
30	Panel B: Summary of Selected Evaluation Criteria					
31			Project S	Project L		
32		NPV	$804.38	$1,048.02		
33		IRR	14.69%	13.79%		
34		MIRR	12.15%	12.78%		
35		PI	1.08	1.10		
36		Payback	2.21	3.39		
37		Discounted Payback	3.21	3.80		

taxes, and salvage values.[3] The investment outlays are shown under Year 0, and they include investments in fixed assets and any necessary working capital. All subsequent cash flows occur at the end of the year. All of the calculations can be done easily with a financial calculator, but since capital budgeting in the real world is generally done using a spreadsheet, we show how problems would be set up in *Excel*.

WEB

See ***Ch12 Tool Kit.xls*** on the textbook's Web site.

We can find the NPVs as follows.

1. Calculate the present value of each cash flow discounted at the project's risk-adjusted cost of capital, which is r = 10% in our example.
2. The sum of the discounted cash flows is defined as the project's NPV.

The equation for the NPV, set up with input data for Project S, is

$$NPV = CF_0 + \frac{CF_1}{(1 + r)^1} + \frac{CF_2}{(1 + r)^2} + \cdots + \frac{CF_N}{(1 + r)^N}$$

$$= \sum_{t=0}^{N} \frac{CF_t}{(1 + r)^t}$$

(12–1)

Applying Equation 12-1 to Project S, we have

$$NPV_S = -\$10,000 + \frac{\$5,300}{(1.10)^1} + \frac{\$4,300}{(1.10)^2} + \frac{\$1,874}{(1.10)^3} + \frac{\$1,500}{(1.10)^4}$$

$$= -\$10,000 + \$4,818.18 + \$3,553.72 + \$1,407.96 + \$1,024.52$$

$$= \$804.38$$

---

3. The most difficult aspect of capital budgeting is estimating the "relevant" cash flows, which are defined as the cash flows generated by the project that are available for distribution to investors. We illustrate this for Project L in Chapter 13.

Here CF_t is the expected net cash flow at Time t, r is the project's risk-adjusted cost of capital (or WACC), and N is its life. Projects generally require an initial investment—for example, developing the product, buying the equipment needed to make it, building a factory, and stocking inventory. The initial investment is a negative cash flow. For Projects S and L, only CF_0 is negative, but for a large project such as an FPL power plant, outflows would occur for several years before cash inflows begin.

Figure 12-2 shows, on Row 51, the cash flow time line for project S as taken from Figure 12-1. The cost is −$10,000, which is not discounted because it occurs at t = 0. The PV of each cash inflow, and the sum of the PVs, is shown in Column B. You could find the PVs of the cash flows with a calculator or with *Excel*, and the end result would be the numbers in Column B of the figure. When we sum the PVs of the inflows and subtract the cost, the result is $804.38, which is NPV_S. The NPV for Project L, $1,048.02, can be found similarly.

The step-by-step procedure shown for Project S is useful for illustrating how the NPV is calculated, but in practice (and on exams) it is far more efficient to use a financial calculator or *Excel*. Different calculators are set up somewhat differently, but (as we discuss in Chapter 28) they all have a "cash flow register" that can be used to evaluate uneven cash flows such as those for Projects S and L. Equation 12-1 is actually programmed into these calculators, and all we need to do is enter the cash flows (with the correct signs) along with r = I/YR = 10. Once the data have been entered, you can press the NPV key to get the answer, 804.38, on the screen.[4] If you are familiar with *Excel*, you can use it to find the NPVs for S and L:

$$NPV_S = \$804.38$$
$$NPV_L = \$1,048.02$$

We provide the model used to obtain these values in the chapter's *Excel Tool Kit*. If you are familiar with *Excel* then you should look at the model, as this is how most people in the real world deal with capital budgeting problems.

Before using these NPVs in the decision process, we need to know whether Projects S and L are **independent** or **mutually exclusive**. Independent projects are those whose cash flows are not affected by other projects. If Wal-Mart were considering a new store in Boise and another in Atlanta, those projects would

WEB

See *Ch12 Tool Kit.xls* on the textbook's Web site.

Figure 12-2   Finding the NPV for Projects S and L

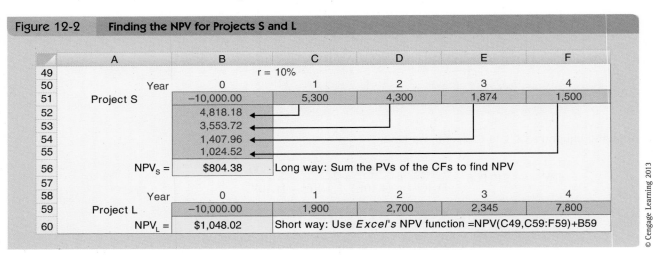

	A	B	C	D	E	F
49			r = 10%			
50		Year	0	1	2	3	4
51	Project S	−10,000.00	5,300	4,300	1,874	1,500
52		4,818.18				
53		3,553.72				
54		1,407.96				
55		1,024.52				
56	NPV_S =	$804.38	Long way: Sum the PVs of the CFs to find NPV			
57						
58		Year	0	1	2	3	4
59	Project L	−10,000.00	1,900	2,700	2,345	7,800
60	NPV_L =	$1,048.02	Short way: Use *Excel's* NPV function =NPV(C49,C59:F59)+B59			

© Cengage Learning 2013

---

4. The keystrokes for finding the NPV are shown for several calculators in the calculator tutorials we provide on the textbook's Web site.

be independent, and if both had positive NPVs, Wal-Mart should accept both. In the case of Projects S and L, GPC is targeting two different heating markets—one for passive solar heating and one for hot water, and so the projects are independent. Mutually exclusive projects, on the other hand, are two different ways of accomplishing the same result, so if one project is accepted then the other must be rejected. A conveyor-belt system to move goods in a warehouse and a fleet of forklifts for the same purpose would be mutually exclusive—accepting one implies rejecting the other. If, instead of two different uses of the nano-coatings, Projects S and L had been two different ways to manufacture the solar water heaters, then they would have been mutually exclusive.

What should the decision be if Projects S and L are independent? In this case, both should be accepted because both have positive NPVs and thus add value to the firm. However, if they are mutually exclusive, then Project L should be chosen because it has the higher NPV and thus adds more value than S. We can summarize these criteria with the following rules.

12.2a NPV Decision Rules

Independent projects: If NPV exceeds zero, accept the project. Since S and L both have positive NPVs, accept them both if they are independent.

Mutually exclusive projects: Accept the project with the highest positive NPV. If no project has a positive NPV, then reject them all. If S and L are mutually exclusive, the NPV criterion would select L.

Projects must be either independent or mutually exclusive, so one or the other of these rules applies to every project.[5]

Self Test

Why is NPV the primary capital budgeting decision criterion?

What is the difference between "independent" and "mutually exclusive" projects?

Projects SS and LL have the following cash flows:

End-of-Year Cash Flows

	0	1	2	3
SS	−700	500	300	100
LL	−700	100	300	600

If the cost of capital is 10%, then what are the projects' NPVs?
($NPV_{SS} = \$77.61$; $NPV_{LL} = \$89.63$)

What project or set of projects would be in your capital budget if SS and LL were (a) independent or (b) mutually exclusive? (**Both; LL**)

12.3 Internal Rate of Return (IRR)

In Chapter 4 we discussed the yield to maturity on a bond, and we explained that if you hold a bond to maturity then you will earn the yield to maturity on your

---

5. This is a simplification. For example, some projects can benefit others—these are "complementary" projects. Other projects harm others—these are called "cannibalizing" projects. These concepts are addressed in Chapter 13.

investment. The YTM is found as the discount rate that forces the present value of the cash inflows to equal the price of the bond. This same concept is used in capital budgeting when we calculate a project's **internal rate of return**, or **IRR**:

A project's IRR is the discount rate that forces the PV of the inflows to equal the initial cost (or to equal the PVs of all the costs if costs are incurred over several years). This is equivalent to forcing the NPV to equal zero. The IRR is an estimate of the project's rate of return, and it is comparable to the YTM on a bond.

To calculate the IRR, we begin with Equation 12-1 for the NPV, replace r in the denominator with the term "IRR," and set the NPV equal to zero. This transforms Equation 12-1 into Equation 12-2, the one used to find the IRR. The rate that forces NPV to equal zero is the IRR.[6]

(12–2)

$$NPV = CF_0 + \frac{CF_1}{(1 + IRR)^1} + \frac{CF_2}{(1 + IRR)^2} + \ldots + \frac{CF_N}{(1 + IRR)^N} = 0$$

$$= \sum_{t=0}^{N} \frac{CF_t}{(1 + IRR)^t} = 0$$

For Project S, we have

$$NPV_s = 0 = -\$10{,}000 + \frac{\$5{,}300}{(1 + IRR)^1} + \frac{\$4{,}300}{(1 + IRR)^2} + \frac{\$1{,}874}{(1 + IRR)^3} + \frac{\$1{,}500}{(1 + IRR)^4}$$

WEB

See *Ch12 Tool Kit.xls* on the textbook's Web site.

Figure 12-3 illustrates the process for finding the IRR of Project S.

Three procedures can be used to find the IRR:

1. *Trial-and-error.* We could use a trial-and-error procedure: Try a discount rate, see if the equation solves to zero, and if it doesn't, try a different rate. Continue until we find the rate that forces the NPV to zero, and that rate will be the IRR. No

Figure 12-3   Finding the IRR

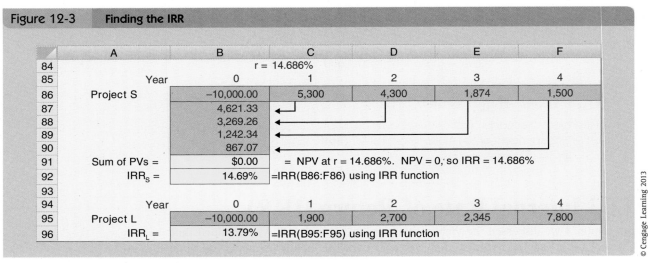

	A	B	C	D	E	F
84		r = 14.686%				
85	Year	0	1	2	3	4
86	Project S	−10,000.00	5,300	4,300	1,874	1,500
87		4,621.33				
88		3,269.26				
89		1,242.34				
90		867.07				
91	Sum of PVs =	$0.00	= NPV at r = 14.686%. NPV = 0, so IRR = 14.686%			
92	IRR$_S$ =	14.69%	=IRR(B86:F86) using IRR function			
93						
94	Year	0	1	2	3	4
95	Project L	−10,000.00	1,900	2,700	2,345	7,800
96	IRR$_L$ =	13.79%	=IRR(B95:F95) using IRR function			

© Cengage Learning 2013

---

6. For a large, complex project like an FPL power plant, costs are incurred for several years before cash inflows begin. That simply means that we have a number of negative cash flows before the positive cash flows begin.

one does this, however. Instead, IRR is always calculated using either a financial calculator or *Excel* (or some other computer program) as described below.

2. *Calculator solution.* Enter the cash flows into the calculator's cash flow register just as we did to find the NPV, and then press the calculator key labeled "IRR." Instantly, you get the internal rate of return. Here are the values for Projects S and L:[7]

$$IRR_S = 14.686\%$$
$$IRR_L = 13.786\%$$

3. *Excel solution.* It is even easier to find IRRs using *Excel,* as we demonstrate in this chapter's *Tool Kit.*[8]

Why is the discount rate that causes a project's NPV to equal zero so special? The reason is that the IRR is an estimate of the project's rate of return. If this return exceeds the cost of the funds used to finance the project, then the difference is a bonus that goes to the firm's stockholders and causes the stock's price to rise. Project S has an estimated return of 14.686% versus a 10% cost of capital, so its bonus is 4.686%. On the other hand, if the IRR is less than the cost of capital then stockholders must make up the shortfall, which would hurt the stock price.

Note again that the IRR formula, Equation 12-2, is simply the NPV formula, Equation 12-1, solved for the particular discount rate that forces the NPV to zero. Thus, the same basic equation is used for both methods. The only difference is that with the NPV method, the discount rate is given and we find the NPV, whereas with the IRR method, the NPV is set equal to zero and we find the interest rate that provides this equality.

If the IRR criterion is used to rank projects, then the decision rules are as follows.

Independent projects: If IRR exceeds the project's WACC, then the project should be accepted. If IRR is less than the project's WACC, reject it. Projects S and L both have positive IRRs, so they would both be accepted by the IRR method. Note that both projects were also accepted by the NPV criterion, so the NPV and IRR criteria provide the same result if the projects are independent.

Mutually exclusive projects: Accept the mutually exclusive project with the highest IRR, provided that the project's IRR is greater than its WACC. Reject any project whose IRR does not exceed the firm's WACC. Since Project S has the higher IRR, it should be accepted (and L rejected) if the projects are mutually exclusive. However, recall that Project L had the larger NPV, so the NPV method ranked L over S and thus would choose L. Therefore, a conflict will exist between the NPV and the IRR criteria if the projects are mutually exclusive.

---

7. See our calculator tutorials on the textbook's Web site. Note that once the cash flows have been entered into the cash flow register, you can find both the NPV and the IRR. To find the NPV, enter the interest rate (I/YR) and then press the NPV key. Then, with no further entries, press the IRR key to find the IRR. Thus, once you set up the calculator to find the NPV, it is easy to find the IRR. This is one reason most firms calculate both the NPV and the IRR. If you calculate one, it is easy to also calculate the other, and both provide information that decision makers find useful. The same is true with *Excel:* After estimating cash flows, it is easy to calculate both NPV and IRR.

8. Note that to calculate the IRR with *Excel* the full data range is specified, because *Excel*'s IRR function assumes that the first cash flow (the negative $10,000) occurs at t = 0. You can use the function wizard if you don't have the formula memorized.

The IRR is logically appealing—it is useful to know the rates of return on proposed investments. However, as we see from Projects L and S, NPV and IRR can produce conflicting conclusions when one is choosing between mutually exclusive projects, and when conflicts occur the NPV criterion is generally better. A simple, but extreme, example should make this very clear. Consider Projects A and B, which are mutually exclusive and each has a 10% cost of capital. Project A costs $1 and will generate cash flows of $0.60 a year for 10 years. Project B costs $100,000 and will generate cash flows of $20,000 a year for 10 years. Project A's IRR is 59.4% and its NPV is $2.60. Project B's IRR is much smaller, only 15.1%, but its NPV is $22,891. Provided the company can obtain the capital it needs to invest in profitable projects, then clearly Project B is better—the company is worth $22,891 more if Project B is selected, but only $2.60 more if Project A is selected, so Project B should be selected despite its lower IRR.

Self Test

In what sense is a project's IRR similar to the YTM on a bond?

The cash flows for Projects SS and LL are as follows:

| | **End-of-Year Cash Flows** | | | |
	0	1	2	3
SS	−700	500	300	100
LL	−700	100	300	600

Assume that the firm's WACC = r = 10%. What are the two projects' IRRs? (**IRR$_{SS}$ = 18.0%; IRR$_{LL}$ = 15.6%**)

Which project would the IRR method select if the firm has a 10% cost of capital and the projects are (a) independent or (b) mutually exclusive? (**Both; SS**)

12.4 Multiple Internal Rates of Return[9]

One problem with the IRR is that, under certain conditions, a project may have more than one IRR. First, note that a project is said to have *normal* cash flows if it has one or more cash outflows (costs) followed by a series of cash inflows. If, however, a cash *outflow* occurs sometime after the inflows have started, meaning that the signs of the cash flows change *more than once*, then the project is said to have *nonnormal* cash flows. Here's an illustration of these concepts:

Normal:	− + + + + +	or − − − + + + + +
Nonnormal:	− + + + + −	or − + + + − + + +

An example of a project with nonnormal flows would be a strip coal mine where the company first spends money to buy the property and prepare the site for mining, has positive inflows for several years, and then spends more money to return the land to its original condition. In this case, the project might have two IRRs—that is, **multiple IRRs**.[10]

---

9. This section is relatively technical, and some instructors may choose to omit it without loss of continuity.

10. Equation 12-2 is a polynomial of degree n, so it has n different roots, or solutions. All except one of the roots are imaginary numbers when investments have normal cash flows (one or more cash outflows followed by cash inflows), so in the normal case only one value of IRR appears. However, the possibility of multiple real roots, and hence of multiple IRRs, arises when negative net cash flows occur after the project has been placed in operation.

To illustrate multiple IRRs, suppose a firm is considering a potential strip mine (Project M) that has a cost of $1.6 million and will produce a cash flow of $10 million at the end of Year 1; then, at the end of Year 2, the firm must spend $10 million to restore the land to its original condition. Therefore, the project's expected net cash flows are as follows (in millions):

	Year 0	End of Year 1	End of Year 2
Cash flows	−$1.6	+$10	−$10

We can substitute these values into Equation 12-2 and then solve for the IRR:

$$NPV = \frac{-\$1.6 \text{ million}}{(1 + IRR)^0} + \frac{\$10 \text{ million}}{(1 + IRR)^1} + \frac{-\$10 \text{ million}}{(1 + IRR)^2} = 0$$

For these cash flows, the NPV equals 0 when IRR = 25%, but it also equals 0 when IRR = 400%.[11] Therefore, Project M has one IRR of 25% and another of 400%, and we don't know which one to use. This relationship is depicted graphically in Figure 12-4.[12] The graph is constructed by plotting the project's NPV at different discount rates.

WEB

See **Ch12 Tool Kit.xls** on the textbook's Web site for all calculations.

Observe that no dilemma regarding Project M would arise if the NPV method were used; we would simply find the NPV at the appropriate cost of capital and use it to evaluate the project. We would see that if Project M's cost of capital were 10% then its NPV would be −$0.774 million and the project should be rejected. If r were between 25% and 400% then the NPV would be positive, but any such number would probably not be realistic or useful for anything. (At such a high cost of capital, the firm's typical projects would have negative NPVs.)

Self Test

What condition regarding cash flows would cause more than one IRR to exist?

Project MM has the following cash flows:

End-of-Year Cash Flows			
0	1	2	3
−$1,000	$2,000	$2,000	−$3,350

Calculate MM's NPV at discount rates of 0%, 10%, 12.2258%, 25%, 122.147%, and 150%. (**−$350; −$46; $0; $165; $0; −$94**)

What are MM's IRRs? (**12.23% and 122.15%**)

If the cost of capital were 10%, should the project be accepted or rejected? (**Reject because NPV < 0**)

---

11. If you attempt to find Project M's IRR with an HP calculator, you will get an error message, whereas TI calculators give only the IRR that's closest to zero. When you encounter either situation, you can find the approximate IRRs by first calculating NPVs using several different values for r = I/YR, constructing a graph with NPV on the vertical axis and cost of capital on the horizontal axis, and then visually determining approximately where NPV = 0. The intersection with the x-axis gives a rough idea of the IRRs' values. With some calculators and also with *Excel*, you can find both IRRs by entering guesses, as we explain in our calculator and *Excel* tutorials.

12. Figure 12-4 is called an *NPV profile*. Profiles are discussed in more detail in Section 12.7.

Figure 12-4   **Graph for Multiple IRRs: Project M (Millions of Dollars)**

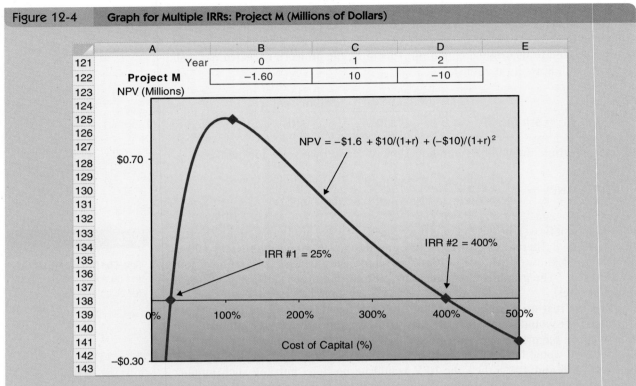

Note:
The data table shown below calculates Project M's NPV at the rates shown in the left column. These data are plotted to form the graph shown above. Notice that NPV = 0 at both 25% and 400%. Since the definition of the IRR is the rate at which the NPV = 0, we see that there are two IRRs.

r	NPV
0%	−$1.600
10%	−$0.774
25%	$0.000 = IRR #1 = 25%
110%	$0.894
400%	$0.000 = IRR #2 = 400%
500%	−$0.211

WEB

See *Ch12 Tool Kit.xls* on the textbook's Web site.

12.5 Reinvestment Rate Assumptions

The NPV calculation is based on the assumption that cash inflows can be reinvested at the project's risk-adjusted WACC, whereas the IRR calculation is based on the assumption that cash flows can be reinvested at the IRR itself. To see why this is so, think about the following diagram, which illustrates the future value of $100 when the interest rate is 5%:

$$0 \quad 5\% \quad 1 \quad 5\% \quad 2 \quad 5\% \quad 3$$

Going from PV to FV: PV = $100.00---▶$105.00---▶$110.25---▶$115.76 = FV

Observe that the FV calculation assumes that the interest earned during each year can itself be reinvested to earn the same 5% in each succeeding year.

Now recall that to find the PV we reversed the process, discounting rather than compounding at the 5% rate. The following diagram can be used to demonstrate this point:

0	5%	1	5%	2	5%	3

Going from FV to PV: PV = $100.00◄---$105.00◄---$110.25◄---$115.76 = FV

We are thus led to the following conclusion: *When we calculate a present value, we are implicitly assuming that cash flows can be reinvested at a specified interest rate* (5% in our example). This applies to Projects S and L: When we calculated their NPVs, we discounted at their WACC of 10%, which means that we assumed that their cash flows could be reinvested at 10%.

Now consider the IRR. In Section 12.3 we presented a cash flow diagram set up to show the PVs of the cash flows when discounted at the IRR. We saw that the sum of the PVs is equal to the cost at a discount rate of 14.686%, so by definition 14.686% is the IRR. Now we can ask this question: What reinvestment rate is built into the IRR?

Because discounting at a given rate assumes that cash flows can be reinvested at that same rate, the IRR assumes that cash flows are reinvested at the IRR itself.

So the NPV assumes reinvestment at the WACC, whereas the IRR assumes reinvestment at the IRR itself. Which assumption is more reasonable? For most firms, assuming reinvestment at the WACC is better, for the following reasons.

- If a firm has reasonably good access to the capital markets then it can raise all the capital it needs at the going rate, which in our example is 10%.
- Since the firm can obtain capital at 10%, if it has investment opportunities with positive NPVs then it should take them on, and it can finance them at a 10% cost.
- If we assume that the firm operates in a reasonably competitive industry, then its return on investment opportunities should be relatively close to its cost of capital; if it were much higher, then new firms would enter the market and drive prices (and thus returns) down to near the cost of capital.
- If the firm uses internally generated cash flows from past projects rather than external capital, this will simply save it the 10% cost of capital. Thus, 10% is the *opportunity cost* of the cash flows, and that is the effective return on reinvested funds.

As an illustration, suppose a project's IRR is 50%, the firm's WACC is 10%, and it has good access to the capital markets and operates in a competitive industry. Thus, the firm can raise all the capital it needs at the 10% rate. Given the existence of competition, the 50% return would attract new entry, which would make it hard to find new projects with a similar high return, which is what the IRR assumes. Moreover, even if the firm does find such projects, it would take them on with external capital that costs 10%. The logical conclusion is that the original project's cash flows will simply save the 10% cost of the external capital and that 10%, not 50%, is the effective return on those flows.

If a firm does not have good access to external capital, and if it also has a lot of potential projects with high IRRs, then it might be reasonable to assume that a project's cash flows could be reinvested at rates close to their IRRs. However, that situation rarely occurs, since firms with good investment opportunities generally *do* have good access to debt and equity markets.

Our conclusion is that the assumption built into the IRR—that cash flows can be reinvested at the IRR, no matter how high it is—is flawed, whereas the assumption built into the NPV—that cash flows can be reinvested at the WACC—is generally correct. Moreover, if the true reinvestment rate is less than the IRR, then the true rate of return on the investment must be less than the calculated IRR; thus the IRR is misleading as a measure of a project's profitability. This point is discussed further in the next section.

Self Test	Why is a reinvestment rate implicitly assumed whenever we find the present value of a future cash flow? Would it be possible to find the PV of a FV without specifying an implicit reinvestment rate?
	What reinvestment rate is built into the NPV calculation? The IRR calculation?
	For a firm that has adequate access to capital markets, is it more reasonable to assume reinvestment at the WACC or the IRR? Why?

12.6 Modified Internal Rate of Return (MIRR)

It is logical for managers to want to know the expected rate of return on investments, and this is what the IRR is supposed to tell us. However, the IRR is based on the assumption that projects' cash flows can be reinvested at the IRR itself, and this assumption is usually wrong: *The IRR overstates the expected return for accepted projects because cash flows cannot generally be reinvested at the IRR itself.* Therefore, the IRR for accepted projects is generally greater than the true expected rate of return. This imparts an upward bias on corporate projections based on IRRs. Given this fundamental flaw, is there a percentage evaluator that is better than the regular IRR? The answer is "yes": *We can modify the IRR to make it a better measure of profitability.*

This new measure, the **Modified IRR (MIRR)**, is illustrated for Project S in Figure 12-5. It is similar to the regular IRR, except it is based on the assumption that cash flows are reinvested at the WACC (or some other explicit rate if that is a more reasonable assumption). Refer to Figure 12-5 as you read about the construction of this measure.

1. Project S has just one outflow, a negative $10,000 at t = 0. Since it occurs at Time 0, it is not discounted, and its PV is −$10,000. If the project had additional outflows, we would find the PV at t = 0 for each one and then sum them for use in the MIRR calculation.

2. Next, we find the future value of each *inflow,* compounded at the WACC out to the "terminal year," which is the year the last inflow is received. We assume that cash flows are reinvested at the WACC. For Project S, the first cash flow, $5,300, is compounded at WACC = 10% for 3 years, and it grows to $7,054. The second inflow, $4,300, grows to $5,203, and the third inflow, $1,874, grows to $2,061. The last inflow, $1,500, is received at the end, so it is not compounded at all. The sum of the future values, $15,819, is called the "terminal value," or TV.

3. We now have the cost at t = 0, −$10,000, and the TV at Year 4, $15,819. There is some discount rate that will cause the PV of the terminal value to equal the cost. *That interest rate is defined as the Modified Internal Rate of Return (MIRR).* In a calculator, enter N = 4, PV = −10000, PMT = 0, and FV = 15819. Then pressing the I/YR key yields the MIRR, 12.15%.

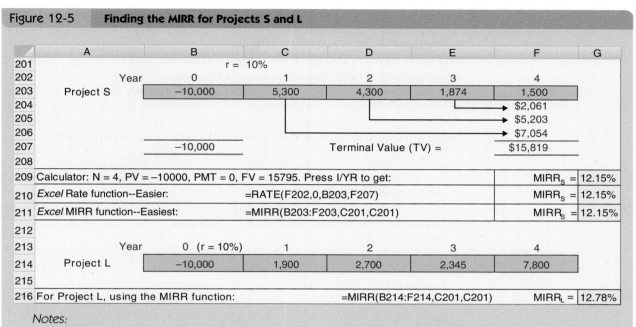

Figure 12-5   Finding the MIRR for Projects S and L

Notes:
1. In this figure we find the rate that forces the present value of the terminal value to equal the project's cost. That rate is defined as the MIRR. We have $10,000 = TV/(1 + MIRR)^N = $15,819/(1 + MIRR)^4$. We can find the MIRR with a calculator or *Excel*.
2. If S and L are independent, then both should be accepted because both MIRRs exceed the cost of capital. If the projects are mutually exclusive, then L should be chosen because it has the higher MIRR.

4. The MIRR can be found in a number of ways. Figure 12-5 illustrates exactly how the MIRR is calculated: We compound each cash inflow, sum them to determine the TV, and then find the rate that causes the PV of the TV to equal the cost. That rate in this example is 12.15%. However, *Excel* and some of the better calculators have a built-in MIRR function that streamlines the process. We explain how to use the MIRR function in our calculator tutorials, and we explain how to find MIRR with *Excel* in this chapter's *Excel* **Tool Kit**.[13]

---

13. If we let COF_t and CIF_t denote cash outflows and inflows, respectively, then Equations 12-2a and 12-2b summarize the steps just described:

$$\sum_{t=0}^{N} \frac{COF_t}{(1+r)^t} = \frac{\sum_{t=0}^{N} CIF_t(1+r)^{N-t}}{(1+MIRR)^N} \qquad (12\text{--}2a)$$

$$PV\ Costs = \frac{TV}{(1+MIRR)^N} \qquad (12\text{--}2b)$$

Also, note that there are alternative definitions for the MIRR. One difference relates to whether negative cash flows after the positive cash flows begin should be compounded and treated as part of the TV or discounted and treated as a cost. A related issue is whether negative and positive flows in a given year should be netted or treated separately. For more discussion, see David M. Shull, "Interpreting Rates of Return: A Modified Rate of Return Approach," *Financial Practice and Education*, Fall 1993, pp. 67–71.

The MIRR has two significant advantages over the regular IRR. First, whereas the regular IRR assumes that the cash flows from each project are reinvested at the IRR itself, the MIRR assumes that cash flows are reinvested at the cost of capital (or some other explicit rate). Since reinvestment at the IRR is generally not correct, the MIRR is usually a better indicator of a project's true profitability. Second, the MIRR eliminates the multiple IRR problem—there can never be more than one MIRR, and it can be compared with the cost of capital when deciding to accept or reject projects.

Our conclusion is that the MIRR is better than the regular IRR; however, this question remains: Is MIRR as good as the NPV? Here is our take on the situation.

- For *independent* projects, the NPV, IRR, and MIRR always reach the same accept–reject conclusion, so the three criteria are equally good when evaluating independent projects.
- However, if projects are *mutually exclusive* and if they differ in size, conflicts can arise. In such cases the NPV is best because it selects the project that maximizes value.[14]
- Our overall conclusions are that (1) the MIRR is superior to the regular IRR as an indicator of a project's "true" rate of return, but (2) NPV is better than either IRR or MIRR when choosing among competing projects. If managers want to know the expected rates of return on projects, it would be better to give them MIRRs rather than IRRs because MIRRs are more likely to be the rates that are actually earned.

Self Test

What's the primary difference between the MIRR and the regular IRR?

Which provides a better estimate of a project's "true" rate of return, the MIRR or the regular IRR? Explain your answer.

Projects A and B have the following cash flows:

	0	1	2
A	−$1,000	$1,150	$100
B	−$1,000	$100	$1,300

The cost of capital is 10%. What are the projects' IRRs, MIRRs, and NPVs? (IRR$_A$ = 23.1%, IRR$_B$ = 19.1%; MIRR$_A$ = 16.8%, MIRR$_B$ = 18.7%; NPV$_A$ = $128.10, NPV$_B$ = $165.29)

Which project would each method select? (IRR: A; MIRR: B; NPV: B)

12.7 NPV Profiles

Figure 12-4 from our discussion of multiple internal rates of return was a **net present value profile** for Project M; to make it, we plotted M's NPV at many different discount rates and connected the values to create a graph. M's (in this case, two different) IRRs were found at the discount rates where the NPV profile crossed the horizontal axis. Figure 12-6 shows the NPV profiles for Projects S and L plotted on the same axes. From this picture, we can observe the following points:

---

14. For projects of equal size but different lives, the MIRR will always lead to the same decision as the NPV if the MIRRs are both calculated using as the terminal year the life of the longer project. (Just fill in zeros for the shorter project's missing cash flows.)

Figure 12-6	NPV Profiles for Projects S and L

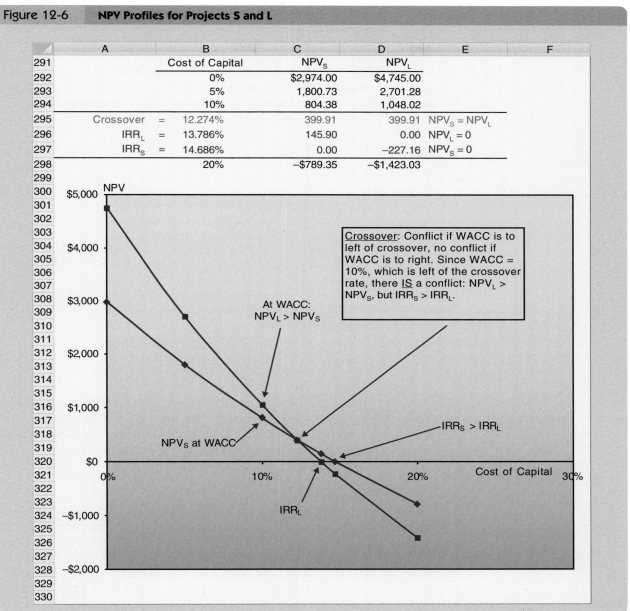

	A	B	C	D	E	F
291		Cost of Capital	NPV_S	NPV_L		
292		0%	$2,974.00	$4,745.00		
293		5%	1,800.73	2,701.28		
294		10%	804.38	1,048.02		
295	Crossover =	12.274%	399.91	399.91	$NPV_S = NPV_L$	
296	IRR_L =	13.786%	145.90	0.00	$NPV_L = 0$	
297	IRR_S =	14.686%	0.00	−227.16	$NPV_S = 0$	
298		20%	−$789.35	−$1,423.03		

Crossover: Conflict if WACC is to left of crossover, no conflict if WACC is to right. Since WACC = 10%, which is left of the crossover rate, there IS a conflict: $NPV_L >$ NPV_S, but $IRR_S > IRR_L$.

At WACC: $NPV_L > NPV_S$

NPV_S at WACC

$IRR_S > IRR_L$

IRR_L

- The NPVs vary depending on the cost of capital. At a zero cost of capital, the NPV is just the sum of all of the cash flows while for a normal project, with a cash outflow at the start and positive cash flows thereafter, the higher the cost of capital, the lower the NPV. Observe also that L's NPV declines faster than does S's with increases in the cost of capital.[15]

WEB

See **Ch12 Tool Kit.xls** on the textbook's Web site.

15. Project M's NPV profile in Figure 12-4 looks different from the NPV profiles for S and L in that it initially increases, reaches a maximum, and then decreases. This is because M has nonnormal cash flows—an outflow followed by an inflow and then an outflow again. Projects S and L have normal cash flows—they only have outflows at the beginning followed by inflows, and so their NPV profiles both slope downward.

- The IRR is the rate at which the NPV profile crosses the horizontal axis and so doesn't depend on the cost of capital at all. Project L's IRR is less than Project S's IRR since L's NPV profile crosses the horizontal axis to the left of where S's NPV profile crosses it.
- The two NPV profile lines cross at a cost of capital of 12.247%, which is called the **crossover rate**. The crossover rate can be found by calculating the IRR of the differences in the projects' cash flows, as demonstrated below:

	0	1	2	3	4
Project S	−$10,000	$5,300	$4,300	$1,874	$1,500
Project L	−10,000	1,900	2,700	2,345	7,800
$\Delta = CF_S - CF_L$	$0	$3,400	$1,600	−$471	−$6,300

IRR Δ = 12.274%

- Project L has the higher NPV if the cost of capital is less than the crossover rate, but S has the higher NPV if the cost of capital is greater than that rate.

Notice that Project L has the steeper slope, indicating that a given increase in the cost of capital causes a larger decline in NPV_L than in NPV_S. To see why this is so, recall the equation for the NPV:

$$NPV = CF_0 + \frac{CF_1}{(1 + r)^1} + \frac{CF_2}{(1 + r)^2} + \cdots + \frac{CF_N}{(1 + r)^N}$$

Now recognize (1) that L's cash flows come in later than those of S, with L's highest cash flows coming when N is large, and (2) that the impact of an increase in the discount rate is much greater on distant than on near-term cash flows. Thus L's NPV is more sensitive to interest rates and so its NPV profile has the steeper slope.

Independent Projects

If an independent project with normal cash flows is being evaluated, then the NPV and IRR criteria always lead to the same accept/reject decision: If NPV says accept then IRR also says accept, and vice versa. To see why this is so, look at Figure 12-6 and notice (1) that the IRR says accept Project S if the cost of capital is less than (or to the left of) the IRR and (2) that if the cost of capital is less than the IRR then the NPV must be positive. Thus, at any cost of capital less than 14.686%, Project S will be recommended by both the NPV and IRR criteria, but both methods reject the project if the cost of capital is greater than 14.686%. A similar statement can be made for Project L, or any other normal project, and we would always reach the same conclusion: *For normal, independent projects, if the IRR says to accept it, then so will the NPV.*

Mutually Exclusive Projects

Now assume that Projects S and L are mutually exclusive rather than independent. Therefore, we can choose either S or L, or we can reject both, but we can't accept both. Now look at Figure 12-6 and note these points.

- $IRR_S > IRR_L$, so the IRR decision rule would say to accept Project S over Project L.

- As long as the cost of capital is *greater than* the crossover rate of 12.274%, both methods agree that Project S is better: $NPV_S > NPV_L$ and $IRR_S > IRR_L$. Therefore, if r is *greater* than the crossover rate, no conflict occurs.
- However, if the cost of capital is *less than* the crossover rate, a conflict arises: NPV ranks L higher, but IRR ranks S higher.

There are two basic conditions that cause NPV profiles to cross and thus lead to conflicts.[16]

1. *Timing differences.* If most of the cash flows from one project come in early while most of those from the other project come in later, then the NPV profiles may cross and result in a conflict. This is the reason for the conflict between our Projects S and L.
2. *Project size (or scale) differences.* If the amount invested in one project is larger than the other, this can also lead to profiles crossing and a resulting conflict. Section 12.3 has an extreme example of this size difference conflict.

When either size or timing differences occur, the firm will have different amounts of funds to invest in other projects in the various years, depending on which of the two mutually exclusive projects it chooses. If it chooses S, then it will have more funds to invest in Year 1 because S has a larger inflow that year. Similarly, if one project costs more than the other, then the firm will have more money to invest at t = 0 if it selects the smaller project.

Given this situation, the rate of return at which differential cash flows can be reinvested is a critical issue. We saw earlier that the NPV assumes reinvestment at the cost of capital, and that this is generally a more reasonable assumption. Therefore, *whenever conflicts exist between mutually exclusive projects, use the NPV method.*

Self Test

Describe in words how an NPV profile is constructed. How does one determine the intercepts for the x-axis and the y-axis?

What is the "crossover rate," and how does it interact with the cost of capital to determine whether or not a conflict exists between NPV and IRR?

What two characteristics can lead to conflicts between the NPV and the IRR when evaluating mutually exclusive projects?

12.8 Profitability Index (PI)

A fourth method used to evaluate projects is the **profitability index (PI)**:

$$PI = \frac{PV \text{ of future cash flows}}{Initial \ cost} = \frac{\sum_{t=1}^{N} \dfrac{CF_t}{(1 + r)^t}}{CF_0} \qquad (12\text{--}3)$$

---

16. Also, if mutually exclusive projects have different lives (as opposed to different cash flow patterns over a common life), this introduces further complications; thus, for meaningful comparisons, some mutually exclusive projects must be evaluated over a common life. This point is discussed later in the chapter.

Here CF_t represents the expected future cash flows and CF_0 represents the initial cost. The PI shows the *relative* profitability of any project, or the present value per dollar of initial cost. As we can see from Figure 12-7, the PI for Project S, based on a 10% cost of capital, is $10,804.38/$10,000 = 1.0804; the PI for Project L is 1.1048. Thus, Project S is expected to produce $1.0804 of present value for each $1 of investment, whereas L should produce $1.1048 for each dollar invested.

A project is acceptable if its PI is greater than 1.0; and the higher the PI, the higher the project's ranking. Therefore, both S and L would be accepted by the PI criterion if they were independent, and L would be ranked ahead of S if they were mutually exclusive.

Mathematically, the NPV, IRR, MIRR, and PI methods will always lead to the same accept/reject decisions for *normal, independent* projects: If a project's NPV is positive, its IRR and MIRR will always exceed r and its PI will always be greater than 1.0. However, these methods can give conflicting rankings for *mutually exclusive* projects if the projects differ in size or in the timing of cash flows. If the PI ranking conflicts with the NPV, then the NPV ranking should be used.

Self Test

Explain how the PI is calculated. What does it measure?

A project has the following expected cash flows: $CF_0 = -\$500$, $CF_1 = \$200$, $CF_2 = \$200$, and $CF_3 = \$400$. If the project's cost of capital is 9%, what is the PI? **(1.32)**

12.9 Payback Period

WEB

See *Ch12 Tool Kit.xls* on the textbook's Web site.

NPV and IRR are the most commonly used methods today, but historically the first selection criterion was the **payback period**, defined as the number of years required to recover the funds invested in a project from its operating cash flows. Equation 12-4 is used for the calculation, and the process is diagrammed in Figure 12-8. We start with the project's cost, a negative number, and then add the cash inflow for each year until the cumulative cash flow turns positive. The payback year is the

---

Figure 12-7   Profitability Index (PI)

	A	B	C	D	E
342	Project S:		PI_S = PV of future cash flows	÷	Initial cost
343			PI_S = $10,804.38	÷	$10,000
344			PI_S = 1.0804		
345					
346	Project L:		PI_L = PV of future cash flows	÷	Initial cost
347			PI_L = $11,048.02	÷	$10,000
348			PI_L = 1.1048		

Notes:
1. If Projects L and S are independent, then both should be accepted because both have PI greater than 1.0. However, if they are mutually exclusive then Project L should be chosen because it has the higher PI.
2. PI and NPV rankings will be consistent if the projects have the same cost, as is true for S and L. However, if they differ in size then conflicts can occur. In the event of a conflict, the NPV ranking should be used.

Figure 12-8	Payback Period					

	A	B	C	D	E	F	G
377		Year	0	1	2	3	4
378	Project S	Cash flow	−10,000	5,300	4,300	1,874	1,500
379		Cumulative cash flow	−10,000	−4,700	−400	1,474	2,974
380	Intermediate calculation for payback		-	-	-	2.21	3.98
381							
382						Intermediate calculation:	
383	Manual calculation of Payback S = 2 + $400/$1,874 =		2.21		=IF(F379>0,E377+ABS(E379/F378),"−")		
384	*Excel* calculation of Payback S =		2.21			2.21	
385							
386		Year	0	1	2	3	4
387	Project L	Cash flow	−10,000	1,900	2,700	2,345	7,800
388		Cumulative cash flow	−10,000	−8,100	−5,400	−3,055	4,745
389							
390	Manual calculation of Payback L = 3 + $3,055/$7,800 =		3.39			Payback is between negative and positive cumulative cash flow.	
391	Alternative *Excel* calculation of Payback L =						
392	=PERCENTRANK(C388:G388,0,6)*G386		3.39				
393							

© Cengage Learning 2013

year *prior to* full recovery, plus a fraction equal to the shortfall at the end of the prior year divided by the cash flow during the year when full recovery occurs:[17]

WEB

See **Ch12 Tool Kit.xls** on the textbook's Web site.

$$\text{Payback} = \begin{array}{c}\text{Number of}\\\text{years prior to}\\\text{full recovery}\end{array} + \frac{\begin{array}{c}\text{Unrecovered cost}\\\text{at start of year}\end{array}}{\begin{array}{c}\text{Cash flow during}\\\text{full recovery year}\end{array}}$$

(12–4)

The cash flows for Projects S and L, together with their paybacks, are shown in Figure 12-8.[18] The shorter the payback, the better the project. Therefore, if the firm requires a payback of 3 years or less, then S would be accepted but L would be rejected. If the projects were mutually exclusive, S would be ranked over L because of its shorter payback.

The regular payback has three flaws: (1) Dollars received in different years are all given the same weight—that is, the time value of money is ignored. (2) Cash flows beyond the payback year are given no consideration whatsoever, regardless of how large they might be. (3) Unlike the NPV or the IRR, which tell us how much wealth a project adds or how much a project's rate of return exceeds the cost of capital, the payback merely tells us how long it takes to recover our investment. There is no necessary relationship between a given payback period and investor wealth, so we don't know how to specify an acceptable payback. The firm might use 2 years, 3 years, or any other number as the minimum acceptable payback, but the choice is purely arbitrary.

To counter the first criticism, financial analysts developed the **discounted payback,** where cash flows are discounted at the WACC and then those discounted cash flows are used to find the payback. In Figure 12-9, we calculate the discounted paybacks for S and L, assuming both have a 10% cost of capital. Each inflow is

---

17. Equation 12-4 assumes that cash flows come in uniformly during the full recovery year.
18. There is not an *Excel* function for payback. But if the cash flows are normal then the PERCENTRANK function can be used to find payback, as illustrated in Figures 12-8 and 12-9.

Figure 12-9   **Discounted Payback**

	A	B	C	D	E	F	G
406		Year	0	1	2	3	4
407	Project S	Cash flow	−10,000.00	5,300.00	4,300.00	1,874.00	1,500.00
408		Discounted cash flow	−10,000.00	4,818.18	3,553.72	1,407.96	1,024.52
409		Cumulative discounted CF	−10,000.00	−5,181.82	−1,628.10	−220.14	804.38
410							
411	Discounted Payback S = 3 + $220.14/$1,024.52 =			3.21		Payback is between negative and positive cumulative discounted cash flow.	
412	*Excel* calculation of Discounted Payback S =						
413	=PERCENTRANK(C409:G409,0,6)*G406			3.21			
414							
415		Year	0	1	2	3	4
416	Project L	Cash flow	−10,000.00	1,900.00	2,700.00	2,345.00	7,800.00
417		Discounted cash flow	−10,000.00	1,727.27	2,231.40	1,761.83	5,327.50
418		Cumulative discounted CF	−10,000.00	−8,272.73	−6,041.32	−4,279.49	1,048.02
419							
420	Discounted Payback L = 3 + $4,279.49/$5,327.50 =			3.80		Payback is between negative and positive cumulative discounted cash flow.	
421	*Excel* calculation of Discounted Payback L =						
422	=PERCENTRANK(C418:G418,0,6)*G415			3.80			
423							

© Cengage Learning 2013

WEB

See **Ch12 Tool Kit.xls** on the textbook's Web site.

divided by $(1 + r)^t = (1.10)^t$, where t is the year in which the cash flow occurs and r is the project's cost of capital, and then those PVs are used to find the payback. Project S's discounted payback is 3.21 years and L's is 3.80 years.

Note that the payback is a "break-even" calculation in the sense that if cash flows come in at the expected rate, then the project will at least break even. However, since the regular payback doesn't consider the cost of capital, it doesn't specify the true break-even year. The discounted payback does consider capital costs, but it still disregards cash flows beyond the payback year, which is a serious flaw. Further, if mutually exclusive projects vary in size, both payback methods can conflict with the NPV, and that might lead to poor decisions. Finally, there is no way to determine how short the payback periods must be to justify accepting a project.

Although the payback methods have faults as ranking criteria, they do provide information about *liquidity* and *risk*. The shorter the payback, other things held constant, the greater the project's liquidity. This factor is often important for smaller firms that don't have ready access to the capital markets. Also, cash flows expected in the distant future are generally riskier than near-term cash flows, so the payback period is also a risk indicator.

Self Test

What two pieces of information does the payback method provide that are absent from the other capital budgeting decision methods?

What three flaws does the regular payback method have? Does the discounted payback method correct all of those flaws? Explain.

Project P has a cost of $1,000 and cash flows of $300 per year for 3 years plus another $1,000 in Year 4. The project's cost of capital is 15%. What are P's regular and discounted paybacks? **(3.10, 3.55)** If the company requires a payback of 3 years or less, would the project be accepted? Would this be a good accept/reject decision, considering the NPV and/or the IRR? **(NPV = $256.72, IRR = 24.78%)**

12.10 Conclusions on Capital Budgeting Methods

We have discussed six capital budgeting decision criteria: NPV, IRR, MIRR, PI, payback, and discounted payback. We compared these methods with one another and highlighted their strengths and weaknesses. In the process, we may have created the impression that "sophisticated" firms should use only one method, the NPV. However, virtually all capital budgeting decisions are analyzed by computer, so it is easy to calculate using all six methods. In making the accept–reject decision, large sophisticated firms such as FPL, GE, and Boeing generally calculate and consider all six measures, because each provides a somewhat different piece of information about the decision.

NPV is the single best criterion because it provides a direct measure of the value a project adds to shareholder wealth. IRR and MIRR measure profitability expressed as a percentage rate of return, which decision makers like to consider. The PI also measures profitability but in relation to the amount of the investment. Further, IRR, MIRR, and PI all contain information concerning a project's "safety margin." To illustrate, consider a firm, whose WACC is 10%, that must choose between these two mutually exclusive projects: SS (for small) has a cost of $10,000 and is expected to return $16,500 at the end of 1 year LL (for large) has a cost of $100,000 and is expected to return $115,550 at the end of 1 year. SS has a huge IRR, 65%, while LL's IRR is a more modest 15.6%. The NPV paints a somewhat different picture: At the 10% cost of capital, SS's NPV is $5,000 while LL's is $5,045. By the NPV rule we would choose LL. However, SS's IRR indicates that it has a much larger margin for error: Even if its cash flow were 39% below the $16,500 forecast, the firm would still recover its $10,000 investment. On the other hand, if LL's inflows fell by only 13.5% from its forecasted $115,550, the firm would not recover its investment. Further, if neither project generated any cash flows at all, the firm would lose only $10,000 on SS but would lose $100,000 by accepting LL.

The modified IRR has all the virtues of the IRR, but it incorporates a better reinvestment rate assumption and also avoids the problem of multiple rates of return. So if decision makers want to know projects' rates of return, the MIRR is a better indicator than the regular IRR.

The PI tells a similar story to the IRR. Here PI_{LL} is only 1.05 while PI_{SS} is 1.50. As with the IRR, this indicates that Project SS's cash inflows could decline by 50% before it loses money, whereas a decline of only 5% in LL's cash flows would result in a loss.

Payback and discounted payback provide indications of a project's *liquidity* and *risk*. A long payback means that investment dollars will be locked up for a long time; hence the project is relatively illiquid. In addition, a long payback means that cash flows must be forecast far into the future, and that probably makes the project riskier than one with a shorter payback. A good analogy for this is bond valuation. An investor should never compare the yields to maturity on two bonds without also considering their terms to maturity, because a bond's risk is significantly influenced by its maturity. The same holds true for capital projects.

In summary, the different measures provide different types of useful information. It is easy to calculate all of them: Simply put the cost of capital and the cash flows into an *Excel* model like the one provided in this chapter's *Tool Kit* and the model will instantly calculate all six criteria. Therefore, most sophisticated companies consider all six measures when making capital budgeting decisions. For most decisions, the greatest weight should be given to the NPV, but it would be foolish to ignore the information provided by the other criteria.

Just as it would be foolish to ignore these capital budgeting methods, it would also be foolish to make decisions based *solely* on them. One cannot know at Time 0 the exact cost of future capital or the exact future cash flows. These inputs are simply estimates, and if they turn out to be incorrect then so will be the calculated NPVs and IRRs. Thus, *quantitative methods provide valuable information, but they should not be used as the sole criteria for accept–reject decisions* in the capital budgeting process. Rather, managers should use quantitative methods in the decision-making process but should also consider the likelihood that actual results will differ from the forecasts. Qualitative factors, such as the chances of a tax increase, or a war, or a major product liability suit, should also be considered. In summary, *quantitative methods such as NPV and IRR should be considered as an aid to informed decisions but not as a substitute for sound managerial judgment.*

In this same vein, managers should ask sharp questions about any project that has a large NPV, a high IRR, or a high PI. In a perfectly competitive economy, there would be no positive-NPV projects—all companies would have the same opportunities, and competition would quickly eliminate any positive NPV. The existence of positive-NPV projects must be predicated on some imperfection in the marketplace, and the longer the life of the project, the longer that imperfection must last. Therefore, managers should be able to identify the imperfection and explain why it will persist before accepting that a project will really have a positive NPV. Valid explanations might include patents or proprietary technology, which is how pharmaceutical and software firms create positive-NPV projects. Pfizer's Lipitor (a cholesterol-reducing medicine) and Microsoft's Windows 7 operating system are examples. Companies can also create positive NPV by being the first entrant into a new market or by creating new products that meet some previously unidentified consumer needs. The Post-it notes invented by 3M are an example. Similarly, Dell developed procedures for direct sales of microcomputers and, in the process, created projects with enormous NPV. Also, companies such as Southwest Airlines have managed to train and motivate their workers better than their competitors, and this has led to positive-NPV projects. In all of these cases, the companies developed some source of competitive advantage, and that advantage resulted in positive-NPV projects.

This discussion suggests three things: (1) If you can't identify the reason a project has a positive projected NPV, then its actual NPV will probably not be positive. (2) Positive-NPV projects don't just happen—they result from hard work to develop some competitive advantage. At the risk of oversimplification, the primary job of a manager is to find and develop areas of competitive advantage. (3) Some competitive advantages last longer than others, with their durability depending on competitors' ability to replicate them. Patents, the control of scarce resources, or large size in an industry where strong economies of scale exist can keep competitors at bay. However, it is relatively easy to replicate product features that cannot be patented. The bottom line is that managers should strive to develop nonreplicable sources of competitive advantage. If such an advantage cannot be demonstrated, then you should question projects with high NPV—especially if they have long lives.

Self Test   Describe the advantages and disadvantages of the six capital budgeting methods.

Should capital budgeting decisions be made solely on the basis of a project's NPV, with no regard to the other criteria? Explain your answer.

What are some possible reasons that a project might have a high NPV?

12.11 Decision Criteria Used in Practice

Over the years, surveys have been designed and administered to find out which of the criteria managers actually use. Surveys prior to 1999 asked companies to indicate which method they gave the most weight, whereas the most recent one (taken in 1999) asked what method or methods managers actually calculated and used. A summary of all these surveys is shown in Table 12-1, and it reveals some interesting trends.

First, the NPV criterion was not used significantly before the 1980s, but by 1999 it was close to the top in usage. Moreover, informal discussions with companies suggest that if a survey were taken in 2012, NPV would be at the top of this list. Second, the IRR method was used slightly more than the NPV at the time of the last survey (1999), but its recent growth is much less dramatic than that of NPV; if a survey were taken today, we believe that the NPV would predominate. Third, payback was the most important criterion years ago, but its use as the primary criterion had fallen drastically by 1980. Companies still use payback because it is easy to calculate and provides some useful information, but it is rarely used as the primary criterion. Fourth, "other methods," primarily the profitability index and the accounting rate of return (the latter of which is explained in this chapter's *Tool Kit*), have been fading due to the increased use of IRR and especially NPV.

These trends are consistent with our evaluation of the various methods. NPV is the best single criterion, but all of the methods provide useful information and are easy to calculate. Hence all are used, along with judgment and common sense. We will have more to say about all this in the next chapter.

What trends in capital budgeting methodology can be seen from Table 12-1?	**Self Test**

12.12 Other Issues in Capital Budgeting

Three other issues in capital budgeting are discussed in this section: (1) how to deal with mutually exclusive projects whose lives differ; (2) the potential advantage of

TABLE 12-1   Capital Budgeting Methods Used in Practice

	Firms' Primary Criterion			Firms Use
	1960	**1970**	**1980**	**1999**
NPV	0%	0%	15%	75%
IRR	20	60	65	76
Payback	35	15	5	57
Discounted Payback	NA	NA	NA	29
Other	45	25	15	NA
Totals	100%	100%	100%	

Sources: The 1999 data are from John R. Graham and Campbell R. Harvey, "The Theory and Practice of Corporate Finance: Evidence from the Field," *Journal of Financial Economics,* 2001, pp. 187–244. Data from prior years are our estimates based on averaging data from these studies: J. S. Moore and A. K. Reichert, "An Analysis of the Financial Management Techniques Currently Employed by Large U.S. Corporations," *Journal of Business Finance and Accounting,* Winter 1983, pp. 623–645; and M. T. Stanley and S. R. Block, "A Survey of Multinational Capital Budgeting," *The Financial Review,* March 1984, pp. 36–51.

© Cengage Learning 2013

terminating a project before the end of its physical life; and (3) the optimal capital budget when the cost of capital rises as the size of the capital budget increases.

12.12a Mutually Exclusive Projects with Unequal Lives

When choosing between two mutually exclusive alternatives with significantly different lives, an adjustment is necessary. For example, suppose a company is planning to modernize its production facilities and is considering either a conveyor system (Project C) or a fleet of forklift trucks (Project F) for moving materials. The first two sections of Figure 12-10 show the expected net cash flows, NPVs, and IRRs for these two mutually exclusive alternatives. We see that Project C, when discounted at the firm's 12% cost of capital, has the higher NPV and thus appears to be the better project.

Although the NPVs shown in Figure 12-10 suggest that Project C should be selected, this analysis is incomplete, and the decision to choose Project C is actually incorrect. If we choose Project F, we will have an opportunity to make a similar investment in 3 years, and if cost and revenue conditions continue at the levels shown in Figure 12-10, then this second investment will also be profitable. However, if we choose Project C, we cannot make this second investment. Two different approaches can be used to correctly compare Projects C and F, as shown in Figure 12-10 and discussed next.

Replacement Chains

The key to the *replacement chain,* or *common life, approach* is to analyze both projects over an equal life. In our example, Project C has a 6-year life, so we assume that Project F will be repeated after 3 years and then analyze it over the same 6-year period. We can then calculate the NPV of C and compare it to the extended-life NPV of Project F. The NPV for Project C, as shown in Figure 12-10, is already based on the 6-year common life. For Project F, however, we must add in a second project to extend the overall life to 6 years. The time line for this extended project, denoted as "All CFs for FF," is shown in Figure 12-10. Here we assume (1) that Project F's cost

WEB

See **Ch12 Tool Kit.xls** on the textbook's Web site.

Figure 12-10   Analysis of Projects C and F (r = 12%)

	A	B	C	D	E	F	G	H
457	WACC = r = 12.0%							
458	Data on Project C, Conveyor System:							
459	Year	0	1	2	3	4	5	6
460	Cash flows for C	($40,000)	$8,000	$14,000	$13,000	$12,000	$11,000	$10,000
461		NPV$_C$ =	$6,491		IRR$_C$ =	17.5%		
462								
463	Data on Project F, Forklifts							
464	Year	0	1	2	3			
465	Cash flows for F	($20,000)	$7,000	$13,000	$12,000			
466		NPV$_F$ =	$5,155		IRR$_F$ =	25.2%		
467								
468	Common Life Approach with F Repeated (Project FF):							
469	Year	0	1	2	3	4	5	6
470	CF$_t$ for 1st F	($20,000)	$7,000	$13,000	$12,000			
471	CF$_t$ for 2nd F				($20,000)	$7,000	$13,000	$12,000
472	All CFs for FF	($20,000)	$7,000	$13,000	($8,000)	$7,000	$13,000	$12,000
473		NPV$_{FF}$ =	$8,824		IRR$_{FF}$ =	25.2%		

and annual cash inflows will not change if the project is repeated in 3 years and (2) that the cost of capital will remain at 12%.

The NPV of this extended Project F is $8,824, and its IRR is 25.2%. (The IRR of two Project Fs is the same as the IRR for one Project F.) However, the $8,824 extended NPV of Project F is greater than Project C's $6,491 NPV, so Project F should be selected.

Alternatively, we could recognize that Project F has an NPV of $5,155 at Time 0 and a second NPV of that same amount at Time 3, then find the PV of the second NPV at Time 0, and sum the two to find Project F's extended-life NPV of $8,824.

Equivalent Annual Annuities (EAA)

Electrical engineers designing power plants and distribution lines were the first to encounter the unequal life problem. They could install transformers and other equipment that had relatively low initial costs but short lives, or they could use equipment that had higher initial costs but longer lives. The services would be required into the indefinite future, so this was the issue: Which choice would result in a higher NPV in the long run? The engineers converted the annual cash flows under the alternative investments into a constant cash flow stream whose NPV was equal to, or equivalent to, the NPV of the initial stream. This was called the **equivalent annual annuity (EAA) method.** To apply the EAA method to Projects C and F, for each project we simply find the constant payment streams that the projects' NPVs ($6,491 for C and $5,155 for F) would provide over their respective lives. Using a financial calculator for Project C, we enter N = 6, I/YR = 12, PV = −6491, and FV = 0. Then, when we press the PMT key, we find $EAA_C = \$1,579$. For Project F, we enter N = 3, I/YR = 12, PV = −5155, and FV = 0; solving for PMT, we find $EAA_F = \$2,146$. Project F would thus produce a higher cash flow stream over the 6 years, so it is the better project.

Conclusions about Unequal Lives

When should we worry about analysis of unequal lives? The unequal life issue (1) does not arise for independent projects but (2) can arise if mutually exclusive projects with significantly different lives are being compared. However, even for mutually exclusive projects, it is not always appropriate to extend the analysis to a common life. This should be done if and only if there is a high probability that the projects will actually be repeated at the end of their initial lives.

We should note several potentially serious weaknesses inherent in this type of analysis. (1) If inflation occurs, then replacement equipment will have a higher price. Moreover, both sales prices and operating costs would probably change. Thus, the static conditions built into the analysis would be invalid. (2) Replacements that occur down the road would probably employ new technology, which in turn might change the cash flows. (3) It is difficult enough to estimate the lives of most projects, and even more so to estimate the lives of a series of projects. In view of these problems, no experienced financial analyst would be too concerned about comparing mutually exclusive projects with lives of, say, 8 years and 10 years. Given all the uncertainties in the estimation process, such projects would, for all practical purposes, be assumed to have the same life. Still, it is important to recognize that a problem exists if mutually exclusive projects have substantially different lives.

When we encounter situations in practice where significant differences in project lives are encountered, we first use a computer spreadsheet to build expected inflation and/or possible efficiency gains directly into the cash flow estimates and then use the replacement chain approach. We prefer the replacement chain approach for two reasons. First, it is easier to explain to those who are responsible for approving capital budgets. Second, it is easier to build inflation and other modifications into a spreadsheet and then go on to make the replacement chain calculations.

12.12b Economic Life versus Physical Life

Projects are normally evaluated under the assumption that the firm will operate them over their full physical lives. However, this may not be the best plan—it may be better to terminate a project before the end of its potential life. For example, the cost of maintenance for trucks and machinery can become quite high if they are used for too many years, so it might be better to replace them before the end of their potential lives.

Figure 12-11 provides data for an asset with a physical life of 3 years. However, the project can be terminated at the end of any year and the asset sold at the indicated salvage values. All of the cash flows are after taxes, and the firm's cost of capital is 10%. The undiscounted cash flows are shown in Columns C and D in the upper part of the figure, and the present values of these flows are shown in Columns E and F. We find the project's NPV under different assumptions about how long it will be operated. If the project is operated for its full 3-year life, it will have a negative NPV. The NPV will be positive if it is operated for 2 years and then the asset is sold for a relatively high salvage value; the NPV will be negative if the asset is disposed after only 1 year of operation. Therefore, the project's optimal life is 2 years.

This type of analysis is used to determine a project's **economic life**, which is the life that maximizes the NPV and thus shareholder wealth. For our project, the economic life is 2 years versus the 3-year **physical**, or **engineering, life**. Note that this analysis was based on the expected cash flows and the expected salvage values, and it should always be conducted as a part of the capital budgeting evaluation if salvage values are relatively high.

WEB

See **Ch12 Tool Kit.xls** on the textbook's Web site.

12.12c The Optimal Capital Budget

The **optimal capital budget** is defined as the set of projects that maximizes the value of the firm. Finance theory states that all independent projects with positive NPVs

---

Figure 12-11   Economic Life versus Physical Life

	A	B	C	D	E	F	G
					PVs of the Cash Flows		
511							
512			Operating Cash		Operating Cash		
513		Year	Flow	Salvage Value	Flow	Salvage Value	
514		0	−$4,800				
515		1	2,000	$3,000	$1,818.18	$2,727.27	
516		2	2,000	1,650	1,652.89	1,363.64	
517		3	1,750	0	1,314.80	0.00	
518	WACC = 10%				PV of		PV of
519	NPV at Different Operating Lives:		Intial Cost	+	Operating Cash	+	Salvage
520					Flows		Value
521	Operate for 3 Years:		−$4,800.00	+	$4,785.88	+	$0.00
522	NPV$_3$:	−$14.12					
523	Operate for 2 Years:		−$4,800.00	+	$3,471.07	+	$1,363.64
524	NPV$_2$:	$34.71					
525	Operate for 1 Year:		−$4,800.00	+	$1,818.18	+	$2,727.27
526	NPV$_1$:	−$254.55					

Note: The project is profitable if and only if it is operated for just 2 years.

should be accepted, as should the mutually exclusive projects with the highest NPVs. Therefore, the optimal capital budget consists of that set of projects. However, two complications arise in practice: (1) The cost of capital might increase as the size of the capital budget increases, making it hard to know the proper discount rate to use when evaluating projects; and (2) sometimes firms set an upper limit on the size of their capital budgets, which is also known as *capital rationing.*

An Increasing Cost of Capital

The cost of capital may increase as the capital budget increases—this is called an *increasing marginal cost of capital.* As we discussed in Chapter 10, flotation costs associated with issuing new equity can be quite high. This means that the cost of capital will increase once a company has invested all of its internally generated cash and must sell new common stock. In addition, once a firm has used up its normal credit lines and must seek additional debt capital, it may encounter an increase in its cost of debt. This means that a project might have a positive NPV if it is part of a $10 million capital budget but the same project might have a negative NPV if it is part of a $20 million capital budget because the cost of capital might increase.

  Fortunately, these problems rarely occur for most firms, especially those that are stable and well established. When a rising cost of capital is encountered, we would proceed as indicated below. You can look at Figure 12-12 as you read through our points.

- Find the IRR (or MIRR) on all potential projects, arrange them in rank order (along with their initial costs), and then plot them on a graph with the IRR on the vertical axis and the cumulative costs on the horizontal axis. The firm's data are shown in Figure 12-12, and the IRRs are plotted in the graph. The line is called the Investment Opportunity Schedule (IOS), and it shows the marginal return on capital.
- Next, determine how much capital can be raised before it is necessary to issue new common stock or go to higher-cost sources of debt, and identify the amounts of higher-cost capital. Use this information to calculate the WACC that corresponds to the different amounts of capital raised. In this example, the firm can raise $300 before the WACC rises, but the WACC increases as additional capital is raised. The increasing WACC represents the marginal cost of capital, and its graph is called the Marginal Cost of Capital (MCC) schedule.
- The intersection of the IOS and MCC schedules indicates the amount of capital the firm should raise and invest, and it is analogous to the familiar marginal cost versus marginal revenue schedule discussed in introductory economics courses. In our example, the firm should have a capital budget of $400; if it uses a WACC of 10% then it will accept projects A, B, C, and D, which have a cumulative cost of $400. The 10% WACC should be used for average-risk projects, but it should be scaled up or down for more or less risky projects as discussed in Chapter 10.

Our example illustrates the case of a firm that cannot raise all the money it needs at a constant WACC. Firms should not try to be too precise with this process—the data are not good enough for precision—but they should be aware of the concept and get at least a rough idea of how raising additional capital will affect the WACC.

Capital Rationing

Armbrister Pyrotechnics, a manufacturer of fireworks and lasers for light shows, has identified 40 potential independent projects, of which 15 have a positive NPV based on the firm's 12% cost of capital. The total investment required to implement these

Figure 12-12   IOS and MCC Schedules

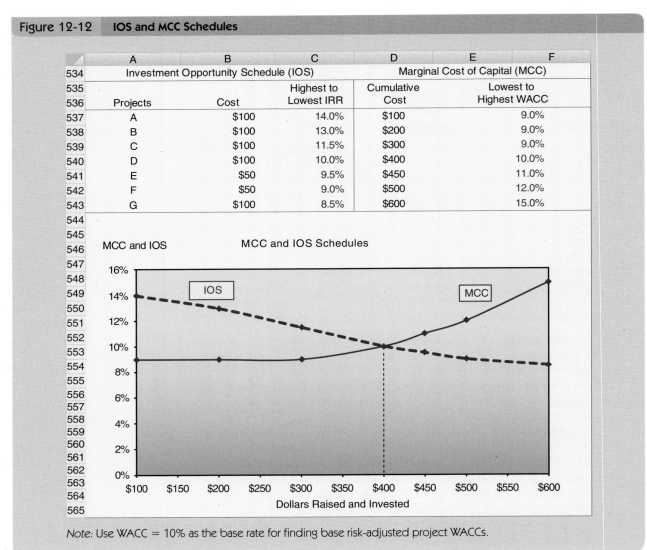

	A	B	C	D	E	F
534	Investment Opportunity Schedule (IOS)			Marginal Cost of Capital (MCC)		
535			Highest to	Cumulative	Lowest to	
536	Projects	Cost	Lowest IRR	Cost	Highest WACC	
537	A	$100	14.0%	$100	9.0%	
538	B	$100	13.0%	$200	9.0%	
539	C	$100	11.5%	$300	9.0%	
540	D	$100	10.0%	$400	10.0%	
541	E	$50	9.5%	$450	11.0%	
542	F	$50	9.0%	$500	12.0%	
543	G	$100	8.5%	$600	15.0%	

Note: Use WACC = 10% as the base rate for finding base risk-adjusted project WACCs.

WEB

See **Ch12 Tool Kit.xls** on the textbook's Web site.

15 projects would be $75 million and so, according to finance theory, the optimal capital budget is $75 million. Thus, Armbrister should accept the 15 projects with positive NPVs and invest $75 million. However, Armbrister's management has imposed a limit of $50 million for capital expenditures during the upcoming year. Because of this restriction, the company must forgo a number of value-adding projects. This is an example of **capital rationing**, defined as a situation in which a firm limits its capital expenditures to an amount less than would be required to fund the optimal capital budget. Despite being at odds with finance theory, this practice is quite common.

Why would any company forgo value-adding projects? Here are some potential explanations, along with some suggestions for better ways to handle these situations.

1. *Reluctance to issue new stock.* Many firms are extremely reluctant to issue new stock, so all of their capital expenditures must be funded out of debt and internally generated cash. Also, most firms try to stay near their target capital

structure, and, when combined with the limit on equity, this limits the amount of debt that can be added during any one year without raising the cost of that debt as well as the cost of equity. The result can be a serious constraint on the amount of funds available for investment in new projects.

The reluctance to issue new stock could be based on some sound reasons: (a) flotation costs can be very expensive; (b) investors might perceive new stock offerings as a signal that the company's equity is overvalued; and (c) the company might have to reveal sensitive strategic information to investors, thereby reducing some of its competitive advantages. To avoid these costs, many companies simply limit their capital expenditures.

However, rather than placing a somewhat artificial limit on capital expenditures, companies might be better off explicitly incorporating the costs of raising external capital into their costs of capital along the lines shown in Figure 12-12. If there still are positive-NPV projects even with the higher cost of capital, then the company should go ahead and raise external equity and accept the projects.

2. *Constraints on nonmonetary resources.* Sometimes a firm simply doesn't have the necessary managerial, marketing, or engineering talent to immediately accept all positive-NPV projects. In other words, the potential projects may be independent from a demand standpoint but not from an internal standpoint, because accepting them all would raise the firm's costs. To avoid potential problems due to spreading existing talent too thinly, many firms simply limit the capital budget to a size that can be accommodated by their current personnel.

A better solution might be to employ a technique called **linear programming**. Each potential project has an expected NPV, and each potential project requires a certain level of support by different types of employees. A linear program can identify the set of projects that maximizes NPV *subject to the constraint* that the total amount of support required for these projects does not exceed the available resources.

3. *Controlling estimation bias.* Many managers become overly optimistic when estimating the cash flows for a project. Some firms try to control this estimation bias by requiring managers to use an unrealistically high cost of capital. Others try to control the bias by limiting the size of the capital budget. Neither solution is generally effective, because managers quickly learn the rules of the game and then increase their own estimates of project cash flows, which might have been biased upward to begin with.

A better solution is to implement a post-audit program and to link the accuracy of forecasts to the compensation of the managers who initiated the projects.

Self Test

Briefly describe the replacement chain (common life) approach and differentiate it from the Equivalent Annual Annuity (EAA) approach.

Differentiate between a project's *physical* life and its *economic* life.

What factors can lead to an increasing marginal cost of capital? How might this affect capital budgeting?

What is capital rationing?

What are three explanations for capital rationing? How might firms otherwise handle these situations?

Summary

This chapter has described six techniques that are used in capital budgeting analysis: NPV, IRR, MIRR, PI, payback, and discounted payback. Each approach provides a different piece of information, so in this age of computers, managers often look at all of them when evaluating projects. However, NPV is the best single measure, and almost all firms now use NPV. The key concepts covered in this chapter are listed below.

- **Capital budgeting** is the process of analyzing potential projects. Capital budgeting decisions are probably the most important ones that managers must make.
- The **net present value (NPV) method** discounts all cash flows at the project's cost of capital and then sums those cash flows. The project should be accepted if the NPV is positive because such a project increases shareholders' value.
- The **internal rate of return (IRR)** is defined as the discount rate that forces a project's NPV to equal zero. The project should be accepted if the IRR is greater than the cost of capital.
- The NPV and IRR methods make the same accept–reject decisions for **independent projects**, but if projects are **mutually exclusive** then ranking conflicts can arise. In such cases, the NPV method should generally be relied upon.
- The NPV method assumes that cash flows will be reinvested at the firm's cost of capital, whereas the IRR method assumes reinvestment at the project's IRR. *Reinvestment at the cost of capital is generally a better assumption* because it is closer to reality.
- The **modified IRR (MIRR) method** corrects some of the problems with the regular IRR. MIRR involves finding the **terminal value (TV)** of the cash inflows, compounding them at the firm's cost of capital, and then determining the discount rate that forces the present value of the TV to equal the present value of the outflows. Thus, the MIRR assumes reinvestment at the cost of capital, not at the IRR. If management wants to know the rate of return on projects, the MIRR is a better estimate than the regular IRR.
- The **profitability index (PI)** is calculated by dividing the present value of cash inflows by the initial cost, so it measures relative profitability—that is, the amount of the present value per dollar of investment.
- The regular **payback period** is defined as the number of years required to recover a project's cost. The regular payback method has three flaws: It ignores cash flows beyond the payback period, it does not consider the time value of money, and it doesn't give a precise acceptance rule. The payback does, however, provide an indication of a project's risk and liquidity, because it shows how long the invested capital will be tied up.
- The **discounted payback** is similar to the regular payback except that it discounts cash flows at the project's cost of capital. It considers the time value of money, but it still ignores cash flows beyond the payback period.
- The chapter's *Tool Kit Excel* model and *Web Extension 12A* describe another but seldom-used evaluation method, the **accounting rate of return**.
- If mutually exclusive projects have **unequal lives**, it may be necessary to adjust the analysis to put the projects on an equal-life basis. This can be done using the **replacement chain (common life) approach** or the **equivalent annual annuity (EAA) approach**.

- A project's true value may be greater than the NPV based on its **physical life** if it can be **terminated** at the end of its **economic life**.
- Flotation costs and increased risk associated with unusually large expansion programs can cause the **marginal cost of capital** to increase as the size of the capital budget increases.
- **Capital rationing** occurs when management places a constraint on the size of the firm's capital budget during a particular period.

Questions

12-1 Define each of the following terms:
     a. Capital budgeting; regular payback period; discounted payback period
     b. Independent projects; mutually exclusive projects
     c. DCF techniques; net present value (NPV) method; internal rate of return (IRR) method; profitability index (PI)
     d. Modified internal rate of return (MIRR) method
     e. NPV profile; crossover rate
     f. Nonnormal cash flow projects; normal cash flow projects; multiple IRRs
     g. Reinvestment rate assumption
     h. Replacement chain; economic life; capital rationing; equivalent annual annuity (EAA)

12-2 What types of projects require the least detailed and the most detailed analysis in the capital budgeting process?

12-3 Explain why the NPV of a relatively long-term project, defined as one for which a high percentage of its cash flows are expected in the distant future, is more sensitive to changes in the cost of capital than is the NPV of a short-term project.

12-4 When two mutually exclusive projects are being compared, explain why the short-term project might be higher ranked under the NPV criterion if the cost of capital is high, whereas the long-term project might be deemed better if the cost of capital is low. Would changes in the cost of capital ever cause a change in the IRR ranking of two such projects?

12-5 In what sense is a reinvestment rate assumption embodied in the NPV, IRR, and MIRR methods? What is the assumed reinvestment rate of each method?

12-6 Suppose a firm is considering two mutually exclusive projects. One has a life of 6 years and the other a life of 10 years. Would the failure to employ some type of replacement chain analysis bias an NPV analysis against one of the projects? Explain.

Problems   Answers Appear in Appendix B

Easy Problems 1–7

12-1 **NPV** A project has an initial cost of $40,000, expected net cash inflows of $9,000 per year for 7 years, and a cost of capital of 11%. What is the project's NPV? (*Hint:* Begin by constructing a time line.)

12-2 **IRR** Refer to Problem 12-1. What is the project's IRR?

12-3 **MIRR** Refer to Problem 12-1. What is the project's MIRR?

12-4 **Profitability Index** Refer to Problem 12-1. What is the project's PI?

12-5 **Payback** Refer to Problem 12-1. What is the project's payback period?

12-6 **Discounted Payback** Refer to Problem 12-1. What is the project's discounted payback period?

12-7 **NPV** Your division is considering two investment projects, each of which requires an up-front expenditure of $15 million. You estimate that the investments will produce the following net cash flows:

Year	Project A	Project B
1	$ 5,000,000	$20,000,000
2	10,000,000	10,000,000
3	20,000,000	6,000,000

   a. What are the two projects' net present values, assuming the cost of capital is 5%? 10%? 15%?

   b. What are the two projects' IRRs at these same costs of capital?

Intermediate Problems 8–18

12-8 **NPVs, IRRs, and MIRRs for Independent Projects** Edelman Engineering is considering including two pieces of equipment, a truck and an overhead pulley system, in this year's capital budget. The projects are independent. The cash outlay for the truck is $17,100 and that for the pulley system is $22,430. The firm's cost of capital is 14%. After-tax cash flows, including depreciation, are as follows:

Year	Truck	Pulley
1	$5,100	$7,500
2	5,100	7,500
3	5,100	7,500
4	5,100	7,500
5	5,100	7,500

Calculate the IRR, the NPV, and the MIRR for each project, and indicate the correct accept–reject decision for each.

12-9 **NPVs and IRRs for Mutually Exclusive Projects** Davis Industries must choose between a gas-powered and an electric-powered forklift truck for moving materials in its factory. Since both forklifts perform the same function, the firm will choose only one. (They are mutually exclusive investments.) The electric-powered truck will cost more, but it will be less expensive to operate; it will cost $22,000, whereas the gas-powered truck will cost $17,500. The cost of capital that applies to both investments is 12%. The life for both types of truck is estimated to be 6 years, during which time the net cash flows for the electric-powered truck will be $6,290 per year and those for the gas-powered truck will be $5,000 per year. Annual net cash flows include depreciation expenses. Calculate the NPV and IRR for each type of truck, and decide which to recommend.

12-10 **Capital Budgeting Methods** Project S has a cost of $10,000 and is expected to produce benefits (cash flows) of $3,000 per year for 5 years. Project L costs $25,000 and is expected to produce cash flows of $7,400 per year for 5 years. Calculate the two projects' NPVs, IRRs, MIRRs, and PIs, assuming a cost of capital of 12%. Which project would be selected, assuming they are mutually exclusive, using each ranking method? Which should actually be selected?

12-11 **MIRR and NPV** Your company is considering two mutually exclusive projects, X and Y, whose costs and cash flows are shown below:

Year	X	Y
0	− $5,000	− $5,000
1	1,000	4,500
2	1,500	1,500
3	2,000	1,000
4	4,000	500

The projects are equally risky, and their cost of capital is 12%. You must make a recommendation, and you must base it on the modified IRR (MIRR). Which project has the higher MIRR?

12-12 **NPV and IRR Analysis** After discovering a new gold vein in the Colorado mountains, CTC Mining Corporation must decide whether to go ahead and develop the deposit. The most cost-effective method of mining gold is sulfuric acid extraction, a process that could result in environmental damage. Before proceeding with the extraction, CTC must spend $900,000 for new mining equipment and pay $165,000 for its installation. The gold mined will net the firm an estimated $350,000 each year for the 5-year life of the vein. CTC's cost of capital is 14%. For the purposes of this problem, assume that the cash inflows occur at the end of the year.

a. What are the project's NPV and IRR?

b. Should this project be undertaken if environmental impacts were not a consideration?

c. How should environmental effects be considered when evaluating this, or any other, project? How might these concepts affect the decision in part b?

12-13 **NPV and IRR Analysis** Cummings Products is considering two mutually exclusive investments whose expected net cash flows are as follows:

Expected Net Cash Flows

Year	Project A	Project B
0	− $400	− $650
1	− 528	235
2	− 219	235
3	− 150	235
4	1,100	235
5	820	235
6	990	235
7	− 325	0

a. Construct NPV profiles for Projects A and B.

b. What is each project's IRR?

c. If you were told that each project's cost of capital was 10%, which project, if either, should be selected? If the cost of capital were 17%, what would be the proper choice?

d. What is each project's MIRR at the cost of capital of 10%? At 17%? (*Hint:* Note that B is a 6-year project.)

e. What is the crossover rate, and what is its significance?

12-14 Timing Differences The Ewert Exploration Company is considering two mutually exclusive plans for extracting oil on property for which it has mineral rights. Both plans call for the expenditure of $10 million to drill development wells. Under Plan A, all the oil will be extracted in 1 year, producing a cash flow at t = 1 of $12 million; under Plan B, cash flows will be $1.75 million per year for 20 years.

a. What are the annual incremental cash flows that will be available to Ewert Exploration if it undertakes Plan B rather than Plan A? (*Hint:* Subtract Plan A's flows from B's.)

b. If the company accepts Plan A and then invests the extra cash generated at the end of Year 1, what rate of return (reinvestment rate) would cause the cash flows from reinvestment to equal the cash flows from Plan B?

c. Suppose a firm's cost of capital is 10%. Is it logical to assume that the firm would take on all available independent projects (of average risk) with returns greater than 10%? Further, if all available projects with returns greater than 10% have been taken, would this mean that cash flows from past investments would have an opportunity cost of only 10%, because all the firm could do with these cash flows would be to replace money that has a cost of 10%? Finally, does this imply that the cost of capital is the correct rate to assume for the reinvestment of a project's cash flows?

d. Construct NPV profiles for Plans A and B, identify each project's IRR, and indicate the crossover rate.

12-15 Scale Differences The Pinkerton Publishing Company is considering two mutually exclusive expansion plans. Plan A calls for the expenditure of $50 million on a large-scale, integrated plant that will provide an expected cash flow stream of $8 million per year for 20 years. Plan B calls for the expenditure of $15 million to build a somewhat less efficient, more labor-intensive plant that has an expected cash flow stream of $3.4 million per year for 20 years. The firm's cost of capital is 10%.

a. Calculate each project's NPV and IRR.

b. Set up a Project Δ by showing the cash flows that will exist if the firm goes with the large plant rather than the smaller plant. What are the NPV and the IRR for this Project Δ?

c. Graph the NPV profiles for Plan A, Plan B, and Project Δ.

d. Give a logical explanation, based on reinvestment rates and opportunity costs, as to why the NPV method is better than the IRR method when the firm's cost of capital is constant at some value such as 10%.

12-16 Unequal Lives Shao Airlines is considering two alternative planes. Plane A has an expected life of 5 years, will cost $100 million, and will produce net cash flows of $30 million per year. Plane B has a life of 10 years, will cost $132 million, and will produce net cash flows of $25 million per year. Shao plans to serve the route for only 10 years. Inflation in operating costs, airplane costs, and fares is expected to be zero, and the company's cost of capital is 12%. By how much would the value of the company increase if it accepted the better project (plane)? What is the equivalent annual annuity for each plane?

12-17 Unequal Lives The Perez Company has the opportunity to invest in one of two mutually exclusive machines that will produce a product it will need for the foreseeable future. Machine A costs $10 million but realizes after-tax inflows of $4 million per year for 4 years. After 4 years, the machine must be replaced. Machine B costs $15 million and realizes after-tax inflows of $3.5 million per year for 8 years, after which it must be replaced. Assume that machine prices are not expected to rise because inflation will be offset by cheaper components used in the machines. The cost of capital is 10%. By how much would the value of the company increase if it accepted the better machine? What is the equivalent annual annuity for each machine?

12-18 Unequal Lives Filkins Fabric Company is considering the replacement of its old, fully depreciated knitting machine. Two new models are available: Machine 190-3, which has a cost of $190,000, a 3-year expected life, and after-tax cash flows (labor savings and depreciation) of $87,000 per year; and Machine 360-6, which has a cost of $360,000, a 6-year life, and after-tax cash flows of $98,300 per year. Knitting machine prices are not expected to rise, because inflation will be offset by cheaper components (microprocessors) used in the machines. Assume that Filkins's cost of capital is 14%. Should the firm replace its old knitting machine? If so, which new machine should it use? By how much would the value of the company increase if it accepted the better machine? What is the equivalent annual annuity for each machine?

Challenging Problems 19–22

12-19 Multiple Rates of Return The Ulmer Uranium Company is deciding whether or not it should open a strip mine whose net cost is $4.4 million. Net cash inflows are expected to be $27.7 million, all coming at the end of Year 1. The land must be returned to its natural state at a cost of $25 million, payable at the end of Year 2.

a. Plot the project's NPV profile.

b. Should the project be accepted if $r = 8\%$? If $r = 14\%$? Explain your reasoning.

c. Can you think of some other capital budgeting situations in which negative cash flows during or at the end of the project's life might lead to multiple IRRs?

d. What is the project's MIRR at $r = 8\%$? At $r = 14\%$? Does the MIRR method lead to the same accept–reject decision as the NPV method?

12-20 Present Value of Costs The Aubey Coffee Company is evaluating the within-plant distribution system for its new roasting, grinding, and packing plant. The two alternatives are (1) a conveyor system with a high initial cost but low annual operating costs, and (2) several forklift trucks, which cost less but have considerably higher operating costs. The decision to construct the plant has already been made, and the choice here will have no effect on the overall revenues of the project. The cost of capital for the plant is 8%, and the projects' expected net costs are listed in the following table:

Expected Net Cost

Year	Conveyor	Forklift
0	−$500,000	−$200,000
1	−120,000	−160,000
2	−120,000	−160,000
3	−120,000	−160,000
4	−120,000	−160,000
5	−20,000	−160,000

a. What is the IRR of each alternative?

b. What is the present value of the costs of each alternative? Which method should be chosen?

12-21 **Payback, NPV, and MIRR** Your division is considering two investment projects, each of which requires an up-front expenditure of $25 million. You estimate that the cost of capital is 10% and that the investments will produce the following after-tax cash flows (in millions of dollars):

Year	Project A	Project B
1	5	20
2	10	10
3	15	8
4	20	6

a. What is the regular payback period for each of the projects?

b. What is the discounted payback period for each of the projects?

c. If the two projects are independent and the cost of capital is 10%, which project or projects should the firm undertake?

d. If the two projects are mutually exclusive and the cost of capital is 5%, which project should the firm undertake?

e. If the two projects are mutually exclusive and the cost of capital is 15%, which project should the firm undertake?

f. What is the crossover rate?

g. If the cost of capital is 10%, what is the modified IRR (MIRR) of each project?

12-22 **Economic Life** The Scampini Supplies Company recently purchased a new delivery truck. The new truck cost $22,500, and it is expected to generate net after-tax operating cash flows, including depreciation, of $6,250 per year. The truck has a 5-year expected life. The expected salvage values after tax adjustments for the truck are given below. The company's cost of capital is 10%.

Year	Annual Operating Cash Flow	Salvage Value
0	−$22,500	$22,500
1	6,250	17,500
2	6,250	14,000
3	6,250	11,000
4	6,250	5,000
5	6,250	0

a. Should the firm operate the truck until the end of its 5-year physical life? If not, then what is its optimal economic life?
b. Would the introduction of salvage values, in addition to operating cash flows, ever *reduce* the expected NPV and/or IRR of a project?

Spreadsheet Problem

12-23 **Build a Model: Capital Budgeting Tools** Start with the partial model in the file *Ch12 P23 Build a Model.xls* on the textbook's Web site. Gardial Fisheries is considering two mutually exclusive investments. The projects' expected net cash flows are as follows:

<table>
<tr><th colspan="3">Expected Net Cash Flows</th></tr>
<tr><th>Year</th><th>Project A</th><th>Project B</th></tr>
<tr><td>0</td><td>−$375</td><td>−$575</td></tr>
<tr><td>1</td><td>−300</td><td>190</td></tr>
<tr><td>2</td><td>−200</td><td>190</td></tr>
<tr><td>3</td><td>−100</td><td>190</td></tr>
<tr><td>4</td><td>600</td><td>190</td></tr>
<tr><td>5</td><td>600</td><td>190</td></tr>
<tr><td>6</td><td>926</td><td>190</td></tr>
<tr><td>7</td><td>−200</td><td>0</td></tr>
</table>

a. If each project's cost of capital is 12%, which project should be selected? If the cost of capital is 18%, what project is the proper choice?
b. Construct NPV profiles for Projects A and B.
c. What is each project's IRR?
d. What is the crossover rate, and what is its significance?
e. What is each project's MIRR at a cost of capital of 12%? At r = 18%? (*Hint:* Note that B is a 6-year project.)
f. What is the regular payback period for these two projects?
g. At a cost of capital of 12%, what is the discounted payback period for these two projects?
h. What is the profitability index for each project if the cost of capital is 12%?

MINI CASE

You have just graduated from the MBA program of a large university, and one of your favorite courses was "Today's Entrepreneurs." In fact, you enjoyed it so much you have decided you want to "be your own boss." While you were in the master's program, your grandfather died and left you $1 million to do with as you please. You are not an inventor, and you do not have a trade skill that you can market; however, you have decided that you would like to purchase at least one established franchise in the fast-foods area, maybe two (if profitable). The problem is that you have never been one to stay with any project for too long, so you figure that your time frame is 3 years. After 3 years you will go on to something else.

You have narrowed your selection down to two choices: (1) Franchise L, Lisa's Soups, Salads, & Stuff, and (2) Franchise S, Sam's Fabulous Fried Chicken. The net cash flows shown below include the price you would receive for selling the franchise in Year 3 and the forecast of how each franchise will do over the 3-year period. Franchise L's cash flows will start off slowly but will increase rather quickly as people become more health-conscious, while Franchise S's cash flows will start off high but will trail off as other chicken competitors enter the marketplace and as people become more health-conscious and avoid fried foods. Franchise L serves breakfast and lunch whereas Franchise S serves only dinner, so it is possible for you to invest in both franchises. You see these franchises as perfect complements to one another: You could attract both the lunch and dinner crowds and the health-conscious and not-so-health-conscious crowds without the franchises directly competing against one another.

Here are the net cash flows (in thousands of dollars):

Expected Net Cash Flows

Year	Franchise L	Franchise S
0	−$100	−$100
1	10	70
2	60	50
3	80	20

Depreciation, salvage values, net working capital requirements, and tax effects are all included in these cash flows.

You also have made subjective risk assessments of each franchise and concluded that both franchises have risk characteristics that require a return of 10%. You must now determine whether one or both of the franchises should be accepted.

a. What is capital budgeting?

b. What is the difference between independent and mutually exclusive projects?

c. (1) Define the term *net present value (NPV)*. What is each franchise's NPV?

   (2) What is the rationale behind the NPV method? According to NPV, which franchise or franchises should be accepted if they are independent? Mutually exclusive?

   (3) Would the NPVs change if the cost of capital changed?

d. (1) Define the term *internal rate of return (IRR)*. What is each franchise's IRR?

   (2) How is the IRR on a project related to the YTM on a bond?

   (3) What is the logic behind the IRR method? According to IRR, which franchises should be accepted if they are independent? Mutually exclusive?

   (4) Would the franchises' IRRs change if the cost of capital changed?

e. (1) Draw NPV profiles for Franchises L and S. At what discount rate do the profiles cross?

   (2) Look at your NPV profile graph without referring to the actual NPVs and IRRs. Which franchise or franchises should be accepted if they are independent? Mutually exclusive? Explain. Are your answers correct at any cost of capital less than 23.6%?

f. (1) What is the underlying cause of ranking conflicts between NPV and IRR?

(2) What is the *reinvestment rate assumption,* and how does it affect the NPV-versus-IRR conflict?

(3) Which method is the best? Why?

g. (1) Define the term *modified IRR (MIRR).* Find the MIRRs for Franchises L and S.

(2) What are the MIRR's advantages and disadvantages vis-à-vis the regular IRR? What are the MIRR's advantages and disadvantages vis-à-vis the NPV?

h. What does the profitability index (PI) measure? What are the PIs of Franchises S and L?

i. (1) What is the payback period? Find the paybacks for Franchises L and S.

(2) What is the rationale for the payback method? According to the payback criterion, which franchise or franchises should be accepted if the firm's maximum acceptable payback is 2 years and if Franchises L and S are independent? If they are mutually exclusive?

(3) What is the difference between the regular and discounted payback periods?

(4) What is the main disadvantage of discounted payback? Is the payback method of any real usefulness in capital budgeting decisions?

j. As a separate project (Project P), you are considering sponsorship of a pavilion at the upcoming World's Fair. The pavilion would cost $800,000, and it is expected to result in $5 million of incremental cash inflows during its single year of operation. However, it would then take another year, and $5 million of costs, to demolish the site and return it to its original condition. Thus, Project P's expected net cash flows look like this (in millions of dollars):

Year	Net Cash Flows
0	− $0.8
1	5.0
2	−5.0

The project is estimated to be of average risk, so its cost of capital is 10%.

(1) What are normal and nonnormal cash flows?

(2) What is Project P's NPV? What is its IRR? Its MIRR?

(3) Draw Project P's NPV profile. Does Project P have normal or nonnormal cash flows? Should this project be accepted?

k. In an unrelated analysis, you have the opportunity to choose between the following two mutually exclusive projects:

Expected Net Cash Flows

Year	Project S	Project L
0	− $100,000	− $100,000
1	60,000	33,500
2	60,000	33,500
3	—	33,500
4	—	33,500

The projects provide a necessary service, so whichever one is selected is expected to be repeated into the foreseeable future. Both projects have a 10% cost of capital.

(1) What is each project's initial NPV without replication?

(2) What is each project's equivalent annual annuity?

(3) Now apply the replacement chain approach to determine the projects' extended NPVs. Which project should be chosen?

(4) Now assume that the cost to replicate Project S in 2 years will increase to $105,000 because of inflationary pressures. How should the analysis be handled now, and which project should be chosen?

l. You are also considering another project that has a physical life of 3 years; that is, the machinery will be totally worn out after 3 years. However, if the project were terminated prior to the end of 3 years, the machinery would have a positive salvage value. Here are the project's estimated cash flows:

Year	Initial Investment and Operating Cash Flows	End-of-Year Net Salvage Value
0	− $5,000	$5,000
1	2,100	3,100
2	2,000	2,000
3	1,750	0

Using the 10% cost of capital, what is the project's NPV if it is operated for the full 3 years? Would the NPV change if the company planned to terminate the project at the end of Year 2? At the end of Year 1? What is the project's optimal (economic) life?

m. After examining all the potential projects, you discover that there are many more projects this year with positive NPVs than in a normal year. What two problems might this extra-large capital budget cause?

Selected Additional Cases

The following cases from TextChoice, *Cengage Learning's online case library, cover many of the concepts discussed in this chapter and are available at* **www.textchoice2.com/casenet.**

Klein-Brigham Series:
Case 11, "Chicago Valve Company."

Brigham-Buzzard Series:
Case 6, "Powerline Network Corporation (Basics of Capital Budgeting)."

Capital Budgeting: Estimating Cash Flows and Analyzing Risk

The basic principles of capital budgeting were covered in Chapter 12. Given a project's expected cash flows, it is easy to calculate its NPV, IRR, MIRR, PI, payback, and discounted payback. Unfortunately, cash flows are rarely just given—rather, managers must estimate them based on information collected from sources both inside and outside the company. Moreover, uncertainty surrounds the cash flow estimates, and some projects are riskier than others. In the first part of this chapter, we develop procedures for estimating the cash flows associated with capital budgeting projects. Then, in the second part, we discuss techniques used to measure and take account of project risk.

WEB

The textbook's Web site contains an *Excel* file that will guide you through the chapter's calculations. The file for this chapter is **Ch13 Tool Kit.xls**, and we encourage you to open the file and follow along as you read the chapter.

Beginning of Chapter Questions

As you read the chapter, consider how you would answer the following questions. You *should not* necessarily be able to answer the questions before you read the chapter. Rather, you should use them to get a sense of the issues covered in the chapter. After reading the chapter, you should be able to give at least partial answers to the questions, and you should be able to give better answers after the chapter has been discussed in class. Note, too, that it is often useful, when answering conceptual questions, to use hypothetical data to illustrate your answer. We illustrate the answers with an *Excel* model that is available on the textbook's Web site. Accessing the model and working through it is a useful exercise, and it provides insights that are useful when answering the questions.

1. How do **project cash flows** as calculated in this chapter affect a firm's **corporate free cash flows** as defined in Chapter 7 and then used in Chapter 11 to calculate a firm's value? How does a proposed project's **estimated NPV** affect the **value of the firm?**

2. Define (a) **externalities** and (b) **sunk costs,** and then give examples of each that might be involved in a proposal by an energy company to build a new coal-fired electric power generating unit. How would these factors be worked into the analysis?

3. If Congress shortened depreciation lives for tax purposes, how would this affect the energy project's NPV, assuming nothing else changes?

4. If the company's capital budgeting analyst decided to show all projected cash flows, both positive and negative, in current dollars rather than inflation-adjusted dollars, would this affect the calculated NPV?

5. Discuss some ways the company could estimate the project's risk, and then explain how risk might be incorporated into the decision analysis.

6. What are **real options,** and why are they important to capital budgeting?

13.1 Conceptual Issues

The most important but also the most difficult step in capital budgeting is estimating **project cash flows.** Many variables are involved, and many individuals and departments participate in the process. For example, the forecasts of unit sales and sales prices are normally made by the marketing group based on their knowledge of price elasticity, advertising effects, the state of the economy, competitors' reactions, and trends in consumers' tastes. Similarly, the capital outlays associated with a new product are generally obtained from the engineering and product development staffs, while operating costs are estimated by cost accountants, production experts, personnel specialists, purchasing agents, and so forth.

A proper analysis includes (1) obtaining information from various departments such as engineering and marketing, (2) ensuring that everyone involved with the forecast uses a consistent set of realistic economic assumptions, and (3) making sure that no biases are inherent in the forecasts. This last point is extremely important, because some managers become emotionally involved with pet projects and others push projects in order to build empires. Both problems cause cash flow forecast biases that make bad projects look good—on paper!

A number of conceptual issues arise in the cash flow estimation process. Some of these are covered in the balance of this section. Some of them are illustrated in the examples we explore in the subsequent sections.

13.1a Cash Flow versus Accounting Income

We saw in Chapter 7 that free cash flow differs from accounting income: Free cash flow is cash flow that is available for distribution to investors; hence free cash flow

CORPORATE VALUATION, CASH FLOWS, AND RISK ANALYSIS

When we estimate a project's cash flows (CF) and then discount them at the project's risk-adjusted cost of capital, r, the result is the project's NPV, which tells us how much the project increases the firm's value. This chapter focuses on how to estimate the size and risk of a project's cash flows.

Note too that project cash flows, once a project has been accepted and placed in operation, are added to the firm's free cash flows from other sources. Therefore, projects' cash flows essentially determine the firm's free cash flows as discussed in Chapter 7 and thus form the basis for the firm's market value and stock price.

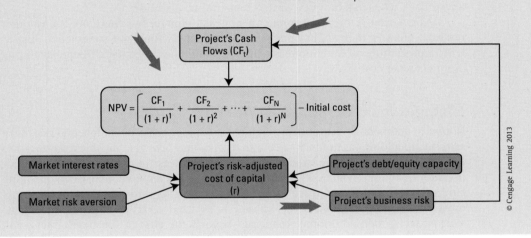

$$NPV = \left[\frac{CF_1}{(1+r)^1} + \frac{CF_2}{(1+r)^2} + \cdots + \frac{CF_N}{(1+r)^N} \right] - \text{Initial cost}$$

© Cengage Learning 2013

is the basis of a firm's value. It is common in the practice of finance to speak of a firm's free cash flow and a project's cash flow (or net cash flow), but these are based on the same concepts. In fact, a project's cash flow is identical to the project's free cash flow, and a firm's total net cash flow from all projects is equal to the firm's free cash flow. We will follow the typical convention and refer to a project's free cash flow simply as project cash flow, but keep in mind that the two concepts are identical.[1]

Because net income is not equal to the cash flow available for distribution to investors, in the last chapter we discounted *net cash flows,* not accounting income, to find projects' NPVs. *For capital budgeting purposes it is the project's net cash flow, not its accounting income, that is relevant.* Therefore, when analyzing a proposed capital budgeting project, disregard the project's net income and focus

---

1. When the financial press refers to a firm's "net cash flow," it is almost always equal to the definition we provide in Chapter 7 (which simply adds back depreciation and any other noncash charges to net income). However, as we explained in Chapter 7, the net cash flow from operations (from the statement of cash flows) and the firm's free cash flow are much more useful measures of cash flow. When financial analysts within a company use the term "a project's net cash flow," they almost always calculate it as we do in this chapter, which is in essence the project's free cash flow. Thus, free cash flow means the same thing whether you calculate it for a firm or for a project. On the other hand, when the financial press talks about a firm's net cash flow or when an internal analyst talks about a project's net cash flow, those "net cash flows" are not the same.

exclusively on its net cash flow.[2] Be especially alert to the following differences between cash flow and accounting income.

The Cash Flow Effect of Asset Purchases and Depreciation

Most projects require assets, and asset purchases represent *negative* cash flows. Even though the acquisition of assets results in a cash outflow, accountants do not show the purchase of fixed assets as a deduction from accounting income. Instead, they deduct a depreciation expense each year throughout the life of the asset. Depreciation shelters income from taxation, and this has an impact on cash flow, but depreciation itself is not a cash flow. Therefore, depreciation must be added back when estimating a project's operating cash flow.

Depreciation is the most common noncash charge, but there are many other noncash charges that might appear on a company's financial statements. Just as with depreciation, all other noncash charges should be added back when calculating a project's net cash flow.

Changes in Net Operating Working Capital

Normally, additional inventories are required to support a new operation, and expanded sales tie up additional funds in accounts receivable. However, payables and accruals increase as a result of the expansion, and this reduces the cash needed to finance inventories and receivables. The difference between the required increase in operating current assets and the increase in operating current liabilities is the change in net operating working capital. If this change is positive, as it generally is for expansion projects, then additional financing—beyond the cost of the fixed assets—will be needed.

Toward the end of a project's life, inventories will be used but not replaced, and receivables will be collected without corresponding replacements. As these changes occur the firm will receive cash inflows; as a result, the investment in net operating working capital will be returned by the end of the project's life.

Interest Charges Are Not Included in Project Cash Flows

Interest is a cash expense, so at first blush it would seem that interest on any debt used to finance a project should be deducted when we estimate the project's net cash flows. However, this is not correct. Recall from Chapter 12 that we discount a project's cash flows by its risk-adjusted cost of capital, which is a weighted average (WACC) of the costs of debt, preferred stock, and common equity, adjusted for the project's risk and debt capacity. This project cost of capital is the rate of return

---

2. This statement is theoretically correct but sometimes an overstatement in the real world. Stockholders in publicly owned companies do look at accounting income; it affects stock prices, and those prices affect the cost of capital. Therefore, if a project would have a negative effect on net income but a positive effect on cash flows, management should focus primarily on cash flows but try to communicate to investors that (1) the adverse effect on net income is temporary and (2) in the long run, the positive effect on cash flows will show up in future net income. Privately owned companies don't have this problem—they can and do focus almost exclusively on cash flows, and that's a significant advantage of private ownership.

necessary to satisfy *all* of the firm's investors, including stockholders and debtholders. A common mistake made by many students and financial managers is to subtract interest payments when estimating a project's cash flows. This is a mistake because the cost of debt is already embedded in the cost of capital, so subtracting interest payments from the project's cash flows would amount to double-counting interest costs. Therefore, *you should not subtract interest expenses when finding a project's cash flows.*[3]

13.1b Timing of Cash Flows: Yearly versus Other Periods

In theory, in capital budgeting analyses we should discount cash flows based on the exact moment when they occur. Therefore, one could argue that daily cash flows would be better than annual flows. However, it would be costly to estimate daily cash flows and laborious to analyze them, and in general the analysis would be no better than one using annual flows because we simply can't make accurate forecasts of daily cash flows more than a couple of months into the future. Therefore, it is generally appropriate to assume that all cash flows occur at the end of the various years. But for projects with highly predictable cash flows, such as constructing a building and then leasing it on a long-term basis (with monthly payments) to a financially sound tenant, we would analyze the project using monthly periods.

13.1c Incremental Cash Flows

The relevant cash flows to be used in project analysis are the difference between the cash flows the firm will have if it implements the project versus the cash flows it will have if it rejects the project. These are called **incremental cash flows**:

$$
\begin{array}{c}
\text{Incremental} \\
\text{cash flows}
\end{array}
=
\begin{array}{c}
\text{Company's cash flows} \\
\textit{with the project}
\end{array}
-
\begin{array}{c}
\text{Company's cash flows} \\
\textit{without the project}
\end{array}
$$

We discuss several types of incremental cash flows in the following sections.

13.1d Expansion Projects and Replacement Projects

Two types of projects can be distinguished: (1) *expansion projects,* in which the firm makes an investment in, for example, a new Home Depot store in Seattle; and (2) *replacement projects*, in which the firm replaces existing assets, generally to reduce costs. In expansion projects, the cash expenditures on buildings, equipment, and required working capital are obviously incremental, as are the sales revenues and operating costs associated with the project. The incremental costs associated with replacement projects are not so obvious. For example, Home Depot might replace some of its delivery trucks to reduce fuel and maintenance expenses. Replacement analysis is complicated by the fact that most of the relevant cash flows are the cash

---

3. Some years ago the interest situation was debated in the academic literature. One position was that interest should be deducted, resulting in the net cash flow to stockholders, and then that cash flow should be discounted at the cost of common equity. It was demonstrated that equity flows discounted at the equity cost and operating flows discounted at the WACC led to the same conclusions. Now most academics recommend the operating cash flow approach, and it is practiced by most companies.

flow differences between the existing project and the replacement project. For example, the fuel bill for a more efficient new truck might be $10,000 per year versus $15,000 for the old truck, and the $5,000 fuel savings would be an incremental cash flow associated with the replacement decision. We analyze an expansion and replacement decision later in the chapter.

13.1e Sunk Costs

A **sunk cost** is an outlay related to the project that was incurred in the past and cannot be recovered in the future regardless of whether or not the project is accepted. Therefore, sunk costs are *not incremental costs* and thus are not relevant in a capital budgeting analysis.

To illustrate, suppose Home Depot spent $2 million to investigate sites for a potential new store in a given area. That $2 million is a sunk cost—the money is gone, and it won't come back regardless of whether or not a new store is built. Therefore, the $2 million should not be included in a capital budgeting decision.

Improper treatment of sunk costs can lead to bad decisions. For example, suppose Home Depot completed the analysis for a new store and found that it must spend an additional (or incremental) $17 million to build and supply the store, on top of the $2 million already spent on the site study. Suppose the present value of future cash flows is $18 million. Should the project be accepted? If the sunk costs are mistakenly included, the NPV is −$2 million + (−$17 million) + $18 million = −$1 million and the project would be rejected. However, *that would be a bad decision*. The real issue is whether the *incremental* $17 million would result in enough *incremental* cash flow to produce a positive NPV. If the $2 million sunk cost were disregarded, as it should be, then the NPV on an incremental basis would be a *positive* $1 million.

13.1f Opportunity Costs Associated with Assets the Firm Already Owns

Another conceptual issue relates to **opportunity costs** related to assets the firm already owns. Continuing our example, suppose Home Depot (HD) owns land with a current market value of $2 million that can be used for the new store if it decides to build the store. If HD goes forward with the project, only another $15 million will be required, not the full $17 million, because it will not need to buy the required land. Does this mean that HD should use the $15 million incremental cost as the cost of the new store? The answer is definitely "no." If the new store is *not* built, then HD could sell the land and receive a cash flow of $2 million. This $2 million is an *opportunity cost*—it is cash that HD would not receive if the land is used for the new store. Therefore, the $2 million must be charged to the new project, and failing to do so would cause the new project's calculated NPV to be too high.

13.1g Externalities

Another conceptual issue relates to **externalities**, which are the effects of a project on other parts of the firm or on the environment. As explained in what follows, there are three types of externalities: negative within-firm externalities, positive within-firm externalities, and environmental externalities.

Negative Within-Firm Externalities

If a retailer like Home Depot opens a new store that is close to its existing stores, then the new store might attract customers who would otherwise buy from the existing stores, reducing the old stores' cash flows. Therefore, the new store's incremental cash flow must be reduced by the amount of the cash flow lost by its other units. This type of externality is called **cannibalization**, because the new business eats into the company's existing business. Many businesses are subject to cannibalization. For example, each new iPod model cannibalizes existing models. Those lost cash flows should be considered, and that means charging them as a cost when analyzing new products.

Dealing properly with negative externalities requires careful thinking. If Apple decided not to come out with a new model of iPod because of cannibalization, another company might come out with a similar new model, causing Apple to lose sales on existing models. Apple must examine the total situation, and this is definitely more than a simple, mechanical analysis. Experience and knowledge of the industry is required to make good decisions in most cases.

One of the best examples of a company getting into trouble as a result of not dealing correctly with cannibalization was IBM's response when personal computers were first developed in the 1970s. IBM's mainframes dominated the computer industry, and they generated huge profits. IBM used its technology to enter the PC market, and initially it was the leading PC company. However, its top managers decided to deemphasize the PC division because they were afraid it would hurt the more profitable mainframe business. That decision opened the door for Apple, Dell, Hewlett Packard, Sony, and Chinese competitors to take PC business away from IBM. As a result, IBM went from being the most profitable firm in the world to one whose very survival was threatened. IBM's experience highlights that, even as it's essential to understand the theory of finance, it is equally important to understand the industry and the long-run consequences of a given decision. Good judgment is an essential element for good financial decisions.

Positive Within-Firm Externalities

As we noted earlier, cannibalization occurs when a new product competes with an old one. However, a new project can also be *complementary* to an old one, in which case cash flows in the old operation will be *increased* when the new one is introduced. For example, Apple's iPod was a profitable product, but when Apple considered an investment in its music store it realized that the store would boost sales of iPods. So, even if an analysis of the proposed music store indicated a negative NPV, the analysis would not be complete unless the incremental cash flows that would occur in the iPod division were credited to the music store. Consideration of positive externalities often changes a project's NPV from negative to positive.

Environmental Externalities

The most common type of negative externality is a project's impact on the environment. Government rules and regulations constrain what companies can do, but firms have some flexibility in dealing with the environment. For example, suppose a manufacturer is studying a proposed new plant. The company could meet current environmental regulations at a cost of $1 million, but the plant would still emit fumes that would cause some bad will in its neighborhood. Those ill feelings would not show up in the cash flow analysis, but they should still be considered. Perhaps a relatively small additional expenditure would reduce the emissions substantially, make the plant look good relative to other plants in the area, and provide goodwill that in the future would help the firm's sales and its negotiations with governmental agencies.

Of course, all firms' profits depend on the Earth remaining healthy, so companies have some incentive to do things that protect the environment even though those actions are not currently required. However, if one firm decides to take actions that are good for the environment but quite costly, then either it must raise its prices or suffer a decline in earnings. If its competitors decide to get by with less costly but environmentally unfriendly processes, they can price their products lower and make more money. Of course, the more environmentally friendly companies can advertise their environmental efforts, and this might—or might not—offset their higher costs. All this illustrates why government regulations are often necessary. Finance, politics, and the environment are all interconnected.

Self Test	Why should companies use a project's net cash flows rather than its accounting income when determining a project's NPV?
	Explain the following terms: incremental cash flow, sunk cost, opportunity cost, externality, cannibalization, and complementary project.
	Provide an example of a "good" externality—that is, one that increases a project's true NPV over what it would be if just its own cash flows were considered.

13.2 Analysis of an Expansion Project

In Chapter 12, we worked with the cash flows associated with Guyton Products Company's expansion project. In this section we show how these cash flows are estimated. Recall that the project is the application of a radically new nano-coating technology to a new type of solar water heater module, which will be manufactured under a 4-year license from a university. It's not clear how well the water heater will work, how strong demand for it will be, how long it will be before the product becomes obsolete, or whether the license can be renewed after the initial 4 years. Still, the water heater has the potential for being quite profitable, though it could also fail miserably. GPC is a relatively large company and this is just one of its projects, so a failure would not bankrupt the firm but would hurt profits and the stock's price.

13.2a Cash Flow Projections: Base Case

WEB

See **Ch13 Tool Kit.xls** on the textbook's Web site.

We used *Excel* to do the analysis. We could have used a calculator and paper, but *Excel* is *much* easier when dealing with realistic capital budgeting problems. You don't need to know *Excel* to understand our discussion, but if you plan to work in finance—or, really, in any business field—you must know how to use *Excel*, so we recommend that you open the *Excel Tool Kit* for this chapter and scroll through it as the textbook explains the analysis.

Figure 13-1 shows the base-case inputs used in the analysis. For example, the cost of required equipment to manufacture the water heaters is $7,750 and is shown in Cell E47 (all dollar values in Figure 13-1 and in our discussion here are reported

Figure 13-1 **Analysis of an Expansion Project: Inputs and Key Results (Thousands of Dollars)**

	A	B	C	D	E	F	G	H	I
44	Part 1. Inputs and Key Results (figures in thousands except units)								
45									
46	Inputs				Base-Case L		Key Results		
47	Equipment cost				$7,750		NPV		$1,048
48	Salvage value, equipment, Year 4				$639		IRR		13.79%
49	Opportunity cost				$0		MIRR		12.78%
50	Externalities (cannibalization)				$0		PI		1.10
51	Units sold, Year 1				10,000		Payback		3.39
52	Annual change in units sold, after Year 1				15.00%		Discounted payback		3.80
53	Sales price per unit, Year 1				$1.50				
54	Annual change in sales price, after Year 1				4.00%				
55	Variable cost per unit (VC), Year 1				$1.07				
56	Annual change in VC, after Year 1				3.00%				
57	Nonvariable cost (Non-VC), Year 1				$2,120.0				
58	Annual change in Non-VC, after Year 1				3.00%				
59	Project WACC				10.00%				
60	Tax rate				40.00%				
61	Working capital as % of next year's sales				15.00%				

in thousands, so the equipment actually costs $7,750,000). If you change the inputs in Cells E47:E61, *Excel* will instantly generate revised cash flows and performance measures (shown in Figure 13-2). We report key results next to the inputs so it is easy to see in real time the effects of changes in assumptions.

The input values from Figure 13-1 are used to calculate cash flows and performance measures, as reported in Figure 13-2. Some values change each year, and we report those in Rows 77 to 82. Annual unit sales are shown on Row 77, and they are projected to grow at 15% per year. The annual sales prices per unit are shown on Row 78, with sales revenue on Row 79. Variable costs per unit are on Row 80, and nonvariable costs are on Row 81. These values are all projected to grow at the rates assumed in Part 1, and the annual values are used in the cash flow forecast. In addition, virtually all projects require working capital, and this one is no exception. For example, raw materials must be purchased and replenished each year as they are used. In Part 1 (Figure 13-1) we assume that GPC must have an amount of net operating working capital on hand equal to 15% of the upcoming year's sales. In Year 0, GPC must have 15%($15,000) = $2,250 in working capital on hand. As sales grow, so does this required working capital, and these amounts are in Row 82.

The initial investments at t = 0 are shown in Cells E85:E87. The initial equipment cost of $7,750 is in Cell E85. As we explained above, an initial investment of working capital of $2,250 is required in Year 0; this is shown in Cell E86.[4] There are no opportunity costs in the base-case scenario, so the entry in Cell E87 is zero.

Projected sales revenues are on Row 89. Variable costs per unit multiplied by the number of module units gives us total variable costs, as shown on Row 90. Nonvariable costs are shown on Row 91, and depreciation is on Row 92 (we explain the depreciation expense later in this section). Subtracting variable costs, nonvariable

WEB

See **Ch13 Tool Kit.xls** on the textbook's Web site.

---

4. Net operating working capital consists of inventories and accounts receivable *less* accounts payable and accruals.

Figure 13-2   Analysis of an Expansion Project: Cash Flows and Performance Measures (Thousands of Dollars)

	A	B	C	D	E	F	G	H	I
75	Part 2. Cash Flows and Performance Measures								
76	Variables Used in the Cash Flow Forecast				0	1	2	3	4
77	Unit sales					10,000	11,500	13,225	15,209
78	Sales price per unit					$1.50	$1.56	$1.62	$1.69
79	Sales revenues = Units × Price/unit					$15,000	$17,940	$21,456	$25,662
80	Variable cost per unit					$1.07	$1.10	$1.14	$1.17
81	Nonvariable costs (excluding depreciation)					$2,120	$2,184	$2,249	$2,317
82	Net working capital$_t$ = 15% × revenues$_{t+1}$				$2,250	$2,691	$3,218	$3,849	$0
83						Cash Flows at End of Year			
84	Investment Outlays at Time = 0				0	1	2	3	4
85	Equipment				−$7,750				
86	Initial investment in working capital				−2,250				
87	Opportunity cost, after taxes				0				
88	Net Cash Flows over the Project's Life								
89	Sales revenues = Units × Price/unit					$15,000	$17,940	$21,456	$25,662
90	Variable costs = Units × Cost/unit					10,700	12,674	15,013	17,782
91	Nonvariable costs (excluding depreciation)					2,120	2,184	2,249	2,317
92	Depreciation: Accelerated, from table below					2,583	3,445	1,148	574
93	Operating profit (EBIT)					−$403	−$363	$3,047	$4,988
94	Taxes on operating profit					−161	−145	1,219	1,995
95	Net operating profit after taxes					−$242	−$218	$1,828	$2,993
96	Add back depreciation					2,583	3,445	1,148	574
97	Opportunity cost, after taxes					0	0	0	0
98	Cannibalization or complementary effects, after taxes					0	0	0	0
99	Salvage value (taxed as ordinary income)								639
100	Tax on salvage value (SV is taxed at 40%)								−256
101	Change in WC: Outflow (−) or recovery (+)					−441	−527	−631	3,849
102	Project net cash flows: Time Line				−$10,000	$1,900	$2,700	$2,345	$7,800
103									
104	Project Evaluation		Accelerated					Straight-Line	
105		Results	Formulas					Results	
106	NPV	$1,048	=NPV(E59,F102:I102)+E102					$925	
107	IRR	13.79%	=IRR(E102:I102)					13.21%	
108	MIRR	12.78%	=MIRR(E102:I102,E59,E59)					12.46%	
109	Profitability index	1.10	=NPV(E59,F102:I102)/(−E102)					1.09	
110	Payback	3.39	=PERCENTRANK(E113:I113,0,6)*I112					3.43	
111	Discounted payback	3.80	=PERCENTRANK(E115:I115,0,6)*I112					3.84	
112	Calculations for Payback			Year:	0	1	2	3	4
113	Cumulative cash flows for payback				−$10,000	−$8,100	−$5,400	−$3,055	$4,745
114	Discounted cash flows for disc. payback				−$10,000	$1,727	$2,231	$1,762	$5,328
115	Cumulative discounted cash flows				−$10,000	−$8,273	−$6,041	−$4,279	$1,048
116			Accelerated Depreciation						
117	Depreciable basis:	$7,750			Rate/year	33.33%	44.45%	14.81%	7.41%
118					Dollars/year	$2,583	$3,445	$1,148	$574

WEB

See **Ch13 Tool Kit.xls** on the textbook's Web site.

costs, and depreciation from sales revenues results in operating profit (EBIT), as shown on Row 93. We calculate taxes on Row 94 and subtract them to get the project's net operating profit after taxes on Row 95. We add back depreciation on Row 96 because it is a noncash expense. There are no annual opportunity costs or cannibalization effects in the base-case scenario; if there were, we would include them on an after-tax basis on Rows 97 and 98.

Because of the license, the project has a 4-year life; at Year 4, the equipment is expected to have a salvage value of $639, which is shown in Cell I99. Because the assets will be fully depreciated by Year 4, the $639 is a gain that is taxed at the firm's ordinary income tax rate of 40%; this tax is shown in Cell I100.[5]

Row 101 shows the incremental investment in working capital required in Years 1 through 4. For example, Cell E82 shows working capital of $2,250 will be needed in Year 0 to support Year 1 sales; we listed this as an initial investment in Cell E86. Cell F82 shows working capital must increase to $2,691 to support Year 2 sales. Thus, GPC must invest $2,691 − $2,250 = $441 in working capital in Year 1, and this is shown as a negative number (since it is an investment) in Cell F101. Then, at the end of Year 4, all of the investments in working capital will be recovered. Inventories will be sold and not replaced, and all receivables will be collected by the end of Year 4. Total net working capital recovered at t = 4 is the sum of the initial investment at t = 0, $2,250, plus the additional investments during Years 1 through 3; the total is $3,849.

We sum Cells E85:E87 to get the total initial investment, and we sum Rows 93 to 101 to get the project's annual net cash flows, set up as a time line on Row 102. These cash flows are then used to calculate NPV, IRR, MIRR, PI, payback, and discounted payback, performance measures that are shown in Cells C106 through C111. (The results in Columns H and I are based on straight-line depreciation and are discussed later.) Based on this analysis, the project looks like it is somewhat profitable, with an NPV of $1,048 as compared with an initial investment of $10,000. Its IRR and MIRR are both greater than the 10% WACC, the PI is just a bit larger than 1.0, and the payback and discounted payback are almost as long as the project's life. However, before the decision is finalized, we need to look at some additional factors. In particular, we must recognize that the actual outcome could be better or worse than the base-case level, that there might be responses management can make to changing conditions, and that there might be qualitative factors to consider. We examine these concerns later in the chapter, but first we address the following issues associated with the base-case analysis.

13.2b Depreciation

The depreciation expense is calculated as the annual rate allowed by the IRS multiplied by the project's depreciable cost basis, which in this case is $7,750.[6] Congress sets the depreciation rates used for tax purposes, which are then used in capital budgeting. The rates for this project are shown on Row 117, and more details are provided in Appendix 13A and in the chapter's *Tool Kit*. Congress permits firms to depreciate assets using either the straight-line method or an accelerated method. The results we have discussed thus far were based on accelerated depreciation. We also analyzed the project using straight-line depreciation with the results reported in Figure 13-2 in H106:H116; the full analysis is in the chapter's *Tool Kit*. The results indicate that the project is worth less when using straight-line depreciation than when using accelerated depreciation. In general, *profitable firms are better off using accelerated depreciation* because more depreciation is taken in the early years under the

WEB

See **Ch13 Tool Kit.xls** on the textbook's Web site.

---

5. If an asset is sold for less than its book value, the resulting "negative" tax is a credit and would increase the cash flow. If an asset is sold for exactly its book value, there will be no gain or loss and hence no tax liability or credit.
6. Regardless of whether accelerated or straight-line depreciation is used, the basis is not adjusted by the expected salvage value when calculating the depreciation expense that is used to determine taxable income.

accelerated method, so taxes are lower in those years and higher in later years. Total depreciation, total cash flows, and total taxes are the same under both depreciation methods, but receiving the cash earlier under the accelerated method results in a higher NPV, IRR, and MIRR.

Suppose Congress wants to encourage companies to increase their capital expenditures and thereby boost economic growth and employment. What changes in depreciation regulations would have the desired effect? The answer is "Make accelerated depreciation even more accelerated." For example, if GPC could write off equipment at rates of 67%, 22%, 7%, and 4% rather than 33.33%, 44.45%, 14.81%, and 7.41%, then its early tax payments would be even lower, early cash flows would be even higher, and the project's NPV would exceed the value shown in Figure 13-2.[7]

13.2c Taxation of Salvage

In our example, GPC's project was fully depreciated by the end of the project. But suppose instead that GPC terminates operations before the equipment is fully depreciated. The after-tax salvage value depends on the price at which GPC can sell the equipment *and* on the book value of the equipment (i.e., the original basis less all previous depreciation charges). The following table shows the calculations of yearly book values.

	Year			
	1	**2**	**3**	**4**
Beginning book value	$7,750	$5,167	$1,722	$574
Annual depreciation	2,583	3,445	1,148	574
Ending book value	$5,167	$1,722	$ 574	$ 0

Suppose GPC terminates at Year 2, at which time the book value is $1,722. We consider two cases, gains and losses. In the first case, the salvage value is $2,200 and so there is a reported gain of $2,200 − $1,722 = $478. This gain is taxed as ordinary income, so the tax is 40%($478) = $191. The after-tax cash flow is equal to the sales price less the tax: $2,200 − $191 = $2,009.

Now suppose the salvage value at Year 2 is only $500. In this case, there is a reported loss: $500 − $1,722 = −$1,222. This is treated as an ordinary expense, so its tax is 40%(−$1,222) = −$489. This "negative" tax acts as a credit if GPC has other taxable income, so the net after-tax cash flow is $500 − (−$489) = $989.

13.2d Externalities: Cannibalization or Complementary Projects

As noted earlier, the solar water heater project does not lead to any cannibalization effects. Suppose, however, that it would reduce the net after-tax cash flows of

---

7. Other than our simplification by rounding, this is exactly what Congress did in 2008 and 2009, in response to the global economic crisis, by establishing a temporary "bonus" depreciation to stimulate investment. The depreciation in the first year is the regular accelerated depreciation plus a bonus of 50% of the original basis. This bonus was increased to 100% of the original basis for 2011, effectively allowing companies to fully expense certain capital expenditures in 2011. The bonus drops back to 50% for 2012. The provisions are set to expire at the end of 2012.

another GPC division by $50 per year and that no other firm could take on this project if GPC turns it down. In this case, we would use the cannibalization line at Row 98, deducting $50 each year. As a result, the project would have a lower NPV. On the other hand, if the project would cause additional inflows to some other GPC division because it was complementary to that other division's products (i.e., if a positive externality exists), then those after-tax inflows should be attributed to the water heater project and thus shown as a positive inflow on Row 98.

13.2e Opportunity Costs

Now suppose the $7,750 initial cost were based on the assumption that the project would use space in a building that GPC now owns and that the space could be leased to another company for $200 per year, after taxes, if the project is rejected. The $200 would be an *opportunity cost*, and it should be reflected in our calculations. We would subtract the $200 per year on Row 97, causing a decrease in NPV.

Sunk Costs

At this point, at time t = 0, GPC is considering whether to make the $10,000 investment on the project. We've determined that the NPV of the investment is $1,048 and that GPC should go ahead with it. Would it make any difference to the decision if you found out that last year GPC had spent $1,500 on a marketing and feasibility study for the project? The answer is no. The money spent last year is a sunk cost and has no impact on the decision today to go forward. Although in total GPC will have lost money on the entire deal if it goes ahead (–$1,500 + 1,048 = –$452), it will lose less than if it forgoes this good investment opportunity (–$1,500), so GPC should go ahead with the project. The way you can tell if a cost is a sunk cost and should be ignored is by asking the question, "Will the company be able to recover this cost if it doesn't undertake the project?" If the answer is no, the cost will still be there whether the company undertakes the project or not, then it is a sunk cost and must be ignored in the decision.

13.2f Other Changes to the Inputs

All of the input variables could be changed, and these changes would alter the calculated project cash flows and thus the NPV and other capital budgeting decision criteria. We could increase or decrease the projected unit sales, the sales price, the variable cost, the nonvariable fixed costs, the initial investment cost, the net working capital requirements, the salvage value, and even the tax rate if we thought Congress was likely to raise or lower taxes. Such changes can be made easily in an *Excel* model, making it possible to immediately see the resulting changes in the decision criteria. This is called *sensitivity analysis*, and we discuss it in Section 13.5.

13.2g The Importance of Incorporating Expected Inflation in Prices and Costs

Notice that the model has inputs for annual changes in prices and costs; in other words, it allows for inflation (or deflation) in prices and costs. In Figure 13-2, the selling price increased by 4% annually, while aggregate variable costs increased by 3%. It is certainly possible that different cost categories (such as energy costs or labor costs) might experience different inflation rates, so our models always include separate line items for the expected inflation in each price or cost. It is easy to overlook inflation, but it is important to include it. For example, had we forgotten to include inflation in the GPC example, then the estimated NPV would have dropped from $1,048 to $225. Forgetting to include inflation in a capital budgeting analysis typically causes the estimated NPV to be lower than the true NPV, which could cause a company to reject a project that it should have accepted.[8]

Self Test

In what way is the setup for finding a project's cash flows similar to the projected income statements for a new, single-product firm? In what way would the two statements be different?

Would a project's NPV for a typical firm be higher or lower if the firm used accelerated rather than straight-line depreciation? Explain.

How could the analysis in Figure 13-2 be modified to consider cannibalization, opportunity costs, and sunk costs?

Why does net working capital appear with both negative and positive values in Figure 13-2?

13.3 Risk Analysis in Capital Budgeting[9]

Projects differ in risk, and risk should be reflected in capital budgeting decisions. There are three separate and distinct types of risk.

1. **Stand-alone risk** is a project's risk assuming (a) that it is the firm's only asset and (b) that each of the firm's stockholders holds only that one stock in his portfolio. Stand-alone risk is based on uncertainty about the project's expected cash flows. It is important to remember that *stand-alone risk ignores diversification by both the firm and its stockholders.*

2. **Within-firm risk** (also called **corporate risk**) is a project's risk to the corporation itself. Within-firm risk recognizes that the project is only one asset in the firm's portfolio of projects; hence some of its risk is eliminated by diversification within the firm. However, *within-firm risk ignores diversification by the firm's stockholders.* Within-firm risk is measured by the project's impact on uncertainty about the firm's future total cash flows.

3. **Market risk** (also called **beta risk**) is the risk of the project as seen by a well-diversified stockholder who recognizes (a) that the project is only one of the firm's projects and (b) that the firm's stock is but one of her stocks. The project's market risk is measured by its effect on the firm's beta coefficient.

Taking on a project with a lot of stand-alone and/or corporate risk will not necessarily affect the firm's beta. However, if the project has high stand-alone risk and if its cash flows are highly correlated with cash flows on the firm's other assets

---

8. The market's estimate of expected inflation is already incorporated into the cost of debt (via the inflation premium) and the cost of equity (via the risk-free rate in the CAPM), so the project's cost of capital includes the effect of expected inflation. If you don't also include the effect of inflation in projected cash flows, then the cash flows will be too low relative to the cost of capital, leading to a downward-biased estimate of NPV.

9. Some professors may choose to cover some of the risk sections and skip others. We offer a range of choices, and we tried to make the exposition clear enough that interested and self-motivated students can read these sections on their own if they are not assigned.

and with cash flows of most other firms in the economy, then the project will have a high degree of all three types of risk. Market risk is, *theoretically*, the most relevant because it is the one that, according to the CAPM, is reflected in stock prices. Unfortunately, market risk is also the most difficult to measure, primarily because new projects don't have "market prices" that can be related to stock market returns.

Most decision makers do a *quantitative* analysis of stand-alone risk and then consider the other two types of risk in a *qualitative* manner. Projects are classified into several categories; then, using the firm's overall WACC as a starting point, a **risk-adjusted cost of capital** is assigned to each category. For example, a firm might establish three risk classes and then assign the corporate WACC to average-risk projects, add a 5% risk premium for higher-risk projects, and subtract 2% for low-risk projects. Under this setup, if the company's overall WACC were 10%, then 10% would be used to evaluate average-risk projects, 15% for high-risk projects, and 8% for low-risk projects. Although this approach is probably better than not making any risk adjustments, these adjustments are highly subjective and difficult to justify. Unfortunately, there's no perfect way to specify how high or low the risk adjustments should be.[10]

WEB

See **Web Extension 13A** on the textbook's Web site for a more detailed discussion on alternative methods for incorporating project risk into the capital budgeting decision process.

Self Test

What are the three types of project risk?

Which type is theoretically the most relevant? Why?

Describe a type of classification scheme that firms often use to obtain risk-adjusted costs of capital.

13.4 Measuring Stand-Alone Risk

A project's stand-alone risk reflects uncertainty about its cash flows. The required dollars of investment, unit sales, sales prices, and operating costs as shown in Figure 13-1 for GPC's project are all subject to uncertainty. First-year sales are projected at 10,000 units to be sold at a price of $1.50 per unit (recall that all dollar values are reported in thousands). However, unit sales will almost certainly be somewhat higher or lower than 10,000, and the price will probably turn out to be different from the projected $1.50 per unit. Similarly, the other variables would probably differ from their indicated values. Indeed, *all the inputs are expected values, not known values, and actual values can and do vary from expected values.* That's what risk is all about!

Three techniques are used in practice to assess stand-alone risk: (1) sensitivity analysis, (2) scenario analysis, and (3) Monte Carlo simulation. We discuss them in the sections that follow.

Self Test

What does a project's stand-alone risk reflect?

What three techniques are used to assess stand-alone risk?

---

10. We should note that the CAPM approach can be used for projects provided there are specialized publicly traded firms in the same business as that of the project under consideration. See the discussion in Chapter 10 regarding techniques for measuring divisional betas.

   For more on risk adjustments, see Tarun K. Mukherjee, "Reducing the Uncertainty-Induced Bias in Capital Budgeting Decisions—A Hurdle Rate Approach," *Journal of Business Finance & Accounting,* September 1991, pp. 747–753.

13.5 Sensitivity Analysis

Intuitively, we know that a change in a key input variable such as units sold or the sales price will cause the NPV to change. **Sensitivity analysis** *measures the percentage change in NPV that results from a given percentage change in an input variable when other inputs are held at their expected values.* This is by far the most commonly used type of risk analysis. It begins with a base-case scenario in which the project's NPV is found using the base-case value for each input variable. GPC's base-case inputs were given in Figure 13-1, but it's easy to imagine changes in the inputs, and any changes would result in a different NPV.

When GPC's senior managers review a capital budgeting analysis, they are interested in the base-case NPV, but they always go on to ask a series of "what if" questions: "What if unit sales fall to 9,000?" "What if market conditions force us to price the product at $1.40, not $1.50?" "What if variable costs are higher than we have forecasted?" Sensitivity analysis is designed to provide answers to such questions. Each variable is increased or decreased by a specified percentage from its expected value, holding other variables constant at their base-case levels. Then the NPV is calculated using the changed input. Finally, the resulting set of NPVs is plotted to show how sensitive NPV is to changes in the different variables.

Figure 13-3 shows GPC's project's sensitivity graph for six key variables. The data below the graph give the NPVs based on different values of the inputs, and those NPVs were then plotted to make the graph. Figure 13-3 shows that, as unit sales and the sales price are increased, the project's NPV increases; in contrast, increases in variable costs, nonvariable costs, equipment costs, and WACC lower the project's NPV. The slopes of the lines in the graph and the ranges in the table below the graph indicate how sensitive NPV is to each input: *The larger the range, the steeper the variable's slope and the more sensitive the NPV is to this variable.* We see that NPV is extremely sensitive to changes in the sales price; fairly sensitive to changes in variable costs, units sold, and fixed costs; and not especially sensitive to changes in the equipment's cost and the WACC. Management should, of course, try especially hard to obtain accurate estimates of the variables that have the greatest impact on the NPV.

If we were comparing two projects, then the one with the steeper sensitivity lines would be riskier (other things held constant), because relatively small changes in the input variables would produce large changes in the NPV. Thus, sensitivity analysis provides useful insights into a project's risk.[11] Note, however, that even though NPV may be highly sensitive to certain variables, if those variables are not likely to change much from their expected values, then the project may not be very risky in spite of its high sensitivity. Also, if several of the inputs change at the same time, the combined effect on NPV can be much greater than sensitivity analysis suggests.

13.5a Tornado Diagrams

Tornado diagrams are another way to present results from sensitivity analysis. The first step is to calculate the range of possible NPVs for each of the input variables

---

11. Sensitivity analysis is tedious with a regular calculator but easy with a spreadsheet. We used the chapter's *Excel Tool Kit* to calculate the NPVs and then to draw the graph in Figure 13-3. To conduct such an analysis by hand would be quite time-consuming, and if the basic data were changed even slightly—say, the cost of the equipment was increased slightly—then all of the calculations would have to be redone. With a spreadsheet, we can simply type over the old input with the new one, and presto, the analysis and the graph change instantaneously.

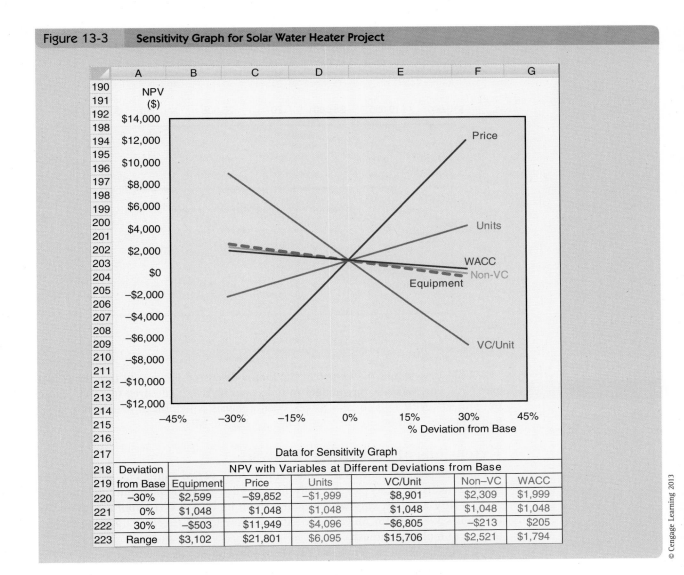

Figure 13-3   **Sensitivity Graph for Solar Water Heater Project**

Data for Sensitivity Graph

Deviation from Base	NPV with Variables at Different Deviations from Base					
	Equipment	Price	Units	VC/Unit	Non–VC	WACC
–30%	$2,599	–$9,852	–$1,999	$8,901	$2,309	$1,999
0%	$1,048	$1,048	$1,048	$1,048	$1,048	$1,048
30%	–$503	$11,949	$4,096	–$6,805	–$213	$205
Range	$3,102	$21,801	$6,095	$15,706	$2,521	$1,794

being changed and rank these ranges. In our example, the range for sales price per unit is the largest and the range for WACC is the smallest. The ranges for each variable are then plotted, with the largest range on top and the smallest range on the bottom. It is also helpful to plot a vertical line showing the base-case NPV. We present a tornado diagram in Figure 13-4. Notice that the diagram is like a tornado in the sense that it is widest at the top and smallest at the bottom; hence its name. The tornado diagram makes it immediately obvious which inputs have the greatest impact on NPV: sales price and variable costs in this case.

WEB

See *Ch13 Tool Kit.xls* on the textbook's Web site.

13.5b NPV Break-Even Analysis

A special application of sensitivity analysis is called **NPV break-even analysis**. In a break-even analysis, we find the level of an input that produces an NPV of exactly zero. We used *Excel*'s Goal Seek feature to do this. See *Ch13 Tool Kit.xls* on the textbook's Web site for an explanation of how to use this *Excel* feature.

Figure 13-4   **Tornado Diagram for Solar Water Heater Project: Range of Outcomes for Input Deviations from Base Case (Thousands of Dollars)**

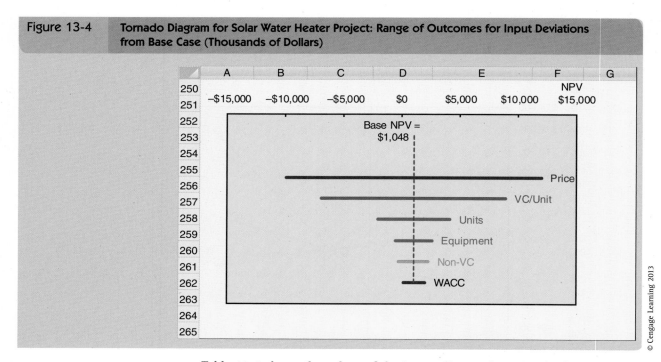

WEB

See **Ch13 Tool Kit.xls** on the textbook's Web site.

Table 13-1 shows the values of the inputs discussed previously that produce a zero NPV. For example, the number of units sold in Year 1 can drop to 8,968 before the project's NPV falls to zero. Break-even analysis is helpful in determining how bad things can get before the project has a negative NPV.

Extensions of Sensitivity Analysis

In our examples, we showed how one output, NPV, varied with a change in a single input. Sensitivity analysis can easily be extended to show how multiple outputs, such as NPV and IRR, vary with a change in an input. See **Ch13 Tool Kit.xls** on the textbook's Web site for an example showing how to use *Excel*'s Data Table feature to present multiple outputs.

It is also possible to use a Data Table to show how a single output, such as NPV, varies for changes in two inputs, such as the number of units sold and the sales price per unit. See **Ch13 Tool Kit.xls** on the textbook's Web site for an example. However, when we examine the impact of a change in more than one input, we usually use scenario analysis, which is described in the following section.

Self Test   What is sensitivity analysis?

Briefly explain the usefulness of a sensitivity graph.

Discuss the following statement: "A project may not be very risky in spite of its high sensitivity to certain variables."

13.6 Scenario Analysis

In the sensitivity analysis just described, we changed one variable at a time. However, it is useful to know what would happen to the project's NPV if several of the inputs turn out to be better or worse than expected, and this is what we do in

TABLE 13-1	NPV Break-Even Analysis (Thousands of Dollars)
Input	**Input Value That Produces Zero NPV Holding All Else Constant**
Sales price per unit, Year 1	$1.457
Variable cost per unit (VC), Year 1	$1.113
Annual change in units sold after Year 1	7.40%
Units sold, Year 1	8,968
Nonvariable cost (Non-VC), Year 1	$2,649
Project WACC	13.79%

a **scenario analysis.** Also, scenario analysis allows us to assign probabilities to the base (or most likely) case, the best case, and the worst case; then we can find the *expected value* of the project's NPV, along with its *standard deviation* and *coefficient of variation,* to get a better idea of the project's risk.

> **WEB**
>
> See **Ch13 Tool Kit.xls** on the textbook's Web site.

In a scenario analysis, we begin with the base-case scenario, which uses the most likely value for each input variable. We then ask marketing, engineering, and other operating managers to specify a worst-case scenario (low unit sales, low sales price, high variable costs, and so on) and a best-case scenario. Often, the best and worst cases are defined as having a 25% probability of occurring, with a 50% probability for the base-case conditions. Obviously, conditions could take on many more than three values, but such a scenario setup is useful to help get some idea of the project's riskiness.

After much discussion with the marketing staff, engineers, accountants, and other experts in the company, a set of worst-case and best-case values were determined for several key inputs. Figure 13-5, taken from Tab 3 of the chapter *Tool Kit* model, shows the probability and inputs assumed for the base-case, worst-case, and best-case scenarios.

The project's cash flows and performance measures under each scenario are calculated; see the *Tool Kit* for the calculations. The cash flows for each scenario are shown in Figure 13-6, along with a probability distribution of the possible outcomes for NPV. If the project is highly successful, then a low initial investment, high sales price, high unit sales, and low production costs would combine to result in a very high NPV, $19,468. However, if things turn out badly, then the NPV would be a *negative* $7,543. This wide range of possibilities, and especially the large potential negative value, suggests that this is a risky project. If bad conditions materialize, the project will not bankrupt the company—this is just one project for a large company. Still, losing $7,543 (actually $7,543,000, since the units are thousands of dollars) would certainly hurt the company's value and the reputation of the project's manager.

If we multiply each scenario's probability by the NPV for that scenario and then sum the products, we will have the project's expected NPV of $3,505, as shown in Figure 13-6. Note that the *expected* NPV differs from the *base-case* NPV. This is not an error—mathematically, they are not equal.[12] We also calculate the standard

---

12. This result occurs for two reasons. First, although in this scenario analysis, the base-case input values happen to be equal to the average of the best- and worst-case values, this is by no means necessary. Best- and worst-case values need not be the same distance from the base case. Second, even though the base-case values are midway between the best- and worst-case values, in our model two uncertain variables, sales volume and sales price, are multiplied together to obtain dollar sales, and this process causes the NPV distribution to be skewed to the right. A large number multiplied by another large number produces a very big number, and this in turn causes the average value (or expected value) to increase.

Figure 13-5   Inputs and Key Results for Each Scenario (Thousands of Dollars)

	A	B	C	D	E	F	G	H	I
34							Scenarios:		
35	Inputs:				Base		Worst		Best
36	Probability of Scenario				50%		25%		25%
37	Equipment cost				$7,750		$8,250		$7,250
38	Salvage value, equipment, Year 4				$639		$639		$639
39	Opportunity cost				$0		$0		$0
40	Externalities (cannibalization)				$0		$0		$0
41	Units sold, Year 1				10,000		8,500		11,500
42	Annual change in units sold, after Year 1				15.00%		5.00%		25.00%
43	Sales price per unit, Year 1				$1.50		$1.25		$1.75
44	Annual change in sales price, after Year 1				4.00%		4.00%		4.00%
45	Variable cost per unit (VC), Year 1				$1.07		$1.17		$0.97
46	Annual change in VC, after Year 1				3.00%		3.00%		3.00%
47	Nonvariable cost (Non-VC), Year 1				$2,120		$2,330		$1,910
48	Annual change in Non-VC, after Year 1				3.00%		3.00%		3.00%
49	Project WACC				10.00%		10.00%		10.00%
50	Tax rate				40.00%		50.00%		30.00%
51	Working capital as % of next year's sales				15.00%		15.00%		15.00%
52	Key Results:				Base		Worst		Best
53	NPV				$1,048		–$7,543		$19,468
54	IRR				13.79%		–29.40%		62.41%
55	MIRR				12.78%		–22.23%		43.49%
56	PI				1.10		0.23		2.90
57	Payback				3.39		Not found		1.83
58	Discounted payback				3.80		Not found		2.07

WEB

See *Ch13 Tool Kit.xls* on the textbook's Web site.

deviation of the expected NPV; it is $9,861. Dividing the standard deviation by the expected NPV yields the coefficient of variation, 2.81, which is a measure of stand-alone risk. The firm's average project has a coefficient of variation of about 1.2, so the 2.815 indicates that this project is riskier than most of GPC's other typical projects.

GPC's corporate WACC is 9%, so that rate should be used to find the NPV of an average-risk project. However, the water heater project is riskier than average, so a higher discount rate should be used to find its NPV. There is no way to determine the "precisely correct" discount rate—this is a judgment call. Management decided to evaluate the project using a 10% rate.[13]

Note that the base-case results are the same in our sensitivity and scenario analyses, but in the scenario analysis the worst case is much worse than in the sensitivity analysis and the best case is much better. This is because in scenario analysis all of the variables are set at their best or worst levels, whereas in sensitivity analysis only one variable is adjusted and all the others are left at their base-case levels.

---

13. One could argue that the best-case scenario should be evaluated with a relatively low WACC, the worst-case scenario with a relatively high WACC, and the base case with the average corporate WACC. However, one could also argue that, at the time of the initial decision, we don't know what case will occur and hence a single rate should be used. Observe that, in the worst-case scenario, all of the cash flows are negative. If we used a high WACC because of this branch's risk, this would lower the PV of these negative cash flows, making the worst case much better than if we used the average WACC. Determining the "right" WACC to use in the analysis is not an easy task!

Figure 13-6	Scenario Analysis: Expected NPV and Its Risk

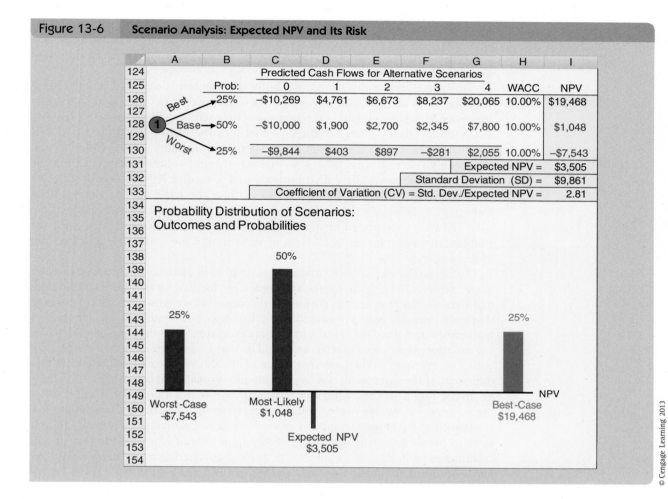

The project has a positive NPV, but its coefficient of variation (CV) is 2.815, which is more than double the 1.2 CV of an average project. With the higher risk, it is not clear if the project should be accepted or not. At this point, GPC's CEO asked the CFO to investigate the risk further by performing a simulation analysis, as described in the next section.

WEB

See **Ch13 Tool Kit.xls** on the textbook's Web site.

Self Test

What is scenario analysis?

Differentiate between sensitivity analysis and scenario analysis. What advantage does scenario analysis have over sensitivity analysis?

13.7 Monte Carlo Simulation[14]

Monte Carlo simulation ties together sensitivities, probability distributions, and correlations among the input variables. It grew out of work in the Manhattan Project to build the first atomic bomb and was so named because it utilized the

---

14. This section is relatively technical, and some instructors may choose to skip it with no loss in continuity.

mathematics of casino gambling. Although Monte Carlo simulation is considerably more complex than scenario analysis, simulation software packages make the process manageable. Many of these packages can be used as add-ons to *Excel* and other spreadsheet programs.

In a simulation analysis, a probability distribution is assigned to each input variable—sales in units, the sales price, the variable cost per unit, and so on. The computer begins by picking a random value for each variable from its probability distribution. Those values are then entered into the model, the project's NPV is calculated, and the NPV is stored in the computer's memory. This is called a trial. After completing the first trial, a second set of input values is selected from the input variables' probability distributions, and a second NPV is calculated. This process is repeated many times. The NPVs from the trials can be charted on a histogram, which shows an estimate of the project's outcomes. The average of the trials' NPVs is interpreted as a measure of the project's expected NPV, with the standard deviation (or the coefficient of variation) of the trials' NPV as a measure of the project's risk.

Using this procedure, we conducted a simulation analysis of GPC's solar water heater project. To compare apples and apples, we focused on the same six variables that were allowed to change in the previously conducted scenario analysis. We assumed that each variable can be represented by its own continuous normal distribution with means and standard deviations that are consistent with the base-case scenario. For example, we assumed that the units sold in Year 1 come from a normal distribution with a mean equal to the base-case value of 10,000. We used the probabilities and outcomes of the three scenarios to estimate the standard deviation (all calculations are in the *Tool Kit*). The standard deviation of units sold is 1,061, as calculated using the scenario values. We made similar assumptions for all variables. In addition, we assumed that the annual change in unit sales will be positively correlated with unit sales in the first year: If demand is higher than expected in the first year, it will continue to be higher than expected. In particular, we assume a correlation of 0.65 between units sold in the first year and growth in units sold in later years. For all other variables, we assumed zero correlation. Figure 13-7 shows the inputs used in the simulation analysis.

Figure 13-7 also shows the current set of random variables that were drawn from the distributions at the time we created the figure for the textbook. We used a two-step procedure to create the random variables for the inputs. First, we used *Excel*'s functions to generate standard normal random variables with a mean of 0 and a standard deviation of 1; these are shown in Cells E38:E51.[15] To create the random values for the inputs used in the analysis, we multiplied a random standard normal variable by the standard deviation and added the expected value. For example, *Excel* drew the value −0.74 for first-year unit sales (Cell E42) from a standard normal distribution. We calculated the value for first-year unit sales to use in the current trial as 10,000 + 1,061(−0.74) = 9,218, which is shown in Cell F42.[16]

We used the inputs in Cells F38:F52 to generate cash flows and to calculate performance measures for the project (the calculations are in the *Tool Kit*). For the trial reported in Figure 13-7, the NPV is $811. We used a Data Table in the *Tool Kit* to generate additional trials. For each trial, the Data Table saved the value of the

---

15. See the *Tool Kit* for detailed explanations on using *Excel* to generate random variables.
16. We used a slightly more complicated procedure to generate a random variable for the annual change in sales to ensure that it had 0.65 correlation with the first-year units sold. See the *Tool Kit* for details.

Figure 13-7   **Inputs and Key Results for the Current Simulation Trial (Thousands of Dollars)**

	A	B	C	D	E	F
31			Inputs for Simulation Probability Distributions		Random Variables Used in Current Simulation Trial	
32						
33						
34			Expected Value of Input	Standard Deviation of Input	Standard Normal Random Variable	Value Used in Current Trial
35						
36						
37	Inputs:					
38	Equipment cost		$7,750	$354	0.12	$7,794
39	Salvage value, equipment, Year 4					$639
40	Opportunity cost					$0
41	Externalities (cannibalization)					$0
42	Units sold, Year 1		10,000	1,061	−0.74	9,218
43	Annual change in units sold, after Year 1		15.00%	7.07%	1.60	26.32%
44	Sales price per unit, Year 1		$1.50	$0.18	−0.79	$1.360
45	Annual change in sales price, after Year 1					4.00%
46	Variable cost per unit (VC), Year 1		$1.07	$0.07	−1.32	$0.98
47	Annual change in VC, after Year 1					3.00%
48	Nonvariable cost (Non-VC), Year 1		$2,120	$148	−0.27	$2.080
49	Annual change in Non-VC, after Year 1					3.00%
50	Project WACC					10.00%
51	Tax rate		40.00%	7.07%	−0.28	38.01%
52	Working capital as % of next year's sales					15.00%
53	Assumed correlation between units sold in Year 1 and annual change in units sold in later years:					
54			$\rho =$	65.00%		
55			Key Results Based on Current Trial			
56						
57			NPV			$811
58			IRR			12.84%
59			MIRR			12.24%
60			PI			1.08
61			Payback			3.48
62			Discounted payback			3.86

input variables and the value of the trial's NPV. Figure 13-8 presents selected results from the simulation for 5,000 trials. (The *Tool Kit* shows only 100 trials because simulating 5,000 trials reduces *Excel*'s speed when performing other calculations in the worksheet.)

After running a simulation, the first thing we do is verify that the results are consistent with our assumptions. The resulting sample mean and standard deviation of units sold in the first year are 10,003 and 1,072, which are virtually identical to our assumptions in Figure 13-7. The same is true for all the other inputs, so we can be reasonably confident that the simulation is doing what we are asking.

Figure 13-8 also reports summary statistics for the project's NPV. The mean is $1,183, which suggests that the project should be accepted. However, the range of outcomes is quite large, from a loss of $17,693 to a gain of $28,610, so the project

WEB

See **Ch13 Tool Kit.xls** on the textbook's Web site.

Figure 13-8   **Summary of Simulation Results (Thousands of Dollars)**

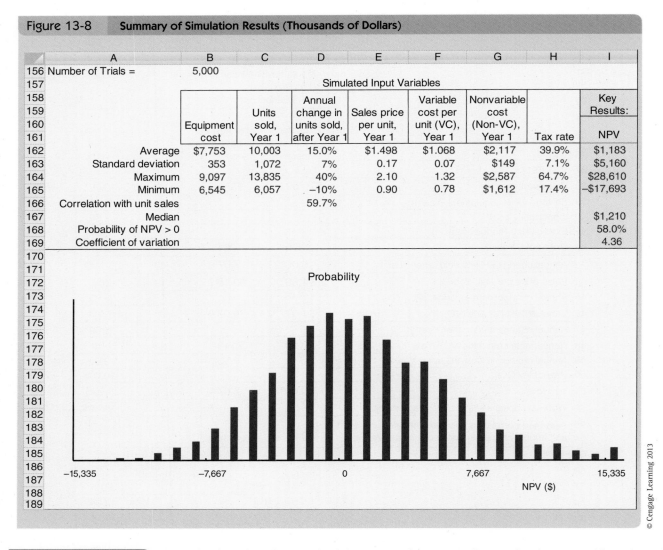

	A	B	C	D	E	F	G	H	I
156	Number of Trials =	5,000							
157				Simulated Input Variables					
158				Annual		Variable	Nonvariable		Key
159			Units	change in	Sales price	cost per	cost		Results:
160		Equipment	sold,	units sold,	per unit,	unit (VC),	(Non-VC),		
161		cost	Year 1	after Year 1	Year 1	Year 1	Year 1	Tax rate	NPV
162	Average	$7,753	10,003	15.0%	$1.498	$1.068	$2,117	39.9%	$1,183
163	Standard deviation	353	1,072	7%	0.17	0.07	$149	7.1%	$5,160
164	Maximum	9,097	13,835	40%	2.10	1.32	$2,587	64.7%	$28,610
165	Minimum	6,545	6,057	−10%	0.90	0.78	$1,612	17.4%	−$17,693
166	Correlation with unit sales			59.7%					
167	Median								$1,210
168	Probability of NPV > 0								58.0%
169	Coefficient of variation								4.36

© Cengage Learning 2013

WEB

See Ch13 Tool Kit.xls on the textbook's Web site.

is clearly risky. The standard deviation of $5,160 indicates that losses could easily occur, which is consistent with this wide range of possible outcomes.[17] Figure 13-8 also reports a median NPV of $1,210, which means that half the time the project will have an NPV of less than $1,210.

A picture is worth a thousand words, and Figure 13-8 shows the probability distribution of the outcomes. Note that the distribution of outcomes is skewed to

---

17. Note that the standard deviation of NPV in the simulation is much smaller than the standard deviation in the scenario analysis. In the scenario analysis, we assumed that all of the poor outcomes would occur together in the worst-case scenario and that all of the positive outcomes would occur together in the best-case scenario. In other words, we implicitly assumed that all of the risky variables were perfectly positively correlated. In the simulation, we assumed that the variables were independent (except for the correlation between unit sales and growth). The independence of variables in the simulation reduces the range of outcomes. For example, in the simulation, sometimes the sales price is high but the sales growth is low. In the scenario analysis, a high sales price is always coupled with high growth. Because the scenario analysis assumption of perfect correlation is unlikely, simulation may provide a better estimate of project risk. However, if the standard deviations and correlations used as inputs in the simulation are inaccurately estimated, then the simulation output will likewise be inaccurate.

THE GLOBAL ECONOMIC CRISIS

Are Bank Stress Tests Stressful Enough?

In late February of 2009, President Obama's newly appointed financial team—consisting of leaders of the Treasury, the Federal Reserve, and the FDIC—announced that the 19 largest U.S. banks (including Citibank, JPMorgan Chase, and Bank of America) would have to undergo "stress tests." If its test indicated that a bank has a high probability of failure under possible conditions, then it would be forced to raise new capital. Investors would be reluctant to provide capital to a bank deemed likely to fail, so the capital would have to come from the Treasury. That would mean that the U.S. government would then own most of the equity and would control the bank, and the bank's top managers would likely be fired.

Just what is a stress test? In medicine, people are connected to a device that monitors their heart, then put on a treadmill, and then tested to see how well their heart takes the stress of a brisk uphill jog. In engineering, beams are subjected to pressure to see how much weight they can hold before breaking. In finance, scenario and simulation analyses like those described in this chapter are conducted to see what would happen under unfavorable conditions. The "worst-case" scenario we described earlier amounts to a stress test for an individual project, and similar tests can be conducted at the corporate level to answer questions like this: "Could we make the required interest and principal payments on our debt if sales fall by 50%?" Well-run companies are constantly stress-testing projects, divisions, and the entire corporation; then, as a result of these tests, managers take actions such as rejecting projects that are too risky or financing with stock rather than debt.

Banks and other financial institutions have been leaders in risk management, which includes stress-testing, but as we know all too well, those tests failed in the 2008–2009 financial crisis. Banks grossly underestimated the combined effects of too much consumer and corporate debt, too much homebuilding, inadequate supervision of mortgage lenders, too many exotic derivatives whose risks the bankers did not fully understand, and so on. In a nutshell, banks throughout the world simply failed to test and plan for the level of economic distress that actually materialized, and the result was a meltdown of the worldwide financial system.

Regulators were determined not to let that situation occur again; hence the administration mandated that the banks undergo stress tests under governmental supervision. Some of the parameters that the banks tested for included a 3.3% decline in GDP in 2009 followed by no growth in 2010, an additional 22% decline in housing prices, and a 10.3% unemployment rate by 2010. These conditions were worse than the consensus of economic forecasters, and worse than what ultimately occurred, but the goal wasn't to predict how the economy was going to fare—it was to see whether the banks could survive another bad, but not completely improbable, downturn. Indeed, a number of analysts think the government's stress test was not nearly stressful enough and that, if "realistic" parameters for a bad-case scenario were used, then most of the large banks would fail. If such information were released, this would set off a panic that would have made the recession worse. Therefore, government officials announced that no banks would be declared to have failed, just that they needed more capital.

A stress test makes sense, but—as with all forecasting—it may or may not do what it is supposed to do. This is true in capital budgeting, and it is even truer for the hugely important job of bank regulation. A failure to develop accurate forecasts of a project's returns could hurt a manager's chances for promotion, but the failure to develop accurate forecasts for our largest banks could do irreparable harm to our entire nation.

---

the right. As the figure shows, the potential downside losses are not as large as the potential upside gains. Our conclusion is that this is a very risky project, as indicated by the coefficient of variation, but it does have a positive expected NPV and the potential to be a "home run."

Self Test

What is Monte Carlo simulation?

13.8 Project Risk Conclusions

We have discussed the three types of risk normally considered in capital budgeting: stand-alone risk, within-firm (or corporate) risk, and market risk. However, two important questions remain: (1) Should firms care at all about stand-alone and corporate risk, given that finance theory says that market (beta) risk is the only relevant risk? (2) What do we do when the stand-alone, within-firm, and market risk assessments lead to different conclusions?

There are no easy answers to these questions. Strict adherents of the CAPM would argue that well-diversified investors are concerned only with market risk, that managers should be concerned only with maximizing stock price, and thus that market (beta) risk ought to be given virtually all the weight in capital budgeting decisions. However, we know that not all investors are well diversified, that the CAPM does not operate exactly as the theory says it should, and that measurement problems keep managers from having complete confidence in the CAPM inputs. In addition, the CAPM ignores bankruptcy costs, even though such costs can be substantial, and the probability of bankruptcy depends on a firm's corporate risk, not on its beta risk. Therefore, even well-diversified investors should want a firm's management to give at least some consideration to a project's corporate risk, and that means giving some consideration to stand-alone project risk.

Although it would be nice to reconcile these problems and to measure risk on some absolute scale, the best we can do in practice is to estimate risk in a somewhat nebulous, relative sense. For example, we can generally say with a fair degree of confidence that a particular project has more, less, or about the same stand-alone risk as the firm's average project. Then, since stand-alone and corporate risks generally are correlated, the project's stand-alone risk is generally a reasonably good measure of its corporate risk. Finally, assuming that market risk and corporate risk are correlated, as is true for most companies, a project with a relatively high or low corporate risk will also have a relatively high or low market risk. We wish we could be more specific, but one simply must use a lot of judgment when assessing projects' risks.

Self Test

In theory, should a firm be equally concerned with stand-alone, corporate, and market risk? Would your answer be the same if we substituted "In practice" for "In theory"? Explain your answers.

If a project's stand-alone, corporate, and market risk are known to be highly correlated, would this make the task of evaluating the project's risk easier or harder? Explain.

CAPITAL BUDGETING PRACTICES IN THE ASIAN/PACIFIC REGION

A survey of executives in Australia, Hong Kong, Indonesia, Malaysia, the Philippines, and Singapore asked several questions about companies' capital budgeting practices. The study yielded the results summarized below.

Techniques for Evaluating Corporate Projects

Consistent with U.S. companies, most companies in this region evaluate projects using IRR, NPV, and payback. For IRR, usage ranges from 96% (in Australia) to 86% (in Hong Kong); NPV usage ranges from 96% (in Australia) to 81% (in the Philippines); and payback usage ranges from 100% (in Hong Kong and the Philippines) to 81% (in Indonesia).

Techniques for Estimating the Cost of Equity Capital

Recall from Chapter 10 that three basic approaches can be used to estimate the cost of equity: CAPM, dividend yield plus growth (DCF), and cost of own debt plus a risk premium. The use of these methods varies considerably from country to country (see Table A). The CAPM is used most often by U.S. firms. This is also true for Australian firms, but not for the other Asian/Pacific firms, which instead more often use the DCF and risk premium approaches.

Techniques for Assessing Risk

Firms in the Asian/Pacific region rely heavily on scenario and sensitivity analyses. They also use decision trees and Monte Carlo simulation, but much less frequently (see Table B).

Table A

Method	Australia	Hong Kong	Indonesia	Malaysia	Philippines	Singapore
CAPM	72.7%	26.9%	0.0%	6.2%	24.1%	17.0%
Dividend yield plus growth rate	16.4	53.8	33.3	50.0	34.5	42.6
Cost of debt plus risk premium	10.9	23.1	53.4	37.5	58.6	42.6

Table B

Risk Assessment Technique	Australia	Hong Kong	Indonesia	Malaysia	Philippines	Singapore
Scenario analysis	96%	100%	94%	80%	97%	90%
Sensitivity analysis	100	100	88	83	94	79
Decision-tree analysis	44	58	50	37	33	46
Monte Carlo simulation	38	35	25	9	24	35

Source: Adapted from George W. Kester et al., "Capital Budgeting Practices in the Asia-Pacific Region: Australia, Hong Kong, Indonesia, Malaysia, Philippines, and Singapore," *Financial Practice and Education,* Vol. 9, No. 1, Spring/Summer 1999, pp. 25–33.

13.9 Replacement Analysis

In the previous sections we assumed that the solar water heater project was an entirely new project, so all of its cash flows were incremental—they would occur if and only if the project were accepted. However, for replacement projects we must find the cash flow *differentials* between the new and old projects, and these differentials are the *incremental cash flows* that we must analyze.

We evaluate a replacement decision in Figure 13-9, which is set up much like Figures 13-1 and 13-2 but with data on both a new, highly efficient machine (which

Figure 13-9   Replacement Analysis

	A	B	C	D	E	F	G	H	I
15						Applies to:			
16	Part I. Inputs:				Both Machines	Old Machine	New Machine		
17	Cost of new machine						$2,000		
18	After-tax salvage value old machine					$400			
19	Sales revenues (fixed)				$2,500				
20	Annual operating costs except depreciation					$1,200	$280		
21	Tax rate				40%				
22	WACC				10%				
23	Depreciation				1	2	3	4	Totals:
24	Depr. rates (new machine)				33.33%	44.45%	14.81%	7.41%	100%
25	Depreciation on new machine				$667	$889	$296	$148	$2,000
26	Depreciation on old machine				$400	$400	$400	$400	$1,600
27	Δ: Change in depreciation				$267	$489	–$104	–$252	$400
28	Part II. Net Cash Flows before Replacement: Old Machine								
29					0	1	2	3	4
30	Sales revenues					$2,500	$2,500	$2,500	$2,500
31	Operating costs except depreciation					1,200	1,200	1,200	1,200
32	Depreciation					400	400	400	400
33	Total operating costs					$1,600	$1,600	$1,600	$1,600
34	Operating income					$900	$900	$900	$900
35	Taxes 40%					360	360	360	360
36	After-tax operating income					$540	$540	$540	$540
37	Add back depreciation					400	400	400	400
38	Net cash flows before replacement				$0	$940	$940	$940	$940
39	Part III. Net Cash Flows after Replacement: New Machine								
40					0	1	2	3	4
41	New machine cost:				–$2,000				
42	After-tax salvage value, old machine				$400				
43	Sales revenues					$2,500	$2,500	$2,500	$2,500
44	Operating costs except depreciation					280	280	280	280
45	Depreciation					667	889	296	148
46	Total operating costs					$947	$1,169	$576	$428
47	Operating income					$1,553	$1,331	$1,924	$2,072
48	Taxes 40%					621	532	770	829
49	After-tax operating income					$932	$799	$1,154	$1,243
50	Add back depreciation					667	889	296	148
51	Net cash flows after replacement				–$1,600	$1,599	$1,688	$1,450	$1,391
52	Part IV. Incremental CF: Row 51 – Row 38				–$1,600	$659	$748	$510	$451
53	Part V. Evaluation			NPV = $308.38		IRR = 19.33%	MIRR = 14.96%		

will be depreciated on an accelerated basis) and data on the old machine (which is being depreciated on a straight-line basis). In Part I we show the key inputs in the analysis, including depreciation on the new and old machines. In Part II we find the cash flows the firm will have if it continues to use the old machine, and in Part III we find the cash flows if the firm replaces the old machine. Then, in Part IV, we subtract the old flows from the new to arrive at the *incremental cash flows*, and we evaluate those flows in Part V to find the NPV, IRR, and MIRR. Replacing the old machine appears to be a good decision.[18]

In some instances, replacements add capacity as well as lower operating costs. In this case, sales revenues in Part III would be increased, and if that leads to a need for more working capital, then this would be shown as a Time-0 expenditure along with a recovery at the end of the project's life. These changes would, of course, be reflected in the incremental cash flows on Row 52.

Self Test

How are incremental cash flows found in a replacement analysis?

If you were analyzing a replacement project and suddenly learned that the old equipment could be sold for $1,000 rather than $400, would this new information make the replacement look better or worse? Explain.

In Figure 13-9 we assumed that output would remain stable if the old machine were replaced. Suppose output would actually double. How would this change be dealt with in the framework of Figure 13-9?

13.10 Real Options

According to traditional capital budgeting theory, a project's NPV is the present value of its expected future cash flows, discounted at a rate that reflects the riskiness of those cash flows. Note, however, that this says nothing about actions that can be taken *after* the project has been accepted and placed in operation that might lead to an increase in the cash flows. In other words, traditional capital budgeting theory assumes that a project is like a roulette wheel. A gambler can choose whether or not to spin the wheel, but once the wheel has been spun, nothing can be done to influence the outcome. Once the game begins, the outcome depends purely on chance, and no skill is involved.

Contrast roulette with a game such as poker. Chance plays a role in poker, and it continues to play a role after the initial deal because players receive additional cards throughout the game. However, poker players are able to respond to their opponents' actions, so skilled players usually win.

Capital budgeting decisions have more in common with poker than roulette because (1) chance plays a continuing role throughout the life of the project, but (2) managers can respond to changing market conditions and to competitors' actions. Opportunities to respond to changing circumstances are called **managerial options** because they give managers a chance to influence the outcome of a project. They are also called **strategic options** because they are often associated with large,

---

18. The same sort of risk analysis discussed in previous sections can be applied to replacement decisions. One of our MBA graduates was hired as a financial analyst with a company that manufactured products for sale to other businesses. He took our *Excel* replacement model, obtained input data from several of his firm's customers, and analyzed how his firm's products would help the customers. In several cases, his analysis helped nail down a sale. He then instructed the firm's sales reps on how to use the model to stimulate sales. This effort was highly successful, so our student got a nice bonus and was promoted in the company.

strategic projects rather than routine maintenance projects. Finally, they are called **real options** to differentiate them from financial options because they involve real, rather than financial, assets. The following sections describe projects with several types of **embedded options**.

13.10a Investment Timing Options

Conventional NPV analysis implicitly assumes that projects either will be accepted or rejected, which implies they will be undertaken now or never. In practice, however, companies sometimes have a third choice—delay the decision until later, when more information is available. Such **investment timing options** can dramatically affect a project's estimated profitability and risk, as we saw in our example of GPC's solar water heater project.

Keep in mind, though, that the *option to delay* is valuable only if it more than offsets any harm that might result from delaying. For example, while one company delays, some other company might establish a loyal customer base that makes it difficult for the first company to enter the market later. The option to delay is usually most valuable to firms with proprietary technology, patents, licenses, or other barriers to entry, because these factors lessen the threat of competition. The option to delay is valuable when market demand is uncertain, but it is also valuable during periods of volatile interest rates, since the ability to wait can allow firms to delay raising capital for a project until interest rates are lower.

13.10b Growth Options

A **growth option** allows a company to increase its capacity if market conditions are better than expected. There are several types of growth options. One lets a company *increase the capacity of an existing product line*. A "peaking unit" power plant illustrates this type of growth option. Such units have high variable costs and are used to produce additional power only if demand, and thus prices, are high.

The second type of growth option allows a company to *expand into new geographic markets*. Many companies are investing in China, Eastern Europe, and Russia even though standard NPV analysis produces negative NPVs. However, if these developing markets really take off, the option to open more facilities could be quite valuable.

The third type of growth option is the opportunity to *add new products,* including complementary products and successive "generations" of the original product. Auto companies are losing money on their first electric autos, but the manufacturing skills and consumer recognition those cars will provide should help turn subsequent generations of electric autos into money makers.

13.10c Abandonment Options

Consider the value of an **abandonment option**. Standard DCF analysis assumes that a project's assets will be used over a specified economic life. But even though some projects must be operated over their full economic life—in spite of deteriorating market conditions and hence lower than expected cash flows—other projects can be abandoned. Smart managers negotiate the right to abandon if a project turns out to be unsuccessful as a condition for undertaking the project.

Note, too, that some projects can be structured so that they provide the option to *reduce capacity* or *temporarily suspend operations*. Such options are common in the natural resources industry, including mining, oil, and timber, and they should be reflected in the analysis when NPVs are being estimated.

13.10d Flexibility Options

Many projects offer **flexibility options** that permit the firm to alter operations depending on how conditions change during the life of the project. Typically, either inputs or outputs (or both) can be changed. BMW's Spartanburg, South Carolina, auto assembly plant provides a good example of output flexibility. BMW needed the plant to produce sports coupes. If it built the plant configured to produce only these vehicles, the construction cost would be minimized. However, the company thought that later on it might want to switch production to some other vehicle type, and that would be difficult if the plant were designed just for coupes. Therefore, BMW decided to spend additional funds to construct a more flexible plant: one that could produce different types of vehicles should demand patterns shift. Sure enough, things did change. Demand for coupes dropped a bit and demand for sport-utility vehicles soared. But BMW was ready, and the Spartanburg plant began spewing out hot-selling SUVs. The plant's cash flows were much higher than they would have been without the flexibility option that BMW "bought" by paying more to build a more flexible plant.

Electric power plants provide an example of input flexibility. Utilities can build plants that generate electricity by burning coal, oil, or natural gas. The prices of those fuels change over time in response to events in the Middle East, changing environmental policies, and weather conditions. Some years ago, virtually all power plants were designed to burn just one type of fuel, because this resulted in the lowest construction costs. However, as fuel cost volatility increased, power companies began to build higher-cost but more flexible plants, especially ones that could switch from oil to gas and back again depending on relative fuel prices.

13.10e Valuing Real Options

A full treatment of real option valuation is beyond the scope of this chapter, but there are some things we can say. First, if a project has an embedded real option, then management should at least recognize and articulate its existence. Second, we know that a financial option is more valuable if it has a long time until maturity or if the underlying asset is very risky. If either of these characteristics applies to a project's real option, then management should know that its value is probably relatively high. Third, management might be able to model the real option along the lines of a decision tree, as we illustrate in the following section.

> **Self Test**
>
> Explain the relevance of the following statement: "Capital budgeting decisions have more in common with poker than roulette."
>
> What are managerial options? Strategic options?
>
> Identify some different types of real options and differentiate among them.

13.11 Phased Decisions and Decision Trees

Up to this point we have focused primarily on techniques for estimating a project's risk. Although this is an integral part of capital budgeting, managers are just as interested in *reducing* risk as in *measuring* it. One way to reduce risk is to structure projects so that expenditures can be made in stages over time rather than all at once. This gives managers the opportunity to reevaluate decisions using new information and then to either invest additional funds or terminate the project. This type of analysis involves the use of *decision trees*.

13.11a The Basic Decision Tree

GPC's analysis of the solar water heater project thus far has assumed that the project cannot be abandoned once it goes into operation, even if the worst-case situation arises. However, GPC is considering the possibility of terminating (abandoning) the project at Year 2 if the demand is low. The net after-tax cash flow from salvage, legal fees, liquidation of working capital, and all other termination costs and revenues is $4,000. Using these assumptions, the GPC ran a new scenario analysis; the results are shown in Figure 13-10, which is a simple decision tree.

Here we assume that, if the worst case materializes, then this will be recognized after the low Year-1 cash flow and GPC will abandon the project. Rather than continue realizing low cash flows in Years 2, 3, and 4, the company will shut down the operation and liquidate the project for $4,000 at t = 2. Now the expected NPV rises from $3,505 to $3,848 and the CV declines from 2.81 to 2.47. So, securing the right to abandon the project if things don't work out raised the project's expected return and lowered its risk. This will give you an approximate value, but keep in mind that you may not have a good estimate of the appropriate discount rate because the real option changes the risk, and hence the required return, of the project. See Chapter 14 for more discussion of real options.[19]

After the management team thought about the decision-tree approach, other ideas for improving the project emerged. The marketing manager stated that for $100,000 she could undertake a study that would give the firm a better idea of demand for the product, and the design engineer stated that he could build a prototype solar water heater that could be used to gauge consumer reactions to the actual product, which would provide even more information about the final demand and production costs. This led the CEO to discuss with the local university the possibility of delaying a final decision on the project until another type of analysis could be done, a full-blown **staged decision-tree analysis**, which is shown in Figure 13-11.

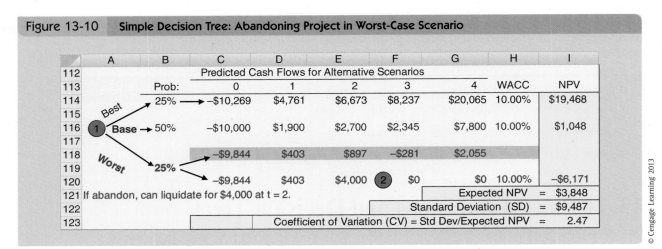

Figure 13-10   Simple Decision Tree: Abandoning Project in Worst-Case Scenario

	A	B	C	D	E	F	G	H	I
112			Predicted Cash Flows for Alternative Scenarios						
113		Prob:	0	1	2	3	4	WACC	NPV
114		25% →	–$10,269	$4,761	$6,673	$8,237	$20,065	10.00%	$19,468
115	Best								
116	1 Base →	50%	–$10,000	$1,900	$2,700	$2,345	$7,800	10.00%	$1,048
117									
118			–$9,844	$403	$897	–$281	$2,055		
119	Worst	25%							
120			–$9,844	$403	$4,000 ②	$0	$0	10.00%	–$6,171
121	If abandon, can liquidate for $4,000 at t = 2.					Expected NPV	=	$3,848
122							Standard Deviation (SD)	=	$9,487
123					Coefficient of Variation (CV) = Std Dev/Expected NPV			=	2.47

---

19. For more on real option valuation, see M. Amram and N. Kulatilaka, *Real Options: Managing Strategic Investment in an Uncertain World* (Boston: Harvard Business School Press, 1999); and H. Smit and L. Trigeorgis, *Strategic Investments: Real Options and Games* (Princeton, NJ: Princeton University Press, 2004).

Figure 13-11	Decision Tree with Multiple Decision Points

Decision trees such as the one in Figure 13-11 are often used to analyze multi-stage, or sequential, decisions. Each circle represents a decision point, also known as a **decision node**. The dollar value to the left of each decision node represents the net cash flow at that point, and the cash flows shown under t = 3, 4, 5, and 6 represent the cash inflows if the project is pushed on to completion. Each diagonal line leads to a **branch** of the decision tree, and each branch has an estimated probability. For example, if the firm decides to "go" with the project at Decision Point 1, then it will spend $100,000 on the marketing study.[20] Management estimates that there is a 0.8 probability that the study will produce *positive* results, leading to the decision to make an additional investment and thus move on to Decision Point 2, and a 0.2 probability that the marketing study will produce *negative* results, indicating that the project should be canceled after Stage 1. If the project is canceled, the cost to the company will be the $100,000 spent on the initial marketing study.

If the marketing study yields positive results, then the firm will spend $500,000 on the prototype water heater module at Decision Point 2. Management estimates (even before making the initial $100,000 investment) that there is a 45% probability of the pilot project yielding good results, a 40% probability of average results, and a 15% probability of bad results. If the prototype works well, then the firm will spend several millions more at Decision Point 3 to build a production plant, buy the necessary inventory, and commence operations. The operating cash flows over the project's 4-year life will be good, average, or bad, and these cash flows are shown under Years 3 through 6.

The column of joint probabilities in Figure 13-11 gives the probability of occurrence of each branch—and hence of each NPV. Each joint probability is obtained by multiplying together all the probabilities on that particular branch. For example, the probability that the company will, if Stage 1 is undertaken, move through Stages 2 and 3, and that a strong demand will produce the indicated cash flows, is (0.8)(0.45) = 0.36 = 36.0%. There is a 32% probability of average results, a 12% probability of building the plant and then getting bad results, and a 20% probability of getting bad initial results and stopping after the marketing study.

WEB

See **Ch13 Tool Kit.xls** on the textbook's Web site.

---

20. GPC might also have to pay the university an additional licensing fee. Such a fee could be added to the $100,000 marketing study cost.

The NPV of the top (most favorable) branch as shown in Column J is $15,534, calculated as follows:

$$\text{NPV} = -\$100 - \frac{\$500}{(1.10)^1} - \frac{\$10,269}{(1.10)^2} + \frac{\$4,761}{(1.10)^3} + \frac{\$6,673}{(1.10)^4} + \frac{\$8,237}{(1.10)^5} + \frac{\$20,065}{(1.10)^6}$$

$$= \$15,534$$

The NPVs for the other branches are calculated similarly.[21]

The last column in Figure 13-11 gives the product of the NPV for each branch times the joint probability of that branch's occurring, and the sum of these products is the project's expected NPV. Based on the expectations used to create Figure 13-11 and a cost of capital of 10%, the project's expected NPV is $5,606, or $5.606 million.[22] In addition, the CV declines from 2.81 to 1.33, and the maximum anticipated loss is a manageable −$555,000. At this point, the solar water heater project looked good, and GPC's management decided to accept it.

Note also that Figure 13-11 illustrates two types of real options. The first real option in the example is a timing option: GPC can delay a decision to spend a large amount of money until it obtains additional information about the likely success of the project. The second real option is an abandonment option, where GPC has the option to abandon the project if continuing with the operation would result in negative cash flows. The analysis could also be extended to illustrate a real growth option. For example, if the project is successful, the company may be able to extend the license, expand production of this project, or develop another profitable solar project. Thus, an additional set of branches might be extended out from Cell I134, where the company would invest in one or more other projects that offer potentially high NPVs. If one or more promising growth options can be identified, then the project's expected NPV might be higher yet.

As this example shows, decision-tree analysis requires managers to explicitly articulate the types of risk a project faces and to develop responses to potential scenarios. Note also that our example could be extended to cover many other types of decisions and could even be incorporated into a simulation analysis. All in all, decision-tree analysis is a valuable tool for analyzing project risks.[23]

Self Test	What is a decision tree? A branch? A node?
	If a firm can structure a project such that expenditures can be made in stages rather than all at the beginning, how would this affect the project's risk and expected NPV? Explain.

21. The calculations in *Excel* use nonrounded annual cash flows, so there may be small differences when calculating by hand with rounded annual cash flows.

22. As we mentioned concerning the abandonment option, the presence of the real options in Figure 13-11 might cause the discount rate to change.

23. In this example we glossed over an important issue: the appropriate cost of capital for the project. Adding decision nodes to a project clearly changes its risk, so we would expect the cost of capital for a project with few decision nodes to have a different risk than one with many nodes. If this is so then the projects should have different costs of capital. In fact, we might expect the cost of capital to change over time as the project moves to different stages, since the stages themselves differ in risk.

Summary

In this chapter, we developed a framework for analyzing a project's cash flows and its risk. The key concepts covered are listed below.

- The most important (and most difficult) step in analyzing a capital budgeting project is **estimating the incremental after-tax cash flows** the project will produce.
- A project's **net cash flow** is different from its accounting income. Project net cash flow reflects (1) cash outlays for fixed assets, (2) sales revenues, (3) operating costs, (4) the tax shield provided by depreciation, and (5) cash flows due to changes in net working capital. A project's net cash flow does *not* include interest payments, since they are accounted for by the discounting process. If we deducted interest and then discounted cash flows at the WACC, this would double-count interest charges.
- In determining incremental cash flows, **opportunity costs** (the cash flows forgone by using an asset) must be included, but **sunk costs** (cash outlays that have been made and that cannot be recouped) are not included. Any **externalities** (effects of a project on other parts of the firm) should also be reflected in the analysis. Externalities can be *positive* or *negative* and may be *environmental*.
- **Cannibalization** is an important type of externality that occurs when a new project leads to a reduction in sales of an existing product.
- **Tax laws** affect cash flow analysis in two ways: (1) taxes reduce operating cash flows, and (2) tax laws determine the depreciation expense that can be taken in each year.
- The incremental cash flows from a typical project can be classified into three categories: (1) **initial investment outlay**, (2) **operating cash flows over the project's life**, and (3) **terminal year cash flows**.
- **Price level changes (inflation** or **deflation)** must be considered in project analysis. The best procedure is to build expected price changes into the cash flow estimates. Recognize that output prices and costs for a product can decline over time even though the economy is experiencing inflation.
- The chapter illustrates both **expansion projects**, in which the investment generates new sales, and **replacement projects**, where the primary purpose of the investment is to operate more efficiently and thus reduce costs.
- We discuss three types of risk: **Stand-alone risk, corporate** (or **within-firm) risk**, and **market** (or **beta) risk**. Stand-alone risk does not consider diversification at all; corporate risk considers risk among the firm's own assets; and market risk considers risk at the stockholder level, where stockholders' own diversification is considered.
- **Risk** is important because it affects the discount rate used in capital budgeting; in other words, a project's WACC depends on its risk.
- Assuming the CAPM holds true, **market risk** is the most important risk because (according to the CAPM) it is the risk that affects stock prices. However, usually *it is difficult to measure a project's market risk*.
- **Corporate risk** is important because it influences the firm's ability to use low-cost debt, to maintain smooth operations over time, and to avoid crises that

might consume management's energy and disrupt its employees, customers, suppliers, and community. Also, a project's corporate risk is generally easier to measure than its market risk; and, because corporate and market risks are generally thought to be correlated, corporate risk can often serve as a proxy for market risk.

- **Stand-alone risk** is easier to measure than either market or corporate risk. Also, most of a firm's projects' cash flows are correlated with one another, and the firm's total cash flows are correlated with those of most other firms. These correlations mean that a project's stand-alone risk can generally be used as a proxy for hard-to-measure market and corporate risk. As a result, most risk analysis in capital budgeting focuses on stand-alone risk.

- **Sensitivity analysis** is a technique that shows how much a project's NPV will change in response to a given change in an input variable, such as sales, when all other factors are held constant.

- **Scenario analysis** is a risk analysis technique in which the best- and worst-case NPVs are compared with the project's base-case NPV.

- **Monte Carlo simulation** is a risk analysis technique that uses a computer to simulate future events and thereby estimate a project's profitability and riskiness.

- The **risk-adjusted discount rate**, or **project cost of capital**, is the rate used to evaluate a particular project. It is based on the corporate WACC, a value that is increased for projects that are riskier than the firm's average project and decreased for less risky projects.

- A **decision tree** shows how different decisions during a project's life can affect its value.

- A **staged decision-tree analysis** divides the analysis into different phases. At each phase a decision is made either to proceed or to stop the project. These decisions are represented on the decision trees by circles and are called **decision nodes**.

- Opportunities to respond to changing circumstances are called **real**, or **managerial, options** because they give managers the option to influence the returns on a project. They are also called **strategic options** if they are associated with large, strategic projects rather than routine maintenance projects. Finally, they are also called "real" options because they involve "real" (or "physical") rather than "financial" assets. Many projects include a variety of these **embedded options** that can dramatically affect the true NPV.

- An **investment timing option** involves the possibility of delaying major expenditures until more information on likely outcomes is known. The opportunity to delay can dramatically change a project's estimated value.

- A **growth option** occurs if an investment creates the opportunity to make other potentially profitable investments that would not otherwise be possible. These include (1) options to expand the original project's output, (2) options to enter a new geographical market, and (3) options to introduce complementary products or successive generations of products.

- An **abandonment option** is the ability to discontinue a project if the operating cash flow turns out to be lower than expected. It reduces the risk of a project and increases its value. Instead of total abandonment, some options allow a company to reduce capacity or temporarily suspend operations.

- A **flexibility option** is the option to modify operations depending on how conditions develop during a project's life, especially the type of output produced or the inputs used.
- The **option value** can be determined by comparing the project's expected NPV with and without the option. If an initial cost is required to obtain a real option, then that cost can be compared to the calculated value of the option as a part of the overall analysis.

Questions

13-1 Define each of the following terms:
 a. Project cash flow; accounting income
 b. Incremental cash flow; sunk cost; opportunity cost; externality; cannibalization; expansion project; replacement project
 c. Net operating working capital changes; salvage value
 d. Stand-alone risk; corporate (within-firm) risk; market (beta) risk
 e. Sensitivity analysis; scenario analysis; Monte Carlo simulation analysis
 f. Risk-adjusted discount rate; project cost of capital
 g. Decision tree; staged decision-tree analysis; decision node; branch
 h. Real options; managerial options; strategic options; embedded options
 i. Investment timing option; growth option; abandonment option; flexibility option

13-2 Operating cash flows, rather than accounting profits, are used in project analysis. What is the basis for this emphasis on cash flows as opposed to net income?

13-3 Why is it true, in general, that a failure to adjust expected cash flows for expected inflation biases the calculated NPV downward?

13-4 Explain why sunk costs should not be included in a capital budgeting analysis but opportunity costs and externalities should be included.

13-5 Explain how net operating working capital is recovered at the end of a project's life and why it is included in a capital budgeting analysis.

13-6 How do simulation analysis and scenario analysis differ in the way they treat very bad and very good outcomes? What does this imply about using each technique to evaluate project riskiness?

13-7 Why are interest charges not deducted when a project's cash flows are calculated for use in a capital budgeting analysis?

13-8 Most firms generate cash inflows every day, not just once at the end of the year. In capital budgeting, should we recognize this fact by estimating daily project cash flows and then using them in the analysis? If we do not, will this bias our results? If it does, would the NPV be biased up or down? Explain.

13-9 What are some differences in the analysis for a replacement project versus that for a new expansion project?

13-10 Distinguish among beta (or market) risk, within-firm (or corporate) risk, and stand-alone risk for a project being considered for inclusion in a firm's capital budget.

13-11 In theory, market risk should be the only "relevant" risk. However, companies focus as much on stand-alone risk as on market risk. What are the reasons for the focus on stand-alone risk?

Problems   Answers Appear in Appendix B

Easy Problems 1–4

13-1 Investment Outlay Talbot Industries is considering launching a new product. The new manufacturing equipment will cost $17 million, and production and sales will require an initial $5 million investment in net operating working capital. The company's tax rate is 40%.

    a. What is the initial investment outlay?

    b. The company spent and expensed $150,000 on research related to the new product last year. Would this change your answer? Explain.

    c. Rather than build a new manufacturing facility, the company plans to install the equipment in a building it owns but is not now using. The building could be sold for $1.5 million after taxes and real estate commissions. How would this affect your answer?

13-2 Operating Cash Flow The financial staff of Cairn Communications has identified the following information for the first year of the rollout of its new proposed service:

Projected sales	$18 million
Operating costs (not including depreciation)	$9 million
Depreciation	$4 million
Interest expense	$3 million

The company faces a 40% tax rate. What is the project's operating cash flow for the first year (t = 1)?

13-3 Net Salvage Value Allen Air Lines must liquidate some equipment that is being replaced. The equipment originally cost $12 million, of which 75% has been depreciated. The used equipment can be sold today for $4 million, and its tax rate is 40%. What is the equipment's after-tax net salvage value?

13-4 Replacement Analysis Although the Chen Company's milling machine is old, it is still in relatively good working order and would last for another 10 years. It is inefficient compared to modern standards, though, and so the company is considering replacing it. The new milling machine, at a cost of $110,000 delivered and installed, would also last for 10 years and would produce after-tax cash flows (labor savings and depreciation tax savings) of $19,000 per year. It would have zero salvage value at the end of its life. The firm's WACC is 10%, and its marginal tax rate is 35%. Should Chen buy the new machine?

Intermediate Problems 5–10

13-5 Depreciation Methods Wendy's boss wants to use straight-line depreciation for the new expansion project because he said it will give higher net income in earlier years and give him a larger bonus. The project will last 4 years and requires $1,700,000 of equipment. The company could use either straight line or the 3-year MACRS accelerated method. Under straight-line depreciation, the cost of the equipment would be depreciated evenly over its 4-year life (ignore the half-year convention for the straight-line method). The applicable MACRS depreciation rates are 33.33%, 44.45%, 14.81%, and 7.41%, as discussed in Appendix 13A. The company's WACC is 10%, and its tax rate is 40%.

a. What would the depreciation expense be each year under each method?

b. Which depreciation method would produce the higher NPV, and how much higher would it be?

c. Why might Wendy's boss prefer straight-line depreciation?

13-6 **New-Project Analysis** The Campbell Company is considering adding a robotic paint sprayer to its production line. The sprayer's base price is $1,080,000, and it would cost another $22,500 to install it. The machine falls into the MACRS 3-year class, and it would be sold after 3 years for $605,000. The machine would require an increase in net working capital (inventory) of $15,500. The sprayer would not change revenues, but it is expected to save the firm $380,000 per year in before-tax operating costs, mainly labor. Campbell's marginal tax rate is 35%.

a. What is the Year-0 net cash flow?

b. What are the net operating cash flows in Years 1, 2, and 3?

c. What is the additional Year-3 cash flow (i.e., the after-tax salvage and the return of working capital)?

d. If the project's cost of capital is 12%, should the machine be purchased?

13-7 **New-Project Analysis** You have been asked by the president of your company to evaluate the proposed acquisition of a new chromatograph for the firm's R&D department. The equipment's basic price is $70,000, and it would cost another $15,000 to modify it for special use by your firm. The chromatograph, which falls into the MACRS 3-year class, would be sold after 3 years for $30,000. Use of the equipment would require an increase in net working capital (spare parts inventory) of $4,000. The spectrometer would have no effect on revenues, but it is expected to save the firm $25,000 per year in before-tax operating costs, mainly labor. The firm's marginal federal-plus-state tax rate is 40%.

a. What is the Year-0 net cash flow?

b. What are the net operating cash flows in Years 1, 2, and 3?

c. What is the additional (nonoperating) cash flow in Year 3?

d. If the project's cost of capital is 10%, should the chromatograph be purchased?

13-8 **Inflation Adjustments** The Rodriguez Company is considering an average-risk investment in a mineral water spring project that has a cost of $150,000. The project will produce 1,000 cases of mineral water per year indefinitely. The current sales price is $138 per case, and the current cost per case is $105. The firm is taxed at a rate of 34%. Both prices and costs are expected to rise at a rate of 6% per year. The firm uses only equity, and it has a cost of capital of 15%. Assume that cash flows consist only of after-tax profits, since the spring has an indefinite life and will not be depreciated.

a. Should the firm accept the project? (*Hint:* The project is a growing perpetuity, so you must use the constant growth formula to find its NPV.)

b. Suppose that total costs consisted of a fixed cost of $10,000 per year plus variable costs of $95 per unit, and suppose that only the variable costs were expected to increase with inflation. Would this make the project better or worse? Continue to assume that the sales price will rise with inflation.

13-9 **Replacement Analysis** The Gilbert Instrument Corporation is considering replacing the wood steamer it currently uses to shape guitar sides. The steamer, purchased just 2 years ago, is being depreciated on a straight-line basis and has 6 years of remaining life. Its current book value is $3,900, and it can be sold on an Internet auction site for $4,500 at this time. Thus, the annual depreciation expense is $4,100/6 = $650 per year. If the old steamer is not replaced, it can be sold for $800 at the end of its useful life.

Gilbert is considering purchasing the *Side Steamer 3000*, a higher-end steamer, which costs $12,000 and has an estimated useful life of 6 years with an estimated salvage value of $1,500. This steamer falls into the MACRS 5-year class, so the applicable depreciation rates are 20.00%, 32.00%, 19.20%, 11.52%, 11.52%, and 5.76%. The new steamer is faster and would allow for an output expansion, so sales would rise by $2,000 per year; even so, the new machine's much greater efficiency would reduce operating expenses by $1,900 per year. To support the greater sales, the new machine would require that inventories increase by $2,900, but accounts payable would simultaneously increase by $700. Gilbert's marginal federal-plus-state tax rate is 40%, and its WACC is 15%. Should it replace the old steamer?

13-10 **Replacement Analysis** St. Johns River Shipyards's welding machine is 15 years old, fully depreciated, obsolete, and has no salvage value. However, even though it is obsolete, it is perfectly functional as originally designed and can be used for quite a while longer. A new welder will cost $182,500 and have an estimated life of 8 years with no salvage value. The new welder will be much more efficient, however, and this enhanced efficiency will increase earnings before depreciation from $27,000 to $74,000 per year. The new machine will be depreciated over its 5-year MACRS recovery period, so the applicable depreciation rates are 20.00%, 32.00%, 19.20%, 11.52%, 11.52%, and 5.76%. The applicable corporate tax rate is 40%, and the firm's WACC is 12%. Should the old welder be replaced by the new one?

Challenging Problems 11–17

13-11 **Scenario Analysis** Shao Industries is considering a proposed project for its capital budget. The company estimates the project's NPV is $12 million. This estimate assumes that the economy and market conditions will be average over the next few years. The company's CFO, however, forecasts there is only a 50% chance that the economy will be average. Recognizing this uncertainty, she has also performed the following scenario analysis:

Economic Scenario	Probability of Outcome	NPV
Recession	0.05	−$70 million
Below average	0.20	−25 million
Average	0.50	12 million
Above average	0.20	20 million
Boom	0.05	30 million

What is the project's expected NPV, its standard deviation, and its coefficient of variation?

13-12 **New-Project Analysis** Madison Manufacturing is considering a new machine that costs $350,000 and would reduce pre-tax manufacturing costs by $110,000 annually. Madison would use the 3-year MACRS method to depreciate the machine, and management thinks the machine would have a value of $33,000 at the end of its 5-year operating life. The applicable depreciation rates are 33.33%, 44.45%, 14.81%, and 7.42%, as discussed in Appendix 13A. Working capital would increase by $35,000 initially, but it would be recovered at the end of the project's 5-year life. Madison's marginal tax rate is 40%, and a 10% WACC is appropriate for the project.

   a. Calculate the project's NPV, IRR, MIRR, and payback.
   b. Assume management is unsure about the $110,000 cost savings—this figure could deviate by as much as plus or minus 20%. What would the NPV be under each of these extremes?
   c. Suppose the CFO wants you to do a scenario analysis with different values for the cost savings, the machine's salvage value, and the working capital (WC) requirement. She asks you to use the following probabilities and values in the scenario analysis:

Scenario	Probability	Cost Savings	Salvage Value	WC
Worst case	0.35	$88,000	$28,000	$40,000
Base case	0.35	110,000	33,000	35,000
Best case	0.30	132,000	38,000	30,000

Calculate the project's expected NPV, its standard deviation, and its coefficient of variation. Would you recommend that the project be accepted?

13-13 **Replacement Analysis** The Everly Equipment Company's flange-lipping machine was purchased 5 years ago for $55,000. It had an expected life of 10 years when it was bought and is being depreciated by the straight-line method by $5,500 per year. As the older flange-lippers are robust and useful machines, it can be sold for $20,000 at the end of its useful life.

A new high-efficiency digital-controlled flange-lipper can be purchased for $120,000, including installation costs. During its 5-year life, it will reduce cash operating expenses by $30,000 per year, although it will not affect sales. At the end of its useful life, the high-efficiency machine is estimated to be worthless. MACRS depreciation will be used, and the machine will be depreciated over its 3-year class life rather than its 5-year economic life, so the applicable depreciation rates are 33.33%, 44.45%, 14.81%, and 7.41%.

The old machine can be sold today for $35,000. The firm's tax rate is 35%, and the appropriate WACC is 16%.

   a. If the new flange-lipper is purchased, what is the amount of the initial cash flow at Year 0?
   b. What are the incremental net cash flows that will occur at the end of Years 1 through 5?
   c. What is the NPV of this project? Should Everly replace the flange-lipper?

13-14 **Replacement Analysis** DeYoung Entertainment Enterprises is considering replacing the latex molding machine it uses to fabricate rubber chickens with a newer, more efficient model. The old machine has a book value of $450,000 and a remaining useful life of 5 years. The current machine would be worn out and worthless in 5 years, but DeYoung can sell it now to a Halloween mask manufacturer for $135,000. The old machine is being depreciated by $90,000 per year, using the straight-line method.

The new machine has a purchase price of $775,000, an estimated useful life and MACRS class life of 5 years, and an estimated salvage value of $105,000. The applicable depreciation rates are 20.00%, 32.00%, 19.20%, 11.52%, 11.52%, and 5.76%. Being highly efficient, it is expected to economize on electric power usage, labor, and repair costs, and, most importantly, to reduce the number of defective chickens. In total, an annual savings of $185,000 will be realized if the new machine is installed. The company's marginal tax rate is 35%, and it has a 12% WACC.

a. What is the initial net cash flow if the new machine is purchased and the old one is replaced?

b. Calculate the annual depreciation allowances for both machines, and compute the change in the annual depreciation expense if the replacement is made.

c. What are the incremental net cash flows in Years 1 through 5?

d. Should the firm purchase the new machine? Support your answer.

e. In general, how would each of the following factors affect the investment decision, and how should each be treated?

1. The expected life of the existing machine decreases.

2. The WACC is not constant but is increasing as DeYoung adds more projects into its capital budget for the year.

13-15 **Risky Cash Flows** The Bartram-Pulley Company (BPC) must decide between two mutually exclusive investment projects. Each project costs $6,750 and has an expected life of 3 years. Annual net cash flows from each project begin 1 year after the initial investment is made and have the following probability distributions:

Project A		Project B	
Probability	Net Cash Flows	Probability	Net Cash Flows
0.2	$6,000	0.2	$ 0
0.6	6,750	0.6	6,750
0.2	7,500	0.2	18,000

BPC has decided to evaluate the riskier project at a 12% rate and the less risky project at a 10% rate.

a. What is the expected value of the annual net cash flows from each project? What is the coefficient of variation (CV)? (*Hint:* $\sigma_B = \$5,798$ and $CV_B = 0.76$.)

b. What is the risk-adjusted NPV of each project?

c. If it were known that Project B is negatively correlated with other cash flows of the firm whereas Project A is positively correlated, how would this affect the decision? If Project B's cash flows were negatively correlated with gross domestic product (GDP), would that influence your assessment of its risk?

13-16 **Simulation** Singleton Supplies Corporation (SSC) manufactures medical products for hospitals, clinics, and nursing homes. SSC may introduce a new type of X-ray scanner designed to identify certain types of cancers in their early stages. There are a number of uncertainties about the proposed project, but the following data are believed to be reasonably accurate.

Probability	Developmental Costs	Random Numbers
0.3	$2,000,000	00–29
0.4	4,000,000	30–69
0.3	6,000,000	70–99

Probability	Project Life	Random Numbers
0.2	3 years	00–19
0.6	8 years	20–79
0.2	13 years	80–99

Probability	Sales in Units	Random Numbers
0.2	100	00–19
0.6	200	20–79
0.2	300	80–99

Probability	Sales Price	Random Numbers
0.1	$13,000	00–09
0.8	13,500	10–89
0.1	14,000	90–99

Probability	Cost per Unit (Excluding Developmental Costs)	Random Numbers
0.3	$5,000	00–29
0.4	6,000	30–69
0.3	7,000	70–99

SSC uses a cost of capital of 15% to analyze average-risk projects, 12% for low-risk projects, and 18% for high-risk projects. These risk adjustments primarily reflect the uncertainty about each project's NPV and IRR as measured by their coefficients of variation. The firm is in the 40% federal-plus-state income tax bracket.

a. What is the expected IRR for the X-ray scanner project? Base your answer on the expected values of the variables. Also, assume the after-tax "profits" figure that you develop is equal to annual cash flows. All facilities are leased, so depreciation may be disregarded. Can you determine the value of σ_{IRR} short of actual simulation or a fairly complex statistical analysis?

b. Assume that SSC uses a 15% cost of capital for this project. What is the project's NPV? Could you estimate σ_{NPV} without either simulation or a complex statistical analysis?

c. Show the process by which a computer would perform a simulation analysis for this project. Use the random numbers 44, 17, 16, 58, 1; 79, 83, 86; and 19, 62, 6 to illustrate the process with the first computer run. Actually calculate the first-run NPV and IRR. Assume the cash flows for each year are independent of cash flows for other years. Also, assume the computer operates as follows: (1) A developmental cost and a project life are estimated for the first run using the first two random numbers.

(2) Next, sales volume, sales price, and cost per unit are estimated using the next three random numbers and used to derive a cash flow for the first year. (3) Then, the next three random numbers are used to estimate sales volume, sales price, and cost per unit for the second year, hence the cash flow for the second year. (4) Cash flows for other years are developed similarly, on out to the first run's estimated life. (5) With the developmental cost and the cash flow stream established, NPV and IRR for the first run are derived and stored in the computer's memory. (6) The process is repeated to generate perhaps 500 other NPVs and IRRs. (7) Frequency distributions for NPV and IRR are plotted by the computer, and the distributions' means and standard deviations are calculated.

13-17 **Decision Tree** The Yoran Yacht Company (YYC), a prominent sailboat builder in Newport, may design a new 30-foot sailboat based on the "winged" keels first introduced on the 12-meter yachts that raced for the America's Cup.

First, YYC would have to invest $10,000 at t = 0 for the design and model tank testing of the new boat. YYC's managers believe there is a 60% probability that this phase will be successful and the project will continue. If Stage 1 is not successful, the project will be abandoned with zero salvage value.

The next stage, if undertaken, would consist of making the molds and producing two prototype boats. This would cost $500,000 at t = 1. If the boats test well, YYC would go into production. If they do not, the molds and prototypes could be sold for $100,000. The managers estimate the probability is 80% that the boats will pass testing and that Stage 3 will be undertaken.

Stage 3 consists of converting an unused production line to produce the new design. This would cost $1 million at t = 2. If the economy is strong at this point, the net value of sales would be $3 million; if the economy is weak, the net value would be $1.5 million. Both net values occur at t = 3, and each state of the economy has a probability of 0.5. YYC's corporate cost of capital is 12%.

a. Assume this project has average risk. Construct a decision tree and determine the project's expected NPV.

b. Find the project's standard deviation of NPV and coefficient of variation of NPV. If YYC's average project had a CV of between 1.0 and 2.0, would this project be of high, low, or average stand-alone risk?

Spreadsheet Problem

13-18 **Build a Model: Issues in Capital Budgeting** Start with the partial model in the file *Ch13 P18 Build a Model.xls* on the textbook's Web site. Webmasters .com has developed a powerful new server that would be used for corporations' Internet activities. It would cost $10 million at Year 0 to buy the equipment necessary to manufacture the server. The project would require net working capital at the beginning of a year in an amount equal to 10% of the year's projected sales: $NOWC_0 = 10\%(Sales_1)$. The servers would sell for $24,000 per unit, and Webmasters believes that variable costs would amount to $17,500 per unit. After Year 1, the sales price and variable costs will increase at the inflation rate of 3%. The company's nonvariable costs would be $1 million at Year 1 and would increase with inflation.

The server project would have a life of 4 years. If the project is undertaken, it must be continued for the entire 4 years. Also, the project's returns are expected to be highly correlated with returns on the firm's other assets. The firm believes it could sell 1,000 units per year.

The equipment would be depreciated over a 5-year period, using MACRS rates. The estimated market value of the equipment at the end of the project's 4-year life is $500,000. Webmasters' federal-plus-state tax rate is 40%. Its cost of capital is 10% for average-risk projects, defined as projects with an NPV coefficient of variation between 0.8 and 1.2. Low-risk projects are evaluated with a WACC of 8% and high-risk projects at 13%.

a. Develop a spreadsheet model, and use it to find the project's NPV, IRR, and payback.

b. Now conduct a sensitivity analysis to determine the sensitivity of NPV to changes in the sales price, variable costs per unit, and number of units sold. Set these variables' values at 10% and 20% above and below their base-case values. Include a graph in your analysis.

c. Now conduct a scenario analysis. Assume that there is a 25% probability that best-case conditions, with each of the variables discussed in part b being 20% better than its base-case value, will occur. There is a 25% probability of worst-case conditions, with the variables 20% worse than base, and a 50% probability of base-case conditions.

d. If the project appears to be more or less risky than an average project, find its risk-adjusted NPV, IRR, and payback.

e. On the basis of information in the problem, would you recommend that the project be accepted?

MINI CASE

Shrieves Casting Company is considering adding a new line to its product mix, and the capital budgeting analysis is being conducted by Sidney Johnson, a recently graduated MBA. The production line would be set up in unused space in Shrieves's main plant. The machinery's invoice price would be approximately $200,000, another $10,000 in shipping charges would be required, and it would cost an additional $30,000 to install the equipment. The machinery has an economic life of 4 years, and Shrieves has obtained a special tax ruling that places the equipment in the MACRS 3-year class. The machinery is expected to have a salvage value of $25,000 after 4 years of use.

The new line would generate incremental sales of 1,250 units per year for 4 years at an incremental cost of $100 per unit in the first year, excluding depreciation. Each unit can be sold for $200 in the first year. The sales price and cost are both expected to increase by 3% per year due to inflation. Further, to handle the new line, the firm's net working capital would have to increase by an amount equal to 12% of sales revenues. The firm's tax rate is 40%, and its overall weighted average cost of capital is 10%.

a. Define "incremental cash flow."

   (1) Should you subtract interest expense or dividends when calculating project cash flow?

   (2) Suppose the firm had spent $100,000 last year to rehabilitate the production line site. Should this be included in the analysis? Explain.

   (3) Now assume the plant space could be leased out to another firm at $25,000 per year. Should this be included in the analysis? If so, how?

   (4) Finally, assume that the new product line is expected to decrease sales of the firm's other

lines by $50,000 per year. Should this be considered in the analysis? If so, how?

b. Disregard the assumptions in part a. What is Shrieves's depreciable basis? What are the annual depreciation expenses?

c. Calculate the annual sales revenues and costs (other than depreciation). Why is it important to include inflation when estimating cash flows?

d. Construct annual incremental operating cash flow statements.

e. Estimate the required net working capital for each year and the cash flow due to investments in net working capital.

f. Calculate the after-tax salvage cash flow.

g. Calculate the net cash flows for each year. Based on these cash flows, what are the project's NPV, IRR, MIRR, PI, payback, and discounted payback? Do these indicators suggest that the project should be undertaken?

h. What does the term "risk" mean in the context of capital budgeting; to what extent can risk be quantified; and, when risk is quantified, is the quantification based primarily on statistical analysis of historical data or on subjective, judgmental estimates?

i. (1) What are the three types of risk that are relevant in capital budgeting?

   (2) How is each of these risk types measured, and how do they relate to one another?

   (3) How is each type of risk used in the capital budgeting process?

j. (1) What is sensitivity analysis?

   (2) Perform a sensitivity analysis on the unit sales, salvage value, and cost of capital for the project. Assume each of these variables can vary from its base-case, or expected, value by ±10%, ±20%,

and ±30%. Include a sensitivity diagram, and discuss the results.

   (3) What is the primary weakness of sensitivity analysis? What is its primary usefulness?

k. Assume that Sidney Johnson is confident in her estimates of all the variables that affect the project's cash flows except unit sales and sales price. If product acceptance is poor, unit sales would be only 900 units a year and the unit price would only be $160; a strong consumer response would produce sales of 1,600 units and a unit price of $240. Johnson believes there is a 25% chance of poor acceptance, a 25% chance of excellent acceptance, and a 50% chance of average acceptance (the base case).

   (1) What is scenario analysis?

   (2) What is the worst-case NPV? The best-case NPV?

   (3) Use the worst-, base-, and best-case NPVs and probabilities of occurrence to find the project's expected NPV, as well as the NPV's standard deviation and coefficient of variation.

l. Are there problems with scenario analysis? Define simulation analysis, and discuss its principal advantages and disadvantages.

m. (1) Assume Shrieves's average project has a coefficient of variation in the range of 0.2 to 0.4. Would the new line be classified as high risk, average risk, or low risk? What type of risk is being measured here?

   (2) Shrieves typically adds or subtracts 3 percentage points to the overall cost of capital to adjust for risk. Should the new line be accepted?

   (3) Are there any subjective risk factors that should be considered before the final decision is made?

n. What is a real option? What are some types of real options?

Selected Additional Cases

The following cases from TextChoice, *Cengage Learning's online case library, cover many of the concepts discussed in this chapter and are available at* www.textchoice2.com/casenet.

Klein-Brigham Series:
Case 12, "Indian River Citrus Company (A)," Case 44, "Cranfield, Inc. (A)," and Case 14, "Robert Montoya, Inc.," focus on cash flow estimation; Case 13, "Indian River Citrus (B)," Case 45, "Cranfield, Inc. (B)," Case 58, "Tasty Foods (B)," Case 60, "Heavenly Foods," and Case 15, "Robert Montoya, Inc. (B)," illustrate project risk analysis; Cases 75, 76, and 77, "The Western Company (A and B)," are comprehensive cases.

Brigham-Buzzard Series:
Case 7, "Powerline Network Corporation (Risk and Real Options in Capital Budgeting)."

Appendix 13A

Tax Depreciation

Companies often calculate depreciation one way when figuring taxes and another way when reporting income to investors: Many use the **straight-line method** for stockholder reporting (or "book" purposes), but they use the fastest rate permitted by law for tax purposes. Under the straight-line method used for stockholder reporting, one normally takes the cost of the asset, subtracts its estimated salvage value, and divides the net amount by the asset's useful economic life. For example, consider an asset with a 5-year life that costs $100,000 and has a $12,500 salvage value; its annual straight-line depreciation charge is ($100,000 − $12,500)/5 = $17,500. Note, however, as we stated earlier, salvage value is a factor in financial reporting but it is *not* considered for tax depreciation purposes.

For tax purposes, Congress changes the permissible tax depreciation methods from time to time. Prior to 1954, the straight-line method was required for tax purposes, but in 1954 **accelerated methods** (double-declining balance and sum-of-years'-digits) were permitted. Then, in 1981, the old accelerated methods were replaced by a simpler procedure known as the Accelerated Cost Recovery System (ACRS). The ACRS system was changed again in 1986 as a part of the Tax Reform Act, and it is now known as the **Modified Accelerated Cost Recovery System (MACRS)**; a 1993 tax law made further changes in this area.

Note that U.S. tax laws are complicated, and in this text we can provide only an overview of MACRS that will give you a basic understanding of the impact of depreciation on capital budgeting decisions. Further, the tax laws change so often that the numbers we present may be outdated before the book is even published. Thus, when dealing with tax depreciation in real-world situations, current Internal Revenue Service (IRS) publications or individuals with expertise in tax matters should be consulted.

For tax purposes, the entire cost of an asset is expensed over its depreciable life. Historically, an asset's depreciable life was set equal to its estimated useful economic life; it was intended that an asset would be fully depreciated at approximately the same time that it reached the end of its useful economic life. However, MACRS totally abandoned that practice and set simple guidelines that created several classes of assets, each with a more-or-less arbitrarily prescribed life called a *recovery period* or *class life*. The MACRS class lives bear only a rough relationship to assets' expected useful economic lives.

A major effect of the MACRS system has been to shorten the depreciable lives of assets, thus giving businesses larger tax deductions early in the assets' lives and thereby increasing the present value of the cash flows. Table 13A-1 describes the types of property that fit into the different class life groups, and Table 13A-2 sets forth the MACRS recovery allowance percentages (depreciation rates) for selected classes of investment property.

TABLE 13A-1   Major Classes and Asset Lives for MACRS

Class	Type of Property
3-year	Certain special manufacturing tools
5-year	Automobiles, light-duty trucks, computers, and certain special manufacturing equipment
7-year	Most industrial equipment, office furniture, and fixtures
10-year	Certain longer-lived types of equipment
27.5-year	Residential rental real property such as apartment buildings
39-year	All nonresidential real property, including commercial and industrial buildings

© Cengage Learning 2013

TABLE 13A-2   Recovery Allowance Percentage for Personal Property

Ownership Year	Class of Investment			
	3-Year	5-Year	7-Year	10-Year
1	33.33%	20.00%	14.29%	10.00%
2	44.45	32.00	24.49	18.00
3	14.81	19.20	17.49	14.40
4	7.41	11.52	12.49	11.52
5		11.52	8.93	9.22
6		5.76	8.92	7.37
7			8.93	6.55
8			4.46	6.55
9				6.56
10				6.55
11				3.28
	100.00%	100.00%	100.00%	100.00%

© Cengage Learning 2013

Notes:

1. We developed these recovery allowance percentages based on the 200% declining balance method prescribed by MACRS, with a switch to straight-line depreciation at some point in the asset's life. For example, consider the 5-year recovery allowance percentages. The straight-line percentage would be 20% per year, so the 200% declining balance multiplier is 2.0(20%) = 40% = 0.4. However, because the half-year convention applies, the MACRS percentage for Year 1 is 20%. For Year 2, there is 80% of the depreciable basis remaining to be depreciated, so the recovery allowance percentage is 0.40(80%) = 32%. In Year 3, 20% + 32% = 52% of the depreciation has been taken, leaving 48%, so the percentage is 0.4(48%) = 19.2%. In Year 4, the percentage is 0.4(28.8%) = 11.52%. After 4 years, straight-line depreciation exceeds the declining balance depreciation, so a switch is made to straight-line (which is permitted under the law). However, the half-year convention must also be applied at the end of the class life, and the remaining 17.28% of depreciation must be taken (amortized) over 1.5 years. Thus, the percentage in Year 5 is 17.28%/1.5 = 11.52%, and in Year 6 it is 17.28% − 11.52% = 5.76%. See the worksheet **7. App. A** in the file **Ch13 Tool Kit.xls** on the textbook's Web site for the exact recovery percentages specified by the IRS for other recovery periods.

2. Residential rental property (apartments) is depreciated over a 27.5-year life, whereas commercial and industrial structures are depreciated over 39 years. In both cases, straight-line depreciation must be used. The depreciation allowance for the first year is based, pro rata, on the month the asset was placed in service, with the remainder of the first year's depreciation being taken in the 28th or 40th year. A half-month convention is assumed; that is, an asset placed in service in February would receive 10.5 months of depreciation in the first year.

Consider Table 13A-1, which gives the MACRS class lives and the types of assets that fall into each category. Property in the 27.5- and 39-year categories (real estate) must be depreciated by the straight-line method, but 3-, 5-, 7-, and 10-year property (personal property) can be depreciated either by the accelerated method set forth in Table 13A-2 or by the straight-line method.[24]

As we saw earlier in the chapter, higher depreciation expenses result in lower taxes in the early years and hence lead to a higher present value of cash flows. Therefore, since a firm has the choice of using straight-line rates or the accelerated rates shown in Table 13A-2, most elect to use the accelerated rates.

The yearly recovery allowance, or depreciation expense, is determined by multiplying each asset's *depreciable basis* by the applicable recovery percentage shown in Table 13A-2. You might be wondering why 4 years of deprecation rates are shown for property in the 3-year class. Under MACRS, the assumption is generally made that property is placed in service in the middle of the first year. Thus, for 3-year-class property, the recovery period begins in the middle of the year the asset is placed in service and ends 3 years later. The effect of the *half-year convention* is to extend the recovery period out one more year, so 3-year-class property is depreciated over 4 calendar years, 5-year property is depreciated over 6 calendar years, and so on. This convention is incorporated into Table 13A-2's recovery allowance percentages.[25]

WEB

See **Ch13 Tool Kit.xls** on the textbook's Web site for all calculations.

Self Test

What do the acronyms ACRS and MACRS stand for?

Briefly describe the tax depreciation system under MACRS.

---

24. The Tax Code currently (for 2011) permits companies to *expense,* which is equivalent to depreciating over 1 year, up to $125,000 of equipment; see IRS Publication 946 for details. This is a benefit primarily for small companies. Thus, if a small company bought one asset worth up to $125,000, it could write the asset off in the year it was acquired. This is called "Section 179 expensing." We shall disregard this provision throughout the book. Also, Congress enacted the Job Creation and Worker Assistance Act of 2002 following the terrorist attacks on the World Trade Center and Pentagon. This act, among other things, temporarily changed how depreciation is charged for property acquired after September 10, 2001, and before September 11, 2004, and put in service before January 1, 2005. We shall disregard this provision throughout the book as well.

25. The half-year convention also applies if the straight-line alternative is used, with half of one year's depreciation taken in the first year, a full year's depreciation taken in each of the remaining years of the asset's class life, and the remaining half-year's depreciation taken in the year following the end of the class life. You should recognize that virtually all companies have computerized depreciation systems. Each asset's depreciation pattern is programmed into the system at the time of its acquisition, and the computer aggregates the depreciation allowances for all assets when the accountants close the books and prepare financial statements and tax returns.

Chapter 14

Real Options

Traditional discounted cash flow (DCF) analysis—in which an asset's cash flows are estimated and then discounted to obtain the asset's NPV—has been the cornerstone for valuing all types of assets since the 1950s. Accordingly, most of our discussion of capital budgeting has focused on DCF valuation techniques. However, in recent years, academics and practitioners have demonstrated that DCF valuation techniques do not always tell the complete story about a project's value and that rote use of DCF can, at times, lead to incorrect capital budgeting decisions.[1]

DCF techniques were originally developed to value securities such as stocks and bonds. Securities are passive investments: Once they have been purchased, most investors have no influence over the cash flows the assets produce. However, real assets are not passive investments because managerial actions after an investment has been made can influence its results. Furthermore, investing in a new project often brings with it the potential for increasing the firm's future investment opportunities. Such opportunities are, in effect, options—the right (but not the obligation) to take some action in the future. As we demonstrate in the next section, options are valuable, so projects that expand the firm's set of opportunities have positive **option values**. Similarly, any project that reduces the set of future opportunities destroys option value. Since a project's impact on the firm's opportunities, or its option value, may not be captured by conventional NPV analysis, this option value should be considered separately, as we do in this chapter.

---

1. For an excellent general discussion of the problems inherent in discounted cash flow valuation techniques as applied to capital budgeting, see Avinash K. Dixit and Robert S. Pindyck, "The Options Approach to Capital Investment," *Harvard Business Review*, May/June 1995, pp. 105–115.

Beginning of Chapter Questions

As you read the chapter, consider how you would answer the following questions. You *should not* necessarily be able to answer the questions before you read the chapter. Rather, you should use them to get a sense of the issues covered in the chapter. After reading the chapter, you should be able to give at least partial answers to the questions, and you should be able to give better answers after the chapter has been discussed in class. Note, too, that it is often useful, when answering conceptual questions, to use hypothetical data to illustrate your answer. We illustrate the answers with an *Excel* model that is available on the textbook's Web site. Accessing the model and working through it is a useful exercise, and it provides insights that are useful when answering the questions.

1. What's the difference between a **financial option** and a **real option?** What are some specific types of real options? Do real options just occur, or can they be "created"?
2. Real options can be analyzed using a **scenario approach** with decision trees or using the **Black-Scholes Option Pricing Model.** What are the pros and cons of the two approaches? Is one procedure "better" than the other?

3. Option values are extinguished when they are exercised. How does this influence capital budgeting decisions? What considerations, or types of analysis, might lead management to "take the plunge" and proceed with a project rather than keep delaying it?
4. Suppose a company uses the NPV method, along with risk-adjusted WACCs, to calculate project NPVs. However, it has not been considering real options in its capital budgeting decisions. Now suppose the company changes its capital budgeting process to take account of four types of real options—**timing, flexibility, growth,** and **abandonment.** Would this decision be likely to affect some of the calculated NPVs? Explain your answer.
5. Good managers not only identify and evaluate real options in projects—they also structure projects so as to create real options. Suppose a company is considering a project to build an electric generating plant. Name some real options that might be built into the project, explain how they could be evaluated, and discuss their effects on the project's NPV.

14.1 Valuing Real Options

Recall from Chapter 13 that real options are opportunities for management to change the timing, scale, or other aspects of an investment in response to changes in market conditions. These opportunities are options in the sense that management can, if it is in the company's best interest, undertake some action; management is not *required* to undertake the action. These opportunities are real (as opposed to financial) because they involve decisions regarding real assets—such as plants, equipment, and land—rather than financial assets like stocks or bonds. Four examples of real options are investment timing options, growth options, abandonment options, and flexibility options. This chapter provides an example of how to value an investment timing option and a growth option. *Web Extension 14A* on the textbook's Web site shows how to value an abandonment option.

Valuing a real option requires judgment, both to formulate the model and to estimate the inputs. Does this mean the answer won't be useful? Definitely not. For example, the models used by NASA only approximate the centers of gravity for the moon, the earth, and other heavenly bodies, yet even with these "errors" in their models, NASA has been able to put astronauts on the moon. As one professor said, "All models are wrong, but some are still quite useful." This is especially true for real options. We might not be able to find the exact value of a real option, but the value we find can be helpful in deciding whether or not to accept the project. Equally important, the process of looking for and then valuing real options often identifies critical issues that might otherwise go unnoticed.

Five possible procedures can be used to deal with real options. Starting with the simplest, they are as follows.

1. Use discounted cash flow (DCF) valuation and ignore any real options by assuming their values are zero.
2. Use DCF valuation and include a qualitative recognition of any real option's value.
3. Use decision-tree analysis.
4. Use a standard model for a financial option.
5. Develop a unique, project-specific model using financial engineering techniques.

The following sections illustrate these procedures.

Self Test

List the five possible procedures for dealing with real options.

14.2 The Investment Timing Option: An Illustration

WEB

All calculations for the analysis of the investment timing option are shown in ***Ch14 Tool Kit.xls*** on the textbook's Web site.

There is frequently an alternative to investing immediately—the decision to invest or not can be postponed until more information becomes available. By waiting, a better-informed decision can be made, and this investment timing option adds value to the project and reduces its risk.

Murphy Systems is considering a project for a new type of handheld device that provides wireless Internet connections. The cost of the project is $50 million, but the future cash flows depend on the demand for wireless Internet connections, which is uncertain. Murphy believes there is a 25% chance that demand for the new device will be high, in which case the project will generate cash flows of $33 million each year for 3 years. There is a 50% chance of average demand, with cash flows of $25 million per year, and a 25% chance that demand will be low and annual cash flows will be only $5 million. A preliminary analysis indicates that the project is somewhat riskier than average, so it has been assigned a cost of capital of 14% versus 12% for an average project at Murphy Systems. Here is a summary of the project's data:

Demand	Probability	Annual Cash Flow
High	0.25	$33 million
Average	0.50	25 million
Low	0.25	5 million
Expected annual cash flow		$22 million
Project's cost of capital		14%
Life of project		3 years
Required investment, or cost of project		$50 million

Murphy could accept the project and implement it immediately; however, since the company has a patent on the device's core modules, it could also choose to delay the decision until next year, when more information about demand will be available. The cost will still be $50 million if Murphy waits, and the project will still be expected to generate the indicated cash flows, but each flow will be pushed back 1 year. However, if Murphy waits then it will know which of the demand conditions—and hence which set of cash flows—will occur. If Murphy waits then it will, of course, make the investment only if demand is sufficient to yield a positive NPV.

Observe that this real timing option resembles a call option on a stock. A call gives its owner the right to purchase a stock at a fixed strike price, but only if the stock's price is higher than the strike price will the owner exercise the option and buy the stock. Similarly, if Murphy defers implementation, then it will have the right to "purchase" the project by making the $50 million investment if the NPV as calculated next year, when new information is available, is positive.

14.2a Approach 1: DCF Analysis Ignoring the Timing Option

Based on probabilities for the different levels of demand, the expected annual cash flows are $22 million per year:

$$\text{Expected cash flow per year} = 0.25(\$33) + 0.50(\$25) + 0.25(\$5)$$
$$= \$22 \text{ million}$$

Ignoring the investment timing option, the traditional NPV is $1.08 million, found as follows:

$$\text{NPV} = -\$50 + \frac{\$22}{(1 + 0.14)^1} + \frac{\$22}{(1 + 0.14)^2} + \frac{\$22}{(1 + 0.14)^3} = \$1.08$$

The present value of the cash inflows is $51.08 million while the cost is $50 million, leaving an NPV of $1.08 million.

Based just on this DCF analysis, Murphy should accept the project. Note, however, that if the expected cash flows had been slightly lower—say, $21.5 million per year—then the NPV would have been negative and the project would have been rejected. Also, note that the project is risky: There is a 25% probability that demand will be weak, in which case the NPV will turn out to be a negative $38.4 million.

14.2b Approach 2: DCF Analysis with a Qualitative Consideration of the Timing Option

The discounted cash flow analysis suggests that the project should be accepted, but just barely, and it ignores the existence of a possibly valuable real option. If Murphy implements the project now, it gains an expected (but risky) NPV of $1.08 million. However, accepting now means that it is also giving up the option to wait and learn more about market demand before making the commitment. Thus, the decision is this: Is the option Murphy would be giving up worth more or less than $1.08 million? If the option is worth more than $1.08 million then Murphy should not give up the option, which means deferring the decision—and vice versa if the option is worth less than $1.08 million.

Based on the discussion of financial options in Chapter 6, what qualitative assessment can we make regarding the option's value? Put another way: Without doing any additional calculations, does it appear that Murphy should go forward now or wait? In thinking about this decision, first note that the value of an option is higher if the current value of the underlying asset is high relative to its strike price, other things held constant. For example, a call option with a strike price of $50 on a stock with a current price of $50 is worth more than if the current price were $20. The strike price of the project is $50 million, and our first guess at the value of its cash flows is $51.08 million. We will calculate the exact value of Murphy's underlying asset later, but the DCF analysis does suggest that the underlying asset's value will be close to the strike price, so the option should be valuable. We also know that an option's value is higher the longer its time to expiration. Here the option has a 1-year life, which is fairly long for an option, and this also suggests that the option is probably valuable. Finally, we know that the value of an option increases with the risk of the underlying asset. The data used in the DCF analysis indicate that the project is quite risky, which again suggests that the option is valuable.

Thus, our qualitative assessment indicates that the option to delay might well be more valuable than the expected NPV of $1.08 if we undertake the project immediately. This conclusion is quite subjective, but the qualitative assessment suggests that Murphy's management should go on to make a quantitative assessment of the situation.

14.2c Approach 3: Scenario Analysis and Decision Trees

Part 1 of Figure 14-1 presents a scenario analysis and decision tree similar to the examples in Chapter 13. Each possible outcome is shown as a "branch" on the tree. Each branch shows the cash flows and probability of a scenario laid out as a time line. Thus, the top line, which gives the payoffs of the high-demand scenario, has positive cash flows of $33 million for the next 3 years, and its NPV is $26.61 million. The average-demand branch in the middle has an NPV of $8.04 million, while the NPV of the low-demand branch is a negative $38.39 million. Since Murphy will suffer a $38.39 million loss if demand is weak and since there is a 25% probability of weak demand, the project is clearly risky.

The expected NPV is the weighted average of the three possible outcomes, where the weight for each outcome is its probability. The sum in the last column in Part 1 shows that the expected NPV is $1.08 million, the same as in the original DCF analysis. Part 1 also shows a standard deviation of $24.02 million for the NPV and a coefficient of variation (defined as the ratio of standard deviation to the expected NPV) of 22.32, which is rather large. Clearly, the project is quite risky under the analysis thus far.

Part 2 is set up similarly to Part 1 except that it shows what happens if Murphy delays the decision and then implements the project only if demand turns out to be high or average. No cost is incurred now at Year 0—here the only action is to wait. Then, if demand is average or high, Murphy will spend $50 million at Year 1 and receive either $33 million or $25 million per year for the following 3 years. If demand is low, as shown on the bottom branch, Murphy will spend nothing at Year 1 and will receive no cash flows in subsequent years. The NPV of the high-demand branch is $23.35 million and that of the average-demand branch is $7.05 million. Because all cash flows under the low-demand scenario are zero, the NPV in this case will also be zero. The expected NPV if Murphy delays the decision is $9.36 million.

This analysis shows that the project's expected NPV will be much higher if Murphy delays than if it invests immediately. Also, since there is no possibility of losing money under the delay option, this decision also lowers the project's risk.

Figure 14-1   DCF and Decision-Tree Analysis for the Investment Timing Option (Millions of Dollars)

	A	B	C	D	E	F	G	H	I
41	Part 1. Scenario Analysis: Proceed with Project Today								
42				Future Cash Flows			NPV of This		Probability
43	Now: Year 0		Year 1	Year 2	Year 3		Scenario[c]	Probability	× NPV
44									
45		0.25	$33	$33	$33		$26.61	0.25	$6.65
46		High							
47	−$50	Average 0.50	$25	$25	$25		$8.04	0.50	$4.02
48		Low							
49		0.25	$5	$5	$5		−$38.39	0.25	−$9.60
50								1.00	
51									
52							Expected value of NPVs =		$1.08
53									
54							Standard deviation[a] =		$24.02
55									
56							Coefficient of variation[b] =		22.32
57									
58	Part 2. Decision-Tree Analysis: Implement in One Year Only if Optimal								
59				Future Cash Flows			NPV of This		Probability
60	Now: Year 0		Year 1	Year 2	Year 3	Year 4	Scenario[d]	Probability	× NPV
61									
62		0.25	−$50	$33	$33	$33	$23.35	0.25	$5.84
63		High							
64	Wait	Average 0.50	−$50	$25	$25	$25	$7.05	0.50	$3.53
65		Low							
66		0.25	$0	$0	$0	$0	$0.00	0.25	$0.00
67								1.00	
68									
69							Expected value of NPVs =		$9.36
70									
71							Standard deviation[a] =		$8.57
72									
73							Coefficient of variation[b] =		0.92

[a]The standard deviation is calculated as explained in Chapter 2.
[b]The coefficient of variation is the standard deviation divided by the expected value.
[c]The WACC is 14%.
[d]The NPV in Part 2 is as of Year 0. Therefore, each of the project cash flows is discounted back one more year than in Part 1.

This plainly indicates that the option to wait is valuable; hence Murphy should wait until Year 1 before deciding whether to proceed with the investment.

Before we conclude the discussion of decision trees, note that we used the same cost of capital, 14%, to discount cash flows in the "proceed immediately" scenario analysis in Part 1 and under the "delay 1 year" scenario in Part 2. However, this is not appropriate for three reasons. First, since there is no possibility of losing money if Murphy delays, the investment under that plan is clearly less risky than if Murphy charges ahead today. Second, the 14% cost of capital might be appropriate for risky cash flows, yet the investment in the project at Year 1 in Part 2 is known with certainty. Perhaps, then, we should discount it at the risk-free rate.[2] Third, the project's cash inflows (excluding the initial investment) are different in Part 2 than in Part 1 because the low-demand cash flows are eliminated. This suggests that if 14% is the appropriate cost of capital in the "proceed immediately" case then some lower rate would be appropriate in the "delay decision" case.

In Figure 14-2, Part 1, we repeat the "delay decision" analysis but with one exception. We continue to discount the operating cash flows in Year 2 through Year 4 at the 14% WACC, but now we discount the project's cost at Year 1 using the risk-free rate of 6%. This increases the PV of the cost, which lowers the NPV from $9.36 million to $6.88 million. Yet we really don't know the precise WACC for this project—the 14% we used might be too high or too low for the operating cash flows in Year 2 through Year 4.[3] Therefore, in Part 2 of Figure 14-2 we show a sensitivity analysis of the NPV in which the discount rates used for both the operating cash flows and for the project's cost vary. This sensitivity analysis shows that, under all reasonable WACCs, the NPV of delaying is greater than $1.08 million. This confirms that the option to wait is more valuable than the $1.08 million NPV resulting from immediate implementation. Therefore, Murphy should wait rather than implement the project immediately.

14.2d Approach 4: Valuing the Timing Option with the Black-Scholes Option Pricing Model

The decision-tree approach, coupled with a sensitivity analysis, may provide enough information for a good decision. However, it is often useful to obtain additional insights into the real option's value, which means using the fourth procedure, an option pricing model. To do this, the analyst must find a standard financial option that resembles the project's real option.[4] As noted earlier, Murphy's option to delay the project is similar to a call option on a stock. Hence, the Black-Scholes option pricing model can be used. This model requires five inputs: (1) the risk-free rate, (2) the time until the option expires, (3) the strike price, (4) the current price of the stock, and (5) the variance of the stock's rate of return. Therefore, we need to estimate values for those five inputs.

First, if we assume that the rate on a 52-week Treasury security is 6%, then this rate can be used as the risk-free rate. Second, Murphy must decide within a year whether or not to implement the project, so there is 1 year until the option expires. Third, it will cost $50 million to implement the project, so $50 million can be used for the strike price. Fourth, we need a proxy for the value of the underlying asset, which in Black-Scholes is the current price of the stock. Note that a stock's current

---

2. For a more detailed explanation of the rationale behind using the risk-free rate to discount the project cost, see Timothy A. Luehrman, "Investment Opportunities as Real Options: Getting Started on the Numbers," *Harvard Business Review,* July/August 1998, pp. 51–67. This paper also provides a discussion of real option valuation. Professor Luehrman also wrote a follow-up paper that provides an excellent discussion of the ways real options affect strategy: "Strategy as a Portfolio of Real Options," *Harvard Business Review,* September/October 1998, pp. 89–99.

3. Murphy might gain information by waiting, which could reduce risk; but if a delay would enable others to enter and perhaps preempt the market, this could increase risk. In our example, we assumed that Murphy has a patent on critical components of the device, precluding the entrance of a competitor that could preempt its position in the market.

4. In theory, financial option pricing models apply only to assets that are continuously traded in a market. Even though real options usually don't meet this criterion, financial option models often provide a reasonably accurate approximation of the real option's value.

Figure 14-2   Decision-Tree and Sensitivity Analysis for the Investment Timing Option (Millions of Dollars)

	A	B	C	D	E	F	G	H	I
85	Part 1. Decision-Tree Analysis: Implement in One Year Only if Optimal								
86	(Discount Cost at theRisk-Free Rate and Operating Cash Flows at the WACC)								
87					Future Cash Flows		NPV of This		Probability
88	Now: Year 0		Year 1	Year 2	Year 3	Year 4	Scenario[c]	Probability	× NPV
89									
90		0.25	−$50	$33	$33	$33	$20.04	0.25	$5.01
91	High								
92	Average	0.50	−$50	$25	$25	$25	$3.74	0.50	$1.87
93	Low								
94		0.25	$0	$0	$0	$0	$0.00	0.25	$0.00
95								1.00	
96									
97							Expected value of NPVs =		$6.88
98									
99							Standard deviation[a] =		$7.75
100									
101							Coefficient of variation[b] =		1.13
102									
103	Part 2. Sensitivity Analysis of NPV to Changes in the Cost of Capital Used to								
104	Discount Cost and Cash Flows								
105					Cost of Capital Used to Discount the Year 1 Cost				
106			3.0%	4.0%	5.0%	6.0%	7.0%	8.0%	9.0%
107		8.0%	$13.11	$13.46	$13.80	$14.14	$14.47	$14.79	$15.11
108		9.0%	$11.78	$12.13	$12.47	$12.81	$13.14	$13.47	$13.78
109		10.0%	$10.50	$10.85	$11.20	$11.53	$11.86	$12.19	$12.51
110		11.0%	$9.27	$9.62	$9.97	$10.30	$10.64	$10.96	$11.28
111		12.0%	$8.09	$8.44	$8.78	$9.12	$9.45	$9.78	$10.09
112		13.0%	$6.95	$7.30	$7.64	$7.98	$8.31	$8.64	$8.95
113		14.0%	$5.85	$6.20	$6.54	$6.88	$7.21	$7.54	$7.85
114		15.0%	$4.79	$5.14	$5.48	$5.82	$6.15	$6.48	$6.79
115		16.0%	$3.77	$4.12	$4.46	$4.80	$5.13	$5.45	$5.77
116		17.0%	$2.78	$3.13	$3.47	$3.81	$4.14	$4.46	$4.78
117		18.0%	$1.83	$2.18	$2.52	$2.86	$3.19	$3.51	$3.83

Cost of Capital Used to Discount the Year-2 through Year-4 Operating Cash Flows

[a]The standard deviation is calculated as explained in Chapter 2.
[b]The coefficient of variation is the standard deviation divided by the expected value.
[c]The operating cash flows in Year 2 through Year 4 are discounted at the WACC of 14%. The cost in Year 1 is discounted at the risk-free rate of 6%.

price is the present value of its expected future cash flows. For Murphy's real option, the underlying asset is the project itself, and its current "price" is the present value of its expected future cash flows. Therefore, as a proxy for the stock price we can use the present value of the project's future cash flows. And fifth, the variance of the project's expected return can be used to represent the variance of the stock's return in the Black-Scholes model.

Figure 14-3 shows how one can estimate the present value of the project's cash inflows. We need to find the current value of the underlying asset—that is, the project. For a stock, the current price is the present value of all expected future cash flows, including those that are expected even if we do not exercise the call option. Note also

Figure 14-3 **Estimating the Input for Stock Price in the Option Analysis of the Investment Timing Option (Millions of Dollars)**

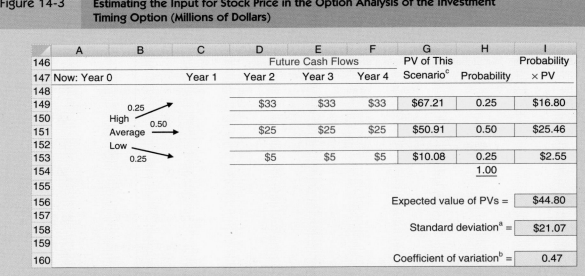

	A	B	C	D	E	F	G	H	I
					Future Cash Flows		PV of This		Probability
146									
147	Now: Year 0		Year 1	Year 2	Year 3	Year 4	Scenario[c]	Probability	× PV
148									
149		0.25		$33	$33	$33	$67.21	0.25	$16.80
150		High							
151		Average 0.50		$25	$25	$25	$50.91	0.50	$25.46
152		Low							
153		0.25		$5	$5	$5	$10.08	0.25	$2.55
154								1.00	
155									
156							Expected value of PVs =		$44.80
157									
158							Standard deviation[a] =		$21.07
159									
160							Coefficient of variation[b] =		0.47

[a]The standard deviation is calculated as explained in Chapter 2.
[b]The coefficient of variation is the standard deviation divided by the expected value.
[c]Here we find the PV, not the NPV, because the project's cost is ignored. The WACC is 14%. All cash flows in this scenario are discounted back to Year 0.

that the strike price for a call option has no effect on the stock's current price.[5] For our real option, the underlying asset is the delayed project, and its current "price" is the present value of all its future expected cash flows. Just as the price of a stock includes all of its future cash flows, so should the present value of the project include all of its possible future cash flows. Moreover, since the price of a stock is not affected by the strike price of a call option, we ignore the project's "strike price," or cost, when we find its present value. Figure 14-3 shows the expected cash flows if the project is delayed. The PV of these cash flows as of now (Year 0) is $44.80 million, and this is the input we should use for the current price in the Black-Scholes model.

The last required input is the variance of the project's return. Three different approaches could be used to estimate this input. First, we could use judgment—an educated guess. Here we would begin by recalling that a company is a portfolio of projects (or assets), with each project having its own risk. Since returns on the company's stock reflect the diversification gained by combining many projects, we might expect the variance of the stock's returns to be lower than the variance of one of its average projects. The variance of an average company's stock return is about 12%, so we might expect the variance for a typical project to be somewhat higher, say, 15% to 25%. Companies in the Internet infrastructure industry are riskier than average, so we might subjectively estimate the variance of Murphy's project to be in the range of 18% to 30%.

The second approach, called the *direct* method, is to estimate the rate of return for each possible outcome and then calculate the variance of those returns. First,

---

5. The company itself is not involved with traded stock options. However, if the option were a warrant issued by the company, then the strike price would affect the company's cash flows and hence its stock price.

Part 1 in Figure 14-4 shows the PV for each possible outcome as of Year 1, the time when the option expires. Here we simply find the present value of all future operating cash flows discounted back to Year 1, using the WACC of 14%. The Year-1 present value is $76.61 million for high demand, $58.04 million for average demand, and $11.61 million for low demand. Then, in Part 2, we show the percentage return from the current time until the option expires for each scenario, based on the $44.80 million starting "price" of the project at Year 0 as calculated in Figure 14-3. If demand is high, we will obtain a return of 71.0%: ($76.61 − $44.80)/$44.80 = 0.710 = 71.0%. Similar calculations show returns of 29.5% for average demand and −74.1% for low demand. The expected percentage return is 14%, the standard deviation is 53.6%, and the variance is 28.7%.[6]

The third approach for estimating the variance is also based on the scenario data, but the data are used in a different manner. First, we know that demand is not really limited to three scenarios; rather, a wide range of outcomes is possible. Similarly, the stock price at the time a call option expires could take one of many values. It is reasonable to assume that the value of the project at the time when we must decide on undertaking it behaves similarly to the price of a stock at the time a call option expires. Under this assumption, we can use the expected value and standard deviation of the project's value to calculate the variance of its rate of return, σ^2, with this formula:[7]

$$\sigma^2 = \frac{\ln(CV^2 + 1)}{t} \tag{14-1}$$

Here CV is the coefficient of variation of the underlying asset's price at the time the option expires, and t is the time until the option expires. Although the three outcomes in the scenarios represent a small sample of the many possible outcomes, we can still use the scenario data to estimate the variance that the project's rate of return would have if there were an infinite number of possible outcomes. For Murphy's project, this indirect method produces the following estimate of the variance of the project's return:

$$\sigma^2 = \frac{\ln(0.47^2 + 1)}{1} = 0.20 = 20\% \tag{14-1a}$$

Which of the three approaches is best? Obviously, they all involve judgment, so an analyst might want to consider all three. In our example, all three methods produce similar estimates, but for illustrative purposes we will simply use 20% as our initial estimate for the variance of the project's rate of return.

In Part 1 of Figure 14-5, we calculate the value of the option to defer investment in the project based on the Black-Scholes model, and the result is $7.04 million.

---

6. Two points should be made about the percentage return. First, for use in the Black-Scholes model, we need a percentage return calculated as shown, not an IRR return. The IRR is not used in the option pricing approach. Second, the expected return comes to 14%, the same as the WACC. This is because the Year-0 price and the Year-1 PVs were all calculated using the 14% WACC and because we measured return over only 1 year. If we measure the compound return over more than 1 year, then the average return generally will not equal 14%.

7. For a more detailed discussion, see David C. Shimko, *Finance in Continuous Time* (Miami, FL: Kolb Publishing, 1992).

Figure 14-4   **Estimating the Input for Variance in the Option Analysis of the Investment Timing Option (Millions of Dollars)**

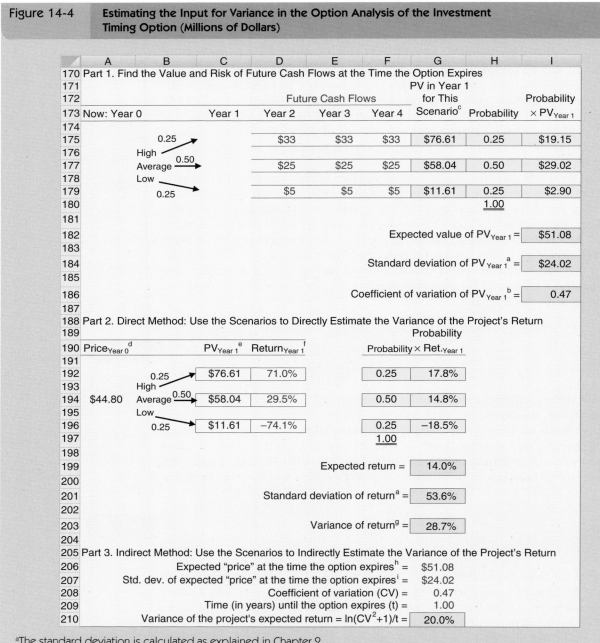

	A	B	C	D	E	F	G	H	I
170	Part 1. Find the Value and Risk of Future Cash Flows at the Time the Option Expires								
171							PV in Year 1		
172					Future Cash Flows		for This		Probability
173	Now: Year 0			Year 1	Year 2	Year 3	Year 4	Scenario[c]	Probability	× PV$_{Year 1}$
174										
175		0.25			$33	$33	$33	$76.61	0.25	$19.15
176		High								
177		Average	0.50		$25	$25	$25	$58.04	0.50	$29.02
178		Low								
179		0.25			$5	$5	$5	$11.61	0.25	$2.90
180									1.00	
181										
182							Expected value of PV$_{Year 1}$ =			$51.08
183										
184							Standard deviation of PV$_{Year 1}$[a] =			$24.02
185										
186							Coefficient of variation of PV$_{Year 1}$[b] =			0.47
187										
188	Part 2. Direct Method: Use the Scenarios to Directly Estimate the Variance of the Project's Return								
189							Probability		
190	Price$_{Year 0}$[d]			PV$_{Year 1}$[e]	Return$_{Year 1}$[f]		Probability × Ret.$_{Year 1}$		
191									
192		0.25		$76.61	71.0%		0.25	17.8%	
193		High							
194	$44.80	Average	0.50	$58.04	29.5%		0.50	14.8%	
195		Low							
196		0.25		$11.61	−74.1%		0.25	−18.5%	
197							1.00		
198									
199					Expected return =		14.0%		
200									
201					Standard deviation of return[a] =		53.6%		
202									
203					Variance of return[g] =		28.7%		
204									
205	Part 3. Indirect Method: Use the Scenarios to Indirectly Estimate the Variance of the Project's Return								
206			Expected "price" at the time the option expires[h] =				$51.08		
207			Std. dev. of expected "price" at the time the option expires[i] =				$24.02		
208			Coefficient of variation (CV) =				0.47		
209			Time (in years) until the option expires (t) =				1.00		
210			Variance of the project's expected return = ln(CV^2+1)/t =				20.0%		

[a]The standard deviation is calculated as explained in Chapter 2.
[b]The coefficient of variation is the standard deviation divided by the expected value.
[c]The WACC is 14%. The Year-2 through Year-4 cash flows are discounted back to Year 1.
[d]The Year-0 price is the expected PV from Figure 14-3.
[e]The Year-1 PVs are from Part 1.
[f]The returns for each scenario are calculated as (PV$_{Year 1}$ − Price$_{Year 0}$)/Price$_{Year 0}$.
[g]The variance of return is the standard deviation squared.
[h]The expected "price" at the time the option expires is taken from Part 1.
[i]The standard deviation of expected "price" at the time the option expires is taken from Part 1.

Figure 14-5   **Estimating the Value of the Investment Timing Option Using a Standard Financial Option (Millions of Dollars)**

	A	B	C	D	E	F	G	H	I
227	Part 1. Find the Value of a Call Option Using the Black-Scholes Model								
228			Real Option						
229		$r_{RF} =$	Risk-free interest rate				=	6%	
230		$t =$	Time until the option expires				=	1	
231		$X =$	Cost to implement the project				=	$50.00	
232		$P =$	Current value of the project				=	$44.80 [a]	
233		$\sigma^2 =$	Variance of the project's rate of return				=	20.0% [b]	
234									
235		$d_1 =$	$\{ \ln (P/X) + [r_{RF} + (\sigma^2 /2)] t \} / (\sigma\, t^{1/2})$				=	0.112	
236		$d_2 =$	$d_1 - \sigma (t^{1/2})$				=	−0.33	
237		$N(d_1) =$					=	0.54	
238		$N(d_2) =$					=	0.37	
239									
240		$V =$	$P[N (d_1)] - Xe^{r_{RF}t} [N (d_2)]$				=	$7.04	
241									
242	Part 2. Sensitivity Analysis of Option Value to Changes in Variance								
243		Variance	Option Value						
244		12.0%	$5.24						
245		14.0%	$5.74						
246		16.0%	$6.20						
247		18.0%	$6.63						
248		20.0%	$7.04						
249		22.0%	$7.42						
250		24.0%	$7.79						
251		26.0%	$8.15						
252		28.0%	$8.49						
253		30.0%	$8.81						
254		32.0%	$9.13						

[a]The current value of the project is taken from Figure 14-3.
[b]The variance of the project's rate of return is taken from Part 3 of Figure 14-4.

Since this is significantly higher than the $1.08 million NPV under immediate implementation and since the option would be forfeited if Murphy goes ahead right now, we conclude as before that the company should defer the final decision until more information is available.

Because judgmental estimates were made at many points in the analysis, it would be useful to see how sensitive the final outcome is to certain of the key inputs. Therefore, in Part 2 of Figure 14-5 we show the sensitivity of the option's value to different estimates of the variance. It is reassuring to see that, for all reasonable estimates of variance, the option to delay remains more valuable than immediate implementation.

14.2e Approach 5: Financial Engineering

Sometimes an analyst might not be satisfied with the results of a decision-tree analysis and cannot find a standard financial option that corresponds to the real option. In such a situation the only alternative is to develop a unique model for the specific real option being analyzed, a process called **financial engineering**.

When financial engineering is applied on Wall Street, where it was developed, the result is a newly designed financial product.[8] When it is applied to real options, the result is the value of a project that contains embedded options.

Although financial engineering was originally developed on Wall Street, many financial engineering techniques have been applied to real options during the last 10 years. We expect this trend to continue, especially in light of the rapid improvements in computer processing speed and spreadsheet software capabilities. One financial engineering technique is called **risk-neutral valuation**. This technique uses simulation, and we discuss it in *Web Extension 14B*. Most other financial engineering techniques are too complicated for a course in financial management, so we leave a detailed discussion of them to a specialized course.

Self Test	What is a decision tree?
	In a qualitative analysis, what factors affect the value of a real option?

14.3 The Growth Option: An Illustration

As we saw with the investment timing option, there is frequently an alternative to merely accepting or rejecting a static project. Many investment opportunities, if successful, lead to other investment opportunities. The production capacity of a successful product line can later be expanded to satisfy increased demand, or distribution can be extended to new geographic markets. A company with a successful name brand can capitalize on its success by adding complementary or new products under the same brand. These growth options add value to a project and explain, for example, why companies are flocking to make inroads into the very difficult business environment in China.

Kidco Corporation designs and manufactures products aimed at the pre-teen market. Most of its products have a very short life, given the rapidly changing tastes of pre-teens. Kidco is now considering a project that will cost $30 million. Management believes there is a 25% chance that the project will "take off" and generate operating cash flows of $34 million in each of the next 2 years, after which pre-teen tastes will change and the project will be terminated. There is a 50% chance of average demand, in which case cash flows will be $20 million annually for 2 years. Finally, there is a 25% chance that the pre-teens won't like the product at all, and it will generate cash flows of only $2 million per year. The estimated cost of capital for the project is 14%.

Based on its experience with other projects, Kidco believes it will be able to launch a second-generation product if demand for the original product is average or above. This second-generation product will cost the same as the first-generation product, $30 million, and the cost will be incurred at Year 2. However, given the success of the first-generation product, Kidco believes that the second-generation product would be just as successful as the first-generation product.

This growth option resembles a call option on a stock, since it gives Kidco the opportunity to "purchase" a successful follow-on project at a fixed cost if the value of the project is greater than the cost. Otherwise, Kidco will let the option expire by not implementing the second-generation product.

---

8. Financial engineering techniques are widely used for the creation and valuation of derivative securities.

The following sections apply the first four valuation approaches: (1) DCF, (2) DCF and qualitative assessment, (3) decision-tree analysis, and (4) analysis with a standard financial option.

14.3a Approach 1: DCF Analysis Ignoring the Growth Option

Based on probabilities for the different levels of demand, the expected annual operating cash flows for the project are $19 million per year:

$$0.25(\$34) + 0.50(\$20) + 0.25(\$2) = \$19.00$$

Ignoring the investment timing option, the traditional NPV is $1.29 million:

$$\text{NPV} = -\$30 + \frac{\$19}{(1 + 0.14)^1} + \frac{\$19}{(1 + 0.14)^2} = \$1.29$$

Based on this DCF analysis, Kidco should accept the project.

14.3b Approach 2: DCF Analysis with a Qualitative Consideration of the Growth Option

Although the DCF analysis indicates that the project should be accepted, it ignores a potentially valuable real option. The option's time to maturity and the volatility of the underlying project provide qualitative insights into the option's value. Kidco's growth option has 2 years until maturity, which is a relatively long time, and the cash flows of the project are volatile. Taken together, this qualitative assessment indicates that the growth option should be quite valuable.

14.3c Approach 3: Decision-Tree Analysis of the Growth Option

Part 1 of Figure 14-6 shows a scenario analysis for Kidco's project. The top line, which describes the payoffs for the high-demand scenario, has operating cash flows of $34 million for the next 2 years. The NPV of this branch is $25.99 million. The NPV of the average-demand branch in the middle is $2.93 million, and it is −$26.71 million for the low-demand scenario. The sum in the last column of Part 1 shows the expected NPV of $1.29 million. The coefficient of variation is 14.54, indicating that the project is very risky.

Part 2 of Figure 14-6 shows a decision-tree analysis in which Kidco undertakes the second-generation product only if demand is average or high. In these scenarios, shown on the top two branches of the decision tree, Kidco will incur a cost of $30 million at Year 2 and receive operating cash flows of either $34 million or $20 million for the next 2 years, depending on the level of demand. If the demand is low, shown on the bottom branch, Kidco has no cost at Year 2 and receives no additional cash flows in subsequent years. All operating cash flows (which do not include the cost of implementing the second-generation project at Year 2) are discounted at the WACC of 14%. Because the $30 million implementation cost is known, it is discounted at the risk-free rate of 6%. As shown in Part 2 of Figure 14-6, the expected NPV is $4.70 million, indicating that the growth option is quite valuable.

Figure 14-6 **Scenario Analysis and Decision-Tree Analysis for the Kidco Project (Millions of Dollars)**

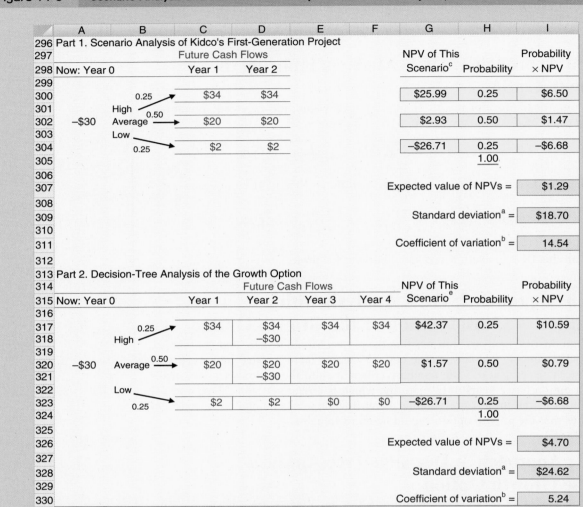

		Part 1. Scenario Analysis of Kidco's First-Generation Project				NPV of This Scenario[c]	Probability	Probability × NPV
		Future Cash Flows						
Now: Year 0		Year 1	Year 2					
	0.25 High	$34	$34			$25.99	0.25	$6.50
−$30	0.50 Average	$20	$20			$2.93	0.50	$1.47
	Low 0.25	$2	$2			−$26.71	0.25	−$6.68
							1.00	
						Expected value of NPVs =		$1.29
						Standard deviation[a] =		$18.70
						Coefficient of variation[b] =		14.54

		Part 2. Decision-Tree Analysis of the Growth Option					NPV of This Scenario[e]	Probability	Probability × NPV
		Future Cash Flows							
Now: Year 0		Year 1	Year 2	Year 3	Year 4				
	0.25 High	$34	$34 −$30	$34	$34		$42.37	0.25	$10.59
−$30	0.50 Average	$20	$20 −$30	$20	$20		$1.57	0.50	$0.79
	Low 0.25	$2	$2	$0	$0		−$26.71	0.25	−$6.68
								1.00	
							Expected value of NPVs =		$4.70
							Standard deviation[a] =		$24.62
							Coefficient of variation[b] =		5.24

[a]The standard deviation is calculated as in Chapter 2.
[b]The coefficient of variation is the standard deviation divided by the expected value.
[c]The operating cash flows are discounted by the WACC of 14%.
[d]The total cash flows at Year 2 are equal to the operating cash flows for the first-generation product minus the $30 million cost to implement the second-generation product, if the firm chooses to do so. For example, the Year-2 cash flow in the high-demand scenario is $34 − $30 = $4 million. Based on Part 1, it makes economic sense to implement the second-generation product only if demand is high or average.
[e]The operating cash flows in Year 1 through Year 2, which do not include the $30 million cost of implementing the second-generation project at Year 2 for the high-demand and average-demand scenarios, are discounted at the WACC of 14%. The $30 million implementation cost at Year 2 for the high-demand and average-demand scenarios is discounted at the risk-free rate of 6%.

The option itself alters the risk of the project, which means that 14% is probably not the appropriate cost of capital. Table 14-1 presents the results of a sensitivity analysis in which the cost of capital for the operating cash flows varies from 8% to 18%. The sensitivity analysis also allows the rate used to discount the implementation

TABLE 14-1   Sensitivity Analysis of the Kidco Decision-Tree Analysis in Figure 14-6
(Millions of Dollars)

	A	B	C	D	E	F	G	H	I
347			Cost of Capital Used to Discount the $30 Million Implementation						
348			Cost in Year 2 of the Second-Generation Project						
349			3.0%	4.0%	5.0%	6.0%	7.0%	8.0%	9.0%
350		8.0%	$10.96	$11.36	$11.76	$12.14	$12.51	$12.88	$13.23
351		9.0%	$9.61	$10.01	$10.41	$10.79	$11.16	$11.52	$11.88
352		10.0%	$8.30	$8.71	$9.10	$9.49	$9.86	$10.22	$10.57
353		11.0%	$7.04	$7.45	$7.84	$8.23	$8.60	$8.96	$9.31
354		12.0%	$5.83	$6.23	$6.63	$7.01	$7.38	$7.75	$8.10
355		13.0%	$4.65	$5.06	$5.45	$5.84	$6.21	$6.57	$6.92
356		14.0%	$3.52	$3.92	$4.32	$4.70	$5.07	$5.44	$5.79
357		15.0%	$2.42	$2.83	$3.22	$3.61	$3.98	$4.34	$4.69
358		16.0%	$1.36	$1.77	$2.16	$2.54	$2.92	$3.28	$3.63
359		17.0%	$0.33	$0.74	$1.13	$1.52	$1.89	$2.25	$2.60
360		18.0%	−$0.66	−$0.25	$0.14	$0.52	$0.90	$1.26	$1.61

Column B label (left margin): Cost of Capital Used to Discount the Year-1 through Year-4 Operating Cash Flows[a]

[a]The operating cash flows do not include the $30 million implementation cost of the second-generation project in Year 2.

cost at Year 2 to vary from 3% to 9%. The resulting NPV is positive for all reasonable combinations of discount rates.

14.3d Approach 4: Valuing the Growth Option with the Black-Scholes Option Pricing Model

The fourth approach is to use a standard model for a corresponding financial option. As we noted earlier, Kidco's growth option is similar to a call option on a stock, so we will use the Black-Scholes model to find the value of the growth option. The time until the growth option expires is 2 years. The rate on a 2-year Treasury security is 6%, and this provides a good estimate of the risk-free rate. Implementing the project will cost $30 million, which is the strike price.

The input for stock price in the Black-Scholes model is the current value of the underlying asset. For the growth option, the underlying asset is the second-generation project, and its current value is the present value of its cash flows. The calculations in Figure 14-7 show that this value is $24.07 million. Because the strike price of $30 million is greater than the current "price" of $24.07 million, the growth option is currently out-of-the-money.

Figure 14-8 shows the estimates for the variance of the project's rate of return using the two methods described earlier in the chapter for the analysis of the investment timing option. The direct method, shown in Part 2 of the figure, produces an estimate of 17.9% for the variance of return. The indirect method, in Part 3, estimates the variance as 15.3%. Both estimates are somewhat higher than the 12% variance of a typical company's stock return, which is consistent with the idea that a project's variance is higher than a stock's because of diversification effects. Thus, an estimated variance of 15% to 20% seems reasonable. We use an initial estimate of 15.3% in our initial application of the Black-Scholes model, shown in Part 1 of Figure 14-9.

Using the Black-Scholes model for a call option, Figure 14-9 shows a $4.34 million value for the growth option. The total NPV is the sum of the first-generation project's NPV and the value of the growth option: Total NPV = $1.29 + $4.34 = $5.63 million,

WEB

See *Ch14 Tool Kit.xls* on the textbook's Web site for all calculations.

Figure 14-7   **Estimating the Input for Stock Price in the Growth Option Analysis of the Investment Timing Option (Millions of Dollars)**

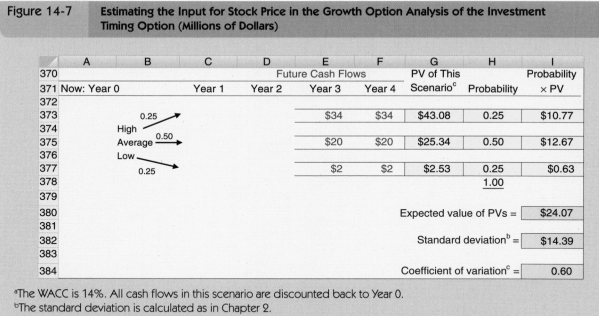

	A	B	C	D	E	F	G	H	I
					Future Cash Flows		PV of This		Probability
371	Now: Year 0		Year 1	Year 2	Year 3	Year 4	Scenario[c]	Probability	× PV
373		0.25			$34	$34	$43.08	0.25	$10.77
374	High								
375	Average	0.50			$20	$20	$25.34	0.50	$12.67
376	Low								
377		0.25			$2	$2	$2.53	0.25	$0.63
378								1.00	
380							Expected value of PVs =		$24.07
382							Standard deviation[b] =		$14.39
384							Coefficient of variation[c] =		0.60

[a]The WACC is 14%. All cash flows in this scenario are discounted back to Year 0.
[b]The standard deviation is calculated as in Chapter 2.
[c]The coefficient of variation is the standard deviation divided by the expected value.

which is much higher than the NPV of the first-generation project alone. As this analysis shows, the growth option adds considerable value to the original project. In addition, the sensitivity analysis in Part 2 of Figure 14-9 indicates that the growth option's value is large for all reasonable values of variance. Kidco should therefore accept the project.

For an illustrative valuation of an abandonment option, see *Web Extension 14A*.

Self Test   Explain how growth options are like call options.

14.4 Concluding Thoughts on Real Options

We don't deny that real options can be pretty complicated. Keep in mind, however, that 50 years ago very few companies used NPV because it seemed too complicated. Now NPV is a basic tool used by virtually all companies and taught in all business schools. A similar but more rapid pattern of adoption is occurring with real options. Ten years ago very few companies used real options, but a recent survey of CFOs reported that more than 26% of companies now use real option techniques when evaluating projects.[9] Just as with NPV, it's only a matter of time before virtually all companies use real option techniques.

We have provided you with some basic tools necessary for evaluating real options, starting with the ability to identify real options and make qualitative assessments

---

9.   See John R. Graham and Campbell R. Harvey, "The Theory and Practice of Corporate Finance: Evidence from the Field," *Journal of Financial Economics*, May 2001, pp. 187–243.

Figure 14-8   Estimating the Input for Stock Return Variance in the Growth Option Analysis (Millions of Dollars)

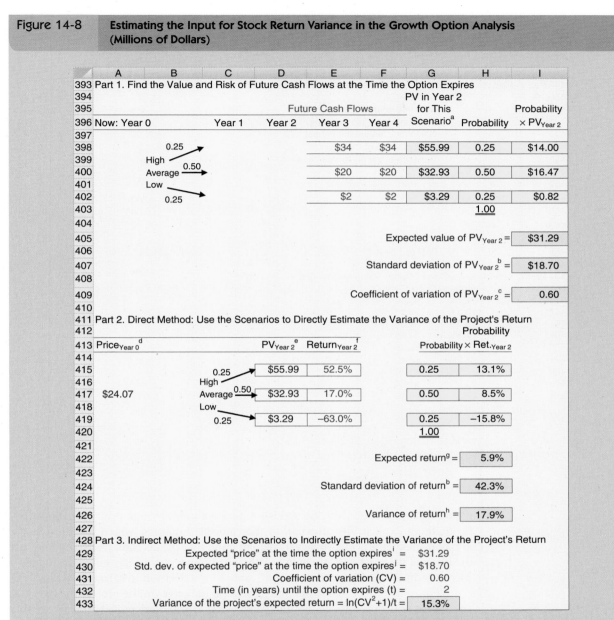

	A	B	C	D	E	F	G	H	I
393	Part 1. Find the Value and Risk of Future Cash Flows at the Time the Option Expires								
394							PV in Year 2		
395					Future Cash Flows		for This		Probability
396	Now: Year 0		Year 1	Year 2	Year 3	Year 4	Scenario[a]	Probability	× PV$_{Year\,2}$
397									
398		0.25			$34	$34	$55.99	0.25	$14.00
399	High								
400	Average	0.50			$20	$20	$32.93	0.50	$16.47
401	Low								
402		0.25			$2	$2	$3.29	0.25	$0.82
403								1.00	
404									
405							Expected value of PV$_{Year\,2}$ =		$31.29
406									
407							Standard deviation of PV$_{Year\,2}$[b] =		$18.70
408									
409							Coefficient of variation of PV$_{Year\,2}$[c] =		0.60
410									
411	Part 2. Direct Method: Use the Scenarios to Directly Estimate the Variance of the Project's Return								
412								Probability	
413	Price$_{Year\,0}$[d]				PV$_{Year\,2}$[e]	Return$_{Year\,2}$[f]		Probability × Ret.$_{Year\,2}$	
414									
415			0.25		$55.99	52.5%		0.25	13.1%
416			High						
417	$24.07		Average	0.50	$32.93	17.0%		0.50	8.5%
418			Low						
419			0.25		$3.29	−63.0%		0.25	−15.8%
420								1.00	
421									
422							Expected return[g] =		5.9%
423									
424							Standard deviation of return[b] =		42.3%
425									
426							Variance of return[h] =		17.9%
427									
428	Part 3. Indirect Method: Use the Scenarios to Indirectly Estimate the Variance of the Project's Return								
429			Expected "price" at the time the option expires[i] =				$31.29		
430			Std. dev. of expected "price" at the time the option expires[j] =				$18.70		
431			Coefficient of variation (CV) =				0.60		
432			Time (in years) until the option expires (t) =				2		
433			Variance of the project's expected return = ln(CV^2+1)/t =				15.3%		

[a]The WACC is 14%. The Year-3 through Year-4 cash flows are discounted back to Year 2.
[b]The standard deviation is calculated as in Chapter 2.
[c]The coefficient of variation is the standard deviation divided by the expected value.
[d]The Year-0 price is the expected PV from Figure 14-7.
[e]The Year-2 PVs are from Part 1.
[f]The annualized returns for each scenario are calculated as $(PV_{Year\,2}/Price_{Year\,0})^{0.5} - 1$.
[g]The expected annualized return is not equal to the cost of capital, 14%. However, if you do the calculations then you'll see that the expected 2-year return is 29.26%, which is equal to the 2-year compounded cost of capital: $(1.14)^2 - 1 = 29.26\%$.
[h]The variance of return is the standard deviation squared.
[i]The expected "price" at the time the option expires is taken from Part 1.
[j]The standard deviation of the expected "price" at the time the option expires is taken from Part 1.

Figure 14-9   Estimating the Value of the Growth Option Using a Standard Financial Option (Millions of Dollars)

	A	B	C	D	E	F	G	H	I
449	Part 1. Find the Value of a Call Option Using the Black-Scholes Model								
450			Real Option						
451		r_{RF} =	Risk-free interest rate				=	6%	
452		t =	Time until the option expires				=	2	
453		X =	Cost to implement the project				=	$30.00	
454		P =	Current value of the project				=	$24.07 [a]	
455		σ^2 =	Variance of the project's rate of return				=	15.3% [b]	
456									
457		d_1 =	$\{ \ln(P/X) + [r_{RF} + (\sigma^2/2)]\, t \} / (\sigma\, t^{1/2})$				=	0.096	
458		d_2 =	$d_1 - \sigma\,(t^{1/2})$				=	−0.46	
459		$N(d_1)$ =					=	0.54	
460		$N(d_2)$ =					=	0.32	
461									
462		V =	$P[N(d_1)] - Xe^{-r_{RF}t}[N(d_2)]$				=	$4.34	
463									
464	Part 2. Sensitivity Analysis of Option Value to Changes in Variance								
465			Variance Option Value						
466			11.3%	$3.60					
467			13.3%	$3.98					
468			15.3%	$4.34					
469			17.3%	$4.68					
470			19.3%	$4.99					
471			21.3%	$5.29					
472			23.3%	$5.74					
473			25.3%	$5.84					
474			27.3%	$6.10					
475			29.3%	$6.35					
476			31.3%	$6.59					

[a]The current value of the project is taken from Figure 14-7.
[b]The variance of the project's rate of return is taken from Part 3 of Figure 14-8.

regarding a real option's value. Decision trees are another important tool, since they facilitate an explicit identification of the embedded options, which is critical in the decision-making process. However, keep in mind that the decision tree should not use the original project's cost of capital. Although finance theory has not yet provided a way to estimate the appropriate cost of capital for a decision tree, sensitivity analysis can identify the effect that different costs of capital have on the project's value.

Many real options can be analyzed using a standard model for an existing financial option, such as the Black-Scholes model for calls and puts. There are also other financial models for a variety of options. These include the option to exchange one asset for another, the option to purchase the minimum or the maximum of two or more assets, the option on an average of several assets, and even an option on an option.[10] In fact, there are entire textbooks that describe even

10. See W. Margrabe, "The Value of an Option to Exchange One Asset for Another," *Journal of Finance,* March 1978, pp. 177–186; R. Stulz, "Options on the Minimum or Maximum of Two Risky Assets: Analysis and Applications," *Journal of Financial Economics,* Vol. 10, 1982, pp. 161–185; H. Johnson, "Options on the Maximum or Minimum of Several Assets," *Journal of Financial and Quantitative Analysis,* September 1987, pp. 277–283; P. Ritchken, L. Sankarasubramanian, and A. M. Vijh, "Averaging Options for Capping Total Costs," *Financial Management,* Autumn 1990, pp. 35–41; and R. Geske, "The Valuation of Compound Options," *Journal of Financial Economics,* March 1979, pp. 63–81.

more options.[11] Given the large number of standard models for existing financial options, it is often possible to find a financial option that resembles the real option being analyzed.

Sometimes there are some real options that don't resemble any financial options. But the good news is that many of these options can be valued using techniques from financial engineering. This is frequently the case if there is a traded financial asset that matches the risk of the real option. For example, many oil companies use oil futures contracts to price the real options that are embedded in various exploration and leasing strategies. With the explosion in the markets for derivatives, there are now financial contracts that span an incredible variety of risks. This means that an ever-increasing number of real options can be valued using these financial instruments. Most financial engineering techniques are beyond the scope of this book, but *Web Extension 14B* on the textbook's Web site describes one particularly useful financial engineering technique called risk-neutral valuation.[12]

Self Test

How widely used is real option analysis?

What techniques can be used to analyze real options?

Summary

In this chapter we discussed some topics that go beyond the simple capital budgeting framework, including the following.

- Investing in a new project often brings with it a potential increase in the firm's future opportunities. Opportunities are, in effect, options—the right but not the obligation to take some future action.
- A project may have an **option value** that is not accounted for in a conventional NPV analysis. Any project that expands the firm's set of opportunities has positive option value.
- **Real options** are opportunities for management to respond to changes in market conditions and involve "real" rather than "financial" assets.

---

11. See John C. Hull, *Options, Futures, and Other Derivatives*, 8th ed. (Boston: Prentice-Hall, 2012).
12. For more on real options, see Martha Amram, *Value Sweep: Mapping Corporate Growth Opportunities* (Boston: Harvard Business School Press, 2002); Martha Amram and Nalin Kulatilaka, *Real Options: Managing Strategic Investment in an Uncertain World* (Boston: Harvard Business School Press, 1999); Michael Brennan and Lenos Trigeorgis, *Project Flexibility, Agency, and Competition: New Developments in the Theory and Application of Real Options* (New York: Oxford University Press, 2000); Eduardo Schwartz and Lenos Trigeorgis, *Real Options and Investment Under Uncertainty* (Cambridge, MA: MIT Press, 2001); Han T. J. Smit and Lenos Trigeorgis, *Strategic Investment: Real Options and Games* (Princeton, NJ: Princeton University Press, 2004); Lenos Trigeorgis, *Real Options in Capital Investment: Models, Strategies, and Applications* (Westport, CT: Praeger, 1995); and Lenos Trigeorgis, *Real Options: Managerial Flexibility and Strategy in Resource Allocation* (Cambridge, MA: MIT Press, 1996).

- There are five possible **procedures for valuing real options:** (1) DCF analysis only, and ignore the real option; (2) DCF analysis and a qualitative assessment of the real option's value; (3) decision-tree analysis; (4) analysis with a standard model for an existing financial option; and (5) financial engineering techniques.
- Many **investment timing options** and **growth options** can be valued using the Black-Scholes call option pricing model.
- See *Web Extension 14A* on the textbook's Web site for an illustration of valuing the **abandonment option.**
- See *Web Extension 14B* on the textbook's Web site for a discussion of **risk-neutral valuation.**

Questions

14-1 Define each of the following terms:
   a. Real option; managerial option; strategic option; embedded option
   b. Investment timing option; growth option; abandonment option; flexibility option
   c. Decision tree

14-2 What factors should a company consider when it decides whether to invest in a project today or to wait until more information becomes available?

14-3 In general, do timing options make it more or less likely that a project will be accepted today?

14-4 If a company has an option to abandon a project, would this tend to make the company more or less likely to accept the project today?

Problems   <small>Answers Appear in Appendix B</small>

Intermediate Problems 1–5

14-1 **Investment Timing Option: Decision-Tree Analysis** Kim Hotels is interested in developing a new hotel in Seoul. The company estimates that the hotel would require an initial investment of $20 million. Kim expects the hotel will produce positive cash flows of $3 million a year at the end of each of the next 20 years. The project's cost of capital is 13%.
   a. What is the project's net present value?
   b. Kim expects the cash flows to be $3 million a year, but it recognizes that the cash flows could actually be much higher or lower, depending on whether the Korean government imposes a large hotel tax. One year from now, Kim will know whether the tax will be imposed. There is a 50% chance that the tax will be imposed, in which case the yearly cash flows will be only $2.2 million. At the same time, there is a 50% chance that the tax will not be imposed, in which case the yearly cash flows will

be $3.8 million. Kim is deciding whether to proceed with the hotel today or to wait a year to find out whether the tax will be imposed. If Kim waits a year, the initial investment will remain at $20 million. Assume that all cash flows are discounted at 13%. Use decision-tree analysis to determine whether Kim should proceed with the project today or wait a year before deciding.

14-2 Investment Timing Option: Decision-Tree Analysis The Karns Oil Company is deciding whether to drill for oil on a tract of land the company owns. The company estimates the project would cost $8 million today. Karns estimates that, once drilled, the oil will generate positive net cash flows of $4 million a year at the end of each of the next 4 years. Although the company is fairly confident about its cash flow forecast, in 2 years it will have more information about the local geology and about the price of oil. Karns estimates that if it waits 2 years then the project would cost $9 million. Moreover, if it waits 2 years, then there is a 90% chance that the net cash flows would be $4.2 million a year for 4 years and a 10% chance that they would be $2.2 million a year for 4 years. Assume all cash flows are discounted at 10%.

    a. If the company chooses to drill today, what is the project's net present value?

    b. Using decision-tree analysis, does it make sense to wait 2 years before deciding whether to drill?

14-3 Investment Timing Option: Decision-Tree Analysis Hart Lumber is considering the purchase of a paper company, which would require an initial investment of $300 million. Hart estimates that the paper company would provide net cash flows of $40 million at the end of each of the next 20 years. The cost of capital for the paper company is 13%.

    a. Should Hart purchase the paper company?

    b. Hart's best guess is that cash flows will be $40 million a year, but it realizes that the cash flows are as likely to be $30 million a year as $50 million. One year from now, it will find out whether the cash flows will be $30 million or $50 million. In addition, Hart could sell the paper company at Year 3 for $280 million. Given this additional information, does decision-tree analysis indicate that it makes sense to purchase the paper company? Again, assume that all cash flows are discounted at 13%.

14-4 Real Options: Decision-Tree Analysis Utah Enterprises is considering buying a vacant lot that sells for $1.2 million. If the property is purchased, the company's plan is to spend another $5 million today (t = 0) to build a hotel on the property. The after-tax cash flows from the hotel will depend critically on whether the state imposes a tourism tax in this year's legislative session. If the tax is imposed, the hotel is expected to produce after-tax cash inflows of $600,000 at the end of each of the next 15 years, versus $1,200,00 if the tax is not imposed. The project has a 12% cost of capital. Assume at the outset that the company does not have the option to delay the project. Use decision-tree analysis to answer the following questions.

    a. What is the project's expected NPV if the tax is imposed?

    b. What is the project's expected NPV if the tax is not imposed?

    c. Given that there is a 50% chance that the tax will be imposed, what is the project's expected NPV if the company proceeds with it today?

d. Although the company does not have an option to delay construction, it does have the option to abandon the project 1 year from now if the tax is imposed. If it abandons the project, it would sell the complete property 1 year from now at an expected price of $6 million. Once the project is abandoned, the company would no longer receive any cash inflows from it. If all cash flows are discounted at 12%, would the existence of this abandonment option affect the company's decision to proceed with the project today?

e. Assume there is no option to abandon or delay the project but that the company has an option to purchase an adjacent property in 1 year at a price of $1.5 million. If the tourism tax is imposed, then the net present value of developing this property (as of t = 1) is only $300,000 (so it wouldn't make sense to purchase the property for $1.5 million). However, if the tax is not imposed, then the net present value of the future opportunities from developing the property would be $4 million (as of t = 1). Thus, under this scenario it would make sense to purchase the property for $1.5 million. Given that cash flows are discounted at 12% and that there's a 50-50 chance the tax will be imposed, how much would the company pay today for the option to purchase this property 1 year from now for $1.5 million?

14-5 **Growth Option: Decision-Tree Analysis** Fethe's Funny Hats is considering selling trademarked, orange-haired curly wigs for University of Tennessee football games. The purchase cost for a 2-year franchise to sell the wigs is $20,000. If demand is good (40% probability), then the net cash flows will be $25,000 per year for 2 years. If demand is bad (60% probability), then the net cash flows will be $5,000 per year for 2 years. Fethe's cost of capital is 10%.

a. What is the expected NPV of the project?

b. If Fethe makes the investment today, then it will have the option to renew the franchise fee for 2 more years at the end of Year 2 for an additional payment of $20,000. In this case, the cash flows that occurred in Years 1 and 2 will be repeated (so if demand was good in Years 1 and 2, it will continue to be good in Years 3 and 4). Write out the decision tree and use decision-tree analysis to calculate the expected NPV of this project, including the option to continue for an additional 2 years. *Note:* The franchise fee payment at the end of Year 2 is known, so it should be discounted at the risk-free rate, which is 6%.

Challenging Problems 6–8

14-6 **Investment Timing Option: Option Analysis** Rework Problem 14-1 using the Black-Scholes model to estimate the value of the option. Assume that the variance of the project's rate of return is 6.87% and that the risk-free rate is 8%.

14-7 **Investment Timing Option: Option Analysis** Rework Problem 14-2 using the Black-Scholes model to estimate the value of the option. Assume that the variance of the project's rate of return is 1.11% and that the risk-free rate is 6%.

14–8 **Growth Option: Option Analysis** Rework Problem 14-5 using the Black-Scholes model to estimate the value of the option. Assume that the variance of the project's rate of return is 20.25% and that the risk-free rate is 6%.

Spreadsheet Problem

14–9 **Build a Model: Real Options** Start with the partial model in the file *Ch14 P09 Build a Model.xls* on the textbook's Web site. Bradford Services Inc. (BSI) is considering a project with a cost of $10 million and an expected life of 3 years. There is a 30% probability of good conditions, in which case the project will provide a cash flow of $9 million at the end of each of the next 3 years. There is a 40% probability of medium conditions, in which case the annual cash flows will be $4 million, and there is a 30% probability of bad conditions with a cash flow of −$1 million per year. BSI uses a 12% cost of capital to evaluate projects like this.

a. Find the project's expected present value, NPV, and the coefficient of variation of the present value.

b. Now suppose that BSI can abandon the project at the end of the first year by selling it for $6 million. BSI will still receive the Year-1 cash flows, but will receive no cash flows in subsequent years.

c. Now assume that the project cannot be shut down. However, expertise gained by taking it on would lead to an opportunity at the end of Year 3 to undertake a venture that would have the same cost as the original project, and the new project's cash flows would follow whichever branch resulted for the original project. In other words, there would be a second $10 million cost at the end of Year 3 followed by cash flows of either $9 million, $4 million, or −$1 million for the subsequent 3 years. Use decision-tree analysis to estimate the value of the project, including the opportunity to implement the new project at Year 3. Assume that the $10 million cost at Year 3 is known with certainty and should be discounted at the risk-free rate of 6%.

d. Now suppose the original project (no abandonment option or additional growth option) could be delayed a year. All the cash flows would remain unchanged, but information obtained during that year would tell the company exactly which set of demand conditions existed. Use decision-tree analysis to estimate the value of the project if it is delayed by 1 year. (*Hint:* Discount the $10 million cost at the risk-free rate of 6% because the cost is known with certainty.)

e. Go back to part c. Instead of using decision-tree analysis, use the Black-Scholes model to estimate the value of the growth option. The risk-free rate is 6%, and the variance of the project's rate of return is 22%.

MINI CASE

Assume you have just been hired as a financial analyst by Tropical Sweets Inc., a mid-sized California company that specializes in creating exotic candies from tropical fruits such as mangoes, papayas, and dates. The firm's CEO, George Yamaguchi, recently returned from an industry corporate executive conference in San Francisco, and one of the sessions he attended addressed real options. Because no one at Tropical Sweets is familiar with the basics of real options, Yamaguchi has asked you to prepare a brief report that the firm's executives can use to gain at least a cursory understanding of the topic.

To begin, you gathered some outside materials on the subject and used these materials to draft a list of pertinent questions that need to be answered. Now that the questions have been drafted, you must develop the answers.

a. What are some types of real options?

b. What are five possible procedures for analyzing a real option?

c. Tropical Sweets is considering a project that will cost $70 million and will generate expected cash flows of $30 million per year for 3 years. The cost of capital for this type of project is 10%, and the risk-free rate is 6%. After discussions with the marketing department, you learn that there is a 30% chance of high demand with associated future cash flows of $45 million per year. There is also a 40% chance of average demand with cash flows of $30 million per year as well as a 30% chance of low demand with cash flows of only $15 million per year. What is the expected NPV?

d. Now suppose this project has an investment timing option, since it can be delayed for a year. The cost will still be $70 million at the end of the year, and the cash flows for the scenarios will still last 3 years. However, Tropical Sweets will know the level of demand and will implement the project only if it adds value to the company. Perform a qualitative assessment of the investment timing option's value.

e. Use decision-tree analysis to calculate the NPV of the project with the investment timing option.

f. Use a financial option pricing model to estimate the value of the investment timing option.

g. Now suppose that the cost of the project is $75 million and the project cannot be delayed. However, if Tropical Sweets implements the project then the firm will have a growth option: the opportunity to replicate the original project at the end of its life. What is the total expected NPV of the two projects if both are implemented?

h. Tropical Sweets will replicate the original project only if demand is high. Using decision-tree analysis, estimate the value of the project with the growth option.

i. Use a financial option model to estimate the value of the project with the growth option.

j. What happens to the value of the growth option if the variance of the project's return is 14.2%? What if it is 50%? How might this explain the high valuations of many start-up high-tech companies that have yet to show positive earnings?

PART IV

Strategic Financing Decisions

Chapter 15

Capital Structure Decisions: Part I

© Nikada/iStockphoto.com

WEB

The textbook's Web site contains an *Excel* file that will guide you through the chapter's calculations. The file for this chapter is ***Ch15 Tool Kit.xls***, and we encourage you to open the file and follow along as you read the chapter.

As we saw in Chapters 9 and 11, growth in sales requires growth in operating capital, often requiring that external funds must be raised through a combination of equity and debt. The firm's mixture of debt and equity is called its **capital structure**. Although actual levels of debt and equity may vary somewhat over time, most firms try to keep their financing mix close to a **target capital structure**. A firm's **capital structure decision** includes its choice of a target capital structure, the average maturity of its debt, and the specific types of financing it decides to use at any particular time. As with operating decisions, managers should make capital structure decisions that are designed to maximize the firm's intrinsic value.

Beginning of Chapter Questions

As you read this chapter, consider how you would answer the following questions. You *should not* necessarily be able to answer the questions before you read the chapter. Rather, you should use them to get a sense of the issues covered in the chapter. After reading the chapter, you should be able to give at least partial answers to the questions, and you should be able to give better answers after the chapter has been discussed in class. Note, too, that it is often useful, when answering conceptual questions, to use hypothetical data to illustrate your answer. We illustrate the answers with an *Excel* model that is available on the textbook's Web site. Accessing the model and working through it is a useful exercise, and it provides insights that are useful when answering the questions.

1. What is **business risk?** List and then discuss some factors that affect business risk.
2. What is **financial risk?** How is it related to business risk?
3. Who are **Modigliani and Miller (MM),** and what were their conclusions regarding the effect of capital structure on a firm's value and cost of capital under the assumption of no corporate taxes? How do their conclusions change when they introduce corporate taxes? If a firm's managers thought that MM were exactly right, and they

wanted to maximize the firm's value, what capital structure would they choose?
4. Does the MM theory appear to be correct according to either empirical research or observations of firms' actual behavior? How do assumptions affect your conclusion about whether the MM theory appears to be correct?
5. What is the **trade-off theory** of capital structure? How does it differ from MM's theory?
6. In general, does the market view the **announcement of a new stock issue** to be a good **signal?** Does the signaling theory lead to the same conclusions regarding the optimal capital structure as the trade-off theory and/or the MM theory?
7. What does it mean to be at the **optimal capital structure?** What is optimized? What is maximized and what is minimized?
8. Should firms focus on **book value** or **market value** capital structures? How would the calculated WACC be affected by the use of book weights rather than market weights?
9. What would you expect to happen to an all-equity firm's stock price if its management announced a **recapitalization** under which debt would be issued and used to repurchase common stock?

15.1 A Preview of Capital Structure Issues

Recall from Chapter 11 that the value of a firm's operations is the present value of its expected future free cash flows (FCF) discounted at its weighted average cost of capital (WACC):

$$V_{op} = \sum_{t=1}^{\infty} \frac{FCF_t}{(1 + WACC)^t}$$ (15–1)

The WACC of a firm financed only by debt and common stock depends on the percentages of debt and common stock (w_d and w_s), the cost of debt (r_d), the cost of stock (r_s), and the corporate tax rate (T):

$$WACC = w_d(1 - T)r_d + w_s r_s$$ (15–2)

CORPORATE VALUATION AND CAPITAL STRUCTURE

A firm's financing choices obviously have a direct effect on the weighted average cost of capital (WACC). Financing choices also have an indirect effect on the costs of debt and equity because they change the risk and required returns of debt and equity. Financing choices can also affect free cash flows if the probability of bankruptcy becomes high. This chapter focuses on the debt–equity choice and its effect on value.

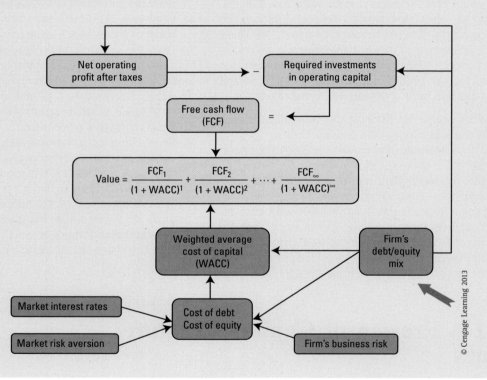

As these equations show, the only way any decision can change a firm's value is by affecting either expected free cash flows or the cost of capital. We discuss below some of the ways that a higher proportion of debt can affect WACC and/or FCF.

15.1a Debt Increases the Cost of Stock, r_s

Debtholders have a claim on the company's cash flows that is prior to shareholders, who are entitled only to any residual cash flow after debtholders have been paid. As we show later in a numerical example, the "fixed" claim of the debtholders causes the "residual" claim of the stockholders to become riskier, and this increases the cost of stock, r_s.

15.1b Debt Reduces the Taxes a Company Pays

Imagine that a company's cash flows are a pie and that three different groups get pieces of the pie. The first piece goes to the government in the form of taxes, the second goes to debtholders, and the third to shareholders. Companies can deduct interest expenses when calculating taxable income, which reduces the government's piece of the pie and leaves more pie available to debtholders and investors. This reduction in taxes reduces the after-tax cost of debt, as shown in Equation 15-2.

15.1c The Risk of Bankruptcy Increases the Cost of Debt, r_d

As debt increases, the probability of financial distress, or even bankruptcy, goes up. With higher bankruptcy risk, debtholders will insist on a higher interest rate, which increases the pre-tax cost of debt, r_d.

15.1d The Net Effect on the Weighted Average Cost of Capital

As Equation 15-2 shows, the WACC is a weighted average of relatively low-cost debt and high-cost equity. If we increase the proportion of debt, then the weight of low-cost debt (w_d) increases and the weight of high-cost equity (w_s) decreases. If all else remained the same, then the WACC would fall and the value of the firm in Equation 15-1 would increase. But the previous paragraphs show that all else doesn't remain the same: Both r_d and r_s increase. It should be clear that changing the capital structure affects all the variables in the WACC equation, but it's not easy to say whether those changes increase the WACC, decrease it, or balance out exactly and thus leave the WACC unchanged. We'll return to this issue later when discussing capital structure theory.

15.1e Bankruptcy Risk Reduces Free Cash Flow

As the risk of bankruptcy increases, some customers may choose to buy from another company, which hurts sales. This, in turn, decreases net operating profit after taxes (NOPAT), thus reducing FCF. Financial distress also hurts the productivity of workers and managers, who spend more time worrying about their next job than attending to their current job. Again, this reduces NOPAT and FCF. Finally, suppliers tighten their credit standards, which reduces accounts payable and causes net operating working capital to increase, thus reducing FCF. Therefore, the risk of bankruptcy can decrease FCF and reduce the value of the firm.

15.1f Bankruptcy Risk Affects Agency Costs

Higher levels of debt may affect the behavior of managers in two opposing ways. First, when times are good, managers may waste cash flow on perquisites and unnecessary expenditures. This is an agency cost, as described in Chapter 11. The good news is that the threat of bankruptcy reduces such wasteful spending, which increases FCF.

But the bad news is that a manager may become gun-shy and reject positive-NPV projects if they are risky. From the stockholder's point of view, it would be unfortunate if a risky project caused the company to go into bankruptcy, but note that other companies in the stockholder's portfolio may be taking on risky projects that turn out to be successful. Since most stockholders are well diversified, they can afford for a manager to take on risky but positive-NPV projects. But a manager's reputation and wealth are generally tied to a single company, so the project may be unacceptably risky from the manager's point of view. Thus, high debt can cause managers to forgo positive-NPV projects unless they are extremely safe. This is called the **underinvestment problem,** and it is another type of agency cost. Notice that debt can reduce one aspect of agency costs (wasteful spending) but may increase another (underinvestment), so the net effect on value isn't clear.

15.1g Issuing Equity Conveys a Signal to the Marketplace

Managers are in a better position to forecast a company's free cash flow than are investors, and academics call this **informational asymmetry.** Suppose a company's stock price is $50 per share. If managers are willing to issue new stock at $50 per share, investors reason that no one would sell anything for less than its true value. Therefore, the true value of the shares as seen by the managers with their superior information must be less than or equal to $50. Thus, investors perceive an equity issue as a negative signal, and this usually causes the stock price to fall.[1]

In addition to affecting investors' perceptions, capital structure choices also affect FCF and risk, as discussed earlier. The following section focuses on the way that capital structure affects risk.

15.1h A Quick Overview of Actual Debt Ratios

For the average company in the S&P 500, the ratio of long-term debt to equity was about 108% in the winter of 2011. This means that the typical company had about $1.08 in debt for every dollar of equity. However, Table 15-1 shows that there are wide divergences in the average ratios for different business sectors and for different companies within a sector. For example, the technology sector has a very low average ratio (13%) while the utilities sector has a much higher ratio (82%). Even so, within each sector there are some companies with low levels of debt and others with high levels. For example, the average debt ratio for the consumer/noncyclical sector is 24%, but in this sector Starbucks has a ratio of 15% while Kellogg has a ratio of 177%. Why do we see such variation across companies and business sectors? Can a company make itself more valuable through its choice of debt ratio? We address those questions in the rest of this chapter, beginning with a description of business risk and financial risk.

Self Test	Briefly describe some ways in which the capital structure decision can affect the WACC and FCF.

15.2 Business Risk and Financial Risk

Business risk and financial risk combine to determine the total risk of a firm's future return on equity, as we explain in the next sections.

---

1. An exception to this rule is any situation with little informational asymmetry, such as a regulated utility. Also, some companies, such as start-ups or high-tech ventures, are unable to find willing lenders and therefore must issue equity; we discuss this later in the chapter.

TABLE 15-1	Long-Term Debt-to-Equity Ratios for Selected Firms and Industries			
Sector and Company	Long-Term Debt-to-Equity Ratio	Sector and Company	Long-Term Debt-to-Equity Ratio	
Technology	**13%**	**Capital Goods**	**24%**	
Microsoft (MSFT)	21	Winnebago Industries (WGO)	0	
Ricoh (RICTEUR.Lp)	64	Caterpillar Inc. (CAT)	207	
Energy	**17**	**Consumer/Noncyclical**	**24**	
ExxonMobil (XOM)	11	Starbucks (SBUX)	15	
Chesapeake Energy (CHK)	75	Kellogg Company (K)	177	
Transportation	**54**	**Services**	**54**	
United Parcel Service (UPS)	102	Administaff Inc. (ASF)	0	
Delta Airlines (DAL)	1,469	Republic Services (RSG)	75	
Basic Materials	**19**	**Utilities**	**82**	
Anglo American PLC (AAUKYN.MX)	37	Genon Energy Inc. (RRI)	51	
Century Aluminum (CENX)	23	CMS Energy (CMS)	220	

© Cengage Learning 2013

Source: For updates on a company's ratio, go to **www.reuters.com** and enter the ticker symbol for a stock quote. Click on Financials tab for updates on the sector ratio.

15.2a Business Risk

Business risk is the risk a firm's common stockholders would face if the firm had no debt. In other words, it is the risk inherent in the firm's operations, which arises from uncertainty about future operating profits and capital requirements.

Business risk depends on a number of factors, beginning with variability in product demand. For example, General Motors has more demand variability than does Kroger: When times are tough, consumers quit buying cars but they still buy food. Second, most firms are exposed to variability in sales prices and input costs. Some firms with strong brand identity like Apple may be able to pass unexpected costs through to their customers, and firms with strong market power like Wal-Mart may be able to keep their input costs low, but variability in prices and costs adds significant risk to most firms' operations. Third, firms that are slower to bring new products to market have greater business risk: Think of GM's relatively sluggish time to bring a new model to the market versus that of Toyota. Being faster to the market allows Toyota to more quickly respond to changes in consumer desires. Fourth, international operations add the risk of currency fluctuations and political risk. Fifth, if a high percentage of a firm's costs are fixed and hence do not decline when demand falls, then the firm has high *operating leverage,* which increases its business risk. We focus on operating leverage in the next section.

15.2b Operating Leverage

A high degree of **operating leverage** implies that a relatively small change in sales results in a relatively large change in EBIT, net operating profits after taxes (NOPAT), and return on invested capital (ROIC). Other things held constant, the higher a firm's fixed costs, the greater its operating leverage. Higher fixed costs are generally

Figure 15-1   **Illustration of Operating and Financial Leverage (Millions of Dollars and Millions of Units, Except Per Unit Data)**

	A	B	C	D	E
23	*Input Data*		Plan A	Plan U	Plan L
24	Required capital		$200	$200	$200
25	Book equity		$200	$200	$150
26	Debt				$50
27	Interest rate		8%	8%	8%
28	Sales price (P)		$2.00	$2.00	$2.00
29	Tax rate (T)		40%	40%	40%
30	Expected units sold (Q)		110	110	110
31	Fixed costs (F)		$20	$60	$60
32	Variable costs (V)		$1.50	$1.00	$1.00
33					
34	*Income Statements*		Plan A	Plan U	Plan L
35	Sales revenue (P×Q)		$220.0	$220.0	$220.0
36	Fixed costs		$20.0	$60.0	$60.0
37	Variable costs (V×Q)		$165.0	$110.0	$110.0
38	EBIT		$35.0	$50.0	$50.0
39	Interest		$0.0	$0.0	$4.0
40	EBT		$35.0	$50.0	$46.0
41	Tax		$14.0	$20.0	$18.4
42	Net income		$21.0	$30.0	$27.6
43					
44	*Key Performance Measures*		Plan A	Plan U	Plan L
45	NOPAT = EBIT(1 − T)		$21.0	$30.0	$30.0
46	ROIC = NOPAT/Capital		10.5%	15.0%	15.0%
47	ROE = NI/Equity		10.5%	15.0%	18.4%

associated with (1) highly automated, capital intensive firms; (2) businesses that employ highly skilled workers who must be retained and paid even when sales are low; and (3) firms with high product development costs that must be maintained to complete ongoing R&D projects.

To illustrate the relative impact of fixed versus variable costs, consider Strasburg Electronics Company, a manufacturer of components used in cell phones. Strasburg is considering several different operating technologies and several different financing alternatives. We will analyze its financing choices in the next section, but for now we focus on its operating plans.

Each of Strasburg's plans requires a capital investment of $200 million; assume for now that Strasburg will finance its choice entirely with equity.[2] Each plan is expected to produce 100 million units (Q) per year at a sales price (P) of $2 per unit. As shown in Figure 15-1, Plan A's technology requires a smaller annual fixed cost (F) than Plan U's, but Plan A has higher variable costs (V). (We denote the second plan with U because it has no financial leverage, and we denote the third plan with L because it does have financial leverage; Plan L is discussed in the next section.) Figure 15-1 also shows the projected income statements and selected performance

---

2. Strasburg has improved its supply chain operations to such an extent that its operating current assets are not larger than its operating current liabilities. In fact, its Op CA = Op CL = $10 million. Recall that net operating working capital (NOWC) is the difference between Op CA and Op CL, so Strasburg has NOWC = 0. Even though Strasburg's plans require $210 million in assets, they also generate $10 million in spontaneous operating liabilities, so Strasburg's investors must put up only $200 million in some combination of debt and equity.

measures for the first year. Notice that Plan U has higher net income, higher net operating profit after taxes (NOPAT), higher return on equity (ROE), and higher return on invested capital than does Plan A. So at first blush it seems that Strasburg should accept Plan U instead of Plan A.

Notice that the projections in Figure 15-1 are based on the 110 million units that are expected to be sold. But what if demand is lower than expected? It often is useful to know how far sales can fall before operating profits become negative. The **operating break-even point** occurs when earnings before interest and taxes (EBIT) equal zero:[3]

$$EBIT = PQ - VQ - F = 0$$

(15–3)

If we solve for the break-even quantity, Q_{BE}, we get this expression:

$$Q_{BE} = \frac{F}{P - V}$$

(15–4)

The break-even quantities for Plans A and U are

$$\text{Plan A: } Q_{BE} = \frac{\$20 \text{ million}}{\$2.00 - \$1.50} = 40 \text{ million units}$$

$$\text{Plan U: } Q_{BE} = \frac{\$60 \text{ million}}{\$2.00 - \$1.00} = 60 \text{ million units}$$

Plan A will be profitable if unit sales are above 40 million, whereas Plan U requires sales of 60 million units before it is profitable. This difference is because Plan U has higher fixed costs, so more units must be sold to cover these fixed costs. Panel a of Figure 15-2 illustrates the operating profitability of these two plans for different levels of unit sales. (We discuss Panel b in the next section.) Suppose sales are at 80 million units. In this case, the NOPAT is identical for each plan. As unit sales begin to climb above 80 million, both plans increase in profitability, but NOPAT increases more for Plan U than for Plan A. If sales fall below 80 million then both plans become less profitable, but NOPAT decreases more for Plan U than for Plan A. This illustrates that the combination of higher fixed costs and lower variable costs of Plan U magnifies its gain or loss relative to Plan A. In other words, because Plan U has higher operating leverage, it also has greater business risk.

Notice that business risk is being driven by variability in the number of units that can be sold. It would be straightforward to estimate a probability for each possible level of sales and then calculate the standard deviation of the resulting NOPATs in exactly the same way that we calculated project risk using scenario analysis in Chapter 13. This would produce a quantitative estimate of business

---

3. This definition of the break-even point does not include any fixed financial costs because it focuses on operating profits. We could also examine net income, in which case a levered firm would have negative net income even at the operating break-even point. We introduce financial costs shortly.

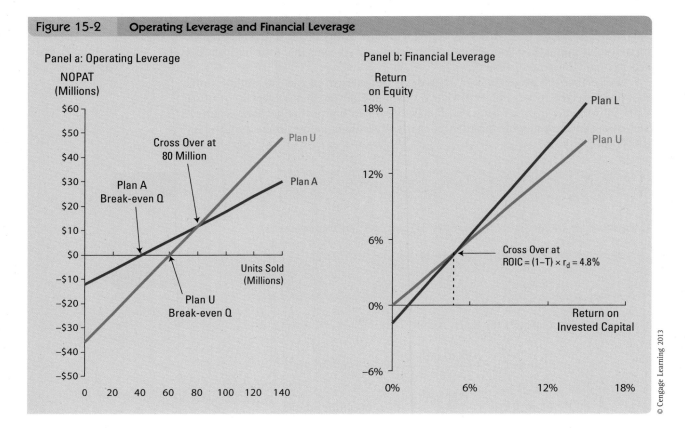

Figure 15-2   Operating Leverage and Financial Leverage

Panel a: Operating Leverage

Panel b: Financial Leverage

risk.[4] However, for most purposes it is sufficient to recognize that business risk increases if operating leverage increases and then use that insight qualitatively rather than quantitatively when evaluating plans with different degrees of operating leverage.

15.2c Financial Risk

Financial risk is the additional risk placed on the common stockholders as a result of the decision to finance with debt.[5] Conceptually, stockholders face a certain amount of risk that is inherent in a firm's operations—this is its business risk, which is defined as the uncertainty in projections of future EBIT, NOPAT, and ROIC. If a firm uses debt (financial leverage), then the business risk is concentrated on the common stockholders. To illustrate, suppose ten people decide to form a corporation to manufacture flash memory drives. There is a certain amount of business risk in the operation. If the firm is capitalized only with common equity and if each person buys 10% of the stock,

---

4. For this example, we could also directly express the standard deviation of NOPAT, σ_{NOPAT}, in terms of the standard deviation of unit sales, σ_Q: $\sigma_{NOPAT} = (P - V)(1 - T) \times \sigma_Q$. We could also express the standard deviation of ROIC as $\sigma_{ROIC} = [(P - V)(1 - T)/Capital] \times \sigma_Q$. As this shows, volatility in NOPAT (and ROIC) is driven by volatility in unit sales, with a bigger spread between price and variable costs leading to higher volatility. Also, there are several other ways to calculate measures of operating leverage, as we explain in *Web Extension 15A*.

5. Preferred stock also adds to financial risk. To simplify matters, we examine only debt and common equity in this chapter.

then each investor shares equally in the business risk. However, suppose the firm is capitalized with 50% debt and 50% equity, with five of the investors putting up their money by purchasing debt and the other five putting up their money by purchasing equity. In this case, the five debtholders are paid before the five stockholders, so *virtually all* of the business risk is borne by the stockholders. Thus, the use of debt, or **financial leverage**, concentrates business risk on stockholders.[6]

To illustrate the impact of financial risk, we can extend the Strasburg Electronics example. Strasburg initially decided to use the technology of Plan U, which is unlevered (financed with all equity), but now it's considering financing the technology with $150 million of equity and $50 million of debt at an 8% interest rate, as shown for Plan L in Figure 15-1 (recall that L denotes leverage). Compare Plans U and L. Notice that the ROIC of 15% is the same for the two plans because the financing choice doesn't affect operations. Plan L has lower net income ($27.6 million versus $30 million) because it must pay interest, but it has a higher ROE (18.4%) because the net income is shared over a smaller equity base.[7]

Suppose Strasburg is a zero-growth company and pays out all net income as dividends. This means that Plan U has net income of $30 million available for distribution to its investors. Plan L has $27.6 million net income available to pay as dividends and it already pays $4 million in interest to its debtholders, so its total distribution is $27.6 + $4 = $31.6 million. How is it that Plan L is able to distribute a larger total amount to investors? Look closely at the taxes paid under the two plans. Plan L pays only $18.4 million in tax while Plan U pays $20 million. The $1.6 million difference is because interest payments are deductible for tax purposes. Because Plan L pays less in taxes, an extra $1.6 million is available to distribute to investors. If our analysis ended here, we would choose Plan L over Plan U because Plan L distributes more cash to investors and provides a higher ROE for its equity holders.

But there is more to the story. Just as operating leverage adds risk, so does financial leverage. We used the Data Table feature in the file *Ch15 Tool Kit.xls* to generate performance measures for plans U and L at different levels of unit sales, which lead to different levels of ROIC. Panel b of Figure 15-2 shows the ROE of Plan L versus its ROIC. (Keep in mind that the ROIC for Plan U is the same as for Plan L because leverage doesn't affect operating performance; also, Plan U's ROE is the same as its ROIC because it has no leverage.)

Notice that for an ROIC of 4.8%, which is the after-tax cost of debt, Plan U (with no leverage) and Plan L (with leverage) have the same ROE. As ROIC increases above 6%, the ROE increases for each plan, but more for Plan L than for Plan U. However, if ROIC falls below 6%, then the ROE falls further for Plan L than for Plan U. Thus, financial leverage magnifies the ROE for good or ill, depending on the ROIC, and so increases the risk of a levered firm relative to an unlevered firm.[8]

We see, then, that using leverage has both good and bad effects: If expected ROIC is greater than the after-tax cost of debt, then higher leverage increases expected ROE but also increases risk.

---

6. Holders of corporate debt generally do bear some business risk, because they may lose some of their investment if the firm goes bankrupt. We discuss this in more depth later in the chapter.

7. Recall that Strasburg's operating CA are equal to its operating CL. Strasburg has no short-term investments, so its book values of debt and equity must sum up to the amount of operating capital it uses.

8. We could also express the standard deviation of ROE, σ_{ROE}, in terms of the standard deviation of ROIC: $\sigma_{ROE} = (\text{Capital/Equity}) \times \sigma_{ROIC} = (\text{Capital/Equity}) \times [(P - V)(1 - T)/\text{Capital}] \times \sigma_Q$. Thus, volatility in ROE is due to the amount of financial leverage, the amount of operating leverage, and the underlying risk in units sold. This is similar in spirit to the Du Pont model discussed in Chapter 8.

15.2d Strasburg's Valuation Analysis

Strasburg decided to go with Plan L, the one with high operating leverage and $50 million in debt financing. This resulted in a stock price of $20 per share. With 10 million shares, Strasburg's market value of equity is $20(10) = $200 million. Strasburg has no short-term investments, so Strasburg's total enterprise value is the sum of its debt and equity: V = $50 + $200 = $250 million. Notice that this is greater than the required investment, which means that the plan has a positive NPV; another way to view this is that Strasburg's Market Value Added (MVA) is positive. In terms of market values, Strasburg's capital structure has 20% debt (w_d = $50/$250 = 0.20) and 80% equity (w_s = $200/$250 = 0.80). These calculations are reported in Figure 15-3.

Is this the optimal capital structure? We will address the question in more detail later, but for now let's focus on understanding Strasburg's current valuation, beginning with its cost of capital. Strasburg has a beta of 1.25. We can use the Capital Asset Pricing Model (CAPM) to estimate the cost of equity. The risk-free rate, r_{RF}, is 6.3% and the market risk premium, RP_M, is 6%, so the cost of equity is

$$r_s = r_{RF} + b(RP_M) = 6.3\% + 1.25(6\%) = 13.8\%$$

Figure 15-3	Strasburg's Valuation Analysis (Millions of Dollars Except Per Share Data)			
	A	**B**	**C**	**D**
104	Input Data (Millions Except Per Share Data)			
105	Tax rate			40.00%
106	Debt (D)			$50.00
107	Number of shares (n)			10.00
108	Stock price per share (P)			$20.00
109	NOPAT			$30.00
110	Free Cash Flow (FCF)			$30.00
111	Growth rate in FCF			0.00%
112				
113	Capital Structure (Millions Except Per Share Data)			
114	Market value of equity (S = P × n)			$200.00
115	Total value (V = D + S)			$250.00
116	Percent financed with debt (w_d = D/V)			20%
117	Percent financed with stock (w_s = S/V)			80%
118				
119	Cost of Capital			
120	Cost of debt (r_d)			8.00%
121	Beta (b)			1.25
122	Risk-free rate (r_{RF})			6.30%
123	Market risk premium (RP_M)			6.00%
124	Cost of equity ($r_s = r_{RF} + b \times RP_M$)			13.80%
125	WACC			12.00%
126				
127	Intrinsic Valuation (Millions Except Per Share Data)			
128	Value of operations:			
129	V_{op} = [FCF(1 + g)]/(WACC – g)			$250.00
130	+ Value of ST investments			$0.00
131	Total intrinsic value of firm			$250.00
132	– Debt			$50.00
133	Intrinsic value of equity			$200.00
134	÷ Number of shares			10.00
135	Intrinsic price per share			$20.00

The weighted average cost of capital is

$$
\begin{aligned}
\text{WACC} &= w_d(1 - T)r_d + w_s r_s \\
&= 20\%(1 - 0.40)(8\%) + 80\%(13.8\%) \\
&= 12\%
\end{aligned}
$$

As shown in Figure 15-1, Plan L has a NOPAT of $30 million. Strasburg expects zero growth, which means there are no required investments in capital. Therefore, FCF is equal to NOPAT. Using the constant growth formula, the value of operations is

$$
V_{op} = \frac{\text{FCF}(1 + g)}{\text{WACC} - g} = \frac{\$30(1 + 0)}{0.12 - 0} = \$250
$$

Figure 15-3 illustrates the calculation of the intrinsic stock price. For Strasburg, the intrinsic stock price and the market price are each equal to $20. Can Strasburg increase its value by changing its capital structure? The next section discusses how the trade-off between risk and return affects the value of the firm, and Section 15.5 estimates the optimal capital structure for Strasburg.

Self Test

What is business risk, and how can it be measured?

What are some determinants of business risk?

How does operating leverage affect business risk?

What is financial risk, and how does it arise?

Explain this statement: "Using leverage has both good and bad effects."

A firm has fixed operating costs of $100,000 and variable costs of $4 per unit. If it sells the product for $6 per unit, what is the break-even quantity? **(50,000)**

15.3 Capital Structure Theory

In the previous section, we showed how capital structure choices affect a firm's ROE and its risk. For a number of reasons, we would expect capital structures to vary considerably across industries. For example, pharmaceutical companies generally have very different capital structures than airline companies. Moreover, capital structures vary among firms within a given industry. What factors explain these differences? In an attempt to answer this question, academics and practitioners have developed a number of theories, and the theories have been subjected to many empirical tests. The following sections examine several of these theories.[9]

---

9. For additional discussion of capital structure theories, see John C. Easterwood and Palani-Rajan Kadapakkam, "The Role of Private and Public Debt in Corporate Capital Structures," *Financial Management,* Autumn 1991, pp. 49–57; Gerald T. Garvey, "Leveraging the Underinvestment Problem: How High Debt and Management Shareholdings Solve the Agency Costs of Free Cash Flow," *Journal of Financial Research,* Summer 1992, pp. 149–166; Milton Harris and Artur Raviv, "Capital Structure and the Informational Role of Debt," *Journal of Finance,* June 1990, pp. 321–349; and Ronen Israel, "Capital Structure and the Market for Corporate Control: The Defensive Role of Debt Financing," *Journal of Finance,* September 1991, pp. 1391–1409.

15.3a Modigliani and Miller: No Taxes

Modern capital structure theory began in 1958, when Professors Franco Modigliani and Merton Miller (MM) published what has been called the most influential finance article ever written.[10] MM's study was based on some strong assumptions, which included the following:

1. There are no brokerage costs.
2. There are no taxes.
3. There are no bankruptcy costs.
4. Investors can borrow at the same rate as corporations.
5. All investors have the same information as management about the firm's future investment opportunities.
6. EBIT is not affected by the use of debt.

Modigliani and Miller imagined two hypothetical portfolios. The first contains all the equity of an unlevered firm, so the portfolio's value is V_U, the value of an unlevered firm. Because the firm has no growth (which means it does not need to invest in any new net assets) and because it pays no taxes, the firm can pay out all of its EBIT in the form of dividends. Therefore, the cash flow from owning this first portfolio is equal to EBIT.

Now consider a second firm that is identical to the unlevered firm *except* that it is partially financed with debt. The second portfolio contains all of the levered firm's stock (S_L) and debt (D), so the portfolio's value is V_L, the total value of the levered firm. If the interest rate is r_d, then the levered firm pays out interest in the amount $r_d D$. Because the firm is not growing and pays no taxes, it can pay out dividends in the amount EBIT − $r_d D$. If you owned all of the firm's debt and equity, your cash flow would be equal to the sum of the interest and dividends: $r_d D$ + (EBIT − $r_d D$) = EBIT. Therefore, the cash flow from owning this second portfolio is equal to EBIT.

Notice that the cash flow of each portfolio is equal to EBIT. Thus, MM concluded that two portfolios producing the same cash flows must have the same value:[11]

$$(15\text{--}5) \qquad V_L = V_U = S_L + D$$

Given their assumptions, MM proved that a firm's value is unaffected by its capital structure.

Recall that the WACC is a combination of the cost of debt and the relatively higher cost of equity, r_s. As leverage increases, more weight is given to low-cost debt but equity becomes riskier, which drives up r_s. Under MM's assumptions,

---

10. Franco Modigliani and Merton H. Miller, "The Cost of Capital, Corporation Finance, and the Theory of Investment," *American Economic Review,* June 1958, pp. 261–297. Modigliani and Miller each won a Nobel Prize for their work.

11. They actually showed that if the values of the two portfolios differed, then an investor could engage in riskless arbitrage: The investor could create a trading strategy (buying one portfolio and selling the other) that had no risk, required none of the investor's own cash, and resulted in a positive cash flow for the investor. This would be such a desirable strategy that everyone would try to implement it. But if everyone tries to buy the same portfolio, its price will be driven up by market demand, and if everyone tries to sell a portfolio, its price will be driven down. The net result of the trading activity would be to change the portfolio's values until they were equal and no more arbitrage was possible.

r_s increases by exactly enough to keep the WACC constant. Put another way: If MM's assumptions are correct, then it doesn't matter how a firm finances its operations and so capital structure decisions are irrelevant.

Even though some of their assumptions are obviously unrealistic, MM's irrelevance result is extremely important. By indicating the conditions under which capital structure is irrelevant, MM also provided us with clues about what is required for capital structure to be relevant and hence to affect a firm's value. The work of MM marked the beginning of modern capital structure research, and subsequent research has focused on relaxing the MM assumptions in order to develop a more realistic theory of capital structure.

Modigliani and Miller's thought process was just as important as their conclusion. It seems simple now, but their idea that two portfolios with identical cash flows must also have identical values changed the entire financial world because it led to the development of options and derivatives. It is no surprise that Modigliani and Miller received Nobel awards for their work.

15.3b Modigliani and Miller II: The Effect of Corporate Taxes

In 1963, MM published a follow-up paper in which they relaxed the assumption that there are no corporate taxes.[12] The Tax Code allows corporations to deduct interest payments as an expense, but dividend payments to stockholders are not deductible. The differential treatment encourages corporations to use debt in their capital structures. This means that interest payments reduce the taxes paid by a corporation, and if a corporation pays less to the government then more of its cash flow is available for its investors. In other words, the tax deductibility of the interest payments shields the firm's pre-tax income.

YOGI BERRA ON THE MM PROPOSITION

When a waitress asked Yogi Berra (Baseball Hall of Fame catcher for the New York Yankees) whether he wanted his pizza cut into four pieces or eight, Yogi replied: "Better make it four. I don't think I can eat eight."[a]

Yogi's quip helps convey the basic insight of Modigliani and Miller. The firm's choice of leverage "slices" the distribution of future cash flows in a way that is like slicing a pizza. MM recognized that holding a company's investment activities fixed is like fixing the size of the pizza; no information costs means that everyone sees the same pizza; no taxes means the IRS gets none of the pie; and no "contracting costs" means nothing sticks to the knife.

So, just as the substance of Yogi's meal is unaffected by whether the pizza is sliced into four pieces or eight, the economic substance of the firm is unaffected by whether the liability side of the balance sheet is sliced to include more or less debt—at least under the MM assumptions.

[a]Lee Green, *Sportswit* (New York: Fawcett Crest, 1984), p. 228.

Source: "Yogi Berra on the MM Proposition," *Journal of Applied Corporate Finance,* Winter 1995, p. 6. Reprinted by permission of Stern Stewart Management.

12. Franco Modigliani and Merton H. Miller, "Corporate Income Taxes and the Cost of Capital: A Correction," *American Economic Review,* June 1963, pp. 433–443.

As in their earlier paper, MM introduced a second important way of looking at the effect of capital structure: The value of a levered firm is the value of an otherwise identical unlevered firm plus the value of any "side effects." While others have expanded on this idea by considering other side effects, MM focused on the tax shield:

$$(15\text{–}6) \qquad V_L = V_U + \text{Value of side effects} = V_U + \text{Present value of tax shield}$$

Under their assumptions, they showed that the present value of the tax shield is equal to the corporate tax rate, T, multiplied by the amount of debt, D:

$$(15\text{–}7) \qquad V_L = V_U + TD$$

With a tax rate of about 40%, this implies that every dollar of debt adds about 40 cents of value to the firm, and this leads to the conclusion that the optimal capital structure is virtually 100% debt. MM also showed that the cost of equity, r_s, increases as leverage increases but that it doesn't increase quite as fast as it would if there were no taxes. As a result, under MM with corporate taxes the WACC falls as debt is added.

15.3c Miller: The Effect of Corporate and Personal Taxes

Merton Miller (this time without Modigliani) later brought in the effects of personal taxes.[13] The income from bonds is generally interest, which is taxed as personal income at rates (T_d) going up to 35%, while income from stocks generally comes partly from dividends and partly from capital gains. Long-term capital gains are taxed at a rate of 15%, and this tax is deferred until the stock is sold and the gain realized. If stock is held until the owner dies, no capital gains tax whatsoever must be paid. So, on average, returns on stocks are taxed at lower effective rates (T_s) than returns on debt.[14]

Because of the tax situation, Miller argued that investors are willing to accept relatively low before-tax returns on stock relative to the before-tax returns on bonds. (The situation here is similar to that with tax-exempt municipal bonds as discussed in Chapter 4 and preferred stocks held by corporate investors as discussed in Chapter 5.) For example, an investor might require a return of 10% on Strasburg's bonds, and if stock income were taxed at the same rate as bond income, the required rate of return on Strasburg's stock might be 16% because of the stock's greater risk. However, in view of the favorable treatment of income on the stock, investors might be willing to accept a before-tax return of only 14% on the stock.

Thus, as Miller pointed out, (1) the *deductibility of interest* favors the use of debt financing, but (2) the *more favorable tax treatment of income from stock* lowers the required rate of return on stock and thus favors the use of equity financing.

---

13. See Merton H. Miller, "Debt and Taxes," *Journal of Finance*, May 1977, pp. 261–275.
14. The Tax Code isn't quite as simple as this. An increasing number of investors face the Alternative Minimum Tax (AMT); see *Web Extension 7A* for a discussion. The AMT imposes a 28% tax rate on most income and an effective rate of 22% on long-term capital gains and dividends. Under the AMT there is still a spread between the tax rates on interest income and stock income, but the spread is narrower. See Leonard Burman, William Gale, Greg Leiserson, and Jeffrey Rohaly, "The AMT: What's Wrong and How to Fix It," *National Tax Journal*, September 2007, pp. 385–405.

Miller showed that the net impact of corporate and personal taxes is given by this equation:

$$V_L = V_U + \left[1 - \frac{(1 - T_c)(1 - T_s)}{(1 - T_d)}\right]D \qquad (15\text{–}8)$$

Here T_c is the corporate tax rate, T_s is the personal tax rate on income from stocks, and T_d is the tax rate on income from debt. Miller argued that the marginal tax rates on stock and debt balance out in such a way that the bracketed term in Equation 15-8 is zero and so $V_L = V_U$, but most observers believe there is still a tax advantage to debt if reasonable values of tax rates are assumed. For example, if the marginal corporate tax rate is 40%, the marginal rate on debt is 30%, and the marginal rate on stock is 12%, then the advantage of debt financing is

$$V_L = V_U + \left[1 - \frac{(1 - 0.40)(1 - 0.12)}{(1 - 0.30)}\right]D \qquad (15\text{–}8a)$$
$$= V_U + 0.25\,D$$

Thus it appears that the presence of personal taxes reduces but does not completely eliminate the advantage of debt financing.

15.3d Trade-off Theory

The results of Modigliani and Miller also depend on the assumption that there are no **bankruptcy costs**. However, bankruptcy can be quite costly. Firms in bankruptcy have very high legal and accounting expenses, and they also have a hard time retaining customers, suppliers, and employees. Moreover, bankruptcy often forces a firm to liquidate or sell assets for less than they would be worth if the firm were to continue operating. For example, if a steel manufacturer goes out of business it might be hard to find buyers for the company's blast furnaces. Such assets are often illiquid because they are configured to a company's individual needs and also because they are difficult to disassemble and move.

Note, too, that the *threat of bankruptcy,* not just bankruptcy per se, causes many of these same problems. Key employees jump ship, suppliers refuse to grant credit, customers seek more stable suppliers, and lenders demand higher interest rates and impose more restrictive loan covenants if potential bankruptcy looms.

Bankruptcy-related problems are most likely to arise when a firm includes a great deal of debt in its capital structure. Therefore, bankruptcy costs discourage firms from pushing their use of debt to excessive levels.

Bankruptcy-related costs have two components: (1) the probability of financial distress and (2) the costs that would be incurred if financial distress does occur. Firms whose earnings are more volatile, all else equal, face a greater chance of bankruptcy and should therefore use less debt than more stable firms. This is consistent with our earlier point that firms with high operating leverage, and thus greater business risk, should limit their use of financial leverage. Likewise, firms that would face high costs in the event of financial distress should rely less heavily on debt.

For example, firms whose assets are illiquid and thus would have to be sold at "fire sale" prices should limit their use of debt financing.

The preceding arguments led to the development of what is called the trade-off theory of leverage, in which firms trade off the benefits of debt financing (favorable corporate tax treatment) against higher interest rates and bankruptcy costs. In essence, the **trade-off theory** says that the value of a levered firm is equal to the value of an unlevered firm plus the value of any side effects, which include the tax shield and the expected costs due to financial distress. A summary of the trade-off theory is expressed graphically in Figure 15-4, and a list of observations about the figure follows here.

1. Under the assumptions of the MM model with corporate taxes, a firm's value increases linearly for every dollar of debt. The line labeled "MM Result Incorporating the Effects of Corporate Taxation" in Figure 15-4 expresses the relationship between value and debt under those assumptions.

2. There is some threshold level of debt, labeled D_1 in Figure 15-4, below which the probability of bankruptcy is so low as to be immaterial. Beyond D_1, however, expected bankruptcy-related costs become increasingly important, and they reduce the tax benefits of debt at an increasing rate. In the range from D_1 to D_2, expected bankruptcy-related costs reduce but do not completely offset the tax benefits of debt, so the stock price rises (but at a decreasing rate) as the debt ratio increases. However, beyond D_2, expected bankruptcy-related costs exceed the tax benefits, so from this point on increasing the debt ratio lowers the value of the stock. Therefore, D_2 is the optimal capital structure. Of course, D_1 and D_2 vary from firm to firm, depending on their business risks and bankruptcy costs.

3. Although theoretical and empirical work confirms the general shape of the curve in Figure 15-4, this graph must be taken as an approximation and not as a precisely defined function.

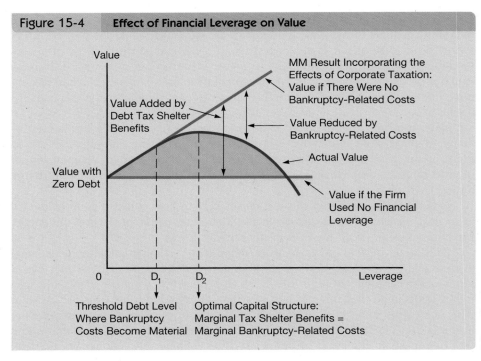

Figure 15-4 **Effect of Financial Leverage on Value**

15.3e Signaling Theory

It was assumed by MM that investors have the same information about a firm's prospects as its managers—this is called **symmetric information**. However, managers in fact often have better information than outside investors. This is called **asymmetric information**, and it has an important effect on the optimal capital structure. To see why, consider two situations, one in which the company's managers know that its prospects are extremely positive (Firm P) and one in which the managers know that the future looks negative (Firm N).

Suppose, for example, that Firm P's R&D labs have just discovered a nonpatentable cure for the common cold. They want to keep the new product a secret as long as possible to delay competitors' entry into the market. New plants must be built to make the new product, so capital must be raised. How should Firm P's management raise the needed capital? If it sells stock then, when profits from the new product start flowing in, the price of the stock would rise sharply and the purchasers of the new stock would make a bonanza. The current stockholders (including the managers) would also do well, but not as well as they would have done if the company had not sold stock before the price increased, because then they would not have had to share the benefits of the new product with the new stockholders. Therefore, *we should expect a firm with very positive prospects to avoid selling stock and instead to raise required new capital by other means, including debt usage beyond the normal target capital structure.*[15]

Now let's consider Firm N. Suppose its managers have information that new orders are off sharply because a competitor has installed new technology that has improved its products' quality. Firm N must upgrade its own facilities, at a high cost, just to maintain its current sales. As a result, its return on investment will fall (but not by as much as if it took no action, which would lead to a 100% loss through bankruptcy). How should Firm N raise the needed capital? Here the situation is just the reverse of that facing Firm P, which did not want to sell stock so as to avoid having to share the benefits of future developments. *A firm with negative prospects would want to sell stock, which would mean bringing in new investors to share the losses!*[16] The conclusion from all this is that firms with extremely bright prospects prefer not to finance through new stock offerings, whereas firms with poor prospects like to finance with outside equity. How should you, as an investor, react to this conclusion? You ought to say: "If I see that a company plans to issue new stock, this should worry me because I know that management would not want to issue stock if future prospects looked good. However, management *would* want to issue stock if things looked bad. Therefore, I should lower my estimate of the firm's value, other things held constant, if it plans to issue new stock."

If you gave this answer then your views are consistent with those of sophisticated portfolio managers. In a nutshell: *The announcement of a stock offering is generally taken as a **signal** that the firm's prospects as seen by its own management are not good; conversely, a debt offering is taken as a positive signal.* Notice that Firm N's managers cannot make a false signal to investors by mimicking Firm P and issuing debt. With its unfavorable future prospects, issuing debt could soon force Firm N into bankruptcy. Given the resulting damage to the personal wealth and reputations of N's managers, they cannot afford to mimic Firm P. All of this

---

15. It would be illegal for Firm P's managers to personally purchase more shares on the basis of their inside knowledge of the new product.

16. Of course, Firm N would have to make certain disclosures when it offered new shares to the public, but it might be able to meet the legal requirements without fully disclosing management's worst fears.

suggests that when a firm announces a new stock offering, more often than not the price of its stock will decline. Empirical studies have shown that this is indeed true.

15.3f Reserve Borrowing Capacity

Because issuing stock sends a negative signal and tends to depress the stock price even if the company's true prospects are bright, a company should try to maintain a **reserve borrowing capacity** so that debt can be used if an especially good investment opportunity comes along. This means that *firms should, in normal times, use more equity and less debt than is suggested by the tax benefit–bankruptcy cost trade-off model depicted in Figure 15-4.*

15.3g The Pecking Order Hypothesis

The presence of flotation costs and asymmetric information may cause a firm to raise capital according to a **pecking order**. In this situation, a firm first raises capital internally by reinvesting its net income and selling its short-term marketable securities. When that supply of funds has been exhausted, the firm will issue debt and perhaps preferred stock. Only as a last resort will the firm issue common stock.[17]

15.3h Using Debt Financing to Constrain Managers

Agency problems may arise if managers and shareholders have different objectives. Such conflicts are particularly likely when the firm's managers have too much cash at their disposal. Managers often use excess cash to finance pet projects or for perquisites such as nicer offices, corporate jets, and sky boxes at sports arenas—none of which have much to do with maximizing stock prices. Even worse, managers might be tempted to pay too much for an acquisition, something that could cost shareholders hundreds of millions of dollars. By contrast, managers with limited "excess cash flow" are less able to make wasteful expenditures.

Firms can reduce excess cash flow in a variety of ways. One way is to funnel some of it back to shareholders through higher dividends or stock repurchases. Another alternative is to shift the capital structure toward more debt in the hope that higher debt service requirements will force managers to be more disciplined. If debt is not serviced as required then the firm will be forced into bankruptcy, in which case its managers would likely lose their jobs. Therefore, a manager is less likely to buy an expensive new corporate jet if the firm has large debt service requirements that could cost the manager his or her job. In short, high levels of debt **bond the cash flow**, since much of it is precommitted to servicing the debt.

A **leveraged buyout (LBO)** is one way to bond cash flow. In an LBO, a large amount of debt and a small amount of cash are used to finance the purchase of a company's shares, after which the firm "goes private." The first wave of LBOs was in the mid-1980s; private equity funds led the buyouts of the late 1990s and early 2000s. Many of these LBOs were specifically designed to reduce corporate waste. As noted, high debt payments force managers to conserve cash by eliminating unnecessary expenditures.

---

17. For more information, see Jonathon Baskin, "An Empirical Investigation of the Pecking Order Hypothesis," *Financial Management*, Spring 1989, pp. 26–35.

Of course, increasing debt and reducing the available cash flow has its downside: It increases the risk of bankruptcy. Ben Bernanke, current (summer 2011) chairman of the Fed, has argued that adding debt to a firm's capital structure is like putting a dagger into the steering wheel of a car.[18] The dagger—which points toward your stomach—motivates you to drive more carefully, but you may get stabbed if someone runs into you—even if you are being careful. The analogy applies to corporations in the following sense: Higher debt forces managers to be more careful with shareholders' money, but even well-run firms could face bankruptcy (get stabbed) if some event beyond their control occurs: a war, an earthquake, a strike, or a recession. To complete the analogy, the capital structure decision comes down to deciding the length of the dagger that stockholders should use to keep managers in line.

Finally, too much debt may overconstrain managers. A large portion of a manager's personal wealth and reputation is tied to a single company, so managers are not well diversified. When faced with a positive-NPV project that is risky, a manager may decide that it's not worth taking on the risk even though well-diversified stockholders would find the risk acceptable. As previously mentioned, this is an underinvestment problem. The more debt the firm has, the greater the likelihood of financial distress and thus the greater the likelihood that managers will forgo risky projects even if they have positive NPVs.

15.3i The Investment Opportunity Set and Reserve Borrowing Capacity

Bankruptcy and financial distress are costly, and, as just reiterated, this can discourage highly levered firms from undertaking risky new investments. If potential new investments, although risky, have positive net present values, then high levels of debt can be doubly costly—the expected financial distress and bankruptcy costs are high, and the firm loses potential value by not making some potentially profitable investments. On the other hand, if a firm has very few profitable investment opportunities then high levels of debt can keep managers from wasting money by investing in poor projects. For such companies, increases in the debt ratio can actually increase the value of the firm.

Thus, in addition to the tax, signaling, bankruptcy, and managerial constraint effects discussed previously, the firm's optimal capital structure is related to its set of investment opportunities. Firms with many profitable opportunities should maintain their ability to invest by using low levels of debt, which is also consistent with maintaining reserve borrowing capacity. Firms with few profitable investment opportunities should use high levels of debt (which have high interest payments) to impose managerial constraint.[19]

15.3j Windows of Opportunity

If markets are efficient, then security prices should reflect all available information; hence they are neither underpriced nor overpriced (except during the time it takes

18. See Ben Bernanke, "Is There Too Much Corporate Debt?" *Federal Reserve Bank of Philadelphia Business Review,* September/October 1989, pp. 3–13.
19. See Michael J. Barclay and Clifford W. Smith, Jr., "The Capital Structure Puzzle: Another Look at the Evidence," *Journal of Applied Corporate Finance,* Spring 1999, pp. 8–20.

prices to move to a new equilibrium caused by the release of new information). The *windows of opportunity theory* states that managers don't believe this and supposes instead that stock prices and interest rates are sometimes either too low or too high relative to their true fundamental values. In particular, the theory suggests that managers issue equity when they believe stock market prices are abnormally high and issue debt when they believe interest rates are abnormally low. In other words, they try to time the market.[20] Notice that this differs from signaling theory because no asymmetric information is involved: These managers aren't basing their beliefs on insider information, just on a difference of opinion with the market consensus.

Self Test	Why does the MM theory with corporate taxes lead to 100% debt?
	Explain how *asymmetric information* and *signals* affect capital structure decisions.
	What is meant by *reserve borrowing capacity,* and why is it important to firms?
	How can the use of debt serve to discipline managers?

15.4 Capital Structure Evidence and Implications

There have been hundreds, perhaps even thousands, of papers testing the capital structure theories described in the previous section. We can cover only the highlights here, beginning with the empirical evidence.[21]

15.4a Empirical Evidence

Studies show that firms do benefit from the tax deductibility of interest payments, with a typical firm increasing in value by about $0.10 for every dollar of debt. This is much less than the corporate tax rate, which supports the Miller model (with corporate and personal taxes) more than the MM model (with only corporate taxes). Recent evidence shows that the cost of bankruptcies can be as much as 10% to 20% of the firm's value.[22] Thus, the evidence shows the existence of tax benefits and financial distress costs, which provides support for the trade-off theory.

A particularly interesting study by Professors Mehotra, Mikkelson, and Partch examined the capital structure of firms that were spun off from their parents.[23] The financing choices of existing firms might be influenced by their past financing choices and by the costs of moving from one capital structure to another, but because spin-offs

---

20. See Malcolm Baker and Jeffrey Wurgler, "Market Timing and Capital Structure," *Journal of Finance,* February 2002, pp. 1–32.

21. This section also draws heavily from Barclay and Smith, "The Capital Structure Puzzle," cited in footnote 19; Jay Ritter, ed., *Recent Developments in Corporate Finance* (Northampton, MA: Edward Elgar Publishing Inc., 2005); and a presentation by Jay Ritter at the 2003 FMA meeting, "The Windows of Opportunity Theory of Capital Structure."

22. The *expected cost* of financial distress is the product of bankruptcy costs and the probability of bankruptcy. At moderate levels of debt with low probabilities of bankruptcy, the expected cost of financial distress would be much less than the actual bankruptcy costs if the firm failed.

23. See V. Mehotra, W. Mikkelson, and M. Partch, "The Design of Financial Policies in Corporate Spin-offs," *Review of Financial Studies,* Winter 2003, pp. 1359–1388.

are newly created companies, managers can choose a capital structure without regard to these issues. The study found that more profitable firms (which have a lower expected probability of bankruptcy) and more asset-intensive firms (which have better collateral and thus a lower cost of bankruptcy should one occur) have higher levels of debt. These findings support the trade-off theory.

However, there is also evidence that is inconsistent with the static optimal target capital structure implied by the trade-off theory. For example, stock prices are volatile, which frequently causes a firm's actual market-based debt ratio to deviate from its target. However, such deviations don't cause firms to immediately return to their target by issuing or repurchasing securities. Instead, firms tend to make a partial adjustment each year, moving about one-third of the way toward their target capital structure.[24] This evidence supports the idea of a more dynamic trade-off theory in which firms have target capital structures but don't strive to maintain them too closely.

If a stock price has a big run-up, which reduces the debt ratio, then the trade-off theory suggests that the firm should issue debt to return to its target. However, firms tend to do the opposite, issuing stock after big run-ups. This is much more consistent with the windows of opportunity theory, with managers trying to time the market by issuing stock when they perceive the market to be overvalued. Furthermore, firms tend to issue debt when stock prices and interest rates are low. The maturity of the issued debt seems to reflect an attempt to time interest rates: Firms tend to issue short-term debt if the term structure is upward sloping but long-term debt if the term structure is flat. Again, these facts suggest that managers try to time the market, which is consistent with the windows of opportunity theory.

Firms issue equity much less frequently than debt. On the surface, this seems to support both the pecking order hypothesis and the signaling hypothesis. The pecking order hypothesis predicts that firms with a high level of informational asymmetry, which causes equity issuances to be costly, should issue debt before issuing equity. Yet we often see the opposite, with high-growth firms (which usually have greater informational asymmetry) issuing more equity than debt. Also, many highly profitable firms could afford to issue debt (which comes before equity in the pecking order) but instead choose to issue equity. With respect to the signaling hypothesis, consider the case of firms that have large increases in earnings that were unanticipated by the market. If managers have superior information, then they will anticipate these upcoming performance improvements and issue debt before the increase. Such firms do, in fact, tend to issue debt slightly more frequently than other firms, but the difference isn't economically meaningful.

Many firms have less debt than might be expected, and many have large amounts of short-term investments. This is especially true for firms with high market/book ratios (which indicate many growth options as well as informational asymmetry). This behavior is consistent with the hypothesis that investment opportunities influence attempts to maintain reserve borrowing capacity. It is also consistent with tax considerations, since low-growth firms (which have more debt) are more likely to benefit from the tax shield. This behavior is not consistent with the pecking order hypothesis, where low-growth firms (which often have high free cash flow) would be able to avoid issuing debt by raising funds internally.

To summarize these results, it appears that firms try to capture debt's tax benefits while avoiding financial distress costs. However, they also allow their debt

---

24. See Mark Flannery and Kasturi Rangan, "Partial Adjustment toward Target Capital Structures," *Journal of Financial Economics,* Vol. 79, 2006, pp. 469–506.

TAKING A LOOK AT GLOBAL CAPITAL STRUCTURES

To what extent does capital structure vary across different countries? The accompanying table, which is taken from a study by Raghuram Rajan and Luigi Zingales, gives the median debt ratios of firms in the largest industrial countries.

Rajan and Zingales show that there is considerable variation in capital structure among firms within each of the seven countries. However, they also show that

capital structures for the firms in each country are generally determined by a similar set of factors: firm size, profitability, market-to-book ratio, and the ratio of fixed assets to total assets. All in all, the Rajan–Zingales study suggests that the points developed in the chapter apply to firms around the world.

MEDIAN PERCENTAGE OF DEBT TO TOTAL ASSETS IN DIFFERENT COUNTRIES

Country	Book Value Debt Ratio
Canada	32%
France	18
Germany	11
Italy	21
Japan	21
United Kingdom	10
United States	25

Source: Raghuram G. Rajan and Luigi Zingales, "What Do We Know about Capital Structure? Some Evidence from International Data," *Journal of Finance*, December 1995, pp. 1421–1460.

ratios to deviate from the static optimal target ratio implied by the trade-off theory. There is a little evidence indicating that firms follow a pecking order and use security issuances as signals, but there is much more evidence in support of the windows of opportunity theory. Finally, it appears that firms often maintain reserve borrowing capacity, especially firms with many growth opportunities or problems with informational asymmetry.[25]

15.4b Implications for Managers

Managers should explicitly consider tax benefits when making capital structure decisions. Tax benefits obviously are more valuable for firms with high tax rates.

---

25. For more on empirical tests of capital structure theory, see Gregor Andrade and Steven Kaplan, "How Costly Is Financial (Not Economic) Distress? Evidence from Highly Leveraged Transactions That Became Distressed," *Journal of Finance*, Vol. 53, 1998, pp. 1443–1493; Malcolm Baker, Robin Greenwood, and Jeffrey Wurgler, "The Maturity of Debt Issues and Predictable Variation in Bond Returns," *Journal of Financial Economics*, November 2003, pp. 261–291; Murray Z. Frank and Vidhan K. Goyal, "Testing the Pecking Order Theory of Capital Structure," *Journal of Financial Economics*, February 2003, pp. 217–248; and Michael Long and Ileen Malitz, "The Investment-Financing Nexus: Some Empirical Evidence," *Midland Corporate Finance Journal*, Fall 1985, pp. 53–59.

Firms can utilize tax loss carryforwards and carrybacks, but the time value of money means that tax benefits are more valuable for firms with stable, positive pre-tax income. Therefore, a firm whose sales are relatively stable can safely take on more debt and incur higher fixed charges than a company with volatile sales. Other things being equal, a firm with less operating leverage is better able to employ financial leverage because it will have less business risk and less volatile earnings.

Managers should also consider the expected cost of financial distress, which depends on the probability and cost of distress. Notice that stable sales and lower operating leverage provide tax benefits but also reduce the *probability* of financial distress. One *cost* of financial distress comes from lost investment opportunities. Firms with profitable investment opportunities need to be able to fund them, either by holding higher levels of marketable securities or by maintaining excess borrowing capacity. An astute corporate treasurer made this statement to the authors:

> *Our company can earn a lot more money from good capital budgeting and operating decisions than from good financing decisions. Indeed, we are not sure exactly how financing decisions affect our stock price, but we know for sure that having to turn down a promising venture because funds are not available will reduce our long-run profitability.*

Another cost of financial distress is the possibility of being forced to sell assets to meet liquidity needs. General-purpose assets that can be used by many businesses are relatively liquid and make good collateral, in contrast to special-purpose assets. Thus, real estate companies are usually highly leveraged, whereas companies involved in technological research are not.

Asymmetric information also has a bearing on capital structure decisions. For example, suppose a firm has just successfully completed an R&D program, and it forecasts higher earnings in the immediate future. However, the new earnings are not yet anticipated by investors and hence are not reflected in the stock price. This company should not issue stock—it should finance with debt until the higher earnings materialize and are reflected in the stock price. Then it could issue common stock, retire the debt, and return to its target capital structure.

Managers should consider conditions in the stock and bond markets. For example, during a recent credit crunch, the junk bond market dried up and there was simply no market at a "reasonable" interest rate for any new long-term bonds rated below BBB. Therefore, low-rated companies in need of capital were forced to go to the stock market or to the short-term debt market, regardless of their target capital structures. When conditions eased, however, these companies sold bonds to get their capital structures back on target.

Finally, managers should always consider lenders' and rating agencies' attitudes. For example, one large utility was recently told by Moody's and Standard & Poor's that its bonds would be downgraded if it issued more debt. This influenced the utility's decision to finance its expansion with common equity. This doesn't mean that managers should never increase debt if it will cause their bond rating to fall, but managers should always factor this into their decision making.[26]

---

26. For some insights into how practicing financial managers view the capital structure decision, see John Graham and Campbell Harvey, "The Theory and Practice of Corporate Finance: Evidence from the Field," *Journal of Financial Economics,* Vol. 60, 2001, pp. 187–243; Ravindra R. Kamath, "Long-Term Financing Decisions: Views and Practices of Financial Managers of NYSE Firms," *Financial Review,* May 1997, pp. 331–356; and Edgar Norton, "Factors Affecting Capital Structure Decisions," *Financial Review,* August 1991, pp. 431–446.

Self Test

Which capital structure theories does the empirical evidence seem to support?

What issues should managers consider when making capital structure decisions?

15.5 Estimating the Optimal Capital Structure

Managers should choose the capital structure that maximizes shareholders' wealth. The basic approach is to consider a trial capital structure, based on the market values of the debt and equity, and then estimate the wealth of the shareholders under this capital structure. This approach is repeated until an optimal capital structure is identified. There are several steps in the analysis of each potential capital structure: (1) Estimate the interest rate the firm will pay. (2) Estimate the cost of equity. (3) Estimate the weighted average cost of capital. (4) Estimate the value of operations, which is the present value of free cash flows discounted by the new WACC. The objective is to find the amount of debt financing that maximizes the value of operations. As we will show, this is also the capital structure that maximizes shareholder wealth and the intrinsic stock price. The following sections explain each of these steps, using the company we considered earlier, Strasburg Electronics.

15.5a Estimating the Cost of Debt, r_d

Recall that Strasburg chose Plan L, with high operating leverage and a capital structure consisting of 20% debt. The CFO asked Strasburg's investment bankers to estimate the cost of debt at different capital structures. The investment bankers began by analyzing industry conditions and prospects. They appraised Strasburg's business risk based on its past financial statements and its current technology and customer base. The bankers also forecasted financial statements with different capital structures and analyzed such key ratios as the current ratio and the times-interest-earned ratio. Finally, they factored in current conditions in the financial markets, including interest rates paid by firms in Strasburg's industry. Based on their analysis and judgment, they estimated interest rates at various capital structures as shown in Row 2 of Figure 15-5, starting with a 7.7% cost of debt for the first dollar of debt. This rate increases to 16% if the firm finances 60% of its capital structure with debt. Strasburg's current situation is in Column D and is shown in blue. (We will explain all the rows in Figure 15-5 in the following discussion.)

15.5b Estimating the Cost of Equity, r_s

An increase in the debt ratio also increases the risk faced by shareholders, and this has an effect on the cost of equity, r_s. Recall from Chapter 2 that a stock's beta is the relevant measure of risk for diversified investors. Moreover, it has been demonstrated, both theoretically and empirically, that beta increases with financial leverage. The Hamada equation specifies the effect of financial leverage on beta:[27]

---

27. See Robert S. Hamada, "Portfolio Analysis, Market Equilibrium, and Corporation Finance," *Journal of Finance*, March 1969, pp. 13–31. For a comprehensive framework, see Robert A. Taggart, Jr., "Consistent Valuation and Cost of Capital Expressions with Corporate and Personal Taxes," *Financial Management*, Autumn 1991, pp. 8–20.

Figure 15-5	Estimating Strasburg's Optimal Capital Structure (Millions of Dollars)

	A	B	C	D				
151				Percent of Firm Financed with Debt (w_d)				
152		0%	10%	20%	30%	40%	50%	60%
153 1.	w_s	100.00%	90.00%	80.00%	70.00%	60.00%	50.00%	40.00%
154 2.	r_d	7.70%	7.80%	8.00%	8.50%	9.90%	12.00%	16.00%
155 3.	b	1.09	1.16	1.25	1.37	1.52	1.74	2.07
156 4.	r_s	12.82%	13.26%	13.80%	14.50%	15.43%	16.73%	18.69%
157 5.	r_d (1–T)	4.62%	4.68%	4.80%	5.10%	5.94%	7.20%	9.60%
158 6.	WACC	12.82%	12.40%	12.00%	11.68%	11.63%	11.97%	13.24%
159 7.	V_{op}	$233.98	$241.96	$250.00	$256.87	$257.86	$250.68	$226.65
160 8.	Debt	$0.00	$24.20	$50.00	$77.06	$103.14	$125.34	$135.99
161 9.	Equity	$233.98	$217.76	$200.00	$179.81	$154.72	$125.34	$90.66
162 10.	# shares	12.72	11.34	10.00	8.69	7.44	6.25	5.13
163 11.	Stock price	$18.40	$19.20	$20.00	$20.69	$20.79	$20.07	$17.66
164 12.	Net income	$30.00	$28.87	$27.60	$26.07	$23.87	$20.98	$16.95
165 13.	EPS	$2.36	$2.54	$2.76	$3.00	$3.21	$3.36	$3.30

Notes:
1. The percent financed with equity is: $w_s = 1 - w_d$.
2. The interest rate on debt, r_d, is obtained from investment bankers.
3. Beta is estimated using Hamada's formula, the unlevered beta of 1.09, and a tax rate of 40%:
   $b = b_U [1 + (1 - T) \times (w_d/w_s)]$.
4. The cost of equity is estimated using the CAPM formula with a risk-free rate of 6.3% and a market risk premium of 6%: $r_s = r_{RF} + (RP_M)b$.
5. The after-tax cost of debt is: $r_d(1 - T)$, where T = 40%.
6. The weighted average cost of capital is calculated as $WACC = w_s r_s + w_d r_d(1 - T)$.
7. The value of the firm's operations is calculated as $V_{op} = [FCF(1 + g)] / (WACC - g)$, where FCF = $30 million and g = 0.
8. Debt = $w_d \times V_{op}$.
9. The intrinsic value of equity after the recapitalization and repurchase is $S_{Post} = V_{op} - Debt = w_s \times V_{op}$.
10. The number of shares after the recap has been completed is found using this equation:
    $n_{Post} = n_{Prior} \times [(V_{opNew} - D_{New}) / (V_{opNew} - D_{Old})]$. The subscript "Old" indicates values from the original capital structure, where $w_d = 20\%$; the subscript "New" indicates values at the current capital structure after the recap and repurchase; and the subscript "Post" indicates values after the recap and repurchase.
11. The price after the recap and repurchase is $P_{Post} = S_{Post}/n_{Post}$, but we can also find the price as $P_{Post} = (V_{opNew} - D_{Old})/n_{Prior}$.
12. EBIT is $50 million; see Figure 15-1. Net income is $NI = (EBIT - r_dD)(1 - T)$.
13. Earnings per share is $EPS = NI/n_{Post}$.

$$b = b_U [1 + (1 - T)(D/S)] \qquad (15\text{–}9)$$

Here D is the market value of the debt and S is the market value of the equity. The Hamada equation shows how increases in the market value debt/equity ratio increase beta. Here b_U is the firm's **unlevered beta** coefficient—that is, the beta it would have if it had no debt. In that case, beta would depend entirely on business risk and thus be a measure of the firm's "basic business risk."

Sometimes it is more convenient to work with the percentages of debt and equity at which the firm is financed (w_d and w_s) rather than the dollar values of D and S. Notice that w_d and w_s are defined as D/(D + S) and S/(D + S), respectively.

This means that the ratio w_d/w_s is equal to the ratio D/S. Substituting these values gives us another form of Hamada's formula:

(15–9a)
$$b = b_U [1 + (1 - T)(w_d/w_s)]$$

Often we know the current capital structure and beta but wish to know the unlevered beta. We find this by rearranging Equation 15-9a as follows:

(15–10)
$$b_U = b/[1 + (1 - T)(w_d/w_s)]$$

For Strasburg, the unlevered beta is

$$b_U = 1.25/[1 + (1 - 0.40)(0.20/0.80)]$$
$$= 1.087$$

Using this unlevered beta, we can then apply Hamada's formula in Equation 15-9a to determine estimates of Strasburg's beta for different capital structures. These results are reported in Line 3 of Figure 15-5.

Recall from Section 15.2 that the risk-free rate is 6.3% and the market risk premium is 6%. We can use the CAPM and the previously estimated betas to estimate Strasburg's cost of equity for different capital structures (which cause Strasburg's beta to change). These results are shown in Line 4 of Figure 15-5. As expected, Strasburg's cost of equity increases as its debt increases. Figure 15-6 graphs Strasburg's required return on equity at different debt ratios. Observe that the cost of

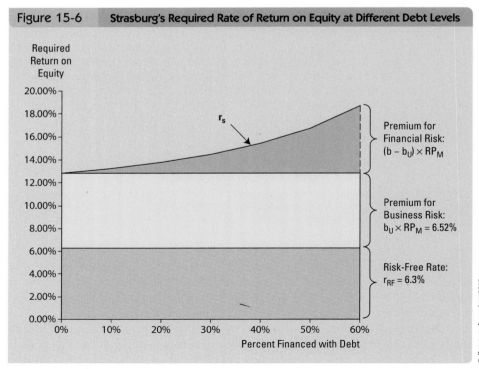

Figure 15-6   Strasburg's Required Rate of Return on Equity at Different Debt Levels

equity consists of the 6.3% risk-free rate, a constant premium for business risk in the amount of $RP_M(b_U) = 6.522\%$, and a premium for financial risk in the amount of $RP_M(b - b_U)$ that starts at zero (because $b = b_U$ for zero debt) but rises at an increasing rate as the debt ratio increases.

15.5c Estimating the Weighted Average Cost of Capital, WACC

Line 6 of Figure 15-5 shows Strasburg's weighted average cost of capital, WACC, at different capital structures. As the debt ratio increases, the costs of both debt and equity rise, at first slowly but then at an accelerating rate. Eventually, the increasing costs of these two components offset the fact that more debt (which is still less costly than equity) is being used. At 40% debt, Strasburg's WACC hits a minimum of 11.63%; Column F is shown in red to indicate that it is the capital structure with the minimum WACC. Notice that the WACC begins to increase for capital structures with more than 40% debt. Figure 15-7 shows how the WACC changes as debt increases.

Note too that, even though the component cost of equity is always higher than that of debt, only using debt would not maximize value. If Strasburg were to issue more than 40% debt, then the costs of both debt and equity would increase in such a way that the overall WACC would increase, because the cost of debt would increase by more than the cost of equity.

15.5d Estimating the Firm's Value

As we showed in Section 15.2, Strasburg currently has a $250 million intrinsic value of operations: $w_d = 20\%$, WACC = 12%, FCF = $30 million, and zero growth in FCF. Using the same approach as in Section 15.2, we can use the data in Figure 15-5 to estimate Strasburg's value of operations at different capital structures; these results are reported in Line 7 of Figure 15-5 and are graphed in Figure 15-8.[28] The maximum

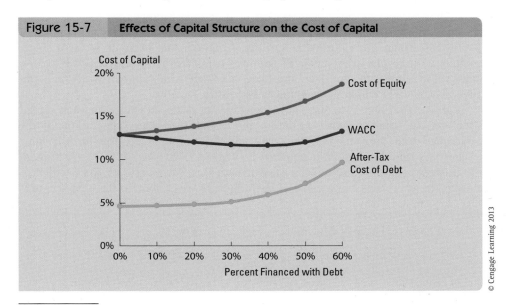

Figure 15-7   Effects of Capital Structure on the Cost of Capital

© Cengage Learning 2013

---

28. In this analysis we assume that Strasburg's expected EBIT and FCF are constant for the various capital structures. In a more refined analysis we might try to estimate any possible declines in FCF at high levels of debt as the threat of bankruptcy becomes imminent.

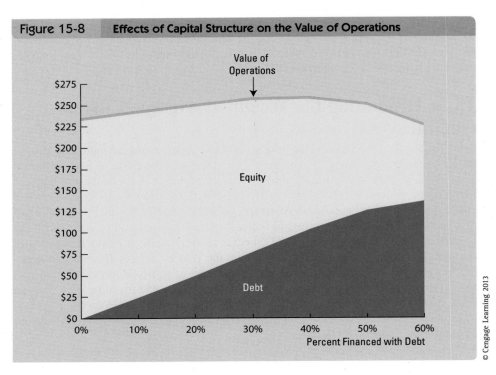

Figure 15-8 **Effects of Capital Structure on the Value of Operations**

value of $257.86 million occurs at a capital structure with 40% debt, which also is the capital structure that minimizes the WACC.

Notice that the value of the firm initially increases but then begins to fall. As discussed earlier, the value initially rises because the WACC initially falls. But the rising costs of equity and debt eventually cause the WACC to increase, causing the value of the firm to fall. Notice how flat the curve is around the optimal level of debt. Thus, it doesn't make a great deal of difference whether Strasburg's capital structure has 30% debt or 40% debt. Also, notice that the maximum value is about 10% greater than the value with no debt. Although this example is for a single company, the results are typical: The optimal capital structure can add 7% to 15% more value relative to zero debt, and there is a fairly wide range of w_d (from about 20% to 50%) over which value changes very little.

Figures 15-5 and 15-8 also show the values of debt and equity for each capital structure. The value of debt is found by multiplying the value of operations by the percentage of the firm that is financed by debt: Debt = $w_d \times V_{op}$. The intrinsic value of equity is found in a similar manner: S = V_{op} − Debt = $w_s \times V_{op}$. Even though the intrinsic value of equity falls as debt increases, the wealth of shareholders is maximized at the maximum value of operations, as we explain in the next section.

Self Test

What happens to the costs of debt and equity when the leverage increases? Explain.

Use the Hamada equation to calculate the unlevered beta for JAB Industries, assuming the following data: Levered beta = b = 1.4; T = 40%; w_d = 45%. **(0.939)**

Suppose r_{RF} = 6% and RP_M = 5%. What would be the cost of equity for JAB Industries if it had no debt? **(10.7%)** If w_d were 45%? **(13.0%)**

15.6 Anatomy of a Recapitalization

Strasburg should **recapitalize**, meaning that it should issue enough additional debt to optimize its capital structure, and then use the debt proceeds to repurchase stock. As shown in Figure 15-5, a capital structure with 40% debt is optimal. But before tackling the **recap**, as it is commonly called, let's consider the sequence of events, starting with the situation before Strasburg issues any additional debt. Figure 15-3 shows the valuation analysis of Strasburg at a capital structure consisting of 20% debt and 80% equity. These results are repeated in Column 1 of Figure 15-9, along with the shareholder wealth, which consists entirely of $200 million in stock before the repurchase. The next step is to examine the impact of Strasburg's debt issuance.

15.6a Strasburg Issues New Debt but Has Not Yet Repurchased Stock

The next step in the recap is to issue debt and announce the firm's intent to repurchase stock with the newly issued debt. At the optimal capital structure of 40% debt, the value of the firm's operations is $257.86 million, as calculated in Figure 15-5 and repeated in Column 2 of Figure 15-9. This value of operations is greater than the $250 million value of operations for $w_d = 20\%$ because the WACC is lower. Notice that Strasburg raised its debt from $50 million to $103.14 million, an increase of $53.14 million. Because Column 2 reports data prior to the repurchase, Strasburg has short-term investments in the amount of $53.14 million, the amount that was raised in the debt issuance but that has not yet been used to repurchase stock.[29] As Figure 15-9 shows, Strasburg's intrinsic value of equity is $207.86 million.

Because Strasburg has not yet repurchased any stock, it still has 10 million shares outstanding. Therefore, the price per share after the debt issue but prior to the repurchase is

$$P_{Prior} = S_{Prior}/n_{Prior}$$
$$= \$207.86/10 = \$20.79$$

Column 2 of Figure 15-9 summarizes these calculations and also shows the wealth of the shareholders. The shareholders own Strasburg's equity, which is worth $207.86 million. Strasburg has not yet made any cash distributions to shareholders, so the total wealth of shareholders is $207.86 million. The new wealth of $207.86 million is greater than the initial wealth of $200 million, so the recapitalization has added value to Strasburg's shareholders. Notice also that the recapitalization caused the intrinsic stock price to increase from $20.00 to $20.79.

Summarizing these results, we see that the issuance of debt and the resulting change in the optimal capital structure caused (1) the WACC to decrease, (2) the value of operations to increase, (3) shareholder wealth to increase, and (4) the stock price to increase.

15.6b Strasburg Repurchases Stock

What happens to the stock price during the repurchase? In Chapter 17 we discuss repurchases and note that a repurchase does not change the stock price. It is true

---

29. These calculations are shown in the *Excel* file **Ch15 Tool Kit.xls** on the textbook's Web site. The values reported in the text are rounded, but the values used in calculations in the spreadsheet are not rounded.

Figure 15-9   Anatomy of a Recapitalization (Millions, Except Per Share Data)

	A	B	C	D	E	F
335					After Debt	
336				Before Issuing	Issue, but Prior	Post
337				Additional Debt	to Repurchase	Repurchase
338				(1)	(2)	(3)
339						
340		Percent financed with debt: w_d		20%	40%	40%
341						
342		Value of operations		$250.00	$257.86	$257.86
343		+ Value of ST investments		0.00	53.14	0.00
344		Total intrinsic value of firm		$250.00	$311.00	$257.86
345		− Debt		50.00	103.14	103.14
346		Intrinsic value of equity		$200.00	$207.86	$154.72
347		÷ Number of shares		10.00	10.00	7.44
348		Intrinsic price per share		$20.00	$20.79	$20.79
349						
350		Value of stock		$200.00	$207.86	$154.72
351		+ Cash distributed in repurchase		0.00	0.00	53.14
352		Wealth of shareholders		$200.00	$207.86	$207.86

Notes:
1. The value of ST investments in Column 1 is equal to the amount of cash raised by issuing additional debt but that has not been used to repurchase shares: ST investments $= D_{New} - D_{Old}$.
2. The value of ST investments in Column 3 is zero because the funds have been used to repurchase shares of stock.
3. The number of shares in Column 3 reflects the shares repurchased: $n_{Post} = n_{Prior} - (Cash_{Rep}/P_{Prior}) = n_{Prior} - [(D_{New} - D_{Old})/P_{Prior}]$.

that the additional debt will change the WACC and the stock price prior to the repurchase (P_{Prior}), but the subsequent repurchase itself will not affect the post-repurchase stock price (P_{Post}).[30] Therefore, $P_{Post} = P_{Prior}$. (Keep in mind that P_{Prior} is the price immediately prior to the repurchase, not the price prior to the event that led to the cash available for the repurchase, such as the issuance of debt in this example.)

Strasburg uses the entire amount of cash raised by the debt issue to repurchase stock. The total cash raised is equal to $D_{New} - D_{Old}$. The number of shares repurchased is equal to the cash raised by issuing debt divided by the repurchase price:

$$(15\text{–}11) \qquad \text{Number of shares repurchased} = \frac{D_{New} - D_{Old}}{P_{Prior}}$$

Strasburg repurchases ($103.14 − $50)/$20.79 = 2.56 million shares of stock.

---

30. As we discuss in Chapter 17, a stock repurchase may be a signal of a company's future prospects or it may be the way a company "announces" a change in capital structure, and either of these situations could have an impact on estimated free cash flows or WACC. However, neither situation applies to Strasburg.

The number of remaining shares after the repurchase, n_{Post}, is equal to the initial number of shares minus the number that is repurchased:

$$n_{Post} = \text{Number of outstanding shares remaining after the repurchase}$$

$$= n_{Prior} - \text{Number of shares repurchased}$$

$$= n_{Prior} - \frac{D_{New} - D_{Old}}{P_{Prior}}$$

(15–12)

For Strasburg, the number of remaining shares after the repurchase is

$$n_{Post} = n_{Prior} - (D_{New} - D_{Old})/P_{Prior}$$

$$= 10 - (\$103.14 - \$50)/\$20.79$$

$$= 7.44 \text{ million}$$

Column 3 of Figure 15-9 summarizes these post-repurchase results. The repurchase doesn't change the value of operations, which remains at $257.86 million. However, the short-term investments are sold and the cash is used to repurchase stock. Strasburg is left with no short-term investments, so the intrinsic value of equity is:

$$S_{Post} = \$257.86 - \$103.14 = \$154.72 \text{ million}$$

After the repurchase, Strasburg has 7.44 million shares of stock. We can verify that the intrinsic stock price has not changed:[31]

$$P_{Post} = S_{Post}/n_{Post} = \$154.72/7.44 = \$20.79$$

Shareholders now own an equity position in the company worth only $154.72 million, but they have received a cash distribution in the amount of $53.14 million, so their total wealth is equal to the value of their equity plus the amount of cash they received: $154.72 + $53.14 = $207.86.

Here are some points worth noting. As shown in Column 3 of Figure 15-9, the change in capital structure clearly added wealth to the shareholders, increased the price per share, and increased the cash (in the form of short-term investments) temporarily held by the company. However, the repurchase itself did not affect shareholder wealth or the price per share. The repurchase did reduce the cash held by the company and the number of shares outstanding, but shareholder wealth stayed constant. After the repurchase, shareholders directly own the funds used in the repurchase; before the repurchase, shareholders indirectly own the funds. In either case, shareholders own the funds. The repurchase simply takes them out of the company's account and puts them into the shareholders' personal accounts.

The approach we've described here is based on the corporate valuation model, and it will always provide the correct value for S_{Post}, and n_{Post}, and P_{Post}. However, there is a quicker way to calculate these values if the firm has no short-term investments

---

31. There may be a small rounding difference due to using rounded numbers in intermediate steps. See the *Excel* file **Ch15 Tool Kit.xls** for the exact calculations.

either before or after the recap (other than the temporary short-term investments held between the time debt was issued and shares repurchased). After the recap is completed, the percentage of equity in the capital structure, based on market values, is equal to $1 - w_d$ if the firm holds no other short-term investments. Therefore, the value of equity after the repurchase is

(15–13)
$$S_{Post} = V_{opNew}(1 - w_d)$$

where we use the subscript "New" to indicate the value of operations at the new capital structure and the subscript "Post" to indicate the post-repurchase intrinsic value of equity.

The post-repurchase number of shares can be found using this equation:

(15–14)
$$n_{Post} = n_{Prior}\left[\frac{V_{opNew} - D_{New}}{V_{opNew} - D_{Old}}\right]$$

Given the value of equity and the number of shares, it is straightforward to calculate the intrinsic price per share as $P_{Post} = S_{Post}/n_{Post}$. But we can also calculate the post-repurchase price using

(15–15)
$$P_{Post} = \frac{V_{opNew} - D_{Old}}{n_{Prior}}$$

Figure 15-5 reports the number of shares and the intrinsic price per share in Lines 9–10. Notice that the number of shares goes down as debt goes up because the debt proceeds are used to buy back stock. Notice also that the capital structure that maximizes stock price, $w_d = 40\%$, is the same capital structure that optimizes the WACC and the value of operations.

Figure 15-5 also reports the earnings per share for the different levels of debt. Figure 15-10 graphs the intrinsic price per share and the earnings per share. Notice that the maximum earnings per share is at 50% debt even though the optimal capital structure is at 40% debt. This means that maximizing EPS will not maximize shareholder wealth.

15.6c Recapitalizations: A Post-Mortem

In Chapter 11, we looked at value-based management and saw how companies can increase their value by improving their operations. Yet there is good news and bad news regarding this connection. The good news is that small improvements in operations can lead to huge increases in value. The bad news is that it's often difficult to improve operations, especially if the company is already well managed and is in a competitive industry.

If instead you seek to increase a firm's value by changing its capital structure, we again have good news and bad news. The good news is that changing capital structure is easy—just call an investment banker and issue debt (or issue equity if

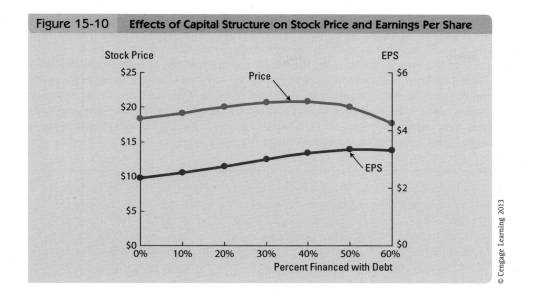

Figure 15-10   **Effects of Capital Structure on Stock Price and Earnings Per Share**

© Cengage Learning 2013

THE GLOBAL ECONOMIC CRISIS

Deleveraging

Many households, nonfinancial businesses, and financial institutions loaded up on easy credit during the run-up to the global economic crisis and found themselves with too much debt during the recession that began in 2007. The process of reducing debt is called *deleveraging*, and it is painful for individuals and the economy.

The debt-to-income ratio for households increased from around 80%–90% during the 1990s to a peak of 133% in 2007. To deleverage, many households are cutting spending on consumer goods and paying off some of their debt. This belt-tightening is difficult for the individual households, but it also is difficult for the economy because decreased spending leads to economic contraction and job losses. Other households are deleveraging by declaring bankruptcy, with over 1.5 million people filing in 2010 and even more expected to file by the end of 2011

Like individuals, businesses can deleverage by paying off debt or by declaring bankruptcy, and many are doing so during this global economic crisis.

But businesses can also deleverage by issuing equity. For example, Dunkin' Brands Group, owner of the Dunkin' Donuts and Baskin-Robbins brands, issued $427 million in stock in July 2011, part of which will be used to pay down debt. And Wells Fargo and Morgan Stanley issued over $12 billion in stock in May of 2009. A problem with deleveraging via stock issuances is that the stock price usually has been beaten down so much by the time of deleveraging that the new investors get a larger stake in the company, which dilutes the existing stockholders. But the bottom line is that dilution is better than bankruptcy!

Sources: Reuven Glick and Kevin J. Lansing, "U.S. Household Deleveraging and Future Consumption Growth," FRBSF Economic Letter, May 15, 2009, **www.frbsf.org/publications/economics /letter/2009/el2009-16.pdf**; and **BankruptcyAction.com**, **www.bankruptcyaction.com/USbankstats.htm**, August 2011.

the firm has too much debt). The bad news is that this will add only a relatively small amount of value. Of course, any additional value is better than none, so it's hard to understand why there are some mature firms with zero debt.

Finally, some firms have more debt than is optimal and should recapitalize to a lower debt level. This is called *deleveraging*. We can use exactly the same approach and the same formulas as we used for Strasburg. The difference is that the debt will go down and the number of shares will go up. In other words, the company will issue new shares of stock and then use the proceeds to pay off debt, resulting in a capital structure with less debt and lower interest payments.

Self Test	A firm's value of operations is equal to $800 million after a recapitalization (the firm had no debt before the recap). The firm raised $200 million in new debt and used this to buy back stock. The firm had no short-term investments before or after the recap. After the recap, $w_d = 25\%$. The firm had 10 million shares before the recap. What is S (the value of equity after the recap)? **($600 million)** What is P (the stock price after the recap)? **($80/share)** What is n (the number of remaining shares after the recap)? **(7.5 million)**

Summary

This chapter examined the effects of financial leverage on stock prices, earnings per share, and the cost of capital. The key concepts covered are listed below.

- A firm's **optimal capital structure** is the mix of debt and equity that maximizes the stock price. At any point in time, management has a specific **target capital structure** in mind, presumably the optimal one, although this target may change over time.
- Several factors influence a firm's capital structure. These include its (1) **business risk**, (2) **tax position**, (3) need for **financial flexibility**, (4) **managerial conservatism or aggressiveness**, and (5) **growth opportunities**.
- **Business risk** is the risk inherent in the firm's operations if it uses no debt. A firm will have little business risk if the demand for its products is stable, if the prices of its inputs and products remain relatively constant, if it can adjust its prices freely if costs increase, and if a high percentage of its costs are variable and hence will decrease if sales decrease. Other things the same, the lower a firm's business risk, the higher its optimal debt ratio.
- **Financial leverage** is the extent to which fixed-income securities (debt and preferred stock) are used in a firm's capital structure. **Financial risk** is the added risk borne by stockholders as a result of financial leverage.
- **Operating leverage** is the extent to which fixed costs are used in a firm's operations. In business terminology, a high degree of operating leverage, other factors held constant, implies that a relatively small change in sales results in a large change in ROIC. *Web Extension 15A* describes additional measures of operating and financial leverage.

- If there are no corporate or personal taxes, Modigliani and Miller showed that the value of a levered firm is equal to the value of an otherwise identical but unlevered firm:

$$V_L = V_U$$

- If there are only corporate taxes, Modigliani and Miller showed that a firm's value increases as it adds debt due to the interest rate deductibility of debt:

$$V_L = V_U + TD$$

- If there are personal and corporate taxes, Miller showed that

$$V_L = V_U + \left[1 - \frac{(1 - T_C)(1 - T_S)}{(1 - T_d)}\right]D$$

- The **Hamada equation** shows the effect of financial leverage on beta as follows:

$$b = b_U[1 + (1 - T)(D/S)]$$

Firms can use their current beta, tax rate, and debt/equity ratio to derive their **unlevered beta, b_U**, as follows:

$$b_U = b/[1 + (1 - T)(D/S)] = b/[1 + (1 - T)(w_d/w_s)]$$

- **The trade-off theory of capital structure** states that debt initially adds value because interest is **tax deductible** but that debt also brings costs associated with actual or potential bankruptcy. The optimal capital structure strikes a balance between the tax benefits of debt and the costs associated with bankruptcy.
- A firm's decision to use debt versus stock to raise new capital sends a **signal** to investors. A stock issue is viewed as a negative signal, whereas a debt issuance is a positive (or at least a neutral) signal. As a result, companies try to avoid having to issue stock by maintaining a **reserve borrowing capacity**, and this means using less debt in "normal" times than the trade-off theory would suggest.
- A firm's owners may decide to use a relatively large amount of debt to constrain the managers. A **high debt ratio raises the threat of bankruptcy**, which not only carries a cost but also forces managers to be more careful and less wasteful with shareholders' money. Many of the corporate takeovers and leveraged buyouts in recent years were designed to improve efficiency by reducing the cash flow available to managers.

Questions

15-1 Define each of the following terms:
- a. Capital structure; business risk; financial risk
- b. Operating leverage; financial leverage; break-even point
- c. Reserve borrowing capacity

15-2 What term refers to the uncertainty inherent in projections of future ROIC?

15-3 Firms with relatively high nonfinancial fixed costs are said to have a high degree of what?

15-4 "One type of leverage affects both EBIT and EPS. The other type affects only EPS." Explain this statement.

15-5 Why is the following statement true? "Other things being the same, firms with relatively stable sales are able to carry relatively high debt ratios."

15-6 Why do public utility companies usually have capital structures that are different from those of retail firms?

15-7 Why is EBIT generally considered to be independent of financial leverage? Why might EBIT actually be influenced by financial leverage at high debt levels?

15-8 If a firm went from zero debt to successively higher levels of debt, why would you expect its stock price to first rise, then hit a peak, and then begin to decline?

Problems   Answers Appear in Appendix B

Easy Problems 1–6

15-1 **Break-even Quantity** Shapland Inc. has fixed operating costs of $500,000 and variable costs of $50 per unit. If it sells the product for $75 per unit, what is the break-even quantity?

15-2 **Unlevered Beta** Counts Accounting has a beta of 1.15. The tax rate is 40%, and Counts is financed with 20% debt. What is Counts's unlevered beta?

15-3 **Premium for Financial Risk** Ethier Enterprise has an unlevered beta of 1.0. Ethier is financed with 50% debt and has a levered beta of 1.6. If the risk-free rate is 5.5% and the market risk premium is 6%, how much is the additional premium that Ethier's shareholders require to be compensated for financial risk?

15-4 **Value of Equity after Recapitalization** Nichols Corporation's value of operations is equal to $500 million after a recapitalization (the firm had no debt before the recap). It raised $200 million in new debt and used this to buy back stock. Nichols had no short-term investments before or after the recap. After the recap, $w_d = 40\%$. What is S (the value of equity after the recap)?

15-5 **Stock Price after Recapitalization** Lee Manufacturing's value of operations is equal to $900 million after a recapitalization (the firm had no debt before the recap). Lee raised $300 million in new debt and used this to buy back stock. Lee had no short-term investments before or after the recap. After the recap, $w_d = 1/3$. The firm had 30 million shares before the recap. What is P (the stock price after the recap)?

15-6 **Shares Remaining after Recapitalization** Dye Trucking raised $150 million in new debt and used this to buy back stock. After the recap, Dye's stock price is $7.50. If Dye had 60 million shares of stock before the recap, how many shares does it have after the recap?

Intermediate Problems 7–8

15-7 **Break-even Point** Schweser Satellites Inc. produces satellite earth stations that sell for $100,000 each. The firm's fixed costs, F, are $2 million, 50 earth stations are produced and sold each year, profits total $500,000, and the firm's assets (all equity financed) are $5 million. The firm estimates that it can change its production process, adding $4 million to investment and $500,000 to fixed operating costs. This change will (1) reduce variable costs per unit by $10,000 and (2) increase output by 20 units, but (3) the sales price on all units will have to be lowered to $95,000 to permit sales of the additional output. The firm has tax loss carryforwards that render its tax rate zero, its cost of equity is 16%, and it uses no debt.

a. What is the incremental profit? To get a rough idea of the project's profit-ability, what is the project's expected rate of return for the next year (defined as the incremental profit divided by the investment)? Should the firm make the investment?

b. Would the firm's break-even point increase or decrease if it made the change?

c. Would the new situation expose the firm to more or less business risk than the old one?

15-8 Capital Structure Analysis The Rivoli Company has no debt outstanding, and its financial position is given by the following data:

Assets (Market value = book value)	$3,000,000
EBIT	$500,000
Cost of equity, r_s	10%
Stock price, P_0	$15
Shares outstanding, n_0	200,000
Tax rate, T (federal-plus-state)	40%

The firm is considering selling bonds and simultaneously repurchasing some of its stock. If it moves to a capital structure with 30% debt based on market values, its cost of equity, r_s, will increase to 11% to reflect the increased risk. Bonds can be sold at a cost, r_d, of 7%. Rivoli is a no-growth firm. Hence, all its earnings are paid out as dividends. Earnings are expected to be constant over time.

a. What effect would this use of leverage have on the value of the firm?

b. What would be the price of Rivoli's stock?

c. What happens to the firm's earnings per share after the recapitalization?

d. The $500,000 EBIT given previously is actually the expected value from the following probability distribution:

Probability	EBIT
0.10	($ 100,000)
0.20	200,000
0.40	500,000
0.20	800,000
0.10	1,100,000

Determine the times-interest-earned ratio for each probability. What is the probability of not covering the interest payment at the 30% debt level?

Challenging Problems 9–11

15-9 Capital Structure Analysis Pettit Printing Company has a total market value of $100 million, consisting of 1 million shares selling for $50 per share and $50 million of 10% perpetual bonds now selling at par. The company's EBIT is $13.24 million, and its tax rate is 15%. Pettit can change its capital structure either by increasing its debt to 70% (based on market values) or decreasing it to 30%. If it decides to *increase* its use of leverage, it must call its old bonds and issue new ones with a 12% coupon. If it decides to *decrease* its leverage, it will call its old bonds and replace them with new 8% coupon bonds. The company will sell or repurchase stock at the new equilibrium price to complete the capital structure change.

The firm pays out all earnings as dividends; hence its stock is a zero-growth stock. Its current cost of equity, r_s, is 14%. If it increases leverage, r_s will be 16%. If it decreases leverage, r_s will be 13%. What is the firm's WACC and total corporate value under each capital structure?

15-10 **Optimal Capital Structure with Hamada** Beckman Engineering and Associates (BEA) is considering a change in its capital structure. BEA currently has $20 million in debt carrying a rate of 8%, and its stock price is $40 per share with 2 million shares outstanding. BEA is a zero-growth firm and pays out all of its earnings as dividends. The firm's EBIT is $14.933 million, and it faces a 40% federal-plus-state tax rate. The market risk premium is 4%, and the risk-free rate is 6%. BEA is considering increasing its debt level to a capital structure with 40% debt, based on market values, and repurchasing shares with the extra money that it borrows. BEA will have to retire the old debt in order to issue new debt, and the rate on the new debt will be 9%. BEA has a beta of 1.0.

    a. What is BEA's unlevered beta? Use market value D/S (which is the same as w_d/w_s) when unlevering.

    b. What are BEA's new beta and cost of equity if it has 40% debt?

    c. What are BEA's WACC and total value of the firm with 40% debt?

15-11 **WACC and Optimal Capital Structure** F. Pierce Products Inc. is considering changing its capital structure. F. Pierce currently has no debt and no preferred stock, but would like to add some debt to take advantage of low interest rates and the tax shield. Its investment banker has indicated that the pre-tax cost of debt under various possible capital structures would be as follows:

Market Debt-to-Value Ratio (w_d)	Market Equity-to-Value Ratio (w_s)	Market Debt-to-Equity Ratio (D/S)	Before-Tax Cost of Debt (r_d)
0.0	1.0	0.00	6.0%
0.2	0.8	0.25	7.0
0.4	0.6	0.67	8.0
0.6	0.4	1.50	9.0
0.8	0.2	4.00	10.0

F. Pierce uses the CAPM to estimate its cost of common equity, r_s and at the time of the analysis the risk-free rate is 5%, the market risk premium is 6%, and the company's tax rate is 40%. F. Pierce estimates that its beta now (which is "unlevered" since it currently has no debt) is 0.8. Based on this information, what is the firm's optimal capital structure, and what would be the weighted average cost of capital at the optimal capital structure?

Spreadsheet Problem

15-12 **Build a Model: WACC and Optimal Capital Structure** Start with the partial model in the file *Ch15 P12 Build a Model.xls* on the textbook's Web site. Reacher Technology has consulted with investment bankers and determined the interest rate it would pay for different capital structures, as shown in the following table. Data for the risk-free rate, the market risk premium, an estimate of Reacher's unlevered beta, and the tax rate are also shown. Based on this information, what is the firm's optimal capital structure, and what is the weighted average cost of capital at the optimal structure?

Percent Financed with Debt (w_d)	Before-Tax Cost Debt (r_d)	Input Data	
0%	6.0%	Risk-free rate	4.5%
10	6.1	Market risk premium	5.5%
20	7.0	Unlevered beta	0.8
30	8.0	Tax rate	40.0%
40	10.0		
50	12.5		
60	15.5		
70	18.0		

 THOMSON REUTERS

Use the Thomson ONE—Business School Edition online database to work this chapter's questions.

Exploring the Capital Structures for Three Global Auto Companies

The following discussion questions demonstrate how we can evaluate the capital structures for three global automobile companies: Ford (F), BMW (BMW), and Toyota (J:TYMO). As you gather information on these companies, be mindful of the currencies in which these companies' financial data are reported.

Discussion Questions

1. To get an overall picture of each company's capital structure, it is helpful to see a chart that summarizes the company's capital structure over the past decade. To obtain this chart, choose a company to start with and select FINANCIALS. Next, select MORE>THOMSON REPORTS & CHARTS>CAPITAL STRUCTURE. This should generate a chart that plots the company's long-term debt, common equity, and total current liabilities over the past decade. What, if any, are the major trends that emerge from looking at these charts? Do these companies tend to have relatively high or relatively low levels of debt? Do these companies have significant levels of current liabilities? Have their capital structures changed over time?

2. To obtain more details about the companies' capital structures over the past 5 years, select FINANCIALS>FINANCIAL RATIOS>THOMSON RATIOS. From here you can select ANNUAL RATIOS and/or 5 YEAR AVERAGE RATIOS REPORT. In each case, you can scroll down and look for Leverage Ratios. Here you will find a variety of leverage ratios for the past 5 years. (Notice that these two pages offer different information. The ANNUAL RATIOS page offers year-end leverage ratios, whereas the 5 YEAR AVERAGE RATIOS REPORT offers the average ratio over the previous 5 years for each calendar date. In other words, the 5 YEAR AVERAGE RATIOS REPORT smoothes the changes in capital structure over the

reporting period.) Do these ratios suggest that the company has significantly changed its capital structure over the past 5 years? If so, what factors could possibly explain this shift? (Financial statements might be useful for detecting any shifts that may have led to the company's changing capital structure. You may also consult the company's annual report to see if there is any discussion and/or explanation for these changes. Both the historical financial statements and annual report information can be found via Thomson ONE).

3. Repeat this procedure for the other auto companies. Do you find similar capital structures for each of the three companies? Do you find that the capital structures have moved in the same direction over the past 5 years, or have the different companies changed their capital structures in different ways over the past 5 years?

4. The financial ratios investigated thus far are based on book values of debt and equity. Determine whether using the market value of equity (market capitalization found on the OVERVIEW page) makes a significant difference in the most recent year's "LT Debt Pct Common Equity" and "Total Debt Pct Total Assets." (*Note:* "LT Debt" is defined by Thomson ONE as the "Long Term Debt" listed on the balance sheet, while "Total Debt" is defined as "Long Term Debt" plus "ST Debt & Current Portion Due LT Debt.") Are there big differences between the capital structures measured on a book or market basis?

5. You can also use Thomson ONE to search for companies with either very large or very small debt ratios. For example, if you want to find the top 50 companies with the highest debt ratio, select: SCREENING & TARGETING > COMPANIES > STEP 1: ALL COMPANIES > STEP 2 DATABASE: THOMSON FINANCIAL > CATEGORIES: RATIOS > LEVERAGE. From here, select "LT Debt Pct Total Cap 5 Yr. Avg." (This will focus in on the average capital structure over the past 5 years, which may give us a better indication of the company's long-run target capital structure.) Once you click on SELECT, you should see the Search Expression Builder screen. From here, you go to Rank and select the top 50 by typing "50" in the box below rank. Next, click in the Expression box below and highlight the expression that was created and copy it by using the Control and the C button together. Now, back under Step 3, click on ADD ITEM > CUSTOM CRITERIA, and paste the expression you copied into the box (using Shift Insert). Next, click ADD, and then SEARCH. You can easily change this to also select the bottom 50 (or perhaps the bottom 5% or 10%). Take a close look at the resulting firms by clicking on SEARCH. Do you observe any differences between the types of firms that have high debt levels and the types of firms that have low debt levels? Are these patterns similar to what you expect after reading the chapter? (As a quick review, you may want to look at the average capital structures for different industries, which are summarized in the text.) *Note:* The searches are cumulative, so that if you ask for the top 10% of the database and follow that by asking for the bottom 5%, you will be shown the bottom 5% of the top 10%. In other words, you would only see a small subset of the firms you are asking for. Hence, *when beginning a new search, clear all existing searches first.*

6. From the submenu just above the list of firms, you may choose a number of options. "List" displays a list of the firms and allows you to access a firm report. "Profiles" provides key information about the firms, such as ticker, country, exchange, and industry code. "Financials" gives a couple of key financial figures (expressed in U.S. dollars) from the firms' balance sheets and income statements. "Market Data" includes the firms' market capitalization, current price, P/E ratio, EPS, and so forth. "Report Writer" allows you to create customized company reports.

MINI CASE

Assume you have just been hired as a business manager of PizzaPalace, a regional pizza restaurant chain. The company's EBIT was $50 million last year and is not expected to grow. The firm is currently financed with all equity, and it has 10 million shares outstanding. When you took your corporate finance course, your instructor stated that most firms' owners would be financially better off if the firms used some debt. When you suggested this to your new boss, he encouraged you to pursue the idea. As a first step, assume that you obtained from the firm's investment banker the following estimated costs of debt for the firm at different capital structures:

Percent Financed with Debt, w_d	r_d
0%	—
20	8.0%
30	8.5
40	10.0
50	12.0

If the company were to recapitalize, then debt would be issued and the funds received would be used to repurchase stock. PizzaPalace is in the 40% state-plus-federal corporate tax bracket, its beta is 1.0, the risk-free rate is 6%, and the market risk premium is 6%.

a. Provide a brief overview of capital structure effects. Be sure to identify the ways in which capital structure can affect the weighted average cost of capital and free cash flows.

b. (1) What is business risk? What factors influence a firm's business risk?

   (2) What is operating leverage, and how does it affect a firm's business risk? Show the operating break-even point if a company has fixed costs of $200, a sales price of $15, and variable costs of $10.

c. Now, to develop an example that can be presented to PizzaPalace's management to illustrate the effects of financial leverage, consider two hypothetical firms: Firm U, which uses no debt financing, and Firm L, which uses $10,000 of 12% debt. Both firms have $20,000 in assets, a 40% tax rate, and an expected EBIT of $3,000.

   (1) Construct partial income statements, which start with EBIT, for the two firms.

   (2) Now calculate ROE for both firms.

   (3) What does this example illustrate about the impact of financial leverage on ROE?

d. Explain the difference between financial risk and business risk.

e. What happens to ROE for Firm U and Firm L if EBIT falls to $2,000? What does this imply about the impact of leverage on risk and return?

f. What does capital structure theory attempt to do? What lessons can be learned from capital structure theory? Be sure to address the MM models.

g. What does the empirical evidence say about capital structure theory? What are the implications for managers?

h. With the preceding points in mind, now consider the optimal capital structure for PizzaPalace.

   (1) For each capital structure under consideration, calculate the levered beta, the cost of equity, and the WACC.

   (2) Now calculate the corporate value for each capital structure.

i. Describe the recapitalization process and apply it to PizzaPalace. Calculate the resulting value of the debt that will be issued, the resulting market value of equity, the price per share, the number of shares repurchased, and the remaining shares. Considering only the capital structures under analysis, what is PizzaPalace's optimal capital structure?

Selected Additional Cases

The following cases from TextChoice, Cengage Learning's online case library, cover many of the concepts discussed in this chapter and are available at **www.textchoice2.com/casenet.**

Klein-Brigham Series:

Case 9, "Kleen Kar, Inc.," Case 43, "Mountain Springs, Inc.," and Case 57, "Greta Cosmetics, Inc.," each present a situation similar to the Strasburg example in the text. Case 74, "The Western Company," and Case 99, "Moore Plumbing Supply," explore capital structure policies.

Brigham-Buzzard Series:

Case 8, "Powerline Network Corporation (Operating Leverage, Financial Leverage, and the Optimal Capital Structure)."

Chapter 16

Capital Structure Decisions: Part II

Chapter 15 presented basic material on capital structure, including an introduction to capital structure theory. We saw that debt concentrates a firm's business risk on its stockholders, thus raising stockholders' risk, but it also increases the expected return on equity. We also saw there is some optimal level of debt that maximizes a company's stock price, and we illustrated this concept with a simple model. Now we go into more detail on capital structure theory. This will give you a deeper understanding of the benefits and costs associated with debt financing.

Beginning of Chapter Questions

As you read the chapter, consider how you would answer the following questions. You *should not* necessarily be able to answer the questions before you read the chapter. Rather, you should use them to get a sense of the issues covered in the chapter. After reading the chapter, you should be able to give at least partial answers to the questions, and you should be able to give better answers after the chapter has been discussed in class. Note, too, that it is often useful, when answering conceptual questions, to use hypothetical data to illustrate your answer. We illustrate the answers with an *Excel* model that is available on the textbook's Web site. Accessing the model and working through it is a useful exercise, and it provides insights that are useful when answering the questions.

1. What is **arbitrage,** and how did Modigliani and Miller use the arbitrage concept in developing their

theory that (with no corporate taxes) capital structure has no effect on value or the cost of capital? What real-world impediments exist to creating one's own "homemade" leverage?

2. What is the essence of Miller's contribution to the theory of capital structure, and how does it relate to the earlier MM with-taxes position?

3. MM and Miller assumed that firms do not grow. If they grow, how would this affect the value of the debt tax shield? What does growth do to the required rate of return on equity and the WACC as a firm increases its use of debt?

4. MM and Miller also assumed that debt is riskless. How does the possibility of default on debt cause equity to take on the characteristics of an option? What types of incentives for shareholders does this lead to?

16.1 Capital Structure Theory: Arbitrage Proofs of the Modigliani-Miller Models

Until 1958, capital structure theory consisted of loose assertions about investor behavior rather than carefully constructed models that could be tested by formal statistical analysis. In what has been called the most influential set of financial papers ever published, Franco Modigliani and Merton Miller (MM) addressed capital structure in a rigorous, scientific fashion, and they set off a chain of research that continues to this day.[1]

16.1a Assumptions

As we explain in this chapter, MM employed the concept of **arbitrage** to develop their theory. Arbitrage occurs if two similar assets—in this case, levered and unlevered stocks—sell at different prices. Arbitrageurs will buy the undervalued stock and simultaneously sell the overvalued stock, earning a profit in the process, and will continue doing so until market forces of supply and demand cause the prices of the two assets to be equal. For arbitrage to work, the assets must be equivalent,

---

1. See Franco Modigliani and Merton H. Miller, "The Cost of Capital, Corporation Finance and the Theory of Investment," *American Economic Review,* June 1958, pp. 261–297; "The Cost of Capital, Corporation Finance and the Theory of Investment: Reply," *American Economic Review,* September 1958, pp. 655–669; "Taxes and the Cost of Capital: A Correction," *American Economic Review,* June 1963, pp. 433–443; and "Reply," *American Economic Review,* June 1965, pp. 524–527. In a survey of Financial Management Association members, the original MM article was judged to have had the greatest impact on the field of finance of any work ever published. See Philip L. Cooley and J. Louis Heck, "Significant Contributions to Finance Literature," *Financial Management,* Tenth Anniversary Issue, 1981, pp. 23–33. Note that both Modigliani and Miller won Nobel Prizes— Modigliani in 1985 and Miller in 1990.

CORPORATE VALUATION AND CAPITAL STRUCTURE DECISIONS

A firm's financing choices obviously have a direct effect on its weighted average cost of capital (WACC). Financing choices also have an indirect effect because they change the risk and required return of debt and equity. This chapter focuses on the debt–equity choice and its effect on value.

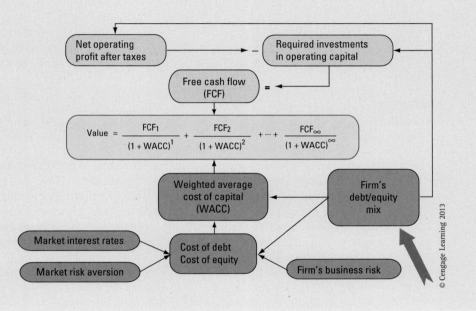

or nearly so. MM show that, under their assumptions, levered and unlevered stocks are sufficiently similar for the arbitrage process to operate.

No one, not even MM, believes their assumptions are sufficiently correct that their models will hold exactly in the real world. However, their models do show how money can be made through arbitrage if one can find ways around problems with the assumptions. Though some of them were later relaxed, here are the initial MM assumptions.

1. There are *no taxes*, either personal or corporate.
2. Business risk can be measured by σ_{EBIT}, and firms with the same degree of business risk are said to be in a *homogeneous risk class*.
3. All present and prospective investors have identical estimates of each firm's future EBIT; that is, investors have *homogeneous expectations* about expected future corporate earnings and the riskiness of those earnings.
4. Stocks and bonds are traded in *perfect capital markets*. This assumption implies, among other things, (a) that there are no brokerage costs and (b) that investors (both individuals and institutions) can borrow at the same rate as corporations.
5. *Debt is riskless.* This applies to both firms and investors, so the interest rate on all debt is the risk-free rate. Further, this situation holds regardless of how much debt a firm (or individual) uses.

6. All cash flows are *perpetuities;* that is, all firms expect zero growth and hence have an "expectationally constant" EBIT, and all bonds are perpetuities. "Expectationally constant" means that the best guess is that EBIT will be constant, although after the fact the realized level could be different from the expected level.

16.1b MM without Taxes

MM first analyzed leverage under the assumption that there are no corporate or personal income taxes. On the basis of their assumptions, they stated and algebraically proved two propositions.[2]

Proposition I

The value of any firm is established by capitalizing its expected net operating income (EBIT) at a constant rate (r_{sU}) that is based on the firm's risk class:

$$(16\text{--}1) \qquad V_L = V_U = \frac{\text{EBIT}}{\text{WACC}} = \frac{\text{EBIT}}{r_{sU}}$$

Here the subscript L designates a levered firm and U designates an unlevered firm. Both firms are assumed to be in the same business risk class, and r_{sU} is the required rate of return for an unlevered (i.e., all-equity) firm of this risk class when there are no taxes. For our purposes, it is easiest to think in terms of a single firm that has the option of financing either with all equity or with some combination of debt and equity. Hence, L designates a firm that uses some amount of debt and U designates a firm that uses no debt.

As established by Equation 16-1, V is a constant; therefore, *under the MM model, if there are no taxes then the value of the firm is independent of its leverage.* As we shall see, this also implies the following statements.

1. The weighted average cost of capital, WACC, is completely independent of a firm's capital structure.
2. Regardless of the amount of debt a firm uses, its WACC is equal to the cost of equity that it would have if it used no debt.

Proposition II

When there are no taxes, the cost of equity to a levered firm, r_{sL}, is equal to (1) the cost of equity to an unlevered firm in the same risk class, r_{sU}, plus (2) a risk premium whose size depends on (a) the difference between an unlevered firm's costs of debt and equity and (b) the amount of debt used:

$$(16\text{--}2) \qquad r_{sL} = r_{sU} + \text{Risk premium} = r_{sU} + (r_{sU} - r_d)(D/S)$$

Here D is the market value of the firm's debt, S is the market value of its equity, and r_d is the constant cost of debt. Equation 16-2 states that, *as debt increases, the cost*

---

2. Modigliani and Miller actually stated and proved three propositions, but the third one is not material to our discussion here.

of equity rises in a mathematically precise manner (even though the cost of debt does not rise).

Taken together, the two MM propositions imply that using more debt in the capital structure will not increase the value of the firm, because the benefits of cheaper debt will be exactly offset by an increase in the riskiness of the equity and hence in its cost. Thus MM argue that, *in a world without taxes, both the value of a firm and its WACC would be unaffected by its capital structure.*

16.1c MM's Arbitrage Proof

Propositions I and II are important because they showed for the first time that any valuation effects due to the use of debt must arise from taxes or other market frictions. The technique that MM used to prove these propositions is equally important, however, so we discuss it in detail here. They used an *arbitrage proof* to support their propositions, and this proof technique was later used in the development of option pricing models that revolutionized the securities industry.[3] Modigliani and Miller showed that, under their assumptions, if two companies differed only (1) in the way they were financed and (2) in their total market values, then investors would sell shares of the higher-valued firm, buy those of the lower-valued firm, and continue this process until the companies had exactly the same market value. To illustrate, assume that two firms, L and U, are identical in all important respects except that Firm L has $4,000,000 of 7.5% debt while Firm U uses only equity. Both firms have EBIT = $900,000, and σ_{EBIT} is the same for both firms, so they are in the same business risk class.

Modigliani and Miller assumed that all firms are in a zero-growth situation. In other words, EBIT is expected to remain constant; this will occur if ROE is constant, all earnings are paid out as dividends, and there are no taxes. Under the constant EBIT assumption, the total market value of the common stock, S, is the present value of a perpetuity, which is found as follows:

$$S = \frac{\text{Dividends}}{r_{sL}} = \frac{\text{Net income}}{r_{sL}} = \frac{\text{EBIT} - r_d D}{r_{sL}}$$ (16-3)

Equation 16-3 is merely the value of a perpetuity, where the numerator is the net income available to common stockholders (all of which is paid out as dividends) and the denominator is the cost of common equity. Since there are no taxes, the numerator is not multiplied by $(1 - T)$, as it was when we calculated NOPAT in Chapters 7 and 11.

Assume that initially, *before any arbitrage occurs,* both firms have the same equity capitalization rate (that is, required rate of return on equity): $r_{sU} = r_{sL} = 10\%$. Under this condition, according to Equation 16-3, the following situation would exist.

---

3. By *arbitrage* we mean the simultaneous buying and selling of essentially identical assets that sell at different prices. The buying increases the price of the undervalued asset, and the selling decreases the price of the overvalued asset. Arbitrage operations will continue until prices have adjusted to the point where the arbitrageur can no longer earn a profit, at which point the market is in equilibrium. In the absence of transaction costs, equilibrium requires that the prices of the two assets be equal.

Firm U:

$$\text{Value of Firm U's stock} = S_U = \frac{\text{EBIT} - r_d D}{r_{sU}}$$

$$= \frac{\$900,000 - \$0}{0.10} = \$9,000,000$$

$$\text{Total market value of Firm U} = V_U = D_U + S_U = \$0 + \$9,000,000$$

$$= \$9,000,000$$

Firm L:

$$\text{Value of Firm L's stock} = S_L = \frac{\text{EBIT} - r_d D}{r_{sL}}$$

$$= \frac{\$900,000 - 0.075(\$4,000,000)}{0.10} = \frac{\$600,000}{10}$$

$$= \$6,000,000$$

$$\text{Total market value of Firm L} = V_L = D_L + S_L = \$4,000,000 + \$6,000,000$$

$$= \$10,000,000$$

Thus, before arbitrage (and assuming that $r_{sU} = r_{sL}$, which implies that capital structure has no effect on the cost of equity), the value of the levered Firm L exceeds that of the unlevered Firm U.

Modigliani and Miller argued that this result is a disequilibrium that cannot persist. To see why, suppose you owned 10% of L's stock and so the market value of your investment was 0.10($6,000,000) = $600,000. According to MM, you could increase your income without increasing your exposure to risk. For example, you could (1) sell your stock in L for $600,000, (2) borrow an amount equal to 10% of L's debt ($400,000), and then (3) buy 10% of U's stock for $900,000. Note that you would receive $1,000,000 from the sale of your 10% of L's stock plus your borrowing, and you would be spending only $900,000 on U's stock. Hence you would have an extra $100,000, which you could invest in riskless debt to yield 7.5%, or $7,500 annually. Now consider your income positions:

Old Portfolio		New Portfolio	
10% of L's $600,000 equity income	$60,000	10% of U's $900,000 equity income	$90,000
		Less 7.5% interest on $400,000 loan	(30,000)
		Plus 7.5% interest on extra $100,000	7,500
Total income	$60,000	Total income	$67,500

Thus, your net income from common stock would be exactly the same as before, $60,000, but you would have $100,000 left over for investment in riskless debt and this would increase your income by $7,500. Therefore, the total return on your $600,000 net worth would rise to $67,500. And your risk, according to MM, would be the same as before, because you would have simply substituted $400,000 of "homemade" leverage for your 10% share of Firm L's $4 million of corporate leverage. Thus, neither your "effective" debt nor your risk would have changed. Therefore, you would have increased your income without raising your risk, which is obviously desirable.

Modigliani and Miller argued that this arbitrage process would actually occur, with sales of L's stock driving its price down and purchases of U's stock driving its price up, until the market values of the two firms were equal. Until this equality was established, gains could be obtained by switching from one stock to the other; hence the profit motive would force equality to be reached. When equilibrium is established, the values of Firms L and U must be equal, which is what Proposition I states. If their values are equal, then Equation 16-1 implies that WACC = r_{sU}. Because there are no taxes, we have

$$WACC = [D/(D+S)]r_d + [S/(D+S)]r_{SL}$$

and a little algebra then yields

$$r_{sL} = r_{sU} + (r_{sU} - r_d)(D/S)$$

which is what Proposition II states. Thus, according to MM, both a firm's value and its WACC must be independent of capital structure.

Note that each of the assumptions listed at the beginning of this section is necessary for the arbitrage proof to work exactly. For example, if the companies did not have identical business risk or if transaction costs were significant, then the arbitrage process could not be invoked. We discuss other implications of the assumptions later in the chapter.

16.1d Arbitrage with Short Sales

Even if you did not own any stock in L, you still could reap benefits if U and L did not have the same total market value. Your first step would be to sell short $600,000 of stock in L. To do this, your broker would let you borrow stock in L from another client. Your broker would then sell the stock for you and give you the proceeds, or $600,000 in cash. You would supplement this $600,000 by borrowing $400,000. With the $1 million total, you would buy 10% of the stock in U for $900,000 and have $100,000 remaining.

Your position would then consist of $100,000 in cash and two portfolios. The first portfolio would contain $900,000 of stock in U, which would generate $90,000 of income. Because you would own the stock, we'll call it the "long" portfolio. The other portfolio would consist of $600,000 of stock in L and $400,000 of debt. The value of this portfolio is $1 million, and it would generate $60,000 of dividends and $30,000 of interest. However, you would not own this second portfolio—you would "owe" it. Since you borrowed the $400,000, you would owe the $30,000 in interest. And since you borrowed the stock in L, you would "owe the stock" to the client from whom it was borrowed. Therefore, you would have to pay your broker the $60,000 of dividends paid by L, which the broker would then pass on to the client from whom the stock was borrowed. Thus your net cash flow from the second portfolio would be a negative $90,000. Because you would "owe" this portfolio, we'll call it the "short" portfolio.

Where would you get the $90,000 that you must pay on the short portfolio? The good news is that this is exactly the amount of cash flow generated by your long portfolio. Because the cash flows generated by each portfolio are the same, the short portfolio "replicates" the long portfolio.

Here is the bottom line. You started out with no money of your own. By selling L short, borrowing $400,000, and purchasing stock in U, you ended up with $100,000 in cash plus the two portfolios. The portfolios mirror one another, so their net cash flow is zero. This is perfect arbitrage: You invest none of your own money, you have no risk, you have no future negative cash flows, but you end up with cash in your pocket.

Not surprisingly, many traders would want to do this. The selling pressure on L would cause its price to fall, and the buying pressure on U would cause its price to rise, until the two companies' values were equal. To put it another way, *if the long and short replicating portfolios have the same cash flows, then arbitrage will force them to have the same value.*

This is one of the most important ideas in modern finance. Not only does it give us insights into capital structure, but it is the fundamental building block underlying the valuation of real and financial options and derivatives as discussed in Chapters 6 and 24. Without the concept of arbitrage, the options and derivatives markets we have today simply would not exist.

16.1e MM with Corporate Taxes

Modigliani and Miller's original work, published in 1958, assumed zero taxes. In 1963, they published a second article that incorporated corporate taxes. With corporate income taxes, they concluded that leverage will increase a firm's value. This occurs because interest is a tax-deductible expense; hence more of a levered firm's operating income flows through to investors.

Later in this chapter we present a proof of the MM propositions when personal taxes as well as corporate taxes are allowed. The situation when there are corporate taxes but no personal taxes is a special instance of the situation with both personal and corporate taxes, so we only present results in this case.

Proposition I

The value of a levered firm is equal to the value of an unlevered firm in the same risk class (V_U) *plus* the value of the tax shield ($V_{\text{Tax shield}}$) due to the tax deductibility of interest expenses. The value of the tax shield, which is often called *the gain from leverage,* is the present value of the annual tax savings. The annual tax saving is equal to the interest payment multiplied by the tax rate, T:

$$\text{Annual tax saving} = r_d D(T)$$

Modigliani and Miller assume a no-growth firm, so the present value of the annual tax saving is the present value of a perpetuity. They assume that the appropriate discount rate for the tax shield is the interest rate on debt, so the value of the tax shield is

$$V_{\text{Tax shield}} = \frac{r_d D(T)}{r_d} = TD$$

Therefore, the value of a levered firm is

(16–4)
$$V_L = V_U + V_{\text{Tax shield}}$$
$$= V_U + TD$$

The important point here is that, when corporate taxes are introduced, the value of the levered firm exceeds that of the unlevered firm by the amount TD. Since the gain from leverage increases as debt increases, this implies that a firm's value is maximized at 100% debt financing.

Because all cash flows are assumed to be perpetuities, the value of the unlevered firm can be found by using Equation 16-3 and incorporating taxes. With zero debt (D = $0), the value of the firm is its equity value:

$$V_U = S = \frac{\text{EBIT}\,(1-T)}{r_{sU}} \qquad (16\text{–}5)$$

Note that the discount rate, r_{sU}, is not necessarily equal to the discount rate in Equation 16-1. The r_{sU} from Equation 16-1 is the required discount rate in a world with no taxes, whereas the r_{sU} in Equation 16-5 is the required discount rate in a world with taxes.

Proposition II

The cost of equity to a levered firm is equal to (1) the cost of equity to an unlevered firm in the same risk class plus (2) a risk premium whose size depends on (a) the difference between the costs of equity and debt to an unlevered firm, (b) the amount of financial leverage used, and (c) the corporate tax rate:

$$r_{sL} = r_{sU} + (r_{sU} - r_d)(1-T)(D/S) \qquad (16\text{–}6)$$

Observe that Equation 16-6 is identical to the corresponding without-tax Equation 16-2 except for the term (1 − T), which appears only in Equation 16-6. Because (1 − T) is less than 1, corporate taxes cause the cost of equity to rise less rapidly with leverage than it would in the absence of taxes. Proposition II, coupled with the reduction (due to taxes) in the effective cost of debt, is what produces the Proposition I result—namely, that the firm's value increases as its leverage increases.

As shown in Chapter 15, Professor Robert Hamada extended the MM analysis to define the relationship between a firm's beta, b, and the amount of leverage it has. The beta of an unlevered firm is denoted by b_U, and Hamada's equation is

$$b = b_U[1 + (1 - T)(D/S)] \qquad (16\text{–}7)$$

Note that beta, like the cost of stock shown in Equation 16-6, increases with leverage.

16.1f Illustration of the MM Models

To illustrate the MM models, assume that the following data and conditions hold for Fredrickson Water Company, an established firm that supplies water to residential customers in several no-growth upstate New York communities.

WEB

See **Ch16 Tool Kit.xls** on the textbook's Web site for all calculations.

1. Fredrickson currently has no debt; it is an all-equity company.
2. Expected EBIT = $2,400,000. This value is not expected to increase over time, so Fredrickson is in a no-growth situation.
3. Because it does not need new capital, Fredrickson pays out all of its income as dividends.

4. If Fredrickson begins to use debt, it can borrow at a rate $r_d = 8\%$. This borrowing rate is constant—it does not increase regardless of the amount of debt used. Any money raised by selling debt would be used to repurchase common stock, so *Fredrickson's assets would remain constant.*

5. The business risk inherent in Fredrickson's assets, and thus in its EBIT, is such that its beta is 0.80; this is called the unlevered beta, b_U, because Fredrickson has no debt. The risk-free rate is 8%, and the market risk premium (RP_M) is 5%. Using the Capital Asset Pricing Model (CAPM), Fredrickson's required rate of return on stock, r_{sU}, is 12% if no debt is used:

$$r_{sU} = r_{RF} + b_U(RP_M) = 8\% + 0.80(5\%) = 12\%$$

With Zero Taxes

To begin, assume that there are no taxes and so $T = 0\%$. At any level of debt, Proposition I (Equation 16-1) can be used to find Fredrickson's value in an MM world, $20 million:

$$V_L = V_U = \frac{EBIT}{r_{sU}} = \frac{\$2.4 \text{ million}}{0.12} = \$20.0 \text{ million}$$

If Fredrickson uses $10 million of debt, then the value of its stock must be $10 million:

$$S = V - D = \$20 \text{ million} - \$10 \text{ million} = \$10 \text{ million}$$

We can also find Fredrickson's cost of equity, r_{sL}, and its WACC at a debt level of $10 million. First, we use Proposition II (Equation 16-2) to find r_{sL}, Fredrickson's levered cost of equity:

$$\begin{aligned} r_{sL} &= r_{sU} + (r_{sU} - r_d)(D/S) \\ &= 12\% + (12\% - 8\%)(\$10 \text{ million}/\$10 \text{ million}) \\ &= 12\% + 4.0\% = 16.0\% \end{aligned}$$

Now we can find the company's weighted average cost of capital:

$$\begin{aligned} WACC &= (D/V)(r_d)(1 - T) + (S/V)r_{sL} \\ &= (\$10/\$20)(8\%)(1.0) + (\$10/\$20)(16.0\%) = 12.0\% \end{aligned}$$

Fredrickson's value and cost of capital based on the MM model without taxes at various debt levels are shown in Panel a on the left side of Figure 16-1. Here we see that, in an MM world without taxes, financial leverage simply does not matter: *The value of the firm and its overall cost of capital are both independent of the amount of debt.*

With Corporate Taxes

To illustrate the MM model with corporate taxes, assume that all of the previous conditions hold except for the following changes:

Figure 16-1	**Effects of Leverage: MM Models (Millions of Dollars)**

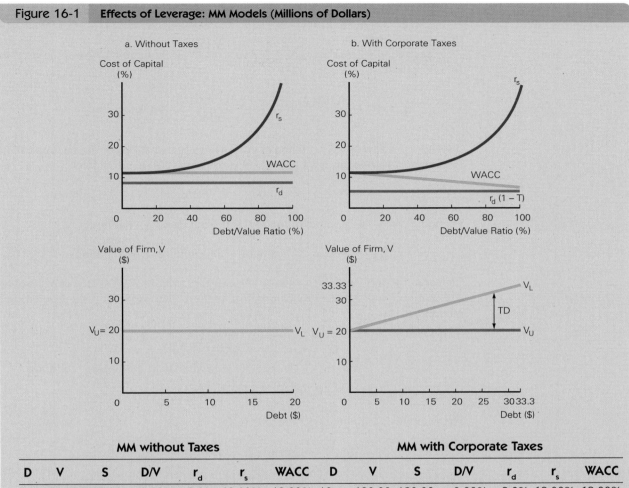

			MM without Taxes							MM with Corporate Taxes			
D	**V**	**S**	**D/V**	**r_d**	**r_s**	**WACC**	**D**	**V**	**S**	**D/V**	**r_d**	**r_s**	**WACC**
$ 0	$20.00	$20.00	0.00%	8.0%	12.00%	12.00%	$0	$20.00	$20.00	0.00%	8.0%	12.00%	12.00%
5	20.00	15.00	25.00	8.0	13.33	12.00	5	22.00	17.00	22.73	8.0	12.71	10.91
10	20.00	10.00	50.00	8.0	16.00	12.00	10	24.00	14.00	41.67	8.0	13.71	10.00
15	20.00	5.00	75.00	8.0	24.00	12.00	15	26.00	11.00	57.69	8.0	15.27	9.23
20	20.00	0.00	100.00	12.0	—	12.00	20	28.00	8.00	71.43	8.0	18.00	8.57
							25	30.00	5.00	83.33	8.0	24.00	8.00
							30	32.00	2.00	93.75	8.0	48.00	7.50
							33.33	33.33	0.00	100.00	12.0	—	12.00

1. Expected EBIT = $4,000,000.[4]
2. Fredrickson has a 40% federal-plus-state tax rate, so T = 40%.

---

4. If we had left Fredrickson's EBIT at $2.4 million, then introducing corporate taxes would have reduced the firm's value from $20 million to $12 million:

$$V_L = \frac{\text{EBIT}(1 - T)}{r_{sU}} = \frac{\$2.4 \text{ million}(0.6)}{0.12} = \$12.0 \text{ million}$$

Corporate taxes reduce the amount of operating income available to investors in an unlevered firm by the factor $(1 - T)$, so the value of the firm would be reduced by the same amount, holding r_{sU} constant.

Other things held constant, the introduction of corporate taxes would lower Fredrickson's net income and hence its value, so we increased EBIT from $2.4 million to $4 million to facilitate comparisons between the two models.

When Fredrickson has zero debt but pays taxes, Equation 16-5 can be used to find its value:

$$V_U = \frac{\text{EBIT}(1 - T)}{r_{sU}} = \frac{\$4 \text{ million}(0.6)}{0.12} = \$2.0 \text{ million}$$

If Fredrickson now uses $10 million of debt in a world with taxes, we see by Proposition I (Equation 16-4) that its total market value rises from $20 to $24 million:

$$V_L = V_U + TD = \$20 \text{ million} + 0.4(\$10 \text{ million}) = \$24 \text{ million}$$

Therefore, the implied value of Fredrickson's equity is $14 million:

$$S = V - D = \$24 \text{ million} - \$10 \text{ million} = \$14 \text{ million}$$

We can also find Fredrickson's cost of equity, r_{sL}, and its WACC at a debt level of $10 million. First, we use Proposition II (Equation 16-6) to find r_{sL}, the levered cost of equity:

$$\begin{aligned} r_{sL} &= r_{sU} + (r_{sU} - r_d)(1 - T)(D/S) \\ &= 12\% + (12\% - 8\%)(0.6)(\$10 \text{ million}/\$14 \text{ million}) \\ &= 12\% + 1.71\% = 13.71\% \end{aligned}$$

The company's weighted average cost of capital is then

$$\begin{aligned} \text{WACC} &= (D/V)(r_d)(1 - T) + (S/V)r_{sL} \\ &= (\$10/\$24)(8\%)(0.6) + (\$14/\$24)(13.71\%) = 10.0\% \end{aligned}$$

Note that we can also find the levered beta and then the levered cost of equity. First, we apply Hamada's equation to find the levered beta:

$$\begin{aligned} b &= b_U[1 + (1 - T)(D/S)] \\ &= 0.80[1 + (1 - 0.4)(\$10 \text{ million}/\$14 \text{ million})] \\ &= 1.1429 \end{aligned}$$

Applying the CAPM then yields the levered cost of equity as

$$r_{sL} = r_{RF} + b(RP_M) = 8\% + 1.1429(5\%) = 0.1371 = 13.71\%$$

Observe that this is the same levered cost of equity that we obtained directly using Equation 16-6.

Fredrickson's value and cost of capital at various debt levels with corporate taxes are shown in Panel b on the right side of Figure 16-1. In an MM world with corporate taxes, financial leverage does matter: The value of the firm is maximized—and its overall cost of capital is minimized—if it uses almost 100% debt financing. The increase in value is due solely to the tax deductibility of interest payments, which lowers both the cost of debt and the equity risk premium by $(1 - T)$.[5]

To conclude this section, compare the "Without Taxes" and "With Corporate Taxes" sections of Figure 16-1. Without taxes, both WACC and the firm's value (V) are constant. With corporate taxes, WACC declines and V rises as more and more debt is used; thus, under MM with corporate taxes, the optimal capital structure is 100% debt.

Self Test

Is there an optimal capital structure under the MM zero-tax model?

What is the optimal capital structure under the MM model with corporate taxes?

How does the Proposition I equation differ between the two models?

How does the Proposition II equation differ between the two models?

Why do taxes result in a "gain from leverage" in the MM model with corporate taxes?

An unlevered firm has a value of $100 million. An otherwise identical but levered firm has $30 million in debt. Under the MM zero-tax model, what is the value of the levered firm? **($100 million)** Under the MM corporate tax model, what is the value of a levered firm if the corporate tax rate is 40%? **($112 million)**

16.2 Introducing Personal Taxes: The Miller Model

Although MM included *corporate taxes* in the second version of their model, they did not extend the model to include *personal taxes*. However, in his presidential address to the American Finance Association, Merton Miller presented a model to show how leverage affects firms' values when both personal and corporate taxes are taken into account.[6] To explain Miller's model, we begin by defining T_c as the

---

5. In the limit case where the firm used 100% debt financing, the bondholders would own the entire company and so would bear all the business risk. (Up until this point, MM assume that stockholders bear all the risk.) If the bondholders bear all the risk, then the capitalization rate on the debt should be equal to the equity capitalization rate at zero debt, $r_d = r_{sU} = 12\%$.

The income stream to the stockholders in the all-equity case was $4,000,000(1 - T) = $2,400,000, and the value of the firm was

$$V_U = \frac{\$2,400,000}{0.12} = \$20,000,000$$

With all debt, the entire $4,000,000 of EBIT would be used to pay interest charges: r_d would be 12%, so I = 0.12(Debt) = $4,000,000. Taxes would be zero, so the investors (bondholders) would get the entire $4,000,000 of operating income (they would not have to share it with the government). Thus, the value of the firm at 100% debt would be

$$V_L = \frac{\$4,000,000}{0.12} = \$33,333,333 = D$$

There is, of course, a transition problem in all this. Modigliani and Miller assume that $r_d = 8\%$ regardless of how much debt the firm has until debt reaches 100%, at which point r_d jumps to 12%, the cost of equity. As we shall see later in the chapter, r_d actually rises as the risk of financial distress increases.

6. See Merton H. Miller, "Debt and Taxes," *Journal of Finance*, May 1977, pp. 261–275.

corporate tax rate, T_s as the personal tax rate on income from stocks, and T_d as the personal tax rate on income from debt. Note that stock returns are expected to come partly as dividends and partly as capital gains, so T_s is a weighted average of the effective tax rates on dividends and capital gains. However, essentially all debt income comes from interest, which is effectively taxed at investors' top rates; thus T_d is higher than T_s.

With personal taxes included and under the same set of assumptions used in the earlier MM models, the value of an unlevered firm is found as follows:

(16–8)

$$V_U = \frac{EBIT(1 - T_c)}{r_{sU}}$$

$$= \frac{EBIT(1 - T_c)(1 - T_s)}{r_{sU}(1 - T_s)}$$

The $(1 - T_s)$ term takes account of personal taxes. Note that, in order to find the value of the unlevered firm, we can either discount pre-personal-tax cash flows at the pre-personal-tax rate of r_{sU} or discount after-personal-tax cash flows at the after-personal-tax rate of $r_{sU}(1 - T_s)$. Therefore, the numerator in the second line of Equation 16-8 shows how much of the firm's operating income is left after the unlevered firm pays corporate income taxes and its stockholders subsequently pay personal taxes on their equity income. Note also that the discount rate, r_{sU}, in Equation 16-8 is not necessarily equal to the discount rate in Equation 16-5. The r_{sU} from Equation 16-5 is the required discount rate in a world with corporate taxes but no personal taxes; the r_{sU} in Equation 16-8 is the required discount rate in a world with both corporate and personal taxes.

Miller's formula can be proved by an arbitrage proof similar to the one we presented earlier. However, the alternative proof shown below is easier to follow. To begin, we partition the levered firm's annual cash flows, CF_L, into those going to stockholders and those going to bondholders *after* corporate and personal taxes:

(16–9)

$$CF_L = \text{Net CF to stockholders} + \text{Net CF to bondholders}$$

$$= (EBIT - I)(1 - T_c)(1 - T_s) + I(1 - T_d)$$

where I is the annual interest payment. Equation 16-9 can be rearranged as follows:

(16–9a) $$CF_L = [EBIT(1 - T_c)(1 - T_s)] - [I(1 - T_c)(1 - T_s)] + [I(1 - T_d)]$$

The first term in Equation 16-9a is identical to the after-personal-tax cash flow of an unlevered firm as shown in the numerator of Equation 16-8, and its present value is found by discounting the perpetual cash flow by $r_{sU}(1 - T_s)$.

The second and third terms reflect leverage and result from the cash flows associated with debt financing, which under the MM assumptions are riskless (because the firm's debt is riskless under those assumptions). We can either discount pre-personal-tax interest payments at the pre-personal-tax rate of r_d or discount after-personal-tax interest payments at the after-personal-tax rate of $r_d(1 - T_d)$.

Because they are after-personal-tax cash flows to debtholders, the present value of the last two right-hand terms in Equation 16-9a can be obtained by discounting at the after-personal-tax cost of debt, $r_d(1 - T_d)$. Combining the present values of the three terms, we obtain this value for the levered firm:

$$V_L = \frac{EBIT(1 - T_c)(1 - T_s)}{r_{sU}(1 - T_s)} - \frac{I(1 - T_c)(1 - T_s)}{r_d(1 - T_d)} + \frac{I(1 - T_d)}{r_d(1 - T_d)} \tag{16-10}$$

The first right-hand term in Equation 16-10 is identical to V_U in Equation 16-8. Recognizing this and consolidating the second two terms, we obtain

$$V_L = V_U + \left[1 - \frac{(1 - T_c)(1 - T_s)}{(1 - T_d)}\right]\left[\frac{I(1 - T_d)}{r_d(1 - T_d)}\right] \tag{16-10a}$$

Now recognize that the after-tax perpetual interest payment divided by the after-tax required rate of return on debt, $I(1 - T_d)/r_d(1 - T_d)$, is equal to the market value of the perpetual debt, D:

$$D = \frac{I}{r_d} = \frac{I(1 - T_d)}{r_d(1 - T_d)} \tag{16-11}$$

Substituting D into Equation 16-10a and rearranging, we obtain the following expression, which is called the **Miller model**:

$$\text{Miller model: } V_L = V_U + \left[1 - \frac{(1 - T_c)(1 - T_s)}{(1 - T_d)}\right]D \tag{16-12}$$

The Miller model provides an estimate of the value of a levered firm in a world with both corporate and personal taxes.

The Miller model has several important implications, as follows.

1. The term in brackets,

$$\left[1 - \frac{(1 - T_c)(1 - T_s)}{(1 - T_d)}\right]$$

when multiplied by D, represents the gain from leverage. The bracketed term thus replaces the corporate tax rate, T, in the earlier MM model with corporate taxes ($V_L = V_U + TD$).
2. If we ignore all taxes (i.e., if $T_c = T_s = T_d = 0$) then the bracketed term is zero, so in this case Equation 16-12 is the same as the original MM model without taxes.
3. If we ignore personal taxes (i.e., if $T_s = T_d = 0$) then the bracketed term reduces to $[1 - (1 - T_c)] = T_c$, so in this case Equation 16-12 is the same as the MM model with corporate taxes.

4. If the effective personal tax rates on stock and bond incomes were equal (i.e., if $T_s = T_d$), then $(1 - T_s)$ and $(1 - T_d)$ would cancel and so the bracketed term would again reduce to T_c.

5. If $(1 - T_c)(1 - T_s) = (1 - T_d)$, then the bracketed term would be zero and so the value of using leverage would also be zero. This implies that the tax advantage of debt to the firm would be exactly offset by the personal tax advantage of equity. Under this condition, capital structure would have no effect on a firm's value or its cost of capital, so we would be back to MM's original zero-tax proposition.

6. Because taxes on capital gains are lower than on ordinary income and can be deferred, the effective tax rate on stock income is normally less than that on bond income. This being the case, what would the Miller model predict as the gain from leverage? To answer this question, assume the tax rate on corporate income is $T_c = 34\%$, the effective rate on bond income is $T_d = 28\%$, and the effective rate on stock income is $T_s = 15\%$. Using these values in the Miller model, we find that a levered firm's value exceeds that of an unlevered firm by 22% of the market value of corporate debt:

$$\text{Gain from leverage} = \left[1 - \frac{(1 - T_c)(1 - T_s)}{(1 - T_d)}\right]D$$

$$= \left[1 - \frac{(1 - 0.34)(1 - 0.15)}{(1 - 0.28)}\right]D$$

$$= (1 - 0.78)D$$

$$= 0.22\,D$$

Note that the MM model with corporate taxes would indicate a gain from leverage of $T_c(D) = 0.34D$, or 34% of the amount of corporate debt. Thus, with these assumed tax rates, adding personal taxes to the model lowers but does not eliminate the benefit from corporate debt. In general, whenever the effective tax rate on income from stock is less than the effective rate on income from bonds, the Miller model produces a lower gain from leverage than is produced by the MM model with taxes.

In his paper, Miller argued that firms in the aggregate would issue a mix of debt and equity securities such that the before-tax yields on corporate securities and the personal tax rates of the investors who bought these securities would adjust until equilibrium was reached. At equilibrium, $(1 - T_d)$ would equal $(1 - T_c)(1 - T_s)$ and so, as we noted in item 5 above, the tax advantage of debt to the firm would be exactly offset by personal taxation and thus capital structure would have no effect on a firm's value or its cost of capital. Hence, according to Miller, the conclusions derived from the original MM zero-tax model are correct!

Others have extended and tested Miller's analysis. Generally, these extensions question Miller's conclusion that there is no advantage to the use of corporate debt. In fact, Equation 16-12 shows that both T_c and T_s must be less than T_d if there is to be zero gain from leverage. For most U.S. corporations and investors, the effective tax rate on income from stock is less than the rate on income from bonds; that is, $T_s < T_d$. However, many corporate bonds are held by tax-exempt institutions, and in those cases T_c is generally greater than T_d. Also, for those high-tax-bracket individuals with $T_d > T_c$, T_s may be large enough that $(1 - T_c)(1 - T_s)$ is less than $(1 - T_d)$; in this case, there would be an advantage to using corporate debt. Still, Miller's work does show that personal taxes offset some of the benefits of corporate debt. This means that the tax advantages of corporate debt are less than were implied by the earlier MM model, where only corporate taxes were considered.

As we discuss in the next section, both the MM and the Miller models are based on strong and unrealistic assumptions, so we should regard our examples as indicating the general effects of leverage on a firm's value and not a precise relationship.

16.3 Criticisms of the MM and Miller Models

The conclusions of the MM and Miller models follow logically from their initial assumptions. However, both academicians and executives have voiced concerns over the validity of the MM and Miller models, and virtually no one believes they hold precisely. The MM zero-tax model leads to the conclusion that capital structure doesn't matter, yet we observe systematic capital structure patterns within industries. Further, when used with "reasonable" tax rates, both the MM model with corporate taxes and the Miller model lead to the conclusion that firms should use 100% debt financing, but real-life firms do not (deliberately) go to that extreme.

People who disagree with the MM and Miller theories generally attack them on the grounds that their assumptions are invalid. Here are the main objections.

1. Both MM and Miller assume that personal and corporate leverage are perfect substitutes. However, an individual investing in a levered firm has less loss exposure as a result of corporate *limited liability* than if she used "homemade" leverage. For example, in our earlier illustration of the MM arbitrage argument, it should be noted that only the $600,000 our investor had in Firm L would be lost if that firm went bankrupt. However, if the investor engaged in arbitrage transactions and employed "homemade" leverage to invest in Firm U, then she could lose $900,000—the original $600,000 investment plus the $400,000 loan less the $100,000 investment in riskless bonds. This increased personal risk exposure would tend to restrain investors from engaging in arbitrage, and that could cause the equilibrium values of V_L, V_U, r_{sL}, and r_{sU} to be different from those specified by MM. Restrictions on institutional investors, who dominate capital markets today, may also hinder the arbitrage process, because many institutional investors cannot legally borrow to buy stocks and hence are prohibited from engaging in homemade leverage.

   However, even though limited liability may present a problem to individuals, it does *not* present a problem to corporations that are set up to undertake **leveraged buyouts (LBOs)**. Thus, after MM's work became widely known, literally hundreds of LBO firms were established whose founders made billions by recapitalizing underleveraged firms. "Junk bonds" were created to aid in the process, and the managers of underleveraged firms who did not want their firms to be taken over increased debt usage on their own. Thus, MM's work raised the level of debt in corporate America, which probably raised the level of economic efficiency.

2. If a levered firm's operating income declined, then it would sell assets and take other measures to raise the cash necessary to meet its interest obligations and thus avoid bankruptcy. If our illustrative unlevered firm experienced the same decline in operating income, it would probably take the less drastic measure of cutting dividends rather than selling assets. But if dividends were cut then investors who employed homemade leverage would not receive cash to pay the interest on their debt. Thus, homemade leverage puts stockholders in greater danger of bankruptcy than does corporate leverage.

3. Brokerage costs were assumed away by MM and Miller, which makes the switch from L to U costless. However, brokerage and other transaction costs do exist, and they also impede the arbitrage process.

4. Modigliani and Miller initially assumed that corporations and investors could borrow at the risk-free rate. Although risky debt has been introduced into the analysis by others, to reach the MM and Miller conclusions it is still necessary to assume that both corporations and investors can borrow at the same rate. Although major institutional investors probably can borrow at the corporate rate, many institutions are not allowed to borrow to buy securities. Furthermore, most individual investors must borrow at higher rates than those paid by large corporations.

5. In his article, Miller concluded that equilibrium would be reached, but to reach his equilibrium the tax benefit from corporate debt must be the same for all firms and must also be constant for an individual firm regardless of the amount of leverage used. However, we know that tax benefits vary from firm to firm: Highly profitable companies gain the maximum tax benefit from leverage, whereas the benefits to firms that are struggling are much smaller. Moreover, some firms have other tax shields (e.g., high depreciation, pension plan contributions, operating loss carryforwards), and these shields reduce the tax savings from interest payments.[7] It also is simplistic to assume that the expected tax shield is unaffected by the amount of debt used. Higher leverage increases the probability that the firm will not be able to use the full tax shield in the future, because higher leverage increases the probability of future unprofitability and consequently lower tax rates. Note also that large, diversified corporations can use losses in one division to offset profits in another. Thus, the tax shelter benefit is more certain in such firms than in smaller, single-product companies. All things considered, it appears likely that the interest tax shield from corporate debt is more valuable to some firms than to others.

6. MM and Miller assume that there are no costs associated with financial distress, and they also ignore agency costs. Further, they assume that all market participants have identical information about firms' prospects, which is clearly an oversimplification.

These six points all suggest that the MM and Miller models lead to questionable conclusions and that the models would be better if certain of their assumptions could be relaxed. We discuss an extension of the models in the next section.

---

7. For a discussion of the impact of tax shields, see Harry DeAngelo and Ronald W. Masulis, "Optimal Capital Structure under Corporate and Personal Taxation," *Journal of Financial Economics,* March 1980, pp. 3–30; Thomas W. Downs, "Corporate Leverage and Nondebt Tax Shields: Evidence on Crowding-Out," *The Financial Review,* November 1993, pp. 549–583; John R. Graham, "Taxes and Corporate Finance: A Review," *Review of Financial Studies,* Winter 2003, pp. 1075–1129; and Jeffrey K. Mackie-Mason, "Do Taxes Affect Corporate Financing Decisions?" *Journal of Finance,* December 1990, pp. 1471–1493.

> Should we accept that one of the models presented thus far (MM with zero taxes, MM with corporate taxes, or Miller) is correct? Why or why not?
>
> Are any of the assumptions used in the models worrisome to you, and what does "worrisome" mean in this context?

Self Test

16.4 An Extension of the MM Model: Nonzero Growth and a Risky Tax Shield

In this section, we discuss an extension of the MM model that incorporates growth and different discount rates for the debt tax shield.[8]

Modigliani and Miller assumed that firms pay out all of their earnings as dividends and therefore do not grow. However, most firms do grow, and growth affects the MM and Hamada results (as found in the first part of this chapter). Recall that, for an unlevered firm, the WACC is just the unlevered cost of equity: WACC = r_{sU}. If g is the constant growth rate and FCF is the expected free cash flow, then the corporate value model from Chapter 11 shows that

$$V_U = \frac{FCF}{r_{sU} - g} \tag{16-13}$$

As shown by Equation 16-4, the value of the levered firm is equal to the value of the unlevered firm plus gain from leverage, which is the value of the tax shield:

$$V_L = V_U + V_{Tax\ shield} \tag{16-4a}$$

However, when there is growth, the value of the tax shield is not equal to TD as it is in the MM model with corporate taxes. If the firm uses debt and if g is positive then, as the firm grows, the amount of debt will increase over time; hence the size of the annual tax shield will also increase at the rate g, provided the debt ratio remains constant. Moreover, the value of this growing tax shield is greater than the value of the constant tax shield in the MM analysis.

Modigliani and Miller assumed that corporate debt was riskless and that the firm would always be able to use its tax savings. Therefore, they discounted the tax savings at the cost of debt, r_d, which is the risk-free rate. However, corporate debt is not risk free—firms do occasionally default on their loans. Also, a firm may not be able to use tax savings from debt in the current year if it already has a pre-tax loss from operations. Therefore, the flow of tax savings to the firm is not risk-free and hence it should be discounted at a higher rate than the risk-free rate. In addition, since debt is safer than equity to an investor because it has a higher priority claim on the firm's cash flows, its discount rate should be no greater than the unlevered cost of equity. For now, assume that the appropriate discount rate for the tax savings

---

8. See Michael C. Ehrhardt and Phillip R. Daves, "Corporate Valuation: The Combined Impact of Growth and the Tax Shield of Debt on the Cost of Capital and Systematic Risk," *Journal of Applied Finance*, Fall/Winter 2002, pp. 31–38.

is r_{TS}, which is greater than or equal to the cost of debt, r_d, and less than or equal to the unlevered cost of equity, r_{sU}.

If r_{TS} is the appropriate discount rate for the tax shield, r_d is the interest rate on the debt, T is the corporate tax rate, and D is the current amount of debt, then the present value of this growing tax shield is

$$(16\text{--}14) \qquad V_{\text{Tax shield}} = \frac{r_d TD}{r_{TS} - g}$$

This formula is similar to the dividend growth formula from Chapter 5, except it has $r_d TD$ as the growing cash flow generated by the tax savings and r_{TS} as the discount rate. Substituting Equation 16-14 into Equation 16-4a yields a valuation expression that incorporates constant growth:

$$(16\text{--}15) \qquad V_L = V_U + \left(\frac{r_d}{r_{TS} - g} \right) TD$$

The difference between Equation 16-15 for the value of the levered firm and the expression given in Equation 16-4 is the $r_d/(r_{TS} - g)$ term in large parentheses, which reflects the added value of the tax shield due to growth. In the MM model, $r_{TS} = r_d = r_{RF}$ and $g = 0$, so the term in parentheses is equal to 1.0.

If $r_{TS} < r_{sU}$, then growth can actually cause the levered cost of equity to be *less* than the unlevered cost of equity.[9] This happens because the combination of rapid growth and a low discount rate for the tax shield causes the value of the tax shield to dominate the unlevered value of the firm. If this were true, then high-growth firms would tend to have larger amounts of debt than low-growth firms. However, this is not consistent with either intuition or what we observe in the market: High-growth firms actually tend to have lower levels of debt. Regardless of the growth rate, firms with more debt should have a higher cost of equity than firms with no debt. These inconsistencies can be resolved if $r_{TS} = r_{sU}$. Given this equality, the value of the levered firm becomes[10]

$$(16\text{--}16) \qquad V_L = V_U + \left(\frac{r_d TD}{r_{sU} - g} \right)$$

In view of this valuation equation, expressions for the levered cost of equity and the levered beta (corresponding to Equations 16-6 and 16-7) become

$$(16\text{--}17) \qquad r_{sL} = r_{sU} + (r_{sU} - r_d)\frac{D}{S}$$

---

9. See the paper by Ehrhardt and Daves cited in footnote 8.
10. For a discussion of the *compressed APV* valuation method, which assumes that $r_{TS} = r_{sU}$, see Steven N. Kaplan and Richard S. Ruback, "The Valuation of Cash Flow Forecasts: An Empirical Analysis," *Journal of Finance,* September 1995, pp. 1059–1093.

and

$$b = b_U + (b_U - b_D)\frac{D}{S}$$

(16–18)

As in Chapter 15, b_U is the beta of an unlevered firm and b is the beta of a levered firm. Because debt is not riskless, it has a beta (b_D).

Although the derivations of Equations 16-17 and 16-18 reflect corporate taxes and growth, neither of these expressions includes the corporate tax rate or the growth rate. This means that the expression for the levered required rate of return, Equation 16-17, is exactly the same as MM's expression for the levered required rate of return *without taxes,* Equation 16-2. And the expression for the levered beta, Equation 16-18, is exactly the same as Hamada's equation (with risky debt) but *without taxes*. The reason the tax rate and the growth rate drop out of these two expressions is that the growing tax shield is discounted at the unlevered cost of equity, r_{sU}, not at the cost of debt as in the MM model. The tax rate drops out because no matter how high the level of T, the total risk of the firm will not be changed: The unlevered cash flows and the tax shield are discounted at the same rate. The growth rate drops out for the same reason: An increasing debt level will not change the riskiness of the entire firm no matter what rate of growth prevails.[11]

Observe that Equation 16-18 includes the term b_D. Since MM and Hamada assumed that corporate debt is riskless, its beta should be zero. However, if corporate debt is not riskless then its beta, b_D, may not be zero. If we assume that bonds lie on the Security Market Line, then a bond's required return, r_d, can be expressed as $r_d = r_{RF} + b_D RP_M$. Solving for b_D then gives $b_D = (r_d - r_{RF})/RP_M$.

16.4a Illustration of the MM Extension with Growth

Earlier in this chapter we examined Fredrickson Water Company, a zero-growth firm with unlevered value of $20 million. To see how growth affects the levered value of the firm and the levered cost of equity, let's look at Peterson Power Inc., which is similar to Fredrickson except that it is growing. Peterson's expected free cash flow is $1 million, which is expected to grow at a rate of 7%. Like Fredrickson, Peterson has an unlevered cost of equity of 12% and faces a 40% tax rate. Peterson's unlevered value is $V_U = (\$1 \text{ million})/(0.12 - 0.07) = \$20$ million, the same as Fredrickson's.

Suppose now that Peterson, like Fredrickson, uses $10 million of debt with a cost of 8%. We see from Equation 16-16 that

$$V_L = \$20\,\text{million} + \left(\frac{0.08 \times 0.40 \times \$10\,\text{million}}{0.12 - 0.07}\right) = \$26.4\,\text{million}$$

---

11. Of course, Equations 16-14, 16-15, and 16-16 also apply to firms that don't happen to be growing. In this special case, the difference between the Ehrhardt and Daves extension and the MM with taxes treatment is that MM assume that the tax shield should be discounted at the risk-free rate, whereas this extension of their model shows it is more reasonable for the tax shield to be discounted at the unlevered cost of equity, r_{sU}. Because r_{sU} is greater than the risk-free rate, the value of a nongrowing tax shield will be lower when discounted at this higher rate, giving a lower value of the levered firm than what MM would predict.

and that the implied value of equity is

$$S = V_L - D = \$26.4 \text{ million} - \$10 \text{ million} = \$16.4 \text{ million}$$

The increase in value due to leverage when there is 7% growth is $6.4 million, compared with the increase in value of only $4 million for Fredrickson. The reason for this difference is that even though the debt tax shield is currently (0.08)(0.40)(10 million) = $0.32 million for each company, this tax shield will grow at an annual rate of 7% for Peterson but will remain fixed over time for Fredrickson. And even though Peterson and Fredrickson have the same initial dollar value of debt, their debt weights, w_d, are not the same. Peterson's w_d is $D/V_L = \$10/\$26.4 = 37.88\%$, whereas Fredrickson's w_d is $\$10/\$24 = 41.67\%$.

With $10 million in debt, Peterson's new cost of equity is given by Equation 16-17:

$$r_{sL} = 12\% + (12\% - 8\%)\frac{0.3788}{0.6212} = 14.44\%$$

This is higher than Fredrickson's levered cost of equity of 13.71%. Finally, Peterson's new WACC is (1.0 − 0.3788)14.44% + 0.3788(1 − 0.40)8% = 10.78% versus Fredrickson's WACC of 10.0%.

In sum, using the MM and Hamada models to calculate the value of a levered firm and its cost of capital when there is growth will: (1) underestimate the value of the levered firm, because these models underestimate the value of the growing tax shield; and (2) underestimate the levered WACC and levered cost of capital because, for a given initial amount of debt, these models overestimate the firm's w_d.

Self Test

Why is the value of the tax shield different when a firm grows?

Why would it be inappropriate to discount tax shield cash flows at the risk-free rate as MM do?

How will your estimates of the levered cost of equity be biased if you use the MM or Hamada models when growth is present? Why does this matter?

An unlevered firm has a value of $100 million. An otherwise identical but levered firm has $30 million in debt. Suppose both firms are growing at a constant rate of 5%, the corporate tax rate is 40%, the cost of debt is 6%, and the unlevered cost of equity is 8% (assume r_{sU} is the appropriate discount rate for the tax shield). What is the value of the levered firm? (**$124 million**) What is the value of the stock? (**$94 million**) What is the levered cost of equity? (**8.64%**)

16.5 Risky Debt and Equity as an Option

In the previous sections, we evaluated equity and debt using the standard discounted cash flow techniques. However, we learned in Chapter 13 that if there is an opportunity for management to make a change as a result of new information after a project or investment has been started, then there might be an option component to the project or investment being evaluated. This is the case with equity. To see why, consider Kunkel Inc., a small manufacturer of electronic wiring harnesses and instrumentation located in Minot, North Dakota. Kunkel's current value (debt plus equity) is $20 million, and its debt consists of $10 million face value of 5-year zero coupon bonds. What decision does management make when the debt comes due? In most cases, it would pay the $10 million that is due. But what if the company has done poorly and the firm is worth only $9 million? In that case, the firm is technically bankrupt, since its value is less than the amount of debt due. Management will choose to default on the loan; in this case, the firm will be liquidated or sold for $9 million, the debtholders will get all $9 million, and the stockholders will get nothing. Of course, if the firm is worth $10 million or more then management will choose to repay the loan. The ability to make this decision—to pay or not to pay—looks very much like an option, and the techniques we developed in Chapter 6 can be used to value it.

16.5a Using the Black-Scholes Option Pricing Model to Value Equity

WEB

See *Ch16 Tool Kit.xls* on the textbook's Web site for all calculations.

To put this decision into an option context, suppose P is Kunkel's total value when the debt matures. Then, if the debt is paid off, Kunkel's stockholders will receive the equivalent of P − $10 million if P > $10 million.[12] They will receive nothing if P ≤ $10 million because management will default on the bond and the bondholders will take over the company. These facts can be summarized as follows:

$$\text{Payoff to stockholders} = \text{MAX}(P - \$10 \text{ million, } 0)$$

This is exactly the same payoff as a European call option on the total value (P) of the firm with a strike price equal to the face value of the debt, $10 million. We can use the Black-Scholes option pricing model from Chapter 6 to determine the value of this asset.

Recall from Chapter 6 that the value of a call option depends on five things: the price of the underlying asset, the strike price, the risk-free rate, the time to expiration, and the volatility of the market value of the underlying asset. Here the underlying asset is the total value of the firm. If we assume that volatility is 40% and that the risk-free rate is 6%, then the inputs for the Black-Scholes model are as follows:

$$\begin{aligned}
P &= \$20 \text{ million} \\
X &= \$10 \text{ million} \\
t &= 5 \text{ years} \\
r_{RF} &= 6\% \\
\sigma &= 40\%
\end{aligned}$$

The value of a European call option, as shown in Chapter 6, is

$$V = P[(N(d_1)] - Xe^{-r_{RF}t}[N(d_2)] \tag{16–19}$$

where

$$d_1 = \frac{\ln(P \,/\, X) + (r_{RF} + \sigma^2/2)t}{\sigma\sqrt{t}} \tag{16–20}$$

---

12. Actually, rather than receive cash of P − $10 million, the stockholders will keep the company (which is worth P − $10 million) rather than turn it over to the bondholders.

and

(16–21)	$$d_2 = d_1 - \sigma\sqrt{t}$$

For Kunkel Inc.,

$$d_1 = \frac{\ln(20/10) + (0.06 + 0.40^2/2)5}{0.40\sqrt{5}} = 1.5576$$

$$d_2 = 1.5576 - 0.40\sqrt{5} = 0.6632$$

Using the *Excel* NORMSDIST function gives $N(d_1) = N(1.5576) = 0.9403$, $N(d_2) = N(0.6632) = 0.7464$, and $V = \$20(0.9403) - \$10e^{-0.06(5)}(0.7464) = \$13.28$ million. So Kunkel's equity is worth $13.28 million, and its debt must be worth what is left over: $20 − $13.28 = $6.72 million. Since this is 5-year, zero coupon debt, its yield must be

$$\text{Yield on debt} = \left(\frac{10}{6.72}\right)^{1/5} - 1 = 0.0827 = 8.27\%$$

Thus, when Kunkel issued the debt, it received $6.72 million and the yield on the debt was 8.27%. Notice that the yield on the debt, 8.27%, is greater than the 6% risk-free rate. This is because the firm might default if its value falls enough, so the bonds are risky. Note also that the yield on the debt depends on the value of the option and hence on the riskiness of the firm. The debt will have a lower value—and a higher yield—the more the option is worth.

16.5b Managerial Incentives

The only decision an investor in a stock option can make, once the option is purchased, is whether and when to exercise it. However, this restriction does not apply to equity when it is viewed as an option on the total value of the firm. Management has some leeway to affect the riskiness of the firm through its capital budgeting and investment decisions, and it can affect the amount of capital invested in the firm through its dividend policy.

16.5c Capital Budgeting Decisions

When Kunkel issued the $10 million face value debt discussed previously, the yield was determined in part by Kunkel's riskiness, which in turn was determined in part by what management intended to do with the $6.72 million it raised. We know from our analysis in Chapter 6 that options are worth more when volatility is higher. This means that if Kunkel's management can find a way to increase its riskiness without decreasing the total value of the firm, then doing so will increase the equity's value while decreasing the debt's value. Management can accomplish this by selecting risky rather than safe investment projects. Table 16-1 shows the value of equity, the value of debt, and the yield on debt for a range of possible volatilities. See *Ch16 Tool Kit.xls* for the calculations.

Kunkel's current volatility is 40%, so its equity is worth $13.28 million and its debt is worth $6.72 million. But if, after incurring the debt, management undertakes projects that increase its riskiness from a volatility of 40% to a volatility of 80%, then the value of Kunkel's equity will increase by $2.53 million to $15.81 million and the value of its debt will decrease by the same amount. This 19% increase in the

TABLE 16-1	The Value of Kunkel's Debt and Equity for Various Levels of Volatility (Millions of Dollars)		
Standard Deviation	**Equity**	**Proceeds from Debt**	**Debt Yield**
20%	$12.62	$7.38	6.25%
30	12.83	7.17	6.89
40	**13.28**	**6.72**	**8.27**
50	13.86	6.14	10.25
60	14.51	5.49	12.74
70	15.17	4.83	15.66
80	15.81	4.19	18.99
90	16.41	3.59	22.74
100	16.96	3.04	26.92
110	17.46	2.54	31.56
120	17.90	2.10	36.68

© Cengage Learning 2013

value of the equity represents a transfer of wealth from bondholders to stockholders. A corresponding transfer of wealth from stockholders to bondholders would occur if Kunkel undertook projects that were safer than originally planned. Table 16-1 shows that if management undertakes safe projects and drives the volatility down to 30%, then stockholders will lose (and bondholders will gain) $0.45 million.

WEB

See **Ch16 Tool Kit.xls** on the textbook's Web site for all calculations.

Such a strategy of investing borrowed funds in risky assets is called **bait and switch** because the firm obtains the money by promising one investment policy and then switching to another policy. The bait-and-switch problem is more severe when a firm's value is low relative to its level of debt. If Kunkel's total value is $20 million, then doubling its volatility from 40% to 80% increases its equity value by 19%. But if Kunkel had done poorly in recent years and its total value were only $10 million, then the impact of increasing volatility would be much greater. Table 16-2 shows that if Kunkel's total value were only $10 million and it issued $10 million face value of 5-year, zero coupon debt, then its equity would be worth $4.46 million at a volatility of 40%. Doubling the volatility to 80% would increase the value of the equity to $6.83 million, or by 53%. The incentive for management to "roll the dice" with borrowed funds can be enormous, and if management owns many stock options then their payoff from rolling the dice is even greater than the payoff to stockholders!

Bondholders are aware of these incentives and write covenants into debt issues that restrict management's ability to invest in riskier projects than originally promised. However, their attempts to protect themselves are not always successful, as the failures of Enron, Lehman Brothers, and AIG demonstrate. The combination of a risky industry, high levels of debt, and option-based compensation has proven to be very dangerous.

16.5d Equity with Risky Coupon Debt

We have analyzed the simple case when a firm has zero coupon debt outstanding. The analysis becomes much more complicated when a firm has debt that requires periodic interest payments, because then management can decide whether or not to default on each interest payment date. For example, suppose Kunkel's $10 million of debt is a 1-year, 8% loan with semiannual payments. The scheduled payments are $400,000 in 6 months, and then $10.4 million at the end of the year. If management makes the

TABLE 16-2 Debt and Equity Values for Various Levels of Volatility When the Firm's Total Value is $10 Million (Millions of Dollars)

Standard Deviation	Equity	Value of Debt	Debt Yield
20%	$3.16	$6.84	7.90%
30	3.80	6.20	10.02
40	**4.46**	**5.54**	**12.52**
50	5.10	4.90	15.35
60	5.72	4.28	18.49
70	6.30	3.70	21.98
80	6.83	3.17	25.81
90	7.31	2.69	30.04
100	7.74	2.26	34.68
110	8.13	1.87	39.77
120	8.46	1.54	45.36

© Cengage Learning 2013

scheduled $400,000 interest payment, then the stockholders will acquire the right to make the next payment of $10.4 million. If it does not make the $400,000 payment, then by defaulting the stockholders lose the right to make that next payment and hence lose the firm.[13] In other words, at the beginning of the year the stockholders have an option to purchase an option. The option they own has an exercise price of $400,000 and it expires in 6 months, and if they exercise it, they will acquire an option to purchase the entire firm for $10.4 million in another 6 months.

If the debt were 2-year debt, then there would be four decision points for management and the stockholders' position would be like an option on an option on an option on an option! These types of options are called **compound options,** and techniques for valuing them are beyond the scope of this book. However, the incentives discussed previously for the case when a firm has risky zero coupon debt still apply when the firm has periodic interest payments to make.[14]

Self Test

Discuss how equity can be viewed as an option. Who has the option and what decision can they make?

Why would management want to increase the riskiness of the firm? Why would this make bondholders unhappy?

What can bondholders do to limit management's ability to bait and switch?

---

13. Actually, bankruptcy is far more complicated than our example suggests. As a firm approaches default it can take a number of actions, and even after filing for bankruptcy the stockholders can substantially delay a takeover by bondholders, during which time the value of the firm can deteriorate further. As a result, stockholders can often extract concessions from bondholders in situations where it would seem that the bondholders should get all of the firm's value. Bankruptcy is discussed in more detail in Chapter 25.

14. For more on viewing equity as an option, see D. Galai and R. Masulis, "The Option Pricing Model and the Risk Factor of Stock," *Journal of Financial Economics,* Vol. 3, 1976, pp. 53–81. For a discussion on compound options, see Robert Geske, "The Valuation of Corporate Liabilities as Compound Options," *Journal of Financial and Quantitative Analysis,* June 1984, pp. 541–552.

16.6 Capital Structure Theory: Our View

The great contribution of the capital structure models developed by MM, Miller, and their followers is that these models identified the specific benefits and costs of using debt: the tax benefits, financial distress costs, and so on. Prior to MM, no capital structure theory existed and so we had no systematic way of analyzing the effects of debt financing.

The trade-off model discussed in Chapter 15 is summarized graphically in Figure 16-2. The top graph shows the relationships between the debt ratio and the cost of debt, the cost of equity, and the WACC. Both r_s and $r_d(1 - T_c)$ rise steadily with increases in leverage, but the rate of increase accelerates at higher debt levels; this reflects agency costs and the increased probability of financial distress. Under increasing leverage the WACC first declines, then hits a minimum at D/V*, and then begins to rise. Note that the value of D in D/V* in the upper graph is D*, the level of debt in the lower graph that maximizes the firm's value. Thus, a firm's WACC is minimized and its value is maximized at the same capital structure. Note also that the general shapes of the curves apply regardless of whether we are using the modified MM with corporate taxes model, the Miller model, or a variant of these models.

Unfortunately, it is impossible to quantify accurately the costs and benefits of debt financing, so it is impossible to pinpoint D/V*, the capital structure that maximizes a firm's value. Most experts believe that such a structure exists for every firm but that it changes over time as a firm's operations and investor preferences change. Most experts also believe that, as shown in Figure 16-2, the relationship between value and leverage is relatively flat over a fairly broad range, so large deviations from the optimal capital structure can occur without materially affecting the stock price.

Now consider signaling theory, which we discussed in Chapter 15. Because of asymmetric information, investors know less about a firm's prospects than its managers know. Furthermore, managers try to maximize value for *current* stockholders, not new ones. Hence, if the firm has excellent prospects then management will not want to issue new shares, but if things look bleak then a new stock offering would benefit current stockholders. Investors therefore view a stock offering as a signal of bad news, so stock prices tend to decline when new issues are announced. As a result, new equity financings are relatively expensive. The net effect of signaling is to motivate firms to maintain a reserve borrowing capacity so that future investment opportunities can be financed by debt if internal funds are not available.

By combining the trade-off and asymmetric information theories, we obtain the following explanation for firms' behavior.

1. Debt financing provides benefits because of the tax deductibility of interest, so firms should have some debt in their capital structures.
2. However, financial distress and agency costs place limits on debt usage—beyond some point, these costs offset the tax advantage of debt. The costs of financial distress are especially harmful to firms whose values consist primarily of intangible growth options, such as research and development. Such firms should have lower levels of debt than firms whose asset bases consist mostly of tangible assets.
3. Because of problems resulting from asymmetric information and flotation costs, low-growth firms should follow a pecking order by raising capital first from internal sources, then by borrowing, and finally by issuing new stock. In fact, such low-growth firms rarely need to issue external equity. High-growth firms whose growth occurs primarily through increases in tangible assets should follow the same pecking order, but usually they will need to issue new stock as well as

| Figure 16-2 | **Effects of Leverage: The Trade-off Models** |

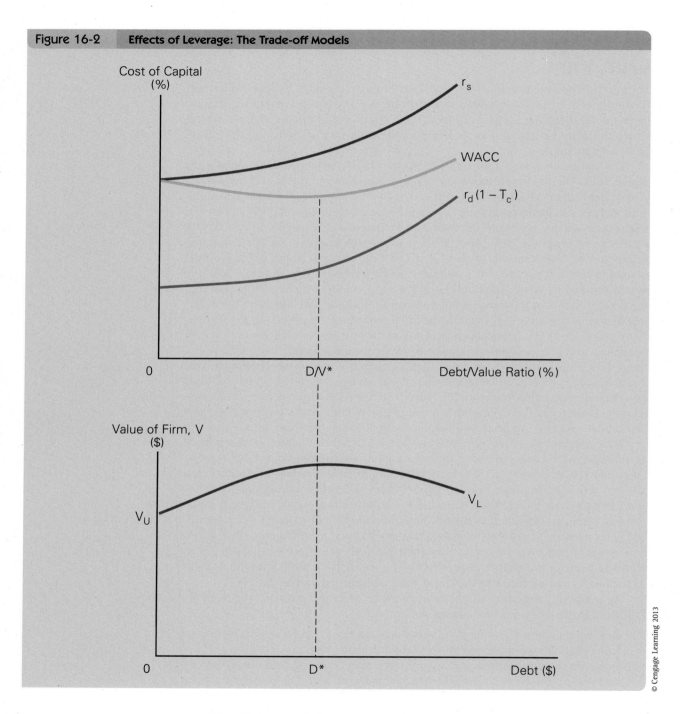

debt. High-growth firms whose values consist primarily of intangible growth options may run out of internally generated cash, but they should emphasize stock rather than debt because of the severe problems that financial distress imposes on such firms.

4. Managers have better information than investors about a firm's prospects. This informational asymmetry causes investors to view a stock issue as a negative signal, which leads to a decline in stock price. To prevent this, firms should maintain

a reserve of borrowing capacity so they can take advantage of investment opportunities without having to issue stock at low prices. This reserve will cause the actual debt ratio to be lower than that suggested by the trade-off models.

There is some evidence that managers do attempt to behave in ways that are consistent with this view of capital structure. In a survey of CFOs, about two-thirds said they follow a "hierarchy in which the most advantageous sources of funds are exhausted before other sources are used." The hierarchy usually followed the pecking order of first internally generated cash flow, then debt, and finally external equity, which is consistent with the predicted behavior of most low-growth firms. But there were occasions in which external equity was the first source of financing, which would be consistent with the theory for either high-growth firms or firms whose agency costs and level of financial distress have exceeded the benefit of tax savings.[15]

Self Test

Summarize the trade-off and signaling theories of capital structure.

Are the trade-off and signaling theories mutually exclusive or might *both* be correct?

Does capital structure theory provide managers with a model that can be used to set a precise optimal capital structure?

Summary

In this chapter we discussed a variety of topics related to capital structure decisions. The key concepts covered are listed below.

- In 1958, **Franco Modigliani and Merton Miller (MM)** proved, under a restrictive set of assumptions including zero taxes, that capital structure is irrelevant; thus, according to the original MM article, a firm's value is not affected by its financing mix.
- Modigliani and Miller later added **corporate taxes** to their model and reached the conclusion that capital structure does matter. Indeed, their model led to the conclusion that firms should use 100% debt financing.
- MM's model with corporate taxes demonstrated that the primary benefit of debt stems from the **tax deductibility of interest payments**.
- Later, Miller extended the theory to include **personal taxes**. The introduction of personal taxes reduces, but does not eliminate, the benefits of debt financing. Thus, the **Miller model** also leads to 100% debt financing.

---

15. For more on capital budgeting issues, see Ravindra R. Kamath, "Long-Term Financing Decisions: Views and Practices of Financial Managers of NYSE Firms," *The Financial Review,* May 1997, pp. 350–356; Michael T. Dugan and Keith A. Shriver, "An Empirical Comparison of Alternative Methods for Estimating the Degree of Operating Leverage," *The Financial Review,* May 1992, pp. 309–321; and Dilip K. Ghosh, "Optimum Capital Structure Redefined," *The Financial Review,* August 1992, pp. 411–429.

- The introduction of growth changes the MM and Hamada results for the levered cost of equity and the levered beta.
- If the firm is growing at a constant rate, the debt tax shield is discounted at r_{sU}, and debt remains a constant proportion of the capital structure, then

$$r_{sL} = r_{sU} + (r_{sU} - r_d)\frac{D}{S}$$

and

$$b = b_U + (b_U - b_D)\frac{D}{S}$$

- When debt is risky, management may choose to default. If the debt is zero coupon debt, then this makes equity like an option on the value of the firm with a strike price equal to the face value of the debt. If the debt has periodic interest payments then the equity is like an option on an option, or a **compound option**.
- When a firm has risky debt and equity is like an option, management has an incentive to increase the firm's risk in order to increase the equity value at the expense of the debt value. This is called **bait and switch**.

Questions

16-1 Define each of the following terms:
   a. MM Proposition I without taxes and with corporate taxes
   b. MM Proposition II without taxes and with corporate taxes
   c. Miller model
   d. Financial distress costs
   e. Agency costs
   f. Trade-off model
   g. Value of debt tax shield
   h. Equity as an option

16-2 Explain, in words, how MM use the arbitrage process to prove the validity of Proposition I. Also, list the major MM assumptions and explain why each of these assumptions is necessary in the arbitrage proof.

16-3 A utility company is allowed to charge prices high enough to cover all costs, including its cost of capital. Public service commissions are supposed to take actions that stimulate companies to operate as efficiently as possible in order to keep costs, and hence prices, as low as possible. Some time ago, AT&T's debt ratio was about 33%. Some individuals (Myron J. Gordon, in particular) argued that a higher debt ratio would lower AT&T's cost of capital and permit it to charge lower rates for telephone service. Gordon thought an optimal debt ratio for AT&T was about 50%. Do the theories presented in the chapter support or refute Gordon's position?

16-4 Modigliani and Miller assumed that firms do not grow. How does positive growth change their conclusions about the value of the levered firm and its cost of capital?

16-5 Your firm's CEO has just learned about options and how your firm's equity can be viewed as an option. Why might he want to increase the riskiness of the firm, and why might the bondholders be unhappy about this?

Problems   Answers Appear in Appendix B

Easy Problems 1–3

16-1 MM Model with Zero Taxes An unlevered firm has a value of $500 million. An otherwise identical but levered firm has $50 million in debt. Under the MM zero-tax model, what is the value of the levered firm?

16-2 MM Model with Corporate Taxes An unlevered firm has a value of $800 million. An otherwise identical but levered firm has $60 million in debt. Assuming the corporate tax rate is 35%, use the MM model with corporate taxes to determine the value of the levered firm.

16-3 Miller Model with Corporate and Personal Taxes An unlevered firm has a value of $600 million. An otherwise identical but levered firm has $240 million in debt. Under the Miller model, what is the value of the levered firm if the corporate tax rate is 34%, the personal tax rate on equity is 10%, and the personal tax rate on debt is 35%?

Intermediate Problems 4–7

16-4 Business and Financial Risk—MM Model Air Tampa has just been incorporated, and its board of directors is currently grappling with the question of optimal capital structure. The company plans to offer commuter air services between Tampa and smaller surrounding cities. Jaxair has been around for a few years, and it has about the same basic business risk as Air Tampa would have. Jaxair's market-determined beta is 1.8, and it has a current market value debt ratio (total debt to total assets) of 50% and a federal-plus-state tax rate of 40%. Air Tampa expects to be only marginally profitable at start-up; hence its tax rate would only be 25%. Air Tampa's owners expect that the total book and market value of the firm's stock, if it uses zero debt, would be $10 million. Air Tampa's CFO believes that the MM and Hamada formulas for the value of a levered firm and the levered firm's cost of capital should be used. (These are given in Equations 16-4, 16-6, and 16-7.)

a. Estimate the beta of an unlevered firm in the commuter airline business based on Jaxair's market-determined beta. (*Hint:* This is a levered beta; use Equation 16-7 and solve for b_U.)

b. Now assume that $r_d = r_{RF} = 10\%$ and that the market risk premium $RP_M = 5\%$. Find the required rate of return on equity for an unlevered commuter airline.

c. Air Tampa is considering three capital structures: (1) $2 million debt, (2) $4 million debt, and (3) $6 million debt. Estimate Air Tampa's r_s for these debt levels.

d. Calculate Air Tampa's r_s at $6 million debt while assuming its federal-plus-state tax rate is now 40%. Compare this with your corresponding answer to part c. (*Hint:* The increase in the tax rate causes V_U to drop to $8 million.)

16-5 MM without Taxes Companies U and L are identical in every respect except that U is unlevered while L has $10 million of 5% bonds outstanding. Assume that (1) there are no corporate or personal taxes, (2) all of the other MM assumptions are met, (3) EBIT is $2 million, and (4) the cost of equity to Company U is 10%.

a. What value would MM estimate for each firm?

b. What is r_s for Firm U? For Firm L?

    c. Find S_L, and then show that $S_L + D = V_L = \$20$ million.

    d. What is the WACC for Firm U? For Firm L?

    e. Suppose $V_U = \$20$ million and $V_L = \$22$ million. According to MM, are these values consistent with equilibrium? If not, explain the process by which equilibrium would be restored.

16-6 MM with Corporate Taxes Companies U and L are identical in every respect except that U is unlevered while L has $10 million of 5% bonds outstanding. Assume that (1) all of the MM assumptions are met, (2) both firms are subject to a 40% federal-plus-state corporate tax rate, (3) EBIT is $2 million, and (4) the unlevered cost of equity is 10%.

    a. What value would MM now estimate for each firm? (*Hint:* Use Proposition I.)

    b. What is r_s for Firm U? For Firm L?

    c. Find S_L, and then show that $S_L + D = V_L$ results in the same value as obtained in part a.

    d. What is the WACC for Firm U? For Firm L?

16-7 Miller Model Companies U and L are identical in every respect except that U is unlevered while L has $10 million of 5% bonds outstanding. Assume that (1) all of the MM assumptions are met, (2) both firms are subject to a 40% federal-plus-state corporate tax rate, (3) EBIT is $2 million, (4) investors in both firms face a tax rate of $T_d = 28\%$ on debt income and $T_s = 20\%$ (on average) on stock income, and (5) the appropriate required pre-personal-tax rate r_{sU} is 10%.

    a. What is the value V_U of the unlevered firm? (Note that V_U is now reduced by the personal tax on stock income, so $V_U = \$12$ million as in Problem 16-6.)

    b. What is the value of V_L?

    c. What is the gain from leverage in this situation? Compare this with the gain from leverage in Problem 16-6.

    d. Set $T_c = T_s = T_d = 0$. What is the value of the levered firm? The gain from leverage?

    e. Now suppose $T_s = T_d = 0$ and $T_c = 40\%$. What are the value of the levered firm and the gain from leverage?

    f. Assume that $T_d = 28\%$, $T_s = 28\%$, and $T_c = 40\%$. Now what are the value of the levered firm and the gain from leverage?

Challenging Problems 8–10

16-8 MM Extension with Growth Schwarzentraub Industries' expected free cash flow for the year is $500,000; in the future, free cash flow is expected to grow at a rate of 9%. The company currently has no debt, and its cost of equity is 13%. Its tax rate is 40%. (*Hint:* Use Equations 16-16 and 16-17.)

    a. Find V_U.

    b. Find V_L and r_{sL} if Schwarzentraub uses $5 million in debt with a cost of 7%. Use the extension of the MM model that allows for growth.

    c. Based on V_U from part a, find V_L and r_{sL} using the MM model (with taxes) if Schwarzentraub uses $5 million in 7% debt.

    d. Explain the difference between your answers to parts b and c.

16-9 MM with and without Taxes International Associates (IA) is about to commence operations as an international trading company. The firm will have book assets of $10 million, and it expects to earn a 16% return on these assets before taxes. However, because of certain tax arrangements with foreign govern-ments, IA will not pay any taxes; that is, its tax rate will be zero. Management is trying to decide how to raise the required $10 million. It is known that the capitalization rate r_U for an all-equity firm in this business is 11%, and IA can borrow at a rate $r_d = 6\%$. Assume that the MM assumptions apply.

a. According to MM, what will be the value of IA if it uses no debt? If it uses $6 million of 6% debt?

b. What are the values of the WACC and r_s at debt levels of D = $0, D = $6 million, and D = $10 million? What effect does leverage have on firm value? Why?

c. Assume the initial facts of the problem ($r_d = 6\%$, EBIT = $1.6 million, $r_{sU} = 11\%$), but now assume that a 40% federal-plus-state corporate tax rate exists. Use the MM formulas to find the new market values for IA with zero debt and with $6 million of debt.

d. What are the values of the WACC and r_s at debt levels of D = $0, D = $6 million, and D = $10 million if we assume a 40% corporate tax rate? Plot the relationship between the value of the firm and the debt ratio as well as that between capital costs and the debt ratio.

e. What is the maximum dollar amount of debt financing that can be used? What is the value of the firm at this debt level? What is the cost of this debt?

f. How would each of the following factors tend to change the values you plotted in your graph?

(1) The interest rate on debt increases as the debt ratio rises.

(2) At higher levels of debt, the probability of financial distress rises.

16-10 **Equity Viewed as an Option** A. Fethe Inc. is a custom manufacturer of gui-tars, mandolins, and other stringed instruments that is located near Knoxville, Tennessee. Fethe's current value of operations, which is also its value of debt plus equity, is estimated to be $5 million. Fethe has $2 million face value, zero coupon debt that is due in 2 years. The risk-free rate is 6%, and the standard deviation of returns for companies similar to Fethe is 50%. Fethe's owners view their equity investment as an option and would like to know the value of their investment.

a. Using the Black-Scholes option pricing model, how much is Fethe's equity worth?

b. How much is the debt worth today? What is its yield?

c. How would the equity value and the yield on the debt change if Fethe's managers could use risk management techniques to reduce its volatility to 30%? Can you explain this?

Spreadsheet Problem

16-11 **Build a Model: Equity Viewed as an Option** Start with the partial model in the file *Ch16 P11 Build a Model.xls* on the textbook's Web site. Rework Problem 16-10 using a spreadsheet model. After completing the problem as it appears, answer the following related questions.

a. Graph the cost of debt versus the face value of debt for values of the face value from $0.5 to $8 million.

b. Graph the values of debt and equity for volatilities from 0.10 to 0.90 when the face value of the debt is $2 million.

c. Repeat part b, but instead using a face value of debt of $5 million. What can you say about the difference between the graphs in part b and part c?

MINI CASE

David Lyons, CEO of Lyons Solar Technologies, is concerned about his firm's level of debt financing. The company uses short-term debt to finance its temporary working capital needs, but it does not use any permanent (long-term) debt. Other solar technology companies average about 30% debt, and Mr. Lyons wonders why they use so much more debt and how it affects stock prices. To gain some insights into the matter, he poses the following questions to you, his recently hired assistant.

a. *BusinessWeek* recently ran an article on companies' debt policies, and the names Modigliani and Miller (MM) were mentioned several times as leading researchers on the theory of capital structure. Briefly, who are MM, and what assumptions are embedded in the MM and Miller models?

b. Assume that Firms U and L are in the same risk class and that both have EBIT = $500,000. Firm U uses no debt financing, and its cost of equity is $r_{sU} = 14\%$. Firm L has $1 million of debt outstanding at a cost of $r_d = 8\%$. There are no taxes. Assume that the MM assumptions hold.
   (1) Find V, S, r_s, and WACC for Firms U and L.
   (2) Graph (a) the relationships between capital costs and leverage as measured by D/V and (b) the relationship between V and D.

c. Now assume that Firms L and U are both subject to a 40% corporate tax rate. Using the data given in part b, repeat the analysis called for in b(1) and b(2) under the MM model with taxes.

d. Suppose investors are subject to the following tax rates: $T_d = 30\%$ and $T_s = 12\%$.
   (1) According to the Miller model, what is the gain from leverage?
   (2) How does this gain compare with the gain in the MM model with corporate taxes?
   (3) What does the Miller model imply about the effect of corporate debt on the value of the firm; that is, how do personal taxes affect the situation?

e. What capital structure policy recommendations do the three theories (MM without taxes, MM with corporate taxes, and Miller) suggest to financial managers? Empirically, do firms appear to follow any one of these guidelines?

f. How is the analysis in part c different if Firms U and L are growing? Assume both firms are growing at a rate of 7% and that the investment in net operating assets required to support this growth is 10% of EBIT.

g. What if L's debt is risky? For the purpose of this example, assume that the value of L's operations is $4 million (the value of its debt plus equity). Assume also that its debt consists of 1-year, zero coupon bonds with a face value of $2 million. Finally, assume that L's volatility, σ, is 0.60 and that the risk-free rate, r_{RF}, is 6%.

h. What is the value of L's stock for volatilities between 0.20 and 0.95? What incentives might the manager of L have if she understands this relationship? What might debtholders do in response?

Selected Additional Cases

The following cases from TextChoice, *Cengage Learning's online case library, cover many of the concepts discussed in this chapter and are available at* **www.textchoice2.com/casenet.**

Klein-Brigham Series:

Case 7, "Seattle Steel Products," Case 9, "Kleen Kar, Inc.," Case 10, "Aspeon Sparkling Water," Case 43, "Mountain Springs," Case 57, "Greta Cosmetics," Case 74, "The Western Company," Case 83, "Armstrong Production Company," and Case 99, "Moore Plumbing Supply Company," focus on capital structure theory. Case 8, "Johnson Window Company," and Case 56, "Isle Marine Boat Company," cover operating and financial leverage.

Brigham-Buzzard Series:

Case 8, "Powerline Network Corporation," covers operating leverage, financial leverage, and the optimal capital structure.

Chapter 17

Distributions to Shareholders: Dividends and Repurchases

WEB

The textbook's Web site contains an *Excel* file that will guide you through the chapter's calculations. The file for this chapter is ***Ch17 Tool Kit.xls***, and we encourage you to open the file and follow along as you read the chapter.

Because a company's value depends on its ability to generate free cash flow (FCF), most of this book has focused on aspects of FCF generation, including measurement, forecasts, and risk analysis. In contrast, this chapter focuses on the use of FCF for cash distributions to shareholders. Here are the central issues addressed in this chapter: Can a company increase its value through its choice of **distribution policy,** defined as (1) the *level* of distributions, (2) the *form* of distributions (cash dividends versus stock repurchases), and (3) the *stability* of distributions? Do different groups of shareholders prefer one form of distribution over the other? Do shareholders perceive distributions as signals regarding a firm's risk and expected future free cash flows?

Before addressing these questions, let's take a look at the big picture regarding cash distributions.

Beginning of Chapter Questions

As you read the chapter, consider how you would answer the following questions. You *should not* necessarily be able to answer the questions before you read the chapter. Rather, you should use them to get a sense of the issues covered in the chapter. After reading the chapter, you should be able to give at least partial answers to the questions, and you should be able to give better answers after the chapter has been discussed in class. Note, too, that it is often useful, when answering conceptual questions, to use hypothetical data to illustrate your answer. We illustrate the answers with an *Excel* model that is available on the textbook's Web site. Accessing the model and working through it is a useful exercise, and it provides insights that are useful when answering the questions.

1. In your judgment, what are some **characteristics of the type of investor** who would likely prefer a **high dividend payout,** and what are some characteristics of one who would prefer a **low payout?** Would you personally prefer to own a stock with a high or a low payout, other things held constant? If you had a low-payout stock that you wanted to keep but you wanted more cash income, what could you do to increase your cash flow? Would those actions cause you to incur costs? What could you do, and what costs would you incur, if you owned a high-payout stock but did not need cash income?

2. Describe the **three theories** that have been advanced regarding whether investors in the aggregate tend to favor high or low dividend payout ratios. What results were reached from **empirical tests** of these theories?

3. How should (a) **signaling** and (b) the **clientele effect** be taken into account by a firm as it considers its dividend decision? Do signaling and clientele effects make it easier or harder to determine if investors prefer high or low payout ratios? Do these factors influence the desirability of a **stable dividend policy** versus one that is **flexible** and thus varies with the company's cash flows and investment opportunities?

4. Describe the **residual dividend model.** Explain how it operates and how firms use it in practice. In your answer, discuss any influences signaling and the clientele effect might have on a firm's decision to use, not use, or modify this model.

5. If a company is thinking about distributing excess cash through a **stock repurchase program** in lieu of continuing to pay regular cash dividends, what are some factors it should consider before making the change?

6. What is a **stock split?** As an investor, would you like to see shares you own be split?

7. In 2003, President Bush proposed a change in the tax law that would have eliminated the tax on dividends received by stockholders. The same proposal also would have increased the basis of stocks by the amount of new retained earnings per share—in effect reducing the capital gains tax to almost zero. In total, the proposal would have, to a large extent, put debt and equity financing on equal footing from a tax standpoint. The proposal did not pass, and instead, the tax rate on dividends was reduced to the rate on capital gains. However, if a similar proposal at some point becomes law, how would it tend to affect (a) corporate capital structures, (b) corporate share repurchases, (c) dividend payout ratios, and (d) any conclusions one might reach regarding the three dividend preference theories?

17.1 An Overview of Cash Distributions

At the risk of stating the obvious, a company must have cash before it can make a cash distribution to shareholders. Occasionally the cash comes from a recapitalization or the sale of an asset, but in most cases it comes from the company's internally generated free cash flow. Recall that FCF is defined as the amount of cash flow available for distribution to investors after expenses, taxes, and the necessary

USES OF FREE CASH FLOW: DISTRIBUTIONS TO SHAREHOLDERS

Free cash flow is generated from operations and is available for distribution to all investors. This chapter focuses on the distributions of FCF to shareholders in the form of dividends and stock repurchases.

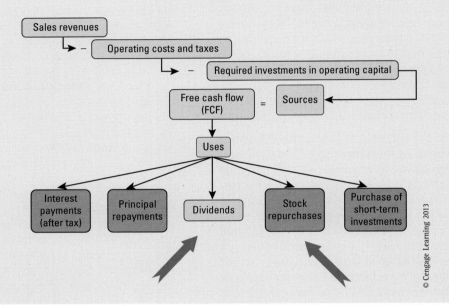

investments in operating capital. Thus, the *source* of FCF depends on a company's investment opportunities and its effectiveness in turning those opportunities into realities. Notice that a company with many opportunities will have large investments in operating capital and might have negative FCF even if the company is profitable. But when growth begins to slow, a profitable company's FCF will be positive and very large. Home Depot and Microsoft are good examples of once-fast-growing companies that are now generating large amounts of free cash flows.

After FCF becomes positive, how should a company use it? There are only five potentially "good" ways to use free cash flow: (1) pay interest expenses, (2) pay down the principal on debt, (3) pay dividends, (4) repurchase stock, or (5) buy nonoperating assets such as Treasury bills or other marketable securities.[1] Let's examine each of these uses.

A company's capital structure choice determines its payments for interest expenses and debt principal. A company's value typically increases over time, even if the company is mature, which implies its debt will also increase over time if the company maintains

---

1. Recall from Chapter 7 that the company's cost of paying interest is on an after-tax basis. Recall also that a company doesn't *spend* FCF on operating assets (such as the acquisition of another company), because those expenditures were already deducted when calculating FCF. In other words, the purchase of an operating asset (even if it is another company) is not a *use* of FCF; instead, it is a *source* of FCF (albeit a "negative source").

a target capital structure. If a company instead were to pay off its debt, then it would lose valuable tax shields associated with the deductibility of interest expenses. Therefore, most companies make net additions to debt over time rather than net repayments, even if FCF is positive. This "negative use" of FCF provides even more FCF for the other uses. We discuss capital structure choices in more detail in Chapter 15.

A company's working capital policies determine its level of marketable securities. Chapter 21 discusses marketable securities in more detail, but for now you should recognize that the decision involves a trade-off between the benefits and costs of having a large investment in marketable securities. In terms of benefits, a large investment in marketable securities reduces the risk of financial distress should there be an economic downturn. Also, if investment opportunities turn out to be better than expected, marketable securities provide a ready source of funding that will not incur the flotation or signaling costs due to raising external funds. However, there is a potential agency cost: If a company has a large investment in marketable securities, then managers might be tempted to squander the money on perks (such as corporate jets) or high-priced acquisitions.

In summary, a company's investment opportunities and operating plans determine its level of FCF. The company's capital structure policy determines the amount of debt and interest payments. Working capital policy determines the investment in marketable securities. The remaining FCF should be distributed to shareholders, with the only question being how much to distribute in the form of dividends versus stock repurchases.

Obviously this is a simplification, since companies (1) sometimes scale back their operating plans for sales and asset growth if such reductions are needed to maintain an existing dividend, (2) temporarily adjust their current financing mix in response to market conditions, and (3) often use marketable securities as shock absorbers for fluctuations in short-term cash flows. Still, there is an interdependence among operating plans (which have the biggest impact on free cash flow), financing plans (which have the biggest impact on the cost of capital), working capital policies (which determine the target level of marketable securities), and shareholder distributions.

WWW

An excellent source of recent dividend news for major corporations is available on the Web site of Corporate Financials Online at **http://cfonews .com/scs**. By clicking the down arrow of the "News Category" box on the left side of the screen, you may select "Dividends" to receive a list of companies with dividend news. Click on any company, and you will see its latest dividend news.

Self Test

What are the five uses of free cash flows?

How do a company's investment opportunities, capital structure, and working capital policies affect its distributions to shareholders?

17.2 Procedures for Cash Distributions

Companies can distribute cash to shareholders via cash dividends or stock repurchases. In this section we describe the actual procedures used to make cash distributions.

17.2a Dividend Payment Procedures

Dividends are normally paid quarterly, and, if conditions permit, the dividend is increased once each year. For example, Katz Corporation paid a $0.50 dividend per share in each quarter of 2012, for an annual dividend per share of $2.00. In common financial parlance, we say that in 2012 Katz's *regular quarterly dividend* was $0.50, and its *annual dividend* was $2.00. In late 2012, Katz's board of directors met, reviewed projections for 2013, and decided to keep the 2013 dividend at $2.00. The directors announced the $2 rate, so stockholders could count on receiving it unless the company experienced unanticipated operating problems.

The actual payment procedure is as follows.

1. *Declaration date.* On the **declaration date**—say, on Thursday, November 15—the directors meet and declare the regular dividend, issuing a statement similar to the following: "On November 15, 2012, the directors of Katz Corporation met and declared the regular quarterly dividend of 50 cents per share, payable to holders of record as of Friday, December 14, payment to be made on Friday, January 4, 2013." For accounting purposes, the declared dividend becomes an actual liability on the declaration date. If a balance sheet were constructed, an amount equal to $0.50 \times n_0$, where n_0 is the number of shares outstanding, would appear as a current liability, and retained earnings would be reduced by a like amount.

2. *Holder-of-record date.* At the close of business on the **holder-of-record date**, December 14, the company closes its stock transfer books and makes up a list of shareholders as of that date. If Katz Corporation is notified of the sale before 5 p.m. on December 14, then the new owner receives the dividend. However, if notification is received after 5 p.m. on December 14, the previous owner gets the dividend check.

3. *Ex-dividend date.* Suppose Jean Buyer buys 100 shares of stock from John Seller on December 11. Will the company be notified of the transfer in time to list Buyer as the new owner and thus pay the dividend to her? To avoid conflict, the securities industry has set up a convention under which the right to the dividend remains with the stock until two business days prior to the holder-of-record date; on the second day before that date, the right to the dividend no longer goes with the shares. The date when the right to the dividend leaves the stock is called the **ex-dividend date**. In this case, the ex-dividend date is two days prior to December 14, which is December 12:

Dividend goes with stock:	Tuesday, December 11
Ex-dividend date:	Wednesday, December 12
	Thursday, December 13
Holder-of-record date:	Friday, December 14

Therefore, if Buyer is to receive the dividend, she must buy the stock on or before December 11. If she buys it on December 12 or later, Seller will receive the dividend because he will be the official holder of record.

Katz's dividend amounts to $0.50, so the ex-dividend date is important. Barring fluctuations in the stock market, we would normally expect the price of a stock to drop by approximately the amount of the dividend on the ex-dividend date. Thus, if Katz closed at $30.50 on December 11, it would probably open at about $30 on December 12.

4. *Payment date.* The company actually pays the dividend on January 4, the **payment date**, to the holders of record.

17.2b Stock Repurchase Procedures

Stock repurchases occur when a company buys back some of its own outstanding stock.[2] Three situations can lead to stock repurchases. First, a company may decide to increase its leverage by issuing debt and using the proceeds to repurchase stock;

---

2. The repurchased stock is called "treasury stock" and is shown as a negative value on the company's detailed balance sheet. On the consolidated balance sheet, treasury shares are deducted to find shares outstanding, and the price paid for the repurchased shares is deducted when determining common equity.

we discuss recapitalizations in more detail in Chapter 15. Second, many firms have given their employees stock options, and companies often repurchase their own stock to sell to employees when employees exercise the options. In this case, the number of outstanding shares reverts to its pre-repurchase level after the options are exercised. Third, a company may have excess cash. This may be due to a one-time cash inflow, such as the sale of a division, or the company may simply be generating more free cash flow than it needs to service its debt.[3]

Stock repurchases are usually made in one of three ways. (1) A publicly owned firm can buy back its own stock through a broker on the open market.[4] (2) The firm can make a tender offer, under which it permits stockholders to send in (that is, "tender") shares in exchange for a specified price per share. In this case, the firm generally indicates it will buy up to a specified number of shares within a stated time period (usually about two weeks). If more shares are tendered than the company wants to buy, purchases are made on a pro rata basis. (3) The firm can purchase a block of shares from one large holder on a negotiated basis. This is a targeted stock repurchase, as discussed in Chapter 11.

17.2c Patterns of Cash Distributions

The occurrence of dividends versus stock repurchases has changed dramatically during the past 30 years. First, total cash distributions as a percentage of net income have remained fairly stable at around 26% to 28%, but the mix of dividends and repurchases has changed.[5] The average dividend payout ratio fell from 22.3% in 1974 to 13.8% in 1998, while the average repurchase payout as a percentage of net income rose from 3.7% to 13.6%. Since 1985, large companies have repurchased more shares than they have issued. Since 1998, more cash has been returned to shareholders in repurchases than as dividend payments.

Second, companies today are less likely to pay a dividend. In 1978, about 66.5% of NYSE, AMEX, and Nasdaq firms paid a dividend. In 1999, only 20.8% paid a dividend. Part of this reduction can be explained by the large number of IPOs in the 1990s, since young firms rarely pay a dividend. However, that doesn't explain the entire story, as many mature firms now do not pay dividends. For example, consider the way in which a maturing firm will make its first cash distribution. In 1973, 73% of firms making an initial distribution did so with a dividend. By 1998, only 19% initiated distributions with dividends.[6]

---

3. See Benton Gup and Doowoo Nam, "Stock Buybacks, Corporate Performance, and EVA," *Journal of Applied Corporate Finance,* Spring 2001, pp. 99–110. The authors show that the firms that repurchase stock have superior operating performance to those that do not buy back stock, which is consistent with the notion that firms buy back stock when they generate additional free cash flow. They also show that operating performance improves in the year after the buyback, indicating that the superior performance is sustainable.

4. Many firms announce their plans to repurchase stock on the open market. For example, a company might announce it plans to repurchase 4 million shares of stock. However, companies usually don't buy back all the shares they announce but instead repurchase only about 80% of the announced number. See Clifford Stephens and Michael Weisbach, "Actual Share Reacquisitions in Open-Market Repurchase Programs," *Journal of Finance,* February 1998, pp. 313–333.

5. See Gustavo Grullon and Roni Michaely, "Dividends, Share Repurchases, and the Substitution Hypothesis," *Journal of Finance,* August 2002, pp. 1649–1684; and Eugene Fama and Kenneth French, "Disappearing Dividends: Changing Firm Characteristics or Lower Propensity to Pay?" *Journal of Applied Corporate Finance,* Spring 2001, pp. 67–79.

6. See Gustavo Grullon and David Ikenberry, "What Do We Know about Stock Repurchases?" *Journal of Applied Corporate Finance,* Spring 2000, pp. 31–51.

Third, the aggregate dividend payouts have become more concentrated in the sense that a relatively small number of older, more established, and more profitable firms accounts for most of the cash distributed as dividends.[7]

Fourth, Table 17-1 shows there is considerable variation in distribution policies, with some companies paying a high percentage of their income as dividends and others paying none. The next section discusses some theories about distribution policies.

<table>
<tr><td>**Self Test**</td><td>Explain the procedures used to actually pay the dividend.

Why is the ex-dividend date important to investors?

What are the three ways in which a company can repurchase stock?</td></tr>
</table>

17.3 Cash Distributions and Firm Value

A company can change its value of operations only if it changes the cost of capital or investors' perceptions regarding expected free cash flow. This is true for all corporate decisions, including the distribution policy. Is there an **optimal distribution policy** that maximizes a company's intrinsic value?

The answer depends in part on investors' preferences for returns in the form of dividend yields versus capital gains. The relative mix of dividend yields and capital gains is determined by the **target distribution ratio**, which is the percentage of net income distributed to shareholders through cash dividends or stock repurchases, and

TABLE 17-1   Dividend Payouts (February 2011)

Company	Industry	Dividend Payout	Dividend Yield
Empire District Electric (EDE)	Electric utility	108%	5.9%
Rayonier Inc. (RYN.N)	Forest products	75	3.60
Regions Financial Corp. (RF)	Regional banks	NM	0.5
Reynolds American Inc. (RAI)	Tobacco products	81	6.1
WD-40 Company (WDFC)	Household products	48	2.7
Harley-Davidson Inc. (HOG)	Recreational products	36	0.97
Ingles Markets Inc. (IMKTA)	Retail (grocery)	46	3.3
Microsoft Corp. (MSFT)	Software and programming	24	2.3
Tiffany and Company (TIF)	Specialty retail	34	1.6
Aaron's Inc. (AAN.N)	Rental and leasing	3	0.3
Papa John's Intl. Inc. (PZZA)	Restaurants	0	NM

Source: **www.reuters.com**, February 2011.
Notes: Regions Financial's payout ratio is not meaningful (NM) because Regions has negative net income. Papa John's dividend yield is not meaningful because it pays no dividend.

7. For example, see Harry DeAngelo, Linda DeAngelo, and Douglas J. Skinner, "Are Dividends Disappearing? Dividend Concentration and the Consolidation of Earnings," *Journal of Financial Economics*, June 2004, pp. 425–456.

the **target payout ratio**, which is the percentage of net income paid as a cash dividend. Notice that the payout ratio must be less than the distribution ratio because the distribution ratio includes stock repurchases as well as cash dividends.

A high distribution ratio and a high payout ratio mean that a company pays large dividends and has small (or zero) stock repurchases. In this situation, the dividend yield is relatively high and the expected capital gain is low. If a company has a large distribution ratio but a small payout ratio, then it pays low dividends but regularly repurchases stock, resulting in a low dividend yield but a relatively high expected capital gain yield. If a company has a low distribution ratio, then it must also have a relatively low payout ratio, again resulting in a low dividend yield and, it is hoped, a relatively high capital gain.

In this section, we examine three theories of investor preferences for dividend yield versus capital gains: (1) the dividend irrelevance theory, (2) the dividend preference theory (also called the "bird-in-the-hand" theory), and (3) the tax effect theory.

17.3a Dividend Irrelevance Theory

The original proponents of the **dividend irrelevance theory** were Merton Miller and Franco Modigliani (MM).[8] They argued that the firm's value is determined only by its basic earning power and its business risk. In other words, MM argued that the value of the firm depends only on the income produced by its assets, not on how this income is split between dividends and retained earnings.

To understand MM's argument, recognize that any shareholder can in theory construct his own dividend policy. For example, if a firm does not pay dividends, a shareholder who wants a 5% dividend can "create" it by selling 5% of his stock. Conversely, if a company pays a higher dividend than an investor desires, the investor can use the unwanted dividends to buy additional shares of the company's stock. If investors could buy and sell shares and thus create their own dividend policy without incurring costs, then the firm's dividend policy would truly be irrelevant.

In developing their dividend theory, MM made a number of important assumptions, especially the absence of taxes and brokerage costs. If these assumptions are not true, then investors who want additional dividends must incur brokerage costs to sell shares and must pay taxes on any capital gains. Investors who do not want dividends must incur brokerage costs to purchase shares with their dividends. Because taxes and brokerage costs certainly exist, dividend policy may well be relevant. We will discuss empirical tests of MM's dividend irrelevance theory shortly.

17.3b Dividend Preference (Bird-in-the-Hand) Theory

The principal conclusion of MM's dividend irrelevance theory is that dividend policy does not affect a stock's value or risk. Therefore, it does not affect the

---

8. See Merton H. Miller and Franco Modigliani, "Dividend Policy, Growth, and the Valuation of Shares," *Journal of Business*, October 1961, pp. 411–433. However, their conclusion is valid only if investors expect managers eventually to pay out the equivalent of the present value of all future free cash flows; see Harry DeAngelo and Linda DeAngelo, "The Irrelevance of the MM Dividend Irrelevance Theorem," *Journal of Financial Economics*, Vol. 79, 2006, pp. 293–315.

required rate of return on equity, r_s. In contrast, Myron Gordon and John Lintner both argued that a stock's risk declines as dividends increase: A return in the form of dividends is a sure thing, but a return in the form of capital gains is risky. In other words, a **bird in the hand** is worth more than two in the bush. Therefore, shareholders prefer dividends and are willing to accept a lower required return on equity.[9]

The possibility of agency costs leads to a similar conclusion. First, high payouts reduce the risk that managers will squander cash because there is less cash on hand. Second, a high-payout company must raise external funds more often than a low-payout company, all else held equal. If a manager knows that the company will receive frequent scrutiny from external markets, then the manager will be less likely to engage in wasteful practices. Therefore, high payouts reduce the risk of agency costs. With less risk, shareholders are willing to accept a lower required return on equity.

17.3c Tax Effect Theory: Capital Gains Are Preferred

Before 2003, individual investors paid ordinary income taxes on dividends but lower rates on long-term capital gains. The Jobs and Growth Act of 2003 changed this, reducing the tax rate on dividend income to the same as on long-term capital gains.[10] However, there are two reasons why stock price appreciation still is taxed more favorably than dividend income. First, an increase in a stock's price isn't taxable until the investor sells the stock, whereas a dividend payment is taxable immediately; a dollar of taxes paid in the future has a lower effective cost than a dollar paid today because of the time value of money. So even when dividends and gains are taxed equally, capital gains are never taxed sooner than dividends. Second, if a stock is held until the shareholder dies, then no capital gains tax is due at all: The beneficiaries who receive the stock can use its value on the date of death as their cost basis and thus completely escape the capital gains tax.

Because dividends are in some cases taxed more highly than capital gains, investors might require a higher pre-tax rate of return to induce them to buy dividend-paying stocks. Therefore, investors may prefer that companies minimize dividends. If so, then investors should be willing to pay more for low-payout companies than for otherwise similar high-payout companies.[11]

---

9. See Myron J. Gordon, "Optimal Investment and Financing Policy," *Journal of Finance,* May 1963, pp. 264–272; and John Lintner, "Dividends, Earnings, Leverage, Stock Prices, and the Supply of Capital to Corporations," *Review of Economics and Statistics,* August 1962, pp. 243–269.

10. Of course, nothing involving taxes is quite this simple. The dividend must be from a domestic company, and the investor must own the stock for more than 60 days during the 120-day period beginning 60 days before the ex-dividend date. There are restrictions for dividends other than regular cash dividends. The Tax Increase Prevention and Reconciliation Act of 2005 cut the long-term capital gains tax rate to zero for low-income investors (that is, those whose marginal tax rate is 15% or less) and kept it at 15% for those with more income. After 2012, unless Congress again extends the provisions, the capital gains rates will revert to 10% and 20%, which were the capital gains rates in effect prior to the 2003 Act. Also, the Alternative Minimum Tax (AMT) increases the effective tax rate on dividends and capital gains by 7% for some moderately high-income earners. See Leonard Burman, William Gale, Greg Leiserson, and Jeffrey Rohaly, "The AMT: What's Wrong and How to Fix It," *National Tax Journal,* September 2007, pp. 385–405.

11. For more on tax-related issues, see Eli Talmor and Sheridan Titman, "Taxes and Dividend Policy," *Financial Management,* Summer 1990, pp. 32–35; and Rosita P. Chang and S. Ghon Rhee, "The Impact of Personal Taxes on Corporate Dividend Policy and Capital Structure Decisions," *Financial Management,* Summer 1990, pp. 21–31.

17.3d Empirical Evidence on Distribution Policies

It is very difficult to construct a perfect empirical test of the relationship between payout policy and the required rate of return on stock. First, all factors other than distribution level should be held constant; that is, the sample companies should differ only in their distribution levels. Second, each firm's cost of equity should be measured with a high degree of accuracy. Unfortunately, we cannot find a set of publicly owned firms that differ only in their distribution levels, nor can we obtain precise estimates of the cost of equity. Therefore, no one has yet identified a completely unambiguous relationship between the distribution level and the cost of equity or firm value.

Although none of the empirical tests is perfect, recent evidence does suggest that firms with higher dividend payouts also have higher required returns.[12] This tends to support the tax effect hypothesis, although the size of the required return is too high to be fully explained by taxes.

Agency costs should be most severe in countries with poor investor protection. In such countries, companies with high dividend payouts should be more highly valued than those with low payouts because high payouts limit the extent to which managers can expropriate shareholder wealth. Recent research shows that this is the case, which supports the dividend preference hypothesis in the case of companies with severe agency problems.[13]

Although the evidence from these studies is mixed as to whether the *average* investor uniformly prefers either higher or lower distribution levels, other research does show that *individual* investors have strong preferences. Also, other research shows that investors prefer stable, predictable dividend payouts (regardless of the payout level) and that they interpret dividend changes as signals about firms' future prospects. We discuss these issues in the next several sections.

Self Test

What did Modigliani and Miller assume about taxes and brokerage costs when they developed their dividend irrelevance theory?

How did the bird-in-the-hand theory get its name?

What have been the results of empirical tests of the dividend theories?

17.4 Clientele Effect

As we indicated earlier, different groups, or *clienteles,* of stockholders prefer different dividend payout policies. For example, retired individuals, pension funds, and university endowment funds generally prefer cash income, so they may want the firm to pay out a high percentage of its earnings. Such investors are often in low or even zero tax brackets, so taxes are of no concern. On the other hand, stockholders in their peak earning years might prefer reinvestment, because they have less need for current investment income and would simply reinvest dividends received—after first paying income taxes on those dividends.

If a firm retains and reinvests income rather than paying dividends, those stockholders who need current income would be disadvantaged. The value of their

---

12. See A. Naranjo, N. Nimalendran, and M. Ryngaert, "Stock Returns, Dividend Yields, and Taxes," *Journal of Finance,* December 1998, pp. 2029–2057.

13. See L. Pinkowitz, R. Stulz, and R. Williamson, "Does the Contribution of Corporate Cash Holdings and Dividends to Firm Value Depend on Governance? A Cross-Country Analysis," *Journal of Finance,* December 2006, pp. 2725–2751.

stock might increase, but they would be forced to go to the trouble and expense of selling some of their shares to obtain cash. Also, some institutional investors (or trustees for individuals) would be legally precluded from selling stock and then "spending capital." On the other hand, stockholders who are saving rather than spending dividends might favor the low-dividend policy: The less the firm pays out in dividends, the less these stockholders will have to pay in current taxes, and the less trouble and expense they will have to go through to reinvest their after-tax dividends. Therefore, investors who want current investment income should own shares in high–dividend payout firms, while investors with no need for current investment income should own shares in low–dividend payout firms. For example, investors seeking high cash income might invest in electric utilities, which averaged a 40% payout in April 2011, while those favoring growth could invest in the semi-conductor industry, which paid out only 5.9% during the same time period.

To the extent that stockholders can switch firms, a firm can change from one dividend payout policy to another and then let stockholders who do not like the new policy sell to other investors who do. However, frequent switching would be inefficient because of (1) brokerage costs, (2) the likelihood that stockholders who are selling will have to pay capital gains taxes, and (3) a possible shortage of investors who like the firm's newly adopted dividend policy. Thus, management should be hesitant to change its dividend policy, because a change might cause current shareholders to sell their stock, forcing the stock price down. Such a price decline might be temporary but might also be permanent—if few new investors are attracted by the new dividend policy, then the stock price would remain depressed. Of course, the new policy might attract an even larger clientele than the firm had before, in which case the stock price would rise.

Evidence from several studies suggests that there is, in fact, a **clientele effect** with, for example, low-tax or tax-free institutions holding relatively more high dividend stocks, and taxable institutions holding fewer high dividend stocks.[14] It's been argued by MM and others that one clientele is as good as another, so the existence of a clientele effect does not necessarily imply that one dividend policy is better than any other. However, MM may be wrong, and neither they nor anyone else can prove that the aggregate makeup of investors permits firms to disregard clientele effects. This issue, like most others in the dividend arena, is still up in the air.

| **Self Test** | Define the clientele effect and explain how it affects dividend policy. |

17.5 Information Content, or Signaling, Hypothesis

When MM set forth their dividend irrelevance theory, they assumed that every-one—investors and managers alike—has identical information regarding a firm's future earnings and dividends. In reality, however, different investors have different views on both the level of future dividend payments and the uncertainty inherent in those payments, and managers have better information about future prospects than public stockholders.

---

14. For example, see R. Richardson Pettit, "Taxes, Transactions Costs and the Clientele Effect of Dividends," *Journal of Financial Economics,* December 1977, pp. 419–436 and William J. Moser and Andy Puckett, "Dividend Tax Clienteles: Evidence from Tax Law Changes," *Journal of the American Taxation Association,* Spring 2009, pp. 1–22.

It has been observed that an increase in the dividend is often accompanied by an increase in the price of a stock and that a dividend cut generally leads to a stock price decline. Some have argued this indicates that investors prefer dividends to capital gains. However, MM saw this differently. They noted the well-established fact that corporations are reluctant to cut dividends, which implies that corporations do not raise dividends unless they anticipate higher earnings in the future. Thus, MM argued that a higher than expected dividend increase is a signal to investors that the firm's management forecasts good future earnings. Conversely, a dividend reduction, or a smaller than expected increase, is a signal that management is forecasting poor earnings in the future. Thus, MM argued that investors' reactions to changes in dividend policy do not necessarily show that investors prefer dividends to retained earnings. Rather, they argue that price changes following dividend actions simply indicate that there is important **information**, or **signaling, content** in dividend announcements.

The initiation of a dividend by a firm that formerly paid no dividend is certainly a significant change in distribution policy. It appears that initiating firms' future earnings and cash flows are less risky than before the initiation. However, the evidence is mixed regarding the future profitability of initiating firms: Some studies find slightly higher earnings after the initiation, but others find no significant change in earnings.[15] What happens when firms with existing dividends unexpectedly increase or decrease the dividend? Early studies, using small data samples, concluded that unexpected dividend changes did not provide a signal about future earnings.[16] However, more recent data with larger samples provide mixed evidence.[17] On average, firms that cut dividends had poor earnings in the years directly preceding the cut but actually improved earnings in subsequent years. Firms that increased dividends had earnings increases in the years preceding the increase but did not appear to have subsequent earnings increases. However, neither did they have subsequent declines in earnings, so it appears that the increase in dividends is a signal that past earnings increases were not temporary. Also, a relatively large number of firms that expect a large permanent increase in cash flow (as opposed to earnings) do in fact increase their dividend payouts in the year prior to the cash flow increase.

All in all, there is clearly some information content in dividend announcements: Stock prices tend to fall when dividends are cut, even if they don't always rise when dividends are increased. However, this doesn't necessarily validate the signaling hypothesis, because it is difficult to tell whether any stock price change following a change in dividend policy reflects only signaling effects or reflects both signaling and dividend preferences.

| Define signaling content, and explain how it affects dividend policy. | Self Test |

---

15. See Edward Dyl and Robert Weigand, "The Information Content of Dividend Initiations: Additional Evidence," *Financial Management,* Autumn 1998, pp. 27–35; P. Asquith and D. Mullins, "The Impact of Initiating Dividend Payments on Shareholders' Wealth," *Journal of Business,* January 1983, pp. 77–96; and P. Healy and K. Palepu, "Earnings Information Conveyed by Dividend Initiations and Omissions," *Journal of Financial Economics,* September 1988, pp. 149–175.

16. For example, see N. Gonedes, "Corporate Signaling, External Accounting, and Capital Market Equilibrium: Evidence of Dividends, Income, and Extraordinary Items," *Journal of Accounting Research,* Spring 1978, pp. 26–79; and R. Watts, "The Information Content of Dividends," *Journal of Business,* April 1973, pp. 191–211.

17. See Shlomo Benartzi, Roni Michaely, and Richard Thaler, "Do Changes in Dividends Signal the Future or the Past?" *Journal of Finance,* July 1997, pp. 1007–1034; and Yaron Brook, William Charlton Jr., and Robert J. Hendershott, "Do Firms Use Dividends to Signal Large Future Cash Flow Increases?" *Financial Management,* Autumn 1998, pp. 46–57.

17.6 Implications for Dividend Stability

The clientele effect and the information content in dividend announcements definitely have implications regarding the desirability of stable versus volatile dividends. For example, many stockholders rely on dividends to meet expenses, and they would be seriously inconvenienced if the dividend stream were unstable. Further, reducing dividends to make funds available for capital investment could send incorrect signals to investors, who might push down the stock price because they interpret the dividend cut to mean that the company's future earnings prospects have been diminished. Thus, maximizing its stock price probably requires a firm to maintain a steady dividend policy. Because sales and earnings are expected to grow for most firms, a stable dividend policy means a company's regular cash dividends should also grow at a steady, predictable rate.[18] But as we explain in the next section, most companies will probably move toward small, sustainable, regular cash dividends that are supplemented by stock repurchases.

Self Test	Why do the clientele effect and the information content hypotheses imply that investors prefer stable dividends?

17.7 Setting the Target Distribution Level: The Residual Distribution Model

When deciding how much cash to distribute to stockholders, two points should be kept in mind: (1) the overriding objective is to maximize shareholder value, and (2) the firm's cash flows really belong to its shareholders, so a company should refrain from retaining income unless its managers can reinvest that income to produce returns higher than shareholders could themselves earn by investing the cash in investments of equal risk. On the other hand, recall from Chapter 10 that internal equity (reinvested earnings) is cheaper than external equity (new common stock issues) because it avoids flotation costs and adverse signals. This encourages firms to retain earnings so as to avoid having to issue new stock.

When establishing a distribution policy, one size does not fit all. Some firms produce a lot of cash but have limited investment opportunities—this is true for firms in profitable but mature industries in which few opportunities for growth exist. Such firms typically distribute a large percentage of their cash to shareholders, thereby attracting investment clienteles that prefer high dividends. Other firms generate little or no excess cash because they have many good investment opportunities. Such firms generally don't distribute much cash but do enjoy rising earnings and stock prices, thereby attracting investors who prefer capital gains.

---

18. For more on announcements and stability, see Jeffrey A. Born, "Insider Ownership and Signals—Evidence from Dividend Initiation Announcement Effects," *Financial Management,* Spring 1988, pp. 38–45; Chinmoy Ghosh and J. Randall Woolridge, "An Analysis of Shareholder Reaction to Dividend Cuts and Omissions," *Journal of Financial Research,* Winter 1988, pp. 281–294; C. Michael Impson and Imre Karafiath, "A Note on the Stock Market Reaction to Dividend Announcements," *Financial Review,* May 1992, pp. 259–271; James W. Wansley, C. F. Sirmans, James D. Shilling, and Young-jin Lee, "Dividend Change Announcement Effects and Earnings Volatility and Timing," *Journal of Financial Research,* Spring 1991, pp. 37–49; and J. Randall Woolridge and Chinmoy Ghosh, "Dividend Cuts: Do They Always Signal Bad News?" *Midland Corporate Finance Journal,* Summer 1985, pp. 20–32.

THE GLOBAL ECONOMIC CRISIS

Will Dividends Ever Be the Same?

The global economic crisis has had dramatic effects on dividend policies. According to Standard & Poor's, companies announcing dividend increases have exceeded those announcing decreases by a factor of 15 to 1 since 1955—at least until the first 5 months of 2009. Out of 7,000 publicly traded companies, only 283 announced dividend increases in the first quarter of 2009, while 367 cut dividends, a stunning reversal in the normal ratio of increasers to decreasers. Even the S&P 500 companies weren't immune to the crisis, with only 74 increasing dividends as compared with 54 cutting dividends and 9 suspending dividend payments altogether. To put this in perspective, only *one* S&P 500 company cut its dividend during the first quarter of 2007. The dividend decreases in 2009 aren't minor cuts, either. Howard Silverblatt, a Senior Index Analyst at Standard & Poor's, estimates the cuts add up to $77 billion.

How has the market reacted to cuts by these companies? JPMorgan Chase's stock price went up on the announcement, presumably because investors thought a stronger balance sheet at JPM would increase its intrinsic value by more than the loss investors incurred because of the lower dividend. On the other hand, GE's stock fell by more than 6% on the news of its 68% dividend cut, perhaps because investors feared this was a signal that GE's plight was worse than they had expected.

One thing is for certain, though: The days of large "permanent" dividends are over!

Sources: "S&P: Q1 Worst Quarter for Dividends Since 1955; Companies Reduce Shareholder Payments by $77 Billion," press release, April 7, 2009; also see **www2.standardandpoors.com/spf/xls/index/INDICATED_RATE_CHANGE.xls.**

As Table 17-1 suggests, dividend payouts and dividend yields for large corporations vary considerably. Generally, firms in stable, cash-producing industries such as utilities, financial services, and tobacco pay relatively high dividends, whereas companies in rapidly growing industries such as computer software tend to pay lower dividends.

For a given firm, the optimal distribution ratio is a function of four factors: (1) investors' preferences for dividends versus capital gains, (2) the firm's investment opportunities, (3) its target capital structure, and (4) the availability and cost of external capital. The last three elements are combined in what we call the **residual distribution model.** Under this model a firm follows these four steps when establishing its target distribution ratio: (1) it determines the optimal capital budget; (2) it determines the amount of equity needed to finance that budget, given its target capital structure (we explain the choice of target capital structures in Chapter 15); (3) it uses reinvested earnings to meet equity requirements to the extent possible; and (4) it pays dividends or repurchases stock only if more earnings are available than are needed to support the optimal capital budget. The word *residual* implies "leftover," and the residual policy implies that distributions are paid out of "leftover" earnings.

If a firm rigidly follows the residual distribution policy, then distributions paid in any given year can be expressed as follows:

$$\text{Distributions} = \text{Net income} - \frac{\text{Retained earnings needed to}}{\text{finance new investments}}$$

$$= \text{Net income} - [(\text{Target equity ratio}) \times (\text{Total capital budget})]$$

 (17–1)

As an illustration, consider the case of Texas and Western (T&W) Transport Company, which has $60 million in net income and a target capital structure of 60% equity and 40% debt.

If T&W forecasts poor investment opportunities, then its estimated capital budget will be only $40 million. To maintain the target capital structure, 40% ($16 million) of this capital must be raised as debt and 60% ($24 million) must be equity. If it followed a strict residual policy, T&W would retain $24 million of its $60 million earnings to help finance new investments and then distribute the remaining $36 million to shareholders:

$$\text{Distributions} = \text{Net income} - [(\text{Target equity ratio})(\text{Total capital budget})]$$
$$= \$60 - [(60\%)(\$40)]$$
$$= \$60 - \$24 = \$36$$

Under this scenario, the company's distribution ratio would be $36 million ÷ $60 million = 0.6 = 60%. These results are shown in Table 17-2.

In contrast, if the company's investment opportunities are average, its optimal capital budget would rise to $70 million. Here it would require $42 million of retained earnings, so distributions would be $60 − $42 = $18 million, for a ratio of $18/$60 = 30%. Finally, if investment opportunities are good then the capital budget would be $150 million, which would require 0.6($150) = $90 million of equity. In this case, T&W would retain all of its net income ($60 million) and thus make no distributions. Moreover, since the required equity exceeds the retained earnings, the company would have to issue some new common stock to maintain the target capital structure.

Because investment opportunities and earnings will surely vary from year to year, a strict adherence to the residual distribution policy would result in unstable distributions. One year the firm might make no distributions because it needs the money to finance good investment opportunities, but the next year it might make a large distribution because investment opportunities are poor and so it does not need to retain much. Similarly, fluctuating earnings could also lead to variable distributions, even if investment opportunities were stable. Until now, we have not said whether distributions should be in the form of dividends, stock repurchases, or some combination. The next sections discuss specific issues associated with dividend payments and stock repurchases; this is followed by a comparison of their relative advantages and disadvantages.

TABLE 17-2   **T&W's Distribution Ratio with $60 Million of Net Income and a 60% Target Equity Ratio When Faced with Different Investment Opportunities (Millions of Dollars)**

	Investment Opportunities		
	Poor	**Average**	**Good**
Capital budget	$40	$70	$150
Net income	60	60	60
Required equity (0.6 × Capital budget)	24	42	90
Distributions paid (NI − Required equity)	$36	$18	−$30[a]
Distribution ratio (Dividend/NI)	60%	30%	0%

[a]With a $150 million capital budget, T&W would retain all of its earnings and also issue $30 million of new stock.

Self Test

Explain the logic of the residual dividend model and the steps a firm would take to implement it.

Hamilton Corporation has a target equity ratio of 65%, and its capital budget is $2 million. If Hamilton has net income of $1.6 million and follows a residual distribution model, how much will its distribution be? **($300,000)**

17.8 The Residual Distribution Model in Practice

If distributions were solely in the form of dividends, then rigidly following the residual policy would lead to fluctuating, unstable dividends. Since investors dislike volatile regular dividends, r_s would be high and the stock price low. Therefore, firms should proceed as follows:

1. Estimate earnings and investment opportunities, on average, for the next 5 or so years.
2. Use this forecasted information and the target capital structure to find the average residual model distributions and dollars of dividends during the planning period.
3. Set a *target payout ratio* based on the average projected data.

Thus, *firms should use the residual policy to help set their long-run target distribution ratios, but not as a guide to the distribution in any one year.*

Companies often use financial forecasting models in conjunction with the residual distribution model discussed here to help understand the determinants of an optimal dividend policy. Most large corporations forecast their financial statements over the next 5 to 10 years. Information on projected capital expenditures and working capital requirements is entered into the model, along with sales forecasts, profit margins, depreciation, and the other elements required to forecast cash flows. The target capital structure is also specified, and the model shows the amount of debt and equity that will be required to meet the capital budgeting requirements while maintaining the target capital structure. Then, dividend payments are introduced. Naturally, the higher the payout ratio, the greater the required external equity. Most companies use the model to find a dividend pattern over the forecast period (generally 5 years) that will provide sufficient equity to support the capital budget without forcing them to sell new common stock or move the capital structure ratios outside their optimal range.

Some companies set a very low "regular" dividend and then supplement it with an "extra" dividend when times are good, such as Microsoft now does. This **low-regular-dividend-plus-extras policy** ensures that the regular dividend can be maintained "come hell or high water" and that stockholders can count on receiving that dividend under all conditions. Then, when times are good and profits and cash flows are high, the company can either pay a specially designated extra dividend or repurchase shares of stock. Investors recognize that the extras might not be maintained in the future, so they do not interpret them as a signal that the companies' earnings are going up permanently; nor do they take the elimination of the extra as a negative signal.

Self Test

Why is the residual model more often used to establish a long-run payout target than to set the actual year-by-year dividend payout ratio?

How do firms use planning models to help set dividend policy?

17.9 A Tale of Two Cash Distributions: Dividends versus Stock Repurchases

Benson Conglomerate, a prestigious publishing house with several Nobel laureates among its authors, recently began generating positive free cash flow and is analyzing the impact of different distribution policies. Benson anticipates extremely stable cash flows and will use the residual model to determine the level of distributions, but it has not yet chosen the form of the distribution. In particular, Benson is comparing distributions via dividends versus repurchases and wants to know the impact the different methods will have on financial statements, shareholder wealth, the number of outstanding shares, and the stock price.

17.9a The Impact on Financial Statements

Consider first the case in which distributions are in the form of dividends. Figure 17-1 shows the most recent financial statements and the inputs we will use to forecast its financial statements. The forecasted financial statements for the next two years are shown in the figure. (The file *Ch17 Tool Kit.xls* shows 4 years of projected statements.) Benson has no debt, so its interest expense is zero.

Calculations to ensure the balance sheets do in fact balance are shown in Panel d of Figure 17-1. Required operating assets are the sum of cash, accounts receivable, inventories, and net plant and equipment. We show balance sheets in Figure 17-1 for both December 30 and 31 of each year; this is to better illustrate the impact of the distribution, which we assume occurs once each year on December 31.[19] Liabilities and equity on December 30 (before the distribution) are the sum of accounts payable, accruals, short-term debt, long-term debt, preferred stock, common stock, the previous year's retained earnings balance, and the current year's net income. The amount of additional funds needed (AFN) is equal to the required operating assets minus liabilities and equity. Notice that a *negative* AFN is projected, which indicates additional funds are available rather than needed.

We assume that the extra funds temporarily are used to purchase short-term investments to be held until the distribution to shareholders. At that time, all short-term investments will be converted to cash and paid out as dividends. Thus, the 2013 short-term investments total $671.6 on December 30 and drop to zero on December 31, when they are distributed to investors.[20] Observe that the retained earnings account also drops by $671.6 on December 31 as funds that were previously retained are paid out as dividends.

Now let's consider the case of stock repurchases. The projected income statements and asset portion of the balance sheets are the same whether the distribution is in the form of dividends or repurchases, but this is not true for the liabilities-and-equity side of the balance sheet. Figure 17-2 reports the case in which distributions are in the form of stock repurchases. As in the case of dividend distributions, the December 30 balance of the retained earnings account is equal to the previous retained earnings balance plus the year's net income, because all income is retained. However, when funds in

---

19. As we noted earlier in the chapter, when dividends are declared, a new current liability called "dividends payable" would be added to current liabilities and then retained earnings would be reduced by that amount. To simplify the example, we ignore that provision and assume that there is no balance sheet effect on the declaration date.

20. As explained previously, there is a difference between the actual payment date and the ex-dividend date. To simplify the example, we assume that the dividends are paid on the ex-dividend date to the shareholder owning the stock the day before it goes ex-dividend.

Figure 17-1 | **Projecting Benson Conglomerate's Financial Statements: Distributions as Dividends (Millions of Dollars)**

	A	B	C	D	E	F	G
79	Panel a: Inputs		Actual	Projected			
80			12/31/2012	2013		2014	
81	Sales growth rate			5%		5%	
82	Costs / Sales		70%	70%		70%	
83	Depreciation / Net PPE		10%	10%		10%	
84	Cash / Sales		1%	1%		1%	
85	Acct. rec. / Sales		15%	15%		15%	
86	Inventories / Sales		12%	12%		12%	
87	Net PPE / Sales		85%	85%		85%	
88	Acct. pay. / Sales		8%	8%		8%	
89	Accruals / Sales		2%	2%		2%	
90	Tax rate		40%	40%		40%	
91							
92	Panel b: Income Statement[a]		12/31/2012	12/31/2013		12/31/2014	
93	Net Sales		$8,000.0	$8,400.0		$8,820.0	
94	Costs (except depreciation)		5,600.0	5,880.0		6,174.0	
95	Depreciation		680.0	714.0		749.7	
96	Earning before int. & tax		$1,720.0	$1,806.0		$1,896.3	
97	Interest expense[b]		0.0	0.0		0.0	
98	Earnings before taxes		$1,720.0	$1,806.0		$1,896.3	
99	Taxes		688.0	722.4		758.5	
100	Net income		$1,032.0	$1,083.6		$1,137.8	
101							
102	Panel c: Balance Sheets			2013		2014	
103	Assets		12/31/2012	12/30	12/31	12/30	12/31
104	Cash		$80.0	$84.0	$84.0	$88.2	$88.2
105	Short-term investments[c]		0.0	671.6	0.0	705.2	0.0
106	Accounts receivable		1,200.0	1,260.0	1,260.0	1,323.0	1,323.0
107	Inventories		960.0	1,008.0	1,008.0	1,058.4	1,058.4
108	Total current assets		$2,240.0	$3,023.6	$2,352.0	$3,174.8	$2,469.6
109	Net plant and equipment		6,800.0	7,140.0	7,140.0	7,497.0	7,497.0
110	Total assets		$9,040.0	$10,163.6	$9,492.0	$10,671.8	$9,966.6
111	Liabilities & Equity						
112	Accounts payable		$640.0	$672.0	$672.0	$705.6	$705.6
113	Accruals		160.0	168.0	168.0	176.4	176.4
114	Short-term debt		0.0	0.0	0.0	0.0	0.0
115	Total current liabilities		$800.0	$840.0	$840.0	$882.0	$882.0
116	Long-term debt		0.0	0.0	0.0	0.0	0.0
117	Total liabilities		$800.0	$840.0	$840.0	$882.0	$882.0
118	Preferred stock		0.0	0.0	0.0	0.0	0.0
119	Common stock		2,400.0	2,400.0	2,400.0	2,400.0	2,400.0
120	Retained earnings[d]		5,840.0	6,923.6	6,252.0	7,389.8	6,684.6
121	Total common equity		$8,240.0	$9,323.6	$8,652.0	$9,789.8	$9,084.6
122	Total liabilities & equity		$9,040.0	$10,163.6	$9,492.0	$10,671.8	$9,966.6
123							
124	Panel d: Plugging to balance			12/30/2013		12/30/2014	
125	Required operating assets:			$9,492.0		$9,966.6	
126	Liabilities & equity before distribution			$10,163.6		$10,671.8	
127	AFN: Addition funds needed			−$671.6		−$705.2	

(Continued)

Figure 17-1	Projecting Benson Conglomerate's Financial Statements: Distributions as Dividends (Millions of Dollars) *(Continued)*

[a]All calculations are in the file **Ch17 Tool Kit.xls**. *Excel* uses all significant digits in calculations, but numbers in the figure are rounded and so columns may not total exactly.

[b]To simplify the example, we assume that any short-term investments are held for only part of the year and earn no interest.

[c]A negative AFN means there are extra funds available. These are held as short-term investments through December 30. The funds are distributed to investors on December 31, so the balance of short-term investments goes to zero on December 31.

[d]Because no funds have been paid out in dividends as of December 30, the retained earnings balance for that date is equal to the previous year's retained earnings balance plus the current year's net income. When short-term investments are sold and their proceeds are used to make the cash dividend payments on December 31, the balance of retained earnings is reduced by the amount of the total dividend payments (which is equal to the reduction in short-term investments).

Figure 17-2	Projecting Benson Conglomerate's Liabilities & Equity: Distributions as Stock Repurchases (Millions of Dollars)

	A	B	C	D	E	F	G
147					Projected		
148				2013		2014	
149	Liabilities & Equity[a]		12/31/2012	12/30	12/31	12/30	12/31
150	Accounts payable		$640.0	$672.0	$672.0	$705.6	$705.6
151	Accruals		160.0	168.0	168.0	176.4	176.4
152	Short-term debt		0.0	0.0	0.0	0.0	0.0
153	Total current liabilities		$800.0	$840.0	$840.0	$882.0	$882.0
154	Long-term debt		0.0	0.0	0.0	0.0	0.0
155	Total liabilities		$800.0	$840.0	840.0	882.0	882.0
156	Preferred stock		0.0	0.0	0.0	0.0	0.0
157	Common stock		2,400.0	2,400.0	2,400.0	2,400.0	2,400.0
158	Treasury stock[b]		0.0	0.0	(671.6)	(671.6)	(1,376.8)
159	Retained earnings[c]		5,840.0	6,923.6	6,923.6	8,061.4	8,061.4
160	Total common equity		$8,240.0	$9,323.6	8,652.0	9,789.8	9,084.6
161	Total liabilities & equity		$9,040.0	$10,163.6	9,492.0	10,671.8	9,966.6

[a]All calculations are in the file **Ch17 Tool Kit.xls**. *Excel* uses all significant digits in calculations, but numbers in the figure are rounded and so columns may not total exactly. See Figure 17-1 for income statements and assets.

[b]When distributions are made as repurchases, the treasury stock account is reduced by the dollar value of the repurchase at the time of the repurchase, which occurs when short-term investments are liquidated and used to repurchase stock.

[c]No funds are paid out in dividends, so the retained earnings balance is equal to the previous balance plus the year's net income (all net income is being retained).

the short-term investments account are used to repurchase stock on December 31, the repurchase is shown as a negative entry in the treasury stock account.

To summarize, the projected income statements and assets are identical whether the distribution is made in the form of dividends or stock repurchases. There also is no difference in liabilities. However, distributions as dividends reduce the retained earnings account, whereas stock repurchases reduce the treasury stock account.

WEB

See **Ch17 Tool Kit.xls** on the textbook's Web site.

17.9b The Residual Distribution Model

Figures 17-1 and 17-2 illustrate the residual distribution model in Equation 17-1 as applied to entire financial statements. The projected capital budget is equal to the net addition to total operating capital from the projected balance sheets in Figure 17-1. For example, for 2013 the capital budget is:

$$
\begin{aligned}
\text{Capital budget} &= (\Delta\text{Cash} + \Delta\text{Accounts receivable} + \Delta\text{Inventories} \\
&\quad + \Delta\text{Net plant \& equipment}) \\
&\quad - (\Delta\text{Accounts payable} + \Delta\text{Accruals}) \\
&= (\$84 - \$80) + (\$1{,}260 - \$1{,}200) + (\$1{,}008 - \$960) \\
&\quad + (\$7{,}140 - \$6{,}800) - (\$672 - \$640) - (\$168 - \$160) \\
&= \$452 - \$40 = \$412
\end{aligned}
$$

With a 100% target equity ratio and net income of $1,083.6, the residual is $1,083.6 − $412 = $671.6, as shown in Figure 17-3. Notice that this is the same as the AFN we calculated in Figure 17-1.

17.9c The Impact of Distributions on Intrinsic Value

What is the impact of cash distributions on intrinsic value? We devote the rest of this section to answering that question.

Free Cash Flow

We begin by calculating expected free cash flows and performance measures as shown in Figure 17-4. Notice that Benson's expected return on invested capital is greater than the cost of capital, indicating that the managers are creating value for their shareholders. Also notice that the company is beyond its high-growth phase, so FCF is positive and growing at a constant rate of 5%. Therefore, Benson has cash flow available for distribution to investors.

The Value of Operations

Figure 17-4 also shows the value of operations for each year. (See the *Tool Kit* for the full 4-year projections.) Recall from Chapter 11 that we can use the projected

WEB

See *Ch17 Tool Kit.xls* on the textbook's Web site.

WEB

See *Ch17 Tool Kit.xls* on the textbook's Web site.

Figure 17-3 **Illustration of the Residual Distribution Model as Applied to Benson Conglomerate (Millions of Dollars): Determining the Level of the Distribution**

	A	B	C	D	E	F	G
179					Projected		
180				12/31/2013		12/31/2014	
181	Capital budget[a]			$412.0		$432.6	
182	Target equity ratio			100%		100%	
183	Net income[b]			$1,083.6		$1,137.8	
184	Required additional equity[c]			$412.0		$432.6	
185	Residual distribution: NI – Req. equ.			$671.6		$705.2	

[a]See Figure 17-1 for balance sheet projections. The capital budget is equal to the net addition to total operating capital: $(\Delta\text{Cash} + \Delta\text{Accts. rec.} + \Delta\text{Inventories} + \Delta\text{Net plant \& equipment}) - (\Delta\text{Accts. pay.} + \Delta\text{Accruals})$.
[b]See Figure 17-1 for income statement projections.
[c]Required additional equity = Capital budget × Target equity ratio.

Figure 17-4   Illustration of the Residual Distribution Model as Applied to Benson Conglomerate (Millions of Dollars): Valuation Analysis

	A	B	C	D	E	F	G
201	WACC = 12.0%						
202					Projected		
203	*Calculation of Free Cash Flow*		12/31/2012		12/31/2013		12/31/2014
204	Operating current assets[a]		$2,240.00		$2,352.00		$2,469.60
205	Operating current liabilities[b]		800.00		840.00		882.00
206	NOWC[c]		$1,440.00		$1,512.00		$1,587.60
207	Net plant & equipment		6,800.00		7,140.00		7,497.00
208	Net operating capital[d]		$8,240.00		$8,652.00		$9,084.60
209	NOPAT[e]		$1,032.00		$1,083.60		$1,137.78
210	Inv. in operating capital[f]				412.00		432.60
211	Free cash flow (FCF)[g]				$671.60		$705.18
212							
213	*Performance Measures*						
214	Expected ROIC[h]				13.15%		13.15%
215	Growth in FCF				na		5.00%
216	Growth in sales				5.00%		5.00%
217							
218	*Valuation*						
219	Horizon value[i]						$10,577.70
220	Value of operations[j]		$9,594.29		$10,074.00		$10,577.70

[a]Sum of cash, accounts receivable, and inventories.
[b]Sum of accounts payable and accruals.
[c]Net operating working capital is equal to operating current assets minus operating current liabilities.
[d]Sum of NOWC and net plant & equipment.
[e]Net operating profit after taxes = (EBIT)(1 − T). In this example, NOPAT is equal to net income because there is no interest expense or interest income.
[f]Change in net operating capital from previous year.
[g]FCF = NOPAT − Investment in operating capital.
[h]Expected return on invested capital = NOPAT divided by beginning capital.
[i]Horizon value at T = $V_{op(T)}$ = [FCF_T(1 + g)]/(WACC − g).
[j]Value of operations before horizon = $V_{op(t)}$ = ($V_{op(t+1)}$ + FCF_{t+1})/(1 + WACC).

FCFs to determine the horizon value at the end of the projections and then estimate the value of operations for each year prior to the horizon. For Benson, the horizon value on December 31, 2014, is

$$V_{op(12/31/14)} = \frac{FCF_{12/31/14}(1 + g)}{WACC - g}$$

$$= \frac{\$705.18(1 + 0.05)}{0.12 - 0.05} = \$10,577.70$$

The value of operations at the end of the previous year is equal to the value of operations 1 year ahead plus the free cash flow 1 year ahead, discounted back 1 year at the cost of capital. For example, the value of operations on December 31, 2013, is

$$V_{op(12/31/13)} = \frac{V_{op(12/31/14)} + FCF_{12/31/14}}{(1 + WACC)}$$

$$= \frac{\$10,577.7 + \$705.18}{1 + 0.12} = \$10,074.00$$

We can repeat this process to obtain the current value of operations (i.e., as of December 31, 2012): $9,549.29.

Notice that the choice of how to distribute the residual does not affect the value of operations because the distribution choice does not affect the projected free cash flows.

The Intrinsic Stock Price: Distributions as Dividends

Figure 17-5 shows the intrinsic stock price each year using the corporate valuation approach described in Chapter 11. Panel a provides calculations assuming cash is distributed via dividends. (See *Ch17 Tool Kit.xls* for projections for 4 years.) Notice that on December 31 the intrinsic value of equity drops because the firm no longer owns the short-term investments. This causes the intrinsic stock price also to drop. In fact, the drop in stock price is equal to the dividend per share. For example, the 2013 dividend per share (DPS) is $0.67 and the drop in stock price is $10.75 − $10.07 = $0.68 ≈ $0.67. (The penny difference here is due to rounding in intermediate steps.)

Notice that if the stock price did *not* fall by the amount of the DPS then there would be an opportunity for arbitrage. If the price were to drop by less than the DPS—say, by $0.50 to $10.25, then you could buy the stock on December 30 for $10.75, receive a DPS of $0.67 on December 31, and then immediately sell the stock for $10.25, reaping a sure profit of −$10.75 + $0.67 + $10.25 = $0.17. Of course, you'd want to implement this strategy with a million shares, not just a single share. But if everyone tried to use this strategy, the increased demand would drive up the stock price on December 30 until there was no more sure profit to be made. The reverse would happen if investors expected the stock price to fall by more than the DPS.[21]

Here is an important observation: Even though the stock price falls, shareholder wealth does not fall. For example, on December 30, a shareholder owns stock worth $10.75. On December 31, the shareholder owns stock worth $10.07 but has cash of $0.67 from the dividend, for total wealth of $10.75 (subject to rounding differences). Thus, the shareholder's wealth is the same before and after the dividend payment, with the only difference being that part of the shareholder's wealth is in the form of cash from the dividend payment.

The Intrinsic Stock Price: Distributions as Repurchases

Panel b of Figure 17-5 provides calculations of intrinsic value for the case in which stock is repurchased. Observe that the intrinsic value of equity is the same for both methods of distributions, but the analysis of a repurchase is a little

---

21. We ignore taxes in this description. Empirical evidence suggests that the actual drop in stock price is equal to about 90% of the DPS, with all pre-tax profit being eliminated by taxes.

Figure 17-5   **Illustration of the Residual Distribution Model as Applied to Benson Conglomerate (Millions of Dollars): Distributions as Dividends versus Stock Repurchases**

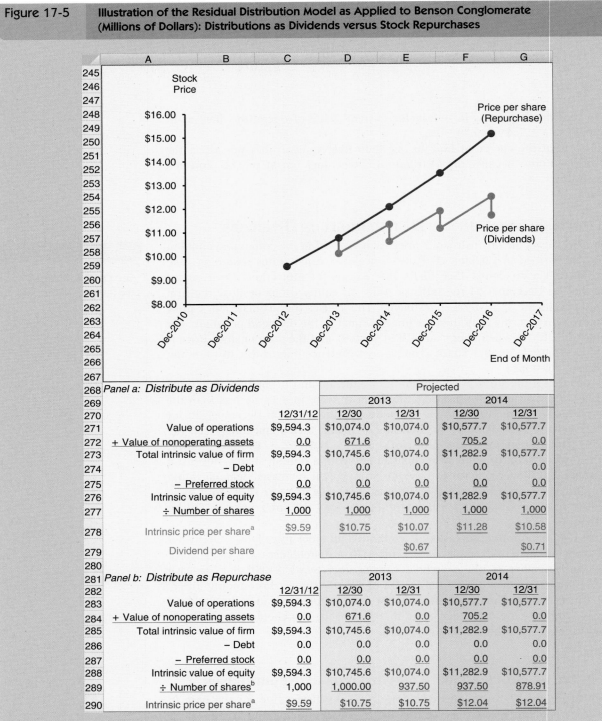

Panel a: Distribute as Dividends			Projected			
			2013		2014	
		12/31/12	12/30	12/31	12/30	12/31
Value of operations		$9,594.3	$10,074.0	$10,074.0	$10,577.7	$10,577.7
+ Value of nonoperating assets		0.0	671.6	0.0	705.2	0.0
Total intrinsic value of firm		$9,594.3	$10,745.6	$10,074.0	$11,282.9	$10,577.7
– Debt		0.0	0.0	0.0	0.0	0.0
– Preferred stock		0.0	0.0	0.0	0.0	0.0
Intrinsic value of equity		$9,594.3	$10,745.6	$10,074.0	$11,282.9	$10,577.7
÷ Number of shares		1,000	1,000	1,000	1,000	1,000
Intrinsic price per share[a]		$9.59	$10.75	$10.07	$11.28	$10.58
Dividend per share				$0.67		$0.71

Panel b: Distribute as Repurchase			2013		2014	
		12/31/12	12/30	12/31	12/30	12/31
Value of operations		$9,594.3	$10,074.0	$10,074.0	$10,577.7	$10,577.7
+ Value of nonoperating assets		0.0	671.6	0.0	705.2	0.0
Total intrinsic value of firm		$9,594.3	$10,745.6	$10,074.0	$11,282.9	$10,577.7
– Debt		0.0	0.0	0.0	0.0	0.0
– Preferred stock		0.0	0.0	0.0	0.0	0.0
Intrinsic value of equity		$9,594.3	$10,745.6	$10,074.0	$11,282.9	$10,577.7
÷ Number of shares[b]		1,000	1,000.00	937.50	937.50	878.91
Intrinsic price per share[a]		$9.59	$10.75	$10.75	$12.04	$12.04

[a]The projected intrinsic stock prices for 4 years are shown in *Ch17 Tool Kit.xls*.

[b]The number of shares after the repurchase is: $n_{Post} = n_{Prior} - (Cash_{Rep}/P_{Prior})$. In this example, the entire amount of ST investments (i.e., the balance of nonoperating assets) is used to repurchase stock.

more complicated because the number of shares changes. The key to solving this additional complexity is to recognize that the repurchase does not change the stock price. If the price did change due to the repurchase, then there would be an arbitrage opportunity. For example, suppose the stock price is expected to increase after the repurchase. If this were true, then it should be possible for an investor to buy the stock the day before the repurchase and then reap a reward the very next day. Current stockholders would realize this and would refuse to sell the stock unless they were paid the price that is expected immediately after the repurchase. Now suppose the stock price is expected to fall immediately after the repurchase. In this case, current shareholders should try to sell the stock prior to the repurchase, but their actions would drive the price down to the price that is expected after the repurchase. As this "thought experiment" shows, the repurchase itself does not change the stock price.

In summary, the events leading up to a repurchase generate cash (the sale of a division, a recapitalization, or the generation of high free cash flows from operations). Generating cash can certainly change the stock price, but the repurchase itself doesn't change the stock price. We can use this fact to determine the number of shares repurchased. First, though, we must define some notation.

n_{Prior} = The number of shares outstanding prior to the repurchase.
n_{Post} = The number of shares outstanding after the repurchase.
S_{Prior} = The intrinsic value of equity prior to the repurchase.
S_{Post} = The intrinsic value of equity after the repurchase.
P_{Prior} = The intrinsic stock price prior to the repurchase.
P_{Post} = The intrinsic stock price after the repurchase.
$P = P_{Prior} = P_{Post}$ = The intrinsic stock price during, before, and after the repurchase.
$Cash_{Rep}$ = The amount of cash used to repurchase shares.

As we explained, the repurchase itself doesn't change the stock price. Therefore, the number of shares repurchased is equal to the amount of cash used to repurchase stocks divided by the stock price:

$$\text{Number of shares repurchased} = n_{Prior} - n_{Post} = \frac{Cash_{Rep}}{P_{prior}} \qquad (17\text{–}2)$$

We can rewrite Equation 17-2 to find an expression for the number of shares after the repurchase:

$$
\begin{aligned}
n_{Post} &= n_{Prior} - \frac{Cash_{Rep}}{P_{Prior}} \\
&= n_{Prior} - \frac{Cash_{Rep}}{S_{Prior} / n_{Prior}} \qquad (17\text{–}3) \\
&= n_{Prior}\left(1 - \frac{Cash_{Rep}}{S_{Prior}}\right)
\end{aligned}
$$

For example, as shown in Panel b of Figure 17-5, the intrinsic stock price on December 30, 2013, the day before the repurchase, is $10.75, and there are 1,000 shares of stock. Using Equation 17-3, the number of shares after the repurchase is equal to:

$$n_{Post} = n_{Prior} - \frac{Cash_{Rep}}{P_{Prior}}$$

$$= 1,000 - \frac{\$671.6}{\$10.75}$$

$$= 1,000 - 62.47 = 937.5$$

Panel b of Figure 17-5 also shows that on December 31, 2013, the intrinsic value of equity prior to the repurchase, S_{Prior}, drops from $10,745.6 to a value after the repurchase, S_{Post}, of $10,074.0. This decrease in the intrinsic value of equity is equal to the amount of the cash used in the repurchase, $671.6. However, the stock price remains at $10.75 after the repurchase because the number of shares also drops:

$$P_{Post} = \frac{S_{Post}}{n_{Post}} = \frac{\$10,074}{93.75} = \$10.75$$

How does the repurchase affect shareholder wealth? The aggregate value of outstanding stock drops after the repurchase, but the aggregate wealth of the shareholders remains unchanged. Before the repurchase, shareholders own a total of equity worth S_{Prior}, $10,745.6. After the repurchase, shareholders own a total of equity worth S_{Post}, $10,074, but they also own cash (received in the repurchase) in the amount of $671.6, for a total wealth of $10,745.6. Thus, the repurchase does not change shareholders' aggregate wealth; it only changes the form in which they hold wealth (all stock versus a combination of stock and cash).

Comparing Intrinsic Stock Prices:
Distributions as Repurchases

The chart at the top of Figure 17-5 shows the projected intrinsic stock prices for the two different distribution methods. Notice that the prices begin at the same level (because Benson has not yet begun making any distributions). The price for the repurchase scenario climbs smoothly and grows to a higher level than does the price for the dividend scenario, which drops by the DPS each time it is paid. However, the number of shares falls in the repurchase scenario. As shown in Rows 277 and 289 of the figure, the intrinsic values of equity are identical for both distribution methods.

This example illustrates three key results: (1) Ignoring possible tax effects and signals, the total market value of equity will be the same whether a firm pays dividends or repurchases stock. (2) The repurchase itself does not change the stock price (compared with using the cash to buy marketable securities) at the time of the repurchase, although it does reduce the number of outstanding shares. (3) Because a company that repurchases stock will have fewer shares than an otherwise identical company that pays dividends, the stock price of a repurchasing company will climb faster than that of the dividend-paying company. However, the total return to the two companies' shareholders will be the same.[22]

Self Test

Explain how a repurchase changes the number of shares but not the stock price.

A firm's most recent FCF was $2.4 million, and its FCF is expected to grow at a constant rate of 5%. The firm's WACC is 14% and it has 2 million shares outstanding. The firm has $12 million in short-term investments that it plans to liquidate and then distribute in a stock repurchase; the firm has no other financial investments or debt. Verify that the value of operations is $28 million. Immediately prior to the repurchase, what are the intrinsic value of equity and the intrinsic stock price? **($40 million; $20/share)** How many shares will be repurchased? **(0.6 million)** How many shares will remain after the repurchase? **(1.4 million)** Immediately after the repurchase, what are the intrinsic value of equity and the intrinsic stock price? **($28 million; $20/share)**

17.10 The Pros and Cons of Dividends and Repurchases

The advantages of repurchases can be listed as follows.

1. Repurchase announcements are viewed as positive signals by investors because the repurchase is often motivated by management's belief that the firm's shares are undervalued.
2. Stockholders have a choice when the firm distributes cash by repurchasing stock—they can sell or not sell. Those stockholders who need cash can sell back some of their shares while others can simply retain their stock. With a cash dividend, on the other hand, stockholders must accept a dividend payment.
3. Dividends are "sticky" in the short run because management is usually reluctant to raise the dividend if the increase cannot be maintained in the future, and cutting cash dividends is always avoided because of the negative signal it gives. Hence, if the excess cash flow is thought to be only temporary, management may prefer making the distribution in the form of a stock repurchase to declaring an increased cash dividend that cannot be maintained.
4. Companies can use the residual model to set a *target cash distribution* level and then divide the distribution into a *dividend component* and a *repurchase component*. The dividend payout ratio will be relatively low, but the dividend itself will be relatively secure, and it will grow as a result of the declining number of shares outstanding. The company has more flexibility in adjusting the total distribution than it would if the entire distribution were in the form of cash dividends, because repurchases can be varied from year to year without

---

22. For more on repurchases, see David J. Denis, "Defensive Changes in Corporate Payout Policy: Share Repurchases and Special Dividends," *Journal of Finance,* December 1990, pp. 1433–1456; Gerald D. Gay, Jayant R. Kale, and Thomas H. Noe, "Share Repurchase Mechanisms: A Comparative Analysis of Efficacy, Shareholder Wealth and Corporate Control Effects," *Financial Management,* Spring 1991, pp. 44–59; Jeffry M. Netter and Mark L. Mitchell, "Stock-Repurchase Announcements and Insider Transactions after the October 1987 Stock Market Crash," *Financial Management,* Autumn 1989, pp. 84–96; William Pugh and John S. Jahera, Jr., "Stock Repurchases and Excess Returns: An Empirical Examination," *The Financial Review,* February 1990, pp. 127–142; and James W. Wansley, William R. Lane, and Salil Sarkar, "Managements' View on Share Repurchase and Tender Offer Premiums," *Financial Management,* Autumn 1989, pp. 97–110.

giving off adverse signals. This procedure, which is what Florida Power & Light employed, has much to recommend it, and it is one reason for the dramatic increase in the total volume of stock repurchases.

5. Repurchases can be used to produce large-scale changes in capital structures. For example, several years ago Consolidated Edison decided to borrow $400 million and use the funds to repurchase some of its common stock. Thus, Con Ed was able to quickly change its capital structure.

6. Companies that use stock options as an important component of employee compensation usually repurchase shares in the secondary market and then use those shares when employees exercise their options. This technique allows companies to avoid issuing new shares and thus diluting earnings.

Repurchases have three principal disadvantages.

1. Stockholders may not be indifferent between dividends and capital gains, and the price of the stock might benefit more from cash dividends than from repurchases. Cash dividends are generally dependable, but repurchases are not.

2. The *selling* stockholders may not be fully aware of all the implications of a repurchase, or they may not have all the pertinent information about the corporation's present and future activities. However, in order to avoid potential stockholder suits, firms generally announce repurchase programs before embarking on them.

3. The corporation may pay too much for the repurchased stock—to the disadvantage of remaining stockholders. If the firm seeks to acquire a relatively large amount of its stock, then the price may be bid above its equilibrium level and then fall after the firm ceases its repurchase operations.

When all the pros and cons on stock repurchases versus dividends have been totaled, where do we stand? Our conclusions may be summarized as follows.

1. Because of the deferred tax on capital gains, repurchases have a tax advantage over dividends as a way to distribute income to stockholders. This advantage is reinforced by the fact that repurchases provide cash to stockholders who want cash while allowing those who do not need current cash to delay its receipt. On the other hand, dividends are more dependable and thus are better suited for those who need a steady source of income.

2. The danger of signaling effects requires that a company not have volatile dividend payments, which would lower investors' confidence in the company and adversely affect its cost of equity and its stock price. However, cash flows vary over time, as do investment opportunities, so the "proper" dividend in the residual model sense varies. To get around this problem, a company can set its dividend low enough to keep dividend payments from constraining operations and then use repurchases on a more or less regular basis to distribute excess cash. Such a procedure will provide regular, dependable dividends plus additional cash flow to those stockholders who want it.

3. Repurchases are also useful when a firm wants to make a large shift in its capital structure, wants to distribute cash from a one-time event such as the sale of a division, or wants to obtain shares for use in an employee stock option plan.

Self Test	What are some advantages and disadvantages of stock repurchases?
	How can stock repurchases help a company operate in accordance with the residual distribution model?

DIVIDEND YIELDS AROUND THE WORLD

Dividend yields vary considerably in different stock markets throughout the world. In 1999, dividend yields in the United States averaged 1.6% for the large blue-chip stocks in the Dow Jones Industrials, 1.2% for a broader sample of stocks in the S&P 500, and 0.3% for stocks in the Nasdaq, where high-tech firms predominate. Outside the United States, average dividend yields ranged from 5.7% in New Zealand to 0.7% in Taiwan. The accompanying table summarizes the dividend picture in 1999.

World Stock Market (Index)	Dividend Yield	World Stock Market (Index)	Dividend Yield
New Zealand	5.7%	United States (Dow Jones Industrials)	1.6%
Australia	3.1	Canada (TSE 300)	1.5
Britain FTSE 100	2.4	United States (S&P 500)	1.2
Hong Kong	2.4	Mexico	1.1
France	2.1	Japan Nikkei	0.7
Germany	2.1	Taiwan	0.7
Belgium	2.0	United States (Nasdaq)	0.3
Singapore	1.7		

Source: From Alexandra Eadie, "On the Grid Looking for Dividend Yield around the World," *The Globe and Mail,* June 23, 1999, p. B16. Eadie's source was Bloomberg Financial Services. Reprinted with permission from *The Globe and Mail.*

17.11 Other Factors Influencing Distributions

In this section, we discuss several other factors that affect the dividend decision. These factors may be grouped into two broad categories: (1) constraints on dividend payments and (2) availability and cost of alternative sources of capital.

17.11a Constraints

Constraints on dividend payments can affect distributions, as the following examples illustrate.

1. *Bond indentures.* Debt contracts often limit dividend payments to earnings generated after the loan was granted. Also, debt contracts often stipulate that no dividends can be paid unless the current ratio, times-interest-earned ratio, and other safety ratios exceed stated minimums.
2. *Preferred stock restrictions.* Typically, common dividends cannot be paid if the company has omitted its preferred dividend. The preferred arrearages must be satisfied before common dividends can be resumed.

3. *Impairment of capital rule.* Dividend payments cannot exceed the balance sheet item "retained earnings." This legal restriction, known as the "impairment of capital rule," is designed to protect creditors. Without the rule, a company in trouble might distribute most of its assets to stockholders and leave its debtholders out in the cold. (*Liquidating dividends* can be paid out of capital, but they must be indicated as such and must not reduce capital below the limits stated in debt contracts.)

4. *Availability of cash.* Cash dividends can be paid only with cash, so a shortage of cash in the bank can restrict dividend payments. However, the ability to borrow can offset this factor.

5. *Penalty tax on improperly accumulated earnings.* To prevent wealthy individuals from using corporations to avoid personal taxes, the Tax Code provides for a special surtax on improperly accumulated income. Thus, if the IRS can demonstrate that a firm's dividend payout ratio is being deliberately held down to help its stockholders avoid personal taxes, the firm is subject to heavy penalties. This factor is generally relevant only to privately owned firms.

17.11b Alternative Sources of Capital

The second factor that influences the dividend decision is the cost and availability of alternative sources of capital.

1. *Cost of selling new stock.* If a firm needs to finance a given level of investment, it can obtain equity by retaining earnings or by issuing new common stock. If flotation costs (including any negative signaling effects of a stock offering) are high then the required return on new equity, r_e, will be well above the required return on internally-generated equity, r_s, making it better to set a low payout ratio and to finance through retention rather than through the sale of new common stock. On the other hand, a high dividend payout ratio is more feasible for a firm whose flotation costs are low. Flotation costs differ among firms—for example, the flotation percentage is generally higher for small firms, so they tend to set low payout ratios.

2. *Ability to substitute debt for equity.* A firm can finance a given level of investment with either debt or equity. As just described, low stock flotation costs permit a more flexible dividend policy because equity can be raised either by retaining earnings or by selling new stock. A similar situation holds for debt policy: If the firm can adjust its debt ratio without raising costs sharply, then it can pay the expected dividend—even if earnings fluctuate—by increasing its debt ratio.

3. *Control.* If management is concerned about maintaining control, it may be reluctant to sell new stock; hence the company may retain more earnings than it otherwise would. However, if stockholders want higher dividends and a proxy fight looms, then the dividend will be increased.

Self Test	What constraints affect dividend policy?
	How do the availability and cost of outside capital affect dividend policy?

17.12 Summarizing the Distribution Policy Decision

In practice, the distribution decision is made jointly with capital structure and capital budgeting decisions. The underlying reason for joining these decisions is asymmetric information, which influences managerial actions in two ways.

1. In general, managers do not want to issue new common stock. First, new common stock involves issuance costs—commissions, fees, and so on—and those costs can be avoided by using retained earnings to finance equity needs. Second, as we explain in Chapter 15, asymmetric information causes investors to view new common stock issues as negative signals and thus lowers expectations regarding the firm's future prospects. The end result is that the announcement of a new stock issue usually leads to a decrease in the stock price. Considering the total costs due to issuance and asymmetric information, managers prefer to use retained earnings as the primary source of new equity.

2. Dividend changes provide signals about managers' beliefs concerning their firms' future prospects. Thus, dividend reductions generally have a significant negative effect on a firm's stock price. Since managers recognize this, they try to set dollar dividends low enough that there is only a remote chance the dividend will have to be reduced in the future.

The effects of asymmetric information suggest that, to the extent possible, managers should avoid both new common stock sales and dividend cuts, because both actions tend to lower the stock price. Thus, in setting distribution policy, managers should begin by considering the firm's future investment opportunities relative to its projected internal sources of funds. The target capital structure also plays a part, but because it is a *range*, firms can vary their actual capital structures somewhat from year to year. Since it is best to avoid issuing new common stock, the target long-term payout ratio should be designed to permit the firm to meet all of its equity capital requirements with retained earnings. In effect, *managers should use the residual model to set dividends, but in a long-term framework*. Finally, the current dollar dividend should be set so that there is an extremely low probability that the dividend, once set, will ever have to be lowered or omitted.

Of course, the dividend decision is made during the planning process, so there is uncertainty about future investment opportunities and operating cash flows. The actual payout ratio in any year will therefore likely be above or below the firm's long-range target. However, the dollar dividend should be maintained, or increased as planned, unless the firm's financial condition deteriorates to the point at which the planned policy simply cannot be maintained. A steady or increasing stream of dividends over the long run signals that the firm's financial condition is under control. Moreover, investor uncertainty is decreased by stable dividends, so a steady dividend stream reduces the negative effect of a new stock issue—should one become absolutely necessary.

In general, firms with superior investment opportunities should set lower payouts, and hence retain more earnings, than firms with poor investment opportunities. The degree of uncertainty also influences the decision. If there is a great deal of uncertainty regarding the forecasts of free cash flows, which are defined here as the firm's operating cash flows minus mandatory equity investments, then it is best to be conservative and to set a lower current dollar dividend. Also, firms with postponable investment opportunities can afford to set a higher dollar dividend, because in times of stress investments can be postponed for a year or two, thus increasing the cash available for dividends. Finally, firms whose cost of capital is largely unaffected by changes in the debt ratio can also afford to set a higher payout ratio, because in times of stress they can more easily issue additional debt to maintain the capital budgeting program without having to cut dividends or issue stock.

The net result of these factors is that many firms' dividend policies are consistent with the life-cycle theory in which younger firms with many investment opportunities but relatively low cash flows reinvest their earnings so that they can avoid the large flotation costs associated with raising external capital.[23] As firms mature and begin to generate more cash flow, they tend to pay more dividends and issue more debt as a way to "bond" their cash flows (as described in Chapter 15) and thereby reduce the agency costs of free cash flow.

What do executives think? A recent survey indicates financial executives believe that it is extremely important to *maintain* dividends but much less important to initiate or increase dividend payments. In general, they view the cash distribution decision as being much less important than capital budgeting decisions. Managers like the flexibility provided by repurchases instead of regular dividends. They tend to repurchase shares when they believe their stock price is undervalued, and they believe that shareholders view repurchases as positive signals. In general, the different taxation of dividends and repurchases is not a major factor when a company chooses how to distribute cash to investors.[24]

Self Test	Describe the decision process for distribution policy and dividend payout. Be sure to discuss all the factors that influence this decision.

17.13 Stock Splits and Stock Dividends

The rationale for stock splits and dividends can best be explained through an example. We will use Porter Electronic Controls Inc., a $700 million electronic components manufacturer, for this purpose. Since its inception, Porter's markets have been expanding, and the company has enjoyed growth in sales and earnings. Some of its earnings have been paid out in dividends, but some are also retained each year, causing its earnings per share and stock price to grow. The company began its life with only a few thousand shares outstanding, and after some years of growth the stock price was high. Porter's CFO thought this high price limited the number of investors who could buy the stock, which reduced demand for the stock and thus kept the firm's total market value below what it could be if there were more shares, at a lower price, outstanding. To correct this situation, Porter "split its stock," as we describe next.

17.13a Stock Splits

Although there is little empirical evidence to support the contention, there is nevertheless a widespread belief in financial circles that an *optimal price range* exists for stocks. "Optimal" means that if the price is within this range, the firm's value will be maximized. Many observers, including Porter's management, believe the best range for most stocks is from $20 to $80 per share. Accordingly, if the price of Porter's stock rose to $80, management would probably declare a 2-for-1 **stock split,** thus doubling the number of shares outstanding, halving the earnings and dividends per share, and thereby lowering the stock price. Each stockholder would have more shares, but each share would be worth less. If the post-split price

---

23. For a test of the life-cycle theory, see Harry DeAngelo, Linda DeAngelo, and René Stulz, "Dividend Policy and the Earned/Contributed Capital Mix: A Test of the Life-Cycle Theory," *Journal of Financial Economics,* August 2006, pp. 227–254.

24. See Alon Brav, John R. Graham, Campbell R. Harvey, and Roni Michaely, "Payout Policy in the 21st Century," *Journal of Financial Economics,* September 2005, pp. 483–527.

were $40, then Porter's stockholders would be exactly as well off as before the split. However, if the stock price were to stabilize above $40, stockholders would be better off. Stock splits can be of any size—for example, the stock could be split 2-for-1, 3-for-1, 1.5-for-1, or in any other way.

Sometimes a company will have a **reverse split.** For example, the financial services company Citigroup (C) was trading in the $55 per share range in 2007 prior to the global financial meltdown. After the meltdown, the stock traded as low as $1 in 2009 and had recovered only to $4.52 per share by May 6, 2011. On May 9, 2011, Citigroup had a 1-10 reverse stock split before trading began, with its shareholders exchanging 10 shares of stock for a single new share. In theory, the stock price should have increased by a factor of 10, to around $45.20, and Citigroup indeed closed that day at a price of $44.16. Even though Citigroup was again trading in the same per-share price range as it did before the global financial meltdown, with only 1/10 the number of shares outstanding, its market value of equity was still less than 10% of what it had been in 2007.

17.13b Stock Dividends

Stock dividends are similar to stock splits in that they "divide the pie into smaller slices" without affecting the fundamental position of the current stockholders. On a 5% stock dividend, the holder of 100 shares would receive an additional 5 shares (without cost); on a 20% stock dividend, the same holder would receive 20 new shares; and so on. Again, the total number of shares is increased, so earnings, dividends, and price per share all decline.

If a firm wants to reduce the price of its stock, should it use a stock split or a stock dividend? Stock splits are generally used after a sharp price run-up to produce a large price reduction. Stock dividends used on a regular annual basis will keep the stock price more or less constrained. For example, if a firm's earnings and dividends

THE GLOBAL ECONOMIC CRISIS

Talk about a Split Personality!

Sun Microsystems once was among the highest of the high-flying companies in the tech boom of the 1990s. Sun went public in 1986 and its stock price grew rapidly, with Sun declaring seven different 2-1 stock splits between 1988 and 2000. Without these splits, Sun's stock price would have grown from about $30 in late 1988 to over $1,700 in mid-2000, a staggering return of over 40% per year! However, Sun's fortunes fell when the tech bubble burst, and Sun never recovered. With its stock price languishing around $5, Sun declared a 1-4 reverse stock split in late 2007, which boosted the stock price to over $20, but subsequently it sank into the $3–$4 range by the

spring of 2009. In April 2009, Sun announced that it had agreed to be acquired by Oracle for about $9.50 per share. This would have been only $2.375 = $9.50/4 if not for the reverse split in 2007, quite a fall from its former highs.

Reverse splits were rare when Sun Microsystems declared its split in 2007, but now Sun might have plenty of company caused by the economic crisis. Such well-known companies as Dynegy and E-Trade effected reverse splits in 2010, and many more are potential candidates. In fact, 58 companies had stock prices of less than a dollar per share in April 2011, including such familiar names as Borders Group, Frederick's of Hollywood, and Jackson Hewitt Tax Service.

were growing at about 10% per year, its stock price would tend to go up at about that same rate, and it would soon be outside the desired trading range. A 10% annual stock dividend would maintain the stock price within the optimal trading range. Note, however, that small stock dividends create bookkeeping problems and unnecessary expenses, so firms today use stock splits far more often than stock dividends.[25]

17.3c Effect on Stock Prices

If a company splits its stock or declares a stock dividend, will this increase the market value of its stock? Many empirical studies have sought to answer this question. Here is a summary of their findings.

1. On average, the price of a company's stock rises shortly after it announces a stock split or a stock dividend.
2. However, these price increases are probably due to signaling rather than a desire for stock splits or dividends per se. Only managers who think future earnings will be higher tend to split stocks, so investors often view the announcement of a stock split as a positive signal. Thus, it is the signal of favorable prospects for earnings and dividends that causes the price to increase.
3. If a company announces a stock split or stock dividend, its price will tend to rise. However, if during the next few months it does not announce an increase in earnings and dividends, then its stock price will drop back to the earlier level.
4. As we noted earlier, brokerage commissions are generally higher in percentage terms on lower-priced stocks. This means that it is more expensive to trade low-priced than high-priced stocks—which, in turn, means that stock splits may reduce the liquidity of a company's shares. This particular piece of evidence suggests that stock splits/dividends might actually be harmful, although a lower price does mean that more investors can afford to trade in round lots (100 shares), which carry lower commissions than do odd lots (fewer than 100 shares).

What can we conclude from all this? From a purely economic standpoint, stock dividends and splits are just additional pieces of paper. However, they provide management with a relatively low-cost way of signaling that the firm's prospects look good.[26] Further, we should note that since few large, publicly owned stocks sell at prices above several hundred dollars, we simply do not know what the effect would be if Microsoft, Wal-Mart, Hewlett-Packard, and other highly successful firms had never split their stocks and consequently sold at prices in the thousands or even tens of thousands of dollars. All in all, it probably makes sense to employ stock splits (or stock dividends) when a firm's

---

25. Accountants treat stock splits and stock dividends somewhat differently. For example, in a 2-for-1 stock split, the number of shares outstanding is doubled and the par value is halved, and that's about all there is to it. With a stock dividend, a bookkeeping entry is made transferring "retained earnings" to "common stock."

26. For more on stock splits and stock dividends, see H. Kent Baker, Aaron L. Phillips, and Gary E. Powell, "The Stock Distribution Puzzle: A Synthesis of the Literature on Stock Splits and Stock Dividends," *Financial Practice and Education,* Spring/Summer 1995, pp. 24–37; Maureen McNichols and Ajay Dravid, "Stock Dividends, Stock Splits, and Signaling," *Journal of Finance,* July 1990, pp. 857–879; and David R. Peterson and Pamela P. Peterson, "A Further Understanding of Stock Distributions: The Case of Reverse Stock Splits," *Journal of Financial Research,* Fall 1992, pp. 189–205.

prospects are favorable, especially if the price of its stock has gone beyond the normal trading range.[27]

What are stock splits and stock dividends?

How do stock splits and dividends affect stock prices?

In what situations should managers consider the use of stock splits?

In what situations should managers consider the use of stock dividends?

Suppose you have 1,000 common shares of Burnside Bakeries. The EPS is $6.00, the DPS is $3.00, and the stock sells for $90 per share. Burnside announces a 3-for-1 split. Immediately after the split, how many shares will you have? **(3,000)** What will the adjusted EPS and DPS be? **($2 and $1)** What would you expect the stock price to be? **($30)**

17.14 Dividend Reinvestment Plans

During the 1970s, most large companies instituted **dividend reinvestment plans (DRIPs)**, under which stockholders can choose to automatically reinvest their dividends in the stock of the paying corporation. Today most large companies offer DRIPs; participation rates vary considerably, but about 25% of the average firm's shareholders are enrolled. There are two types of DRIPs: (1) plans that involve only "old stock" that is already outstanding and (2) plans that involve newly issued stock. In either case, the stockholder must pay taxes on the amount of the dividends, even though stock rather than cash is received.

Under both types of DRIPs, stockholders choose between continuing to receive dividend checks or having the company use the dividends to buy more stock in the corporation. Under the "old stock" type of plan, if a stockholder elects reinvestment then a bank, acting as trustee, takes the total funds available for reinvestment, purchases the corporation's stock on the open market, and allocates the shares purchased to the participating stockholders' accounts on a pro rata basis. The transaction costs of buying shares (brokerage costs) are low because of volume purchases, so these plans benefit small stockholders who do not need cash dividends for current consumption.

The "new stock" type of DRIP uses the reinvested funds to buy newly issued stock; hence these plans raise new capital for the firm. AT&T, Union Carbide, and many other companies have used new stock plans to raise substantial amounts of new equity capital. No fees are charged to stockholders, and many companies offer stock at a discount of 3% to 5% below the actual market price. The companies offer discounts as a trade-off against flotation costs that would have been incurred if new stock had been issued through investment bankers instead of through the dividend reinvestment plans.

One interesting aspect of DRIPs is that they cause corporations to re-examine their basic dividend policies. A high participation rate in a DRIP suggests that

---

27. It is interesting to note that Berkshire Hathaway (controlled by billionaire Warren Buffett) has never had a stock split, and its stock (BRKa) sold on the NYSE for $111,495 per share in June 2011. Yet in response to investment trusts that were being formed in 1996 to sell fractional units of the stock and thus—in effect—split it, Buffett himself created a new class of Berkshire Hathaway stock (Class B) worth about 1/30 of a Class A (regular) share.

stockholders might be better off if the firm simply reduced cash dividends, which would save stockholders some personal income taxes. Quite a few firms are surveying their stockholders to learn more about their preferences and to find out how they would react to a change in dividend policy. A more rational approach to basic dividend policy decisions may emerge from this research.

Note that companies start or stop using new stock DRIPs depending on their need for equity capital. For example, Union Carbide and AT&T recently stopped offering new stock DRIPs with a 5% discount because their needs for equity capital declined.

Some companies have expanded their DRIPs by moving to "open enrollment," whereby anyone can purchase the firm's stock directly and thus bypass brokers' commissions. ExxonMobil not only allows investors to buy their initial shares at no fee but also lets them pick up additional shares through automatic bank account withdrawals. Several plans, including ExxonMobil's, offer dividend reinvestment for individual retirement accounts, and some, such as U.S. West's, allow participants to invest weekly or monthly rather than on the quarterly dividend schedule. In all of these plans, and many others, stockholders can invest more than the dividends they are forgoing—they simply send a check to the company and buy shares without a broker-age commission. According to First Chicago Trust, which handles the paperwork for 13 million shareholder DRIP accounts, at least half of all DRIPs will offer open enrollment, extra purchases, and other expanded services within the next few years.

Self Test	What are dividend reinvestment plans?
	What are their advantages and disadvantages from both the stockholders' and the firm's perspectives?

Summary

- **Distribution policy** involves three issues: (1) What fraction of earnings should be distributed? (2) Should the distribution be in the form of cash dividends or stock repurchases? (3) Should the firm maintain a steady, stable dividend growth rate?
- The **optimal distribution policy** strikes a balance between current dividends and future growth so as to maximize the firm's stock price.
- Miller and Modigliani (MM) developed the **dividend irrelevance theory,** which holds that a firm's dividend policy has no effect on either the value of its stock or its cost of capital.
- The **dividend preference theory,** also called the **bird-in-the-hand theory,** holds that the firm's value will be maximized by a high dividend payout ratio, because investors regard cash dividends as being less risky than potential capital gains.

- The **tax effect theory** states that because long-term capital gains are subject to lower taxes than dividends, investors prefer to have companies retain earnings rather than pay them out as dividends.
- Dividend policy should take account of the **information content of dividends (signaling)** and the **clientele effect.** The information content, or signaling, effect stems from investors regarding an unexpected dividend change as a signal of management's forecast of future earnings. The clientele effect suggests that a firm will attract investors who like the firm's dividend payout policy. Both factors should be taken into account by firms that are considering a change in dividend policy.
- In practice, dividend-paying firms follow a policy of paying a **steadily increasing dividend.** This policy provides investors with stable, dependable income, and departures from it give investors signals about management's expectations for future earnings.
- Most firms use the **residual distribution model** to set the long-run target distribution ratio at a level that will permit the firm to meet its equity requirements with retained earnings.
- Under a **stock repurchase plan,** a firm buys back some of its outstanding stock, thereby decreasing the number of shares but leaving the stock price unchanged.
- Legal constraints, investment opportunities, availability and cost of funds from other sources, and taxes are also considered when firms establish dividend policies.
- A **stock split** increases the number of shares outstanding. Normally, splits reduce the price per share in proportion to the increase in shares because splits merely "divide the pie into smaller slices." However, firms generally split their stocks only if (1) the price is quite high and (2) management thinks the future is bright. Therefore, stock splits are often taken as positive signals and thus boost stock prices.
- A **stock dividend** is a dividend paid in additional shares rather than in cash. Both stock dividends and splits are used to keep stock prices within an "optimal" trading range.
- A **dividend reinvestment plan (DRIP)** allows stockholders to have the company automatically use dividends to purchase additional shares. DRIPs are popular because they allow stockholders to acquire additional shares without brokerage fees.

Questions

17-1 Define each of the following terms:
    a. Optimal distribution policy
    b. Dividend irrelevance theory; bird-in-the-hand theory; tax effect theory
    c. Information content, or signaling, hypothesis; clientele effect
    d. Residual distribution model; extra dividend
    e. Declaration date; holder-of-record date; ex-dividend date; payment date
    f. Dividend reinvestment plan (DRIP)
    g. Stock split; stock dividend; stock repurchase

17-2 How would each of the following changes tend to affect aggregate payout ratios (that is, the average for all corporations), other things held constant? Explain your answers.

a. An increase in the personal income tax rate

b. A liberalization of depreciation for federal income tax purposes—that is, faster tax write-offs

c. A rise in interest rates

d. An increase in corporate profits

e. A decline in investment opportunities

f. Permission for corporations to deduct dividends for tax purposes as they now do interest charges

g. A change in the Tax Code so that both realized and unrealized capital gains in any year were taxed at the same rate as dividends

17-3 What is the difference between a stock dividend and a stock split? As a stockholder, would you prefer to see your company declare a 100% stock dividend or a 2-for-1 split? Assume that either action is feasible.

17-4 One position expressed in the financial literature is that firms set their dividends as a residual after using income to support new investments. Explain what a residual policy implies (assuming that all distributions are in the form of dividends), illustrating your answer with a table showing how different investment opportunities could lead to different dividend payout ratios.

17-5 Indicate whether the following statements are true or false. If the statement is false, explain why.

a. If a firm repurchases its stock in the open market, the shareholders who tender the stock are subject to capital gains taxes.

b. If you own 100 shares in a company's stock and the company's stock splits 2-for-1, then you will own 200 shares in the company following the split.

c. Some dividend reinvestment plans increase the amount of equity capital available to the firm.

d. The Tax Code encourages companies to pay a large percentage of their net income in the form of dividends.

e. A company that has established a clientele of investors who prefer large dividends is unlikely to adopt a residual dividend policy.

f. If a firm follows a residual dividend policy then, holding all else constant, its dividend payout will tend to rise whenever the firm's investment opportunities improve.

Problems Answers Appear in Appendix B

Easy Problems 1–5

17-1 **Residual Distribution Model** Puckett Products is planning for $5 million in capital expenditures next year. Puckett's target capital structure consists of 60% debt and 40% equity. If net income next year is $3 million and Puckett follows a residual distribution policy with all distributions as dividends, what will be its dividend payout ratio?

17-2 Residual Distribution Policy Petersen Company has a capital budget of $1.2 million. The company wants to maintain a target capital structure which is 60% debt and 40% equity. The company forecasts that its net income this year will be $600,000. If the company follows a residual distribution model and pays all distributions as dividends, what will be its payout ratio?

17-3 Dividend Payout The Wei Corporation expects next year's net income to be $15 million. The firm's debt ratio is currently 40%. Wei has $12 million of profitable investment opportunities, and it wishes to maintain its existing debt ratio. According to the residual distribution model (assuming all payments are in the form of dividends), how large should Wei's dividend payout ratio be next year?

17-4 Stock Repurchase A firm has 10 million shares outstanding with a market price of $20 per share. The firm has $25 million in extra cash (short-term investments) that it plans to use in a stock repurchase; the firm has no other financial investments or any debt. What is the firm's value of operations, and how many shares will remain after the repurchase?

17-5 Stock Split JPix management is considering a stock split. JPix currently sells for $120 per share, and a 3-for-2 stock split is contemplated. What will be the company's stock price following the stock split assuming that the split has no effect on the total market value of JPix's equity?

Intermediate Problems 6–9

17-6 External Equity Financing Gardial GreenLights, a manufacturer of energy efficient lighting solutions, has had such success with its new products that it is planning to substantially expand its manufacturing capacity with a $15 million investment in new machinery. Gardial plans to maintain its current 30% debt-to-total-assets ratio for its capital structure and to maintain its dividend policy in which at the end of each year it distributes 55% of the year's net income. This year's net income was $8 million. How much external equity must Gardial seek now to expand as planned?

17-7 Stock Split Suppose you own 2,000 common shares of Laurence Incorporated. The EPS is $10.00, the DPS is $3.00, and the stock sells for $80 per share. Laurence announces a 2-for-1 split. Immediately after the split, how many shares will you have, what will the adjusted EPS and DPS be, and what would you expect the stock price to be?

17-8 Stock Split Fauver Enterprises declared a 3-for-1 stock split last year, and this year its dividend is $1.50 per share. This total dividend payout represents a 6% increase over last year's pre-split total dividend payout. What was last year's dividend per share?

17-9 Residual Distribution Policy Harris Company must set its investment and dividend policies for the coming year. It has three independent projects from which to choose, each of which requires a $3 million investment. These projects have different levels of risk, and therefore different costs of capital. Their projected IRRs and costs of capital are as follows:

Project A: Cost of capital = 17%; IRR = 20%
Project B: Cost of capital = 13%; IRR = 10%
Project C: Cost of capital = 7%; IRR = 9%

Harris intends to maintain its 35% debt and 65% common equity capital structure, and its net income is expected to be $4,750,000. If Harris maintains its residual dividend policy (with all distributions in the form of dividends), what will its payout ratio be?

Challenging Problems 10–12

17-10 **Alternative Dividend Policies** Boehm Corporation has had stable earnings growth of 8% a year for the past 10 years, and in 2012 Boehm paid dividends of $2.6 million on net income of $9.8 million. However, in 2013 earnings are expected to jump to $12.6 million, and Boehm plans to invest $7.3 million in a plant expansion. This one-time unusual earnings growth won't be maintained, though, and after 2013 Boehm will return to its previous 8% earnings growth rate. Its target debt ratio is 35%.

    a. Calculate Boehm's total dividends for 2013 under each of the following policies:

       (1) Its 2013 dividend payment is set to force dividends to grow at the long-run growth rate in earnings.

       (2) It continues the 2012 dividend payout ratio.

       (3) It uses a pure residual policy with all distributions in the form of dividends (35% of the $7.3 million investment is financed with debt).

       (4) It employs a regular-dividend-plus-extras policy, with the regular dividend being based on the long-run growth rate and the extra dividend being set according to the residual policy.

    b. Which of the preceding policies would you recommend? Restrict your choices to the ones listed, but justify your answer.

    c. Does a 2013 dividend of $9 million seem reasonable in view of your answers to parts a and b? If not, should the dividend be higher or lower?

17-11 **Residual Distribution Model** Kendra Brown is analyzing the capital requirements for Reynolds Corporation for next year. Kendra forecasts that Reynolds will need $15 million to fund all of its positive-NPV projects, and her job is to determine how to raise the money. Reynolds's net income is $11 million, and it has paid a $2 dividend per share (DPS) for the past several years (1 million shares of common stock are outstanding); its shareholders expect the dividend to remain constant for the next several years. The company's target capital structure is 30% debt and 70% equity.

    a. Suppose Reynolds follows the residual model and makes all distributions as dividends. How much retained earnings will it need to fund its capital budget?

    b. If Reynolds follows the residual model with all distributions in the form of dividends, what will be its dividend per share and payout ratio for the upcoming year?

    c. If Reynolds maintains its current $2 DPS for next year, how much retained earnings will be available for the firm's capital budget?

    d. Can Reynolds maintain its current capital structure, maintain its current dividend per share, and maintain a $15 million capital budget *without* having to raise new common stock?

    e. Suppose Reynolds's management is firmly opposed to cutting the dividend; that is, it wishes to maintain the $2 dividend for the next year.

Suppose also that the company is committed to funding all profitable projects and is willing to issue more debt (along with the available retained earnings) to help finance the company's capital budget. Assume the resulting change in capital structure has a minimal impact on the company's composite cost of capital, so that the capital budget remains at $15 million. What portion of this year's capital budget would have to be financed with debt?

f. Suppose once again that Reynolds's management wants to maintain the $2 DPS. In addition, the company wants to maintain its target capital structure (30% debt, 70% equity) and its $15 million capital budget. What is the minimum dollar amount of new common stock the company would have to issue in order to meet all of its objectives?

g. Now consider the case in which Reynolds's management wants to maintain the $2 DPS and its target capital structure but also wants to avoid issuing new common stock. The company is willing to cut its capital budget in order to meet its other objectives. Assuming the company's projects are divisible, what will be the company's capital budget for the next year?

h. If a firm follows the residual distribution policy, what actions can it take when its forecasted retained earnings are less than the retained earnings required to fund its capital budget?

17-12 Stock Repurchase Bayani Bakery's most recent FCF was $48 million; the FCF is expected to grow at a constant rate of 6%. The firm's WACC is 12%, and it has 15 million shares of common stock outstanding. The firm has $30 million in short-term investments, which it plans to liquidate and distribute to common shareholders via a stock repurchase; the firm has no other nonoperating assets. It has $368 million in debt and $60 million in preferred stock.

a. What is the value of operations?

b. Immediately prior to the repurchase, what is the intrinsic value of equity?

c. Immediately prior to the repurchase, what is the intrinsic stock price?

d. How many shares will be repurchased? How many shares will remain after the repurchase?

e. Immediately after the repurchase, what is the intrinsic value of equity? The intrinsic stock price?

Spreadsheet Problem

17-13 Build a Model: Distributions as Dividends or Repurchases Start with the partial model in the file *Ch17 P13 Build a Model.xls* on the textbook's Web site. J. Clark Inc. (JCI), a manufacturer and distributor of sports equipment, has grown until it has become a stable, mature company. Now JCI is planning its first distribution to shareholders. (See the file for the most recent year's financial statements and projections for the next year, 2013; JCI's fiscal year ends on June 30.) JCI plans to liquidate and distribute $500 million of its short-term securities on July 1, 2013, the first day of the next fiscal year, but has not yet decided whether to distribute with dividends or with stock repurchases.

a. Assume first that JCI distributes the $500 million as dividends. Fill in the missing values in the file's balance sheet column for July 1, 2013, that is labeled "Distribute as Dividends." (*Hint:* Be sure that the balance sheets balance after you fill in the missing items.) Assume that JCI did not have to establish an account for dividends payable prior to the distribution.

b. Now assume that JCI distributes the $500 million through stock repurchases. Fill in the missing values in the file's balance sheet column for July 1, 2013, that is labeled "Distribute as Repurchase." (*Hint:* Be sure that the balance sheets balance after you fill in the missing items.)

c. Calculate JCI's projected free cash flow; the tax rate is 40%.

d. What is JCI's current intrinsic stock price (the price on 6/30/2012)? What is the projected intrinsic stock price for 6/30/2013?

e. What is the projected intrinsic stock price on 7/1/2013 if JCI distributes the cash as dividends?

f. What is the projected intrinsic stock price on 7/1/2013 if JCI distributes the cash through stock repurchases? How many shares will remain outstanding after the repurchase?

THOMSON REUTERS

Use the Thomson ONE—Business School Edition online database to work this chapter's questions.

Microsoft's Dividend Policy

Let's find out what has happened to Microsoft's (MSFT) dividend policy since its 2003 announcement to initiate dividends. We can address this issue by relying on the data that are provided to you in Thomson ONE.

Discussion Questions

1. To get information about MSFT's dividend policy, enter its ticker and select OVERVIEW>FULL REPORTS>WORLDSCOPE FULL REPORTS>FULL COMPANY REPORT. Click on STOCK & EARNINGS DATA, and scroll down to the Annual Historical Data section. What has happened to MSFT's dividend per share, dividend yield, and dividend payout over the past 5 years? Do you have any explanations?

2. Compare this with other firms in the same industry. To see how MSFT stacks up against its peers, select COMPARABLES>OVERVIEWS>PER SHARE DATA to get MSFT's peers' last annual dividends. Accessing COMPARABLES>OVERVIEWS>ABSOLUTE RANKINGS will give their dividend yields. You can also get this information from the VALUATION COMPARISON in this same section. Has MSFT behaved differently from its peers, or have there been industry-wide shifts?

3. Refer back to the FULL COMPANY REPORT used in Question 1. Manually plot earnings and dividends over time. In the text, we point out that dividends are often much more stable than earnings. Do you see a similar pattern for MSFT?

4. In the Interim Financial Data section of the FULL COMPANY REPORT, identify the dividend declared date, the ex-dividend date, and the pay date. Explain the significance of these dates. Go back to Overview and access the Interactive Price Chart. Can you observe price shifts around these dates? Explain what price shifts you might expect to see.

5. Investors are more concerned with future dividends than historical dividends, so go to ESTIMATES and scroll down to the Consensus Estimates section. Click on the Available Measures menu to toggle between earnings per share and dividends per share. What do analysts expect MSFT's payout policy to be in the future?

6. Refer back to the FULL COMPANY REPORT, and scroll down to the 5 Yr Annual Balance Sheet section. Does it appear that MSFT has been repurchasing any stock, or has it been issuing new stock?

MINI CASE

Integrated Waveguide Technologies Inc. (IWT) is a 6-year-old company founded by Hunt Jackson and David Smithfield to exploit metamaterial plasmonic technology to develop and manufacture miniature microwave frequency directional transmitters and receivers for use in mobile Internet and communications applications. The technology, although highly advanced, is relatively inexpensive to implement, and their patented manufacturing techniques require little capital in comparison to many electronics fabrication ventures. Because of the low capital requirement, Jackson and Smithfield have been able to avoid issuing new stock and thus own all of the shares. Because of the explosion in demand for its mobile Internet applications, IWT must now access outside equity capital to fund its growth, and Jackson and Smithfield have decided to take the company public. Until now, Jackson and Smithfield have paid themselves reasonable salaries but routinely reinvested all after-tax earnings in the firm, so dividend policy has not been an issue. However, before talking with potential outside investors, they must decide on a dividend policy.

Your new boss at the consulting firm Flick and Associates, which has been retained to help IWT prepare for its public offering, has asked you to make a presentation to Jackson and Smithfield in which you review the theory of dividend policy and discuss the following issues.

a. (1) What is meant by the term "distribution policy"? How has the mix of dividend payouts and stock repurchases changed over time?

(2) The terms "irrelevance," "dividend preference, or bird-in-the-hand," and "tax effect" have been used to describe three major theories regarding the way dividend payouts affect a firm's value. Explain what these terms mean, and briefly describe each theory.

(3) What do the three theories indicate regarding the actions management should take with respect to dividend payouts?

(4) What results have empirical studies of the dividend theories produced? How does all this affect what we can tell managers about dividend payouts?

b. Discuss (1) the information content, or signaling, hypothesis, (2) the clientele effect, and (3) their effects on distribution policy.

c. (1) Assume that IWT has completed its IPO and has a $112.5 million capital budget planned for the coming year. You have determined that its present capital structure (80% equity and 20% debt) is optimal, and its net income is forecasted at $140 million. Use the residual distribution approach to determine IWT's total dollar distribution. Assume for now that the distribution is in the form of a dividend. Suppose IWT has 100 million shares of stock outstanding. What is the forecasted dividend payout ratio? What is the forecasted dividend per share? What would happen to the payout ratio and DPS if net income were forecasted to decrease to $90 million? To increase to $160 million?

   (2) In general terms, how would a change in investment opportunities affect the payout ratio under the residual distribution policy?

   (3) What are the advantages and disadvantages of the residual policy? (*Hint:* Don't neglect signaling and clientele effects.)

d. (1) Describe the procedures a company follows when it make a distribution through dividend payments.

   (2) What is a stock repurchase? Describe the procedures a company follows when it make a distribution through a stock repurchase.

e. Discuss the advantages and disadvantages of a firm repurchasing its own shares.

f. Suppose IWT has decided to distribute $50 million, which it presently is holding in very liquid short-term investments. IWT's value of operations is estimated to be about $1,937.5 million, and it has $387.5 million in debt (it has no preferred stock). As mentioned previously, IWT has 100 million shares of stock outstanding.

   (1) Assume that IWT has not yet made the distribution. What is IWT's intrinsic value of equity? What is its intrinsic stock price per share?

   (2) Now suppose that IWT has just made the $50 million distribution in the form of dividends. What is IWT's intrinsic value of equity? What is its intrinsic stock price per share?

   (3) Suppose instead that IWT has just made the $50 million distribution in the form of a stock repurchase. Now what is IWT's intrinsic value of equity? How many shares did IWT repurchase? How many shares remained outstanding after the repurchase? What is its intrinsic stock price per share after the repurchase?

g. Describe the series of steps that most firms take when setting dividend policy.

h. What are stock splits and stock dividends? What are the advantages and disadvantages of each?

i. What is a dividend reinvestment plan (DRIP), and how does it work?

Selected Additional Cases

The following cases from TextChoice, Cengage Learning's online case library, cover many of the concepts discussed in this chapter and are available at **www.textchoice2.com/casenet.**

Klein-Brigham Series:

Case 19, "Georgia Atlantic Company," Case 20, "Bessemer Steel Products, Inc.," Case 47, "Floral Fragrance, Inc.," and Case 80, "The Western Company," all illustrate the dividend policy decision.

Brigham-Buzzard Series:

Case 9, "Powerline Network Corporation (Dividend Policy)."

PART V

Tactical Financing Decisions

Chapter 18

Initial Public Offerings, Investment Banking, and Financial Restructuring

WEB

The textbook's Web site contains an *Excel* file that will guide you through the chapter's calculations. The file for this chapter is **Ch18 Tool Kit.xls,** and we encourage you to open the file and follow along as you read the chapter.

Previous chapters described how a company makes capital structure and dividend policy decisions. Those decisions affect a firm's need for new capital and the form or forms in which this capital is raised. We now discuss the actual process of raising capital, including the roles played by investment banks and regulatory agencies.

Beginning of Chapter Questions

As you read the chapter, consider how you would answer the following questions. You *should not* necessarily be able to answer the questions before you read the chapter. Rather, you should use them to get a sense of the issues covered in the chapter. After reading the chapter, you should be able to give at least partial answers to the questions, and you should be able to give better answers after the chapter has been discussed in class. Note, too, that it is often useful, when answering conceptual questions, to use hypothetical data to illustrate your answer. We illustrate the answers with an *Excel* model that is available on the textbook's Web site. Accessing the model and working through it is a useful exercise, and it provides insights that are useful when answering the questions.

1. What are some reasons why companies decide to **go public?** If going public is a good idea, why don't all companies do so?
2. On the day an IPO comes out, the market price can rise above the offering price or fall below that price. Is it more common for the market price to close above or below the offering price on the day of an IPO? If a company's market price rises above the IPO price, does that suggest that the company **left money on the table** and thus received less for its shares than it should have received? If most companies do leave money on the table, does that indicate the IPO market is inefficient? How might systematic underpricing be explained? Has the amount of underpricing been constant over time? Explain.
3. What's the difference between an IPO and an SEO? Would you view purchasing a stock in an SEO as more or less risky than purchasing a stock in an IPO? Would you expect the same first day returns for an SEO purchase as for an IPO purchase? Why?
4. How do companies decide whether or not to **refund their outstanding bonds?** If the NPV as calculated in a bond refunding analysis is positive, does that mean that the company should call and refund the bond? What is the effect of calling a bond on its bondholders?

18.1 The Financial Life Cycle of a Start-up Company

Most businesses begin life as proprietorships or partnerships, and if they become successful and grow, at some point they find it desirable to become corporations. Initially, most corporate stock is owned by the firms' founding managers and key employees. Even start-up firms that are ultimately successful usually begin with negative free cash flows because of their high growth rates and product development costs; hence, they must raise capital during these high-growth years. If the founding owner-managers have invested all of their own financial resources in the company, then they must turn to outside sources of capital. Start-up firms generally have high growth opportunities relative to assets-in-place, and they suffer from especially large problems with asymmetric information. Therefore, as we discussed in Chapter 15, they must raise external capital primarily as equity rather than debt.

To protect investors from fraudulent stock issues, in 1933 Congress enacted the Securities Act, which created the **Securities and Exchange Commission (SEC)** to regulate the financial markets.[1] The Securities Act regulates interstate public offerings, which we explain later in this section, but it also provides several exemptions that allow companies to issue securities through **private placements** that

---

1. In addition to federal statutes, which affect transactions that cross state borders, states have "Blue Sky" laws that regulate securities sold just within the state. These laws were designed to prevent unscrupulous dealers from selling something of little worth, such as blue sky, to naïve investors.

are not registered with the SEC. The rules governing these exemptions are quite complex, but in general they restrict the number and type of investors who may participate in an issue. **Accredited investors** include the officers and directors of the company, high-wealth individuals, and institutional investors. In a non-registered private placement, the company may issue securities to an unlimited number of accredited investors but to only 35 nonaccredited investors. In addition, none of the investors can sell their securities in the secondary market to the general public.

For most start-ups, the first round of external financing comes through a private placement of equity to one or two individual investors, called **angels**. In return for a typical investment in the range of $50,000 to $400,000, the angels receive stock and perhaps also a seat on the board of directors. Because angels can influence the strategic direction of the company, it is best when they bring experience and industry contacts to the table, not just cash.

As the company grows, its financing requirements may exceed the resources of individual investors, in which case it is likely to turn to a **venture capital fund**. A venture capital fund is a private limited partnership, which typically raises $30 million to $80 million from a relatively small group of primarily institutional investors, including pension funds, college endowments, and corporations.[2] The managers of a venture capital fund, called **venture capitalists**, or **VCs**, are usually very knowledgeable and experienced in a particular industry, such as health care or biotechnology. They screen hundreds of companies and ultimately fund around a dozen, called **portfolio companies**. The venture fund buys shares of the portfolio companies, and the VCs sit on the companies' boards of directors. The venture capital fund usually has a prespecified life of 7 to 10 years, after which it is dissolved, either by selling the portfolio companies' stock and distributing the proceeds to the funds' investors or by directly distributing the stock to the investors.

Self Test

What is a private placement?

What is an angel?

What is a venture capital fund? A VC?

18.2 The Decision to Go Public

Going public means selling some of a company's stock to outside investors in an initial public offering (IPO) and then letting the stock trade in public markets. For example, the health care company HCA, Nielsen Holdings, Kinder Morgan, and many other companies took this step in 2011. The advantages and disadvantages of public stock ownership are discussed next.

---

2. The typical venture capital fund is a private limited partnership, with limited partners and a general partner. The limited partners contribute cash but are prohibited from being involved in the partnership's decision making. Because of their limited participation, they are not held liable for any of the partnership's liabilities, except to the extent of their original investment. The general partner usually contributes a relatively modest amount of cash but acts as the partnership's manager. In return, the general partner normally receives annual compensation equal to 1% to 2% of the fund's assets plus a 20% share of the fund's eventual profits.

18.2a Advantages of Going Public

There are many advantages to going public, as we detail in the following list.

1. *Increases liquidity and allows founders to harvest their wealth.* The stock of a private, or closely held, corporation is illiquid. It may be hard for one of the owners who wants to sell some shares to find a ready buyer, and even if a buyer is located, there is no established price on which to base the transaction.

2. *Permits founders to diversify.* As a company grows and becomes more valuable, its founders often have most of their wealth tied up in the company. By selling some of their stock in a public offering, they can diversify their holdings, thereby reducing the riskiness of their personal portfolios.

3. *Facilitates raising new corporate cash.* If a privately held company wants to raise cash by selling new stock, it must either go to its existing owners, who may not have any money or may not want to put more eggs in this particular basket, or else shop around for wealthy investors. However, it is usually quite difficult to get outsiders to put money into a closely held company: If the outsiders do not have voting control (more than 50% of the stock), then the inside stockholders/managers can take advantage of them. Going public, which brings with it both public disclosure of information and regulation by the SEC, greatly reduces this problem and thus makes people more willing to invest in the company, which makes it easier for the firm to raise capital.

4. *Establishes a value for the firm.* If a company wants to give incentive stock options to key employees, it is useful to know the exact value of those options. Employees much prefer to own stock, or options on stock, that is publicly traded and therefore liquid. Also, when the owner of a privately owned business dies, state and federal tax appraisers must set a value on the company for estate tax purposes. Often these appraisers set a higher value than that of a similar publicly traded company.

5. *Facilitates merger negotiations.* Having an established market price helps when a company either is being acquired or is seeking to acquire another company in which the payment will be with stock.

6. *Increases potential markets.* Many companies report that it is easier to sell their products and services to potential customers after they become publicly traded.

18.2b Disadvantages of Going Public

There are also a number of disadvantages associated with going public, as follows.

1. *Cost of reporting.* A publicly owned company must file quarterly and annual reports with the SEC and/or various state agencies. These reports can be a costly burden, especially for small firms. In addition, compliance with the Sarbanes-Oxley Act often requires considerable expense and manpower.

2. *Disclosure.* Management may not like the idea of reporting operating data, because these data will then be available to competitors. Similarly, the owners of the company may not want people to know their net worth. But since a publicly owned company must disclose the number of shares owned by its officers, directors, and major stockholders, it is easy enough for anyone to multiply shares held by price per share to estimate the net worth of the insiders.

3. *Inactive market and/or low price.* If the firm is very small and if its shares are not traded frequently, then its stock will not really be liquid and so the market price may not represent the stock's true value. Security analysts and stockbrokers simply

will not follow the stock, because there will not be sufficient trading activity to generate enough brokerage commissions to cover the costs of following it.

4. *Control.* Because of possible tender offers and proxy fights, the managers of publicly owned firms who do not have voting control must be concerned about maintaining control. Further, there is pressure on such managers to produce annual earnings gains, even when it might be in the shareholders' best long-term interests to adopt a strategy that reduces short-term earnings but raises them in future years. These factors have led a number of public companies to "go private" in leveraged buyout deals, where the managers borrow the money to buy out the nonmanagement stockholders. We discuss the decision to go private in a later section.

5. *Investor relations.* Public companies must keep investors abreast of current developments. Many CFOs of newly public firms report that they spend two full days a week talking with investors and analysts.

18.2c Conclusions on Going Public

There are no hard-and-fast rules regarding if or when a company should go public. This is an individual decision that should be made on the basis of the company's and stockholders' own unique circumstances. If a company does decide to go public, either by selling newly issued stock to raise new capital or by selling stock of the current owners, the key issue is setting the price at which shares will be offered to the public. The company and its current owners should want to set the price as high as possible: The higher the offering price, the smaller the fraction of the company the current owners will have to give up to obtain any specified amount of money. On the other hand, potential buyers want the price set as low as possible. We return to the establishment of the offering price later in the chapter, after we describe some other aspects of common stock financing.

Self Test	What are the major advantages of going public?
	What are the major disadvantages?

18.3 The Process of Going Public: An Initial Public Offering

As the following sections show, an initial public offering is a lot more complicated, expensive, and time-consuming than simply making the decision to go public.

18.3a Selecting an Investment Bank

After a company decides to go public, it faces the problem of how to sell its stock to a large number of investors. Although most companies know how to sell their products, few have experience in selling securities. To help in this process, the company will interview a number of different **investment banks,** also called **underwriters,** and then select one to be the lead underwriter. To understand the factors that affect this choice, it helps to understand exactly what investment banks do.

First, the investment bank helps the firm determine the preliminary offering price, or price range, for the stock and the number of shares to be sold. The investment bank's reputation and experience in the company's industry are critical in convincing potential investors to purchase the stock at the offering price. In effect, the investment bank implicitly certifies that the stock is not overpriced, which obviously comforts investors. Second, the investment bank actually sells the shares to its existing clients, which include a mix of institutional investors and retail (that is, individual) customers. Third, the investment bank, through its associated brokerage house, will have an analyst "cover" the stock after it is issued. This analyst will regularly distribute reports to investors describing the stock's prospects, which will help to maintain an interest in the stock. Well-respected analysts increase the likelihood that there will be a liquid secondary market for the stock and that its price will reflect the company's true value.

18.3b The Underwriting Syndicate

The firm and its investment bank must next decide whether the bank will work on a **best efforts basis** or will **underwrite** the issue. In a best efforts sale, the bank does not guarantee that the securities will be sold or that the company will get the cash it needs, only that it will put forth its "best efforts" to sell the issue. On an underwritten issue, in contrast, the company does get a guarantee: The bank agrees to buy the entire issue and then resell the stock to its customers. Therefore, the bank bears significant risks in underwritten offerings. For example, on one IBM bond issue interest rates rose sharply and bond prices fell after the deal had been set but before the investment banks could sell the bonds to the ultimate purchasers. The banks lost somewhere between $10 million and $20 million. Had the offering been on a best efforts basis, IBM would have been the loser.

Except for extremely small issues, virtually all IPOs are underwritten. Investors are required to pay for securities within 10 days, and the investment bank must pay the issuing firm within 4 days of the official commencement of the offering. Typically, the bank sells the stock within a day or two after the offering begins, but on occasion the bank miscalculates, sets the offering price too high, and thus is unable to move the issue. At other times, the market declines during the offering period, forcing the bank to reduce the price of the stock or bonds. In either instance, on an underwritten offering the firm receives the price that was agreed upon, so the bank must absorb any losses that are incurred.

Because they are exposed to large potential losses, investment banks typically do not handle the purchase and distribution of issues single-handedly unless the issue is a very small one. If the sum of money involved is large, then investment banks form **underwriting syndicates** in an effort to minimize the risk each individual bank faces. The banking house that sets up the deal is called the **lead,** or **managing, underwriter.** Syndicated offerings are usually covered by more analysts, which contributes to greater liquidity in the post-IPO secondary market. Thus, syndication provides benefits to both underwriters and issuers.

In addition to the underwriting syndicate, on larger offerings still more investment banks are included in a **selling group,** which handles the distribution of securities to individual investors. The selling group includes all members of the underwriting syndicate plus additional dealers who take relatively small percentages of the total issue from the members of the underwriting syndicate. Thus, the underwriters act as wholesalers while members of the selling group act as retailers. The number of brokerage houses in a selling group depends partly on the size of the issue, but it is normally in the range of 10 to 15.

A new selling procedure has recently emerged that takes advantage of the trend toward institutional ownership of stock. In this type of sale, called an **unsyndicated stock offering,** the managing underwriter—acting alone—sells the issue entirely to a group of institutional investors, thus bypassing both retail stockbrokers and individual investors. In recent years, about 50% of all stock sold has been by unsyndicated offerings. Behind this phenomenon is a simple motivating force: money. The fees that issuers pay on a syndicated offering, which include commissions paid to retail brokers, can run a full percentage point higher than those on unsyndicated offerings. Moreover, although total fees are lower in unsyndicated offerings, managing underwriters usually come out ahead because they do not have to share the fees with an underwriting syndicate. However, some types of stock do not appeal to institutional investors, so not all firms can use unsyndicated offers.

18.3c Regulation of Securities Sales

Sales of new securities, and also sales in the secondary markets, are regulated by the Securities and Exchange Commission and, to a lesser extent, by each of the 50 states. There are four primary elements of SEC regulation.

1. *Jurisdiction.* The SEC has jurisdiction over all **interstate public offerings** in amounts of $1.5 million or more.
2. *Registration.* Newly issued securities (stocks and bonds) must be registered with the SEC at least 20 days before they are publicly offered. The **registration statement,** called Form S-1, provides financial, legal, and technical information about the company to the SEC. A **prospectus,** which is embedded in the S-1, summarizes this information for investors. The SEC's lawyers and accountants analyze both the registration statement and the prospectus; if the information is inadequate or misleading, the SEC will delay or stop the public offering.[3]
3. *Prospectus.* After the SEC declares the registration to be effective, new securities may be advertised, but all sales solicitations must be accompanied by the prospectus. **Preliminary,** or **"red herring," prospectuses** may be distributed to potential buyers during the 20-day waiting period after the registration is effective, but no sales may be finalized during this time. The "red herring" prospectus (so called because it has a standard legal disclaimer printed in red across its cover) contains all the key information that will appear in the final prospectus except the final price, which is generally set after the market closes the day before the new securities are actually offered to the public.
4. *Truth in reporting.* If the registration statement or prospectus contains **misrepresentations** or **omissions** of material facts, then any purchaser who suffers a loss may sue for damages. Severe penalties may be imposed on the issuer or its officers, directors, accountants, engineers, appraisers, underwriters, and all others who participated in the preparation of the registration statement or prospectus.

www

The SEC Web site allows users to search for any filings by a company, including Form S-1. See **www.sec.gov/edgar .shtml**.

---

3. With the Internet, it is extremely easy to obtain the S-1 form, which typically has 50 to 200 pages of financial statements in addition to a detailed discussion of the firm's business, the risks and opportunities the firm faces, its principal stockholders and managers, what will be done with the funds raised, and the like. This statement is filed with the SEC and is immediately available, through the Internet, to investors. The SEC staff reviews the filed S-1, and amendments may be issued (labeled S-1A, S-1B, etc.). The likely range for the offering price will be reported— for example, $13 to $15 per share. If the market strengthens or weakens while the stock is undergoing SEC review, the price may be increased or decreased right up until the last day. The SEC Web site with these and other filings is **www.sec.gov**.

18.3d The Roadshow and Book-Building

After the registration statement has been filed, the senior management team, the investment banker, and the company's lawyers go on a **roadshow**. The management team will make three to seven presentations each day to potential institutional investors, who typically are existing clients of the underwriters. The institutional investors ask questions during the presentation, but the management team may not give any information that is not in the registration statement. Nor may the management team make any forecasts or express any opinions about the value of their company. These provisions are due to the SEC-mandated **quiet period**. This quiet period begins when the registration statement is made effective and lasts for 40 days after the stock begins trading. Its purpose is to create a level playing field for all investors by ensuring that they all have access to the same information. It is not uncommon for the SEC to delay an IPO if managers violate the quiet period rules. The typical roadshow may last 10 to 14 days, with stops in 10 to 20 different cities. In many ways the process resembles a coming-out party for the company, but it is much more grueling and has much higher stakes.

After a presentation, the investment banker asks the investor for an indication of interest, based on the offering price range shown in the registration statement. The investment banker records the number of shares each investor is willing to buy, which is called **book-building**. As the roadshow progresses, an investment bank's "book" shows how demand for the offering is building. Many IPOs are **oversubscribed**, with investors wishing to purchase more shares than are available. In such a case, the investment bank will allocate shares to the investors on a pro rata basis.[4] If demand is high enough, the banks may increase the offering price; if demand is low, they will either reduce the offering price or withdraw the IPO. Sometimes low demand is specifically due to concern over the company's future prospects, but sometimes low demand is caused by a fall in the general stock market. Thus, the timing of the roadshow and offering date are important. As the old saying goes, sometimes it is better to be lucky than good.

If all goes well with the roadshow, the investment bank will finalize the offering price on the evening before the actual offering date.

18.3e The First Day of Trading

The first day of trading for many IPOs is wild and exciting. Table 18-1 shows the largest first-day returns for IPOs during the 12 months ending March 31, 2011. Some stocks end the day with large gains, such as the 161.3% price increase of Youku.com Inc., as shown in Line 1 of the table. Others have a sharp run-up and then fall back by the end of the day. A few IPOs actually end their first day with a loss.

According to a study of IPOs during 1990–1998 by Professors Tim Loughran and Jay Ritter, about 27.3% of the IPOs had an offer price that was lower than the low range in their initial registration filing, and these stocks had an average first-day return of 4.0%.[5] Even though the average return was positive, 47% of these stocks actually ended the day with a loss or no gain. About 48.4% of IPOs had an offering price that was within the range of their initial filing. For such companies,

---

4. Most underwriting agreements contain an "overallotment option" that permits the underwriter to purchase additional shares from the company up to 15% of the issue size to cover promises made to potential buyers. This is called a "green shoe" agreement because it was first used in the 1963 underwriting of a company named Green Shoe.

5. See Tim Loughran and Jay R. Ritter, "Why Don't Issuers Get Upset about Leaving Money on the Table in IPOs?" *Review of Financial Studies*, 2002, pp. 413-444.

TABLE 18-1 Highest First-Day IPO Returns in 2011[a]

Rank	Company (Symbol)	Offering Price	First-Day Closing Price	Gain
1	Youku.com Inc. (YOUKU)	$12.80	$34.44	161.3%
2	Qihoo 360 Technology (QIHU)	14.50	34.00	134.5
3	ChinaCache International (CCIH)	13.90	27.15	95.32
4	MakeMyTrip Limited (MMYT)	14.00	26.45	88.93
5	E-Commerce China Dangdang (DANG)	16.00	29.91	86.93
6	SouFun Holdings Limited (SFUN)	42.50	73.50	72.94
7	Mecox Lane Ltd. (MCOX)	11.00	17.26	56.91
8	Vera Bradley Inc. (VRA)	16.00	24.85	53.31
9	SemiLEDs Corporation (LEDS)	17.00	25.76	51.53
10	TAL Education Group (XRS)	10.00	15.00	50.00

[a]These are the highest first-day IPO returns in the 4 quarters ending March 31, 2011.

Source: Compiled from **http://moneycentral.hoovers.com/global/msn/index.xhtml?pageid510021**.

the average first-day return was 10.8%. As a result of high demand during the roadshow, 24.3% of IPOs had a final offer price that exceeded their original range. These stocks had an average first-day return of 31.9%. Overall, the average first-day return was 14.1% during 1990–1998, with 75% of all IPOs having a positive return. During 1999, the average first-day return was an astronomical 70%!

You're probably asking yourself two questions: (1) How can you get in on these deals? (2) Why is the offering price so low? First, you probably can't get the chance to buy an IPO at its offering price, especially not a "hot" one. Virtually all sales go to institutional investors and preferred retail customers. There are a few Web-based investment banks who are trying to change this, such as the OpenIPO of W. R. Hambrecht & Co., but right now it is difficult for small investors to get in on the better first-day IPOs.

Various theories have been put forth to explain IPO underpricing. As long as issuing companies don't complain, investment banks have strong incentives to underprice the issue. First, underpricing increases the likelihood of oversubscription, which reduces the risk to the underwriter. Second, most investors who get to purchase the IPO at its offering price are preferred customers of the investment bank, and they became preferred customers by generating lots of commissions in the investment bank's sister brokerage company. Therefore, the IPO is an easy way for the underwriter to reward customers for past and future commissions. Third, the underwriter needs an honest indication of interest when building the book prior to the offering, and underpricing is a possible way to secure this information from the institutional investors.

But why don't issuing companies object to underpricing? Some do, and they are seeking alternative ways to issue securities, such as OpenIPO. However, most seem content to leave some money on the table. The best explanations seem to be that (1) the company wants to create excitement, and a price run-up on the first day does that; (2) only a small percentage of the company's stock is generally offered to the public, so current stockholders lose less to underpricing than appears at first glance; and (3) IPO companies generally plan to have additional offerings in the future, and the best way to ensure future success is to have a successful IPO, which underpricing guarantees.

Although IPOs on average provide large first-day returns, their long-term returns over the following 3 years are below average. For example, if you could not get in at the IPO price but purchased a portfolio of IPO stocks on their second day of trading, your 3-year return would have been lower than the return on a portfolio of similar but seasoned stocks. In summary, the offering price appears to be too low, but the first-day run-up is generally too high.

18.3f The Costs of Going Public

During recent years, virtually all investment banks have charged a 7% **spread** between the price they pay the issuing company and the price at which they sell shares to the public. Thus, they keep 7% of the offering price as their compensation. For example, Epocrates (EPOC), a developer of clinical information tools for health care professionals, went public in 2011. EPOC sold 3.574 million shares at an offering price of $16.00 per share to the public (founders and other shareholders also sold 1.785 million of their own shares). In this IPO, the underwriters' direct compensation was $1.12 per share, which means that the stock was sold at a price of $16 to the public but EPOC received only $16.00 − $1.12 = $14.88 per share. For the 3.574 million shares issued by EPOC, these direct underwriting costs totaled about $1.12(3.574) = $4.003 million; the underwriters also made the same amount on the shares they sold for founders and other existing shareholders.

But there are other direct costs, such as lawyers' fees, accountants' costs, printing, engraving, and so on. EPOC estimated that these fees totaled about $2.8 million.

Last but not least are the indirect costs. The money left on the table, which is equal to the number of shares multiplied by the difference in the closing price and the offering price, can be quite large. EPOC experienced a first-day run-up to $21.96 from an offering price of $16.00, so its indirect costs totaled 3.574($21.96 − $16.00) = $21.30 million. In addition, senior managers spend an enormous amount of time working on the IPO rather than managing the business, which certainly carries a high cost even if it cannot be easily measured.

Thus, EPOC received proceeds of 3.574($16 − $1.12) = $53.2 million, the underwriters and their sales forces received $4.0 million, other expenses totaled about $2.8 million, and $21.3 million was left on the table. There were undoubtedly other indirect costs due to the diversion of the management team. As you can see, an IPO is quite expensive.[6]

18.3g The Importance of the Secondary Market

An active secondary market after the IPO provides the pre-IPO shareholders with a chance to convert some of their wealth into cash, makes it easier for the company to raise additional capital later, makes employee stock options more attractive, and makes it easier for the company to use its stock to acquire other companies. Without an active secondary market, there would be little reason to have an IPO. Thus, companies should

---

6. For more on IPOs, see Roger G. Ibbotson, Jody L. Sindelar, and Jay R. Ritter, "The Market's Problems with the Pricing of Initial Public Offerings," *Journal of Applied Corporate Finance*, Spring 1994, pp. 66–74; Chris J. Muscarella and Michael R. Vetsuypens, "The Underpricing of 'Second' Initial Public Offerings," *Journal of Financial Research*, Fall 1989, pp. 183–192; Jay R. Ritter, "The Long-Run Performance of Initial Public Offerings," *Journal of Finance*, March 1991, pp. 3–27; and Jay R. Ritter, "Initial Public Offerings," *Contemporary Finance Digest*, Spring 1998, pp. 5–30.

try to ensure that their stock will trade in an active secondary market before they incur the high costs of an IPO.

There are several types of secondary markets: physical stock exchanges, dealer markets, and bulletin boards. We discuss each of these below.

The physical exchanges, such as the NYSE and AMEX, conduct their trading in an actual location. In general, the NYSE and AMEX provide excellent liquidity. In order to have its stock listed, a company must apply to an exchange, pay a relatively small fee, and meet the exchange's minimum requirements. These requirements relate to the size of the company's net income, its market value, and its "float," which is the number of shares outstanding and in the hands of outsiders (as opposed to the number held by insiders, who generally do not actively trade their stock). Also, the company must agree to disclose certain information to the exchange and to help the exchange track trading patterns and thus ensure that no one is attempting to manipulate the stock's price. The size qualifications increase as a company moves from the AMEX to the NYSE.

Assuming a company qualifies, many believe that listing is beneficial to the company and to its stockholders. Listed companies receive a certain amount of free advertising and publicity, and their status as listed companies may enhance their prestige and reputation, which often leads to higher sales. Investors respond favorably to increased information, increased liquidity, and the confidence that the quoted price is not being manipulated. Listing provides investors with these benefits, which may help managers lower their firms' cost of equity and increase the value of their stock.[7]

The advantages of physical exchanges have been eroded—some would say eliminated—by computers and the Internet, which have benefited the dealer markets. The primary equity dealer markets are administered by Nasdaq, and they include the Nasdaq National Market and the Nasdaq SmallCap Market. Almost 85% of new IPO stocks trade in these markets. Unlike the physical exchanges, these consist of a network of dealers, with each dealer making a market in one or more stocks. A dealer makes a market in a company's stock by holding an inventory of the shares and then making offers to buy or sell the stock. Many stocks have excellent liquidity in these markets and remain there even though they easily meet the requirements for listing on the NYSE. Examples include Microsoft, Intel, Apple, and Cisco Systems.

Investment banks generally agree to make a market in a company's stock as part of their IPO duties. The diligence with which they carry out this task can have a huge effect on the stock's liquidity in the secondary market and thus on the success of the IPO.

Although the requirements for listing on the Nasdaq National Market or SmallCap Market are not as stringent as for the NYSE, some companies fail to maintain them and hence are "delisted." For these companies, offers to buy or sell the stock may be posted on the OTC Bulletin Board, an electronic bulletin board administered by Nasdaq. However, there is very little liquidity in these stocks, and an IPO would be considered a failure if the company's stock ended up on the OTC Bulletin Board.

18.3h Regulating the Secondary Market

As we stated earlier, a liquid and crime-free secondary market is critical to the success of an IPO or any other publicly traded security. So, in addition to regulating the

---

7. For additional discussion on the benefits of listing, see H. Kent Baker and Richard B. Edelman, "AMEX-to-NYSE Transfers, Market Microstructure, and Shareholder Wealth," *Financial Management*, Winter 1992, pp. 60–72; and Richard B. Edelman and H. Kent Baker, "Liquidity and Stock Exchange Listing," *The Financial Review*, May 1990, pp. 231–249.

process for issuing securities, the Securities and Exchange Commission also has responsibilities in the secondary markets. The primary elements of SEC regulation are set forth below.

1. *Stock exchanges.* The SEC *regulates all national stock exchanges,* and companies whose securities are listed on an exchange must file annual reports similar to the registration statement with both the SEC and the exchange.
2. *Insider trading.* The SEC has control over trading by corporate *insiders.* Officers, directors, and major stockholders must file monthly reports of changes in their holdings of the stock of the corporation. Any short-term profits from such transactions must be turned over to the corporation.
3. *Market manipulation.* The SEC has the power to *prohibit manipulation* by such devices as pools (large amounts of money used to buy or sell stocks to artificially affect prices) or wash sales (sales between members of the same group to record artificial transaction prices).
4. *Proxy statements.* The SEC has *control over the proxy statement* and the way the company uses it to solicit votes.

Control over credit used to buy securities is exercised by the Federal Reserve Board through **margin requirements,** which specify the maximum percentage of the purchase price someone can borrow. If a great deal of margin borrowing has persisted, then a decline in stock prices can result in inadequate coverages. This could force stockbrokers to issue **margin calls,** which require investors either to put up more money or have their margined stock sold to pay off their loans. Such forced sales further depress the stock market and thus can set off a downward spiral. The required margin at the time a stock is purchased has been 50% since 1974 (subsequent "maintenance margins" are lower and are generally set by individual lenders).

The securities industry itself realizes the importance of stable markets, sound brokerage firms, and the absence of stock manipulation.[8] Therefore, the various exchanges work closely with the SEC to police transactions and to maintain the integrity and credibility of the system. Similarly, the **National Association of Securities Dealers (NASD)** cooperates with the SEC to police trading in its dealer and OTC markets. These industry groups also cooperate with regulatory authorities to set net worth and other standards for securities firms, to develop insurance programs to protect the customers of failed brokerage houses, and the like.

In general, government regulation of securities trading, as well as industry self-regulation, is designed to ensure that (1) investors receive information that is as accurate as possible, (2) no one artificially manipulates the market price of a given stock, and (3) corporate insiders do not take advantage of their position to profit in their companies' stocks at the expense of other stockholders. Neither the SEC, the state regulators, nor the industry itself can prevent investors from making foolish decisions or from having "bad luck," but they can and do help investors obtain the best data possible for making sound investment decisions.

---

8. It is illegal for anyone to attempt to manipulate the price of a stock. During the 1920s and earlier, syndicates would buy and sell stocks back and forth at rigged prices so the public would believe that a particular stock was worth more or less than its true value. The exchanges, with the encouragement and support of the SEC, utilize sophisticated computer programs to help spot any irregularities that suggest manipulation, and they require disclosures to help identify manipulators. This same system helps to identify illegal insider trading. It is now illegal to manipulate a stock's price by spreading false news on the Internet.

18.3i Questionable IPO Practices

Among the many revelations to come out during 2002 regarding investment banking was the practice by some investment banking houses of letting CEOs and other high-ranking corporate executives in on "hot" IPOs. In these deals, the demand for the new stock was far greater than supply at the offering price, so the investment banks were virtually certain that the stock would soar far above the offering price.

Some investment banks systematically allocated shares of hot IPOs to executives of companies that were issuing stocks and bonds—and thus generating fees to the banks who underwrote the deals. Bernie Ebbers, the chairman and CEO of WorldCom—one of the biggest sources of underwriting fees for investment banks—was given huge allocations in hot IPOs, and he made millions on these deals. Ebbers is just one example; a lot of this was going on in the late 1990s, at the height of the tech/dot-com bubble.

Government regulators have been investigating this practice, called "spinning," and corporate executives and investment bankers have been charged with something that amounts to a kickback scheme under which those executives who favored particular investment banks were rewarded with allocations in hot IPOs. Indeed, in 2003 ten Wall Street securities firms agreed to pay $1.4 billion in fines to settle charges of investor abuse, including spinning. Although the practice may or may not be illegal (this has yet to be determined), it is certainly unethical. The corporate executives were paid to work for their stockholders, so they should have turned over any IPO profits to their companies—not kept those profits for themselves.

This kind of unethical and perhaps illegal behavior may help to explain IPO underpricing and "money left on the table." An executive might be more interested in getting a future hot IPO allocation than in whether or not the company gets the best terms from its investment bank. This situation would be exacerbated if the investment banks' analysts overstated prospects for the company and thereby pumped up its price just prior to the time when executives were to receive and exercise stock options.

In summary, we have a hard time justifying IPO underpricing during the late 1990s on rational economic grounds. People have come up with explanations for why companies let their investment banks price their stocks too low in IPOs, but those reasons seem rather weak. However, when coupled with what may have been a kickback scheme, the underpricing is less puzzling (but ethically troubling). Before closing, though, we should make it clear that relatively few corporate executives were corrupt. However, just as one rotten apple can spoil an entire barrel, a few bad executives—when combined with lax regulation—can help a bad practice become "the industry standard" and thus become widespread.

Self Test

What is the difference between *best efforts* and *underwriting*?

What are some SEC regulations regarding sales of new securities?

What is a roadshow? What is book-building?

What is underpricing? Leaving money on the table?

What are some of the costs of going public?

A company is planning an IPO. Its underwriters have said the stock will sell at $50 per share. The underwriters will charge a 7% spread. How many shares must the company sell to net $93 million, ignoring any other expenses? (**2 million**)

18.4 Equity Carve-outs: A Special Type of IPO

In 2009, Bristol-Myers Squibb sold to the public about 15% of the equity in its wholly owned subsidiary, Mead Johnson Nutrition. In this transaction, the subsidiary, like the parent, became publicly owned, but the parent retained full control of the subsidiary by keeping about 85% of the subsidiary's common stock. (Parent companies typically retain at least 80% of the subsidiary's common stock to preserve their ability to file a consolidated tax return.) This type of transaction is called an **equity carve-out** (or **partial public offering**, or **spin-out**).[9] The market's response to Mead Johnson's carve-out was positive—the stock price rose almost 10% during the first day of trading. Equity carve-outs raise an interesting question: Why do carve-out announcements typically result in stock price increases while the announcements of new stock issues by parent corporations generally decrease stock prices?

One possible answer is that carve-outs facilitate the evaluation of corporate growth opportunities on a line-of-business basis. Thus, analysts might have an easier time evaluating Mead Johnson as a separate company than when it was a part of Bristol-Myers. This also applies to providers of capital—Mead Johnson might be able to raise capital more effectively as a stand-alone company because investors are better able to evaluate its prospects. A third advantage to carve-outs is that they improve the ability of the parent to offer incentives to a subsidiary's managers. Thus, Mead Johnson can now offer equity incentives to its managers based on its own stock price rather than that of Bristol-Myers.

Equity carve-outs do have some associated costs. First, the underwriting commission involved in a carve-out is larger than for an equity offering by the parent. Second, because an equity carve-out is a type of initial public offering, there is a potential for underpricing the new offering. Third, key managers of the subsidiary must spend a significant amount of time marketing the new stock. Fourth, there are costs associated with the minority interest that is created in the carve-out. For example, the subsidiary's new board of directors must monitor all transactions between the subsidiary and the parent to ensure that the minority investors are not being exploited. Finally, there are additional costs such as annual reports, SEC filings, analyst presentations, and so on, which now must be borne both by parent and subsidiary.

> **Self Test**
>
> Explain what is meant by an equity carve-out.
>
> On average, equity carve-outs have increased shareholder wealth. What are some potential explanations for this observed phenomenon?

18.5 Other Ways to Raise Funds in the Capital Markets

IPOs are exciting and play a vital role in stimulating the entrepreneurship and innovation that are vital for economic growth. However, the funds raised through IPOs

---

9. For more information on equity carve-outs, see Roni Michaely and Wayne H. Shaw, "The Choice of Going Public: Spin-offs vs. Carve-outs," *Financial Management*, Autumn 1995, pp. 5–21; and Anand Vijh, "Long-Term Returns from Equity Carve-outs," *Journal of Financial Economics*, Vol. 51, 1999, pp. 273–308.

are only a small fraction of the total funding that companies raise from commercial banks and capital markets. We discuss other ways that firms raise cash from capital markets in the following sections.[10]

18.5a Preliminary Decisions

Before raising capital, a firm must make some initial, preliminary decisions, which include the following.

1. *Dollars to be raised.* How much new capital is needed?
2. *Type of securities used.* Should common, preferred, bonds, hybrid securities, or a combination be used? If common stock is to be issued, should it be done as a preemptive rights offering to current shareholders or by a direct sale to the general public?
3. *Competitive bid versus a negotiated deal.* Should the company simply offer a block of its securities for sale to the highest bidder, or should it negotiate a deal with an investment bank? These two procedures are called **competitive bids** and **negotiated deals,** respectively. Only about 100 of the largest firms listed on the NYSE, whose securities are already well known to the investment banking community, are in a position to use the competitive bidding process. The investment banks must do a great deal of investigative work ("due diligence") to bid on an issue unless they are already quite familiar with the firm, and such costs would be too high to make it worthwhile unless the bank was sure of getting the deal. Therefore, except for the largest firms, offerings of stock and bonds are generally on a negotiated basis.
4. *Selection of an investment bank.* Most deals are negotiated, so the firm must select an investment bank. This can be an important decision for a firm that is going public. On the other hand, an older firm that has already "been to market" will have an established relationship with an investment bank. However, it is easy to change banks if the firm is dissatisfied. Different investment banking houses are better suited for different companies. For example, Goldman Sachs and Morgan Stanley are the leading tech-IPO underwriters. Investment banking houses sell new issues largely to their own regular brokerage customers, so the nature of these customers has a major effect on the ability of the house to do a good job for corporate issuers. Finally, a major factor in choosing an underwriter is the reputation of the analyst who will cover the stock in the secondary market, since a strong buy recommendation from a well-respected analyst can trigger a sharp price run-up.

18.5b Seasoned Equity Offerings

When a company with publicly traded stock issues additional shares, this is called a **seasoned equity offering,** also known as a *secondary* or *follow-on offering.* Because the stock is already publicly traded, the offering price will be based upon the existing market price of the stock. Typically, the investment bank buys the securities at a prescribed number of points below the closing price on the last day of registration. For example, suppose that in August 2012 the stock of Microwave

---

10. For an excellent discussion of the various procedures used to raise capital, see Jay R. Ritter, "Investment Banking and Securities Issuance," in *North-Holland Handbook of the Economics of Finance*, George Constantinides, Milton Harris, and René Stulz, eds. (Amsterdam: North-Holland, 2002). Also see Claudio Loderer, John W. Cooney, and Leonard D. Van Drunen, "The Price Elasticity of Demand for Common Stock," *Journal of Finance*, June 1991, pp. 621–651.

Telecommunications Inc. (MTI) had a price of $28.60 per share and that the stock had traded between $25 and $30 per share during the previous 3 months. Suppose further that MTI and its underwriter agreed that the investment bank would buy 10 million new shares at $1 per share below the closing price on the last day of registration. If the stock closed at $25 on the day the SEC released the issue, then MTI would receive $24 per share. Typically, such agreements have an escape clause that provides for the contract to be voided if the price of the securities drops below some predetermined figure. In the illustrative case, this "upset" price might be set at $24 per share. Thus, if the closing price of the shares on the last day of registration had been $23.50, MTI would have had the option of withdrawing from the agreement.

The investment bank will have an easier job if the issue is priced relatively low. However, the issuer naturally wants as high a price as possible. A conflict of interest on price therefore arises between the investment bank and the issuer. If the issuer is financially sophisticated and makes comparisons with similar security issues, the investment bank will be forced to price close to the market.

As we discussed in Chapter 15, the announcement of a new stock offering by a mature firm is often taken as a negative signal—if the firm's prospects were good, management would not want to issue new stock and thus share the rosy future with new stockholders. Therefore, the announcement of a new offering is taken as bad news. Consequently, the price will probably fall when the announcement is made, so the offering price will probably have to be set at a price below the pre-announcement market price.

One final point is that *if negative signaling effects drive down the price of the stock then all shares outstanding, not just the new shares, are affected.* Thus, if MTI's stock should fall from $28.60 to $25 per share as a result of the financing and if the price remains at the new level, then the company would incur a loss of $3.60 on each of the 50 million shares previously outstanding, or a total market value loss of $180 million. This loss, like underwriting expenses, is a flotation cost, and it should be considered as a cost associated with the stock issue. Of course, if the company's prospects really were poorer than investors thought, then the price decline would have occurred sooner or later anyway. On the other hand, if the company's prospects are really not all that bad (the signal was incorrect), then over time MTI's price should move back to its previous level. Yet even if the price does revert to its former level, there will have been a transfer of wealth from the original shareholders to the new shareholders. To prevent this, companies occasionally sell additional shares of stock through a rights offering (also called a preemptive rights offering), which we explain in *Web Extension 18A*.

WEB

See **Web Extension 18A** on the textbook's Web site for a discussion of rights offerings.

18.5c Shelf Registrations

The selling procedures described so far, including the 20-day waiting period after registration with the SEC, apply to most security sales. However, under the SEC's Rule 415, large, well-known public companies that issue securities frequently may file a master registration statement with the SEC and then update it with a short-form statement just prior to each individual offering. Under this procedure, a company can decide at 10 a.m. to sell securities and have the sale completed before noon. This procedure is known as **shelf registration** because, in effect, the company puts its new securities "on the shelf" and then sells them to investors when it feels the market is "right." Firms with less than $150 million in stock held by outside investors cannot use shelf registrations. The rationale for this distinction is to protect investors who may not be able to obtain adequate financial data about a little-known company in the short time between announcement of a shelf issue and its sale. Shelf registrations have two advantages over standard registrations: (1) lower flotation costs and (2) more control over the timing of the issue.[11]

18.5d Private Placements

In a *private placement,* securities are sold to one or a few investors, generally institutional investors. Private placements are most common with bonds, but they also occur with stocks. The primary advantages of private placements are (1) lower flotation costs and (2) greater speed, since the shares do not have to go through the SEC registration process.

Sometimes it is a privately held firm that makes a private placement. For example, Facebook, the social media company, placed $1 billion of common stock with non-U.S. investors in 2011. At other times it is a public company making a private placement. For example, General Growth Properties, which develops real estate properties like shopping malls, raised $6.8 billion by selling stock directly to a consortium of investment funds, including Pershing Square Capital Management and Blackstone Group. Since GGP is a publicly held company, this is called a **private placement of public equity**, or a **PIPE**. The most common type of private placement occurs when a company places securities directly with a financial institution, often an insurance company or a pension fund.

Many large companies make equity investments in suppliers or in start-up companies that are developing a related technology. For example, Microsoft's 2010 annual report showed $6.6 billion of investments in the common and preferred stock of other companies.

A potential disadvantage of a private placement is that if the securities are not registered with the SEC, they cannot be resold except to another large, "sophisticated" purchaser. However, many institutions meet this qualification, so there is a large potential market for the securities. In addition, companies are increasingly choosing to register the securities they privately place in order to improve their marketability after placement. With improved marketability, private placements are popular: More than $41 billion of debt was placed privately in the United States during 2010.

18.5e Securitization

In Chapter 1 we discussed securitization in the context of mortgage markets, and now we discuss it in the context of capital formation. As the term is generally used, a **security** refers to a publicly traded financial instrument as opposed to a privately placed instrument. Thus, securities have greater liquidity than otherwise similar instruments that are not traded in an open market. In recent years, procedures have been developed to **securitize** various types of debt instruments, thus increasing their liquidity, lowering the cost of capital to borrowers, and generally increasing the efficiency of the financial markets.

Securitization occurs in two ways. First, a debt instrument that formerly was rarely traded becomes actively traded, usually because the size of the market increases and the terms of the debt instrument become more standardized. For example, this has occurred with commercial paper and junk bonds, both of which are now considered to be securities.

---

11. In 2005, the SEC began allowing very large firms, known as "well known seasoned issuers" or WKSIs, even greater flexibility in selling shelf-registered shares. WKSIs may now bypass SEC review and automatically shelf-register an unspecified number of securities to sell at times of their choosing. This speeds up the process even more for these large issuers. For more on shelf registrations, see David J. Denis, "The Costs of Equity Issues Since Rule 415: A Closer Look," *Journal of Financial Research,* Spring 1993, pp. 77–88.

Second, a security can be created by the pledging of specific assets. This is called **asset securitization,** resulting in the creation of **asset-backed securities.** The oldest type of asset securitization was in the mortgage industry, as we described in Chapter 1. Today, many different types of assets are used as collateral, including auto loans, credit card balances, and even the royalties from David Bowie's music!

The asset securitization process involves the pooling and repackaging of loans secured by relatively homogeneous, small-dollar assets (such as an automobile) into liquid securities. Usually several different financial institutions are involved, with each playing a different functional role. For example, an auto dealer might sell a car, the auto manufacturer's lending operation might originate the loan, an investment bank might pool similar car loans and structure the security, a federal agency might insure against credit risk, a second investment bank might sell the securities, and a pension fund might supply the final capital.

A similar process can occur with equipment leases. For example, CIT Group provides lease financing for equipment used by small and mid-sized companies. In 2009, CIT sold $954 million in notes securitized by equipment leases. The notes qualify for the Fed's Term Asset-Backed Securities Loan Facility (TALF), which means that the investor, usually a bank, can use these notes as collateral for loans from the New York Fed. If you trace the money, it could easily be the case that the Fed is financing a new dishwashing machine for a restaurant in Milwaukee.

The process of securitization lowers costs and increases the availability of funds to borrowers, with the risk being transferred to the investor. But as we described in Chapter 1, if loans are originated to borrowers with high credit risk, then the cash flows received by the ultimate investor are likely to be low.

Self Test

What is the difference between a competitive bid and a negotiated deal?

What is a private placement?

What is shelf registration?

What is securitization? What are its advantages to borrowers? What are its advantages to lenders?

BOWIE BONDS CH-CH-CHANGE ASSET SECURITIZATION

In 1997, asset securitization was already booming, with bonds being backed by mortgages, car loans, credit cards, and student loans. But David Bowie juiced it up even more by issuing Bowie Bonds, which were backed by future royalties on more than 250 of his older songs. These bonds had a 10-year maturity and paid an interest rate of 7.9%. In a private placement, Prudential Insurance bought the entire issue for $55 million in order to receive a whopping $4.345 million in interest payment each year (assuming the songs generated enough in royalties). At the time of issue, Moody's Investor Service was bullish on Bowie, since it gave his issue a rating of A3, high enough that the bonds were issued with an interest rate only 1.53 percentage points higher than 10-year Treasury bonds. However, in response to declining industry sales, Moody's downgraded the bonds to Baa3 in 2004. The bonds matured in 2007 and royalties reverted to Bowie.

Sources: "Bowie Ch-Ch-Changes the Market," *CFO,* April 1997, p. 20; and **www.moodys.com**.

18.6 Investment Banking Activities and Their Role in the Global Economic Crisis

Investment banks underwrite IPOs, underwrite seasoned equity offerings, and manage debt offerings. In other words, investment banks help firms raise capital, and lots of it: Table 18-2 shows that investment banks helped firms raise just over *$6.9 trillion* during 2010, and that was a down year. Investment banks also engage in other activities. Because of increasingly relaxed regulations that culminated with the repeal of the Glass-Stegall Act in 1999, there is no longer a clear delineation between investment banks, brokerage firms, and commercial banks. In the following sections we discuss activities that are primarily associated with the investment banking arm of the financial conglomerates.

18.6a Mergers and Acquisitions

Many investment banks are actively involved in mergers and acquisitions (M&As) through three activities.

1. *Matchmaking.* Investment banks often find potential targets for acquirers, sometimes earning a finder's fee if the deal is successful.
2. *Advising.* Both the target and acquirer must document that the deal is "fair" for their stockholders by performing a due diligence valuation analysis. Investment banks often provide consulting advice during this stage of the M&A.
3. *Underwriting.* Most M&As require that new capital be raised. Investment banks underwrite these new issues.

Underwriting is the most lucrative of these activities, but if the deal falls through then no new securities will be underwritten. This makes one wonder how unbiased investment bankers are when finding targets and providing advice during negotiations.

18.6b Securitization

Investment banks often provide advice to financial institutions regarding the securitization of the institutions' loans or leases. In fact, investment banks frequently provide turnkey service by purchasing an institution's loans, securitizing the loans, and selling the newly created securities. Thus, the investment bank becomes the securitizer, not just the advisor. During the build-up to the global economic crisis,

TABLE 18-2	Top Five Underwriters of Global Debt and Equity in 2010
Manager	**Proceeds (Billions)**
JPMorgan	$ 504.5
Barclays Capital	486.7
Deutsche Bank AG	444.4
Bank of America Merrill Lynch	434.5
UBS	351.3
Industry total	$6,932.6

Source: The Wall Street Journal Online, January 3, 2011.

many investment banks were unable to sell all the mortgage-backed securities they created and were left holding some of them in their own portfolios. When the original borrowers began defaulting, the values of these securities owned by the investment banks plummeted, contributing to the downfall of Bear Stearns, Lehman Brothers, and Merrill Lynch.

18.6c Asset Management

Many investment banking companies create investment funds, such as a limited partnership (LP) that might invest in real estate in developing nations or an LP that might seek to exploit mispricing in various asset classes. In other words, they run their own hedge funds, which can be quite lucrative. Like any other hedge fund, they raise capital for these funds from a variety of sources. But unlike other hedge funds, investment banks often have access to a special source—their own clients!

Here is how that works. Many investment banks have "wealth management" divisions or subsidiaries that provide investment advice to wealthy individuals or institutions such as pension funds. As advisors, they recommend investment strategies, including specific investments, to their clients. Some of these investments might be individual securities or mutual funds managed by other organizations. However, some of the recommended investments might be funds managed by the advisor's own investment bank. These might be great investments, but there is at least the appearance of a conflict of interest when advisors recommend funds managed by their own company.

In addition to managing clients' money, investment banks also invest their own money (actually, the money of their own stockholders and creditors) in financial securities. Sometimes the choice of investment is intentional, but sometimes it is not—as we mentioned previously, some investment banks were unable to sell all the mortgage-backed securities they created and were left holding some in their own portfolios.

18.6d Trading Operations

Many investment banking companies have trading operations through which they actively trade on the behalf of clients. For example, a client might need help in selling a large block of debt. Also, investment banking companies usually make a market in the stock of companies that they took public. Thus, these activities can be viewed as services provided to clients.

However, many investment banks also view their trading operations as profit centers. In other words, the traders try to buy low and sell high, and in the process they sometimes accumulate large positions that become difficult to unload.

What are some investment banking activities?   **Self Test**

18.7 The Decision to Go Private

In a **going private** transaction, the entire equity of a publicly held firm is purchased by a small group of investors, with the firm's current senior management usually maintaining or increasing their ownership stakes. The outside investors typically place directors on the now-private firm's board and arrange for the financing needed to purchase the publicly held stock. When the financing involves substantial borrowing, as it usually does, it is known as a **leveraged buyout (LBO)**. In some cases, the

THE GLOBAL ECONOMIC CRISIS

What Was The Role of Investment Banks?

There is plenty of blame to spread around for the cause of the global economic crisis, but investment banks certainly played a special role.

Among their many strategic errors, investment banks morphed from organizations that earned money primarily through fee-generating activities into organizations that earned money as highly levered investors. Investing is an inherently risky business, especially when the investments include extremely complicated mortgage-backed securities and credit default swaps. Investing becomes even riskier when you borrow $33 for every $1 of equity, as many investment banks did. This strategy works great if you earn more than you owe on your debt because leverage magnifies returns, and these magnified returns generated gigantic bonuses for senior managers at the investment banks. But it doesn't take too much of a decline in asset values and investment income to cause failure. In essence, the investment bankers were willing to risk it all for the chance of mind-boggling bonuses.

In addition to selling toxic investments (such as complex mortgage-backed securities) to pension funds and other financial institutions, the interconnectedness of failing investment banks threatened the entire world economy. Lehman Brothers had been borrowing short-term in the commercial paper market and investing long-term in risky assets. When those assets failed, Lehman

defaulted on its commercial paper obligations, many of which were owned by money market funds. This caused some funds, like the large Reserve fund, to "break the buck," which means that their reported net asset value dropped below $1, something that none of their investors ever expected. This led to a run on many money market funds and a huge disruption in the financial commercial paper markets.

Investment banks also were major players in the market for credit default swaps (CDS). If investment banks defaulted on their CDS, then it would cause potentially bankrupting financial distress at many other financial institutions.

Because many investment banks are subsidiaries of bank holding companies, the failure of the investment banks threatened the viability of the holding company and its other subsidiaries, such as commercial banks, which began limiting the credit they provided to their borrowers. In short, the financial crisis spread to the nonfinancial sector as financial institutions began cutting back on the credit they provided to the nonfinancial sector.

The investment banking landscape has certainly changed during the global economic crisis. Bear Stearns was acquired by JP Morgan, Lehman Brothers went bankrupt and was sold piecemeal, Merrill Lynch was acquired by Bank of America, and several investment banks, including Goldman Sachs, rechartered themselves as banks to qualify for TARP funds.

current management group raises the financing and acquires all of the equity of the company; these are called management buyouts (MBOs).

The outside equity in a buyout often comes from a **private equity (PE) fund,** which is a limited liability partnership created to own and manage investments in nontraded equity. Private equity funds raise money from wealthy investors and institutions like university endowments, pension funds, and insurance companies. The PE funds then take public firms private or invest in firms that already are privately held. Most PE funds plan on improving the companies' performance and then harvesting their investments by selling the company, perhaps in an IPO.[12]

---

12. For more information on private equity, see Steve Kaplan, "Private Equity: Past, Present and Future," *Journal of Applied Corporate Finance,* Summer 2007, pp. 8–16; "Morgan Stanley Roundtable on Private Equity and Its Import for Public Companies," *Journal of Applied Corporate Finance,* Summer 2006, pp. 8–37; and Stephen D. Prowse, "The Economics of the Private Equity Market," *Economic Review,* third quarter 1998, pp. 21–33.

Regardless of the deal's structure, going private initially affects the right-hand side of the balance sheet, the liabilities and capital, and not the assets: Going private simply rearranges the ownership structure. Thus, going private involves no obvious operating economies, yet the new owners are generally willing to pay a large premium over the stock's current price in order to take the firm private. For example, in 2006 HCA Inc., a large health care corporation, was taken private by the original family owners, the Frists, and a group of private equity firms and investment banks, including Bain Capital and Kohlberg Kravis Roberts & Co., for $51 per share. The stock had been selling in the low $40s the month prior to the announcement. The investors put up about $4.9 billion in equity and borrowed about $28 billion to fund the purchase of equity and refinance some of the company's debt. It is hard to believe that these sophisticated investors and managers would knowingly pay too much for the firm. Thus, the investors and managers must have regarded the firm as being grossly undervalued, even at $51 per share, or else thought that they could significantly boost the firm's value under private ownership. In fact, after four years as a private company HCA went public again in 2011. The owners received $4.3 billion in dividends during 2010 and an additional $1.1 billion in cash from shares they sold in the IPO, almost completely recovering their initial investment. After the IPO the stock was worth about $16 billion, with about 25% of the company in public hands, and 75%, or about $12 billion, remaining with the private equity fund. Although the total return the investors ultimately earn depends on how much they receive for the shares they still hold in the company, the $4.9 billion investment has currently reaped cash and stock worth some $16 billion. Not a bad return for a 4-year investment!

This suggests that going private can increase the value of some firms sufficiently to enrich both managers and public stockholders. Other large companies going private recently include Jo-Ann Stores (2011), J Crew (2011), Gymboree Corp (2010), and Burger King (2010).

The primary advantages to going private are (1) administrative cost savings, (2) increased managerial incentives, (3) increased managerial flexibility, (4) increased shareholder oversight and participation, and (5) increased use of financial leverage, which of course reduces taxes. We discuss each of these advantages in more detail in the following paragraphs.

1. *Administrative cost savings.* Because going private takes the stock of a firm out of public hands, it saves on the time and costs associated with securities registration, annual reports, SEC and exchange reporting, responding to stockholder inquiries, and so on.

2. *Increased managerial incentives.* Managers' increased ownership and equity incentive plans mean that managers benefit more directly from their own efforts; hence managerial efficiency tends to increase after going private. If the firm is highly successful then its managers can easily see their personal net worth increase twentyfold, but if the firm fails then its managers end up with nothing.

3. *Increased managerial flexibility.* Managers at private companies do not have to worry about what a drop in the next quarter's earnings will do to the firm's stock price, so they can focus on long-term, strategic actions that ultimately will have the greatest positive impact on the firm's value. Managerial flexibility concerning asset sales is also greater in a private firm, since such sales need not be justified to a large number of shareholders with potentially diverse interests.

4. *Increased shareholder oversight and participation.* Going private typically results in replacing a dispersed, largely passive group of public shareholders with a small group of investors who take a much more active role in managing the firm. These new equity investors have a substantial position in the private firm; hence they

have a greater motivation to monitor management and to provide incentives to management than do the typical stockholders of a public corporation. Further, the new nonmanagement equity investors—frequently private equity firms, such as Kohlberg Kravis Roberts & Company (KKR), Carlyle Group, or Blackstone Group— are typically represented on the board, and they bring sophisticated industry and financial expertise and hard-nosed attitudes to the new firm.

5. *Increased financial leverage.* Going private usually entails a drastic increase in the firm's use of debt financing, which has two effects. First, the firm's taxes are reduced because of the increase in deductible interest payments, so more of the operating income flows through to investors. Second, the increased debt service requirements force managers to hold costs down to ensure that the firm has sufficient cash flow to meet its obligations—a highly leveraged firm simply cannot afford any fat.

One might ask why all firms are not privately held. The answer is that, although there are real benefits to private ownership, there are also benefits to being publicly owned. Most notably, public corporations have access to large amounts of equity capital on favorable terms, and for most companies, the advantage of access to public capital markets dominates the advantages of going private. Also, note that most companies that go private end up going public again after several years of operation as private firms. In addition to HCA, for example, Celanese AG, a global chemical company, went public in 1999. It was taken private in 2004 by Blackstone Capital Partners, a PE firm, and taken public in 2005.

Self Test	What is meant by the term "going private"?
	What is a private equity fund?
	What are the main benefits of going private?
	Why don't all firms go private to capture these benefits?

18.8 Managing the Maturity Structure of Debt

Chapters 15 and 16 describe the capital structure decision. But after a firm chooses the total amount of debt in its capital structure, it must still choose the maturities of the various securities that make up its debt. The following sections explain the factors associated with the choice of maturity structure.

18.8a Maturity Matching

Assume that Consolidated Tools, a Cincinnati machine tool manufacturer, made the decision to float a $25 million nonconvertible bond issue to help finance its 2012 capital budget. It must choose a maturity for the issue, taking into consideration the shape of the yield curve, management's own expectations about future interest rates, and the maturity of the assets being financed. To illustrate how asset maturities affect the choice of debt maturities, suppose Consolidated's capital projects consist primarily of new milling machinery. This machinery has an expected economic life of 10 years (even though it falls into the MACRS 5-year class life). Should Consolidated use debt with a 5-year, 10-year, 20-year, 30-year, or some other maturity?

Note that some of the new capital will come from common equity, which is permanent capital. On the other hand, debt maturities can be specified at the time of issue. If Consolidated financed its capital budget with 10-year sinking fund bonds, it would be matching asset and liability maturities. The cash flows resulting from the new machinery could be used to make the interest and sinking fund payments on the issue, so the bonds would be retired as the machinery wore out. If Consolidated used 1-year debt, then it would have to pay off this debt with cash flows derived from assets other than the machinery in question.

Of course, the 1-year debt could probably be rolled over year after year, out to the 10-year asset maturity. However, if interest rates rose then Consolidated would have to pay a higher rate when it rolled over its debt, and if the company experienced difficulties then it might not be able to refund the debt at a reasonable rate. Conversely, if it used 20-year or 30-year debt, it would have to service the debt long after the assets that were purchased with the funds had been scrapped and had ceased providing cash flows. This would worry lenders.

For all these reasons, *the safest all-around financing strategy is to match debt maturities with asset maturities.* In recognition of this fact, firms generally place great emphasis on maturity matching, and this factor often dominates the debt maturity decision.

Some firms use zero coupon bonds as a tool in matching maturities. We explain these bonds in *Web Extension 4A.*

WEB

See *Web Extension 4A* on the textbook's Web site for more on zero coupon bonds.

18.8b Effects of Interest Rate Levels and Forecasts

Financial managers also consider interest rate levels and forecasts, both absolute and relative, when making financing decisions. For example, if long-term interest rates are high by historical standards and are expected to fall, managers will be reluctant to issue long-term debt, which would lock in those costs for long periods. We already know that one solution to this problem is to use a call provision, since callability permits refunding should interest rates drop. This flexibility comes at a cost, however, because of the call premium and also because the firm must set a higher coupon on callable debt. Floating-rate debt could be used, but another alternative would be to finance with short-term debt whenever long-term rates are historically high, and then, assuming that interest rates subsequently fall, sell a long-term issue to replace the short-term debt. Of course, this strategy has its risks: If interest rates move even higher, the firm will be forced to renew its short-term debt at higher and higher rates or to replace the short-term debt with a long-term bond that costs even more than it would have when the original decision was made.

We could argue that capital markets are efficient and hence that it's not possible to predict future interest rates, because these rates will be determined by information that is not now known. Thus, under the efficient markets hypothesis, it would be unproductive for firms to try to "beat the market" by forecasting future capital costs and then acting on these forecasts. According to this view, financial managers ought to arrange their capital structures in such a manner that they can ride out almost any economic storm, and this generally calls for (1) using some "reasonable" mix of debt and equity and (2) using debt with maturities that more or less match the maturities of the assets being financed.

18.8c Information Asymmetries

In Chapter 4, we discussed bond ratings and the effects of changes in ratings on the cost and availability of capital. If a firm's current financial condition is poor, then its managers may be reluctant to issue new long-term debt because (1) a new debt issue would probably trigger a review by the rating agencies, and (2) debt issued when a firm is in poor financial shape would probably cost more and be subject to more severe restrictive covenants than debt issued from strength. Furthermore, in Chapters 15 and 16 we point out that firms are reluctant to use new common stock financing, especially when this might be taken as a negative signal. Thus, a firm that is in a weakened condition but whose internal forecasts indicate greater financial strength in the future would be inclined to delay long-term financing of any type until things improved. Such a firm would be motivated to use short-term debt even to finance long-term assets, with the expectation of replacing the short-term debt in the future with cheaper, higher-rated long-term debt.

Conversely, a firm that is strong now but that forecasts a potentially bad time in the period just ahead would be motivated to finance long term now rather than to wait. Each of these scenarios implies either that the capital markets are inefficient or that investors do not have the same information regarding the firm's future as does its financial manager. The second situation undoubtedly is true at times, and the first one possibly is true at times.

The firm's earnings outlook and the extent to which forecasted higher earnings per share are reflected in stock prices also have an effect on the choice of securities. If a successful R&D program has just been concluded and causes management to forecast higher earnings than do most investors, then the firm would not want to issue common stock. It would use debt and then, once earnings rise and push up the stock price, sell common stock to restore the capital structure to its target level.

18.8d Amount of Financing Required

Obviously, the amount of financing required will influence the financing decision. This is mainly because of flotation costs. A $5 million debt financing, which is small in Wall Street terms, would most likely be done with a term loan or a privately placed bond issue, whereas a firm seeking $2 billion of new debt would most likely use a public offering of long-term bonds.

18.8e Availability of Collateral

Generally, secured debt is less costly than unsecured debt. Thus, firms with large amounts of marketable fixed assets are likely to use a relatively large amount of long-term debt, especially mortgage bonds. Additionally, each year's financing decision would be influenced by the amount of qualified assets available as security for new bonds.

Self Test	What are some factors that financial managers consider when choosing the maturity structure of their debt? How do information asymmetries affect financing decisions?

18.9 Refunding Operations

A great deal of corporate debt was sold during the late 1990s. Because the call protection on much of this debt has ended and because interest rates have fallen since the debt was issued, many companies are analyzing the pros and cons of bond refundings. The basic approach is to estimate the incremental after-tax cash flows associated with the refunding. The cash flows in a refunding decision are due to the presence of debt, so the cash flows should be discounted at the after-tax cost of debt.

The best way to examine the refunding decision is through an example. Microchip Computer Company has a $60 million bond issue outstanding that has a 12% annual coupon interest rate and 20 years remaining to maturity. This issue, which was sold 5 years ago, had flotation costs of $3 million that the firm has been amortizing on a straight-line basis over the 25-year original life of the issue. The bond has a call provision that makes it possible for the company to retire the issue at this time by calling the bonds in at a 10% call premium. Investment banks have assured the company that it could sell an additional $60 million to $70 million worth of new 20-year bonds at an interest rate of 9%. To ensure that the funds required to pay off the old debt will be available, the new bonds will be sold 1 month before the old issue is called; thus, for 1 month the company will have to pay interest on two issues. Current short-term interest rates are 6%. Predictions are that long-term interest rates are unlikely to fall below 9%.[13] Flotation costs on a new refunding issue will amount to $2,650,000, and the firm's marginal federal-plus-state tax rate is 40%. Should the company refund the $60 million of 12% bonds?

The following steps outline the decision process; they are summarized in the spreadsheet in Figure 18-1. This spreadsheet is part of the spreadsheet model, *Ch18 Tool Kit.xls*, developed for this chapter. The range of cells from A17 through H23 shows input data needed for the analysis, which were just discussed.

WEB

See **Ch18 Tool Kit.xls** on the textbook's Web site for details.

18.9a Step 1: Determine the Investment Outlay Required to Refund the Issue

Row 26

Call premium on old issue:

$$\text{Before tax: } 0.10(\$60,000,000) = \$6,000,000$$
$$\text{After tax: } \$6,000,000(1 - T) = \$6,000,000(0.6)$$
$$= \$3,600,000$$

Although Microchip must spend $6 million on the call premium, this is a deductible expense in the year the call is made. Because the company is in the 40% tax bracket, it saves $2.4 million in taxes; therefore, the after-tax cost of the call is only $3.6 million.

Row 27

Flotation costs on new issue: Flotation costs on the new issue will be $2,650,000. This amount cannot be expensed for tax purposes, so it provides no immediate tax benefit.

Row 28

Flotation costs on old issue: The old issue has an unamortized flotation cost of $(20/25)(\$3,000,000) = \$2,400,000$ at this time. If the issue is retired then the unamortized flotation cost may be recognized immediately as an expense, thus creating an after-tax savings of $\$2,400,000(T) = \$960,000$. Because this is a cash inflow, it is shown as a positive number.

---

13. The firm's management has estimated that interest rates will probably remain at their present level of 9% or else rise; there is only a 25% probability that they will fall further.

Figure 18-1   Spreadsheet for the Bond Refunding Decision

	A	B	C	D	E	F	G	H
15	Input Data (in thousands of dollars)							
16	Existing bond issue		=	$60,000		New bond issue	=	$60,000
17	Original flotation cost		=	$3,000		New flotation cost	=	$2,650
18	Maturity of original debt		=	25		New bond maturity	=	20
19	Years since old debt issue		=	5		New cost of debt	=	9.0%
20	Call premium (%)		=	10.0%				
21	Original coupon rate		=	12.0%		Tax rate	=	40.0%
22	After-tax cost of new debt		=	5.4%		Short-term interest rate	=	6.0%
23								
24	Schedule of cash flows							
25	Investment Outlay					Before-tax	After-tax	
26	Call premium on the old bond					($6,000.0)	($3,600.0)	
27	Flotation costs on new issue					($2,650.0)	($2,650.0)	
28	Immediate tax savings on old flotation cost expense					$2,400.0	$960.0	
29	Extra interest paid on old issue					($600.0)	($360.0)	
30	Interest earned on short-term investment					$300.0	$180.0	
31	Total after-tax investment						($5,470.0)	
32								
33	Annual Flotation Cost Tax Effects: t = 1 to 20							
34	Annual tax savings from new-issue flotation costs					$132.5	$53.0	
35	Annual lost tax savings from old-issue flotation costs					($120.0)	($48.0)	
36	Net flotation cost tax savings					$12.5	$5.0	
37								
38	Annual Interest Savings Due to Refunding: t = 1 to 20							
39	Interest on old bond					$7,200.0	$4,320.0	
40	Interest on new bond					($5,400.0)	($3,240.0)	
41	Net interest savings					$1,800.0	$1,080.0	
42								
43	Calculating the annual flotation cost tax effects and the annual interest savings							
44	Annual Flotation Cost Tax Effects					Annual Interest Savings		
45	Maturity of the new bond (Nper)			20		Maturity of the new bond (Nper)		20
46	After-tax cost of new debt (Rate)			5.4%		After-tax cost of new debt (Rate)		5.4%
47	Annual flotation cost tax savings (Pmt)			$5		Annual interest savings (Pmt)		$1,080
48								
49	Since the annual flotation cost tax effects and interest savings occur for the next 20 years, they represent							
50	annuities. To evaluate this project, we must find the present values of these savings. Using the function							
51	wizard and solving for present value, we find that the present values of these annuities are:							
52								
53	NPV of annual flotation cost savings			$60.251		NPV of annual interest savings		$13,014.174
54								
55	Hence, the net present value of this bond refunding project will be the sum of the initial outlay and the present							
56	values of the annual flotation cost tax effects and interest savings.							
57								
58	Bond Refunding NPV = Initial Outlay				+	PV of flotation costs	+	PV of interest savings
59	Bond Refunding NPV = ($5,470.000)				+	$60.251	+	$13,014.174
60								
61	Bond Refund NPV = $7,604.425							

WEB

See *Ch18 Tool Kit.xls* on the textbook's Web site for details.

Rows 29 and 30

Additional interest: One month's "extra" interest on the old issue, after taxes, costs $360,000:

$$\text{Interest cost} = (\text{Dollar amount})(1/12 \text{ of } 12\%)(1 - T)$$
$$= (\$60,000,000)(0.01)(0.6) = \$360,000$$

However, the proceeds from the new issue can be invested in short-term securities for 1 month. Thus, $60 million invested at a rate of 6% will return $180,000 in after-tax interest:

$$\text{Interest earned} = (\$60{,}000{,}000)(1/12 \text{ of } 6\%)(1 - T)$$

$$= (\$60{,}000{,}000)(0.005)(0.6) = \$180{,}000$$

Row 31

Total after-tax investment: The total investment outlay required to refund the bond issue, which will be financed by debt, is thus $5,470,000:[14]

Call premium	($3,600,000)
Flotation costs, new	(2,650,000)
Flotation costs, old, tax savings	960,000
Net additional interest	(180,000)
Total investment	($5,470,000)

18.9b Step 2: Calculate the Annual Flotation Cost Tax Effects

Row 34

Tax savings on flotation costs on the new issue: For tax purposes, flotation costs must be amortized over the life of the new bond, which is 20 years. Therefore, the annual tax deduction is

$$\frac{\$2{,}650{,}000}{20} = \$132{,}500$$

Since our spreadsheet shows dollars in thousands, this number appears as $132.5 on the spreadsheet. Because the firm is in the 40% tax bracket, it has a tax savings of $132,500(0.4) = $53,000 a year for 20 years. This is an annuity of $53,000 for 20 years.

Row 35

Tax benefits lost on flotation costs on the old issue: The firm, however, will no longer receive a tax deduction of $120,000 a year for 20 years, so it loses an after-tax benefit of $48,000 a year.

---

14. The investment outlay (in this case, $5,470,000) is usually obtained by increasing the amount of the new bond issue. In the example given, the new issue would be $65,470,000. However, the interest on the additional debt *should not* be deducted at Step 3 because the $5,470,000 itself will be deducted at Step 4. If additional interest on the $5,470,000 were deducted at Step 3 then interest would, in effect, be deducted twice. The situation here is exactly like that in regular capital budgeting decisions. Even though some debt may be used to finance a project, interest on that debt is not subtracted when developing the annual cash flows. Instead, the annual cash flows are *discounted* at the project's cost of capital.

Row 36

Net flotation amortization tax effect: The after-tax difference between the amortization tax effects of flotation on the new and old issues is $5,000 a year for 20 years.

18.9c Step 3: Calculate the Annual Interest Savings

Row 39

Interest on old bond, after tax: The annual after-tax interest on the old issue is $4.32 million:

$$(\$60,000,000)(0.12)(0.6) = \$4,320,000$$

Row 40

Interest on new bond, after tax: The new issue has an annual after-tax cost of $3,240,000:

$$(\$60,000,000)(0.09)(0.6) = \$3,240,000$$

Row 43

Net annual interest savings: Thus, the net annual interest savings is $1,080,000:

Interest on old bonds, after tax	$4,320,000
Interest on new bonds, after tax	(3,240,000)
Annual interest savings, after tax	$1,080,000

18.9d Step 4: Determine the NPV of the Refunding

Row 53

PV of the benefits: The PV of the annual after-tax flotation cost benefit can be found using a financial calculator, with N = 20, I/YR = 5.4, PMT = 5000, and FV = 0. Solving for PV shows that the flotation cost savings have a present value equal to $60,251. The PV of the $1,080,000 annual after-tax interest savings is found with N = 20, I/YR = 5.4, PMT = 1080000 and FV = 0; solving for PV shows that the present value of after-tax interest cost savings is $13,014,174.

These values are used in Row 61 when finding the NPV of the refunding operation:

Amortization tax effects	$ 60,251
Interest savings	13,014,174
Net investment outlay	(5,470,000)
NPV from refunding	$ 7,604,425

Because the net present value of the refunding is positive, it would be profitable to refund the old bond issue.

TVA RATCHETS DOWN ITS INTEREST EXPENSES

In 1998, TVA raised $575 million in 30-year debt. If it had issued fixed-rate debt, it would be stuck with high coupon payments if interest rates in the market fall. If it had issued floating-rate debt, it would be stuck with high coupon payments if interest rates rise. If it had issued callable debt, then it could refinance if interest rates fall. But the costs of refunding are high, and TVA would have to agonize over the decision of whether to refund or wait in the hopes that rates will fall. None of these three choices seemed desirable, so TVA issued a new type of security that finesses these problems.

The new bonds are officially called Putable Automatic Rate Reset Securities (PARRS), but they are commonly known as ratchet bonds. These bonds have a feature that resets the coupon rate each year, starting in 2003, to 94 basis points over the rate on the prevailing 30-year Treasury bond—provided the new coupon would be lower than the ratchet bond's current coupon. In other words, the coupon on the bond will fall if interest rates fall, but it will never increase from year to year, allowing TVA to lock in the lowest interest rates that prevail during the bond's life. In essence, TVA gets to refund its debt in any year when rates fall, hence the term "ratchet."

The 94-basis-point spread is higher than the spread over Treasuries that normally exists on TVA's noncallable bonds, given its bond rating. However, if the bond rating deteriorates, then investors can "put" the bond by selling it back to TVA. The net effect is that investors are exposed to interest rate risk but not to credit risk, and they are compensated for interest rate risk by the relatively high spread.

These bonds were originally issued with a 6.750% coupon, and on the first reset date (June 1, 2003) the rate ratcheted down to 5.952%, reflecting the decline in long-term interest rates since 1998. By June 1, 2009, long-term interest rates had fallen so that the coupon rate on the PARRS was ratcheted down to 4.728%.

Sources: Andrew Kalotay and Leslie Abreo, "Ratchet Bonds: Maximum Refunding Efficiency at Minimum Transaction Cost," *Journal of Applied Corporate Finance,* Vol. 41, No. 1, Spring 1999, pp. 40–47; and TVA's Web site, **www.tva.gov**.

We can summarize the data shown in Figure 18-1 using a time line (amounts in thousands) as shown below:

	0	5.4%	1	2	20
After-tax investment	−5,470				
Flotation cost tax effects			5	5	5
Interest savings			1,080	1,080	1,080
Net cash flows	−5,470		1,085	1,085	1,085

$NPV_{5.4\%} = \$7,604$

Several other points should be made. First, because the cash flows are based on differences between contractual obligations, their risk is the same as that of the underlying obligations. Therefore, the present values of the cash flows should be found by discounting at the firm's least risky rate—its after-tax cost of marginal debt. Second, since the refunding operation is advantageous to the firm, it must be disadvantageous to bondholders; they must give up their 12% bonds and reinvest in new ones yielding 9%. This points out the danger of the call provision to bondholders, and it also explains why noncallable bonds command higher prices than callable bonds with the same coupon rate. Third, although it is not emphasized in the example, we assumed that the firm raises the investment required to undertake the refunding operation (the $5,470,000 shown in Row 33 of Figure 18-1) as debt. This should be feasible because the refunding operation will improve the interest coverage ratio, even though a larger amount of debt is outstanding. Fourth, we set up our example in such a way that the new issue had the same maturity as the remaining life of the old one. Often, the old bonds have a relatively short time to maturity (say, 5 to 10 years), whereas the new bonds have a much longer maturity (say, 25 to 30 years). In such a situation, the analysis should be set up similarly to a replacement chain analysis in capital budgeting, which was discussed in Chapter 12. Fifth, refunding decisions are well suited for analysis with a computer spreadsheet program. Spreadsheets such as the one shown in Figure 18-1 are easy to set up, and once the model has been constructed, it is easy to vary the assumptions (especially the assumption about the interest rate on the refunding issue) and to see how such changes affect the NPV.

One final point should be addressed: Although our analysis shows that the refunding would increase the firm's value, would refunding *at this time* truly maximize the firm's expected value? If interest rates continue to fall then the company might be better off waiting, for this would increase the NPV of the refunding operation even more. The mechanics of calculating the NPV in a refunding are easy, but the decision of *when* to refund is not at all simple because it requires a forecast of future interest rates. Thus, the final decision on refunding now versus waiting for a possibly more favorable time is a judgment call.

To illustrate the timing decision, assume Microchip's managers forecast that long-term interest rates have a 50% probability of remaining at their present level of 9% over the next year. However, there is a 25% probability that rates could fall to 7% and a 25% probability they could rise to 11%. Further, assume that short-term rates are expected to remain 3 percentage points below long-term rates and that the call premium would be reduced by 5% if the call were delayed for 1 year.

The refunding analysis could then be repeated, as previously, but as if it were a year later. Thus, the old bonds would have only 19 years remaining to maturity. We performed the analysis and found the NPV distribution of refunding 1 year from now:

Probability	Long-Term Interest Rate	NPV of Refunding 1 Year from Now
25%	7%	$17,947,071
50	9	7,390,083
25	11	(1,359,939)

At first blush, it would seem reasonable to calculate the expected NPV of refunding next year in terms of the probability distribution. However, that would not be correct. If interest rates did rise to 11%, Microchip would not refund the issue; therefore, the actual NPV if rates rose to 11% would be zero. The expected NPV from refunding 1 year hence is therefore $0.25(\$17,947,071) + 0.50(\$7,390,083) + 0.25(\$0) = \$8,181,809$, versus $7,604,425 if refunding occurred today.

Even though the expected NPV of refunding in 1 year is higher, Microchip's managers would probably decide to refund today. The $7,604,425 represents a sure increase in firm value, whereas the $8,181,809 is risky. Also, proper comparison requires that the $8,181,809 be discounted back 1 year to today. Microchip's managers should opt to delay refunding only if the expected NPV from later refunding is sufficiently above today's sure NPV to compensate for the risk and time value involved.

Clearly, the decision to refund now versus refund later is complicated by the fact that there would be numerous opportunities to refund in the future rather than just a single opportunity 1 year from now. Furthermore, the decision must be based on a large set of interest rate forecasts, a daunting task in itself. Fortunately, financial managers making bond refunding decisions can now use the values of derivative securities to estimate the value of the bond issue's embedded call option. If the call option is worth more than the NPV of refunding today, the issue should not be immediately refunded. Rather, the issuer should either delay the refunding to take advantage of the information obtained from the derivative market or actually create a derivative transaction to lock in the value of the call option.[15]

How is bond refunding like a capital budgeting project?	Self Test

18.10 Managing the Risk Structure of Debt with Project Financing

Historically, many large projects such as the Alaska pipeline have been financed by what is called **project financing**.[16] We can only present an overview of the concept, for in practice it involves complicated provisions and can take on many forms.

Project financing has been used to finance energy explorations, oil tankers, refineries, and electric generating plants. Generally, one or more firms will sponsor the project, putting up the required equity capital, while the remainder of the financing is furnished by lenders or lessors. Most often, a separate legal entity is formed to operate the project. Normally, the project's creditors do not have full recourse against the sponsors. In other words, the lenders and lessors must be paid from the project's cash flows and from the sponsors' equity in the project, because the creditors have no claims against the sponsors' other assets or cash flows. Often the sponsors write "comfort" letters, giving general assurances that they will strive diligently to make the project successful. However, these letters are not legally binding, so in project financing the lenders and lessors must focus their analysis on the inherent merits of the project and on the equity cushion provided by the sponsors.[17]

Project financing is not a new development. Indeed, back in 1299 the English Crown negotiated a loan with Florentine merchant banks that was to be repaid with

15. For more information on derivatives in general, see Chapter 24. For more information on the use of derivatives to help make call decisions, see Andrew J. Kalotay and George O. Williams, "How to Succeed in Derivatives without Really Buying," *Journal of Applied Corporate Finance*, Fall 1993, pp. 100–103. For more on bond refunding, see Raymond C. Chiang and M. P. Narayanan, "Bond Refunding in Efficient Markets: A Dynamic Analysis with Tax Effects," *Journal of Financial Research*, Winter 1991, pp. 287–302; David C. Mauer, "Optimal Bond Call Policies under Transactions Costs," *Journal of Financial Research*, Spring 1993, pp. 23–37; and Janet S. Thatcher and John G. Thatcher, "An Empirical Test of the Timing of Bond-Refunding Decisions," *Journal of Financial Research*, Fall 1992, pp. 219–230.

16. For an excellent discussion of project financing, see Benjamin C. Esty, "Petrozuata: A Case Study on the Effective Use of Project Finance," *Journal of Applied Corporate Finance*, Fall 1999, pp. 26–42.

17. In another type of project financing, each sponsor guarantees its share of the project's debt obligations. Here the creditors also consider the creditworthiness of the sponsors in addition to the project's own prospects. It should be noted that project financing with multiple sponsors in the electric utility industry has led to problems when one or more of the sponsors has landed in financial trouble. For example, Long Island Lighting, one of the sponsors in the Nine Mile Point nuclear project, became unable to meet its commitments to the project, which forced other sponsors to shoulder an additional burden or else see the project cancelled and lose all their investment up to that point. The risk of such default makes many companies reluctant to enter into similar projects.

1 year's output from the Devon silver mines. Essentially, the Italians were allowed to operate the mines for 1 year, paying all the operating costs and mining as much ore as they could. The Crown made no guarantees as to how much ore could be mined or the value of the refined silver. A more current example involved GE Capital, the credit arm of General Electric, which recently financed a $72 million project to build an aluminum can plant. The plant is owned by several beverage makers but it is operated independently, and GE Capital must depend on the cash flows from the plant to repay the loan. About half of all project financings in recent years have been for electric generating plants, including plants owned by electric utilities and cogeneration plants operated by industrial companies. Project financings are generally characterized by large size and a high degree of complexity. However, because project financing is tied to a specific project, it can be tailored to meet the specific needs of both the creditors and the sponsors. In particular, the financing can be structured so that both the funds provided during the construction phase and the subsequent repayments match the timing of the project's projected cash outflows and inflows.

Project financing offers several potential benefits over conventional debt financing. For one, project financing usually restricts the use of the project's cash flows, which means that the lenders—rather than the managers—can decide whether excess cash flows should be reinvested or instead used to reduce the loan balance by more than the minimum required. Conferring this power on the lenders reduces their risks. Project financings also have advantages for borrowers. First, because risks to the lenders are reduced, the interest rate built into a project financing deal may be relatively low. Second, because suppliers of project financing capital have no recourse against the sponsoring firms' other assets and cash flows, project financings insulate the firms' other assets from risks associated with the project being financed. Managers may be more willing to take on a large, risky project if they know that the company's existence would not be threatened if it fails.

Project financings increase the number and type of investment opportunities; hence they make capital markets "more complete." At the same time, project financings reduce the costs to investors of obtaining information and monitoring the borrower's operations. To illustrate, consider an oil and gas exploration project that is funded using project financing. If the project were financed as an integral part of the firm's normal operations, investors in all the firm's outstanding securities would need information on the project. By isolating the project, the need for information is confined to the investors in the project financing, who need to monitor only the project's operations and not those of the entire firm.

Project financings also permit firms whose earnings are below the minimum requirements specified in their existing bond indentures to obtain additional debt financing. In such situations, lenders look only at the merits of the new project, and its cash flows may support additional debt even though the firm's overall situation does not. Project financings also permit managers to reveal proprietary information to a smaller group of investors, so project financings increase the ability of a firm to maintain confidentiality. Finally, project financings can improve incentives for key managers by enabling them to take direct ownership stakes in the operations under their control. By establishing separate projects, companies can provide incentives that are much more directly based on individual performance than is typically possible within a large corporation.

Self Test   What is project financing? What are its advantages and disadvantages?

Summary

- The **Securities and Exchange Commission (SEC)** regulates securities markets.
- **Private placements** are securities offerings to a limited number of investors and are exempt from registration with the SEC.
- **Accredited investors** include the officers and directors of a company, high-wealth individuals, and institutional investors. These investors are eligible to buy securities in private placements.
- An **angel** is a wealthy individual who makes an equity investment in a start-up company.
- The managers of a **venture capital fund** are called **venture capitalists,** or **VCs.** They raise money from investors and make equity investments in start-up companies, called **portfolio companies.**
- **Going public** in an **initial public offering (IPO)** facilitates stockholder diversification, increases liquidity of the firm's stock, makes it easier for the firm to raise capital, establishes a value for the firm, and makes it easier for a firm to sell its products. However, reporting costs are high, operating data must be disclosed, management self-dealings are harder to arrange, the price may sink to a low level if the stock is not traded actively, and public ownership may make it harder for management to maintain control.
- **Investment banks** assist in issuing securities by helping the firm determine the size of the issue and the type of securities to be used, by establishing the selling price, by selling the issue, and, in some cases, by maintaining an after-market for the stock.
- An investment bank may sell a security issue on a **best efforts basis,** or it may guarantee the sale by **underwriting** the issue.
- Before an IPO, the investment bank and management team go on a **roadshow** and make presentations to potential institutional investors.
- An IPO is **oversubscribed** if investors are willing to purchase more shares than are being offered at the IPO price.
- The **spread** is the difference between the price at which an underwriter sells a security and the proceeds that the underwriter gives to the issuing company. In recent years the spread for almost all IPOs has been 7%.
- An **equity carve-out** (also called a **partial public offering** or **spin-out**) is a special IPO in which a publicly traded company converts a subsidiary into a separately traded public company by selling shares of stock in the subsidiary. The parent typically retains a controlling interest.
- SEC Rule 415, also known as **shelf registration,** allows a company to register an issue and then sell that issue in pieces over time rather than all at once.
- A **seasoned equity offering** occurs when a public company issues additional shares of stock.
- A **private equity fund** is a limited liability partnership created to own and manage investments in the nontraded equity of firms.
- A company **goes private** when a small group of investors, including the firm's senior management, purchases all of the equity in the company. Such deals usually involve high levels of debt and are commonly called **leveraged buyouts (LBOs).**

- If a bond has a call provision, then the issuer may **refund (call)** the bond prior to maturity and pay for it with a new debt issue at a lower interest rate.
- In **project financing,** the payments on debt are secured by the cash flows of a particular project.
- **Asset securitization** occurs when assets such as mortgages or credit card receivables are bundled together into a pool. Then bonds are created that use the payments in the pool to make interest and principal payments on the bonds.
- *Web Extension 18A* describes a **rights offering.**

Questions

18-1 Define each of the following terms:
   a. Going public; new issue market; initial public offering (IPO)
   b. Public offering; private placement
   c. Venture capitalists; roadshow; spread
   d. Securities and Exchange Commission (SEC); registration statement; shelf registration; margin requirement; insiders
   e. Prospectus; "red herring" prospectus
   f. National Association of Securities Dealers (NASD)
   g. Best efforts arrangement; underwritten arrangement
   h. Refunding; project financing; securitization; maturity matching

18-2 Is it true that the "flatter" (more nearly horizontal) the demand curve for a particular firm's stock and the less important investors regard the signaling effect of the offering, the more important the role of investment banks when the company sells a new issue of stock?

18-3 The SEC attempts to protect investors who are purchasing newly issued securities by making sure that the information put out by a company and its investment banks is correct and is not misleading. However, the SEC does not provide an opinion about the real value of the securities; hence an investor might pay too much for some new stock and consequently lose heavily. Do you think the SEC should, as a part of every new stock or bond offering, render an opinion to investors on the proper value of the securities being offered? Explain.

18-4 How do you think each of the following items would affect a company's ability to attract new capital and the flotation costs involved in doing so?
   a. A decision of a privately held company to go public
   b. The increasing institutionalization of the "buy side" of the stock and bond markets
   c. The trend toward financial conglomerates as opposed to stand-alone investment banking houses
   d. Elimination of the preemptive right
   e. The introduction in 1981 of shelf registration of securities

18-5 Before entering a formal agreement, investment banks carefully investigate the companies whose securities they underwrite; this is especially true of the issues of firms going public for the first time. Since the banks do not themselves plan to hold the securities but intend to sell them to others as soon as possible, why are they so concerned about making careful investigations?

Problems   Answers Appear in Appendix B

Easy Problems 1–2

18-1 **Profit or Loss on New Stock Issue** Security Brokers Inc. specializes in underwriting new issues by small firms. On a recent offering of Beedles Inc., the terms were as follows:

Price to public	$5 per share
Number of shares	3 million
Proceeds to Beedles	$14,000,000

The out-of-pocket expenses incurred by Security Brokers in the design and distribution of the issue were $300,000. What profit or loss would Security Brokers incur if the issue were sold to the public at the following average price?
a. $5 per share
b. $6 per share
c. $4 per share

18-2 **Underwriting and Flotation Expenses** The Beranek Company, whose stock price is now $25, needs to raise $20 million in common stock. Underwriters have informed the firm's management that they must price the new issue to the public at $22 per share because of signaling effects. The underwriters' compensation will be 5% of the issue price, so Beranek will net $20.90 per share. The firm will also incur expenses in the amount of $150,000.

How many shares must the firm sell to net $20 million after underwriting and flotation expenses?

Intermediate Problem 3

18-3 **New Stock Issue** Bynum and Crumpton Inc. (B&C), a small jewelry manufacturer, has been successful and has enjoyed a good growth trend. Now B&C is planning to go public with an issue of common stock, and it faces the problem of setting an appropriate price for the stock. The company and its investment banks believe that the proper procedure is to conduct a valuation and select several similar firms with publicly traded common stock and to make relevant comparisons.

Several jewelry manufacturers are reasonably similar to B&C with respect to product mix, asset composition, and debt/equity proportions. Of these companies, Abercrombie Jewelers and Gunter Fashions are most similar. When analyzing the following data, assume that the most recent year has been reasonably "normal" in the sense that it was neither especially good nor especially bad in terms of sales, earnings, and free cash flows. Abercrombie is listed on the AMEX and Gunter on the NYSE, while B&C will be traded in the Nasdaq market.

Company Data	Abercrombe	Gunter	B&C
Shares outstanding	5 million	10 million	1,000
Price per share	$35.00	$47.00	NA
Earnings per share	$2.20	$3.75	$1,332.50
Free cash flow per share	$1.54	$2.25	$976.00
Book value per share	$16.00	$21.00	$7,500.00
Total assets	$115 million	$260 million	$11.5 million
Total debt	$35 million	$50 million	$4 million

a. B&C is a closely held corporation with only 1,000 shares outstanding. Free cash flows have been low and in some years negative due to B&C's recent high sales growth rates, but as its expansion phase comes to an end B&C's free cash flows should increase. B&C anticipates the following free cash flows over the next 5 years:

Year	1	2	3	4	5
FCF	1,025,000	1,076,000	1,237,000	1,1361,000	1,497,000

After Year 5, free cash flow growth will be stable at 7% per year. Currently, B&C has no non-operating assets, has $4 million in debt, and its WACC is 12%. Calculate B&C's value of equity and per share value of equity using the corporate valuation model.

b. Calculate debt to total assets, P/E, market to book, P/FCF, and ROE for Abercrombe, Gunter, and B&C. For calculations that require a price for B&C, use the per share price you obtained with the corporate valuation model in part a.

c. On the basis of your answer to parts a and b, do you think B&C stock would sell at a price in the same "ballpark" as that of Abercrombe and Gunter—that is, in the range of $25 to $100 per share?

d. Using Abercrombe's and Gunter's P/E, Market/Book, and Price/FCF ratios, calculate the range of prices for B&C's stock that would be consistent with these ratios. For example, if you multiply B&C's earnings per share by Abercrombe's P/E ratio you get a price. What range of prices do you get? How does this compare with the price you get using the corporate valuation model?

e. Assuming B&C's management can split the stock so that the 1,000 shares could be changed to 10,000 shares, 100,000 shares, or any other number, would such an action make sense in this case? Why or why not?

f. Should B&C split the stock and at what price do you think B&C shares should be offered to the public? You will want to select a price that will be low enough to induce investors to buy the stock but not so low that it will rise sharply immediately after it is issued. Think about the corporate valuation model and the multiples and ROEs from part d.

Challenging Problems 4–5

18-4 **Refunding Analysis** Jan Volk, financial manager of Green Sea Transport (GST), has been asked by her boss to review GST's outstanding debt issues for possible bond refunding. Five years ago, GST issued $40,000,000 of 11%,

25-year debt. The issue, with semiannual coupons, is currently callable at a premium of 11%, or $110 for each $1,000 par value bond. Flotation costs on this issue were 6%, or $2,400,000.

Volk believes that GST could issue 20-year debt today with a coupon rate of 8%. The firm has placed many issues in the capital markets during the last 10 years, and its debt flotation costs are currently estimated to be 4% of the issue's value. GST's federal-plus-state tax rate is 40%.

Help Volk conduct the refunding analysis by answering the following questions.

a. What is the total dollar call premium required to call the old issue? Is it tax deductible? What is the net after-tax cost of the call?

b. What is the dollar flotation cost on the new issue? Is it immediately tax deductible? What is the after-tax flotation cost?

c. What amounts of old-issue flotation costs have not been expensed? Can these deferred costs be expensed immediately if the old issue is refunded? What is the value of the tax savings?

d. What is the net after-tax cash outlay required to refund the old issue?

e. What is the semiannual tax savings that arises from amortizing the flotation costs on the new issue? What is the forgone semiannual tax savings on the old-issue flotation costs?

f. What is the semiannual after-tax interest savings that would result from the refunding?

g. Thus far, Volk has identified two future cash flows: (1) the net of new-issue flotation cost tax savings and old-issue flotation cost tax savings that are lost if refunding occurs and (2) after-tax interest savings. What is the sum of these two semiannual cash flows? What is the appropriate discount rate to apply to these future cash flows? What is their present value?

h. What is the NPV of refunding? Should GST refund now or wait until later?

18-5 **Refunding Analysis** Mullet Technologies is considering whether or not to refund a $75 million, 12% coupon, 30-year bond issue that was sold 5 years ago. It is amortizing $5 million of flotation costs on the 12% bonds over the issue's 30-year life. Mullet's investment banks have indicated that the company could sell a new 25-year issue at an interest rate of 10% in today's market. Neither they nor Mullet's management anticipate that interest rates will fall below 10% any time soon, but there is a chance that rates will increase.

A call premium of 12% would be required to retire the old bonds, and flotation costs on the new issue would amount to $5 million. Mullet's marginal federal-plus-state tax rate is 40%. The new bonds would be issued 1 month before the old bonds are called, with the proceeds being invested in short-term government securities returning 6% annually during the interim period.

a. Perform a complete bond refunding analysis. What is the bond refunding's NPV?

b. What factors would influence Mullet's decision to refund now rather than later?

Spreadsheet Problem

18-6 **Build a Model: Bond Refunding** Start with the partial model in the file *Ch18 P06 Build a Model.xls* on the textbook's Web site. Schumann Shoe Manufacturer is considering whether or not to refund a $70 million, 10% coupon, 30-year bond issue that was sold 8 years ago. It is amortizing $4.5 million of flotation costs on the 10% bonds over the issue's 30-year life. Schumann's investment bankers have indicated that the company could sell a new 22-year issue at an interest rate of 8% in today's market. Neither they nor Schumann's management anticipate that interest rates will fall below 6% anytime soon, but there is a chance that interest rates will increase.

   a. Perform a complete bond refunding analysis. What is the bond refunding's NPV?

   b. At what interest rate on the new debt is the NPV of the refunding no longer positive?

MINI CASE

Randy's, a family-owned restaurant chain operating in Alabama, has grown to the point that expansion throughout the entire Southeast is feasible. The proposed expansion would require the firm to raise about $15 million in new capital. Because Randy's currently has a debt ratio of 50% and because family members already have all their personal wealth invested in the company, the family would like to sell common stock to the public to raise the $15 million. However, the family wants to retain voting control. You have been asked to brief family members on the issues involved by answering the following questions.

   a. What agencies regulate securities markets?

   b. How are start-up firms usually financed?

   c. Differentiate between a private placement and a public offering.

   d. Why would a company consider going public? What are some advantages and disadvantages?

   e. What are the steps of an initial public offering?

   f. What criteria are important in choosing an investment bank?

   g. Would companies going public use a negotiated deal or a competitive bid?

   h. Would the sale be on an underwritten or best efforts basis?

   i. Without actually doing any calculations, describe how the preliminary offering range for the price of an IPO would be determined.

   j. What is a roadshow? What is book-building?

   k. Describe the typical first-day return of an IPO and the long-term returns to IPO investors.

   l. What are the direct and indirect costs of an IPO?

   m. What are equity carve-outs?

   n. Describe some ways other than an IPO that companies can use to raise funds from the capital markets.

   o. What are some other investment banking activities? How did these increase investment banks' risk?

   p. What is meant by "going private"? What are some advantages and disadvantages? What role do private equity funds play?

   q. How do companies manage the maturity structure of their debt?

   r. Under what conditions would a firm exercise a bond call provision?

   s. Explain how firms manage the risk structure of their debt with project financing.

Selected Additional Cases

The following cases from TextChoice, *Cengage Learning's online case library, cover many of the concepts discussed in this chapter and are available at* **www.textchoice2.com/casenet.**

Klein-Brigham Series:

Case 21, "Sun Coast Savings Bank," illustrates the decision to go public; Case 22, "Precision Tool Company," emphasizes the investment banking process; Case 23, "Art Deco Reproductions, Inc.," focuses on the analysis of a rights offering; and Case 24, "Bay Area Telephone Company," Case 24A, "Shenandoah Power Company," and Case 24B, "Tucson Entertainment, Inc.," illustrate the bond refunding decision.

Chapter 19

Lease Financing

© Nikada/iStockphoto.com

WEB

The textbook's Web site contains an *Excel* file that will guide you through the chapter's calculations. The file for this chapter is ***Ch19 Tool Kit.xls***, and we encourage you to open the file and follow along as you read the chapter.

Firms generally own fixed assets and report them on their balance sheets, but it is the use of assets that is important, not their ownership per se. One way to obtain the *use* of facilities and equipment is to buy them, but an alternative is to lease them. Prior to the 1950s, leasing was generally associated with real estate—land and buildings. Today, however, it is possible to lease virtually any kind of fixed asset, and currently over 30% of all new capital equipment is financed through lease arrangements.[1] In fact, the Equipment Leasing Association estimates that about 20,000 equipment leases are signed each day in the United States, with around $220 billion in equipment held in the form of leases.[2] Because leases are so frequently used by virtually all businesses, it is important for every manager to understand them.

---

1. For a detailed treatment of leasing, see James S. Schallheim, *Lease or Buy? Principles for Sound Decision Making* (Boston: Harvard Business School Press, 1994).
2. See Tammy Whitehouse, "FASB to Revisit Lease Accounting," Compliance Week, May 9, 2006, www.complianceweek.com/article/2488/fasb-to-revisit-lease-accounting.

Beginning of Chapter Questions

As you read the chapter, consider how you would answer the following questions. You *should not* necessarily be able to answer the questions before you read the chapter. Rather, you should use them to get a sense of the issues covered in the chapter. After reading the chapter, you should be able to give at least partial answers to the questions, and you should be able to give better answers after the chapter has been discussed in class. Note, too, that it is often useful, when answering conceptual questions, to use hypothetical data to illustrate your answer. We illustrate the answers with an *Excel* model that is available on the textbook's Web site. Accessing the model and working through it is a useful exercise, and it provides insights that are useful when answering the questions.

1. Differentiate between an **operating lease,** a **capital** (or **financial**) **lease,** and a **sale-and-leaseback arrangement.** How might investors be misled by firms that use lease financing extensively, and what rules have accountants put in place in an effort to mitigate this problem?
2. What is a **synthetic lease?** How are such leases structured, and what is their primary purpose?

Is it likely that the use of synthetic leases will increase or decrease?
3. How do **IRS regulations** affect leasing decisions?
4. Assuming that **FASB Statement 13** is working as it is supposed to work, should traditional leasing arrangements enable a firm to use more financial leverage than it otherwise could? How did synthetic leases alter the situation? How do FASB Statement 13 and synthetic leases affect the rate at which cash flows are discounted in a lease analysis?
5. Define the term **NAL** as it is used in lease analysis, and then explain how the NAL is calculated.
6. Is leasing a **zero sum game** in the sense that any gain to the lessee is a cost to the lessor? If not, how might both parties gain from a lease transaction? In your answer, explain how the lessee and the lessor analyze the situation, why they might use different inputs in their analyses, and how those input differences could affect the outcome. To help you with this analysis, the Beginning-of-Chapter *Excel* model for this chapter has a "negotiation graph" that should help tie things together.

19.1 Types of Leases

Lease transactions involve two parties: the lessor, who owns the property, and the lessee, who obtains use of the property in exchange for one or more lease, or rental, payments. (Note that the term *lessee* is pronounced "less-ee," not "lease-ee," and *lessor* is pronounced "less-or.") Because both parties must agree before a lease transaction can be completed, this chapter discusses leasing from the perspectives of both the lessor and the lessee.

Leasing takes several different forms, of which the five most important are: (1) operating leases; (2) financial, or capital, leases; (3) sale-and-leaseback arrangements; (4) combination leases; and (5) synthetic leases.

19.1a Operating Leases

Operating leases generally provide for both *financing* and *maintenance.* IBM was one of the pioneers of the operating lease contract, and computers and office copying machines—together with automobiles, trucks, and aircraft—are the primary types of equipment involved in operating leases. Ordinarily, operating leases require the lessor to maintain and service the leased equipment, and the cost of the maintenance is built into the lease payments.

Another important characteristic of operating leases is the fact that they are *not fully amortized.* In other words, the rental payments required under the lease contract are not sufficient for the lessor to recover the full cost of the asset. However, the lease contract is written for a period considerably shorter than the expected economic life of the asset, so the lessor can expect to recover all costs either by subsequent renewal payments, by re-leasing the asset to another lessee, or by selling the asset.

A final feature of operating leases is that they often contain a *cancellation clause* that gives the lessee the right to cancel the lease and return the asset before the expiration of the basic lease agreement. This is an important consideration to the lessee, for it means that the asset can be returned if it is rendered obsolete by technological developments or is no longer needed because of a change in the lessee's business.

19.1b Financial, or Capital, Leases

Financial leases, sometimes called capital leases, differ from operating leases in that they (1) *do not* provide for maintenance service, (2) *are not* cancellable, and (3) *are* fully amortized (that is, the lessor receives rental payments equal to the full price of the leased equipment plus a return on invested capital). In a typical arrangement, the firm that will use the equipment (the lessee) selects the specific items it requires and negotiates the price with the manufacturer. The user firm then arranges to have a leasing company (the lessor) buy the equipment from the manufacturer and simultaneously executes a lease contract. The terms of the lease generally call for full amortization of the lessor's investment, plus a rate of return on the unamortized balance that is close to the percentage rate the lessee would have paid on a secured loan. For example, if the lessee had to pay 10% for a loan, then a rate of about 10% would be built into the lease contract.

The lessee is generally given an option to renew the lease at a reduced rate upon expiration of the basic lease. However, the basic lease usually cannot be cancelled unless the lessor is paid in full. Also, the lessee generally pays the property taxes and insurance on the leased property. Since the lessor receives a return *after,* or *net of,* these payments, this type of lease is often called a "net, net" lease.

19.1c Sale-and-Leaseback Arrangements

Under a sale-and-leaseback arrangement, a firm that owns land, buildings, or equipment sells the property to another firm and simultaneously executes an agreement to lease the property back for a stated period under specific terms. The capital supplier could be an insurance company, a commercial bank, a specialized leasing company, the finance arm of an industrial firm, a limited partnership, or an individual investor. The sale-and-leaseback plan is an alternative to a mortgage.

Note that the seller immediately receives the purchase price put up by the buyer. At the same time, the seller-lessee retains the use of the property. The parallel to borrowing is carried over to the lease payment schedule. Under a mortgage loan arrangement, the lender would normally receive a series of equal payments just sufficient to amortize the loan and to provide a specified rate of return on the outstanding loan balance. Under a sale-and-leaseback arrangement, the lease payments are set up exactly the same way—the payments are just sufficient to return the full purchase price to the investor plus a stated return on the lessor's investment.

Sale-and-leaseback arrangements are almost the same as financial leases; the major difference is that the leased equipment is used, not new, and the lessor buys it from the user-lessee instead of a manufacturer or a distributor. A sale-and-leaseback is thus a special type of financial lease.

19.1d Combination Leases

Many lessors offer a wide variety of terms. Therefore, in practice leases often do not fit exactly into the operating lease or financial lease category but combine some features of each. Such leases are called **combination leases.** To illustrate, cancellation clauses are normally associated with operating leases, but many of today's financial leases also contain cancellation clauses. However, in financial leases these clauses generally include prepayment provisions whereby the lessee must make penalty payments sufficient to enable the lessor to recover the unamortized cost of the leased property.

19.1e Synthetic Leases

A fifth type of lease, the *synthetic lease,* should also be mentioned. These leases were first used in the early 1990s, and they became very popular in the mid- to late-1990s when companies such as Enron and Tyco, as well as "normal" companies, discovered that synthetic leases could be used to keep debt off their balance sheets. In a typical **synthetic lease,** a corporation that wanted to acquire an asset—generally real estate, with a very long life—with debt would first establish a **special purpose entity,** or **SPE.** The SPE would then obtain financing, typically 97% debt provided by a financial institution and 3% equity provided by a party other than the corporation itself.[3] The SPE would then use the funds to acquire the property, and the corporation would lease the asset from the SPE, generally for a term of 3 to 5 years but with an option to extend the lease, which the firm generally expected to exercise. Because of the relatively short term of the lease, it was deemed to be an operating lease and hence did not have to be capitalized and shown on the balance sheet.

A corporation that set up an SPE was required to do one of three things when the lease expired: (1) pay off the SPE's 97% loan; (2) refinance the loan at the current interest rate, if the lender was willing to refinance at all; or (3) sell the asset and make up any shortfall between the sale price and the amount of the loan. Thus, the corporate user was guaranteeing the loan, yet it did not have to show an obligation on its balance sheet.

Synthetic leases stayed under the radar until 2001. As we discuss in the next section, long-term leases must be capitalized and shown on the balance sheet. Synthetic leases were designed to get around this requirement, and neither the corporations that used them (such as Enron and Tyco) nor the accounting firms that approved them (such as Arthur Andersen) wanted anyone to look closely at them. However, the scandals of the early 2000s led security analysts, the SEC, banking regulators, the FASB, and even corporate boards of directors to begin seriously discussing SPEs and synthetic leases. Investors and bankers subjectively downgraded companies that made heavy use of them, and boards of directors began to tell their CFOs to stop using them and to close down the ones that existed. In 2003, the FASB put in place rules that require companies to report on their balance sheets most

---

3. Enron's CFO, Andy Fastow, and other insiders provided the equity for many of Enron's SPEs. Also, a number of Merrill Lynch's executives provided SPE equity, allegedly to enable Merrill Lynch to obtain profitable investment banking deals. The very fact that SPEs are so well suited to conceal what is going on helped those who used them engage in shady deals that would have at least raised eyebrows had they been disclosed. In fact, Fastow pled guilty to two counts of conspiracy in connection to Enron's accounting fraud and ultimate bankruptcy. For more on this subject, see W. R. Pollert and E. J. Glickman, "Synthetic Leases Under Fire," at **www.strategicfinancemag.com**, October 2002.

special purpose entities and synthetic leases of the type Enron abused, limiting management's opportunity to hide these particular transactions from shareholders.

Self Test

Who are the two parties to a lease transaction?

What is the difference between an operating lease and a financial, or capital, lease?

What is a sale-and-leaseback transaction?

What is a combination lease?

What is a synthetic lease?

19.2 Tax Effects

The full amount of the lease payments is a tax-deductible expense for the lessee *provided the Internal Revenue Service agrees that a particular contract is a genuine lease and not simply a loan called a lease.* This makes it important that a lease contract be written in a form acceptable to the IRS. A lease that complies with all IRS requirements is called a **guideline,** or **tax-oriented, lease,** and the tax benefits of ownership (depreciation and any investment tax credits) belong to the lessor. The main provisions of the tax guidelines are as follows:

1. The lease term (including any extensions or renewals at a fixed rental rate) must not exceed 80% of the estimated useful life of the equipment at the commencement of the lease transaction. Thus, an asset with a 10-year life can be leased for no more than 8 years. Further, the remaining useful life must not be less than 1 year. Note that an asset's expected useful life is normally much longer than its MACRS depreciation class life.
2. The equipment's estimated residual value (in constant dollars without adjustment for inflation) at the expiration of the lease must be at least 20% of its value at the start of the lease. This requirement can have the effect of limiting the maximum lease term.
3. Neither the lessee nor any related party can have the right to purchase the property at a predetermined fixed price. However, the lessee can be given an option to buy the asset at its fair market value.
4. Neither the lessee nor any related party can pay or guarantee payment of any part of the price of the leased equipment. Simply put, the lessee cannot make any investment in the equipment other than through the lease payments.
5. The leased equipment must not be "limited use" property, defined as equipment that can be used only by the lessee or a related party at the end of the lease.

The reason for the IRS's concern about lease terms is that, without restrictions, a company could set up a "lease" transaction calling for very rapid payments, which would be tax deductible. The effect would be to depreciate the equipment over a much shorter period than its MACRS class life. For example, suppose a firm planned to acquire a $2 million computer that had a 3-year MACRS class life. The annual depreciation allowances would be $666,600 in Year 1, $889,000 in Year 2, $296,200 in Year 3, and $148,200 in Year 4. If the firm were in the 40% federal-plus-state tax bracket, the depreciation would provide a tax savings of $266,640 in Year 1, $355,600 in Year 2, $118,480 in Year 3, and $59,280 in Year 4, for a total savings of $800,000. At a 6% discount rate, the present value of these tax savings would be $714,463.

Now suppose the firm could acquire the computer through a 1-year lease arrangement with a leasing company for a payment of $2 million, with a $1 purchase option. If the $2 million payment were treated as a lease payment, it would be fully deductible, so it would provide a tax savings of 0.4($2,000,000) = $800,000 versus a present value of only $714,463 for the depreciation shelters. Thus, the lease payment and the depreciation would both provide the same total amount of tax savings (40% of $2,000,000, or $800,000), but the savings would come in faster with the 1-year lease, giving it a higher present value. Therefore, if just any type of contract could be called a lease and given tax treatment as a lease, then the timing of the tax shelters could be speeded up as compared with ownership depreciation tax shelters. This speedup would benefit companies, but it would be costly to the government. For this reason, the IRS has established the rules just described for defining a lease for tax purposes.

Even though leasing can be used only within limits to speed up the effective depreciation schedule, there are still times when very substantial tax benefits can be derived from a leasing arrangement. For example, if a firm has incurred losses and hence has no current tax liabilities, then its depreciation shelters are not very useful. In this case, a leasing company set up by profitable companies such as GE or Philip Morris can buy the equipment, receive the depreciation shelters, and then share these benefits with the lessee by charging lower lease payments. This will be discussed in detail later in the chapter, but the point now is that if firms are to obtain tax benefits from leasing, the lease contract must be written in a manner that will qualify it as a true lease under IRS guidelines. If there is any question about the legal status of the contract, the financial manager must be sure to have the firm's lawyers and accountants check the latest IRS regulations.

Note that a lease that does not meet the tax guidelines is called a **non–tax-oriented lease**. For this type of lease, the lessee (1) is the effective owner of the leased property, (2) can depreciate it for tax purposes, and (3) can deduct only the interest portion of each lease payment.

Self Test

What is the difference between a tax-oriented lease and a non–tax-oriented lease?

What are some lease provisions that would cause a lease to be classified as a non–tax-oriented lease?

Why does the IRS place limits on lease provisions?

19.3 Financial Statement Effects

Under certain conditions, neither the leased assets nor the liabilities under the lease contract appear directly on the firm's balance sheet. For this reason, leasing is often called **off–balance sheet financing**. This point is illustrated in Table 19-1 by the balance sheets of two hypothetical firms, B (for "borrow") and L (for "lease"). Initially, the balance sheets of both firms are identical, and they both have debt ratios of 50%. Next, each firm decides to acquire a fixed asset costing $100. Firm B borrows $100 and buys the asset, so both an asset and a liability go on its balance sheet, and its debt ratio rises from 50% to 75%. Firm L leases the equipment. The lease may call for fixed charges as high as or even higher than the loan, and the obligations assumed under the lease may be equally or more dangerous from the standpoint of potential bankruptcy, but the firm's debt ratio remains at only 50%.

TABLE 19-1 Balance Sheet Effects of Leasing

Panel a: Before Asset Increase

Firms B and L

Current assets	$ 50	Debt	$ 50
Fixed assets	50	Equity	50
	$100		$100
Debt/assets ratio:			50%

Panel b: After Asset Increase

Firm B, Which Borrows and Buys				**Firm L, Which Leases**			
Current assets	$ 50	Debt	$150	Current assets	$ 50	Debt	$ 50
Fixed assets	150	Equity	50	Fixed assets	50	Equity	50
	$200		$200		$100		$100
Debt/assets ratio:		75%					50%

© Cengage Learning 2013

To correct this problem, the Financial Accounting Standards Board (FASB) issued FASB Statement 13, which requires that, for an unqualified audit report, firms entering into financial (or capital) leases must restate their balance sheets and report the leased asset as a fixed asset and the present value of the future lease payments as a liability. This process is called **capitalizing the lease**, and its net effect is to cause Firms B and L to have similar balance sheets—both of which will, in essence, resemble the one shown for Firm B.[4]

The logic behind Statement 13 is as follows: If a firm signs a financial lease contract, its obligation to make lease payments is just as binding as if it had signed a loan agreement—the failure to make lease payments can bankrupt a firm just as fast as the failure to make principal and interest payments on a loan. Therefore, for all intents and purposes, a financial lease is identical to a loan.[5] This being the case, if a firm signs a financial lease agreement then the effect is to raise its true debt ratio, and hence its true capital structure is changed. Therefore, if the firm had previously established a target capital structure and if there is no reason to think the optimal capital structure has changed, then lease financing requires additional equity support, just as debt financing does.

---

4. FASB Statement 13, "Accounting for Leases," spells out in detail both the conditions under which the lease must be capitalized and the procedures for capitalizing it. See also Chapter 4 of Schallheim's *Lease or Buy?* (cited in footnote 1) for more on the accounting treatment of leases.

5. There are, however, certain legal differences between loans and leases. In the event of liquidation in bankruptcy, a lessor is entitled to take possession of the leased asset, and if the value of the asset is less than the required payments under the lease, the lessor can enter a claim (as a general creditor) for 1 year's lease payments. Also, after bankruptcy has been declared but before the case has been resolved, lease payments may be continued, whereas all payments on debts are generally stopped. In a reorganization, the lessor receives the asset plus 3 years' lease payments if needed to cover the value of the lease. The lender under a secured loan arrangement has a security interest in the asset; this means that, if the asset is sold, then the lender will be given the proceeds and the full unsatisfied portion of the lender's claim will be treated as a general creditor obligation. It is not possible to state, as a general rule, whether a supplier of capital is in a stronger position as a secured creditor or as a lessor. However, in certain situations, lessors may bear less risk than secured lenders if financial distress occurs.

If disclosure of the lease in our Table 19-1 example were not made, then Firm L's investors could be deceived into thinking its financial position is stronger than it really is. Thus, even before FASB Statement 13 was issued, firms were required to disclose the existence of long-term leases in footnotes to their financial statements. At that time, it was debated as to whether or not investors recognized fully the impact of leases and, in effect, would see that Firms B and L were in essentially the same financial position. Some people argued that leases were not fully recognized, even by sophisticated investors. If this were the case, then leasing could alter the capital structure decision in a significant manner—a firm could increase its true leverage through a lease arrangement, and this procedure would have a smaller effect on its cost of conventional debt, r_d, and on its cost of equity, r_s, than if it had borrowed directly and reflected this fact on its balance sheet. These benefits of leasing would accrue to existing investors at the expense of new investors, who would be deceived because the firm's balance sheet did not reflect its true financial leverage.

The question of whether investors were truly deceived was debated but never resolved. Those who believed strongly in efficient markets thought investors were not deceived and that footnotes were sufficient, while those who questioned market efficiency thought all leases should be capitalized. Statement 13 represents a compromise between these two positions, though one that is tilted heavily toward those who favor capitalization.

A lease is classified as a capital lease—and hence must be capitalized and shown directly on the balance sheet—if one or more of the following conditions exist.

1. Under the terms of the lease, ownership of the property is effectively transferred from the lessor to the lessee.
2. The lessee can purchase the property at less than its true market value when the lease expires.
3. The lease runs for a period equal to or greater than 75% of the asset's life. Thus, if an asset has a 10-year life and the lease is written for 8 years, the lease must be capitalized.
4. The present value of the lease payments is equal to or greater than 90% of the initial value of the asset.[6]

These rules, together with strong footnote disclosure rules for operating leases, were supposed to be sufficient to ensure that no one would be fooled by lease financing. Thus, leases should be regarded as debt for capital structure purposes, and they should have the same effects as debt on r_d and r_s. Therefore, leasing is not likely to permit a firm to use more financial leverage than could be obtained with conventional debt.

Self Test

Why is lease financing sometimes referred to as off–balance sheet financing?

What is the intent of FASB Statement 13?

What is the difference in the balance sheet treatment of a lease that is capitalized versus one that is not?

---

6. The discount rate used to calculate the present value of the lease payments must be the lower of (1) the rate used by the lessor to establish the lease payments (this rate is discussed later in the chapter) or (2) the rate of interest that the lessee would have to pay for new debt with a maturity equal to that of the lease. Also, note that any maintenance payments embedded in the lease payment must be stripped out prior to checking this condition.

OFF–BALANCE SHEET FINANCING: IS IT GOING TO DISAPPEAR?

There is currently (mid-2011) a movement to standardize global accounting regulations, with the IASB (International Accounting Standards Board) and the FASB working toward this goal. One element of any agreement will be the treatment of leases. It appears likely that the FASB and IASB will require all leases to be capitalized, even those that are now classified as operating leases. This could have a huge impact on many companies' financial statements. For example, Credit Suisse estimated that the S&P 500 firms use about $369 billion in assets that are in the form of operating leases. As such, these are not shown as either assets or liabilities and instead are off the balance sheets. Putting these leases on the balance sheets by capitalizing them would boost the average liabilities by about 2%, but the impact would be much higher for some companies. This might be painful for businesses, but it certainly would help investors identify a company's obligations and liabilities.

19.4 Evaluation by the Lessee

WEB

See **Ch19 Tool Kit.xls** on the textbook's Web site for all calculations.

Leases are evaluated by both the lessee and the lessor. The lessee must determine whether leasing an asset is less costly than buying it, and the lessor must decide whether the lease payments provide a satisfactory return on the capital invested in the leased asset. This section focuses on the lessee's analysis.

In the typical case, the events leading to a lease arrangement follow the sequence described below. We should note that a degree of uncertainty exists regarding the theoretically correct way to evaluate lease-versus-purchase decisions, and some very complex decision models have been developed to aid in the analysis. However, the simple analysis given here leads to the correct decision in all the cases we have ever encountered.

WEB

See **Web Extension 19A** on the textbook's Web site for more information on such feedback effects.

1. When the firm decides to acquire a particular building or piece of equipment, the decision is based on regular capital budgeting procedures. Whether or not to acquire the asset is *not* part of the typical lease analysis—in a lease analysis, we are concerned simply with whether to obtain the use of the machine by lease or by purchase. Thus, for the lessee, the lease decision is typically just a financing decision. However, if the effective cost of capital obtained by leasing is substantially lower than the cost of debt, then the cost of capital used in the capital budgeting decision would have to be recalculated, and perhaps projects formerly deemed unacceptable might become acceptable. Such feedback effects usually are very small and can safely be ignored.
2. Once the firm has decided to acquire the asset, the next question is how to finance it. Well-run businesses do not have excess cash lying around, so capital to finance new assets must be obtained from some source.
3. Funds to purchase the asset could be obtained from internally generated cash flows, by borrowing, or by selling new equity. Alternatively, the asset could be leased. Because of the capitalization/disclosure provision for leases, leasing normally has the same capital structure effect as borrowing.
4. As indicated earlier, a lease is comparable to a loan in the sense that the firm is required to make a specified series of payments, and a failure to meet these payments could result in bankruptcy. If a company has a target capital structure, then $1 of lease financing displaces $1 of debt financing.

Thus, the most appropriate comparison is lease financing versus debt financing. Note that the analysis should compare the cost of leasing with the cost of debt financing *regardless* of how the asset purchase is actually financed. The asset may be purchased with available cash or with cash raised by issuing stock, but since leasing is a substitute for debt financing and has the same capital structure effect, the appropriate comparison would still be with debt financing.

To illustrate the basic elements of lease analysis, consider this simplified example. (See *Ch19 Tool Kit.xls* on the textbook's Web site for this analysis.) The Thompson-Grammatikos Company (TGC) needs a 2-year asset that costs $100 million, and the company must choose between leasing and buying the asset. TGC's tax rate is 40%. If the asset is purchased, the bank would lend TGC the $100 million at a rate of 10% on a 2-year, simple interest loan. Thus, the firm would have to pay the bank $10 million in interest at the end of each year *and* return the $100 million of principal at the end of Year 2. For simplicity, assume that: (1) TGC could depreciate the asset over 2 years for tax purposes by the straight-line method if it is purchased, resulting in tax depreciation of $50 million and tax savings of T(Depreciation) = 0.4($50) = $20 million in each year; and (2) the asset's value at the end of 2 years will be $0.

WEB

See *Ch19 Tool Kit.xls* on the textbook's Web site for this analysis.

Alternatively, TGC could lease the asset under a guideline lease (by a special IRS ruling) for 2 years for a payment of $55 million at the end of each year. The analysis for the lease-versus-borrow decision consists of (1) estimating the cash flows associated with borrowing and buying the asset—that is, the flows associated with debt financing; (2) estimating the cash flows associated with leasing the asset; and (3) comparing the two financing methods to determine which has the lower present value costs. Figure 19-1 reports the borrow-and-buy flows, set up to produce a cash flow time line for owning option.

The net cash flow for owning is zero in Year 0, positive in Year 1, and negative in Year 2. The operating cash flows are not shown, but they must, of course, have a PV greater than the PV of the financing costs or else TGC would not want to acquire the asset. Because the operating cash flows will be the same regardless of whether the asset is leased or purchased, they can be ignored.

Figure 19-1 also shows the cash flows associated with leasing. Note that the two sets of cash flows reflect the tax deductibility of interest and depreciation if the asset is purchased or the deductibility of lease payments if it is leased. Thus, the net cash flows include the tax savings from these items.[7]

To compare the cost streams of buying versus leasing, we must put them on a present value basis. As we explain later, the correct discount rate is the after-tax cost of debt, which for TGC is 10%(1 − 0.4) = 6.0%. Applying this rate, we find the present value of the ownership cash flows to be $63.33 million versus a present value of leasing cash flows of $60.50 million. The cost of ownership and leasing are the negatives of the PVs: The PVs are based on cash flows, and a cost is a negative cash flow.

We define the **net advantage to leasing (NAL)** as follows:

$$\text{NAL} = \text{PV cost of owning} - \text{PV cost of leasing} \qquad (19\text{–}1)$$

For TGC, the NAL is $63.33 − $60.50 = $2.83 million.

---

7. If the lease had not met IRS guidelines, then ownership would effectively reside with the lessee, and TGC would depreciate the asset for tax purposes whether it was leased or purchased. However, only the implied interest portion of the lease payment would be tax deductible. Thus, the analysis for a nonguideline lease would consist of simply comparing the after-tax financing flows on the loan with the after-tax lease payment stream.

Figure 19-1   **Analysis of the TGC Lease-versus-Buy Decision (Millions of Dollars)**

	A	B	C	D	E
79				Year	
80			0	1	2
81	*Cost of Owning*				
82	Equipment cost		($100.00)		
83	Loan amount		$100.00		
84	Interest expense			($10.00)	($10.00)
85	Tax savings from interest			$4.00	$4.00
86	Principal repayment				($100.00)
87	Tax savings from depr.			$20.00	$20.00
88	Net cash flow		$0.00	$14.00	($86.00)
99	PV ownership CF @ 6%		($63.33)		
90	Cost of ownership		$63.33		
91					
92	*Cost of Leasing*				
93	Lease payment			($55.00)	($55.00)
94	Tax savings from lease			$22.00	$22.00
95	Net cash flow		$0.00	($33.00)	($33.00)
96	PV of leasing CF @ 6%		($60.50)		
97	Cost of leasing		$60.50		
98					
99	*Net advantage to leasing (NAL)*				
100	NAL = Cost of ownership – cost of leasing =				$2.83

WEB

See *Ch19 Tool Kit.xls* on the textbook's Web site for all calculations.

Now we examine a more realistic example, one from the Anderson Company, which is conducting a lease analysis on some assembly line equipment it will procure during the coming year. (See *Ch19 Tool Kit.xls* on the textbook's Web site for this analysis.) The following data have been collected.

1. Anderson plans to acquire automated assembly line equipment with a 10-year life at a cost of $10 million, delivered and installed. However, Anderson plans to use the equipment for only 5 years and then discontinue the product line.
2. Anderson can borrow the required $10 million at a pre-tax cost of 10%.
3. The equipment's estimated scrap value is $50,000 after 10 years of use, but its estimated salvage value after only 5 years of use is $2,000,000. Thus, if Anderson buys the equipment, it would expect to receive $2,000,000 before taxes when the equipment is sold in 5 years. In leasing, the asset's value at the end of the lease is called its **residual value.**
4. Anderson can lease the equipment for 5 years for an annual rental charge of $2,600,000, payable at the beginning of each year, but the lessor will own the equipment upon the expiration of the lease. (The lease payment schedule is established by the potential lessor, as described in the next section, and Anderson can accept it, reject it, or negotiate modifications.)
5. The lease contract stipulates that the lessor will maintain the equipment at no additional charge to Anderson. However, if Anderson borrows and buys, it will have to bear the cost of maintenance, which will be done by the equipment manufacturer at a fixed contract rate of $500,000 per year, payable at the beginning of each year.

6. The equipment falls in the MACRS 5-year class, Anderson's marginal tax rate is 35%, and the lease qualifies as a guideline lease.

Figure 19-2 shows the steps involved in the analysis. Part I of the table is devoted to the costs of borrowing and buying. The company borrows $10 million and uses it to pay for the equipment, so these two items net out to zero and thus are not shown in the figure. Then, the company makes the *after-tax* payments shown in Line 1. In Year 1, the after-tax interest charge is 0.10($10 million)(0.65) = $650,000, and other payments are calculated similarly. The $10 million loan is repaid at the end of Year 5. Line 2 shows the maintenance cost. Line 3 gives the maintenance tax savings. Line 4 contains the annual depreciation tax savings, which are the depreciation expenses multiplied by the tax rate. The notes to Figure 19-2 explain the depreciation calculation. Lines 5 and 6 contain the residual (or salvage) value cash flows. The tax is on the excess of the residual value over the asset's book value, not on the full residual value. Line 7 contains the net cash flows, and Line 8 shows the net present value of these flows discounted at 6.5%. Line 9 reports the cost of owning (which is the negative of the PV of cash flows).

WEB

See **Ch19 Tool Kit.xls** on the textbook's Web site for all calculations.

Figure 19-2 Anderson Company: Lease Analysis (Thousands of Dollars)

	A B	C	D	E	F	G	H
140				Year			
141		0	1	2	3	4	5
142	I. Cost of Owning						
143	1. After-tax loan payments		($650)	($650)	($650)	($650)	($10,650)
144	2. Maintenance cost	($500)	(500)	(500)	(500)	(500)	
145	3. Maintenance tax savings	175	175	175	175	175	
146	4. Depreciation tax savings		700	1,120	672	403	403
147	5. Residual value						2,000
148	6. Tax on residual value						(498)
149	7. Net cash flow	($325)	($275)	$145	($303)	($572)	($8,745)
150	8. PV ownership CF @ 6.5%	($7,534)					
151	9. Cost of ownership	$7,534					
152							
153	II. Cost of Leasing						
154	10. Lease payment	($2,600)	($2,600)	($2,600)	($2,600)	($2,600)	
155	11. Tax savings from lease	910	910	910	910	910	
156	12. Net cash flow	($1,690)	($1,690)	($1,690)	($1,690)	($1,690)	$0
157	13. PV of leasing CF @ 6.5%	($7,480)					
158	14. Cost of leasing	$7,480					
159							
160	III. Net advantage to leasing (NAL)						
161	15. NAL = Cost of ownership – cost of leasing	=		$54			

Notes:
(1) The after-tax loan payments consist of after-tax interest for Years 1–4 and after-tax interest plus the principal amount in Year 5.
(2) The net cash flows shown in Lines 7 and 11 are discounted at the lessee's after-tax cost of debt, 6.5%.
(3) The MACRS depreciation allowances are 0.20, 0.32, 0.192, 0.1152, and 0.1152 in Years 1 through 5, respectively. Thus, the depreciation expense is 0.20($10,000) = $2,000 in Year 1, and so on. The depreciation tax savings in each year is 0.35(Depreciation).
(4) The residual value is $2,000, while the book value is $576. Thus, Anderson would have to pay 0.35($2,000 − $576) = $498.4 in taxes, producing a net after-tax residual value of $2,000 − $498.4 = $1,501.6. These amounts are shown in Lines 5 and 6 in the cost-of-owning analysis.

Part II of Figure 19-2 analyzes the lease. The lease payments, shown in Line 10, are $2,600,000 per year; this rate, which includes maintenance, was established by the prospective lessor and offered to Anderson Equipment. If Anderson accepts the lease then the full amount will be a deductible expense, so the annual tax savings, shown in Line 11, are 0.35(Lease payment) = 0.35($2,600,000) = $910,000. Thus, the after-tax cost of the lease payment is Lease payment − Tax savings = $2,600,000 − $910,000 = $1,690,000. This amount is shown in Line 12 for Years 0 through 4.

The next step is to compare the net cost of owning with the net cost of leasing. However, we must first put the annual cash flows of leasing and borrowing on a common basis. This requires converting them to present values, which brings up the question of the proper rate at which to discount the costs. Because leasing is a substitute for debt, most analysts recommend that the company's cost of debt be used, and this rate seems reasonable in our example. Moreover, because the cash flows are after taxes, *we should use the **after-tax cost of debt***, which is 10%(1 − T) = 10%(0.65) = 6.5%. Accordingly, we discount the net cash flows in Lines 7 and 12 using a rate of 6.5%. We then convert the PVs to costs of owning and leasing, shown in Lines 9 and 14: The resulting present values are $7,534,000 for the cost of owning and $7,480,000 for the cost of leasing. The financing method that produces the smaller present value of costs is the one that should be selected. Here the net advantage to leasing is

$$\text{NAL} = \text{PV cost of owning} - \text{PV cost of leasing}$$
$$= \$7,534,000 - \$7,480,000$$
$$= \$54,000$$

The PV cost of owning exceeds the PV cost of leasing, so the NAL is positive. Therefore, Anderson should lease the equipment.[8]

In this example, Anderson did not plan on using the equipment beyond Year 5. But if Anderson instead had planned on using the equipment after Year 5, the analysis would be modified. For example, suppose Anderson planned on using the equipment for 10 years and the lease allowed Anderson to purchase the equipment at the residual value. First, how do we modify the cash flows due to owning? Lines 5 and 6 (for residual value and tax on residual value) in Figure 19-2 will be zero at Year 5, because Anderson will not sell the equipment then.[9] However, there will be the additional remaining year of depreciation tax savings in Line 4 for Year 6. There will be no entries for Years 6–10 for Line 1, the after-tax loan payments, because the loan is completely repaid at Year 5. Also, there will be no incremental maintenance costs and tax savings in Lines 2 and 3 for Years 6–10, because Anderson will have to perform its own maintenance on the equipment in those years whether it initially purchases the equipment or whether it leases the equipment for 5 years and then purchases it. Either way, Anderson will own the equipment in Years 6–10 and must pay for its own maintenance.

Second, how do we modify the cash flows if Anderson leases the equipment and then purchases it at Year 5? There will be a negative cash flow at Year 5 reflecting

---

8. The more complicated methods that exist for analyzing leasing generally focus on the issue of what discount rate should be used to discount the cash flows—especially the residual value, since its risk might be different from the risk of the other cash flows. For more on residual value risk, see Chapter 8 of Schallheim's *Lease or Buy?* (cited in footnote 1).
9. There might be a salvage value in Line 5 at Year 10 (and a corresponding tax adjustment in Line 6) if the equipment is not completely worn out or obsolete.

the purchase. Because the equipment was originally classified with a MACRS 5-year life, Anderson will be allowed to depreciate the purchased equipment (even though it is not new) with a MACRS 5-year life. Therefore, in Years 6–10, there will be after-tax savings due to depreciation.[10] Given the modified cash flows, we can calculate the NAL just as we did in Figure 19-2.

In this section, we focused on the dollar cost of leasing versus borrowing and buying, which is analogous to the NPV method used in capital budgeting. A second method that lessees can use to evaluate leases focuses on the percentage cost of leasing and is analogous to the IRR method used in capital budgeting.

WEB

The percentage approach is discussed in **Web Extension 19B** on the textbook's Web site.

Self Test

Explain how the cash flows are structured in order to estimate the net advantage to leasing.

What discount rate should be used to evaluate a lease? Why?

Define the term *net advantage to leasing* (NAL).

19.5 Evaluation by the Lessor

Thus far, we have considered leasing only from the lessee's viewpoint. It is also useful to analyze the transaction as the lessor sees it: Is the lease a good investment for the party who must put up the money? The lessor will generally be a specialized leasing company, a bank or bank affiliate, an individual or group of individuals organized as a limited partnership or limited liability corporation, or a manufacturer such as IBM or GM that uses leasing as a sales tool. The specialized leasing companies are often owned by profitable companies such as General Electric, which owns General Electric Capital, the largest leasing company in the world. Investment banking houses such as Merrill Lynch also set up and/or work with specialized leasing companies, where brokerage clients' money is made available to leasing customers in deals that permit the investors to share in tax shelters provided by leases.

Any potential lessor needs to know the rate of return on the capital invested in the lease, and this information is also useful to the prospective lessee: Lease terms on large leases are generally negotiated, so the lessee should know what return the lessor is earning. The lessor's analysis involves (1) determining the net cash outlay, which is usually the invoice price of the leased equipment less any lease payments made in advance; (2) determining the periodic cash inflows, which consist of the lease payments minus both income taxes and any maintenance expense the lessor must bear; (3) estimating the after-tax residual value of the property when the lease expires; and (4) determining whether the rate of return on the lease exceeds the lessor's opportunity cost of capital or, equivalently, whether the NPV of the lease exceeds zero.

19.5a Analysis by the Lessor

To illustrate the lessor's analysis, we assume the same facts as for the Anderson Company lease, plus the following: (1) The potential lessor is a wealthy individual whose current income is in the form of interest and whose marginal federal-plus-state income tax rate, T, is 40%. (2) The investor can buy 5-year bonds that have a 9%

---

10. There will also be an after-tax cash flow at Year 10 that depends on the salvage value of the equipment at that date.

yield to maturity, providing an after-tax yield of $(9\%)(1 - T) = (9\%)(0.6) = 5.4\%$. This is the after-tax return the investor can obtain on alternative investments of similar risk. (3) The before-tax residual value is $2,000,000. Because the asset will be depreciated to a book value of $600,000 at the end of the 5-year lease, $1,400,000 of this $2 million will be taxable at the 40% rate by the depreciation recapture rule, so the lessor can expect to receive $2,000,000 - 0.4(\$1,400,000) = \$1,440,000$ after taxes from the sale of the equipment after the lease expires.

The lessor's cash flows are developed in Figure 19-3. Here we see that the lease as an investment has a net present value of $81,000. On a present value basis, the investor who invests in the lease rather than in the 9% bonds (5.4% after taxes) is better off by $81,000, indicating that he or she should be willing to write the lease. As we saw earlier, the lease is also advantageous to Anderson Company, so the transaction should be completed.

The investor can also calculate the lease investment's internal rate of return based on the net cash flows shown in Line 9 of Figure 19-3. The IRR of the lease, which is that discount rate that forces the NPV of the lease to zero, is 5.8%. Thus, the lease provides a 5.8% after-tax return to this 40% tax rate investor, which exceeds the 5.4% after-tax return on 9% bonds. So, using either the IRR or the NPV method, the lease would appear to be a satisfactory investment.[11]

19.5b Setting the Lease Payment

So far we have evaluated leases assuming that the lease payments have already been specified. However, in large leases the parties generally sit down and work out

Figure 19-3 Lease Analysis from the Lessor's Viewpoint (Thousands of Dollars)

	A	B	C	D	E	F	G	H
220						Year		
221			0	1	2	3	4	5
222	*Cost of Owning*							
223	1. Net purchase price		($10,000)					
224	2. Maintenance cost		(500)	($500)	($500)	($500)	($500)	
225	3. Maintenance tax savings		200	200	200	200	200	
226	4. Depreciation tax savings[a]			800	1,280	768	461	$461
227	5. Lease payment		2,600	2,600	2,600	2,600	2,600	
228	6. Tax on lease payment		(1,040)	(1,040)	(1,040)	(1,040)	(1,040)	
229	7. Residual value							2,000
230	8. Tax on residual value[b]							(570)
231	9. Net cash flow		($8,740)	$2,060	$2,540	$2,028	$1,721	$1,891
232	10. NPV @ 5.4%	=	$81					
233	11. IRR	=	5.8%					
234	12. MIRR	=	5.6%					

[a]Depreciation tax savings = Depreciation × (Tax rate).
[b](Residual value − Book value) × (Tax rate).

---

11. Note that the lease investment is actually slightly more risky than the alternative bond investment because the residual value cash flow is less certain than a principal repayment. Thus, the lessor might require an expected return somewhat above the 5.4% promised on a bond investment.

an agreement on the size of the lease payments, with these payments being set so as to provide the lessor with some specific rate of return. In situations in which the lease terms are not negotiated, which is often the case for small leases, the lessor must still go through the same type of analysis, setting terms that provide a target rate of return and then offering these terms to the potential lessee on a take-it-or-leave-it basis.

To illustrate all this, suppose the potential lessor described earlier, after examining other alternative investment opportunities, decides that the 5.4% after-tax bond return is too low to use for evaluating the lease and that the required after-tax return on the lease should be 6.0%. What lease payment schedule would provide this return?

To answer this question, note again that Figure 19-3 contains the lessor's cash flow analysis. We used the *Excel* Goal Seek function to set the lessor's IRR equal to 6% by changing the lease payment; see the analysis in ***Ch19 Tool Kit.xls***. We found that the lessor must set the lease payment at $2,621,278 to obtain an after-tax rate of return of 6.0%. If this lease payment is not acceptable to the lessee, Anderson Company, then it may not be possible to strike a deal. Naturally, competition among leasing companies forces lessors to build market-related returns into their lease payment schedules.[12]

If the inputs to the lessee and the lessor are identical, then a positive NAL to the lessee implies an equal but negative NPV to the lessor. However, *conditions are often such that leasing can provide net benefits to both parties. This situation arises because of differentials in taxes, in borrowing rates, in estimated residual values, or in the ability to bear the residual value risk.* We will explore these issues in detail in the next section.

Note that the lessor can, under certain conditions, increase the return on the lease by borrowing some of the funds used to purchase the leased asset. Such a lease is called a **leveraged lease.** Whether or not a lease is leveraged has no effect on the lessee's analysis, but it can have a significant effect on the cash flows to the lessor and hence on the lessor's expected rate of return.

WEB

We discuss leveraged leases in more detail in ***Web Extension 19C*** on the textbook's Web site.

Self Test

What discount rate is used in a lessor's NPV analysis?

Under what conditions will the lessor's NPV be the negative of the lessee's NAL?

19.6 Other Issues in Lease Analysis

The basic methods of analysis used by lessees and lessors were presented in the previous sections. However, some other issues warrant discussion.[13]

19.6a Estimated Residual Value

It is important to note that the lessor owns the property upon expiration of a lease, so the lessor has claim to the asset's residual value. Superficially, it would appear that if residual values are expected to be large, then owning would have

---

12. For a discussion of realized returns on lease contracts, see Ronald C. Lease, John J. McConnell, and James S. Schallheim, "Realized Returns and the Default and Prepayment Experience of Financial Leasing Contracts," *Financial Management,* Summer 1990, pp. 11–20.

13. For a description of lease analysis in practice as well as a comprehensive bibliography of the leasing literature, see Tarun K. Mukherjee, "A Survey of Corporate Leasing Analysis," *Financial Management,* Autumn 1991, pp. 96–107.

an advantage over leasing. However, this apparent advantage does not hold up. If expected residual values are large—as they may be under inflation for certain types of equipment and also if real estate is involved—then competition between leasing companies and other financing sources, as well as competition among leasing companies themselves, will force leasing rates down to the point where potential residual values are fully recognized in the lease contract. Thus, the existence of large residual values is not likely to result in materially higher costs for leasing.

19.6b Increased Credit Availability

As noted earlier, leasing is sometimes said to be advantageous for firms that are seeking to increase their financial leverage. First, it is sometimes argued that firms can obtain more money, and for longer terms, under a lease arrangement than under a loan secured by a specific piece of equipment. Second, since some leases do not appear on the balance sheet, lease financing has been said to give the firm a stronger appearance in a *superficial* credit analysis and thus to permit the firm to use more leverage than would be possible if it did not lease.

There may be some truth to these claims for smaller firms. However, since firms are required to capitalize financial leases and to report them on their balance sheets,

WHAT YOU DON'T KNOW CAN HURT YOU!

A leasing decision seems to be pretty straightforward, at least from a financial perspective: Calculate the NAL for the lease and undertake it if the NAL is positive. Right? But tracking down all the financial implications from lease contract provisions can be difficult, requiring the lessee to make assumptions about future costs that are not explicitly spelled out in the lease contract. For example, consider the purchase option embedded in the lease that Rojacks Food Stores undertook with GE Capital for restaurant equipment. Upon expiration, the lease allowed Rojacks either to return the equipment or purchase it at the current market value. When the lease expired, GE set a purchase price that was much higher than Rojacks expected. Rojacks needed the equipment for its day-to-day operations so it couldn't just return the equipment without disrupting its business. Ultimately, Rojacks hired an independent appraiser for the equipment and negotiated a lower purchase price—but without the appraiser, Rojacks would have been stuck with the price GE decided to set for the equipment.

The Rojacks–GE situation isn't that unusual. Lessors often use high expected residual values or high expected penalties to offset low lease payments. In addition, some contracts may require that (1) all of the equipment covered under a lease must either be purchased or returned in its entirety, (2) equipment that is moved must be purchased, (3) large fees must be paid even for minor damage or missing parts, and/or (4) equipment must be returned in its original packaging. These conditions impose costs on the lessee when the lease is terminated and should be considered explicitly when making the leasing decision.

The moral of the story for lessees is to read the fine print and request changes to objectionable terms before signing the lease. Here are some ways to reduce the likelihood of unanticipated costs: (1) specify residual value as a percentage of the initial cost of the equipment; (2) allow for portions of the equipment to be returned and portions to be purchased at the end of the lease; and (3) specify that disagreements will be adjudicated by arbitration.

Source: Linda Corman, "(Don't) Look Deep into My Lease," *CFO,* July 2006, pp. 71–75.

this point is of questionable validity for any firm large enough to have audited financial statements. However, leasing can be a way to circumvent existing loan covenants. If restrictive covenants prohibit a firm from issuing more debt but fail to restrict lease payments, then the firm could effectively increase its leverage by leasing additional assets. Also, firms that are in poor financial condition and face possible bankruptcy may be able to obtain lease financing at a lower cost than comparable debt financing because (1) lessors often have a more favorable position than lenders should the lessee actually go bankrupt, and (2) lessors that specialize in certain types of equipment may be in a better position to dispose of repossessed equipment than banks or other lenders.

19.6c Real Estate Leases

Most of our examples have focused on equipment leasing. However, leasing originated with real estate, and such leases still constitute a huge segment of total lease financing. (We distinguish between housing rentals and long-term business leases; our concern is with business leases.) Retailers lease many of their stores. In some situations, retailers have no choice but to lease—this is true of locations in malls and certain office buildings. In other situations, they have a choice of building and owning versus leasing. Law firms and accounting firms, for example, can choose between buying their own facilities or leasing on a long-term basis (up to 20 or more years).

The type of lease-versus-purchase analysis we discussed in this chapter is just as applicable for real estate as for equipment—conceptually, there is no difference. Of course, such things as maintenance, who the other tenants will be, what alterations can be made, who will pay for alterations, and the like become especially important with real property, but the analytical procedures upon which the lease-versus-buy decision is based are no different from any other lease analysis.

19.6d Vehicle Leases

Vehicle leasing is very popular today both for large corporations and for individuals, especially professionals such as MBAs, doctors, lawyers, and accountants. For corporations, the key factor involved with transportation is often maintenance and disposal of used vehicles—the leasing companies are specialists here, and many businesses prefer to "outsource" services related to autos and trucks. For individuals, leasing is often more convenient, and it may be easier to justify tax deductions on leased than on owned vehicles. Also, most auto leasing to individuals is through dealers. These dealers (and manufacturers) use leasing as a sales tool, and they often make the terms quite attractive—especially when it comes to the down payment, which may be nonexistent in the case of a lease.

Vehicle leasing also permits many individuals to drive more expensive cars than would otherwise be possible. For example, the monthly payment on a new BMW might be $1,500 when financed with a 3-year loan, but the same car, if leased for 3 years, might cost only $749 a month. At first glance, it appears that leasing is less expensive than owning because the monthly payment is so much lower. However, such a simplistic analysis ignores the fact that payments end after the loan is paid off but continue indefinitely under leasing. By using the techniques described in this chapter, individuals can assess the true costs associated with auto leases and then rationally judge the merits of each type of auto financing.

19.6e Leasing and Tax Laws[14]

The ability to structure leases that are advantageous to both lessor and lessee depends in large part on tax laws. The four major tax factors that influence leasing are (1) investment tax credits, (2) depreciation rules, (3) tax rates, and (4) the alternative minimum tax. In this section, we briefly discuss each of these factors and how they influence leasing decisions.

The investment tax credit (ITC), when it is allowed, is a direct reduction of taxes that occurs when a firm purchases new capital equipment. Prior to 1987, firms could immediately deduct up to 10% of the cost of new capital investments from their corporate tax bills. Thus, a company that bought a $1,000,000 mainframe computer system would get a $100,000 reduction in current-year taxes. Because the ITC goes to the owner of the capital asset, low-tax-bracket companies that could not

LEASE SECURITIZATION

Compared with many markets, the leasing market is fragmented and inefficient. There are millions of potential lessees, including all equipment users. Some are in high tax brackets, some are in low brackets. Some are financially sophisticated, some are not. Some have excellent credit ratings, some have poor credit. On the other side of the market are millions of potential lessors—including equipment manufacturers, banks, and individual investors—with different tax brackets and risk tolerances. If each lessee had to negotiate a separate deal for each lease, then information and search costs would be so high that few leases would be written.

Tax laws complicate the picture. For example, the alternative minimum tax (AMT) often has the effect of limiting the amount of depreciation a firm can utilize. In addition, a firm can't take a full half-year's depreciation on purchases in the fourth quarter if those purchases amount to more than 40% of total annual purchases. In this case the firm can take only a half-quarter's depreciation, which is the equivalent of one-eighth of a year's depreciation.

Lease brokers have for many years served as facilitators in this complicated and inefficient market. Working with many different equipment manufacturers and lenders, brokers are in a position to match lessees with appropriate lessors in such a way that the full benefit of tax laws can be utilized.

Lease securitization, a new procedure, is the ultimate method of matching lessees with appropriate lessors. The first step is to create a portfolio consisting of numerous leases. The second step is to divide the leasing cash flows into different streams of income, called *tranches*. For example, one tranche might contain only lease payments, which would appeal to an investor in a low tax bracket. A second tranche might consist of depreciation, which a high-tax-bracket investor could use to shelter income from other sources. A third might contain the residual cash flows, which will occur in the future when the leases end. This tranche would appeal to a high-tax-bracket investor who can take some risk. Tranches can also be allocated according to the credit rating of the lessees, allowing investors with different risk tolerances to take on their desired level of risk.

In addition, a company might obtain a lease in its fourth quarter, but if this is the third quarter of the *lessor's* fiscal year, the lessor can take a full half-year's depreciation.

Sound complicated? It is, but it's an efficient answer to an inefficient market.

Source: SMG Fairfax, Knoxville, Tennessee.

---

14. See Chapters 3 and 6 of Schallheim's *Lease or Buy?* (cited in footnote 1) for an in-depth discussion of tax effects on leasing.

otherwise use the ITC could use leasing as a vehicle to pass immediate tax savings to high–tax–bracket lessors. The ITC is not currently in effect, but it could be reinstated in the future. If the ITC is put back into law, leasing will become especially attractive to low-tax-bracket firms.

Owners recover their investments in capital assets through depreciation, which is a tax-deductible expense. Because of the time value of money, the faster an asset can be depreciated, the greater the tax advantages of ownership. Recent tax law changes have tended to slow depreciation write-offs, thus reducing the value of ownership. This has also reduced the advantage to leasing by low-tax-bracket lessees from high-tax-bracket lessors. Any move to liberalize depreciation rules would tend to make leasing more desirable in many situations. The value of depreciation also depends on the firm's tax rate, because the depreciation tax saving equals the amount of depreciation multiplied by the tax rate. Thus, higher corporate tax rates mean greater ownership tax savings and hence more incentive for tax-driven leases.

Finally, the alternative minimum tax (AMT) also affects leasing activity. Corporations are permitted to use accelerated depreciation and other tax shelters on their tax books but then use straight-line depreciation for reporting results to shareholders. Thus, some firms report to the IRS that they are doing poorly, and hence pay little or no taxes, but report high earnings to shareholders. The corporate AMT, which is roughly computed by applying a 20% tax rate to the profits reported to shareholders, is designed to force highly profitable companies to pay at least some taxes even if they have tax shelters that push their taxable income to zero. In effect, all firms (and individuals) must compute the "regular" tax and the AMT tax, and then pay the higher of the two.

Companies with large AMT liabilities look for ways to reduce their tax bills by lowering reported income. Leasing can be beneficial here—a relatively short-term lease with high annual payments will increase reported expenses and thus lower reported profits. Note that the lease does not have to qualify as a guideline lease and be deducted for regular tax purposes—all that is needed is to lower reported income as shown on the income statement.

We see that tax laws and differential tax rates between lessors and lessees can be a motivating force for leasing. However, as we discuss in the next section, there are some sound nontax economic reasons why firms lease plants and equipment.

Self Test

Does leasing lead to increased credit availability?

How do tax laws affect leasing?

19.7 Other Reasons for Leasing

Up to this point, we have noted that tax rate or other differentials are generally necessary to make leasing attractive to both the lessee and lessor. If the lessee and lessor are facing different tax situations, including the alternative minimum tax, then it is often possible to structure a lease that is beneficial to both parties. However, there are other reasons that firms might want to lease an asset rather than buy it.

More than half of all commercial aircraft are leased, and smaller airlines, especially in developing nations, lease an especially high percentage of their planes. One of the reasons for this is that airlines can reduce their risks by leasing. If an airline purchased all its aircraft, it would be hampered in its ability to respond to changing market conditions. Because they have become specialists at matching airlines with available aircraft, the aircraft lessors (which are multibillion-dollar concerns) are quite good at managing the changing demand for different types of aircraft. This permits them to offer attractive lease terms. In this situation, *leasing provides operating flexibility.* Leasing is not necessarily less expensive than buying, but the operating flexibility is quite valuable.

Leasing is also an attractive alternative for many high-technology items that are subject to rapid and unpredictable technological obsolescence. Suppose a small rural hospital wants to buy a magnetic resonance imaging (MRI) device. If it buys the MRI equipment, then it is exposed to the risk of technological obsolescence. In a short time some new technology might lower the value of the current system and thus render the project unprofitable. Since it does not use much equipment of this nature, the hospital would bear a great deal of risk if it bought the MRI device. However, a lessor that specializes in state-of-the-art medical equipment would be exposed to significantly less risk. By purchasing and then leasing many different items, the lessor benefits from diversification. Of course, over time some items will probably lose more value than the lessor expected, but this will be offset by other items that retain more value than expected. Also, because such a leasing company will be especially familiar with the market for used medical equipment, it can refurbish the equipment and then get a better price in the resale market than could a remote rural hospital. For these reasons, leasing can reduce the risk of technological obsolescence.

Leasing can also be attractive when a firm is uncertain about the demand for its products or services and thus about how long the equipment will be needed. Again, consider the hospital industry. Hospitals often offer services that are dependent on a single staff member—for example, a physician who does liver transplants. To support the physician's practice, the hospital might have to invest millions in equipment that can be used only for this particular procedure. The hospital will charge for the use of the equipment, and if things go as expected, the investment will be profitable. However, if the physician leaves the hospital and if no replacement can be recruited, then the project is dead and the equipment becomes useless to the hospital. In this case, a lease with a cancellation clause would permit the hospital to simply return the equipment. The lessor would charge something for the cancellation clause, and this would lower the expected profitability of the project, but it would provide the hospital with an option to abandon the equipment, and the value of the option could easily exceed the incremental cost of the cancellation clause. The leasing company would be willing to write this option because it is in a better position to remarket the equipment, either by writing another lease or by selling it outright.

The leasing industry recently introduced a type of lease that even transfers some of a project's operating risk from the lessee to the lessor and also motivates the lessor to maintain the leased equipment in good working order. Instead of making a fixed rental payment, the lessee pays a fee each time the leased equipment is used. This type of lease originated with copy machines, where the lessee pays so much per month plus an additional amount per copy made. If the machine breaks down, no copies are made and the lessor's rental income declines. This motivates the lessor to repair the machine quickly.

This type of lease is also used in the health care industry, where it is called a "per-procedure lease." For example, a hospital might lease an X-ray machine for a fixed fee per X-ray, say, $5. If demand for the machine's X-rays is less than expected by the hospital, then revenues will be lower than expected but so will the machine's capital costs. Conversely, high demand would lead to higher than expected lease costs, but these would be offset by higher than expected revenues. By using a per-procedure lease, the hospital is converting a fixed cost for the equipment into a variable cost and thereby reducing the machine's operating leverage and break-even point. The net effect is to reduce the project's risk. Of course, the expected cost of a per-procedure lease might be more than the cost of a conventional lease, but the risk reduction benefit could be worth the cost. Note too that if the lessor writes a large number of per-procedure leases then much of the riskiness inherent in such leases can be eliminated by diversification, so the risk premiums that lessors build into per-procedure lease payments could be low enough to attract potential lessees.

Some companies also find leasing attractive because the lessor is able to provide servicing on favorable terms. For example, Virco Manufacturing, a company that makes school desks and other furniture, recently leased 25 truck tractors and 140 trailers that it uses to ship furniture from its plant. The lease agreement, with a large leasing company that specializes in purchasing, maintaining, and then reselling trucks, permitted the replacement of an aging fleet that Virco had built up over the years. "We are pretty good at manufacturing furniture, but we aren't very good at maintaining a truck fleet," said Virco's CFO.

There are other reasons that might cause a firm to lease an asset rather than buy it. Often these reasons are difficult to quantify and so cannot be easily incorporated into an NPV or IRR analysis. Nevertheless, a sound lease decision must begin with a quantitative analysis, and then qualitative factors can be considered before making the final lease-or-buy decision.[15]

Self Test

Describe some economic factors that might provide an advantage to leasing.

Summary

In the United States, more than 30% of all equipment is leased, as is a great deal of real estate. Consequently, leasing is an important financing vehicle. In this chapter, we discussed the leasing decision from the standpoints of both the lessee and lessor. The key concepts covered are listed below.

- The five most important types of lease agreement are the (1) **operating lease**; (2) **financial**, or **capital, lease**; (3) **sale-and-leaseback**; (4) **combination lease**; and (5) **synthetic lease**.
- The IRS has specific guidelines that apply to lease arrangements. A lease that meets these guidelines is called a **guideline**, or **tax-oriented, lease,** because the IRS permits the lessor to deduct the asset's depreciation and allows the lessee

---

15. For more on leasing, see Thomas J. Finucane, "Some Empirical Evidence on the Use of Financial Leases," *The Journal of Financial Research,* Fall 1988, pp. 321–333; and Lawrence D. Schall, "The Evaluation of Lease Financing Opportunities," *Midland Corporate Finance Journal,* Spring 1985, pp. 48–65.

to deduct the lease payments. A lease that does not meet the IRS guidelines is called a **non–tax-oriented lease,** in which case ownership for tax purposes resides with the lessee rather than the lessor.

- **FASB Statement 13** spells out the conditions under which a lease must be **capitalized** (shown directly on the balance sheet) as opposed to shown only in the notes to the financial statements. Generally, leases that run for a period equal to or greater than 75% of the asset's life must be capitalized.
- The lessee's analysis consists basically of a comparison of the PV of costs associated with leasing versus the PV of costs associated with owning. The difference in these costs is called the **net advantage to leasing (NAL).**
- One of the key issues in the lessee's analysis is the appropriate discount rate. A lease is a substitute for debt, cash flows in a lease analysis are stated on an after-tax basis, and cash flows are known with relative certainty, so the appropriate discount rate is the **lessee's after-tax cost of debt.** A higher discount rate may be used on the **residual value** if it is substantially riskier than the other flows.
- The lessor evaluates the lease as an **investment.** If the lease's NPV is greater than zero or if its IRR is greater than the lessor's opportunity cost, then the lease should be written.
- Leasing is motivated by various differences between lessees and lessors. Three of the most important reasons for leasing are (1) **tax rate differentials,** (2) leases in which the lessor is better able than the lessee to bear the **residual value risk,** and (3) situations in which the lessor can maintain the leased equipment more efficiently than the lessee can.
- *Web Extension 19A* explains **leasing feedback effects**; *Web Extension 19B* explains the **percentage cost of leasing**; and *Web Extension 19C* explains **leveraged leases.**

Questions

19-1 Define each of the following terms:
   a. Lessee; lessor
   b. Operating lease; financial lease; sale-and-leaseback; combination lease; synthetic lease; SPE
   c. Off–balance sheet financing; capitalizing
   d. FASB Statement 13
   e. Guideline lease
   f. Residual value
   g. Lessee's analysis; lessor's analysis
   h. Net advantage to leasing (NAL)
   i. Alternative minimum tax (AMT)

19-2 Distinguish between operating leases and financial leases. Would you be more likely to find an operating lease employed for a fleet of trucks or for a manufacturing plant?

19-3 Are lessees more likely to be in higher or lower income tax brackets than lessors?

19-4 Commercial banks moved heavily into equipment leasing during the early 1970s, acting as lessors. One major reason for this invasion of the leasing industry was to gain the benefits of accelerated depreciation and the investment tax credit on leased equipment. During this same period, commercial banks were investing heavily in municipal securities, and they were also making loans to real estate investment trusts (REITs). In the mid-1970s, these REITs got into such serious difficulty that many banks suffered large losses on their REIT loans. Explain how its investments in municipal bonds and REITs could reduce a bank's willingness to act as a lessor.

19-5 One advantage of leasing voiced in the past is that it kept liabilities off the balance sheet, thus making it possible for a firm to obtain more leverage than it otherwise could have. This raised the question of whether or not both the lease obligation and the asset involved should be capitalized and shown on the balance sheet. Discuss the pros and cons of capitalizing leases and related assets.

19-6 Suppose there were no IRS restrictions on what constituted a valid lease. Explain, in a manner a legislator might understand, why some restrictions should be imposed. Illustrate your answer with numbers.

19-7 Suppose Congress enacted new tax law changes that would (1) permit equipment to be depreciated over a shorter period, (2) lower corporate tax rates, and (3) reinstate the investment tax credit. Discuss how each of these potential changes would affect the relative volume of leasing versus conventional debt in the U.S. economy.

19-8 In our Anderson Company example, we assumed that the lease could not be cancelled. What effect would a cancellation clause have on the lessee's analysis? On the lessor's analysis?

Problems   Answers Appear in Appendix B

Easy Problems 1–2

19-1 **Balance Sheet Effects** Reynolds Construction needs a piece of equipment that costs $200. Reynolds can either lease the equipment or borrow $200 from a local bank and buy the equipment. If the equipment is leased, the lease would *not* have to be capitalized. Reynolds's balance sheet prior to the acquisition of the equipment is as follows:

Current assets	$300	Debt	$400
Net fixed assets	500	Equity	400
Total assets	$800	Total claims	$800

    a. (1) What is Reynolds's current debt ratio?
        (2) What would be the company's debt ratio if it purchased the equipment?
        (3) What would be the debt ratio if the equipment were leased?
    b. Would the company's financial risk be different under the leasing and purchasing alternatives?

19-2 **Lease versus Buy** Consider the data in Problem 19-1. Assume that Reynolds's tax rate is 40% and that the equipment's depreciation would be $100 per year. If the company leased the asset on a 2-year lease, the payment would be $110 at the beginning of each year. If Reynolds borrowed and bought, the bank would charge 10% interest on the loan. In either case, the equipment is worth nothing after 2 years and will be discarded. Should Reynolds lease or buy the equipment?

Intermediate Problems 3–4

19-3 Balance Sheet Effects Two companies, Energen and Hastings Corporation, began operations with identical balance sheets. A year later, both required additional fixed assets at a cost of $50,000. Energen obtained a 5-year, $50,000 loan at an 8% interest rate from its bank. Hastings, on the other hand, decided to lease the required $50,000 capacity for 5 years, and an 8% return was built into the lease. The balance sheet for each company, before the asset increases, follows:

Current assets	$ 25,000	Debt	$ 50,000
Fixed assets	125,000	Equity	100,000
Total assets	$150,000	Total claims	$150,000

a. Show the balance sheets for both firms after the asset increases, and calculate each firm's new debt ratio. (Assume that the lease is not capitalized.)

b. Show how Hastings's balance sheet would look immediately after the financing if it capitalized the lease.

19-4 Lease versus Buy Big Sky Mining Company must install $1.5 million of new machinery in its Nevada mine. It can obtain a bank loan for 100% of the purchase price, or it can lease the machinery. Assume that the following facts apply.

(1) The machinery falls into the MACRS 3-year class.

(2) Under either the lease or the purchase, Big Sky must pay for insurance, property taxes, and maintenance.

(3) The firm's tax rate is 40%.

(4) The loan would have an interest rate of 15%.

(5) The lease terms call for $400,000 payments at the end of each of the next 4 years.

(6) Big Sky Mining has no use for the machine beyond the expiration of the lease, and the machine has an estimated residual value of $250,000 at the end of the 4th year.

What is the NAL of the lease?

Challenging Problem 5

19-5 Lease versus Buy Sadik Industries must install $1 million of new machinery in its Texas plant. It can obtain a bank loan for 100% of the required amount. Alternatively, a Texas investment banking firm that represents a group of investors believes it can arrange for a lease financing plan. Assume that the following facts apply.

(1) The equipment falls in the MACRS 3-year class.

(2) Estimated maintenance expenses are $50,000 per year.

(3) The firm's tax rate is 34%.

(4) If the money is borrowed, the bank loan will be at a rate of 14%, amortized in three equal installments at the end of each year.

(5) The tentative lease terms call for payments of $320,000 at the end of each year for 3 years. The lease is a guideline lease.

(6) Under the proposed lease terms, the lessee must pay for insurance, property taxes, and maintenance.

(7) Sadik must use the equipment if it is to continue in business, so it will almost certainly want to acquire the property at the end of the lease. If it does, then under the lease terms it can purchase the machinery at its fair market value at that time. The best estimate of this market value is $200,000, but it could be much higher or lower under certain circumstances.

To assist management in making the proper lease-versus-buy decision, you are asked to answer the following questions.

a. Assuming the lease can be arranged, should the firm lease or borrow and buy the equipment? Explain. (*Hint:* In this situation, the firm plans to use the asset beyond the term of the lease. Thus, the residual value becomes a *cost* to leasing in Year 3. The firm will depreciate the equipment it purchases under the purchase option starting in Year 3, using the MACRS 3-year class schedule. Depreciation will begin in the year in which the equipment is purchased, which is Year 3.)

b. Consider the $200,000 estimated residual value. Is it appropriate to discount it at the same rate as the other cash flows? Are the other cash flows all equally risky? (*Hint:* Riskier cash flows are normally discounted at higher rates, but when the cash flows are *costs* rather than *inflows*, the normal procedure must be reversed.)

Spreadsheet Problem

19-6 **Build a Model: Lessee's Analysis** Start with the partial model in the file *Ch19 P06 Build a Model.xls* on the textbook's Web site. As part of its overall plant modernization and cost reduction program, Western Fabrics's management has decided to install a new automated weaving loom. In the capital budgeting analysis of this equipment, the IRR of the project was found to be 20% versus the project's required return of 12%.

The loom has an invoice price of $250,000, including delivery and installation charges. The funds needed could be borrowed from the bank through a 4-year amortized loan at a 10% interest rate, with payments to be made at the end of each year. In the event the loom is purchased, the manufacturer will contract to maintain and service it for a fee of $20,000 per year paid at the end of each year. The loom falls in the MACRS 5-year class, and Western's marginal federal-plus-state tax rate is 40%.

Aubey Automation Inc., maker of the loom, has offered to lease the loom to Western for $70,000 upon delivery and installation (at t = 0) plus four additional annual lease payments of $70,000 to be made at the end of Years 1 to 4. (Note that there are five lease payments in total.) The lease agreement includes maintenance and servicing. Actually, the loom has an expected life of 8 years, at which time its expected salvage value is zero; however, after 4 years its market value is expected to equal its book value of $42,500. Western plans to build an entirely new plant in 4 years, so it has no interest in either leasing or owning the proposed loom for more than that period.

a. Should the loom be leased or purchased?
b. The salvage value is clearly the most uncertain cash flow in the analysis. What effect would a salvage value risk adjustment have on the analysis? (Assume that the appropriate salvage value pre-tax discount rate is 15%.)
c. Assuming that the after-tax cost of debt should be used to discount all anticipated cash flows, at what lease payment would the firm be indifferent to either leasing or buying?

MINI CASE

Lewis Securities Inc. has decided to acquire a new market data and quotation system for its Richmond home office. The system receives current market prices and other information from several online data services and then either displays the information on a screen or stores it for later retrieval by the firm's brokers. The system also permits customers to call up current quotes on terminals in the lobby.

The equipment costs $1,000,000 and, if it were purchased, Lewis could obtain a term loan for the full purchase price at a 10% interest rate. Although the equipment has a 6-year useful life, it is classified as a special-purpose computer and therefore falls into the MACRS 3-year class. If the system were purchased, a 4-year maintenance contract could be obtained at a cost of $20,000 per year, payable at the beginning of each year. The equipment would be sold after 4 years, and the best estimate of its residual value is $200,000. However, because real-time display system technology is changing rapidly, the actual residual value is uncertain.

As an alternative to the borrow-and-buy plan, the equipment manufacturer informed Lewis that Consolidated Leasing would be willing to write a 4-year guideline lease on the equipment, including maintenance, for payments of $260,000 at the beginning of each year. Lewis's marginal federal-plus-state tax rate is 40%. You have been asked to analyze the lease-versus-purchase decision and, in the process, to answer the following questions.

a. (1) Who are the two parties to a lease transaction?
   (2) What are the five primary types of leases, and what are their characteristics?
   (3) How are leases classified for tax purposes?
   (4) What effect does leasing have on a firm's balance sheet?
   (5) What effect does leasing have on a firm's capital structure?

b. (1) What is the present value cost of owning the equipment? (Hint: Set up a time line that shows the net cash flows over the period $t = 0$ to $t = 4$, and then find the PV of these net cash flows, or the PV cost of owning.)
   (2) Explain the rationale for the discount rate you used to find the PV.

c. What is Lewis's present value cost of leasing the equipment? (Hint: Again, construct a time line.)

d. What is the net advantage to leasing (NAL)? Does your analysis indicate that Lewis should buy or lease the equipment? Explain.

e. Now assume that the equipment's residual value could be as low as $0 or as high as $400,000 but $200,000 is the expected value. Since the residual value is riskier than the other relevant cash flows, this differential risk should be incorporated into the analysis. Describe how this could be accomplished. (No calculations are necessary, but explain how you would modify the analysis if calculations were required.) What effect would the residual value's increased uncertainty have on Lewis's lease-versus-purchase decision?

f. The lessee compares the cost of owning the equipment with the cost of leasing it. Now put yourself in the lessor's shoes. In a few sentences, how should you analyze the decision to write or not to write the lease?

g. (1) Assume that the lease payments were actually $280,000 per year, that Consolidated Leasing is also in the 40% tax bracket, and that it also forecasts a $200,000 residual value. Also, to furnish the maintenance support, Consolidated would have to purchase a maintenance contract from the manufacturer at the same $20,000 annual cost, again paid in advance. Consolidated Leasing can obtain an expected 10% pre-tax return on investments of similar risk. What would

be Consolidated's NPV and IRR of leasing under these conditions?

(2) What do you think the lessor's NPV would be if the lease payment were set at $260,000 per year? (*Hint:* The lessor's cash flows would be a "mirror image" of the lessee's cash flows.)

h. Lewis's management has been considering moving to a new downtown location, and they are concerned that these plans may come to fruition prior to the equipment lease's expiration. If the move occurs then Lewis would buy or lease an entirely new set of equipment, so management would like to include a cancellation clause in the lease contract. What effect would such a clause have on the riskiness of the lease from Lewis's standpoint? From the lessor's standpoint? If you were the lessor, would you insist on changing any of the other lease terms if a cancellation clause were added? Should the cancellation clause contain provisions similar to call premiums or any restrictive covenants and/or penalties of the type contained in bond indentures?

Selected Additional Cases

The following cases from TextChoice, *Cengage Learning's online case library, cover many of the concepts discussed in this chapter and are available at* **www.textchoice2.com/casenet.**

Klein-Brigham Series:
Case 25, "Environmental Sciences, Inc.," Case 49, "Agro Chemical Corporation," Case 69, "Friendly Food Stores, Inc.," and Case 26, "Prudent Solutions, Inc.," all examine the lease decision from the perspectives of both the lessee and the lessor.

Brigham-Buzzard Series:
Case 12, "Powerline Network Corporation (Leasing)."

Chapter 20

Hybrid Financing: Preferred Stock, Warrants, and Convertibles

WEB

The textbook's Web site contains an *Excel* file that will guide you through the chapter's calculations. The file for this chapter is ***Ch20 Tool Kit.xls,*** and we encourage you to open the file and follow along as you read the chapter.

In previous chapters, we examined common stocks and various types of long-term debt. In this chapter, we examine three other securities used to raise long-term capital: (1) *preferred stock,* which is a hybrid security that represents a cross between debt and common equity, (2) *warrants,* which are derivative securities issued by firms to facilitate the issuance of some other type of security, and (3) *convertibles,* which combine the features of debt (or preferred stock) and warrants.

Beginning of Chapter Questions

As you read this chapter, consider how you would answer the following questions. You *should not* necessarily be able to answer the questions before you read the chapter. Rather, you should use them to get a sense of the issues covered in the chapter. After reading the chapter, you should be able to give at least partial answers to the questions, and you should be able to give better answers after the chapter has been discussed in class. Note, too, that it is often useful, when answering conceptual questions, to use hypothetical data to illustrate your answer. We illustrate the answers with an *Excel* model that is available on the textbook's Web site. Accessing the model and working through it is a useful exercise, and it provides insights that are useful when answering the questions.

1. Why do companies use so many different types of instruments to raise capital? Why not just use debt and common stock?
2. If a company is thinking about issuing **preferred stock** to raise capital, what are some factors that it should consider? What factors should an investor consider before buying preferred stock?
3. What is a **warrant?** If a company decides to raise capital by issuing bonds with warrants, how would the terms on both the bond and the warrant be set? Consider in particular how the coupon rate and maturity of the bond would be related to the exercise price and life of the warrant, together with any other factors that might affect the decision.

4. What is a **convertible?** If a company decides to raise capital by issuing convertible bonds, how would the terms on the bond be set? Consider specifically the maturity, coupon rate, and call features of the bond, as well as the conversion price (or conversion ratio), together with any other parameters required for the analysis.
5. Suppose you just bought a convertible bond at its par value. Your broker gives you information on the bond's conversion ratio, coupon rate, maturity, years of call protection, and the yield on nonconvertible bonds of similar risk and maturity. The company has a well-established payout ratio, and you also know the stock's price, beta, and expected ROE. You also know the risk-free rate and the market risk premium.
   a. How could you use this information to determine how much you are paying for the option to convert?
   b. How would you determine the expected rate of return on the convertible, along with the expected return on the common stock and the straight bonds?
   c. Now suppose the company unexpectedly announced (1) an increase in its target dividend payout ratio from, say, 25% to 75% and (2) an increase in the dividend from $1 to $3 to conform to the new policy. Would the new dividend policy help or hurt you and other holders of the convertible bond? Explain.

20.1 Preferred Stock

Preferred stock is a hybrid—it is similar to bonds in some respects and to common stock in other ways. Accountants classify preferred stock as equity; hence they show it on the balance sheet as an equity account. However, from a finance perspective preferred stock lies somewhere between debt and common equity: It imposes a fixed charge and thus increases the firm's financial leverage, yet omitting the preferred dividend does not force a company into bankruptcy. Also, unlike interest on debt, preferred dividends are not deductible by the issuing corporation, so preferred stock has a higher cost of capital than does debt. We first describe the basic features of preferred stock, after which we discuss the types of preferred stock and the advantages and disadvantages of preferred stock.

20.1a Basic Features

Preferred stock has a par (or liquidating) value, often either $25 or $100. The dividend is stated as either a percentage of par, as so many dollars per share, or both ways.

For example, several years ago Klondike Paper Company sold 150,000 shares of $100 par value perpetual preferred stock for a total of $15 million. This preferred stock had a stated annual dividend of $12 per share, so the preferred dividend yield was $12/$100 = 0.12, or 12%, at the time of issue. The dividend was set when the stock was issued; it will not be changed in the future. Therefore, if the required rate of return on preferred, r_{ps}, changes from 12% after the issue date—as it did—then the market price of the preferred stock will go up or down. Currently, r_{ps} for Klondike Paper's preferred is 9%, and the price of the preferred has risen from $100 to $12/0.09 = $133.33.

If the preferred dividend is not earned, the company does not have to pay it. However, most preferred issues are **cumulative,** meaning that the cumulative total of unpaid preferred dividends must be paid before dividends can be paid on the common stock. Unpaid preferred dividends are called **arrearages.** Dividends in arrears do not earn interest; thus, arrearages do not grow in a compound interest sense, they only grow from additional nonpayments of the preferred dividend. Also, many preferred stocks accrue arrearages for only a limited number of years—so that, for example, the cumulative feature may cease after 3 years. However, the dividends in arrears continue in force until they are paid.

Preferred stock normally has no voting rights. However, most preferred issues stipulate that the preferred stockholders can elect a minority of the directors—say, three out of ten—if the preferred dividend is passed (omitted). Some preferreds even entitle their holders to elect a majority of the board.

Although nonpayment of preferred dividends will not trigger bankruptcy, corporations issue preferred stock with every intention of paying the dividend. Even if passing the dividend does not give the preferred stockholders control of the company, failure to pay a preferred dividend precludes payment of common dividends. In addition, passing the dividend makes it difficult to raise capital by selling bonds and virtually impossible to sell more preferred or common stock except at rock-bottom prices. However, having preferred stock outstanding does give a firm the chance to overcome its difficulties: If bonds had been used instead of preferred stock, a company could be forced into bankruptcy before it could straighten out its problems. Thus, *from the viewpoint of the issuing corporation, preferred stock is less risky than bonds.*

For an investor, however, preferred stock is riskier than bonds: (1) preferred stock-holders' claims are subordinated to those of bondholders in the event of liquidation, and (2) bondholders are more likely to continue receiving income during hard times than are preferred stockholders. Accordingly, investors require a higher after-tax rate of return on a given firm's preferred stock than on its bonds. However, since 70% of preferred dividends is exempt from corporate taxes, preferred stock is attractive to corporate investors. Indeed, high-grade preferred stock, on average, sells on a lower pre-tax yield basis than high-grade bonds. As an example, Alcoa has preferred stock with an annual dividend of $3.75 (a 3.75% rate applied to $100 par value). In April 2011, Alcoa's preferred stock had a price of $73.11, for a market yield of about $3.75/$73.11 = 5.13%. Alcoa's long-term bonds that mature in 2037 provided a yield of 5.86%, which is 0.73 percentage points *more* than its preferred. The tax treatment accounted for this differential; the *after-tax yield* to corporate investors was greater on the preferred stock than on the bonds because 70% of the dividend may be excluded from taxation by a corporate investor.[1]

About half of all preferred stock issued in recent years has been convertible into common stock. We discuss convertibles in Section 20.3.

www

For updates, go to **finance.yahoo.com** and get quotes for AA-P, Alcoa's 3.75% preferred stock. For an updated bond yield, use the bond screener and search for Alcoa bonds.

---

1. The after-tax yield on an 8.1% bond to a corporate investor in the 34% marginal tax rate bracket is 8.1%(1 − T) = 5.3%. The after-tax yield on a 7.0% preferred stock is 7.0%(1 − Effective T) = 7.0% [1 − (0.30)(0.34)] = 6.3%. Also, note that tax law prevents arbitrage. If a firm issues debt and uses the proceeds to purchase another firm's preferred stock, then the 70% dividend exclusion is voided.

THE ROMANCE HAD NO CHEMISTRY, BUT IT HAD A LOT OF PREFERRED STOCK!

On April 1, 2009, Dow Chemical Company merged with Rohm & Haas after a bitter dispute over the interpretation of their previous merger agreement. So even though the two companies make a lot of chemicals, there apparently wasn't much chemistry by the time the merger was completed.

To raise cash for the $78.97 per share purchase of Rohm & Haas's outstanding shares, Dow borrowed over $9 billion from Citibank and also issued $4 billion in convertible preferred stock to Berkshire Hathaway and The Kuwait Investment Authority.

The Haas Family Trusts and Paulson & Company were large shareholders in Rohm & Haas. As part of the deal, they sold their shares to Dow with one hand and bought $3 billion in preferred stock from Dow with the other. This preferred stock pays a cash dividend of 7%. It also pays an 8% "dividend" that can either be in cash or in additional shares of the preferred stock, with the choice left to Dow; this is called a payment-in-kind (PIK) dividend.

These terms mean that Dow can conserve cash if it runs into difficult times: Dow can pay the 8% in additional stock and Dow can even defer payment of the 7% cash dividend without risk of bankruptcy. But if this happens, a troubled marriage is likely to cause even more grief.

Source: 8-K reports from the SEC filed on March 12, 2009 and April 1, 2009.

Some preferred stocks are similar to perpetual bonds in that they have no maturity date, but most new issues now have specified maturities. For example, many preferred shares have a sinking fund provision that calls for the retirement of 2% of the issue each year, meaning the issue will "mature" in a maximum of 50 years. Also, many preferred issues are callable by the issuing corporation, which can also limit the life of the preferred.[2]

Nonconvertible preferred stock is virtually all owned by corporations, which can take advantage of the 70% dividend exclusion to obtain a higher after-tax yield on preferred stock than on bonds. Individuals should not own preferred stocks (except convertible preferreds)—they can get higher yields on safer bonds, so it is not logical for them to hold preferreds.[3] As a result of this ownership

---

2. Prior to the late 1970s, virtually all preferred stock was perpetual and almost no issues had sinking funds or call provisions. Then insurance company regulators, worried about the unrealized losses the companies had been incurring on preferred holdings as a result of rising interest rates, made changes essentially mandating that insurance companies buy only limited life preferreds. From that time on, virtually no new preferred has been perpetual. This example illustrates the way securities change as a result of changes in the economic environment.

3. Since 2003, qualified dividends received by individuals are taxed at a capital gains rate rather than as ordinary income. This makes preferred stock more attractive relative to bonds, putting individual investors in much the same boat as corporations. For example, a corporation in the 35% tax bracket with a 70% dividend exclusion faces a $(0.35)(1 - 0.70) = 10.5\%$ tax rate on dividend income as compared to a 35% rate on interest income. Most individuals face a dividend tax rate of 15%, and high income earners would face a 35% tax on ordinary income. Thus there is a tax advantage for dividend income for both individuals and corporations, although the advantage is larger for corporations.

   Also, some financially engineered preferred stock has "dividends" that the paying company can deduct for tax purposes in the same way that interest payments are deductible. Therefore, the company is able to pay a higher rate on such preferred stock, making it potentially attractive to individual investors. These securities trade under a variety of colorful names, including MIPS (Modified Income Preferred Securities), QUIPS (Quarterly Income Preferred Securities), TOPrS (Trust Originated Preferred Stock), and QUIDS (Quarterly Income Debt Securities). However, dividends from these hybrid securities are not subject to the 70% corporate exclusion and are taxed as ordinary income for individual investors.

pattern, the volume of preferred stock financing is geared to the supply of money in the hands of corporate investors. When the supply of such money is plentiful, the prices of preferred stocks are bid up, their yields fall, and investment bankers suggest that companies in need of financing consider issuing preferred stock.

For issuers, preferred stock has a tax *disadvantage* relative to debt: Interest expense is deductible, but preferred dividends are not. Still, firms with low tax rates may have an incentive to issue preferred stock that can be bought by high–tax-rate corporate investors, who can take advantage of the 70% dividend exclusion. If a firm has a lower tax rate than potential corporate buyers, then the firm might be better off issuing preferred stock than debt. The key here is that the tax advantage to a high–tax-rate corporation is greater than the tax disadvantage to a low–tax-rate issuer. As an illustration, assume that risk differentials between debt and preferred would require an issuer to set the interest rate on new debt at 10% and the dividend yield on new preferred stock 2% higher, or at 12% in a no-tax world. However, when taxes are considered, a corporate buyer with a high tax rate—say, 40%—might be willing to buy the preferred stock if it has an 8% before-tax yield. This would produce an 8%(1 − Effective T) = 8%[1 − 0.30(0.40)] = 7.04% after-tax return on the preferred versus 10%(1 − 0.40) = 6.0% on the debt. If the issuer has a low tax rate—say, 10%—then its after-tax costs would be 10%(1 − T) = 10%(0.90) = 9% on the bonds and 8% on the preferred. Thus, the security with lower risk to the issuer, preferred stock,

HYBRIDS AREN'T ONLY FOR CORPORATIONS

The Cooperative Regions of Organic Producer Pools (CROPP) is a Section 521 agricultural cooperative organization in the Midwest that markets organic produce under such brand names as Organic Valley and Organic Prairie and is a supplier to Stonyfield. It's not a corporation or a partnership. Rather, a cooperative is an organization that provides services for its owner/members. In this case, CROPP purchases produce from its members, processes it, and then resells it. Profits are re-distributed to the owner/members as dividends.

With the beginnings of the financial recovery and an overall increase in the demand for organic products, CROPP's sales grew 18% in 2009 to over $600 million and, partly as a result of this growth, it found itself in need of some $14 million in additional financing. CROPP decided to raise the funds by issuing preferred stock to members and non-members. CROPP had successfully issued preferred stock in the past and this issue was a $50 par, 6% cumulative dividend, non-voting preferred stock, and was sold for $50 per share.

CROPP chose not to use an investment banker for this issue; the co-op's investor relations manager was in charge of marketing and selling the preferred stock and CROPP saved quite a bit of money in fees with issuance costs totaling about 4.5% rather than the 7% or more charged by an investment bank.

Unlike preferred stock issued by corporations, dividends on preferred stock issued by a Section 521 cooperative such as CROPP can be deducted from its pre-tax income, and the dividend recipient treats it as ordinary income for tax purposes. Therefore this preferred stock is treated like perpetual debt for tax purposes. Why then would CROPP issue preferred stock rather than debt? The simple reason is that preferred stock is non-recourse. If CROPP misses a dividend payment, the dividend accrues, but the preferred stockholder cannot force CROPP into bankruptcy. This flexibility is valuable, especially in an industry as volatile as farming!

also has a lower cost. Such situations can make preferred stock a logical financing choice.[4]

20.1b Other Types of Preferred Stock

In addition to "plain vanilla" preferred stock, there are two other variations: adjustable rate and market auction preferred stock.

Adjustable Rate Preferred Stock

Instead of paying fixed dividends, **adjustable rate preferred stocks (ARPs)** have their dividends tied to the rate on Treasury securities. ARPs are issued mainly by utilities and large commercial banks. When ARPs were first developed, they were touted as nearly perfect short-term corporate investments because (1) only 30% of the dividends are taxable to corporations, and (2) the floating-rate feature was supposed to keep the issue trading at near par. The new security proved to be so popular as a short-term investment for firms with idle cash that mutual funds designed just to invest in them sprouted like weeds (and shares of these funds, in turn, were purchased by corporations). However, the ARPs still had some price volatility due to (1) changes in the riskiness of the issuers (some big banks that had issued ARPs, such as Continental Illinois, ran into serious loan default problems) and (2) fluctuations in Treasury yields between dividend rate adjustment dates. Therefore, the ARPs had too much price instability to be held in the liquid asset portfolios of many corporate investors.

Market Auction Preferred Stock

In 1984, investment bankers introduced **money market preferred,** which is also called **market auction preferred.**[5] Here the underwriter conducts an auction on the issue every 7 weeks (to get the 70% exclusion from taxable income, buyers must hold the stock for at least 46 days). Holders who want to sell their shares can put them up for auction at par value. Buyers then submit bids in the form of the yields they are willing to accept over the next 7-week period. The yield set on the issue for the coming period is the lowest yield sufficient to sell all the shares being offered at that auction. The buyers pay the sellers the par value; hence holders are virtually assured that their shares can be sold at par. The issuer then must pay a dividend rate over the next 7-week period as determined by the auction. From the holder's standpoint, market auction preferred is a low-risk, largely tax-exempt, 7-week maturity security that can be sold between auction dates at close to par.

In practice, things may not go quite so smoothly. If there are few potential buyers, then an excessively high yield might be required to clear the market. To protect the issuing firms or mutual funds from high dividend payments, the securities have a cap on the allowable dividend yield. If the market-clearing yield is higher than this

---

4. For more on preferred stock, see Arthur L. Houston Jr. and Carol Olson Houston, "Financing with Preferred Stock," *Financial Management,* Autumn 1990, pp. 42–54; and Michael J. Alderson and Donald R. Fraser, "Financial Innovations and Excesses Revisited: The Case of Auction Rate Preferred Stock," *Financial Management,* Summer 1993, pp. 61–75.

5. Confusingly, market auction preferred stock is frequently referred to as *auction-rate preferred* stock and with the acronym ARP as well.

cap then the next dividend yield will be set equal to this cap rate, but the auction will fail and the owners of the securities who wish to sell will not be able to do so. This happened in February 2008, and many market auction preferred stockholders were left holding securities they wanted to liquidate.

20.1c Advantages and Disadvantages of Preferred Stock

There are both advantages and disadvantages to financing with preferred stock. Here are the major advantages from the issuer's standpoint.

1. In contrast to bonds, the obligation to pay preferred dividends is not firm, and passing (not paying) a preferred dividend cannot force a firm into bankruptcy.
2. By issuing preferred stock, the firm avoids the dilution of common equity that occurs when common stock is sold.
3. Since preferred stock sometimes has no maturity and since preferred sinking fund payments (if present) are typically spread over a long period, preferred issues reduce the cash flow drain from repayment of principal that occurs with debt issues.

There are two major disadvantages, as follows.

1. Preferred stock dividends are not normally deductible to the issuer, so the after-tax cost of preferred is typically higher than the after-tax cost of debt. However, the tax advantage of preferreds to corporate purchasers lowers its pre-tax cost and thus its effective cost.
2. Although preferred dividends can be passed, investors expect them to be paid and firms intend to pay them if conditions permit. Thus, preferred dividends are considered to be a fixed cost. As a result, their use—like that of debt—increases financial risk and hence the cost of common equity.

Self Test

Should preferred stock be considered as equity or debt? Explain.

Who are the major purchasers of nonconvertible preferred stock? Why?

Briefly explain the mechanics of adjustable rate and market auction preferred stock.

What are the advantages and disadvantages of preferred stock to the issuer?

A company's preferred stock has a pre-tax dividend yield of 7%, and its debt has a pre-tax yield of 8%. If an investor is in the 34% marginal tax bracket, what are the after-tax yields of the preferred stock and debt? **(6.29% and 5.28%)**

20.2 Warrants

A **warrant** is a certificate issued by a company that gives the holder the right to buy a stated number of shares of the company's stock at a specified price for some specified length of time. Generally, warrants are issued along with debt, and they are used to induce investors to buy long-term debt with a lower coupon rate than would otherwise be required. For example, when Infomatics Corporation, a rapidly growing high-tech company, wanted to sell $50 million of 20-year bonds in 2012, the company's investment bankers informed the financial vice president that the bonds would be difficult to sell and that a coupon rate of 10% would be required. However, as an alternative the bankers suggested that investors might be willing to buy the bonds with a coupon rate of only 8% if the company would offer 20 warrants with each $1,000 bond, each warrant entitling the holder to buy one share of common stock at a strike price (also called an *exercise price*) of $22 per share. The stock was selling for $20 per share at the time, and the warrants would expire in the year 2022 if they had not been exercised previously.

Why would investors be willing to buy Infomatics's bonds at a yield of only 8% in a 10% market just because warrants were also offered as part of the package? It's because the warrants are long-term *call options* that have value, since holders can buy the firm's common stock at the strike price regardless of how high the market price climbs. This option offsets the low interest rate on the bonds and makes the package of low-yield bonds plus warrants attractive to investors. (See Chapter 6 for a discussion of options.)

20.2a Initial Market Price of a Bond with Warrants

If the Infomatics bonds had been issued as straight debt, they would have carried a 10% interest rate. However, with warrants attached, the bonds were sold to yield 8%. Someone buying the bonds at their $1,000 initial offering price would thus be receiving a package consisting of an 8%, 20-year bond plus 20 warrants. Because the going interest rate on bonds as risky as those of Infomatics was 10%, we can find the straight-debt value of the bonds, assuming an annual coupon for ease of illustration, as follows:

0	10%	1	2	3	20
PV		80	80	80	80
					1,000

Using a financial calculator, input N = 20, I/YR = 10, PMT = 80, and FV = 1000. Then press the PV key to obtain the bond's value of $829.73, or approximately $830. Thus, a person buying the bonds in the initial underwriting would pay $1,000 and receive in exchange a straight bond worth about $830 plus 20 warrants that are presumably worth about $1,000 − $830 = $170:

$$\text{Price paid for bond with warrants} = \text{Straight-debt value of bond} + \text{Value of warrants} \qquad (20\text{--}1)$$

$$\$1,000 = \$830 + \$170$$

Because investors receive 20 warrants with each bond, each warrant has an implied value of $170/20 = $8.50.

The key issue in setting the terms of a bond-with-warrants deal is valuing the warrants. The straight-debt value can be estimated quite accurately, as we have shown. However, it is more difficult to estimate the value of the warrants. The Black-Scholes option pricing model (OPM), discussed in Chapter 6, can be used to find the value of a call option. There is a temptation to use this model to find the value of a warrant, since call options are similar to warrants in many respects: Both give the investor the right to buy a share of stock at a fixed strike price on or before the expiration date. However, there are major differences between call options and warrants. When call options are exercised, the stock provided to the option holder comes from the secondary market, but when warrants are exercised, the stock provided to the warrant holders is either newly issued shares or treasury stock the company has previously purchased. This means that the exercise of warrants dilutes the value of the original equity, which could cause the value of the original warrant to differ from the value of a similar call option. Also, call options typically have a life of just a few months, whereas warrants often have lives of 10 years or more. Finally, the Black-Scholes model assumes that the underlying stock pays no dividend, which is not unreasonable over a short period but is unreasonable for 5 or 10 years. Therefore, investment bankers cannot use the original Black-Scholes model to determine the value of warrants.

Even though the original Black-Scholes model cannot be used to determine a precise value for a warrant, there are more sophisticated models that work reasonably well.[6] In addition, investment bankers can simply contact portfolio managers of mutual funds, pension funds, and other organizations that would be interested in buying the securities to get an indication of how many they would buy at different prices. In effect, the bankers hold a presale auction and determine the set of terms that will just clear the market. If they do this job properly then they will, in effect, be letting the market determine the value of the warrants.

20.2b Use of Warrants in Financing

Warrants generally are used by small, rapidly growing firms as **sweeteners** when they sell debt or preferred stock. Such firms frequently are regarded by investors as being highly risky, so their bonds can be sold only at extremely high coupon rates and with very restrictive indenture provisions. To avoid such restrictions, firms like Infomatics often offer warrants along with the bonds.

Getting warrants along with bonds enables investors to share in the company's growth, assuming it does in fact grow and prosper. Therefore, investors are willing to accept a lower interest rate and less restrictive indenture provisions. A bond with warrants has some characteristics of debt and some characteristics of equity. It is a hybrid security that provides the financial manager with an opportunity to expand the firm's mix of securities and thereby appeal to a broader group of investors.

Virtually all warrants issued today are **detachable.** In other words, after a bond with attached warrants is sold, the warrants can be detached and traded separately

---

6. For example, see John C. Hull, *Options, Futures, and Other Derivatives,* 8th ed. (Boston: Prentice-Hall, 2012). Hull shows that if there are m warrants outstanding, each of which can be converted into γ shares of common stock at an exercise price of X, as well as n shares of common stock outstanding, then the price γ of a warrant is given by this modification of the Black-Scholes option pricing formula from Chapter 6:

$$\omega = \left(\frac{n\gamma}{n+m\gamma}\right)\left[S^*N(d_1^*) - Xe^{-r_{RF}(T-t)}N(d_2^*)\right] \text{ where } d_1^* = \frac{\ln(S^*/X)+(r_{RF}+\sigma_0^2/2)(T-t)}{\sigma_0\sqrt{T-t}}$$

Here $d_2^* = d_1^* - \sigma_0(T-t)^{1/2}$ and $S^* = S + m\omega/n$, where S is the underlying stock price, T is the maturity date, r_{RF} is the risk free rate, σ_0 is the volatility of the stock and the warrants together, and $N(\cdot)$ is the cumulative normal distribution function. See Chapter 6 for more on the Black-Scholes option pricing formula. If $\gamma = 1$ and n is very much larger than m, so that the number of warrants issued is very small compared to the number of shares of stock outstanding, then this simplifies to the standard Black-Scholes option pricing formula.

from the bond. Further, even after the warrants have been exercised, the bond (with its low coupon rate) remains outstanding.

The strike price on warrants is generally set some 20% to 30% above the market price of the stock on the date the bond is issued. If the firm grows and prospers, causing its stock price to rise above the strike price at which shares may be purchased, then warrant holders could exercise their warrants and buy stock at the stated price. However, without some incentive, warrants would never be exercised prior to maturity—their value in the open market would be greater than their value if exercised, so holders would sell warrants rather than exercise them. There are three conditions that cause holders to exercise their warrants: (1) Warrant holders will surely exercise and buy stock if the warrants are about to expire and the market price of the stock is above the exercise price. (2) Warrant holders will exercise voluntarily if the company raises the dividend on the common stock by a sufficient amount. No dividend is earned on the warrant, so it provides no current income. However, if the common stock pays a high dividend, then it provides an attractive dividend yield but limits stock price growth. This induces warrant holders to exercise their option to buy the stock. (3) Warrants sometimes have stepped-up strike prices (also called stepped-up exercise prices), which prod owners into exercising them. For example, Williamson Scientific Company has warrants outstanding with a strike price of $25 until December 31, 2016, at which time the strike price rises to $30. If the price of the common stock is over $25 just before December 31, 2016, many warrant holders will exercise their options before the stepped-up price takes effect and the value of the warrants falls.

Another desirable feature of warrants is that they generally bring in funds only if funds are needed. If the company grows, it will probably need new equity capital. At the same time, growth will cause the price of the stock to rise and the warrants to be exercised; hence the firm will obtain the cash it needs. If the company is not successful and it cannot profitably employ additional money, then the price of its stock will probably not rise enough to induce exercise of the warrants.

20.2c The Component Cost of Bonds with Warrants

When Infomatics issued its bonds with warrants, the firm received $1,000 for each bond. The pre-tax cost of debt would have been 10% if no warrants had been attached, but each Infomatics bond has 20 warrants, each of which entitles its holder to buy one share of stock for $22. The presence of warrants also allows Infomatics to pay only 8% interest on the bonds, obligating it to pay $80 interest for 20 years plus $1,000 at the end of 20 years. What is the percentage cost of each $1,000 bond with warrants? As we shall see, the cost is well above the 8% coupon rate on the bonds.

The best way to approach this analysis is to break the $1,000 into two components, one consisting of an $830 bond and the other consisting of $170 of warrants. Thus, the $1,000 bond-with-warrants package consists of $830/$1,000 = 0.83 = 83% straight debt and $170/$1,000 = 0.17 = 17% warrant. Our objective is to find the cost of capital for the straight bonds and the cost of capital for the warrant, then weight them to derive the cost of capital for the bond-with-warrants package.

The pre-tax cost of debt is 10% because this is the pre-tax cost of debt for a straight bond, so our task is to estimate the cost of capital for a warrant. Estimating the cost of capital for a warrant is fairly complicated, but we can use the following procedure to obtain a reasonable approximation.[7] The basic idea is to estimate the firm's expected cost of satisfying the warrant holders at the time the warrants expire. To do this, we need to estimate the value of the firm, the value of the debt, the intrinsic value of equity, and the stock price at the time of expiration.

Assume that the total value of Infomatics's operations and investments, which is $250 million immediately after issuing the bonds with warrants, is expected to grow at 9% per year. When the warrants are due to expire in 10 years, the total value of Infomatics is expected to be $250(1.09)^{10} = $591.841 million.

Infomatics will receive $22 per warrant when exercised; with 1 million warrants, this results in a cash flow to Infomatics of $22 million. The total value of Infomatics will be equal to the value of operations plus the value of this cash. This will make the total value of Infomatics equal to $591.841 + $22 = $613.841 million.

When the warrants expire, the bonds will have 10 years remaining until maturity with a fixed coupon payment of $80. If the expected market interest rate is still 10%, then the time line of cash flows will be

Using a financial calculator, input N = 10, I/YR = 10, PMT = 80, and FV = 1000; then press the PV key to obtain the bond's value, $877.11. The total value of all of the bonds is 50,000($877.11) = $43.856 million.

The intrinsic value of equity is equal to the total value of the firm minus the value of debt: $613.841 − $43.856 = $569.985 million.

Infomatics had 10 million shares outstanding prior to the warrants' exercise, so it will have 11 million after the 1 million options are exercised. The previous warrant holders will now own 1/11 of the equity, for a total of $569.985(1/11) = $51.82 million dollars. We can also estimate the predicted intrinsic stock price, which is equal to the intrinsic value of equity divided by the number of shares: $569.985/11 = $51.82 per share.[8] These calculations are summarized in Table 20-1.

To find the component cost of the warrants, consider that Infomatics will have to issue one share of stock worth $51.82 for each warrant exercised and, in return, Infomatics will receive the strike price, $22. Thus, a purchaser of the bonds with warrants, if she holds the complete package, would expect to realize a profit in Year 10 of $51.82 − $22 = $29.82 for each warrant exercised.[9] Since each bond has 20 warrants attached and since each warrant entitles the holder to buy one share of common stock, it follows that warrant holders will have an expected cash flow of 20($29.82) = $596.40 per bond at the end of Year 10. Here is a time line of the expected cash flow stream to a warrant holder:

---

7. For an exact solution, see P. Daves and M. Ehrhardt, "Convertible Securities, Employee Stock Options, and the Cost of Equity," *The Financial Review*, Vol. 42, 2007, pp. 267–288.

8. If the stock price had been less than the strike price of $22 at expiration, then the warrants would not have been exercised. Based on the expected growth in the firm's value, there is little chance that the stock price will not be greater than $22.

9. It is not strictly accurate to say that the expected profit from the warrant position is the expected stock price less the strike price: $29.82 = $51.82 − $22. This is because if the stock price drops below the strike price, in this case $22, then the warrant profit is $0, regardless of how low the stock price goes. Thus the expected payoff will be somewhat more than $29.82. Although this expectation can be calculated using options techniques similar to those in Chapter 6, it is beyond the scope of this chapter. However, if there is a very small probability that the stock price will drop below the exercise price, then $29.82 is very close to the true expected payoff.

TABLE 20-1	Valuation Analysis after Exercise of Warrants in 10 Years (Millions of Dollars, Except for Per Share Data)	
		Warrants Are Exercised
Expected value of operations and investments[a]		$591.841
Plus new cash from exercise of warrants[b]		22.000
Total value of firm		$613.841
Minus value of bonds		43.856
Value remaining for shareholders		$569.985
Divided by shares outstanding[c]		11.0
Price per share		$ 51.82

© Cengage Learning 2013

[a]The value of operations and investments is expected to grow from its current $250 million at a rate of 9%: $250(1.09)^{10} = $591.841 million.

[b]The warrants will be exercised only if the stock price at expiration is above $22. If the stock price is less than $22, then the warrants will expire worthless and there will be no new capital. Our calculations show that the expected stock price is much greater than $22, so the warrants are expected to be exercised.

[c]Before the warrants are exercised, there are 10 million shares of stock. After the warrants are exercised, there will be 10 + 1 = 11 million shares outstanding.

0	10%	1	2	3	10
−170		0	0	0	$596.40

The IRR of this stream is 13.35%, which is an approximation of the warrant holder's expected return on the warrants (r_w) in the bond with warrants. The overall pre-tax cost of capital for the bonds with warrants is the weighted average of the cost of straight debt and the cost of warrants:

$$\text{Pre-tax cost of bonds with warrants} = r_d(\$830/\$1{,}000) + r_w(\$170/\$1{,}000)$$

$$= 10\%(0.83) + 13.35\%(0.17) = 10.57\%$$

The cost of the warrants is higher than the cost of debt because warrants are riskier than debt; in fact, the cost of warrants is greater than the cost of equity because warrants also are riskier than equity. Thus, the cost of capital for a bond with warrants is weighted between the cost of debt and the much higher cost of equity. This means the overall cost of capital for the bonds with warrants will be greater than the cost of straight debt and will be much higher than the 8% coupon rate on the bonds-with-warrants package.[10]

---

10. In order to estimate the after-tax cost of capital, the after-tax cost of each component must be estimated. The after-tax cost of the warrant is the same as the pre-tax cost because warrants do not affect the issuer's tax liability. This is not true for the bond component. Because the straight bond is worth only $830 at the time of issue, it has an original issue discount (OID). This means that the after-tax cost of debt is not exactly equal to $r_d(1 - T)$. For long-term bonds, such as the one in this example, the difference is small enough to be neglected. See *Web Extension 4A* on the textbook's Web site for a general discussion of the after-tax cost of debt for zero coupon bonds and OID bonds. The *Ch20 Tool Kit.xls* calculates the after-tax cost of Infomatics's bond component, which is 6.3% rather than 10%(1 − 0.40) = 6%, assuming a 40% tax rate.

Bonds with warrants and preferred stock with warrants have become an important source of funding for companies during the global economic crisis. But as our example shows, this form of financing has a much higher cost of capital than its low coupon and preferred dividend might lead you to think.[11]

Self Test	What is a warrant?
	Describe how a new bond issue with warrants is valued.
	How are warrants used in corporate financing?
	The use of warrants lowers the coupon rate on the corresponding debt issue. Does this mean that the component cost of a debt-plus-warrants package is less than the cost of straight debt? Explain.
	Shanton Corporation could issue 15-year straight debt at a rate of 8%. Instead, Shanton issues 15-year debt with a coupon rate of 6%, but each bond has 25 warrants attached. The bonds can be issued at par ($1,000 per bond). Assuming annual interest payments, what is the implied value of each warrant? **($6.85)**

20.3 Convertible Securities

Convertible securities are bonds or preferred stocks that, under specified terms and conditions, can be exchanged for (that is, converted into) common stock at the option of the holder. Unlike the exercise of warrants, which brings in additional funds to the firm, conversion does not provide new capital; debt (or preferred stock) is simply replaced on the balance sheet by common stock. Of course, reducing the debt or preferred stock will improve the firm's financial strength and make it easier to raise additional capital, but that requires a separate action.

20.3a Conversion Ratio and Conversion Price

WEB

See **Ch20 Tool Kit.xls** on the textbook's Web site for details.

The **conversion ratio, CR,** for a convertible security is defined as the number of shares of stock a bondholder will receive upon conversion. The **conversion price, P_c,** is defined as the effective price investors pay for the common stock when conversion occurs. The relationship between the conversion ratio and the conversion price can be illustrated by Silicon Valley Software Company's convertible debentures issued at their $1,000 par value in July of 2012. At any time prior to maturity on July 15, 2032, a debenture holder can exchange a bond for 18 shares of common stock. Therefore, the conversion ratio, CR, is 18. The bond cost a purchaser $1,000, the par value, when it was issued. Dividing the $1,000 par value by the 18 shares received gives a conversion price of $55.56 a share:

---

11. For more on warrant pricing, see Michael C. Ehrhardt and Ronald E. Shrieves, "The Impact of Warrants and Convertible Securities on the Systematic Risk of Common Equity," *Financial Review,* November 1995, pp. 843–856; Beni Lauterbach and Paul Schultz, "Pricing Warrants: An Empirical Study of the Black-Scholes Model and Its Alternatives," *Journal of Finance,* September 1990, pp. 1181–1209; David C. Leonard and Michael E. Solt, "On Using the Black-Scholes Model to Value Warrants," *Journal of Financial Research,* Summer 1990, pp. 81–92; and Katherine L. Phelps, William T. Moore, and Rodney L. Roenfeldt, "Equity Valuation Effects of Warrant-Debt Financing," *Journal of Financial Research,* Summer 1991, pp. 93–103.

$$\text{Conversion price} = P_c = \frac{\text{Par value of bond given up}}{\text{Shares received}} \qquad (20\text{--}2)$$

$$= \frac{\$1,000}{\text{CR}} = \frac{\$1,000}{18} = \$55.56$$

Conversely, by solving for CR, we obtain the conversion ratio:

$$\text{Conversion ratio} = \text{CR} = \frac{\$1,000}{P_c} \qquad (20\text{--}3)$$

$$= \frac{\$1,000}{\$55.56} = 18 \text{ shares}$$

Once CR is set, the value of P_c is established, and vice versa.

Like a warrant's exercise price, the conversion price is typically set some 20% to 30% above the prevailing market price of the common stock on the issue date. Generally, the conversion price and conversion ratio are fixed for the life of the bond, like those of Silicon Valley Software. Some companies, like Breedon Industries, however, have convertibles with a stepped-up conversion price. For example, Breedon's 2012 convertible debentures are convertible into 12.5 shares until 2021, into 11.76 shares from 2022 until 2032, and into 11.11 shares from 2032 until maturity in 2042. The conversion price thus starts at $80, rises to $85, and then goes to $90. Breedon's convertibles, like most, have a 10-year call-protection period.

Another factor that may cause a change in the conversion price and ratio is a standard feature of almost all convertibles—the clause protecting the convertible against dilution from stock splits, stock dividends, and the sale of common stock at prices below the conversion price. The typical provision states that if common stock is sold at a price below the conversion price, then the conversion price must be lowered (and the conversion ratio raised) to the price at which the new stock was issued. Also, if the stock is split or if a stock dividend is declared, the conversion price must be lowered by the percentage amount of the stock dividend or split. For example, if Breedon Industries were to have a 2-for-1 stock split during the first 10 years of its convertible's life, then the conversion ratio would automatically be adjusted from 12.5 to 25 and the conversion price lowered from $80 to $40. If this protection were not contained in the contract, then a company could completely thwart conversion by the use of stock splits and stock dividends. Warrants are similarly protected against dilution.

However, this standard protection against dilution from selling new stock at prices below the conversion price can get a company into trouble. For example, assume that Breedon's stock was selling for $65 per share at the time the convertible was issued. Then suppose that the market went sour and that Breedon's stock price dropped to $30 per share. If Breedon needed new equity to support operations, a new common stock sale would require the company to lower the conversion price on the convertible debentures from $80 to $30. That would raise the value of the convertibles and, in effect, transfer wealth from current shareholders to the convertible holders. This transfer would amount to a de facto additional flotation cost on the new common stock. Potential problems such as this must be kept in mind by firms considering the use of convertibles or bonds with warrants.

WEB

See *Ch20 Tool Kit.xls* on the textbook's Web site for details.

WEB

For a more detailed discussion of call strategies, see *Web Extension 20A* on the textbook's Web site.

20.3b The Component Cost of Convertibles

In the spring of 2012, Silicon Valley Software was evaluating the use of the convertible bond issue described earlier. The issue would consist of 20-year convertible bonds that would sell at a price of $1,000 per bond; this $1,000 would also be the bond's par (and maturity) value. The bonds would pay an 8% annual coupon interest rate, which is $80 per year. Each bond would be convertible into 18 shares of stock, so the conversion price would be $1,000/18 = $55.56. The stock was expected to pay a dividend of $1.40 during the coming year, and it sold at $35 per share. Further, the stock price was expected to grow at a constant rate of 9% per year. Therefore, $\hat{r}_s = D_1/P_0 + g = \$1.40/\$35 + 9\% = 4\% + 9\% = 13\%$. If the bonds were not made convertible then they would have to provide a yield of 10%, given their risk and the general level of interest rates. The convertible bonds would not be callable for 10 years, after which they could be called at a price of $1,050, with this price declining by $5 per year thereafter. If, after 10 years, the conversion value exceeded the call price by at least 20%, management would probably call the bonds.

Figure 20-1 shows the expectations of both an average investor and the company. Refer to the figure as you consider the following points.

1. The horizontal dashed line at $1,000 represents the par (and maturity) value. Also, $1,000 is the price at which the bond is initially offered to the public.
2. The bond is protected against a call for 10 years. It is initially callable at a price of $1,050, and the call price declines thereafter by $5 per year, as shown by the pink line in Figure 20-1.
3. Since the convertible has an 8% coupon rate and since the yield on a nonconvertible bond of similar risk is 10%, it follows that the expected "straight-bond" value of the convertible, B_t, must be less than par. At the time of issue and assuming an annual coupon, B_0 is $830:

(20–4)

$$\text{Pure-debt value at time of issue} = B_0 = \sum_{t=1}^{N} \frac{\text{Coupon interest}}{(1+r_d)^t} + \frac{\text{Maturity value}}{(1+r_d)^N}$$

$$= \sum_{t=1}^{20} \frac{\$80}{(1.10)^t} + \frac{\$1,000}{(1.10)^{20}} = 830$$

Note, however, that the bond's straight-debt value must be $1,000 at maturity, so the straight-debt value rises over time; this is plotted by the brown line in Figure 20-1.

4. The bond's initial **conversion value, C_t**, or the value of the stock an investor would receive if the bonds were converted at t = 0, is $P_0(CR) = \$35(18 \text{ shares}) = \$630$. Since the stock price is expected to grow at a 9% rate, the conversion value should rise over time. For example, in Year 5 it should be $P_5(CR) = \$35(1.09)^5(18) = \$969$. The expected conversion value is shown by the green line in Figure 20-1.
5. If the market price dropped below the straight-bond value, then those who wanted bonds would recognize the bargain and buy the convertible as a bond. Similarly, if the market price dropped below the conversion value, people would buy the convertibles, exercise them to get stock, and then sell the stock at a profit. Therefore, the higher of the bond value and conversion value curves in the graph represents a *floor price* for the bond. In Figure 20-1, the floor price is represented by the red line.

Figure 20-1	Silicon Valley Software: Convertible Bond Model

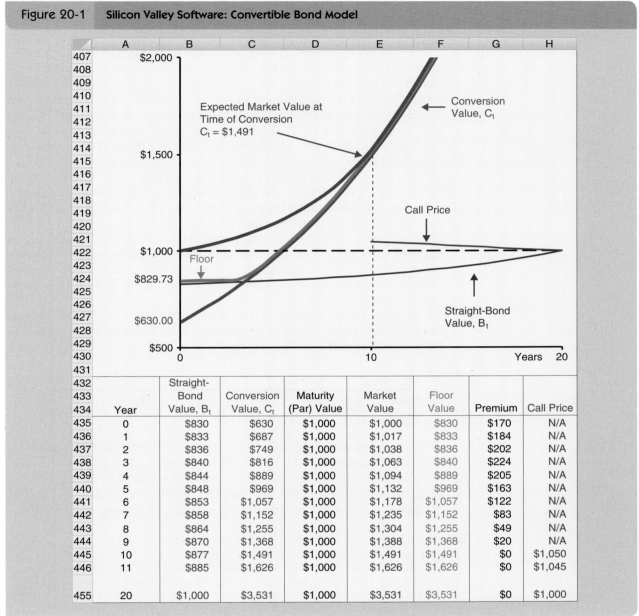

Year	Straight-Bond Value, B_t	Conversion Value, C_t	Maturity (Par) Value	Market Value	Floor Value	Premium	Call Price
0	$830	$630	$1,000	$1,000	$830	$170	N/A
1	$833	$687	$1,000	$1,017	$833	$184	N/A
2	$836	$749	$1,000	$1,038	$836	$202	N/A
3	$840	$816	$1,000	$1,063	$840	$224	N/A
4	$844	$889	$1,000	$1,094	$889	$205	N/A
5	$848	$969	$1,000	$1,132	$969	$163	N/A
6	$853	$1,057	$1,000	$1,178	$1,057	$122	N/A
7	$858	$1,152	$1,000	$1,235	$1,152	$83	N/A
8	$864	$1,255	$1,000	$1,304	$1,255	$49	N/A
9	$870	$1,368	$1,000	$1,388	$1,368	$20	N/A
10	$877	$1,491	$1,000	$1,491	$1,491	$0	$1,050
11	$885	$1,626	$1,000	$1,626	$1,626	$0	$1,045
20	$1,000	$3,531	$1,000	$3,531	$3,531	$0	$1,000

6. The convertible bond's market price will exceed the straight-bond value because the option to convert is worth something—an 8% bond with conversion possibilities is worth more than an 8% bond without this option. The convertible's price will also exceed its conversion value because holding the convertible is equivalent to holding a call option and, prior to expiration, the option's true value is higher than its exercise (or conversion) value. Without using financial engineering models, we cannot say exactly where the market value line will lie, but as a rule it will be above the floor, as shown by the blue line in Figure 20-1.

7. If the stock price continues to increase, then it becomes more and more likely that the bond will be converted. As this likelihood increases, the market value line will begin to converge with the conversion value line.

   After the bond becomes callable, its market value cannot exceed the higher of the conversion value and the call price without exposing investors to the danger of a call. For example, suppose that 10 years after issue (when the bonds become callable) the market value of the bond is $1,600, the conversion value is $1,500, and the call price is $1,050. If the company called the bonds the day after you bought one for $1,600, you would choose to convert them to stock worth only $1,500 (rather than let the company buy the bond from you at the $1,050 call price), so you would suffer a loss of $100. Recognizing this danger, you and other investors would refuse to pay a premium over the higher of the call price or the conversion value after the bond becomes callable. Therefore, in Figure 20-1, we assume that the market value line hits the conversion value line in Year 10, when the bond becomes callable.

8. In our example, the call-protection period ends in 10 years. At this time, the expected stock price is so high that the conversion value is almost certainly going to be greater than the call price; hence we assume that the bond will be converted immediately prior to the company calling the bond, which would happen in 10 years.

9. The expected market value at Year 10 is $35(1.09)^{10}(18) = \$1,491$. An investor can find the expected rate of return on the convertible bond, r_c, by finding the IRR of the following cash flow stream:

With a financial calculator, we set $N = 10$, $PV = -1000$, $PMT = 80$, and $FV = 1491$; we then solve for $I/YR = r_c = IRR = 10.94\%$.[12]

10. A convertible is riskier than straight debt but less risky than stock, so its cost of capital should be somewhere between the cost of straight debt and the cost of equity. This is true in our example: $r_d = 10\%$, $r_c = 10.94\%$, and $r_s = 13\%$.[13]

---

12. As in the case with warrants, the expected conversion value is not precisely equal to the expected stock price multiplied by the conversion ratio. Here is the reason. If after 10 years the stock price happens to be low, so that the conversion value is less than the call price, then the bondholders would not choose to convert—instead, they would surrender their bonds if the company called them. In this example, conversion does not occur if the stock price is less than $1,050/18 = \$58.33$ after 10 years. Since the company makes a call in order to force conversion, it won't call the bonds if the stock price is less than $58.33. So when the stock price is low, the bondholders will keep the bonds, whose value will depend primarily on interest rates at that time. Finding the expected value in this situation is a difficult problem (and is beyond the scope of this text)! However, if the expected stock price is much greater than the conversion price when the bonds are called (in this case, $35[1.09]^{10} = \$82.86$ is much more than $58.33), then the difference between the true expected conversion value and the conversion value that we calculated using the expected stock price will be very small. Therefore, we can approximate the component cost reasonably accurately with the approach used in the example.

13. To find the after-tax cost of the convertible, you can replace the pre-tax coupons with the after-tax coupons paid by the company. If the corporate tax rate is 40%, then we have $N = 10$, $PV = -1000$, $PMT = 80(1 - 0.40) = 48$, and $FV = 1491$; we solve for $I/YR = r_{c,AT} = 8.16\%$. Notice that this after-tax cost is not equal to $r_c(1 - T)$.

20.3c Use of Convertibles in Financing

Convertibles have two important advantages from the issuer's standpoint: (1) Convertibles, like bonds with warrants, offer a company the chance to sell debt with a low coupon rate in exchange for giving bondholders a chance to participate in the company's success if it does well. (2) In a sense, convertibles provide a way to sell common stock at prices higher than those currently prevailing. Some companies actually want to sell common stock, not debt, but feel that the price of their stock is temporarily depressed. Management may know, for example, that earnings are depressed because of start-up costs associated with a new project, but they expect earnings to rise sharply during the next year or so, pulling the price of the stock up with them. Thus, if the company sold stock now, it would be giving up more shares than necessary to raise a given amount of capital. However, if it set the conversion price 20% to 30% above the present market price of the stock, then 20% to 30% fewer shares would be given up when the bonds were converted than if stock were sold directly at the current time. Note, however, that management is counting on the stock's price to rise above the conversion price, thus making the bonds attractive in conversion. If earnings do not rise and pull the stock price up, so that conversion does *not* occur, then the company will be saddled with debt in the face of low earnings, which could be disastrous.

How can the company be sure that conversion will occur if the price of the stock rises above the conversion price? Typically, convertibles contain a call provision that enables the issuing firm to force holders to convert. Suppose the conversion price is $50, the conversion ratio is 20, the market price of the common stock has risen to $60, and the call price on a convertible bond is $1,050. If the company calls the bond, bondholders can either convert into common stock with a market value of $20($60) = $1,200 or allow the company to redeem the bond for $1,050. Naturally, bondholders prefer $1,200 to $1,050, so conversion would occur. The call provision thus gives the company a way to force conversion, provided the market price of the stock is greater than the conversion price. Note, however, that most convertibles have a fairly long period of call protection—10 years is typical. Therefore, if the company wants to be able to force conversion fairly early, it will have to set a short call-protection period. This will, in turn, require that it set a higher coupon rate or a lower conversion price.

From the standpoint of the issuer, convertibles have three important disadvantages: (1) Even though the use of a convertible bond may give the company the opportunity to sell stock at a price higher than the price at which it could be sold currently, if the stock greatly increases in price then the firm would be better off if it had used straight debt (in spite of its higher cost) and then later sold common stock and refunded the debt. (2) Convertibles typically have a low coupon interest rate, and the advantage of this low-cost debt will be lost when conversion occurs. (3) If the company truly wants to raise equity capital and if the price of the stock does not rise sufficiently after the bond is issued, then the company will be stuck with debt.

20.3d Convertibles and Agency Costs

A potential agency conflict between bondholders and stockholders is asset substitution, also known as "bait and switch." Suppose a company has been investing in low-risk projects, and because risk is low, bondholders charge a low interest rate. What happens if the company is considering a very risky but highly profitable venture that potential lenders don't know about? The company might decide to raise low–interest-rate debt without revealing that the funds will be invested in a risky project. After the funds have been raised and the investment is made, the value of the debt should fall because its interest rate will be too low to compensate debtholders for the high risk they bear. This is a "heads I win, tails you lose" situation, and it results in a wealth transfer from bondholders to stockholders.

Let's use some numbers to illustrate this scenario. The value of a company, based on the present value of its future free cash flows, is $800 million. It has $300 million of debt, based on market values. Therefore, its equity is worth $800 − $300 = $500 million. The company now undertakes some projects with high but risky expected returns, and its expected NPV remains unchanged. In other words, the actual NPV will probably end up much higher or much lower than under the old situation, but the firm still has the same expected value. Even though its total value is still $800 million, the value of the debt falls because its risk has increased. Note that the debtholders don't benefit if the venture's value is higher than expected, because the most they can receive is the contracted coupon and the principal repayment. However, they will suffer if the value of the projects turns out to be lower than expected, since they might not receive the full value of their contracted payments. In other words, risk doesn't give them any upside potential but does expose them to downside losses, so the bondholders' expected value must decline.

With a constant total firm value, if the value of the debt falls from $300 to $200 million, then the value of equity must increase from $500 to $800 − $200 = $600 million. Thus, the bait-and-switch tactic causes a wealth transfer of $100 million from debtholders to stockholders.

If debtholders think a company might employ the bait-and-switch tactic, they will charge a higher interest rate, and this higher interest rate is an agency cost. Debtholders will charge this higher rate even if the company has no intention of engaging in bait-and-switch behavior, since they can't know the company's true intentions. Therefore, they assume the worst and charge a higher interest rate.

Convertible securities are one way to mitigate this type of agency cost. Suppose the debt is convertible and the company does take on the high-risk project. If the value of the company turns out to be higher than expected, then bondholders can convert their debt to equity and benefit from the successful investment. Therefore, bondholders are willing to charge a lower interest rate on convertibles, and this serves to minimize the agency costs.

Note that if a company does not engage in bait-and-switch behavior by swapping low-risk projects for high-risk projects, then the chance of "hitting a home run" is reduced. Because there is less chance of a home run, the convertible bond is less likely to be converted. In this situation, the convertible bonds are actually similar to nonconvertible debt, except that they carry a lower interest rate.

Now consider a different agency cost, one due to asymmetric information between the managers and potential new stockholders. Suppose a firm's managers know that its future prospects are not as good as the market believes, which means the current stock price is too high. Acting in the interests of existing stockholders, managers can issue stock at the current high price. When the poor future prospects are eventually revealed, the stock price will fall, causing a transfer of wealth from the new shareholders to old shareholders.

To illustrate this, suppose the market estimates an $800 million present value of future free cash flows. For simplicity, assume the firm has no nonoperating assets and no debt, so the total value of both the firm and the equity is $800 million. However, its managers know the market has overestimated the future free cash flows and that the true value is only $700 million. When investors eventually discover this, the value of the company will drop to $700 million. But before this happens, suppose the company raises $200 million of new equity. The company uses this new cash to invest in projects with a present value of $200 million, which shouldn't be too hard, since these are projects with a zero NPV. Right after the new stock is sold, the company will have a market value of $800 + $200 = $1,000 million, based on the market's overly optimistic estimate of the company's future prospects. Observe that the new shareholders own 20% of the company ($200/$1,000 = 0.20) and the original shareholders own 80%.

As time passes, the market will realize that the previously estimated value of $800 million for the company's original set of projects was too high and that these projects are worth only $700 million. The new projects are still worth $200 million, so the total value of the company will fall to $700 + $200 = $900 million. The original shareholders' value is now 80% of $900 million, which is $720 million. Note that this is $20 million *more* than it would have been if the company had issued no new stock. The new shareholders' value is now 0.20($900) = $180 million, which is $20 million *less* than their original investment. The net effect is a $20 million wealth transfer from the new shareholders to the original shareholders.

Because potential shareholders know this might occur, they interpret an issue of new stock as a signal of poor future prospects, which causes the stock price to fall. Note also that this will occur even for companies whose future prospects are actually quite good, because the market has no way of distinguishing between companies with good versus poor prospects.

A company with good future prospects might want to issue equity, but it knows the market will interpret this as a negative signal. One way to obtain equity and yet avoid this signaling effect is to issue convertible bonds. Because the company knows its true future prospects are better than the market anticipates, it knows the bonds will likely end up being converted to equity. Thus, a company in this situation is issuing equity "through the back door" when it issues convertible debt.

In summary, convertibles are logical securities to use in at least two situations. First, if a company would like to finance with straight debt but lenders are afraid the funds will be invested in a manner that increases the firm's risk profile, then convertibles are a good choice. Second, if a company wants to issue stock but thinks such a move would cause investors to interpret a stock offering as a signal of tough times ahead, then again convertibles would be a good choice.[14]

---

14. See Craig M. Lewis, Richard J. Rogalski, and James K. Seward, "Understanding the Design of Convertible Debt," *Journal of Applied Corporate Finance,* Vol. 11, No. 1, Spring 1998, pp. 45–53. For more insights into convertible pricing and use, see Paul Asquith and David W. Mullins Jr., "Convertible Debt: Corporate Call Policy and Voluntary Conversion," *Journal of Finance,* September 1991, pp. 1273–1289; Randall S. Billingsley and David M. Smith, "Why Do Firms Issue Convertible Debt?" *Financial Management,* Summer 1996, pp. 93–99; Douglas R. Emery, Mai E. Iskandar-Datta, and Jong-Chul Rhim, "Capital Structure Management as a Motivation for Calling Convertible Debt," *Journal of Financial Research,* Spring 1994, pp. 91–104; T. Harikumar, P. Kadapakkam, and Ronald F. Singer, "Convertible Debt and Investment Incentives," *Journal of Financial Research,* Spring 1994, pp. 15–29; and V. Sivarama Krishnan and Ramesh P. Rao, "Financial Distress Costs and Delayed Calls of Convertible Bonds," *Financial Review,* November 1996, pp. 913–925.

What is a conversion ratio? A conversion price? A straight-bond value?

What is meant by a convertible's *floor value*?

What are the advantages and disadvantages of convertibles to issuers? To investors?

How do convertibles reduce agency costs?

A convertible bond has a par value of $1,000 and a conversion price of $25. The stock currently trades for $22 a share. What are the bond's conversion ratio and conversion value at t = 0? **(40, $880)**

20.4 A Final Comparison of Warrants and Convertibles

Convertible debt can be thought of as straight debt with nondetachable warrants. Thus, at first blush, it might appear that debt with warrants and convertible debt are more or less interchangeable. However, a closer look reveals one major and several minor differences between these two securities.[15] First, as we discussed previously, the exercise of warrants brings in new equity capital, whereas the conversion of convertibles results only in an accounting transfer.

A second difference involves flexibility. Most convertibles contain a call provision that allows the issuer either to refund the debt or to force conversion, depending on the relationship between the conversion value and call price. However, most warrants are not callable, so firms must wait until maturity for the warrants to generate new equity capital. Generally, maturities also differ between warrants and convertibles. Warrants typically have much shorter maturities than convertibles, and warrants typically expire before their accompanying debt matures. Warrants also provide for fewer future common shares than do convertibles, because with convertibles all of the debt is converted to stock, whereas debt remains outstanding when warrants are exercised. Together, these facts suggest that debt-plus-warrant issuers are actually more interested in selling debt than in selling equity.

In general, firms that issue debt with warrants are smaller and riskier than those that issue convertibles. One possible rationale for the use of option securities, especially the use of debt with warrants by small firms, is the difficulty investors have in assessing the risk of small companies. If a start-up with a new, untested product seeks debt financing, then it's difficult for potential lenders to judge the riskiness of the venture and so it's difficult to set a fair interest rate. Under these circumstances, many potential investors will be reluctant to invest, making it necessary to set a very high interest rate to attract debt capital. By issuing debt with warrants, investors obtain a package that offers upside potential to offset the risks of loss.

Finally, there is a significant difference in issuance costs between debt with warrants and convertible debt. Bonds with warrants typically require issuance costs that are about 1.2 percentage points more than the flotation costs for convertibles. In general, bond-with-warrant financings have underwriting fees that approximate

---

15. For a more detailed comparison of warrants and convertibles, see Michael S. Long and Stephen F. Sefcik, "Participation Financing: A Comparison of the Characteristics of Convertible Debt and Straight Bonds Issued in Conjunction with Warrants," *Financial Management*, Autumn 1990, pp. 23–34.

the weighted average of the fees associated with debt and equity issues, whereas underwriting costs for convertibles are more like those associated with straight debt.

Self Test

What are some differences between debt-with-warrant financing and convertible debt?

Explain how bonds with warrants might help small, risky firms sell debt securities.

20.5 Reporting Earnings When Warrants or Convertibles Are Outstanding

If warrants or convertibles are outstanding, the Financial Accounting Standard Board requires that a firm report basic earnings per share and diluted earnings per share.[16]

1. *Basic EPS* is calculated as earnings available to common stockholders divided by the average number of shares actually outstanding during the period.
2. *Diluted EPS* is calculated as the earnings that would have been available to common shareholders divided by the average number of shares that would have been outstanding if "dilutive" securities had been converted. The rules governing the calculation of diluted EPS are quite complex; here we present a simple illustration using convertible bonds. If the bonds had been converted at the beginning of the accounting period, then the firm's interest payments would have been lower because it would not have had to pay interest on the bonds, and this would have caused earnings to be higher. But the number of outstanding shares of stock also would have increased because of the conversion. If the higher earnings and higher number of shares caused EPS to fall, then the convertible bonds would be defined as dilutive securities because their conversion would decrease (or dilute) EPS. All convertible securities with a net dilutive effect are included when calculating diluted EPS. Therefore, this definition means that diluted EPS always will be lower than basic EPS. In essence, the diluted EPS measure is an attempt to show how the presence of convertible securities reduces common shareholders' claims on the firm.

Under SEC rules, firms are required to report both basic and diluted EPS. For firms with large amounts of option securities outstanding, there can be a substantial difference between the basic and diluted EPS figures. This makes it easier for investors to compare the performance of U.S. firms with their foreign counterparts, which tend to use basic EPS.

---

16. FAS 128 was issued in February of 1997. It simplified the calculations required by firms, made U.S. standards more consistent with international standards, and required the presentation of both basic EPS and diluted EPS for those firms with significant amounts of convertible securities. In addition, it replaced a measure called *primary EPS* with basic EPS. In general, the calculation of primary EPS required the company to estimate whether or not a security was "likely to be converted in the near future" and to base the calculation of EPS on the assumption that those securities would in fact have been converted. In June 2008 the FASB issued FSP APB 14-1, which (although not changing how EPS is reported under FAS 128) requires that convertibles be split into their implied equity and debt components for accounting purposes, in much the same way as we analyze them in this chapter.

Self Test

What are the three possible methods for reporting EPS when warrants and convertibles are outstanding?

Which methods are most used in practice?

Why should investors be concerned about a firm's outstanding warrants and convertibles?

Summary

Although common stock and long-term debt provide most of the capital used by corporations, companies also use several forms of "hybrid securities." The hybrids include preferred stock, convertibles, and warrants, and they generally have some characteristics of debt and some of equity. The key concepts covered are listed below.

- **Preferred** stock is a hybrid—it is similar to bonds in some respects and to common stock in other ways.
- **Adjustable rate preferred stocks (ARPs)** pay dividends tied to the rate on Treasury securities. **Market auction (money market) preferred stocks** are low-risk, largely tax-exempt securities of 7-week maturity that can be sold between auction dates at close to par.
- A **warrant** is a long-term call option issued along with a bond. Warrants are generally detachable from the bond, and they trade separately in the market. When warrants are exercised, the firm receives additional equity capital, and the original bonds remain outstanding.
- A **convertible** security is a bond or preferred stock that can be exchanged for common stock at the option of the holder. When a security is converted, debt or preferred stock is replaced with common stock, and no money changes hands.
- Warrant and convertible issues generally are structured so that the **strike price** (also called the **exercise price**) or **conversion price** is 20% to 30% above the stock's price at time of issue.
- Although both warrants and convertibles are option securities, there are several differences between the two, including **separability, impact when exercised, callability, maturity,** and **flotation costs.**
- Warrants and convertibles are **sweeteners** used to make the underlying debt or preferred stock issue more attractive to investors. Although the coupon rate or dividend yield is lower when options are part of the issue, the overall cost of the issue is higher than the cost of straight debt or preferred, because option-related securities are riskier.
- For a more detailed discussion of **call strategies** see *Web Extension 20A* on the textbook's Web site.

Questions

20-1 Define each of the following terms.
   a. Preferred stock
   b. Cumulative dividends; arrearages
   c. Warrant; detachable warrant
   d. Stepped-up price
   e. Convertible security
   f. Conversion ratio; conversion price; conversion value
   g. Sweetener

20-2 Is preferred stock more like bonds or common stock? Explain.

20-3 What effect does the trend in stock prices (subsequent to issue) have on a firm's ability to raise funds through (a) convertibles and (b) warrants?

20-4 If a firm expects to have additional financial requirements in the future, would you recommend that it use convertibles or bonds with warrants? What factors would influence your decision?

20-5 How does a firm's dividend policy affect each of the following?
   a. The value of its long-term warrants
   b. The likelihood that its convertible bonds will be converted
   c. The likelihood that its warrants will be exercised

20-6 Evaluate the following statement: "Issuing convertible securities is a means by which a firm can sell common stock for more than the existing market price."

20-7 Suppose a company simultaneously issues $50 million of convertible bonds with a coupon rate of 10% and $50 million of straight bonds with a coupon rate of 14%. Both bonds have the same maturity. Does the convertible issue's lower coupon rate suggest that it is less risky than the straight bond? Is the cost of capital lower on the convertible than on the straight bond? Explain.

Problems   Answers Appear in Appendix B

Easy Problems 1–2

20-1 **Warrants** Neubert Enterprises recently issued $1,000 par value 15-year bonds with a 5% coupon paid annually and warrants attached. These bonds are currently trading for $1,000. Neubert also has outstanding $1,000 par value 15-year straight debt with a 7% coupon paid annually, also trading for $1,000. What is the implied value of the warrants attached to each bond?

20-2 **Convertibles** Breuer Investment's convertible bonds have a $1,000 par value and a conversion price of $50 a share. What is the convertible issue's conversion ratio?

Intermediate Problems 3–4

20-3 **Warrants** Maese Industries Inc. has warrants outstanding that permit the holders to purchase 1 share of stock per warrant at a price of $25.

a. Calculate the exercise value of the firm's warrants if the common sells at each of the following prices: (1) $20, (2) $25, (3) $30, (4) $100. (*Hint:* A warrant's exercise value is the difference between the stock price and the purchase price specified by the warrant if the warrant were to be exercised.)

b. Assume the firm's stock now sells for $20 per share. The company wants to sell some 20-year, $1,000 par value bonds with interest paid annually. Each bond will have attached 50 warrants, each exercisable into 1 share of stock at an exercise price of $25. The firm's straight bonds yield 12%. Assume that each warrant will have a market value of $3 when the stock sells at $20. What coupon interest rate, and dollar coupon, must the company set on the bonds with warrants if they are to clear the market? (*Hint:* The convertible bond should have an initial price of $1,000.)

20-4 Convertible Premiums The Tsetsekos Company was planning to finance an expansion. The principal executives of the company all agreed that an industrial company such as theirs should finance growth by means of common stock rather than by debt. However, they felt that the current $42 per share price of the company's common stock did not reflect its true worth, so they decided to sell a convertible security. They considered a convertible debenture but feared the burden of fixed interest charges if the common stock did not rise enough in price to make conversion attractive. They decided on an issue of convertible preferred stock, which would pay a dividend of $2.10 per share.

a. The conversion ratio will be 1.0; that is, each share of convertible preferred can be converted into a single share of common. Therefore, the convertible's par value (and also the issue price) will be equal to the conversion price, which in turn will be determined as a premium (i.e., the percentage by which the conversion price exceeds the stock price) over the current market price of the common stock. What will the conversion price be if it is set at a 10% premium? At a 30% premium?

b. Should the preferred stock include a call provision? Why?

Challenging Problems 5–7

20-5 Convertible Bond Analysis Fifteen years ago, Roop Industries sold $400 million of convertible bonds. The bonds had a 40-year maturity, a 5.75% coupon rate, and paid interest annually. They were sold at their $1,000 par value. The conversion price was set at $62.75, and the common stock price was $55 per share. The bonds were subordinated debentures and were given an A rating; straight nonconvertible debentures of the same quality yielded about 8.75% at the time Roop's bonds were issued.

a. Calculate the premium on the bonds—that is, the percentage excess of the conversion price over the stock price at the time of issue.

b. What is Roop's annual before-tax interest savings on the convertible issue versus a straight-debt issue?

c. At the time the bonds were issued, what was the value per bond of the conversion feature?

d. Suppose the price of Roop's common stock fell from $55 on the day the bonds were issued to $32.75 now, 15 years after the issue date (also assume the stock price never exceeded $62.75). Assume interest rates remained constant. What is the current price of the straight-bond portion of the convertible bond? What is the current value if a bondholder converts a bond? Do you think it is likely that the bonds will be converted?

e. The bonds originally sold for $1,000. If interest rates on A-rated bonds had remained constant at 8.75% and if the stock price had fallen to $32.75, then what do you think would have happened to the price of the convertible bonds? (Assume no change in the standard deviation of stock returns.)

f. Now suppose that the price of Roop's common stock had fallen from $55 on the day the bonds were issued to $32.75 at present, 15 years after the issue. Suppose also that the interest rate on similar straight debt had fallen from 8.75% to 5.75%. Under these conditions, what is the current price of the straight-bond portion of the convertible bond? What is the current value if a bondholder converts a bond? What do you think would have happened to the price of the bonds?

20-6 **Warrant/Convertible Decisions** The Howland Carpet Company has grown rapidly during the past 5 years. Recently, its commercial bank urged the company to consider increasing its permanent financing. Its bank loan under a line of credit has risen to $250,000, carrying an 8% interest rate. Howland has been 30 to 60 days late in paying trade creditors.

Discussions with an investment banker have resulted in the decision to raise $500,000 at this time. Investment bankers have assured the firm that the following alternatives are feasible (flotation costs will be ignored).

- *Alternative 1:* Sell common stock at $8.
- *Alternative 2:* Sell convertible bonds at an 8% coupon, convertible into 100 shares of common stock for each $1,000 bond (i.e., the conversion price is $10 per share).
- *Alternative 3:* Sell debentures at an 8% coupon, each $1,000 bond carrying 100 warrants to buy common stock at $10.

John L. Howland, the president, owns 80% of the common stock and wishes to maintain control of the company. There are 100,000 shares outstanding. The following are extracts of Howland's latest financial statements:

Balance Sheet

		Current liabilities	$400,000
		Common stock, par $1	100,000
		Retained earnings	50,000
Total assets	$550,000	Total claims	$550,000

Income Statement

Sales	$1,100,000
All costs except interest	990,000
EBIT	$ 110,000
Interest	20,000
EBT	$ 90,000
Taxes (40%)	36,000
Net income	$ 54,000
Shares outstanding	100,000
Earnings per share	$ 0.54
Price/earnings ratio	15.83
Market price of stock	$ 8.55

a. Show the new balance sheet under each alternative. For Alternatives 2 and 3, show the balance sheet after conversion of the bonds or exercise of the warrants. Assume that half of the funds raised will be used to pay off the bank loan and half to increase total assets.

b. Show Mr. Howland's control position under each alternative, assuming that he does not purchase additional shares.

c. What is the effect on earnings per share of each alternative, assuming that profits before interest and taxes will be 20% of total assets?

d. What will be the debt ratio (TL/TA) under each alternative?

e. Which of the three alternatives would you recommend to Howland, and why?

20-7 **Convertible Bond Analysis** Niendorf Incorporated needs to raise $25 million to construct production facilities for a new type of USB memory device. The firm's straight nonconvertible debentures currently yield 9%. Its stock sells for $23 per share, has an expected constant growth rate of 6%, and has an expected dividend yield of 7%, for a total expected return on equity of 13%. Investment bankers have tentatively proposed that the firm raise the $25 million by issuing convertible debentures. These convertibles would have a $1,000 par value, carry a coupon rate of 8%, have a 20-year maturity, and be convertible into 35 shares of stock. Coupon payments would be made annually. The bonds would be noncallable for 5 years, after which they would be callable at a price of $1,075; this call price would decline by $5 per year in Year 6 and each year thereafter. For simplicity, assume that the bonds may be called or converted only at the end of a year, immediately after the coupon and dividend payments. Also assume that management would call eligible bonds if the conversion value exceeded 20% of par value (not 20% of call price).

a. At what year do you expect the bonds will be forced into conversion with a call? What is the bond's value in conversion when it is converted at this time? What is the cash flow to the bondholder when it is converted at this time? (*Hint:* The cash flow includes the conversion value and the coupon payment, because the conversion occurs immediately after the coupon is paid.)

b. What is the expected rate of return (i.e., the before-tax component cost) on the proposed convertible issue?

Spreadsheet Problem

20-8 **Build a Model: Convertible Bond Analysis** Start with the partial model in the file *Ch20 P08 Build a Model.xls* on the textbook's Web site. Maggie's Magazines (MM) has straight nonconvertible bonds that currently yield 9%. MM's stock sells for $22 per share, has an expected constant growth rate of 6%, and has a dividend yield of 4%. MM plans on issuing convertible bonds that will have a $1,000 par value, a coupon rate of 8%, a 20-year maturity, and a conversion ratio of 32 (i.e., each bond could be convertible into 32 shares of stock). Coupon payments will be made annually. The bonds will be noncallable for 5 years, after which they will be callable at a price of $1,090; this call price would decline by $6 per year in Year 6 and each year thereafter. For simplicity, assume that the bonds may be called or converted only at the end of a year, immediately after the coupon and dividend payments.

Management will call the bonds when their conversion value exceeds 25% of their par value (not their call price).

a. For each year, calculate (1) the anticipated stock price, (2) the anticipated conversion value, (3) the anticipated straight-bond price, and (4) the cash flow to the investor assuming conversion occurs. At what year do you expect the bonds will be forced into conversion with a call? What is the bond's value in conversion when it is converted at this time? What is the cash flow to the bondholder when it is converted at this time? (*Hint:* The cash flow includes the conversion value and the coupon payment, because the conversion occurs immediately after the coupon is paid.)

b. What is the expected rate of return (i.e., the before-tax component cost) on the proposed convertible issue?

c. Assume that the convertible bondholders require a 9% rate of return. If the coupon rate remains unchanged, then what conversion ratio will give a bond price of $1,000?

MINI CASE

Paul Duncan, financial manager of EduSoft Inc., is facing a dilemma. The firm was founded 5 years ago to provide educational software for the rapidly expanding primary and secondary school markets. Although EduSoft has done well, the firm's founder believes an industry shake-out is imminent. To survive, EduSoft must grab market share now, and this will require a large infusion of new capital.

Because he expects earnings to continue rising sharply and looks for the stock price to follow suit, Mr. Duncan does not think it would be wise to issue new common stock at this time. On the other hand, interest rates are currently high by historical standards, and the firm's B rating means that interest payments on a new debt issue would be prohibitive. Thus, he has narrowed his choice of financing alternatives to (1) preferred stock, (2) bonds with warrants, or (3) convertible bonds.

As Duncan's assistant, you have been asked to help in the decision process by answering the following questions.

a. How does preferred stock differ from both common equity and debt? Is preferred stock more risky than common stock? What is floating rate preferred stock?

b. How can a knowledge of call options help a financial manager to better understand warrants and convertibles?

c. Mr. Duncan has decided to eliminate preferred stock as one of the alternatives and focus on the others. EduSoft's investment banker estimates that EduSoft could issue a bond-with-warrants package consisting of a 20-year bond and 27 warrants. Each warrant would have a strike price of $25 and 10 years until expiration. It is estimated that each warrant, when detached and traded separately, would have a value of $5. The coupon on a similar bond but without warrants would be 10%.

(1) What coupon rate should be set on the bond with warrants if the total package is to sell at par ($1,000)?

(2) When would you expect the warrants to be exercised? What is a stepped-up exercise price?

(3) Will the warrants bring in additional capital when exercised? If EduSoft issues 100,000 bond-with-warrant packages, how much cash will EduSoft receive when the warrants are exercised? How many shares of stock will be

outstanding after the warrants are exercised? (EduSoft currently has 20 million shares outstanding.)

(4) Because the presence of warrants results in a lower coupon rate on the accompanying debt issue, shouldn't all debt be issued with warrants? To answer this, estimate the anticipated stock price in 10 years when the warrants are expected to be exercised, then estimate the return to the holders of the bond-with-warrants packages. Use the corporate valuation model to estimate the expected stock price in 10 years. Assume that EduSoft's current value of operations is $500 million and it is expected to grow at 8% per year.

(5) How would you expect the cost of the bond with warrants to compare with the cost of straight debt? With the cost of common stock (which is 13.4%)?

(6) If the corporate tax rate is 40%, what is the after-tax cost of the bond with warrants?

d. As an alternative to the bond with warrants, Mr. Duncan is considering convertible bonds. The firm's investment bankers estimate that EduSoft could sell a 20-year, 8.5% coupon (paid annually), callable convertible bond for its $1,000 par value, whereas a straight-debt issue would require a 10% coupon (paid annually). The convertibles would be call protected for 5 years, the call price would be $1,100, and the company would probably call the bonds as soon as possible after their conversion value exceeds $1,200. Note, though, that the call must occur on an issue-date anniversary. EduSoft's current stock price is $20, its last dividend was $1, and the dividend is expected to grow at a constant 8% rate. The convertible could be converted into 40 shares of EduSoft stock at the owner's option.

(1) What conversion price is built into the bond?

(2) What is the convertible's straight-debt value? What is the implied value of the convertibility feature?

(3) What is the formula for the bond's expected conversion value in any year? What is its conversion value at Year 0? At Year 10?

(4) What is meant by the "floor value" of a convertible? What is the convertible's expected floor value at Year 0? At Year 10?

(5) Assume that EduSoft intends to force conversion by calling the bond as soon as possible after its conversion value exceeds 20% above its par value, or 1.2($1,000) = $1,200. When is the issue expected to be called? (Hint: Recall that the call must be made on an anniversary date of the issue.)

(6) What is the expected cost of capital for the convertible to EduSoft? Does this cost appear to be consistent with the riskiness of the issue?

(7) What is the after-tax cost of the convertible bond?

e. Mr. Duncan believes that the costs of both the bond with warrants and the convertible bond are close enough to call them even and also are consistent with the risks involved. Thus, he will make his decision based on other factors. What are some of the factors that he should consider?

f. How do convertible bonds help reduce agency costs?

Selected Additional Cases

The following cases from TextChoice, Cengage Learning's online case library, cover many of the concepts discussed in this chapter and are available at **www.textchoice2.com/casenet.**

Klein-Brigham Series:

Case 27, "Virginia May Chocolate Company," which illustrates convertible bond valuation, and Case 98, "Levinger Organic Snack," which illustrates the use of convertibles and warrants.

PART VI

Working Capital Management

Chapter 21

Working Capital Management

WEB

The textbook's Web site contains an *Excel* file that will guide you through the chapter's calculations. The file for this chapter is **Ch21Tool Kit.xls**, and we encourage you to open the file and follow along as you read the chapter.

Working capital management involves two basic questions: (1) What is the appropriate amount of working capital, both in total and for each specific account, and (2) how should working capital be financed? Note that sound working capital management goes beyond finance. Indeed, improving the firm's working capital position generally comes from improvements in the operating divisions. For example, experts in logistics, operations management, and information technology often work with engineers and production specialists to develop ways to speed up the manufacturing process and thus reduce the goods-in-process inventory. Similarly, marketing managers and logistics experts cooperate to develop better ways to deliver the firm's products to its customers. Finance comes into play in evaluating how effective the firm's operating departments are relative to other firms in its industry and also in evaluating the profitability of alternative proposals for improving working capital management. In addition, financial managers decide how much cash their companies should keep on hand and how much short-term financing should be used to finance their working capital.

Here are some basic definitions and concepts.

1. **Working capital,** sometimes called *gross working capital,* simply refers to current assets used in operations.[1]
2. **Net working capital** is defined as current assets minus all current liabilities.
3. **Net operating working capital (NOWC)** is defined as operating current assets minus operating current liabilities. Generally, NOWC is equal to cash required in operations, accounts receivable, and inventories, less accounts payable and accruals. Marketable securities not used in operations, cash in excess of operating needs, and other short-term investments are generally not considered to be operating current assets, so they are typically excluded when NOWC is calculated. The firm itself determines how much of its cash is required for operations, but all of the cash of most firms is used in operations.

---

1. The term "working capital" originated with the old Yankee peddler, who would load his wagon with pots and pans and then take off to peddle his wares. His horse and wagon were his fixed assets, while his merchandise was sold, or turned over at a profit, and thus was called his *working capital.*

Beginning of Chapter Questions

As you read this chapter, consider how you would answer the following questions. You *should not* necessarily be able to answer the questions before you read the chapter. Rather, you should use them to get a sense of the issues covered in the chapter. After reading the chapter, you should be able to give at least partial answers to the questions, and you should be able to give better answers after the chapter has been discussed in class. Note, too, that it is often useful, when answering conceptual questions, to use hypothetical data to illustrate your answer. We illustrate the answers with an *Excel* model that is available on the textbook's Web site. Accessing the model and working through it is a useful exercise, and it provides insights that are useful when answering the questions.

1. What is the **cash conversion cycle (CCC)?** Why is it better, other things held constant, to have a shorter rather than a longer CCC? Suppose you know a company's annual sales, average inventories, average accounts receivable, average accounts payable, and annual cost of goods sold. How could you use that information to determine the company's CCC? If you also knew its cost of capital, how could you determine its annual cost of carrying working capital? How could you determine how much the company would save if it could reduce the CCC by, say,

5 days? What are some actions it might take to reduce the CCC?

2. What is a **cash budget,** and how is this statement used by a business? How is the cash budget affected by the CCC? By credit policy?

3. Differentiate between **free** and **costly trade credit.** What is the formula for determining the **nominal annual cost rate** associated with a credit policy? What is the formula for the **effective annual cost rate?** How would these cost rates be affected if a firm buying on credit could "stretch" either the discount days or the net payment days— that is, take discounts on payments made after the discount period or else pay later than the stated payment date?

4. What are some advantages of **matching the maturities** of claims against assets with the lives of the assets financed by those claims? Is it feasible for a firm to match perfectly the maturities of all assets and claims against assets? Why might a firm deliberately mismatch some asset and claim maturities?

5. Define the terms **aggressive** and **conservative** when applied to financing, give examples of each, and then discuss the pros and cons of each approach. Would you expect to find entrenched firms in monopolistic (or oligopolistic) industries leaning more toward the aggressive or the conservative approach?

21.1 Current Asset Holdings

Current assets can be divided into two categories, operating and nonoperating. Operating current assets consist of cash plus marketable securities held as a substitute for operating cash, inventories, and accounts receivable. These are assets that are necessary to operate the business. Nonoperating current assets consist of any other current assets, principally short-term securities in excess of what is required in operations, funds held in case a good merger opportunity arises, cash from the sale of a stock or bond issue before the funds can be invested in fixed assets, or funds held in case the firm loses a lawsuit and is required to compensate the winning party. *Our focus in this section is strictly on operating current assets.*

The amount of operating current assets held is a policy decision, and one that affects profitability. Figure 21-1 shows three alternative policies regarding the size of the firm's operating current assets. The top line has the steepest slope, which indicates that the firm holds a lot of cash, marketable securities, receivables, and inventories relative to its sales. If receivables are high, the firm has a liberal credit

CORPORATE VALUATION AND WORKING CAPITAL MANAGEMENT

Superior working capital management can dramatically reduce required investments in operating capital, which can lead in turn to larger free cash flows and greater firm value.

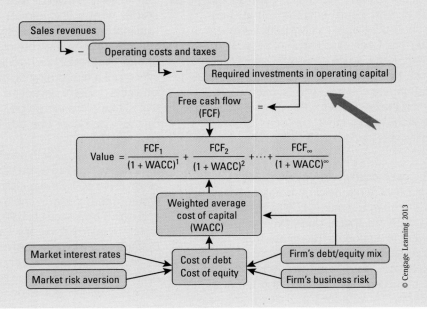

policy that results in a high level of accounts receivable. This is a **relaxed policy.** On the other hand, if a firm has a **restricted policy,** holdings of current assets are minimized and we say that the firm's policy is *tight* or *"lean-and-mean."* A **moderate policy** lies between the two extremes.

We can use the Du Pont equation to demonstrate how working capital management affects the return on equity:

$$\text{ROE} = \text{Profit margin} \times \text{Total assets turnover} \times \text{Equity multiplier}$$

$$= \frac{\text{Net income}}{\text{Sales}} \times \frac{\text{Sales}}{\text{Assets}} \times \frac{\text{Assets}}{\text{Equity}}$$

A relaxed policy means a high level of assets and hence a low total assets turnover ratio; this results in a low ROE, other things held constant. Conversely, a restricted policy results in low current assets, a high turnover, and hence a relatively high ROE. However, the restricted policy exposes the firm to risk, because shortages can lead to work stoppages, unhappy customers, and serious long-run problems. The moderate policy falls between the two extremes. The optimal strategy is the one that management believes will maximize the firm's long-run free cash flow and thus the stock's intrinsic value.

Figure 21-1 **Current Asset Investment Policies (Millions of Dollars)**

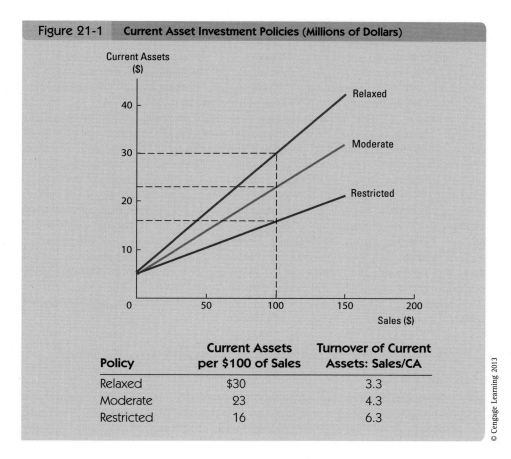

Policy	Current Assets per $100 of Sales	Turnover of Current Assets: Sales/CA
Relaxed	$30	3.3
Moderate	23	4.3
Restricted	16	6.3

© Cengage Learning 2013

Note that changing technologies can lead to changes in the optimal policy. For example, if a new technology makes it possible for a manufacturer to produce a given product in 5 rather than 10 days, then work-in-progress inventories can be cut in half. Similarly, retailers such as Wal-Mart and Home Depot have inventory management systems that use bar codes on all merchandise. These codes are read at the cash register; this information is transmitted electronically to a computer that adjusts the remaining stock of the item; and the computer automatically places an order with the supplier's computer when the stock falls to a specified level. This process lowers the "safety stocks" that would otherwise be necessary to avoid running out of stock. Such systems have dramatically lowered inventories and thus boosted profits.

Self Test

Identify and explain three alternative current asset investment policies.

Use the Du Pont equation to show how working capital policy can affect a firm's expected ROE.

What are the reasons for not wanting to hold too little working capital? For not wanting to hold too much?

21.2 Current Assets Financing Policies

Investments in operating current assets must be financed, and the primary sources of funds include bank loans, credit from suppliers (accounts payable), accrued liabilities, long-term debt, and common equity. Each of those sources has advantages and disadvantages, so a firm must decide which sources are best for it.

To begin, note that most businesses experience seasonal and/or cyclical fluctuations. For example, construction firms tend to peak in the summer, retailers peak around Christmas, and the manufacturers who supply both construction companies and retailers follow related patterns. Similarly, the sales of virtually all businesses increase when the economy is strong, so they increase operating current assets during booms but let inventories and receivables fall during recessions. However, current assets rarely drop to zero—companies maintain some **permanent operating current assets**, which are the operating current assets needed even at the low point of the business cycle. For a growing firm in a growing economy, permanent current assets tend to increase over time. Also, as sales increase during a cyclical upswing, current assets are increased; these extra current assets are defined as **temporary operating current assets** as opposed to permanent current assets. The way permanent and temporary current assets are financed is called the firm's **operating current assets financing policy**. Three alternative policies are discussed next.

21.2a Maturity Matching, or "Self-Liquidating," Approach

The **maturity matching,** or **"self-liquidating," approach** calls for matching asset and liability maturities as shown in Panel a of Figure 21-2. All of the fixed assets plus the permanent current assets are financed with long-term capital, but temporary current assets are financed with short-term debt. Inventory expected to be sold in 30 days would be financed with a 30-day bank loan; a machine expected to last for 5 years would be financed with a 5-year loan; a 20-year building would be financed with a 20-year mortgage bond; and so on. Actually, two factors prevent an exact maturity matching: (1) The lives of assets are uncertain. For example, a firm might finance inventories with a 30-day bank loan, expecting to sell the inventories and use the cash to retire the loan. But if sales are slow, then the cash would not be forthcoming and the firm might not be able to pay off the loan when it matures. (2) Some common equity must be used, and common equity has no maturity. Still, if a firm attempts to match or come close to matching asset and liability maturities, this is defined as a *moderate current asset financing policy.*

21.2b Aggressive Approach

Panel b of Figure 21-2 illustrates the situation for a more aggressive firm that finances some of its permanent assets with short-term debt. Note that we used the term "relatively" in the title for Panel b because there can be different *degrees* of aggressiveness. For example, the dashed line in Panel b could have been drawn *below* the line designating fixed assets, indicating that all of the current assets—both permanent and temporary—and part of the fixed assets were financed with short-term credit. This policy would be a highly aggressive, extremely nonconservative position, and the firm would be subject to dangers from loan renewal as well as rising interest rate problems. However, short-term interest rates are generally lower than long-term rates, and some firms are willing to gamble by using a large amount of low-cost, short-term debt in hopes of earning higher profits.

Figure 21-2   Alternative Operating Current Assets Financing Policies

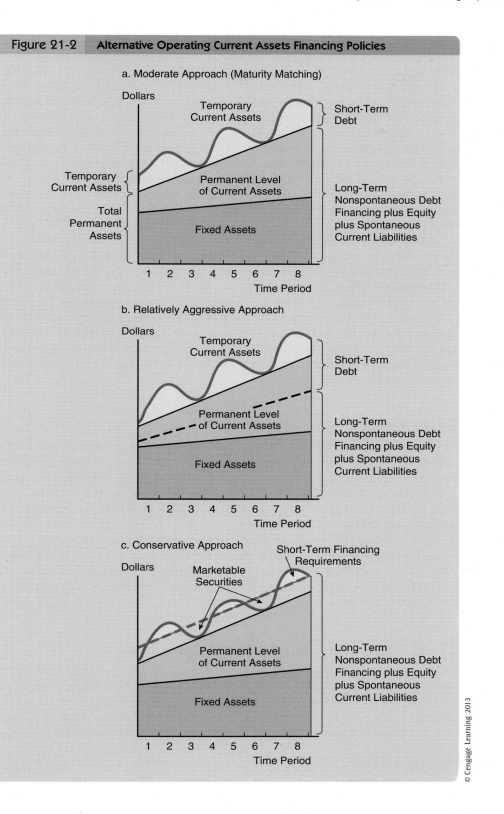

a. Moderate Approach (Maturity Matching)

- Dollars
- Temporary Current Assets
- Short-Term Debt
- Temporary Current Assets
- Permanent Level of Current Assets
- Total Permanent Assets
- Fixed Assets
- Long-Term Nonspontaneous Debt Financing plus Equity plus Spontaneous Current Liabilities
- Time Period (1 2 3 4 5 6 7 8)

b. Relatively Aggressive Approach

- Dollars
- Temporary Current Assets
- Short-Term Debt
- Permanent Level of Current Assets
- Fixed Assets
- Long-Term Nonspontaneous Debt Financing plus Equity plus Spontaneous Current Liabilities
- Time Period (1 2 3 4 5 6 7 8)

c. Conservative Approach

- Dollars
- Marketable Securities
- Short-Term Financing Requirements
- Permanent Level of Current Assets
- Fixed Assets
- Long-Term Nonspontaneous Debt Financing plus Equity plus Spontaneous Current Liabilities
- Time Period (1 2 3 4 5 6 7 8)

A possible reason for adopting the aggressive policy is to take advantage of an upward sloping yield curve, for which short-term rates are lower than long-term rates. However, as many firms learned during the financial crisis of 2009, a strategy of financing long-term assets with short-term debt is really quite risky. As an illustration, suppose a company borrowed $1 million on a 1-year basis and used the funds to buy machinery that would lower labor costs by $200,000 per year for 10 years.[2] Cash flows from the equipment would not be sufficient to pay off the loan at the end of only one year, so the loan would have to be renewed. If the economy were in a recession like that of 2009, the lender might refuse to renew the loan, and that could lead to bankruptcy. Had the firm matched maturities and financed the equipment with a 10-year loan, then the annual loan payments would have been lower and better matched with the cash flows, and the loan renewal problem would not have arisen.

Under some circumstances, even maturity matching can be risky, as many firms that thought they were conservatively financed learned in 2009. If a firm borrowed on a 30-day bank loan to finance inventories that it expected to sell within 30 days but then sales dropped, as they did for many firms in 2009, the funds needed to pay off the maturing bank loan might not be available. Then the bank might not extend the loan, and if it did not then the firm could be forced into bankruptcy. This happened to many firms in 2009, and it was exacerbated by the banks' own problems. The banks had lost billions on mortgages, mortgage-backed bonds, and other bad investments, which led banks to restrict credit to their normal business customers in order to conserve their own cash.

21.2c Conservative Approach

Panel c of the figure shows the dashed line *above* the line designating permanent current assets, indicating that long-term capital is used to finance all permanent assets and also to meet some seasonal needs. In this situation, the firm uses a small amount of short-term credit to meet its peak requirements, but it also meets a part of its seasonal needs by "storing liquidity" in the form of marketable securities. The humps above the dashed line represent short-term financings, while the troughs below the dashed line represent short-term security holdings. This conservative financing policy is fairly safe, and the wisdom of using it was demonstrated in 2009: When credit dried up, firms with adequate cash holdings were able to operate more effectively than those that were forced to cut back their operations because they couldn't order new inventories or pay their normal workforce.

21.2d Choosing among the Approaches

Because the yield curve is normally upward sloping, *the cost of short-term debt is generally lower than that of long-term debt*. However, *short-term debt is riskier to the borrowing firm* for two reasons: (1) If a firm borrows on a long-term basis then its interest costs will be relatively stable over time, but if it uses short-term credit then its interest expense can fluctuate widely—perhaps reaching such high levels that

---

2. We are oversimplifying here. Few lenders would explicitly lend money for 1 year to finance a 10-year asset. What would actually happen is that the firm would borrow on a 1-year basis for "general corporate purposes" and then actually use the money to purchase the 10-year machinery.

profits are extinguished.[3] (2) If a firm borrows heavily on a short-term basis, then a temporary recession may adversely affect its financial ratios and render it unable to repay its debt. Recognizing this fact, the lender may not renew the loan if the borrower's financial position is weak, which could force the borrower into bankruptcy.

Note also that *short-term loans can generally be negotiated much faster* than long-term loans. Lenders need to make a thorough financial examination before extending long-term credit, and the loan agreement must be spelled out in great detail because a lot can happen during the life of a 10- to 20-year loan.

Finally, *short-term debt generally offers greater flexibility.* If the firm thinks that interest rates are abnormally high and due for a decline, it may prefer short-term credit because prepayment penalties are often attached to long-term debt. Also, if its needs for funds are seasonal or cyclical, then the firm may not want to commit itself to long-term debt because of its underwriting costs and possible prepayment penalties. Finally, long-term loan agreements generally contain provisions, or *covenants,* that constrain the firm's future actions in order to protect the lender, whereas short-term credit agreements generally have fewer restrictions.

All things considered, it is not possible to state that either long-term or short-term financing is generally better. The firm's specific conditions will affect its decision, as will the risk preferences of managers. Optimistic and/or aggressive managers will lean more toward short-term credit to gain an interest cost advantage, whereas more conservative managers will lean toward long-term financing to avoid potential renewal problems. The factors discussed here should be considered, but the final decision will reflect managers' personal preferences and subjective judgments.

Self Test

Differentiate between permanent operating current assets and temporary operating current assets.

What does maturity matching mean, and what is the logic behind this policy?

What are some advantages and disadvantages of short-term versus long-term debt?

21.3 The Cash Conversion Cycle

All firms follow a "working capital cycle" in which they purchase or produce inventory, hold it for a time, and then sell it and receive cash. This process is known as the **cash conversion cycle (CCC)**.

21.3a Calculating the Target CCC

Assume that Great Basin Medical Equipment (GBM) is just starting in business, buying orthopedic devices from a manufacturer in China and selling them through distributors in the United States, Canada, and Mexico. Its business plan calls for it to purchase $10,000,000 of merchandise at the start of each month and have

---

3. The prime interest rate—the rate banks charge very good customers—hit 21% in the early 1980s. This produced a level of business bankruptcies that was not seen again until 2009. The primary reason for the very high interest rate was that the inflation rate was up to 13%, and high inflation must be compensated by high interest rates. Also, the Federal Reserve was tightening credit in order to hold down inflation, and it was encouraging banks to restrict their lending.

it sold within 50 days. The company will have 40 days to pay its suppliers, and it will give its customers 60 days to pay for their purchases. GBM expects to just break even during its first few years and so its monthly sales will be $10,000,000, the same as its purchases (or cost of goods sold). For simplicity, assume that there are no administrative costs. Also, any funds required to support operations will be obtained from the bank, and those loans must be repaid as soon as cash becomes available.

This information can be used to calculate GBM's target, or theoretical, cash conversion cycle, which "nets out" the three time periods described below.[4]

1. **Inventory conversion period.** For GBM, this is the 50 days it expects to take to sell the equipment, converting it from equipment to accounts receivable.[5]
2. **Average collection period (ACP).** This is the length of time customers are given to pay for goods following a sale. The ACP is also called the *days sales outstanding* (DSO). GBM's business plan calls for an ACP of 60 days based on its 60-day credit terms. This is also called the *receivables conversion period,* as it is supposed to take 60 days to collect and thus convert receivables to cash.
3. **Payables deferral period.** This is the length of time GBM's suppliers give it to pay for its purchases, which in our example is 40 days.

On Day 1, GBM expects to buy merchandise, and it expects to sell the goods and thus convert them to accounts receivable within 50 days. It should then take 60 days to collect the receivables, making a total of 110 days between receiving merchandise and collecting cash. However, GBM is able to defer its own payments for only 40 days.

We can combine these three periods to find the theoretical, or target, cash conversion cycle, shown below as an equation and diagrammed in Figure 21-3.

(21–1)

$$\begin{array}{ccccc} \text{Inventory} & \text{Average} & \text{Payables} & & \text{Cash} \\ \text{conversion} + & \text{collection} - & \text{deferral} = & \text{conversion} \\ \text{period} & \text{period} & \text{period} & & \text{cycle} \end{array}$$

$$50 \quad + \quad 60 \quad - \quad 40 \quad = \quad 70 \text{ days}$$

Although GBM is supposed to pay its suppliers $10,000,000 after 40 days, it does not expect to receive any cash until $50 + 60 = 110$ days into the cycle. Therefore, it will have to borrow the $10,000,000 cost of the merchandise from its bank on Day 40, and it does not expect to be able to repay the loan until it collects on Day 110. Thus, for $110 - 40 = 70$ days—which is the theoretical cash conversion cycle (CCC)—it will owe the bank $10,000,000 and it will be paying interest on this debt. The shorter the cash conversion cycle the better, because a shorter CCC means lower interest charges.

Observe that if GBM could sell goods faster, collect receivables faster, or defer its payables longer without hurting sales or increasing operating costs, then its CCC would decline, its expected interest charges would be reduced, and its expected profits and stock price would be improved.

---

4. See Verlyn D. Richards and Eugene J. Laughlin, "A Cash Conversion Cycle Approach to Liquidity Analysis," *Financial Management*, Spring 1980, pp. 32–38.
5. If GBM were a manufacturer, the inventory conversion period would be the time required to convert raw materials into finished goods and then to sell those goods.

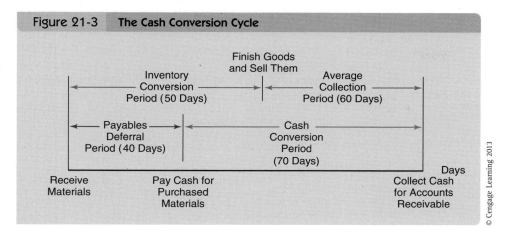

Figure 21-3   **The Cash Conversion Cycle**

21.3b Calculating the Actual CCC from Financial Statements

So far we have illustrated the CCC from a theoretical standpoint. However, in practice we would generally calculate the CCC based on the firm's financial statements, and the actual CCC would almost certainly differ from the theoretical value because of real-world complexities such as shipping delays, sales slowdowns, and slow-paying customers. Moreover, a firm such as GBM would be continually starting new cycles before the earlier ones ended, and this too would muddy the waters.

To see how the CCC is calculated in practice, assume that GBM has been in business for several years and is in a stable position, placing orders, making sales, receiving payments, and making its own payments on a recurring basis. The following data were taken from its latest financial statements, in millions:

Annual sales	$1,216.7
Cost of goods sold	1,013.9
Inventories	140.0
Accounts receivable	445.0
Accounts payable	115.0

Thus, its net operating working capital due to inventory, receivables, and payables is $140 + $445 − $115 = $470 million, and that amount must be financed—in GBM's case, through bank loans at a 10% interest rate. Therefore, its interest expense is $47 million per year.

We can analyze the situation more closely. First, consider the inventory conversion period:[6]

$$\text{Inventory conversion period} = \frac{\text{Inventory}}{\text{Cost of goods sold per day}} \qquad (21\text{--}2)$$

$$= \frac{\$140.0}{\$1,013.9/365} = 50.4 \text{ days}$$

---

6. In past editions of this book we divided inventories by daily sales to be consistent with many reported data sources. We believe that dividing by daily cost of goods sold provides a more meaningful cash conversion period, so we changed the formula in this edition.

Thus, it takes GBM an average of 50.4 days to sell its merchandise, which is very close to the 50 days called for in the business plan. Note also that inventory is carried at cost, which explains why the denominator in Equation 21-2 is the cost of goods sold per day, not daily sales.

The average collection period (or days sales outstanding) is calculated next:

(21–3)
$$\text{Average collection period} = \text{ACP (or DSO)} = \frac{\text{Receivables}}{\text{Sales}/365}$$

$$= \frac{\$445.0}{\$1,216.7/365} = 133.5 \text{ days}$$

Thus, it takes GBM 133.5 days after a sale to receive cash, not the 60 days called for in its business plan. Because receivables are recorded at the sales price, we use daily sales (rather than the cost of goods sold per day) in the denominator for the ACP.

The payables deferral period is found as follows, again using daily cost of goods sold in the denominator because payables are recorded at cost:

(21–4)
$$\frac{\text{Payables}}{\text{deferral period}} = \frac{\text{Payables}}{\text{Purchases per day}} = \frac{\text{Payables}}{\text{Cost of goods sold}/365}$$

$$= \frac{\$115.0}{\$1,013.9/365} = 41.4 \text{ days}$$

GBM is supposed to pay its suppliers after 40 days, but it actually pays on average just after Day 41. This slight delay is normal, since mail delays and time for checks to be cashed generally slow payments down a bit.

We can now combine the three periods to calculate GBM's actual cash conversion cycle:

Cash conversion cycle (CCC) = 50.4 days + 133.5 days − 41.4 days = 142.5 days

WEB

See *Ch21 Tool Kit.xls* on the textbook's Web site for details.

Figure 21-4 summarizes all of these calculations and then analyzes why the actual CCC exceeds the theoretical CCC by such a large amount. It is clear from the figure that the firm's inventory control is working as expected in that sales match the inflow of new inventory items quite well. Also, its own payments match reasonably well the terms under which it buys. However, its accounts receivable are much higher than they should be, indicating that its customers are not paying on time. In fact, they are paying 73.5 days late, which is increasing GBM's working capital. Because working capital must be financed, the collections delay is lowering the firm's profits and presumably hurting its stock price.

When the CFO reviewed the situation, she discovered that GBM's customers—doctors, hospitals, and clinics—were themselves reimbursed by insurance companies and government units, and those organizations were paying late. The credit manager was doing everything he could to collect faster, but the customers said that they just could not make their own payments until they themselves were paid. If GBM wanted to keep making sales, it seemed that it would have to accept late-paying

Figure 21-4	**Summary of the Cash Conversion Cycle (Millions of Dollars)**

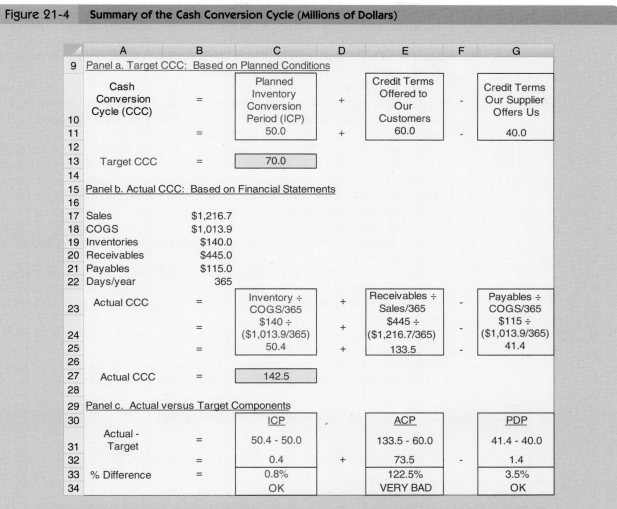

Note: GBM's inventories are in line with its plans, and it's paying its suppliers nearly on time. However, some of its customers are paying quite late, so its average collection period (or DSO) is 133.5 days even though all customers are supposed to pay by Day 60.

customers. However, the CFO wondered if collections might come in faster if GBM offered substantial discounts for early payments. We will take up this issue later in the chapter.

21.3c Benefits of Reducing the CCC

As we have seen, GBM currently has a CCC of 142.5 days, which results in $470 million being tied up in net operating working capital. Assuming that its cost of debt to carry working capital is 10%, this means that the firm is incurring interest charges of $47 million per year to carry its working capital. Now suppose the company can speed up its sales enough to reduce the inventory conversion period from 50.4 to 35.0 days. In addition, it begins to offer discounts for early payment and thereby reduces its average collection period to 40 days. Finally, assume that it could negotiate a change in its own payment terms from 40 to 50 days. The "New" column of Figure 21-5 shows the net effects of these improvements: a 117.5-day reduction in the cash conversion cycle and a reduction in net operating working capital from $470.0 to $91.7 million, which saves $37.8 million of interest.

Recall also that free cash flow (FCF) is equal to NOPAT minus the net new investment in operating capital. Therefore, if working capital *decreases* by a given amount while other things remain constant, then FCF *increases* by that same amount—$378.3 million in the GBM example. If sales remained constant in the following years, then this reduction in working capital would simply be a one-time cash inflow. However, suppose sales grow in future years. When a company improves its working capital management, the components (inventory conversion period, collection period, and payments period) usually remain at their improved levels, which means the NOWC-to-Sales ratio remains at its new level. With an improved NOWC-to-Sales ratio, less working capital will be required to support future sales, leading to higher annual FCFs than would have otherwise existed.

Thus, an improvement in working capital management creates a large one-time increase in FCF at the time of the improvement as well as higher FCF in future years. Therefore, an improvement in working capital management is a gift that keeps on giving.

These benefits can add substantial value to the company. Professors Hyun-Han Shin and Luc Soenen studied more than 2,900 companies over a 20-year period, finding a strong relationship between a company's cash conversion cycle and its stock performance.[7] For an average company, a 10-day improvement in its CCC

Figure 21-5   **Benefits from Reducing the Cash Conversion Cycle (Millions of Dollars)**

	A	B	C	D	E	F	G
					Old (Actual)		New (Target)
44							
45	Inventory conversion period (ICP, days)				50.4		35.0
46	Average collection period (ACP, days)				133.5		40.0
47	Payable deferral period (PDP, days)				-41.4		-50.0
48	Cash Collection Cycle (CCC, days)				142.5		25.0
49							
50	Reduction in CCC					117.5	
51							
52	Effects of the CCC Reduction						
53	Annual sales				$1,216.7		$1,216.7
54	Costs of goods sold (COGS)				$1,013.9		$1,013.9
55	Inventory = Actual Old, New = new ICP(COGS/365)				$140.0		$97.2
56	Receivables = Actual Old, New = new ACP(Sales/365)				445.0		133.3
57	Payables = Actual Old, New = new PDP(COGS/365)				-115.0		-138.9
58	Net operating WC = Inv + Receivables – Payables				$470.0		$91.7
59							
60	Reduction in NOWC					$378.3	
61	Reduction in interest expense @ 10%					$37.8	

---

7. Hyun-Han Shin and Luc Soenen, "Efficiency of Working Capital Management and Corporate Profitability," *Financial Practice and Education*, Fall/Winter 1998, pp. 37–45.

SOME FIRMS OPERATE WITH NEGATIVE WORKING CAPITAL!

Some firms are able to operate with zero or even negative net working capital. Dell Computer and Amazon.com are examples. When customers order computers from Dell's Web site or books from Amazon, they must provide a credit card number. Dell and Amazon then receive next-day cash, even before the product is shipped and even before they have paid their own suppliers. This results in a negative CCC, which means that working capital *provides* cash rather than using it.

In order to grow, companies normally need cash for working capital. However, if the CCC is negative then growth in sales *provides* cash rather than *uses* it. This cash can be invested in plant and equipment, research and development, or for any other corporate purpose. Analysts recognize this point when they value Dell and Amazon, and it certainly helps their stock prices.

was associated with an increase in pre-tax operating profit margin from 12.76% to 13.02%. Moreover, companies with cash conversion cycles 10 days shorter than the average for their industry had annual stock returns that were 1.7 percentage points higher than the average company. Given results like these, it's no wonder firms place so much emphasis on working capital management![8]

Self Test

Define the following terms: inventory conversion period, average collection period, and payables deferral period. Give the equation for each term.

What is the cash conversion cycle? What is its equation?

What should a firm's goal be regarding the cash conversion cycle, holding other things constant? Explain your answer.

What are some actions a firm can take to shorten its cash conversion cycle?

A company has $20 million of inventory, $5 million of receivables, and $4 million of payables. Its annual sales revenue is $80 million, and its cost of goods sold is $60 million. What is its CCC? **(120.15)**

21.4 The Cash Budget

Firms must forecast their cash flows. If they are likely to need additional cash then they should line up funds well in advance, yet if they are likely to generate surplus cash then they should plan for its productive use. The primary forecasting tool is the cash budget, illustrated in Figure 21-6, which is a screenshot from the chapter's *Excel Tool Kit* model. The illustrative company is Educational Products Corporation (EPC), which supplies educational materials to schools and retailers in the Midwest. Sales are cyclical, peaking in September and then declining for the balance of the year.

WEB

See *Ch21 Tool Kit.xls* on the textbook's Web site for details.

---

8. For more on the CCC, see James A. Gentry, R. Vaidyanathan, and Hei Wai Lee, "A Weighted Cash Conversion Cycle," *Financial Management*, Spring 1990, pp. 90–99.

Figure 21-6   **EPC's Cash Budget, July–December 2013 (Millions of Dollars)**

	A	B	C	D	E	F	G	H	I	J	K	L	M	N
						May	June	July	August	Sept	Oct	Nov	Dec	Jan
73	Base Case													
74	*Forecasted gross sales (manual inputs):*					$200.0	$250.0	$300.0	$400.0	$500.0	$350.0	$250.0	$200.0	$200.0
75	Adjustment: % deviation from forecast					0%	0%	0%	0%	0%	0%	0%	0%	0%
76	Adjusted gross sales forecast					$200.0	$250.0	$300.0	$400.0	$500.0	$350.0	$250.0	$200.0	$200.0
77														
78	*Collections on sales:*													
79	During sales' month:	0.2	(Sales)(1 – discount %)					$58.8	$78.4	$98.0	$68.6	$49.0	$39.2	
80	During 2nd month:	0.7	(prior month's sales)					175.0	210.0	280.0	350.0	245.0	175.0	
81	Due in 3rd month:	0.1	(sales 2 months ago)					20.0	25.0	30.0	40.0	50.0	35.0	
82	Less bad debts (BD% × Sales 2 months ago)							0.0	0.0	0.0	0.0	0.0	0.0	
83	Total collections							$253.8	$313.4	$408.0	$458.6	$344.0	$249.2	
84														
85	*Purchases: 60% of next month's sales*					$180.0	$240.0	$300.0	$210.0	$150.0	$120.0	$120.0		
86	*Payments*													
87	Pmt for last month's purchases (30 days of credit)						$180.0	$240.0	$300.0	$210.0	$150.0	$120.0		
88	Wages and salaries							30.0	40.0	50.0	40.0	30.0	30.0	
89	Lease payments							30.0	30.0	30.0	30.0	30.0	30.0	
90	Other payments (interest on LT bonds, dividends, etc.)							30.0	30.0	30.0	30.0	30.0	30.0	
91	Taxes									30.0			30.0	
92	Payment for plant construction									150.0				
93	Total payments							$270.0	$340.0	$590.0	$310.0	$240.0	$240.0	
94														
95	*Net cash flows:*													
96	Assumed <u>excess</u> cash on hand at start of forecast period							$0.0						
97	Net cash flow (NCF): Total collections – Total pmts							-16.2	-26.6	-182.0	148.6	104.0	9.2	
98	Cumulative NCF: Prior month cum plus this month's NCF							-$16.2	-$42.8	-$224.8	-$76.2	$27.8	$37.0	
99														
100	*Cash surplus (or loan requirement)*													
101	Target cash balance							$10.0	$10.0	$10.0	$10.0	$10.0	$10.0	
102	Surplus cash or loan needed: Cum NCF – Target cash							-$26.2	-$52.8	-$234.8	-$86.2	$17.8	$27.0	
103														
104	Max required loan (most <u>negative</u> on Row 102)				$234.8									
105	Max investable funds (most <u>positive</u> on Row 102)				$27.0									

Notes:
1. Although the budget period is July through December, sales and purchases data for May and June are needed to determine collections and payments during July and August.
2. Firms can both borrow and pay off commercial loans on a daily basis, so the $26.2 million loan needed for July would likely be gradually borrowed as needed on a daily basis, and during October the $234.8 million loan that presumably existed at the beginning of the month would be reduced daily to the $86.2 million ending balance—which, in turn, would be completely paid off sometime during November.
3. The data in the figure are for EPC's base-case forecast. Data for alternative scenarios are shown in the chapter's *Excel Tool Kit* model.

21.4a Monthly Cash Budgets

Cash budgets can be of any length, but EPC and most companies use a monthly cash budget such as the one in Figure 21-6, but set up for 12 months. We used only 6 months for the purpose of illustration. The monthly budget is used for longer-range planning, but a daily cash budget is also prepared at the start of each month to provide a more precise picture of the daily cash flows for use in scheduling actual payments on a day-by-day basis.

The cash budget focuses on cash flows, but it also includes information on forecasted sales, credit policy, and inventory management. Since the statement is a forecast and not a report on historical results, actual results could vary from the figures given. Therefore, the cash budget is generally set up as an expected, or base-case, forecast, but it is created with a model that makes it easy to generate alternative forecasts to see what would happen under different conditions.

Figure 21-6 begins with a forecast of sales for each month on Row 74. Then, on Row 75, it shows possible percentage deviations from the forecasted sales. Since we are showing the base-case forecast, no adjustments are made, but the model is set up to show the effects if sales increase or decrease and so result in "adjusted sales" that are above or below the forecasted levels.

The company sells on terms of "2/10, net 60." This means that a 2% discount is given if payment is made within 10 days; otherwise, the full amount is due in 60 days. However, like most companies, EPC finds that some customers pay late. Experience shows that 20% of customers pay during the month of the sale and take the discount. Another 70% pay during the month immediately following the sale, and 10% are late, paying in the second month after the sale.[9]

The statement (Line 85) next shows forecasted materials purchases, which equal 60% of the following month's sales. EPC buys on terms of net 30, meaning that it receives no discounts and is required to pay for its purchases within 30 days of the purchase date. The purchases information is followed by forecasted payments for materials, labor, leases, other payments such as dividends and interest on long-term bonds, taxes (due in September and December), and a payment of $150 million in September for a new plant that is being constructed.

When the total forecasted payments are subtracted from the forecasted collections, the result is the expected net cash gain or loss for each month. This gain or loss is added to or subtracted from the excess cash on hand at the start of the forecast (which we assume was zero), and the result—the *cumulative net cash flow*—is the amount of cash the firm would have on hand at the end of the month if it neither borrowed nor invested.

EPC's target cash balance is $10 million, and it plans either to borrow to meet this target or to invest surplus funds if it generates more cash than it needs. How the target cash balance is determined is discussed later in the chapter, but EPC believes that it needs $10 million.

By subtracting the target cash balance from the cumulative cash flow, we calculate the *loan needed or surplus cash,* as shown on Row 102. A negative number indicates that we need a loan, whereas a positive number indicates that we forecast surplus cash that is available for investment or other uses.

If we total the net cash flows on Row 97 then the sum is $37 million, the cumulative NCF as shown in Cell M98. Because this number is positive, it indicates that EPC's cash flow is positive. Also, note that EPC borrows on a basis that allows it to borrow or repay loans on a daily basis. Thus, it would borrow a total of $26.2 million in July, increasing the loan daily, and would continue to build up the loan through September. Then, when its cash flows turn positive in October, it would start repaying

---

9. A negligible percentage of sales results in bad debts. The low bad-debt losses evident here result from EPC's careful screening of customers and its generally tight credit policies. However, the cash budget model is able to show the effects of bad debts, so EPC's CFO could show top management how cash flows would be affected if the firm relaxed its credit policy in order to stimulate sales or if the recession worsened and more customers were forced to delay payments.

the loan on a daily basis and completely pay it off sometime in November, assuming that everything works out as forecasted.

Note that our cash budget is incomplete in that it shows neither interest paid on the working capital loans nor interest earned on the positive cash balances. These amounts could be added to the budget simply by adding rows and including them. Similarly, if the firm makes quarterly dividend payments, principal payments on its long-term bonds, or any other payments, or if it has investment income, then those cash flows also could be added to the statement. In our simplified statement, we just lumped all such payments into "other payments."

Under the base-case forecast, the CFO will need to arrange a line of credit so that the firm can borrow up to $234.8 million, increasing the loan over time as funds are needed and repaying it later when cash flows become positive. The treasurer would show the cash budget to the bankers when negotiating for the line of credit. Lenders would want to know how much the firm expects to need, when the funds will be needed, and when the loan will be repaid. The lenders—and EPC's top executives—would question the treasurer about the budget, and they would want to know how the forecasts would be affected if sales were higher or lower than those projected, how changes in customers' payment times would affect the forecasts, and the like. The focus would be on these two questions: *How accurate is the forecast likely to be? What would be the effects of significant errors?* The first question could best be answered by examining historical forecasts, and the second by running different scenarios as we do in the *Excel Tool Kit* model.

No matter how hard we try, no forecast will ever be exactly correct, and this includes cash budgets. You can imagine the bank's reaction if the company negotiated a loan of $235 million and then came back a few months later saying that it had underestimated its requirements and needed to boost the loan to say $260 million. The banker might well refuse, thinking the company was not very well managed. Therefore, EPC's treasurer would undoubtedly want to build a cushion into the line of credit—say, a maximum commitment of $260 million rather than the forecasted requirement of $234.8 million. However, as we discuss later in the chapter, banks charge commitment fees for guaranteed lines of credit; thus, the higher the cushion built into the line of credit, the more costly the credit will be. This is another reason why it is important to develop accurate forecasts.

WEB

See **Ch21 Tool Kit.xls** on the textbook's Web site for details.

21.4b Cash Budgets versus Income Statements and Free Cash Flows

If you look at the cash budget, it looks similar to an income statement. However, the two statements are quite different. Here are some key differences: (1) In an income statement, the focus would be on sales, not collections. (2) An income statement would show accrued taxes, wages, and so forth, not the actual payments. (3) An income statement would show depreciation as an expense, but it would not show expenditures on new fixed assets. (4) An income statement would show a cost for goods purchased when those goods were sold, not for when they were ordered or paid.

These are obviously large differences, so it would be a big mistake to confuse a cash budget with an income statement. Also, the cash flows shown on the cash budget are different from the firm's free cash flows, because FCF reflects after-tax operating income and the investments required to maintain future operations whereas the cash budget reflects only the actual cash inflows and outflows during a particular period.

The bottom line is that cash budgets, income statements, and free cash flows are all important and are related to one another, but they are also quite different.

Each is designed for a specific purpose, and the main purpose of the cash budget is to forecast the firm's liquidity position, not its profitability.

21.4c Daily Cash Budgets

Note that if cash inflows and outflows do not occur uniformly during each month, then the actual funds needed might be quite different from the indicated amounts. The data in Figure 21-6 show the situation on the last day of each month, and we see that the maximum projected loan during the forecast period is $234.8 million. Yet if all payments had to be made on the 1st of the month but most collections came on the 30th, then EPC would have to make $270 million of payments in July before it received the $253.8 million from collections. In that case, the firm would need to borrow about $270 million in July, not the $26.2 million shown in Figure 21-6. This would make the bank unhappy—perhaps so unhappy that it would not extend the requested credit. A daily cash budget would have revealed this situation.

Figure 21-6 was prepared using *Excel*, which makes it easy to change the assumptions. In the *Tool Kit* model we examine the cash flow effects of changes in sales, in customers' payment patterns, and so forth. Also, the effects of changes in credit policy and inventory management could be examined through the cash budget.

WEB

See *Ch21 Tool Kit.xls* on the textbook's Web site for details.

Self Test

How could the cash budget be used when negotiating the terms of a bank loan?

How would a shift from a tight credit policy to a relaxed policy be likely to affect a firm's cash budget?

How would the cash budget be affected if our firm's suppliers offered us terms of "2/10, net 30," rather than "net 30," and we decided to take the discount?

Suppose a firm's cash flows do not occur uniformly throughout the month. What effect would this have on the accuracy of the forecasted borrowing requirements based on a monthly cash budget? How could the firm deal with this problem?

21.5 Cash Management and the Target Cash Balance

Cash is needed to pay for labor and raw materials, to purchase fixed assets, to pay taxes, to service debt, to pay dividends, and so on, but cash itself (and the money in most commercial checking accounts) earns no interest. Thus, the goal of the cash manager is to minimize the cash amount the firm must hold for conducting its normal business activities while continuing to maintain a sufficient cash reserve to (1) take trade discounts, (2) pay promptly and thus maintain its credit rating, and (3) meet any unexpected cash needs. We begin our analysis with a discussion of the traditional reasons for holding cash.

21.5a Reasons for Holding Cash

Firms hold cash for two primary reasons:

1. *Transactions, both routine and precautionary.* Cash balances are necessary in business operations. Payments must be made in cash, and receipts are deposited in

THE *CFO* CASH MANAGEMENT SCORECARD

Each year, *CFO Magazine* publishes a cash management scorecard, prepared by REL Consultancy Group, based on the 1,000 largest publicly traded U.S. companies. On the one hand, if a company holds more cash than needed to support its operations, its return on invested capital (ROIC) will be dragged down because cash earns a low rate of return. On the other hand, if a company doesn't have enough cash, then it might experience financial distress if there is an unexpected downturn in business. How much cash is enough?

Although the optimum level of cash depends on a company's unique set of circumstances, REL defines industry benchmarks as that quartile of firms in an industry that have the lowest cash/sales ratios—on the theory that these firms have the best cash management procedures. A recent average benchmark cash/sales ratio was 5.6%, whereas the average firm had a ratio of 10.4%. This suggests that many firms had a lot more cash than they actually needed.

It's one thing to talk about reducing cash, but how can a company do it? A good relationship with its banks is one key to keeping low cash levels. Jim Hopwood, treasurer of Wickes, says, "We have a credit revolver if we ever need it." The same is true at Havertys Furniture, where CFO Dennis Fink says that if you have solid bank commitments, "You don't have to worry about predicting short-term fluctuations in cash flow."

Sources: Randy Myers, "Tight Makes Right," *CFO*, December 2008, pp. 64–70; D. M. Katz, "Cash Scorecard: Unleash the Hoards," *CFO.com*, October 17, 2006, **www.cfo.com/article.cfm/8048654?f=search**; Randy Myers, "Stuck on Yellow," *CFO*, October 2005, pp. 81–90; and S. L. Mintz, "Lean Green Machine," *CFO*, July 2000, pp. 76–94. For updates, go to **www.cfo.com** and search for "cash management."

the cash account. Cash balances associated with routine payments and collections are known as **transactions balances**. Cash inflows and outflows are unpredictable, and the degree of predictability varies among firms and industries. Therefore, firms need to hold some cash to meet random, unforeseen fluctuations in inflows and outflows. These "safety stocks" are called **precautionary balances,** and the less predictable the firm's cash flows, the larger such balances should be.

2. *Compensation to banks for providing loans and services.* A bank makes money by lending out funds that have been deposited with it, so the larger its deposits, the better the bank's profit position. If a bank is providing services to a customer, then it may require that customer to leave a minimum balance on deposit to help offset the costs of providing those services. Also, banks may require borrowers to hold their transactions deposits at the bank. Both types of deposits are called **compensating balances**. In a 1979 survey, 84.7% of responding companies reported they were required to maintain compensating balances to help pay for bank services; only 13.3% reported paying direct fees for banking services.[10] By 1996, those findings were reversed: Only 28% paid for bank services with compensating balances, while 83% paid direct fees.[11] Although the use of compensating balances to pay for services has declined,

---

10. See Lawrence J. Gitman, E. A. Moses, and I. T. White, "An Assessment of Corporate Cash Management Practices," *Financial Management,* Spring 1979, pp. 32–41.

11. See Charles E. Maxwell, Lawrence J. Gitman, and Stephanie A. M. Smith, "Working Capital Management and Financial-Service Consumption Preferences of US and Foreign Firms: A Comparison of 1979 and 1996 Preferences," *Financial Practice and Education,* Fall/Winter 1998, pp. 46–52.

these balances improve a firm's relationship with its bank and are still a reason why some companies hold additional cash.

In addition to holding cash for transactions, precautionary, and compensating balances, it is essential that the firm have sufficient cash to take **trade discounts**. Suppliers frequently offer customers discounts for early payment of bills. As we will see later in this chapter, the cost of not taking discounts is sometimes very high, so firms should have enough cash to permit payment of bills in time to take discounts.

Finally, for a number of reasons firms often hold short-term investments in excess of the cash needed to support operations. We discuss short-term investments later in the chapter.

Why is cash management important?	**Self Test**
What are the primary motives for holding cash?	

21.6 Cash Management Techniques

In terms of dollar volume, most business is conducted by large firms, many of which operate nationally or globally. They collect cash from many sources and make payments from a number of different cities or even countries. For example, companies such as IBM, General Electric, and Hewlett-Packard have manufacturing plants all around the world, even more sales offices, and bank accounts in virtually every city where they do business. Their collection centers follow sales patterns. However, while some disbursements are made from local offices, most are made in the cities where manufacturing occurs or else from the home office. Thus, a major corporation might have hundreds or even thousands of bank accounts located in cities all over the globe, but there is no reason to think that inflows and outflows will balance in each account. Therefore, a system must be in place to transfer funds from where they come in to where they are needed, to arrange loans to cover net corporate shortfalls, and to invest net corporate surpluses without delay. Some commonly used techniques for accomplishing these tasks are discussed next.[12]

21.6a Synchronizing Cash Flow

If you as an individual were to receive income once a year, then you would probably put it in the bank, draw down your account periodically, and have an average balance for the year equal to about half of your annual income. If instead you received income weekly and paid rent, tuition, and other charges on a daily basis, then your average bank balance would still be about half of your periodic receipts and thus only 1/52 as large as if you received income only once annually.

Exactly the same situation holds for businesses: By timing their cash receipts to coincide with their cash outlays, firms can hold their transactions balances to a minimum. Recognizing this fact, firms such as utilities, oil companies, and credit card companies arrange to bill customers—and to pay their own bills—on regular "billing cycles" throughout the month. This **synchronization of cash flows** provides cash when it is needed and thus enables firms to reduce their average cash balances.

---

12. For more information on cash management, see Bruce J. Summers, "Clearing and Payment Systems: The Role of the Central Bank," *Federal Reserve Bulletin*, February 1991, pp. 81–91.

21.6b Speeding Up the Check-Clearing Process

When a customer writes and mails a check, the funds are not available to the receiving firm until the **check-clearing process** has been completed. First, the check must be delivered through the mail. Checks received from customers in distant cities are especially subject to mail delays.

When a customer's check is written on one bank and a company deposits the check in another bank, the company's bank must verify that the check is valid before the payee can use those funds. Checks are generally cleared through the Federal Reserve System or through a clearinghouse set up by the banks in a particular city.[13] Before 2004, this process sometimes took 2 to 5 days. But with the passage of a federal law in 2004 known as "Check 21," banks can exchange digital images of checks. This means that most checks now clear in a single day.

21.6c Using Float

Float is defined as the difference between the balance shown in a firm's (or individual's) checkbook and the balance on the bank's records. Suppose a firm writes, on average, checks in the amount of $5,000 each day, and suppose it takes 6 days for these checks to clear and be deducted from the firm's bank account. This will cause the firm's own checkbook to show a balance that is $30,000 smaller than the balance on the bank's records; this difference is called **disbursement float**. Now suppose the firm also receives checks in the amount of $5,000 daily but that it loses 4 days while those checks are being deposited and cleared. This will result in $20,000 of **collections float**. In total, the firm's **net float**—the difference between the $30,000 positive disbursement float and the $20,000 negative collections float—will be $10,000. In sum, collections float is bad, disbursement float is good, and positive net float is even better.

Delays that cause float will occur because it takes time for checks to (1) travel through the mail (mail float), (2) be processed by the receiving firm (processing float), and (3) clear through the banking system (clearing, or availability, float). Basically, the size of a firm's net float is a function of its ability to speed up collections on checks it receives and to slow down collections on checks it writes. Efficient firms go to great lengths to speed up the processing of incoming checks, thus putting the funds to work faster, and they try to stretch their own payments out as long as possible, sometimes by disbursing checks from banks in remote locations.

21.6d Speeding Up Collections

Two major techniques are used to speed collections and to get funds where they are needed: lockboxes and electronic transfers.

Lockboxes

A **lockbox system** is one of the oldest cash management tools. In a lockbox system, incoming checks are sent to post office boxes rather than to the firm's corporate headquarters. For example, a firm headquartered in New York City might have its

---

13. For example, suppose a check for $100 is written on Bank A and deposited at Bank B. Bank B will usually contact either the Federal Reserve System or a clearinghouse to which both banks belong. The Fed or the clearinghouse will then verify with Bank A that the check is valid and that the account has sufficient funds to cover the check. Bank A's account with the Fed or the clearinghouse is then reduced by $100, and Bank B's account is increased by $100. Of course, if the check is deposited in the same bank on which it was drawn, that bank merely transfers funds by bookkeeping entries from one depositor to another.

West Coast customers send their payments to a post office box in San Francisco, its customers in the Southwest send their checks to Dallas, and so on, rather than having all checks sent to New York City. Several times a day, a local bank will empty the lockbox and deposit the checks into the company's local account. The bank then provides the firm with a daily record of the receipts collected, usually via an electronic data transmission system in a format that permits online updating of the firm's accounts receivable records.

A lockbox system reduces the time required to receive incoming checks, to deposit them, and to get them cleared through the banking system and available for use. Lockbox services can make funds available as many as 2 to 5 days faster than via the "regular" system.

Payment by Wire or Automatic Debit

Firms are increasingly demanding payments of larger bills by wire or by automatic electronic debits. Under an electronic debit system, funds are automatically deducted from one account and added to another. This is, of course, the ultimate in a speeded-up collection process, and computer technology is making such a process increasingly feasible and efficient, even for retail transactions.

Self Test

What is float? How do firms use float to increase cash management efficiency?

What are some methods firms can use to accelerate receipts?

YOUR CHECK ISN'T IN THE MAIL

Issuing payroll checks to thousands of employees is expensive—in both the time and resources it takes the company to print, process, and deliver the checks, and in the time it takes the employee to deposit or cash the check. Paper checks cost a company between $1 and $2 each, and multiply that by thousands of employees, some of whom are paid weekly or biweekly, it adds up to a lot of money every year! Direct deposit of payroll checks into the employee's checking account reduces these costs, but there are still many employees, especially seasonal, temporary, part-time, or young employees, who don't have a checking account.

A growing solution to high check costs and the needs of these "unbanked" employees is the payroll debit card. Companies, in partnership with a bank, issue the employee a debit card that is automatically filled each payday. The employee either uses the debit card to make purchases or withdraws cash at an ATM. The cost to load a debit card is around $0.20, and so saves the companies 80% to 90% of the cost to print a check, and saves the unbanked employee from paying the frequently usurious check cashing fees that can be 10% or more. In fact, because debit card transactions that are processed as a credit card result in fees to the merchant, there is a small amount of money available to provide a rebate to the employer. For example, Premier Pay Cards offers a 0.1% rebate to the employer on certain purchases the employee makes with the debit card.

Although the use of a debit card for payroll eliminates the float that would occur with check-based pay, for many companies the reduced processing costs and increased employee satisfaction more than outweigh the reduction in float.

Sources: "The End of the Paycheck," *Fortune Small Business Magazine*, December 5, 2006, and **www.premierpaycards .com**.

21.7 Inventory Management

Inventory management techniques are covered in depth in production management courses. Still, financial managers have a responsibility for raising the capital needed to carry inventory and for overseeing the firm's overall profitability, so it is appropriate that we cover the financial aspects of inventory management here.

The twin goals of inventory management are (1) to ensure that the inventories needed to sustain operations are available, but (2) to hold the costs of ordering and carrying inventories to the lowest possible level. While analyzing improvements in the cash conversion cycle, we identified some of the cash flows associated with a reduction in inventory. In addition to the points made earlier, lower inventory levels reduce costs due to storage and handling, insurance, property taxes, spoilage, and obsolescence.

Before the computer age, companies used such simple inventory control techniques as the "red line" system, where a red line was drawn around the inside of a bin holding inventory items; when the actual stock declined to the level where the red line showed, inventory would be reordered. But now computers have taken over, and supply chains have been established that provide inventory items just before

SUPPLY CHAIN MANAGEMENT

Herman Miller Inc. manufactures a wide variety of office furniture, and a typical order from a single customer might require work at five different plants. Each plant uses components from different suppliers, and each plant works on orders for many customers. Imagine all the coordination that is required. The sales force generates the order, the purchasing department orders components from suppliers, and the suppliers must order materials from their own suppliers. The suppliers make and then ship the components to Herman Miller, the factory builds the products, the different products are gathered together to complete the order, and then the order is shipped to the customer. If one part of that process malfunctions, then the order will be delayed, inventory will pile up, extra costs to expedite the order will be incurred, and the customer's goodwill will be damaged, hurting future growth.

To prevent such consequences, many companies employ supply chain management (SCM). The key element in SCM is sharing information all the way back from the retailer where the product is sold, to the company's own plant, then back to the firm's suppliers, and even back to the suppliers' suppliers. SCM requires special computer software, but even more important is that it requires cooperation among the different companies and departments in the supply chain. This culture of open communication is often difficult for many companies, which can be reluctant to divulge operating information. For example, EMC Corp., a manufacturer of data storage systems, has become deeply involved in the design processes and financial controls of its key suppliers. Many of EMC's suppliers were initially wary of these new relationships. However, SCM has been a win–win proposition, with higher profits for both EMC and its suppliers.

The same is true at many other companies. After implementing SCM, Herman Miller was able to reduce its days of inventory on hand by a week and to cut 2 weeks off of delivery times to customers. It was also able to operate its plants at a 20% higher volume without additional capital expenditures, because downtime due to inventory shortages was virtually eliminated. As another example, Heineken USA can now get beer from its Dutch breweries to its customers' shelves in less than 6 weeks, compared with 10 to 12 weeks before implementing SCM. As these and other companies have found, SCM increases free cash flows, and that leads to more profits and higher stock prices.

Sources: Elaine L. Appleton, "Supply Chain Brain," *CFO*, July 1997, pp. 51–54; and Kris Frieswick, "Up Close and Virtual," *CFO*, April 1998, pp. 87–91.

they are needed—the *just-in-time* system. For example, consider Trane Corporation, which makes air conditioners and currently uses just-in-time procedures. In the past, Trane produced parts on a steady basis, stored them as inventory, and had them ready whenever the company received an order for a batch of air conditioners. However, the company's inventory eventually covered an area equal to three football fields, and it still could take as long as 15 days to fill an order. To make matters worse, occasionally some of the necessary components simply could not be located; in other instances, the components were located but found to have been damaged from long storage.

Then Trane adopted a new inventory policy—it began producing components only after receiving an order and then sending the parts directly from the machines that make them to the final assembly line. The net effect: Inventories fell nearly 40% even as sales were increasing by 30%.

Such improvements in inventory management can free up considerable amounts of cash. For example, suppose a company has sales of $120 million and an inventory turnover ratio of 3. This means the company has an inventory level of

$$\text{Inventory} = \text{Sales/(Inventory turnover ratio)}$$
$$= \$120/3 = \$40 \text{ million}$$

If the company can improve its inventory turnover ratio to 4, then its inventory will fall to

$$\text{Inventory} = \$120/4 = \$30 \text{ million}$$

This $10 million reduction in inventory boosts free cash flow by $10 million.

However, there are costs associated with holding too little inventory, and these costs can be severe. If a business lowers its inventories then it must reorder frequently, which increases ordering costs. Even worse, if stocks become depleted then firms can miss out on profitable sales and also suffer lost goodwill, which may lead to lower future sales. Therefore, it is important to have enough inventory on hand to meet customer demands but not so much as to incur the costs we discussed previously. Inventory optimization models have been developed, but the best approach—and the one most firms today are following—is to use supply chain management and monitor the system closely.[14]

Self Test

What are some costs associated with high inventories? With low inventories?

What is a "supply chain," and how are supply chains related to just-in-time inventory procedures?

A company has $20 million in sales and an inventory turnover ratio of 2.0. If it can reduce its inventory and improve its inventory turnover ratio to 2.5 with no loss in sales, by how much will FCF increase? **($2 million)**

---

14. For additional insights into the problems of inventory management, see Richard A. Followill, Michael Schellenger, and Patrick H. Marchard, "Economic Order Quantities, Volume Discounts, and Wealth Maximization," *The Financial Review*, February 1990, pp. 143–152.

21.8 Receivables Management

Firms would, in general, rather sell for cash than on credit, but competitive pressures force most firms to offer credit for substantial purchases, especially to other businesses. Thus, goods are shipped, inventories are reduced, and an **account receivable** is created.[15] Eventually, the customer will pay the account, at which time (1) the firm will receive cash and (2) its receivables will decline. Carrying receivables has both direct and indirect costs, but selling on credit also has an important benefit: increased sales.

Receivables management begins with the firm's credit policy, but a monitoring system is also important to keep tabs on whether the terms of credit are being observed. Corrective action is often needed, and the only way to know whether the situation is getting out of hand is with a good receivables control system.[16]

21.8a Credit Policy

The success or failure of a business depends primarily on the demand for its products—as a rule, high sales lead to larger profits and a higher stock price. Sales, in turn, depend on a number of factors: Some, like the state of the economy, are exogenous, but others are under the firm's control. The major controllable factors are sales prices, product quality, advertising, and the firm's **credit policy**. Credit policy, in turn, consists of the following four variables.

1. *Credit period.* A firm might sell on terms of "net 30," which means that the customer must pay within 30 days.
2. *Discounts.* If the credit terms are stated as "2/10, net 30," then buyers may deduct 2% of the purchase price if payment is made within 10 days; otherwise, the full amount must be paid within 30 days. Thus, these terms allow a discount to be taken.
3. *Credit standards.* How much financial strength must a customer show to qualify for credit? Lower credit standards boost sales, but they also increase bad debts.
4. *Collection policy.* How tough or lax is a company in attempting to collect slow-paying accounts? A tough policy may speed up collections, but it might also anger customers and cause them to take their business elsewhere.

The credit manager is responsible for administering the firm's credit policy. However, because of the pervasive importance of credit, the credit policy itself is normally established by the executive committee, which usually consists of the president plus the vice presidents of finance, marketing, and production.

---

15. Whenever goods are sold on credit, two accounts are created—an asset item entitled *accounts receivable* appears on the books of the selling firm, and a liability item called *accounts payable* appears on the books of the purchaser. At this point, we are analyzing the transaction from the viewpoint of the seller, so we are concentrating on the variables under its control (i.e., the receivables). We examine the transaction from the viewpoint of the purchaser later in this chapter, where we discuss accounts payable as a source of funds and consider their cost.
16. For more on credit policy and receivables management, see Shehzad L. Mian and Clifford W. Smith, "Extending Trade Credit and Financing Receivables," *Journal of Applied Corporate Finance,* Spring 1994, pp. 75–84; and Paul D. Adams, Steve B. Wyatt, and Yong H. Kim, "A Contingent Claims Analysis of Trade Credit," *Financial Management,* Autumn 1992, pp. 104–112.

21.8b The Accumulation of Receivables

The total amount of accounts receivable outstanding at any given time is determined by two factors: (1) the credit sales per day and (2) the average length of time it takes to collect cash on accounts receivable:

$$\text{Accounts receivable} = \text{Credit sales per day} \times \text{Length of collection period} \qquad (21\text{--}5)$$

For example, suppose Boston Lumber Company (BLC), a wholesale distributor of lumber products, opens a warehouse on January 1 and, starting the first day, makes sales of $1,000 each day. For simplicity, we assume that all sales are on credit and that customers are given 10 days to pay. At the end of the first day, accounts receivable will be $1,000; they will rise to $2,000 by the end of the second day; and by January 10, they will have risen to 10($1,000) = $10,000. On January 11, another $1,000 will be added to receivables, but payments for sales made on January 1 will be collected and thus will reduce receivables by $1,000, so total accounts receivable will remain constant at $10,000. Once the firm's operations have stabilized, the following situation will exist:

$$\begin{aligned}
\text{Accounts receivable} &= \text{Credit sales per day} \times \text{Length of collection period} \\
&= \$1,000 \quad \times \quad 10 \text{ days} \quad = \$10,000
\end{aligned}$$

If either credit sales or the collection period changes, these changes will be reflected in the accounts receivable balance.

21.8c Monitoring the Receivables Position

Both investors and bank loan officers should pay close attention to accounts receivable, because what you see on a financial statement is not necessarily what you end up getting. To see why, consider how the accounting system operates. When a credit sale is made, these events occur: (1) inventories are reduced by the cost of goods sold; (2) accounts receivable are increased by the sales price; and (3) the difference is reported as a profit, which is adjusted for taxes and then added to the previous retained earnings balance. If the sale is for cash, then the cash from the sale has actually been received by the firm and the scenario just described is completely valid. If the sale is on credit, however, then the firm will not receive the cash from the sale unless and until the account is collected. Firms have been known to encourage "sales" to weak customers in order to report high current profits. This could boost the firm's stock price—but only for a short time. Eventually, credit losses will lower earnings, at which time the stock price will fall. This is another example of how differences between a firm's stock price and its intrinsic value can arise, and it is something that security analysts must keep in mind.

An analysis along the lines suggested in the following sections will detect any such questionable practice, and it will also help a firm's management learn of problems that might be arising. Such early detection helps both investors and bankers avoid losses, and it also helps a firm's management maximize intrinsic values.

SUPPLY CHAIN FINANCE

In our global economy, companies purchase parts and materials from suppliers located all over the world. For small and mid-size suppliers, especially those in less developed economies, selling to international customers can lead to cash flow problems. First, many suppliers have no way of knowing when their invoices have been approved by their customers. Second, they have no way of knowing when they will actually receive payment from their customers. With a 4–5-month lag between the time an order is received and the time the payment occurs, many suppliers resort to expensive local financing that can add as much as 4% to their costs. Even worse, some suppliers go out of business, which reduces competition and ultimately leads to higher prices.

Although most companies now work very hard with their suppliers to improve their supply chain operations, which is at the heart of supply management, a recent poll shows that only 13% actively use supply chain finance (SCF) techniques. However, that figure is likely to rise in the near future.

For example, Big Lots joined a Web-based service operated by Prime-Revenue that works like this: First, invoices received by Big Lots are posted to the system as soon as they are approved. The supplier doesn't need specialized software but can check its invoices using a Web browser. Second, the supplier has the option of selling the approved invoices at a discount to financial institutions and banks that have access to the PrimeRevenue network. A further advantage to the supplier is that it receives cash within a day of the invoices' approval. In addition, the effective interest rate built into the discounted price is based on the credit rating of Big Lots, not that of the supplier.

As Big Lots treasurer Jared Poff puts it, this allows vendors to "compete on their ability to make the product and not on their ability to access financing."

Source: Kate O'Sullivan, "Financing the Chain," *CFO*, February 2007, pp. 46–53.

Days Sales Outstanding (DSO)

Suppose Super Sets Inc., a television manufacturer, sells 200,000 television sets a year at a price of $198 each. Assume that all sales are on credit under the terms 2/10, net 30. Finally, assume that 70% of the customers take the discount and pay on Day 10 and that the other 30% pay on Day 30.[17]

Super Sets's **days sales outstanding (DSO)**, sometimes called the *average collection period (ACP)*, is 16 days:

$$DSO = ACP = 0.7(10 \text{ days}) + 0.3(30 \text{ days}) = 16 \text{ days}$$

Super Sets's *average daily sales (ADS)* is $108,493:

$$(21\text{-}6) \qquad ADS = \frac{\text{Annual sales}}{365} = \frac{(\text{Units sold})(\text{Sales price})}{365}$$

$$= \frac{200,000(\$198)}{365} = \frac{\$39,600,000}{365} = \$108,493$$

---

17. Unless otherwise noted, we assume throughout that payments are made either on the *last day* for taking discounts or on the *last day* of the credit period. It would be foolish to pay on (say) the 5th day or on the 20th day if the credit terms were 2/10, net 30.

Super Sets's accounts receivable—assuming a constant, uniform rate of sales throughout the year—will at any point in time be $1,735,888:

$$\text{Receivables} = (\text{DSO})(\text{ADS}) \qquad (21\text{--}7)$$

$$= (\$108,493)(16) = \$1,735,888$$

Note that DSO, or average collection period, is a measure of the average length of time it takes the firm's customers to pay off their credit purchases. Super Sets's DSO is 16 days versus an industry average of 25 days, so either Super Sets has a higher percentage of discount customers or else its credit department is exceptionally good at ensuring prompt payment.

Finally, note that you can derive both the annual sales and the receivables balance from the firm's financial statements, so you can calculate DSO as follows:

$$\text{DSO} = \frac{\text{Receivables}}{\text{Sales per day}} = \frac{\$1,735,888}{\$108,493} = 16 \text{ days}$$

The DSO can also be compared with the firm's own credit terms. For example, suppose Super Sets's DSO had been averaging 35 days. With a 35-day DSO, some customers obviously are taking more than 30 days to pay their bills. In fact, if many customers are paying by Day 10 to take advantage of the discount, then the others must be taking, on average, *much* longer than 35 days. A way to check this possibility is to use an aging schedule, as described next.

Aging Schedules

An **aging schedule** breaks down a firm's receivables by age of account. Table 21-1 shows the December 31, 2012, aging schedules of two television manufacturers, Super Sets and Wonder Vision. Both firms offer the same credit terms, and they have the same total receivables. Super Sets's aging schedule indicates that all of its customers pay on time: 70% pay by Day 10 and 30% pay by Day 30. In contrast, Wonder Vision's schedule, which is more typical, shows that many of its customers are not paying on time: 27% of its receivables are more than 30 days old, even though Wonder Vision's credit terms call for full payment by Day 30.

TABLE 21-1 Aging Schedules

	Super Sets		Wonder Vision	
Age of Account (Days)	Value of Account	Percentage of Total Value	Value of Account	Percentage of Total Value
0–10	$1,215,122	70%	$ 815,867	47%
11–30	520,766	30	451,331	26
31–45	0	0	260,383	15
46–60	0	0	173,589	10
Over 60	0	0	34,718	2
Total receivables	$1,735,888	100%	$1,735,888	100%

Aging schedules cannot be constructed from the type of summary data reported in financial statements; rather, they must be developed from the firm's accounts receivable ledger. However, well-run firms have computerized their accounts receivable records, so it is easy to determine the age of each invoice, to sort electronically by age categories, and thus to generate an aging schedule.

Management should constantly monitor both the DSO and the aging schedule to detect any trends, to see how the firm's collections experience compares with its credit terms, and to see how effectively the credit department is operating in comparison with other firms in the industry. If the DSO starts to lengthen or the aging schedule begins to show an increasing percentage of past-due accounts, then the credit manager should examine why these changes are occurring.

Although increases in the DSO and the aging schedule are warning signs, this does not necessarily indicate the firm's credit policy has weakened. If a firm experiences sharp seasonal variations or if it is growing rapidly, then both the aging schedule and the DSO may be distorted. To see this point, note that the DSO is calculated as follows:

$$\text{DSO} = \frac{\text{Accounts receivable}}{\text{Annual sales}/365}$$

Receivables at any point in time reflect sales in the past 1 or 2 months, but sales as shown in the denominator are for the past 12 months. Therefore, a seasonal increase in sales will increase the numerator more than the denominator and hence will raise the DSO, even if customers continue to pay just as quickly as before. Similar problems arise with the aging schedule, because if sales are rising then the percentage in the 0–10-day category will be high, and the reverse will occur if sales are falling. Therefore, a change in either the DSO or the aging schedule should be taken as a signal to investigate further; it is not necessarily a sign that the firm's credit policy has weakened.

Self Test

Explain how a new firm's receivables balance is built up over time.

Define days sales outstanding (DSO). What can be learned from it? How is it affected by sales fluctuations?

What is an aging schedule? What can be learned from it? How is it affected by sales fluctuations?

A company has annual sales of $730 million. If its DSO is 35, what is its average accounts receivables balance? (**$70 million**).

21.9 Accruals and Accounts Payable (Trade Credit)

Recall that net operating working capital is equal to operating current assets minus operating current liabilities. The previous sections discussed the management of operating current assets (cash, inventory, and accounts receivable), and the following sections discuss the two major types of operating current liabilities: accruals and accounts payable.[18]

---

18. For more on accounts payable management, see James A. Gentry and Jesus M. De La Garza, "Monitoring Accounts Payables," *Financial Review*, November 1990, pp. 559–576.

21.9a Accruals

Firms generally pay employees on a weekly, biweekly, or monthly basis, so the balance sheet will typically show some accrued wages. Similarly, the firm's own estimated income taxes, employment and income taxes withheld from employees, and sales taxes collected are generally paid on a weekly, monthly, or quarterly basis. Therefore, the balance sheet will typically show some accrued taxes along with accrued wages.

These **accruals** can be thought of as short-term, interest-free loans from employees and taxing authorities, and they increase automatically (that is, *spontaneously*) as a firm's operations expand. However, a firm cannot ordinarily control its accruals: The timing of wage payments is set by economic forces and industry norms, and tax payment dates are established by law. Thus, firms generally use all the accruals they can, but they have little control over the levels of these accounts.

21.9b Accounts Payable (Trade Credit)

Firms generally make purchases from other firms on credit, recording the debt as an *account payable*. Accounts payable, or **trade credit**, is the largest single operating current liability, representing about 40% of the current liabilities for an average non-financial corporation. The percentage is somewhat larger for smaller firms: Because small companies often have difficulty obtaining financinsg from other sources, they rely especially heavily on trade credit.

Trade credit is a spontaneous source of financing in the sense that it arises from ordinary business transactions. For example, suppose a firm makes average purchases of $2,000 a day on terms of net 30, meaning that it must pay for goods

A WAG OF THE FINGER OR TIP OF THE HAT? THE COLBERT REPORT AND SMALL BUSINESS PAYMENT TERMS

On February 17, 2011, The Colbert Report featured an interview with Jeffrey Leonard. During a spirited exchange with Stephen Colbert, Leonard accused many large businesses of imposing onerous payment terms on their small suppliers. According to Leonard, when Cisco Systems sells to the U.S. government, Cisco receives its payment in 30 days, the standard credit terms used by the federal government. Yet Cisco changed its own credit policy in 2010 to "net 60," meaning that Cisco's suppliers don't get paid for 60 days. In other words, many small companies essentially are helping Cisco finance its working capital, even though Cisco has over $39 billion in cash. Cisco isn't alone in delaying its payments: Dell, Wal-Mart, and AB InBev (the owner of Anheuser-Busch) also pay slower than 30 days.

Colbert and Leonard agreed on the facts, but interpreted them differently. Leonard suggested that the government

help small businesses by requiring its own supplier companies to offer their vendors the same terms as the government does. Colbert, however, suggested (perhaps with tongue-in-cheek) that this was just the natural result of free markets and that no government interference was warranted.

You be the judge. When big companies legally take what they can from smaller companies, should they receive a wag of the finger or a tip of the hat?

Sources: **www.washingtonmonthly.com/features/2011/ 1101.leonard.html,www.colbertnation.com/the-colbert-report-videos/374633/february-17-2011/jeffrey-leonard,** and **www.allbusiness.com/company-activities-manage ment/management-benchmarking/15472247-1.html.**

30 days after the invoice date. On average, it will owe 30 times $2,000, or $60,000, to its suppliers. If its sales, and consequently its purchases, were to double, then its accounts payable would also double, to $120,000. So simply by growing, the firm would spontaneously generate an additional $60,000 of financing. Similarly, if the terms under which the firm buys were extended from 30 to 40 days, then its accounts payable would expand from $60,000 to $80,000 even with no growth in sales. Thus, both expanding sales and lengthening the credit period generate additional amounts of financing via trade credit.

21.9c The Cost of Trade Credit

Firms that sell on credit have a *credit policy* that includes their *terms of credit*. For example, Microchip Electronics sells on terms of 2/10, net 30: It gives customers a 2% discount if they pay within 10 days of the invoice date, but the full invoice amount is due and payable within 30 days if the discount is not taken.

The "true price" of Microchip's products is the net price, or 0.98 times the list price, because any customer can purchase an item at that price as long as payment is made within 10 days. Now consider Personal Computer Company (PCC), which buys its memory chips from Microchip. One chip is listed at $100, so its "true" price to PCC is $98. Now if PCC wants an additional 20 days of credit beyond the 10-day discount period, it must incur a finance charge of $2 per chip for that credit. Thus, the $100 list price consists of two components:

$$\text{List price} = \$98 \text{ true price} + \$2 \text{ finance charge}$$

The question PCC must ask before it turns down the discount to obtain the additional 20 days of credit is this: Could credit be obtained at a lower cost from a bank or some other lender?

Now assume that PCC buys $11,923,333 of memory chips from Microchip each year at the net, or true, price. This amounts to $11,923,333/365 = $32,666.67 per day. For simplicity, assume that Microchip is PCC's only supplier. If PCC decides not to take the additional 20 days of trade credit—that is, if it pays on the 10th day and takes the discount—then its payables will average 10($32,666.67) = $326,667. Thus, PCC will be receiving $326,667 of credit from Microchip.

Now suppose PCC decides to take the additional 20 days credit and so must pay the full list price. Since PCC will now pay on the 30th day, its accounts payable will increase to 30($32,666.67) = $980,000.[19] Microchip will now be supplying PCC with an additional $980,000 − $326,667 = $653,333 of credit, which PCC could use to build up its cash account, to pay off debt, to expand inventories, or even to extend credit to its own customers, hence increasing its own accounts receivable.

Thus the additional trade credit offered by Microchip has a cost: PCC must pay a finance charge equal to the 2% discount it is forgoing. PCC buys $11,923,333 of chips at the true price, so the added finance charge would increase the total cost to $11,923,333/0.98 = $12,166,666. Therefore, the annual financing cost is $12,166,666 − $11,923,333 = $243,333. Dividing the $243,333 financing cost by

---

19. A question arises here: Should accounts payable reflect gross purchases or purchases net of discounts? Generally accepted accounting principles permit either treatment if the difference is not material, but if the discount is material then the transaction must be recorded net of discounts, or at "true" prices. Then, the higher payment that results from not taking discounts is reported as an expense called "discounts lost." Therefore, *we show accounts payable net of discounts even if the company does not expect to take discounts.*

the $653,333 of additional credit, we calculate the nominal annual cost rate of the additional trade credit to be 37.2%:

$$\text{Nominal annual costs} = \frac{\$243,333}{\$653,333} = 37.2\%$$

If PCC can borrow from its bank (or some other source) at an interest rate less than 37.2%, then it should take the 2% discount and forgo the additional trade credit.

The following equation can be used to calculate the nominal cost (on an annual basis) of not taking discounts, illustrated with terms of 2/10, net 30:

$$\frac{\text{Nominal cost}}{\text{of trade credit}} = \text{Cost per period} \times \text{Number of periods per year}$$

$$\frac{\text{Nominal cost}}{\text{of trade credit}} = \frac{\text{Discount percentage}}{100 - \frac{\text{Discount}}{\text{percentage}}} \times \frac{365}{\frac{\text{Days credit is}}{\text{outstanding}} - \frac{\text{Discount}}{\text{period}}} \qquad (21\text{--}8)$$

$$= \frac{2}{98} \times \frac{365}{20} = 2.04\% \times 18.25 = 37.2\%$$

The numerator of the first term, Discount percentage, is the cost per dollar of credit, while the denominator, 100 − Discount percentage, represents the funds made available by not taking the discount. Thus, the first term, 2.04%, is the cost per period for the trade credit. The denominator of the second term is the number of days of extra credit obtained by not taking the discount, so the entire second term shows how many times each year the cost is incurred—18.25 times in this example.

This nominal annual cost formula does not consider the compounding of interest. In terms of effective annual interest, the cost of trade credit is even higher:

$$\text{Effective annual rate} = (1.0204)^{18.25} - 1.0 = 1.4459 - 1.0 = 44.6\%$$

Thus, the 37.2% nominal cost calculated with Equation 21-8 actually understates the true cost.

Note, however, that the calculated cost of trade credit can be reduced by paying late. Thus, if PCC could get away with paying in 60 days rather than the specified 30 days, then the effective credit period would become 60 − 10 = 50 days, the number of times the discount would be lost would fall to 365/50 = 7.3, and the nominal cost would drop from 37.2% to 2.04% × 7.3 = 14.9%. Then the effective annual rate would drop from 44.6% to 15.9%:

$$\text{Effective annual rate} = (1.0204)^{7.3} - 1.0 = 1.1589 - 1.0 = 15.9\%$$

In periods of excess capacity, firms may be able to get away with deliberately paying late, or **stretching accounts payable**. However, they will also suffer a variety of problems associated with being a "slow payer." These problems are discussed later in the chapter.

The costs of the additional trade credit from forgoing discounts under some other purchase terms are taken from the chapter's *Excel Tool Kit* model and shown here as Figure 21-7. As these numbers indicate, the cost of not taking discounts can be substantial.

WEB

See *Ch21 Tool Kit.xls* on the textbook's Web site for details.

Figure 21-7 **Varying Credit Terms and Their Associated Costs**

	A	B	C	D	E	F
32		Days in year: 365			Cost of additional credit	
33						
34	Credit terms	Discount	Discount period	Net period	Nominal	Effective
35	1/10, net 20	1%	10	20	36.87%	44.32%
36	1/10, net 30	1%	10	30	18.43%	20.13%
37	1/10, net 90	1%	10	90	4.61%	4.69%
38	2/10, net 20	2%	10	20	74.49%	109.05%
39	2/10, net 30	2%	10	30	37.24%	44.59%
40	3/15, net 45	3%	15	45	37.63%	44.86%

On the basis of the preceding discussion, trade credit can be divided into two components: (1) **free trade credit**, which involves credit received during the discount period, and (2) **costly trade credit**, which involves credit in excess of the free trade credit and whose cost is an implicit one based on the forgone discounts. *Firms should always use the free component, but they should use the costly component only after analyzing the cost of this capital to make sure it is less than the cost of funds that could be obtained from other sources.* Under the terms of trade found in most industries, the costly component is relatively expensive, so stronger firms generally avoid using it.

Note, though, that firms sometimes offer favorable credit terms in order to stimulate sales. For example, suppose a firm has been selling on terms of 2/10, net 30, with a nominal cost of 37.24%, but a recession has reduced sales and the firm now has excess capacity. It wants to boost the sales of its product without cutting the list price, so it might offer terms of 1/10, net 90, which implies a nominal cost of additional credit of only 4.61%. In this situation, its customers would probably be wise to take the additional credit and reduce their reliance on banks and other lenders. So, turning down discounts is not always a bad decision.

Self Test

What are accruals? How much control do managers have over accruals?

What is trade credit?

What's the difference between free trade credit and costly trade credit?

How does the cost of costly trade credit generally compare with the cost of short-term bank loans?

A company buys on terms of 2/12, net 28. What is its nominal cost of trade credit? (**46.6%**) The effective cost? (**58.5%**)

21.10 Short-Term Marketable Securities

Short-term marketable securities are held for two separate and distinct purposes: (1) to provide liquidity, as a substitute for cash; and (2) as a nonoperating investment, generally on a temporary basis while awaiting deployment for long-term, permanent investments. Of course, it is difficult to separate these two purposes, because securities held while awaiting reinvestment are available for liquidity purposes.

With regard to operating funds, companies typically lump liquid marketable securities in with currency and bank demand deposits and call the total "cash and cash equivalents." These are the current assets that the firm needs to carry in its operations on an uninterrupted basis. If the company needs to write checks in amounts greater than its demand deposits, it simply makes a phone call to a broker and places a market sell order; the broker in turn will sell the securities, and almost immediately the sale proceeds will be deposited in the firm's bank account. Because cash and most commercial checking accounts yield nothing whereas marketable securities provide at least a modest return, firms choose to hold part of their liquid assets as marketable securities rather than pure cash balances.

Note also that firms' cash and equivalents holdings can be reduced by having unused credit lines with banks. A firm can negotiate a line of credit under which it can borrow immediately if it needs cash for transactions. It can simply call the bank, ask to "take down" a portion of its line, and the bank will immediately deposit funds in its account that can then be used for writing checks. This ready source of funds proved to be not quite so reliable for some firms during the financial crisis of 2008 and 2009 and the credit crunch that led up to it as banks refused to renew or extend lines of credit. Even today (mid-year 2011) banks are stricter in their lending practices than they were before the financial crisis. As a result, some companies are holding higher cash and marketable securities balances rather than relying as much on lines of credit.

There are both benefits and costs associated with holding marketable securities. The benefits are twofold: (1) the firm reduces risk and transaction costs, because it won't have to issue securities or borrow as frequently to raise cash; and (2) it will have ready cash to take advantage of bargain purchases or growth opportunities. Funds held for the second reason are called **speculative balances**. The primary disadvantage is that the after-tax return on short-term securities is very low. Thus, firms face a trade-off between benefits and costs.

Recent research supports this trade-off hypothesis as an explanation for firms' cash holdings.[20] Firms with high growth opportunities suffer the most if they don't have ready cash to quickly take advantage of an opportunity, and the data show that these firms do hold relatively high levels of marketable securities. Firms with volatile cash flows are the ones most likely to run low on cash, so they tend to hold high levels of cash. In contrast, cash holdings are less important to large firms with high credit ratings, because they have quick and inexpensive access to capital markets. As expected, such firms hold relatively low levels of cash. Of course, there will always be outliers such as Microsoft, which is large, strong, and cash-rich, but volatile firms with good growth opportunities are still the ones that hold the most marketable securities, on average.

	Self Test

Why might a company hold low-yielding marketable securities when it could earn a much higher return on operating assets?

---

20. See Tim Opler, Lee Pinkowitz, René Stulz, and Rohan Williamson, "The Determinants and Implications of Corporate Cash Holdings," *Journal of Financial Economics,* 1999, pp. 3–46. For additional insights into maturity choice, see Karlyn Mitchell, "The Debt Maturity Choice: An Empirical Investigation," *Journal of Financial Research,* Winter 1993, pp. 309–320.

21.11 Short-Term Financing

The three possible short-term financing policies described earlier in the chapter were distinguished by the relative amounts of short-term debt used under each policy. The aggressive policy called for the greatest use of short-term debt, and the conservative policy called for using the least; maturity matching fell in between. Although short-term credit is generally riskier than long-term credit, using short-term funds does have some significant advantages. The pros and cons of short-term financing are considered in this section.

21.11a Advantages of Short-Term Financing

First, a short-term loan can be obtained much faster than long-term credit. Lenders will insist on a more thorough financial examination before extending long-term credit, and the loan agreement will have to be spelled out in considerable detail because a lot can happen during the life of a 10- to 20-year loan. Therefore, if funds are needed in a hurry, the firm should look to the short-term markets.

Second, if its needs for funds are seasonal or cyclical, then a firm may not want to commit itself to long-term debt. There are three reasons for this: (1) Flotation costs are higher for long-term debt than for short-term credit. (2) Although long-term debt can be repaid early (provided the loan agreement includes a prepayment provision), prepayment penalties can be expensive. Accordingly, if a firm thinks its need for funds will diminish in the near future, it should choose short-term debt. (3) Long-term loan agreements always contain provisions, or covenants, that constrain the firm's future actions. Short-term credit agreements are generally less restrictive.

The third advantage is that, because the yield curve is normally upward sloping, interest rates are generally lower on short-term debt. Thus, under normal conditions, interest costs at the time the funds are obtained will be lower if the firm borrows on a short-term rather than a long-term basis.

21.11b Disadvantages of Short-Term Debt

Even though short-term rates are often lower than long-term rates, using short-term credit is riskier for two reasons: (1) If a firm borrows on a long-term basis then its interest costs will be relatively stable over time, but if it uses short-term credit then its interest expense will fluctuate widely, at times going quite high. For example, the rate banks charged large corporations for short-term debt more than tripled over a 2-year period in the 1980s, rising from 6.25% to 21%. Many firms that had borrowed heavily on a short-term basis simply could not meet their rising interest costs; as a result, bankruptcies hit record levels during that period. (2) If a firm borrows heavily on a short-term basis, a temporary recession may render it unable to repay this debt. If the borrower is in a weak financial position then the lender may not extend the loan, which could force the firm into bankruptcy.

Self Test   What are the advantages and disadvantages of short-term debt compared with long-term debt?

21.12 Short-Term Bank Loans

Loans from commercial banks generally appear on balance sheets as notes payable. A bank's importance is actually greater than it appears from the dollar amounts shown on balance sheets because banks provide *nonspontaneous* funds. As a firm's financing needs increase, it requests additional funds from its bank. If the request is denied, the firm may be forced to abandon attractive growth opportunities. The key features of bank loans are discussed in the following paragraphs.

21.12a Maturity

Although banks do make longer-term loans, *the bulk of their lending is on a short-term basis*—about two-thirds of all bank loans mature in a year or less. Bank loans to businesses are frequently written as 90-day notes, so the loan must be repaid or renewed at the end of 90 days. Of course, if a borrower's financial position has deteriorated then the bank may refuse to renew the loan. This can mean serious trouble for the borrower.

21.12b Promissory Notes

When a bank loan is approved, the agreement is executed by signing a **promissory note**. The note specifies (1) the amount borrowed, (2) the interest rate, (3) the re-payment schedule, which can call for either a lump sum or a series of installments, (4) any collateral that might have to be put up as security for the loan, and (5) any other terms and conditions to which the bank and the borrower have agreed. When the note is signed, the bank credits the borrower's checking account with the funds; hence both cash and notes payable increase on the borrower's balance sheet.

21.12c Compensating Balances

Banks sometimes require borrowers to maintain an average demand deposit (checking account) balance of 10% to 20% of the loan's face amount. This is called a compen-sating balance, and such balances raise the effective interest rate on the loans. For example, if a firm needs $80,000 to pay off outstanding obligations but it must maintain a 20% compensating balance, then it must borrow $100,000 to obtain a usable $80,000. If the stated annual interest rate is 8%, the effective cost is actually 10%: $8,000 interest divided by $80,000 of usable funds equals 10%.[21]

As we noted earlier in the chapter, recent surveys indicate that compensating balances are much less common now than earlier. In fact, compensating balances are now illegal in many states. Despite this trend, some small banks in states where compensating balances are legal still require their customers to maintain them.

21.12d Informal Line of Credit

A **line of credit** is an informal agreement between a bank and a borrower indicating the maximum credit the bank will extend to the borrower. For example, on December 31, a bank loan officer might indicate to a financial manager that the bank regards the firm as being "good" for up to $80,000 during the forthcoming year, provided the borrower's financial condition does not deteriorate. If on January 10 the finan-cial manager signs a 90-day promissory note for $15,000, this would be called

---

21. Note, however, that the compensating balance may be set as a minimum monthly *average,* and if the firm would maintain this average anyway then the compensating balance requirement would not raise the effective interest rate. Also, note that these loan compensating balances are *added to* any compensating balances that the firm's bank may require for services performed, such as clearing checks.

"taking down" $15,000 of the total line of credit. This amount would be credited to the firm's checking account at the bank, and the firm could borrow additional amounts up to a total of $80,000 outstanding at any one time.

21.12e Revolving Credit Agreement

A **revolving credit agreement** is a formal line of credit often used by large firms. To illustrate, suppose in 2012 Texas Petroleum Company negotiated a revolving credit agreement for $100 million with a group of banks. The banks were formally committed for 4 years to lend the firm up to $100 million if the funds were needed. Texas Petroleum, in turn, paid an annual commitment fee of 0.25% on the unused balance of the commitment to compensate the banks for making the commitment. Thus, if Texas Petroleum did not take down any of the $100 million commitment during a year, it would still be required to pay a $250,000 annual fee, normally in monthly installments of $20,833.33. If it borrowed $50 million on the first day of the agreement, then the unused portion of the line of credit would fall to $50 million and the annual fee would fall to $125,000. Of course, interest would also have to be paid on the money Texas Petroleum actually borrowed. As a general rule, the interest rate on "revolvers" is pegged to the London Interbank Offered Rate (LIBOR), the T-bill rate, or some other market rate, so the cost of the loan varies over time as interest rates change. The interest that Texas Petroleum must pay was set at the prime lending rate plus 1.0%.

Observe that a revolving credit agreement is similar to an informal line of credit but has an important difference: The bank has a *legal obligation* to honor a revolving credit agreement, and it receives a commitment fee. Neither the legal obligation nor the fee exists under the informal line of credit.

Often a line of credit will have a **cleanup clause** that requires the borrower to reduce the loan balance to zero at least once a year. Keep in mind that a line of credit typically is designed to help finance seasonal or cyclical peaks in operations, not as a source of permanent capital. For example, our cash budget for Educational Products Corporation showed negative flows from July through September but positive flows from October through December. Also, the cumulative net cash flow goes positive in November, indicating that the firm could pay off its loan at that time. If the cumulative flows were always negative, this would indicate that the firm was using its credit lines as a permanent source of financing.

21.12f Costs of Bank Loans

The costs of bank loans vary for different types of borrowers at any given point in time and for all borrowers over time. Interest rates are higher for riskier borrowers, and rates are also higher on smaller loans because of the fixed costs involved in making and servicing loans. If a firm can qualify as a "prime credit" because of its size and financial strength, it can borrow at the **prime rate**, which at one time was the lowest rate banks charged. Rates on other loans are generally scaled up from the prime rate. Loans to large, strong customers are made at rates tied to LIBOR; and the costs of such loans are generally well below prime:

Rates on March 3, 2011	
Prime	3.25%
1-Year LIBOR	0.79%

The rate to smaller, riskier borrowers is generally stated something like "prime plus 1.0%"; but for a larger borrower it is generally stated as something like "LIBOR plus 1.5%."

Bank rates vary widely over time depending on economic conditions and Federal Reserve policy. When the economy is weak, loan demand is usually slack, inflation is low, and the Fed makes plenty of money available to the system. As a result, rates on all types of loans are relatively low. Conversely, when the economy is booming, loan demand is typically strong, the Fed restricts the money supply to fight inflation, and the result is high interest rates. As an indication of the kinds of fluctuations that can occur, the prime rate during 1980 rose from 11% to 21% in just 4 months; during 1994, it rose from 6% to 9%.

Calculating Banks' Interest Charges: Regular (or "Simple") Interest

Banks calculate interest in several different ways. In this section, we explain the procedure used for most business loans. For illustration purposes, we assume a loan of $10,000 at the prime rate, currently 3.25%, with a 360-day year. Interest must be paid monthly, and the principal is payable "on demand" if and when the bank wants to end the loan. Such a loan is called a **regular interest** loan; it is also called a **simple interest** loan.

We begin by dividing the nominal interest rate (3.25% in this case) by 360 to obtain the rate per day. This rate is expressed as a *decimal fraction,* not as a percentage:

$$\text{Simple interest rate per day} = \frac{\text{Nominal rate}}{\text{Days in year}}$$

$$= 0.0325/360 = 0.000090278$$

To find the monthly interest payment, the daily rate is multiplied by the amount of the loan, then by the number of days during the payment period. For our illustrative loan, the daily interest charge would be $0.902777778, and the total for a 30-day month would be $27.08:

$$\text{Interest charge for month} = (\text{Rate per day})(\text{Amount of loan})(\text{Days in month})$$

$$= (0.000090278)(\$10,000)(30 \text{ days}) = \$27.08$$

The *effective interest rate* on a loan depends on how frequently interest must be paid—the more frequently interest is paid, the higher the effective rate. If interest is paid once per year, then the nominal rate is also the effective rate. However, if interest must be paid monthly, then the effective rate is $(1 + 0.0325/12)^{12} - 1 = 3.2989\%$.

Calculating Banks' Interest Charges: Add-on Interest

Banks and other lenders typically use **add-on interest** for automobiles and other types of installment loans. The term *add-on* means that the interest is calculated and then added to the amount borrowed to determine the loan's face value. To illustrate, suppose you borrow $10,000 on an add-on basis at a nominal rate of 7.25% to buy a car, with the loan to be repaid in 12 monthly installments. At a 7.25% add-on rate, you would make total interest payments of $10,000(0.0725) = $725. However, since the loan is paid off in monthly installments, you would have the use of the full $10,000 for only the first month; then the outstanding balance would decline until, during the last month, only 1/12 of the original loan was still outstanding. Thus, you would be paying $725 for the use of only about half the loan's face amount, since the average usable funds would be only about $5,000. Therefore, we can calculate the approximate annual rate as 14.5%:

(21–9)

$$\text{Approximate annual rate}_{\text{Add-on}} = \frac{\text{Interest paid}}{(\text{Amount received})/2}$$

$$= \frac{\$725}{\$10,000/2} = 14.5\%.$$

The annual percentage rate (APR) the bank would provide to the borrower would be 13.12%, and the true effective annual rate would be 13.94%.[22] Both of these rates are much higher than the nominal 7.25%.

Self Test

What is a promissory note, and what are some terms that are normally included in promissory notes?

What is a line of credit? A revolving credit agreement?

What's the difference between simple interest and add-on interest?

Explain how a firm that expects to need funds during the coming year might make sure that the needed funds will be available.

How does the cost of costly trade credit generally compare with the cost of short-term bank loans?

If a firm borrowed $500,000 at a rate of 10% simple interest with monthly interest payments and a 365-day year, what would be the required interest payment for a 30-day month? **($4,109.59)** If interest must be paid monthly, what would be the effective annual rate? **(10.47%)**

If this loan had been made on a 10% add-on basis, payable in 12 end-of-month installments, what would be the monthly payment amount? **($45,833.33)** What is the annual percentage rate? **(17.97%)** The effective annual rate? **(19.53%)**

---

www

For updates on the outstanding balances of commercial paper, go to **www.federalreserve.gov/ econresdata/releases/ statisticsdata.htm** and check out the volume statistics for Commercial Paper and the weekly releases for Assets and Liabilities of Commercial Banks in the United States.

21.13 Commercial Paper

Commercial paper is a type of unsecured promissory note issued by large, strong firms and sold primarily to other business firms, to insurance companies, to pension funds, to money market mutual funds, and to banks. In July 2011, there was approximately $1.1 trillion of commercial paper outstanding, versus nearly $1.3 trillion of commercial and industrial bank loans. Most, but not all, commercial paper outstanding is issued by financial institutions.

---

22. To find the annual percentage rate and the effective rate on an add-on loan, we first find the payment per month, $10,725/12 = $893.75. With a financial calculator, enter N = 12, PV = 10000, PMT = −893.75, and FV = 0; then press I/YR to obtain 1.093585%. This is a monthly rate, so multiply by 12 to get 13.12%, which is the APR the bank would report to the borrower. The effective annual rate would then be $(1.010936)^{12} − 1 = 13.94\%$, quite a bit above the APR.

21.13a Maturity and Cost

Maturities of commercial paper generally vary from 1 day to 9 months, with an average of about 5 months.[23] The interest rate on commercial paper fluctuates with supply and demand conditions—it is determined in the marketplace, varying daily as conditions change. Recently, commercial paper rates have ranged from 1.5 to 3.5 percentage points below the stated prime rate and up to half of a percentage point above the T-bill rate. For example, in March 2011, the average rate on 3-month commercial paper was 0.25%, the prime rate was 3.25%, and the 3-month T-bill rate was 0.13%.

21.13b Use of Commercial Paper

The use of commercial paper is restricted to a comparatively small number of very large concerns that are exceptionally good credit risks. Dealers prefer to handle the paper of firms whose net worth is $100 million or more and whose annual borrowing exceeds $10 million. One potential problem with commercial paper is that a debtor who is in temporary financial difficulty may receive little help because commercial paper dealings are generally less personal than are bank relationships. Thus, banks are generally more able and willing to help a good customer weather a temporary storm than is a commercial paper dealer. On the other hand, using commercial paper permits a corporation to tap a wide range of credit sources, including financial institutions outside its own area and industrial corporations across the country, and this can reduce interest costs.

WWW

For current rates, see **www.federalreserve.gov/econresdata/releases/statisticsdata.htm** and look at the Daily Releases for Selected Interest Rates.

Self Test

What is commercial paper?

What types of companies can use commercial paper to meet their short-term financing needs?

How does the cost of commercial paper compare with the cost of short-term bank loans? With the cost of Treasury bills?

21.14 Use of Security in Short-Term Financing

Thus far, we have not addressed the question of whether or not short-term loans should be secured. Commercial paper is never secured, but other types of loans can be secured if this is deemed necessary or desirable. Other things held constant, it is better to borrow on an unsecured basis, since the bookkeeping costs of **secured loans** are often high. However, firms often find that they can borrow only if they put up some type of collateral to protect the lender or that, by using security, they can borrow at a much lower rate.

Several different kinds of collateral can be employed, including marketable stocks or bonds, land or buildings, equipment, inventory, and accounts receivable. Marketable securities make excellent collateral, but few firms that need loans also

---

23. The maximum maturity without SEC registration is 270 days. Also, commercial paper can be sold only to "sophisticated" investors; otherwise, SEC registration would be required even for maturities of 270 days or less.

WEB

For a more detailed discussion of secured financing, see **Web Extension 21A** on the textbook's Web site.

hold portfolios of stocks and bonds. Similarly, real property (land and buildings) and equipment are good forms of collateral, but they are generally used as security for long-term loans rather than for working capital loans. Therefore, most secured short-term business borrowing involves the use of accounts receivable and inventories as collateral.

To understand the use of security, consider the case of a Chicago hardware dealer who wanted to modernize and expand his store. He requested a $200,000 bank loan. After examining the business's financial statements, his bank indicated that it would lend him a maximum of $100,000 and that the effective interest rate would be 9%. The owner had a substantial personal portfolio of stocks, and he offered to put up $300,000 of high-quality stocks to support the $200,000 loan. The bank then granted the full $200,000 loan at the prime rate of 3.25%. The store owner might also have used his inventories or receivables as security for the loan, but processing costs would have been high.[24]

Self Test	What is a secured loan?
	What are some types of current assets that are pledged as security for short-term loans?

Summary

This chapter discussed working capital management and short-term financing. The key concepts covered are listed below.

- **Working capital** refers to current assets used in operations, and **net working capital** is defined as current assets minus all current liabilities. **Net operating working capital** is defined as operating current assets minus operating current liabilities.
- Under a **relaxed working capital policy**, a firm would hold relatively large amounts of each type of current asset. Under a **restricted working capital policy**, the firm would hold minimal amounts of these items.
- A **moderate** approach to short-term financing involves matching, to the extent possible, the maturities of assets and liabilities, so that temporary operating current assets are financed with short-term debt and permanent operating current assets and fixed assets are financed with long-term debt or equity. Under an **aggressive** approach, some permanent operating current assets, and perhaps even some fixed assets, are financed with short-term debt. A **conservative** approach would be to use long-term sources to finance all permanent operating capital and some of the temporary operating current assets.

---

24. The term "asset-based financing" is often used as a synonym for "secured financing." In recent years, accounts receivable have been used as security for long-term bonds, permitting corporations to borrow from lenders such as pension funds rather than just from banks and other traditional short-term lenders.

- **Permanent operating current assets** are the operating current assets the firm holds even during slack times, whereas **temporary operating current assets** are the additional operating current assets needed during seasonal or cyclical peaks. The methods used to finance permanent and temporary operating current assets define the firm's **short-term financing policy.**
- The **inventory conversion period** is the average time required to convert materials into finished goods and then to sell those goods:

  Inventory conversion period = Inventory ÷ Cost of goods sold per day

- The **average collection period** is the average length of time required to convert the firm's receivables into cash—that is, to collect cash following a sale:

  Average collection period = DSO = Receivables ÷ (Sales/365)

- The **payables deferral period** is the average length of time between the purchase of materials and labor and the payment of cash for them:

  Payables deferral period = Payables ÷ Cost of goods sold per day

- The **cash conversion cycle (CCC)** is the length of time between the firm's actual cash expenditures to pay for productive resources (materials and labor) and its own cash receipts from the sale of products (that is, the length of time between paying for labor and materials and collecting on receivables):

$$\begin{matrix} \text{Cash} & & \text{Inventory} & & \text{Average} & & \text{Payables} \\ \text{conversion} & = & \text{conversion} & + & \text{collection} & - & \text{deferral} \\ \text{cycle} & & \text{period} & & \text{period} & & \text{period} \end{matrix}$$

- A **cash budget** is a schedule showing projected cash inflows and outflows over some period. The cash budget is used to predict cash surpluses and deficits, and it is the primary cash management planning tool.
- The **primary goal of cash management** is to minimize the amount of cash the firm must hold for conducting its normal business activities while at the same time maintaining a sufficient cash reserve to take discounts, pay bills promptly, and meet any unexpected cash needs.
- The **transactions balance** is the cash necessary to conduct routine day-to-day business; **precautionary balances** are cash reserves held to meet random, unforeseen needs. A **compensating balance** is a minimum checking account balance that a bank requires as compensation either for services provided or as part of a loan agreement.
- The twin goals of **inventory management** are (1) to ensure that the inventories needed to sustain operations are available, but (2) to hold the costs of ordering and carrying inventories to the lowest possible level.
- When a firm sells goods to a customer on credit, an **account receivable** is created.
- A firm can use an **aging schedule** and the **days sales outstanding (DSO)** to monitor its receivables balance and to help avoid an increase in bad debts.
- A firm's **credit policy** consists of four elements: (1) credit period, (2) discounts given for early payment, (3) credit standards, and (4) collection policy.
- **Accounts payable**, or **trade credit**, arises spontaneously as a result of credit purchases. Firms should use all the **free trade credit** they can obtain, but they

should use **costly trade credit** only if it is less expensive than other forms of short-term debt. Suppliers often offer discounts to customers who pay within a stated period. The following equation may be used to calculate the nominal cost, on an annual basis, of not taking such discounts:

$$\begin{array}{l}\text{Nominal} \\ \text{annual cost of} = \\ \text{trade credit}\end{array} = \frac{\text{Discount percentage}}{100 - \begin{array}{c}\text{Discount}\\\text{percentage}\end{array}} \times \frac{365}{\begin{array}{c}\text{Days credit is}\\\text{outstanding}\end{array} - \begin{array}{c}\text{Discount}\\\text{period}\end{array}}$$

- The advantages of short-term credit are (1) the **speed** with which short-term loans can be arranged, (2) increased **flexibility,** and (3) generally **lower interest rates** than with long-term credit. The principal disadvantage of short-term credit is the **extra risk** the borrower must bear because (1) the lender can demand payment on short notice, and (2) the cost of the loan will increase if interest rates rise.
- **Bank loans** are an important source of short-term credit. When a bank loan is approved, a **promissory note** is signed. It specifies: (1) the amount borrowed, (2) the percentage interest rate, (3) the repayment schedule, (4) the collateral, and (5) any other conditions to which the parties have agreed.
- Banks sometimes require borrowers to maintain **compensating balances,** which are deposit requirements set at between 10% and 20% of the loan amount. Compensating balances raise the effective interest rate on bank loans.
- A **line of credit** is an informal agreement between the bank and the borrower indicating the maximum amount of credit the bank will extend to the borrower.
- A **revolving credit agreement** is a formal line of credit often used by large firms; it involves a **commitment fee.**
- A **simple interest** loan is one in which interest must be paid monthly and the principal is payable "on demand" if and when the bank wants to end the loan.
- An **add-on interest loan** is one in which interest is calculated and added to the funds received to determine the face amount of the installment loan.
- **Commercial paper** is unsecured short-term debt issued by large, financially strong corporations. Although the cost of commercial paper is lower than the cost of bank loans, it can be used only by large firms with exceptionally strong credit ratings.
- Sometimes a borrower will find it is necessary to borrow on a **secured basis,** in which case the borrower pledges assets such as real estate, securities, equipment, inventories, or accounts receivable as collateral for the loan. For a more detailed discussion of secured financing, see *Web Extension 21A.*

Questions

21-1 Define each of the following terms:
   a. Working capital; net working capital; net operating working capital
   b. Relaxed policy; restricted policy; moderate policy
   c. Permanent operating current assets; temporary operating current assets
   d. Moderate (maturity matching) financing policy; aggressive financing policy; conservative financing policy
   e. Inventory conversion period; average collection period; payables deferral period; cash conversion cycle

f. Cash budget; target cash balance

g. Transactions balances; compensating balances; precautionary balances

h. Trade discounts

i. Credit policy; credit period; credit standards; collection policy; cash discounts

j. Account receivable; days sales outstanding; aging schedule

k. Accruals; trade credit

l. Stretching accounts payable; free trade credit; costly trade credit

m. Promissory note; line of credit; revolving credit agreement

n. Commercial paper; secured loan

21-2 What are the two principal reasons for holding cash? Can a firm estimate its target cash balance by summing the cash held to satisfy each of the two reasons?

21-3 Is it true that, when one firm sells to another on credit, the seller records the transaction as an account receivable while the buyer records it as an account payable and that, disregarding discounts, the receivable typically exceeds the payable by the amount of profit on the sale?

21-4 What are the four elements of a firm's credit policy? To what extent can firms set their own credit policies as opposed to accepting policies that are dictated by its competitors?

21-5 What are the advantages of matching the maturities of assets and liabilities? What are the disadvantages?

21-6 From the standpoint of the borrower, is long-term or short-term credit riskier? Explain. Would it ever make sense to borrow on a short-term basis if short-term rates were above long-term rates?

21-7 Discuss this statement: "Firms can control their accruals within fairly wide limits."

21-8 Is it true that most firms are able to obtain some free trade credit and that additional trade credit is often available, but at a cost? Explain.

21-9 What kinds of firms use commercial paper?

Problems   Answers Appear in Appendix B

Easy Problems 1–5

21-1 **Cash Management** Williams & Sons last year reported sales of $10 million and an inventory turnover ratio of 2. The company is now adopting a new inventory system. If the new system is able to reduce the firm's inventory level and increase the firm's inventory turnover ratio to 5 while maintaining the same level of sales, how much cash will be freed up?

21-2 **Receivables Investment** Medwig Corporation has a DSO of 17 days. The company averages $3,500 in credit sales each day. What is the company's average accounts receivable?

21-3 **Cost of Trade Credit** What is the nominal and effective cost of trade credit under the credit terms of 3/15, net 30?

21-4 **Cost of Trade Credit** A large retailer obtains merchandise under the credit terms of 1/15, net 45, but routinely takes 60 days to pay its bills. (Because the retailer is an important customer, suppliers allow the firm to stretch its credit terms.) What is the retailer's effective cost of trade credit?

21-5 **Accounts Payable** A chain of appliance stores, APP Corporation, purchases inventory with a net price of $500,000 each day. The company purchases the inventory under the credit terms of 2/15, net 40. APP always takes the discount but takes the full 15 days to pay its bills. What is the average accounts payable for APP?

Intermediate Problems 6–12

21-6 **Receivables Investment** Snider Industries sells on terms of 2/10, net 45. Total sales for the year are $1,500,000. Thirty percent of customers pay on the 10th day and take discounts; the other 70% pay, on average, 50 days after their purchases.
  a. What is the days sales outstanding?
  b. What is the average amount of receivables?
  c. What would happen to average receivables if Snider toughened its collection policy with the result that all nondiscount customers paid on the 45th day?

21-7 **Cost of Trade Credit** Calculate the nominal annual cost of nonfree trade credit under each of the following terms. Assume that payment is made either on the discount date or on the due date.
  a. 1/15, net 20
  b. 2/10, net 60
  c. 3/10, net 45
  d. 2/10, net 45
  e. 2/15, net 40

21-8 **Cost of Trade Credit**
  a. If a firm buys under terms of 3/15, net 45, but actually pays on the 20th day and *still takes the discount,* what is the nominal cost of its nonfree trade credit?
  b. Does it receive more or less credit than it would if it paid within 15 days?

21-9 **Cost of Trade Credit** Grunewald Industries sells on terms of 2/10, net 40. Gross sales last year were $4,562,500 and accounts receivable averaged $437,500. Half of Grunewald's customers paid on the 10th day and took discounts. What are the nominal and effective costs of trade credit to Grunewald's nondiscount customers? (*Hint:* Calculate daily sales based on a 365-day year, then calculate average receivables of discount customers, and then find the DSO for the nondiscount customers.)

21-10 **Effective Cost of Trade Credit** The D.J. Masson Corporation needs to raise $500,000 for 1 year to supply working capital to a new store. Masson buys from its suppliers on terms of 3/10, net 90, and it currently pays on the 10th day and takes discounts. However, it could forgo the discounts, pay on the 90th day, and thereby obtain the needed $500,000 in the form of costly trade credit. What is the effective annual interest rate of this trade credit?

21-11 **Cash Conversion Cycle** Negus Enterprises has an inventory conversion period of 50 days, an average collection period of 35 days, and a payables deferral period of 25 days. Assume that cost of goods sold is 80% of sales.
  a. What is the length of the firm's cash conversion cycle?
  b. If Negus's annual sales are $4,380,000 and all sales are on credit, what is the firm's investment in accounts receivable?
  c. How many times per year does Negus Enterprises turn over its inventory?

21-12 **Working Capital Cash Flow Cycle** Strickler Technology is considering changes in its working capital policies to improve its cash flow cycle. Strickler's sales last year were $3,250,000 (all on credit), and its net profit margin was 7%. Its inventory turnover was 9.0 times during the year, and its DSO was 41 days. Its annual cost of goods sold was $1,895,000. The firm had fixed assets totaling $535,000. Strickler's payables deferral period is 45 days.

   a. Calculate Strickler's cash conversion cycle.
   b. Assuming Strickler holds negligible amounts of cash and marketable securities, calculate its total assets turnover and ROA.
   c. Suppose Strickler's managers believe the annual inventory turnover can be raised to 12 times without affecting sales. What would Strickler's cash conversion cycle, total assets turnover, and ROA have been if the inventory turnover had been 12 for the year?

Challenging Problems 13–17

21-13 **Working Capital Policy** Payne Products's sales last year were an anemic $1.6 million, but with an improved product mix it expects sales growth to be 25% this year, and Payne would like to determine the effect of various current assets policies on its financial performance. Payne has $1 million of fixed assets and intends to keep its debt ratio at its historical level of 60%. Payne's debt interest rate is currently 8%. You are to evaluate three different current asset policies: (1) a tight policy in which current assets are 45% of projected sales, (2) a moderate policy with 50% of sales tied up in current assets, and (3) a relaxed policy requiring current assets of 60% of sales. Earnings before interest and taxes is expected to be 12% of sales. Payne's tax rate is 40%.

   a. What is the expected return on equity under each current asset level?
   b. In this problem, we have assumed that the level of expected sales is independent of current asset policy. Is this a valid assumption?
   c. How would the overall riskiness of the firm vary under each policy?

21-14 **Cash Budgeting** Dorothy Koehl recently leased space in the Southside Mall and opened a new business, Koehl's Doll Shop. Business has been good, but Koehl has frequently run out of cash. This has necessitated late payment on certain orders, which is beginning to cause a problem with suppliers. Koehl plans to borrow from the bank to have cash ready as needed, but first she needs a forecast of just how much she should borrow. Accordingly, she has asked you to prepare a cash budget for the critical period around Christmas, when needs will be especially high.

   Sales are made on a cash basis only. Koehl's purchases must be paid for during the following month. Koehl pays herself a salary of $4,800 per month, and the rent is $2,000 per month. In addition, she must make a tax payment of $12,000 in December. The current cash on hand (on December 1) is $400, but Koehl has agreed to maintain an average bank balance of $6,000—this is her target cash balance. (Disregard the amount in the cash register, which is insignificant because Koehl keeps only a small amount on hand in order to lessen the chances of robbery.)

The estimated sales and purchases for December, January, and February are shown below. Purchases during November amounted to $140,000.

	Sales	Purchases
December	$160,000	$40,000
January	40,000	40,000
February	60,000	40,000

a. Prepare a cash budget for December, January, and February.
b. Now suppose that Koehl starts selling on a credit basis on December 1, giving customers 30 days to pay. All customers accept these terms, and all other facts in the problem are unchanged. What would the company's loan requirements be at the end of December in this case? (*Hint:* The calculations required to answer this part are minimal.)

21-15 Cash Discounts Suppose a firm makes purchases of $3.65 million per year under terms of 2/10, net 30, and takes discounts.
a. What is the average amount of accounts payable net of discounts? (Assume the $3.65 million of purchases is net of discounts—that is, gross purchases are $3,724,489.80, discounts are $74,489.80, and net purchases are $3.65 million.)
b. Is there a cost of the trade credit the firm uses?
c. If the firm did not take discounts but did pay on the due date, what would be its average payables and the cost of this nonfree trade credit?
d. What would be the firm's cost of not taking discounts if it could stretch its payments to 40 days?

21-16 Trade Credit The Thompson Corporation projects an increase in sales from $1.5 million to $2 million, but it needs an additional $300,000 of current assets to support this expansion. Thompson can finance the expansion by no longer taking discounts, thus increasing accounts payable. Thompson purchases under terms of 2/10, net 30, but it can delay payment for an additional 35 days—paying in 65 days and thus becoming 35 days past due—without a penalty because its suppliers currently have excess capacity. What is the effective, or equivalent, annual cost of the trade credit?

21-17 Bank Financing The Raattama Corporation had sales of $3.5 million last year, and it earned a 5% return (after taxes) on sales. Recently, the company has fallen behind in its accounts payable. Although its terms of purchase are net 30 days, its accounts payable represents 60 days' purchases. The company's treasurer is seeking to increase bank borrowings in order to become current in meeting its trade obligations (that is, to have 30 days' payables outstanding). The company's balance sheet is as follows (in thousands of dollars):

Cash	$ 100	Accounts payable	$ 600
Accounts receivable	300	Bank loans	700
Inventory	1,400	Accruals	200
Current assets	$1,800	Current liabilities	$1,500
Land and buildings	600	Mortgage on real estate	700
Equipment	600	Common stock, $0.10 par	300
		Retained earnings	500
Total assets	$3,000	Total liabilities and equity	$3,000

a. How much bank financing is needed to eliminate the past-due accounts payable?
b. Assume that the bank will lend the firm the amount calculated in part a. The terms of the loan offered are 8%, simple interest, and the bank uses a 360-day year for the interest calculation. What is the interest charge for 1 month? (Assume there are 30 days in a month.)
c. Now ignore part b and assume that the bank will lend the firm the amount calculated in part a. The terms of the loan are 7.5%, add-on interest, to be repaid in 12 monthly installments.
    1. What is the total loan amount?
    2. What are the monthly installments?
    3. What is the APR of the loan?
    4. What is the effective rate of the loan?
d. Would you, as a bank loan officer, make this loan? Why or why not?

Spreadsheet Problem

21-18 **Build a Model: Cash Budgeting** Start with the partial model in the file *Ch21 P18 Build a Model.xls* on the textbook's Web site. Rusty Spears, CEO of Rusty's Renovations, a custom building and repair company, is preparing documentation for a line of credit request from his commercial banker. Among the required documents is a detailed sales forecast for parts of 2013 and 2014:

	Sales	Labor and Raw Materials
May 2013	$60,000	$ 75,000
June	100,000	90,000
July	130,000	95,000
August	120,000	70,000
September	100,000	60,000
October	80,000	50,000
November	60,000	20,000
December	40,000	20,000
January 2014	30,000	NA

Estimates obtained from the credit and collection department are as follows: collections within the month of sale, 15%; collections during the month following the sale, 65%; collections the second month following the sale, 20%. Payments for labor and raw materials are typically made during the month following the one in which these costs were incurred. Total costs for labor and raw materials are estimated for each month as shown in the table.

General and administrative salaries will amount to approximately $15,000 a month; lease payments under long-term lease contracts will be $5,000 a month; depreciation charges will be $7,500 a month; miscellaneous expenses will be $2,000 a month; income tax payments of $25,000 will be due in both September and December; and a progress payment of $80,000 on a new office suite must be paid in October. Cash on hand on July 1 will amount to $60,000, and a minimum cash balance of $40,000 will be maintained throughout the cash budget period.

a. Prepare a monthly cash budget for the last 6 months of 2013.

b. Prepare an estimate of the required financing (or excess funds)—that is, the amount of money Rusty's Renovations will need to borrow (or will have available to invest)—for each month during that period.

c. Assume that receipts from sales come in uniformly during the month (i.e., cash receipts come in at the rate of 1/30 each day) but that all outflows are paid on the 5th of the month. Will this have an effect on the cash budget—in other words, would the cash budget you have prepared be valid under these assumptions? If not, what can be done to make a valid estimate of peak financing requirements? No calculations are required, although calculations can be used to illustrate the effects.

d. Rusty's Renovations produces on a seasonal basis, just ahead of sales. Without making any calculations, discuss how the company's current ratio and debt ratio would vary during the year assuming all financial requirements were met by short-term bank loans. Could changes in these ratios affect the firm's ability to obtain bank credit?

e. If its customers began to pay late, this would slow down collections and thus increase the required loan amount. Also, if sales dropped off, this would have an effect on the required loan amount. Perform a sensitivity analysis that shows the effects of these two factors on the maximum loan requirement.

MINI CASE

Karen Johnson, CFO for Raucous Roasters (RR), a specialty coffee manufacturer, is rethinking her company's working capital policy in light of a recent scare she faced when RR's corporate banker, citing a nationwide credit crunch, balked at renewing RR's line of credit. Had the line of credit not been renewed, RR would not have been able to make payroll, potentially forcing the company out of business. Although the line of credit was ultimately renewed, the scare has forced Johnson to examine carefully each component of RR's working capital to make sure it is needed, with the goal of determining whether the line of credit can be eliminated entirely. In addition to (possibly) freeing RR from the need for a line of credit, Johnson is well aware that reducing working capital can also add value to a company by improving its EVA (Economic Value Added). In her corporate finance course Johnson learned that EVA is calculated by taking net operating profit after taxes (NOPAT) and then subtracting the dollar cost of all the capital the firm uses:

$$EVA = NOPAT - \text{Capital costs}$$
$$= EBIT(1 - T) - WACC(\text{Total capital employed})$$

If EVA is positive then the firm's management is creating value. On the other hand, if EVA is negative, then the firm is not covering its cost of capital and stockholders' value is being eroded. If RR could generate its current level of sales with fewer assets, it would need less capital. This would, other things held constant, lower capital costs and increase its EVA.

Historically, RR has done little to examine working capital, mainly because of poor communication among business functions. In the past, the production manager resisted Johnson's efforts to question his holdings of raw materials, the marketing manager resisted questions about finished goods, the sales staff resisted questions about credit policy (which affects accounts receivable), and the treasurer did not want to talk about the cash and securities balances. However, with the recent credit scare, this resistance became unacceptable and Johnson has undertaken a company-wide examination of cash, marketable securities, inventory, and accounts receivable levels.

Johnson also knows that decisions about working capital cannot be made in a vacuum. For example, if inventories could be lowered without adversely affecting operations, then less capital would be required, the dollar cost of capital would decline, and EVA would increase. However, lower raw materials inventories might lead to production slowdowns and higher costs, and lower finished goods inventories might lead to stock-outs and loss of sales. So, before inventories are changed, it will be necessary to study operating as well as financial effects. The situation is the same with regard to cash and receivables. Johnson has begun her investigation by collecting the ratios shown below. (The partial cash budget shown after the ratios is used later in this mini case.)

a. Johnson plans to use the preceding ratios as the starting point for discussions with RR's operating team. She wants everyone to think about the pros and cons of changing each type of current asset and how changes would interact to affect profits and EVA. Based on the data, does RR seem to be following a relaxed, moderate, or restricted working capital policy?

b. How can one distinguish between a relaxed but rational working capital policy and a situation in which a firm simply has excessive current assets because it is inefficient? Does RR's working capital policy seem appropriate?

c. Calculate the firm's cash conversion cycle given that annual sales are $660,000 and cost of goods sold represents 90% of sales. Assume a 365-day year.

d. What might RR do to reduce its cash without harming operations?

In an attempt to better understand RR's cash position, Johnson developed a cash budget. Data for the first 2 months of the year are shown above. (Note that Johnson's preliminary cash budget does not account for interest income or interest expense.) She has the figures for the other months, but they are not shown.

e. Should depreciation expense be explicitly included in the cash budget? Why or why not?

f. In her preliminary cash budget, Johnson has assumed that all sales are collected and thus that RR has no bad debts. Is this realistic? If not, how would bad debts be dealt with in a cash budgeting sense? (*Hint:* Bad debts will affect collections but not purchases.)

	RR	Industry
Current	1.75	2.25
Quick	0.92	1.16
Total liabilities/assets	58.76%	50.00%
Turnover of cash and securities	16.67	22.22
Days sales outstanding (365-day basis)	45.63	32.00
Inventory turnover	12.00	20.00
Fixed assets turnover	7.75	13.22
Total assets turnover	2.08	3.00
Profit margin on sales	2.07%	3.50%
Return on equity (ROE)	10.45%	21.00%
Payables deferral period	30.00	33.00

Cash Budget (Thousands of Dollars)	Nov	Dec	Jan	Feb	Mar	Apr
Sales Forecast						
(1) Sales (gross)	$71,218.00	$68,212.00	$65,213.00	$52,475.00	$42,909.00	$30,524.00
Collections						
(2) During month of sale: (0.2)(0.98)(month's sales)			12,781.75	10,285.10		
(3) During first month after sale: (0.7)(previous month's sales)			47,748.40	45,649.10		
(4) During second month after sale: (0.1)(sales 2 months ago)			7,121.80	6,821.20		
(5) Total collections (Lines 2 + 3 + 4)			$67,651.95	$62,755.40		
Purchases						
(6) (0.85)(forecasted sales 2 months from now)		$44,603.75	$36,472.65	$25,945.40		
Payments						
(7) Payments (1-month lag)			44,603.75	36,472.65		
(8) Wages and salaries			6,690.56	5,470.90		
(9) Rent			2,500.00	2,500.00		
(10) Taxes						
(11) Total payments			$53,794.31	$44,443.55		
NCFs						
(12) Cash on hand at start of forecast			$3,000.00			
(13) NCF: Coll. − Pmts. = Line 5 − Line 11			$13,857.64	$18,311.85		
(14) Cum NCF: Prior + this mos. NCF			$16,857.64	$35,169.49		
Cash Surplus (or Loan Requirement)						
(15) Target cash balance			1,500.00	1,500.00		
(16) Surplus cash or loan needed			$15,357.64	$33,669.49		

g. Johnson's cash budget for the entire year, although not given here, is based heavily on her forecast for monthly sales. Sales are expected to be extremely low between May and September but then to increase dramatically in the fall and winter. November is typically the firm's best month, when RR ships its holiday blend of coffee. Johnson's forecasted cash budget indicates that the company's cash holdings will exceed the targeted cash balance every month except for October and November, when shipments will be high but collections will not be coming in until later. Based on the ratios shown earlier, does it appear that RR's target cash balance is appropriate? In addition to possibly lowering the target cash balance, what actions might RR take to better improve its cash management policies, and how might that affect its EVA?

h. What reasons might RR have for maintaining a relatively high amount of cash?

i. Is there any reason to think that RR may be holding too much inventory? If so, how would that affect EVA and ROE?

j. If the company reduces its inventory without adversely affecting sales, what effect should this have on the company's cash position (1) in the short run and (2) in the long run? Explain in terms of the cash budget and the balance sheet.

k. Johnson knows that RR sells on the same credit terms as other firms in its industry. Use the ratios presented earlier to explain whether RR's customers pay more or less promptly than those of its competitors. If there are differences, does that suggest RR should tighten or loosen its credit policy? What four variables make up a firm's credit policy, and in what direction should each be changed by RR?

l. Does RR face any risks if it tightens its credit policy?

m. If the company reduces its DSO without seriously affecting sales, what effect would this have on its cash position (1) in the short run and (2) in the long run? Answer in terms of the cash budget and the balance sheet. What effect should this have on EVA in the long run?

In addition to improving the management of its current assets, RR is also reviewing the ways in which it finances its current assets. With this concern in mind, Johnson is also trying to answer the following questions.

n. Is it likely that RR could make significantly greater use of accruals?

o. Assume that RR purchases $200,000 (net of discounts) of materials on terms of 1/10, net 30, but that it can get away with paying on the 40th day if it chooses not to take discounts. How much free trade credit can the company get from its equipment supplier, how much costly trade credit can it get, and what is the nominal annual interest rate of the costly credit? Should RR take discounts?

p. RR tries to match the maturity of its assets and liabilities. Describe how RR could adopt either a more aggressive or a more conservative financing policy.

q. What are the advantages and disadvantages of using short-term debt as a source of financing?

r. Would it be feasible for RR to finance with commercial paper?

Selected Additional Cases

The following cases from TextChoice, Cengage Learning's online case library, cover many of the concepts discussed in this chapter and are available at www.textchoice2.com/casenet.

Klein-Brigham Series:
Case 29, "Office Mates, Inc.," which illustrates how changes in current asset policy affect expected profitability and risk; Case 32, "Alpine Wear, Inc.," which illustrates the mechanics of the cash budget and the rationale behind its use; Case 33, "Upscale Toddlers, Inc.," which deals with credit policy changes; Case 34, "Texas Rose Company," which focuses on receivables management; Case 50, "Toy World, Inc.," and Case 66, "Sorenson Stove Company," which deal with cash budgeting.

Brigham-Buzzard Series:
Case 11, "Powerline Network Corporation (Working Capital Management)."

Chapter 22

Providing and Obtaining Credit

WEB

The textbook's Web site contains an *Excel* file that will guide you through the chapter's calculations. The file for this chapter is ***Ch22 Tool Kit.xls***, and we encourage you to open the file and follow along as you read the chapter.

Chapter 21 covered the basics of working capital management, including a brief discussion of trade credit from the standpoint of firms that grant credit and report it as accounts receivable and also from the standpoint of firms that use credit and report it as accounts payable. In this chapter, we expand the discussion of this important topic and also discuss the cost of the other major source of short-term financing, bank loans.

Beginning of Chapter Questions

As you read the chapter, consider how you would answer the following questions. You *should not* necessarily be able to answer the questions before you read the chapter. Rather, you should use them to get a sense of the issues covered in the chapter. After reading the chapter, you should be able to give at least partial answers to the questions, and you should be able to give better answers after the chapter has been discussed in class. Note, too, that it is often useful, when answering conceptual questions, to use hypothetical data to illustrate your answer. We illustrate the answers with an *Excel* model that is available on the textbook's Web site. Accessing the model and working through it is a useful exercise, and it provides insights that are useful when answering the questions.

1. How do each of the items in a firm's **credit policy**—defined to include the credit period, the discount and discount period, the credit standards used, and the collection policy—affect its sales, the level of its accounts receivable, and its profitability?

2. Does its management typically have complete control over a firm's credit policy? As a general rule, is it more likely that a company would increase its profitability if it tightened or loosened its credit policy?

3. How does credit policy affect the cash conversion cycle as discussed in the last chapter?

4. Suppose a company's current credit terms are 1/10, net 30, but management is considering changing its terms to 2/10, net 40, relaxing its credit standards, and putting less pressure on slow-paying customers. How would you expect these changes to affect (a) sales, (b) the percentage of customers who take discounts, (c) the percentage of customers who pay late, and (d) the percentage of customers who end up as bad debts?

5. How would you decide whether or not to make the change described in question 4? Assume you also have information on the company's cost of capital, tax rate, and variable costs. How would the company's capacity utilization affect the decision?

6. What are some ways banks can state their charges, and how should the cost of bank debt be analyzed? In the early 1970s, Congress debated the need for new legislation, and it ended up passing a "Truth in Lending" law. One part of the law was the requirement that banks disclose their **APR**. How is the APR calculated? Do you think the Truth in Lending law was really necessary?

22.1 Credit Policy

As we stated in Chapter 21, the success or failure of a business depends primarily on the demand for its products: As a rule, the higher its sales, the larger its profits and the higher its stock price. Sales, in turn, depend on a number of factors, some exogenous but others under the firm's control. The major controllable determinants of demand are sales price, product quality, advertising, and the firm's **credit policy**. Credit policy, in turn, consists of these four variables:

1. *Credit period,* which is the length of time buyers are given to pay for their purchases.
2. *Discounts* given for early payment, including the discount percentage and how rapidly payment must be made to qualify for the discount.
3. *Credit standards,* which refer to the required financial strength of acceptable credit customers.
4. *Collection policy,* which is measured by the firm's toughness or laxity in attempting to collect on slow-paying accounts.

The credit manager is responsible for administering the firm's credit policy. However, because of the pervasive importance of credit, the credit policy itself is normally established by the executive committee, which usually consists of the president plus the vice presidents of finance, marketing, and production.

22.2 Setting the Credit Period and Standards

A firm's regular **credit terms**, which include the **credit period** and **discount**, might call for sales on a 2/10, net 30 basis to all "acceptable" customers. Here customers are required to pay within 30 days, but they are given a 2% discount if they pay by the 10th day. The firm's *credit standards* would be applied to determine which customers qualify for the regular credit terms and the amount of credit available to each customer.

22.2a Credit Standards

Credit standards refer to the financial strength and creditworthiness a customer must exhibit in order to qualify for credit. A customer that does not qualify for the regular credit terms can still purchase from the firm but only under more restrictive terms. For example, a firm's "regular" credit terms might call for payment within 30 days, and these terms might be offered to all qualified customers; the firm's credit standards are applied when determining which customers qualify. The major factors considered when setting credit standards concern the likelihood that a given customer will pay slowly or perhaps end up as a bad-debt loss.

Setting credit standards requires a measurement of *credit quality,* which is defined in terms of the probability of a customer's default. The probability estimate for a given customer is, for the most part, a subjective judgment. Nevertheless, credit evaluation is a well-established practice, and a good credit manager can make reasonably accurate judgments of the probability of default by different classes of customers.

Managing a credit department requires fast, accurate, and up-to-date information. To help get such information, the National Association of Credit Management (a group with 43,000 member firms) persuaded TRW, a large credit-reporting agency, to develop a computer-based telecommunications network for the collection, storage, retrieval, and distribution of credit information. A typical business credit report would include the following pieces of information:

1. A summary balance sheet and income statement.
2. A number of key ratios, including trend information.
3. Information obtained from the firm's suppliers telling whether it pays promptly or slowly and whether it has recently failed to make any payments.
4. A verbal description of the physical condition of the firm's operations.
5. A verbal description of the backgrounds of the firm's owners, including any previous bankruptcies, lawsuits, divorce settlement problems, and the like.
6. A summary rating, ranging from A for the best credit risks down to F for those deemed likely to default.

Consumer credit is appraised similarly, using income, years of employment, ownership of home, and past credit history (pays on time or has defaulted) as criteria.

Although a great deal of credit information is available, it must still be processed in a judgmental manner. Computerized information systems can assist in making better credit decisions, but, in the final analysis, most credit decisions are really exercises in informed judgment.[1]

22.3 Setting the Collection Policy

Collection policy refers to the procedures the firm follows to collect past-due accounts. For example, a letter might be sent to customers when a bill is 10 days past due; a more severe letter, followed by a telephone call, would be sent if payment is not received within 30 days; and the account would be turned over to a collection agency after 90 days.

The collection process can be expensive in terms of both out-of-pocket expenditures and lost goodwill—customers dislike being turned over to a collection agency. However, at least some firmness is needed to prevent an undue lengthening of the collection period and to minimize outright losses. A balance must be struck between the costs and benefits of different collection policies.

Changes in collection policy influence sales, the collection period, and the bad-debt loss percentage. All of this should be taken into account when setting the credit policy.

22.4 Cash Discounts

The last element in the credit policy decision, the use of **cash discounts** for early payment, is analyzed by balancing the costs and benefits of different cash discounts. For example, a firm might decide to change its credit terms from "net 30," which means that customers must pay within 30 days, to "2/10, net 30," in which a 2% discount is given if payment is made within 10 days. This change should produce two benefits: (1) it should attract new customers who consider the discount to be a price reduction; and (2) it should lead to a reduction in the days sales outstanding (DSO), because some existing customers will pay more promptly in order to get the discount. Offsetting these benefits is the dollar cost of the discounts. The optimal discount percentage is established at the point at which the marginal costs and benefits are exactly offsetting.

---

1. Credit analysts use procedures ranging from highly sophisticated, computerized "credit-scoring" systems, which actually calculate the statistical probability that a given customer will default, to informal procedures, which involve going through a checklist of factors that should be considered when processing a credit application. The credit-scoring systems use various financial ratios such as the current ratio and the debt ratio (for businesses) and income, years with the same employer, and the like (for individuals) to determine the statistical probability of default. Credit is then granted to those with low default probabilities. The informal procedures often involve examining the "5 C's of Credit": character, capacity, capital, collateral, and conditions. Character is obvious; capacity is a subjective estimate of ability to repay; capital means how much net worth the borrower has; collateral means assets pledged to secure the loan; and conditions refers to business conditions that affect ability to repay.

If sales are seasonal, a firm may use **seasonal dating** on discounts. For example, Slimware Inc., a swimsuit manufacturer, sells on terms of 2/10, net 30, May 1 dating. This means that the effective invoice date is May 1, even if the sale was made back in January. The discount may be taken up to May 10; otherwise, the full amount must be paid by May 30. Slimware produces throughout the year, but retail sales of bathing suits are concentrated in the spring and early summer. By offering seasonal dating, the company induces some of its customers to stock up early, saving Slimware some storage costs and also "nailing down sales."

Self Test	How can cash discounts be used to influence sales volume and the DSO? What is seasonal dating?

22.5 Other Factors Influencing Credit Policy

In addition to the factors discussed in previous sections, two other points should be made regarding credit policy: the potential for profit and the legal considerations.

22.5a Profit Potential

We have emphasized the costs of granting credit. However, *if it is possible to sell on credit and also to impose a carrying charge on receivables that are outstanding, then credit sales can actually be more profitable than cash sales.* This is especially true for consumer durables (autos, appliances, and so on), but it is also true for certain types of industrial equipment.[2]

The carrying charges on outstanding credit are generally about 18% on a nominal basis: 1.5% per month, so $1.5\% \times 12 = 18\%$. This is equivalent to an effective annual rate of $(1.015)^{12} - 1.0 = 19.6\%$. Having receivables outstanding that earn more than 18% is highly profitable unless there are too many bad-debt losses.

22.5b Legal Considerations

It is illegal, under the Robinson-Patman Act, for a firm to charge prices that discriminate between customers unless these differential prices are cost-justified. The same holds true for credit—it is illegal to offer more favorable credit terms to one customer or class of customers than to another unless the differences are cost-justified.

Self Test	How do profit potential and legal considerations affect a firm's credit policy?

22.6 The Payments Pattern Approach to Monitoring Receivables

In Chapter 21, we discussed two methods for monitoring a firm's receivables position: days sales outstanding and aging schedules. These procedures are useful, particularly

---

2. Companies that do a large volume of sales financing typically set up subsidiary companies called *captive finance companies* to do the actual financing.

for monitoring an individual customer's account, but neither is totally suitable for monitoring the aggregate payment performance of all credit customers, especially for a firm that experiences fluctuating credit sales. In this section, we present another way to monitor receivables, the **payments pattern approach**.

The primary point in analyzing the aggregate accounts receivable situation is to see if customers, on average, are paying more slowly. If so, then accounts receivable will build up, as will the cost of carrying receivables. Furthermore, the payment slowdown may signal a decrease in the quality of the receivables and hence an increase in bad-debt losses down the road. The DSO and aging schedules are useful in monitoring credit operations, but both are affected by increases and decreases in the level of sales. Thus, changes in sales levels, including normal seasonal or cyclical changes, can change a firm's DSO and aging schedule even though its customers' payment behavior has not changed at all. For this reason, a procedure called the *payments pattern approach* has been developed to measure any changes that might be occurring in customers' payment behavior. To illustrate the payments pattern approach, consider the Hanover Company, a small manufacturer of hand tools that commenced operations in January 2012. Table 22-1 contains Hanover's credit sales and receivables data for 2012. Column 2 shows that Hanover's credit sales are seasonal, with the lowest sales in the fall and winter months and the highest during the summer.

Now assume that 10% of Hanover's customers pay in the month the sale is made, 30% pay in the first month following the sale, 40% pay in the second month, and the remaining 20% pay in the third month. Further, assume that Hanover's customers have the same payment behavior throughout the year; that is, they always take the same length of time to pay. Column 3 of Table 22-1 contains Hanover's receivables

TABLE 22-1	Hanover Company: Receivables Data for 2012 (Thousands of Dollars)						
			Based on Quarterly Sales Data		Based on Year-to-Date Sales Data		
Month (1)	Credit Sales for Month (2)	Receivables at End of Month (3)	ADS[a] (4)	DSO[b] (5)	ADS[c] (6)	DSO[c] (7)
January	$ 60	$ 54				
February	60	90				
March	60	102	$1.98	52 days	$1.98	52 days
April	60	102				
May	90	129				
June	120	174	2.97	59	2.47	70
July	120	198				
August	90	177				
September	60	132	2.97	44	2.64	50
October	60	108				
November	60	102				
December	60	102	1.98	52	2.47	41

[a]ADS = Average daily sales.
[b]DSO = Days sales outstanding.
[c]We assume that each quarter is 91 days long.

balance at the end of each month. For example, during January Hanover had $60,000 in sales. Because 10% of the customers paid during the month of sale, the receivables balance at the end of January was $60,000 − 0.1($60,000) = (1.0 − 0.1)($60,000) = 0.9($60,000) = $54,000. By the end of February, 10% + 30% = 40% of the customers had paid for January's sales and 10% had paid for February's sales. Thus, the receivables balance at the end of February was 0.6($60,000) + 0.9($60,000) = $90,000. By the end of March, 80% of January's sales had been collected, 40% of February's sales had been collected, and 10% of March's sales had been collected, so the receivables balance was 0.2($60,000) + 0.6($60,000) + 0.9($60,000) = $102,000, and so on.

Columns 4 and 5 give Hanover's average daily sales (ADS) and days sales outstanding (DSO), respectively, as these measures would be calculated from quarterly financial statements. For example, in the April–June quarter, ADS = ($60,000 + $90,000 + $120,000)/91 = $2,967, and the end-of-quarter (June 30) DSO = $174,000/$2,967 = 58.6 days. Columns 6 and 7 also show ADS and DSO, but here they are calculated on the basis of accumulated sales throughout the year. For example, at the end of June ADS = $450,000/182 = $2,473 and DSO = $174,000/$2,473 = 70 days. (For the entire year, sales are $900,000; ADS = $2,466 and DSO at year-end = 41 days. These last two figures are shown at the bottom of the last two columns.)

The data in Table 22-1 illustrate two major points. First, fluctuating sales lead to changes in the DSO, which suggests that customers are paying faster or slower even though we know that customers' payment patterns are not changing at all. The rising monthly sales trend causes the calculated DSO to rise, whereas declining sales (as in the third quarter) cause the calculated DSO to fall, even though nothing is changing with regard to when customers actually pay. Second, we see that the DSO depends on an averaging procedure; however, regardless of whether quarterly, semiannual, or annual data are used, the DSO is unstable even when payment patterns are *not* changing. Therefore, it is inadvisable to use the DSO as a monitoring device if the firm's sales exhibit seasonal or cyclical patterns.

Seasonal or cyclical variations also make it difficult to interpret aging schedules. Table 22-2 contains Hanover's aging schedules at the end of each quarter. At the end of June, Table 22-2 shows that Hanover's receivables balance was $174,000: 0.2($60,000) + 0.6($90,000) + 0.9($120,000) = $174,000. Note again that Hanover's customers had not changed their payment patterns. However, rising sales during the second quarter created the impression of faster payments when judged by the percentage aging schedule, and declining sales after July created the opposite appearance. Thus, neither the DSO nor the aging schedule provides an accurate picture of customers' payment patterns if sales fluctuate during the year or are trending up or down.

With this background, we can now examine another basic tool, the *uncollected balances schedule,* as shown in Table 22-3. At the end of each quarter, the dollar amount of receivables remaining from each of the 3 month's sales is divided by that

TABLE 22-2	Hanover Company: Quarterly Aging Schedules for 2012 (Thousands of Dollars)							
Ages of Accounts (Days)	Value and Percentage of Total Accounts Receivable at the End of Each Quarter							
	March 31		June 30		September 30		December 31	
0–30	$ 54	53%	$108	62%	$ 54	41%	$ 54	53%
31–60	36	35	54	31	54	41	36	35
61–90	12	12	12	7	24	18	12	12
	$102	100%	$174	100%	$132	100%	$102	100%

Quarter	Monthly Sales	Remaining Receivables at End of Quarter	Remaining Receivables as a Percentage of Month's Sales at End of Quarter
Quarter 1:			
January	$ 60	$ 12	20%
February	60	36	60
March	60	54	90
		$102	170%
Quarter 2:			
April	$ 60	$ 12	20%
May	90	54	60
June	120	108	90
		$174	170%
Quarter 3:			
July	$120	$ 24	20%
August	90	54	60
September	60	54	90
		$132	170%
Quarter 4:			
October	$ 60	$ 12	20%
November	60	36	60
December	60	54	90
		$102	170%

TABLE 22-3 Hanover Company: Quarterly Uncollected Balances Schedules for 2012 (Thousands of Dollars)

© Cengage Learning 2013

month's sales to obtain three receivables-to-sales ratios. For example, at the end of the first quarter, $12,000 of the $60,000 January sales, or 20%, are still outstanding, 60% of February sales are still out, and 90% of March sales are uncollected. Exactly the same situation is revealed at the end of each of the next three quarters. Thus, Table 22-3 shows that Hanover's customers' payment behavior has remained constant.

Recall that, at the beginning of the example, we assumed the existence of a constant payments pattern. In a normal situation, the firm's customers' payments pattern would probably vary somewhat over time. Such variations would be shown in the last column of the uncollected balances schedule. For example, suppose customers began to pay their accounts more slowly in the second quarter. That might cause the second-quarter uncollected balances schedule to look like this (in thousands of dollars):

Quarter 2, 2012	Sales	New Remaining Receivables	New Receivables/Sales
April	$ 60	$ 16	27%
May	90	70	78
June	120	110	92
		$196	197%

We see that the receivables-to-sales ratios are now higher than in the corresponding months of the first quarter. This causes the total uncollected balances percentage to rise from 170% to 197%, which should alert Hanover's managers that customers are paying more slowly than they did earlier in the year.

The uncollected balances schedule permits a firm to monitor its receivables better, and it can also be used to forecast future receivables balances. When Hanover's projected 2013 quarterly balance sheets are constructed, management can use the historical receivables-to-sales ratios, coupled with 2013 sales estimates, to project each quarter's receivables balance. For example, with projected sales as given below and using the same payments pattern as in 2012, Hanover's projected end-of-June 2013 receivables balance would be as follows:

Quarter 2, 2013	Projected Sales	Receivables/Sales	Projected Receivables
April	$ 70	20%	$ 14
May	100	60	60
June	140	90	126
		Total projected receivables =	$200

The payments pattern approach permits us to remove the effects of seasonal and/or cyclical sales variation and to construct a more accurate measure of customers' payments patterns. Thus, it provides financial managers with better aggregate information than the days sales outstanding or the aging schedule. Managers should use the payments pattern approach to monitor collection performance as well as to project future receivables requirements.

Except possibly in the inventory and cash management areas, nowhere in the typical firm have computers had more of an effect than in accounts receivable management. A well-run business will use a computer system to record sales, to send out bills, to keep track of when payments are made, to alert the credit manager when an account becomes past due, and to take action automatically to collect past-due accounts (for example, to prepare form letters requesting payment). Additionally, the payment history of each customer can be summarized and used to help establish credit limits for customers and classes of customers, and the data on each account can be aggregated and used for the firm's accounts receivable monitoring system. Finally, historical data can be stored in the firm's database and used to develop inputs for studies related to credit policy changes, as we discuss in the next section.

Self Test

Define days sales outstanding. What can be learned from it? Does it have any deficiencies when used to monitor collections over time?

What is an aging schedule? What can be learned from it? Does it have any deficiencies when used to monitor collections over time?

What is the uncollected balances schedule? What advantages does it have over the DSO and the aging schedule for monitoring receivables? How can it be used to forecast a firm's receivables balance?

22.7 Analyzing Proposed Changes in Credit Policy

In Chapter 21, our discussion of credit policy included setting the credit period, credit standards, collection policy, and discount percentage as well as the factors that influence credit policy. A firm's credit policy is reviewed periodically, and policy changes may be proposed. However, before a new policy is adopted, it should be analyzed to determine whether it is indeed preferable to the existing policy. In this section, we discuss procedures for analyzing proposed changes in credit policy.

If a firm's credit policy is *eased* by such actions as lengthening the credit period, relaxing credit standards, following a less tough collection policy, or offering cash discounts, then sales should increase: *Easing the credit policy stimulates sales.* Of course, if credit policy is eased and sales rise, then costs will also rise because more labor, materials, and other inputs will be required to produce the additional goods. Additionally, receivables outstanding will also increase, which will increase carrying costs. Moreover, bad debts and/or discount expenses may also rise. Thus, the key question when deciding on a proposed credit policy change is this: Will sales revenues increase more than costs, including credit-related costs, or will the increase in sales revenues be more than offset by higher costs?

Table 22-4 illustrates the general idea behind the analysis of credit policy changes. Column 1 shows the projected income statement for Monroe Manufacturing under the assumption that the firm's current credit policy is maintained throughout the upcoming year. Column 2 shows the expected effects of easing the credit policy by extending the credit period, offering larger discounts, relaxing

TABLE 22-4	Monroe Manufacturing Company: Analysis of Changing Credit Policy (Millions of Dollars)		
	Projected 2013 Net Income under Current Credit Policy (1)	Effect of Credit Policy Change (2)	Projected 2013 Net Income under New Credit Policy (3)
Gross sales	$400	+ $130	$530
Less discounts	2	+ 4	6
Net sales	$398	+ $126	$524
Production costs, including overhead	280	+ 91	371
Profit before credit costs and taxes	$118	+ $ 35	$153
Credit-related costs:			
Cost of carrying receivables	3	+ 2	5
Credit analysis and collection expenses	5	− 3	2
Bad-debt losses	10	+ 22	32
Profit before taxes	$100	+ 14	$114
State-plus-federal taxes (50%)	50	+ 7	57
Net income	$ 50	+ $ 7	$ 57

Note: The table reports only those cash flows that are related to the credit policy decision.

credit standards, and easing collection efforts. Specifically, Monroe is analyzing the effects of changing its credit terms from 1/10, net 30, to 2/10, net 40, relaxing its credit standards, and putting less pressure on slow-paying customers. Column 3 shows the projected 2013 income statement incorporating the expected effects of easing the credit policy. The generally looser policy is expected to increase sales and lower collection costs, but discounts and several other types of costs would rise. The overall, bottom-line effect is a $7 million increase in projected net income. In the following paragraphs, we explain how the numbers in the table were calculated.

Monroe's annual sales are $400 million. Under its current credit policy, 50% of those customers who pay do so on Day 10 and take the discount, 40% pay on Day 30, and 10% pay late, on Day 40. Thus, Monroe's days sales outstanding is (0.5)(10) + (0.4)(30) + (0.1)(40) = 21 days, and discounts total (0.01)($400,000,000)(0.5) = $2,000,000.

The cost of carrying receivables is equal to the average receivables balance multiplied by the variable cost ratio times the cost of money used to carry receivables. The firm's variable cost ratio is 70%, and its pre-tax cost of capital invested in receivables is 20%. Thus, its annual cost of carrying receivables is $3 million:

$$(\text{DSO})\left(\frac{\text{Sales}}{\text{per day}}\right)\left(\frac{\text{Variable}}{\text{cost ratio}}\right)\left(\frac{\text{Cost of}}{\text{funds}}\right) = \text{Cost of carrying receivables}$$

$$(21)(\$400,000,000/365)(0.70)(0.20) = \$3,221,918 \approx \$3 \text{ million}$$

Only variable costs enter this calculation, because this is the only cost element in receivables that must be financed. We are seeking the cost of carrying receivables, and variable costs represent the firm's investment in the cost of goods sold.

Even though Monroe spends $5 million annually to analyze accounts and to collect bad debts, 2.5% of sales will never be collected. Bad-debt losses therefore amount to (0.025)($400,000,000) = $10,000,000.

Monroe's new credit policy would be 2/10, net 40 versus the old policy of 1/10, net 30, so it would call for a larger discount and a longer payment period in addition to a relaxed collection effort and lower credit standards. The company believes these changes will lead to a $130 million increase in sales to $530 million per year. Under the new terms, management believes that 60% of the customers who pay will take the 2% discount, so discounts will increase to (0.02)($530,000,000)(0.60) = $6,360,000 ≈ $6 million. Half of the nondiscount customers will pay on Day 40 and the remainder on Day 50. The new DSO is thus estimated to be 24 days:

$$(0.6)(10) + (0.2)(40) + (0.2)(50) = 24 \text{ days}$$

Also, the cost of carrying receivables will increase to $5 million[3]:

$$(24)(\$530,000,000/365)(0.70)(0.20) = \$4,878,904 \approx \$5 \text{ million}$$

---

3. Since the credit policy change will result in a longer DSO, the firm will have to wait longer to receive its profit on the goods it sells. Therefore, the firm will incur an opportunity cost due to not having the cash from these profits available for investment. The dollar amount of this opportunity cost is equal to the old sales per day multiplied by the change in DSO times the contribution margin (1 − Variable cost ratio) times the firm's cost of carrying receivables, or

   Opportunity cost = (Old sales/365)(ΔDSO)(1 − V)(r)
   = ($400/365)(3)(0.3)(0.20)
   = $0.197 = $197,000

   For simplicity, we have ignored this opportunity cost in our analysis. However, we consider opportunity costs in the next section, where we discuss incremental analysis.

The company plans to reduce its annual credit analysis and collection expenditures to $2 million. The reduced credit standards and the relaxed collection effort are expected to raise bad-debt losses to about 6% of sales, or to (0.06)($530,000,000) = $31,800,000 ≈ $32,000,000, which is an increase of $22 million from the previous level.

The combined effect of all the changes in credit policy is a projected $7 million annual increase in net income. There would, of course, be corresponding changes on the projected balance sheet—the higher sales would necessitate somewhat larger cash balances, inventories, and (depending on the capacity situation) perhaps more fixed assets. Accounts receivable would, of course, also increase. Because these asset increases would have to be financed, certain liabilities and/or equity would have to be increased.

The $7 million expected increase in net income is, of course, an estimate, and the actual effects of the change could be quite different. In the first place, there is uncertainty—perhaps quite a lot—about the projected $130 million increase in sales. Indeed, if the firm's competitors matched its changes then sales might not rise at all. Similar uncertainties must be attached to the number of customers who would take discounts, to production costs at higher or lower sales levels, to the costs of carrying additional receivables, and to bad-debt losses. In the final analysis, the decision will be based on judgment, especially concerning the risks involved, but the type of quantitative analysis set forth in this section is essential to the process.

Describe the procedure for evaluating a change in credit policy using the income statement approach.

Do you think that credit policy decisions are made more on the basis of numerical analyses or on judgmental factors?

22.8 Analyzing Proposed Changes in Credit Policy: Incremental Analysis

To evaluate a proposed change in credit policy, one could compare alternative projected income statements, as we did in Table 22-4. Alternatively, one could develop the data in Column 2, which shows the incremental effect of the proposed change, without first developing the projected financial statements. This second approach is often preferable: Given that firms usually change their credit policies in specific divisions or on specific products, and not across the board, it may not be feasible to develop complete corporate income statements. Of course, the two approaches are based on exactly the same data, so they should produce identical results.

In an incremental analysis, we attempt to determine the increase or decrease in both sales and costs associated with a given easing or tightening of credit policy. The difference between incremental sales and incremental costs is defined as **incremental profit**. If the expected incremental profit is positive and if it is sufficiently large to compensate for the risks involved, then the proposed credit policy change should be accepted.

22.8a The Basic Equations

In order to ensure that all relevant factors are considered, it is useful to set up some equations for analyzing changes in credit policy. We begin by defining the following terms and symbols:

S_0 = Current gross sales.

S_N = New gross sales after the change in credit policy; note that S_N can be greater or less than S_0.

$S_N - S_0$ = Incremental (change in) gross sales.

V = Variable costs as a percentage of gross sales; V includes production costs, inventory carrying costs, the cost of administering the credit department, and all other variable costs *except* bad-debt losses, financing costs associated with carrying the investment in receivables, and costs of giving discounts.

$1 - V$ = Contribution margin, or the percentage of each gross sales dollar that goes toward covering overhead and increasing profits; the contribution margin is sometimes called the *gross profit* margin.

r = Cost of financing the investment in receivables.

DSO_0 = Days sales outstanding prior to the change in credit policy.

DSO_N = New days sales outstanding after the credit policy change.

B_0 = Average bad-debt loss at the current sales level as a percentage of current gross sales.

B_N = Average bad-debt loss at the new sales level as a percentage of new gross sales.

P_0 = Percentage of total customers (by dollar amount) who take discounts under the current credit policy; in other words, the percentage of gross sales that is discount sales.

P_N = Percentage of total customers (by dollar amount) that will take discounts under the new credit policy.

D_0 = Discount percentage offered at the present time.

D_N = Discount percentage offered under the new credit policy.

With these definitions in mind, we can calculate values for the incremental change in the level of the firm's investment in receivables, ΔI, and the incremental change in pre-tax profits, ΔP. The formula for calculating ΔI differs depending on whether the change in credit policy results in an increase or decrease in sales. Here we simply present the equations; we discuss and explain them shortly, through use of examples, once all the equations have been set forth.

If the change is expected to *increase* sales—either additional sales to old customers or sales to newly attracted customers, or both—then we have the following situation.

Formula for ΔI if Sales Increase:

$$\Delta I = \begin{pmatrix} \text{Increased investment in} \\ \text{receivables associated} \\ \text{with original sales} \end{pmatrix} + \begin{pmatrix} \text{Increased investment in} \\ \text{receivables associated} \\ \text{with incremental sales} \end{pmatrix}$$

$$= \begin{pmatrix} \text{Change in} \\ \text{days sales} \\ \text{outstanding} \end{pmatrix} \begin{pmatrix} \text{Old} \\ \text{sales} \\ \text{per day} \end{pmatrix} + V \begin{pmatrix} DSO_N \begin{pmatrix} \text{Incremental} \\ \text{sales} \\ \text{per day} \end{pmatrix} \end{pmatrix}$$

$$= [(DSO_N - DSO_0)(S_0/365)] + V[(DSO_N)(S_N - S_0)/365]$$

(22–1)

However, if the change in credit policy is expected to *decrease* sales, then the change in the level of investment in receivables is calculated as follows.

Formula for ΔI if Sales Decrease:

$$\Delta I = \begin{pmatrix} \text{Decreased investment in} \\ \text{receivables associated with} \\ \text{remaining original customers} \end{pmatrix} + \begin{pmatrix} \text{Decreased investment in} \\ \text{receivables associated} \\ \text{with customers who left} \end{pmatrix}$$

$$= \begin{pmatrix} \text{Change in} \\ \text{days sales} \\ \text{outstanding} \end{pmatrix} \begin{pmatrix} \text{Remaining} \\ \text{sales} \\ \text{per day} \end{pmatrix} + V \begin{pmatrix} DSO_0 \begin{pmatrix} \text{Incremental} \\ \text{sales} \\ \text{per day} \end{pmatrix} \end{pmatrix}$$

$$= [(DSO_N - DSO_0)(S_N/365)] + V[(DSO_0)(S_N - S_0)/365]$$

(22–2)

Having calculated the change in receivables investment, we can now analyze the pre-tax profitability of the proposed change.

Formula for ΔP:

$$\Delta P = \begin{pmatrix} \text{Change in} \\ \text{gross} \\ \text{profit} \end{pmatrix} - \begin{pmatrix} \text{Change in cost} \\ \text{of carrying} \\ \text{receivables} \end{pmatrix} - \begin{pmatrix} \text{Change in} \\ \text{bad-debt} \\ \text{losses} \end{pmatrix} - \begin{pmatrix} \text{Change in} \\ \text{cost of} \\ \text{discounts} \end{pmatrix}$$

$$= (S_N - S_0)(1 - V) - r(\Delta I) - (B_N S_N - B_0 S_0) - (D_N S_N P_N - D_0 S_0 P_0)$$

(22–3)

Thus, changes in credit policy are analyzed by using either Equation 22-1 or 22-2, depending on whether the proposed change is expected to increase or decrease sales, together with Equation 22-3. The rationale behind these equations will become clear as we work through several illustrations. Note that all the terms in Equation 22-3 need not be used in a particular analysis. For example, a change in credit policy might not affect discount sales or bad-debt losses, in which case the last two terms of the equation would both be zero. Note also that the form of the equations depends on the way in which the variables are first defined.[4]

---

4. For example, P_0 and P_N are defined as the percentage of *total* customers who take discounts. If P_0 and P_N were defined as the percentage of *paying* customers (excluding bad debts) who take discounts, then Equation 22-3 would become

$$\Delta P = (S_N - S_0)(1 - V) - r(\Delta I) - (B_N S_N - B_0 S_0) - [D_N S_N P_N (1 - B_N) - D_0 S_0 P_0 (1 - B_0)]$$

Similarly, changing the definitions of B_0 and B_N would affect the third term of Equation 22-3, as we discuss later.

28.8b Changing the Credit Period

In this section, we examine the effects of changing the credit period, and in the subsequent sections we consider changes in credit standards, collection policy, and cash discounts. Throughout, we illustrate the situation with data on Stylish Fashions Inc.

Lengthening the Credit Period

Stylish Fashions currently sells on a cash-only basis. Since it extends no credit, the company has no funds tied up in receivables, no bad-debt losses, and no credit expenses of any kind. On the other hand, its sales volume is lower than it would be if credit terms were offered. Stylish is now considering offering credit on 30-day terms. Current sales are $100,000 per year, variable costs are 60% of sales, excess production capacity exists (so no new fixed costs would be incurred as a result of expanded sales), and the cost of capital invested in receivables is 10%. Stylish estimates sales would increase to $150,000 per year if credit were extended and that bad-debt losses would be 2% of total sales. Thus, we have the following:

S_0 = $100,000
S_N = $150,000
V = 60% = 0.6
$1 - V$ = 1 − 0.6 = 0.4
r = 10% = 0.10
DSO_0 = 0 days
DSO_N = 30 days. Here we assume that all customers will pay on time, so DSO = specified credit period. Generally, some customers pay late, so in most cases DSO is greater than the specified credit period.
B_0 = 0% = 0.00. There are currently no bad-debt losses.
B_N = 2% = 0.02. These losses apply to the entire $150,000 new level of sales.
D_0 = D_N = 0%. No discounts are given under either the current or the proposed credit policies.

Because sales are expected to increase, Equation 22-1 is used to determine the change in the investment in receivables:

$$\Delta I = [(DSO_N - DSO_0)(S_0/365)] + V[(DSO_N)(S_N - S_0)/365]$$
$$= [(30 - 0)(\$100,000/365)] + 0.6[30(\$150,000 - \$100,000)/365]$$
$$= \$8,219 + \$2,466 = \$10,685$$

Note that the first term, the increased investment in accounts receivable associated with *old sales,* is based on the full amount of the receivables, whereas the second term, the investment associated with *incremental sales,* consists of incremental receivables multiplied by V, the variable cost percentage. This difference reflects that (1) the firm invests only its variable cost in incremental receivables, but (2) it would have collected the full sales price on the old sales earlier had it not made the credit policy change. There is an *opportunity cost* on the profit and a *direct financing cost* associated with the $8,219 additional investment in receivables from old sales, but only a direct financing cost associated with the $2,466 investment in receivables from incremental sales.

Looking at this another way, incremental sales will generate an actual increase in receivables of $(DSO_N)(S_N - S_0)/365 = 30(\$50,000/365) = \$4,110$. However, the only part of that increase that must be financed (by bank borrowing or from other sources) and reported as a liability on the right-hand side of the balance sheet is the cash outflow required to support the incremental sales—that is, the variable costs $V(\$4,110) = 0.6(\$4,110) = \$2,466$. The remainder of the receivables increase, $\$1,644$ of accrued before-tax profit, is reflected on the balance sheet not as some type of credit used to finance receivables but rather as an increase in retained earnings generated by the sales. On the other hand, the old receivables level was zero, meaning that the original sales produced cash of $\$100,000/365 = \$273.97$ per day, which was immediately available for investing in assets or for reducing capital from other sources. The change in credit policy will cause a delay in the collection of these funds and hence will require the firm (1) to borrow to cover the variable costs of the sales and (2) to forgo a return on the retained earnings portion, which would have been available immediately had the credit policy change not been made.

Given ΔI, we may now use Equation 22-3 to determine the incremental profit, ΔP, associated with the proposed credit period change:

$$\Delta P = (S_N - S_0)(1 - V) - r(\Delta I) - (B_N S_N - B_0 S_0) - (D_N S_N P_N - D_0 S_0 P_0)$$
$$= (\$50,000)(0.4) - 0.10(\$10,685) - [0.02(\$150,000) - 0.00(\$100,000)] - \$0$$
$$= \$20,000 - \$1,069 - \$3,000 = \$15,931$$

Since pre-tax profits are expected to increase by $\$15,931$, the credit policy change appears to be desirable.

Two simplifying assumptions that were made in our analysis should be noted: We assumed (1) that all customers paid on time (DSO = credit period) and (2) that there were no current bad-debt losses. The assumption of prompt payment can be relaxed quite easily—we can simply use the actual days sales outstanding (say, 40 days), rather than the 30-day credit period, to calculate the investment in receivables and then use this new (higher) value of ΔI in Equation 22-3 to calculate ΔP. Thus, if DSO_N were 40 days then the increased investment in receivables would be

$$\Delta I = [(40 - 0)(\$100,000/365)] + 0.6[40(\$50,000/365)]$$
$$= \$10,959 + \$3,288 = \$14,247$$

and the change in pre-tax profits would be

$$\Delta P = \$50,000(0.4) - 0.10(\$14,247) - 0.02(\$150,000)$$
$$= \$20,000 - \$1,425 - \$3,000 = \$15,575$$

The longer collection period causes incremental profits to fall slightly, but they are still positive and so the credit policy should probably be relaxed.

If the company had been selling on credit initially and therefore incurring some bad-debt losses, then this information would need to be included in Equation 22-3. In our example, $B_0 S_0$ was equal to zero because Stylish Fashions did not previously sell on credit; therefore, the change in bad-debt losses was equal to $B_N S_N$.

Note that B_N is defined as the average credit loss as a percentage of total sales, not of incremental sales. Bad debts might be higher for new customers attracted by the credit terms than for old customers who take advantage of them, but B_N is an average of these two groups. However, if one wanted to keep the two groups separate, it would be easy enough to define B_N as the bad-debt percentage of the incremental sales only.

Other factors could also be introduced into the analysis. For example, the company could consider a further easing of credit by extending the credit period to 60 days, or it could analyze the effects of a sales expansion so great that fixed assets, and hence fixed costs, had to be added. Or the variable cost ratio might change as sales increased, falling if economies of scale were present or rising if diseconomies were present. Adding such factors complicates the analysis, but the basic principles are the same; just bear in mind that we are seeking to determine the *incremental sales revenues,* the *incremental costs,* and consequently the *incremental before-tax profit* associated with a given change in credit policy.

Shortening the Credit Period

Suppose that a year after Stylish Fashions began offering 30-day credit terms its management decided to consider the possibility of shortening the credit period from 30 to 20 days. It was believed that sales would decline by $20,000 per year from the current level of $150,000, so $S_N = \$130,000$. It was also believed that the bad-debt percentage on these lost sales would be 2%, the same as on other sales, and that all other values would remain as given in the previous section.

We first calculate the incremental investment in receivables. Because the change in credit policy is expected to decrease sales, Equation 22-2 is used:

$$\Delta I = [(DSO_N - DSO_0)(S_N/365)] + V[(DSO_0)(S_N - S_0)/365]$$
$$= [(20 - 30)(\$130,000/365)] + 0.6[30(\$130,000 - \$150,000)/365]$$
$$= (-10)(\$356.16) + 0.6[(30)(-\$54.79)]$$
$$= -\$3,562 - \$986 = -\$4,548$$

With a shorter credit period, there is a shorter collection period, so sales are collected sooner. There is also a smaller volume of business, and hence a smaller investment in receivables. The first term captures the speedup in collections, while the second reflects the reduced sales and hence the lower receivables investment (at variable cost).

Note that V is included in the second term but not in the first. The logic here is similar to the logic underlying Equation 22-1: V is included in the second term because, by shortening the credit period, Stylish Fashions will drive off some customers and forgo sales of $20,000 per year, or $54.79 per day. The firm's investment in those sales was only 60% of the average receivables outstanding, or 0.6(30)($54.79) = $986. However, the situation is different for the remaining customers. They would have paid their full purchase price—variable cost plus profit—after 30 days. Now, however, they will have to pay this amount 10 days sooner, so those funds will be available to meet operating costs or for investment. Therefore, the first term should not be reduced by the variable cost factor. In total, then, reducing the credit period would result in a $4,548 reduction in the investment in receivables, consisting of a $3,562 decline in receivables associated with continuing customers and a further $986 decline in investment as a result of the reduced sales volume.

Having calculated the change in investment, we can now use Equation 22-3 to analyze the profitability of the proposed change:

$$\Delta P = (S_N - S_0)(1 - V) - r(\Delta I) - (B_N S_N - B_0 S_0) - (D_N S_N P_N - D_0 S_0 P_0)$$
$$= (\$130,000 - \$150,000)(0.4) - 0.10(-\$4,548)$$
$$\quad - [(0.02)(\$130,000) - (0.02)(\$150,000)] - \$0$$
$$= -\$8,000 + \$455 + \$400 = -\$7,145$$

Because the expected incremental pre-tax profits are negative, the firm should not reduce its credit period from 30 to 20 days.

28.8c Changes in Other Credit Policy Variables

In the preceding section, we examined the effects of changes in the credit period. Changes in other credit policy variables may be analyzed similarly. In general, we would follow these steps.

Step 1 Estimate the effect of the policy change on sales, on DSO, on bad-debt losses, and so on.

Step 2 Determine the change in the firm's investment in receivables. If the change will increase sales, use Equation 22-1 to calculate ΔI. Conversely, if the change will decrease sales then use Equation 22-2.

Step 3 Use Equation 22-3, or one of its variations, to calculate the effect of the change on pre-tax profits. If profits are expected to increase, the policy change should be made—unless it is judged to increase the firm's risk by a disproportionate amount.

28.8d Simultaneous Changes in Policy Variables

In the preceding discussion, we considered the effects of changes in only one credit policy variable. The firm could, of course, change several or even all policy variables simultaneously. An almost endless variety of equations could be developed, depending on which policy variables are manipulated and on the assumed effects on sales, discounts taken, the collection period, bad-debt losses, the existence of excess capacity, changes in credit department costs, changes in the variable cost percentage, and so on. The analysis would get "messy" and the incremental profit equation would be complex, but the principles we have developed could be used to handle any type of policy change.

> **Self Test**
>
> Describe the incremental analysis approach for evaluating a proposed credit policy change.
>
> How can risk be incorporated into the analysis?

22.9 The Cost of Bank Loans

In Chapter 21, we discussed the various short-term bank loans that are typically available: promissory notes, informal lines of credit, and revolving credit agreements. We provide a more in-depth and comprehensive discussion here.

The terms on a short-term bank loan to a business are spelled out in the promissory note. Here are the key elements contained in most promissory notes.

1. *Interest-only versus amortized.* Loans are either *interest-only,* meaning that only interest is paid during the life of the loan and the principal is repaid when the loan matures, or *amortized,* meaning that some of the principal is repaid on each payment date. Amortized loans are called *installment loans.* Note, too, that loans can be fully or partially amortized. For example, a loan may mature after 10 years, but payments may be based on 20 years, so an unpaid balance will still exist at the end of the 10th year. Such a loan is called a "balloon" loan.

2. *Collateral.* If a short-term loan is secured by some specific collateral, generally accounts receivable or inventories, then this fact is indicated in the note. If the collateral is to be kept on the premises of the borrower, then a form called a

UCC-1 (Uniform Commercial Code-1) is filed with the Secretary of State for the state in which the collateral resides, along with a *Security Agreement* (also part of the Uniform Commercial Code) that describes the nature of the agreement. These filings prevent the borrower from using the same collateral to secure loans from different lenders, and they spell out conditions under which the lender can seize the collateral.

3. *Loan guarantees.* If the borrower is a small corporation, its bank will probably insist that the larger stockholders *personally guarantee* the loan. Banks have often seen a troubled company's owner divert assets from the company to some other entity he or she owned, so banks protect themselves by insisting on personal guarantees. However, stockholder guarantees are virtually impossible to secure in the case of larger corporations that have many stockholders. Also, guarantees are unnecessary for proprietorships or partnerships because in those cases the owners are already personally liable for the businesses' debts.

4. *Nominal, or stated, interest rate.* The interest rate can be either *fixed* or *floating.* If it floats, then it is generally indexed to LIBOR. Most loans of any size ($25,000 and up) have floating rates if their maturities are greater than 90 days. The note will also indicate whether the bank uses a *360- or 365-day year* for purposes of calculating interest.

5. *Frequency of interest payments.* If the note is on an interest-only basis, it will indicate *how frequently interest must be paid.* Interest is typically calculated on a daily basis but paid monthly.

6. *Maturity.* Long-term loans always have specific maturity dates. A short-term loan may or may not have a specified maturity. For example, a loan may mature in 30 days, 90 days, 6 months, or 1 year; or it may call for "payment on demand," in which case the loan can remain outstanding as long as the borrower wants to continue using the funds and the bank agrees. Banks virtually never call demand notes unless the borrower's creditworthiness deteriorates, so some "short-term loans" remain outstanding for years, with the interest rate floating with rates in the economy.

7. *Calculation and payment of interest.* For most loans, interest is paid after it is earned. But not all loans follow this convention, and the method by which interest is calculated and paid affects the overall cost of credit. One alternate method is *discount interest.* A *discount loan* requires that interest be paid in advance. If the loan is on a discount basis, the borrower actually receives less than the face amount of the loan, and this increases the loan's effective cost. We discuss discount loans in a later section. Another method is used in an *add-on basis installment loan.* Auto loans and other types of consumer installment loans are generally set up on an "add-on basis," which means that interest over the life of the loan is calculated and then added to the face amount of the loan. Thus, the borrower signs a note for the funds received plus the interest. The add-on feature also raises the effective cost of a loan, as we demonstrate in a later section.

8. *Other cost elements.* Some commercial loans require the borrower to keep a percentage of the borrowed funds in an account at the lending bank. These held funds are called *compensating balances.* In addition, revolving credit agreements often require *commitment fees* in which the borrower pays interest on the amount actually drawn plus a separate fee based either on the total size of the line of credit or on the unused credit. Both of these conditions will be spelled out in the loan agreement, and both raise the effective cost of a loan above its stated nominal rate.

9. The **annual percentage rate (APR)**. The various fees and methods of calculating interest mean that the nominal, or stated, interest rate may not reflect the true cost of the loan. The APR calculation incorporates all of the costs of borrowing and reports a single nominal rate that reflects all of these costs. However, this rate is required to be reported only for consumer loans.

10. *Key-person insurance.* Often the success of a small company is linked to its owner or to a few important managers. It's a sad fact, but many small companies fail when one of these key individuals dies. Therefore, banks often require small companies to take out *key-person insurance* on their most important managers as part of the loan agreement. Usually the loan becomes due and payable should there be an untimely demise, with the insurance benefits being used to repay the loan. This makes the best of a bad situation—the bank gets its money, and the company reduces its debt burden without having to use any of its operating cash.

In the following sections, we explain how to calculate the effective cost of different bank loans. For illustrative purposes, we assume a loan of $10,000 at a nominal interest rate of 12% and with a 365-day year.

22.9a Regular, or Simple, Interest

In Chapter 21, we explained **simple interest**, which is also called **regular interest**. We review that discussion here. Most short-term business lending is with interest-only loans. The first step is to divide the nominal interest rate, 12% in this case, by 365 (or 360 in some cases) to obtain the rate per day:

$$\frac{\text{Interest rate}}{\text{per day}} = \frac{\text{Nominal rate}}{\text{Days in year}} \qquad (22\text{-}4)$$

$$= 0.12/365 = 0.00032876712$$

This rate is then multiplied by the number of days during the specific payment period and then by the amount of the loan. For example, if the loan is interest-only with monthly payments, then the interest payment for January would be $101.92:

$$\frac{\text{Interest charge}}{\text{for period}} = (\text{Days in period})(\text{Rate per day})(\text{Amount of loan}) \qquad (22\text{-}5)$$

$$= (31 \text{ days})(0.00032876712)(\$10,000) = \$101.92$$

If interest were payable quarterly and if there were 91 days in the quarter, then the interest payment would be $299.18. The annual interest would be $365 \times 0.00032876712 \times \$10,000 = \$1,200.00$. Note that if the bank had based the interest calculation on a 360-day year, as most banks do, then the interest charges would have been slightly higher and the annual charge would have been $1,216.67. Obviously, banks use a 360-day year to boost their earnings.

The effective interest rate on a loan depends on how frequently interest must be paid—the more frequently, the higher the effective rate. We demonstrate this point with two time lines, one for interest paid once a year and one for quarterly payments:

Interest Paid Annually:

0	0.25	0.5	0.75	1.0
10,000	0	0	0	−1,200.00
				−10,000.00
				−11,200.00

The borrower gets $10,000 at t = 0 and pays $11,200 at t = 1. On a financial calculator, enter N = 1, PV = 10000, PMT = 0, and FV = −11200; then press I/YR to get the effective cost of the loan, 12%.

Interest Paid Quarterly:

0	0.25	0.5	0.75	1.0
10,000	−299.18	−299.18	−302.47	−299.18
				−10,000.00
				−10,299.18

Note that the third quarter has 92 days. After entering the data in the cash flow register of a financial calculator (being sure to use the +/− key to enter −299.18), we find the periodic rate to be 2.9999%. The effective annual rate is 12.55%:

$$\text{Effective annual rate, quarterly} = (1 + 0.029999)^4 - 1 = 12.55\%$$

Had the loan called for interest to be paid monthly then the effective rate would have been 12.68%, and if interest had been paid daily then the rate would have been 12.75%. These rates would be higher if the bank used a 360-day year.

In these examples, we assumed that the loan matured in 1 year but that interest was paid at various times during the year. The rates we calculated would have been exactly the same even if the loan had matured on each interest payment date. In other words, the effective rate on a monthly payment loan would be 12.68% regardless of whether it matured after 1 month, 6 months, 1 year, or 10 years, providing the stated rate remained at 12%.

22.9b Discount Interest

In a **discount interest** loan, the bank deducts the interest in advance (*discounts* the loan). Thus, the borrower receives less than the face value of the loan. On a 1-year, $10,000 loan with a 12% (nominal) rate and discount basis, the interest is $10,000(0.12) = $1,200. Therefore, the borrower obtains the use of only $10,000 − $1,200 = $8,800. If the loan were for less than a year then the interest charge (the discount) would be lower; in our example, it would be $600 if the loan were for 6 months and so the amount received would be $9,400.

The effective rate on a discount loan is always higher than the rate on an otherwise similar simple interest loan. To illustrate, consider the situation for a discounted 12% loan for 1 year, as follows.

Discount Interest, Paid Annually:

```
        0          0.25        0.5         0.75        1.0
        |------------+-----------+-----------+-----------|
    10,000           0           0           0      -10,000.00
    -1,200
    ------
     8,800
```

On a financial calculator, enter N = 1, PV = 8800, PMT = 0, and FV = −10000; then press I/YR to get the effective cost of the loan, 13.64%.[5]

If a discount loan matures in less than a year—say, after 1 quarter—then we have the following situation.

Discount Interest, One Quarter:

```
        0          0.25        0.5         0.75        1.0
        |------------+-----------+-----------+-----------|
    10,000      -10,000          0           0           0
     -300
    ------
     9,700
```

Enter N = 1, PV = 9700, PMT = 0, and FV = −10000, and then press I/YR to find the periodic rate, 3.092784% per quarter, that corresponds to an effective annual rate of 12.96%. Thus, shortening the period of a discount loan lowers the effective rate of interest.

22.9c Effects of Compensating Balances

If the bank requires a compensating balance and if the amount of the required balance exceeds the amount the firm would normally hold on deposit, then the excess must be deducted at t = 0 and then added back when the loan matures. This has the effect of raising the effective rate on the loan. To illustrate, here is the setup for a 1-year discount loan requiring a 20% compensating balance that the firm would not otherwise hold on deposit.

---

5. Note that the firm actually receives less than the face amount of the loan:

   Funds received = (Face amount of loan)(1.0 − Nominal interest rate)

   We can solve for the face amount as follows:

   $$\text{Face amount of loan} = \frac{\text{Funds received}}{1.0 - \text{Nominal interest rate}}$$

   Therefore, if the borrowing firm actually requires $10,000 of cash, it must borrow $11,363.64:

   $$\text{Face value} = \frac{\$10,000}{1.0 - 0.12} = \frac{\$10,000}{0.88} = \$11,363.64$$

   Now the borrower will receive $11,363.64 − 0.12($11,363.64) = $10,000. Increasing the face value of the loan does not change the effective rate of 13.64% on the $10,000 of usable funds.

Discount Interest, Paid Annually, with 20% Compensating Balance:

0	0.25	0.5	0.75	1.0
10,000	0	0	0	−10,000
−1,200				2,000
−2,000				
6,800				−8,000

Note that the bank initially gives, and the borrower gets, $10,000 at time 0. However, the bank takes out the $1,200 of interest in advance, and the company must leave $2,000 in the bank as a compensating balance; hence the borrower's effective net cash flow at t = 0 is $6,800. At t = 1, the borrower must repay the $10,000, but $2,000 is already in the bank (the compensating balance), so the company must repay a net amount of $8,000.

On a financial calculator, enter N = 1, PV = 6800, PMT = 0, and FV = −8000; then press I/YR to get the effective cost of the discount loan with a compensating balance, 17.65%.

Note that banks recently have moved away from requiring compensating balances for fear of violating anti-trust regulations. Tying deposit services to lending services can be viewed as anti-competitive.

29.9d Installment Loans: Add-on Interest

Lenders typically charge **add-on interest** on automobile and other types of installment loans. The term "add-on" means the interest is calculated and then added to the amount received to determine the loan's face value. To illustrate, suppose you borrow $10,000 on an add-on basis at a nominal rate of 12% to buy a car, with the loan to be repaid in 12 monthly installments. At a 12% add-on rate, you will pay a total interest charge of $10,000(0.12) = $1,200. However, since the loan is paid off in monthly installments, you have the use of the full $10,000 for only the first month; then the outstanding balance declines until, during the last month, only one-twelfth of the original loan is still outstanding. Thus, you are paying $1,200 for the use of only about half the loan's face amount, as the average usable funds are only about $5,000. Therefore, we can calculate the approximate annual rate as follows:

(22–6)
$$\text{Approximate annual rate}_{\text{Add-on}} = \frac{\text{Interest paid}}{(\text{Amount received})/2}$$

$$= \frac{\$1,200}{\$10,000/2} = 24.0\%$$

To determine the effective rate of an add-on loan, we proceed as follows.

1. The total amount to be repaid is $10,000 of principal, plus $1,200 of interest, or $11,200.
2. The monthly payment is $11,200/12 = $933.33.

3. You are, in effect, paying off a 12-period annuity of $933.33 in order to receive $10,000 today, so $10,000 is the present value of the annuity. Here is the time line:

```
    0    i = ?    1           2         11      12 Months
    |      |      |           |          |          |
  10,000        −933.33   −933.33  ... −933.33   −933.33
```

4. On a financial calculator, enter N = 12, PV = 10000, PMT = −933.33, and FV = 0; then press I/YR to obtain 1.7880%. However, this is a monthly rate.

5. The effective annual rate is found as follows:[6]

$$\text{Effective annual rate}_{\text{Add-on}} = (1 + r_d)^n - 1.0 \qquad\qquad (22\text{–}7)$$

$$= (1.01788)^{12} - 1.0$$

$$= 1.2370 - 1.0 = 23.7\%$$

29.9e Annual Percentage Rate

The various ways of calculating interest (simple, discount, add-on), together with the various costs that are also frequently associated with smaller loans (e.g., credit report, loan processing and origination fees), cause the effective annual rate to differ even for loans that have identical stated interest rates. For example, although the add-on interest rate in our example above is 12%, its effective rate is 23.7%. If the loan used discount interest paid quarterly then the effective rate would be 12.96%, and if the loan used monthly simple interest the effective rate would be $(1.01)^{12} - 1.0 = 12.68\%$. In order to attempt to bring some consistency to reporting the cost of credit across various loan types, Congress passed the Truth in Lending Act in 1968. This legislation required that the **annual percentage rate (APR)** for all "consumer loans" be stated in bold print on the loan agreement.

The APR is the annual nominal effective cost of the credit, taking into account fees and the timing of payments:

$$\text{APR} = (\text{Periods per year})(\text{Rate per period})$$

So for a loan with 1% monthly simple interest, the APR would be 12(1%) = 12%. For the 12% add-on loan with monthly payments, the APR would be 12(1.788%) = 21.46%. For the 12% discount loan with quarterly payments, the APR would be 4(3.093%) = 12.37%. In most cases, this means that the effective annual rate can easily be calculated from the APR by compounding:

$$\text{Effective annual rate} = (1 + \text{APR}/n)^n - 1$$

where n is the number of periods per year.

The truth-in-lending laws apply primarily to consumer (not business) loans, so the APR does not necessarily appear on a business loan. In these cases the all-in borrowing cost must be calculated by the borrower.

---

6. Note that if an installment loan is paid off ahead of schedule, additional complications arise. For the classic discussion of this point, see Dick Bonker, "The Rule of 78," *Journal of Finance*, June 1976, pp. 877–888.

22.10 Choosing a Bank

Individuals whose only contact with their bank is through the use of its checking services generally choose a bank for the convenience of its location and the competitive cost of its services. However, a business that borrows from banks must look at other criteria and recognize that important differences exist among banks. Some of these differences are considered next.

22.10a Willingness to Assume Risks

Banks have different basic policies toward risk. Some follow relatively conservative lending practices, while others engage in what are properly termed "creative banking practices." These policies reflect partly the personalities of bank officers and partly the characteristics of the bank's deposit liabilities. Thus, a bank with fluctuating deposit liabilities in a static community will tend to be a conservative lender, whereas a bank whose deposits are growing with little interruption may follow more liberal credit policies. Similarly, a large bank with broad diversification over geographic regions and across industries can obtain the benefit of combining and averaging risks. Thus, marginal credit risks that might be unacceptable to a small or specialized bank can be pooled by a branch banking system to reduce the overall risk of a group of marginal accounts.[7]

22.10b Advice and Counsel

Some bank loan officers are active in providing counsel and in granting loans to firms in their early and formative years. Certain banks have specialized departments that make loans to firms that are expected to grow and thus to become more important customers. The personnel of these departments can provide valuable counseling to customers: The bankers' experience with other firms in growth situations may enable them to spot, and then to warn their customers about, developing problems.

22.10c Loyalty to Customers

Banks differ in their support of borrowers in bad times. This characteristic is referred to as the degree of *loyalty* of the bank. Some banks may put great pressure on a business to liquidate its loans when the firm's outlook becomes clouded, whereas others will stand by the firm and work diligently to help it get back on its feet.

---

7. Bank deposits are insured by a federal agency, and banks are required to pay premiums toward the cost of this insurance. Logically, riskier banks should pay higher premiums, but to date political forces have limited the use of risk-based insurance premiums. As an alternative, banks with riskier loan portfolios are required to have more equity capital per dollar of deposits than less risky banks. Until the 1980s, the savings and loan industry had federal insurance, no differential capital requirements, and lax regulations. As a result, some S&L operators wrote risky loans at high interest rates using low-cost, insured deposits. If the loans paid off, the S&L owners would get rich. If they went into default, the taxpayers would have to pay off the deposits. Those government policies ended up costing taxpayers more than $100 billion.

An especially dramatic illustration of this point was Bank of America's bailout of Memorex Corporation. The bank could have forced Memorex into bankruptcy, but instead it loaned the company additional capital and helped it survive a bad period. Memorex's stock price subsequently rose from $1.50 to $68, so Bank of America's help was indeed beneficial.

22.10d Specialization

Banks differ greatly in their degrees of loan specialization. Larger banks have separate departments that specialize in different kinds of loans—for example, real estate loans, farm loans, and commercial loans. Within these broad categories there may be a specialization by line of business, such as steel, machinery, cattle, or textiles. The strengths of banks are also likely to reflect the nature of the businesses and the economic environment in the areas in which they operate. For example, some California banks have become specialists in lending to electronics companies, while many Midwestern banks are agricultural specialists. A sound firm can obtain more creative cooperation and more active support by going to a bank that has experience and familiarity with its particular type of business. Therefore, a bank that is excellent for one firm may be unsatisfactory for another.

22.10e Maximum Loan Size

The size of a bank can be an important factor. Since the maximum loan a bank can make to any one customer is limited to 15% of the bank's capital accounts (capital stock plus retained earnings), it is generally not appropriate for large firms to develop borrowing relationships with small banks.

22.10f Other Services

Banks also provide cash management services, assist with electronic funds transfers, help firms obtain foreign exchange, and the like; and the availability of such services should be taken into account when selecting a bank. Also, if the firm is a small business whose manager owns most of its stock, the bank's willingness and ability to provide trust and estate services should be considered.

| What are some factors that should be considered when choosing a bank? | **Self Test** |

Summary

This chapter discussed granting credit and the conventions for interest rates on bank loans. It is important to monitor the results of credit policy by monitoring accounts receivable. A firm can affect its level of accounts receivable by changing its credit and collections policy, but doing so also affects sales. Therefore, a complete analysis of the effects of changes in credit policy is necessary. The key concepts covered in this chapter are listed below.

- A firm's credit policy consists of four elements: (1) **credit period**, (2) **discounts** given for early payment, (3) **credit standards**, and (4) **collection policy**. The first two, when combined, are called the **credit terms**.
- Additional factors that influence a firm's overall credit policy are **profit potential** and **legal considerations**.
- The basic objective of the credit manager is to increase profitable sales by extending credit to worthy customers and therefore adding value to the firm.
- Firms can use **days sales outstanding (DSO)** and **aging schedules** to help monitor their receivables position, but the best way to monitor aggregate receivables is the **payments pattern approach**. The primary tool in this approach is the **uncollected balances schedule**.
- If a firm **eases its credit policy** by lengthening the credit period, relaxing its credit standards and collection policy, and offering (or raising) its cash discount, then its sales should increase; however, its costs will also increase. A firm should ease its credit policy only if the costs of doing so will be offset by higher expected revenues. In general, credit policy changes should be evaluated on the basis of incremental profits.
- Changes in credit policy can be analyzed in two ways. First, **projected income statements** can be constructed for both the current and the proposed policies. Second, equations can be used to estimate the **incremental change** in profits resulting from a proposed new credit policy.
- With a **regular**, or **simple, interest loan**, interest is not compounded; that is, interest is not earned on interest.
- In a **discount interest loan**, the bank deducts the interest in advance. Interest is calculated on the face amount of the loan but it is paid in advance.
- Installment loans are typically **add-on interest loans**. Interest is calculated and added to the funds received to determine the face amount of the loan.
- The **annual percentage rate (APR)** is a rate reported by banks and other lenders on consumer loans that reflects all of the various loan fees and the timing of interest and principal payments.

Questions

22-1 Define each of the following terms:
   a. Cash discounts
   b. Seasonal dating
   c. Aging schedule; days sales outstanding (DSO)
   d. Payments pattern approach; uncollected balances schedule
   e. Simple interest; discount interest; add-on interest
22-2 Suppose a firm makes a purchase and receives the shipment on February 1. The terms of trade as stated on the invoice read "2/10, net 40, May 1 dating." What is the latest date on which payment can be made and the discount still be taken? What is the date on which payment must be made if the discount is not taken?
22-3 Is it true that, if a firm calculates its days sales outstanding, it has no need for an aging schedule?

22-4 Firm A had no credit losses last year, but 1% of Firm B's accounts receivable proved to be uncollectible and resulted in losses. Should Firm B fire its credit manager and hire A's?

22-5 Indicate by a (+), (–), or (0) whether each of the following events would probably cause accounts receivable (AR), sales, and profits to increase, decrease, or be affected in an indeterminate manner:

	AR	Sales	Profits
The firm tightens its credit standards.	_____	_____	_____
The terms of trade are changed from 2/10, net 30, to 3/10, net 30.	_____	_____	_____
The terms are changed from 2/10, net 30, to 3/10, net 40.	_____	_____	_____
The credit manager gets tough with past-due accounts.	_____	_____	_____

Problems   Answers Appear in Appendix B

Easy Problems 1–4

22-1 **Cost of Bank Loan** On March 1, Minnerly Motors obtains a business loan from a local bank. The loan is a $25,000 interest-only loan with a nominal rate of 11%. Interest is calculated on a simple interest basis with a 365-day year. What is Minnerly's interest charge for the first month (assuming 31 days in the month)?

22-2 **Cost of Bank Loan** Mary Jones recently obtained an equipment loan from a local bank. The loan is for $15,000 with a nominal interest rate of 11%. However, this is an installment loan, so the bank also charges add-on interest. Mary must make monthly payments on the loan, and the loan is to be repaid in 1 year. What is the effective annual rate on the loan (assuming a 365-day year)?

22-3 **Cost of Bank Loans** Del Hawley, owner of Hawley's Hardware, is negotiating with First City Bank for a 1-year loan of $50,000. First City has offered Hawley the alternatives listed below. Calculate the effective annual interest rate for each alternative. Which alternative has the lowest effective annual interest rate?

  a. A 12% annual rate on a simple interest loan, with no compensating balance required and interest due at the end of the year

  b. A 9% annual rate on a simple interest loan, with a 20% compensating balance required and interest due at the end of the year

  c. An 8.75% annual rate on a discounted loan, with a 15% compensating balance

  d. Interest figured as 8% of the $50,000 amount, *payable at the end of the year,* but with the loan amount repayable in monthly installments during the year

22-4 **Cost of Bank Loans** Gifts Galore Inc. borrowed $1.5 million from National City Bank. The loan was made at a simple annual interest rate of 9% a year for 3 months. A 20% compensating balance requirement raised the effective interest rate.

  a. The nominal annual rate on the loan was 11.25%. What is the true effective rate?

b. What would be the effective cost of the loan if the note required discount interest?

c. What would be the nominal annual interest rate on the loan if the bank did not require a compensating balance but required repayment in three equal monthly installments?

Intermediate Problems 5–7

22-5 **Relaxing Collection Efforts** The Boyd Corporation has annual credit sales of $1.6 million. Current expenses for the collection department are $35,000, bad-debt losses are 1.5%, and the days sales outstanding is 30 days. The firm is considering easing its collection efforts such that collection expenses will be reduced to $22,000 per year. The change is expected to increase bad-debt losses to 2.5% and to increase the days sales outstanding to 45 days. In addition, sales are expected to increase to $1,625,000 per year.

Should the firm relax collection efforts if the opportunity cost of funds is 16%, the variable cost ratio is 75%, and taxes are 40%?

22-6 **Tightening Credit Terms** Kim Mitchell, the new credit manager of the Vinson Corporation, was alarmed to find that Vinson sells on credit terms of net 90 days while industry-wide credit terms have recently been lowered to net 30 days. On annual credit sales of $2.5 million, Vinson currently averages 95 days of sales in accounts receivable. Mitchell estimates that tightening the credit terms to 30 days would reduce annual sales to $2,375,000, but accounts receivable would drop to 35 days of sales and the savings on investment in them should more than overcome any loss in profit.

Vinson's variable cost ratio is 85%, and taxes are 40%. If the interest rate on funds invested in receivables is 18%, should the change in credit terms be made?

22-7 **Effective Cost of Short-Term Credit** Yonge Corporation must arrange financing for its working capital requirements for the coming year. Yonge can: (a) borrow from its bank on a simple interest basis (interest payable at the end of the loan) for 1 year at a 12% nominal rate; (b) borrow on a 3-month, but renewable, loan basis at an 11.5% nominal rate; (c) borrow on an installment loan basis at a 6% add-on rate with 12 end-of-month payments; or (d) obtain the needed funds by no longer taking discounts and thus increasing its accounts payable. Yonge buys on terms of 1/15, net 60. What is the effective annual cost (*not* the nominal cost) of the *least expensive* type of credit, assuming 360 days per year?

Challenging Problems 8–10

22-8 **Monitoring of Receivables** The Russ Fogler Company, a small manufacturer of cordless telephones, began operations on January 1. Its credit sales for the first 6 months of operations were as follows:

Month	Credit Sales
January	$ 50,000
February	100,000
March	120,000
April	105,000
May	140,000
June	160,000

Throughout this entire period, the firm's credit customers maintained a constant payments pattern: 20% paid in the month of sale, 30% paid in the first month following the sale, and 50% paid in the second month following the sale.

a. What was Fogler's receivables balance at the end of March and at the end of June?

b. Assume 90 days per calendar quarter. What were the average daily sales (ADS) and days sales outstanding (DSO) for the first quarter and for the second quarter? What were the cumulative ADS and DSO for the first half-year?

c. Construct an aging schedule as of June 30. Use account ages of 0–30, 31–60, and 61–90 days.

d. Construct the uncollected balances schedule for the second quarter as of June 30.

22-9 Short-Term Financing Analysis Malone Feed and Supply Company buys on terms of 1/10, net 30, but it has not been taking discounts and has actually been paying in 60 rather than 30 days. Assume that the accounts payable are recorded at full cost, not net of discounts. Malone's balance sheet follows (thousands of dollars):

Cash	$ 50	Accounts payable	$ 500
Accounts receivable	450	Notes payable	50
Inventory	750	Accruals	50
Current assets	$1,250	Current liabilities	$ 600
		Long-term debt	150
Fixed assets	750	Common equity	1,250
Total assets	$2,000	Total liabilities and equity	$2,000

Malone's suppliers are threatening to stop shipments unless the company begins making prompt payments (that is, paying within 30). The firm can borrow on a 1-year note (call this a current liability) from its bank at a rate of 15% discount interest with a 20% compensating balance required. (Malone's $50,000 of cash is needed for transactions; it cannot be used as part of the compensating balance.)

a. How large would the accounts payable balance be if Malone takes discounts? If it does not take discounts and pays in 30 days?

b. How large must the bank loan be if Malone takes discounts? If Malone doesn't take discounts?

c. What are the nominal and effective costs of costly trade credit? What is the effective cost of the bank loan? Based on these costs, what should Malone do?

d. Assume Malone forgoes the discount and borrows the amount needed to become current on its payables. Construct a projected balance sheet based on this decision. (*Hint:* You will need to include an account called "prepaid interest" under current assets.)

e. Now assume that the $500,000 shown on the balance sheet is recorded net of discounts. How much would Malone have to pay its suppliers in order to reduce its accounts payable to $250,000? If Malone's tax rate is 40%, then what is the effect on its net income due to the lost discount when it reduces its accounts payable to $250,000? How much would Malone have to borrow? (*Hint:* Malone will receive a tax deduction due to the lost discount, which will affect the amount it must borrow.) Construct a projected balance sheet based on this scenario. (*Hint:* You will need to include an account called "prepaid interest" under current assets and then adjust retained earnings by the after-tax amount of the lost discount.)

22-10 **Alternative Financing Arrangements** Suncoast Boats Inc. estimates that, because of the seasonal nature of its business, it will require an additional $2 million of cash for the month of July. Suncoast Boats has the following four options available for raising the needed funds.

(1) Establish a 1-year line of credit for $2 million with a commercial bank. The commitment fee will be 0.5% per year on the unused portion, and the interest charge on the used funds will be 11% per annum. Assume the funds are needed only in July and that there are 30 days in July and 360 days in the year.

(2) Forgo the trade discount of 2/10, net 40, on $2 million of purchases during July.

(3) Issue $2 million of 30-day commercial paper at a 9.5% annual interest rate. The total transaction fee (including the cost of a backup credit line) for using commercial paper is 0.5% of the amount of the issue.

(4) Issue $2 million of 60-day commercial paper at a 9% annual interest rate plus a transaction fee of 0.5%. Since the funds are required for only 30 days, the excess funds ($2 million) can be invested in 9.4% per annum marketable securities for the month of August. The total transaction costs of purchasing and selling the marketable securities is 0.4% of the amount of the issue.

   a. What is the dollar cost of each financing arrangement?

   b. Is the source with the lowest expected cost necessarily the one to select? Why or why not?

Spreadsheet Problem

22-11 **Build a Model: Short-Term Financing Analysis** Start with the partial model in the file *Ch22 P11 Build a Model.xls* on the textbook's Web site. Rework parts a through d of Problem 22-9 using a spreadsheet model. Then answer the following related question.

   f. Using interest rates in the range of 5% to 25% and compensating balances in the range of 0% to 30%, perform a sensitivity analysis that shows how the size of the bank loan would vary with changes in the interest rate and the compensating balance percentage.

MINI CASE

Rich Jackson, a recent finance graduate, is planning to go into the wholesale building supply business with his brother, Jim, who majored in building construction. The firm would sell primarily to general contractors, and it would start operating next January. Sales would be slow during the cold months, rise during the spring, and then fall off again in the summer, when new construction in the area slows. Sales estimates for the first 6 months are as follows (in thousands of dollars):

January	$100	March	$300	May	$200
February	200	April	300	June	100

The terms of sale are net 30 but, because of special incentives, the brothers expect 30% of the customers (by dollar value) to pay on the 10th day following the sale, 50% to pay on the 40th day, and the remaining 20% to pay on the 70th day. No bad-debt losses are expected because Jim, the building construction expert, knows which contractors are having financial problems.

a. Discuss, in general, what it means for the brothers to set a credit and collections policy.

b. Assume that, on average, the brothers expect annual sales of 18,000 items at an average price of $100 per item. (Use a 365-day year.)

 (1) What is the firm's expected days sales outstanding (DSO)?

 (2) What is its expected average daily sales (ADS)?

 (3) What is its expected average accounts receivable (AR) level?

 (4) Assume the firm's profit margin is 25%. How much of the receivables balance must be financed? What would the firm's balance sheet figures be for accounts receivable, notes payable, and retained earnings at the end of 1 year if notes payable are used to finance the investment in receivables? Assume that the cost of carrying receivables had been deducted when the 25% profit margin was calculated.

 (5) If bank loans have a cost of 12%, what is the annual dollar cost of carrying the receivables?

c. What are some factors that influence (1) a firm's receivables level and (2) the dollar cost of carrying receivables?

d. Assuming the monthly sales forecasts given previously are accurate and that customers pay exactly as predicted, what would the receivables level be at the end of each month? To reduce calculations, assume that 30% of the firm's customers pay in the month of sale, 50% pay in the month following the sale, and the remaining 20% pay in the second month following the sale. (*Note:* This is a different assumption than was made earlier.) Also assume there are 91 days in each quarter. Use the following format to answer parts d and e:

Month	Sales	End-of-Month Receivables	Quarterly Sales	ADS	DSO = (AR) ÷ (ADS)
January	$100	$ 70			
February	200	160			
March	300	250	$600	$6.59	37.9
April	300				
May	200				
June	100				

e. What is the firm's forecasted average daily sales for the first 3 months? For the entire half-year? The days sales outstanding is commonly used to measure receivables performance. What DSO is expected at the end of March? At the end of June? What does the DSO indicate about customers' payments? Is DSO a good management tool in this situation? If not, why not?

f. Construct aging schedules for the end of March and the end of June (use the format given below). Do these schedules properly measure customers' payment patterns? If not, why not?

Age of Account (Days)	March		June	
	AR	%	AR	%
0–30	$210	84%		
31–60	40	16		
61–90	0	0	___	___
	$250	100%		

g. Construct the uncollected balances schedules for the end of March and the end of June. Use the format given below. Do these schedules properly measure customers' payment patterns?

	March				June		
Month	Sales	Contribution to AR	AR-to-Sales Ratio	Month	Sales	Contribution to AR	AR-to-Sales Ratio
January	$100	$ 0	0%	April			
February	200	40	20	May			
March	300	210	70	June		___	___

h. Assume that it is now July of Year 1 and that the brothers are developing projected financial statements for the following year. Further, assume that sales and collections in the first half-year matched the predicted levels. Use the Year-2 sales forecasts shown below to estimate next year's receivables levels for the end of March and for the end of June.

Month	Predicted Sales	Predicted AR-to-Sales Ratio	Predicted Contribution to Receivables
January	$150	0%	$ 0
February	300	20	60
March	500	70	350
		Projected March 31 AR balance =	$410
April	$400		
May	300		
June	200		
		Projected June 30 AR balance =	___

i. Now assume that it is several years later. The brothers are concerned about the firm's current credit terms of net 30, which means that contractors buying building products from the firm are not offered a discount and are supposed to pay the full amount in 30 days. Gross sales are now running $1,000,000 a year, and 80% (by dollar volume) of the firm's *paying* customers generally pay the full amount on Day 30; the other 20% pay, on average, on Day 40. Of the firm's gross sales, 2% ends up as bad-debt losses.

The brothers are now considering a change in the firm's credit policy. The change would entail (1) changing the credit terms to 2/10, net 20, (2) employing stricter credit standards before granting credit, and (3) enforcing collections with greater vigor than in the past. Thus, cash customers and those paying within 10 days would receive a 2% discount, but all others would have to pay the full amount after only 20 days. The brothers believe the discount would both attract additional customers and encourage some existing customers to purchase more from the firm—after all, the discount amounts to a price reduction. Of course, these customers would take the discount and hence would pay in only 10 days. The net expected result is for sales to increase to $1,100,000; for 60% of the paying customers to take the discount and pay on the 10th day; for 30% to pay the full amount on Day 20; for

10% to pay late on Day 30; and for bad-debt losses to fall from 2% to 1% of gross sales. The firm's operating cost ratio will remain unchanged at 75%, and its cost of carrying receivables will remain unchanged at 12%.

To begin the analysis, describe the four variables that make up a firm's credit policy and explain how each of them affects sales and collections. Then use the information given in part h to answer parts j through q.

j. Under the current credit policy, what is the firm's days sales outstanding? What would the expected DSO be if the credit policy change were made?

k. What is the dollar amount of the firm's current bad-debt losses? What losses would be expected under the new policy?

l. What would be the firm's expected dollar cost of granting discounts under the new policy?

m. What is the firm's current dollar cost of carrying receivables? What would it be after the proposed change?

n. What is the incremental after-tax profit associated with the change in credit terms? Should the company make the change? (Assume a tax rate of 40%.)

o. Suppose the firm makes the change but its competitors react by making similar changes to their own credit terms, with the net result being that gross sales remain at the current $1,000,000 level. What would be the impact on the firm's after-tax profitability?

	New	Old	Difference
Gross sales		$1,000,000	
Less discounts	_____	0	_____
Net sales		$1,000,000	
Production costs	_____	750,000	_____
Profit before credit costs and taxes		$ 250,000	
Credit-related costs:			
Carrying costs		8,000	
Bad-debt losses	_____	20,000	_____
Profit before taxes		$ 222,000	
Taxes (40%)	_____	88,800	_____
Net income	======	$ 133,200	======

p. The brothers need $100,000 and are considering a 1-year bank loan with a quoted annual rate of 8%. The bank is offering the following alternatives: (1) simple interest, (2) discount interest, (3) discount interest with a 10% compensating balance, and (4) add-on interest on a 12-month installment loan. What is the

effective annual cost rate for each alternative? For the first three of these assumptions, what is the effective rate if the loan is for 90 days but renewable? How large must the face value of the loan amount actually be in each of the four alternatives to provide $100,000 in usable funds at the time the loan is originated?

Selected Additional Cases

The following cases from TextChoice, *Cengage Learning's online case library, cover many of the concepts discussed in this chapter and are available at* **www.textchoice2.com/casenet.**

Klein-Brigham Series:
Case 33, "Upscale Toddlers, Inc.," which deals with credit policy changes; Case 34, "Texas Rose Company," and Case 67, "Bridgewater Pool Company," which focus on receivables management; Case 79, "Mitchell Lumber Company," which deals with credit policy; Case 88, "Chef's Selection," which deals with short-term financing; and Case 96, "Lifeline Health Products," which deals with credit policy.

Chapter 23

Other Topics in Working Capital Management

Chapters 21 and 22 presented the basic elements of current asset management and short-term financing. This chapter provides a more in-depth treatment of several working capital topics, including (1) the target cash balance, (2) inventory control systems, (3) accounting treatments for inventory, and (4) the EOQ model.

WEB

The textbook's Web site contains an *Excel* file that will guide you through the chapter's calculations. The file for this chapter is ***Ch23 Tool Kit.xls***, and we encourage you to open the file and follow along as you read the chapter.

Beginning of Chapter Questions

As you read the chapter, consider how you would answer the following questions. You *should not* necessarily be able to answer the questions before you read the chapter. Rather, you should use them to get a sense of the issues covered in the chapter. After reading the chapter, you should be able to give at least partial answers to the questions, and you should be able to give better answers after the chapter has been discussed in class. Note, too, that it is often useful, when answering conceptual questions, to use hypothetical data to illustrate your answer. We illustrate the answers with an *Excel* model that is available on the textbook's Web site. Accessing the model and working through it is a useful exercise, and it provides insights that are useful when answering the questions.

1. Explain briefly what the **EOQ model** is and how it can be used to help establish an optimal inventory policy. Is the EOQ concept consistent with **just-in-time** procedures for managing inventories?

2. Explain how the EOQ inventory model can be modified and used to help determine the optimal size of a firm's cash balances. Do you think the EOQ approach to cash management is more or less relevant today than it was in precomputer, preelectronic communications days?

3. What four methods are used to account for inventory? What are the financial implications of one method over another? How does the choice of inventory accounting method affect the order in which actual items in inventory are sold? Is it possible for the choice of accounting method for inventory to affect the free cash flow value of a firm as discussed in Chapter 11? How?

23.1 The Concept of Zero Working Capital

At first glance, it might seem that working capital management is not as important as capital budgeting, dividend policy, and other decisions that determine a firm's long-term direction. However, in today's world of intense global competition, working capital management is receiving increasing attention from managers striving for peak efficiency. In fact, the goal of many leading companies today is *zero working capital*. Proponents of the zero working capital concept claim that a movement toward this goal not only generates cash but also speeds up production and helps businesses make more timely deliveries and operate more efficiently. The concept has its own definition of working capital: Inventories + Receivables − Payables. The rationale here is (1) that inventories and receivables are the keys to making sales, but (2) that inventories can be financed by suppliers through accounts payable.

Companies generally use about 20 cents of working capital for each dollar of sales. So, on average, working capital is turned over five times per year. Reducing working capital and thus increasing turnover has two major financial benefits. First, every dollar freed up by reducing inventories or receivables, or by increasing payables, results in a one-time contribution to cash flow. Second, a movement toward zero working capital permanently raises a company's earnings. Like all capital, funds invested in working capital cost money, so reducing those funds yields permanent savings in capital costs. In addition to the financial benefits, reducing working capital forces a company to produce and deliver faster than its competitors, which helps it gain new business and charge premium prices for providing good services. As inventories disappear, warehouses can be sold off, both labor and handling equipment needs are reduced, and obsolete and/or out-of-style goods are minimized.

The most important factor in moving toward zero working capital is increased speed. If the production process is fast enough, companies can produce items as they are ordered rather than having to forecast demand and build up large inventories that are managed by bureaucracies. The best companies are able to start production after an order is received yet still meet customer delivery requirements. This system is known as *demand flow,* or *demand-based management,* and it builds on the just-in-time method of inventory control discussed later in this chapter. However, demand flow management is broader than just-in-time, because it requires that all elements of a production system operate quickly and efficiently.

Achieving zero working capital requires that every order and part move at maximum speed, which generally means replacing paper with electronic data. Then, orders streak from the processing department to the plant, where flexible production lines produce each product every day and finished goods flow directly from the production line onto waiting trucks or rail cars. Instead of cluttering plants or warehouses with inventories, products move directly into the pipeline. As efficiency rises, working capital dwindles.

Clearly, it is not possible for most firms to achieve zero working capital and infinitely efficient production. Still, a focus on minimizing cash, receivables, and inventories while maximizing payables will help a firm lower its investment in working capital and achieve financial and production economies.

> **Self Test**
>
> What is the basic idea of zero working capital, and how is working capital defined for this purpose?

23.2 Setting the Target Cash Balance

Recall from Chapter 21 that firms hold cash balances primarily for two reasons: to pay for *transactions* they must make in their day-to-day operations and to maintain *compensating balances* that banks may require in return for loans. In addition, firms maintain additional cash balances as a *precaution* against unforeseen fluctuations in cash flows and in order to take advantage of *trade discounts*. Given that cash is necessary for these purposes but is also a nonearning asset, the primary goal of cash management is to minimize the amount of cash a firm holds while maintaining a sufficient *target cash balance* to conduct business.

In Chapter 21, when we discussed Educational Products Corporation's cash budget, we took as a given the $10 million target cash balance. We also discussed how lockboxes, synchronizing inflows and outflows, and float can reduce the required cash balance. Now we consider how target cash balances are set in practice.

Note that (1) cash per se earns no return, (2) cash is an asset that appears on the left side of the balance sheet, (3) cash holdings must be financed by raising either debt or equity, and (4) both debt and equity capital have a cost. If cash holdings could be reduced without hurting sales or other aspects of a firm's operations, then this reduction would permit a reduction in either debt or equity or both, which would increase the return on capital and thus boost the value of the firm's stock. Therefore, *the general operating goal of the cash manager is to minimize the amount of cash held subject to the constraint that enough cash be held to enable the firm to operate efficiently.*

For most firms, cash as a percentage of assets and/or sales has declined sharply over the last couple of decades as a direct result of technological developments in computers and telecommunications. Years ago, it was difficult to move money from one location to another, and it was also difficult to forecast exactly how much cash would be needed in different locations at different points in time. As a result, firms had to hold relatively large "safety stocks" of cash to be sure they had enough when and where it was needed. Also, they held relatively large amounts of short-term securities as a backup, and they also had backup lines of credit that permitted them to borrow on short notice to build up the cash account if it became depleted.

Think about how computers and telecommunications now affect the situation. With a good computer system tied together with good telecommunications links, a company can get real-time information on its cash balances regardless of whether it operates in a single location or all over the world. Furthermore, it can use statistical procedures to forecast cash inflows and outflows, and good forecasts reduce the need for safety stocks. Finally, improvements in telecommunications systems make it possible for a treasurer to replenish the firm's cash accounts within minutes simply by calling a lender and stating that the firm wants to borrow a given amount under its line of credit. The lender then wires the funds to the desired location. Similarly, marketable securities can be sold with close to the same speed and with the same minimal transactions costs. This trend toward lower cash levels, however, was reversed in the wake of the financial crisis in 2008 and 2009 when firms found it difficult to obtain or renew lines of credit. As they became profitable moving out of the accompanying recession, many firms have squirreled away relatively larger amounts of cash as a safeguard against turmoil in the banking industry.

Super Cell, a provider of cell phone services, can be used to illustrate the impact of computers and high-speed telecommunications on cash management. Super Cell knows exactly how much it must pay and when, and it can forecast quite accurately when it will receive checks. For example, the treasurer of Super Cell's Florida operation knows when the major employers in Tampa pay their workers and how long after that people generally pay their phone bills. Armed with this information, Super Cell's Florida treasurer can forecast with great accuracy any cash surpluses or deficits on a daily basis. Of course, no forecast will be exact, so slight overages or underages will occur. But this presents no problem. The treasurer knows by 11 a.m. the checks that must be covered by 4 p.m. that day, how much cash has come in, and consequently how much of a cash surplus or deficit will exist. Then, with a single phone call, the company borrows to cover any deficit or buys securities (or pays off outstanding loans) with any surplus. Thus, Super Cell can maintain cash balances that are very close to zero, a situation that would have been impossible a few years ago.

Today, cash management in reasonably sophisticated firms is largely a job for systems people. Except for the very largest firms, it is generally most efficient to have a bank handle the actual operations of the cash management system. When it comes to operating a cash management system, banks have extensive experience and are able to capture economies of scale that are unobtainable by individual nonfinancial firms. Also, many banks are willing and able to offer such services, so competition has driven the cost of cash management down to a reasonable level. Still, it is essential that corporate treasurers know enough about cash management procedures to be able to negotiate and then work with the banks to ensure that they get the best price (interest rate) on credit lines, the best yield on short-term investments, and a reasonable cost for other banking services. To provide perspective on these issues, we next discuss a theoretical model for cash balances as well as a practical approach to setting the target cash balance.

23.2a The Baumol Model

William Baumol first noted that cash balances are, in many respects, similar to inventories and that the EOQ inventory model, which will be developed in a later section, can be used to establish a target cash balance.[1] Baumol's model assumes that the firm uses cash at a steady, predictable rate—say, $1,000,000 per week—and that the firm's cash inflows from operations also occur at a steady, predictable rate—say, $900,000 per week. Therefore, the firm's net cash outflows, or net need for cash, also occur at a steady rate—in this case, $100,000 per week.[2] Under these steady-state assumptions, the firm's cash position will resemble the situation shown in Figure 23-1.

If our illustrative firm started at Time 0 with a cash balance of C = $300,000 and if its outflows exceeded its inflows by $100,000 per week, then its cash balance would drop to zero at the end of Week 3 and its average cash balance would be C/2 = $300,000/2 = $150,000. Therefore, at the end of Week 3, the firm would have to replenish its cash balance by selling marketable securities (if it had any) or by borrowing.

If C were set at a higher level—say, $600,000—then the cash supply would last longer (6 weeks) and the firm would have to sell securities (or borrow) less frequently. However, its average cash balance would rise from $150,000 to $300,000. Brokerage or some other type of transaction costs must be incurred to sell securities (or to borrow), so holding larger cash balances will lower the transaction costs associated with obtaining cash. On the other hand, cash provides no income, so larger average

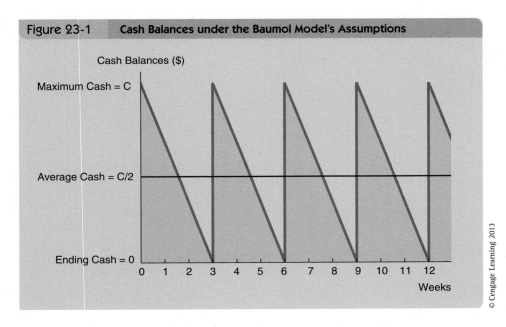

Figure 23-1   Cash Balances under the Baumol Model's Assumptions

© Cengage Learning 2013

---

1. William J. Baumol, "The Transactions Demand for Cash: An Inventory Theoretic Approach," *Quarterly Journal of Economics,* November 1952, pp. 545–556.
2. Our hypothetical firm is experiencing a $100,000 weekly cash shortfall, but this does not necessarily imply it is headed for bankruptcy. The firm could, for example, be highly profitable and be enjoying high earnings yet be expanding so rapidly that it experiences chronic cash shortages that must be made up by borrowing or by selling common stock. Or the firm could be in the construction business and therefore receive major cash inflows at widely spaced intervals but still have net cash outflows of $100,000 per week between these inflows.

cash balances entail a higher opportunity cost, which is the return that could have been earned on securities or other assets held in lieu of cash. Thus, we have the situation graphed in Figure 23-2. The optimal cash balance is found by using the following variables and equations:

C = Amount of cash raised by selling marketable securities or by borrowing.

C/2 = Average cash balance.

C* = Optimal amount of cash to be raised by selling marketable securities or by borrowing.

C*/2 = Optimal average cash balance.

F = Fixed costs of selling securities or of obtaining a loan.

T = Total amount of net new cash needed for transactions during the entire period (usually a year).

r = Opportunity cost of holding cash, set equal to either the rate of return forgone on marketable securities or the cost of borrowing to hold cash.

The total costs of cash balances consist of holding (or opportunity) costs plus transactions costs:[3]

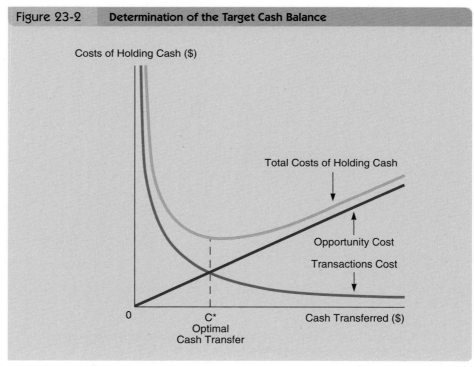

Figure 23-2   Determination of the Target Cash Balance

Costs of Holding Cash ($)

Total Costs of Holding Cash

Opportunity Cost

Transactions Cost

0

C*
Optimal
Cash Transfer

Cash Transferred ($)

---

3. Total costs can be expressed on either a before-tax or an after-tax basis. Both methods lead to the same conclusions regarding target cash balances and comparative costs. For simplicity, we present the model here on a before-tax basis.

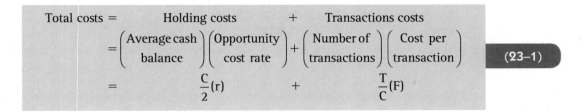

$$\text{Total costs} = \text{Holding costs} + \text{Transactions costs}$$

$$= \left(\begin{array}{c}\text{Average cash}\\ \text{balance}\end{array}\right)\left(\begin{array}{c}\text{Opportunity}\\ \text{cost rate}\end{array}\right) + \left(\begin{array}{c}\text{Number of}\\ \text{transactions}\end{array}\right)\left(\begin{array}{c}\text{Cost per}\\ \text{transaction}\end{array}\right)$$

$$= \frac{C}{2}(r) + \frac{T}{C}(F)$$ (23–1)

The minimum total costs are achieved when C is set equal to C*, the optimal cash transfer. The value of C* is found as follows:[4]

$$C^* = \sqrt{\frac{2(F)(T)}{r}}$$ (23–2)

Equation 23-2 is the **Baumol model** for determining optimal cash balances. To illustrate its use, suppose F = $150, T = 52 weeks × $100,000/week = $5,200,000, and r = 15% = 0.15. Then

$$C^* = \sqrt{\frac{2(\$150)\,(\$5,200,000)}{0.15}} = \$101,980$$

Therefore, the firm should sell securities (or borrow if it does not hold securities) in the amount of $101,980 when its cash balance approaches zero, thus building its cash balance back up to $101,980. Dividing T by C* yields the number of transactions per year: $5,200,000/$101,980 = 50.99 ≈ 51, or about once a week. The firm's average cash balance is $101,980/2 = $50,990 ≈ $51,000.

Note that the optimal cash balance increases less than proportionately with increases in the amount of cash needed for transactions. For example, if the firm's size, and consequently its net new cash needs, doubled from $5,200,000 to $10,400,000 per year, then average cash balances would increase by only 41%, from $51,000 to $72,000. This suggests that there are economies of scale in holding cash balances, and this, in turn, gives larger firms an edge over smaller ones.[5]

Of course, the firm would probably want to hold a safety stock of cash designed to reduce the probability of a cash shortage. However, if the firm is able to sell securities or to borrow on short notice—and most larger firms can do so in a matter of minutes simply by making a telephone call—then the safety stock can be quite low.

The Baumol model is obviously simplistic. Most important, it assumes relatively stable, predictable cash inflows and outflows, and it does not take into account seasonal or cyclical trends. Other models have been developed to deal both with uncertainty and with trends, but all of them have limitations and are more useful as conceptual models than for actually setting target cash balances.

---

4. Equation 23-1 is differentiated with respect to C. The derivative is set equal to zero, and we then solve for C = C* to derive Equation 23-2. This model, applied to inventories and called the EOQ model, is discussed further in a later section.

5. This edge may, of course, be more than offset by other factors—after all, cash management is only one aspect of running a business.

23.2b Monte Carlo Simulation

Although the Baumol model and other theoretical models provide insights into the optimal cash balance, they are generally not practical for actual use. Rather, firms generally set their target cash balances based on some "safety stock" of cash that holds the risk of running out of money to some acceptably low level. One commonly used procedure is **Monte Carlo simulation**. To illustrate, consider the cash budget for Educational Products Corporation (EPC) presented in Figure 21-6 in Chapter 21. Sales and collections are the driving forces in the cash budget and, of course, are subject to uncertainty. In the cash budget, we used expected values for sales and collections as well as for all other cash flows. However, it would be relatively easy to use Monte Carlo simulation, first discussed in Chapter 13, to introduce uncertainty. If the cash budget were constructed using a spreadsheet program with Monte Carlo add-in software, then the key uncertain variables could be specified as continuous probability distributions rather than point values.

The end result of the simulation would be a distribution for each month's net cash flow instead of the single values shown on Row 97 of Figure 21-6. Suppose September's net cash flow distribution looked like this (in millions):

September Net Cash Flow	Probability of This Cash Flow or Less
−$208	10%
−200	20
−193	30
−187	40
−182 Expected CF	50
−177	60
−171	70
−164	80
−156	90

Now suppose EPC's managers want to be 90% confident that the firm will not run out of cash during September, since they don't want to borrow to cover any shortfall. They would set the beginning-of-month target balance at $200 million, well above the current target balance of $10 million, because there is only a 10% probability that September's cash flow will be worse than a $200 million outflow. With a balance of $200 million at the beginning of the month, there would be only a 10% chance that EPC would run out of cash during September. Of course, Monte Carlo simulation could be applied to the remaining months in the Figure 21-6 cash budget, and the amounts so obtained to match a given confidence level could be used to set each month's target cash balance instead of using a fixed target across all months.

The same type of analysis could be used to determine the amount of short-term securities to hold or the size of a requested line of credit. Of course, as in all simulations, the hard part is estimating the probability distributions for sales, collections, and the other highly uncertain variables. If these inputs are not good representations of the actual uncertainty facing the firm, then the resulting target balances will not offer the protection against cash shortages implied by the simulation. There is no substitute for experience, and cash managers will adjust the target balances obtained by Monte Carlo simulation on a judgmental basis.

How has technology changed the way target cash balances are set?

What is the Baumol model, and how is it used?

Explain how Monte Carlo simulation can be used to help set a firm's target cash balance.

23.3 Inventory Control Systems

Inventory management requires the establishment of an *inventory control system*. Inventory control systems run the gamut from very simple to extremely complex, depending on the size of the firm and the nature of its inventory. For example, one simple control procedure is the **red-line method**—inventory items are stocked in a bin, a red line is drawn around the inside of the bin at the level of the reorder point, and the inventory clerk places an order when the red line shows. The **two-bin method** has inventory items stocked in two bins. When the working bin is empty, an order is placed and inventory is drawn from the second bin. These procedures work well for parts such as bolts in a manufacturing process or for many items in retail businesses.

23.3a Computerized Systems

Most companies today employ **computerized inventory control systems.** The computer starts with an inventory count in memory. As withdrawals are made, they are recorded by the computer, and the inventory balance is revised. When the reorder point is reached, the computer automatically places an order, and when the order is received, the recorded balance is increased. As we noted earlier, retailers such as Wal-Mart have carried this system quite far: Each item has a bar code and, as an item is checked out, the code is read, a signal is sent to the computer, and the inventory balance is adjusted at the same time the price is fed into the cash register tape. When the balance drops to the reorder point, an order is placed. In Wal-Mart's case, the order goes directly from its computers to those of its suppliers.

A good inventory control system is dynamic, not static. A company such as Wal-Mart or General Motors stocks hundreds of thousands of different items. The sales (or use) of individual items can rise or fall quite separately from rising or falling overall corporate sales. As the usage rate for an individual item begins to rise or fall, the inventory manager must adjust its balance to avoid running short or ending up with obsolete items. If the change in the usage rate appears to be permanent, then the safety stock level should be reconsidered and the computer model used in the control process should be reprogrammed.

23.3b Just-in-Time Systems

An approach to inventory control called the **just-in-time (JIT) system** was developed by Japanese firms but is now used throughout the world. Toyota provides a good example of the just-in-time system. Many of Toyota's suppliers are located near its factories. Delivery of components is tied to the speed of the assembly line, and parts are generally delivered no more than a few hours before they are used. The just-in-time system reduces the need for Toyota and other manufacturers to carry large inventories, but it requires a great deal of coordination between the manufacturer and its suppliers—both in the timing of deliveries and the quality of the parts. The component parts must be perfect, because a few bad parts could stop the entire production line. Therefore, JIT inventory management has been developed in conjunction with total quality management (TQM).

The close coordination required between the parties using JIT procedures has led to an overall reduction of inventory throughout the production–distribution system and to a general improvement in economic efficiency. This point is borne out by economic statistics, which show that inventory as a percentage of sales has been declining since the use of just-in-time procedures began. Also, with smaller inventories in the system, economic recessions have become shorter and less severe.

23.3c Outsourcing

Another important development related to inventory is **outsourcing**, which is the practice of purchasing components rather than making them in-house. Thus, GM has been moving toward buying radiators, axles, and other parts from suppliers rather than making them itself, so it has been increasing its use of outsourcing. Outsourcing is often combined with just-in-time systems to reduce inventory levels. However, perhaps the major reason for outsourcing has nothing to do with inventory policy: A bureaucratic, unionized company like GM can often buy parts from a smaller, nonunionized supplier at a lower cost than it can make them itself.

23.3d The Relationship between Production Scheduling and Inventory Levels

A final point relating to inventory levels is the relationship between production scheduling and inventory levels. For example, a greeting card manufacturer has highly seasonal sales. Such a firm could produce on a steady, year-round basis, or it could let production rise and fall with sales. If it established a level production schedule, its inventory would rise sharply during periods when sales were low and then decline during peak sales periods, but its average inventory would be substantially higher than if production rose and fell with sales.

Our discussions of just-in-time systems, outsourcing, and production scheduling all point out the necessity of coordinating inventory policy with manufacturing/procurement policies. Companies try to minimize *total production and distribution costs,* and inventory costs are just one part of total costs. Still, they are an important cost, and financial managers should be aware of the determinants of inventory costs and how those costs can be minimized.

Self Test

Describe some inventory control systems that are used in practice.

What are just-in-time systems? What are their advantages? Why is quality especially important if a JIT system is used?

What is outsourcing?

Describe the relationship between production scheduling and inventory levels.

23.4 Accounting for Inventory

When finished goods are sold, the firm must assign a cost of goods sold. The cost of goods sold appears on the income statement as an expense for the period, and the balance sheet inventory account is reduced by a like amount. Four methods can be used to value the cost of goods sold and hence to value the remaining inventory: (1) specific identification, (2) first-in, first-out (FIFO), (3) last-in, first-out (LIFO), and (4) weighted average.

23.4a Specific Identification

Under **specific identification**, a unique cost is attached to each item in inventory. Then, when an item is sold, the inventory value is reduced by that specific amount. This method is used only when the items are high cost and move relatively slowly, such as cars for an automobile dealer.

23.4b First-In, First-Out (FIFO)

In the **FIFO** method, the units sold during a given period are assumed to be the first units that were placed in inventory. As a result, the cost of goods sold is based on the cost of the oldest inventory items, and the remaining inventory consists of the newest goods.

23.4c Last-In, First-Out (LIFO)

LIFO is the opposite of FIFO. The cost of goods sold is based on the last units placed in inventory, while the remaining inventory consists of the first goods placed in inventory. Note that this is purely an accounting convention—the actual physical units sold could be either the earlier or the later units placed in inventory, or some combination. For example, Del Monte has in its LIFO inventory accounts catsup bottled in the 1920s, but all the catsup in its warehouses was bottled in 2011 or 2012. Note, however, that once international financial reporting standards (IFRS) are adopted for U.S. companies, LIFO accounting for inventory will no longer be allowed. Adoption of IFRS by U.S. companies has been delayed until at least 2015.

23.4d Weighted Average

The **weighted average** method involves calculating the weighted average unit cost of goods available for sale from inventory; the average is then used to determine the cost of goods sold. This method results in a cost of goods sold and an ending inventory that fall somewhere between the FIFO and LIFO methods.

23.4e Comparison of Inventory Accounting Methods

To illustrate these methods and their effects on financial statements, assume that Custom Furniture Inc. manufactured five identical faux antique dining tables during a 1-year accounting period. During the year, a new labor contract and dramatically increasing mahogany prices caused manufacturing costs to almost double, resulting in the following inventory costs:

Table Number:	1	2	3	4	5	Total
Cost:	$10,000	$12,000	$14,000	$16,000	$18,000	$70,000

There were no tables in stock at the beginning of the year, and Tables 1, 3, and 5 were sold during the year.

If Custom used the specific identification method, then the cost of goods sold would be reported as $10,000 + $14,000 + $18,000 = $42,000 and the end-of-period inventory value would be $70,000 − $42,000 = $28,000. If Custom used the FIFO method, then its cost of goods sold would be $10,000 + $12,000 + $14,000 = $36,000 and ending inventory would be $70,000 − $36,000 = $34,000. If Custom used the LIFO method, then its cost of goods sold would be $48,000 and its ending inventory would be $22,000. Finally, if Custom used the weighted average method, then its average cost per unit of inventory would be $70,000/5 = $14,000, its cost of goods sold would be 3($14,000) = $42,000, and its ending inventory would be $70,000 − $42,000 = $28,000.

If Custom's actual sales revenues from the tables were $80,000, or an average of $26,667 per unit sold, and if its other costs were minimal, then the following table summarizes the effects of the four methods:

Method	Sales	Cost of Goods Sold	Reported Profit	Ending Inventory Value
Specific identification	$80,000	$42,000	$38,000	$28,000
FIFO	80,000	36,000	44,000	34,000
LIFO	80,000	48,000	32,000	22,000
Weighted average	80,000	42,000	38,000	28,000

If we ignore taxes, then Custom's cash flows would not be affected by its choice of inventory methods, yet its balance sheet and reported profits would vary with each method. In an inflationary period such as in our example, FIFO gives the lowest cost of goods sold and thus the highest net income. FIFO also shows the highest inventory value, so it produces the strongest apparent liquidity position as measured by net working capital or the current ratio. On the other hand, LIFO produces the highest cost of goods sold, the lowest reported profits, and the weakest apparent liquidity position. However, when taxes are considered, LIFO provides the greatest tax deductibility and therefore results in the lowest tax burden. Consequently, after-tax cash flows are highest when LIFO is used.

Of course, these results apply only to periods when costs are increasing. If costs were constant then all four methods would produce the same cost of goods sold, ending inventory, taxes, and cash flows. However, inflation has been a fact of life in recent years, so most firms use LIFO to take advantage of its greater tax and cash flow benefits.

Self Test	What are the four methods used to account for inventory?
	What effect does each method used have on the firm's reported profits? On ending inventory levels?
	Which method should be used if management anticipates a period of inflation? Why?

23.5 The Economic Ordering Quantity (EOQ) Model

As discussed in Chapter 21, inventories are obviously necessary, but it is equally obvious that a firm's profitability will suffer if it has too much or too little inventory.

Most firms take a pragmatic approach to setting inventory levels in which past experience plays a major role. However, as a starting point in the process, it is useful for managers to consider the insights provided by the **Economic Ordering Quantity (EOQ) model.** The EOQ model first specifies the costs of ordering and carrying inventories and then combines these costs to obtain the total costs associated with inventory holdings. Finally, optimization techniques are used to find the order quantity, and hence inventory level, that minimizes total costs. Note that a third category of inventory costs, the costs of running short (stock-out costs), is not considered in our initial discussion. These costs are dealt with by adding safety stocks, as we discuss later. Similarly, we shall discuss quantity discounts in a later section. The costs that remain for consideration at this stage are carrying costs and ordering, shipping, and receiving costs.

23.5a Carrying Costs

Carrying costs generally rise in direct proportion to the average amount of inventory carried. Inventories carried, in turn, depend on the frequency with which orders are placed. To illustrate, suppose a firm sells S units per year and places equal-sized orders N times per year; then S/N units will be purchased with each order. If the inventory is used evenly over the year and if no safety stocks are carried, then the average inventory, A, will be

$$A = \frac{\text{Units per order}}{2} = \frac{S/N}{2} \qquad (23\text{--}3)$$

For example, if S = 120,000 units in a year and N = 4, then the firm will order 30,000 units at a time and its average inventory will be 15,000 units:

$$A = \frac{S/N}{2} = \frac{120,000/4}{2} = \frac{30,000}{2} = 15,000 \text{ units}$$

Just after a shipment arrives, the inventory will be 30,000 units; just before the next shipment arrives, it will be zero; and on average, 15,000 units will be carried.

Now assume the firm purchases its inventory at a price P = $2 per unit. The average inventory value is thus (P)(A) = $2(15,000) = $30,000. If the firm has a cost of capital of 10%, it will incur $3,000 in financing charges to carry the inventory for 1 year. Further, assume that each year the firm incurs $2,000 of storage costs (space, utilities, security, taxes, and so forth), that its inventory insurance costs are $500, and that it must mark down inventories by $1,000 because of depreciation and obsolescence. The firm's total cost of carrying the $30,000 average inventory is thus $3,000 + $2,000 + $500 + $1,000 = $6,500, and the annual percentage cost of carrying the inventory is $6,500/$30,000 = 0.217 = 21.7%.

Defining the annual percentage carrying cost as C, we can, in general, find the annual total carrying cost, TCC, as the percentage carrying cost (C) multiplied by the price per unit (P) times the average number of units (A):

$$\text{Total carrying cost} = \text{TCC} = (C)(P)(A) \qquad (23\text{--}4)$$

In our example,

$$TCC = (0.217)(\$2)(15,000) \approx \$6,500$$

23.5b Ordering Costs

Although we assume that carrying costs are entirely variable and rise in direct proportion to the average size of inventories, *ordering costs* are often fixed. For example, the costs of placing and receiving an order—interoffice memos, long-distance telephone calls, setting up a production run, and taking delivery—are essentially fixed regardless of the size of an order, so this part of inventory cost is simply the fixed cost of placing and receiving orders multiplied by the number of orders placed per year.[6] We define the fixed costs associated with ordering inventories as F, and if we place N orders per year then the total ordering cost is given by Equation 23-5:

(23–5)

$$\text{Total ordering cost} = \text{TOC} = (F)(N)$$

Here TOC = total ordering cost, F = fixed costs per order, and N = number of orders placed per year.

Equation 23-3 may be rewritten as N = S/2A and then substituted into Equation 23-5:

(23–6)

$$\text{Total ordering cost} = \text{TOC} = F\left(\frac{S}{2A}\right)$$

To illustrate the use of Equation 23-6, let F = \$100, S = 120,000 units, and A = 15,000 units. Then TOC, the total annual ordering cost, is \$400:

$$TOC = \$100\left(\frac{120,000}{30,000}\right) = \$100(4) = \$400$$

23.5c Total Inventory Costs

Total carrying cost, TCC, as defined in Equation 23-4, and total ordering cost, TOC, as defined in Equation 23-6, may be combined to find *total inventory costs,* TIC, as follows:

---

6. Note that, in reality, both carrying and ordering costs can have variable and fixed-cost elements—at least over certain ranges of average inventory. For example, security and utilities charges are probably fixed in the short run over a wide range of inventory levels. Similarly, labor costs in receiving inventory could be tied to the quantity received and hence could be variable. To simplify matters, we treat all carrying costs as variable and all ordering costs as fixed. However, if these assumptions do not fit the situation at hand, the cost definitions can be changed. For example, one could add another term for shipping costs if there are economies of scale in shipping such that the cost of shipping a unit is smaller if shipments are larger. However, in most situations shipping costs are not sensitive to order size, so total shipping costs are simply the shipping cost per unit times the units ordered (and sold) during the year. Under this condition, shipping costs are not influenced by inventory policy; hence they may be disregarded for purposes of determining the optimal inventory level and the optimal order size.

$$\text{Total inventory costs} = \text{TIC} = \text{TCC} + \text{TOC}$$

$$= (C)(P)(A) + F\left(\frac{S}{2A}\right) \tag{23-7}$$

Recognizing that the average inventory carried is A = Q/2, or one-half the size of each order quantity, Q, we may rewrite Equation 23-7 as

$$\text{TIC} = \text{TCC} + \text{TOC}$$

$$= (C)(P)\left(\frac{Q}{2}\right) + (F)\left(\frac{S}{Q}\right) \tag{23-8}$$

Here we see that total carrying cost equals average inventory in units, Q/2, multiplied by unit price, P, times the percentage annual carrying cost, C. Total ordering cost equals the number of orders placed per year, S/Q, multiplied by the fixed cost of placing and receiving an order, F. Finally, total inventory costs equal the sum of total carrying cost plus total ordering cost. We will use this equation in the next section to develop the optimal inventory ordering quantity.

23.5d Derivation of the EOQ Model

Figure 23-3 illustrates the basic premise on which the EOQ model is built—namely, that some costs rise with larger inventories while other costs decline and there is an optimal order size (and associated average inventory) that minimizes the total costs of inventories. First, as noted earlier, the average investment in inventories depends on how frequently orders are placed and the size of each order—if we fill orders every day, then average inventories will be much smaller than if we fill orders once a year. Further, as Figure 23-3 shows, the firm's carrying costs rise with larger orders; larger orders mean larger average inventories and so warehousing costs, interest on funds tied up in inventory, insurance, and obsolescence costs will all increase. However, ordering costs decline with larger orders and inventories; the cost of placing orders, suppliers' production setup costs, and order-handling costs will all decline if we order infrequently and consequently hold larger quantities.

If the carrying and ordering cost curves in Figure 23-3 are added, the sum represents total inventory costs, TIC. The point at which the TIC is minimized represents the Economic Ordering Quantity, and this, in turn, determines the optimal average inventory level.

The EOQ is found by differentiating Equation 23-8 with respect to ordering quantity, Q, and setting the derivative equal to zero:

$$\frac{d(\text{TIC})}{dQ} = \frac{(C)(P)}{2} - \frac{(F)(S)}{Q^2} = 0$$

Now, solving for Q, we obtain:

$$\frac{(C)(P)}{2} = \frac{(F)(S)}{Q^2}$$

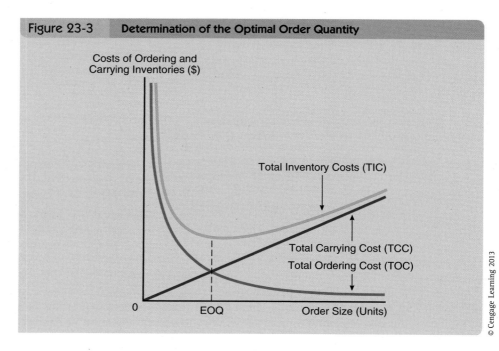

Figure 23-3   Determination of the Optimal Order Quantity

© Cengage Learning 2013

$$Q^2 = \frac{2(F)(S)}{(C)(P)}$$

(23–9)

$$Q = EOQ = \sqrt{\frac{2(F)(S)}{(C)(P)}}$$

Here:

EOQ = Economic Ordering Quantity—the optimal quantity to be ordered each time an order is placed.

F = Fixed costs of placing and receiving an order.

S = Annual sales in units.

C = Annual carrying costs expressed as a percentage of average inventory value.

P = Purchase price the firm must pay per unit of inventory.

Equation 23-9 is the EOQ model.[7] The assumptions of the model, which will be relaxed shortly, include the following: (1) sales can be forecasted perfectly, (2) sales are evenly distributed throughout the year, and (3) orders are received when expected.

---

7. The EOQ model can also be written as

$$EOQ = \sqrt{\frac{2(F)(S)}{C^*}}$$

where C* is the annual carrying cost per unit expressed in dollars.

23.5e EOQ Model Illustration

As an illustration of the EOQ model, consider the following data supplied by Cotton Tops Inc., a distributor of budget-priced, custom-designed T-shirts that it sells to concessionaires at various theme parks in the United States:

> S = Annual sales = 26,000 shirts per year.
>
> C = Percentage carrying cost = 25% of inventory value.
>
> P = Purchase price per shirt = \$4.92 per shirt. (The sales price is \$9, but this is irrelevant for our purposes here.)
>
> F = Fixed cost per order = \$1,000. Cotton Tops designs and distributes the shirts, but the actual production is done by another company. The bulk of this \$1,000 cost is the labor cost for setting up the equipment for the production run, which the manufacturer bills separately from the \$4.92 cost per shirt.

Substituting these data into Equation 23-9, we obtain an EOQ of 6,500 units:

$$EOQ = \sqrt{\frac{2(F)(S)}{(C)(P)}} = \sqrt{\frac{(2)(\$1,000)(26,000)}{(0.25)(\$4.92)}}$$
$$= \sqrt{42,276,423} \approx 6,500 \text{ units}$$

With an EOQ of 6,500 shirts and annual usage of 26,000 shirts, Cotton Tops will place 26,000/6,500 = 4 orders per year. Note that average inventory holdings depend directly on the EOQ. This relationship is illustrated graphically in Figure 23-4, where we see that average inventory = EOQ/2. Immediately after an order is received, 6,500 shirts are in stock. The usage rate, or sales rate, is 500 shirts per week (26,000/52 weeks), so inventories are drawn down by this amount each week. Thus, the actual number of units held in inventory will vary from 6,500 shirts just after an order is received to zero just before a new order arrives. With a 6,500 beginning balance, a zero ending balance, and a uniform sales rate, inventories will average one-half the EOQ, or 3,250 shirts, during the year. At a cost of \$4.92 per shirt, the average investment in inventories will be (3,250)(\$4.92) $\approx$ \$16,000. If inventories are financed by bank loans then the loan will vary from a high of \$32,000 to a low of \$0, but the average amount outstanding over the course of a year will be \$16,000.

Note that the EOQ, and hence the average inventory holdings, rises with the square root of sales. Therefore, a given increase in sales will result in a less-than-proportionate increase in inventories, so the inventory/sales ratio will tend to decline as a firm grows. For example, Cotton Tops's EOQ is 6,500 shirts at an annual sales level of 26,000, and the average inventory is 3,250 shirts, or \$16,000. However, if sales were to increase by 100% to 52,000 shirts per year, then the EOQ would rise only to 9,195 units or by 41%, and the average inventory would rise by this same percentage. This suggests there are economies of scale in holding inventories.[8]

---

8. Note, however, that these scale economies relate to each particular item, not to the entire firm. Thus, a large distributor with \$500 million of sales might have a higher inventory/sales ratio than a much smaller distributor if the small firm has only a few items with high sales volume and the large firm distributes a great many low-volume items.

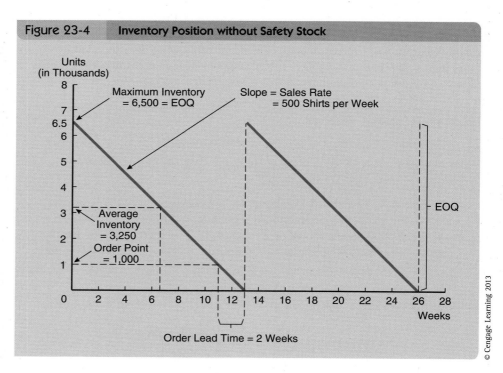

Figure 23-4 Inventory Position without Safety Stock

© Cengage Learning 2013

Finally, look at Cotton Tops's total inventory costs for the year, assuming that the EOQ is ordered each time. Using Equation 23-8, we find that total inventory costs are $8,000:

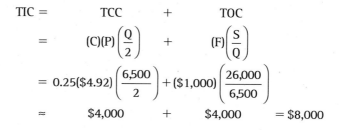

$$\text{TIC} = \text{TCC} + \text{TOC}$$
$$= (C)(P)\left(\frac{Q}{2}\right) + (F)\left(\frac{S}{Q}\right)$$
$$= 0.25(\$4.92)\left(\frac{6,500}{2}\right) + (\$1,000)\left(\frac{26,000}{6,500}\right)$$
$$\approx \$4,000 + \$4,000 = \$8,000$$

Note these two points: (1) The $8,000 total inventory cost represents the total of carrying costs and ordering costs, but this amount does *not* include the 26,000 ($4.92) = $127,920 annual purchasing cost of the inventory itself. (2) As we see both in Figure 23-3 and in the calculation above, at the EOQ, total carrying cost (TCC) equals total ordering cost (TOC). This property is not unique to our Cotton Tops illustration; it always holds.

23.5f Setting the Order Point

If a 2-week lead time is required for production and shipping, what is Cotton Tops's order point level? Cotton Tops sells 26,000/52 = 500 shirts per week. Thus, if a 2-week lag occurs between placing an order and receiving goods, Cotton Tops must place the order when there are 2(500) = 1,000 shirts on hand. During the 2-week production and shipping period, the inventory balance will continue to decline at the rate of 500 shirts per week, and the inventory balance will hit zero just as the order of new shirts arrives.

If Cotton Tops knew for certain that both the sales rate and the order lead time would never vary, then it could operate exactly as shown in Figure 23-4. However, sales do change, and production and/or shipping delays are sometimes encountered. To guard against these events, the firm must carry additional inventories, or safety stocks, as discussed in the next section.

23.6 EOQ Model Extensions

The basic EOQ model was derived under several restrictive assumptions. In this section we relax some of these assumptions and, in the process, extend the model to make it more useful.

23.6a The Concept of Safety Stocks

The concept of a **safety stock** is illustrated in Figure 23-5. First, note that the slope of the sales line measures the expected rate of sales. The company *expects* to sell 500 shirts per week, but let us assume that the maximum likely sales rate is twice this amount, or 1,000 units each week. Further, assume that Cotton Tops sets the safety stock at 1,000 shirts, so it initially orders 7,500 shirts, the EOQ of 6,500 plus the 1,000-unit safety stock. Subsequently, it reorders the EOQ whenever the inventory level falls to 2,000 shirts, the safety stock of 1,000 shirts plus the 1,000 shirts expected to be used while awaiting delivery of the order.

Note that the company could, over the 2-week delivery period, sell 1,000 units a week, or double its normal expected sales. This maximum rate of sales is shown by the steeper dashed line in Figure 23-5. The condition that makes this higher sales rate possible is the safety stock of 1,000 shirts.

The safety stock is also useful to guard against delays in receiving orders. The expected delivery time is 2 weeks, but with a 1,000-unit safety stock, the company could maintain sales at the expected rate of 500 units per week for an additional 2 weeks if something should delay an order.

However, carrying a safety stock has a cost. The average inventory is now EOQ/2 plus the safety stock, or $6,500/2 + 1,000 = 3,250 + 1,000 = 4,250$ shirts, and the average inventory value is now $(4,250)(\$4.92) = \$20,910$. This increase in average inventory causes an increase in annual inventory carrying costs equal to (Safety stock)(P)(C) = $1,000(\$4.92)(0.25) = \$1,230$.

The optimal safety stock varies from situation to situation, but in general it *increases* (1) with the uncertainty of demand forecasts, (2) with the costs (in terms

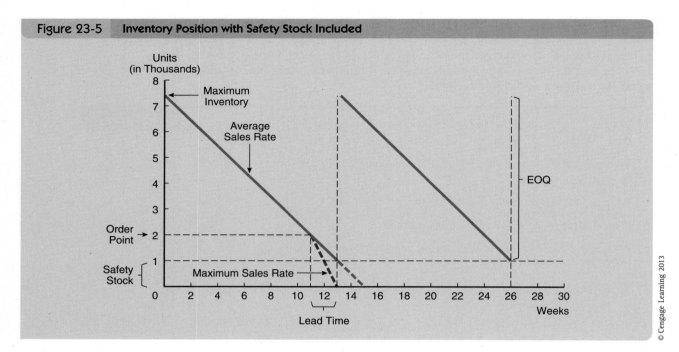

Figure 23-5   Inventory Position with Safety Stock Included

of lost sales and lost goodwill) that result from inventory shortages, and (3) with the probability that delays will occur in receiving shipments. The optimal safety stock *decreases* as the cost of carrying this additional inventory increases.

23.6b Setting the Safety Stock Level

The critical question with regard to safety stocks is this: How large should the safety stock be? To answer this question, first examine Table 23-1, which contains the probability distribution of Cotton Tops's unit sales for an average 2-week period, the time it takes to receive an order of 6,500 T-shirts. Note that the expected sales over an average 2-week period are 1,000 units. Why do we focus on a 2-week period? Because shortages can occur only during the 2 weeks it takes for an order to arrive.

Cotton Tops's managers have estimated that the annual carrying cost is 25% of inventory value. Because each shirt has an inventory value of $4.92, the annual carrying cost per unit is 0.25($4.92) = $1.23 and the carrying cost for each 13-week inventory period is $1.23(13/52) = $0.308 per unit. Even though shortages can occur only during the 2-week order period, safety stocks must be carried over the

TABLE 23-1	Two-Week Sales Probability Distribution
Probability	**Unit Sales**
0.1	0
0.2	500
0.4	1,000
0.2	1,500
0.1	2,000
1.0	Expected sales = 1,000

full 13-week inventory cycle. Next, Cotton Tops's managers must estimate the cost of shortages. Assume that when shortages occur, 50% of Cotton Tops's buyers are willing to accept back orders but 50% of its potential customers simply cancel their orders. Remember that each shirt sells for $9.00, so each one-unit shortage produces expected lost profits of 0.5($9.00 − $4.92) = $2.04. With this information, the firm can calculate the expected costs of different safety stock levels. This is done in Table 23-2.

For each safety stock level, we determine the expected cost of a shortage based on the sales probability distribution in Table 23-1. There is an expected shortage cost of $408 if no safety stock is carried; $102 if the safety stock is set at 500 units; and no expected shortage, hence no shortage cost, with a safety stock of 1,000 units. The cost of carrying each safety level is merely the cost of carrying a unit of inventory over the 13-week inventory period, $0.308, multiplied by the safety stock; for example, the cost of carrying a safety stock of 500 units is $0.308(500) = $154. Finally, we sum the expected shortage cost in Column 6 and the safety stock carrying cost in Column 7 to obtain the total cost figures given in Column 8. Because the 500-unit safety stock has the lowest expected total cost, Cotton Tops should carry this safety level.

Of course, the optimal safety level is highly sensitive to the estimates of the sales probability distribution and shortage costs. Errors here could result in incorrect

TABLE 23-2   Safety Stock Analysis

Safety Stock (1)	Sales During 2-Week Delivery Period (2)	Probability (3)	Shortage[a] (4)	Shortage Cost (Lost Profits): $2.04 × (4) = (5)	Expected Shortage Cost: (3) × (5) = (6)	Safety Stock Carrying Cost: $0.308 × (1) = (7)	Expected Total Cost: (6) + (7) = (8)
0	0	0.1	0	$ 0	$ 0		
	500	0.2	0	0	0		
	1,000	0.4	0	0	0		
	1,500	0.2	500	1,020	204		
	2,000	0.1	1,000	$2,040	204		
		1.0		Expected shortage cost = $408		$ 0	$408
500	0	0.1	0	$ 0	$ 0		
	500	0.2	0	0	0		
	1,000	0.4	0	0	0		
	1,500	0.2	0	0	0		
	2,000	0.1	500	1,020	102		
		1.0		Expected shortage cost = $102		$154	$256
1,000	0	0.1	0	$ 0	$ 0		
	500	0.2	0	0	0		
	1,000	0.4	0	0	0		
	1,500	0.2	0	0	0		
	2,000	0.1	0	0	0		
		1.0		Expected shortage cost = $ 0		$308	$308

[a]Shortage = Actual sales − (1,000 Stock at order point − Safety stock); positive values only.

safety stock levels. Note also that, in calculating the shortage cost of $2.04 per unit, we implicitly assumed that a lost sale in one period would not result in lost sales in future periods. If shortages cause customer ill will, the result could be permanent sales reductions. Then the situation would be much more serious, stock-out costs would be far higher, and the firm should consequently carry a larger safety stock.

The stock-out example is just one example of the many judgments required in inventory management—the mechanics are relatively simple, but the inputs are judgmental and difficult to obtain.

23.6c Quantity Discounts

Now suppose the T-shirt manufacturer offered Cotton Tops a **quantity discount** of 2% on large orders. If the quantity discount applied to orders of 5,000 or more, then Cotton Tops would continue to place the EOQ order of 6,500 shirts and take the quantity discount. However, if the quantity discount required orders of 10,000 or more, then Cotton Tops would have to compare the savings in purchase price that would result if its ordering quantity were increased to 10,000 units with the increase in total inventory costs caused by deviating from the 6,500-unit EOQ.

First, consider the total costs associated with Cotton Tops's EOQ of 6,500 units. We found earlier that total inventory costs are $8,000:

$$
\begin{aligned}
\text{TIC} &= \qquad \text{TCC} \qquad + \qquad \text{TOC} \\
&= \qquad (C)(P)\left(\frac{Q}{2}\right) \qquad + \qquad (F)\left(\frac{S}{Q}\right) \\
&= 0.25(\$4.92)\left(\frac{6{,}500}{2}\right) + (\$1{,}000)\left(\frac{26{,}000}{6{,}500}\right) \\
&\approx \qquad \$4{,}000 \qquad + \qquad \$4{,}000 \qquad = \$8{,}000
\end{aligned}
$$

Now, what would total inventory costs be if Cotton Tops ordered 10,000 units instead of 6,500? The answer is $8,625:

$$
\begin{aligned}
\text{TIC} &= 0.25(\$4.82)\left(\frac{10{,}000}{2}\right) + (\$1{,}000)\left(\frac{26{,}000}{10{,}000}\right) \\
&\approx \qquad \$6{,}025 \qquad + \qquad \$2{,}600 \qquad = \$8{,}625
\end{aligned}
$$

Note that when the discount is taken, the price, P, is reduced by the amount of the discount; the new price per unit would be 0.98($4.92) = $4.82. Also note that, when the ordering quantity is increased, carrying costs *increase* (because the firm is carrying a larger average inventory) but ordering costs *decrease* (because the number of orders per year decreases). If we were to calculate total inventory costs at an ordering quantity less than the EOQ—say, 5,000—then we would find carrying costs to be less than $4,000 and ordering costs to be more than $4,000; however, the total inventory costs would be more than $8,000 because they are at a minimum when only 6,500 units are ordered.[9]

Thus, inventory costs would increase by $8,625 − $8,000 = $625 if Cotton Tops were to increase its order size to 10,000 shirts. However, *this cost increase must be*

---

9. At an ordering quantity of 5,000 units, total inventory costs are $8,275:

$$
\text{TIC} = (0.25)(\$4.92)\left(\frac{5{,}000}{2}\right) + (\$1{,}000)\left(\frac{26{,}000}{5{,}000}\right)
$$
$$
= \$3{,}075 + \$5{,}200 = \$8{,}275
$$

compared with Cotton Tops's savings if it takes the discount. Taking the discount would save 0.02($4.92) = $0.0984 per unit. Over the year, Cotton Tops orders 26,000 shirts, so the annual savings is $0.0984(26,000) ≈ $2,558. Here is a summary:

Reduction in purchase price = 0.02($4.92)(26,000)	= $2,558
Increase in total inventory cost	= 625
Net savings from taking discounts	$1,933

Obviously, the company should order 10,000 units at a time and take advantage of the quantity discount.

23.6d Inflation

Moderate inflation—say, 3% per year—can largely be ignored for purposes of inventory management, but higher rates of inflation must be explicitly considered. If the rate of inflation in the types of goods the firm stocks tends to be relatively constant, then it can be dealt with quite easily: Simply deduct the expected annual rate of inflation from the carrying cost percentage, C, in Equation 23-9; then use this modified version of the EOQ model to establish the ordering quantity. The reason for making this deduction is that inflation causes the value of the inventory to rise, thus offsetting somewhat the effects of depreciation and other carrying costs. Now C will be smaller, assuming other factors are held constant, so the calculated EOQ and the average inventory will increase. However, higher rates of inflation usually mean higher interest rates, and this will cause C to increase, thus lowering the EOQ and average inventory.

On balance, there is no evidence that inflation either raises or lowers the optimal inventories of firms in the aggregate. Inflation should still be explicitly considered, however, for it will raise the individual firm's optimal holdings if the rate of inflation for its own inventories is above average (and is greater than the effects of inflation on interest rates), and vice versa.

23.6e Seasonal Demand

For most firms, it is unrealistic to assume that the demand for an inventory item is uniform throughout the year. What happens when there is seasonal demand, as would hold true for an ice cream company? Here the standard annual EOQ model is obviously not appropriate. However, it does provide a point of departure for setting inventory parameters, which are then modified to fit the particular seasonal pattern. We divide the year into the seasons in which annualized sales are relatively constant (e.g., summer, spring and fall, and winter); then the EOQ model is applied separately to each period. During the transitions between seasons, inventories would be either run down or else built up with special seasonal orders.

23.6f EOQ Range

Thus far, we have interpreted the EOQ and the resulting inventory values as single-point estimates. It can be easily demonstrated that small deviations from the EOQ do not appreciably affect total inventory costs and consequently that the optimal ordering quantity should be viewed more as a range than as a single value.[10]

---

10. This is somewhat analogous to the optimal capital structure in that small changes in capital structure around the optimum do not have much effect on the firm's weighted average cost of capital.

TABLE 23-3   EOQ Sensitivity Analysis

Ordering Quantity	Total Inventory Costs	Percentage Deviation from Optimal
3,000	$10,512	+31.4%
4,000	8,960	+12.0
5,000	8,275	+3.4
6,000	8,023	+0.3
6,500	8,000	0.0
7,000	8,019	+0.2
8,000	8,170	+2.1
9,000	8,423	+5.3
10,000	8,750	+9.1

© Cengage Learning 2013

To illustrate this point, we examine the sensitivity of total inventory costs to ordering quantity for Cotton Tops. Table 23-3 contains the results. We conclude that the ordering quantity could range from 5,000 to 8,000 units without affecting total inventory costs by more than 3.4%. Thus, managers can adjust the ordering quantity within a fairly wide range without significantly increasing total inventory costs.

Self Test

Why are safety stocks required?

Conceptually, how would you evaluate a quantity discount offer from a supplier?

What effect does inflation typically have on the EOQ?

Can the EOQ model be used when a company faces seasonal demand fluctuations?

What is the effect of minor deviations from the EOQ on total inventory costs?

Summary

This chapter discussed the goals of cash management and how a company might determine its optimal cash balance using the Baumol model. It also discussed how an optimal inventory policy might be identified using the Economic Ordering Quantity (EOQ) model. The key concepts covered are listed below.

- A policy that strives for **zero working capital** not only generates cash but also speeds up production and helps businesses operate more efficiently. This concept has its own definition of working capital: Inventories +

Receivables – Payables. The rationale is that inventories and receivables are the keys to making sales and that inventories can be financed by suppliers through accounts payable.

- The primary goal of cash management is to minimize the amount of cash a firm holds while maintaining a sufficient **target cash balance** to conduct business.

- The **Baumol model** provides insights into the optimal cash balance. The model balances the opportunity cost of holding cash against the transaction costs associated with obtaining cash either by selling marketable securities or by borrowing:

$$\text{Optimal cash infusion} = \sqrt{\frac{2(F)(T)}{r}}$$

- Firms generally set their target cash balances at the level that holds the risk of running out of cash to some acceptable level. **Monte Carlo simulation** can be helpful in setting the target cash balance.

- Firms use inventory control systems such as the **red-line method**, the **two-bin method**, and **computerized inventory control systems** to help them keep track of actual inventory levels and to ensure that inventory levels are adjusted as sales change. **Just-in-time (JIT) systems** are used to hold down inventory costs and, simultaneously, to improve the production process. **Outsourcing** is the practice of purchasing components rather than making them in-house.

- Inventory can be accounted for in four different ways: (1) **specific identification**, (2) **first-in, first-out (FIFO)**, (3) **last-in, first-out (LIFO)**, and (4) **weighted average**.

- **Inventory costs** can be divided into three parts: carrying costs, ordering costs, and stock-out costs. In general, **carrying costs** increase as the level of inventory rises, but **ordering costs** and **stock-out costs** decline with larger inventory holdings.

- **Total carrying cost (TCC)** is equal to the percentage cost of carrying inventory (C) multiplied by the purchase price per unit of inventory (P) times the average number of units held (A): TCC = (C)(P)(A).

- **Total ordering cost (TOC)** is equal to the fixed cost of placing an order (F) multiplied by the number of orders placed per year (N): TOC = (F)(N).

- **Total inventory costs (TIC)** equal total carrying cost (TCC) plus total ordering cost (TOC): TIC = TCC + TOC.

- The **Economic Ordering Quantity (EOQ) model** is a formula for determining the order quantity that will minimize total inventory costs:

$$\text{EOQ} = \sqrt{\frac{2(F)(S)}{(C)(P)}}$$

Here F is the fixed cost per order, S is annual sales in units, C is the percentage cost of carrying inventory, and P is the purchase price per unit.

- The **order point** is the inventory level at which new items must be ordered.

- **Safety stocks** are held to avoid shortages, which can occur if (1) sales increase more than was expected or (2) shipping delays are encountered on inventory ordered. The cost of carrying a safety stock, which is separate from that based on the EOQ model, is equal to the percentage cost of carrying inventory multiplied by the purchase price per unit times the number of units held as the safety stock.

Questions

23–1 Define each of the following terms:
   a. Baumol model
   b. Total carrying cost; total ordering cost; total inventory costs
   c. Economic Ordering Quantity (EOQ); EOQ model; EOQ range
   d. Reorder point; safety stock
   e. Red-line method; two-bin method; computerized inventory control system
   f. Just-in-time system; outsourcing

23–2 Indicate by a (+), (–), or (0) whether each of the following events would probably cause average annual inventory holdings to rise, fall, or be affected in an indeterminate manner:
   a. Our suppliers change from delivering by train to air freight. _____
   b. We change from producing just-in-time to meet seasonal demand to steady, year-round production. _____
   c. Competition in the markets in which we sell increases. _____
   d. The general rate of inflation rises. _____
   e. Interest rates rise; other things are constant. _____

23–3 Assuming the firm's sales volume remained constant, would you expect it to have a higher cash balance during a tight-money period or during an easy-money period? Why?

23–4 Explain how each of the following factors would probably affect a firm's target cash balance if all other factors were held constant.
   a. The firm institutes a new billing procedure that better synchronizes its cash inflows and outflows.
   b. The firm develops a new sales forecasting technique that improves its forecasts.
   c. The firm reduces its portfolio of U.S. Treasury bills.
   d. The firm arranges to use an overdraft system for its checking account.
   e. The firm borrows a large amount of money from its bank and also begins to write far more checks than it did in the past.
   f. Interest rates on Treasury bills rise from 5% to 10%.

Problems   Answers Appear in Appendix B

Intermediate Problems 1–2

23–1 Economic Ordering Quantity The Gentry Garden Center sells 90,000 bags of lawn fertilizer annually. The optimal safety stock (which is on hand initially) is 1,000 bags. Each bag costs the firm $1.50, inventory carrying costs are 20%, and the cost of placing an order with its supplier is $15.

a. What is the Economic Ordering Quantity?

b. What is the maximum inventory of fertilizer?

c. What will be the firm's average inventory?

d. How often must the company order?

23-2 **Optimal Cash Transfer** Barenbaum Industries projects that cash outlays of $4.5 million will occur uniformly throughout the year. Barenbaum plans to meet its cash requirements by periodically selling marketable securities from its portfolio. The firm's marketable securities are invested to earn 12%, and the cost per transaction of converting securities to cash is $27.

a. Use the Baumol model to determine the optimal transaction size for transfers from marketable securities to cash.

b. What will be Barenbaum's average cash balance?

c. How many transfers per year will be required?

d. What will be Barenbaum's total annual cost of maintaining cash balances? What would the total cost be if the company maintained an average cash balance of $50,000 or of $0 (it deposits funds daily to meet cash requirements)?

Spreadsheet Problem

23-3 **Build a Model: Inventory Management** Start with the partial model in the file *Ch23 P03 Build a Model.xls* on the textbook's Web site. The following inventory data have been established for the Adler Corporation.

(1) Orders must be placed in multiples of 100 units.

(2) Annual sales are 338,000 units.

(3) The purchase price per unit is $3.

(4) Carrying cost is 20% of the purchase price of goods.

(5) Cost per order placed is $24.

(6) Desired safety stock is 14,000 units; this amount is on hand initially.

(7) Two weeks are required for delivery.

a. What is the EOQ?

b. How many orders should the firm place each year?

c. At what inventory level should a reorder be made? *Hint:* Reorder point = (Safety stock + Weeks to deliver × Weekly usage) − Goods in transit.

d. Calculate the total costs of ordering and carrying inventories if the order quantity is (1) 4,000 units, (2) 4,800 units, or (3) 6,000 units. What are the total costs if the order quantity is the EOQ?

e. What are the EOQ and total inventory costs if the following were to occur?

(1) Sales increase to 500,000 units.

(2) Fixed order costs increase to $30; sales remain at 338,000 units.

(3) Purchase price increases to $4; sales and fixed costs remain at original values.

MINI CASE

Andria Mullins, financial manager of Webster Electronics, has been asked by the firm's CEO, Fred Weygandt, to evaluate the company's inventory control techniques and to lead a discussion of the subject with the senior executives. Andria plans to use as an example one of Webster's "big ticket" items, a customized computer microchip that the firm uses in its laptop computers. Each chip costs Webster $200, and it must also pay its supplier a $1,000 setup fee on each order; the minimum order size is 250 units. Webster's annual usage forecast is 5,000 units, and the annual carrying cost of this item is estimated to be 20% of the average inventory value.

Andria plans to begin her session with the senior executives by reviewing some basic inventory concepts, after which she will apply the EOQ model to Webster's microchip inventory. As her assistant, you have been asked to help her by answering the following questions:

a. Why is inventory management vital to the financial health of most firms?

b. What assumptions underlie the EOQ model?

c. Write out the formula for the total costs of carrying and ordering inventory, and then use the formula to derive the EOQ model.

d. What is the EOQ for custom microchips? What are total inventory costs if the EOQ is ordered?

e. What is Webster's added cost if it orders 400 units at a time rather than the EOQ quantity? What if it orders 600 units?

f. Suppose it takes 2 weeks for Webster's supplier to set up production, make and test the chips, and deliver them to Webster's plant. Assuming certainty in delivery times and usage, at what inventory level should Webster reorder? (Assume a 52-week year, and assume Webster orders the EOQ amount.)

g. Of course, there is uncertainty in Webster's usage rate as well as in delivery times, so the company must carry a safety stock to avoid running out of chips and having to halt production. If a 200-unit safety stock is carried, what effect would this have on total inventory costs? What is the new reorder point? What protection does the safety stock provide if usage increases or if delivery is delayed?

h. Now suppose Webster's supplier offers a discount of 1% on orders of 1,000 or more. Should Webster take the discount? Why or why not?

i. For many firms, inventory usage is not uniform throughout the year but instead follows some seasonal pattern. Can the EOQ model be used in this situation? If so, how?

j. How would these factors affect an EOQ analysis?

   (1) The use of just-in-time procedures.

   (2) The use of air freight for deliveries.

   (3) The use of a computerized inventory control system, in which an electronic system automatically reduced the inventory account as units were removed from stock and, when the order point was hit, automatically sent an electronic message to the supplier placing an order. The electronic system would ensure that inventory records are accurate and that orders are placed promptly.

   (4) The manufacturing plant is redesigned and automated. Computerized process equipment and state-of-the-art robotics are installed, making the plant highly flexible in the sense that the company can quickly switch from the production of one item to another at a minimum cost. This makes short production runs more feasible than under the old plant setup.

k. Webster runs a $100,000 per month cash deficit, requiring periodic transfers from its portfolio of marketable securities. Broker fees are $32 per transaction, and Webster earns 7% on its investment portfolio. How can Andria use the EOQ model to determine how Webster should liquidate part of its portfolio to provide cash?

Selected Additional Cases

The following cases from TextChoice, *Cengage Learning's online case library, cover many of the concepts discussed in this chapter and are available at* **www.textchoice2.com/casenet.**

Klein-Brigham Series:

Case 33, "Upscale Toddlers, Inc.," Case 34, "Texas Rose Company," Case 67, "Bridgewater Pool Company," and Case 79, "Mitchell Lumber Co.," all of which focus on receivables management.

PART VII

Special Topics

Chapter 24

Derivatives and Risk Management

© Nikada/iStockphoto.com

In this chapter, we discuss risk management, an important topic for financial managers. The term *risk management* can mean many things, but in business it involves identifying events that could have adverse financial consequences and then taking actions to prevent or minimize the damage caused by these events. Years ago, corporate risk managers dealt primarily with insurance—they made sure the firm was adequately insured against fire, theft, and other casualties and also that it had adequate liability coverage. More recently, the scope of risk management has been broadened to include controlling the costs of key inputs like petroleum by purchasing oil futures as well as protecting against changes in interest rates or exchange rates through transactions in the interest rate or foreign exchange markets. In addition, risk managers try to ensure that actions intended to hedge against risk are not actually increasing risks.

Also, since the September 11, 2001, attacks on the World Trade Center and the Pentagon, insurance against terrorist attacks has become a major issue. Unless possible terrorist targets—including large malls, office buildings, oil refineries, airlines, and ships—can be insured against attacks, lenders may refuse to provide mortgage financing, and that would crimp the economy. Private insurance companies are reluctant to insure these projects, at least without charging prohibitive premiums, so the federal government has been asked to step in and provide terrorist insurance.[1] However, losses due to terrorist attacks are potentially so large that they could bankrupt even strong insurance companies. Therefore, Congress passed the Terrorism Risk Insurance Act (TRIA) in 2002 and extended it in 2007 through 2014. Under the TRIA, the federal government and private insurers will share the cost of benefits paid on insured losses caused by terrorists.

---

1. Most insurance policies exclude claims that result from acts of war.

Beginning of Chapter Questions

As you read this chapter, consider how you would answer the following questions. You *should not* necessarily be able to answer the questions before you read the chapter. Rather, you should use them to get a sense of the issues covered in the chapter. After reading the chapter, you should be able to give at least partial answers to the questions, and you should be able to give better answers after the chapter has been discussed in class. Note, too, that it is often useful, when answering conceptual questions, to use hypothetical data to illustrate your answer. We illustrate the answers with an *Excel* model that is available on the textbook's Web site. Accessing the model and working through it is a useful exercise, and it provides insights that are useful when answering the questions.

1. What does it mean to "manage" **risks?** Should its stockholders want a firm to "manage" all the risks it faces?

2. What types of risks are **interest rate and exchange rate swaps** designed to mitigate? Why might one company prefer fixed-rate payments while another company prefers floating-rate payments, or payments in one currency versus another?

3. SafeCo can issue floating-rate debt at **LIBOR** + 1% or fixed-rate debt at 8%, but it would prefer to use fixed-rate debt. RiskyCo can issue floating-rate debt at LIBOR + 2% or fixed-rate debt at 8.8%, but it would prefer to use floating-rate debt. Explain why both companies might be better off if SafeCo issues floating-rate debt, RiskyCo issues fixed-rate debt, and they then swap payment streams. Assume that if they do arrange a swap, SafeCo will make a fixed payment of 6.9 percent to RiskyCo, and RiskyCo will make a payment of LIBOR (which is currently 6%) to SafeCo.

4. What is a **futures contract,** and how are futures used to manage risk? What are you protecting against if you buy Treasury futures contracts? What if you sell Treasury futures short?

5. Stohs Semiconductor Corporation plans to issue $50 million of 20-year bonds in 6 months. The interest rate would be 9% if the bonds were issued today. How can Stohs set up a hedge against an increase in interest rates over the next 6 months? Assume that 6-month futures sell for 100'22.

24.1 Reasons to Manage Risk

We know investors dislike risk. We also know that most investors hold well-diversified portfolios, so at least in theory the only "relevant risk" is systematic risk. Therefore, if you asked corporate executives what type of risk worries them most, you might expect their answer to be "beta." However, this is almost certainly not the answer you would get. If you asked a CEO to define risk, the most likely answer would be: "Risk is the possibility that our future earnings and free cash flows will be significantly lower than we expect." For example, consider Plastics Inc., which manufactures dashboards, interior door panels, and other plastic components used by auto companies. Petroleum is the key feedstock for plastic and thus makes up a large percentage of its costs. Plastics has a 3-year contract with an auto company to deliver 500,000 door panels each year at a price of $20 each. When the company recently signed this contract, oil sold for $100 per barrel and was expected to stay at that level for the next 3 years. If oil prices fell during this time, Plastics would have higher than expected profits and free cash flows, but if oil prices rose, profits would fall. Since Plastics's value depends on its profits and free cash flows, a change in the price of oil would cause stockholders to earn either more or less than they anticipated.

Now suppose that, shortly after signing the contract with its door panel supplier, Plastics announces that it plans to lock in a 3-year supply of oil at a guaranteed

CORPORATE VALUATION AND RISK MANAGEMENT

All companies are exposed to risk from volatility in product prices, demand, input costs, and other sources of business risk, such as the risk stemming from the choice of production technology. Many companies also are exposed to risk from volatility in exchange rates and interest rates. Risk management can reduce firm risk, preventing catastrophes and leading to a lower cost of capital. In some instances, derivatives such as swaps can actually reduce the effective interest rate paid by a corporation, again reducing its cost of capital.

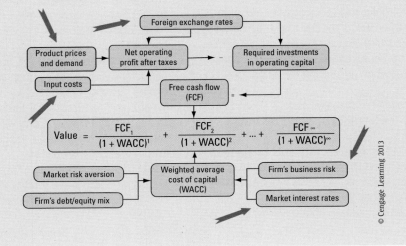

price of $100 per barrel *and* that the cost of this guarantee is zero. Would that cause its stock price to rise? At first glance, it seems that the answer should be "yes," but maybe that's not correct. Recall that the value of a stock depends on the present value of its expected future free cash flows, discounted at the weighted average cost of capital (WACC). Locking in the cost of oil will cause an increase in Plastics's stock price if and only if (1) it causes the expected future free cash flows to increase or (2) it causes the WACC to decline.

Consider first the free cash flows. Before the announcement of guaranteed oil costs, investors had formed an estimate of the expected future free cash flows based on an expected oil price of $100 per barrel. Locking in the cost of oil at $100 per barrel will lower the *risk* of the expected future free cash flows, but it might not change the expected *size* of these cash flows because investors already expected a price of $100 per barrel. Of course, smaller than expected cash flows can disrupt a firm's operation and that disruption can, in turn, adversely affect cash flows.

Now what about the WACC? It will change only if locking in the cost of oil causes a change either in the cost of debt or equity or in the target capital structure. If the foreseeable increases in the price of oil are not enough to increase the threat of bankruptcy, then Plastics's cost of debt should not change and neither should its target capital structure. Regarding the cost of equity, recall from Chapter 2 that most investors hold well-diversified portfolios, which means that the cost of equity should depend only on systematic risk. Moreover, even though an increase in oil prices would have a negative effect on Plastics's stock price, it would not have a negative effect on all stocks. Indeed, oil producers should have higher than expected returns and stock prices. Assuming that Plastics's investors hold well-diversified portfolios that include stocks of oil-producing companies, we should have little reason to expect its cost of equity to decrease. The bottom line is this: If Plastics's expected future cash flows and WACC will not change significantly as a consequence of eliminating the risk of oil price increases, then neither should the value of its stock.

We discuss futures contracts and hedging in detail in the next section, but for now let's assume that Plastics has *not* locked in oil prices. Therefore, if oil prices increase, its stock price will fall. However, if its stockholders know this, they can build portfolios that contain oil futures whose values will rise or fall with oil prices and thus offset changes in the price of Plastics's stock. By choosing the correct amount of futures contracts, investors can thus "hedge" their portfolios and completely eliminate the risk due to changes in oil prices. There will be a cost to hedging, but that cost to large investors should be about the same as the cost to Plastics. Since stockholders can hedge away oil price risk themselves, why should they pay a higher price for Plastics's stock just because the company itself hedged away that risk?

The previous points notwithstanding, companies clearly believe that active risk management is important. A 1998 survey reported that 83% of firms with market values greater than $1.2 billion engage in risk management.[2] A more recent 2005 survey of CFOs reported that 90% of the international and domestic firms responding considered risk in the planning process. The average of the estimates of the contribution that risk management made to the market value of the firm was 3.8%.[3] There are many reasons why companies manage their risks.

1. *Debt capacity.* Risk management can reduce the volatility of cash flows, which decreases the probability of bankruptcy. As we discussed in Chapter 15, firms with lower operating risks can use more debt, and this can lead to higher stock prices due to the interest tax savings.

2. *Maintaining the optimal capital budget over time.* Recall from Chapter 15 that firms are reluctant to raise external equity because of high flotation costs and market pressure. This means that the capital budget must generally be financed with a combination of debt and internally generated funds. In bad years, internal cash flows may be too low to support the optimal capital budget, causing firms to either slow investment below the optimal rate or else incur the high costs associated with external equity. By smoothing out the cash flows, risk management can alleviate this problem. This issue is most relevant for firms with large growth opportunities. A study by Professors Gerald Gay and Jouahn Nam found that such firms do in fact use derivatives more than low-growth firms.[4] Thus, maintaining an optimal capital budget is an important determinant of firms' risk management practices.

3. *Financial distress.* The stages of financial distress can range from stockholder concern and higher interest rates on debt to customer defections and bankruptcy. Any serious level of financial distress causes a firm to have lower cash

---

2. See Gordon M. Bodnar, Gregory S. Hayt, and Richard C. Marston, "1998 Wharton Survey of Financial Risk Management by U.S. Non-Financial Firms," *Financial Management,* Winter 1998, pp. 70–91.

3. See Henri Servaes, Ane Tamayo, and Peter Tufano, "The Theory and Practice of Corporate Risk Management," *Journal of Applied Corporate Finance,* Fall 2009, pp. 60–78.

4. See Gerald D. Gay and Jouahn Nam, "The Underinvestment Problem and Corporate Derivatives Use," *Financial Management,* Winter 1998, pp. 53–69.

flows than expected. Risk management can reduce the likelihood of low cash flows and hence of financial distress.

4. *Comparative advantages in hedging.* Most investors cannot hedge as efficiently as a company. First, firms generally incur lower transaction costs because of their larger volume of hedging activities. Second, there is the problem of asymmetric information: Managers know more about the firm's risk exposure than do outside investors, so managers can create more effective hedges. And third, effective risk management requires specialized skills and knowledge that firms are more likely to have.

5. *Borrowing costs.* As discussed later in the chapter, firms can sometimes reduce input costs—especially the interest rate on debt—through the use of derivative instruments called "swaps." Any such cost reduction adds value to the firm.

6. *Tax effects.* The present value of taxes paid by companies with volatile earnings is higher than the present value of taxes paid by stable companies; this is because of the treatment of tax credits and the rules governing corporate loss carryforwards and carrybacks. Moreover, if volatile earnings cause a company to declare bankruptcy, then the company usually completely loses its tax loss carryforwards. Therefore, using risk management to stabilize earnings can reduce the present value of a company's tax burden.

7. *Compensation systems.* Many compensation systems establish "floors" and "ceilings" on bonuses and also reward managers for meeting targets. To illustrate, suppose a firm's compensation system calls for a manager to receive no bonus if net income is below $1 million, a bonus of $10,000 if income is between $1 million and $2 million, or a bonus of $20,000 if income is $2 million or more. The manager will also receive an additional $10,000 if actual income is at least 90% of the forecasted level, which is $1 million. Now consider the following two situations. First, if income is stable at $2 million each year then the manager receives a $30,000 bonus each year, for a 2-year total of $60,000. However, if income is zero the first year and $4 million the second, the manager gets no bonus the first year and $30,000 the second, for a 2-year total of $30,000. So, even though the company has the same total income ($4 million) over the two years, the manager's bonus is higher if earnings are stable. Therefore, even if hedging does not add much value for stockholders, it may still benefit managers.

Perhaps the most important tool for risk management is the use of derivative securities. The next section explains **derivatives**, which are securities whose values are determined by the market price of some other asset. Derivatives include *options* (which we discussed in Chapter 6), whose values depend on the price of some underlying asset; *interest rate and exchange rate futures and swaps*, whose values depend on interest rate and exchange rate levels; and *commodity futures*, whose values depend on commodity prices.

Self Test

Explain why finance theory, combined with well-diversified investors and "homemade hedging," might suggest that risk management should not add much value to a company.

List and explain some reasons companies might employ risk management techniques.

24.2 Background on Derivatives

www

See the CME Group's Web site, **www.cmegroup.com**, for a wealth of information on the operation and history of the exchange.

A historical perspective helps in understanding derivatives. One of the first formal markets for derivatives was the futures market for wheat. Farmers were concerned about the price they would receive for their wheat when they sold it in the fall, and millers were concerned about the price they would have to pay. Each party soon realized that the risks they faced could be reduced if they established a price earlier in the year. Accordingly, mill agents began going out to the Wheat Belt with contracts that called for the farmers to deliver grain at a predetermined price, and both parties benefited from the transaction in the sense that their risks were reduced. The farmers could concentrate on growing their crop without worrying about the price of grain, and the millers could concentrate on their milling operations. Thus, *hedging with futures* lowered aggregate risk in the economy.

These early futures dealings were between two parties who arranged transactions between themselves. Soon, though, intermediaries came into the picture, and *trading* in futures was established. The Chicago Board of Trade, founded in 1848 and now a member of the CME Group, was an early marketplace where *futures dealers* helped make a market in futures contracts. Thus, farmers could sell futures on the exchange and millers could buy them there. This improved the efficiency and lowered the cost of hedging operations.

A third group, *speculators,* soon entered the scene. As we see in the next section, most derivatives—including futures—are highly leveraged, which means that a small change in the value of the underlying asset will produce a large change in the price of the derivative. This leverage appealed to speculators. At first blush, one might think that the appearance of speculators would increase risk, but this is not true. Speculators add capital and players to the market, which tends to stabilize the market. Of course, derivatives markets are inherently volatile because of the leverage involved; hence risk to the speculators themselves is high. Still, the speculators bear much of the risk, which makes the derivatives markets more stable for hedgers.

Natural hedges, defined as situations in which aggregate risk can be reduced by derivatives transactions between two parties (called *counterparties*), exist for many commodities, for foreign currencies, for interest rates on securities with different maturities, and even for common stocks where investors want to "hedge their bets." Natural hedges occur when futures are traded between cotton farmers and cotton mills, copper mines and copper fabricators, importers and foreign manufacturers for currency exchange rates, electric utilities and coal mines, and oil producers and oil users. In all such situations, hedging reduces aggregate risk and thus benefits the economy.

Hedging can also be done in situations in which no natural hedge exists. Here one party wants to reduce some type of risk, and another party agrees to write a contract that protects the first party from that specific event or situation. Insurance is an obvious example of this type of hedge. However, with these types of hedges, risks are generally *transferred* rather than *eliminated*. Even here, though, insurance companies can reduce certain types of risk through diversification.

The derivatives markets have grown more rapidly than any other major market in recent years for a number of reasons. First, analytical techniques such as the Black-Scholes Option Pricing Model (discussed in Chapter 6) have been developed to help establish "fair" prices, and having a good, transparent basis for pricing hedges makes the counterparties more comfortable with deals. Second, computers and electronic communications make it much easier for counterparties to deal with one another. Third, globalization has greatly increased the importance of currency markets and the need for reducing the exchange rate risks brought on by global trade. Recent trends and developments are sure to continue if not accelerate, so the use of derivatives for risk management is bound to grow.[5]

24.3 Derivatives in the News

Although derivatives are important tools for corporate risk management, they also have a potential downside. These instruments are highly leveraged, so small miscalculations can lead to huge losses. They are also complicated and misunderstood by most people. This makes mistakes more likely than with less complex instruments, which makes it harder for a firm's top management to understand and exercise proper control over derivatives transactions. This potential for miscalculation and misuse has led to highly publicized losses for some large and well-respected companies in the past several years. Procter & Gamble (P&G), Gibson Greetings, Metallgesellschaft, Barings Bank, Long Term Capital Management (LTCM), Enron, and Orange County, California, all experienced losses that were either attributed to or associated with inappropriate use of derivatives. In the Barings Bank case, one relatively low-level 28-year-old employee operating in the Far East entered into transactions that led to the bankruptcy of Britain's oldest bank, the institution that held the accounts of the Queen of England.

The widespread use (and misuse) of credit default swaps (CDS) was a major factor in the failures of financial institution such as AIG, Lehman Brothers, Merrill Lynch, and Bear Stearns in the global economic crisis that began in 2007. Following are more detailed explanations of Enron Corporation's failure and the role of derivatives in the global economic crisis.

24.3a Enron and Other Energy Traders

Most segments of the electric power industry were deregulated during the 1990s. Previously, all power users were required to buy from their local utility, but after deregulation large users, which account for about 65% of electricity usage, could buy from other suppliers. Independent power producers then built plants and began competing with the older utilities. Power users could buy electricity on the "spot" market at prices that fluctuated depending on supply and demand, or they could contract with independent producers to buy at a fixed price for delivery in the future. Thus, the electricity market was transformed from a regulated monopoly into a competitive market that was something akin to the wheat market, where farmers worked with grain merchants to deliver wheat to milling companies.

However, there is a major difference between wheat and electricity—wheat can be stored efficiently, and stored wheat mitigates the effects of fluctuations in supply

---

5. For more information on the derivatives markets, see Don M. Chance and Robert Brooks, *An Introduction to Derivatives and Risk Management, 8th Edition* (Mason, OH: South-Western, Cengage Learning, 2010); and Alger B. "Duke" Chapman, "Future of the Derivatives Markets: Products, Technology, and Participants," *Financial Practice and Education*, Fall/Winter 1994, pp. 124–128.

and demand on prices. Electricity cannot be stored, so supply and demand fluctuations result in wide price swings, which disrupt both users and producers. It did not take long for users and producers to realize that all parties would benefit by hedging with long-term supply contracts at fixed prices. Users would have an assured supply at a known price, and producers would have a guaranteed market for their power. Thus, hedging would help all parties, just as it helped wheat farmers and millers.

Enron Corporation was one of the first companies to get into the electricity trading business. Enron owned a few generating plants, but it operated primarily as a marketer, buying from merchant generators and reselling to large users. Enron would sign a multiyear contract to supply specific amounts of electricity at a fixed price to a customer such as General Motors. For example, it might agree to build a new plant, expecting to produce power at a cost of 3 cents per kilowatt-hour (kWh) and simultaneously contract to sell the plant's output at 3.1¢/kWh. The 0.1¢/kWh margin would cover administrative costs and provide a "normal" profit. Under those conditions, the PV of the expected revenues would be about equal to the PV of the expected costs, so the NPV of the new plant would be slightly above zero.[6]

Now suppose conditions changed so that the cost of producing power fell below 3.0¢/kWh—say, to 2 cents—but the price remained at 3.1 cents. In that case, the expected cash flows from the new plant would rise, causing the contract's net present value to increase. Enron would report the increase in the contract's value as profit and add it to operating income. The higher profit would then boost the stock price and trigger executive bonuses.

Such a development would be legal, but Enron cheated. Its executives wanted to report higher profits in order to trigger bonuses and more stock options, so it inflated its profits by forecasting unreasonably high sales prices, unreasonably low purchase costs, and thus unreasonably high profits. It also downplayed the risk inherent in the contracts and discounted the overstated cash flows at unreasonably low discount rates. All of this should have been caught by its auditor, Arthur Andersen, but Andersen let Enron get away with it, resulting in reported profits that were far too high.

Note, too, that California environmentalists had for years prevented the construction of new plants. The growing demand for power caught up with a fixed supply in 2000, and a shortage resulted. This led to huge price spikes and enormous profits for generators and traders such as Enron. California then relaxed its restrictions on construction, and Enron's wonderful reported profits attracted other companies into considering construction of new plants and getting into the energy trading business. Some made careful forecasts and concluded that something was fishy because their forecasts did not produce results anywhere close to those reported by Enron. These companies wisely avoided the new market. However, others decided that if Enron could do it, so could they, and they charged ahead with new plant construction, financed primarily with debt.

When all the new capacity came online, it greatly exceeded demand. This led to huge price declines, and the builders of new plants found themselves in trouble. A new plant might have cost $100 million and shown an NPV of $10 million based on output prices when construction began. However, when the new plant came online the new low prices might have led to an actual NPV of *negative* $50 million. Similarly, a trading company that had contracted to buy power for a long period at,

---

6. Similarly, Enron might sign a long-term contract to buy electricity at 3¢/kWh, expecting to sell it on the spot market at 3.1 cents. The initial NPV of the contract would be close to zero. However, if demand for power rose sharply, then the spot price would rise above 3.1 cents, the expected cash flows would rise, and the contract's NPV would also rise.

say, 4¢/kWh, expecting to sell it in the spot market for 5 cents, might have found that it could only sell the power for 3 cents; this would also result in a *negative* NPV for the contract. Those results had to be reflected in the financial statements, so there were massive reported losses and huge write-downs, which lowered stockholder equity on the balance sheets. This, in turn, raised the companies' debt ratios, lowered their coverage ratios, and generally reduced their financial strength.

No one wants to sign a long-term contract with a party that might default if things go badly, so energy traders must have letters of credit that assure counterparties that they can make good on their contracts. They are required to maintain their financial ratios at specified levels, and if the covenants are violated then they must put up additional collateral. Many could not do so, and that led to bankruptcies, including Enron's in late 2001.

Some old-line utilities also built merchant plants and thus got into trouble. Examples include Duke Power and TECO Energy, both of which saw their stock prices decline by 50% or more in 2002. Southern Company, like several other utilities, put its merchant plants and trading business into a separate subsidiary (Mirant Corporation) and then spun it off to Southern's stockholders. That spin-off insulated Southern from the debacle, so its stock price dropped by only 12% during 2002, about the same as the general market. However, Mirant itself experienced a huge drop after the Enron troubles hit in 2001, falling from $47.20 to $1.90. If Southern had retained Mirant, it probably would have experienced a decline similar to that of TECO and Duke.

24.3b The Credit Crisis and Mortgage-Backed Securities

The years 2007 and 2008 saw the meltdown of U.S. and international credit markets. Banks cut back on lending, and consumers and businesses cut back on spending, slowing the economy. The driving force behind this meltdown was the bursting of the U.S. housing market bubble that had developed over the previous decade. Mortgage-backed securities (discussed in more detail later in this chapter) played a significant role in this crisis because, as housing prices declined, homeowners who wanted to move or refinance were unable to do so. This bumped up the default rate on the home mortgages on which the mortgage-backed securities were based, causing their values to plummet. Banks had invested huge amounts in these securities, and as the securities tanked the banks' equity positions declined, forcing them to scale back on their lending. This further limited the supply of funds for new mortgages, further depressing home prices.

As discussed in Chapter 1, purchasers of mortgage-backed securities (MBS) also often bought credit default swaps in which a counterparty promised to pay the purchaser if the debt defaulted. However, the counterparties, such as AIG and Lehman Brothers, failed to hedge their own risk. Thus, when mortgage-backed securities began defaulting, many of the counterparties went bankrupt. And because the "insurance" bought by the MBS purchasers didn't pay up, many MBS purchasers themselves went bankrupt.

Financial institutions' losses and failures rippled throughout the global economy and were major contributors to the global economic crisis of 2007.

24.3c Are Derivatives Too Dangerous?

Scandals and widespread failures—such as those at Enron, AIG, and Lehman Brothers—make the headlines, causing some people to argue that derivatives should be regulated out of existence to "protect the public." However, derivatives are used far more often to hedge risks than to speculate, and these beneficial hedging transactions never make the headlines. The horror stories point out the need for (1) top managers to exercise control over the personnel who deal with derivatives; (2) more transparent information about the details and obligations of derivative contracts; (3) better information about the creditworthiness of the counterparties; and (4) additional regulation of the amount of capital that financial institutions are required to set aside when they purchase risky assets. In our opinion, however, the disasters do not justify the elimination of derivatives.

In the balance of this chapter, we discuss how firms can manage risks and how derivatives are used in risk management.

Describe some examples of the misuse of derivatives.	**Self Test**

24.4 Other Types of Derivatives

We discussed put and call options in Chapter 6. They represent an important class of derivative securities, but there are many other types of derivatives, including forward contracts, futures, swaps, structured notes, inverse floaters, and a host of other "exotic" contracts.

24.4a Forward Contracts versus Futures Contracts

Forward contracts are agreements in which one party agrees to buy a commodity at a specific price on a specific future date and the other party agrees to sell the product. *Goods are actually delivered under forward contracts.* Unless both parties are morally and financially strong, there is a danger that one party will default on the contract, especially if the price of the commodity changes markedly after the agreement is reached.

A **futures contract** is similar to a forward contract, but with three key differences: (1) Futures contracts are marked-to-market on a daily basis, meaning that gains and losses are noted and money must be put up to cover losses. This greatly reduces the risk of default that exists with forward contracts. (2) With futures, physical delivery of the underlying asset is virtually never taken—the two parties simply settle up with cash for the difference between the contracted price and the actual price on the expiration date. (3) Futures contracts are generally standardized instruments that are traded on exchanges, whereas forward contracts are usually tailor-made, negotiated between two parties, and not traded after they have been signed.

Futures and forward contracts were originally used for commodities such as wheat; farmers would sell forward contracts to millers, enabling both parties to lock in prices and thus reduce their risk exposure. Commodities contracts are still important, but today more trading is done in foreign exchange and interest rate futures. To illustrate how foreign exchange contracts are used, suppose GE arranges to buy electric motors from a European manufacturer on terms that call for GE to pay 10 million euros in 180 days. GE would not want to give up the free trade credit, but if the euro appreciated against the dollar during the next 6 months then the dollar cost of the 10 million euros would rise. GE could hedge the transaction by buying a forward contract under which it agreed to buy the 10 million euros in 180 days at a fixed dollar price, which would lock in the dollar cost of the motors. This transaction would probably be conducted through a money center bank, which would try to find a European company (a "counterparty") that needed dollars in 6 months. Alternatively, GE could buy a futures contract on an exchange. Foreign exchange forward contracts such as these are discussed in more detail in Chapter 27.

Interest rate futures represent another huge and growing market. For example, suppose Simonset Corporation decides to build a new plant at a cost of $200 million. It plans to finance the project with 20-year bonds that would carry an 8% interest rate if they were issued today. However, the company will not need the money for about 6 months. Simonset could go ahead and sell 20-year bonds now, locking in the 8% rate, but it would have the money (and would have to pay interest on the money) before it was needed, so it would have to invest in short-term securities that would yield less than 8%. However, if Simonset waits 6 months to sell the bond issue then interest rates might be higher than they are today, in which case the value of the plant would be reduced—perhaps to the point of making it unprofitable.

One solution to Simonset's dilemma involves *interest rate futures,* which are based on a hypothetical 20-year Treasury bond with a 6% semiannual coupon. If interest rates in the economy go up, the value of the hypothetical T-bond will go down, and vice versa. In our example, Simonset is worried about an increase in interest rates. Should rates rise, the hypothetical Treasury bond's value would decline. Therefore, Simonset could sell T-bond futures for delivery in 6 months to hedge its position. If interest rates rise, Simonset will have to pay a higher interest rate when it issues its own bonds. However, it will make a profit on its futures position because it will have presold the bonds at a higher price than it will have to pay to cover (repurchase) them. Of course, if interest rates decline then Simonset will lose on its futures position, but this will be offset by the lower interest rate paid when it issues its bonds.

Our examples show that forward contracts and futures can be used to hedge, or reduce, risks. It has been estimated that more than 95% of all such transactions are indeed designed as hedges, with banks and futures dealers serving as intermediaries between hedging counterparties. Interest rate and exchange rate futures can, of course, be used for speculative as well as hedging purposes. A hedger can buy a T-bond contract on $100,000 of bonds with only $2,700 collateral (this is called the **margin** or the **performance bond**). With such small initial investments, even a minor change in interest rates will result in a very large gain or loss. Still, the primary motivation behind the vast majority of these transactions is to hedge risks, not to create them.

www

For current margin requirements, go to **www.cmegroup.com**, and select Performance Bond/Margins under the Featured Links section. The T-bond futures contract is Product Code 17.

24.4b Swaps

A **swap** is just what the name implies—two parties agree to swap something, generally obligations to make specified payment streams. Most swaps today involve either interest payments or currencies, but just about anything can be swapped, including equity swaps, credit spread swaps, and commodity swaps.[7] To illustrate an interest rate swap, suppose that Company S has a 20-year, $100 million floating-rate bond outstanding and that Company F has a $100 million, 20-year, fixed-rate issue outstanding. Thus, each company has an obligation to make a stream of interest payments, but one payment stream is fixed while the other will vary as interest rates change in the future. This situation is shown in the top part of Figure 24-1.

---

7. In an equity swap, the cash flow based on an equity index is swapped for some other cash flow. In a commodity swap, the swapped cash flow is based on commodity prices. In a credit swap, the cash flow usually is based on the spread between a risky bond and a U.S. Treasury bond.

Figure 24-1	Cash Flows under a Swap

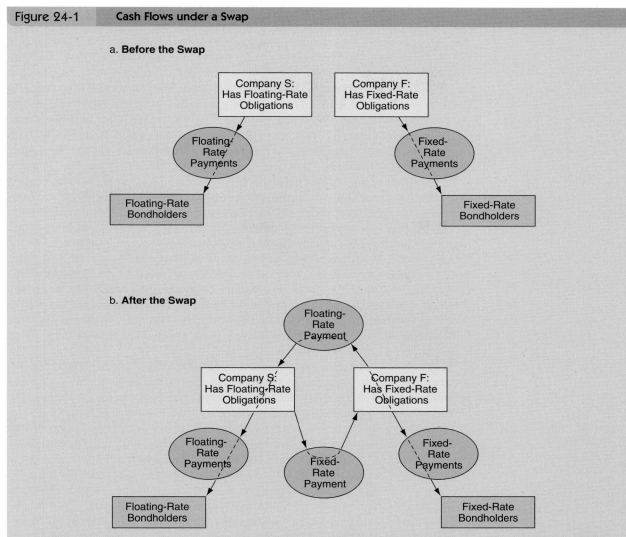

a. **Before the Swap**

b. **After the Swap**

Note: In Panel a, Company S must make floating-rate payments out of its own internal cash flows; but in Panel b, it uses the floating payments from Company F to pay its bondholders. Company F has a reversed position. After the swap, S has de facto fixed payments, which are consistent with its stable internal flows, and F has floating payments, which are consistent with its fluctuating flows.

Now suppose that Company S has stable cash flows and wants to lock in its cost of debt. Company F has cash flows that fluctuate with the economy, rising when the economy is strong and falling when it is weak. Recognizing that interest rates also move up and down with the economy, Company F has concluded it would be better off with variable-rate debt. If the companies swapped their payment obligations, an *interest rate swap* would occur. The bottom half of Figure 24-1 shows that the net cash flows for Company S are at a fixed rate and those for Company F are based on a floating rate. Company S would now have to make fixed payments, which are consistent with its stable cash inflows, and Company F would have a floating obligation, which for it is less risky.

Our example illustrates how swaps can reduce risks by allowing each company to match the variability of its interest payments with that of its cash flows. However, there are also situations in which swaps can reduce both the riskiness and the effective cost of debt. For example, Antron Corporation, which has a high credit rating, can issue either floating-rate debt at LIBOR + 1% or fixed-rate debt at 10%.[8] Bosworth Industries is less creditworthy, so its cost for floating-rate debt is LIBOR + 1.5% and its fixed-rate cost is 10.4%. Owing to the nature of Antron's operations, its CFO has decided that the firm would be better off with fixed-rate debt; meanwhile, Bosworth's CFO prefers floating-rate debt. Paradoxically, both firms can benefit by issuing the type of debt they do not want and then swapping their payment obligations.

First, each company will issue an identical amount of debt, which is called the **notional principal**. Even though Antron wants fixed-rate debt, it issues floating-rate debt at LIBOR + 1%, and Bosworth issues fixed-rate debt at 10.4%. Next, the two companies enter into an interest rate swap.[9] Assume the debt maturities are 5 years, which means the length of this swap will also be 5 years. By convention, the floating-rate payments of most swaps are based on LIBOR, with the fixed rate adjusted upward or downward to reflect credit risk and the term structure. The riskier the company that will receive the floating-rate payments, the higher the fixed-rate payment it must make. In our example, Antron will be receiving floating-rate payments from Bosworth, and those payments will be set at LIBOR multiplied by the notional principal. Then, payments will be adjusted every 6 months to reflect changes in the LIBOR rate.

The fixed payment that Antron must make to Bosworth is set (that is, "fixed") for the duration of the swap at the time the contract is signed, and it depends primarily on two factors: (1) the level of fixed interest rates at the time of the agreement and (2) the relative creditworthiness of the two companies.

In our example, assume interest rates and creditworthiness are such that 8.95% is the appropriate fixed swap rate for Antron, so it will make 8.95% fixed-rate payments to Bosworth. In turn, Bosworth will pay the LIBOR rate to Antron. Table 24-1 shows the net rates paid by each participant, and Figure 24-2 graphs the flows. Note that Antron ends up making fixed payments, which it desires, but because of the swap the rate paid is 9.95% versus the 10% rate it would have paid had it issued fixed-rate debt directly. At the same time, the swap leaves

TABLE 24-1	Anatomy of an Interest Rate Swap		
Antron's Payments: Borrows Floating, Swaps for Fixed		**Bosworth's Payments: Borrows Fixed, Swaps for Floating**	
Payment to lender	− (LIBOR + 1%)	Payment to lender	− 10.40% fixed
Payment from Bosworth	+ LIBOR	Payment from Antron	+ 8.95% fixed
Payment to Bosworth	− 8.95% fixed	Payment to Antron	− LIBOR
Net payment by Antron	− 9.95% fixed	Net payment by Bosworth	− (LIBOR + 1.45%)

© Cengage Learning 2013

8. LIBOR stands for the London Interbank Offered Rate, the rate charged on interbank dollar loans in the Eurodollar market.
9. Actually, such transactions are generally arranged by large money center banks, and payments are made to the bank, which in turn pays the interest on the original loans. The bank assumes the credit risk and guarantees the payments should one of the parties default. For its services, the bank receives a percentage of the payments as its fee.

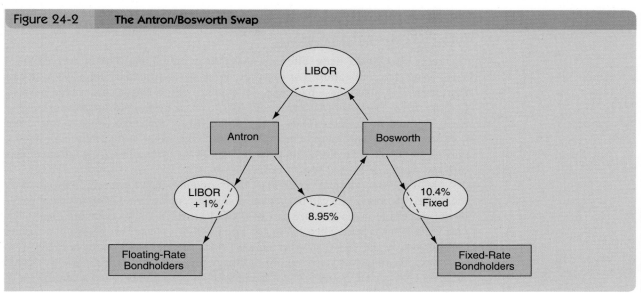

Figure 24-2   The Antron/Bosworth Swap

Bosworth with floating-rate debt, which it wants, but at a rate of LIBOR + 1.45% versus the LIBOR + 1.50% it would have paid on directly issued floating-rate debt. As this example illustrates, swaps can sometimes lower the interest rate paid by each party.

Currency swaps are similar to interest rate swaps. To illustrate, suppose Company A, an American firm, had issued $100 million of dollar-denominated bonds in the United States to fund an investment in Germany. Meanwhile, Company G, a German firm, had issued $100 million of euro-denominated bonds in Germany to make an investment in the United States. Company A would earn euros but be required to make payments in dollars, and Company G would be in the opposite situation. Thus, both companies would be exposed to exchange rate risk. However, both companies' risks would be eliminated if they swapped payment obligations.

Originally, swaps were arranged between companies by money center banks, which would match up counterparties. Such matching still occurs, but today most swaps are between companies and banks, with the banks then taking steps to ensure that their own risks are hedged. For example, Citibank might arrange a swap with Company A. Company A would agree to make specified payments in euros to Citibank, while Citibank made dollar payments to Company A. Citibank would charge a fee for setting up the swap, and these charges would reflect the creditworthiness of Company A. To protect itself against exchange rate movements, the bank would hedge its position, either by lining up a European company that needed to make dollar payments or else by using currency futures.[10]

---

10. For more information on swaps, see Keith C. Brown and Donald J. Smith, "Default Risk and Innovations in the Design of Interest Rate Swaps," *Financial Management,* Summer 1993, pp. 94–105; Robert Einzig and Bruce Lange, "Swaps at Transamerica: Applications and Analysis," *Journal of Applied Corporate Finance,* Winter 1990, pp. 48–58; John F. Marshall, Vipul K. Bansal, Anthony F. Herbst, and Alan L. Tucker, "Hedging Business Cycle Risk with Macro Swaps and Options," *Journal of Applied Corporate Finance,* Winter 1992, pp. 103–108; and Laurie S. Goodman, "The Uses of Interest Rate Swaps in Managing Corporate Liabilities," *Journal of Applied Corporate Finance,* Winter 1990, pp. 35–47.

24.4c Structured Notes and Collateralized Mortgage Obligations

The term **structured note** often means a debt obligation that is derived from some other debt obligation. For example, Wall Street firms buy large packages of mortgages and place these packages, or "pools," with a trustee. Then bonds called *Collateralized Mortgage Obligations (CMOs),* backed by the mortgage pool held in trust, are sold to pension funds, hedge funds, university endowments, and other investors who are willing to invest in CMOs but who would not purchase individual mortgages. There is an entire industry devoted to creating and selling various types of these *mortgage-backed securities (MBS).*

CMOs are more difficult to evaluate than straight bonds for several reasons. First, the underlying mortgages can be prepaid at any time, and when this occurs the prepayment proceeds are used to retire part of the CMO security itself. Therefore, the holder of a CMO is never sure when his or her bond will be called. This situation is further complicated by the fact that, when interest rates decline, bond prices normally rise. However, declining rates also lead to mortgage prepayments, which cause the CMOs to be called especially rapidly, and it is not good to have bonds called when the funds must be reinvested at a lower rate. And as we learned in 2007 and 2008 during the global economic crisis, default risk can be very high for mortgage-backed securities.

It should also be noted that a variety of structured notes can be created, ranging from notes whose cash flows can be predicted with virtual certainty to other notes whose payment streams are highly uncertain. For example, investment bankers can (and do) create notes called *IOs* (for *Interest Only*), which provide cash flows from the interest component of the mortgage amortization payments, and *POs* (for *Principal Only*), which are paid from the principal repayment stream. In each case, the value of the note is found as the present value of an expected payment stream, but the length and size of the stream are uncertain. Suppose, for example, you are offered an IO that you expect to provide payments of $100 for 10 years (you expect the mortgages to be refinanced after 10 years, at which time your payments will cease). Suppose further that you discount the expected payment stream at a rate of 10% and determine the value is $614.46. You have $614.46 to invest, so you buy the IO, expecting to earn 10% on your money.

Now suppose interest rates decline. If rates fall, the discount rate would drop, and that would normally imply an increase in the IO's value. However, if rates decline sharply, this would lead to a rash of mortgage refinancings, in which case your payments, which come from interest only, would cease (or be greatly reduced), and the value of your IO would fall sharply. On the other hand, a sharp increase in interest rates would reduce refinancing, lengthen your expected payment stream, and probably increase the value of your IO.

Investment bankers can slice and dice a pool of mortgages into a bewildering array of structured notes, ranging from "plain vanilla" ones with highly predictable cash flows to "exotic" ones (sometimes called "toxic waste") whose risks are almost incalculable but are surely large.

Securitizing mortgages through CMOs serves a useful economic function—it provides an investment outlet for pension funds and others with money to invest, and it makes more money available to homeowners at a reasonable cost. Also, some investors want relatively safe investments, while others are willing to buy more speculative securities for the higher expected returns they provide. Structured notes permit a partitioning of risks to give investors what they want. There are dangers, though, as the global economic crisis demonstrated, in which "toxic waste" led to numerous bankruptcies and contributed to a global recession.

24.4d Inverse Floaters

A floating-rate note has an interest rate that rises and falls with some interest rate index. For example, if the prime rate were currently 8.5%, then the interest rate on a $100,000 note at prime plus 1% would be 9.5% and the note's rate would move up and down with the prime rate. Because both the cash flows associated with the note and the discount rate used to value it would rise and fall together, the market value of the note would be relatively stable.

With an **inverse floater,** the rate paid on the note moves *counter* to market rates. Thus, if interest rates in the economy rise, the interest rate paid on an inverse floater will fall, reducing its cash interest payments. At the same time, the discount rate used to value the inverse floater's cash flows will rise along with other rates. The combined effect of lower cash flows and a higher discount rate would lead to a large decline in the value of the inverse floater. Thus, inverse floaters are exceptionally vulnerable to increases in interest rates. Of course, if interest rates fall then the value of an inverse floater will soar.

Could an inverse floater be used for hedging purposes? The answer is "yes, perhaps quite effectively." These securities have a magnified effect, so not many are required to hedge a given position. However, because they are so volatile, they could make what is supposed to be a hedged position actually quite risky.

We have discussed the most important types of derivative securities, but certainly not all types. Even so, this discussion should give you a good idea of how and why derivatives are created and how they can be used and misused.

> **Self Test**
>
> Briefly describe the following types of derivative securities: (1) futures and forward contracts, (2) swaps, (3) structured notes and CMOs, and (4) inverse floaters.
>
> Messman Corporation issues fixed-rate debt at a rate of 9.00%. Messman agrees to an interest rate swap in which it pays LIBOR to Moore Inc. and Moore pays 8.75% to Messman. What is Messman's resulting net payment? **(LIBOR + 0.25%)**

24.5 Corporate Risk Management

As businesses become increasingly complex, it is becoming more and more difficult for CEOs and directors to know what problems might lie in wait. Therefore, companies need to have someone systematically look for potential problems and design safeguards to minimize potential damage. With this in mind, most large firms have a designated "risk manager" who reports to the chief financial officer, and the CFOs of smaller firms personally assume risk management responsibilities. In any event, **risk management** is becoming increasingly important, and it is something finance students should understand. Therefore, in the remainder of this chapter we discuss the basics of risk management, with particular emphasis on how derivatives can be used to hedge financial risks.[11]

---

11. For an excellent overview of risk management, see Brian Nocco and Rene Stultz, "Enterprise Risk Management, Theory and Practice," *Journal of Applied Corporate Finance,* Fall 2008, pp. 8–20; Kenneth A. Froot, David S. Scharfstein, and Jeremy Stein, "A Framework for Risk Management," *Journal of Applied Corporate Finance,* Fall 1994, pp. 22–32; Walter Dolde, "The Trajectory of Corporate Financial Risk Management," *Journal of Applied Corporate Finance,* Fall 1993, pp. 33–41; and Marshall Blake and Nelda Mahady, "How Mid-Sized Companies Manage Risk," *Journal of Applied Corporate Finance,* Spring 1991, pp. 59–65.

24.5a Types of Risk

It is useful to begin our discussion of risk management by defining some commonly used terms that describe different risks. Some of these risks can be mitigated, or managed, and that is what risk management is all about.

1. *Pure risks* are risks that offer only the prospect of a loss. Examples include the risk that a plant will be destroyed by fire or that a product liability suit will result in a large judgment against the firm.
2. *Speculative risks* are situations that offer the chance of a gain but might result in a loss. Investments in new projects and marketable securities involve speculative risks.
3. *Demand risks* are associated with the demand for a firm's products or services. Because sales are essential to all businesses, demand risk is one of the most significant risks that firms face.
4. *Input risks* are risks associated with input costs, including both labor and materials. Thus, a company that uses copper as a raw material in its manufacturing process faces the risk that the cost of copper will increase and that it will not be able to pass this increase on to its customers.
5. *Financial risks* are risks that result from financial transactions. As we have seen, if a firm plans to issue new bonds then it faces the risk that interest rates will increase before the bonds can be brought to market. Similarly, if the firm enters into contracts with foreign customers or suppliers, it faces the risk that fluctuations in exchange rates will result in unanticipated losses.
6. *Property risks* are associated with destruction of productive assets. Thus, the threats of fire, floods, and riots impose property risks on a firm.
7. *Personnel risks* are risks that result from employees' actions. Examples include the risks associated with employee fraud or embezzlement and suits based on charges of age or sex discrimination.
8. *Environmental risks* include risks associated with polluting the environment. Public awareness in recent years, coupled with the huge costs of environmental cleanup, has increased the importance of this risk.
9. *Liability risks* are associated with products, services, or employee actions. Examples include the very large judgments assessed against asbestos manufacturers and some health care providers as well as costs incurred as a result of improper actions of employees, such as driving corporate vehicles in a reckless manner.
10. *Insurable risks* are risks that can be covered by insurance. In general, property, personnel, environmental, and liability risks can be transferred to insurance companies. Note, though, that the *ability* to insure a risk does not necessarily mean that the risk *should be* insured. Indeed, a major function of risk management involves evaluating all alternatives for managing a particular risk, including self-insurance, and then choosing the optimal alternative.

WEB

For a more detailed discussion of corporate insurance programs, see **Web Extension 24A** on the textbook's Web site.

Note that the risk classifications we used are somewhat arbitrary, and different classifications are commonly used in different industries. However, the list does give an idea of the wide variety of risks to which a firm can be exposed.

24.5b An Approach to Risk Management

Firms often use the following process for managing risks.

1. *Identify the risks faced by the firm.* Here the risk manager identifies the potential risks faced by his or her firm.

2. *Measure the potential effect of each risk.* Some risks are so small as to be immaterial, whereas others have the potential for dooming the company. It is useful to segregate risks by potential effect and then to focus on the most serious threats.

3. *Decide how each relevant risk should be handled.* In most situations, risk exposure can be reduced through one of the following techniques.

   a. *Transfer the risk to an insurance company.* Often, it is advantageous to insure against, and hence transfer, a risk. However, insurability does not necessarily mean that a risk should be covered by insurance. In many instances, it might be better for the company to *self-insure,* which means bearing the risk directly rather than paying another party to bear it.

   b. *Transfer the function that produces the risk to a third party.* For example, suppose a furniture manufacturer is concerned about potential liabilities arising from its ownership of a fleet of trucks used to transfer products from its manufacturing plant to various points across the country. One way to eliminate this risk would be to contract with a trucking company to do the shipping, thus passing the risks to a third party.

   c. *Purchase derivative contracts to reduce risk.* As we indicated earlier, firms use derivatives to hedge risks. Commodity derivatives can be used to reduce input risks. For example, a cereal company may use corn or wheat futures to hedge against increases in grain prices. Similarly, financial derivatives can be used to reduce risks that arise from changes in interest rates and exchange rates.

   d. *Reduce the probability of occurrence of an adverse event.* The expected loss arising from any risk is a function of both the probability of occurrence and the dollar loss if the adverse event occurs. In some instances, it is possible to reduce the probability that an adverse event will occur. For example, the probability that a fire will occur can be reduced by instituting a fire prevention program, by replacing old electrical wiring, and by using fire-resistant materials in areas with the greatest fire potential.

   e. *Reduce the magnitude of the loss associated with an adverse event.* Continuing with the fire risk example, the dollar cost associated with a fire can be reduced by such actions as installing sprinkler systems, designing facilities with self-contained fire zones, and locating facilities close to a fire station.

   f. *Totally avoid the activity that gives rise to the risk.* For example, a company might discontinue a product or service line because the risks outweigh the rewards, as with the decision by Dow Corning to discontinue its manufacture of silicone breast implants.

Risk management decisions, like all corporate decisions, should be based on a cost–benefit analysis for each feasible alternative. For example, suppose it would cost $50,000 per year to conduct a comprehensive fire safety training program for all personnel in a high-risk plant. Presumably, this program would reduce the expected value of future fire losses. An alternative to the training program would be to place $50,000 annually in a reserve fund set aside to cover future fire losses. Both alternatives involve expected cash flows, and from an economic standpoint the choice should be made on the basis of the lowest present value of future costs. Thus, the same financial management techniques applied to other corporate decisions can also be applied to risk management decisions. However, if a fire occurs and a life is lost, the trade-off between fire prevention and expected losses may not sit well with a jury. The same thing holds true for product liability—as Firestone, Ford, GM, and others have learned.

Self Test

Define the following terms: pure risks, speculative risks, demand risks, input risks, financial risks, property risks, personnel risks, environmental risks, liability risks, insurable risks, and self-insurance.

Should a firm insure itself against all of the insurable risks it faces? Explain.

ENTERPRISE RISK MANAGEMENT AND VALUE AT RISK

Throughout this book, we have emphasized the goal of maximizing a company's intrinsic value. At the risk of simplification, risk management seeks to identify and control threats to intrinsic value.

A company's total intrinsic value is the sum of the intrinsic values of all its projects and business units. But if each business unit performs its own capital budgeting analysis without considering the impacts on other business units, then total intrinsic value almost certainly will not be maximized. For example, the costs of better sales forecasting systems might be borne by the marketing department while the benefits of lower inventory and smoother production would accrue to factory and warehouse managers. Therefore, maximizing total intrinsic value often requires using a corporate valuation model such as the one described in Chapter 11.

Similar reasoning applies to risk management: It is suboptimal for each business unit to be solely responsible for managing its own risk in isolation from other business units. Therefore, many companies now use *enterprise resource management (ERM)* to coordinate and control total risk. The more complex an organization is, the more important it is to have effective ERM. For example, many large financial institutions failed from 2007 to 2009 partly because they did not understand or coordinate the risks from their wide scope of activities, which included investment banking, trading, and insurance in addition to commercial banking. On the other hand, many small commercial banks weathered this environment partly because they engaged in a fairly limited set of activities, which enabled the small banks to understand their risk exposure.

How should a company measure its enterprise risk? One common metric is called *value at risk*, or *VaR*. To estimate VaR, many companies use scenario analysis or Monte Carlo simulation. The process begins by identifying sources of risk and estimating the sources' probability distributions. For example, sources might include foreign exchange rate volatility, changes in consumer demand, or access to credit markets. The next step is to estimate the impact that these sources have on a particular output, such as cash flow, earnings, or total intrinsic value. In particular, the goal is to estimate the resulting probability distribution for the output. The third step is to identify an acceptable risk threshold; for example, many companies use 5% or 1%. The final step is to identify the value at risk, which is the value of the output corresponding to the threshold. For example, suppose a company uses a 1% threshold and estimates a −$100 million VaR for its projected cash flow for the upcoming quarter. In other words, there is a 1% probability that the company will have a quarterly cash flow lower than −$100 million. If this VaR is unacceptable, then management must take actions to reduce the risk.

In 2009, the government subjected 19 large banks to stress tests designed to determine whether the banks had enough capital to withstand potential deterioration in the economy. After conducting these tests, the government essentially decided that the VaR was unacceptable for 10 of the banks and told them they needed to raise $75 billion in capital.

24.6 Using Derivatives to Reduce Risks

Firms are subject to numerous risks related to interest rate, stock price, and exchange rate fluctuations in the financial markets. For an investor, one of the most obvious ways to reduce financial risks is to hold a broadly diversified portfolio of stocks and debt securities, including international securities and debt of varying maturities. However, derivatives can also be used to reduce the risks associated with financial and commodity markets.[12]

24.6a Hedging with Futures

One of the most useful tools for reducing interest rate, exchange rate, and commodity risk is to hedge in the futures markets. Most financial and real asset transactions occur in what is known as the *spot,* or *cash, market,* where the asset is delivered immediately (or within a few days). *Futures,* or *futures contracts,* on the other hand, call for the purchase or sale of an asset at some future date but at a price that is fixed today.

Today, futures contracts are available on hundreds of real and financial assets traded on dozens of U.S. and international exchanges, the largest of which are the Chicago Board of Trade (CBOT) and the Chicago Mercantile Exchange (CME), both of which are now part of the CME Group. Futures contracts are divided into two classes, **commodity futures** and **financial futures**. Commodity futures—which cover oil, various grains, oilseeds, livestock, meats, fibers, metals, and wood—were first traded in the United States in the mid-1800s. Financial futures, which were first traded in 1975, include Treasury bills, notes, bonds, certificates of deposit, Eurodollar deposits, foreign currencies, and stock indexes.

To illustrate how futures contracts work, consider the CBOT's contract on Treasury bonds. The basic contract is for $100,000 of a hypothetical 6% coupon, semiannual payment Treasury bond with 20 years to maturity.[13] Table 24-2 shows Treasury bond futures data from the Chicago Board of Trade.

The first column of the table gives the delivery month, and the next three columns give the opening, high, and low prices for the day. Column 5 shows the last price of the day, also called the *settlement* price, and the next column shows the change in price from the previous day. For example, the last price for the December 2011 contract, 123'30.0, means 123 plus $^{30.0}/_{32}$, or 123.9375%, of par. The change was –0'01, which means the December 2011 contract's last price of the day was $^{1}/_{32}$ lower than the previous day's last trade, which must have been at 123'31.0. Column 7 shows the day's estimated trading volume. Notice that most of the trading occurs in the contract with the nearest delivery date. Finally, Column 8 shows the "open interest," which is the number of contracts outstanding.

---

12. In Chapter 27 we discuss the risks involved with holding foreign currencies as well as procedures for reducing such risks.
13. The coupon rate on the hypothetical bond was changed to 6% from 8% in March 2000. The CBOT contract doesn't actually specify a 20-year bond but instead allows delivery of any noncallable bond with a remaining maturity greater than 15 years (or callable bond that is not callable for at least 15 years) and less than 25 years. Rather than simply deliver a bond, which might have an interest rate other than 6%, the actual bond price is adjusted by a conversion feature to make it equivalent to a 6% bond that is trading at par. Because the average maturity of bonds that are eligible for delivery is about 20 years, we use a 20-year maturity for the hypothetical bond in the futures contract. For even longer maturity hedging, the CBOT also has the Ultra T-Bond contract, which allows for delivery of a Treasury bond of at least 25 years to maturity.

TABLE 24-2 Futures Prices (Treasury Bonds: $100,000; Pts. 32nds of 100%)

Delivery Month (1)	Open (2)	High (3)	Low (4)	Settle (5)	Change (6)	Estimated Volume (7)	Open Interest (8)
Sep 2011	125'13.0	126'00.0	125'04.0	125'12.0	−'01.0	561,806	645,452
Dec 2011	124'01.0	124'13.0	123'31.0	123'30.0	−'01.0	n.a.	45

Source: The Wall Street Journal Online, **www.wsj.com**, settlement prices for June 22, 2011.

WEB

See ***Ch24 Tool Kit.xls*** on the textbook's Web site for all calculations.

To illustrate, we focus on the Treasury bonds for December delivery. The settlement price was 123.9375% of the $100,000 contract value. Thus, the price at which one could buy $100,000 face value of 6%, 20-year Treasury bonds to be delivered in December was 123.9375%($100,000) = $123,937.50. The contract price decreased by $\frac{1}{32}$ of 1% of $100,000 from the previous day, so if you had bought the contract yesterday, you would have lost $31.250 = ($\frac{1}{32}$) (0.01) ($100,000). There were 45 contracts outstanding, representing a total value of about 45($123,937.50) = $5,577,187.50.

Note that the contract decreased by $\frac{1}{32}$ of a percent on this particular day. Why would the value of the bond futures contract decrease? Bond prices decrease when interest rates rise, so interest rates must have risen on that day. Moreover, we can calculate the implied rate inherent in the futures price. Recall that the contract relates to a hypothetical 20-year, semiannual payment, 6% coupon bond. The settlement price was 123.9375% of par, so a $1,000 par bond would have a price of 123.9375%($1,000) = $123,937.50. We can solve for r_d by using the following equation:

$$\sum_{t=1}^{40} \frac{\$30}{(1 + r_d/2)^t} + \frac{\$1,000}{(1 + r_d/2)^{40}} = \$123,937.50$$

Using a financial calculator, input N = 40, PV = −1239.375, PMT = 30, and FV = 1000; then solve for I/YR = 2.1082%. This is the semiannual rate, which is equivalent to a nominal annual rate of 4.2165%, or approximately 4.22%. The previous day's last (settlement) price was 123^{31}⁄$_{32}$. Setting N = 40, PV = −1239.6875, PMT = 30, and FV = 1000 and then solving for I/YR = 2.1072 implies an annual yield of 4.2145%, or approximately 4.21%. Therefore, interest rates fell by about 1 basis point from the previous day, but that was enough to decrease the value of the contract by $31.25.

In June 2011, when the data in Table 24-2 were gathered, the yield on a 20-year T-bond was about 3.84%. But as we just calculated, the implied yield on the December 2011 futures contract was about 4.22%. The December yield reflects investors' beliefs as to what the interest rate level will be in December: The marginal trader in the futures market was predicting a 38-basis-point increase in yields between June and December. That prediction could, of course, turn out to be incorrect.

Now suppose that 3 months later, in September, implied yields in the futures market had fallen from the earlier levels—say, from 4.22% to 3.72%. Inputting N = 40, I/YR = 3.72/2 = 1.860, PMT = 30, and FV = 1000 and then solving for PV = −1319.6485 shows that the December contract would be worth about $131,964.85 in September if implied yields fell to 3.72%. Thus, the contract's value would have increased by $131,964.85 − $123,937.50 ≈ $8,027.

When futures contracts are purchased, the purchaser does not have to put up the full amount of the purchase price; instead, the purchaser need only post an initial *margin,* which for CBOT Treasury bond contracts is $2,700 per $100,000 contract.[14] However, investors are required to maintain a certain value in the margin account, called a *maintenance margin.* If the value of the contract declines, then the owner may be required to add additional funds to the margin account, and the more the contract value falls, the more money must be added. The value of the contract is checked at the end of every working day, and margin account adjustments are made at that time. This is called "marking to market." If an investor purchased our illustrative contract and then sold it later for $131,964.85, then she would have made a profit of $8,027 on a $2,700 investment, or a return of 197% in only 3 months. Thus it is clear that futures contracts offer a considerable amount of leverage. Of course, if interest rates had risen, then the value of the contract would have fallen and the investor could easily have lost her $2,700, or more. Futures contracts are rarely settled by delivery of the securities involved. Rather, the transaction is completed by reversing the trade, which amounts to selling the contract back to the original seller.[15] The actual gains and losses on the contract are realized when the futures contract is closed.

Futures contracts and options are similar to one another—so similar that people often confuse the two. Therefore, it is useful to compare the two instruments. A *futures contract* is a definite agreement on the part of one party to buy something on a specific date and at a specific price, and the other party agrees to sell on the same terms. No matter how low or how high the price goes, the two parties must settle the contract at the agreed-upon price and the losses of one party are exactly equal to the gains of the other. In addition, a dollar increase in the futures price has exactly the opposite effect of a dollar decrease in the futures price. A hedge constructed using futures contracts is called a *symmetric hedge* because of this feature; the payoff from an increase in the futures price is exactly opposite the payoff from a decrease in the futures price. For this reason, symmetric hedges are typically used to provide a fixed transaction price at some date in the future. For example, suppose an investor wants to sell a Treasury bond in 6 months but is worried about a decline in Treasury bond prices and so sells a Treasury bond futures contract maturing in 6 months as a hedge. If the Treasury bond price (and hence also the Treasury bond futures price) decreases over the 6 months, then the investor will receive less when selling the bond but will make up the difference when closing out the futures contract. And if the Treasury bond price increases, then the investor will make more money when selling the bond in 6 months but will lose money when closing out the futures contract. In this way the ending value of the position doesn't depend on the Treasury bond price in 6 months, and so the amount received for selling the bond in 6 months is locked in.

An *option,* on the other hand, gives someone the right to buy (call) or sell (put) an asset, but the holder of the option does not have to complete the transaction. The payoff from a hedge constructed using options will be different from a futures hedge because of this option feature. As discussed in Chapter 6, the payoff from

WWW

For current margin requirements, go to **www.cmegroup.com/ clearing/margins**.

---

14. This is the margin requirement for hedgers. Speculators have a higher margin requirement.
15. The buyers and sellers of most financial futures contracts do not actually trade with one another—each trader's contractual obligation is with a futures exchange. This feature helps to guarantee the fiscal integrity of the trade. Incidentally, commodities futures traded on the exchanges are settled in the same way as financial futures, but in the case of commodities much of the contracting is done off the exchange, between farmers and processors, as *forward contracts,* in which case actual deliveries occur.

a call option increases as the price of the underlying asset increases, but if the underlying asset price decreases, then the most the option holder can lose is the amount invested in the option. That is, upside gains are unlimited but downside losses are capped at the amount invested in the option. For this reason, an option is said to create an *asymmetric hedge*—it hedges price changes in one direction more than price changes in the other.

Asymmetric hedges tend to behave like insurance, hedging away downside risk while leaving upside potential intact. In the Treasury bond example above, our investor could, instead, have purchased a Treasury bond futures put option expiring in 6 months to hedge the Treasury bond position. Then if the price of the Treasury bond decreased the value of the put option would increase, and the profits on the option would offset the loss from selling the bond at the lower price, thus protecting from a decrease in Treasury bond prices. However, if Treasury bond prices increased, then the investor would let the put option expire and simply sell the bond at the higher price. Thus when using an asymmetric hedge, the investor gets to participate in profits when bond prices increase, but is insured against a loss when bond prices decrease. Of course this protection comes at a cost. The investor must purchase the put option and if the maturity is long, the option could be quite expensive.

Note also that options exist both for individual stocks, for "bundles" of stocks such as those in the S&P and *Value Line* indexes, and for futures contracts (called *options on futures*), but generally not for commodities themselves. Futures, on the other hand, are used for commodities, debt securities, and stock indexes. Both of these two types of instruments can be used for hedging. One is not necessarily better or worse than the other—they are simply different.[16]

24.6b Security Price Exposure

All investors are exposed to losses due to changes in security prices when securities are held in investment portfolios, and firms are also exposed during times when securities are being issued. In addition, firms are exposed to risk if they use floating-rate debt to finance an investment that produces a fixed income stream. Risks such as these can often be mitigated by using derivatives. As we discussed earlier, derivatives are securities whose value stems, or is derived, from the values of other assets. Thus, options and futures contracts are derivatives, because their values depend on the prices of some underlying asset. Now we will explore further the use of two types of derivatives, futures and swaps, to help manage certain types of risk.

Futures

Futures are used for both speculation and hedging. **Speculation** involves betting on future price movements, and futures are used because of the leverage inherent in the contract. **Hedging**, on the other hand, is done by a firm or individual to protect against a price change that would otherwise negatively affect profits. For example, rising interest rates and commodity (raw material) prices can hurt profits, as can adverse currency fluctuations. If two parties have mirror-image risks, then they can enter into a transaction that eliminates, rather than transfers, risks. This is a "natural hedge." Of course, one party to a futures contract could be a speculator, the other a

---

16. For additional insights into the use of financial futures for hedging, see Mark G. Castelino, Jack C. Francis, and Avner Wolf, "Cross-Hedging: Basis Risk and Choice of the Optimal Hedging Vehicle," *The Financial Review,* May 1991, pp. 179–210.

hedger. Thus, to the extent that speculators broaden the market and make hedging possible, they help decrease risk for those who seek to avoid it.

There are two basic types of hedges: (1) **long hedges**, in which futures contracts are *bought* in anticipation of (or to guard against) price increases, and (2) **short hedges**, where a firm or individual *sells* futures contracts to guard against price declines. Recall that rising interest rates lower bond prices and thus decrease the value of bond futures contracts. Therefore, if a firm or individual needs to guard against an *increase* in interest rates, a futures contract that makes money if rates rise should be used. That means selling, or going short, on a Treasury bond futures contract. To illustrate, assume that in August Carson Foods is considering a plan to issue $10,000,000 of 20-year bonds in December to finance a capital expenditure program. The interest rate would be 9% paid semiannually if the bonds were issued today, and at that rate the project would have a positive NPV. However, interest rates may rise, and when the issue is actually sold, the interest rate might be substantially above 9%, which would make the project a bad investment. Carson can protect itself against a rise in rates by hedging in the futures market.

In this situation, Carson would be hurt by an increase in interest rates, so it would use a short hedge. It would choose a futures contract on the security most similar to the one it plans to issue, long-term bonds, and so would probably hedge with December Treasury bond futures. We can see from Table 24-2 that each December contract has a value of 123'30.0, so the total value of one contract is $123,937.50. Because it plans to issue $10,000,000 of bonds and because each contract is worth $123,937.50, Carson will sell $10,000,000/$123,937.50 = 80.69 ≈ 81 contracts for delivery in December. It will have to put up 81($2,700) = $218,700 in margin money and also pay brokerage commissions. The total value of the 81 contracts is 81($123,937.50) = $10,038,938.00, which is very close to the value of the bonds Carson wants to issue.

WEB

See **Ch24 Tool Kit.xls** on the textbook's Web site for all calculations.

RISK MANAGEMENT IN THE CYBER ECONOMY

In the old bricks-and-mortar economy, most of a company's value was due to its tangible assets. Not so in the cyber economy, where value is due to intellectual property and networks that manage knowledge bases. Insurance companies are rapidly developing new types of insurance policies to protect these valuable cyber assets.

Intellectual property (IP) insurance now covers "all intellectual property—patents, trademarks, trade secrets, copyright—and includes defense, as well as enforcement, of intellectual property rights," according to Judith Pearson, director of Aon Corp.'s financial services group. These policies can cover losses in excess of $200 million, with premiums ranging from 1% to 5% of the coverage.

Insurers also provide coverage for breaches in network security. For example, companies can buy insurance to cover cases of cyberextortion, such as the demand for $100,000 by the hacker "Maxus" in exchange for not publicly releasing 300,000 credit card numbers stolen from CD Universe. Other policies cover content defamation, copyright and trademark infringement, denial-of-service attacks, viruses, theft of information, and destruction or alteration of data. Costs of insurance have fallen to between 1% and 3% of the policy's coverage, but most insurers subject applicants to a thorough review of their current security measures before granting coverage.

Sources: John P. Mello, Jr., "Blanketing Intellectual Risk," *CFO*, May 2000, p. 16; and Russ Banham, "Hacking It," *CFO*, August 2000, pp. 115–118.

Now suppose that in December, when Carson issues its bonds, renewed fears of inflation push interest rates up by 100 basis points. What would the bond proceeds be if Carson still tried to issue 9% coupon bonds when the market requires a 10% rate of return? We can find the total value of the offering with a financial calculator, inputting N = 40, I/YR = 5, PMT = −450000, and FV = −10000000 and then solving for PV = 9142046. Therefore, bonds with a 9% coupon, based upon its original plans, would bring proceeds of only $9,142,046, because investors now require a 10% return. Because Carson would have to issue $10 million worth of bonds at a 10% rate, Carson's cost would go up by $857,954 = $10,000,000 − $9,142,046 as a result of delaying the financing.

However, the increase in interest rates would also bring about a change in the value of Carson's short position in the futures market. When interest rates increase, the value of the futures contract will fall. If the interest rate on the futures contract also increased by the same full percentage point, from 4.2165% to 5.2165%, then the new contract value can be found by inputting N = 40, I/YR = 5.2165/2 = 2.60825, PMT = −3000, and FV = −100000 and then solving for PV = 109657.13 per contract. With 81 contracts, the total value of the position is thus $8,882,228.00 = 81($109,657.13). Carson would then close its position in the futures market by repurchasing for $8,882,228.00 the contracts that it earlier sold for $10,038,938.00, giving it a profit of $1,156,710.00 (less commissions).

Thus, Carson would offset the loss on the bond issue if we ignore commissions and the opportunity cost of the margin money. In fact, in our example Carson more than offsets the loss, pocketing an additional $298,756 = $1,156,710 − $857,954. Of course, if interest rates had fallen then Carson would have lost on its futures position, but this loss would have been offset because Carson could now sell its bonds with a lower coupon.

If futures contracts existed on Carson's own debt and if interest rates moved identically in the spot and futures markets, then the firm could construct a **perfect hedge** in which gains on the futures contract would exactly offset losses on the bonds. In reality, it is virtually impossible to construct perfect hedges, because in most cases the underlying asset is not identical to the futures asset; and even when the assets are, prices (and interest rates) may not move exactly together in the spot and futures markets.[17]

Observe also that if Carson had been planning an equity offering and if its stock tended to move fairly closely with one of the stock indexes, then the company could have hedged against falling stock prices by selling the index future. Even better, if options on Carson's stock were traded in the options market, then it could use options rather than futures to hedge against falling stock prices.

The futures and options markets permit flexibility in the timing of financial transactions: The firm can be protected, at least partially, against changes that occur between the time a decision is reached and the time when the transaction is completed. However, this protection has a cost—the firm must pay commissions. Whether or not the protection is worth the cost is a matter of judgment. The decision to

---

17. In this example, Carson hedged a 20-year bond with a T-bond futures contract. Rather than simply matching on maturity, it would be more accurate to match on duration (see *Web Extension 4C*, available on the textbook's Web site, for a discussion of duration). A matching duration in the futures contacts could be accomplished by taking positions in the T-bond futures contract and in another financial futures contract, such as the 10-Year Treasury note contract. Because Carson's bond had a 20-year maturity, matching on maturity instead of duration provided a good hedge. If Carson's bond had a different maturity, then it would be essential to match on duration.

hedge also depends on management's risk aversion and on the company's strength and ability to assume the risk in question.

Swaps

A *swap* is another method for reducing financial risks. As we noted earlier, a swap is an exchange of cash payment obligations in which each party prefers the payment type or pattern of the other party. Generally, one party has a fixed-rate obligation and the other a floating-rate obligation, or one has an obligation denominated in one currency and the other in another currency.

Major changes have occurred over time in the swaps market. First, standardized contracts have been developed for the most common types of swaps, which has had two effects: (1) Standardized contracts lower the time and effort involved in arranging swaps, and this lowers transactions costs. (2) The development of standardized contracts has led to a secondary market for swaps, which has increased the liquidity and efficiency of the swaps market. A number of international banks now make markets in swaps and offer quotes on several standard types. Also, as noted previously, the banks now take counterparty positions in swaps, so it is not necessary to find another firm with mirror-image needs before a swap transaction can be completed. The bank would generally find a final counterparty for the swap at a later date, so its positioning helps make the swap market more operationally efficient.

To further illustrate a swap transaction, consider the following situation. An electric utility recently issued a 5-year floating-rate note tied to the prime rate. The prime rate could rise significantly over the period, so the note carries a high degree of interest rate risk. The utility could, however, enter into a swap with a counterparty (say, Citibank) in which the utility would pay Citibank a fixed series of interest payments over the 5-year period and Citibank would make the company's required floating-rate payments. As a result, the utility would have converted a floating-rate loan to a fixed-rate loan, and the risk of rising interest rates would have been passed from the utility to Citibank. Such a transaction can lower both parties' risks—because banks' revenues rise as interest rates rise, Citibank's risk would actually be lower if it had floating-rate obligations.

Longer-term swaps can also be made. For example, Citibank entered into a 17-year swap in an electricity cogeneration project financing deal. The project's sponsors were unable to obtain fixed-rate financing on reasonable terms, and they were afraid interest rates would increase and make the project unprofitable. However, the project's sponsors were able to borrow from local banks on a floating-rate basis and then arrange a simultaneous swap with Citibank for a fixed-rate obligation.

Credit default swaps (CDS) are called swaps but are actually more like insurance. An investor might purchase a CDS by making an annual payment to a counterparty to insure a particular bond against default (it is not necessary that the purchaser actually own the bond); if the bond defaults, the counterparty pays the purchaser the amount of the defaulted bond that was insured.

When banks and other major financial institutions take positions in swaps and CDS, they are themselves exposed to various risks, especially if their counterparties cannot meet their obligations. Furthermore, swaps are off–balance sheet transactions, making it impossible to tell just how large the swap market is or who has what obligation. Well before the financial crisis that began in 2007, academics had speculated that the size of the swap markets, the interconnectedness of so many financial institutions through the swap markets, and the overall lack of transparency made for a volatile mix capable of disrupting the entire global financial system. These worries were confirmed in 2007 and 2008 when mortgage-backed securities began defaulting and counterparties for CDS, like AIG, could not cover their obligations. Congress, the Federal Reserve, and the Treasury are currently (June 2011) debating how the swap markets should be regulated to prevent future meltdowns.

24.6c Commodity Price Exposure

As we noted earlier, futures markets were established for many commodities long before they began to be used as financial instruments. We can use Porter Electronics, which uses large quantities of copper as well as several precious metals, to illustrate inventory hedging. Suppose that in May 2012, Porter foresaw a need for 100,000 pounds of copper in March 2013 for use in fulfilling a fixed-price contract to supply solar power cells to the U.S. government. Porter's managers are concerned that a strike by Chilean copper miners will occur, which could raise the price of copper in world markets and possibly turn the expected profit into a loss.

Porter could, of course, go ahead and buy the copper it will need to fulfill the contract, but doing so will incur substantial carrying costs. As an alternative, the company could hedge against increasing copper prices in the futures market. The New York Commodity Exchange trades standard copper futures contracts of 25,000 pounds each. Thus, Porter could buy four contracts (go long) for delivery in March 2013. Assume these contracts were trading in May for about $4.10 per pound and that the spot price at that date was about $4.08 per pound. If copper prices do rise appreciably over the next 10 months then the value of Porter's long position in copper futures would increase, thus offsetting some of the price increase in the commodity itself. Of course, if copper prices fall then Porter would lose money on its futures contracts, but the company would be buying the copper on the spot market at a cheaper price, so it would make a higher than anticipated profit on its sale of solar cells. Thus, hedging in the copper futures market locks in the cost of raw materials and removes some risk to which the firm would otherwise be exposed.

Many other companies, such as Alcoa with aluminum and Archer Daniels Midland with grains, routinely use the futures markets to reduce the risks associated with price volatility.

24.6d The Use and Misuse of Derivatives

Most of the news stories about derivatives are related to financial disasters. Much less is heard about the benefits of derivatives. However, because of these benefits, more than 83% of large U.S. companies use derivatives on a regular basis. In today's market, sophisticated investors and analysts are demanding that firms use derivatives to hedge certain risks. For example, Compaq Computer (now a part of Hewlett-Packard) was sued by a shareholder group for failing to properly hedge its foreign exchange exposure. The shareholders lost the suit, but Compaq got the message and now uses currency futures to hedge its international operations. In another example, Prudential Securities reduced its earnings estimate for Cone Mills, a North Carolina textile company, because Cone did not sufficiently hedge its exposure to changing cotton prices. These examples lead to one conclusion: If a company can safely and inexpensively hedge its risks, it should do so.

There can, however, be a downside to the use of derivatives. Hedging is invariably cited by authorities as a "good" use of derivatives, whereas speculating with derivatives is often cited as a "bad" use. Some people and organizations can afford to bear the risks involved in speculating with derivatives, but others are either not sufficiently knowledgeable about the risks or else should not be taking those risks in the first place. Most would agree that the typical corporation should use derivatives only to hedge risks, not to speculate in an effort to increase profits. Hedging allows a manager to concentrate on running his core business without having to worry about interest rate, currency, and commodity price variability. However, big problems can arise if hedges are improperly constructed or if a corporate treasurer, eager to report relatively high returns, uses derivatives for speculative purposes.

One interesting example of a derivatives debacle involved Kashima Oil, a Japanese firm that imports oil. It pays with U.S. dollars but then sells oil in the Japanese market for yen. Kashima began by using currency futures to hedge, but it later started to speculate on dollar–yen price movements, hoping to increase profits. When the currency markets moved against Kashima's speculative position, lax accounting rules permitted it to avoid reporting the losses by simply rolling over the contract. By the time Kashima bit the bullet and closed its position, it had lost $1.5 billion. Other companies have experienced similar problems.

Our belief is that derivatives can and should be used to hedge against certain risks but that the leverage inherent in derivatives contracts makes them potentially dangerous. Also, CFOs, CEOs, and board members should be reasonably knowledgeable about the derivatives their firms use, should establish policies regarding when they can and cannot be used, and should establish audit procedures to ensure that the policies are carried out. Moreover, a firm's derivatives position should be reported to stockholders, because stockholders have a right to know when situations such as the one involving Kashima might arise.

Self Test

What is a futures contract?

Explain how a company can use the futures market to hedge against rising interest rates.

What is a swap? Describe the mechanics of a fixed-rate to floating-rate swap.

Explain how a company can use the futures market to hedge against rising raw materials prices.

How should derivatives be used in risk management? What problems can occur?

A Treasury bond futures contract is selling for 94'16. What is the implied annual yield? **(6.5%)**

Summary

Companies every day face a variety of risks, for it is hard to operate a successful business without taking some chances. Back in Chapter 2, we discussed the trade-off between risk and return. If some action can lower risk without lowering returns too much, then the action can enhance value. With this in mind, we described in this chapter the various types of risks that companies face, and we discussed the basic principles of corporate risk management. One important tool for managing risk is the derivatives market. Consequently, this chapter has also provided an introduction to derivative securities. The key concepts covered are listed below.

- There are several reasons **risk management** might increase the value of a firm. Risk management allows corporations (1) to increase their **use of debt,** (2) to maintain their **capital budget** over time, (3) to avoid costs associated with **financial distress,** (4) to utilize their **comparative advantages in hedging** relative to the hedging ability of individual investors, (5) to reduce both the risks and costs of borrowing by using **swaps,** and (6) to reduce the **higher taxes** that result from fluctuating earnings. Managers may also want to stabilize earnings in order to boost their own compensation.
- A **derivative** is a security whose value is determined by the market price or interest rate of some other security.
- A **hedge** is a transaction that lowers risk. A **natural hedge** is a transaction between two **counterparties** whose risks are mirror images of each other.
- A **futures contract** is a standardized contract that is traded on an exchange and is marked-to-market daily, although physical delivery of the underlying asset usually does not occur.
- Under a **forward contract**, one party agrees to buy a commodity at a specific price and a specific future date and the other party agrees to make the sale; delivery does occur.
- A **structured note** is a debt obligation derived from another debt obligation.
- A **swap** is an exchange of cash payment obligations. Swaps occur because the parties involved prefer the other's payment stream.
- In general, **risk management** involves the management of unpredictable events that have adverse consequences for the firm.
- The three key steps in risk management are as follows: (1) **identify** the risks faced by the company, (2) **measure** the potential impacts of these risks, and (3) **decide** how each relevant risk should be dealt with.
- In most situations, risk exposure can be dealt with by one or more of the following techniques: (1) **transfer the risk** to an insurance company, (2) **transfer the function** that produces the risk to a third party, (3) **purchase a derivative contract,** (4) **reduce the probability** of occurrence of an adverse event, (5) **reduce the magnitude** of the loss associated with an adverse event, and (6) totally **avoid** the activity that gives rise to the risk.
- **Financial futures** permit firms to create hedge positions to protect themselves against fluctuating interest rates, stock prices, and exchange rates.
- **Commodity futures** can be used to hedge against input price increases.
- **Long hedges** involve buying futures contracts to guard against price increases.
- **Short hedges** involve selling futures contracts to guard against price declines.
- **Symmetric hedges** protect against price increases and price decreases. Futures contracts are frequently used for symmetric hedges.
- **Asymmetric hedges** protect against price movements in one direction more than movements in another. Options are frequently used for asymmetric hedges.

- A **perfect hedge** occurs when the gain or loss on the hedged transaction exactly offsets the loss or gain on the unhedged position.

Questions

24-1 Define each of the following terms:
  a. Derivative
  b. Corporate risk management
  c. Financial futures; forward contract
  d. Hedging; natural hedge; long hedge; short hedge; perfect hedge; symmetric hedge; asymmetric hedge
  e. Swap; structured note
  f. Commodity futures

24-2 Give two reasons stockholders might be indifferent between owning the stock of a firm with volatile cash flows and that of a firm with stable cash flows.

24-3 List six reasons why risk management might increase the value of a firm.

24-4 Discuss some of the techniques available to reduce risk exposures.

24-5 Explain how the futures markets can be used to reduce interest rate risk and input price risk.

24-6 How can swaps be used to reduce the risks associated with debt contracts?

Problems Answers Appear in Appendix B

Easy Problems 1–2

24-1 **Swaps** Zhao Automotive issues fixed-rate debt at a rate of 7.00%. Zhao agrees to an interest rate swap in which it pays LIBOR to Lee Financial and Lee pays 6.8% to Zhao. What is Zhao's resulting net payment?

24-2 **Futures** A Treasury bond futures contract has a settlement price of 89'08. What is the implied annual yield?

Intermediate Problems 3–4

24-3 **Futures** What is the implied interest rate on a Treasury bond ($100,000) futures contract that settled at 100'16? If interest rates increased by 1%, what would be the contract's new value?

24-4 **Swaps** Carter Enterprises can issue floating-rate debt at LIBOR + 2% or fixed-rate debt at 10%. Brence Manufacturing can issue floating-rate debt at LIBOR + 3.1% or fixed-rate debt at 11%. Suppose Carter issues floating-rate debt and Brence issues fixed-rate debt. They are considering a swap in which Carter makes a fixed-rate payment of 7.95% to Brence and Brence makes a payment of LIBOR to Carter. What are the net payments of Carter and Brence if they engage in the swap? Would Carter be better off if it issued fixed-rate debt or if it issued floating-rate debt and engaged in the swap? Would Brence be better off if it issued floating-rate debt or if it issued fixed-rate debt and engaged in the swap?

Challenging Problem 5

24-5 Hedging The Zinn Company plans to issue $10,000,000 of 20-year bonds in June to help finance a new research and development laboratory. The bonds will pay interest semiannually. It is now November, and the current cost of debt to the high-risk biotech company is 11%. However, the firm's financial manager is concerned that interest rates will climb even higher in coming months. The following data are available:

Futures Prices: Treasury Bonds—$100,000; Pts. 32nds of 100%

Delivery Month (1)	Open (2)	High (3)	Low (4)	Settle (5)	Change (6)	Open Interest (7)
Dec	94'28	95'13	94'22	95'05	+0'07	591,944
Mar	96'03	96'03	95'13	95'25	+0'08	120,353
June	95'03	95'17	95'03	95'17	+0'08	13,597

a. Use the given data to create a hedge against rising interest rates.
b. Assume that interest rates in general increase by 200 basis points. How well did your hedge perform?
c. What is a perfect hedge? Are any real-world hedges perfect? Explain.

Spreadsheet Problem

24-6 Build a Model: Hedging Start with the partial model in the file *Ch24 P06 Build a Model.xls* on the textbook's Web site. Use the information and data below.

F. Pierce Products Inc. is financing a new manufacturing facility with the issue in March of $20,000,000 of 20-year bonds with semiannual interest payments. It is now October, and if Pierce were to issue the bonds now, the yield would be 10% because of Pierce's high risk. Pierce's CFO is concerned that interest rates will climb even higher in coming months and is considering hedging the bond issue. The following data are available:

Futures Prices: Treasury Bonds—$100,000; Pts. 32nds of 100%

Delivery Month (1)	Open (2)	High (3)	Low (4)	Settle (5)	Change (6)	Open Interest (7)
Dec	93'28	94'13	93'22	94'05	+0'06	723,946
Mar	95'03	95'03	94'13	94'25	+0'07	97,254

a. Create a hedge with the futures contract for Pierce's planned March debt offering of $20 million using the March Treasury Bond futures contract. What is the implied yield on the bond underlying the futures contract?
b. Suppose that interest rates fall by 300 basis points. What are the dollar savings from issuing the debt at the new interest rate? What is the dollar

change in value of the futures position? What is the total dollar value change of the hedged position?

c. Create a graph showing the effectiveness of the hedge if the change in interest rates, in basis points, is −300, −200, −100, 0, 100, 200, or 300. Show the dollar cost (or savings) from issuing the debt at the new interest rates, the dollar change in value of the futures position, and the total dollar value change.

MINI CASE

Assume you have just been hired as a financial analyst by Tennessee Sunshine Inc., a mid-sized Tennessee company that specializes in creating exotic sauces from imported fruits and vegetables. The firm's CEO, Bill Stooksbury, recently returned from an industry corporate executive conference in San Francisco, and one of the sessions he attended was on the pressing need for smaller companies to institute corporate risk management programs. Since no one at Tennessee Sunshine is familiar with the basics of derivatives and corporate risk management, Stooksbury has asked you to prepare a brief report that the firm's executives could use to gain at least a cursory understanding of the topics.

To begin, you gathered some outside materials on derivatives and corporate risk management and used these materials to draft a list of pertinent questions that need to be answered. In fact, one possible approach to the paper is to use a question-and-answer format. Now that the questions have been drafted, you have to develop the answers.

a. Why might stockholders be indifferent to whether or not a firm reduces the volatility of its cash flows?

b. What are six reasons risk management might increase the value of a corporation?

c. What is corporate risk management? Why is it important to all firms?

d. Risks that firms face can be categorized in many ways. Define the following types of risk:
   (1) Speculative risks
   (2) Pure risks
   (3) Demand risks
   (4) Input risks
   (5) Financial risks
   (6) Property risks
   (7) Personnel risks
   (8) Environmental risks
   (9) Liability risks
   (10) Insurable risks

e. What are the three steps of corporate risk management?

f. What are some actions that companies can take to minimize or reduce risk exposures?

g. What is financial risk exposure? Describe the following concepts and techniques that can be used to reduce financial risks:
   (1) Derivatives
   (2) Futures markets
   (3) Hedging
   (4) Swaps

h. Describe how commodity futures markets can be used to reduce input price risk.

i. It is January, and Tennessee Sunshine is considering issuing $5 million in bonds in June to raise capital for an expansion. Currently, the firm can issue 20-year bonds with a 7% coupon (with interest paid semiannually), but interest rates are on the rise and Stooksbury is concerned that long-term interest rates might rise by as much as 1% before June. You looked online and found that June T-bond futures are trading at 111'25. What are the risks of not hedging, and how might TS hedge this exposure? In your analysis, consider what would happen if interest rates all increased by 1%.

Chapter 25

Bankruptcy, Reorganization, and Liquidation

Thus far, we have dealt with issues faced by growing, successful enterprises. However, many firms encounter financial difficulties, and some—including such big names as General Motors, Chrysler, Delta Air Lines, and Lehman Brothers—are forced into bankruptcy. When a firm encounters financial distress, its managers must try to ward off a total collapse and thereby minimize losses. The ability to hang on during rough times often means the difference between forced liquidation versus rehabilitation and eventual success. An understanding of bankruptcy is also critical to the executives of healthy firms, because they must know the best actions to take when their customers or suppliers face the threat of bankruptcy.

Beginning of Chapter Questions

As you read the chapter, consider how you would answer the following questions. You *should not* necessarily be able to answer the questions before you read the chapter. Rather, you should use them to get a sense of the issues covered in the chapter. After reading the chapter, you should be able to give at least partial answers to the questions, and you should be able to give better answers after the chapter has been discussed in class. Note, too, that it is often useful, when answering conceptual questions, to use hypothetical data to illustrate your answer. (There is no model on the textbook's Web site for these Beginning of Chapter Questions.)

1. Is **bankruptcy** a fairly common occurrence among large companies, or is it restricted primarily to small firms?
2. How can a company use a bankruptcy to abrogate labor contracts? Has this occurred in certain industries in recent years?
3. In your answers to the following set of questions, assume that Ross Corporation has $200 million of assets at book value, $150 million of liabilities owed to 500 different creditors, and $50 million of common equity book value. Also, assume that Ross has failed to make timely payments on its debt. The assets are worth less than the $200 million shown on the balance sheet, although their actual market value is uncertain. The company issued mortgage bonds that are held by public bondholders and are secured by real estate, and 15 different banks hold loans secured by all of the company's accounts receivable, inventories, and equipment. There are also some

250 general (unsecured) creditors, including accounts payable, accrued wages and taxes, and pension plan obligations. Answer the following questions:

   a. Should Ross attempt to resolve its problems using **informal procedures,** or should it file for bankruptcy? Why?
   b. What are the two key **chapters** in the bankruptcy code, and what is the primary effect of each one?
   c. Who is more likely to initiate **formal bankruptcy proceedings**—the company or its creditors? What exactly would be filed to start the bankruptcy process?
   d. If the company initiated the proceedings, would it be more likely to seek relief under **Chapter 7** or **Chapter 11?** Would the same be true if a creditor initiated the proceedings? Explain.
   e. What is the **common pool problem**, and would it be likely to arise in Ross's case in the absence of a bankruptcy filing?
   f. What is the **automatic stay,** and is it likely that it would be applied in this case?
   g. What is a **pre-pack,** and is it likely that one would be used in this case?
   h. What is a **cramdown,** and is it likely that one would be used in this case?
   i. Define the terms **absolute priority doctrine** and **relative priority doctrine.**
   j. If the assets were sold at auction and the company **liquidated,** how would the proceeds be divided up?
   k. If the company were **reorganized,** who would get what in the reorganization?

25.1 Financial Distress and Its Consequences

We begin with some background on financial distress and its consequences.[1]

25.1a Causes of Business Failure

A company's intrinsic value is the present value of its expected future free cash flows. There are many factors that can cause this value to decline. These factors

---

1. Much of the current academic work in the area of financial distress and bankruptcy is based on writings by Edward I. Altman. See Edward I. Altman and Edith Hotchkiss, *Corporate Financial Distress and Bankruptcy: Predict and Avoid Bankruptcy, Analyze and Invest in Distressed Debt* (Hoboken, NJ: Wiley, 2006).

include general economic conditions, industry trends, and company-specific problems such as shifting consumer tastes, obsolete technology, and changing demographics in existing retail locations. Financial factors, such as too much debt and unexpected increases in interest rates, can also cause business failures. The importance of the different factors varies over time, and most business failures occur because a number of factors combine to make the business unsustainable. Further, case studies show that financial difficulties are usually the result of a series of errors, misjudgments, and interrelated weaknesses that can be attributed directly or indirectly to management. In a few cases, such as Enron and WorldCom, fraud leads to bankruptcy.

As you might guess, signs of potential financial distress are generally evident in a ratio analysis long before the firm actually fails, and researchers use ratio analysis to estimate the probability that a given firm will go bankrupt. Financial analysts constantly are seeking ways to assess a firm's likelihood of going bankrupt. We discuss one method, **multiple discriminant analysis (MDA)**, in *Web Extension 25A.*

25.1b The Business Failure Record

Although bankruptcy is more frequent among smaller firms, it is clear from Table 25-1 that large firms are not immune. This is especially true in the current global economic crisis: Six of the largest bankruptcies occurred in 2008 and 2009.

Bankruptcy obviously is painful for a company's shareholders, but it also can be harmful to the economy if the company is very large or is in a critical sector. For example, the failure of Lehman Brothers in September 2008 sparked a global run on financial institutions that froze credit markets and contributed to the ensuing global recession. It is not clear whether the damage to the world economy could have been mitigated if the government had intervened to prevent Lehman's failure, but the government subsequently decided not to take chances with many other troubled financial institutions. For example, the government helped arrange the 2008 acquisition of Wachovia by Wells Fargo, the 2008 acquisition of Bear Sterns by JPMorgan Chase, and the 2009 acquisition of Merrill Lynch by Bank of America (despite Bank of America's misgivings). In addition, the government provided

TABLE 25-1	**The Ten Largest Bankruptcies since 1980 (Billions of Dollars)**		
Company	**Business**	**Assets**	**Date**
Lehman Brothers Holdings Inc.	Investment banking	$691.1	September 15, 2008
Washington Mutual Inc.	Financial services	327.9	September 26, 2008
WorldCom Inc.	Telecommunications	103.9	July 21, 2002
General Motors Corporation	Auto manufacturing	91.0	June 1, 2009
CIT Group Inc.	Financial services	80.4	November 1, 2009
Enron Corp.	Energy trading	63.4	December 2, 2001
Conseco Inc.	Financial services	61.4	December 17, 2002
Chrysler LLC	Auto manufacturing	39.3	April 30, 2009
Thornburg Mortgage Inc.	Residential mortgage	36.5	May 1, 2009
Pacific Gas and Electric Co.	Energy	36.1	April 6, 2001

Source: **BankruptcyData.com**, a division of New Generation Research, July 2011.

billions of dollars of capital to many major financial institutions in 2008, including AIG. In each of these cases, the government decided that a complete failure of these institutions might cause the entire financial system to collapse.

In other cases, the government has decided that a company was too important to the nonfinancial side of the economy to be allowed to go through liquidation. For example, in 2008 and 2009 the government provided billions of dollars of financing to General Motors and Chrysler. Even though these companies subsequently went through bankruptcy proceedings in 2009, they avoided liquidation, still have a significant number of employees, and remain major players in the automobile industry. In past years, the government also has intervened to support troubled firms in other critical sectors, such as Lockheed and Douglas Aircraft in the defense industry.

Self Test

What are the major causes of business failure?

Do business failures occur evenly over time?

Which size of firm, large or small, is most prone to business failure? Why?

25.2 Issues Facing a Firm in Financial Distress

Financial distress begins when a firm is unable to meet scheduled payments or when cash flow projections indicate that it will soon be unable to do so. As the situation develops, five central issues arise.

1. Is the firm's inability to meet scheduled debt payments a temporary cash flow problem, or is it a permanent problem caused by asset values having fallen below debt obligations?
2. If the problem is a temporary one, then an agreement with creditors that gives the firm time to recover and to satisfy everyone may be worked out. However, if basic long-run asset values have truly declined, then economic losses have occurred. In this event, who should bear the losses, and who should get whatever value remains?
3. Is the company "worth more dead than alive"? That is, would the business be more valuable if it were liquidated and sold off in pieces or if it were maintained and continued in operation?
4. Should the firm file for protection under Chapter 11 of the Bankruptcy Act, or should it try to use informal procedures? (Both reorganization and liquidation can be accomplished either informally or under the direction of a bankruptcy court.)
5. Who should control the firm while it is being liquidated or rehabilitated? Should the existing management be left in charge, or should a trustee be placed in charge of operations?

In the remainder of the chapter, we discuss these issues in turn.

Self Test

What five major issues must be addressed when a firm faces financial distress?

25.3 Settlements without Going through Formal Bankruptcy

When a firm experiences financial distress, its managers and creditors must decide whether the problem is temporary and the firm is really financially viable or whether a permanent problem exists that endangers the firm's life. Then the parties must decide whether to try to solve the problem informally or under the direction of a bankruptcy court. Because of costs associated with formal bankruptcy—including the disruptions that occur when a firm's customers, suppliers, and employees learn that it has filed under the Bankruptcy Act—it is preferable to reorganize (or liquidate) outside of formal bankruptcy. We first discuss informal settlement procedures and then the procedures under a formal bankruptcy.

25.3a Informal Reorganization

In the case of an economically sound company whose financial difficulties appear to be temporary, creditors are generally willing to work with the company to help it recover and reestablish itself on a sound financial basis. Such voluntary plans, commonly called **workouts**, usually require a **restructuring** of the firm's debt, because current cash flows are insufficient to service the existing debt. Restructuring typically involves extension and/or composition. In an **extension**, creditors postpone the dates of required interest or principal payments, or both. In a **composition**, creditors voluntarily reduce their fixed claims on the debtor by accepting a lower principal amount, by reducing the interest rate on the debt, by taking equity in exchange for debt, or by some combination of these changes.

A debt restructuring begins with a meeting between the failing firm's managers and creditors. The creditors appoint a committee consisting of four or five of the largest creditors plus one or two of the smaller ones. This meeting is often arranged and conducted by an **adjustment bureau** associated with and run by a local credit managers' association.[2] The first step is for management to draw up a list of creditors that shows the amounts of debt owed. There are typically different classes of debt, ranging from first-mortgage holders to unsecured creditors. Next, the company develops information showing the value of the firm under different scenarios. Typically, one scenario is going out of business, selling off the assets, and then distributing the proceeds to the various creditors in accordance with the priority of their claims, with any surplus going to the common stockholders. The company may hire an appraiser to get an appraisal of the value of the firm's property to use as a basis for this scenario. Other scenarios include continued operations, frequently with some improvements in capital equipment, marketing, and perhaps some management changes.

This information is then shared with the firm's bankers and other creditors. Frequently, it can be demonstrated that the firm's debts exceed its liquidating value, and the legal fees and other costs associated with a formal liquidation under federal bankruptcy procedures will materially lower the net proceeds available to creditors. Furthermore, it generally takes at least a year (and often several years) to resolve matters in a formal proceeding, so the present value of the eventual proceeds will be lower still. This information, when presented in a credible manner, often convinces

---

2. There is a nationwide group called the National Association of Credit Management, which consists of bankers and industrial companies' credit managers. This group sponsors research on credit policy and problems, conducts seminars on credit management, and operates local chapters in cities throughout the nation. These local chapters frequently operate adjustment bureaus.

creditors they would be better off accepting something less than the full amount of their claims rather than holding out for the full face amount. If management and the major creditors agree that the problems can probably be resolved, then a more formal plan is drafted and presented to all the creditors, along with the reasons creditors should be willing to compromise on their claims.

In developing the reorganization plan, creditors prefer an extension because it promises eventual payment in full. In some cases, creditors may agree not only to postpone the date of payment but also to subordinate existing claims to vendors who are willing to extend new credit during the workout period. Similarly, creditors may agree to accept a lower interest rate on loans during the extension, perhaps in exchange for a pledge of collateral. Because of the sacrifices involved, the creditors must have faith that the debtor firm will be able to solve its problems.

In a composition, creditors agree to reduce their claims. Typically, creditors receive cash and/or new securities that have a combined market value that is less than the amounts owed them. The cash and securities, which might have a value of only 10% of the original claim, are taken as full settlement of the original debt. Bargaining will take place between the debtor and the creditors over the savings that result from avoiding the costs of legal bankruptcy: administrative costs, legal fees, investigative costs, and so on. In addition to escaping such costs, the debtor gains because the stigma of bankruptcy may be avoided. As a result, the debtor may be induced to part with most of the savings from avoiding formal bankruptcy.

Often, the bargaining process will result in a restructuring that involves both extension and composition. For example, the settlement may provide for a cash payment of 25% of the debt immediately plus a new note promising six future installments of 10% each, for a total payment of 85%.

Voluntary settlements are both informal and simple; they are also relatively inexpensive, because legal and administrative expenses are held to a minimum. Thus, voluntary procedures generally result in the largest return to creditors. Although creditors do not obtain immediate payment and may even have to accept less than is owed them, they generally recover more money, and sooner, than if the firm were to file for bankruptcy.

In recent years, the fact that restructurings can sometimes help creditors avoid showing a loss has motivated some creditors, especially banks and insurance companies, to agree to voluntary restructurings. Thus, a bank "in trouble" with its regulators over weak capital ratios may agree to extend loans that are used to pay the interest on earlier loans—in order to keep the bank from having to write down the value of those earlier loans. This particular type of restructuring depends on (1) the willingness of the regulators to go along with the process, and (2) whether the bank is likely to recover more in the end by restructuring the debt than by forcing the borrower into bankruptcy immediately.

We should point out that informal voluntary settlements are not reserved for small firms. International Harvester (now Navistar International) avoided formal bankruptcy proceedings by getting its creditors to agree to restructure more than $3.5 billion of debt. Likewise, Chrysler's creditors accepted both an extension and a composition to help it through its bad years in the late 1970s before it merged with Daimler-Benz. The biggest problem with informal reorganizations is getting all the parties to agree to the voluntary plan. This problem, called the *holdout* problem, is discussed in a later section.

25.3b Informal Liquidation

When it is obvious that a firm is more valuable dead than alive, informal procedures can also be used to **liquidate** the firm. **Assignment** is an informal procedure for liquidating a firm, and it usually yields creditors a larger amount than they would get in a formal bankruptcy liquidation. However, assignments are feasible only if the firm is small and its affairs are not too complex. An assignment calls for title to the debtor's assets to be transferred to a third party, known as an **assignee** or trustee. The assignee is instructed to liquidate the assets through a private sale or public auction and then to distribute the proceeds among the creditors on a pro rata basis. The assignment does not automatically discharge the debtor's obligations. However, the debtor may have the assignee write the requisite legal language on the check to each creditor so that endorsement of the check constitutes acknowledgment of full settlement of the claim.

Assignment has some advantages over liquidation in federal bankruptcy courts in terms of time, legal formality, and expense. The assignee has more flexibility in disposing of property than does a federal bankruptcy trustee, so action can be taken sooner, before inventory becomes obsolete or machinery rusts. Also, because the assignee is often familiar with the debtor's business, better results may be achieved. However, an assignment does not automatically result in a full and legal discharge of all the debtor's liabilities, nor does it protect the creditors against fraud. Both of these problems can be reduced by formal liquidation in bankruptcy, which we discuss in a later section.

Self Test	Define the following terms: (1) restructuring, (2) extension, (3) composition, (4) assignment, and (5) assignee (trustee).
	What are the advantages of liquidation by assignment versus a formal bankruptcy liquidation?

25.4 Federal Bankruptcy Law

U.S. bankruptcy laws were first enacted in 1898. They were modified substantially in 1938 and again in 1978, and some fine-tuning was done in 1986. In 2005, Congress further modified the bankruptcy code, speeding up bankruptcy proceedings for companies and making it more difficult for consumers to take advantage of provisions that can wipe out certain debts. The primary purpose of the bankruptcy law is to prevent individual creditors from forcing the liquidation of firms that are worth more as ongoing concerns, and thus causing harm to other stakeholders.

Currently, our bankruptcy law consists of eight odd-numbered chapters, plus one even-numbered chapter. (The old even-numbered chapters were deleted when the act was revised in 1978.) Chapters 1, 3, and 5 contain general provisions applicable to the other chapters. **Chapter 11**, which deals with business reorganization, is the most important section from a financial management viewpoint. **Chapter 7** details the procedures to be followed when liquidating a firm; generally, Chapter 7 does not come into play unless it has been determined that reorganization under Chapter 11 is not feasible. Chapter 9 deals with financially distressed municipalities; Chapter 12 covers special procedures for family-owned farms; Chapter 13 covers the adjustment of debts for "individuals with regular income"; and Chapter 15 sets up a system of trustees who help administer proceedings under the act.

A firm is officially bankrupt when it files for bankruptcy with a federal court. When you read that a company such as General Motors has "filed for court protection under Chapter 11," this means the company is attempting to reorganize under the supervision of a bankruptcy court. Formal bankruptcy proceedings are designed to protect both the firm and its creditors. On the one hand, if the problem is temporary insolvency, then the firm may use bankruptcy proceedings to gain time to solve its cash flow problems without asset seizure by its creditors. On the other hand, if the firm is truly bankrupt in the sense that liabilities exceed assets, then creditors can use bankruptcy procedures to stop the firm's managers from continuing to operate, lose more money, and thus deplete assets that should go to creditors.

Bankruptcy law is flexible in that it provides scope for negotiations between a company, its creditors, its labor force, and its stockholders. A case is opened by filing a petition with one of the 291 bankruptcy courts serving 90 judicial districts. The petition may be either **voluntary** or **involuntary**; that is, it may be filed either by the firm's management or by its creditors. After a filing, a committee of unsecured creditors is then appointed by the Office of the U.S. Trustee to negotiate with management for a reorganization, which may include the restructuring of debt. Under Chapter 11, a **trustee** will be appointed to take over the company if the court deems current management incompetent or if fraud is suspected. Normally, though, the existing management retains control. If no fair and feasible reorganization can be worked out, the bankruptcy judge will order that the firm be liquidated under procedures spelled out in Chapter 7 of the Bankruptcy Act, in which case a trustee will always be appointed.[3]

Self Test

Define the following terms: bankruptcy law, Chapter 11, Chapter 7, trustee, voluntary bankruptcy, and involuntary bankruptcy.

How does a firm formally declare bankruptcy?

25.5 Reorganization in Bankruptcy

It might appear that most reorganizations should be handled informally because informal reorganizations are faster and less costly than formal bankruptcy. However, two problems often arise to stymie informal reorganizations and thus force debtors into Chapter 11 bankruptcy: the common pool problem and the holdout problem.[4]

To illustrate these problems, consider a firm that is having financial difficulties. It is worth $9 million as a going concern (this is the present value of its expected future operating cash flows) but only $7 million if it is liquidated. The firm's debt totals $10 million at face value—ten creditors with equal priority each have a $1 million claim. Now suppose the firm's liquidity deteriorates to the point that it defaults on one of its loans. The holder of that loan has the contractual right to *accelerate* the claim, which means the creditor can *foreclose* on the loan and demand payment of the entire balance. Further, since most debt agreements have *cross-default provisions*, defaulting on one loan effectively places all loans in default.

---

3. For a discussion of European bankruptcy laws, see Kevin M. J. Kaiser, "European Bankruptcy Laws: Implications for Corporations Facing Financial Distress," *Financial Management,* Autumn 1996, pp. 67–85.

4. The issues discussed in this section are covered in more detail in Thomas H. Jackson, *The Logic and Limits of Bankruptcy Law* (Frederick, MD: Beard Group, 2001). Also see Stuart C. Gilson, "Managing Default: Some Evidence on How Firms Choose between Workouts and Chapter 11," *Journal of Applied Corporate Finance,* Summer 1991, pp. 62–70; and Yehning Chen, J. Fred Weston, and Edward I. Altman, "Financial Distress and Restructuring Models," *Financial Management,* Summer 1995, pp. 57–75.

The firm's market value is less than the $10 million face value of debt, regardless of whether it remains in business or liquidates. Therefore, it would be impossible to pay off all of the creditors in full. However, the creditors in total would be better off if the firm is not shut down, because they could ultimately recover $9 million if the firm remains in business but only $7 million if it is liquidated. The problem here, which is called the **common pool problem,** is that in the absence of protection under the Bankruptcy Act, individual creditors would have an incentive to foreclose on the firm even though it is worth more as an ongoing concern.

An individual creditor would have the incentive to foreclose because it could then force the firm to liquidate a portion of its assets to pay off that particular creditor's $1 million claim in full. The payment to that creditor would probably require the liquidation of vital assets, which might cause a shutdown of the firm and thus lead to a total liquidation. Therefore, the value of the remaining creditors' claims would decline. Of course, all the creditors would recognize the gains to be had from this strategy, so they would storm the debtor with foreclosure notices. Even those creditors who understand the merits of keeping the firm alive would be forced to foreclose, because the foreclosures of the other creditors would reduce the payoff to those who do not. In our hypothetical example, if seven creditors foreclosed and forced liquidation, they would be paid in full, and the remaining three creditors would receive nothing.

With many creditors, as soon as a firm defaults on one loan, there is the potential for a disruptive flood of foreclosures that would make the creditors collectively worse off. In our example, the creditors would lose $9 − $7 = $2 million in value if a flood of foreclosures were to force the firm to liquidate. If the firm had only one creditor—say, a single bank loan—then the common pool problem would not exist. If a bank had loaned the company $10 million, it would not force liquidation to get $7 million when it could keep the firm alive and eventually realize $9 million.

Chapter 11 of the Bankruptcy Act provides a solution to the common pool problem through its **automatic stay** provision. *An automatic stay, which is forced on all creditors in a bankruptcy, limits the ability of creditors to foreclose to collect their individual claims.* However, the creditors can collectively foreclose on the debtor and force liquidation.

Although bankruptcy gives the firm a chance to work out its problems without the threat of creditor foreclosure, management does not have a completely free rein over the firm's assets. First, bankruptcy law requires the debtor firm to request permission from the court to take many actions, and the law also gives creditors the right to petition the bankruptcy court to block almost any action the firm might take while in bankruptcy. Second, **fraudulent conveyance** statutes, which are part of debtor–creditor law, protect creditors from unjustified transfers of property by a firm in financial distress.

To illustrate fraudulent conveyance, suppose a holding company is contemplating bankruptcy protection for one of its subsidiaries. The holding company might be tempted to sell some or all of the subsidiary's assets to itself (the parent company) for less than the true market value. This transaction would reduce the value of the subsidiary by the difference between the true market value of its assets and the amount paid, and the loss would be borne primarily by the subsidiary's creditors. Such a transaction would be voided by the courts as a fraudulent conveyance. Note also that transactions favoring one creditor at the expense of another can be voided under the same law. For example, a transaction in which an asset is sold and the proceeds are used to pay one creditor in full at the expense of other creditors could be voided. Thus, fraudulent conveyance laws also protect creditors from each other.[5]

The second problem that is mitigated by bankruptcy law is the **holdout problem.** To illustrate this, consider again our example firm with ten creditors owed $1 million each but with assets worth only $9 million. The goal of the firm is to avoid liquidation by remedying the default. In an informal workout, this would require a reorganization plan that is agreed to by each of the ten creditors. Suppose the firm offers each creditor new debt with a face value of $850,000 in exchange for the old $1,000,000 face value debt. If each of the creditors accepted the offer, the firm could be successfully reorganized. The reorganization would leave the equity holders with some value—the market value of the equity would be $9,000,000 − 10($850,000) = $500,000. Further, the creditors would have claims worth $8.5 million, much more than the $7 million value of their claims in liquidation.

Although such an exchange offer seems to benefit all parties, it might not be accepted by the creditors. Here's why: Suppose seven of the ten creditors tender their bonds; thus, seven creditors each now have claims with a face value of $850,000 each, or $5,950,000 in total, while the three creditors that did not tender their bonds each still have a claim with a face value of $1 million. The total face value of the debt at this point is $8,950,000, which is less than the $9 million value of the firm. In this situation, the three holdout creditors would receive the full face value of their debt. However, this probably would not happen, because (1) all of the creditors would be sophisticated enough to realize this could happen, and (2) each creditor would want to be one of the three holdouts that gets paid in full. Thus, it is likely that none of the creditors would accept the offer. The holdout problem makes it difficult to restructure the firm's debts. Again, if the firm had a single creditor, there would be no holdout problem.

The holdout problem is mitigated in bankruptcy proceedings by the bankruptcy court's ability to lump creditors into classes. Each class is considered to have accepted a reorganization plan if two-thirds of the amount of debt and one-half the number of claimants vote for the plan, and the plan will be approved by the court if it is deemed to be "fair and equitable" to the dissenting parties. This procedure, in which the court mandates a reorganization plan in spite of dissent, is called a **cramdown,** because the court crams the plan down the throats of the dissenters. The ability of the court to force acceptance of a reorganization plan greatly reduces the incentive for creditors to hold out. Thus, in our example, if the reorganization plan offered each creditor a new claim worth $850,000 in face value along with information that each creditor would probably receive only $700,000 under the liquidation alternative, then reorganization would have a good chance of success.

It is easier for a firm with few creditors to reorganize informally than it is for a firm with many creditors. A 1990 study examined 169 publicly traded firms that experienced severe financial distress from 1978 to 1987.[6] About half of the firms reorganized without filing for bankruptcy, while the other half were forced to reorganize in bankruptcy. The firms that reorganized without filing for bankruptcy owed most of their debt to a few banks and had fewer creditors. Generally, bank

---

5. The bankruptcy code requires that all transactions undertaken by the firm in the 6 months prior to a bankruptcy filing be reviewed by the court for fraudulent conveyance, and the review can go back as far as 3 years.
6. See Stuart Gilson, Kose John, and Larry Lang, "Troubled Debt Restructurings: An Empirical Study of Private Reorganization of Firms in Default," *Journal of Financial Economics,* October 1990, pp. 315–354.

debt can be reorganized outside of bankruptcy, but a publicly traded bond issue held by thousands of individual bondholders makes reorganization difficult.

Filing for bankruptcy under Chapter 11 has several other features that help the bankrupt firm.

1. Interest and principal payments, including interest on delayed payments, may be delayed without penalty until a reorganization plan is approved, and the plan itself may call for even further delays. This permits cash generated from operations to be used to sustain operations rather than be paid to creditors.

2. The firm is permitted to issue **debtor-in-possession (DIP) financing**. DIP financing enhances the ability of the firm to borrow funds for short-term liquidity purposes, because such loans are, under the law, senior to all previous unsecured debt.

3. The debtor firm's managers are given the exclusive right for 120 days after filing for bankruptcy protection to submit a reorganization plan, plus another 60 days to obtain agreement on the plan from the affected parties. The court may also extend these dates up to 18 months. After management's first right to submit a plan has expired, any party to the proceedings may propose its own reorganization plan.

Under the early bankruptcy laws, most formal reorganization plans were guided by the **absolute priority doctrine**.[7] This doctrine holds that creditors should be compensated for their claims in a rigid hierarchical order and that senior claims must be paid in full before junior claims can receive even a dime. If there were any chance that a delay would lead to losses by senior creditors, then the firm would be shut down and liquidated. However, an alternative position, the **relative priority doctrine,** holds that more flexibility should be allowed in a reorganization and that a balanced consideration should be given to all claimants. The current law represents a movement away from absolute priority toward relative priority.

The primary role of the bankruptcy court in a reorganization is to determine the **fairness** and the **feasibility** of the proposed plan of reorganization. The basic doctrine of fairness states that claims must be recognized in the order of their legal and contractual priority. Feasibility means that there is a reasonable chance that the reorganized company will be viable. Carrying out the concepts of fairness and feasibility in a reorganization involves the following steps.

1. Future sales must be estimated.
2. Operating conditions must be analyzed so that future earnings and cash flows can be predicted.
3. The appropriate capitalization rate must be determined.
4. This capitalization rate must then be applied to the estimated cash flows to obtain an estimate of the company's value.[8]

---

7. For more on absolute priority, see Lawrence A. Weiss, "The Bankruptcy Code and Violations of Absolute Priority," *Journal of Applied Corporate Finance,* Summer 1991, pp. 71–78; William Beranek, Robert Boehmer, and Brooke Smith, "Much Ado about Nothing: Absolute Priority Deviations in Chapter 11," *Financial Management,* Autumn 1996, pp. 102–109; and Allan C. Eberhart, William T. Moore, and Rodney Roenfeldt, "Security Pricing and Deviations from the Absolute Priority Rule in Bankruptcy Proceedings," *Journal of Finance,* December 1990, pp. 1457–1469.

8. Several different approaches can be used to estimate a company's value. Market-determined multiples such as the price/earnings ratio, which are obtained from an analysis of comparable firms, can be applied to some measure of the company's earnings or cash flow. Alternatively, discounted cash flow techniques may be used. The key point here is that fairness requires the value of a company facing reorganization to be estimated so that potential offers can be evaluated rationally by the bankruptcy court.

5. An appropriate capital structure for the company after it emerges from Chapter 11 must be determined.
6. The reorganized firm's securities must be allocated to the various claimants in a fair and equitable manner.

The primary test of feasibility in a reorganization is whether the fixed charges after reorganization will be adequately covered by earnings. Adequate coverage generally requires an improvement in earnings, a reduction of fixed charges, or both. Among the actions that must generally be taken are the following.

1. Debt maturities are usually lengthened, interest rates may be lowered, and some debt is usually converted into equity.
2. When the quality of management has been substandard, a new team must be given control of the company.
3. If inventories have become obsolete or depleted, they must be replaced.
4. Sometimes the plant and equipment must be modernized before the firm can operate and compete successfully.
5. Reorganization may also require an improvement in production, marketing, advertising, and/or other functions.
6. It is sometimes necessary to develop new products or markets to enable the firm to move from areas where economic trends are poor into areas with more potential for growth.
7. Labor unions must agree to accept lower wages and less restrictive work rules. This was a major issue for United Airlines in 2003 as it attempted to emerge from Chapter 11 bankruptcy protection. By threatening liquidation, UAL was able to squeeze a $6.6 billion reduction in payroll costs from its pilots over 6 years and another $2.6 billion from its ground-crew workers. This wasn't enough, though, and UAL didn't emerge from bankruptcy for another 3 years.

These actions usually require at least some new money, so most reorganization plans include new investors who are willing to put up new capital.

It might appear that stockholders have very little to say in a bankruptcy situation in which the firm's assets are worth less than the face value of its debt. Under the absolute priority rule, stockholders in such a situation should get nothing of value under a reorganization plan. In fact, however, stockholders may be able to extract some of the firm's value. This occurs because (1) stockholders generally continue to control the firm during the bankruptcy proceedings, (2) stockholders have the first right (after management's 120-day window) to file a reorganization plan, and (3) for the creditors, developing a plan and taking it through the courts would be expensive and time-consuming. Given this situation, creditors may support a plan under which they are not paid off in full and where the old stockholders will control the reorganized company, just because the creditors want to get the problem behind them and to get some money in the near future.

25.5a Illustration of a Reorganization

Reorganization procedures may be illustrated with an example involving the Columbia Software Company, a regional firm that specializes in selling, installing, and servicing accounting software for small businesses.[9] Table 25-2 gives Columbia's

---

9. This example is based on an actual reorganization, although the company name has been changed and the numbers have been changed slightly to simplify the analysis.

TABLE 25-2	Columbia Software Company: Balance Sheet as of March 31, 2012 (Millions of Dollars)	
Assets		
Current assets		$ 3.50
Net fixed assets		12.50
Other assets		0.70
Total assets		$16.70
Liabilities and Equity		
Accounts payable		$ 1.00
Accrued taxes		0.25
Notes payable		0.25
Other current liabilities		1.75
7.5% first-mortgage bonds, due 2020		6.00
9% subordinated debentures, due 2015[a]		7.00
Total liabilities		$16.25
Common stock ($1 par)		1.00
Paid-in capital		3.45
Retained earnings		(4.00)
Total liabilities and equity		$16.70

[a]The debentures are subordinated to the notes payable.

balance sheet as of March 31, 2012. The company had been suffering losses running to $2.5 million a year, and (as the following discussion will make clear) the asset values in the balance sheet are overstated relative to their market values. The firm was **insolvent,** which means that the book values of its liabilities were greater than the market values of its assets, so it filed a petition with a federal court for reorganization under Chapter 11. Management filed a plan of reorganization with the court on June 13, 2012. The plan was subsequently submitted for review by the SEC.[10]

The plan concluded that the company could not be internally reorganized and that the only feasible solution would be to combine Columbia with a larger, nationwide software company. Accordingly, management solicited the interest of a number of software companies. Late in July 2012, Moreland Software showed an interest in Columbia. On August 3, 2012, Moreland made a formal proposal to take over Columbia's $6 million of 7.5% first-mortgage bonds, to pay the $250,000 in taxes owed by Columbia, and to provide 40,000 shares of Moreland common stock to satisfy the remaining creditor claims. Since the Moreland stock had a market price of $75 per share, the value of the stock was $3 million. Thus, Moreland was offering $3 million of stock plus assuming $6 million of loans and $250,000 of taxes—a total of $9.25 million for assets that had a book value of $16.7 million.

---

10. Reorganization plans must be submitted to the Securities and Exchange Commission (SEC) if (1) the securities of the debtor are publicly held and (2) total indebtedness exceeds $3 million. However, in recent years the only bankruptcy cases that the SEC has become involved in are those that are either precedent-setting or involve issues of national interest.

TABLE 25-3	Columbia Software Company: Reorganization Plan

Senior Claims

Taxes	$ 250,000	Paid off by Moreland
Mortgage bonds	$6,000,000	Assumed by Moreland

The reorganization plan for the remaining $10 million of liabilities, based on 40,000 shares at a price of $75 for a total market value of $3 million, or 30% of the remaining liabilities, is as follows:

Junior Claims (1)	Original Amount (2)	30% of Claim Amount (3)	Claim after Subordination (4)	Number of Shares of Common Stock (5)	Percentage of Original Claim Received (6)
Notes payable	$ 250,000	$ 75,000	$ 250,000[a]	3,333	100%
Unsecured creditors	2,750,000	825,000	825,000	11,000	30
Subordinated debentures	7,000,000	2,100,000	1,925,000[a]	25,667	28
	$10,000,000	$ 3,000,000	$3,000,000	40,000	30

[a]Because the debentures are subordinated to the notes payable, $250,000 − $75,000 = $175,000 must be redistributed from the debentures to the notes payable; this leaves a claim of $2,100,000 − $175,000 = $1,925,000 for the debentures.

Moreland's plan is shown in Table 25-3. As in most Chapter 11 plans, the secured creditors' claims are paid in full (in this case, the mortgage bonds are taken over by Moreland Software). However, the total remaining unsecured claims equal $10 million against only $3 million of Moreland stock. Thus, each unsecured creditor would be entitled to receive 30% before the adjustment for subordination. Before this adjustment, holders of the notes payable would receive 30% of their $250,000 claim, or $75,000 in stock. However, the debentures are subordinated to the notes payable, so an additional $175,000 must be allocated to notes payable (see footnote a in Table 25-3). In Column 5, the dollar claims of each class of debt are restated in terms of the number of shares of Moreland common stock received by each class of unsecured creditors. Finally, Column 6 shows the percentage of the original claim that each group received. Of course, both the taxes and the secured creditors were paid off in full, while the stockholders received nothing.[11]

The bankruptcy court first evaluated the proposal from the standpoint of fairness. The court began by considering the value of Columbia Software as estimated by the unsecured creditors' committee and by a subgroup of debenture holders. After discussions with various experts, one group had arrived at estimated post-reorganization sales of $25 million per year. It further estimated that the profit margin on sales would equal 6%, thus producing estimated future annual earnings of $1.5 million.

This subgroup analyzed price/earnings ratios for comparable companies and arrived at 8 times future earnings for a capitalization factor. Multiplying 8 by

---

11. We do not show it, but $365,000 of fees for Columbia's attorneys and $123,000 of fees for the creditors' committee lawyers were also deducted. The current assets shown in Table 25-2 were net of these fees. Creditors joke (often bitterly) about the "lawyers first" rule in payouts in bankruptcy cases. It is often said, with much truth, that the only winners in bankruptcy cases are the attorneys.

$1.5 million gave an indicated equity value of the company of $12 million. This value was 4 times that of the 40,000 shares of Moreland stock offered for the remainder of the company. Thus, the subgroup concluded that the plan for reorganization did not meet the test of fairness. Note that, under both Moreland's plan and the subgroup's plan, the holders of common stock were to receive nothing, which is one of the risks of ownership, while the holders of the first-mortgage bonds were to be assumed by Moreland, which amounts to being paid in full.

The bankruptcy judge examined management's plan for feasibility, observing that in the reorganization Moreland Software would take over Columbia's properties. The court judged that the direction and aid of Moreland would remedy the deficiencies that had troubled Columbia. Whereas the debt/assets ratio of Columbia Software had become unbalanced, Moreland had only a moderate amount of debt. After consolidation, Moreland would still have a relatively low 27% debt ratio.

Moreland's net income before interest and taxes had been running at a level of approximately $15 million. The interest on its long-term debt after the merger would be $1.5 million and, taking short-term borrowings into account, would total a maximum of $2 million per year. The $15 million in earnings before interest and taxes would therefore provide an interest charge coverage of 7.5 times, exceeding the norm of 5 times for the industry.

Note that the question of feasibility would have been irrelevant if Moreland had offered $3 million in cash (rather than in stock) and payment of the bonds (rather than assuming them). It is the court's responsibility to protect the interests of Columbia's creditors. Because the creditors are being forced to take common stock or bonds guaranteed by another firm, the law requires the court to look into the feasibility of the transaction. However, if Moreland had made a cash offer, then the feasibility of its own operation after the transaction would not have been a concern.

Moreland Software was told of the subgroup's analysis and concern over the fairness of the plan. Further, Moreland was asked to increase the number of shares it offered. Moreland refused, and no other company offered to acquire Columbia. Because no better offer could be obtained and since the only alternative to the plan was liquidation (with an even lower realized value), Moreland's proposal was ultimately accepted by the creditors despite some disagreement with the valuation.

One interesting aspect of this case concerned an agency conflict between Columbia's old stockholders and its management. Columbia's management knew when it filed for bankruptcy that the company was probably worth less than the amount of its debt and hence that stockholders would probably receive nothing. Indeed, that situation did materialize. If management has a primary responsibility to the stockholders, then why would it file for bankruptcy knowing that the stockholders would receive nothing? In the first place, management did not know for certain that stockholders would receive nothing. But they were certain that, if they did not file for bankruptcy protection, then creditors would foreclose on the company's property and shut the company down, which would surely lead to liquidation and a total loss to stockholders. Second, if the company were liquidated, then managers and workers would lose their jobs and the managers would have a black mark on their records. Finally, Columbia's managers thought (correctly) that there was nothing they could do to protect the stockholders, so they might as well do what was best for the workforce, the creditors, and themselves—and that meant realizing the most value possible for the company's assets.

Some of the stockholders felt betrayed by management—they thought management should have taken more heroic steps to protect them, regardless of the cost to other parties. One stockholder suggested management should have sold off assets, taken the cash to Las Vegas, and rolled the dice. Then, if they won, they should have paid off the debt and had something left for stockholders, leaving debtholders holding the bag if they lost. Actually, management had done something a bit like this in the year preceding the bankruptcy. Management realized the company was floundering, was likely to sink under its current operating plan, and that only a "big winner" project would save the company. Hence they took on several risky, "bet the company" projects with negative expected NPVs but at least some chance for high profits. Unfortunately, those projects did not work out.

25.5b Prepackaged Bankruptcies

In recent years, a new type of reorganization that combines the advantages of both the informal workout and formal Chapter 11 reorganization has become popular. This hybrid is called a **prepackaged bankruptcy,** or **pre-pack.**[12]

In an informal workout, a debtor negotiates a restructuring with its creditors. Even though complex workouts typically involve corporate officers, lenders, lawyers, and investment bankers, workouts are still less expensive and less damaging to reputations than are Chapter 11 reorganizations. In a prepackaged bankruptcy, the debtor firm gets all, or most, of the creditors to agree to the reorganization plan *prior* to filing for bankruptcy. Then, a reorganization plan is filed along with, or shortly after, the bankruptcy petition. If enough creditors have signed on before the filing, a cramdown can be used to bring reluctant creditors along.

A logical question arises: Why would a firm that can arrange an informal reorganization want to file for bankruptcy? The three primary advantages of a prepackaged bankruptcy are (1) reduction of the holdout problem, (2) preserving creditors' claims, and (3) taxes. Perhaps the biggest benefit of a prepackaged bankruptcy is the reduction of the holdout problem, because a bankruptcy filing permits a cramdown that would otherwise be impossible. By eliminating holdouts, bankruptcy forces all creditors in each class to participate on a pro rata basis, which preserves the relative value of all claimants. Also, filing for formal bankruptcy can at times have positive tax implications. First, in an informal reorganization in which the debtholders trade debt for equity, if the original equity holders end up with less than 50% ownership then the company loses its accumulated tax losses. In formal bankruptcy, in contrast, the firm may get to keep its loss carryforwards. Second, in a workout, when (say) debt worth $1,000 is exchanged for debt worth $500, the reduction in debt of $500 is considered to be taxable income to the corporation. However, if this same situation occurs in a Chapter 11 reorganization, the difference is not treated as taxable income.[13]

All in all, prepackaged bankruptcies make sense in many situations. If sufficient agreement can be reached among creditors through informal negotiations, a

---

12. For more information on prepackaged bankruptcies, see John J. McConnell and Henri Servaes, "The Economics of Pre-Packaged Bankruptcy," *Journal of Applied Corporate Finance,* Summer 1991, pp. 93–97; Brian L. Betker, "An Empirical Examination of Prepackaged Bankruptcy," *Financial Management,* Spring 1995, pp. 3–18; Sris Chatterjee, Upinder S. Dhillon, and Gabriel G. Ramirez, "Resolution of Financial Distress: Debt Restructurings via Chapter 11, Prepackaged Bankruptcies, and Workouts," *Financial Management,* Spring 1996, pp. 5–18; and John J. McConnell, Ronald C. Lease, and Elizabeth Tashjian, "Prepacks as a Mechanism for Resolving Financial Distress," *Journal of Applied Corporate Finance,* Winter 1996, pp. 99–106.

13. Note that in both tax situations—loss carryforwards and debt value reductions—favorable tax treatment can be available in workouts if the firm is deemed to be legally insolvent—that is, if the market value of its assets is demonstrated to be less than the face value of its liabilities.

subsequent filing can solve the holdout problem and result in favorable tax treatment. For these reasons, the number of prepackaged bankruptcies has grown dramatically in recent years.

25.5c Reorganization Time and Expense

The time, expense, and headaches involved in a reorganization are almost beyond comprehension. Even in a small bankruptcy, such as one with assets valued between $2 million and $5 million, many people and groups are involved: lawyers representing the company, the U.S. Bankruptcy Trustee, each class of secured creditor, the general creditors as a group, tax authorities, and the stockholders if they are upset with management. There are time limits within which things are supposed to be done, but the process generally takes at least a year and usually much longer. The company must be given time to file its plan, and creditor groups must be given time to study and seek clarifications to it and then file counterplans, to which the company must respond. Also, different creditor classes often disagree among themselves as to how much each class should receive, and hearings must be held to resolve such conflicts.

Management will want to remain in business, whereas some well-secured creditors may want the company liquidated as quickly as possible. Often, some party's plan will involve selling the business to another concern, as was the case with Columbia Software in our earlier example. Obviously, it can take months to seek out and negotiate with potential merger candidates.

The typical bankruptcy case takes about 2 years from the time the company files for protection under Chapter 11 until the final reorganization plan is approved or rejected. While all of this is going on, the company's business suffers. Sales certainly won't be helped, key employees may leave, and the remaining employees will be worrying about their jobs rather than concentrating on their work. Further, management will be spending much of its time on the bankruptcy rather than running the business, and it won't be able to take any significant action without court approval, which requires filing a formal petition with the court and giving all parties involved a chance to respond.

Even if its operations do not suffer, the company's assets surely will be reduced by its own legal fees and the required court and trustee costs. Good bankruptcy lawyers charge from $200 to $400 or more per hour, depending on the location, so those costs are not trivial. The creditors also will be incurring legal costs. Indeed, the sound of all of those meters ticking at $400 or so an hour in a slow-moving hearing can be deafening.

Note that creditors also lose the time value of their money. A creditor with a $100,000 claim and a 10% opportunity cost who ends up getting $50,000 after 2 years would have been better off settling for $41,500 initially. When the creditor's legal fees, executive time, and general aggravation are taken into account, it might make sense to settle for $25,000 or even $20,000.

Both the troubled company and its creditors know the drawbacks of formal bankruptcy, or their lawyers will inform them. Armed with knowledge of how bankruptcy works, management may be in a strong position to persuade creditors to accept a workout that may seem to be unfair and unreasonable. Or, if a Chapter 11 case has already begun, creditors may at some point agree to settle just to stop the bleeding.

One final point should be made before closing this section. In most reorganization plans, creditors with claims of less than $1,000 are paid off in full. Paying off these "nuisance claims" does not cost much money, and it saves time and gets votes to support the plan.[14]

Define the following terms: common pool problem, holdout problem, automatic stay, cramdown, fraudulent conveyance, absolute priority doctrine, relative priority doctrine, fairness, feasibility, debtor-in-possession financing, and prepackaged bankruptcy.

What are the advantages of a formal reorganization under Chapter 11?

What are some recent trends regarding absolute versus relative priority doctrines?

How do courts assess the fairness and feasibility of reorganization plans?

Why have prepackaged bankruptcies become so popular in recent years?

25.6 Liquidation in Bankruptcy

If a company is "too far gone" to be reorganized, then it must be liquidated. Liquidation should occur when the business is worth more dead than alive, or when the possibility of restoring it to financial health is remote and the creditors are exposed to a high risk of greater loss if operations are continued. Earlier we discussed assignment, which is an informal liquidation procedure. Now we consider **liquidation in bankruptcy,** which is carried out under the jurisdiction of a federal bankruptcy court.

Chapter 7 of the Federal Bankruptcy Reform Act of 1978 deals with liquidation. It (1) provides safeguards against fraud by the debtor, (2) provides for an equitable distribution of the debtor's assets among the creditors, and (3) allows insolvent debtors to discharge all their obligations and thus be able to start new businesses unhampered by the burdens of prior debt. However, formal liquidation is time-consuming and costly, and it extinguishes the business.

The distribution of assets in a liquidation under Chapter 7 is governed by the following priority of claims.

1. *Past-due property taxes.*
2. *Secured creditors, who are entitled to the proceeds of the sale of specific property pledged for a lien or a mortgage.* If the proceeds from the sale of the pledged property do not fully satisfy a secured creditor's claim, the remaining balance is treated as a general creditor claim (see Item 10 below).[15]
3. *Legal fees and other expenses to administer and operate the bankrupt firm.* These costs include legal fees incurred in trying to reorganize.

---

14. For more information on bankruptcy costs, see Daryl M. Guffey and William T. Moore, "Direct Bankruptcy Costs: Evidence from the Trucking Industry," *The Financial Review,* May 1991, pp. 223–235.
15. When a firm or individual who goes bankrupt has a bank loan, the bank will attach any deposit balances. The loan agreement may stipulate that the bank has a first-priority claim on any deposits. If so, then the deposits are used to offset all or part of the bank loan—in legal terms, "the right of offset." In this case, the bank will not have to share the deposits with other creditors. Loan contracts often designate compensating balances as security against a loan. Even if the bank has no explicit claim against deposits, the bank will attach the deposits and hold them for the general body of creditors, including the bank itself. Without an explicit statement in the loan agreement, the bank does not receive preferential treatment with regard to attached deposits.

4. *Expenses incurred after an involuntary case has begun but before a trustee is appointed.*

5. *Wages due workers if earned within 3 months prior to the filing of the petition for bankruptcy.* The amount of wages is limited to $2,000 per employee.

6. *Claims for unpaid contributions to employee pension plans that should have been paid within 6 months prior to filing.* These claims, plus wages in Item 5, may not exceed the limit of $2,000 per wage earner.

7. *Unsecured claims for customer deposits.* These claims are limited to a maximum of $900 per individual.

8. *Taxes due to federal, state, county, and other government agencies.*

9. *Unfunded pension plan liabilities.* These liabilities have a claim above that of the general creditors for an amount up to 30% of the common and preferred equity, and any remaining unfunded pension claims rank with the general creditors.[16]

10. *General, or unsecured, creditors.* Holders of trade credit, unsecured loans, the unsatisfied portion of secured loans, and debenture bonds are classified as general creditors. Holders of subordinated debt also fall into this category, but they must turn over required amounts to the senior debt.

11. *Preferred stockholders.* These stockholders can receive an amount up to the par value of their stock.

12. *Common stockholders.* These stockholders receive any remaining funds.[17]

To illustrate how this priority system works, consider the balance sheet of Whitman Inc., shown in Table 25-4. Assets have a book value of $90 million. The claims are shown on the right-hand side of the balance sheet. Note that the debentures are subordinated to the notes payable to banks. Whitman filed for bankruptcy under Chapter 11, but since no fair and feasible reorganization could be arranged, the trustee is liquidating the firm under Chapter 7.

The assets as reported in the balance sheet are greatly overstated; they are, in fact, worth less than half the $90 million that is shown. The following amounts are realized on liquidation:

From sale of current assets	$28,000,000
From sale of fixed assets	5,000,000
Total receipts	$33,000,000

---

16. Pension plan liabilities have a significant bearing on bankruptcy settlements. As we discuss in **Web Chapter 30**, pension plans may be funded or unfunded. With a *funded* plan, the firm makes cash payments to an insurance company or to a trustee (generally a bank), which then uses these funds (and the interest earned on them) to pay retirees' pensions. With an *unfunded* plan, the firm is obligated to make payments to retirees, but it does not provide cash in advance. Many plans are actually partially funded—some money has been paid in advance but not enough to provide full pension benefits to all employees.

    If a firm goes bankrupt, the funded part of the pension plan remains intact and is available for retirees. Prior to 1974, employees had no explicit claims for unfunded pension liabilities, but under the Employees' Retirement Income Security Act of 1974 (ERISA), an amount up to 30% of the equity (common and preferred) is earmarked for employees' pension plans and has a priority over the general creditors, with any remaining pension claims having status equal to that of the general creditors. This means, in effect, that the funded portion of a bankrupt firm's pension plan is completely secured, whereas the unfunded portion ranks just above the general creditors. Obviously, unfunded pension liabilities should be of great concern to a firm's unsecured creditors.

17. Note that if different classes of common stock have been issued, then differential priorities may exist in stockholder claims.

TABLE 25-4	Whitman Inc.: Balance Sheet at Liquidation (Millions of Dollars)		
Current assets	$80.0	Accounts payable	$20.0
Net fixed assets	10.0	Notes payable (to banks)	10.0
		Accrued wages (1,400 @ $500)	0.7
		Federal taxes	1.0
		State and local taxes	0.3
		Current liabilities	$32.0
		First mortgage	6.0
		Second mortgage	1.0
		Subordinated debentures[a]	8.0
		Total long-term debt	$15.0
		Preferred stock	2.0
		Common stock	26.0
		Paid-in capital	4.0
		Retained earnings	11.0
		Total equity	$43.0
Total assets	$90.0	Total liabilities and equity	$90.0

[a]The debentures are subordinated to the notes payable.

The distribution of proceeds from the liquidation is shown in Table 25-5. The first-mortgage holders receive the $5 million in net proceeds from the sale of fixed property, leaving $28 million available to the remaining creditors, including a $1 million unsatisfied claim of the first-mortgage holders. Next are the fees and expenses of administering the bankruptcy, which are typically about 20% of gross proceeds (including the bankrupt firm's own legal fees); in this example, they are assumed to be $6 million. Next in priority are wages due workers, which total $700,000, and taxes due, which amount to $1.3 million. Thus far, the total amount of claims paid from the $33 million received from the asset sale is $13 million, leaving $20 million for the general creditors. In this example, we assume there are no claims for unpaid benefit plans or unfunded pension liabilities.

The claims of the general creditors total $40 million. Since $20 million is available, claimants will be allocated 50% of their claims initially, as shown in Column 3. However, the subordination adjustment requires that the subordinated debentures turn over to the notes payable all amounts received until the notes are satisfied. In this situation, the claim of the notes payable is $10 million but only $5 million is available; the deficiency is therefore $5 million. After transfer of $4 million from the subordinated debentures, there remains a deficiency of $1 million on the notes; this amount will remain unsatisfied.

Note that 90% of the bank claim is satisfied, whereas a maximum of 50% of other unsecured claims will be satisfied. These figures illustrate the usefulness of the subordination provision to the security to which the subordination is made.

Because no other funds remain, the claims of the holders of preferred and common stocks, as well as the subordinated debentures, are completely wiped out. Studies of the proceeds in bankruptcy liquidations reveal that unsecured creditors receive, on the average, about 15 cents on the dollar, while common stockholders generally receive nothing.

TABLE 25-5	Whitman Inc.: Distribution of Liquidation Proceeds (Millions of Dollars)	
Distribution to Priority Claimants		
Proceeds from the sale of assets	$33.0	
Less:		
1. First mortgage (paid from the sale of fixed assets)	5.0	
2. Fees and expenses of bankruptcy	6.0	
3. Wages due to workers within 3 months of bankruptcy	0.7	
4. Taxes due to federal, state, and local governments	1.3	
Funds available for distribution to general creditors	$20.0	

		Distribution to General Creditors		
General Creditors' Claims (1)	**Amount of Claim[a] (2)**	**Pro Rata Distribution[b] (3)**	**Distribution after Subordination Adjustment[c] (4)**	**Percentage of Original Claim Received[d] (5)**
Unsatisfied portion of first mortgage	$ 1.0	$ 0.5	$ 0.5	92%
Second mortgage	1.0	0.5	0.5	50
Notes payable (to banks)	10.0	5.0	9.0	90
Accounts payable	20.0	10.0	10.0	50
Subordinated debentures	8.0	4.0	0.0	0
Total	$40.0	$20.0	$20.0	

[a]Column 2 is the claim of each class of general creditor. Total claims equal $40.0 million.
[b]From the top section of the table, we see that $20 million is available for distribution to general creditors. Since there is $40 million worth of general creditor claims, the pro rata distribution will be $20/$40 = 0.50, or 50 cents on the dollar.
[c]The debentures are subordinate to the notes payable, so up to $5 million could be reallocated from debentures to notes payable. However, only $4 million is available to the debentures, so this entire amount is reallocated.
[d]Column 5 shows the results of dividing the Column 4 final allocation by the original claim shown in Column 2—except for the first mortgage, where the $5 million received from the sale of fixed assets is included in the calculation.

© Cengage Learning 2013

Self Test

Describe briefly the priority of claims in a formal liquidation.

What is the impact of subordination on the final allocation of proceeds from liquidation?

In general, how much do unsecured creditors receive from a liquidation? How much do stockholders receive?

25.7 Other Motivations for Bankruptcy

Normally, bankruptcy proceedings do not commence until a company has become so financially weak that it cannot meet its current obligations. However, bankruptcy law also permits a company to file for bankruptcy if its financial forecasts indicate that a continuation of current conditions would lead to insolvency.

A NATION OF DEFAULTERS?

Big corporate bankruptcies like those of Lehman Brothers and General Motors get the headlines, but they represent a small portion of the many bankruptcies each year, as shown in the accompanying table. Most business bankruptcies are liquidations (Chapter 7) of small businesses, and they rose steadily from 2006 through 2009 and then declined slightly in 2010. Although there are fewer business reorganizations than liquidations, reorganizations also increased steadily from 2006 through 2009, and then dropped off slightly in 2010.

Personal bankruptcies can be liquidations (Chapter 7) or reorganizations (Chapter 13). In a Chapter 7 bankruptcy, an individual can keep a small amount of exempt personal property, and the nonexempt property is sold to satisfy creditors. In a Chapter 13 bankruptcy, an individual is allowed to keep nonexempt personal property but typically must repay the debt within 3 to 5 years. A change in bankruptcy laws in 2005 made it more difficult for individuals to declare bankruptcy, but there has been a dramatic increase in personal bankruptcies since 2006, with liquidations leading the way.

Napoleon Bonaparte reputedly scorned England as "a nation of shopkeepers." If he had been able to see current U.S. bankruptcy statistics, would he have called modern America "a nation of defaulters"?

| | Business | | | | | Personal | | | |
Year	Ch. 7	Ch. 11	Ch. 12	Ch. 13	Total	Ch. 7	Ch. 11	Ch. 13	Total
2010	39,485	11,774	723	4,174	56,282	1,100,116	1,939	434,739	1,536,799
2009	41,962	13,683	544	4,500	60,837	1,008,870	1,506	402,462	1,412,838
2008	30,035	9,272	345	3,815	43,546	714,389	888	358,947	1,074,225
2007	18,751	5,736	376	3,412	28,322	500,613	617	321,359	822,590
2006	11,878	4,643	348	2,749	19,695	349,012	520	248,430	597,965
2005	28,006	5,923	380	4,808	39,201	1,631,011	877	407,322	2,039,214
2004	20,192	9,186	108	4,701	34,317	1,117,766	946	444,428	1,563,145

Source: **www.uscourts.gov/Statistics/BankruptcyStatistics.aspx.**

Bankruptcy law has also been used to hasten settlements in major product liability suits. The Manville asbestos case is an example. The company was being bombarded by thousands of lawsuits, and the very existence of such huge contingent liabilities made normal operations impossible. Further, it was relatively easy to prove (1) that if the plaintiffs won, the company would be unable to pay the full amount of the claims, (2) that a larger amount of funds would be available to the claimants if the company continued to operate rather than liquidate, (3) that continued operations were possible only if the suits were brought to a conclusion, and (4) that a timely resolution of all the suits was impossible because of their vast number and variety. Manville filed for bankruptcy in 1982, at that time the largest U.S. bankruptcy ever. The bankruptcy statutes were used to consolidate all the suits and to reach settlements under which the plaintiffs obtained more money than they otherwise would have received, and Manville was able to stay in business. (It was acquired in 2001 by Berkshire Hathaway.) The stockholders did poorly under these plans because most of the companies' future cash flows were assigned to the plaintiffs, but even so, the stockholders probably fared better than they would have if the suits had been concluded through the jury system.

What are some situations other than immediate financial distress that lead firms to file for bankruptcy?

25.8 Some Criticisms of Bankruptcy Laws

Although bankruptcy laws, for the most part, exist to protect creditors, many critics claim that current laws are not doing what they were intended to do. Before 1978, most bankruptcies ended quickly in liquidation. Then Congress rewrote the laws, giving companies more opportunity to stay alive on the grounds that this was best for managers, employees, creditors, and stockholders. Before the reform, 90% of Chapter 11 filers were liquidated, but now that percentage is less than 80%, and the average time between filing and liquidation has almost doubled. Indeed, large public corporations with the ability to hire high-priced legal help can avoid (or at least delay) liquidation, often at the expense of creditors and shareholders.

Critics believe that bankruptcy is great for businesses these days—especially for consultants, lawyers, and investment bankers, who reap hefty fees during bankruptcy proceedings, and for managers, who continue to collect their salaries and bonuses as long as the business is kept alive. The problem, according to critics, is that bankruptcy courts allow cases to drag on too long, depleting assets that could be sold to pay off creditors and shareholders. Too often, quick resolution is impossible because bankruptcy judges are required to deal with issues such as labor disputes, pension plan funding, and environmental liability—social questions that could be solved by legislative action rather than by bankruptcy courts.

Critics contend that bankruptcy judges ought to realize that some sick companies should be allowed to die—and die quickly. Maintaining companies on life support does not serve the interests of the parties that the bankruptcy laws were designed to protect. The 2005 changes to the bankruptcy code addressed this issue by limiting to 18 months the time that management has to file a reorganization plan. Prior to the change, judges could extend this time almost indefinitely. Now, creditors may propose a plan if an acceptable plan hasn't been filed by management within 18 months.

Other critics think the entire bankruptcy system of judicial protection and supervision needs to be scrapped. Some even have proposed a kind of auction procedure, where shareholders and creditors would have the opportunity to gain control of a bankrupt company by raising the cash needed to pay the bills. The rationale here is that the market is a better judge than a bankruptcy court as to whether a company is worth more dead or alive.

According to critics, what are some problems with the bankruptcy system?

Summary

This chapter discussed the main issues involved in bankruptcy and financial distress in general. The key concepts are listed below.

- The fundamental issue that must be addressed when a company encounters financial distress is whether it is "worth more dead than alive"; that is, would the business be more valuable if it continued in operation or if it were liquidated and sold off in pieces?

- In the case of a fundamentally sound company whose financial difficulties appear to be temporary, creditors will frequently work directly with the company, helping it to recover and reestablish itself on a sound financial basis. Such voluntary reorganization plans are called **workouts**.

- Reorganization plans usually require some type of **restructuring** of the firm's debts; this may involve an **extension**, which postpones the date of required payment of past-due obligations, and/or a **composition**, by which the creditors voluntarily reduce their claims on the debtor or the interest rate on their claims.

- When it is obvious that a firm is worth more dead than alive, informal procedures can sometimes be used to **liquidate** the firm. **Assignment** is an informal procedure for liquidating a firm, and it usually yields creditors a larger amount than they would receive in a formal bankruptcy liquidation. However, assignments are feasible only if the firm is small and its affairs are not too complex.

- Current **bankruptcy law** consists of nine chapters, designated by Arabic numbers. For businesses, the most important chapters are **Chapter 7**, which details the procedures to be followed when liquidating a firm, and **Chapter 11**, which contains procedures for formal reorganizations.

- Since the first bankruptcy laws, most formal reorganization plans have been guided by the **absolute priority doctrine**. This doctrine holds that creditors should be compensated for their claims in a rigid hierarchical order and that senior claims must be paid in full before junior claims can receive even a dime.

- Another position, the **relative priority doctrine**, holds that more flexibility should be allowed in a reorganization and that a balanced consideration should be given to all claimants. In recent years, there has been a shift away from absolute priority toward relative priority. The primary effect of this shift has been to delay liquidations, giving managements more time to rehabilitate companies in an effort to provide value to junior claimants.

- The primary role of the bankruptcy court in a reorganization is to determine the **fairness** and the **feasibility** of proposed plans of reorganization.

- Even if some creditors or stockholders dissent and do not accept a reorganization plan, the plan may still be approved by the court if the plan is deemed to be "fair and equitable" to all parties. This procedure, in which the court mandates a reorganization plan in spite of dissent, is called a **cramdown**.

- In the last few years, a new type of reorganization that combines the advantages of both the informal workout and formal Chapter 11 reorganization has become popular. This new hybrid is called a **prepackaged bankruptcy**, or **pre-pack.**
- The distribution of assets in a **liquidation** under Chapter 7 of the Bankruptcy Act is governed by a specific priority of claims.
- **Multiple discriminant analysis (MDA)** is a method to identify firms with high bankruptcy risk. We discuss MDA in *Web Extension 25A.*

Questions

25-1 Define each of the following terms:
   a. Informal restructuring; reorganization in bankruptcy
   b. Assignment; liquidation in bankruptcy; fairness; feasibility
   c. Absolute priority doctrine; relative priority doctrine
   d. Bankruptcy Reform Act of 1978; Chapter 11; Chapter 7
   e. Priority of claims in liquidation
   f. Extension; composition; workout; cramdown; prepackaged bankruptcy; holdout

25-2 Why do creditors usually accept a plan for financial rehabilitation rather than demand liquidation of the business?

25-3 Would it be a sound rule to liquidate whenever the liquidation value is above the value of the corporation as a going concern? Discuss.

25-4 Why do liquidations usually result in losses for the creditors or the owners, or both? Would partial liquidation or liquidation over a period limit their losses? Explain.

25-5 Are liquidations likely to be more common for public utility, railroad, or industrial corporations? Why?

Problems   Answers Appear in Appendix B

Easy Problem 1

25-1 **Liquidation** Southwestern Wear Inc. has the following balance sheet:

Current assets	$1,875,000	Accounts payable	$ 375,000
Fixed assets	1,875,000	Notes payable	750,000
		Subordinated debentures	750,000
		Total debt	$1,875,000
		Common equity	1,875,000
Total assets	$3,750,000	Total liabilities and equity	$3,750,000

The trustee's costs total $281,250, and the firm has no accrued taxes or wages. The debentures are subordinated only to the notes payable. If the firm goes bankrupt and liquidates, how much will each class of investors receive if a total of $2.5 million is received from sale of the assets?

Intermediate Problem 2

25-2 Reorganization The Verbrugge Publishing Company's 2012 balance sheet and income statement are as follows (in millions of dollars):

Balance Sheet

Current assets	$168	Current liabilities	$ 42
Net fixed assets	153	Advance payments	78
Goodwill	15	Reserves	6
		$6 preferred stock, $112.50 par value (1,200,000 shares)	135
		$10.50 preferred stock, no par, callable at $150 (60,000 shares)	9
		Common stock, $1.50 par value (6,000,000 shares)	9
		Retained earnings	57
Total assets	$336	Total claims	$336

Income Statement

Net sales	$ 540.0
Operating expense	516.0
Net operating income	$ 24.0
Other income	3.0
EBT	$ 27.0
Taxes (50%)	13.5
Net income	$ 13.5
Dividends on $6 preferred	7.2
Dividends on $10.50 preferred	0.6
Income available to common stockholders	$ 5.7

Verbrugge and its creditors have agreed upon a voluntary reorganization plan. In this plan, each share of the $6 preferred will be exchanged for one share of $2.40 preferred with a par value of $37.50 plus one 8% subordinated income debenture with a par value of $75. The $10.50 preferred issue will be retired with cash.

a. Construct the projected balance sheet while assuming that reorganization takes place. Show the new preferred stock at its par value.

b. Construct the projected income statement. What is the income available to common shareholders in the proposed recapitalization?

c. *Required earnings* is defined as the amount that is just enough to meet fixed charges (debenture interest and/or preferred dividends). What are the required pre-tax earnings before and after the recapitalization?

d. How is the debt ratio affected by the reorganization? If you were a holder of Verbrugge's common stock, would you vote in favor of the reorganization?

Challenging Problems 3–4

25-3 Liquidation At the time it defaulted on its interest payments and filed for bankruptcy, the McDaniel Mining Company had the balance sheet shown below (in thousands of dollars). The court, after trying unsuccessfully to reorganize the firm, decided that the only recourse was liquidation under Chapter 7. Sale of the fixed assets, which were pledged as collateral to the mortgage bondholders, brought in $400,000, while the current assets were sold for another $200,000. Thus, the total proceeds from the liquidation sale were $600,000. The trustee's costs amounted to $50,000; no single worker was due more than $2,000 in wages; and there were no unfunded pension plan liabilities.

Current assets	$ 400	Accounts payable	$ 50
Net fixed assets	600	Accrued taxes	40
		Accrued wages	30
		Notes payable	180
		Total current liabilities	$ 300
		First-mortgage bonds[a]	300
		Second-mortgage bonds[a]	200
		Debentures	200
		Subordinated debentures[b]	100
		Common stock	50
		Retained earnings	(150)
Total assets	$1,000	Total claims	$1,000

[a] All fixed assets are pledged as collateral to the mortgage bonds.
[b] Subordinated to notes payable only.

a. How much will McDaniel's shareholders receive from the liquidation?
b. How much will the mortgage bondholders receive?
c. Who are the other priority claimants (in addition to the mortgage bond-holders)? How much will they receive from the liquidation?
d. Who are the remaining general creditors? How much will each receive from the distribution before subordination adjustment? What is the effect of adjusting for subordination?

25-4 Liquidation The following balance sheet represents Boles Electronics Corporation's position at the time it filed for bankruptcy (in thousands of dollars):

Cash	$ 10	Accounts payable	$ 1,600
Receivables	100	Notes payable	500
Inventories	890	Wages payable	150
		Taxes payable	50
Total current assets	$ 1,000	Total current liabilities	$ 2,300
Net plant	4,000	Mortgage bonds	2,000
Net equipment	5,000	Subordinated debentures	2,500
		Preferred stock	1,500
		Common stock	1,700
Total assets	$10,000	Total claims	$10,000

The mortgage bonds are secured by the plant but not by the equipment. The subordinated debentures are subordinated to notes payable. The firm was unable to reorganize under Chapter 11; therefore, it was liquidated under Chapter 7.

The trustee, whose legal and administrative fees amounted to $200,000, sold off the assets and received the following proceeds (in thousands of dollars):

Asset	Proceeds
Plant	$1,600
Equipment	1,300
Receivables	50
Inventories	240
Total	$3,190

In addition, the firm had $10,000 in cash available for distribution. No single wage earner had over $2,000 in claims, and there were no unfunded pension plan liabilities.

   a. What is the total amount available for distribution to all claimants? What is the total of creditor and trustee claims? Will the preferred and common stockholders receive any distributions?

   b. Determine the dollar distribution to each creditor and to the trustee. What percentage of each claim is satisfied?

Spreadsheet Problem

25-5 Liquidation Start with the partial model in the file *Ch25 P05 Build a Model .xls* on the textbook's Web site. Duchon Industries had the following balance sheet at the time it defaulted on its interest payments and filed for liquidation under Chapter 7. Sale of the fixed assets, which were pledged as collateral to the mortgage bondholders, brought in $900 million, while the current assets were sold for another $401 million. Thus, the total proceeds from the liquidation sales were $1,300 million. The trustee's costs amounted to $1 million; no single worker was due more than $2,000 in wages; and there were no unfunded pension plan liabilities. Determine the amount available for distribution to shareholders and all claimants.

Duchon Industries's Balance Sheets (Millions of Dollars)

Current assets	$ 400	Accounts payable	$ 50
Net fixed assets	600	Accrued taxes	40
		Accrued wages	30
		Notes payable	180
		Total current liabilities	$ 300
		First-mortgage bonds[a]	300
		Second-mortgage bonds[a]	200
		Debentures	200
		Subordinated debentures[b]	100
		Common stock	50
		Retained earnings	(150)
Total assets	$1,000	Total claims	$1,000

[a]All fixed assets are pledged as collateral to the mortgage bonds.
[b]Subordinated to notes payable only.

MINI CASE

Kimberly MacKenzie—president of Kim's Clothes Inc., a medium-sized manufacturer of women's casual clothing—is worried. Her firm has been selling clothes to Russ Brothers Department Store for more than 10 years, and she has never experienced any problems in collecting payment for the merchandise sold. Currently, Russ Brothers owes Kim's Clothes $65,000 for spring sportswear that was delivered to the store just 2 weeks ago. Kim's concern arose from reading an article in yesterday's The Wall Street Journal that indicated Russ Brothers was having serious financial problems. Moreover, the article stated that Russ Brothers's management was considering filing for reorganization, or even liquidation, with a federal bankruptcy court.

Kim's immediate concern was whether or not her firm would collect its receivables if Russ Brothers went bankrupt. In pondering the situation, Kim also realized that she knew nothing about the process that firms go through when they encounter severe financial distress. To learn more about bankruptcy, reorganization, and liquidation, Kim asked Ron Mitchell, the firm's chief financial officer, to prepare a briefing on the subject for the entire board of directors. In turn, Ron asked you, a newly hired financial analyst, to do the groundwork for the briefing by answering the following questions.

a. (1) What are the major causes of business failure?
   (2) Do business failures occur evenly over time?
   (3) Which size of firm, large or small, is more prone to business failure? Why?
b. What key issues must managers face in the financial distress process?
c. What informal remedies are available to firms in financial distress? In answering this question, define the following terms:
   (1) Workout
   (2) Restructuring
   (3) Extension
   (4) Composition
   (5) Assignment
   (6) Assignee (trustee)
d. Briefly describe U.S. bankruptcy law, including the following terms:

(1) Chapter 11
(2) Chapter 7
(3) Trustee
(4) Voluntary bankruptcy
(5) Involuntary bankruptcy

e. What are the major differences between an informal reorganization and reorganization in bankruptcy? In answering this question, be sure to discuss the following items:
   (1) Common pool problem
   (2) Holdout problem
   (3) Automatic stay
   (4) Cramdown
   (5) Fraudulent conveyance
f. What is a prepackaged bankruptcy? Why have prepackaged bankruptcies become more popular in recent years?
g. Briefly describe the priority of claims in a Chapter 7 liquidation.
h. Assume that Russ Brothers did indeed fail, and that it had the following balance sheet when it was liquidated (in millions of dollars):

Current assets	$40.0	Accounts payable	$10.0
Net fixed assets	5.0	Notes payable (to banks)	5.0
		Accrued wages	0.3
		Federal taxes	0.5
		State and local taxes	0.2
		Current liabilities	$16.0
		First-mortgage bonds	3.0
		Second-mortgage bonds	0.5
		Subordinated debentures[a]	4.0
		Total long-term debt	$ 7.5
		Preferred stock	1.0
		Common stock	13.0
		Paid-in capital	2.0
		Retained earnings	5.5
		Total equity	$21.5
Total assets	$45.0	Total claims	$45.0

[a]The debentures are subordinated to the notes payable.

The liquidation sale resulted in the following proceeds:

From sale of current assets	$14,000,000
From sale of fixed assets	2,500,000
Total receipts	$16,500,000

For simplicity, assume there were no trustee's fees or any other claims against the liquidation proceeds. Also, assume that the mortgage bonds are secured by the entire amount of fixed assets. What would each claimant receive from the liquidation distribution?

Selected Additional Case

The following cases from TextChoice, *Cengage Learning's online case library, cover many of the concepts discussed in this chapter and are available at* **www.textchoice2.com/casenet.**

Klein-Brigham Series:

Case 39, "Mark X Company (B)," which examines the allocation of proceeds under bankruptcy.

Chapter 26

Mergers, LBOs, Divestitures, and Holding Companies

WEB

The textbook's Web site contains an *Excel* file that will guide you through the chapter's calculations. The file for this chapter is ***Ch26 Tool Kit.xls***, and we encourage you to open the file and follow along as you read the chapter.

Most corporate growth occurs by *internal expansion,* which takes place when a firm's existing divisions grow through normal capital budgeting activities. However, the most dramatic examples of growth result from mergers, the first topic covered in this chapter. *Leveraged buyouts,* or *LBOs,* occur when a firm's stock is acquired by a small group of investors rather than by another operating company. Conditions change over time, causing firms to sell off, or divest, major divisions to other firms that can better utilize the divested assets. Divestitures are also discussed in the chapter. Finally, we discuss the *holding company* form of organization, wherein one corporation owns the stock of one or more other companies.

Beginning of Chapter Questions

As you read this chapter, consider how you would answer the following questions. You *should not* necessarily be able to answer the questions before you read the chapter. Rather, you should use them to get a sense of the issues covered in the chapter. After reading the chapter, you should be able to give at least partial answers to the questions, and you should be able to give better answers after the chapter has been discussed in class. Note, too, that it is often useful, when answering conceptual questions, to use hypothetical data to illustrate your answer. We illustrate the answers with an *Excel* model that is available on the textbook's Web site. Accessing the model and working through it is a useful exercise, and it provides insights that are useful when answering the questions.

1. What are **horizontal, vertical, congeneric,** and **conglomerate mergers?** Are the different types of mergers equally likely to pass muster with the Justice Department?

2. What is **synergy?** What are some factors that might lead to synergy? How is the amount of synergy in a proposed merger measured, and how is it allocated between the two firms' stockholders? Would the four types of mergers as discussed in Question 1 be equally likely to produce synergy?

3. Many companies have serious discussions about merging. Sometimes these discussions lead to mergers, sometimes not. What are some factors that should be considered and that affect the likelihood of a merger actually being completed?

4. Explain how the **market multiples method** is used to determine the value of a target firm to a potential acquirer. Give several examples of this procedure.

5. Explain how the **corporate valuation model** and the **adjusted present value (APV) method** are used to estimate the value of a target company. If someone did a complete and careful analysis of a given target using both of these methods, would they produce the same results? Explain why, under certain growth and capital structure conditions, it is better to use the APV method.

6. If you were conducting a merger analysis, would you give the multiples method or one of the DCF methods (that is, the APV or corporate valuation model) more weight in your decision? Explain.

7. Explain how **purchase accounting** is implemented in a merger. Does the accounting profession now require this method? How is any premium that the acquiring firm paid over the acquired firm's book value treated subsequent to a merger?

8. Acquisitions can have important tax consequences depending on (a) whether the acquiring firm purchases the target's stock or just its assets, (b) whether cash or stock is used for the payment, and (c) how the acquirer records the target's assets on its books after the merger. Suppose a target's assets have a value of $50 million, but the appraised value of those assets is $80 million. The target firm is in the 20% tax bracket. Here are four possible situations:

   (1) Acquirer pays $100 million in cash for the target's stock in a tender offer and records assets at their book value.

   (2) Same as in part (1) but acquirer records assets at their appraised value.

   (3) Acquirer pays $100 million worth of stock in exchange for the target's stock.

   (4) Acquirer pays $100 million in cash to the target for its assets.

   In each situation, answer the following questions. (*Hint:* The tax situation is complicated, but Figure 26-1 would be helpful in answering these questions.)

   a. How much would the target's shareholders receive from the acquirer, and how much of that total would be taxable?

   b. How much would the target's shareholders receive from the target firm, and how much of that total would be taxable?

   c. How much in taxes would the target firm have to pay on any gains it realizes?

   d. What would the total depreciable value of the target be once it has been acquired?

26.1 Rationale for Mergers

Many reasons have been proposed by financial managers and theorists to account for the high level of U.S. merger activity. The primary motives behind corporate **mergers** are presented in this section.[1]

26.1a Synergy

The primary motivation for most mergers is to increase the value of the combined enterprise. If Companies A and B merge to form Company C and if C's value exceeds that of A and B taken together, then **synergy** is said to exist, and such a merger should be beneficial to both A's and B's stockholders.[2] Synergistic effects can arise from five sources: (1) *operating economies,* which result from economies of scale in management, marketing, production, or distribution; (2) *financial economies,* including lower transaction costs and better coverage by security analysts; (3) *tax effects,* in which case the combined enterprise pays less in taxes than the separate firms would pay; (4) *differential efficiency,* which implies that the management of one firm is more efficient and that the weaker firm's assets will be more productive after the merger; and (5) *increased market power* due to reduced competition. Operating and financial economies are socially desirable, as are mergers that increase managerial efficiency, but mergers that reduce competition are socially undesirable and illegal.[3]

Expected synergies are not always realized. For example, when AOL acquired Time Warner, it believed that Time Warner's extensive content library could be sold to AOL's Internet subscribers and that AOL subscribers could be shifted over to Time Warner's cable system. When the merger was announced, the new management estimated that such synergies would increase operating income by $1 billion per year. However, things didn't work out as expected, and in 2002 Time Warner had to write off about $100 billion in lost value associated with the merger.

Merrill Lynch (ML) was facing bankruptcy in late 2008, so federal officials encouraged Bank of America (BoA) to save ML from bankruptcy by acquiring it, creating one of the world's largest (if not the largest) financial conglomerate. But BoA tried to back out of the deal as it learned more about ML's situation. Under pressure from the government, BoA went through with the merger and almost immediately reported over $21 billion in associated losses.

As these examples illustrate, often it is blemishes and not synergies that materialize after a merger.

---

1. As we use the term, *merger* means any combination that forms one economic unit from two or more previous ones. For legal purposes, there are distinctions among the various ways these combinations can occur, but our focus is on the fundamental economic and financial aspects of mergers.

2. If synergy exists, then the whole is greater than the sum of the parts. Synergy is also called the "2 plus 2 equals 5 effect." The distribution of the synergistic gain between A's and B's stockholders is determined by negotiation. This point is discussed later in the chapter.

3. In the 1880s and 1890s, many mergers occurred in the United States, and some of them were obviously directed toward gaining market power rather than increasing efficiency. As a result, Congress passed a series of acts designed to ensure that mergers are not used to reduce competition. The principal acts include the Sherman Act (1890), the Clayton Act (1914), and the Celler Act (1950). These acts make it illegal for firms to combine if the combination tends to lessen competition. The acts are enforced by the antitrust division of the Justice Department and by the Federal Trade Commission.

26.1b Tax Considerations

Tax considerations have stimulated a number of mergers. For example, a profitable firm in the highest tax bracket could acquire a firm with large accumulated tax losses. These losses could then be turned into immediate tax savings rather than carried forward and used in the future.[4]

Also, mergers can serve as a way of minimizing taxes when disposing of excess cash. For example, if a firm has a shortage of internal investment opportunities compared with its free cash flow, it could (1) pay an extra dividend, (2) invest in marketable securities, (3) repurchase its own stock, or (4) purchase another firm. If it pays an extra dividend, its stockholders would have to pay immediate taxes on the distribution. Marketable securities often provide a good temporary parking place for money, but they generally earn a rate of return less than that required by stockholders. A stock repurchase might result in a capital gain for the selling stockholders. However, using surplus cash to acquire another firm would avoid all these problems, and this has motivated a number of mergers. Still, as we discuss later, the tax savings are often less than the premium paid in the acquisition. Thus, mergers motivated only by tax considerations often reduce the acquiring shareholders' wealth.

26.1c Purchase of Assets below Their Replacement Cost

Sometimes a firm will be touted as an acquisition candidate because the cost of replacing its assets is considerably higher than its market value. This is especially true in the natural resources industry; for example, an oil company's reserves might be worth more on paper than the company's stock. (Of course, converting paper value to monetary value isn't always as easy as it sounds.)

26.1d Diversification

Managers often cite diversification as a reason for mergers. They contend that diversification helps stabilize a firm's earnings and thus benefits its owners. Stabilization of earnings is certainly beneficial to employees, suppliers, and customers, but its value to stockholders is less certain. Why should Firm A acquire Firm B to stabilize earnings when stockholders can simply buy the stocks of both firms? Indeed, research suggests that in most cases diversification does not increase the firm's value. In fact, many studies find that diversified firms are worth significantly *less* than the sum of their individual parts.[5]

Of course, if you were the owner-manager of a closely held firm, it might be nearly impossible to sell part of your stock to diversify. Also, selling your stock would probably lead to a large capital gains tax. So, a diversification merger might be the best way to achieve personal diversification for a privately held firm.

---

4. Mergers undertaken only to use accumulated tax losses would probably be challenged by the IRS. In recent years, Congress has made it increasingly difficult for firms to pass along tax savings after mergers.

5. See, for example, Philip Berger and Eli Ofek, "Diversification's Effect on Firm Value," *Journal of Financial Economics,* 1995, pp. 37–65; and Larry Lang and René Stulz, "Tobin's Q, Corporate Diversification, and Firm Performance," *Journal of Political Economy,* December 1994, pp. 1248–1280.

26.1e Managers' Personal Incentives

Financial economists like to think that business decisions are based only on economic considerations, especially maximization of firms' values. However, many business decisions are based more on managers' personal motivations than on economic analyses. Business leaders like power, and more power is attached to running a larger corporation than a smaller one. Most likely, no executive would admit that his or her ego was the primary reason behind a merger, but egos do play a prominent role in many mergers.[6]

It has also been observed that executive salaries are highly correlated with company size—the bigger the company, the higher the salaries of its top officers. This, too, could obviously cause unnecessary acquisitions.

Personal considerations deter as well as motivate mergers. After most takeovers, some managers of the acquired companies lose their jobs, or at least their autonomy. Therefore, managers who own less than 51% of their firms' stock look to devices that will lessen the chances of a takeover, and a merger can serve as such a device. In 2005, for example, MCI's board of directors, over the objection of large shareholders, turned down repeated acquisition offers from Qwest, at the time the nation's fourth-largest local phone company, in favor of substantially smaller offers from Verizon, the nation's largest phone company. MCI's management viewed Verizon as a stronger, more stable partner than Qwest even though Qwest's bid was at times 20% higher than Verizon's. In response to management's refusal to accept the higher bid, the holders of some 28% of MCI's stock withheld their votes to re-elect the board of directors as a protest. Nonetheless, management proceeded with the Verizon merger negotiations, and the two companies merged in June of 2006. In such cases, management always argues that synergy, not a desire to protect their own jobs, is the motivation for the choice. However, it is difficult to rationalize rejecting a 20% larger bid for undocumented synergies, and some observers suspect that this merger—like many others—was ultimately designed to benefit managers rather than shareholders.

26.1f Breakup Value

Some takeover specialists estimate a company's **breakup value**, which is the value of the individual parts of the firm if they were sold off separately. If this value is higher than the firm's current market value, then a takeover specialist could acquire the firm at or even above its current market value, sell it off in pieces, and earn a profit.

Self Test	Define *synergy*. Is synergy a valid rationale for mergers? Describe several situations that might produce synergistic gains.
	Suppose your firm could purchase another firm for only half of its replacement value. Would that be a sufficient justification for the acquisition?
	Discuss the pros and cons of diversification as a rationale for mergers.
	What is breakup value?

6. See Randall Morck, Andrei Shleifer, and Robert W. Vishny, "Do Managerial Objectives Drive Bad Acquisitions?" *Journal of Finance,* March 1990, pp. 31–48.

26.2 Types of Mergers

Economists classify mergers into four types: (1) horizontal, (2) vertical, (3) congeneric, and (4) conglomerate. A **horizontal merger** occurs when one firm combines with another in its same line of business—the 2005 Sprint–Nextel merger is an example as is the 2009 Wachovia–Wells Fargo merger. An example of a **vertical merger** would be a steel producer's acquisition of one of its own suppliers, such as an iron or coal mining firm, or an oil producer's acquisition of a petrochemical firm that uses oil as a raw material. *Congeneric* means "allied in nature or action"; hence a **congeneric merger** involves related enterprises but not producers of the same product (horizontal) or firms in a producer–supplier relationship (vertical). The AOL and Time Warner merger is an example. A **conglomerate merger** occurs when unrelated enterprises combine.

Operating economies (and also anticompetitive effects) are at least partially dependent on the type of merger involved. Vertical and horizontal mergers generally provide the greatest synergistic operating benefits, but they are also the ones most likely to be attacked by the Department of Justice as being anticompetitive.[7] In any event, it is useful to think of these economic classifications when analyzing prospective mergers.

What are the four economic types of mergers?   **Self Test**

26.3 Level of Merger Activity

Five principal "merger waves" have occurred in the United States. The first was in the late 1800s, when consolidations occurred in the oil, steel, tobacco, and other basic industries. The second was in the 1920s, when the stock market boom helped financial promoters consolidate firms in a number of industries, including utilities, communications, and autos. The third was in the 1960s, when conglomerate mergers were the rage. The fourth occurred in the 1980s, when LBO firms and others began using junk bonds to finance all manner of acquisitions. The fifth, which involves strategic alliances designed to enable firms to compete better in the global economy, is in progress today.

As can be seen from Table 26-1, some huge mergers have occurred in recent years. Most recent mergers have been strategic in nature—companies are merging to gain economies of scale or scope and thus be better able to compete in the world economy. Indeed, many recent mergers have involved companies in the financial, defense, media, computer, telecommunications, and health care industries, all of which are experiencing structural changes and intense competition.

In the 1980s, cash was the preferred method of payment, because large cash payments could convince even the most reluctant shareholder to approve the deal. However, the cash was generally obtained by borrowing, leaving the consolidated company with a heavy debt burden, which often led to difficulties. Through the mid-2000s, stock replaced borrowed cash as the merger currency for two reasons: (1) Many of the 1980s mergers were financed with junk bonds that later went into default. These defaults, along with the demise of Drexel Burnham, the leading junk bond dealer, have made it difficult to arrange debt-financed mergers. (2) Many

---

7. For interesting insights into antitrust regulations and mergers, see B. Espen Eckbo, "Mergers and the Value of Antitrust Deterrence," *Journal of Finance,* July 1992, pp. 1005–1029.

TABLE 26-1	The Ten Largest Completed Mergers Worldwide through December 31, 2010		
Buyer	**Target**	**Completion Date**	**Value (Billions of U.S. Dollars)**
Vodafone AirTouch	Mannesmann	April 12, 2000	$161
Pfizer	Warner-Lambert	June 19, 2000	116
America Online	Time Warner	January 11, 2001	106
RFS Holdings	ABN-AMRO Holding	October 5, 2007	99
Exxon	Mobil	November 30, 1999	81
Glaxo Wellcome	SmithKline Beecham	December 27, 2000	74
Royal Dutch Petroleum	Shell Transport and Trading	July 20, 2005	74
ATT	BellSouth	December 29, 2006	73
SBC Communications	Ameritech	October 8, 1999	72
VodafoneGroup	AirTouch	June 30, 1999	69

Sources: "A Look at the Top 10 Global Mergers," *Associated Press Newswires,* January 11, 2001; *The Wall Street Journal,* "Year-End Review of Markets and Finance World-Wide Deals," various issues.

of the mergers during that time were for strategic reasons, such as Eli Lilly's $6.5 billion acquisition of ImClone Systems in 2008. Most of these mergers have been friendly, and stock swaps are easier to arrange in friendly mergers than in hostile ones. Global merger activity has declined significantly since the 2007–2008 financial crisis and subsequent recession, and much of the activity that took place from 2009 to 2011 again consisted of cash deals, such as the 2011 $2.2 billion acquisition of Novell by the private IT company, Attachmate.

There has also been an increase in cross-border mergers. For example, in 2011 the Swiss automation technology company ABB acquired Baldor Electric Company, a U.S.-based industrial motors manufacturer. Also in early 2011, Pepsico acquired a 66% interest in the Russian food company, Wimm-Bill-Dann Foods, with purchase of the remaining shares slated for late 2011.

Self Test	What five major "merger waves" have occurred in the United States?
	What are some reasons for the current wave?

26.4 Hostile versus Friendly Takeovers

In the vast majority of merger situations, one firm (generally the larger of the two) simply decides to buy another company, negotiates a price with the management of the target firm, and then acquires the target company. Occasionally, the acquired firm will initiate the action, but it is much more common for a firm to seek companies to acquire than to seek to be acquired. Following convention, we call a company that seeks to acquire another firm the **acquiring company** and the one that it seeks to acquire the **target company.**

Once an acquiring company has identified a possible target, it must (1) establish a suitable price, or range of prices, and (2) decide on the terms of payment—will it offer cash, its own common stock, bonds, or some combination? Next, the acquiring firm's managers must decide how to approach the target company's managers. If the acquiring firm has reason to believe that the target's management will approve the merger, then one CEO will contact the other, propose a merger, and then try to work out suitable terms. If an agreement is reached, then the two management groups will issue statements to their stockholders indicating that they approve the merger, and the target firm's management will recommend to its stockholders that they agree to the merger. Generally, the stockholders are asked to *tender* (or send in) their shares to a designated financial institution, along with a signed power of attorney that transfers ownership of the shares to the acquiring firm. The target firm's stockholders then receive the specified payment, either common stock of the acquiring company (in which case the target company's stockholders become stockholders of the acquiring company), cash, bonds, or some mix of cash and securities. This is a **friendly merger.** Kraft's acquisition of the British firm Cadbury in 2010 is an example of a friendly merger, even though Cadbury initially rejected an earlier offer by Kraft for being too low.

Often, however, the target company's management resists the merger. Perhaps they feel that the price offered is too low, or perhaps they simply want to keep their jobs. Regardless of the reasons, in this case the acquiring firm's offer is said to be **hostile** rather than friendly, and the acquiring firm must make a direct appeal to the target firm's stockholders. In a hostile merger, the acquiring company will again make a **tender offer,** and again it will ask the stockholders of the target firm to tender their shares in exchange for the offered price. This time, though, the target firm's managers will urge stockholders not to tender their shares, generally stating that the price offered (cash, bonds, or stocks in the acquiring firm) is too low. For example, in late 2010 the board of directors for the biotech company Genzyme refused to consider a $69 per share offer from French pharmaceutical giant Sanofi. To encourage the board to actively consider the offer, Sanofi appealed directly to Genzyme's shareholders with a tender offer at $69 per share. The tender offer got the attention of Genzyme's board and in early 2011, Sanofi increased the cash component of the offer to $74 and added a security called a contingent value right (CVR) to the mix. The CVR would pay up to $14 per share more to the selling shareholders, depending on performance of one of Genzyme's drugs, and the merger was finally approved by management.[8]

Although most mergers are friendly, there are cases in which high-profile firms have attempted hostile takeovers. For example, Wachovia, before its acquisition by Wells Fargo during the financial crisis in 2008, defeated a hostile bid by SunTrust and was acquired, instead, by First Union. Looking overseas, Olivetti successfully conducted a hostile takeover of Telecom Italia, and, in another hostile telecommunications merger, Britain's Vodafone AirTouch acquired its German rival, Mannesmann AG.

Perhaps not surprisingly, hostile bids often fail. However, an all-cash offer that is high enough will generally overcome any resistance by the target firm's management. A hostile merger often begins with a "preemptive" or "blowout" bid. The idea is to offer such a high premium over the pre-announcement price that (a) no other bidders will be willing to jump into the fray and (b) the target company's board cannot simply reject the bid. If a hostile bid is eventually accepted by the target's board then the deal ends up as "friendly," despite any acrimony during the hostile phase.

What is the difference between a hostile and a friendly merger?   **Self Test**

---

8. See www.bloomberg.com/news/2011-02-16/sanofi-aventis-agrees-to-buy-genzyme-for-74-a-share-in-19-2-billion-deal.html for more information on the Sanofi-Genzyme acquisition.

26.5 Merger Regulation

Prior to the mid-1960s, friendly acquisitions generally took place as simple exchange-of-stock mergers, and a proxy fight was the primary weapon used in hostile control battles. In the mid-1960s, however, corporate raiders began to operate differently. First, it took a long time to mount a proxy fight—raiders had to first request a list of the target company's stockholders, be refused, and then get a court order forcing management to turn over the list. During that time, the target's management could think through and then implement a strategy to fend off the raider. As a result, management won most proxy fights.

Then raiders thought, "If we could bring the decision to a head quickly, before management can take countermeasures, that would greatly increase our probability of success." That led the raiders to turn from proxy fights to tender offers, which had a much shorter response time. For example, the stockholders of a company whose stock was selling for $20 might be offered $27 per share and be given 2 weeks to accept. The raider, meanwhile, would have accumulated a substantial block of the shares in open market purchases, and additional shares might have been purchased by institutional friends of the raider who promised to tender their shares in exchange for the tip that a raid was to occur.

Faced with a well-planned raid, managements were generally overwhelmed. The stock might actually be worth more than the offered price, but management simply did not have time to get this message across to stockholders or to find a competing bidder. This situation seemed unfair, so Congress passed the Williams Act in 1968. This law had two main objectives: (1) to regulate the way acquiring firms can structure takeover offers and (2) to force acquiring firms to disclose more information about their offers. In essence, Congress wanted to put target managements in a better position to defend against hostile offers. Additionally, Congress believed that shareholders needed easier access to information about tender offers—including information on any securities that might be offered in lieu of cash—in order to make rational tender-versus-don't-tender decisions.

The Williams Act placed the following four restrictions on acquiring firms: (1) Acquirers must disclose their current holdings and future intentions within 10 days of amassing at least 5% of a company's stock. (2) Acquirers must disclose the source of the funds to be used in the acquisition. (3) The target firm's shareholders must be allowed at least 20 days to tender their shares; that is, the offer must be "open" for at least 20 days. (4) If the acquiring firm increases the offer price during the 20-day open period, then all shareholders who tendered prior to the new offer must receive the higher price. In total, these restrictions were intended to reduce the acquiring firm's ability to surprise management and to stampede target shareholders into accepting an inadequate offer. Prior to the Williams Act, offers were generally made on a first-come, first-served basis, and they were often accompanied by an implicit threat to lower the bid price after 50% of the shares were in hand. The legislation also gave the target more time to mount a defense, and it gave rival bidders and white knights a chance to enter the fray and thus help a target's stockholders obtain a better price.

Many states have also passed laws designed to protect firms in their states from hostile takeovers. In 1987 the U.S. Supreme Court upheld an Indiana law that radically changed the rules of the takeover game. Specifically, the Indiana law first defined "control shares" as enough shares to give an investor 20% of the vote. It went on to state that when an investor buys control shares, those shares can be voted only after approval by a majority of "disinterested shareholders," defined as those who are neither officers nor inside directors of the company nor associates of the raider. The law also gives the buyer of control shares the right to insist that a shareholders' meeting be called within 50 days to decide whether the shares may be voted. The Indiana law dealt a major blow to raiders, mainly because it slows down the action and thus gives the target firm time to mount a defense. Delaware (the state in which most large companies are incorporated) later passed a similar bill, as did New York and a number of other important states.

The state laws also have some features that protect target stockholders from their own managers. Included are limits on the use of golden parachutes, onerous debt financing plans, and some types of takeover defenses. Because these laws do not regulate tender offers per se but rather govern the practices of firms in the state, they have withstood all legal challenges to date. But when companies such as IBM offer 100% premiums for companies such as Lotus, it is hard for any defense to hold them off.

Is there a need to regulate mergers? Explain.

Do the states play a role in merger regulation, or is it all done at the national level? Explain.

Self Test

26.6 Overview of Merger Analysis

An acquiring firm must answer two questions. First, how much would the target be worth after being incorporated into the acquirer? Notice that this may be quite different from the target's current value, which does not reflect any post-merger synergies or tax benefits. Second, how much should the acquirer offer for the target? A low price is obviously better for the acquirer, but the target won't take the offer if it is too low. However, a higher offer price could scare off potential rival bidders. Later sections discuss setting the offer's price and structure (cash versus stock), but for now we focus on estimating the post-merger value of the target.

There are two basic approaches used in merger valuation: discounted cash flow (DCF) techniques and market multiple analysis.[9] Survey evidence shows that 49.3% of firms use only discounted cash flow techniques, 33.3% use both DCF and market multiples, and 12.0% use only market multiples. The market multiple approach assumes that a target is directly comparable to the average firm in its industry. Therefore, this procedure provides at best a ballpark estimate. Because it is less accurate and less frequently used than DCF approaches, we will focus on DCF methods.[10]

There are three widely used DCF methods: (1) the corporate valuation method, (2) the adjusted present value method, and (3) the equity residual method, which is also called the "free cash flow to equity" method. Chapter 11 explained the corporate

---

9. See Chapter 5 for an explanation of market multiple analysis.
10. For recent survey evidence on merger valuation methods, see Tarun K. Mukherjee, Halil Kiymaz, and H. Kent Baker, "Merger Motives and Target Valuation: A Survey of Evidence from CFOs," *Journal of Applied Finance,* Fall/Winter 2004, pp. 7–23. For evidence on the effectiveness of market multiples and DCF approaches, see S. N. Kaplan and R. S. Ruback, "The Market Pricing of Cash Flow Forecasts: Discounted Cash Flow vs. the Method of 'Comparables,'" *Journal of Applied Corporate Finance,* Winter 1996, pp. 45–60. Also see Samuel C. Weaver, Robert S. Harris, Daniel W. Bielinski, and Kenneth F. MacKenzie, "Merger and Acquisition Valuation," *Financial Management,* Summer 1991, pp. 85–96; and Nancy Mohan, M. Fall Ainina, Daniel Kaufman, and Bernard J. Winger, "Acquisition/Divestiture Valuation Practices in Major U.S. Firms," *Financial Practice and Education,* Spring 1991, pp. 73–81.

valuation model, Section 26.7 explains the adjusted present value model, and Section 26.8 explains the equity residual model. Section 26.8 also provides a numerical illustration for a company with a constant capital structure and shows that all three models, when properly applied, produce identical valuations if the capital structure is held constant. However, in many situations, there will be a nonconstant capital structure in years immediately following the merger. For example, this often occurs if an acquisition is financed with a temporarily high level of debt that will be reduced to a sustainable level as the merger is digested. In such situations, it is extremely difficult to apply the corporate valuation model or the equity residual model correctly because the cost of equity and the cost of capital are changing as the capital structure changes. Fortunately, the adjusted present value model is ideally suited for such situations, as we show in the next section.

What are the two questions that an acquirer must answer?

What are four methods for estimating a target's value?

26.7 The Adjusted Present Value (APV) Approach

Recall from Chapter 15 that interest payments are tax deductible. This means that the government receives less tax revenue from a levered firm than from an otherwise identical but unlevered firm, which leaves more money available for the levered firm's investors. More money for investors increases a firm's value, all else equal. In other words, the value of a levered firm is equal to the value of an unlevered firm plus an *adjustment* for tax savings. The **adjusted present value (APV) approach** explicitly employs this concept by expressing the value of operations as the sum of two components: (1) the unlevered value of the firm's operations (i.e., as though the firm had no debt), plus (2) the present value of the interest tax savings, also known as the **interest tax shield**:

(26–1)
$$V_{Operations} = V_{Unlevered} + V_{Tax\ shield}$$

The value of an unlevered firm's operations is the present value of the firm's free cash flows discounted at the unlevered cost of equity (r_{sU}), and the value of the tax shield is the present value of all of the interest tax savings (TS), discounted at the unlevered cost of equity:[11]

(26–2)
$$V_{Unlevered} = \sum_{t=1}^{\infty} \frac{FCF_t}{(1 + r_{sU})^t}$$

---

11. Although some analysts discount the tax shield at the cost of debt or some other rate, we believe that the unlevered cost of equity is the appropriate discount rate for the interest tax savings. See Chapter 16 for a detailed explanation.

and

$$V_{\text{Tax shield}} = \sum_{t=1}^{\infty} \frac{TS_t}{(1 + r_{sU})^t}$$

(26–3)

Before we can apply Equations 26-2 and 26-3, the FCF and TS must eventually stabilize at a constant growth rate. When they do so, we can use an approach similar to the ones we used for the nonconstant dividend model in Chapter 5 and the corporate valuation model in Chapter 11. In those approaches, we explicitly projected the years with nonconstant growth rates, found the horizon value at the end of the nonconstant growth period, and then calculated the present value of the horizon value and the cash flows during the forecast period.

Here is a detailed description of how to apply that approach in the APV model.

1. Calculate the target's unlevered cost of equity, r_{sU}, based upon its current capital structure at the time of the acquisition. In other words, you "unlever" the target's cost of equity. Chapter 16 shows that a firm's levered cost of equity, r_{sL}, is a function of its unlevered cost of equity, its cost of debt (r_d), and the amount of debt (D) and equity (S) in its capital structure:

$$r_{sL} = r_{sU} + (r_{sU} - r_d)(D/S)$$

(26–4)

Because the weights of debt and equity in a capital structure, w_d and w_s, are defined as D/(D + S) and S/(D + S), respectively, the ratio of D/S can be expressed as w_d/w_s. We make this substitution in Equation 26-4 and then solve for the unlevered cost of equity:

$$r_{sU} = w_s r_{sL} + w_d r_d$$

(26–5)

Keep in mind that r_{sL}, r_d, w_d, and w_s are based upon the target's capital structure immediately before the acquisition.

2. Project the free cash flows, FCF_t, and the annual interest tax savings, TS_t. The tax savings are equal to the projected interest payments multiplied by the tax rate:[12]

$$\text{Tax savings} = (\text{Interest expense})(\text{Tax rate})$$

(26–6)

---

12. The tax shield is based only on interest expense, not the net value of interest expense and interest income. This is because the impact of interest income is taken into account when the value of short-term investments is added later to the value of operations; hence, including the impact of interest income in the tax shield would amount to "double counting." In other words, there are no "side effects" due to owning a short-term investment: The value of the investment to the company is just the reported value. This is in contrast to debt, which does have a "side effect" in the sense that the cost to the company is less than the reported value because of the tax shield provided by the debt.

You must project enough years so that the FCF and the tax savings are expected to grow at a constant rate (g) after the horizon, which is at Year N. This means that the capital structure must become constant at Year N − 1 to ensure that the projected interest payment at Year N will grow at a constant rate after Year N. See *Web Extension 26A* for a detailed explanation of how to project financial statements that reflect a constant capital structure. For the remainder of this chapter, we will assume that your trusty assistant has made such projections.

Observe that the APV approach does not require a constant capital structure in each and every year of the analysis; it requires only that the capital structure eventually become stable in the post-horizon period.

3. Calculate the horizon value of an unlevered firm at Year N ($HV_{U,N}$), which is the value of all free cash flows beyond the horizon discounted back to the horizon at the unlevered cost of equity. Also calculate the horizon value of the tax shield at Year N ($HV_{TS,N}$), which is the value of all tax shields beyond the horizon discounted back to the horizon at the unlevered cost of equity. Because FCF and TS are growing at a constant rate of g in the post-horizon period, we can use the constant growth formula:

WEB

See **Web Extension 26A** on the textbook's Web site.

(26–7)
$$\text{Horizon value of unlevered firm} = HV_{U,N} = \frac{FCF_{N+1}}{r_{sU} - g} = \frac{FCF_N(1 + g)}{r_{sU} - g}$$

and

(26–8)
$$\text{Horizon value of tax shield} = HV_{TS,N} = \frac{TS_{N+1}}{r_{sU} - g} = \frac{TS_N(1 + g)}{r_{sU} - g}$$

The unlevered horizon value is the horizon value of the company if it had no debt. The tax shield horizon value is the contribution the tax savings after Year N make to the horizon value of the levered firm. Therefore, the horizon value of the levered firm is the sum of the unlevered horizon value and the tax shield horizon value.

4. Calculate the present value of the free cash flows and their horizon value. This is the value of operations for the unlevered firm—that is, the value it would have if it had no debt. Also calculate the present value of the yearly tax savings during the forecast period and the horizon value of tax savings. This is the value that the interest tax shield contributes to the firm. The sum of the value of unlevered operations and the value of the tax shield is equal to the value of operations for the levered firm:

(26–9)
$$V_{Unlevered} = \sum_{t=1}^{N} \frac{FCF_t}{(1 + r_{sU})^t} + \frac{HV_{U,N}}{(1 + r_{sU})^N}$$

(26–10)
$$V_{Tax\ shield} = \sum_{t=1}^{N} \frac{TS_t}{(1 + r_{sU})^t} + \frac{HV_{TS,N}}{(1 + r_{sU})^N}$$

(26–11)
$$V_{Operations} = V_{Unlevered} + V_{Tax\ shield}$$

5. To find the total value of the firm, add the value of operations to the value of any nonoperating assets, such as marketable securities. To find the value of equity, subtract the value of the debt before the merger from the total value of the firm.

$$
\begin{array}{r}
\text{Unlevered value of operations} \\
\underline{+\ \text{Value of tax shield}} \\
\text{Value of operations} \\
\underline{+\ \text{Value of nonoperating assets}} \\
\text{Total value of firm} \\
\underline{-\ \text{Value of debt}} \\
\text{Value of equity}
\end{array}
$$

To find the stock price per share, divide the value of equity by the number of shares.

The APV technique is especially useful for valuing acquisition targets. Many acquisitions are difficult to value using the corporate valuation model because (1) acquiring firms frequently assume the debt of the target firm, so old debt at different coupon rates is often part of the deal; and (2) the acquisition is usually financed partially by new debt that will be paid down rapidly, so the proportion of debt in the capital structure changes during the years immediately following the acquisition. Thus, the debt cost and capital structure associated with a merger are generally more complex than for a typical firm. The easiest way to handle these complexities is to specify each year's expected interest expense and use the APV method to find the value of the unlevered firm and the interest tax shields separately, and then sum those values.

> Why is the adjusted present value approach appropriate for situations with a changing capital structure?
>
> Describe the steps required to apply the APV approach.

Self Test

26.8 The Free Cash Flow to Equity (FCFE) Approach

Free cash flow is the cash flow available for distribution to *all* investors. In contrast, **free cash flow to equity (FCFE)** is the cash flow available for distribution to *common shareholders*. Because FCFE is available for distribution only to shareholders, it should be discounted at the levered cost of equity, r_{sL}. Therefore, the **free cash flow to equity approach,** also called the **equity residual model,** discounts the projected FCFEs at the cost of equity to determine the value of the equity from operations.

Because FCFE is the cash flow available for distribution to shareholders, it may be used to pay common dividends, repurchase stock, purchase financial assets, or some combination of these uses. In other words, the uses of FCFE include all those of FCF except for distributions to debtholders. Therefore, one way to calculate FCFE is to start with FCF and reduce it by the net after-tax distributions to debtholders:

$$
\begin{aligned}
\text{FCFE} &= \begin{array}{c}\text{Free}\\\text{cash flow}\end{array} - \begin{array}{c}\text{After-tax}\\\text{interest expense}\end{array} - \begin{array}{c}\text{Principal}\\\text{payments}\end{array} + \begin{array}{c}\text{Newly issued}\\\text{debt}\end{array} \\[2mm]
&= \begin{array}{c}\text{Free}\\\text{cash flow}\end{array} - \begin{array}{c}\text{Interest}\\\text{expense}\end{array} + \begin{array}{c}\text{Interest}\\\text{tax shield}\end{array} + \begin{array}{c}\text{Net change}\\\text{in debt}\end{array}
\end{aligned}
$$

(26–12)

Alternatively, the FCFE can be calculated as

$$
\text{(26-12a)} \qquad \text{FCFE} = \text{Net income} - \frac{\text{Net investment in}}{\text{operating capital}} + \frac{\text{Net change}}{\text{in debt}}
$$

Both calculations provide the same value for FCFE, but Equation 26-12 is used more often because analysts don't always estimate the net income for a target after it has been acquired.

Given projections of FCFE, the value of a firm's equity due to operations, V_{FCFE}, is

$$
\text{(26-13)} \qquad V_{FCFE} = \sum_{t=1}^{\infty} \frac{FCFE_t}{(1 + r_{sL})^t}
$$

If we assume constant growth beyond the horizon, then the horizon value of the value of equity due to operations, $HV_{FCFE,N}$, is

$$
\text{(26-14)} \qquad HV_{FCFE,N} = \frac{FCFE_{N+1}}{r_{sL} - g} = \frac{FCFE_N(1+g)}{r_{sL} - g}
$$

The value of equity due to operations is the present value of the horizon value and the FCFE during the forecast period:

$$
\text{(26-15)} \qquad V_{FCFE} = \sum_{t=1}^{N} \frac{FCFE_t}{(1 + r_{sL})^t} + \frac{HV_{FCFE,N}}{(1 + r_{sL})^N}
$$

The total value of a company's equity, S, is the value of the equity from operations plus the value of any nonoperating assets:

$$
\text{(26-16)} \qquad S = V_{FCFE} + \text{Nonoperating assets}
$$

To get a per share price, simply divide the total value of equity by the shares outstanding.[13] Like the corporate valuation model, the FCFE model can be applied only when the capital structure is constant.

Table 26-2 summarizes the three cash flow valuation methods and their assumptions.

---

13. The FCFE model is similar to the dividend growth model in that cash flows are discounted at the cost of equity. The cash flows in the FCFE model are those that are generated from operations, while the cash flows in the dividend growth model (i.e., the dividends) also contain cash flows due to interest earned on nonoperating assets.

TABLE 26-2   Summary of Cash Flow Approaches

	Approach		
	Corporate Valuation Model	**Free Cash Flow to Equity Model**	**APV Model**
Cash flow definition	FCF = NOPAT − Net investment in operating capital	FCFE = FCF − Interest expense + Interest tax shield + Net change in debt	(1) FCF and (2) Interest tax savings
Discount rate	WACC	r_{sL} = Cost of equity	r_{sU} = Unlevered cost of equity
Result of present value calculation	Value of operations	Value of equity due to operations	(1) Value of unlevered operations and (2) Value of the tax shield; together, these are the value of operations
How to get equity value	Value of operations + Value of nonoperating assets − Value of debt	Value of equity due to operations + Value of nonoperating assets	Value of operations + Value of nonoperating assets − Value of debt
Assumption about capital structure during forecast period	Capital structure is constant	Capital structure is constant	None
Requirement for analyst to project interest expense	No interest expense projections needed	Projected interest expense must be based on the assumed capital structure	Interest expense projections are unconstrained
Assumption at horizon	FCF grows at constant rate g	FCFE grows at constant rate g	FCF and interest tax savings grow at constant rate g

© Cengage Learning 2013

What cash flows are discounted in the FCFE model, and what is the discount rate?   **Self Test**

How do the FCFE, corporate valuation, and APV models differ? How are they similar?

26.9 Illustration of the Three Valuation Approaches for a Constant Capital Structure

To illustrate the three valuation approaches, consider Caldwell Inc., a large technology company, as it evaluates the potential acquisition of Tutwiler Controls. If the acquisition takes place, it will occur on January 1, 2013, and so each valuation will be as of that date and will be based on the capital structure and synergies expected after the acquisition. Tutwiler currently has a $62.5 million market value of equity and $27 million in debt, for a total market value of $89.5 million. Thus, Tutwiler's capital structure consists of $27/($62.5 + $27) = 30.17% debt. Caldwell intends to finance the acquisition with this same proportion of debt and plans to maintain this constant capital structure throughout the projection period and thereafter. Tutwiler is a publicly traded company, and its market-determined pre-merger beta was 1.2. Given a risk-free rate of 7% and a 5% market risk premium, the Capital Asset Pricing Model produces a pre-merger required rate of return on equity, r_{sL}, of

$$r_{sL} = 7\% + 1.2(5\%) = 13\%$$

Tutwiler's cost of debt is 9%. Its WACC is

$$\begin{aligned} WACC &= w_d(1 - T)r_d + w_s r_{sL} \\ &= 0.3017(0.60)(9\%) + 0.6983(13\%) \\ &= 10.707\% \end{aligned}$$

How much would Tutwiler be worth to Caldwell after the merger? The following sections illustrate the application of the corporate valuation model, the APV model, and the FCFE model. All three models produce an identical value of equity, but keep in mind this is only because the capital structure is constant. If the capital structure were to change during the projection period before becoming stable, then only the APV model could be used. Section 26.11 illustrates the APV in the case of a nonconstant capital structure.

WEB

See *Ch26 Tool Kit.xls* for details.

26.9a Projecting Post-Merger Cash Flows

The first order of business is to estimate the post-merger cash flows that Tutwiler will produce. This is by far the most important task in any merger analysis. In a **pure financial merger,** defined as one in which no operating synergies are expected, the incremental post-merger cash flows are simply the target firm's expected cash flows. In an **operating merger,** in which the two firms' operations are to be integrated, forecasting future cash flows is obviously more difficult, because potential synergies must be estimated. People from marketing, production, human resources, and accounting play leading roles here, with financial managers focusing on financing the acquisition and doing an analysis designed to determine whether the projected cash flows are worth the cost. In this chapter, we take the projections as given and concentrate on how they are analyzed. See *Web Extension 26A*, available on the textbook's Web site, for a discussion that focuses on projecting financial statements in a merger analysis.

Table 26-3 shows the post-merger projections for Tutwiler, taking into account all expected synergies and maintaining a constant capital structure. Both Caldwell and Tutwiler are in the 40% marginal federal-plus-state tax bracket. The cost of debt after the acquisition will remain at 9%. The projections assume that growth in the post-horizon period will be 6%.

Panel A of Table 26-3 shows selected items from the projected financial statements. Panel B shows the calculations for free cash flow, which is used in the corporate valuation model. Row 9 shows net operating profit after taxes (NOPAT), which is equal to EBIT(1 − T). Row 10 shows the net investment in operating capital, which is the annual change in the total net operating capital in Row 8. Free cash flow, shown

TABLE 26-3	Post-Merger Projections for the Tutwiler Subsidiary (Millions of Dollars)					
	1/1/13	**12/31/13**	**12/31/14**	**12/31/15**	**12/31/16**	**12/31/17**
Panel A: Selected Items from Projected Financial Statements[a]						
1. Net sales		$105.0	$126.0	$151.0	$174.0	$191.0
2. Cost of goods sold		80.0	94.0	113.0	129.3	142.0
3. Selling and administrative expenses		10.0	12.0	13.0	15.0	16.0
4. Depreciation		8.0	8.0	9.0	9.0	10.0
5. EBIT		$ 7.0	$ 12.0	$ 16.0	$ 20.7	$ 23.0
6 Interest expense[b]		3.0	3.2	3.5	3.7	3.9
7 Debt[c]	$ 33.2	35.8	38.7	41.1	43.6	46.2
8. Total net operating capital	116.0	117.0	121.0	125.0	131.0	138.0
Panel B: Corporate Valuation Model Cash Flows						
9. NOPAT = EBIT(1 − T)		$ 4.2	$ 7.2	$ 9.6	$ 12.4	$ 13.8
10. Less net investment in operating capital		1.0	4.0	4.0	6.0	7.0
11. Free cash flow		$ 3.2	$ 3.2	$ 5.6	$ 6.4	$ 6.8
Panel C: APV Model Cash Flows						
12. Free cash flow		$ 3.2	$ 3.2	$ 5.6	$ 6.4	$ 6.8
13. Interest tax saving = Interest(T)		$ 1.2	$ 1.3	$ 1.4	$ 1.5	$ 1.6
Panel D: FCFE Model Cash Flows						
14. Free cash flow		$ 3.2	$ 3.2	$ 5.6	$ 6.4	$ 6.8
15. Less A-T interest = Interest(1 − T)		1.8	1.9	2.1	2.2	2.4
16. Plus change in debt[d]	6.2	2.6	2.9	2.5	2.5	2.6
17. FCFE	$ 6.2	$ 4.0	$ 4.1	$ 6.0	$ 6.7	$ 7.1

© Cengage Learning 2013

[a] Rounded figures are presented here, but the full nonrounded values are used in all calculations. The tax rate is 40%.
[b] Interest payments are based on Tutwiler's existing debt, new debt to be issued to finance the acquisition, and additional debt required to finance annual growth.
[c] Debt is existing debt plus additional debt required to maintain a constant capital structure. Caldwell will increase Tutwiler's debt by $6.2 million, from $27 million to $33.2 million, at the time of the acquisition in order to keep the capital structure constant. This increase occurs because the post-merger synergies make Tutwiler more valuable to Caldwell than it was on a stand-alone basis. Therefore, it can support more dollars of debt and still maintain the constant debt ratio.
[d] The increase in debt at the time of acquisition is a source of free cash flow to equity.

in Row 11, is equal to NOPAT less the net investment in operating capital. Panel C shows the cash flows that will be used in the APV model. In particular, Row 13 shows the annual tax shield, which is equal to the interest expense multiplied by the tax rate. Panel D provides the calculations for FCFE, based upon Equation 26-12.

Of course, the post-merger cash flows are extremely difficult to estimate, and in merger valuations—just as in capital budgeting analysis—sensitivity, scenario, and simulation analyses should be conducted.[14] Indeed, in a friendly merger the acquiring firm would send a team consisting of literally dozens of financial analysts, accountants, engineers, and so forth to the target firm's headquarters. They would go over its

---

14. We purposely kept the cash flows simple in order to focus on key analytical issues. In actual merger valuations, the cash flows would be much more complex, normally including such items as tax loss carryforwards, tax effects of plant and equipment valuation adjustments, and cash flows from the sale of some of the subsidiary's assets.

books, estimate required maintenance expenditures, set values on assets such as real estate and petroleum reserves, and the like. Such an investigation, which is one example of **due diligence,** is an essential part of any merger analysis.

Following are valuations of Tutwiler using all three methods, beginning with the corporate valuation model.

26.9b Valuation Using the Corporate Valuation Model

WEB

See **Ch26 Tool Kit.xls** on the textbook's Web site for all calculations. Note that rounded intermediate values are shown in the text, but all calculations are performed in *Excel* using nonrounded values.

Because Caldwell does not plan on changing Tutwiler's capital structure, the post-merger WACC will be equal to the pre-merger WACC of 10.707% that we calculated previously. Tutwiler's free cash flows are shown in Row 11 of Table 26-3. The horizon value of Tutwiler's operations as of 2017 can be calculated with the constant growth formula that we used in Chapter 11:

$$HV_{Operations,2017} = \frac{FCF_{2018}}{WACC - g} = \frac{FCF_{2017}(1 + g)}{WACC - g}$$

$$= \frac{\$6.800(1.06)}{0.10707 - 0.06} = \$153.1 \text{ million}$$

The value of operations as of January 1, 2013, is the present value of the cash flows in the forecast period and the horizon value:

$$V_{Operations} = \frac{\$3.2}{(1 + 0.10707)^1} + \frac{\$3.2}{(1 + 0.10707)^2} + \frac{\$5.6}{(1 + 0.10707)^3}$$

$$+ \frac{\$6.4}{(1 + 0.10707)^4} + \frac{\$6.8 + \$153.1}{(1 + 0.10707)^5}$$

$$= \$110.1$$

There are no nonoperating assets, so the value of equity to Caldwell if Tutwiler is acquired is equal to the value of operations less the value of Tutwiler's debt:[15]

$$\$110.1 - \$27 = \$83.1 \text{ million}$$

26.9c Valuation Using the APV Approach

The APV approach requires an estimate of Tutwiler's unlevered cost of equity. Inputting Tutwiler's capital structure, cost of equity, and cost of debt, Equation 26-5 can be used to estimate the unlevered cost of equity:

(26–5a)

$$r_{sU} = w_s r_{sL} + w_d r_d$$

$$= 0.6983(13\%) + 0.3017(9\%)$$

$$= 11.793\%$$

In other words, if Tutwiler had no debt, its cost of equity would be 11.793%.

---

15. Notice that we subtract the $27 million value of Tutwiler's debt, not the $33.2 million of debt supported *after* the merger, because $27 million is the amount that must be paid off or assumed by Caldwell.

The horizon value of Tutwiler's unlevered cash flows ($HV_{U,2017}$) and tax shield ($HV_{TS,2017}$) can be calculated using the constant growth formula with the unlevered cost of equity as the discount rate, as shown in Equations 26-7 and 26-8:[16]

$$HV_{U,2017} = \frac{FCF_{2018}}{r_{sU} - g} = \frac{FCF_{2017}(1 + g)}{r_{sU} - g} = \frac{\$6.800(1.06)}{0.11793 - 0.06} = \$124.4 \text{ million}$$

$$HV_{TS,2017} = \frac{TS_{2018}}{r_{sU} - g} = \frac{TS_{2017}(1 + g)}{r_{sU} - g} = \frac{\$1.57(1.06)}{0.11793 - 0.06} = \$28.7 \text{ million}$$

The sum of the two horizon values is $124.4 + $28.7 = $153.1 million. This is the horizon value of operations, which is the same as the horizon value calculation we reached with the corporate valuation model.

Row 11 in Table 26-3 shows the projected free cash flows. The unlevered value of operations is calculated as the present value of the free cash flows during the forecast period and the horizon value of the free cash flows:

$$\begin{aligned} V_{Unlevered} &= \frac{\$3.2}{(1 + 0.11793)^1} + \frac{\$3.2}{(1 + 0.11793)^2} + \frac{\$5.6}{(1 + 0.11793)^3} \\ &+ \frac{\$6.4}{(1 + 0.11793)^4} + \frac{\$6.8 + \$124.4}{(1 + 0.11793)^5} \\ &= \$88.7 \text{ million} \end{aligned}$$

This shows that Tutwiler's operations would be worth $88.7 million if it had no debt.

Row 13 shows the yearly interest tax savings. The value of the tax shield is calculated as the present value of the yearly tax savings and the horizon value of the tax shield:

$$\begin{aligned} V_{Tax\ shield} &= \frac{\$1.2}{(1 + 0.11793)^1} + \frac{\$1.3}{(1 + 0.11793)^2} + \frac{\$1.4}{(1 + 0.11793)^3} \\ &+ \frac{\$1.5}{(1 + 0.11793)^4} + \frac{\$1.57 + \$28.7}{(1 + 0.11793)^5} \\ &= \$21.4 \text{ million} \end{aligned}$$

Thus, Tutwiler's operations would be worth only $88.7 million if it had no debt, but its capital structure contributes $21.4 million in value due to the tax deductibility of its interest payments. Since Tutwiler has no nonoperating assets, the total value of the firm is the sum of the unlevered value of operations, $88.7 million, and the value of the tax shield, $21.4 million, for a total of $110.1 million. The value of the equity is this total value less Tutwiler's outstanding debt of $27 million: $110.1 − $27 = $83.1 million. Note that this is the same value we obtained using the corporate valuation model.

---

16. Note that we report two decimal places for the 2017 tax shield even though Table 26-3 reports only one decimal place. All calculations are performed in *Excel*, which uses the full nonrounded values.

26.9d Valuation Using the FCFE Model

The horizon value of Tutwiler's free cash flows to equity can be calculated using the constant growth formula of Equation 26-14:[17]

$$HV_{FCFE,2017} = \frac{FCF_{2017}(1+g)}{r_{sL}-g} = \frac{\$7.06(1.06)}{0.13-0.06} = \$106.9 \text{ million}$$

Notice that this horizon value is different from the APV and corporate valuation horizon values. That is because the FCFE horizon value is only for equity, whereas the other two horizon values are for the total value of operations. If the 2017 debt of $46.2 million shown in Row 7 of Table 26-3 is added to the $HV_{FCFE,2017}$, the result is the same $153.1 million horizon value of operations obtained with the corporate valuation model and APV model.

Row 17 in Table 26-3 shows the yearly projections of FCFE. When discounted at the 13% cost of equity, the present value of these yearly FCFEs and the horizon value is the value of equity due to operations, which is $83.1 million:[18]

$$V_{FCFE} = \$6.2 + \frac{\$4.0}{(1+0.13)^1} + \frac{\$4.1}{(1+0.13)^2} + \frac{\$6.0}{(1+0.13)^3}$$

$$+ \frac{\$6.7}{(1+0.13)^4} + \frac{\$7.1 + \$106.9}{(1+0.13)^5}$$

$$= \$83.1 \text{ million}$$

If Tutwiler had any nonoperating assets, we would add them to V_{FCFE} to determine the total value of equity. Since Tutwiler has no nonoperating assets, its total equity value is equal to the V_{FCFE} of $83.1 million. Notice that this is the same value given by the corporate valuation model and the APV approach.

All three models agree that the estimated equity value is $83.1 million, which is more than the $62.5 million current market value of Tutwiler's equity. This means that Tutwiler is more valuable as a part of Caldwell than as a stand-alone corporation being run by its current managers.

Self Test	Why is the adjusted present value approach appropriate for situations with a changing capital structure?
	Describe the steps required to apply the APV approach.
	How do the FCFE, APV, and corporate valuation approaches differ from one another?

---

17. Note that we report two decimal places for the 2017 FCFE even though Table 26-3 reports only one decimal place. All calculations are performed in *Excel*, which uses the full nonrounded values.

18. Row 16 in Table 26-3 shows that debt is forecast to increase from its pre-merger $27 million to $33.2 million at the acquisition date. This is because Tutwiler is more valuable after the merger, so it can support more dollars of debt while still maintaining 30% debt in its capital structure. The increase in debt of $33.2 – $27 = $6.2 million is a FCFE that is immediately available to Caldwell and so is not discounted.

26.10 Setting the Bid Price

Under the acquisition plan, Caldwell would assume Tutwiler's debt and would also take on additional short-term debt as necessary to complete the purchase. The valuation models show that $83.1 million is the most it should pay for Tutwiler's stock. If it paid more, then Caldwell's own value would be diluted. On the other hand, if it could get Tutwiler for less than $83.1 million, Caldwell's stockholders would gain value. Therefore, Caldwell should bid something less than $83.1 million when it makes an offer for Tutwiler.

Now consider the target company. As stated earlier, Tutwiler's value of equity as an independent operating company is $62.5 million. If Tutwiler were acquired at a price greater than $62.5 million then its stockholders would gain value, whereas they would lose value at any lower price.

The difference between $62.5 million and $83.1 million, or $20.6 million, represents **synergistic benefits** expected from the merger. If there were no synergistic benefits, the maximum bid would be the current value of the target company. The greater the synergistic gains, the greater the gap between the target's current price and the maximum the acquiring company could pay.

The issue of how to divide the synergistic benefits is critically important. Obviously, both parties would want to get the best deal possible. In our example, if it knew the maximum price Caldwell could pay, Tutwiler's management would argue for a price close to $83.1 million. Caldwell, on the other hand, would try to get Tutwiler at a price as close to $62.5 million as possible.

Where, within the range of $62.5 to $83.1 million, will the actual price be set? The answer depends on a number of factors, including whether Caldwell offers to pay with cash or securities, the negotiating skills of the two management teams, and, most importantly, the bargaining positions of the two parties as determined by fundamental economic conditions. Let's first consider bargaining power and then examine the mechanics of a cash offer versus a stock offer.

26.10a Relative Bargaining Power

To illustrate the relative bargaining power of the target and the acquirer, assume there are many companies similar to Tutwiler that Caldwell could acquire, but suppose that no company other than Caldwell could gain synergies by acquiring Tutwiler. In this case, Caldwell would probably make a relatively low, take-it-or-leave-it offer, and Tutwiler would probably take it because some gain is better than none. On the other hand, if Tutwiler has some unique technology or other asset that many companies want, then once Caldwell announces its offer, others would probably make competing bids and the final price would probably be close to (or even above) $83.1 million. A price above $83.1 million presumably would be paid by some other company with a better synergistic fit or with a management that is more optimistic about Tutwiler's cash flow potential.

Caldwell would, of course, want to keep its maximum bid secret, and it would plan its bidding strategy carefully. If it thought other bidders would emerge or that Tutwiler's management might resist in order to preserve their jobs, it might make a high preemptive bid in hopes of scaring off competing bids or management resistance. On the other hand, it might make a lowball bid in hopes of "stealing" the company.[19]

---

19. For an interesting discussion of the aftereffects of losing a bidding contest, see Mark L. Mitchell and Kenneth Lehn, "Do Bad Bidders Become Good Targets?" *Journal of Applied Corporate Finance,* Summer 1990, pp. 60–69.

26.10b Cash Offers versus Stock Offers

Most target stockholders prefer to sell their shares for cash rather than to exchange them for stock in the post-merger company. Following is a brief description of each payment method.

Cash Offers

Tutwiler's pre-merger equity is worth $62.5 million. With 10 million shares outstanding, Tutwiler's stock price is $62.5/10 = $6.25. If the synergies are realized, then Tutwiler's equity will be worth $83.1 million to Caldwell, so $83.1/10 = $8.31 is the maximum price per share that Caldwell should be willing to pay to Tutwiler's stockholders. For example, Caldwell might offer $7.25 cash for each share of Tutwiler stock.

Stock Offers

In a stock offer, Tutwiler's stockholders exchange their Tutwiler shares for new shares in the post-merger company, which will be named CaldwellTutwiler. Targets typically prefer cash offers to stock offers, so perhaps Caldwell must offer a package worth $7.50 per share. With 10 million outstanding Tutwiler shares, the Tutwiler shareholders must end up owning $7.50 × 10 million = $75 million worth of stock in the post-merger company.

Suppose Caldwell has 20 million shares of stock outstanding (n_{Old}) prior to the merger and the stock price per share is $15. Then the total pre-merger value of Caldwell's equity is $15 × 20 million = $300 million. As calculated previously, the post-merger value of Tutwiler to Caldwell is $83.1 million. Therefore, the total post-merger value of CaldwellTutwiler will be $300 + $83.1 = $383.1 million.

After the merger, Tutwiler's former stockholders should own $75/$383.1 = 0.196 = 19.58% of the post-merger CaldwellTutwiler. With 20 million Caldwell shares outstanding, Caldwell must issue enough new shares, n_{New}, to the Tutwiler stockholders (in exchange for the Tutwiler shares) so that Tutwiler's former stockholders will own 19.6% of the shares of CaldwellTutwiler:

$$\text{Percent required by target stockholders} = \frac{n_{New}}{n_{New} + n_{Old}}$$

$$19.58\% = \frac{n_{New}}{n_{New} + 20}$$

$$n_{New} = \frac{20 \times 0.1958}{1 - 0.1958} = 4.87 \text{ million}$$

Tutwiler's former stockholders will exchange 10 million shares of stock in Tutwiler for 4.87 million shares of stock in the combined CaldwellTutwiler. Thus, the exchange ratio is 4.87/10 = 0.487.

After the merger, there will be 4.87 million new shares for a total of 24.87 million shares. With a combined intrinsic equity value of $383.1 million, the resulting price per share will be $383.1/24.87 = $15.40. The total value owned by Tutwiler's shareholders is this price multiplied by their shares: $15.40 × 4.87 million = $75 million. Also notice that the price will increase from $15.00 per share before the merger to $15.40 after the merger, so the merger will benefit Caldwell's shareholders if the synergies are realized.

26.11 Analysis When There Is a Permanent Change in Capital Structure

Tutwiler currently has equity worth $62.5 million and debt of $27 million, giving it a capital structure financed with about 30% debt: $27.0/($62.5 + $27.0) = 0.302 = 30.2%. Suppose Caldwell has decided to increase Tutwiler's debt from 30% to 50% over the next 5 years and to maintain the capital structure at that level from 2017 on. How would this affect Tutwiler's valuation? The free cash flows will not change, but the interest tax shield, the WACC, and the bid price will all change.[20] At a 30% debt level, the interest rate on Tutwiler's debt was 9%. However, at a 50% debt level, Tutwiler is more risky, and its interest rate would rise to 9.5% to reflect this additional risk. Because the capital structure is changing, we will use only the APV for this analysis.

26.11a The Effect on the Tax Shield

It is reasonable to assume that Caldwell will use more debt during the first 5 years of the acquisition if its long-run target capital structure is 50% debt. With more debt and a higher interest rate, the interest payments will be higher than those shown in Table 26-3, thus increasing the tax savings shown in Line 15. The interest payments and tax savings with more debt and a higher interest rate are projected as follows:

	2013	2014	2015	2016	2017
Interest	$5.00	$6.00	$7.00	$7.50	$8.30
Interest tax savings	2.00	2.40	2.80	3.00	3.32

In these projections, Tutwiler will reach its target capital structure of 50% debt and 50% equity by the start of 2017.[21]

26.11b The Effect on the Bid Price

The new capital structure would affect the maximum bid price by changing the value of Tutwiler to Caldwell. Based on the new tax shields, the unlevered and tax shield horizon values in 2017 are calculated as

$$HV_{U,2017} = \frac{FCF_{2018}}{r_{sU} - g} = \frac{FCF_{2017}(1 + g)}{r_{sU} - g} = \frac{\$6.800(1.06)}{0.11793 - 0.06} = \$124.4$$

WEB

For more information on projecting financial statements, see **Web Extension 26A** and **Ch26 Tool Kit.xls** on the textbook's Web site.

20. We are assuming for simplicity that Tutwiler has no more expected bankruptcy costs at 50% debt than at 30% debt. If Tutwiler's risk of bankruptcy and hence its expected bankruptcy costs are larger at this higher level of debt, then its projected free cash flows should be reduced by these expected costs. In practice it is extremely difficult to estimate expected bankruptcy costs. However, these costs can be significant and should be considered when a high degree of leverage is being used.

21. The last year's projected interest expense must be consistent with the assumed capital structure in order to use the relation $TS_{N+1} = TS_N(1 + g)$ in calculating the tax shield horizon value.

$$HV_{TS,2017} = \frac{TS_{2018}}{r_{sU} - g} = \frac{TS_{2017}(1 + g)}{r_{sU} - g} = \frac{\$3.32(1.06)}{0.11793 - 0.06} = \$60.7$$

Based on the new interest payments and horizon values, the cash flows to be discounted at the unlevered cost of equity are as follows:

	2013	2014	2015	2016	2017
Free cash flow	$3.2	$3.2	$5.6	$6.4	$ 6.8
Unlevered horizon value					124.4
FCF plus horizon value	$3.2	$3.2	$5.6	$6.4	$131.2
Interest tax saving	2.0	2.4	2.8	3.0	3.3
Tax shield horizon value					$ 60.7
TS$_t$ plus horizon value	$2.0	$2.4	$2.8	$3.0	$ 64.0

The present value of the free cash flows and their horizon value is $88.7 million, just as it was under the 30% debt policy; the unlevered value of operations is not impacted by the change in capital structure:

$$V_{Unlevered} = \frac{\$3.2}{(1 + 0.11793)^1} + \frac{\$3.2}{(1 + 0.11793)^2} + \frac{\$5.6}{(1 + 0.11793)^3}$$
$$+ \frac{\$6.4}{(1 + 0.11793)^4} + \frac{\$6.8 + \$124.4}{(1 + 0.11793)^5}$$
$$= \$88.7 \text{ million}$$

The present value of the tax shields and their horizon value is $44.3 million, which is $22.9 million more than the value of the tax shield under the 30% debt policy:

$$V_{Tax shield} = \frac{\$2.0}{(1 + 0.11793)^1} + \frac{\$2.4}{(1 + 0.11793)^2} + \frac{\$2.8}{(1 + 0.11793)^3}$$
$$+ \frac{\$3.0}{(1 + 0.11793)^4} + \frac{\$3.3 + \$60.7}{(1 + 0.11793)^5}$$
$$= \$44.3 \text{ million}$$

Thus, Tutwiler is worth almost $23 million more to Caldwell if it is financed with 50% rather than 30% debt because of the added value of the tax shields.

The value of operations under the new 50% debt policy is the sum of the unlevered value of operations and the value of the tax shields, or $133.0 million. There are no nonoperating assets to add, and subtracting the debt of $27 million leaves the value of Tutwiler's equity at $106.0 million. Because Tutwiler has 10 million shares outstanding, the maximum amount Caldwell should be willing to pay per share, given a post-merger target capital structure of 50% debt, is $10.60. This is more than the $8.31 maximum price if the capital structure had 30% debt. The difference, $2.29 per share, reflects the added value of the interest tax shields under the higher-debt plan.

Self Test	How does a change in capital structure affect the valuation analysis?

26.12 Taxes and the Structure of the Takeover Bid

In a merger, the acquiring firm can either buy the target's assets or buy shares of stock directly from the target's shareholders. If the offer is for the target's assets then the target's board of directors will make a recommendation to the shareholders, who will vote either to accept or reject the offer. If they accept the offer, the payment goes directly to the target corporation, which pays off any debt not assumed by the acquiring firm, pays any corporate taxes that are due, and then distributes the remainder of the payment to the shareholders, often in the form of a liquidating dividend. In this situation, the target firm is usually dissolved and no longer continues to exist as a separate legal entity, although its assets and work force may continue to function as a division or as a wholly owned subsidiary of the acquiring firm. The acquisition of assets is a common form of takeover for small and medium-sized firms, especially those that are not publicly traded. A major advantage of this method compared with the acquisition of the target's stock is that the acquiring firm simply acquires assets and is not saddled with any hidden liabilities. In contrast, if the acquiring firm buys the target's stock, then it is responsible for any legal contingencies against the target, even for those that might have occurred prior to the takeover.

An offer for a target's stock rather than its assets can be made either directly to the shareholders, as is typical in a hostile takeover, or indirectly through the board of directors, which in a friendly deal makes a recommendation to the shareholders to accept the offer. In a successful offer, the acquiring firm will end up owning a controlling interest or perhaps even all of the target's stock. Sometimes the target retains its identity as a separate legal entity and is operated as a subsidiary of the acquiring firm, and sometimes its corporate status is dissolved and it is operated as one of the acquiring firm's divisions.

The payment offered by the acquiring firm can be in the form of cash, stock of the acquiring firm, debt of the acquiring firm, or some combination. The structure of the bid affects (1) the capital structure of the post-merger firm, (2) the tax treatment of both the acquiring firm and the target's stockholders, (3) the ability of the target firm's stockholders to benefit from future merger-related gains, and (4) the types of federal and state regulations to which the acquiring firm will be subjected.

The tax consequences of the merger depend on whether it is classified as a *taxable offer* or a *nontaxable offer.*[22] In general, a nontaxable offer is one in which the form of payment is predominately stock, although the application of this simple principle is much more complicated in practice. The Internal Revenue Code views a mostly stock merger as an exchange rather than a sale, making it a nontaxable event. However, if the offer includes a significant amount of cash or bonds, then the IRS views it as a sale, and it is a taxable transaction just like any other sale.

In a nontaxable deal, target shareholders who receive shares of the acquiring company's stock do not have to pay any taxes at the time of the merger. When they eventually sell their stock in the acquiring company, they must pay a tax on the gain. The amount of the gain is the sales price of their stock in the acquiring

---

22. For more details, see J. Fred Weston, Mark L. Mitchell, and Harold Mulherin, *Takeovers, Restructuring, and Corporate Governance,* 4th ed. (Upper Saddle River, NJ: Prentice-Hall, 2004), especially Chapter 4. Also see Kenneth E. Anderson, Thomas R. Pope, and John L. Kramer, eds., *Prentice Hall's Federal Taxation: Corporations, Partnerships, Estates, and Trusts,* 2006 ed. (Upper Saddle River, NJ: Prentice-Hall, 2006), especially Chapter 7.

TEMPEST IN A TEAPOT?

In 2001, amid a flurry of warnings and lobbying, the Financial Accounting Standards Board (FASB) in its Statement 141 eliminated the use of pooling for merger accounting, requiring that purchase accounting be used instead. Because the change would otherwise have required that all purchased goodwill be amortized and reported earnings be reduced, the FASB also issued Statement 142, which eliminated the regular amortization of purchased goodwill, replacing it with an "impairment test." The impairment test requires that companies evaluate annually their purchased goodwill and write it down if its value has declined. This impairment test resulted in Time Warner's unprecedented 2002 write-down of $54 billion of goodwill associated with the AOL merger.

So what exactly is the effect of the change? First and foremost, the change does *nothing* to the firm's actual cash flows. Purchased goodwill may still be amortized for federal income tax purposes, so the change does not affect the actual taxes a company pays, nor does it affect the company's operating cash flows. However, it does affect the earnings that companies report to their shareholders. Firms that used to have large goodwill charges from past acquisitions have seen their reported earnings increase because they no longer have to amortize the remaining goodwill. Firms whose acquisitions have fared badly, such as Time Warner, must make large write-downs. Executives facing an earnings boost hope—and executives facing a write-down fear—that investors will not see through these accounting changes. However, evidence suggests that investors realize that a company's assets have deteriorated long before the write-down actually occurs, and they build this information into the price of the stock. For example, Time Warner's announcement of its $54 billion charge in January 2002 resulted in only a blip in its stock price at that time, even though the write-down totaled more than a third of its market value. The market had recognized the decline in value months earlier, and by the time of the announcement Time Warner had already lost more than $100 billion in market value.

company minus the price at which they purchased their original stock in the target company.[23] In a taxable offer, the gain between the offer price and the original purchase price of the target stock is taxed in the year of the merger.[24]

All other things equal, stockholders prefer nontaxable offers, since they may then postpone taxes on their gains. Furthermore, if the target firm's stockholders receive stock, they will benefit from any synergistic gains produced by the merger. Most target shareholders are thus willing to give up their stock for a lower price in a nontaxable offer than in a taxable one. As a result, one might expect nontaxable bids to dominate. However, this is not the case: Roughly half of all mergers have been taxable. The reason for this is explained in the following paragraphs.

The form of the payment also has tax consequences for the acquiring and target firms. To illustrate, consider the following situation. The target firm has assets with a book value of $100 million, but these assets have an appraised value of $150 million. The offer by the acquiring firm is worth $225 million. If it is a nontaxable

---

23. This is a capital gain if it has been at least 1 year since they purchased their original stock in the target.
24. Even in nontaxable deals, taxes must be paid in the year of the merger by any stockholders who receive cash.

offer, then after the merger the acquiring firm simply adds the $100 million book value of the target's assets to its own assets and continues to depreciate them according to their previous depreciation schedules. To keep the example simple, we assume the target has no debt.

The situation is more complicated for a taxable offer, and the treatment is different depending on whether the offer is for the target's assets or for its stock. If the acquiring firm offers $225 million for the target's assets, then the target firm must pay a tax on the gain of $225 − $100 = $125 million. Assuming a corporate tax rate of 40%, this tax is 0.40($125) = $50 million. This leaves the target with $225 − $50 = $175 million to distribute to its shareholders upon liquidation. Adding insult to injury, the target's shareholders must also pay individual taxes on any of their own gains.[25] This is truly a taxable transaction, with taxes assessed at both the corporate and individual levels!

In contrast to the tax disadvantages for the target and its shareholders, the acquiring firm receives two major tax advantages. First, it records the acquired assets at their appraised value and depreciates them accordingly. Thus, it will depreciate $150 million of assets in this taxable transaction versus only $100 million in a nontaxable transaction. Second, it will create $75 million in a new asset account called **goodwill,** which is the difference between the purchase price of $225 million and the appraised value of $150 million. Tax laws that took effect in 1993 permit companies to amortize this goodwill over 15 years using the straight-line method and also to deduct the amortization from taxable income. The net effect is that the full purchase price of $225 million can be written off in a taxable merger versus only the original book value of $100 million in a nontaxable transaction.

Now suppose the acquiring firm offers $225 million for the target's stock, rather than just its assets as in the preceding example, in a taxable offer. After completing the merger, the acquiring firm must choose between two tax treatments. Under the first alternative, it will record the assets at their book value of $100 million and continue depreciating them using their current schedules. This treatment does not create any goodwill. Under the second alternative, it will record the assets at their appraised value of $150 million and create $75 million of goodwill. As described earlier for the asset purchase, this allows the acquiring firm to effectively depreciate the entire purchase price of $225 million for tax purposes. However, there will also be an immediate tax liability on the $125 million gain, just as when the firm purchased assets.[26] Therefore, many companies choose not to mark up the assets. Figure 26-1 illustrates the tax implications for the various types of transactions.

If you think this is complicated, you are right! At this point, you should know enough to talk with specialized accountants and lawyers or be ready to delve into tax accounting texts, but merger taxation is too complex a subject to be covered thoroughly in a general finance textbook.

Securities laws also have an effect on the offer's construction. The SEC has oversight over the issuance of new securities, including stock or debt issued in

---

25. Our example assumes that the target is a publicly owned firm, which means that it must be a "C corporation" for tax purposes. However, if it is privately held then it might be an "S corporation," in which case only the stockholders would be taxed. This helps smaller firms to use mergers as an exit strategy.

26. Technically speaking, it is the target firm that is responsible for this tax on the write-up. Keep in mind, however, that the acquiring firm previously purchased the stock in the target and so, in reality, must bear the brunt of the tax.

Figure 26-1   Merger Tax Effects

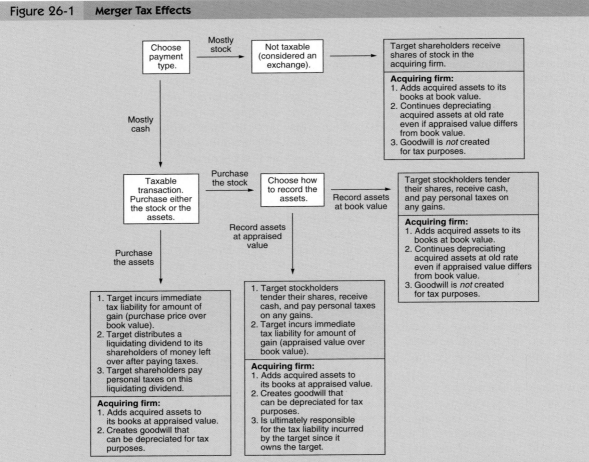

Note: These are actual cash tax effects. However, the tax effects reported to shareholders will be different because shareholder statements must conform to GAAP conventions, not to federal Tax Code conventions. For example, purchased goodwill can no longer be deducted for shareholder reporting under GAAP, even though it is still deductible for federal tax purposes. See the box entitled "Tempest in a Teapot?" which deals with changes in the accounting treatment of mergers and goodwill.

connection with a merger. Therefore, whenever a corporation bids for control of another firm through the exchange of equity or debt, the entire process must take place under the scrutiny of the Securities and Exchange Commission. The time required for such reviews allows target managements to implement defensive tactics and other firms to make competing offers; as a result, nearly all hostile tender offers are for cash rather than securities.

Self Test

What are some alternative ways of structuring takeover bids?

How do taxes influence the payment structure?

How do securities laws affect the payment structure?

26.13 Financial Reporting for Mergers

Although a detailed discussion of financial reporting is best left to accounting courses, the accounting implications of mergers cannot be ignored. Currently, mergers are handled using **purchase accounting**.[27] Keep in mind, however, that all larger companies are required to keep two sets of books. The first is for the IRS, and it reflects the tax treatment of mergers as described in the previous section. The second is for financial reporting, and it reflects the treatment described here. As you will see, the rules for financial reporting differ from those for the IRS.

26.13a Purchase Accounting

Table 26-4 illustrates purchase accounting. Here, Firm A is assumed to have "bought" Firm B using the stock of the acquiring company. If the price paid is exactly equal to the acquired firm's *net asset value,* which is defined as its total assets minus its liabilities, then the consolidated balance sheet will be as if the two statements were merged. Normally, though, there is an important difference. If the price paid *exceeds* the net asset value, then asset values will be increased to reflect the price actually paid, whereas if the price paid is *less* than the net asset value, then assets must be written down when preparing the consolidated balance sheet.

Note that Firm B's net asset value is $30, which is also its reported common equity value. This $30 book value could be equal to the market value (which is determined by investors based on the firm's earning power), but book value could also be more or less than the market value. Three situations are considered in Table 26-4. First, in Column 3 we assume that Firm A gives stock worth $20 for Firm B. Thus, B's assets as reported on its balance sheet were overvalued, and A pays less than B's net asset value. The overvaluation could be in either fixed or current assets; an appraisal would be made, but we assume it is fixed assets that are overvalued. Accordingly, we reduce B's fixed assets and also its common equity by $10 before constructing the consolidated balance sheet shown in Column 3. Next, in Column 4, we assume that A pays exactly the net asset value for B. In this case, the financial statements are simply combined.

Finally, in Column 5 we assume that A pays more than the net asset value for B: $50 is paid for $30 of net assets. This excess is assumed to be partly attributable to undervalued assets (land, buildings, machinery, and inventories) and so, to reflect this undervaluation, current and fixed assets are each increased by $5. In addition, we assume that $10 of the $20 excess of market value over book value is due to a superior sales organization or to some other intangible factor, and we post this excess as goodwill. Firm B's common equity is increased by $20, the sum of the increases in current and fixed assets plus goodwill, and this markup is also reflected in Firm A's post-merger equity account.[28]

---

27. In 2001, the Financial Accounting Standards Board (FASB) issued Statement 141, which eliminated the use of *pooling* accounting.

28. This example assumes that additional debt was not issued to help finance the acquisition. If the acquisition were totally debt financed, then the post-merger balance sheet would show an increase in debt rather than an increase in the equity account. If it were financed by a mix of debt and equity, both accounts would increase. If the acquisition were paid for with cash on hand, then current assets would decrease by the amount paid and the equity account would not increase.

TABLE 26-4	Accounting for Mergers: Firm A Acquires Firm B with Stock				
			Post-Merger: Firm A		
	Firm A	**Firm B**	**$20 Paid[a]**	**$30 Paid[a]**	**$50 Paid[a]**
	(1)	**(2)**	**(3)**	**(4)**	**(5)**
Current assets	$ 50	$25	$ 75	$ 75	$ 80[b]
Fixed assets	50	25	65[c]	75	80[b]
Goodwill[d]	0	0	0	0	10[d]
Total assets	$100	$50	$140	$150	$170
Liabilities	$ 40	$20	$ 60	$ 60	$ 60
Equity	60	30	80[e]	90	110[f]
Total claims	$100	$50	$140	$150	$170

© Cengage Learning 2013

[a]The price paid is the *net asset value*—that is, total assets minus liabilities.
[b]Here we assume that Firm B's current and fixed assets are both increased to $30.
[c]Here we assume that Firm B's fixed assets are written down from $25 to $15 before constructing the consolidated balance sheet.
[d]*Goodwill* refers to the excess paid for a firm above the appraised value of the physical assets purchased. Goodwill represents payment both for intangibles such as patents and for "organization value," such as that associated with having an effective sales force. Beginning in 2001, purchased goodwill such as this may not be amortized for financial statement reporting purposes.
[e]Firm B's common equity is reduced by $10 prior to consolidation to reflect the fixed asset write-off.
[f]Firm B's equity is increased to $50 to reflect the above-book purchase price.

26.13b Income Statement Effects

A merger can have a significant effect on reported profits. If asset values are increased, as they often are under a purchase, then this must be reflected in higher depreciation charges (and also in a higher cost of goods sold if inventories are written up). This, in turn, will further reduce reported profits. Prior to 2001, goodwill was also amortized over its expected life. Now, however, goodwill is subject to an "annual impairment test." If the fair market value of the goodwill has declined over the year, then the amount of the decline must be charged to earnings. If not, then there is no charge, but gains in goodwill cannot be added to earnings.

Table 26-5 illustrates the income statement effects of the write-up of current and fixed assets. We assume A purchased B for $50, creating $10 of goodwill and $10 of higher physical asset value. As Column 3 indicates, the asset markups cause reported profits to be lower than the sum of the individual companies' reported profits.

The asset markup is also reflected in earnings per share. In our hypothetical merger, we assume that nine shares exist in the consolidated firm. (Six of these shares went to A's stockholders, and three went to B's.) The merged company's EPS is $2.33, whereas each of the individual companies' EPS was $2.40.

WEB

See *Ch26 Tool Kit.xls* on the textbook's Web site for details.

Self Test

What is purchase accounting for mergers?

What is goodwill? What impact does goodwill have on the firm's balance sheet? On its income statement?

TABLE 26-5	**Income Statement Effects**		
	Pre-Merger		**Post-Merger: Firm A**
	Firm A	**Firm B**	**Merged**
	(1)	**(2)**	**(3)**
Sales	$100.0	$50.0	$150.0
Operating costs	72.0	36.0	109.0[a]
Operating income	$ 28.0	$14.0	$ 41.0[a]
Interest (10%)	4.0	2.0	6.0
Taxable income	$ 24.0	$12.0	$ 35.0
Taxes (40%)	9.6	4.8	14.0
Net income	$ 14.4	$ 7.2	$ 21.0
EPS[b]	$ 2.40	$ 2.40	$ 2.33

[a]Operating costs are $1 higher than they otherwise would be; this reflects the higher reported costs (depreciation and cost of goods sold) caused by the physical asset markup at the time of purchase.
[b]Before the merger, Firm A had six shares and Firm B had three shares. Firm A gives one of its shares for each of Firm B's, so A has nine shares outstanding after the merger.

26.14 Analysis for a "True Consolidation"

Most of our analysis in the preceding sections assumed that one firm plans to acquire another. However, in many situations it is hard to identify an "acquirer" and a "target"— the merger appears to be a true "merger of equals," as was the case with the Exxon–Mobil and First Union–Wachovia mergers. In such cases, how is the analysis handled?

The first step is to estimate the value of the combined enterprise, incorporating any synergies, tax effects, or capital structure changes. The second step is to decide how to allocate the new company's stock between the two sets of old stockholders. Because of synergy, one would normally expect the consolidated value to exceed the sum of the pre-announcement values of the two companies. For example, Company A might have had a pre-merger equity value of $10 billion, found as (Number of shares)(Price per share), and Company B might have had a pre-merger value of $15 billion. If the post-merger value of new Company AB is estimated to be $30 billion, then that value must be allocated. Company A's stockholders must receive enough shares to give them a projected value of at least $10 billion, and Company B's stockholders must receive at least $15 billion. But how will the remaining $5 billion of synergistically induced value be divided?

This is a key issue, requiring intense negotiation between the two management groups. There is no rule or formula that can be applied, but one basis for the allocation is the relative pre-announcement values of the two companies. For example, in our hypothetical merger of A and B to form AB, the companies might agree to give $10/$25 = 40% of the new stock to A's stockholders and 60% to B's stockholders. Unless a case could be made for giving a higher percentage of the shares to one of the companies because it was responsible for more of the synergistic value, then the pre-merger value proportions would seem to be a "fair" solution. In any event, the pre-merger proportions will probably be given the greatest weight in reaching the final decision.

It should also be noted that control of the consolidated company is always an issue. Generally, the companies hold a press conference and announce that the CEO of one firm will be chairman of the new company, that the other CEO will be president, that the new board will consist of directors from both old boards, and that power will be shared. With huge mergers such as those we have been seeing lately, there is plenty of power to be shared.

Self Test	How does merger analysis differ in the case of a large company acquiring a smaller one versus a "true merger of equals"?
	Do you think the same guidelines for allocating synergistic gains would be used in both types of mergers?

26.15 The Role of Investment Bankers

Investment bankers are involved with mergers in a number of ways: (1) they help arrange mergers, (2) they help target companies develop and implement defensive tactics, (3) they help value target companies, (4) they help finance mergers, and (5) they invest in the stocks of potential merger candidates.

26.15a Arranging Mergers

The major investment banking firms have merger and acquisition groups that operate within their corporate finance departments. (Corporate finance departments offer advice, as opposed to underwriting or brokerage services, to business firms.) Members of these groups identify firms with excess cash that might want to buy other firms, companies that might be willing to be bought, and firms that might, for a number of reasons, be attractive to others. Sometimes dissident stockholders of firms with poor track records work with investment bankers to oust management by helping to arrange a merger.

26.15b Developing Defensive Tactics

Target firms that do not want to be acquired generally enlist the help of an investment banking firm along with a law firm that specializes in mergers. Defenses include such tactics as (1) changing the bylaws so that only one-third of the directors are elected each year and/or so that a 75% approval (a *super majority*) rather than a simple majority is required to approve a merger, (2) trying to convince the target firm's stockholders that the price being offered is too low, (3) raising antitrust issues in the hope that the Justice Department will intervene, (4) repurchasing stock in the open market in an effort to push the price above that being offered by the potential acquirer, (5) finding a **white knight** who is acceptable to the target firm's management to compete with the potential acquirer, and (6) finding a **white squire** who is friendly to current management and can buy enough of the target firm's shares to block the merger.

26.15c Establishing a Fair Value

If a friendly merger is being worked out between two firms' managements, then it is important to document that the agreed-upon price is a fair one; otherwise, the stockholders of either company may sue to block the merger. Therefore, in most large mergers, each side will hire an investment banking firm to evaluate the target company and to help establish the fair price. Even if the merger is not friendly, investment bankers may still be asked to help establish a price. If a surprise tender offer is to be made, then the acquiring firm will want to know the lowest price at which it might be able to acquire the stock while the target firm may seek help in "proving" that the price being offered is too low.

26.15d Financing Mergers

To be successful in the mergers and acquisitions (M&A) business, an investment banker must be able to offer a financing package to clients—whether they are acquirers who need capital to take over companies or target companies trying to finance stock repurchase plans or other defenses against takeovers. In fact, the fees that investment banks generate through issuing merger-related debt often dwarf their other merger-related fees.

26.16e Arbitrage Operations

Arbitrage generally means simultaneously buying and selling the same commodity or security in two different markets at different prices and pocketing a risk-free return. However, the major brokerage houses, as well as some wealthy private investors, are engaged in a different type of arbitrage called *risk arbitrage*. The *arbitrageurs,* or "arbs," speculate in the stocks of companies that are likely takeover targets. Vast amounts of capital are required to speculate in a large number of securities and thus reduce risk, and also to make money on narrow spreads. Yet the large investment bankers have the wherewithal to play this game. To be successful, arbs must be able to sniff out likely targets, assess the probability of offers reaching fruition, and move in and out of the market quickly and with low transaction costs.

What are some defensive tactics that firms can use to resist hostile takeovers?	**Self Test**
What is the difference between pure arbitrage and risk arbitrage?	

26.16 Who Wins: The Empirical Evidence

The magnitude of the merger market raises two questions: (1) Do corporate acquisitions create value? (2) If so, how is the value shared between the parties?

Most researchers agree that takeovers increase the wealth of the shareholders of target firms, for otherwise they would not agree to the offer. However, there is a debate as to whether mergers benefit the acquiring firm's shareholders. In particular, managements of acquiring firms may be motivated by factors other than maximizing shareholder wealth. For example, they may want to merge merely to increase the size of the corporations they manage, because increased size usually brings larger salaries plus job security, perquisites, power, and prestige.

The question of who gains from corporate acquisitions can be tested by examining the stock price changes that occur around the time of a merger or takeover announcement. Changes in the stock prices of the acquiring and target firms represent market participants' beliefs about the value created by the merger and about how that value will be divided between the target and acquiring firms' shareholders. Therefore, examining a large sample of stock price movements can shed light on the issue of who gains from mergers.

One cannot simply examine stock prices around merger announcement dates, because other factors influence stock prices. For example, if a merger was announced on a day when the entire market advanced, then a rise in the target firm's price would not necessarily signify that the merger was expected to create value. Hence, studies examine *abnormal returns* associated with merger announcements, where abnormal returns are defined as that part of a stock price change caused by factors other than changes in the general stock market.

These "event studies" have examined both acquiring and target firms' stock price responses to mergers and tender offers.[29] Jointly, they have covered nearly every acquisition involving publicly traded firms from the early 1960s to the present, and they are remarkably consistent in their results: On average, the stock prices of target firms increase by about 30% in hostile tender offers, whereas in friendly mergers the average increase is about 20%. However, for both hostile and friendly

MERGER MISTAKES

Academics have long known that acquiring firms' shareholders rarely reap the benefits of mergers. However, this important information never seemed to make it up to the offices of corporate America's decision makers; the 1990s saw bad deal after bad deal and with no apparent learning on the part of acquisitive executives. *BusinessWeek* published an analysis of 302 large mergers from 1995 to 2001, and it found that 61% of them led to losses by the acquiring firms' shareholders. Indeed, those losing shareholders' returns during the first post-merger year averaged 25 percentage points less than the returns on other companies in their industry. The average returns for all the merging companies, both winners and losers, were 4.3% below industry averages and 9.2% below the S&P 500.

The article cited four common mistakes:

1. The acquiring firms often overpaid. Generally, the acquirers gave away all of the synergies from the mergers to the acquired firms' shareholders, and then some.
2. Management overestimated the synergies (cost savings and revenue gains) that would result from the merger.
3. Management took too long to integrate operations between the merged companies. This irritated customers and employees alike, and it postponed any gains from the integration.
4. Some companies cut costs too deeply at the expense of maintaining sales and production infrastructures.

The worst performance came from companies that paid for their acquisitions with stock. The best performance, albeit a paltry 0.3% better than industry averages, came from companies that used cash for their acquisitions. On the bright side, the shareholders of the companies that were acquired fared quite well, earning on average 19.3% more than their industry peers, and all of those gains came in the two weeks surrounding the merger announcement.

Source: David Henry, "Mergers: Why Most Big Deals Don't Pay Off," *BusinessWeek*, October 14, 2002, pp. 60–70.

---

29. For more on the effects of mergers on value, see Bernard S. Black and Joseph A. Grundfest, "Shareholder Gains from Takeovers and Restructurings between 1981 and 1986: $162 Billion Is a Lot of Money," *Journal of Applied Corporate Finance,* Spring 1988, pp. 5–15; and James W. Wansley, William R. Lane, and Ho C. Yang, "Abnormal Returns to Acquired Firms by Type of Acquisition and Method of Payment," *Financial Management,* Autumn 1983, pp. 16–22.

deals, the stock prices of acquiring firms, on average, remain constant. Thus, the event study evidence strongly indicates (1) that acquisitions do create value but (2) that shareholders of target firms reap virtually all the benefits.

The event study evidence suggests that mergers benefit targets but not acquirers—and hence that an acquiring firm's stockholders should be skeptical of its managers' plans for acquisitions. This evidence cannot be dismissed out of hand, but neither is it entirely convincing. There are undoubtedly many good mergers, just as there are many poorly conceived ones. Like most of finance, merger decisions should be studied carefully, and it is best not to judge the outcome of a specific merger until the actual results start to come in.

Self Test

Explain how researchers can study the effects of mergers on shareholder wealth.

Do mergers create value? If so, who profits from this value?

Do the research results discussed in this section seem logical? Explain.

26.17 Corporate Alliances

Mergers are one way for two companies to join forces, but many companies are striking cooperative deals, called **corporate,** or **strategic, alliances,** which stop far short of merging. Whereas mergers combine all of the assets of the firms involved, as well as their ownership and managerial expertise, alliances allow firms to create combinations that focus on specific business lines that offer the most potential synergies. These alliances take many forms, from simple marketing agreements to joint ownership of worldwide operations.

One form of corporate alliance is the **joint venture,** in which parts of companies are joined to achieve specific, limited objectives. A joint venture is controlled by a management team consisting of representatives of the two (or more) parent companies. A study of 345 corporate alliances found that the stock prices of both partners in an alliance tended to increase when the alliance was announced, with an average abnormal return of about 0.64% on the day of the announcement.[30] About 43% of the alliances were marketing agreements, 14% were R&D agreements, 11% were for licensing technology, 7% for technology transfers, and 25% were for some combination of these four reasons. Although most alliances were for marketing agreements, the market reacted most favorably when the alliance was for technology sharing between two firms in the same industry. The study also found that the typical alliance lasted at least 5 years and that the allied firms had better operating performance than their industry peers during this period.

Self Test

What is the difference between a merger and a corporate alliance?

What is a joint venture? Give some reasons why joint ventures may be advantageous to the parties involved.

---

30. See Su Han Chan, John W. Kensinger, Arthur J. Keown, and John D. Martin, "When Do Strategic Alliances Create Shareholder Value?" *Journal of Applied Corporate Finance,* Winter 1999, pp. 82–87.

26.18 Leveraged Buyouts

In a **leveraged buyout (LBO)**, a small group of investors, often led by a private equity fund, acquires a firm in a transaction financed largely by debt. The debt is serviced with funds generated by the acquired company's operations and often by the sale of some of its assets. Generally, the acquiring group keeps the current management team and provides them with incentive compensation plans. The objective is to run the acquired company for a number of years, boost its value, and then take it public again as a stronger company. In other instances, the acquiring firm plans to sell off divisions to other firms that can gain synergies. In either case, the acquiring group expects to make a substantial profit from the LBO, but the inherent risks are great owing to the heavy use of financial leverage.[31]

Self Test	What is an LBO?

26.19 Divestitures

There are four types of **divestitures**. **Sale to another firm** generally involves the sale of an entire division or unit, usually for cash but sometimes for stock in the acquiring firm. In a **spin-off**, the firm's existing stockholders are given new stock representing separate ownership rights in the division that was divested. The division establishes its own board of directors and officers, and it becomes a separate company. The stockholders end up owning shares of two firms instead of one, but no cash has been transferred. In a **carve-out**, a minority interest in a corporate subsidiary is sold to new shareholders, so the parent gains new equity financing yet retains control. In a **liquidation**, the assets of a division are sold off piecemeal to many purchasers rather than as a single operating entity to one purchaser. To illustrate the different types of divestitures, we now present some examples.

In 2011, Ralcorp Holdings proposed splitting the company into a Post Foods piece and a private-label business. The reason for the spin-off was to allow the two divisions to focus on their different product markets and also to allow ConAgra, which had been pursuing Ralcorp for its private-label business, to make a more limited acquisition. In 2009, Time Warner announced that it planned to spin off AOL, the dissolution of a merger that had never worked. And in 2008, Cadbury Schweppes decided to focus on its chocolate and candy businesses, so it spun off soft-drink brands into a separately traded company, the Dr Pepper Snapple Group.

As these examples illustrate, the reasons for divestitures vary widely. Sometimes the market feels more comfortable when firms "stick to their knitting," as the Cadbury Schweppes divestiture illustrates. Sometimes companies need cash either to finance expansion in their primary business lines or to reduce a large debt burden, and divestitures can be used to raise this cash; for example, AMD spun off its manufacturing operations in 2009. The divestitures also show that running a business is

---

31. For more on LBOs, see Martin S. Fridson, "What Went Wrong with the Highly Leveraged Deals? (Or, All Variety of Agency Costs)," *Journal of Applied Corporate Finance,* Fall 1991, pp. 47–57. Also see Jay R. Allen, "LBOs—The Evolution of Financial Strategies and Structures," *Journal of Applied Corporate Finance,* Winter 1996, pp. 18–29; George P. Baker, "Beatrice: A Study in the Creation and Destruction of Value," *Journal of Finance,* July 1992, pp. 1081–1119; and George P. Baker and Karen H. Wruck, "Lessons from a Middle Market LBO: The Case of O. M. Scott," *Journal of Applied Corporate Finance,* Spring 1991, pp. 46–58.

a dynamic process—conditions change, corporate strategies change in response, and consequently firms alter their asset portfolios by acquisitions and/or divestitures. Some divestitures are designed to unload losing assets that would otherwise drag the company down, such as Time Warner's planned spin-off of AOL.

In general, the empirical evidence shows that the market reacts favorably to divestitures, with the divesting company typically having a small increase in stock price on the day of the announcement. The announcement-day returns are largest for companies that "undo" previous conglomerate mergers by divesting businesses in unrelated areas.[32] Studies also show that divestitures generally lead to superior operating performance for both the parent and the divested company.[33]

Self Test

What are some types of divestitures?

What are some motives for divestitures?

26.20 Holding Companies

Holding companies date from 1889, when New Jersey became the first state to pass a law permitting corporations to be formed for the sole purpose of owning the stocks of other companies. Many of the advantages and disadvantages of holding companies are identical to those of any large-scale organization. Whether a company is organized on a divisional basis or with subsidiaries kept as separate companies does not affect the basic reasons for conducting a large-scale, multiproduct, multiplant operation.

26.20a Advantages and Disadvantages of Holding Companies

There are two principal advantages of a holding company.

1. *Control with fractional ownership.* Through a holding company operation, a firm may buy 5%, 10%, or 50% of the stock of another corporation. Such fractional ownership may be sufficient to give the holding company effective working control over the operations of the company in which it has acquired stock ownership. Working control is often considered to entail more than 25% of the common stock, but it can be as low as 10% if the stock is widely distributed. One financier says that the attitude of management is more important than the number of shares owned: "If management thinks you can control the company, then you do." In addition, control on a very slim margin can be held through relationships with large stockholders outside the holding company group.

2. *Isolation of risks.* Because the various **operating companies** in a holding company system are separate legal entities, the obligations of any one unit are

---

32. For details, see Jeffrey W. Allen, Scott L. Lummer, John J. McConnell, and Debra K. Reed, "Can Takeover Losses Explain Spin-off Gains?" *Journal of Financial and Quantitative Analysis,* December 1995, pp. 465–485.

33. See Shane A. Johnson, Daniel P. Klein, and Verne L. Thibodeaux, "The Effects of Spin-offs on Corporate Investment and Performance," *Journal of Financial Research,* Summer 1996, pp. 293–307. Also see Steven Kaplan and Michael S. Weisbach, "The Success of Acquisitions: Evidence from Divestitures," *Journal of Finance,* March 1992, pp. 107–138.

separate from those of the other units. Therefore, catastrophic losses incurred by one unit of the holding company system may not be translatable into claims on the assets of the other units. However, we should note that while this is a customary generalization, it is not always valid. First, the **parent company** may feel obligated to make good on the subsidiary's debts, even though it is not legally bound to do so, in order to keep its good name and to retain customers. Second, a parent company may feel obligated to supply capital to an affiliate in order to protect its initial investment. And third, when lending to one of the units of a holding company system, an astute loan officer may require a guarantee by the parent holding company. To some degree, then, the assets in the various elements of a holding company are not really separate.

The main disadvantage of a holding company involves *partial multiple taxation.* Provided the holding company owns at least 80% of a subsidiary's voting stock, the IRS permits the filing of consolidated returns, in which case dividends received by the parent are not taxed. However, if less than 80% of the stock is owned, then tax returns cannot be consolidated. Firms that own more than 20% but less than 80% of another corporation can deduct 80% of the dividends received, whereas firms that own less than 20% may deduct only 70% of the dividends received. This partial double taxation somewhat offsets the benefits of holding company control with limited ownership, but whether the tax penalty is sufficient to offset other possible advantages varies from case to case.

26.20b Holding Companies as a Leveraging Device

The holding company vehicle has been used to obtain huge degrees of financial leverage. In the 1920s, several tiers of holding companies were established in the electric utility, railroad, and other industries. In those days, an operating company at the bottom of the pyramid might have $100 million of assets, financed by $50 million of debt and $50 million of equity. Then, a first-tier holding company might own the stock of the operating firm as its only asset and be financed with $25 million of debt and $25 million of equity. A second-tier holding company, which owned the stock of the first-tier company, might be financed with $12.5 million of debt and $12.5 million of equity. Such systems were extended to five or six levels. With six holding companies, $100 million of operating assets could be controlled at the top by only $0.78 million of equity, and the operating assets would have to provide enough cash income to support $99.22 million of debt. *Such a holding company system is highly leveraged—its consolidated debt ratio is 99.22%, even though each of the individual components shows only a 50% debt/assets ratio.* Because of this consolidated leverage, even a small decline in profits at the operating company level could bring the whole system down like a house of cards. This situation existed in the electric utility industry in the 1920s, and the Depression of the 1930s wreaked such havoc with the holding companies that federal legislation was enacted that constrained holding companies in that industry.

Self Test	What is a holding company?
	What are some of the advantages of holding companies? Identify a disadvantage.

Summary

- A **merger** occurs when two firms combine to form a single company. The primary motives for mergers are (1) synergy, (2) tax considerations, (3) purchase of assets below their replacement costs, (4) diversification, (5) gaining control over a larger enterprise, and (6) breakup value.
- Mergers can provide economic benefits through **economies of scale** and through putting assets in the hands of **more efficient managers.** However, mergers also have the potential for reducing competition, and for this reason they are carefully regulated by government agencies.
- In most mergers, one company (the **acquiring company**) initiates action to take over another (the **target company**).
- A **horizontal merger** occurs when two firms in the same line of business combine.
- A **vertical merger** combines a firm with one of its customers or suppliers.
- A **congeneric merger** involves firms in related industries but where no customer–supplier relationship exists.
- A **conglomerate merger** occurs when firms in totally different industries combine.
- In a **friendly merger,** the managements of both firms approve the merger, whereas in a **hostile merger,** the target firm's management opposes it.
- An **operating merger** is one in which the operations of the two firms are combined. A **financial merger** is one in which the firms continue to operate separately; hence no operating economies are expected.
- In a typical **merger analysis,** the key issues to be resolved are (1) the price to be paid for the target firm and (2) the employment/control situation. If the merger is a consolidation of two relatively equal firms, at issue is the percentage of ownership that each merger partner's shareholders will receive.
- Four methods are commonly used to determine the **value of the target firm:** (1) **market multiple analysis,** (2) the **corporate valuation model,** (3) the **free cash flow to equity (FCFE) model,** and (4) the **adjusted present value (APV) model.** The three cash flow models give the same value if implemented correctly, but the APV model is the easiest to implement correctly and should be used when the capital structure is changing.
- For accounting purposes, mergers are handled as a **purchase.**
- A **joint venture** is a **corporate alliance** in which two or more companies combine some of their resources to achieve a specific, limited objective.
- A **leveraged buyout (LBO)** is a transaction in which a firm's publicly owned stock is acquired in a mostly debt-financed tender offer, resulting in a privately owned, highly leveraged firm. Often, the firm's own management initiates the LBO.
- A **divestiture** is the sale of some of a company's operating assets. A divestiture may involve (1) selling an operating unit to another firm, (2) **spinning off** a unit as a separate company, (3) **carving out** a unit by selling a minority interest, or (4) the outright **liquidation** of a unit's assets.

- The **reasons for divestiture** include (1) to settle antitrust suits, (2) to improve the transparency of the resulting companies so that investors can more easily evaluate them, (3) to enable management to concentrate on a particular type of activity, and (4) to raise the capital needed to strengthen the corporation's core business.
- A **holding company** is a corporation that owns sufficient stock in another firm to control it. The holding company is also known as the **parent company,** and the companies that it controls are called **subsidiaries,** or **operating companies.**
- Holding company operations are advantageous because (1) control can often be obtained for a smaller cash outlay, (2) risks may be segregated, and (3) regulated companies can operate separate subsidiaries for their regulated and unregulated businesses.
- A major disadvantage to holding company operations is the possibility of multiple taxation.

Questions

26-1 Define each of the following terms:
   a. Synergy; merger
   b. Horizontal merger; vertical merger; congeneric merger; conglomerate merger
   c. Friendly merger; hostile merger; defensive merger; tender offer; target company; breakup value; acquiring company
   d. Operating merger; financial merger
   e. Adjusted present value (APV) model
   f. Free cash flow to equity
   g. Purchase accounting
   h. White knight; proxy fight
   i. Joint venture; corporate alliance
   j. Divestiture; spin-off; leveraged buyout (LBO)
   k. Holding company; operating company; parent company
   l. Arbitrage; risk arbitrage

26-2 Four economic classifications of mergers are (1) horizontal, (2) vertical, (3) conglomerate, and (4) congeneric. Explain the significance of these terms in merger analysis with regard to (a) the likelihood of governmental intervention and (b) possibilities for operating synergy.

26-3 Firm A wants to acquire Firm B. Firm B's management agrees that the merger is a good idea. Might a tender offer be used?

26-4 Distinguish between operating mergers and financial mergers.

26-5 Distinguish between the APV, FCFE, and corporate valuation models.

Problems   Answers Appear in Appendix B

The following information is required to work Problems 26-1 through 26-4.

Hastings Corporation is interested in acquiring Vandell Corporation. Vandell has 1 million shares outstanding and a target capital structure consisting of 30% debt. Vandell's debt interest rate is 8%. Assume that the risk-free rate of interest is 5% and the market risk premium is 6%. Both Vandell and Hastings face a 40% tax rate.

Easy Problem 1

26-1 **Valuation** Vandell's free cash flow (FCF_0) is $2 million per year and is expected to grow at a constant rate of 5% a year; its beta is 1.4. What is the value of Vandell's operations? If Vandell has $10.82 million in debt, what is the current value of Vandell's stock? (*Hint:* Use the corporate valuation model from Chapter 11.)

Intermediate Problems 2–3

26-2 **Merger Valuation** Hastings estimates that if it acquires Vandell, interest payments will be $1.5 million per year for 3 years, after which the current target capital structure of 30% debt will be maintained. Interest in the fourth year will be $1.472 million, after which interest and the tax shield will grow at 5%. Synergies will cause the free cash flows to be $2.5 million, $2.9 million, $3.4 million, and $3.57 million in Years 1 through 4, respectively, after which the free cash flows will grow at a 5% rate. What is the unlevered value of Vandell, and what is the value of its tax shields? What is the per share value of Vandell to Hastings Corporation? Assume that Vandell now has $10.82 million in debt.

26-3 **Merger Bid** On the basis of your answers to Problems 26-1 and 26-2, indicate the range of possible prices that Hastings could bid for each share of Vandell common stock in an acquisition.

Challenging Problems 4–6

26-4 **Merger Valuation with Change in Capital Structure** Assuming the same information as for Problem 26-2, suppose Hastings will increase Vandell's level of debt at the end of Year 3 to $30.6 million so that the target capital structure is now 45% debt. Assume that with this higher level of debt the interest rate would be 8.5%, and assume that interest payments in Year 4 are based on the new debt level from the end of Year 3 and a new interest rate. Again, free cash flows and tax shields are projected to grow at 5% after Year 4. What are the values of the unlevered firm and the tax shield, and what is the maximum price that Hastings would bid for Vandell now?

26-5 **Merger Analysis** Marston Marble Corporation is considering a merger with the Conroy Concrete Company. Conroy is a publicly traded company, and its beta is 1.30. Conroy has been barely profitable, so it has paid an average of only 20% in taxes during the last several years. In addition, it uses little debt; its target ratio is just 25%, with the cost of debt 9%.

If the acquisition were made, Marston would operate Conroy as a separate, wholly owned subsidiary. Marston would pay taxes on a consolidated basis, and the tax rate would therefore increase to 35%. Marston also would increase the debt capitalization in the Conroy subsidiary to $w_d = 40\%$, for a total of $22.27 million in debt by the end of Year 4, and pay 9.5% on the debt. Marston's acquisition department estimates that Conroy, if acquired, would generate the following free cash flows and interest expenses (in millions of dollars) in Years 1–5:

Year	Free Cash Flows	Interest Expense
1	$1.30	$1.2
2	1.50	1.7
3	1.75	2.8
4	2.00	2.1
5	2.12	?

In Year 5, Conroy's interest expense would be based on its beginning-of-year (that is, the end-of-Year-4) debt, and in subsequent years both interest expense and free cash flows are projected to grow at a rate of 6%.

These cash flows include all acquisition effects. Marston's cost of equity is 10.5%, its beta is 1.0, and its cost of debt is 9.5%. The risk-free rate is 6%, and the market risk premium is 4.5%.

a. What is the value of Conroy's unlevered operations, and what is the value of Conroy's tax shields under the proposed merger and financing arrangements?

b. What is the dollar value of Conroy's operations? If Conroy has $10 million in debt outstanding, how much would Marston be willing to pay for Conroy?

26-6 **Merger Valuation with Change in Capital Structure** VolWorld Communications Inc., a large telecommunications company, is evaluating the possible acquisition of Bulldog Cable Company (BCC), a regional cable company. VolWorld's analysts project the following post-merger data for BCC (in thousands of dollars, with a year end of December 31):

	2012	2013	2014	2015	2016	2017
Net sales		$450	$518	$ 555	$ 600	$ 643
Selling and administrative expense		45	53	60	68	73
Interest		40	45	47	52	54
Total net operating capital	$800	850	930	1,005	1,075	1,150
Tax rate after merger: 35%						
Cost of goods sold as a percent of sales: 65%						
BCC's pre-merger beta: 1.40						
Risk-free rate: 6%						
Market risk premium: 4%						
Terminal growth rate of free cash flows: 7%						

If the acquisition is made, it will occur on January 1, 2013. All cash flows shown in the income statements are assumed to occur at the end of the year. BCC currently has a capital structure of 40% debt, which costs 10%, but over the next 4 years VolWorld would increase that to 50%, and the target capital structure would be reached by the start of 2017. BCC, if independent, would pay taxes at 20%, but its income would be taxed at 35% if it were consolidated. BCC's current market-determined beta is 1.4. The cost of goods sold is expected to be 65% of sales.

a. What is the unlevered cost of equity for BCC?

b. What are the free cash flows and interest tax shields for the first 5 years?

c. What is BCC's horizon value of interest tax shields and unlevered horizon value?

d. What is the value of BCC's equity to VolWorld's shareholders if BCC has $300,000 in debt outstanding now?

Spreadsheet Problem

26-7 **Build a Model: Merger Analysis** Start with the partial model in the file *Ch26 P07 Build a Model.xls* on the textbook's Web site. Wansley Portal Inc., a large Internet service provider, is evaluating the possible acquisition of Alabama Connections Company (ACC), a regional Internet service provider. Wansley's analysts project the following post-merger data for ACC (in thousands of dollars):

	2013	2014	2015	2016	2017
Net sales	$500	$600	$700	$760	$806
Selling and administrative expense	60	70	80	90	96
Interest	30	40	45	60	74

If the acquisition is made, it will occur on January 1, 2013. All cash flows shown in the income statements are assumed to occur at the end of the year. ACC currently has a capital structure of 30% debt, which costs 9%, but Wansley would increase that over time to 40%, costing 10%, if the acquisition were made. ACC, if independent, would pay taxes at 30%, but its income would be taxed at 35% if it were consolidated. ACC's current market-determined beta is 1.4. The cost of goods sold, which includes depreciation, is expected to be 65% of sales, but it could vary somewhat. Required gross investment in operating capital is approximately equal to the depreciation charged, so there will be no investment in net operating capital. The risk-free rate is 7%, and the market risk premium is 6.5%. Wansley currently has $400,000 in debt outstanding.

a. What is the unlevered cost of equity?

b. What are the horizon value of the tax shields and the horizon value of the unlevered operations? What are the value of ACC's operations and the value of ACC's equity to Wansley's shareholders?

MINI CASE

Hager's Home Repair Company, a regional hardware chain that specializes in "do it yourself" materials and equipment rentals, is cash rich because of several consecutive good years. One of the alternative uses for the excess funds is an acquisition. Doug Zona, Hager's trea-

surer and your boss, has been asked to place a value on a potential target, Lyons Lighting (LL), a chain that operates in several adjacent states, and he has enlisted your help.

The table below indicates Zona's estimates of LL's earnings potential if it came under Hager's management (in millions of dollars). The interest expense listed here includes the interest (1) on LL's existing debt, which is $55 million at a rate of 9%, and (2) on new debt expected to be issued over time to help finance expansion within the new "L division," the code name given to the target firm. If acquired, LL will face a 40% tax rate.

Security analysts estimate LL's beta to be 1.3. The acquisition would not change Lyons's capital structure, which is 20% debt. Zona realizes that Lyons Lighting's business plan also requires certain levels of operating capital and that the annual investment could be significant. The required levels of total net operating capital are listed in the table.

Zona estimates the risk-free rate to be 7% and the market risk premium to be 4%. He also estimates that free cash flows after 2017 will grow at a constant rate of 6%. Following are projections for sales and other items.

Hager's management is new to the merger game, so Zona has been asked to answer some basic questions about mergers as well as to perform the merger analysis. To structure the task, Zona has developed the following questions, which you must answer and then defend to Hager's board.

a. Several reasons have been proposed to justify mergers. Among the more prominent are (1) tax considerations, (2) risk reduction, (3) control, (4) purchase of assets at below replacement cost, (5) synergy, and (6) globalization. In general, which of the reasons are economically justifiable? Which are not? Which fit the situation at hand? Explain.

	2012	2013	2014	2015	2016	2017
Net sales		$ 60.00	$ 90.00	$112.50	$127.50	$139.70
Cost of goods sold (60%)		36.00	54.00	67.50	76.50	83.80
Selling/administrative expense		4.50	6.00	7.50	9.00	11.00
Interest expense		5.00	6.50	6.50	7.00	8.16
Total net operating capital	$150.00	150.00	157.50	163.50	168.00	173.00

b. Briefly describe the differences between a hostile merger and a friendly merger.

c. What are the steps in valuing a merger?

d. Use the data developed in the table to construct the L division's free cash flows for 2013 through 2017. Why are we identifying interest expense separately when it is not normally included in calculating free cash flows or in a capital budgeting cash flow analysis? Why is investment in net operating capital included when calculating the free cash flow?

e. Conceptually, what is the appropriate discount rate to apply to the cash flows developed in part c? What is your actual estimate of this discount rate?

f. What is the estimated horizon, or continuing, value of the acquisition; that is, what is the estimated value of the L division's cash flows beyond 2017? What is LL's value to Hager's shareholders? Suppose another firm were evaluating LL as an acquisition candidate. Would it obtain the same value? Explain.

g. Assume that LL has 20 million shares outstanding. These shares are traded relatively infrequently, but the last trade (made several weeks ago) was at a price of $11 per share. Should Hager's make an offer for Lyons Lighting? If so, how much should it offer per share?

h. How would the analysis be different if Hager's intended to recapitalize LL with 40% debt costing 10% at the end of 4 years? This amounts to $221.6 million in debt as of the end of 2016.

i. There has been considerable research undertaken to determine whether mergers really create value and, if so, how this value is shared between the parties involved. What are the results of this research?

j. What method is used to account for mergers?

k. What merger-related activities are undertaken by investment bankers?

l. What is a leveraged buyout (LBO)? What are some of the advantages and disadvantages of going private?

m. What are the major types of divestitures? What motivates firms to divest assets?

n. What are holding companies? What are their advantages and disadvantages?

Selected Additional Cases

The following cases from TextChoice, *Cengage Learning's online case library, cover many of the concepts discussed in this chapter and are available at* **www.textchoice2.com/casenet.**

Klein-Brigham Series:
Case 40, "Nina's Fashions, Inc."; Case 53, "Nero's Pasta, Inc."; and Case 70, "Computer Concepts/CompuTech."

Chapter 27

Multinational Financial Management[*]

WEB

The textbook's Web site contains an *Excel* file that will guide you through the chapter's calculations. The file for this chapter is ***Ch27 Tool Kit.xls***, and we encourage you to open the file and follow along as you read the chapter.

Managers of multinational companies must deal with a wide range of issues that are not present when a company operates in a single country. In this chapter, we highlight the key differences between multinational and domestic corporations, and we discuss the effects these differences have on the financial management of multinational businesses.

---

[*] Earlier editions of this chapter benefited from the help of Professor Roy Crum of the University of Florida and Subu Venkataraman of Morgan Stanley.

Beginning of Chapter Questions

As you read this chapter, consider how you would answer the following questions. You *should not* necessarily be able to answer the questions before you read the chapter. Rather, you should use them to get a sense of the issues covered in the chapter. After reading the chapter, you should be able to give at least partial answers to the questions, and you should be able to give better answers after the chapter has been discussed in class. Note, too, that it is often useful, when answering conceptual questions, to use hypothetical data to illustrate your answer. We illustrate the answers with an *Excel* model that is available on the textbook's Web site. Accessing the model and working through it is a useful exercise, and it provides insights that are useful when answering the questions.

1. How is **multinational financial management** different from financial management as practiced by a firm that has no direct contacts with foreign firms or customers? What special problems and challenges do multinational firms face? What factors cause companies to "go multinational"?
2. What is an **exchange rate?** What is the difference between **direct** and **indirect rates?** What is a **cross rate?**

3. What is the difference between a **spot rate** and a **forward rate?** How can forward rates be used for **hedging** purposes? Why would hedging occur?
4. What is **interest rate parity?** How might the treasurer of a multinational firm use the interest rate parity concept (a) when deciding how to invest the firm's surplus cash and (b) when deciding where to borrow funds on a short-term basis?
5. What is **purchasing power parity?** How might a firm use this concept in its operations?
6. Suppose IBM signed a contract to buy a supply of computer chips from a German firm. The price is 10 million euros, and the chips will be delivered immediately, but IBM can delay payment for 6 months if it wants to. What risk would IBM be exposed to if it delays payment? Can it hedge this risk? Should it pay now or delay payment?
7. Much has been made about the sweeping changes that are occurring in Europe as a result of the **euro.** Will the euro help European firms become more efficient? Will it change the way multinational corporations manage cash? Manage exchange risk? Borrow funds in local markets? What effects will the euro have on non-European firms?

27.1 Multinational, or Global, Corporations

The terms **multinational corporations, transnational corporations,** and **global corporations** are used to describe firms that operate in an integrated fashion in a number of countries. Rather than merely buying resources from and selling goods to foreign nations, multinational firms often make direct investments in fully integrated operations, from extraction of raw materials, through the manufacturing process, and to distribution to consumers throughout the world. Today, multinational corporate networks control a large and growing share of the world's technological, marketing, and productive resources.

Companies "go global" for many reasons, including the following.

1. *To broaden their markets.* After a company has saturated its home market, growth opportunities are often better in foreign markets. Thus, such homegrown firms as Coca-Cola and McDonald's are aggressively expanding into overseas markets, and foreign firms such as Sony and Toshiba now dominate the U.S. consumer electronics market.
2. *To seek raw materials.* Many U.S. oil companies, such as ExxonMobil, have major subsidiaries around the world to ensure access to the basic resources needed to sustain the companies' primary business lines.

CORPORATE VALUATION IN A GLOBAL CONTEXT

The intrinsic value of a firm is determined by the size, timing, and risk of its expected future free cash flows (FCF). This is true for foreign as well as domestic operations, but the FCF of a foreign operation is affected by exchange rates, cultural differences, and the host country's regulatory environment. In addition, global financial markets and political risk can affect the cost of capital.

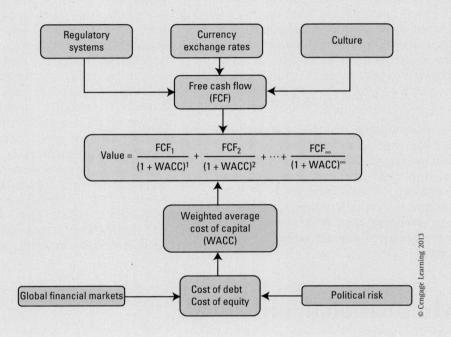

© Cengage Learning 2013

3. *To seek new technology.* No single nation holds a commanding advantage in all technologies, so companies scour the globe for leading scientific and design ideas. For example, Xerox has introduced more than 80 different office copiers in the United States that were engineered and built by its Japanese joint venture, Fuji Xerox.

4. *To seek production efficiency.* Companies in high-cost countries are shifting production to low-cost regions. For example, GE has production and assembly plants in Mexico, South Korea, and Singapore; Japanese manufacturers are shifting some of their production to lower-cost countries in the Pacific Rim.

5. *To avoid political and regulatory hurdles.* For example, when Germany's BASF launched biotechnology research at home, it confronted legal and political challenges from the environmentally conscious Green movement. In response, BASF shifted its cancer and immune system research to two laboratories in the Boston suburbs. This location is attractive not only because of its large number of engineers and scientists but also because the Boston area has resolved many controversies involving safety, animal rights, and the environment.

6. *To diversify.* By establishing worldwide production facilities and markets, firms can cushion the impact of adverse economic trends in any single country. In

www

Interesting reports about the effect of trade on the U.S. economy can be found on the United States Trade Representative's home page at **www.ustr.gov**.

general, geographic diversification helps because the economic ups and downs of different countries are not perfectly correlated.

What is a multinational corporation?

Why do companies "go global"?

27.2 Multinational versus Domestic Financial Management

In theory, the concepts and procedures discussed in earlier chapters are valid for both domestic and multinational operations. However, six major factors distinguish financial management in firms operating entirely within a single country from that of firms operating globally.

1. *Different currency denominations.* Cash flows in various parts of a multinational corporate system will be denominated in different currencies. Hence, the effects of exchange rates must be addressed in all financial analyses.

2. *Economic and legal ramifications.* Each country has its own unique economic and legal systems, and these differences can cause significant problems when a corporation tries to coordinate and control its worldwide operations. For example, differences in tax laws among countries can cause a given economic transaction to have strikingly different after-tax consequences, depending on where the transaction occurs. Similarly, differences in legal systems of host nations, such as the Common Law of Great Britain versus the French Civil Law, complicate matters ranging from the simple recording of business transactions to the role played by the judiciary in resolving conflicts. Such differences can restrict multinational corporations' flexibility in deploying resources and can even make procedures that are required in one part of the company illegal in another part. These differences also make it difficult for executives trained in one country to move easily to another.

3. *Language differences.* The ability to communicate is critical in all business transactions, and here U.S. citizens are often at a disadvantage because they are generally fluent only in English, whereas European and Japanese business-people are usually fluent in several languages, including English.

4. *Cultural differences.* Even within geographic regions that are considered relatively homogeneous, different countries have unique cultural heritages that shape values and influence the conduct of business. Multinational corporations find that matters such as defining the appropriate goals of the firm, attitudes toward risk, dealings with employees, and the ability to curtail unprofitable operations vary dramatically from one country to the next.

5. *Role of governments.* In a foreign country, the terms under which companies compete, the actions that must be taken or avoided, and the terms of trade on various transactions often are determined not in the marketplace but by direct negotiation between host governments and multinational corporations.

6. *Political risk.* A nation might place constraints on the transfer of corporate resources or even expropriate assets within its boundaries. This is political risk, and it varies from country to country. Another aspect of political risk is terrorism against U.S. firms or executives. For example, U.S. and Japanese executives are at risk of being kidnapped in Mexico and several South American countries.

These factors complicate financial management, and they increase the risks faced by multinational firms. However, the prospects for high returns and better diversification make it worthwhile for firms to accept these risks and learn how to manage them.

Identify and briefly discuss six major factors that complicate financial management in multinational firms.

27.3 Exchange Rates

www

The Bloomberg World Currency Values site provides up-to-the-minute foreign currency values versus the U.S. dollar. The site can be accessed at **www.bloomberg.com/ markets/currencies**.

An **exchange rate** specifies the number of units of a given currency that can be purchased with one unit of another currency. Exchange rates appear daily in the financial sections of newspapers, such as *The Wall Street Journal,* and on financial Web sites, such as www.bloomberg.com. The values shown in Column 1 of Table 27-1 are the number of U.S. dollars required to purchase one unit of a foreign currency; this is called a **direct quotation**. Direct quotations have a dollar sign in their quotation and state the number of dollars per foreign currency unit, such as dollars per euro. Thus, the direct U.S. dollar quotation for the euro is $1.3903, because one euro could be bought for 1.3903 dollars.

The exchange rates given in Column 2 represent the number of units of a foreign currency that can be purchased for one U.S. dollar; these are called **indirect quotations**. Indirect quotations often begin with the foreign currency's equivalent to the dollar sign and express the foreign currency per dollar, such as euros per dollar. Thus, the indirect quotation for the euro is €0.7193. (The "€" stands for *euro,* and it is analogous to the symbol "$.")

Normal practice in currency trading centers is to use the indirect quotations (Column 2) for all currencies other than British pounds and euros, for which the direct quotations are given. Thus, we speak of the pound as "selling at 1.6085 dollars, or at $1.6085," and the euro as "selling at $1.3903." For all other currencies, the normal convention is to use indirect quotations. For example, for the Japanese yen, we would quote the dollar as "being at ¥81.8930," where the "¥" stands for *yen.*

TABLE 27-1	**Selected Exchange Rates**	
	Direct Quotation: U.S. Dollars Required to Buy One Unit of Foreign Currency **(1)**	**Indirect Quotation: Number of Units of Foreign Currency per U.S. Dollar** **(2)**
Canadian dollar	1.0298	0.9711
Japanese yen	0.0122	81.8930
Mexican peso	0.0839	11.9180
Swiss franc	1.0761	0.9293
U.K. (British) pound	1.6085	0.6217
Euro	1.3903	0.7193

Note: The financial press usually quotes British pounds and euros as direct quotations, so Column 2 equals 1.0 divided by Column 1 for these currencies. The financial press usually quotes all other currencies as indirect quotations, so Column 1 equals 1.0 divided by Column 2 for these currencies.
Source: The Wall Street Journal, **online.wsj.com**; quotes for March 11, 2011.

This convention eliminates confusion when comparing quotations from one trading center—say, New York—with those from another—say, London or Zurich.

We can use the data in Table 27-1 to show how to work with exchange rates. Suppose a tourist flies from New York to London, then to Paris, and then on to Geneva. She then flies to Montreal, and finally back to New York. Her tour includes lodging, food, and transportation, but she must pay for any other expenses. When she arrives at London's Heathrow Airport, she goes to the bank to check the foreign exchange listings. The rate she observes for U.S. dollars is $1.6085, which means that £1 will cost $1.6085. Assume that she exchanges $3,000. How many pounds will she get?

WEB

See **Ch27 Tool Kit.xls** on the textbook's Web site for all calculations.

$$\text{Pounds} = \frac{\text{Dollars}}{\text{Dollars/pound}}$$

$$= \frac{\$3,000}{\$1.6085 \text{ per pound}} = £1,865.09$$

She then enjoys a week's vacation in London, ending with £1,000.

After taking a train under the Channel to France, she realizes that she needs to exchange her 1,000 remaining pounds for euros. However, what she sees on the board is the direct quotation for dollars per pound and the direct quotation for dollars per euro. The exchange rate between any two currencies other than dollars is called a **cross rate**. Cross rates are actually calculated on the basis of various currencies relative to the U.S. dollar. For example, the cross rate between British pounds and euros is computed as follows:

$$\text{Cross rate of euros per pound} = \frac{\text{Dollars/Pound}}{\text{Dollars/Euro}} = \frac{\text{Euros}}{\text{Pound}}$$

$$= \frac{\$1.6085 \text{ per pound}}{\$1.3903 \text{ per euro}} = 1.1569 \text{ euros per pound}$$

She would receive 1.1569 euros for every British pound, so she would receive 1,156.90 euros = (1.1569 euros/pound)(1,000 pounds).

She has 800 euros remaining when she finishes touring in France and arrives in Geneva. She again needs to determine a cross rate, this time between euros and Swiss francs. The quotes she sees, as shown in Table 27-1, are a direct quote for euros ($1.3903 per euro) and an indirect quote for Swiss francs (SFr 0.9293 per dollar). To find the cross rate for Swiss francs per euro, she makes the following calculation:

www

For a nice currency calculator to determine the exchange rate between any two currencies, see **finance.yahoo.com/ currency**.

$$\text{Cross rate of Swiss francs per euro} = \left(\frac{\text{Swiss francs}}{\text{Dollar}}\right)\left(\frac{\text{Dollars}}{\text{Euro}}\right)$$

$$= (\text{SFr } 0.9293 \text{ per dollar})(\$1.3903 \text{ per euro})$$

$$= 1.2920 \text{ Swiss francs per euro}$$

Therefore, for every euro she would receive 1.2920 Swiss francs, so she would receive 1,033.60 Swiss francs = (1.2920 Swiss francs per euro)(800 euros).

She has 500 Swiss francs remaining when she leaves Geneva and arrives in Montreal. She again needs to determine a cross rate, this time between Swiss francs and Canadian dollars. The quotes she sees, as shown in Table 27-1, are an indirect quote for Swiss francs (SFr 0.9293 per dollar) and an indirect quote for Canadian dollars (0.9711 Canadian dollars per U.S. dollar). To find the cross rate for Canadian dollars per Swiss franc, she makes the following calculation:

$$\begin{array}{l} \text{Cross rate of Canadian dollars} \\ \text{per Swiss franc} \end{array} = \dfrac{\left(\dfrac{\text{Canadian dollars}}{\text{U.S. dollar}}\right)}{\left(\dfrac{\text{Swiss francs}}{\text{U.S. dollar}}\right)}$$

$$= \dfrac{0.9711 \text{ Canadian dollars per U.S. dollar}}{\text{SFr } 0.9293 \text{ per U.S. dollar}}$$

$$= 1.045 \text{ Canadian dollars per Swiss franc}$$

Therefore, she would receive 522.5 Canadian dollars = (1.045 Canadian dollars per Swiss franc)(500 Swiss francs).

After leaving Montreal and arriving at New York, she has 100 Canadian dollars remaining. She sees the indirect quote for Canadian dollars and converts the 100 Canadian dollars to U.S. dollars as follows:

$$100 \text{ Canadian dollars} = \dfrac{100 \text{ Canadian dollars}}{0.9711 \text{ Canadian dollars per U.S. dollar}} = \$102.98$$

In this example, we made three assumptions. First, we assumed that our traveler had to calculate all of the cross rates. For retail transactions, it is customary to display the cross rates directly instead of a series of dollar rates. Second, we assumed that exchange rates remain constant over time. Actually, exchange rates vary every day, often dramatically. We will have more to say about exchange rate fluctuations in the next section. Finally, we assumed that there were no transaction costs involved in exchanging currencies. In reality, small retail exchange transactions such as those in our example usually involve fixed and/or sliding-scale fees that can easily consume 5% or more of the transaction amount. However, credit card purchases minimize these fees.

Major business publications, such as *The Wall Street Journal,* and Web sites, such as **www.bloomberg.com**, regularly report cross rates among key currencies. A set of cross rates is given in Table 27-2. When examining the table, note the following points.

1. Column 1 gives indirect quotes for dollars—that is, units of a foreign currency that can be bought with one U.S. dollar. Examples: $1 will buy 0.7193 euro or 0.9293 Swiss francs. This is consistent with Table 27-1, Column 2.
2. Other columns show number of units of other currencies that can be bought with one pound, one Swiss franc, etc. For example, the euro column shows that 1 euro will buy 1.3501 Canadian dollars, 113.8558 Japanese yen, or 1.3903 U.S. dollars.
3. The rows show direct quotes—that is, the number of units of the currency of the country listed in the left column required to buy one unit of the currency listed in the top row. The bottom row is particularly important for U.S. companies, as it shows the direct quotes for the U.S. dollar. This row is consistent with Column 1 of Table 27-1.
4. Observe that the values on the bottom row of Table 27-2 are reciprocals of the corresponding values in the first column. For example, the U.K. row in the first column shows 0.6217 pound per dollar, and the pound column in the bottom row shows $1/0.6217 = 1.6085$ dollars per pound.
5. By reading down the euro column, you can see that 1 euro is worth 1.2920 Swiss francs. This is the same cross rate that we calculated for the U.S. tourist in our example.

TABLE 27-2	Key Currency Cross Rates						
	Dollar	**Euro**	**Pound**	**SFranc**	**Peso**	**Yen**	**CdnDlr**
Canada	0.9711	1.3501	1.5620	1.0450	0.0815	0.0119	....
Japan	81.8930	113.8558	131.7249	88.1233	6.8714	....	84.3301
Mexico	11.9180	16.5696	19.1701	12.8247	....	0.1455	12.2727
Switzerland	0.9293	1.2920	1.4948	....	0.0780	0.0113	0.9570
United Kingdom	0.6217	0.8643	....	0.6690	0.0522	0.0076	0.6402
Euro	0.7193	....	1.1569	0.7740	0.0604	0.0088	0.7407
United States	....	1.3903	1.6085	1.0761	0.0839	0.0122	1.0298

© Cengage Learning 2013

Source: Derived from Table 27-1; quotes for March 11, 2011.

The tie-in with the dollar ensures that all currencies are related to one another in a consistent manner—if this consistency did not exist, then currency traders could profit by buying undervalued and selling overvalued currencies. This process, known as *arbitrage,* works to bring about an equilibrium wherein the same relationship described earlier exists. Currency traders are constantly operating in the market, seeking small inconsistencies from which they can profit. The traders' existence enables the rest of us to assume that currency markets are in equilibrium and that, at any moment in time, cross rates are all internally consistent.[1]

Self Test

What is an exchange rate?

Explain the difference between direct and indirect quotations.

What is a cross rate?

Assume that the indirect quote is for 10.0 Mexican pesos per U.S. dollar. What is the direct quote for dollars per peso? **(0.10 dollars/peso)**

Assume that the indirect quote is for 115 Japanese yen per U.S. dollar and that the direct quote is for 1.25 U.S. dollars per euro. What is the yen per euro exchange rate? **(143.75 yen per euro)**

27.4 Exchange Rates and International Trade

Just as the demand for consumer goods such as Tommy Hilfiger clothing and Nike shoes changes over time, so does the demand for currency. One factor affecting currency demand is the balance of trade between two countries. For example, U.S. importers must buy yen to pay for Japanese goods, whereas Japanese importers

---

1. For more discussion of exchange rates, see Jongmoo Jay Choi and Anita Mehra Prasad, "Exchange Risk Sensitivity and Its Determinants: A Firm and Industry Analysis of U.S. Multinationals," *Financial Management,* Autumn 1995, pp. 77–88; Jerry A. Hammer, "Hedging Performance and Hedging Objectives: Tests of New Performance Measures in the Foreign Currency Market," *Journal of Financial Research,* Winter 1990, pp. 307–323; and William C. Hunter and Stephen G. Timme, "A Stochastic Dominance Approach to Evaluating Foreign Exchange Hedging Strategies," *Financial Management,* Autumn 1992, pp. 104–112.

must buy U.S. dollars to pay for U.S. goods. If U.S. imports from Japan were to exceed U.S. exports to Japan, then the United States would have a **trade deficit** with Japan, and there would be a greater demand for yen than for dollars. Capital movements also affect currency demand. For example, suppose interest rates in the United States were higher than those in Japan. To take advantage of high U.S. interest rates, Japanese banks, corporations, and sophisticated individuals would buy dollars with yen and then use those dollars to purchase high-yielding U.S. securities. This would create greater demand for dollars than for yen.

Without any government intervention, the relative prices of yen and dollars would fluctuate in response to changes in supply and demand in much the same way that prices of consumer goods fluctuate. For example, if U.S. consumers were to increase their demand for Japanese electronic products, then the accompanying increase in demand for the yen would cause its value to increase relative to the dollar. In this situation, the strong yen would be due to fundamental economic forces.

However, governments can and do intervene. A country's central bank can artificially prop up its currency by using its reserves of gold or foreign currencies to purchase its own currency in the open market. This creates artificial demand for its own currency, thus causing its value to be artificially high. A central bank can also keep its currency at an artificially low value by selling its own currency in the open markets. This increases the currency's supply, which reduces its price.

Why might an artificially low currency be a problem? After all, a cheap currency makes it less expensive for other nations to purchase the country's goods, which creates jobs in the exporting country. However, an artificially low currency value raises the cost of imports, which increases inflation. In addition, high import prices allow competing domestic manufacturers to raise their prices as well, further boosting inflation. The government intervention that causes the artificially low value also contributes to inflation: When a government creates currency to sell in the open markets, this increases the money supply, and, all else held constant, an increasing money supply leads to still more inflation. Thus, artificially holding down the value of a currency stimulates exports but at the expense of potentially overheating and inflating the economy. Also, other countries—whose economies are being weakened because their manufacturers cannot compete against the artificially low prices—may retaliate and impose tariffs or other restrictions on the country that is holding its currency value down.

For example, China had for many years artificially held down the value of the yuan (also called the rinminbi). This helped make China the world's largest exporter and greatly stimulated its economy. However, by 2004 the Chinese economy was growing at an unsustainably high rate, and inflation was rising rapidly. The United States and other nations began urging the Chinese government to allow the yuan to rise, which would help their economies by slowing Chinese exports and stimulating their own exports to China. On July 21, 2005, the Chinese government suddenly announced that it was changing the exchange rate to allow the yuan's value to rise by 2.1%. The Chinese government has continued to allow the yuan to appreciate slowly, and it now (May 2011) stands at about 0.1540 dollars/yuan versus 0.1217 dollars/yuan in June 2005. Notice that this change has made it somewhat cheaper for Chinese to buy from America (a yuan now buys more dollars) and more expensive for Americans to buy from China.

A currency that is artificially high has the opposite effects: Inflation will be held down and citizens can purchase imported goods at low domestic prices, but exporting industries are hurt, as are domestic industries that compete with the cheap imports. Because there is relatively little external demand for the currency, the government will have to create demand by purchasing its own currency, paying with either gold or foreign currencies held by its central bank. Over time, supporting an inflated currency can deplete the gold and foreign currency reserves, making it impossible to continue propping up the currency.

The following sections describe ways that governments handle changes in currency demands.

Self Test

What is the effect on a country's economy of an artificially low exchange rate? Of an artificially high exchange rate?

27.5 The International Monetary System and Exchange Rate Policies

www

The International Monetary Fund reports a full listing of exchange rate arrangements. See **www .imf.org/external/pubs/ ft/aa/aa04.htm**. The IMF also publishes a more detailed listing in its *Annual Report on Exchange Arrangements and Exchange Restrictions.* For another listing of world currencies, **see fx.sauder .ubc.ca/currency_table .html**.

Every nation has a monetary system and a monetary authority. In the United States, the Federal Reserve is our monetary authority, and its task is to hold down inflation while promoting economic growth and raising our national standard of living. Moreover, if countries are to trade with one another, we must have some sort of system designed to facilitate payments between nations. The international monetary system is the framework within which exchange rates are determined. As we describe in this section, there are several different policies used by various countries to determine exchange rates.[2]

27.5a A Short History Lesson: The Bretton Woods Fixed Exchange Rate System

From the end of World War II until August 1971, most of the industrialized world operated under the Bretton Woods **fixed exchange rate system** administered by the International Monetary Fund (IMF). Under this system, the U.S. dollar was linked to gold (at $35 per ounce), and other currencies were then tied to the dollar. The United States took actions to keep the price of gold at $35 per ounce, and central banks acted to keep exchange rates between other currencies and the dollar within narrow limits. For example, when the demand for pounds was falling, the Bank of England would step in and buy pounds to push up their price, offering gold or foreign currencies in exchange for pounds. Conversely, when the demand for pounds was too high, the Bank of England would sell pounds for dollars or gold. The Federal Reserve in the United States performed the same functions, and central banks of other countries operated similarly. These actions artificially matched supply and demand, keeping exchange rates stable, but they didn't address the underlying imbalance. For example, if the high demand for pounds occurred because British productivity

---

2. For a comprehensive history of the international monetary system and details of how it has evolved, consult one of the many economics books on the subject, which include Robert Carbaugh, *International Economics,* 13th ed. (Mason, OH: South-Western Cengage Learning, 2011); Mordechai Kreinin, *International Economics: A Policy Approach,* 10th ed. (Mason, OH: Thomson/South-Western, 2006); Jeff Madura, *International Financial Management,* 11th ed. (Mason, OH: Thomson/South-Western, 2012); and Joseph P. Daniels and David D. Van Hoose, *International Monetary and Financial Economics,* 3rd ed. (Mason, OH: South-Western, 2005).

was rising and British goods were improving in quality, then the underlying demand for pounds would continue in spite of central bank intervention. In such a situation, the Bank of England would find it necessary to continually sell pounds. If the central bank stopped selling pounds then their value would rise; that is, the pound would strengthen and exceed the agreed-upon limits.

Many countries found it difficult and economically painful to maintain the fixed exchange rates required by Bretton Woods. This system began to crumble in August 1971, and it was abandoned completely by the end of 1973. The following sections describe several modern exchange rate systems.

27.5b Freely, or Independently, Floating Rates

In the early 1970s, the U.S. dollar was cut loose from the gold standard and, in effect, allowed to "float" in response to supply and demand caused by international trade and international investing activities. According to the International Monetary Fund, about 42 countries currently operate under a system of **floating exchange rates**, whereby currency prices are allowed to seek their own levels, with only modest central bank intervention to smooth out extreme exchange rate fluctuations. The IMF reports that about 31 currencies have freely, or independently, floating exchange rates; these currencies include the dollar, euro, pound, and yen.

Currency Appreciation and Depreciation

Suppose the dollar cost of a pound is $1.6085, as shown in Table 27-1. If there were increased demand for pounds caused by a U.S. trade deficit with Great Britain, then the price of pounds might increase to $2.0. In this situation the pound is said to be *appreciating,* because a pound would now buy more dollars. In other words, a pound would now be worth more than it previously was. This is called **currency appreciation**. Conversely, the dollar would be *depreciating* because the dollar now buys fewer pounds (a dollar would previously buy 1/1.6085 = 0.6217 pounds, but afterward it would buy only 1/2.0 = 0.5 pounds). This is called **currency depreciation**. Notice that the more costly pound would make British imports more expensive to U.S. consumers, which would reduce imports—and, consequently, the demand for pounds—until the exchange rate reached equilibrium.

Exchange Rate Risk

Exchange rate fluctuations can have a profound effect on profits and trade. For example, in 2002 the euro exchange rate was about $0.87 (i.e., 0.87 dollars per euro). In 2011, the exchange rate was about $1.39. Consider the impact this has on profits and trade. For example, a hand-blown glass from the Italian island of Murano cost about €50 in 2002. Ignoring shipping costs and taxes, a consumer in the United States could have purchased this glass for €50($0.87/€) = $43.50. Assuming the price in 2011 still was €50, it would cost €50($1.39/€) = $60.47. Thus, the change in exchange rates obviously hurt Italian exports to the United States.

On the other hand, U.S. vintners were able to export wines to Italy much more profitably in 2011 than in 2002. For example, suppose a bottle of Pinot Noir cost a California vineyard $10 to produce in 2002 but could be sold for €17 in Europe. In 2002, the profit would have been €17($0.87/€) – $10 = $14.79 – $10 = $4.79. Assuming no change in production costs, the bottle's profit in 2011 is €17($1.39/€) – $10 = $23.63 – $10 = $13.63. Thus, U.S. exporters to Europe have benefited by the change in exchange rates.

The volatility of exchange rates under a floating system increases the uncertainty of the cash flows for a multinational corporation. Because its cash flows are generated in many parts of the world, they are denominated in many different currencies. When exchange rates change, the dollar-equivalent value of the company's consolidated cash flows also fluctuates. This is known as **exchange rate risk**, and it is a major factor differentiating a global company from a purely domestic one.

27.5c Managed Floating Rates

In a **managed floating rate** system, there is significant government intervention to manage the exchange rate by manipulating the currency's supply and demand. The government rarely reveals its target exchange rate levels if it uses a managed float regime because this would make it too easy for currency speculators to profit. According to the IMF, about 48 countries have a managed floating rate system, including Colombia, India, Singapore, and Burundi.

27.5d Pegged Exchange Rates

In a **pegged exchange rates** system, a country locks, or "pegs," its currency's exchange rate to another currency or basket of currencies. It is common for a country with a pegged exchange rate to allow its currency to vary within specified limits or bands (often set at ±1% of the target rate) before the country intervenes to force the currency back within the limits. Examples in which a currency is pegged to another country's currency include Bhutan's ngultrum, which is pegged to the Indian rupee; the Falkland Islands' pound, which is pegged to the British pound; and Barbados's dollar, which is pegged to the U.S. dollar. An example of a currency being pegged to a basket is China, where the yuan is no longer just pegged to the U.S. dollar but rather to a basket of currencies. The Chinese government will not reveal exactly which currencies make up the basket, but the U.S. dollar, the euro, the yen, and the South Korean won are certainly components.

Currency Devaluation and Revaluation

As indicated previously, countries with pegged exchange rates establish a fixed exchange rate with some other major currency or basket of currencies. When a government reduces its target fixed exchange rate, the result is a currency **devaluation**; increasing the rate results in a currency **revaluation**. For example, from 1991 through early 2002, Argentina had a fixed exchange rate of 1 peso per U.S. dollar. Imports were high, exports were low, and the Argentinean government had to purchase huge amounts of pesos to maintain that artificially high exchange rate. The government borrowed heavily to finance these purchases, and eventually it was unable to continue supporting the peso. (Indeed, the government defaulted on some of its obligations.) As a result, the government had to devalue the peso to 1.4 pesos per dollar in early 2002. Notice that this made the peso weaker: Before the devaluation, 1 peso would buy 1 dollar, but afterward 1 peso would buy only 71 cents (1.4 pesos per dollar = 1/1.4 = 0.71 dollar per peso). The devaluation lowered the prices of Argentine goods on the world market, which helped its exporters, but prices rose for imported goods, including oil. The initial shock to the Argentine economy was severe, as employment fell in those industries that were not exporters. The problem was exacerbated because many Argentine companies and individuals had incurred debt that was denominated in dollars, which instantly cost much more to service. However, the economy gradually improved, aided by increased exports, tourism, and employment rates. Still, the initial pain caused by devaluation helps explain why many countries with fixed exchange rates tend to postpone needed measures until economic pressures build to explosive levels.

Given the expense of maintaining an artificially high exchange rate and the pain of large devaluations, many countries that once had pegged exchange rates now allow their currencies to float. For example, Mexico had a pegged exchange rate prior to 1994, but it depleted its foreign reserves trying to support the peso and was forced to devalue it. Mexico's currency now floats, as does that of Argentina.

Convertible versus Nonconvertible Securities

A pegged exchange rate isn't necessarily a deterrent to direct investment in the country by foreign corporations—as long as the local government's central bank supports the currency and devaluations are unlikely. This was generally the case in the Bretton Woods era, so those currencies were considered to be **convertible** because the nation that issued them allowed them to be traded in the currency markets and was willing to redeem them at market rates. This is true today for all floating-rate currencies, which are also called **hard currencies** because of their convertibility. Some pegged currencies are also at least partially convertible, because their central banks will redeem them at market rates under specified conditions.

However, some countries set the exchange rate but do not allow their currencies to be traded on world markets. For example, the Chinese yuan is allowed to float in a very narrow band against a basket of securities. However, the yuan can be legally used and exchanged only within China. Furthermore, the Chinese government imposes restrictions on both residents and nonresidents from freely converting their holdings of yuans into another currency. Thus, the yuan is a **nonconvertible currency**, also called a **soft currency**. When official exchange rates differ from "market rates" or when there are restrictions on convertibility, a black market will often arise. For example, in early 2011 Venezuela's official exchange rate was about 4.3 bolivars per dollar, but black market prices were estimated to be around 8.3.

A nonconvertible currency creates problems for foreign companies looking to make direct investments. Consider the situation faced by Pizza Hut when it wanted to open a chain of restaurants in the former Soviet Union. The Russian ruble was not convertible, so Pizza Hut could not take the profits from its restaurants out of the Soviet Union in the form of dollars. Because there was no mechanism to exchange the rubles it earned in Russia for dollars, it seemed that investing in the Soviet Union was essentially worthless to a U.S. company. However, Pizza Hut arranged to use the ruble profit from the restaurants to buy Russian vodka, which it then shipped to the United States and sold for dollars. Pizza Hut managed to find a solution, but lack of convertibility significantly inhibits the ability of a country to attract foreign investment.

27.5e No Local Currency

A few countries don't have their own separate legal tender but instead use the currency of another nation. For example, Ecuador has used the U.S. dollar since September 2000. Other countries belong to a monetary union, such as the 17 European Monetary Union nations in 2011 whose currency is the euro, which is allowed to float. In contrast, member nations of the Eastern Caribbean Currency Union, the West African Economic and Monetary Union (WAEMU), and the Central African Economic and Monetary Community (CAEMC) use their respective union's currency, which is itself pegged to some other currency. For example, the Eastern Caribbean dollar is pegged to the U.S. dollar, and the CFA franc (used by both the WAEMU and CAEMC) is pegged to the euro.[3]

What is the difference between a fixed exchange rate system and a floating rate system?

What are pegged exchange rates?

What does it mean to say that the dollar is depreciating with respect to the euro?

What is a convertible currency?

27.6 Trading in Foreign Exchange

Importers, exporters, tourists, and governments buy and sell currencies in the foreign exchange market. For example, when a U.S. trader imports automobiles from Japan, payment will probably be made in Japanese yen. The importer buys yen (through its bank) in the foreign exchange market, much as one buys common stocks on the New York Stock Exchange or pork bellies on the Chicago Mercantile Exchange. However, whereas stock and commodity exchanges have organized trading floors, the foreign exchange market consists of a network of brokers and banks based in New York, London, Tokyo, and other financial centers. Most buy and sell orders are conducted by computer and telephone.

27.6a Spot Rates and Forward Rates

The exchange rates shown in Tables 27-1 and 27-2 are known as **spot rates**, which means the rate paid for delivery of the currency "on the spot" or, in reality, no more than 2 days after the day of the trade. For most of the world's major currencies, it is also possible to buy (or sell) currencies for delivery at some agreed-upon future date, usually 30, 90, or 180 days from the day the transaction is negotiated. This rate is known as the **forward exchange rate**.

For example, suppose that a U.S. firm must pay 500 million yen to a Japanese firm in 30 days and that the current spot rate is 81.8930 yen per dollar. If spot rates remain constant, then the U.S. firm will pay the Japanese firm the equivalent of $6.106 million (500 million yen divided by 81.8930 yen per dollar) in 30 days. But if the spot rate falls to, say, 74 yen per dollar, then the U.S. firm will have to pay the equivalent of $5/(74 ¥/$) = $6.757 million. If the spot rate increases to 90, the firm will pay only $5/(90 ¥/$) = $5.556 million. The treasurer of the U.S. firm can avoid this variability by entering into a 30-day forward exchange contract. Suppose this contract promises delivery of yen to the U.S. firm in 30 days at a guaranteed price

www

Currency futures prices are available from the Chicago Mercantile Exchange (CME) on its Web site at **www.cme.com**. Currency spot and forward rates are available from the Bank of Montreal Financial Group at **www.bmo.com**.

---

3. A few countries, such as Bosnia and Herzegovina, have currency board arrangements. Under this system, a country technically has its own currency but commits to exchange it for a specified foreign money unit at a fixed exchange rate. This requires it to impose domestic currency restrictions unless it has the foreign currency reserves to cover requested exchanges.

of 81.8700 yen per dollar. No cash changes hands at the time the treasurer signs the forward contract, although the U.S. firm might have to put some collateral down as a guarantee against default. Yet because the firm can use an interest-bearing instrument for the collateral, this requirement is not costly. The counterparty to the forward contract must deliver the yen to the U.S. firm in 30 days, and the U.S. firm is obligated to purchase the 500 million yen at the previously agreed-upon rate of 81.8700 yen per dollar. Therefore, the treasurer of the U.S. firm is able to lock in a payment equivalent to $6.107 million = (¥500 million)/(81.8700 ¥/$), no matter what happens to spot rates. This technique is called *hedging*.

Forward rates for 30-, 90-, and 180-day delivery, along with the current spot rates for some commonly traded currencies, are given in Table 27-3. If you can obtain *more* of the foreign currency for a dollar in the forward than in the spot market, then the forward currency is less valuable than the spot currency and the forward currency is said to be selling at a **discount**. In other words, if the foreign currency is expected to depreciate (based on the forward rates), then the forward currency is at a discount. Conversely, since a dollar would buy *fewer* yen and francs in the forward than in the spot market, the forward yen and francs are selling at a **premium**.

Self Test	Differentiate between spot and forward exchange rates.
	Explain what it means for a forward currency to sell at a discount and at a premium.

27.7 Interest Rate Parity

Market forces determine whether a currency sells at a forward premium or a discount, and the general relationship between spot and forward exchange rates is specified by a concept called "interest rate parity."

Interest rate parity means that investors should expect to earn the same return on security investments in all countries after adjusting for risk. It recognizes that when you invest in a country other than your home country, you are affected by two

TABLE 27-3	Selected Spot and Forward Exchange Rates, Indirect Quotation: Number of Units of Foreign Currency per U.S. Dollar				
		Forward Rates[a]			
	Spot Rate	**30 Days**	**90 days**	**180 days**	**Forward Rate at a Premium or Discount[b]**
Britain (Pound)	0.6217	0.6219	0.6224	0.6233	Discount
Canada (Dollar)	0.9711	0.9717	0.9730	0.9755	Discount
Japan (Yen)	81.8930	81.8700	81.8300	81.7500	Premium
Switzerland (Franc)	0.9293	0.9290	0.9285	0.9280	Premium

[a]These are representative quotes as provided by a sample of New York banks. Forward rates for other currencies and for other lengths of time can often be negotiated.
[b]When it takes more units of a foreign currency to buy a dollar in the future, then the value of the foreign currency is less in the forward market than in the spot market; hence the forward rate is at a *discount* to the spot rate. When it takes fewer units of a foreign currency to buy a dollar in the future, the forward rate is at a *premium*.
Source: *The Wall Street Journal*, **online.wsj.com**; quotes for March 11, 2011.

forces—returns on the investment itself and changes in the exchange rate. It follows that your overall return will be higher than the investment's stated return if the currency in which your investment is denominated appreciates relative to your home currency. Likewise, your overall return will be lower if the foreign currency that you receive declines in value.

To illustrate interest rate parity, consider the case of a U.S. investor who can buy default-free 180-day Swiss bonds that promise a 4% nominal annual return. The 180-day foreign (Swiss) interest rate, r_f, is $4\% \div 2 = 2\%$ because 180 days is one-half of a 360-day year. Assume also that the indirect quotation for the spot exchange rate is 0.9293 Swiss francs per dollar, as shown in Table 27-3. Finally, assume that the 180-day forward exchange rate is 0.9280 Swiss francs per dollar, which means that in 180 days the investor can exchange 1 dollar for 0.9280 Swiss francs.

The U.S. investor could receive a 4% annualized return denominated in Swiss francs, but if he ultimately wants to consume goods in the United States, then those Swiss francs must be converted to dollars. The dollar return on the investment depends, therefore, on what happens to exchange rates over the next 6 months. However, the investor can lock in the dollar return by selling the foreign currency in the forward market. For example, the investor could simultaneously do the following:

1. Convert $1,000 to 929.30 Swiss francs in the spot market: $1,000(0.9293 Swiss francs per dollar) = 929.30 Swiss francs.
2. Invest the Swiss francs in a 180-day Swiss bond that has a 4% annual return, or a 2% semiannual return. This investment will pay 929.30(1.02) = 947.89 Swiss francs in 180 days.
3. Agree today to exchange the Swiss francs in 180 days at the forward rate of 0.9280 Swiss francs per dollar, for a total of (947.89 Swiss francs) ÷ (0.9280 Swiss francs per dollar) = $1,021.43.

Hence this investment has an expected 180-day return in dollars of $21.43/$1,000 = 2.143%, which translates into a nominal annual return of 2(2.143%) = 4.286%. In this case, the expected 4.286% return consists of 4% from the Swiss bond itself plus 0.286% because the market believes that the Swiss franc will strengthen relative to the dollar. Observe that, by locking in the forward rate today, the investor has eliminated all exchange rate risk. And since the Swiss bond is assumed to be default-free, the investor is certain to earn a 4.286% annual dollar return.

Interest rate parity implies that an investment in the United States with the same risk as the Swiss bond should also have a return of 4.286%. When we express interest rates as periodic rates, we can express interest rate parity by the following equation (later in the chapter we will use a slightly different version of interest rate parity when we consider multi-year cash flows):

$$\frac{\text{Forward exchange rate}}{\text{Spot exchange rate}} = \frac{1 + r_h}{1 + r_f} \qquad (27\text{--}1)$$

Here r_h is the periodic interest rate in the home country, r_f is the periodic interest rate in the foreign country, and the forward and exchange rates are expressed as direct quotations (that is, dollars per foreign currency).

Using Table 27-3, the direct spot quotation is 1.07608 dollar per Swiss franc = (1/0.9293 Swiss francs per dollar), and the direct 180-day forward quotation is

1.07759 = (1/0.9280). Using Equation 27-1, we can solve for the equivalent home rate, r_h:

$$\frac{\text{Forward exchange rate}}{\text{Spot exchange rate}} = \frac{1 + r_h}{1 + r_f} = \frac{1 + r_h}{1 + 0.02} = \frac{1.07759}{1.07608}$$

(27–1a)

$$1 + r_h = \left(\frac{1.07759}{1.07608}\right)(1 + 0.02) = 1.02143$$

The periodic home interest rate is 2.143%, and the annualized home interest rate is (2.143%)(2) = 4.286%, the same value we found before excepting a slight difference due to rounding.

After accounting for exchange rates, interest rate parity states that bonds in the home country and the foreign country must have the same actual rate of return in the investor's currency. In this example, the U.S. bond must yield 4.286% to provide the same return as the 4% Swiss bond. If one bond provides a higher return, then investors will sell their low-return bond and flock to the high-return bond. This activity will cause the price of the low-return bond to fall (which pushes up its yield) and the price of the high-return bond to increase (driving down its yield). These effects will continue until the two bonds again have the same returns after accounting for exchange rates.

In other words, interest rate parity implies that an investment in the United States with the same risk as a Swiss bond should have a dollar value return of 4.286%. Solving for r_h in Equation 27-1, we indeed find that the predicted interest rate in the United States is 4.286%, the same return except for the slight rounding difference.

Interest rate parity shows why a particular currency might be at a forward premium or discount. Note that a currency is at a forward premium whenever domestic interest rates are higher than foreign interest rates. Discounts prevail if domestic interest rates are lower than foreign interest rates. If these conditions do not hold, then arbitrage will soon force interest rates and exchange rates back to parity.

Self Test

What is interest rate parity?

Assume that interest rate parity holds. When a currency trades at a forward premium, what does that imply about domestic rates relative to foreign interest rates? What does it imply when a currency trades at a forward discount?

Assume that 90-day U.S. securities have a 4.5% annualized interest rate whereas 90-day Swiss securities have a 5% annualized interest rate. In the spot market, 1 U.S. dollar can be exchanged for 1.2 Swiss francs. If interest rate parity holds, what is the 90-day forward rate exchange between U.S. and Swiss francs? **(0.8323 $/SFr or 1.2015 SFr/$)**

On the basis of your answer to the previous question, is the Swiss franc selling at a premium or discount on the forward rate? **(Discount)**

27.8 Purchasing Power Parity

We have discussed exchange rates in some detail, and we have considered the relationship between spot and forward exchange rates. However, we have not yet addressed the fundamental question: What determines the spot level of exchange rates in each country? Although exchange rates are influenced by a multitude of factors that are difficult to predict, particularly on a day-to-day basis, market forces over the long run work to ensure that similar goods sell for similar prices in different countries after taking exchange rates into account. This relationship is known as "purchasing power parity."

Purchasing power parity (PPP), sometimes referred to as the *law of one price,* implies that the levels of exchange rates and prices adjust so as to cause identical goods to cost the same amount in different countries. For instance, if a pair of tennis shoes costs $150 in the United States and 100 pounds in Britain, then PPP implies that the exchange rate must be $1.50 per pound. Consumers could purchase the shoes in Britain for 100 pounds, or they could exchange their 100 pounds for $150 and then purchase the same shoes in the United States at the same effective cost (assuming no transaction or transportation costs). Here is the equation for purchasing power parity:

$$P_h = (P_f)(\text{Spot rate}) \tag{27-2}$$

or

$$\text{Spot rate} = \frac{P_h}{P_f} \tag{27-3}$$

Here

P_h = The price of the good in the home country ($150 in our example, assuming the United States is the home country).

P_f = The price of the good in the foreign country (100 pounds).

Note that the spot market exchange rate is expressed as the number of units of home currency that can be exchanged for one unit of foreign currency ($1.50 per pound).

Purchasing power parity assumes that market forces will eliminate situations in which the same product sells at a different price overseas. For example, if the shoes cost $140 in the United States then importers/exporters could purchase them in the United States for $140, sell them for 100 pounds in Britain, exchange the 100 pounds for $150 in the foreign exchange market, and earn a profit of $10 on every pair of shoes. Ultimately, this trading activity would increase the demand for shoes in the United States and thus raise P_h, increase the supply of shoes in Britain and thus reduce P_f, and increase the demand for dollars in the foreign exchange market and thus reduce the spot rate. Each of these actions works to restore PPP.

Note that PPP assumes that there are no transportation or transaction costs and no import restrictions, all of which limit the ability to ship goods between countries. In many cases, these assumptions are incorrect, which explains why PPP is often violated. An additional problem for empirical tests of the PPP theorem is that products in different countries are rarely identical. There are frequently real or perceived differences in quality that can lead to price differences in different countries.

Still, the concepts of interest rate parity and purchasing power parity are vitally important to those engaged in international activities. Companies and investors must anticipate changes in interest rates, inflation, and exchange rates, and they often try to hedge the risks of adverse movements in these factors. The parity relationships are extremely useful when anticipating future conditions.

HUNGRY FOR A BIG MAC? GO TO UKRAINE!

Purchasing power parity (PPP) implies that the same product will sell for the same price in every country after adjusting for current exchange rates. One problem when testing to see if PPP holds is that it assumes that goods consumed in different countries are of the same quality. For example, if you find that a product is more expensive in Switzerland than it is in Canada, one explanation is that PPP fails to hold, but another explanation is that the product sold in Switzerland is of a higher quality and therefore deserves a higher price.

One way to test for PPP is to find goods that have the same quality worldwide. With this in mind, *The Economist* magazine occasionally compares the prices of a well-known good whose quality is the same in nearly 120 different countries: the McDonald's Big Mac hamburger.

The accompanying table provides information collected during mid-2010. The second column shows the price of a Big Mac in local currency. For example, a Big Mac costs 71 rubles in Russia. The second column shows the cost in dollars (based on the actual exchange rate in the fourth column), which is the amount you would pay in that country if you exchanged dollars for local currency and then purchased a Big Mac at the local price. For example, the exchange rate is 30.4 rubles per dollar, which

means that a Big Mac in Russia costs \$2.33 = (71 rubles) ÷ (30.4 rubles per dollar), subject to rounding in the exchange rate used by *The Economist*.

The third column backs out the implied exchange rate that would hold under PPP. For example, the 71-ruble price of a Big Mac in Russia compared to the \$3.73 price in the United States gives us the implied PPP exchange rate of (71 rubles per Big Mac) ÷ (\$3.73 per Big Mac) = 19.0 rubles per dollar. The last column shows how much the local currency is overvalued or undervalued relative to the dollar. The ruble is undervalued by 38%: (19.0 − 30.4)/30.4 = −0.38.

The evidence suggests that strict PPP does not hold, but the Big Mac test may shed some insights about where exchange rates are headed. Most European currencies are overvalued against the dollar, while most other currencies are undervalued. The Big Mac 2010 test suggests that European currencies will fall over the next year or so but that most others will rise.

One last benefit of the Big Mac test is that it tells us the cheapest places to find a Big Mac. According to the data, if you are looking for a Big Mac, head to Ukraine and avoid Norway.

The Big Mac Index

	Big Mac prices*		Implied PPP† of the dollar	Actual dollar exchange rate July 21st	Under(−)/over(+) valuation against the dollar, %
	in local currency	in dollars			
United States‡	\$3.73	3.73			
Argentina	Peso 14.0	3.56	3.75	3.93	−5
Australia	A\$ 4.35	3.84	1.17	1.13	3
Brazil	Real 8.71	4.91	2.33	1.77	31
Britain	£ 2.29	3.48	1.63§	1.52§	−7
Canada	C\$ 4.17	4.00	1.12	1.04	7
Chile	Peso 1,750	3.34	469	524	−10
China	Yuan 13.2	1.95	3.54	6.78	−48
Colombia	Peso 8,200	4.39	2,196	1,868	18
Costa Rica	Colones 2,000	3.83	536	522	3
Czech Republic	Koruna 67.6	3.43	18.1	19.7	−8

(Continued)

The Big Mac Index (*Continued*)

	Big Mac prices*		Implied PPP† of the dollar	Actual dollar exchange rate July 21st	Under(−)/over(+) valuation against the dollar, %
	in local currency	in dollars			
Denmark	DK 28.5	4.90	7.63	5.81	31
Egypt	Pound 13.0	2.28	3.48	5.70	−39
Estonia	Kroon 32.0	2.62	8.57	12.2	−30
Euro area**	€ 3.38	4.33	1.10††	1.28††	16
Hong Kong	HK$ 14.8	1.90	3.96	7.77	−49
Hungary	Forint 740	3.33	198	222	−11
Indonesia	Rupiah 22,780	2.51	6,102	9,063	−33
Israel	Shekel 14.9	3.86	3.99	3.86	3
Japan	¥ 320	3.67	85.7	87.2	−2
Latvia	Lats 1.55	2.80	0.42	0.55	−25
Lithuania	Litas 7.30	2.71	1.96	2.69	−27
Malaysia	Ringgit 7.05	2.19	1.89	3.21	−41
Mexico	Peso 32.0	2.50	8.57	12.8	−33
New Zealand	NZ$ 5.00	3.59	1.34	1.39	−4
Norway	Kroner 45.0	7.20	12.1	6.25	93
Pakistan	Rupee 210	2.46	56.3	85.5	−34
Peru	Sol 10.0	3.54	2.68	2.83	−5
Philippines	Peso 102	2.19	27.3	46.5	−41
Poland	Zloty 8.30	2.60	2.22	3.20	−30
Russia	Rouble 71.0	2.33	19.0	30.4	−38
Saudi Arabia	Riyal 10.0	2.67	2.68	3.75	−29
Singapore	S$ 4.23	3.08	1.13	1.37	−18
South Africa	Rand 18.5	2.45	4.94	7.54	−34
South Korea	Won 3,400	2.82	911	1,204	−24
Sri Lanka	Rupee 210	1.86	56.3	113	−50
Sweden	SKr 48.4	6.56	13.0	7.37	76
Switzerland	SFr 6.50	6.19	1.74	1.05	66
Taiwan	NT$ 75.0	2.34	20.1	32.1	−37
Thailand	Baht 70.0	2.17	18.8	32.3	−42
Turkey	Lira 5.95	3.89	1.59	1.53	4
UAE	Dirhams 11.0	2.99	2.95	3.67	−20
Ukraine	Hryvnia 14.5	1.84	3.88	7.90	−51
Uruguay	Peso 79.0	3.74	21.2	21.1	*nil*

*At current exchange rates †Purchasing-power parity; local price divided by price in United States ‡Average of Atlanta, Chicago, New York and San Francisco §Dollars per pound **Weighted average of prices in euro area ††Dollars per euro

Sources: McDonalds; *The Economist*, July 22, 2010, **www.economist.com**.

Self Test

What is meant by purchasing power parity?

A computer sells for $1,500 U.S. dollars. In the spot market, $1 = 115 Japanese yen. If purchasing power parity holds, what should be the price (in yen) of the same computer in Japan? **(¥172,500)**

27.9 Inflation, Interest Rates, and Exchange Rates

Relative inflation rates, or the rates of inflation in foreign countries compared with that in the home country, have many implications for multinational financial decisions. Obviously, relative inflation rates will greatly influence future production costs at home and abroad. Equally important, inflation has a dominant influence on relative interest rates and exchange rates. Both of these factors influence decisions by multinational corporations for financing their foreign investments, and both have an important effect on the profitability of foreign investments.

www

For current international interest rates, go to **www .bloomberg.com** and select Market Data. Then select Rates and Bonds.

The currencies of countries with higher inflation rates than that of the United States will by definition *depreciate* over time against the dollar. Countries where this has occurred include Mexico and all the South American nations. On the other hand, the currencies of Switzerland and Japan, which have had less inflation than the United States, have generally *appreciated* against the dollar. In fact, *a foreign currency will, on average, depreciate or appreciate against the U.S. dollar at a percentage rate approximately equal to the amount by which its inflation rate exceeds or is less than the U.S. rate.*

Relative inflation rates also affect interest rates. The interest rate in any country is largely determined by its inflation rate. Therefore, countries currently experiencing higher rates of inflation than the United States also tend to have higher interest rates. The reverse is true for countries with lower inflation rates.

It is tempting for a multinational corporation to borrow in countries with the lowest interest rates. However, this is not always a good strategy. Suppose, for example, that interest rates in Switzerland are lower than those in the United States because of Switzerland's lower inflation rate. A U.S. multinational firm could therefore save interest by borrowing in Switzerland. However, because of relative inflation rates, the Swiss franc will probably appreciate in the future, causing the dollar cost of annual interest and principal payments on Swiss debt to rise over time. Thus, *the lower interest rate could be more than offset by losses from currency appreciation.* Similarly, multinational corporations should not necessarily avoid borrowing in a country such as Brazil, where interest rates have been very high, because future depreciation of the Brazilian real could make such borrowing end up being relatively inexpensive.

Self Test

What effects do relative inflation rates have on relative interest rates?

What happens over time to the currencies of countries with higher inflation rates than that of the United States? To those with lower inflation rates?

Why might a multinational corporation decide to borrow in a country such as Brazil, where interest rates are high, rather than in a country like Switzerland, where interest rates are low?

27.10 International Money and Capital Markets

One way for U.S. citizens to invest in world markets is to buy the stocks of U.S. multinational corporations that invest directly in foreign countries. Another way is to purchase foreign securities—stocks, bonds, or money market instruments issued by foreign companies. Security investments are known as *portfolio investments,* and they are distinguished from *direct investments* in physical assets by U.S. corporations.

From World War II through the 1960s, the U.S. capital markets dominated world markets. Today, however, the value of U.S. securities represents less than one-fourth the value of all securities. Given this situation, it is important for both corporate managers and investors to have an understanding of international markets. Moreover, these markets often offer better opportunities for raising or investing capital than are available domestically.

27.10a Eurodollar Market

A **Eurodollar** is a U.S. dollar deposited in a bank outside the United States. (Although they are called Eurodollars because they originated in Europe, Eurodollars are actually any dollars deposited in any part of the world other than the United States.) The bank in which the deposit is made may be a non-U.S. bank, such as Barclays Bank in London; the foreign branch of a U.S. bank, such as Citibank's Paris branch; or

GREASING THE WHEELS OF INTERNATIONAL BUSINESS

What do bribery and tax shelters have in common? Both are targets of international regulation.

Thirty-seven countries have now signed the Organization for Economic Cooperation and Development's Anti-Bribery Convention. This requires each country to pass legislation making it a crime for companies to bribe public officials. The United States, which signed the convention, has been the most aggressive in prosecuting violators. It is interesting that this prosecution has not been limited to U.S. companies but also has extended to foreign companies whose stocks are listed in the United States. For example, Statoil, a Norwegian firm, was fined $10.5 million in 2006 for bribing Iranian officials. Subsidiaries of Vetco International, headquartered in the United Kingdom, were fined $26 million in 2007 for bribing Nigerian officials. Siemens, a German company, holds the record for the largest fine paid to date (2009), with over *$1.6 billion* paid to regulatory agencies in the United States and Germany.

Among the international organizations striving to reform global taxation and eliminate tax-shelter abuse are the Joint International Tax Shelter Information Centre, the Seven Country Working Group, and the Leeds Castle Group. Their goals include improving transparency, eliminating double taxation, and abolishing tax havens.

What does the reformation of tax havens have in common with the elimination of bribery? First, both of these problems distract companies from focusing on their core business issues, and both create uneven playing fields where providing the best product at the best price isn't as important as who you know (and bribe!) or how clever your lawyers are. Second, these problems reduce transparency in capital markets, making it harder for investors to identify the best firms. When investors are uncertain about a company, the cost of capital goes up. Thus, there is a direct link between transparency and a company's ability to raise capital at a fair price.

Sources: Janet Kersnar, "View from Europe," *CFO,* June 2007, p. 25; and Kayleigh Karutis, *CFO,* "Global Norming," May 2007, p. 22.

even a foreign branch of a third-country bank, such as Barclays's Munich branch. Most Eurodollar deposits are for $500,000 or more, and they have maturities ranging from overnight to about 1 year.

The major difference between Eurodollar deposits and regular U.S. time deposits is their geographic locations. The two types of deposits do not involve different currencies—in both cases, dollars are on deposit. However, Eurodollars are outside the direct control of the U.S. monetary authorities, so U.S. banking regulations, including reserve requirements and FDIC insurance premiums, do not apply. The absence of these costs means that the interest rate paid on Eurodollar deposits can be higher than domestic U.S. rates on equivalent instruments.

The dollar is the leading international currency. However, British pounds, euros, Swiss francs, Japanese yen, and other currencies are also deposited outside their home countries; these *Eurocurrencies* are handled in exactly the same way as Eurodollars.

Eurodollars are borrowed by U.S. and foreign corporations for various purposes but especially to pay for goods imported from the United States and to invest in U.S. security markets. Also, U.S. dollars are used as an international currency or medium of exchange, and many Eurodollars are also used for this purpose. It is interesting to note that Eurodollars were actually "invented" by the Soviets in 1946. International merchants did not trust the Soviets or their rubles, so the Soviets bought some dollars (for gold), deposited them in a Paris bank, and then used these dollars to buy goods in the world markets. Others found it convenient to use dollars this same way, and soon the Eurodollar market was in full swing.

Eurodollars are usually held in interest-bearing accounts. The interest rate paid on these deposits depends (1) on the bank's lending rate, since the interest a bank earns on loans determines its willingness and ability to pay interest on deposits, and (2) on rates of return available on U.S. money market instruments. If money market rates in the United States were above Eurodollar deposit rates then these dollars would be sent back and invested in the United States, whereas if Eurodollar deposit rates were significantly above U.S. rates, which is more often the case, then more dollars would be sent out of the United States to become Eurodollars. Given the existence of the Eurodollar market and the electronic flow of dollars to and from the United States, it is easy to see why interest rates in the United States cannot be insulated from those in other parts of the world.

Interest rates on Eurodollar deposits (and loans) are tied to a standard rate known by the acronym **LIBOR**, which stands for **London Interbank Offered Rate**. LIBOR is the rate of interest offered by the largest and strongest London banks on dollar deposits of significant size. On May 26, 2011, LIBOR rates were just a little above domestic U.S. bank rates on time deposits of the same maturity—0.20% for 3-month CDs versus 0.25% for LIBOR CDs. The Eurodollar market is essentially a short-term market; most loans and deposits are for less than 1 year.

27.10b International Bond Markets

Any bond sold outside the country of the borrower is called an *international bond*. However, there are two important types of international bonds: foreign bonds and Eurobonds. **Foreign bonds** are bonds sold by a foreign borrower but denominated in the currency of the country in which the issue is sold. For instance, Nortel Networks (a Canadian company) may need U.S. dollars to finance the operations of its subsidiaries in the United States. If it decides to raise the needed capital in the United States, then the bond would be underwritten by a syndicate of U.S. investment bankers, denominated in U.S. dollars, and sold to U.S. investors in accordance with SEC and applicable state regulations. Except for the foreign origin of the borrower, this bond would be indistinguishable from those issued by equivalent U.S. corporations. However, since Nortel is a foreign corporation, the bond would be a foreign bond. Furthermore, because it is denominated in dollars and sold in the United States under SEC regulations, it is also called a **Yankee bond**. In contrast, if Nortel issued bonds in Mexico that were denominated in pesos then they would be foreign bonds, not Yankee bonds.

The term **Eurobond** is used to designate any bond issued in one country but denominated in the currency of some other country. Examples include a Ford Motor Company issue denominated in dollars and sold in Germany and a British firm's sale of euro-denominated bonds in Switzerland. The institutional arrangements by which Eurobonds are marketed are different than those for most other bond issues, with the most important distinction being a far lower level of required disclosure than is usually found for bonds issued in domestic markets, particularly in the United States. Governments tend to be less strict when regulating securities denominated in foreign currencies, because the bonds' purchasers are generally more "sophisticated." The lower disclosure requirements result in lower total transaction costs for Eurobonds.

Eurobonds appeal to investors for several reasons. Generally, they are issued in bearer form rather than as registered bonds, so the names and nationalities of investors are not recorded. Individuals who desire anonymity, whether for privacy reasons or for tax avoidance, like Eurobonds. Similarly, most governments do not withhold taxes on interest payments associated with Eurobonds. If the investor requires an effective yield of 10%, then a Eurobond that is exempt from tax withholding would simply need a coupon rate of 10%. Another type of bond—for instance, a domestic issue subject to a 30% withholding tax on interest paid to foreigners—would need a coupon rate of 14.3% to yield an after-withholding rate of 10%. Investors who desire secrecy would not want to file for a refund of the tax, so they would prefer to hold the Eurobond.

More than half of all Eurobonds are denominated in dollars. Bonds in Japanese yen, German marks, and Dutch guilders account for most of the rest. Although centered in Europe, Eurobonds are truly international. Their underwriting syndicates include investment bankers from all parts of the world, and the bonds are sold to investors not only in Europe but also in such faraway places as Bahrain and Singapore. Up to a few years ago, Eurobonds were issued solely by multinational firms, by international financial institutions, or by national governments. Today, however, the Eurobond market is also being tapped by purely domestic U.S. firms, which often find they can lower their debt costs by borrowing overseas.

27.10c International Stock Markets

New issues of stock are sold in international markets for a variety of reasons. For example, a non-U.S. firm might sell an equity issue in the United States because it can tap a much larger source of capital than in its home country. Also, a U.S. firm might tap a foreign market because it wants to create an equity market presence to accompany its operations in that country. Large multinational companies also occasionally issue new stock simultaneously in multiple countries. For example, Alcan Aluminum, a Canadian company, issued new stock in Canada, Europe, and the United States simultaneously, using different underwriting syndicates in each market.

In addition to new issues, outstanding stocks of large multinational companies are increasingly being listed on multiple international exchanges. For example, Coca-Cola's stock is traded on six stock exchanges in the United States, four stock exchanges in Switzerland, the Frankfurt stock exchange in Germany, the Lima stock exchange in Peru, and the Mexican stock exchange in Mexico City. Some 500 foreign stocks are listed in the United States—an example here is Royal Dutch Petroleum, which is listed on the New York Stock Exchange. U.S. investors can also invest in foreign companies through American Depository Receipts (ADRs), which are certificates representing ownership of foreign stock held in trust. About 1,700 ADRs are now available in the United States, with most of them traded on the over-the-counter

(OTC) market. However, more and more ADRs are being listed on the NYSE, including England's British Airways, Japan's Honda Motors, and Italy's Fiat Group.[4]

Self Test

Differentiate between foreign portfolio investments and direct foreign investments.

What are Eurodollars?

Has the development of the Eurodollar market made it easier or more difficult for the Federal Reserve to control U.S. interest rates?

Differentiate between foreign bonds and Eurobonds.

Why do Eurobonds appeal to investors?

STOCK MARKET INDICES AROUND THE WORLD

In the United States, the Dow Jones Industrial Average (^DJI) is the most well-known stock market index. Similar indices also exist for each major world financial center. As shown in the accompanying table, India's market has had the strongest performance during the past 10 years while Japan's has had the weakest.

Hong Kong (^HSI)
In Hong Kong, the primary stock index is the Hang Seng. Created by HSI Services Limited, the Hang Seng index is composed of 33 large stocks.

Great Britain (^FTSE)
The FT-SE 100 Index (pronounced "footsie") is the most widely followed indicator of equity investments in Great Britain. It is a value-weighted index composed of the 100 largest companies on the London Stock Exchange.

Japan (^N225)
In Japan, the principal barometer of stock performance is the Nikkei 225 Index. The index consists of highly liquid equity issues thought to be representative of the Japanese economy.

Germany (^GDAXI)
The Deutscher Aktienindex, commonly called the DAX, is an index composed of the 30 largest companies trading on the Frankfurt Stock Exchange.

India (^BSESN)
Of the 22 stock exchanges in India, the Bombay Stock Exchange (BSE) is the largest, with more than 6,000 listed stocks and approximately two-thirds of the country's total trading volume. Established in 1875, the exchange is also the oldest in Asia. Its yardstick is the BSE Sensex, an index of 30 publicly traded Indian stocks that account for one-fifth of the BSE's market capitalization.

Note: For easy access to world indices, see **finance .yahoo.com/m2** and use the ticker symbols shown above in parentheses.

Relative 10-Year Performance (Starting Values = 100)

	United States	Germany	Great Britain	Hong Kong	India	Japan
July 2001	100	100	100	100	100	100
July 2011	107	122	105	182	547	83

---

4. For an interesting discussion of ADRs and the costs faced by listing companies when the ADR is underwritten by investment banks, see Hsuen-Chi Chen, Larry Fauver, and Pei-Ching Yang, "What Do Investment Banks Charge to Underwrite American Depository Receipts?" *Journal of Banking and Finance,* April 2009, pp. 609–618.

27.11 Multinational Capital Budgeting

Until now we've discussed the general environment in which multinational firms operate. In the remainder of the chapter, we see how international factors affect key corporate decisions, beginning with capital budgeting. Although the same basic principles apply to capital budgeting for both foreign and domestic operations, there are some key differences. These include the types of risks faced by the firm, cash flow estimation, and project analysis.[5]

27.11a Risk Exposure

Foreign projects may be more or less risky than equivalent domestic projects, and that can lead to differences in the cost of capital. Higher risk for foreign projects tends to result from two primary sources: (1) exchange rate risk and (2) political risk. However, international diversification might result in a lower risk.

Exchange rate risk concerns the value of the basic cash flows in the parent company's home currency. Foreign currency cash flows turned over to the parent must be converted into U.S. dollars, so projected cash flows must be translated to dollars at the expected future exchange rates. An analysis should be conducted to ascertain the effects of exchange rate variations on dollar cash flows; then, on the basis of this analysis, an exchange rate risk premium should be added to the domestic cost of capital. It is sometimes possible to hedge against exchange rate risk, but it may not be possible to hedge completely, especially on long-term projects. If hedging is used, then the costs of doing so must be subtracted from the project's operating cash flows.

Political risk refers to potential actions by a host government that would reduce the value of a company's investment. It includes at one extreme expropriation of the subsidiary's assets without compensation, but it also includes less drastic actions that reduce the value of the parent firm's investment in the foreign subsidiary.[6] Included here are higher taxes, tighter repatriation or currency controls, and restrictions on prices charged. The risk of expropriation is small in traditionally friendly and stable countries such as Great Britain or Switzerland. However, in Latin America, Africa, the Far East, and Eastern Europe, the risk may be substantial. Past expropriations include those of ITT and Anaconda Copper in Chile; Gulf Oil in Bolivia; Occidental Petroleum in Libya; Enron Corporation in Peru; BP, ConocoPhillips, ExxonMobil, and Chevron in Venezuela; and the assets of many companies in Iraq, Iran, and Cuba.

Note that companies can take steps to reduce the potential loss from expropriation, including one or more of the following.

1. Finance the subsidiary with local capital.
2. Structure operations so that the subsidiary has value only as a part of the integrated corporate system.
3. Obtain insurance against economic losses from expropriation from a source such as the Overseas Private Investment Corporation (OPIC).

---

5. Many domestic companies form joint ventures with foreign companies; see Insup Lee and Steve B. Wyatt, "The Effects of International Joint Ventures on Shareholder Wealth," *Financial Review,* November 1990, pp. 641–649. For a discussion of the Japanese cost of capital, see Jeffrey A. Frankel, "The Japanese Cost of Finance," *Financial Management,* Spring 1991, pp. 95–127. For a discussion of financial practices in the Pacific basin, see George W. Kester, Rosita P. Chang, and Kai-Chong Tsui, "Corporate Financial Policy in the Pacific Basin: Hong Kong and Singapore," *Financial Practice and Education,* Spring/Summer 1994, pp. 117–127.

6. For an interesting article on expropriation, see Arvind Mahajan, "Pricing Expropriation Risk," *Financial Management,* Winter 1990, pp. 77–86.

CONSUMER FINANCE IN CHINA

The financial frontier for consumer finance is in China, where applicants must often wait more than a month to get a credit card and even longer for car loans or home mortgages. But that is changing quickly, as GE Money (formerly known as GE Capital) is among a host of financial players looking to partner with or become part owners of Chinese banks. Other foreign investors include financial institutions from all over the world, such as Citigroup (United States), ING Group (Netherlands), Hang Seng Bank (Hong Kong), and the Royal Bank of Scotland. Even investment banks (Goldman Sachs) and private equity firms (Newbridge Capital) are in the hunt.

What makes Chinese banks attractive? First, China is now allowing foreign-owned banks to make direct loans to Chinese customers. Second, China has a huge consumer base with a growing middle class that is purchasing homes, cars, and other consumer goods. Third, many Chinese banks might be considered "fixer-uppers" because they hold too many uncollectible loans (up to 9.2% of their loan portfolios), have weak information technology systems, and provide poor customer service.

These problems are viewed as opportunities by GE Money, which brings considerable business expertise (in addition to cash) to the partnership. For example, GE Money helped Shenzhen Development Bank (SDB) introduce a Wal-Mart credit card, an Auchen credit card (Auchen is a large French retailer), and various mortgage services. All the results aren't yet in, but GE has helped SDB reduce the time to get a credit card from over a month to just 5 days.

Investing in China isn't without risks, with an estimated 60% of partnerships not providing the return that was anticipated at the deal's inception. Problems include insufficient pre-deal planning, a lack of focus and traction in the immediate post-deal period, a failure to integrate cultures, and a lack of flexibility in adapting to local conditions. Still, the potential rewards are enormous, so you should expect to see more foreign investment in China.

Source: Don Durfee, "Give Them Credit," *CFO*, July 2007, pp. 50–57.

If OPIC insurance is purchased, then the premiums paid must be added to the project's cost.

Several organizations rate countries according to different aspects of risk. For example, Transparency International (TI) ranks countries based on perceived corruption, which is an important part of political risk. Table 27-4 shows selected countries. Denmark, New Zealand, and Sweden are rated by TI as the most honest countries, while Somalia is the most dishonest. The United States is ranked twenty-second.

27.11b Cash Flow Estimation

Cash flow estimation is more complex for foreign than domestic investments. Most multinational firms set up separate subsidiaries in each foreign country in which they operate, and the relevant cash flows for the parent company are the dividends and royalties paid by the subsidiaries to the parent, translated into dollars. Dividends and royalties are normally taxed by both foreign and home country governments, although the home country may allow credits for some or all of the foreign taxes paid. Furthermore, a foreign government may restrict the amount of the cash that may be **repatriated** to the parent company. For example, some governments place a ceiling, stated as a percentage of the company's net worth, on the amount of cash dividends that a subsidiary can pay to its parent. Such restrictions are normally intended to force multinational firms to reinvest earnings in the foreign country, although restrictions are sometimes imposed to prevent large currency outflows, which might disrupt the exchange rate.

TABLE 27-4	The 2010 Transparency International Corruption Perceptions Index (CPI)				
Top-Ranked Countries			**Bottom-Ranked Countries**		
Rank	**Country**	**2010 CPI Score**	**Rank**	**Country**	**2010 CPI Score**
1 (tie)	Denmark	9.3	127	Syria	2.5
	New Zealand	9.3	134	Zimbabwe	2.4
	Singapore	9.3	143	Pakistan	2.3
2 (tie)	Sweden	9.2	146	Libya	2.2
	Finland	9.2	154 (tie)	Russia	2.1
8	Switzerland	8.7		Tajikistan	2.1
11 (tie)	Iceland	8.5		Laos	2.1
	Luxembourg	8.5		Kenya	2.1
15 (tie)	Austria	7.9		Cambodia	2.1
	Germany	7.9	164	Venezuela	2.0
17	Japan	7.8	170	Burundi	1.8
20	United Kingdom	7.6	172	Sudan	1.6
22	United States	7.1	176	Afghanistan	1.4
26	Estonia	6.5	178	Somalia	1.1

Source: **www.transparency.org**.

Whatever the host country's motivation for blocking repatriation of profits, the result is that the parent corporation cannot use cash flows blocked in the foreign country to pay dividends to its shareholders or to invest elsewhere in the business. Hence, from the perspective of the parent organization, the cash flows relevant for foreign investment analysis are the cash flows that the subsidiary is actually expected to send back to the parent. Note, though, that if returns on investments in the foreign country are attractive and if blockages are expected to be lifted in the future, then current blockages may not be bad; however, dealing with this situation does complicate the process of cash flow estimation.

Some companies attempt to circumvent repatriation restrictions (and to lower their taxes) through the use of transfer pricing. For example, a foreign subsidiary might obtain raw materials or other input components from the parent. The price the subsidiary pays the parent is called a **transfer price**. If the transfer price is high then the foreign subsidiary's costs will be high, leaving little or no profit to repatriate. However, the parent's profit will be higher because it sold to the subsidiary at an inflated transfer price. The net result is that the parent receives cash flows from the subsidiary via transfer pricing rather than as repatriated dividends. Transfer pricing can also be used to shift profits from high-tax to low-tax jurisdictions. Of course, governments are well aware of these possibilities, so governmental auditors are on guard to prevent abusive transfer pricing.

27.11c Project Analysis

First, consider a domestic project that requires foreign raw materials, or one where the finished product will be sold in a foreign market. Because the operation is based in the United States, any projected nondollar cash flows—costs in the first example and revenues in the second—should be converted into dollars. This conversion does not present much of a problem for cash flows to be paid or received in the short run, but there is a significant problem in estimating exchange rates for converting long-term foreign cash flows into dollars because forward exchange rates are usually not available for more than 180 days into the future. However, long-term expected forward exchange rates can be estimated using the idea behind the interest rate parity relationship. For example, if a foreign cash flow is expected to occur in 1 year, then the 1-year forward exchange rate can be estimated using domestic and foreign government bonds maturing in 1 year. Similarly, the 2-year exchange rate can be estimated using 2-year bonds. Thus, foreign cash flows can be converted into dollars and added to the project's other projected cash flows, and then the project's NPV can be calculated based on its cost of capital.

Now consider a project to be based overseas, so that most expected future cash flows will be denominated in a foreign currency. Two approaches can be used to estimate such a project's NPV. Both begin by forecasting the future cash flows denominated in the foreign currency and then determining the annual repatriations to the United States, denominated in the foreign currency. Under the first approach, we convert the expected future repatriations to dollars (as described earlier) and then find the NPV using the project's cost of capital. Under the second approach, we take the projected repatriations (denominated in the foreign currency) and then discount them at the foreign cost of capital, which reflects foreign interest rates and relevant risk premiums. This produces an NPV denominated in the foreign currency, which can be converted into a dollar-denominated NPV using the spot exchange rate.

The following example illustrates the first approach. A U.S. company has the opportunity to lease a manufacturing facility in Great Britain for 3 years. The company must spend £20 million initially to refurbish the plant. The expected net cash flows from the plant for the next 3 years, in millions, are $CF_1 = £7$, $CF_2 = £9$, and $CF_3 = £11$. A similar project in the United States would have a risk-adjusted cost of capital of 10%. The first step is to estimate the expected exchange rates at the end of 1, 2, and 3 years using the multi-year interest rate parity equation:

$$(27\text{-}4) \qquad \text{Expected t-year forward exchange rate} = (\text{Spot exchange rate})\left(\frac{1+r_h}{1+r_f}\right)^t$$

where the exchange rates are expressed in direct quotations and the interest rates are expressed as annual rates, not periodic rates. We are using the interest rate parity equation to estimate expected forward rates because market-based forward rates for maturities longer than a year are generally not available.

Suppose the spot exchange rate is 1.8000 dollars per pound. Interest rates on U.S. and U.K. government bonds are shown below, along with the expected forward rate implied by the multi-year interest rate parity relationship in Equation 27-4:

	Maturity (Years)		
	1	2	3
r_h (annualized)	2.0%	2.8%	3.5%
r_f (annualized)	4.6%	5.0%	5.2%
Spot rate ($/£)	1.8000	1.8000	1.8000
Expected forward rate based on Equation 27-4 ($/£)	1.7553	1.7254	1.7141

TABLE 27-5 Net Present Value of International Investment (Cash Flows in Millions)

	Year			
	0	**1**	**2**	**3**
Cash flows in pounds	−£20	£7	£9	£11
Expected exchange rates (dollars/pound)	1.8000	1.7553	1.7254	1.7141
Cash flows in dollars	−$36.00	$12.29	$15.53	$18.86
Project cost of capital	10%			
NPV	$2.18			

© Cengage Learning 2013

The current dollar cost of the project is £20(1.8000 $/£) = $36 million. The Year-1 cash flow in dollars is £7(1.7553 $/£) = $12.29 million. Table 27-5 shows the complete time line and the net present value of $2.18 million.

List some key differences in capital budgeting as applied to foreign versus domestic operations.

What are the relevant cash flows for an international investment: the cash flow produced by the subsidiary in the country where it operates, or the cash flows in dollars that it sends to its parent company?

Why might the cost of capital for a foreign project differ from that of an equivalent domestic project? Could it be lower?

What adjustments might be made to the domestic cost of capital for a foreign investment that are due to exchange rate risk and political risk?

27.12 International Capital Structures

Companies' capital structures vary among countries. For example, the Organization for Economic Cooperation and Development (OECD) recently reported that, on average, Japanese firms use 85% debt to total assets (in book value terms), German firms use 64%, and U.S. firms use 55%. One problem when interpreting these numbers is that different countries often use different accounting conventions with regard to (1) reporting assets on the basis of historical versus replacement cost, (2) the treatment of leased assets, (3) pension plan funding, and (4) capitalizing versus expensing R&D costs. These differences make it difficult to compare capital structures.

A study by Raghuram Rajan and Luigi Zingales of the University of Chicago attempted to account for differences in accounting practices. In their study, Rajan and Zingales used a database that covered fewer firms than the OECD but that provided a more complete breakdown of balance sheet data. They concluded that differences in accounting practices can explain much of the cross-country variation in capital structures.

Rajan and Zingales's results are summarized in Table 27-6. There are a number of different ways to measure capital structure. One measure is the average ratio of total liabilities to total assets—this is similar to the measure used by the OECD, and it is reported in Column 1. Based on this measure, German and Japanese firms appear to be more highly levered than U.S. firms. However, if you look at Column 2, where capital structure is measured by interest-bearing debt to total assets, it appears that German

TABLE 27-6	Median Capital Structures among Large Industrialized Countries (Measured in Terms of Book Value)				
Country	**Total Liabilities to Total Assets (Unadjusted for Accounting Differences)** **(1)**	**Interest-Bearing Debt to Total Assets (Unadjusted for Accounting Differences)** **(2)**	**Total Liabilities to Total Assets (Adjusted for Accounting Differences)** **(3)**	**Debt to Total Assets (Adjusted for Accounting Differences)** **(4)**	**Times-Interest-Earned (TIE) Ratio** **(5)**
Canada	56%	32%	48%	32%	1.55
France	71	25	69	18	2.64
Germany	73	16	50	11	3.20
Italy	70	27	68	21	1.81
Japan	69	35	62	21	2.46
United Kingdom	54	18	47	10	4.79
United States	58	27	52	25	2.41
Mean	64%	26%	57%	20%	2.69
Standard deviation	8%	7%	10%	8%	1.07

Source: Raghuram Rajan and Luigi Zingales, "What Do We Know about Capital Structure? Some Evidence from International Data," *Journal of Finance*, December 1995, pp. 1421–1460.

firms use less leverage than U.S. and Japanese firms. What explains these conflicting results? Rajan and Zingales argue that much of the difference is explained by the way German firms account for pension liabilities. German firms generally include all pension liabilities (and their offsetting assets) on the balance sheet, whereas firms in other countries (including the United States) generally "net out" pension assets and liabilities on their balance sheets. To see the importance of this difference, consider a firm with $10 million in liabilities (not including pension liabilities) and $20 million in assets (not including pension assets). Assume that the firm has $10 million in pension liabilities that are fully funded by $10 million in pension assets. Therefore, net pension liabilities are zero. If this firm were in the United States, it would report a ratio of total liabilities to total assets equal to 50% ($10 million/$20 million). By contrast, if this firm operated in Germany, both its pension assets and liabilities would be reported on the balance sheet. The firm would have $20 million in liabilities and $30 million in assets—or a 67% ($20 million/$30 million) ratio of total liabilities to total assets. Total debt is the sum of short-term debt and long-term debt and *excludes* other liabilities, including pension liabilities. Therefore, the measure of total debt to total assets provides a more comparable measure of leverage across different countries.

Rajan and Zingales also make a variety of adjustments that attempt to control for other differences in accounting practices. The effects of these adjustments are reported in Columns 3 and 4. Overall, the evidence suggests that companies in Germany and the United Kingdom tend to have less leverage, and that firms in Canada appear to have more leverage, than firms in the United States, France, Italy, and Japan. This conclusion is supported by data in the final column, which shows the average times-interest-earned ratio for firms in a number of different countries. Recall from Chapter 8 that the times-interest-earned ratio is the ratio of operating income (EBIT) to interest expense. This measure indicates how much cash the firm has available to service its interest expense. In general, firms with more leverage have a lower times-interest-earned ratio. The data indicate that this ratio is highest in the United Kingdom and Germany and lowest in Canada.

Are there international differences in firms' financial leverage? Explain.   **Self Test**

27.13 Multinational Working Capital Management

Working capital management in a multinational setting involves more complexity than purely domestic working capital management. We discuss some of these differences in this section.

27.13a Cash Management

The goals of cash management in a multinational corporation are similar to those in a purely domestic corporation: (1) to speed up collections, slow down disbursements, and thus maximize net float; (2) to shift cash as rapidly as possible from those parts of the business where it is not needed to those parts where it is needed; and (3) to maximize the risk-adjusted, after-tax rate of return on temporary cash balances. Multinational companies use the same general procedures for achieving these goals as domestic firms, but the longer distances and more serious mail delays make such devices as lockbox systems and electronic funds transfers especially important.

Although multinational and domestic corporations have the same objectives and use similar procedures, multinational corporations face a far more complex task. As noted earlier in our discussion of political risk, foreign governments often place restrictions on transfers of funds out of the country. So even though IBM can transfer money from its Salt Lake City office to its New York concentration bank just by pressing a few buttons, a similar transfer from its Buenos Aires office is far more complex. Buenos Aires funds must be converted to dollars before the transfer. If there is a shortage of dollars in Argentina or if the Argentinean government wants to conserve dollars so they will be available for the purchase of strategic materials, then conversion, and hence the transfer, may be blocked. Even if no dollar shortage exists in Argentina, the government may still restrict funds outflows if those funds represent profits or depreciation rather than payments for purchased materials or equipment, because many countries—especially those that are less developed—want profits reinvested in the country in order to stimulate economic growth.

Once it has been determined what funds can be transferred, the next task is to get those funds to locations where they will earn the highest returns. Whereas domestic corporations tend to think in terms of domestic securities, multinationals are more likely to be aware of investment opportunities all around the world. Most multinational corporations use one or more global concentration banks, located in money centers such as London, New York, Tokyo, Zurich, or Singapore, and their staffs in those cities, working with international bankers, are able to take advantage of the best rates available anywhere in the world.

27.13b Credit Management

Consider the international cash conversion cycle for a foreign company importing from the United States: The order is placed, the goods are shipped, an account payable is created for the importer and an account receivable is created for the exporter, the goods arrive in the foreign country, the importer sells them, and the importer collects on the sales. At some point in this process, the importer pays off the account payable, which is usually before the importer collects on its own sales. Notice that the importer must finance the transaction from the time it pays the account payable until it collects on its sales. In many poorer, less-developed nations, the capital markets are not adequate to enable the importer to finance the cash conversion cycle. Even when foreign capital markets are available, the additional shipping time might lengthen the cash conversion cycle to such an extent that the importer can't afford the financing costs. Thus, there is enormous pressure on the exporter to grant credit, often with very lengthy payment periods.

But now consider the situation from the exporter's point of view. First, it is much more difficult for the exporter to perform a credit analysis on a foreign customer. Second, the exporter must also worry about exchange-rate fluctuations between the time of the sale and the time the receivable is collected. For example, if IBM sold a computer to a Japanese customer for 90 million yen when the exchange rate was 90 yen to the dollar, IBM would obtain $90,000,000/90 = \$1,000,000$ for the computer. However, if it sold the computer on terms of net/6 months and if the yen then fell against the dollar, so that 1 dollar would now buy 112.5 yen, IBM would end up realizing only $90,000,000/112.5 = \$800,000$ when it collected the receivable. Hedging with forward contracts can reduce this exchange rate risk, but what about the credit risk?

One possibility is for the importer to obtain a letter of credit from its bank whereby the bank certifies that the importer will meet the terms of the account payable or else the bank will pay. However, the importer often must pay the bank a relatively large fee for the letter of credit, and letters of credit might not be available to companies in developing countries.

A second option is for the importer to essentially write a check to the exporter at the time of the purchase, but one that is postdated so that it cannot be cashed until the account payable's due date. If the importer's bank promises that it will "accept" the check even if there are insufficient funds in the importer's account, then the check becomes a financial instrument that is called a **banker's acceptance**. If the bank is strong, then this virtually eliminates the credit risk. In addition, the exporter can then sell this banker's acceptance in the secondary market if it needs funds immediately. Of course, it must sell the banker's acceptance at a discount to reflect the time value of money, because the banker's acceptance is essentially a short-term financial security that pays no interest, similar to a T-bill. Financing an international transaction via a banker's acceptance has many benefits for the exporter, but the importer often must pay the bank a relatively large fee, and this service might not be available to companies in developing countries.

A third alternative is for the exporter to purchase export credit insurance, in which an insurer makes a commitment to pay the exporter even if the importer defaults. Sometimes the "insurer" is a government agency, such as the Japanese Ministry of International Trade and Industry (MITI) or the United States Export-Import Bank. Other times, the insurer is a private insurance company. These large insurance companies have developed expertise in international credit analysis, and they can spread the risk over a large number of customers. These advantages allow them to offer credit insurance at rates that often make it less costly than either letters of credit or bankers' acceptances. In fact, export credit insurance has been so success-ful that it has virtually killed the market for bankers' acceptances and has become the primary method companies use to manage the credit risk of international sales.

27.13c Inventory Management

As with most other aspects of finance, inventory management for a firm in a multinational setting is similar to but more complex than for a purely domestic firm. First, there is the matter of the physical location of inventories. For example, where should ExxonMobil keep its stockpiles of crude oil and refined products? It has refineries and marketing centers located worldwide, and one alternative is to keep items concentrated in a few strategic spots from which they can then be shipped as needs arise. Such a strategy might minimize the total amount of inventories needed and thus might minimize the investment in inventories. Note, though, that consideration will have to be given to potential delays in getting goods from central storage locations to user locations all around the world. Both working stocks and safety stocks would have to be maintained at each user location as well as at the strategic storage centers. Problems like the Iraqi occupation of Kuwait in 1990 and the subsequent trade embargo, which brought with it the potential for a shutdown of production of about 25% of the world's oil supply, complicate matters further.

Exchange rates also influence inventory policy. If a local currency—say, the Danish krone—were expected to rise in value against the dollar, then a U.S. company operating in Denmark would want to increase stocks of local products before the rise in the krone, and vice versa if the krone were expected to fall.

Another factor that must be considered is the possibility of import or export quotas or tariffs. For example, Apple Computer Company was buying certain memory chips from Japanese suppliers at a bargain price. Then U.S. chipmakers accused the Japanese of dumping chips in the U.S. market at prices below cost, and they sought to force the Japanese to raise their prices.[7] This led Apple to increase its chip inventory. Then computer sales slacked off, and Apple ended up with an oversupply of obsolete computer chips. As a result, Apple's profits were hurt and its stock price fell, demonstrating once more the importance of careful inventory management.

As mentioned earlier, another danger in certain countries is the threat of expropriation. If that threat is large, then inventory holdings will be minimized and goods will be brought in only as needed. Similarly, if the operation involves extraction of raw materials such as oil or bauxite, processing plants may be moved offshore rather than located close to the production site.

Taxes have two effects on multinational inventory management. First, countries often impose property taxes on assets, including inventories; when this is done, the tax is based on holdings as of a specific date, such as January 1 or March 1. Such rules make it advantageous for a multinational firm (1) to schedule production so that inventories are low on the assessment date, and (2) if assessment dates vary among countries in a region, to hold safety stocks in different countries at different times during the year.

---

7. The term "dumping" warrants explanation, because the practice can be so important in international markets. Suppose Japanese chipmakers have excess capacity. A particular chip has a variable cost of $25, and its "fully allocated cost," which is the $25 plus total fixed cost per unit of output, is $40. Now suppose the Japanese firm can sell chips in the United States at $35 per unit, but if it charges $40 then it won't make any sales because U.S. chipmakers sell for $35.50. If the Japanese firm sells at $35, it will cover variable costs plus make a contribution to fixed overhead, so selling at $35 makes sense. Continuing, if the Japanese firm can sell in Japan at $40 but U.S. firms are excluded from Japanese markets by import duties or other barriers, then the Japanese will have a huge advantage over U.S. manufacturers. This practice of selling goods at lower prices in foreign markets than at home is called "dumping." U.S. firms are required by antitrust laws to offer the same price to all customers and, therefore, cannot engage in dumping.

Finally, multinational firms may consider the possibility of at-sea storage. Oil, chemical, grain, and other companies that deal in a bulk commodity that must be stored in some type of tank can often buy tankers at a cost not much greater—or perhaps even less, considering land cost—than land-based facilities. Loaded tankers can then be kept at sea or at anchor in some strategic location. This eliminates the danger of expropriation, minimizes the property tax problem, and maximizes flexibility with regard to shipping to areas where needs are greatest or prices highest.

This discussion has only scratched the surface of inventory management in the multinational corporation—the task is much more complex than for a purely domestic firm. However, the greater the degree of complexity, the greater the rewards from superior performance, so if you are willing to take challenges along with potentially high rewards then look to the international arena.

Self Test

What are some factors that make cash management more complicated in a multinational corporation than in a purely domestic corporation?

Why is granting credit riskier in an international context?

Why is inventory management especially important for a multinational firm?

Summary

Multinational companies have more opportunities but also face different risks than do companies that operate only in their home market. This chapter discussed many of the key trends affecting the global markets today, and it described the most important differences between multinational and domestic financial management. The key concepts are listed below.

- **International operations** are becoming increasingly important to individual firms and to the national economy. A multinational, transnational, or **global corporation** is a firm that operates in an integrated fashion in a number of countries.
- Companies "go global" for these reasons: (1) to expand their markets, (2) to obtain raw materials, (3) to seek new technology, (4) to lower production costs, (5) to avoid trade barriers, and (6) to diversify.
- Several major factors distinguish financial management as practiced by domestic firms from that practiced by multinational corporations: (1) different currency denominations, (2) different economic and legal structures, (3) languages, (4) cultural differences, (5) role of governments, and (6) political risk.
- When discussing **exchange rates,** the number of U.S. dollars required to purchase one unit of a foreign currency is called a **direct quotation,** while the number of units of foreign currency that can be purchased for one U.S. dollar is an **indirect quotation.**

- **Exchange rate fluctuations** make it difficult to estimate the dollars that overseas operations will produce.
- Prior to August 1971, the world was on a **fixed exchange rate system** whereby the U.S. dollar was linked to gold and other currencies were then tied to the dollar. After August 1971, the world monetary system changed to a **floating system** under which major world currency rates float with market forces, largely unrestricted by governmental intervention. The central bank of each country does operate in the foreign exchange market, buying and selling currencies to smooth out exchange rate fluctuations, but only to a limited extent.
- **Pegged exchange rates** occur when a country establishes a fixed exchange rate with a major currency. Consequently, the values of pegged currencies move together over time.
- A **convertible currency** is one that may be readily exchanged for other currencies.
- **Spot rates** are the rates paid for delivery of currency "on the spot," whereas the **forward exchange rate** is the rate paid for delivery at some agreed-upon future date—usually 30, 90, or 180 days from the day the transaction is negotiated. The forward rate can be at either a **premium** or a **discount** to the spot rate.
- **Interest rate parity** holds that investors should expect to earn the same risk-free return in all countries after adjusting for exchange rates.
- **Purchasing power parity**, sometimes referred to as the *law of one price,* implies that the level of exchange rates adjusts so that identical goods cost the same in different countries.
- Granting credit is more risky in an international context because, in addition to the normal risks of default, the multinational firm must worry about **exchange rate changes** between the time a sale is made and the time a receivable is collected.
- Credit policy is important for a multinational firm for two reasons: (1) Much trade is with less-developed nations, and in such situations granting credit is a necessary condition for doing business. (2) The governments of nations such as Japan, whose economic health depends on exports, often help their firms compete by granting credit to foreign customers.
- Foreign investments are similar to domestic investments, but political risk and exchange rate risk must be considered. **Political risk** is the risk that the foreign government will take some action that will decrease the value of the investment; **exchange rate risk** is the risk of losses due to fluctuations in the value of the dollar relative to the values of foreign currencies.
- Investments in **international capital projects** expose firms to exchange rate risk and political risk. The relevant cash flows in international capital budgeting are the dollars that can be **repatriated** to the parent company.
- **Eurodollars** are U.S. dollars deposited in banks outside the United States. Interest rates on Eurodollars are tied to **LIBOR**, the **London Interbank Offered Rate**.
- U.S. firms often find that they can raise long-term capital at a lower cost outside the United States by selling bonds in the **international capital markets**. International bonds may be either **foreign bonds**, which are exactly like regular domestic bonds except that the issuer is a foreign company, or **Eurobonds**, which are bonds sold in a foreign country but denominated in the currency of the issuing company's home country.

Questions

27-1 Define each of the following terms:
   a. Multinational corporation
   b. Exchange rate; fixed exchange rate system; floating exchange rates
   c. Trade deficit; devaluation; revaluation
   d. Exchange rate risk; convertible currency; pegged exchange rates
   e. Interest rate parity; purchasing power parity
   f. Spot rate; forward exchange rate; discount on forward rate; premium on forward rate
   g. Repatriation of earnings; political risk
   h. Eurodollar; Eurobond; international bond; foreign bond
   i. The euro

27-2 Under the fixed exchange rate system, what was the currency against which all other currency values were defined? Why?

27-3 Exchange rates fluctuate under both the fixed exchange rate and floating exchange rate systems. What, then, is the difference between the two systems?

27-4 If the Swiss franc depreciates against the U.S. dollar, can a dollar buy more or fewer Swiss francs as a result?

27-5 If the United States imports more goods from abroad than it exports, then foreigners will tend to have a surplus of U.S. dollars. What will this do to the value of the dollar with respect to foreign currencies? What is the corresponding effect on foreign investments in the United States?

27-6 Why do U.S. corporations build manufacturing plants abroad when they could build them at home?

27-7 Should firms require higher rates of return on foreign projects than on identical projects located at home? Explain.

27-8 What is a Eurodollar? If a French citizen deposits $10,000 in Chase Bank in New York, have Eurodollars been created? What if the deposit is made in Barclays Bank in London? Chase's Paris branch? Does the existence of the Eurodollar market make the Federal Reserve's job of controlling U.S. interest rates easier or more difficult? Explain.

27-9 Does interest rate parity imply that interest rates are the same in all countries?

27-10 Why might purchasing power parity fail to hold?

Problems   Answers Appear in Appendix B

Easy Problems 1–4

27-1 **Cross Rates** At today's spot exchange rates 1 U.S. dollar can be exchanged for 9 Mexican pesos or for 111.23 Japanese yen. You have pesos that you would like to exchange for yen. What is the cross rate between the yen and the peso; that is, how many yen would you receive for every peso exchanged?

27-2 **Interest Rate Parity** The nominal yield on 6-month T-bills is 7%, while default-free Japanese bonds that mature in 6 months have a nominal rate of 5.5%. In the spot exchange market, 1 yen equals $0.009. If interest rate parity holds, what is the 6-month forward exchange rate?

27-3 **Purchasing Power Parity** A computer costs $500 in the United States. The same model costs 550 euros in France. If purchasing power parity holds, what is the spot exchange rate between the euro and the dollar?

27-4 **Exchange Rate** If euros sell for $1.50 (U.S.) per euro, what should dollars sell for in euros per dollar?

Intermediate Problems 5–8

27-5 **Currency Appreciation** Suppose that 1 Swiss franc could be purchased in the foreign exchange market for 60 U.S. cents today. If the franc appreciated 10% tomorrow against the dollar, how many francs would a dollar buy tomorrow?

27-6 **Cross Rates** Suppose the exchange rate between U.S. dollars and the Swiss franc is SFr1.6 = $1 and the exchange rate between the dollar and the British pound is £1 = $1.50. What then is the cross rate between francs and pounds?

27-7 **Interest Rate Parity** Assume that interest rate parity holds. In both the spot market and the 90-day forward market, 1 Japanese yen equals 0.0086 dollar. In Japan, 90-day risk-free securities yield 4.6%. What is the yield on 90-day risk-free securities in the United States?

27-8 **Purchasing Power Parity** In the spot market, 7.8 pesos can be exchanged for 1 U.S. dollar. A pair of headphones costs $15 in the United States. If purchasing power parity holds, what should be the price of the same headphones in Mexico?

Challenging Problems 9–14

27-9 **Exchange Gains and Losses** Your Boston-headquartered manufacturing company, Wruck Enterprises, obtained a 50 million peso loan from a Mexico City bank last month to fund the expansion of your Monterrey, Mexico plant. When you took out the loan the exchange rate was 10 U.S. cents per peso, but since then, the exchange rate has dropped to 9 U.S. cents per peso. Has Wruck Enterprises made a gain or a loss due to the exchange rate change, and how much? Note that your shareholders live in the United States.

27-10 **Results of Exchange Rate Changes** In 1983 the Japanese yen-U.S. dollar exchange rate was 245 yen per dollar, and the dollar cost of a compact Japanese-manufactured car was $8,000. Thirty years later, the exchange rate is 80 yen per dollar. Assume there has been no inflation in the yen cost of an automobile so that all price changes are due to exchange rate changes.
   a. Has the price (in dollars) of the automobile increased or decreased since 1983 because of changes in the exchange rate?
   b. What would the dollar price of the car be, assuming the car's price changes only with exchange rates?

27-11 **Spot and Forward Rates** Boisjoly Watch Imports has agreed to purchase 15,000 Swiss watches for 1 million francs at today's spot rate. The firm's financial manager, James Desreumaux, has noted the following current spot and forward rates:

	U.S. Dollar/Franc	Franc/U.S. Dollar
Spot	1.6590	0.6028
30-day forward	1.6540	0.6046
90-day forward	1.6460	0.6075
180-day forward	1.6400	0.6098

On the same day, Desreumaux agrees to purchase 15,000 more watches in 3 months at the same price of 1 million francs.

    a. What is the price of the watches, in U.S. dollars, if purchased at today's spot rate?

    b. What is the cost, in dollars, of the second 15,000 batch if payment is made in 90 days and the spot rate at that time equals today's 90-day forward rate?

    c. If the exchange rate for the Swiss franc is 0.50 to $1 in 90 days, how much will Desreumaux have to pay (in dollars) for the watches?

27-12 Interest Rate Parity Assume that interest rate parity holds and that 90-day risk-free securities yield 5% in the United States and 5.3% in Germany. In the spot market, 1 euro equals $1.40.

    a. Is the 90-day forward rate trading at a premium or a discount relative to the spot rate?

    b. What is the 90-day forward rate?

27-13 Foreign Investment Analysis Chapman, Inc.'s Mexican subsidiary, V. Gomez Corporation, is expected to pay to Chapman 50 pesos in dividends this year after all foreign and U.S. taxes have been subtracted. The exchange rate at the end of the year is expected to be $0.10, and because of the differential inflation rates in the United States and Mexico, the peso is expected to depreciate against the dollar at a rate of 4% a year, indefinitely. The peso-denominated dividend is expected to grow at a rate of 8% a year indefinitely. Chapman owns 10 million shares of V. Gomez. What is the present value of the dividend stream, in dollars, assuming V. Gomez's cost of equity is 13%?

27-14 Foreign Capital Budgeting The South Korean multinational manufacturing firm, Nam Sung Industries, is debating whether to invest in a 2-year project in the United States. The project's expected dollar cash flows consist of an initial investment of $1 million with cash inflows of $700,000 in Year 1 and $600,000 in Year 2. The risk-adjusted cost of capital for this project is 13%. The current exchange rate is 1,050 won per U.S. dollar. Risk-free interest rates in the United States and S. Korea are:

	1-Year	2-Year
United States	4.0%	4.25%
S. Korea	3.0%	3.25%

    a. If this project were instead undertaken by a similar U.S.-based company with the same risk-adjusted cost of capital, what would be the net present value and rate of return generated by this project?

    b. What is the expected forward exchange rate 1 year from now and 2 years from now?

    c. If Nam Sung undertakes the project, what is the net present value and rate of return of the project for Nam Sung?

Spreadsheet Problem

27-15 Build a Model: Multinational Financial Management Start with the partial model in the file *Ch27 P15 Build a Model.xls* on the textbook's Web site. Mark Collins, luthier and businessman, builds and sells custom-made acoustic and electric stringed instruments. Although located in Maryville, Tennessee, he purchases raw materials from around the globe. For example, his top-of-the line acoustic guitar with onboard electronics, the MC-28, is constructed from rosewood and mahogany imported from a distributor in Mexico, spruce harvested in and imported from Canada, and ebony and the electronics imported from a Japanese distributor. Other parts are obtained in the United States. When broken down on a per-guitar basis, the component and finishing costs are as follows:

Rosewood and mahogany: 2,750 Mexican pesos
Spruce: 200 Canadian dollars
Ebony and electronics: 12,400 Japanese yen
Other parts plus woodworking labor: $600

Collins sells some of this model in the United States, but the majority of the units are sold in England, where he has developed a loyal following and the guitars have become something of a cult symbol. There, his guitars fetch £1,600, excluding shipping. Mark is concerned about the effect of exchange rates on his materials costs and profit.

You will find Tables 27-1, 27-2, and 27-3 useful for this problem.

a. How much, in dollars, does it cost for Mark Collins to produce his MC-28? What is the dollar sale price of the MC-28 sold in England?

b. What is the dollar profit that Collins makes on the sale of the MC-28? What is the percentage profit?

c. If the U.S. dollar were to weaken by 10% against all foreign currencies, what would be the dollar profit for the MC-28?

d. If the U.S. dollar were to weaken by 10% only against the pound and remained constant relative to all other foreign currencies, what would be the dollar and percentage profits for the MC-28?

e. Using the forward exchange information from Table 27-3, calculate the return on 90-day securities in England if the rate of return on 90-day securities in the United States is 3.9%.

f. Assuming that purchasing power parity (PPP) holds, what would be the sale price of the MC-28 if it were sold in France rather than in England?

MINI CASE

With the growth in demand for exotic foods, Possum Products's CEO Michael Munger is considering expanding the geographic footprint of its line of dried and smoked low-fat opossum, ostrich, and venison jerky snack packs. Historically, jerky products have performed well in the southern United States, but there are indications of a growing demand for these unusual delicacies in Europe. Munger recognizes that the expansion carries some risk—Europeans may not be as accepting of

opossum jerky as initial research suggests—so the expansion will proceed in steps. The first step will be to set up sales subsidiaries in France and Sweden (the two countries with the highest indicated demand), and the second is to set up a production plant in France with the ultimate goal of product distribution throughout Europe.

Possum Products's CFO, Kevin Uram, although enthusiastic about the plan, is nonetheless concerned about how an international expansion and the additional risk that entails will affect the firm's financial management process. He has asked you, the firm's most recently hired financial analyst, to develop a 1-hour tutorial package that explains the basics of multinational financial management. The tutorial will be presented at the next board of directors meeting. To get you started, Uram has supplied you with the following list of questions.

a. What is a multinational corporation? Why do firms expand into other countries?

b. What are the six major factors that distinguish multinational financial management from financial management as practiced by a purely domestic firm?

c. Consider the following illustrative exchange rates.

**U.S. Dollars Required to Buy
1 Unit of Foreign Currency**

Euro	1.2500
Swedish krona	0.1481

(1) Are these currency prices direct quotations or indirect quotations?

(2) Calculate the indirect quotations for euros and kronor (the plural of krona is kronor).

(3) What is a cross rate? Calculate the two cross rates between euros and kronor.

(4) Assume Possum Products can produce a package of jerky and ship it to France for $1.75. If the firm wants a 50% markup on the product, what should the jerky sell for in France?

(5) Now assume that Possum Products begins producing the same package of jerky in France. The product costs 2 euros to produce and ship to Sweden, where it can be sold for 20 kronor. What is the dollar profit on the sale?

(6) What is exchange rate risk?

d. Briefly describe the current international monetary system. How does the current system differ from the system that was in place prior to August 1971?

e. What is a convertible currency? What problems arise when a multinational company operates in a country whose currency is not convertible?

f. What is the difference between spot rates and forward rates? When is the forward rate at a premium to the spot rate? At a discount?

g. What is interest rate parity? Currently, you can exchange 1 euro for 1.25 dollars in the 180-day forward market, and the risk-free rate on 180-day securities is 6% in the United States and 4% in France. Does interest rate parity hold? If not, which securities offer the highest expected return?

h. What is purchasing power parity? If a package of jerky costs $2 in the United States and purchasing power parity holds, what should be the price of the jerky package in France?

i. What effect does relative inflation have on interest rates and exchange rates?

j. Briefly discuss the international capital markets.

k. To what extent do average capital structures vary across different countries?

l. Briefly describe special problems that occur in multinational capital budgeting, and describe the process for evaluating a foreign project. Now consider the following project: A U.S. company has the opportunity to lease a manufacturing facility in Japan for 2 years. The company must spend ¥1 billion initially to refurbish the plant. The expected net cash flows from the plant for the next 2 years, in millions, are $CF_1 = ¥500$ and $CF_2 = ¥800$. A similar project in the United States would have a risk-adjusted cost of capital of 10%. In the United States, a 1-year government bond pays 2% interest and a 2-year bond pays 2.8%. In Japan, a 1-year bond pays 0.05% and a 2-year bond pays 0.26%. What is the project's NPV?

m. Briefly discuss special factors associated with the following areas of multinational working capital management:

(1) Cash management

(2) Credit management

(3) Inventory management

Selected Additional Case

The following case from TextChoice, Cengage Learning's online case library, covers many of the concepts discussed in this chapter and is available at **www.textchoice2.com/casenet.**

Klein-Brigham Series:
Case 18, "Alaska Oil Corporation."

Appendix A

Values of the Areas under the Standard Normal Distribution Function

TABLE A-1	Values of the Areas under the Standard Normal Distribution Function								
z	0.00	0.01	0.02	0.03	0.04	0.05	0.06	0.07	0.08	0.09
0.0	.0000	.0040	.0080	.0120	.0160	.0199	.0239	.0279	.0319	.0359
0.1	.0398	.0438	.0478	.0517	.0557	.0596	.0636	.0675	.0714	.0753
0.2	.0793	.0832	.0871	.0910	.0948	.0987	.1026	.1064	.1103	.1141
0.3	.1179	.1217	.1255	.1293	.1331	.1368	.1406	.1443	.1480	.1517
0.4	.1554	.1591	.1628	.1664	.1700	.1736	.1772	.1808	.1844	.1879
0.5	.1915	.1950	.1985	.2019	.2054	.2088	.2123	.2157	.2190	.2224
0.6	.2257	.2291	.2324	.2357	.2389	.2422	.2454	.2486	.2517	.2549
0.7	.2580	.2611	.2642	.2673	.2704	.2734	.2764	.2794	.2823	.2852
0.8	.2881	.2910	.2939	.2967	.2995	.3023	.3051	.3078	.3106	.3133
0.9	.3159	.3186	.3212	.3238	.3264	.3289	.3315	.3340	.3365	.3389
1.0	.3413	.3438	.3461	.3485	.3508	.3531	.3554	.3577	.3599	.3621
1.1	.3643	.3665	.3686	.3708	.3729	.3749	.3770	.3790	.3810	.3830
1.2	.3849	.3869	.3888	.3907	.3925	.3944	.3962	.3980	.3997	.4015
1.3	.4032	.4049	.4066	.4082	.4099	.4115	.4131	.4147	.4162	.4177
1.4	.4192	.4207	.4222	.4236	.4251	.4265	.4279	.4292	.4306	.4319
1.5	.4332	.4345	.4357	.4370	.4382	.4394	.4406	.4418	.4429	.4441
1.6	.4452	.4463	.4474	.4484	.4495	.4505	.4515	.4525	.4535	.4545
1.7	.4554	.4564	.4573	.4582	.4591	.4599	.4608	.4616	.4625	.4633
1.8	.4641	.4649	.4656	.4664	.4671	.4678	.4686	.4693	.4699	.4706
1.9	.4713	.4719	.4726	.4732	.4738	.4744	.4750	.4756	.4761	.4767
2.0	.4773	.4778	.4783	.4788	.4793	.4798	.4803	.4808	.4812	.4817
2.1	.4821	.4826	.4830	.4834	.4838	.4842	.4846	.4850	.4854	.4857
2.2	.4861	.4864	.4868	.4871	.4875	.4878	.4881	.4884	.4887	.4890
2.3	.4893	.4896	.4898	.4901	.4904	.4906	.4909	.4911	.4913	.4916
2.4	.4918	.4920	.4922	.4925	.4927	.4929	.4931	.4932	.4934	.4936
2.5	.4938	.4940	.4941	.4943	.4945	.4946	.4948	.4949	.4951	.4952
2.6	.4953	.4955	.4956	.4957	.4959	.4960	.4961	.4962	.4963	.4964
2.7	.4965	.4966	.4967	.4968	.4969	.4970	.4971	.4972	.4973	.4974
2.8	.4974	.4975	.4976	.4977	.4977	.4978	.4979	.4979	.4980	.4981
2.9	.4981	.4982	.4982	.4982	.4984	.4984	.4985	.4985	.4986	.4986
3.0	.4987	.4987	.4987	.4988	.4988	.4989	.4989	.4989	.4990	.4990

Answers to End-of-Chapter Problems

We present here some intermediate steps and final answers to selected end-of-chapter problems. Please note that your answer may differ slightly from ours because of rounding differences. Also, although we hope not, some of the problems may have more than one correct solution, depending on what assumptions are made when working the problem. Finally, many of the problems involve some verbal discussion as well as numerical calculations; this verbal material is not presented here.

2-1 $b = 1.08$.

2-2 $r_s = 10.40\%$.

2-3 $r_M = 12\%$; $r_{sB} = 16.9\%$.

2-4 $\hat{r} = 11.40\%$; $\sigma = 26.69\%$;
$CV = 2.34$.

2-5 a. $\hat{r}_M = 13.5\%$; $\hat{r}_j = 11.6\%$.
b. $\sigma_M = 3.85\%$; $\sigma_j = 6.22\%$.
c. $CV_M = 0.29$; $CV_j = 0.54$.

2-6 a. $b_A = 1.40$.
b. $r_A = 15\%$.

2-7 a. $r_i = 14.8\%$.
b. (1) $r_M = 13\%$; $r_i = 15.8\%$.
(2) $r_M = 11\%$; $r_i = 13.8\%$.
c. (1) $r_i = 17.6\%$.
(2) $r_i = 13.4\%$.

2-8 $b_N = 1.25$.

2-9 $b_p = 0.7625$; $r_p = 12.1\%$.

2-10 $b_N = 1.1250$.

2-11 4.5%.

2-12 a. $\bar{r}_A = 11.80\%$; $\bar{r}_B = 11.80\%$.
b. $\bar{r}_p = 11.80\%$.
c. $\sigma_A = 25.3\%$; $\sigma_B = 24.3\%$;
$\sigma_p = 16.3\%$.

d. $CV_A = 2.14$; $CV_B = 2.06$;
$CV_p = 1.38$.

2-13 a. $b_X = 1.3471$; $b_Y = 0.6508$.
b. $r_X = 12.7355\%$; $r_Y = 9.254\%$.
c. $r_p = 12.04\%$.

3-1 1.4.

3-2 12%.

3-3 15.96%.

3-4 16.2%; 45.9%.

3-5 a. $r_i = r_{RF} + (r_M - r_{RF})\dfrac{p_{iM}\sigma_i}{\sigma_M}$

3-6 a. 14.15%.
b. 16.45%.

3-7 a. $b = 0.56$.
b. X: 10.6%; 13.1%.
M: 12.1%; 22.6%.
c. 8.6%.

3-8 a. $b = 0.62$.

4-1 928.39.

4-2 12.48%.

4-3 8.55%.

4-4 7%; 7.33%.

4-5 2.5%.

4-6 0.3%.

4-7 $1,085.80$.

4-8 YTM $= 6.62\%$; YTC $= 6.49\%$.

4-9 a. 5%: $V_L = 1,518.98$;
$V_S = 1,047.62$.

8%: $V_L = \$1,171.19$;

$V_S = \$1,018.52$.

12%: $V_L = \$863.78$;

$V_S = \$982.14$.

4-10 a. YTM at $829 = 13.98\%$;

YTM at $1,104 = 6.50\%$.

4-11 14.82%.

4-12 a. 10.37%.

b. 10.91%.

c. −0.54%.

d. 10.15%.

4-13 8.65%.

4-14 10.78%.

4-15 YTC = 6.47%.

4-16 a. 10-year, 10% coupon = 6.75%;

10-year zero = 9.75%;

5-year zero = 4.76%;

30-year zero = 32.19%;

$100 perpetuity = 14.29%.

4-17 $C_0 = \$1,012.79$; $Z_0 = \$693.04$;

$C_1 = \$1,010.02$; $Z_1 = \$759.57$;

$C_2 = \$1,006.98$; $Z_2 = \$832.49$;

$C_3 = \$1,003.65$; $Z_3 = \$912.41$;

$C_4 = \$1,000.00$; $Z_4 = \$1,000.00$.

4-18 5.8%.

4-19 1.5%.

4-20 6.0%.

4-21 a. $1,251.22.

b. $898.94.

4-22 a. 8.02%.

b. 7.59%.

4-23 a. $r_1 = 9.20\%$; $r_5 = 7.20\%$.

5-1 $D_1 = \$1.5750$; $D_3 = \$1.7364$;

$D_5 = \$2.1011$.

5-2 $\hat{P}_0 = \$21.43$.

5-3 $\hat{P}_1 = \$24.20$; $\hat{r}s = 16.00\%$.

5-4 $r_{ps} = 10\%$.

5-5 $50.50.

5-6 $g = 9\%$.

5-7 $\hat{P}_3 = \$43.08$.

5-8 a. 11.67%.

b. 8.75%.

c. 7.00%.

d. 5.00%.

5-9 $32.00.

5-10 a. $r_C = 10.6\%$; $r_D = 7\%$.

5-11 $25.03.

5-12 $\hat{P}_0 = \$10.76$.

5-13 a. $125.

b. $83.33.

5-14 a. 7%.

b. 5%.

c. 12%.

5-15 a. (1) $15.83.

(2) $23.08.

b. (1) Undefined.

5-16 a. $\hat{P}_0 = \$21.43$.

b. $\hat{P}_0 = \$26.47$.

c. $\hat{P}_0 = \$32.14$.

d. $\hat{P}_0 = \$40.54$.

5-17 b. PV = $3.97.

d. $22.71.

5-18 a. $D_5 = \$3.52$.

b. $\hat{P}_0 = \$39.42$.

c. $D_1/P_0 = 5.10\%$;

$D_6/P_5 = 7.00\%$.

5-19 $\hat{P}_0 = \$78.35$.

6-1 $5; $2.

6-2 $27.00; $37.00.

6-3 $1.67.

6-4 $3.70.

6-5 $1.90.

6-6 $2.39.

6-7 $1.91.

7-1 5.8%.

7-2 25%.

7-3 $3,000,000.

7-4 $2,000,000.

7-5 $3,600,000.

7-6 $25,000,000.

7-7   Tax = $107,855;

      NI = $222,145;

      Marginal tax rate = 39%;

      Average tax rate = 33.8%.

7-8   a. Tax = $3,575,000.

      b. Tax = $350,000.

      c. Tax = $105,000.

7-9   AT&T bond = 4.875%;

      AT&T preferred stock = 5.37%;

      Florida bond = 5%.

7-10   NI = $450,000;

      NCF = $650,000.

7-11   a. $2,400,000.

      b. NI = $0;

        NCF = $3,000,000.

      c. NI = $1,350,000;

        NCF = $2,100,000.

7-12   a. NOPAT = $756 million.

      b. $NOWC_{11}$ = $3.0 billion;

        $NOWC_{12}$ = $3.3 billion.

      c. Op. capital$_{11}$ = $6.5 billion;

        Op. capital$_{12}$ = $7.15 billion.

      d. FCF = $106 million.

      e. ROIC = 10.57%.

      f. Answers in millions:

        A-T int. = $72.

        Inc. in debt = −$284.

        Div. = $220.

        Rep. stock = $88.

        Purch. ST inv. = $10.

7-13   Refund = $120,000.

      Future taxes = $0; $0; $40,000; $60,000;

             $60,000.

8-1   AR = $400,000.

8-2   D/A = 60%.

8-3   M/B = 10.

8-4   P/E = 16.0.

8-5   ROE = 12%.

8-6   S/TA = 2.4; TA/E = 1.67.

8-7   CL = $2,000,000;

      Inv = $1,000,000.

8-8   Net profit margin = 3.33%;

      D/A = 42.9%.

8-9 $262,500; 1.19.

8-10   TIE = 4.13.

8-11   AP = $110,000;

      Inv. = $120,000;

      FA = $192,000.

8-12   Sales = $2,592,000;

      DSO = 36.33 days.

8-13   a. Current ratio = 2.01;

        DSO = 77 days;

        TA turnover = 1.75;

        Debt ratio = 59.0%.

8-14   a. Quick ratio = 0.8;

        DSO = 37 days;

        ROE = 13.1%;

        Debt ratio = 54.8%.

9-1   AFN = $283,800.

9-2   AFN = $583,800.

9-3   AFN = $63,000.

9-4   ΔS = $202,312.

9-5   a. $590,000; $1,150,000.

      b. $238,563.

9-6   AFN = $360.

9-7   a. $13.44 million.

      b. 6.38%.

      c. Notes payable = $31.44 million.

9-8   a. Total assets = $33,534;

        AFN = $2,128.

      b. Notes payable = $4,228.

9-9   a. AFN = $128,783.

      b. Notes payable = $284,783.

10-1 a. 13%.

 b. 10.4%.

 c. 8.45%.

10-2 5.2%.

10-3 9%.

10-4 5.41%.

10-5 13.33%.

10-6 10.4%.

10-7 9.17%.

10-8 13%.

10-9 7.2%.

10-10 a. 16.3%.

 b. 15.4%.

 c. 16%.

10-11 a. 8%.

 b. $2.81.

 c. 15.81%.

10-12 a. g = 3%.

 b. EPS_1 = $5.562.

10-13 16.1%.

10-14 $(1 - T)r_d$ = 5.57%.

10-15 a. $15,000,000.

 b. 8.4%.

10-16 Short-term debt = 11.14%;

 Long-term debt = 22.03%;

 Common equity = 66.83%.

10-17 $w_{d(Short)}$ = 0%; $w_{d(Long)}$ = 20%;

 w_{ps} = 4%; w_s = 76%;

 r_d(After-tax) = 7.2%;

 r_{ps} = 11.6%; r_s ≈ 17.5%.

11-1 FCF = $37.0.

11-2 V_{op} = $6,000,000.

11-3 V_{op} at 2014 = $15,000.

11-4 V_{op} = $160,000,000;

 MVA = −$40,000,000.

11-5 $259,375,000.

11-6 a. HV_2 = $2,700,000.

 b. $2,303,571.43.

11-7 a. $713.33.

 b. $527.89.

 c. $43.79.

11-8 $416 million.

11-9 $46.90.

11-10 a. $34.96 million.

 b. $741.152 million.

 c. $699.20 million.

 d. $749.10 million.

 e. $50.34.

12-1 NPV = $2,409.77.

12-2 IRR = 12.84%.

12-3 MIRR = 11.93%.

12-4 PI = 1.06.

12-5 4.44 years.

12-6 6.44 years.

12-7 5%: NPV_A = $16,108,952;

 NPV_B = $18,300,939.

 10%: NPV_A = $12,836,213;

 NPV_B = $15,954,170.

 15%: NPV_A = $10,059,587;

 NPV_B = $13,897,838.

12-8 NPV_T = $409; IRR_T = 15%;

 $MIRR_T$ = 14.54%; Accept.

 NPV_P = $3,318; IRR_P = 20%;

 $MIRR_P$ = 17.19%; Accept.

12-9 NPV_E = $3,861; IRR_E = 18%;

 NPV_G = $3,057; IRR_G = 18%;

 Purchase electric-powered forklift

 because it has a higher NPV.

12-10 NPV_S = $814.33; NPV_L = $1,675.34;

 IRR_S = 15.24%; IRR_L = 14.67%;

 $MIRR_S$ = 13.77%; $MIRR_L$ = 13.46%;

 PI_S = 1.081; PI_L = 1.067.

12-11 $MIRR_X$ = 17.49%;

 $MIRR_Y$ = 18.39%.

12-12 a. NPV = $136,578;

 IRR = 19.22%.

12-13   b. IRR_A = 20.7%;

   IRR_B = 27.9%.

   c. 10%: NPV_A = \$478.83;

   NPV_B = \$373.49.

   17%: NPV_A = \$133.76;

   NPV_B = \$193.46.

   d. (1) $MIRR_A$ = 14.91%;

   $MIRR_B$ = 17.37%.

   (2) $MIRR_A$ = 18.65%;

   $MIRR_B$ = 22.19%.

   e. Crossover rate = 14.07%.

12-14   a. \$0; −\$10,250,000; \$1,750,000.

   b. 16.07%.

12-15   a. NPV_A = \$18,108,510;

   NPV_B = \$13,946,117;

   IRR_A = 15.03%; IRR_B = 22.26%.

   b. NPV_Δ = \$4,162,393;

   IRR_Δ = 11.71%.

12-16   Extended NPV_A = \$12.76 million;

   Extended NPV_B = \$9.26 million.

   EAA_A = \$2.26 million;

   EAA_B = \$1.64 million.

12-17   Extended NPV_A = \$4.51 million.

   EAA_A = \$0.85 million;

   EAA_B = \$0.69 million.

12-18   NPV of 360-6 = \$22,256.

   Extended NPV of 190-3 = \$20,070.

   EAA of 360-6 = \$5,723.30;

   EAA of 190-3 = \$5,161.02.

12-19   d. 7.61%; 15.58%.

12-20   a. Undefined.

   b. NPV_C = −\$911,067;

   NPV_F = −\$838,834.

12-21   a. A = 2.67 years;

   B = 1.5 years.

   b. A = 3.07 years;

   B = 1.825 years.

   c. NPV_A = \$12,739,908;

   Choose both.

   d. NPV_A = \$18,243,813;

   Choose A.

   e. NPV_B = \$8,643,390;

   Choose B.

   f. 13.53%.

   g. $MIRR_A$ = 21.93%;

   $MIRR_B$ = 20.96%.

12-22   a. 3 years.

   b. No.

13-1   a. \$22,000,000.

   b. No.

   c. Charge it against project and add \$1.5 million to initial investment outlay.

13-2   \$7,000,000.

13-3   \$3,600,000.

13-4   NPV = \$6,746.78

13-5   a. Straight line: \$425,000 per year.

   MACRS: \$566,610; \$755,650; \$251,770; \$125,970.

   b. MACRS; \$27,043.62 higher.

13-6   a. −\$1,118,000.

   b. \$375,612; \$418,521; \$304,148.

   c. \$437,343.

   d. NPV = \$78,790; Purchase.

13-7   a. −\$89,000.

   b. \$26,332; \$30,113; \$20,035.

   c. \$24,519.

   d. NPV = −\$6,700; Don't purchase.

13-8   a. NPV = \$106,520.

13-9   NPV of replace = \$2,377.21.

13-10   NPV of replace = \$11,468.48.

13-11   E(NPV) = \$3 million;

   s_{NPV} = \$23.622 million;

   CV_{NPV} = 7.874.

13-12   a. NPV = \$15,732; IRR = 11.64%; MIRR = 10.88%; Payback = 3.75 years.

   b. \$65,770; −\$34,307.

   c. E(NPV) = \$13,042; σ_{NPV} = \$43,289; CV = 3.32.

13-13 a. −$87,625.

b. $31,574; $36,244; $23,795; $20,687; $4,575.

c. NPV = −$4,623.

13-14 a. −$529,750.

b. New depreciation: $155,000; $248,000; $148,000; $89,280; $89,280.

c. Net incremental cash flows: $143,000; $175,550; $140,830; $119,998; $203,872.

d. NPV = $30,059.

13-15 a. Expected CF_A = $6,750; Expected CF_B = $7,650; CV_A = 0.0703.

b. NPV_A = $10,036; NPV_B = $11,624.

13-16 a. E(IRR) ≈ 15.3%.

b. NPV = $38,589.

13-17 a. E(NPV) = $117,779.

b. σ_{NPV} = $445,060; CV_{NPV} = 3.78.

14-1 a. $1.074 million.

b. $2.96 million.

14-2 a. $4.6795 million.

b. $3.208 million.

14-3 a. −$19 million.

b. $9.0981 million.

14-4 a. −$2.113 million.

b. $1.973 million.

c. −$70,222.

d. $565,090.

e. $1.116 million.

14-5 a. $2,562.

b. E[NPV] = $9,786; Value of growth option = $7,224.

14-6 P = $18.646 million; X = $20 million; t = 1; r_{RF} = 0.08; σ^2 = 0.0687; V = $2.028 million.

14-7 P = $10.479 million; X = $9 million; t = 2; r_{RF} = 0.06; σ^2 = 0.0111; V = $2.514 million.

14-8 P = $18,646; X = $20,000; t = 2; V = $5,009.

15-1 20,000.

15-2 1.0.

15-3 3.6%.

15-4 $300 million.

15-5 $30.

15-6 40 million.

15-7 a. ΔProfit = $850,000; Return = 21.25% > r_s = 15%.

b. $Q_{BE,Old}$ = 40; $Q_{BE,New}$ = 45.45.

15-8 a. V = $3,348,214.

b. $16.74.

c. $1.84.

d. 10%.

15-9 30% debt: WACC = 11.14%; V = $101.023 million.

50% debt: WACC = 11.25%; V = $100 million.

70% debt: WACC = 11.94%; V = $94.255 million.

15-10 a. 0.870.

b. b = 1.218; r_s = 10.872%.

c. WACC = 8.683%; V = $103.188 million.

15-11 WACC at optimal debt level: 8.89%.

16-1 $500 million.

16-2 $821 million.

16-3 $620.68 million.

16-4 a. b_U = 1.13.

b. r_{sU} = 15.625%.

c. 16.62%; 18.04%; 20.23%.

d. 20.23%.

16-5 a. V_U = V_L = $20 million.

b. r_{sU} = 10%; r_{sL} = 15%.

c. S_L = $10 million.

d. $WACC_U$ = 10%; $WACC_L$ = 10%.

16-6 a. V_U = $12 million; V_L = $16 million.

b. r_{sU} = 10%; r_{sL} = 15%.

c. S_L = $6 million.

d. $WACC_U$ = 10%; $WACC_L$ = 7.5%.

16-7 a. V_U = $12 million.

b. V_L = $15.33 million.

c. $3.33 million versus $4 million.

d. V_L = $20 million; $0.

e. V_L = $16 million; $4 million.

f. V_L = $16 million; $4 million.

16-8 a. V_U = $12.5 million.

b. V_L = $16 million; r_{sL} = 15.7%.

c. V_L = $14.5 million; r_{sL} = 14.9%.

16-9 a. $V_U = V_L$ = $14,545,455.

b. At D = $6 million: r_{sL} = 14.51%; WACC = 11.0%.

c. V_U = $8,727,273; V_L = $11,127,273.

d. At D = $6 million: r_{sL} = 14.51%; WACC = 8.63%.

e. D = V = $14,545,455.

16-10 a. V = $3.29 million.

b. D = $1.71 million; Yield = 8.1%.

c. V = $3.23 million; D = $1.77 million; Yield = 6.3%.

17-1 Payout = 33.33%.

17-2 Payout = 20%.

17-3 Payout = 52%.

17-4 V_{op} = $175 million; n = 8.75 million.

17-5 P_0 = $80.

17-6 $6,900,000.

17-7 n = 4,000; EPS = $5.00; DPS = $1.50; P = $40.00.

17-8 D_0 = $4.25.

17-9 Payout = 17.89%.

17-10 a. (1) $2,808,000.

(2) $3,342,857.

(3) $7,855,000.

(4) Regular = $2,808,000;

Extra = $5,047,000.

17-11 a. $10,500,000.

b. DPS = $0.50; Payout = 4.55%.

c. $9,000,000.

d. No.

e. 40%.

f. $1,500,000.

g. $12,875,143.

17-12 a. $848 million.

b. $450 million.

c. $30.

d. 1 million; 14 million.

e. $420 million; $30.

18-1 a. $700,000.

b. $3,700,000.

c. −$2,300,000.

18-2 964,115 shares.

18-3 a. $18,545,783; $18,545.78 per share.

b. Abercrombe: D/A 30.43%; P/E 15.91; M/B 2.19; P/FCF 22.73; ROE 13.8%

c. No.

d. Price based on: Abercrombe P/E $21,199; Gunter P/E $16,701.

Price based on: Abercrombe M/B $16,406; Gunter M/B $16,768.

18-4 a. After-tax call cost = $2,640,000.

b. Flotation cost = $1,600,000.

c. $1,920,000; $768,000.

d. $3,472,000.

e. New tax savings = $16,000;

Lost tax savings = $19,200.

f. $360,000.

g. PV = $9,109,413.

h. $5,637,413.

18-5 a. NPV = $2,717,128.

19-1 a. (1) 50%.

(2) 60%.

(3) 50%.

19-2 Cost of owning = −$127;

Cost of leasing = −$128.

19-3 a. Energen: Debt/TA = 50%;

Hastings: Debt/TA = 33%.

b. TA = $200.

19-4 a. NAL = $108,147.

19-5 a. Cost of leasing = $637,702;

Cost of owning = $713,300.

20-1 $182.16.

20-2 20 shares.

20-3 a. (1) $0.

(2) $0.

(3) $5.

(4) $75.

b. 10%; $100.

20-4 Premium = 10%: $46.20;

Premium = 30%: $54.60.

20-5 a. 14.1%.

b. $12 million before tax.

c. $331.89.

d. Value as a straight bond = $699.25;
Value in conversion = $521.91.

f. Value as a straight bond = $1,000.00;
Value in conversion = $521.91.

20-6 b. Plan 1: 49%; Plan 2: 53%; Plan 3: 53%.

c. Plan 1: $0.59; Plan 2: $0.64; Plan 3: $0.88.

d. Plan 1: 19%; Plan 2: 19%; Plan 3: 50%.

20-7 a. Year = 7;

CV_7 = $1,210.422;

CF_7 = $1,290.422.

b. 10.2%.

21-1 $3,000,000.

21-2 AR = $59,500.

21-3 r_{NOM} = 75.26%; EAR = 109.84%.

21-4 EAR = 8.49%.

21-5 $7,500,000.

21-6 a. DSO = 38 days.

b. AR = $156,164.

c. AR = $141,781.

21-7 a. 73.74%.

b. 14.90%.

c. 32.25%.

d. 21.28%.

e. 29.80%.

21-8 a. 45.15%.

21-9 Nominal cost = 14.90%;

Effective cost = 15.89%.

21-10 14.91%.

21-11 a. 60 days.

b. $420,000.

c. 9.1.

21-12 a. 65.6 days.

b. (1) 2.577.

(2) 18.04%.

c. (1) 48.2 days.

(2) 2.78.

(3) 19.4%.

21-13 a. ROE_T = 11.75%;

ROE_M = 10.80%;

ROE_R = 9.16%.

21-14 a. Feb. surplus = $2,000.

b. $164,400.

21-15 a. $100,000.

c. (1) $300,000.

(2) Nominal cost = 37.24%;

Effective cost = 44.59%.

d. Nominal cost = 24.83%;

Effective cost = 27.86%.

21-16 a. 14.35%.

21-17 a. $300,000.

b. $2,000.

c. (1) $322,500.

(2) $26,875.

(3) 13.57%.

(4) 14.44%.

22-1 $233.56.

22-2 EAR = 21.60%.

22-3   a. 12%.

     b. 11.25%.

     c. 11.48%.

     d. 14.47%; Alternative b has the lowest interest rate.

22-4   a. 11.73%.

     b. 12.09%.

     c. 13.45%.

22-5 $\Delta NI = -\$3,381$.

22-6 $\Delta NI = +\$27,577$.

22-7   d. 8.3723%.

22-8   a. March: $146,000; June: $198,000.

     b. Q1: ADS = $3,000; DSO = 48.7 days.

       Q2: ADS = $4,500; DSO = 44.0 days.

       Cumulative: ADS = $3,750; DSO = 52.8 days.

     c. 0–30 days: 65%; 31–60 days: 35%.

     d. Receivables/Sales = 130%.

22-9   a. With discount = $83.33;

       Without discount = $250.

     b. With discount = $641.03;

       Without discount = $384.62.

     c. Nominal cost of trade credit = 18.18%.

       Effective cost of trade credit = 19.83%.

       Bank cost = 23.08%.

     d. Cash = $126.90; NP = $434.60.

22-10   a. (1) $27,500.

        (3) $25,833.

23-1   a. 3,000 bags.

     b. 4,000 bags.

     c. 2,500 bags.

     d. Every 12 days.

23-2   b. $22,500.

     c. 100 transfers per year.

24-1   Net payment = LIBOR + 0.2%.

24-2 $r_d = 7.01\%$.

24-3 $r_d = 5.96\%$.

24-4   Net to Carter = 9.95% fixed;

     Net to Brence = LIBOR + 3.05% floating.

24-5   a. Sell 105 contracts.

     b. Bond = −$1,414,552.69;

       Futures = $1,951,497.45;

       Net = +$536,944.76.

25-1   AP = $375,000; NP = $750,000; SD = $750,000; Stockholders = $343,750.

25-2   a. Total assets: $327 million.

     b. Income: $7 million.

     c. Before: $15.6 million;

       After: $13.0 million.

     d. Before: 35.7%;

       After: 64.2%.

25-3   a. $0.

     b. First mortgage holders: $300,000; Second mortgage holders: $100,000 plus $12,700 as a general claimant.

     c. Trustee's expenses: $50,000;

       Wages due: $30,000;

       Taxes due: $40,000.

     d. *Before subordination:*

       Accounts payable = $6,350;

       Notes payable = $22,860;

       Second mortgage = $12,700 + $100,000;

       Debentures = $25,400;

       Sub. debentures = $12,700.

       After subordination:

       Notes payable = $35,560;

       Sub. debentures = $0.

25-4   a. $0 for stockholders.

     b. AP = 24%; NP = 100%; WP = 100%; TP = 100%; Mortgage = 85%; Subordinated debentures = 9%; Trustee = 100%.

26-1 $P_0 = \$25.26$.

26-2 $P_0 = \$41.54$.

26-3 $25.26 to $41.54.

26-4   Value of equity = $46.30 million.

26-5 a. $V_{op\ Unlevered}$ = \$32.02 million;

   $V_{Tax\ shields}$ = \$11.50 million.

   b. V_{op} = \$43.52 million;

   max = \$33.52 million.

26-6 a. 10.96%.

   b. (All in millions) FCF_1 = \$23.12, TS_1 = \$14.00; FCF_3 = \$12.26, TS_3 = \$16.45; FCF_5 = \$23.83, TS_5 = \$18.90.

   c. HV_{TS} = \$510.68 million;

   HV_{UL} = \$643.89 million.

   d. Value of equity = \$508.57 million.

27-1 12.358 yen per peso.

27-2 f_t = \$0.00907.

27-3 1 euro = \$0.9091 or \$1 = 1.1 euros.

27-4 0.6667 euros per dollar.

27-5 1.5152 SFr.

27-6 2.4 Swiss francs per pound.

27-7 $r_{NOM-U.S.}$ = 4.6%.

27-8 117 pesos.

27-9 +\$500,000.

27-10 b. \$24,500.

27-11 a. \$1,659,000.

   b. \$1,646,000.

   c. \$2,000,000.

27-12 b. f_t = \$1.3990.

27-13 \$327,731,092.

27-14 a. \$89,357; 20%.

   b. 1,039.9 won per U.S. dollar and 1030.0 won per U.S. dollar.

   c. 78,150,661 won; 18.85%.

Selected Equations

Chapter 1

$$\text{Value} = \frac{FCF_1}{(1+WACC)^1} + \frac{FCF_2}{(1+WACC)^2} + \frac{FCF_3}{(1+WACC)^3} + \cdots + \frac{FCF_\infty}{(1+WACC)^\infty}$$

Chapter 2

$$\text{Expected rate of return} = \hat{r} = \sum_{i=1}^{n} P_i r_i$$

$$\text{Historical average, } \overline{r}_{Avg} = \frac{\sum_{t=1}^{n} \overline{r}_t}{n}$$

$$\text{Variance} = \sigma^2 = \sum_{i=1}^{n} (r_i - \hat{r})^2 P_i$$

$$\text{Standard deviation} = \sigma = \sqrt{\sum_{i=1}^{n} (r_i - \hat{r})^2 P_i}$$

$$\text{Historical estimated } \sigma = S = \sqrt{\frac{\sum_{t=1}^{n} (\overline{r}_t - \overline{r}_{Avg})^2}{n-1}}$$

$$CV = \frac{\sigma}{\hat{r}}$$

$$\hat{r}_p = \sum_{i=1}^{n} w_i \hat{r}_i$$

$$\sigma_p = \sqrt{\sum_{i=1}^{n} (r_{pi} - \hat{r}_p)^2 P_i}$$

$$\text{Estimated } \rho = R = \frac{\sum_{t=1}^{n} (\overline{r}_{i,t} - \overline{r}_{i,Avg})(\overline{r}_{j,t} - \overline{r}_{j,Avg})}{\sqrt{\sum_{t=1}^{n} (\overline{r}_{i,t} - \overline{r}_{i,Avg})^2 \sum_{t=1}^{n} (\overline{r}_{j,t} - \overline{r}_{j,Avg})^2}}$$

$$\text{COV}_{iM} = \rho_{iM} \sigma_i \sigma_M$$

$$b_i = \left(\frac{\sigma_i}{\sigma_M}\right) \rho_{iM} = \frac{\text{COV}_{iM}}{\sigma_M^2}$$

$$b_p = \sum_{i=1}^{n} w_i b_i$$

Required return on stock market $= r_M$

Market risk premium $= RP_M = r_M - r_{RF}$

$$RP_i = (r_M - r_{RF})b_i = (RP_M)b_i$$

$$SML = r_i = r_{RF} + (r_M - r_{RF})b_i = r_{RF} + RP_M b_i$$

Chapter 3

$$\hat{r}_p = w_A \hat{r}_A + (1 - w_A)\hat{r}_B$$

$$\text{Portfolio SD} = \sigma_p = \sqrt{w_A^2 \sigma_A^2 + (1 - w_A)^2 \sigma_B^2 + 2w_A(1 - w_A)\rho_{AB}\sigma_A\sigma_B}$$

$$\text{Minimum-risk portfolio: } w_A = \frac{\sigma_B(\sigma_B - \rho_{AB}\sigma_A)}{\sigma_A^2 + \sigma_B^2 - 2\rho_{AB}\sigma_A\sigma_B}$$

$$\hat{r}_p = \sum_{i=1}^{N} (w_i \hat{r}_i)$$

$$\sigma_p^2 = \sum_{i=1}^{N} \sum_{j=1}^{N} (w_i w_j \sigma_i \sigma_j \rho_{ij})$$

$$\sigma_p^2 = \sum_{i=1}^{N} w_i^2 \sigma_i^2 + \sum_{i=1}^{N} \sum_{\substack{j=1 \\ j \neq i}}^{N} w_i \sigma_i \, w_j \sigma_j \rho_{ij}$$

$$\sigma_p = \sqrt{(1 - w_{RF})^2 \sigma_M^2} = (1 - w_{RF})\sigma_M$$

$$\text{CML: } \hat{r}_p = r_{RF} + \left(\frac{\hat{r}_M - r_{RF}}{\sigma_M}\right)\sigma_p$$

$$r_i = r_{RF} + \frac{(r_M - r_{RF})}{\sigma_M}\left(\frac{\text{Cov}(r_i, r_M)}{\sigma_M}\right) = r_{RF} + (r_M - r_{RF})\left(\frac{\text{Cov}(r_i, r_M)}{\sigma_M^2}\right)$$

$$b_i = \frac{\text{Covariance between Stock i and the market}}{\text{Variance of market returns}} = \frac{\text{Cov}(r_i, r_M)}{\sigma_M^2} = \frac{\rho_{iM}\sigma_i\sigma_M}{\sigma_M^2} = \rho_{iM}\left(\frac{\sigma_i}{\sigma_M}\right)$$

$$\text{SML} = r_i = r_{RF} + (r_M - r_{RF})b_i = r_{RF} + (RP_M)b_i$$

$$\sigma_i^2 = b_i^2\sigma_M^2 + \sigma_{e_i}^2$$

$$\text{APT: } r_i = r_{RF} + (r_1 - r_{RF})b_{i1} + \cdots + (r_j - r_{RF})b_{ij}$$

$$\text{Fama-French: } r_i = r_{RF} + a_i + b_i(r_M - r_{RF}) + c_i(r_{SMB}) + d_i(r_{HML})$$

Chapter 4

$$V_B = \sum_{t=1}^{N} \frac{\text{INT}}{(1+r_d)^t} + \frac{M}{(1+r_d)^N}$$

$$\text{Semiannual payments: } V_B = \sum_{t=1}^{2N} \frac{\text{INT}/2}{(1+r_d/2)^t} + \frac{M}{(1+r_d/2)^{2N}}$$

$$\text{Yield to maturity: Bond price} = \sum_{t=1}^{N} \frac{\text{INT}}{(1+\text{YTM})^t} + \frac{M}{(1+\text{YTM})^N}$$

$$\text{Price of callable bond (if called at N)} = \sum_{t=1}^{N} \frac{\text{INT}}{(1+r_d)^t} + \frac{\text{Call price}}{(1+r_d)^N}$$

$$\text{Current yield} = \frac{\text{Annual interest}}{\text{Bond's current price}}$$

$$\text{Current yield} + \text{Capital gains yield} = \text{Yield to maturity}$$

$$r_d = r^* + IP + DRP + LP + MRP$$

$$r_{RF} = r^* + IP$$

$$r_d = r_{RF} + DRP + LP + MRP$$

$$IP_N = \frac{I_1 + I_2 + \cdots + I_N}{N}$$

Chapter 5

$$\hat{P}_0 = \text{PV of expected future dividends} = \sum_{t=1}^{\infty} \frac{D_t}{(1+r_s)^t}$$

$$\text{Constant growth: } \hat{P}_0 = \frac{D_0(1+g)}{r_s - g} = \frac{D_1}{r_s - g}$$

$$\hat{r}_s = \frac{D_1}{P_0} + g$$

$$\text{Capital gains yield} = \frac{\hat{P}_1 - P_0}{P_0}$$

$$\text{Dividend yield} = \frac{D_1}{P_0}$$

$$\text{For a zero growth stock, } \hat{P}_0 = \frac{D}{r_s}$$

$$\text{Horizon value} = \text{Terminal value} = \hat{P}_N = \frac{D_{N+1}}{r_s - g} = \frac{D_N(1+g)}{r_s - g}$$

$$V_{ps} = \frac{D_{ps}}{r_{ps}}$$

$$\hat{r}_{ps} = \frac{D_{ps}}{V_{ps}}$$

$$\bar{r}_s = \text{Actual dividend yield} + \text{Actual capital gains yield}$$

Chapter 6

Exercise value = MAX[Current price of stock − Strike price, 0]

$$\text{Number of stock shares in hedged portfolio} = N = \frac{C_u - C_d}{P_u - P_d}$$

$$V_C = P[N(d_1)] - Xe^{-r_{RF}t}[N(d_2)]$$

$$d_1 = \frac{\ln(P/X) + [r_{RF} + (\sigma^2/2)]t}{\sigma\sqrt{t}}$$

$$d_2 = d_1 - \sigma\sqrt{t}$$

Put–call parity: Put option $= V_C - P + Xe^{-r_{RF}t}$

$$V \text{ of put} = P[N(d_1) - 1] - Xe^{-r_{RF}t}[N(d_2) - 1]$$

Chapter 7

EBIT = Earnings before interest and taxes = Sales revenues − Operating costs

EBITDA = Earnings before interest, taxes, depreciation and amortization

$\qquad$ = EBIT + Depreciation + Amortization

Net cash flow = Net income + Depreciation and amortization

NOWC = Net operating working capital

$\qquad$ = Operating current assets − Operating current liabilities

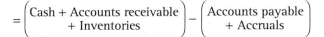

$$= \left(\begin{array}{c}\text{Cash + Accounts receivable}\\ \text{+ Inventories}\end{array}\right) - \left(\begin{array}{c}\text{Accounts payable}\\ \text{+ Accruals}\end{array}\right)$$

Total net operating capital = Net operating working capital + Operating long-term assets

NOPAT = Net operating profit after taxes = EBIT(1 − Tax rate)

Free cash flow (FCF) = NOPAT − Net investment in operating capital

$$= \text{NOPAT} - \left(\begin{array}{cc} \text{Current year's total} & \text{Previous year's total} \\ \text{net operating capital} & \text{net operating capital} \end{array} \right)$$

Operating cash flow = NOPAT + Depreciation and amortization

$$\begin{array}{c} \text{Gross investment in} \\ \text{operating capital} \end{array} = \begin{array}{c} \text{Net investment in} \\ \text{operating capital} \end{array} + \text{Depreciation}$$

$$\text{FCF} = \text{Operating cash flow} - \begin{array}{c} \text{Gross investment} \\ \text{in operating capital} \end{array}$$

$$\text{Return on invested capital (ROIC)} = \frac{\text{NOPAT}}{\text{Total net operating capital}}$$

MVA = Market value of stock − Equity capital supplied by shareholders

= (Shares outstanding)(Stock price) − Total common equity

MVA = Total market value − Total investor-supplied capital

$$= \left(\begin{array}{c} \text{Market value of stock} \\ + \text{Market value of debt} \end{array} \right) - \text{Total investor-supplied capital}$$

$$\text{EVA} = \left(\begin{array}{c} \text{Net operating profit} \\ \text{after taxes (NOPAT)} \end{array} \right) - \left(\begin{array}{c} \text{After-tax dollar cost of capital} \\ \text{used to support operations} \end{array} \right)$$

= EBIT(1 − Tax rate) − (Total net operating capital)(WACC)

EVA = (Total net operating capital)(ROIC − WACC)

Chapter 8

$$\text{Current ratio} = \frac{\text{Current assets}}{\text{Current liabilities}}$$

$$\text{Quick, or acid test, ratio} = \frac{\text{Current assets} - \text{Inventories}}{\text{Current liabilities}}$$

$$\text{Inventory turnover ratio} = \frac{\text{Sales}}{\text{Inventories}}$$

$$\text{DSO} = \text{Days sales outstanding} = \frac{\text{Receivables}}{\text{Average sales per day}} = \frac{\text{Receivables}}{\text{Annual sales}/365}$$

$$\text{Fixed assets turnover ratio} = \frac{\text{Sales}}{\text{Net fixed assets}}$$

$$\text{Total assets turnover ratio} = \frac{\text{Sales}}{\text{Total assets}}$$

$$\text{Debt ratio} = \frac{\text{Total liabilities}}{\text{Total assets}}$$

$$\text{Market debt ratio} = \frac{\text{Total liabilities}}{\text{Total liabilities} + \text{Market value of equity}}$$

$$\text{Debt-to-equity ratio} = \frac{\text{Total liabilities}}{\text{Total assets} - \text{Total liabilities}}$$

$$\text{Debt-to-equity} = \frac{\text{Debt ratio}}{1 - \text{Debt ratio}} \quad \text{and Debt ratio} = \frac{\text{Debt-to-equity}}{1 + \text{Debt-to-equity}}$$

$$\text{Equity multiplier} = \frac{\text{Total assets}}{\text{Common equity}}$$

$$\text{Debt ratio} = 1 - \frac{1}{\text{Equity multiplier}}$$

$$\text{Times-interest-earned (TIE) ratio} = \frac{\text{EBIT}}{\text{Interest charges}}$$

$$\text{EBITDA coverage ratio} = \frac{\text{EBITDA} + \text{Lease payments}}{\text{Interest} + \text{Principal payments} + \text{Lease payments}}$$

$$\text{Net profit margin} = \frac{\text{Net income available to common stockholders}}{\text{Sales}}$$

$$\text{Operating profit margin} = \frac{\text{EBIT}}{\text{Sales}}$$

$$\text{Gross profit margin} = \frac{\text{Sales} - \text{Cost of goods sold}}{\text{Sales}}$$

$$\text{Return on total assets (ROA)} = \frac{\text{Net income available to common stockholders}}{\text{Total assets}}$$

$$\text{Basic earning power (BEP) ratio} = \frac{\text{EBIT}}{\text{Total assets}}$$

$$\text{ROA} = \text{Profit margin} \times \text{Total assets turnover} = \frac{\text{Net income}}{\text{Sales}} \times \frac{\text{Sales}}{\text{Total assets}}$$

$$\text{Return on common equity (ROE)} = \frac{\text{Net income available to common stockholders}}{\text{Common equity}}$$

$$\text{ROE} = \text{ROA} \times \text{Equity multiplier}$$

$$= \text{Profit margin} \times \text{Total assets turnover} \times \text{Equity multiplier}$$

$$= \frac{\text{Net income}}{\text{Sales}} \times \frac{\text{Sales}}{\text{Total assets}} \times \frac{\text{Total assets}}{\text{Common equity}}$$

$$\text{Price/earnings (P/E) ratio} = \frac{\text{Price per share}}{\text{Earnings per share}}$$

$$\text{Price/cash flow ratio} = \frac{\text{Price per share}}{\text{Cash flow per share}}$$

$$\text{Book value per share} = \frac{\text{Common equity}}{\text{Shares outstanding}}$$

$$\text{Market/book (M/B) ratio} = \frac{\text{Market price per share}}{\text{Book value per share}}$$

Chapter 9

$$\begin{array}{ccccc} \text{Additional} & \text{Required} & \text{Spontaneous} & & \text{Increase in} \\ \text{funds} & = \text{asset} & - \text{liability} & - & \text{retained} \\ \text{needed} & \text{increase} & \text{increase} & & \text{earnings} \end{array}$$

$$\text{AFN} = (A^*/S_0)\Delta S - (L^*/S_0)\Delta S - MS_1(1 - \text{Payout ratio})$$

$$\begin{array}{c} \text{Full} \\ \text{capacity} \\ \text{sales} \end{array} = \frac{\text{Actual sales}}{\begin{array}{c}\text{Percentage of capacity} \\ \text{at which fixed assets} \\ \text{were operated}\end{array}}$$

$$\text{Target fixed assets/Sales} = \frac{\text{Actual fixed assets}}{\text{Full capacity sales}}$$

$$\begin{array}{c}\text{Required level} \\ \text{of fixed assets}\end{array} = (\text{Target fixed assets/Sales})(\text{Projected sales})$$

Chapter 10

$$\text{After-tax component cost of debt} = r_d(1 - T)$$

$$M(1 - F) = \sum_{t=1}^{N} \frac{\text{INT}(1-T)}{[1 + r_d(1-T)]^t} + \frac{M}{[1 + r_d(1-T)]^N}$$

$$r_{ps} = \frac{D_{ps}}{P_{ps}(1 - F)}$$

$$\text{Market equilibrium: } \begin{array}{c}\text{Expected rate} \\ \text{of return}\end{array} = \hat{r}_M = \frac{D_1}{P_0} + g = r_{RF} + RP_M = r_M = \begin{array}{c}\text{Required} \\ \text{rate of return}\end{array}$$

Note: D_1, P_0, and g are for the market, not an individual company.

Rep/Div = ratio of payouts via repurchases to payouts via dividends

$$r_M = \hat{r}_M = (1 + \text{Rep/Div})\frac{D_1}{P_0} + g$$

Note: g is long-term growth rate in total payouts for the market, and D_1 and P_0 are for the market, not an individual company

CAPM: $r_s = r_{RF} + b_i(RP_M)$

DCF: $r_s = \hat{r}_s = \dfrac{D_1}{P_0} + \text{Expected g in dividends per share}$

Own-bond yield-plus-judgmental-risk-premium: $r_s = \dfrac{\text{Company's own}}{\text{bond yield}} + \dfrac{\text{Judgmental risk}}{\text{premium}}$

g = (Retention rate)(ROE) = (1.0 − Payout rate)(ROE)

$r_e = \hat{r}_e = \dfrac{D_1}{P_0(1-F)} + g$

$\text{WACC} = w_d r_d (1 - T) + w_{ps} r_{ps} + w_s r_s$

Chapter 11

V_{op} = Value of operations

= PV of expected future free cash flows

$$= \sum_{t=1}^{\infty} \frac{FCF_1}{(1 + WACC)^t}$$

Horizon value: $V_{op(\text{at time N})} = \dfrac{FCF_{N+1}}{WACC - g} = \dfrac{FCF_N(1+g)}{WACC - g}$

Total value = V_{op} + Value of nonoperating assets

Value of equity = Total value − Preferred stock − Debt

Operating profitability (OP) = NOPAT/Sales

Capital requirements (CR) = Operating capital/Sales

$EROIC_N$ = Expected return on invested capital

$= NOPAT_{N+1}/Capital_N$

$= NOPAT_N(1 + g)/Capital_N$

$= OP_{N+1}/CR_N$

For constant growth:

$$V_{op(\text{at time N})} = Capital_N + \left\{ \left[\frac{Sales_N(1+g)}{WACC - g} \right] \left[OP - WACC \left(\frac{CR}{1+g} \right) \right] \right\}$$

$$= Capital_N + \frac{Capital_N(EROIC_N - WACC)}{WACC - g}$$

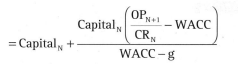

$$= \text{Capital}_N + \frac{\text{Capital}_N \left(\dfrac{OP_{N+1}}{CR_N} - WACC \right)}{WACC - g}$$

Chapter 12

$$NPV = CF_0 + \frac{CF_1}{(1+r)^1} + \frac{CF_2}{(1+r)^2} + \cdots + \frac{CF_N}{(1+r)^N}$$

$$= \sum_{t=0}^{N} \frac{CF_t}{(1+r)^t}$$

$$IRR: CF_0 + \frac{CF_1}{(1+IRR)^1} + \frac{CF_2}{(1+IRR)^2} + \cdots + \frac{CF_N}{(1+IRR)^N} = 0$$

$$NPV = \sum_{t=0}^{N} \frac{CF_t}{(1+IRR)^t} = 0$$

MIRR: PV of costs = PV of terminal value

$$\sum_{t=0}^{N} \frac{COF_t}{(1+r)^t} = \frac{\displaystyle\sum_{t=0}^{N} CIF_t (1+r)^{N-t}}{(1+MIRR)^N}$$

$$PV \text{ of costs} = \frac{\text{Terminal value}}{(1+MIRR)^N}$$

$$PI = \frac{PV \text{ of future cash flows}}{\text{Initial cost}} = \frac{\displaystyle\sum_{t=1}^{N} \frac{CF_t}{(1+r)^t}}{CF_0}$$

$$\text{Payback} = \begin{array}{c}\text{Number of}\\\text{years prior to}\\\text{full recovery}\end{array} + \frac{\begin{array}{c}\text{Unrecovered cost}\\\text{at start of year}\end{array}}{\begin{array}{c}\text{Cash flow durirg}\\\text{full recovery year}\end{array}}$$

Chapter 13

$$\text{Project cash flow} = FCF = \begin{array}{c}\text{Investment outlay}\\\text{cash flow}\end{array} + \begin{array}{c}\text{Operating}\\\text{cash flow}\end{array} + \begin{array}{c}\text{NOWC}\\\text{cash flow}\end{array} + \begin{array}{c}\text{Salvage}\\\text{cash flow}\end{array}$$

$$\text{Expected NPV} = \sum_{i=1}^{n} P_i(NPV_i)$$

$$\sigma_{NPV} = \sqrt{\sum_{i=1}^{n} P_i(NPV_i - \text{Expected NPV})^2}$$

$$CV_{NPV} = \frac{\sigma_{NPV}}{E(NPV)}$$

Chapter 14

$$CV = \frac{\sigma(\text{PV of future CF})}{E(\text{PV of future CF})}$$

Variance of project's rate of return: $\sigma^2 = \dfrac{\ln(CV^2 + 1)}{t}$

Chapter 15

$$V_{op} = \sum_{t=1}^{\infty} \frac{FCF_t}{(1 + WACC)^t}$$

$$WACC = w_d(1 - T)r_d + w_s r_s$$

$$ROIC = \frac{NOPAT}{Capital} = \frac{EBIT(1 - T)}{Capital}$$

$$EBIT = PQ - VQ - F$$

$$Q_{BE} = \frac{F}{P - V}$$

$$V_L = S_L + D$$

MM, no taxes: $V_L = V_U$

MM, corporate taxes: $V_L = V_U + TD$

Miller, corporate and personal taxes: $V_L = V_U + \left[1 - \dfrac{(1 - T_c)(1 - T_s)}{(1 - T_d)}\right]D$

$$b = b_U[1 + (1 - T)(D/S)] = b_U[1 + (1 - T)(w_d/w_s)]$$

$$b_U = b/[1 + (1 - T)(D/S)] = b/[1 + (1 - T)(w_d/w_s)]$$

$$r_s = r_{RF} + RP_M(b)$$

$$r_s = r_{RF} + \text{Premium for business risk} + \text{Premium for financial risk}$$

If $g = 0$: $V_{op} = \dfrac{FCF}{WACC} = \dfrac{NOPAT}{WACC} = \dfrac{EBIT(1 - T)}{WACC}$

Total corporate value = V_{op} + Value of short-term investments

S = Total corporate value − Value of all debt

$$D = w_d V_{op}$$

$$S = (1 - w_d) V_{op}$$

Cash raised by issuing debt = $D - D_0$

$$P_{Prior} = S_{Prior}/n_{Prior}$$

$P_{Post} = P_{Prior}$

$n_{Post} = n_{Prior} \left[\dfrac{V_{opNew} - D_{New}}{V_{opNew} - D_{Old}} \right]$

$n_{Post} = n_{Prior} - (D_{New} - D_{Old})/P_{Prior}$

$P_{Post} = \dfrac{V_{opNew} - D_{Old}}{n_{Prior}}$

$NI = (EBIT - r_d D)(1 - T)$

$EPS = NI/n$

Chapter 16

MM, no taxes:

$$V_L = V_U = \dfrac{EBIT}{WACC} = \dfrac{EBIT}{r_{sU}}$$

$$r_{sL} = r_{sU} + \text{Risk premium} = r_{sU} + (r_{sU} - r_d)(D/S)$$

MM, corporate taxes:

$$V_L = V_U + TD$$

$$V_U = S = \dfrac{EBIT(1 - T)}{r_{sU}}$$

$$r_{sL} = r_{sU} + (r_{sU} - r_d)(1 - T)(D/S)$$

Miller, personal taxes:

$$V_U = \dfrac{EBIT(1 - T_c)}{r_{sU}} = \dfrac{EBIT(1 - T_c)(1 - T_s)}{r_{sU}(1 - T_s)}$$

$$CF_L = (EBIT - I)(1 - T_c)(1 - T_s) + I(1 - T_d)$$

$$V_L = V_U + \left[1 - \dfrac{(1 - T_c)(1 - T_s)}{(1 - T_d)} \right] D$$

Ehrhardt & Daves, impact of growth:

$$V_U = \dfrac{FCF}{r_{sU} - g}$$

General case:

$$V_L = V_U + V_{Tax\ shield}$$

$$V_{Tax\ shield} = \dfrac{r_d TD}{r_{TS} - g}$$

$$V_L = V_U + \left(\frac{r_d}{r_{TS} - g}\right)TD$$

Case for $r_{TS} = r_{sU}$:

$$V_L = V_U + \left(\frac{r_d\,TD}{r_{sU} - g}\right)$$

$$r_{sL} = r_{sU} + (r_{sU} - r_d)\frac{D}{S}$$

$$b = b_U + (b_U - b_D)\frac{D}{S}$$

Chapter 17

Residual distribution = Net income − [(Target equity ratio)(Total capital budget)]

$$\text{Number of shares repurchased} = n_{Prior} - n_{Post} = \frac{\text{Cash}_{Rep}}{P_{Prior}}$$

$$n_{Post} = n_{Prior} - \frac{\text{Cash}_{Rep}}{P_{Prior}} = n_{Prior} - \frac{\text{Cash}_{Rep}}{S_{Prior}/n_{Prior}} = n_{Prior}\left(1 - \frac{\text{Cash}_{Rep}}{S_{Prior}}\right)$$

Chapter 18

Amount left on table = (Closing price − Offer price)(Number of shares)

Chapter 19

NAL = PV cost of owning − PV cost of leasing

Chapter 20

$$\frac{\text{Price paid for}}{\text{bond with warrants}} = \frac{\text{Straight-debt}}{\text{value of bond}} + \frac{\text{Value of}}{\text{warrants}}$$

$$\text{Conversion price} = P_c = \frac{\text{Par value of bond given up}}{\text{Shares received}}$$

$$= \frac{\text{Par value of bond given up}}{\text{CR}}$$

$$\text{Conversion ratio} = CR = \frac{\text{Par value of bond given up}}{P_c}$$

Chapter 21

$$\text{Inventory conversion period} = \frac{\text{Inventory}}{\text{Cost of goods sold}/365}$$

$$\text{Receivables collection period} = \text{DSO} = \frac{\text{Receivables}}{\text{Sales}/365}$$

$$\text{Payables deferral period} = \frac{\text{Payables}}{\text{Cost of goods sold}/365}$$

$$\begin{array}{c}\text{Cash} \\ \text{conversion} \\ \text{cycle}\end{array} = \begin{array}{c}\text{Inventory} \\ \text{conversion} \\ \text{period}\end{array} + \begin{array}{c}\text{Average} \\ \text{collection} \\ \text{period}\end{array} - \begin{array}{c}\text{Payables} \\ \text{deferral} \\ \text{period}\end{array}$$

$$\begin{array}{c}\text{Accounts} \\ \text{receivable}\end{array} = \begin{array}{c}\text{Credit sales} \\ \text{per day}\end{array} \times \begin{array}{c}\text{Length of} \\ \text{collection period}\end{array}$$

$$\text{ADS} = \frac{(\text{Units sold})(\text{Sales price})}{365} = \frac{\text{Annual sales}}{365}$$

$$\text{Receivables} = (\text{ADS})(\text{DSO})$$

$$\begin{array}{c}\text{Nominal annual cost} \\ \text{of trade credit}\end{array} = \frac{\text{Discount percentage}}{100 - \begin{array}{c}\text{Discount} \\ \text{percentage}\end{array}} \times \frac{365}{\begin{array}{c}\text{Days credit is} \\ \text{outstanding}\end{array} - \begin{array}{c}\text{Discount} \\ \text{period}\end{array}}$$

Chapter 22

$$\Delta I \text{ for increase in sales} = [(\text{DSO}_N - \text{DSO}_0)(S_0/365)] + V[(\text{DSO}_N)(S_N - S_0)/365]$$

$$\Delta I \text{ for decrease in sales} = [(\text{DSO}_N - \text{DSO}_0)(S_N/365)] + V[(\text{DSO}_0)(S_N - S_0)/365]$$

$$\Delta P = (S_N - S_0)(1 - V) - r(\Delta I) - (B_N S_N - B_0 S_0) - (D_N S_N P_N - D_0 S_0 P_0)$$

$$\text{Cost of carrying receivables} = (\text{DSO})\left(\frac{\text{Sales}}{\text{per day}}\right)\left(\frac{\text{Variable}}{\text{cost ratio}}\right)\left(\frac{\text{Cost of}}{\text{funds}}\right)$$

$$\text{Simple interest rate per day} = \frac{\text{Nominal rate}}{\text{Days in year}}$$

$$\text{Simple interest charge for period} = (\text{Days in period})(\text{Rate per day})(\text{Amount of loan})$$

$$\text{Face value}_{\text{Discount}} = \frac{\text{Funds received}}{1.0 - \text{Nominal rate (decimal)}}$$

$$\text{APR rate} = (\text{Periods per year})(\text{Rate per period})$$

Chapter 23

Total costs = Holding costs + Transactions costs

$$= \frac{C}{2}(r) + \frac{T}{C}(F)$$

$$C^* = \sqrt{\frac{2(F)(T)}{r}}$$

$$A = \frac{\text{Units per order}}{2} = \frac{S/N}{2}$$

$$TCC = (C)(P)(A)$$

$$TOC = (F)(N)$$

$$TIC = TCC + TOC$$

$$= (C)(P)(A) + F\left(\frac{S}{2A}\right)$$

$$= (C)(P)(Q/2) + (F)(S/Q)$$

$$EOQ = \sqrt{\frac{2(F)(S)}{(C)(P)}}$$

Chapter 26

$$r_{sL} = r_{sU} + (r_{sU} - r_d)(D/S)$$

$$r_{sU} = w_s r_{sL} + w_d r_d$$

Tax savings = (Interest expense)(Tax rate)

$$\text{Horizon value of unlevered firm} = HV_{U,N} = \frac{FCF_{N+1}}{r_{sU} - g} = \frac{FCF_N(1+g)}{r_{sU} - g}$$

$$\text{Horizon value of tax shield} = HV_{TS,N} = \frac{TS_{N+1}}{r_{sU} - g} = \frac{TS_N(1+g)}{r_{sU} - g}$$

$$V_{\text{Unlevered}} = \sum_{t=1}^{N} \frac{FCF_t}{(1+r_{sU})^t} + \frac{HV_{U,N}}{(1+r_{sU})^N}$$

$$V_{\text{Tax shield}} = \sum_{t=1}^{N} \frac{TS_t}{(1+r_{sU})^t} + \frac{HV_{TS,N}}{(1+r_{sU})^N}$$

$$\text{Value of operations} = V_{op} = V_{\text{Unlevered}} + V_{\text{Tax shield}}$$

$$FCFE = \frac{\text{Free}}{\text{cash flow}} - \frac{\text{After-tax}}{\text{interest expense}} - \frac{\text{Principal}}{\text{payments}} + \frac{\text{Newly issued}}{\text{debt}}$$

$$= \frac{\text{Free}}{\text{cash flow}} - \frac{\text{Interest}}{\text{expense}} + \frac{\text{Interest}}{\text{tax shield}} + \frac{\text{Net change}}{\text{in debt}}$$

$$FCFE = \text{Net income} - \frac{\text{Net investment in}}{\text{operating capital}} + \frac{\text{Net change}}{\text{in debt}}$$

$$HV_{FCFE,N} = \frac{FCFE_{N+1}}{r_{sL} - g} = \frac{FCFE_N(1+g)}{r_{sL} - g}$$

$$V_{FCFE} = \sum_{t=1}^{N} \frac{FCFE_t}{(1+r_{sL})^t} + \frac{HV_{FCFE,N}}{(1+r_{sL})^N}$$

$$S = V_{FCFE} + \text{Nonoperating assets}$$

$$\frac{\text{Total value of shares to target shareholders}}{\text{Total post-merger value of equity}} = \frac{\text{Percent required by}}{\text{target stockholders}} = \frac{n_{New}}{n_{New} + n_{Old}}$$

Chapter 27

$$\frac{\text{Single-period interest}}{\text{rate parity}} : \frac{\text{Forward exchange rate}}{\text{Spot exchange rate}} = \frac{1+r_h}{1+r_f}$$

$$\frac{\text{Expected t-year}}{\text{forward exchange rate}} = (\text{Spot rate})\left(\frac{1+r_h}{1+r_f}\right)^t$$

$$P_h = (P_f)(\text{Spot rate})$$

$$\text{Spot rate} = \frac{P_h}{P_f}$$

Glossary

501(c)(3) corporation A charitable organization that meets the IRS requirements for tax-exempt status under the tax code section 501(c)(3).

abandonment option Allows a company to reduce the capacity of its output in response to changing market conditions. This includes the option to contract production or abandon a project if market conditions deteriorate too much.

absolute priority doctrine States that claims must be paid in strict accordance with the priority of each claim, regardless of the consequence to other claimants.

account receivable Created when a good is shipped or a service is performed and payment for that good is made on a credit basis, not on a cash basis.

accounting income Income as defined by Generally Accepted Accounting Principles (GAAP).

accounting profit A firm's net income as reported on its income statement.

acquiring company A company that seeks to acquire another firm.

actual, or realized, rate of return, $\bar{r}_s$ The rate of return that was actually realized at the end of some holding period.

actuarial rate of return The discount rate used to determine the present value of future benefits under a defined benefits pension plan.

additional funds needed (AFN) Those funds required from external sources to increase the firm's assets to support a sales increase. A sales increase will normally require an increase in assets. However, some of this increase is usually offset by a spontaneous increase in liabilities as well as by earnings retained in the firm. Those funds that are required but not generated internally must be obtained from external sources.

add-on basis installment loan Interest is calculated over the life of the loan and then added on to the loan amount. This total amount is paid in equal installments. This raises the effective cost of the loan.

agency cost or problem An expense, either direct or indirect, that is borne by a principal as a result of having delegated authority to an agent. An example is the costs borne by shareholders to encourage managers to maximize a firm's stock price rather than act in their own self-interests. These costs may also arise from lost efficiency and the expense of monitoring management to ensure that debtholders' rights are protected.

agency debt Debt issued by federal agencies. Agency debt is not officially backed by the full faith and credit of the U.S. government, but investors assume that the government implicitly guarantees this debt, so these bonds carry interest rates only slightly higher than Treasury bonds.

aggressive short-term financing policy Refers to a policy in which a firm finances all of its fixed assets with long-term capital but part of its permanent current assets with short-term, nonspontaneous credit.

aging schedule Breaks down accounts receivable according to how long they have been outstanding. This gives the firm a more complete picture of the structure of accounts receivable than that provided by days sales outstanding.

alternative minimum tax (AMT) A provision of the U.S. Tax Code that requires profitable firms to pay at least some taxes if such taxes are greater than the amount due under standard tax accounting.

amortization A noncash charge against intangible assets, such as goodwill.

amortization schedule A table that breaks down the periodic fixed payment of an installment loan into its principal and interest components.

amortized loan A loan that is repaid in equal periodic amounts (or "killed off") over time.

anchoring bias Occurs when predictions of future events are influenced too heavily by recent events.

animal spirits John Maynard Keynes, writing during the 1920s and 1930s, suggested that—after a period of rising prosperity and stock prices—investors begin to think that the good times will last forever, a feeling that is driven by happy talk and high spirits rather than cool reasoning.

annual report A report issued annually by a corporation to its stockholders. It contains basic financial statements as well as management's opinion of the past year's operations and the firm's future prospects.

annual vesting A certain percentage of the options in a grant vest each year. For example, one-third of the options in the grant might vest each year.

annuity A series of payments of a fixed amount for a specified number of periods.

annuity due An annuity with payments occurring at the beginning of each period.

APR The nominal annual interest rate is also called the annual percentage rate, or APR.

arbitrage The simultaneous buying and selling of the same commodity or security in two different markets at different prices, thus yielding a risk-free return.

Arbitrage Pricing Theory (APT) An approach to measuring the equilibrium risk–return relationship for a given stock as a function of multiple factors, rather than the single factor (the market return) used by the CAPM. The APT is based on complex mathematical and statistical theory, and it can account for several factors (such as GNP and the level of inflation) in determining the required return for a particular stock.

arrearages Preferred dividends that have not been paid and hence are "in arrears."

asset allocation models Used by pension fund managers to make funding and investment decisions; these models use computer simulations to examine the risk/return characteristics of portfolios with various mixes of assets.

asset management ratios A set of ratios that measure how effectively a firm is managing its assets.

assets-in-place Refers to the land, buildings, machines, and inventory that the firm uses in its operations to produce its products and services. Also known as operating assets.

assignment An informal procedure for liquidating debts that transfers title to a debtor's assets to a third person, known as an assignee or trustee.

asymmetric information theory Assumes managers have more complete information than investors and leads to a preferred "pecking order" of financing: (1) retained earnings, followed by

(2) debt, and then (3) new common stock. Also known as signaling theory.

average stock's beta, $b_A = b_M$ The beta coefficient (b) is a measure of a stock's market risk. It measures the stock's volatility relative to an average stock, which has a beta of 1.0.

average tax rate Calculated by taking the total amount of tax paid divided by taxable income.

balance sheet A statement of the firm's financial position at a specific point in time. The firm's assets are listed on the left-hand side of the balance sheet; the right-hand side shows its liabilities and equity, or the claims against these assets.

banker's acceptance Created when an importer's bank promises to accept a postdated check written to an exporter even if there are insufficient funds in the importer's account. If the bank is strong, then this financial instrument virtually eliminates credit risk.

Bankruptcy Reform Act of 1978 Enacted to speed up and streamline bankruptcy proceedings. This law represented a shift to a relative priority doctrine of creditors' claims.

basic earning power (BEP) ratio Calculated by dividing earnings before interest and taxes by total assets. This ratio shows the raw earning power of the firm's assets before the influence of taxes and leverage.

Baumol model A model for establishing the firm's target cash balance that closely resembles the economic ordering quantity model used for inventory. The model assumes (1) that the firm uses cash at a steady, predictable rate, (2) that the firm's cash inflows from operations also occur at a steady, predictable rate, and (3) that its net cash outflows therefore also occur at a steady rate. The model balances the opportunity cost of holding cash against the transactions costs associated with replenishing the cash account.

behavioral finance A field of study that analyzes investor behavior as a result of psychological traits. It does not assume that investors necessarily behave rationally.

benchmarking When a firm compares its ratios to other leading companies in the same industry.

best efforts arrangement A type of contract with an investment banker when issuing stock. In a best efforts sale, the investment banker is only committed to making every effort to sell the stock at the offering price. In this case, the issuing firm bears the risk that the new issue will not be fully subscribed.

beta coefficient, b A measure of a stock's market risk, or the extent to which the returns on a given stock move with the stock market.

bird-in-the-hand theory Assumes that investors value a dollar of dividends more highly than a dollar of expected capital gains, because a certain dividend is less risky than a possible capital gain. This theory implies that a high-dividend stock has a higher price and lower required return, all else held equal.

Black-Scholes option pricing model A model to estimate the value of a call option. It is widely used by options traders.

board of trustees Group of community leaders who control a tax-exempt, charitable organization. Members of the board of trustees must have no direct economic interest in the organization.

bond A promissory note issued by a business or a governmental unit.

bond insurance Protects investors against default by the issuer and provides credit enhancement to the bond issue.

book value per share Common equity divided by the number of shares outstanding.

break-even point The level of unit sales at which costs equal revenues.

breakup value A firm's value if its assets are sold off in pieces.

business risk The risk inherent in the operations of the firm, prior to the financing decision. Thus, business risk is the uncertainty inherent in future operating income or earnings before interest and taxes. Business risk is caused by many factors; two of the most important are sales variability and operating leverage.

call option An option that allows the holder to buy the asset at some predetermined price within a specified period of time.

call provision Gives the issuing corporation the right to call the bonds for redemption. The call provision generally states that if the bonds are called then the company must pay the bondholders an amount greater than the par value, or a call premium. Most bonds contain a call provision.

capacity option Allows a company to change the capacity of its output in response to changing market conditions. This includes the option to contract or expand production. It also includes

the option to abandon a project if market conditions deteriorate too much.

Capital Asset Pricing Model (CAPM) A model based on the proposition that any stock's required rate of return is equal to the risk-free rate of return plus a risk premium reflecting only the risk remaining after diversification. The CAPM equation is $r_i = r_{RF} + b_i(r_M - r_{RF})$.

capital budget Outlines the planned expenditures on fixed assets.

capital budgeting The whole process of analyzing projects and deciding whether they should be included in the capital budget.

capital gain (loss) The profit (loss) from the sale of a capital asset for more (less) than its purchase price.

capital gains yield Results from changing prices and is calculated as $(P_1 - P_0)/P_0$, where P_0 is the beginning-of-period price and P_1 is the end-of-period price.

capital intensity ratio The dollar amount of assets required to produce a dollar of sales. The capital intensity ratio is the reciprocal of the total assets turnover ratio.

capital market Capital markets are the financial markets for long-term debt and corporate stocks. The New York Stock Exchange is an example of a capital market.

capital rationing Occurs when management places a constraint on the size of the firm's capital budget during a particular period.

capital structure The manner in which a firm's assets are financed; that is, the right side of the balance sheet. Capital structure is normally expressed as the percentage of each type of capital used by the firm such as debt, preferred stock, and common equity.

capitalizing Incorporating the lease provisions into the balance sheet by reporting the leased asset under fixed assets and reporting the present value of future lease payments as debt.

cash balance plan A type of defined benefits plan in which benefits are defined in terms of the cash balance in the employee's account rather than monthly salary.

cash budget A schedule showing cash flows (receipts, disbursements, and cash balances) for a firm over a specified period.

cash conversion cycle The length of time between the firm's actual cash expenditures on productive resources (materials and labor) and its own cash receipts from the sale of products (that is, the length of time between paying for labor and materials and collecting on receivables). Thus, the cash conversion cycle equals the length of time the firm has funds tied up in current assets.

cash discounts The amount by which a seller is willing to reduce the invoice price in order to be paid immediately, rather than in the future. A cash discount might be 2/10, net 30, which means a 2% discount if the bill is paid within 10 days and otherwise the entire amount is due within 30 days.

CDO, collateralized debt obligation Created when large numbers of mortgages are bundled into pools to create new securities that are then sliced into tranches; the tranches are re-combined and re-divided into securities called CDOs.

CDS, credit default swap Derivative in which a counterparty pays if a specified debt instrument goes into default; similar to insurance on a bond.

Chapter 7 The chapter of the Bankruptcy Reform Act that provides for the liquidation of a firm to repay creditors.

Chapter 11 The business reorganization chapter of the Bankruptcy Reform Act. The chapter provides for the reorganization, rather than the liquidation, of a business.

characteristic line Obtained by regressing the historical returns on a particular stock against the historical returns on the general stock market. The slope of the characteristic line is the stock's beta, which measures the amount by which the stock's expected return increases for a given increase in the expected return on the market.

charitable contributions One way that not-for-profit businesses raise equity capital. Individuals and firms make these contributions for a variety of reasons including concern for the well-being of others, the recognition that accompanies large donations, and tax deductibility.

charter The legal document that is filed with the state to incorporate a company.

check-clearing process When a customer's check is written upon one bank and a company deposits the check in its own bank, the company's bank must verify that the check is valid before the company can use those funds. Checks are generally cleared through the Federal Reserve System or through a clearinghouse set up by the banks in a particular city.

classified boards A board of directors with staggered terms. For example, a board with one-third of the

seats filled each year and directors serving three-year terms.

classified stock Sometimes created by a firm to meet special needs and circumstances. Generally, when special classifications of stock are used, one type is designated "Class A," another as "Class B," and so on. For example, Class A might be entitled to receive dividends before dividends can be paid on Class B stock. Class B might have the exclusive right to vote.

cleanup clause A clause in a line of credit that requires the borrower to reduce the loan balance to zero at least once a year.

clientele effect The attraction of companies with specific dividend policies to those investors whose needs are best served by those policies. Thus, companies with high dividends will have a clientele of investors with low marginal tax rates and strong desires for current income. Conversely, companies with low dividends will have a clientele of investors with high marginal tax rates and little need for current income.

cliff vesting All the options in a grant vest on the same date.

closely held corporation Refers to companies that are so small that their common stocks are not actively traded; they are owned by only a few people, usually the companies' managers.

coefficient of variation, CV Equal to the standard deviation divided by the expected return; it is a standardized risk measure that allows comparisons between investments having different expected returns and standard deviations.

collection policy The procedure for collecting accounts receivable. A change in collection policy will affect sales, days sales outstanding, bad debt losses, and the percentage of customers taking discounts.

collections float Float created while funds from customers' checks are being deposited and cleared through the check collection process.

combination lease Combines some aspects of both operating and financial leases. For example, a financial lease that contains a cancellation clause—normally associated with operating leases—is a combination lease.

commercial paper Unsecured, short-term promissory notes of large firms, usually issued in denominations of $100,000 or more and having an interest rate somewhat below the prime rate.

commodity futures Futures contracts that involve the sale or purchase of various commodities, including grains, oilseeds, livestock, meats, fiber, metals, and wood.

common stockholders' equity (net worth) The capital supplied by common stockholders—capital stock, paid-in capital, retained earnings, and (occasionally) certain reserves. Paid-in capital is the difference between the stock's par value and what stockholders paid when they bought newly issued shares.

comparative ratio analysis Compares a firm's own ratios to other leading companies in the same industry. This technique is also known as benchmarking.

compensating balance (CB) A minimum checking account balance that a firm must maintain with a bank to compensate the bank for services rendered or for making a loan; generally equal to 10%–20% of the loans outstanding.

composition Creditors voluntarily reduce their fixed claims on the debtor by accepting a lower principal amount, reducing the interest rate on the debt, accepting equity in place of debt, or some combination of these changes.

compounding The process of finding the future value of a single payment or series of payments.

computer/telephone network A computer/telephone network, such as Nasdaq, consists of all the facilities that provide for security transactions not conducted at a physical location exchange. These facilities are, basically, the communications networks that link buyers and sellers.

congeneric merger Involves firms that are interrelated but do not have identical lines of business. One example is Prudential's acquisition of Bache & Company.

conglomerate merger Occurs when unrelated enterprises combine, such as Mobil Oil and Montgomery Ward.

conservative short-term financing policy Refers to using permanent capital to finance all permanent asset requirements as well as to meet some or all of the seasonal demands.

consol A type of perpetuity. Consols were originally bonds issued by England in the mid-1700s to consolidate past debt.

continuous probability distribution Contains an infinite number of outcomes and is graphed from $-\infty$ and $+\infty$.

conversion price The effective price per share of stock if conversion occurs; the par value of the convertible security divided by the conversion ratio.

conversion ratio The number of shares of common stock received upon conversion of one convertible security.

conversion value The value of the stock that the investor would receive if conversion occurred; the market price per share times the conversion ratio.

convertible bond Security that is convertible into shares of common stock, at a fixed price, at the option of the bondholder.

convertible currency A currency that can be traded in the currency markets and can be redeemed at current market rates.

convertible security Bonds or preferred stocks that can be exchanged for (converted into) common stock, under specific terms, at the option of the holder. Unlike the exercise of warrants, conversion of a convertible security does not provide additional capital to the issuer.

corporate alliance A cooperative deal that stops short of a merger; also called a strategic alliance.

corporate beta (b) The quantitative measure of corporate risk of a project; the slope of the corporate characteristic line.

corporate bond Debt issued by corporations and exposed to default risk. Different corporate bonds have different levels of default risk, depending on the issuing company's characteristics and on the terms of the specific bond.

corporate characteristic line The regression line that results when the project's returns are plotted on the Y axis and the returns on the firm's total operations are plotted on the X axis.

corporate governance The set of rules that control a company's behavior toward its directors, managers, employees, shareholders, creditors, customers, competitors, and community.

corporate risk management Managing unpredictable events that have adverse consequences for the firm. This effort involves reducing the consequences of risk to the point where there would be no significant adverse impact on the firm's financial position.

corporate valuation model Defines the total value of a company as the value of operations plus the value of nonoperating assets plus the value of growth options.

corporation A corporation is a legal entity created by a state. The corporation is separate and distinct from its owners and managers.

correlation The tendency of two variables to move together.

correlation coefficient, ρ (rho) A standardized measure of how two random variables covary. A correlation coefficient (ρ) of +1.0 means that the two variables move up and down in perfect synchronization, whereas a coefficient of –1.0 means the variables always move in opposite directions. A correlation coefficient of zero suggests that the two variables are not related to one another; that is, they are independent.

cost of common stock, r_s The return required by the firm's common stockholders. It is usually calculated using Capital Asset Pricing Model or the dividend growth model.

cost of new external common equity, r_e A project financed with external equity must earn a higher rate of return because it must cover the flotation costs. Thus, the cost of new common equity is higher than that of common equity raised internally by reinvesting earnings.

cost of preferred stock, r_{ps} The return required by the firm's preferred stockholders. The cost of preferred stock, r_{ps}, is the cost to the firm of issuing new preferred stock. For perpetual preferred, it is the preferred dividend, D_{ps}, divided by the net issuing price, P_n.

costly trade credit Credit taken (in excess of free trade credit) whose cost is equal to the discount lost.

coupon interest rate Stated rate of interest on a bond; defined as the coupon payment divided by the par value.

coupon payment Dollar amount of interest paid to each bondholder on the interest payment dates.

coverage ratio Similar to the times-interest-earned ratio, but it recognizes that many firms lease assets and also must make sinking fund payments. It is found by adding earnings before interest, taxes, depreciation, amortization (EBITDA), and lease payments and then dividing this total by interest charges, lease payments, and sinking fund payments over 1 – T (where T is the tax rate).

cramdown Reorganization plans that are mandated by the bankruptcy court and binding on all parties.

credit enhancement Enables a bond's rating to be upgraded to AAA when the issuer purchases bond insurance. The bond insurance company guarantees that bondholders will receive the promised interest and principal payments. Therefore, the bond carries the credit rating of the insurance company rather than that of the issuer.

credit period The length of time for which credit is extended. If the credit period is lengthened then sales will generally increase, as will accounts receivable. This will increase the firm's financing needs and possibly increase bad debt losses. A shortening of the credit period will have the opposite effect.

credit policy The firm's policy on granting and collecting credit. There are four elements of credit policy, or credit policy variables: credit period, credit standards, collection policy, and discounts.

credit standards The financial strength and creditworthiness that qualifies a customer for a firm's regular credit terms.

credit terms Statements of the credit period and any discounts offered—for example, 2/10, net 30.

cross rate The exchange rate between two non-U.S. currencies.

crossover rate The cost of capital at which the NPV profiles for two projects intersect.

cumulative preferred dividends A protective feature on preferred stock that requires all past preferred dividends to be paid before any common dividends can be paid.

currency appreciation Occurs when a particular currency is worth more than it previously was.

currency depreciation Occurs when a particular currency is worth less than it previously was.

current ratio Indicates the extent to which current liabilities are covered by those assets expected to be converted to cash in the near future; it is found by dividing current assets by current liabilities.

current yield (on a bond) The annual coupon payment divided by the current market price.

days sales outstanding (DSO) Used to appraise accounts receivable and indicates the length of time the firm must wait after making a sale before receiving cash. It is found by dividing receivables by average sales per day.

DCF (discounted cash flow) techniques The net present value (NPV) and internal rate of return (IRR) techniques are discounted cash flow (DCF) evaluation techniques. These are called DCF methods because they explicitly recognize the time value of money.

dealer market In a dealer market, a dealer holds an inventory of the security and makes a market by offering to buy or sell. Others who wish to buy or sell can see the offers made by the dealers and can contact the dealer of their choice to arrange a transaction.

debenture An unsecured bond; as such, it provides no lien against specific property as security for the obligation. Debenture holders are therefore general creditors whose claims are protected by property not otherwise pledged.

debt ratio The ratio of total liabilities to total assets; it measures the percentage of funds provided by creditors.

debt service requirements The total amount of principal and interest that must be paid on a bond issue.

debt-to-equity ratio Ratio of debt divided by equity.

decision trees A form of scenario analysis in which different actions are taken in different scenarios.

declaration date The date on which a firm's directors issue a statement declaring a dividend.

default risk The risk that a borrower may not pay the interest and/or principal on a loan when it becomes due. If the issuer defaults, investors receive less than the promised return on the bond. Default risk is influenced by the financial strength of the issuer and also by the terms of the bond contract, especially whether collateral has been pledged to secure the bond. The greater the default risk, the higher the bond's yield to maturity.

default risk premium (DRP) The premium added to the real risk-free rate to compensate investors for the risk that a borrower may fail to pay the interest and/or principal on a loan when they become due.

defensive merger Occurs when one company acquires another to help ward off a hostile merger attempt.

defined benefit plan Under this type of pension plan, employers agree to give retirees a specifically defined benefit.

defined contribution plan Under this type of pension plan, employers agree to make specific payments into a retirement fund and retirees receive benefits that depend on the plan's investment success.

depreciation A noncash charge against tangible assets, such as buildings or machines. It is taken for the purpose of showing an asset's estimated dollar cost of the capital equipment used up in the production process.

derivatives Claims whose value depends on what happens to the value of some other asset. Futures and options are two important types of derivatives, and their values depend on what happens

to the prices of other assets. Therefore, the value of a derivative security is derived from the value of an underlying real asset or other security.

detachable warrant A warrant that can be detached and traded separately from the underlying security. Most warrants are detachable.

devaluation The lowering, by governmental action, of the price of its currency relative to another currency. For example, in 1967 the British pound was devalued from $2.80 per pound to $2.50 per pound.

development bond A tax-exempt bond sold by state and local governments whose proceeds are made available to corporations for specific uses deemed (by Congress) to be in the public interest.

direct quotation When discussing exchange rates, the number of U.S. dollars required to purchase one unit of a foreign currency.

disbursement float Float created before checks written by a firm have cleared and been deducted from the firm's account; disbursement float causes the firm's own checkbook balance to be smaller than the balance on the bank's records.

discount bond Bond prices and interest rates are inversely related; that is, they tend to move in the opposite direction from one another. A fixed-rate bond will sell at par when its coupon interest rate is equal to the going rate of interest, r_d. When the going rate of interest is above the coupon rate, a fixed-rate bond will sell at a "discount" below its par value. If current interest rates are below the coupon rate, a fixed-rate bond will sell at a "premium" above its par value.

discount interest Interest that is calculated on the face amount of a loan but is paid in advance.

discount on forward rate Occurs when the forward exchange rate differs from the spot rate. When the forward rate is below the spot rate, the forward rate is said to be at a discount.

discounted cash flow (DCF) method A method of valuing a business that involves the application of capital budgeting procedures to an entire firm rather than to a single project.

discounted payback period The number of years it takes a firm to recover its project investment based on discounted cash flows.

discounting The process of finding the present value of a single payment or series of payments.

distribution policy The policy that sets the level of distributions and the form of the distributions (dividends and stock repurchases).

diversifiable risk Refers to that part of a security's total risk associated with random events not affecting the market as a whole. This risk can be eliminated by proper diversification. Also known as company-specific risk.

divestiture The opposite of an acquisition. That is, a company sells a portion of its assets—often a whole division—to another firm or individual.

dividend irrelevance theory Holds that dividend policy has no effect on either the price of a firm's stock or its cost of capital.

dividend reinvestment plan (DRIP) Allows stockholders to automatically purchase shares of common stock of the paying corporation in lieu of receiving cash dividends. There are two types of plans: One involves only stock that is already outstanding; the other involves newly issued stock. In the first type, the dividends of all participants are pooled and the stock is purchased on the open market. Participants benefit from lower transaction costs. In the second type, the company issues new shares to the participants. Thus, the company issues stock in lieu of the cash dividend.

dividend yield Defined as either the end-of-period dividend divided by the beginning-of-period price or as the ratio of the current dividend to the current price. Valuation formulas use the former definition.

Du Pont chart A chart designed to show the relationships among return on investment, asset turnover, the profit margin, and leverage.

Du Pont equation A formula showing that the rate of return on equity can be found as the profit margin multiplied by the product of total assets turnover and the equity multiplier.

EBITDA Earnings before interest, taxes, depreciation, and amortization.

ECN In an ECN (electronic communications network), orders from potential buyers and sellers are automatically matched and the transaction is automatically completed.

economic life The number of years a project should be operated to maximize its net present value; often less than the maximum potential life.

economic ordering quantity (EOQ) The order quantity that minimizes the costs of ordering and carrying inventories.

Economic Value Added (EVA) A method used to measure a firm's true profitability. EVA is found by taking the firm's after-tax operating profit and subtracting the annual cost of all the capital a firm uses. If the firm generates a positive EVA, its management has created value for its shareholders. If the EVA is negative, management has destroyed shareholder value.

effective (or equivalent) annual rate (EAR or EFF%) The effective annual rate is the rate that, under annual compounding, would have produced the same future value at the end of 1 year as was produced by more frequent compounding, say quarterly. If the compounding occurs annually, then the effective annual rate and the nominal rate are the same. If compounding occurs more frequently, then the effective annual rate is greater than the nominal rate.

efficient frontier The set of efficient portfolios out of the full set of potential portfolios. On a graph, the efficient frontier constitutes the boundary line of the set of potential portfolios.

Efficient Markets Hypothesis (EMH) States (1) that stocks are always in equilibrium and (2) that it is impossible for an investor to consistently "beat the market." The EMH assumes that all important information regarding a stock is reflected in the price of that stock.

efficient portfolio Provides the highest expected return for any degree of risk. The efficient portfolio also provides the lowest degree of risk for any expected return.

embedded options Options that are a part of another project. Also called real options, managerial options, and strategic options.

Employee Retirement Income Security Act (ERISA) The basic federal law governing the structure and administration of corporate pension plans.

entrenchment Occurs when a company has such a weak board of directors and has such strong anti-takeover provisions in its corporate charter that senior managers feel there is little chance of being removed.

EOQ model The equation used to find the economic ordering quantity.

EOQ range The range around the optimal ordering quantity that may be ordered without significantly affecting total inventory costs.

equilibrium The condition under which the intrinsic value of a security is equal to its price; also, when a security's expected return is equal to its required return.

equity premium, RP_M Expected market return minus the risk-free rate; also called market risk premium or equity risk premium.

equity risk premium, RP_M Expected market return minus the risk-free rate; also called market risk premium or equity premium.

EROIC Expected return on invested capital (EROIC) is equal to expected NOPAT divided by the amount of capital that is available at the beginning of the year.

ESOP (employee stock ownership plan) A type of retirement plan in which employees own stock in the company.

euro The currency used by nations in the European Monetary Union.

Eurobond Any bond sold in some country other than the one in whose currency the bond is denominated. Thus, a U.S. firm selling dollar bonds in Switzerland is selling Eurobonds.

Eurodollar A U.S. dollar on deposit in a foreign bank or a foreign branch of a U.S. bank. Eurodollars are used to conduct transactions throughout Europe and the rest of the world.

exchange rate Specifies the number of units of a given currency that can be purchased for one unit of another currency.

exchange rate risk Refers to the fluctuation in exchange rates between currencies over time.

ex-dividend date The date when the right to the dividend leaves the stock. This date was established by stockbrokers to avoid confusion, and it is four business days prior to the holder-of-record date. If the stock sale is made prior to the ex-dividend date, then the dividend is paid to the buyer; if the stock is bought on or after the ex-dividend date, the dividend is paid to the seller.

exercise price The price stated in the option contract at which the security can be bought (or sold). Also called the strike price.

exercise value Equal to the current price of the stock (underlying the option) minus the strike price of the option.

expectations theory States that the slope of the yield curve depends on expectations about future inflation rates and interest rates. Thus, if the annual rate of inflation and future interest rates are expected to increase, then the yield curve will be upward sloping; the curve will be downward sloping if the annual rates are expected to decrease.

expected rate of return, $\hat{r}_s$ The rate of return expected on a stock given its current price and expected future cash flows. If the stock is in equilibrium, the required rate of return will equal the expected rate of return.

extension A form of debt restructuring in which creditors postpone the dates of required interest or principal payments, or both.

extra dividend A dividend paid, in addition to the regular dividend, when earnings permit. Firms with volatile earnings may have a low regular dividend that can be maintained even in years of low profit (or high capital investment) but is supplemented by an extra dividend when excess funds are available.

fairness The standard of fairness states that claims must be recognized in the order of their legal and contractual priority. In simpler terms, the reorganization must be fair to all parties.

Fama-French three-factor model Includes one factor for the excess market return (the market return minus the risk-free rate), a second factor for size (defined as the return on a portfolio of small firms minus the return on a portfolio of big firms), and a third factor for the book-to-market effect (defined as the return on a portfolio of firms with a high book-to-market ratio minus the return on a portfolio of firms with a low book-to-market ratio).

FASB Financial Accounting Standards Board Promulgates standards for issues pertaining to private organizations.

FASB Statement 13 The Financial Accounting Standards Board statement that spells out the conditions under which a lease must be capitalized and the specific procedures to follow.

feasibility The standard of feasibility states that there must be a reasonably high probability of successful rehabilitation and profitable future operations.

feasible set Represents all portfolios that can be constructed from a given set of stocks; also known as the attainable set.

financial distress costs Incurred when a leveraged firm facing a decline in earnings is forced to take actions to avoid bankruptcy. These costs may be the result of delays in the liquidation of assets, legal fees, the effects on product quality from cutting costs, and evasive actions by suppliers and customers.

financial futures Provide for the purchase or sale of a financial asset at some time in the future, but at a price that is established today. Financial futures exist for Treasury bills, Treasury notes and bonds, certificates of deposit, Eurodollar deposits, foreign currencies, and stock indexes.

financial intermediary Intermediary that buys securities with funds that it obtains by issuing its own securities. An example is a common stock mutual fund that buys common stocks with funds obtained by issuing shares in the mutual fund.

financial lease Covers the entire expected life of the equipment; does not provide for maintenance service, is not cancellable and is fully amortized.

financial leverage The extent to which fixed-income securities (debt and preferred stock) are used in a firm's capital structure. If a high percentage of a firm's capital structure is in the form of debt and preferred stock, then the firm is said to have a high degree of financial leverage.

financial merger A merger in which the companies will not be operated as a single unit and for which no operating economies are expected.

financial risk The risk added by the use of debt financing. Debt financing increases the variability of earnings before taxes (but after interest); thus, along with business risk, it contributes to the uncertainty of net income and earnings per share. Business risk plus financial risk equals total corporate risk.

financial service corporation A corporation that offers a wide range of financial services such as brokerage operations, insurance, and commercial banking.

financing feedback Circularity created when additional debt causes additional interest expense, which reduces the addition to retained earnings, which in turn requires a higher level of debt, which causes still more interest expense, causing the cycle to be repeated.

fixed assets turnover ratio The ratio of sales to net fixed assets; it measures how effectively the firm uses its plant and equipment.

fixed exchange rate system The system in effect from the end of World War II until August 1971. Under the system, the U.S. dollar was linked to gold at the rate of $35 per ounce, and other currencies were then tied to the dollar.

floating exchange rates The system currently in effect, where the forces of supply and demand are allowed to determine currency prices with little government intervention.

floating-rate bond A bond whose coupon payment may vary over time. The coupon rate is usually linked to the rate on some other security, such as a Treasury security, or to some other rate, such as the prime rate or LIBOR.

flotation cost, F Those costs occurring when a company issues a new security, including fees to an investment banker and legal fees.

forecasted financial statements approach A method of forecasting financial statements to determine the additional funds needed. Many items on the income statement and balance sheets are assumed to increase proportionally with sales. As sales increase, these items that are tied to sales also increase, and the values of these items for a particular year are estimated as percentages of the forecasted sales for that year. The first step in forecasting financial statements is to forecast the future sales growth rate.

foreign bond A bond sold by a foreign borrower but denominated in the currency of the country in which the issue is sold. Thus, a U.S. firm selling bonds denominated in Swiss francs in Switzerland is selling foreign bonds.

foreign trade deficit A deficit that occurs when businesses and individuals in the United States import more goods from foreign countries than are exported.

forward contract A contract to buy or sell some item at some time in the future at a price established when the contract is entered into.

forward exchange rate The prevailing exchange rate for exchange (delivery) at some agreed-upon future date, which is usually 30, 90, or 180 days from the day the transaction is negotiated.

founders' shares Stock owned by the firm's founders that have sole voting rights but restricted dividends for a specified number of years.

free cash flow (FCF) The cash flow actually available for distribution to all investors after the company has made all investments in fixed assets and working capital necessary to sustain ongoing operations.

free trade credit Credit received during the discount period.

friendly merger Occurs when the target company's management agrees to the merger and recommends that shareholders approve the deal.

fully funded pension plan The present value of all expected retirement benefits is equal to assets on hand.

fund capital Not-for-profit business equivalent of equity capital. It consists of retained profits and charitable contributions.

funding strategy Necessary for a defined benefit plan and involves two decisions: how fast should any unfunded liability be reduced and what rate of return should be assumed in the actuarial calculations.

FVA$_N$ The future value of a stream of annuity payments, where N is the number of payments of the annuity.

FVIFA$_{I,N}$ The future value interest factor for an ordinary annuity of N periodic payments paying I percent interest per period.

FVIF$_{I,N}$ The future value interest factor for a lump sum left in an account for N periods paying I percent interest per period.

FV$_N$ The future value of an initial single cash flow, where N is the number of periods the initial cash flow is compounded.

GAAP, Generally Accepted Accounting Principles A set of standards for financial reporting established by the accounting profession.

GASB, Government Accounting Standards Board Promulgates standards for issues pertaining to governmental entities.

general obligation bonds Type of municipal bonds which are secured by the full faith and credit of a government unit; that is, backed by the full taxing authority of the issuer.

going public The act of selling stock to the public at large by a closely held corporation or its principal stockholders.

golden parachute A payment made to executives who are forced out when a merger takes place.

greenmail Targeted share repurchases that occur when a company buys back stock from a potential acquirer at a higher than fair-market price. In return, the potential acquirer agrees not to attempt to take over the company.

gross profit margin Ratio of gross profit (sales minus cost of goods sold) divided by sales.

growth option Occurs if an investment creates the opportunity to make other potentially profitable investments that would not otherwise be possible, including options to expand output, to enter a new geographical market, and to introduce complementary products or successive generations of products.

GSE (government-sponsored entity) debt Debt issued by government-sponsored entities (GSEs) such as the Tennessee Valley Authority or the Small Business Administration; not officially backed by the full faith and credit of the U.S. government.

guideline lease Meets all of the Internal Revenue Service (IRS) requirements for a genuine lease.

If a lease meets the IRS guidelines, the IRS allows the lessor to deduct the asset's depreciation and allows the lessee to deduct the lease payments. Also called a tax-oriented lease.

hard currencies Currencies considered to be convertible because the nation that issues them allows them to be traded in the currency markets and is willing to redeem them at market rates.

hedging A transaction that lowers a firm's risk of damage due to fluctuating commodity prices, interest rates, and exchange rates.

herding instinct When one group of investors does well, other investors begin to emulate them, acting like a herd of sheep.

holder-of-record date If a company lists the stockholder as an owner on the holder-of-record date, then the stockholder receives the dividend.

holding company A corporation formed for the sole purpose of owning stocks in other companies. A holding company differs from a stock mutual fund in that holding companies own sufficient stock in their operating companies to exercise effective working control.

holdout A problematic characteristic of informal reorganizations whereby all of the involved parties do not agree to the voluntary plan. Holdouts are usually made by creditors in an effort to receive full payment on claims.

horizon value The value of operations at the end of the explicit forecast period. It is equal to the present value of all free cash flows beyond the forecast period, discounted back to the end of the forecast period at the weighted average cost of capital.

horizontal merger A merger between two companies in the same line of business.

hostile merger Occurs when the management of the target company resists the offer.

hurdle rate The project cost of capital, or discount rate. It is the rate used to discount future cash flows in the net present value method or to compare with the internal rate of return.

improper accumulation The retention of earnings by a business for the purpose of enabling stockholders to avoid personal income taxes on dividends.

income bond Pays interest only if the interest is earned. These securities cannot bankrupt a company, but from an investor's standpoint, they are riskier than "regular" bonds.

income statement Summarizes the firm's revenues and expenses over an accounting period. Net sales are shown at the top of each statement, after which various costs, including income taxes, are subtracted to obtain the net income available to common stockholders. The bottom of the statement reports earnings and dividends per share.

incremental cash flow Those cash flows that arise solely from the asset that is being evaluated.

indentures A legal document that spells out the rights of both bondholders and the issuing corporation.

independent projects Projects that can be accepted or rejected individually.

indexed, or purchasing power, bond The interest rate of such a bond is based on an inflation index such as the consumer price index (CPI), so the interest paid rises automatically when the inflation rate rises, thus protecting the bondholders against inflation.

indifference curve The risk–return trade-off function for a particular investor; reflects that investor's attitude toward risk. An investor would be indifferent between any pair of assets on the same indifference curve. In risk–return space, the greater the slope of the indifference curve, the greater is the investor's risk aversion.

indirect quotation When discussing exchange rates, the number of units of foreign currency that can be purchased for one U.S. dollar.

inflation premium (IP) The premium added to the real risk-free rate of interest to compensate for the expected loss of purchasing power. The inflation premium is the average rate of inflation expected over the life of the security.

informal debt restructuring An agreement between a troubled firm and its creditors to change existing debt terms. An extension postpones the required payment date; a composition is a reduction in creditor claims.

information content, or signaling, hypothesis A theory that holds that investors regard dividend changes as "signals" of management forecasts. Thus, when dividends are raised, this is viewed by investors as recognition by management of future earnings increases. Therefore, if a firm's stock price increases with a dividend increase, the reason may not be investor preference for dividends but rather expectations of higher future earnings. Conversely, a dividend reduction may signal that management is forecasting poor earnings in the future.

initial public offering (IPO) Occurs when a closely held corporation or its principal stockholders sell stock to the public at large.

initial public offering (IPO) market Going public is the act of selling stock to the public at large by a closely held corporation or its principal stockholders, and this market is often termed the initial public offering market.

I_{NOM} The nominal, or quoted, interest rate.

insiders The officers, directors, and major stockholders of a firm.

interest coverage ratio Also called the times-interest-earned (TIE) ratio; determined by dividing earnings before interest and taxes by the interest expense.

interest rate parity Holds that investors should expect to earn the same return in all countries after adjusting for risk.

interest rate risk Arises from the fact that bond prices decline when interest rates rise. Under these circumstances, selling a bond prior to maturity will result in a capital loss; the longer the term to maturity, the larger the loss.

interlocking boards of directors Occur when the CEO of Company A sits on the board of Company B while B's CEO sits on A's board.

internal rate of return (IRR) method The discount rate that equates the present value of the expected future cash inflows and outflows. IRR measures the rate of return on a project, but it assumes that all cash flows can be reinvested at the IRR rate.

international bond Any bond sold outside of the country of the borrower. There are two types of international bonds: Eurobonds and foreign bonds.

intrinsic (or fundamental) value, P_0 The present value of a firm's expected future free cash flows.

inventory conversion period The average length of time to convert materials into finished goods and then to sell them; calculated by dividing total inventory by sales per day.

inventory turnover ratio Sales divided by inventories.

inverted (abnormal) yield curve A downward-sloping yield curve.

investment bank A firm that assists in the design of an issuing firm's corporate securities and in the sale of the new securities to investors in the primary market.

investment grade bond Securities with ratings of Baa/BBB or above.

investment strategy Deals with the question of how the pension assets portfolio should be structured given the assumed actuarial rate of return.

investment timing option Gives companies the option to delay a project rather than implement it immediately. This option to wait allows a company to reduce the uncertainty of market conditions before it decides to implement the project.

Jensen's alpha Measures the vertical distance of a portfolio's return above or below the Security Market Line; first suggested by Professor Michael Jensen, it became popular because of its ease of calculation.

joint venture Involves the joining together of parts of companies to accomplish specific, limited objectives. Joint ventures are controlled by the combined management of the two (or more) parent companies.

junk bond High-risk, high-yield bond issued to finance leveraged buyouts, mergers, or troubled companies.

lessee The party leasing the property.

lessee's analysis Involves determining whether leasing an asset is less costly than buying the asset. The lessee will compare the present value cost of leasing the asset with the present value cost of purchasing the asset (assuming the funds to purchase the asset are obtained through a loan). If the present value cost of the lease is less than the present value cost of purchasing, then the asset should be leased. The lessee can also analyze the lease using the IRR approach or the equivalent loan method.

lessor The party receiving the payments from the lease (that is, the owner of the property).

lessor's analysis Involves determining the rate of return on the proposed lease. If the internal rate of return of the lease cash flows exceeds the lessor's opportunity cost of capital, then the lease is a good investment. This is equivalent to analyzing whether the net present value of the lease is positive.

leveraged buyout (LBO) A transaction in which a firm's publicly owned stock is acquired in a mostly debt-financed tender offer, resulting in a privately owned, highly leveraged firm. Often, the firm's own management initiates the LBO.

leveraged lease The lessor borrows a portion of the funds needed to buy the equipment to be leased.

LIBOR (London Interbank Offered Rate) The rate that U.K. banks charge one another.

limited liability partnership A limited liability partnership (LLP), sometimes called a limited liability company (LLC), combines the limited liability advantage of a corporation with the tax advantages of a partnership.

limited partnership A partnership in which limited partners' liabilities, investment returns, and control are limited; general partners have unlimited liability and control.

line of credit An arrangement in which a bank agrees to lend up to a specified maximum amount of funds during a designated period.

liquidation in bankruptcy The sale of the assets of a firm and the distribution of the proceeds to the creditors and owners in a specific priority.

liquidity Liquidity refers to a firm's cash and marketable securities position and to its ability to meet maturing obligations. A liquid asset is any asset that can be quickly sold and converted to cash at its "fair" value. Active markets provide liquidity.

liquidity premium (LP) A liquidity premium is added to the real risk-free rate of interest, in addition to other premiums, if a security is not liquid.

liquidity ratio A ratio that shows the relationship of a firm's cash and other current assets to its current liabilities.

lockbox plan A cash management tool in which incoming checks for a firm are sent to post office boxes rather than to corporate headquarters. Several times a day, a local bank will collect the contents of the lockbox and deposit the checks into the company's local account.

long hedges Occur when futures contracts are bought in anticipation of (or to guard against) price increases.

low-regular-dividend-plus-extras policy Dividend policy in which a company announces a low regular dividend that it is sure can be maintained; if extra funds are available, the company pays a specially designated extra dividend or repurchases shares of stock.

lumpy assets Those assets that cannot be acquired smoothly and instead require large, discrete additions. For example, an electric utility that is operating at full capacity cannot add a small amount of generating capacity, at least not economically.

managerial options Options that give opportunities to managers to respond to changing market conditions. Also called real options.

margin requirement The margin is the percentage of a stock's price that an investor has borrowed in order to purchase the stock. The Securities and Exchange Commission sets margin requirements, which is the maximum percentage of debt that can be used to purchase a stock.

marginal tax rate The tax rate on the last unit of income.

market multiple method Multiplies a market-determined ratio (called a multiple) by some value of the target firm to estimate the target's value. The market multiple can be based on net income, earnings per share, sales, book value, or number of subscribers.

market portfolio A portfolio consisting of all stocks.

market risk That part of a security's total risk that cannot be eliminated by diversification; measured by the beta coefficient.

market risk premium, RP$_M$ The difference between the expected return on the market and the risk-free rate.

Market Value Added (MVA) The difference between the market value of the firm (that is, the sum of the market value of common equity, the market value of debt, and the market value of preferred stock) and the book value of the firm's common equity, debt, and preferred stock. If the book values of debt and preferred stock are equal to their market values, then MVA is also equal to the difference between the market value of equity and the amount of equity capital that investors supplied.

market value ratios Relate the firm's stock price to its earnings and book value per share.

marketable securities Can be converted to cash on very short notice and provide at least a modest return.

maturity date The date when the bond's par value is repaid to the bondholder. Maturity dates generally range from 10 to 40 years from the time of issue.

maturity matching short-term financing policy A policy that matches asset and liability maturities. It is also referred to as the moderate, or self-liquidating, approach.

maturity risk premium (MRP) The premium that must be added to the real risk-free rate of interest to compensate for interest rate risk, which depends on a bond's maturity. Interest rate risk arises from the fact that bond prices decline when interest rates rise. Under these circumstances, selling a

bond prior to maturity will result in a capital loss; the longer the term to maturity, the larger the loss.

merger The joining of two firms to form a single firm.

Miller model Introduces the effect of personal taxes into the valuation of a levered firm, which reduces the advantage of corporate debt financing.

MM Proposition I with corporate taxes $V_L = V_U + TD$. Thus, firm value increases with leverage and the optimal capital structure is virtually all debt.

MM Proposition I without taxes $V_L = V_U = EBIT/r_{sU}$. Since both EBIT and r_{sU} are constant, firm value is also constant and capital structure is irrelevant.

MM Proposition II with corporate taxes $r_{sL} = r_{sU} + (r_{sU} - r_d)(1 - T)(D/S)$. Here the increase in equity costs is less than the zero-tax case, and the increasing use of lower-cost debt causes the firm's cost of capital to decrease. In this case, the optimal capital structure is virtually all debt.

MM Proposition II without taxes $r_{sL} = r_{sU} - (r_{sU} - r_d)(D/S)$. Thus, r_s increases in a precise way as leverage increases. In fact, this increase is just sufficient to offset the increased use of lower-cost debt.

moderate net operating working capital policy A policy that matches asset and liability maturities. It is also referred to as maturity matching or the self-liquidating approach.

Modified Internal Rate of Return (MIRR) method Assumes that cash flows from all projects are reinvested at the cost of capital, not at the project's own IRR. This makes the modified internal rate of return a better indicator of a project's true profitability.

money market A financial market for debt securities with maturities of less than 1 year (short-term). The New York money market is the world's largest.

money market fund A mutual fund that invests in short-term debt instruments and offers investors check-writing privileges; thus, it amounts to an interest-bearing checking account.

Monte Carlo simulation analysis A risk analysis technique in which a computer is used to simulate probable future events and thus to estimate the likely profitability and risk of a project.

mortgage bond A bond for which a corporation pledges certain assets as security. All such bonds are written subject to an indenture.

multinational (or global) corporation A corporation that operates in two or more countries.

municipal bond Issued by state and local governments. The interest earned on most municipal bonds is exempt from federal taxes and also from state taxes if the holder is a resident of the issuing state.

municipal bond insurance An insurance company guarantees to pay the coupon and principal payments should the issuer of the bond (the municipality) default. This reduces the risk to investors who are willing to accept a lower coupon rate for an insured bond issue compared to an uninsured issue.

mutual fund A corporation that sells shares in the fund and uses the proceeds to buy stocks, long-term bonds, or short-term debt instruments. The resulting dividends, interest, and capital gains are distributed to the fund's shareholders after the deduction of operating expenses. Some funds specialize in certain types of securities, such as growth stocks, international stocks, or municipal bonds.

mutually exclusive projects Projects that cannot be performed at the same time. A company could choose either Project 1 or Project 2, or it can reject both, but it cannot accept both projects.

National Association of Securities Dealers (NASD) An industry group primarily concerned with the operation of the over-the-counter (OTC) market.

natural hedge A transaction between two counterparties where both parties' risks are reduced.

net advantage to leasing (NAL) The dollar value of the lease to the lessee. It is, in a sense, the net present value of leasing versus owning.

net cash flow The sum of net income plus noncash adjustments.

net float The difference between a firm's disbursement float and collections float.

net operating working capital (NOWC) Operating current assets minus operating current liabilities. Operating current assets are the current assets used to support operations, such as cash, accounts receivable, and inventory. They do not include short-term investments. Operating current liabilities are the current liabilities that are a natural consequence of the firm's operations, such as accounts payable and accruals. They do not include notes payable or any other short-term debt that charges interest.

net present value (NPV) method Used to assess the present value of the project's expected future cash flows, discounted at the appropriate cost of capital. NPV is a direct measure of the value of the project to shareholders.

net working capital Current assets minus current liabilities.

new issue market The market for stock of companies that go public.

nominal (quoted) interest rate, I_{NOM} The rate of interest stated in a contract. If the compounding occurs annually, the effective annual rate and the nominal rate are the same. If compounding occurs more frequently, the effective annual rate is greater than the nominal rate. The nominal annual interest rate is also called the annual percentage rate, or APR.

nominal rate of return, r_n Includes an inflation adjustment (premium). Thus, if nominal rates of return are used in the capital budgeting process, then the net cash flows must also be nominal.

nominal risk-free rate of interest, r_{RF} The real risk-free rate plus a premium for expected inflation. The short-term nominal risk-free rate is usually approximated by the U.S. Treasury bill rate, and the long-term nominal risk-free rate is approximated by the rate on U.S. Treasury bonds.

nonnormal cash flow projects Projects with a large cash outflow either sometime during or at the end of their lives. A common problem encountered when evaluating projects with nonnormal cash flows is multiple internal rates of return.

nonoperating assets Include investments in marketable securities and noncontrolling interests in the stock of other companies.

nonpecuniary benefits Perks that are not actual cash payments, such as lavish offices, memberships at country clubs, corporate jets, and excessively large staffs.

NOPAT (net operating profit after taxes) The amount of profit a company would generate if it had no debt and no financial assets.

normal cash flow project A project with one or more cash outflows (costs) followed by a series of cash inflows.

normal yield curve When the yield curve slopes upward it is said to be "normal," because it is like this most of the time.

not-for-profit corporation A tax-exempt charitable organization. The tax code defines a charitable organization as any corporation, community chest, fund, or foundation that is organized and operated exclusively for religious, charitable, scientific, public safety, literary, or educational purposes. This standard may be expanded to include an organization that provides health care services provided other requirements are met.

off–balance sheet financing A financing technique in which a firm uses partnerships and other arrangements to (in effect) borrow money while not reporting the liability on its balance sheet. For example, for many years neither leased assets nor the liabilities under lease contracts appeared on the lessees' balance sheets. To correct this problem, the Financial Accounting Standards Board issued FASB Statement 13.

official statement Contains information about municipal bond issues. It is prepared before the issue is brought to market.

open outcry auction A method of matching buyers and sellers in which the buyers and sellers are face-to-face, all stating a price at which they will buy or sell.

operating capital The sum of net operating working capital and operating long-term assets, such as net plant and equipment. Operating capital also is equal to the net amount of capital raised from investors. This is the amount of interest-bearing debt plus preferred stock plus common equity minus short-term investments. Also called total net operating capital, net operating capital, or net operating assets.

operating company A company controlled by a holding company.

operating current assets The current assets used to support operations, such as cash, accounts receivable, and inventory. It does not include short-term investments.

operating current liabilities The current liabilities that are a natural consequence of the firm's operations, such as accounts payable and accruals. It does not include notes payable or any other short-term debt that charges interest.

operating lease Provides for both financing and maintenance. Generally, the operating lease contract is written for a period considerably shorter than the expected life of the leased equipment and contains a cancellation clause; sometimes called a service lease.

operating leverage The extent to which fixed costs are used in a firm's operations. If a high percentage of a firm's total costs are fixed costs, then the firm is said to have a high degree of operating leverage. Operating leverage is a measure of one element of business risk but does not include the second major element, sales variability.

operating merger Occurs when the operations of two companies are integrated with the expectation of obtaining synergistic gains. These may occur in response to economies of scale, management efficiency, or a host of other factors.

operating profit margin Ratio of earnings before interest and taxes divided by sales.

opportunity cost A cash flow that a firm must forgo in order to accept a project. For example, if the project requires the use of a building that could otherwise be sold, then the market value of the building is an opportunity cost of the project.

opportunity cost rate The rate of return available on the best alternative investment of similar risk.

optimal distribution policy The distribution policy that maximizes the value of the firm by choosing the optimal level and form of distributions (dividends and stock repurchases).

optimal dividend policy The dividend policy that strikes a balance between current dividends and future growth and maximizes the firm's stock price.

optimal portfolio The point at which the efficient set of portfolios—the efficient frontier—is just tangent to the investor's indifference curve. This point marks the highest level of satisfaction an investor can attain given the set of potential portfolios.

option A contract that gives its holder the right to buy or sell an asset at some predetermined price within a specified period of time.

ordinary (deferred) annuity An annuity with a fixed number of equal payments occurring at the end of each period.

original issue discount (OID) bond In general, any bond originally offered at a price that is significantly below its par value.

overfunded pension plan The assets on hand exceed the present value of all expected retirement benefits.

par value The nominal or face value of a stock or bond. The par value of a bond generally represents the amount of money that the firm borrows and promises to repay at some future date. The par value of a bond is often $1,000, but it can be $5,000 or more.

parent company Another name for a holding company. A parent company will often have control over many subsidiaries.

partnership A partnership exists when two or more persons associate to conduct a business.

payables deferral period The average length of time between a firm's purchase of materials and labor and the payment of cash for them. It is calculated by dividing accounts payable by credit purchases per day (i.e., cost of goods sold ÷ 365).

payback period The number of years it takes a firm to recover its project investment. Payback does not capture a project's entire cash flow stream and is thus not the preferred evaluation method. Note, however, that the payback does measure a project's liquidity, so many firms use it as a risk measure.

payment date The date on which a firm actually mails dividend checks.

payment, PMT Equal to the dollar amount of an equal or constant cash flow (an annuity).

payments pattern approach A method of monitoring accounts receivable that looks for changes in a customers' payment pattern. This takes into account the seasonal nature of customer orders.

pegged exchange rates Rates that are fixed against a major currency such as the U.S. dollar. Consequently, the values of the pegged currencies move together over time.

Pension Benefit Guarantee Corporation Established by ERISA to insure corporate defined benefits plans; PBGC steps in and takes over payments to retirees of bankrupt companies with underfunded pension plans.

perfect hedge A hedge in which the gain or loss on the hedged transaction exactly offsets the loss or gain on the unhedged position.

periodic rate, I_{PER} The rate charged by a lender or paid by a borrower each period. It can be a rate per year, per 6-month period, per quarter, per month, per day, or per any other time interval (usually 1 year or less).

permanent net operating working capital The NOWC required when the economy is weak and seasonal sales are at their low point. Thus, this level of NOWC always requires financing and can be regarded as permanent.

perpetuity A series of payments of a fixed amount that continue indefinitely.

physical location exchanges Exchanges, such as the New York Stock Exchange, that facilitate trading of securities at a particular location.

plug technique Technique used in financial forecasting to "plug" in enough new liabilities or assets to make the balance sheets balance.

poison pills Shareholder rights provisions that allow existing shareholders in a company to purchase additional shares of stock at a lower-than-market value if a potential acquirer purchases a controlling stake in the company.

political risk Refers to the possibility of expropriation and the unanticipated restriction of cash flows to the parent by a foreign government.

pooling of interests A method of accounting for a merger in which the consolidated balance sheet is constructed by simply adding together the balance sheets of the merged companies. This is no longer allowed.

portability A portable pension plan is one that the employee can carry from one employer to another.

portfolio A group of individual assets held in combination. An asset that would be relatively risky if held in isolation may have little or no risk if held in a well-diversified portfolio.

post-audit The final aspect of the capital budgeting process. The post-audit is a feedback process in which the actual results are compared with those predicted in the original capital budgeting analysis. The post-audit has several purposes, of which the most important are to improve forecasts and operations.

precautionary balance A cash balance held in reserve for random, unforeseen fluctuations in cash inflows and outflows.

preemptive right Gives the current shareholders the right to purchase any new shares issued in proportion to their current holdings. The preemptive right enables current owners to maintain their proportionate share of ownership and control of the business.

preferred stock A hybrid security that is similar to bonds in some respects and to common stock in other respects. Preferred dividends are similar to interest payments on bonds in that they are fixed in amount and generally must be paid before common stock dividends can be paid. If the preferred dividend is not earned, the directors can omit it without throwing the company into bankruptcy.

premium bond Bond prices and interest rates are inversely related; that is, they tend to move in the opposite direction from one another. A fixed-rate bond will sell at par when its coupon interest rate is equal to the going rate of interest, r_d. When the going rate of interest is above the coupon rate, a fixed-rate bond will sell at a "discount" below its par value. If current interest rates are below the coupon rate, a fixed-rate bond will sell at a "premium" above its par value.

premium on forward rate Occurs when the forward exchange rate differs from the spot rate. When the forward rate is above the spot rate, it is said to be at a premium.

prepackaged bankruptcy (or pre-pack) A type of reorganization that combines the advantages of informal workouts and formal Chapter 11 reorganization.

price/cash flow ratio Calculated by dividing price per share by cash flow per share. This shows how much investors are willing to pay per dollar of cash flow.

price/earnings (P/E) ratio Calculated by dividing price per share by earnings per share. This shows how much investors are willing to pay per dollar of reported profits.

price/EBITDA ratio The ratio of price per share divided by per share earnings before interest, depreciation, and amortization.

primary market Markets in which newly issued securities are sold for the first time.

priority of claims in liquidation Established in Chapter 7 of the Bankruptcy Act. It specifies the order in which the debtor's assets are distributed among the creditors.

private markets Markets in which transactions are worked out directly between two parties and structured in any manner that appeals to them. Bank loans and private placements of debt with insurance companies are examples of private market transactions.

private placement The sale of stock to only one or a few investors, usually institutional investors. The advantages of private placements are lower flotation costs and greater speed, since the shares issued are not subject to Securities and Exchange Commission registration.

probability distribution A listing, chart, or graph of all possible outcomes, such as expected rates of return, with a probability assigned to each outcome.

professional corporation (PC) Has most of the benefits of incorporation but the participants are not relieved of professional (malpractice) liability; known in some states as a professional association (PA).

profit margin on sales Calculated by dividing net income by sales; gives the profit per dollar of sales.

profit sharing plan Under this type of pension plan, employers make payments into the retirement fund but the payments to retirees vary with the level of corporate profits.

profitability index Found by dividing the project's present value of future cash flows by its initial cost. A profitability index greater than 1 is equivalent to a project's having positive net present value.

profitability ratios Ratios that show the combined effects of liquidity, asset management, and debt on operations.

progressive tax A tax system in which the higher one's income, the larger the percentage paid in taxes.

project cash flows The incremental cash flows of a proposed project.

project cost of capital The risk-adjusted discount rate for that project.

project financing Financing method in which the project's creditors do not have full recourse against the borrowers; the lenders and lessors must be paid from the project's cash flows and equity.

projected (pro forma) financial statement Shows how an actual statement would look if certain assumptions are realized.

promissory note A document specifying the terms and conditions of a loan, including the amount, interest rate, and repayment schedule.

proprietorship A business owned by one individual.

prospectus Summarizes information about a new security issue and the issuing company.

proxy A document giving one person the authority to act for another, typically the power to vote shares of common stock.

proxy fight An attempt to take over a company in which an outside group solicits existing shareholders' proxies, which are authorizations to vote shares in a shareholders' meeting, in an effort to overthrow management and take control of the business.

public markets Markets in which standardized contracts are traded on organized exchanges. Securities that are issued in public markets, such as common stock and corporate bonds, are ultimately held by a large number of individuals.

public offering An offer of new common stock to the general public.

publicly owned corporation Corporation in which the stock is owned by a large number of investors, most of whom are not active in management.

purchase accounting A method of accounting for a merger in which the merger is handled as a purchase. In this method, the acquiring firm is assumed to have "bought" the acquired company in much the same way it would buy any capital asset.

purchasing power parity Implies that the level of exchange rates adjusts so that identical goods cost the same in different countries. Sometimes referred to as the "law of one price."

put option Allows the holder to sell the asset at some predetermined price within a specified period of time.

PV The value today of a future payment, or stream of payments, discounted at the appropriate rate of interest. PV is also the beginning amount that will grow to some future value.

PVA$_N$ The value today of a future stream of N equal payments at the end of each period (an ordinary annuity).

PVIFA$_{I,N}$ The present value interest factor for an ordinary annuity of N periodic payments discounted at I percent interest per period.

PVIF$_{I,N}$ The present value interest factor for a lump sum received N periods in the future discounted at I percent per period.

quick, or acid test, ratio Found by taking current assets less inventories and then dividing by current liabilities.

real options Occur when managers can influence the size and risk of a project's cash flows by taking different actions during the project's life. They are referred to as real options because they deal with real as opposed to financial assets. They are also called managerial options because they give opportunities to managers to respond to changing market conditions. Sometimes they are called strategic options because they often deal with strategic issues. Finally, they are also called embedded options because they are a part of another project.

real rate of return, r$_r$ Contains no adjustment for expected inflation. If net cash flows from a project do not include inflation adjustments,

then the cash flows should be discounted at the real cost of capital. In a similar manner, the internal rate of return resulting from real net cash flows should be compared with the real cost of capital.

real risk-free rate of interest, r* The interest rate on a risk-free security in an economy with zero inflation. The real risk-free rate could also be called the pure rate of interest since it is the rate of interest that would exist on very short-term, default-free U.S. Treasury securities if the expected rate of inflation were zero.

realized rate of return, r̄ The actual return an investor receives on his or her investment. It can be quite different than the expected return.

receivables collection period The average length of time required to convert a firm's receivables into cash. It is calculated by dividing accounts receivable by sales per day.

red herring (preliminary) prospectus A preliminary prospectus that may be distributed to potential buyers prior to approval of the registration statement by the Securities and Exchange Commission. After the registration has become effective, the securities—accompanied by the prospectus—may be offered for sale.

redeemable bond Gives investors the right to sell the bonds back to the corporation at a price that is usually close to the par value. If interest rates rise, then investors can redeem the bonds and reinvest at the higher rates.

refunding Occurs when a company issues debt at current low rates and uses the proceeds to repurchase one of its existing high–coupon rate debt issues. Often these are callable issues, which means the company can purchase the debt at a call price lower than the market price.

registration statement Required by the Securities and Exchange Commission before a company's securities can be offered to the public. This statement is used to summarize various pieces of financial and legal information about the company.

reinvestment rate risk Occurs when a short-term debt security must be "rolled over." If interest rates have fallen, then the reinvestment of principal will be at a lower rate with correspondingly lower interest payments and ending value.

relative priority doctrine More flexible than absolute priority. Gives a more balanced consideration to all claimants in a bankruptcy reorganization than does the absolute priority doctrine.

relaxed net operating working capital policy A policy under which relatively large amounts of cash, marketable securities, and inventories are carried and under which sales are stimulated by a liberal credit policy, resulting in a high level of receivables.

reorder point The inventory level at which a new order is placed.

reorganization in bankruptcy A court-approved attempt to keep a company alive by changing its capital structure in lieu of liquidation. A reorganization must adhere to the standards of fairness and feasibility.

repatriation of earnings The cash flow, usually in the form of dividends or royalties, from the foreign branch or subsidiary to the parent company. These cash flows must be converted to the currency of the parent and thus are subject to future exchange rate changes. A foreign government may restrict the amount of cash that may be repatriated.

replacement chain (common life) approach A method of comparing mutually exclusive projects that have unequal lives. Each project is replicated so that they will both terminate in a common year. If projects with lives of 3 years and 5 years are being evaluated, then the 3-year project would be replicated 5 times and the 5-year project replicated 3 times; thus, both projects would terminate in 15 years.

required rate of return, r_s The minimum acceptable rate of return, considering both its risk and the returns available on other investments.

reserve borrowing capacity Exists when a firm uses less debt under "normal" conditions than called for by the trade-off theory. This allows the firm some flexibility to use debt in the future when additional capital is needed.

residual distribution model In this model, firms should pay dividends only when more earnings are available than needed to support the optimal capital budget.

residual value The market value of the leased property at the expiration of the lease. The estimate of the residual value is one of the key elements in lease analysis.

restricted charitable contributions Donations that can be used only for designated purposes.

restricted net operating working capital policy A policy under which holdings of cash, securities, inventories, and receivables are minimized.

restricted voting rights A provision that automatically deprives a shareholder of voting rights if the shareholder owns more than a specified amount of stock.

retained earnings The portion of the firm's earnings that have been saved rather than paid out as dividends.

retiree health benefits A major issue for employers because of the escalating costs of health care and a recent FASB ruling forcing companies to accrue the retiree health care liability rather than expensing the cash flows as they occur.

return on common equity (ROE) Found by dividing net income by common equity.

return on invested capital (ROIC) Net operating profit after taxes divided by the operating capital.

return on total assets (ROA) The ratio of net income to total assets.

revaluation Occurs when the relative price of a currency is increased. It is the opposite of devaluation.

revenue bonds Type of municipal bonds which are secured by the revenues derived from projects such as roads and bridges, airports, water and sewage systems, and not-for-profit health care facilities.

reverse split Situation in which shareholders exchange a particular number of shares of stock for a smaller number of new shares.

revolving credit agreement A formal, committed line of credit extended by a bank or other lending institution.

rights offering Occurs when a corporation sells a new issue of common stock to its existing stockholders. Each stockholder receives a certificate, called a stock purchase right, giving the stockholder the option to purchase a specified number of the new shares. The rights are issued in proportion to the amount of stock that each shareholder currently owns.

risk arbitrage The practice of purchasing stock in companies (in the context of mergers) that may become takeover targets.

risk aversion A risk-averse investor dislikes risk and requires a higher rate of return as an inducement to buy riskier securities.

risk premium for Stock i, RP_i The extra return that an investor requires to hold risky Stock i instead of a risk-free asset.

risk-adjusted discount rate Incorporates the risk of the project's cash flows. The cost of capital to the firm reflects the average risk of the firm's existing projects. Thus, new projects that are riskier than existing projects should have a higher risk-adjusted discount rate. Conversely, projects with less risk should have a lower risk-adjusted discount rate.

roadshow Before an IPO, the senior management team and the investment banker make presentations to potential investors. They make three to five presentations daily over a 2-week period in 10 to 20 cities.

S corporation A small corporation that, under Subchapter S of the Internal Revenue Code, elects to be taxed as a proprietorship or a partnership yet retains limited liability and other benefits of the corporate form of organization.

safety stock Inventory held to guard against larger-than-normal sales and/or shipping delays.

sale-and-leaseback A type of financial lease in which the firm owning the property sells it to another firm, often a financial institution, while simultaneously entering into an agreement to lease the property back from the firm.

salvage value The market value of an asset after its useful life.

scenario analysis A shorter version of simulation analysis that uses only a few outcomes. Often the outcomes are for three scenarios: optimistic, pessimistic, and most likely.

seasonal effects on ratios Seasonal factors can distort ratio analysis. At certain times of the year, a firm may have excessive inventories in preparation of a "season" of high demand. Therefore, an inventory turnover ratio taken at this time will be radically different than one taken after the season.

secondary market Markets in which securities are resold after initial issue in the primary market. The New York Stock Exchange is an example.

secured loan A loan backed by collateral, which is often in the form of inventories or receivables.

Securities and Exchange Commission (SEC) A government agency which regulates the sales of new securities and the operations of securities exchanges. The SEC, along with other government agencies and self-regulation, helps ensure stable markets, sound brokerage firms, and the absence of stock manipulation.

securitization The process whereby financial instruments that were previously thinly traded are converted to a form that creates greater liquidity. Securitization also applies to the situation where specific assets are pledged as collateral for securities, thus creating asset-backed securities. One example of the former is junk bonds; an example of the latter is mortgage-backed securities.

Security Market Line (SML) Represents, in a graphical form, the relationship between the risk of an asset as measured by its beta and the required rates of return for individual securities. The SML equation is one of the key results of the CAPM: $r_i = r_{RF} + b_i(r_M - r_{RF})$.

semistrong form of market efficiency States that current market prices reflect all publicly available information. Therefore, the only way to gain abnormal returns on a stock is to possess inside information about the company's stock.

sensitivity analysis Indicates exactly how much net present value will change in response to a given change in an input variable, other things held constant. Sensitivity analysis is sometimes called "what if" analysis because it answers this type of question.

shareholder rights provision Also known as a poison pill, it allows existing shareholders to purchase additional shares of stock at a price that is lower than the market value if a potential acquirer purchases a controlling stake in the company.

shelf registration Frequently, companies will file a master registration statement and then update it with a short-form statement just before an offering. This procedure is termed shelf registration because companies put new securities "on the shelf" and then later sell them when the market is right.

short hedges Occur when futures contracts are sold to guard against price declines.

simple interest The situation when interest is not compounded; that is, interest is not earned on interest. Also called regular interest. Divide the nominal interest rate by 365 and multiply by the number of days the funds are borrowed to find the interest for the term borrowed.

sinking fund Facilitates the orderly retirement of a bond issue. This can be achieved in one of two ways: (1) the company can call in for redemption (at par value) a certain percentage of bonds each year; or (2) the company may buy the required amount of bonds on the open market.

social value Projects of not-for-profit businesses are expected to provide a social value in addition to an economic value.

soft currencies Currencies of countries that set the exchange rate but do not allow their currencies to be traded on world markets.

special tax bonds Type of municipal bonds which are secured by a specified tax, such as a tax on utility services.

speculative balances Funds held by a firm in order to have cash for taking advantage of bargain purchases or growth opportunities.

spin-off Occurs when a holding company distributes the stock of one of the operating companies to its shareholders, thus passing control from the holding company to the shareholders directly.

spontaneously generated funds Funds generated if a liability account increases spontaneously (automatically) as sales increase. An increase in a liability account is a source of funds, thus funds have been generated. Two examples of spontaneous liability accounts are accounts payable and accrued wages. Notes payable, although a current liability account, is not a spontaneous source of funds because an increase in notes payable requires a specific action between the firm and a creditor.

spot rate The exchange rate that applies to "on the spot" trades or, more precisely, to exchanges that occur two days following the day of trade (in other words, current exchanges).

spread The difference between the price at which an underwriter sells the stock in an initial public offering and the proceeds that the underwriter passes on to the issuing firm; the fee collected by the underwriter. It is often about 7% of the offering price.

stakeholders All parties that have an interest, financial or otherwise, in a not-for-profit business.

stand-alone risk The risk an investor takes by holding only one asset.

standard deviation, σ A statistical measure of the variability of a set of observations. It is the square root of the variance.

statement of cash flows Reports the impact of a firm's operating, investing, and financing activities on cash flows over an accounting period.

statement of stockholders' equity Statement showing the beginning stockholders' equity, any changes due to stock issues/repurchases, the amount of net income that is retained, and the ending stockholders' equity.

stepped-up strike (or exercise) price A provision in a warrant that increases the strike price over time. This provision is included to encourage owners to exercise their warrants.

stock dividend Increases the number of shares outstanding but at a slower rate than splits. Current shareholders receive additional shares on some proportional basis. Thus, a holder of 100 shares would receive 5 additional shares at no cost if a 5% stock dividend were declared.

stock option Allows its owner to purchase a share of stock at a fixed price, called the strike price or the exercise price, no matter what the actual price of the stock is. Stock options always have an expiration date, after which they cannot be exercised.

stock repurchase Occurs when a firm repurchases its own stock. These shares of stock are then referred to as treasury stock.

stock split Current shareholders are given some number (or fraction) of shares for each stock share owned. Thus, in a 3-for-1 split, each shareholder would receive three new shares in exchange for each old share, thereby tripling the number of shares outstanding. Stock splits usually occur when the stock price is outside of the optimal trading range.

strategic options Options that often deal with strategic issues. Also called real options, embedded options, and managerial options.

stretching accounts payable The practice of deliberately paying accounts late.

strike (or exercise) price The price stated in the option contract at which the security can be bought (or sold).

strong form of market efficiency Assumes that all information pertaining to a stock, whether public or inside information, is reflected in current market prices. Thus, no investors would be able to earn abnormal returns in the stock market.

structured note A debt obligation derived from another debt obligation. Permits a partitioning of risks to give investors what they want.

subordinated debenture Debentures that have claims on assets, in the event of bankruptcy, only after senior debt (as named in the subordinated debt's indenture) has been paid off. Subordinated debentures may be subordinated to designated notes payable or to all other debt.

sunk cost A cost that has already occurred and is not affected by the capital project decision. Sunk costs are not relevant to capital budgeting decisions.

swap An exchange of cash payment obligations. Usually occurs because the parties involved prefer someone else's payment pattern or type.

sweetener A feature that makes a security more attractive to some investors, thereby inducing them to accept a lower current yield. Convertible features and warrants are examples of sweeteners.

synchronization of cash flows Occurs when firms are able to time cash receipts to coincide with cash requirements.

synergy Occurs when the whole is greater than the sum of its parts. When applied to mergers, a synergistic merger occurs when the post-merger earnings exceed the sum of the separate companies' pre-merger earnings.

takeover An action whereby a person or group succeeds in ousting a firm's management and taking control of the company.

tapping fund assets Deals with the issue of allowing a corporation to invest its pension fund assets to the corporation's own advantage.

target capital structure The relative amount of debt, preferred stock, and common equity that the firm desires. The weighted average cost of capital should be based on these target weights.

target cash balance The desired cash balance that a firm plans to maintain in order to conduct business.

target company A firm that another company seeks to acquire.

target distribution ratio Percentage of net income distributed to shareholders through cash dividends or stock repurchases.

target payout ratio Percentage of net income paid as a cash dividend.

targeted share repurchases Also known as greenmail, occurs when a company buys back stock from a potential acquirer at a price that is higher than the market price. In return, the potential acquirer agrees not to attempt to take over the company.

tax loss carryback and carryforward Ordinary corporate operating losses can be carried backward for 2 years or forward for 20 years to offset taxable income in a given year.

tax preference theory Proposes that investors prefer capital gains over dividends, because capital gains taxes can be deferred into the future but taxes on dividends must be paid as the dividends are received.

taxable income Gross income less a set of exemptions and deductions that are spelled out in the instructions to the tax forms that individuals must file.

technical analysts Stock analysts who believe that past trends or patterns in stock prices can be used to predict future stock prices.

temporary net operating working capital The NOWC required above the permanent level when the economy is strong and/or seasonal sales are high.

tender offer The offer of one firm to buy the stock of another by going directly to the stockholders, frequently over the opposition of the target company's management.

term structure of interest rates The relationship between yield to maturity and term to maturity for bonds of a single risk class.

terminal value Value of operations at the end of the explicit forecast period; equal to the present value of all free cash flows beyond the forecast period, discounted back to the end of the forecast period at the weighted average cost of capital.

time line A graphical representation used to show the timing of cash flows.

times-interest-earned (TIE) ratio Determined by dividing earnings before interest and taxes by the interest charges. This ratio measures the extent to which operating income can decline before the firm is unable to meet its annual interest costs.

total assets turnover ratio Measures the turnover of all the firm's assets; it is calculated by dividing sales by total assets.

total carrying cost The costs of carrying inventory.

total inventory costs The sum of ordering and carrying costs.

total net present value (TNPV) Equal to net present value plus net present social value in a not-for-profit business.

total ordering cost The costs of ordering inventory.

trade credit Debt arising from credit sales and recorded as an account receivable by the seller and as an account payable by the buyer.

trade deficit Occurs when a country imports more goods from abroad than it exports.

trade discounts Price reductions that suppliers offer customers for early payment of bills.

trade-off model The addition of financial distress and agency costs to either the MM tax model or the Miller model. In this model, the optimal capital structure can be visualized as a trade-off between the benefit of debt (the interest tax shelter) and the costs of debt (financial distress and agency costs).

transactions balance The cash balance associated with payments and collections; the balance necessary for day-to-day operations.

Treasury bond Bonds issued by the federal government; sometimes called T-bonds or government bonds. Treasury bonds have no default risk.

trend analysis An analysis of a firm's financial ratios over time. It is used to estimate the likelihood of improvement or deterioration in its financial situation.

uncollected balances schedule Helps a firm monitor its receivables better and also forecast future receivables balances; an integral part of the payments pattern approach.

underfunded pension plan The present value of expected retirement benefits exceeds the assets on hand.

underinvestment problem A type of agency problem in which high debt can cause managers to forgo positive NPV projects unless they are extremely safe.

underwritten arrangement Contract between a firm and an investment banker when stock is issued. An investment banker agrees to buy the entire issue at a set price and then resells the stock at the offering price. Thus, the risk of selling the issue rests with the investment banker.

value drivers The four value drivers are the growth rate in sales (g), operating profitability (OP = NOPAT/Sales), capital requirements (CR= Capital/Sales), and the weighted average cost of capital (WACC).

value of operations (V_{op}) The present value of all expected future free cash flows when discounted at the weighted average cost of capital.

value-based management Managing a firm with shareholder value in mind. It typically involves use of a model of shareholder value, such as the corporate value model.

variance, σ^2 A measure of the distribution's variability. It is the sum of the squared deviations about the expected value.

venture capitalist The manager of a venture capital fund. The fund raises most of its capital from institutional investors and invests in start-up companies in exchange for equity.

vertical merger Occurs when a company acquires another firm that is "upstream" or "downstream"; for example, an automobile manufacturer acquires a steel producer.

vesting If an employee has the right to receive pension benefits even if they leave the company prior to retirement, their rights are said to be vested.

vesting period Period during which employee stock options cannot be exercised.

warrant A call option, issued by a company, that allows the holder to buy a stated number of shares of stock from the company at a specified price. Warrants are generally distributed with debt, or preferred stock, to induce investors to buy those securities at lower cost.

weak form of market efficiency Assumes that all information contained in past price movements is fully reflected in current market prices. Thus, information about recent trends in a stock's price is of no use in selecting a stock.

weighted average cost of capital (WACC) The weighted average of the after-tax component costs of capital—debt, preferred stock, and common equity. Each weighting factor is the proportion of that type of capital in the optimal, or target, capital structure.

white knight A friendly competing bidder that a target management likes better than the company making a hostile offer; the target solicits a merger with the white knight as a preferable alternative.

window dressing Techniques employed by firms to make their financial statements look better than they really are.

working capital A firm's investment in short-term assets—cash, marketable securities, inventory, and accounts receivable.

workout Voluntary reorganization plans arranged between creditors and generally sound companies experiencing temporary financial difficulties. Workouts typically require some restructuring of the firm's debt.

Yankee bonds Bond issued by a foreign borrower denominated in dollars and sold in the United States under SEC regulations.

yield curve The curve that results when yield to maturity is plotted on the y-axis with term to maturity on the x-axis.

yield to call (YTC) The rate of interest earned on a bond if it is called. If current interest rates are well below an outstanding callable bond's coupon rate, then the YTC may be a more relevant estimate of expected return than the YTM because the bond is likely to be called.

yield to maturity (YTM) The rate of interest earned on a bond if it is held to maturity.

zero coupon bond Pays no coupons at all but is offered at a substantial discount below its par value and hence provides capital appreciation rather than interest income.

Name Index

Subject Index

Development bonds, **143**
Differential efficiency, 972
Diluted earnings per share (EPS), 781
DIP (debtor-in-possession) financing, 950
Direct quotation, 1020
Disbursement float, 809
Discount bonds, 129
Discount interest loans, 860, 862–863
Discounted cash flow (DCF) method, 375–378, **376**, 549f
  historical growth rates, 376
  merger analysis, 979
  overview, 378
  retention growth model, 376–377
  security analyst forecasts, 377
Discounted dividend model, 169
Discounted payback, 473–474, 474f, 477t
Discounts
  cash, 845–846
  credit policy, 814, 843–**844**
  quantity, 898–899
  selling currency at, **1030**
  trade, 809, 879
Distribution policy, 648–690
  cash distributions, 649–654, 654t, 664–673
  clientele effect, 657–658
  comparison of dividends and repurchases, 673–675
  dividend reinvestment plans, 681–682
  factors affecting, 675–676
  free cash flows, 649–651
  information content hypothesis, 658–659
  residual distribution model, 660–663
  stock dividends, 679–681
  stock splits, 678–681
Diversifiable (company-specific; unsystematic) risk, 51–53, **52**, 52n
Diversification, 48–50, 53, 973
Divestitures, 1006–1007
Dividend growth model, 413–415

Dividend irrelevance theory, 655
Dividend preference (bird-in-the-hand) theory, 655–**656**
Dividend reinvestment plans (DRIPs), 681–682
Dividend yields, 171, 675
Dividends. *See* **Stock dividends**
Dollar General, 154
Douglas Aircraft, 943
Dow Chemical Company, 763
Dow Corning, 925
Dr Pepper Snapple Group, 1006
Drexel Burnham Lambert, 153
DRIPs (dividend reinvestment plans), 681–682
DRP. *See* Default risk premium (DRP)
DSO (days sales outstanding; average collection period [ACP]), 285–286, 296t, **798**, 799f, **816**–817
Du Pont equation, 299–301
Duke Power, 916
Dumping, 1049, 1049n
Dun and Bradstreet (D&B), 301
Dunkin' Brands Group, 603
Dynegy, 679

E

EAA (equivalent annual annuity) method, 479
Earnings (net income), 238, 240
Earnings before interest and taxes (EBIT), 291–292, 292n
Earnings before interest, taxes, depreciation, and amortization (EBITDA), 184, 238, 289–290
Earnings per share (EPS), 175–176
  basic, 781
  diluted, 781
  effect of capital structure on, 603f
EBIT (earnings before interest and taxes), 291–292, 292n
EBITDA (earnings before interest, taxes, depreciation, and

amortization), 184, **238**, 289–290
EBITDA coverage ratio, 289, 289n, 296t
E-Commerce China Dangdang, 700t
Economic crisis. *See* Global economic crisis
Economic life, 480, 480f
Economic Ordering Quantity (EOQ) model, 888–895, **889**
  carrying costs, 889
  derivation of, 891–892
  extensions for, 895–900, 900t
  illustration of, 893–894, 894f
  ordering costs, 890
  setting order point, 894–895
  total inventory costs, 890–891
Economic Value Added (EVA), 256n, **257**–260, 257n, 258t
The Economist, 1034–1035
Efficient frontier, 86
Efficient Markets Hypothesis (EMH), 110–112, **189**–193
  discussion of, 190–191
  financial decisions and, 191–193
  semistrong-form efficiency, 189–190
  strong-form efficiency, 190
  weak-form efficiency, 189
Efficient portfolios, 80–88
  efficient frontier, 86
  expected rate of return on, 91
  for investors, 88
  N-asset case, 84–85
  risk–return indifference curves, 86–88
  two-asset case, 80–84
Eli Lilly, 976
Embedded (historical) rate, 361
Embedded options, 524
EMC Corp., 812
EMH. *See* **Efficient Markets Hypothesis (EMH)**
Empire District Electric, 56t, 654t
Employee stock options, 209, 224, 430–432
Employee stock ownership plans (ESOPs), 438–441
Employees' Retirement Income Security Act (ERISA), 958n